The fifty-five delegates meeting in the stuffy Pennsylvania state house from May to September 1787 had no idea that Chickasaws were leveraging peace as power against American expansion, that Creeks and Indigenous peoples of the Ohio Valley were gaining ground in recruiting more Cherokees into their military alliance, and that Tennessee Valley settlers were planning further invasions of Native land. But they would have been little surprised. Delegates traveled to Philadelphia because they believed the very survival of the United States depended on governmental centralization that could prevent internal disorder. Many were uncertain whether their effort would succeed. "I still think," reported William Blount, one of North Carolina's five representatives at the Constitutional Convention, "we shall ultimately and not many Years first be separated and distinct Governments perfectly independent of each other." Blount had little faith in the Constitution's lasting impact.[4]

From the distance of over two centuries, Blount's prediction appears ludicrous. The constitutional government of the United States not only survived but laid the foundation for a continental empire that expanded from the thirteen original colonies along the Atlantic Coast to the Pacific Ocean. Most scholars agree that the national authority granted to the federal government in the Constitution made expansion possible. The reorganized national state brought stability to North America's interior though military campaigns against Native peoples, treaties with European empires, the distribution of public land, and the admission of new state governments into the Union.[5]

Many U.S. leaders, particularly Federalist officials in Washington's cabinet, favored orderly, controlled American expansion. They wanted access to Native territory but only through negotiated land cessions or justified military action. The new nation could ill afford constant conflict with Indigenous peoples perpetuated by frontier whites' unending invasion of Native territory. The 1790 organization of the Southwest Territory to provide direct national administration of the Tennessee Country epitomized the federal government's attempt to supervise the process of national expansion.[6]

This veneer of national authority obscures federal powerlessness. White settlers and speculators demanded unchecked access to Chickasaw and Cherokee territory, and they actively disrupted U.S. negotiations that jeopardized their claims to Indigenous land. Chickasaw and Cherokee leaders welcomed greater federal oversight of the Tennessee Country, seeing the United States as a potential ally against neighboring white settlers. Yet the federal government was unprepared to enforce Native boundaries. In 1790, the entire U.S. army consisted of only 800 men, compared to an estimated 2,500 Cherokee and 1,000 Chickasaw soldiers. The difficulty of creating an orderly empire in the Tennessee Country was not lost on the nation's first president. Writing only two years after the creation of the Southwest Territory, Washington lamented that "the difficulty of deciding between lawless Settlers & greedy (land) Speculators on one side, and the jealousies of the Indian Nations & their banditti on the other, becomes more and more obvious every day." The federal government, according to Washington, was powerless to enact its own agenda in the Tennessee Country.[7] American leaders' vision for an orderly empire may have held true north of the Ohio River, but inhabitants of the Tennessee Country experienced a vastly different relationship with the U.S. government.

For their part, Chickasaws and Cherokees confronted federal powerlessness with a renewed commitment to their national borders. Though they did not resort to violence, Chickasaws took greater pains to redefine their boundaries with the United States as well as with other Native nations. They demanded that all peoples recognize their sovereignty. Cherokees began to police their nation against white intruders, which reignited simmering tension with neighboring American settlers. Cherokee diplomats' ongoing negotiations regarding boundary lines complicated the Native nation's fitful political centralization. For much of the eighteenth century, Cherokees' decentralized, town-based government shaped their imagined geographies and their defense of national lands. Women and men made decisions concerning territory only within their part of the Cherokee Nation. Over the course of the 1790s, however, Cherokees began to see their borders as a national issue, even if negotiated boundaries did not include territory near their individual towns. This was most evident in the Tennessee County, as Chickamauga Cherokees slowly returned to national diplomatic councils. It remains unquestionably true that the 1787 Constitutional Convention established the foundation for future U.S. imperialism. Yet decisions made at Long Town and Nashville, Ustanali and Jonesborough long remained more significant for inhabitants of the Tennessee Country than anything done in distant Philadelphia.

The First Failed Attempt at Federal Order

"I am happy to hear of so much Unanimity in the late Convention & have sanguine Hopes you have adopted a plan of Government that will add dignity to the Rising Greatness and Happiness of our American Empire," wrote John Sevier to Benjamin Franklin in November 1787. The State of Franklin's governor had initiated this correspondence with his government's namesake in hopes that Benjamin Franklin would aid Franklinites' ongoing struggle for federal recognition. Rather than lend his support, however, Franklin lectured Sevier that "there are only two Things that Humanity induces me to wish you may succeed in: The Accommodating your Misunderstanding with the Government of North Carolina by amicable Means; and the Avoiding an Indian War by preventing Encroachments on their Lands." Franklin advised Sevier to reorganize American settlements in the Tennessee Valley into orderly townships, both to provide better defense from potential Native attacks and to promote greater civilization among residents. "In our Way of sparse and remote Settlements," explained Franklin, "we are in danger of bringing up a Sett of Savages of our own Colour." Not only did the American statesman criticize Franklinites' geographical expansion, but he also implied that Tennessee Valley whites risked cultural degeneration if they refused to turn from their disorderly ways.[8]

Sevier surely found Franklin's advice disappointing. By early 1788, North Carolina legislators had refused, once again, to sanction Franklin's independence; several former Franklinites had accepted civil and military appointments from North Carolina; and Sevier's faction had suffered an embarrassing defeat in a skirmish with anti-Franklin settlers in February. Neither could Franklin leaders gain traction with Congress. Benjamin Franklin's stern response to Sevier was emblematic of numerous national leaders' views of the breakaway government. Alexander Hamilton even referenced "the late revolt of a part of the State of North Carolina" as a reason for Americans to ratify the Constitution, which he argued would prevent similar "dissensions between the States themselves, and from domestic factions and convulsions." Proponents of national centralization preferred stable relations with the Chickasaw and Cherokee Nations to the disorderly State of Franklin.[9]

To compound Franklinites' frustration, Cherokees succeeded in pressuring the federal government for new treaty negotiations to acknowledge their sovereignty in the Tennessee Country. While the Ustanali conference debated war in the summer of 1787, Upper Town Cherokees sent Sconetoyah to Congress to convince the federal government to enforce their Hopewell Treaty boundaries against white intruders. Though Sconetoyah met only with Constitutional Convention delegates in Philadelphia, Congress responded to the Cherokees' request. Congressmen knew from past experience how much states resented federal involvement with Native peoples living within their chartered boundaries. Upon the recommendation of secretary of war Henry Knox, however, they decided to treat Cherokees as "the common friends or enemies of the United States," similar to "foreign powers." The federal government under the Articles of Confederation, they insisted, possessed the authority to negotiate with Native nations because white encroachment could result in war. With this jurisdictional foundation, Congress approved treaty negotiations with Cherokees and Creeks, whose territories included land claimed by North Carolina, South Carolina, and Georgia.[10]

Congress's projection of federal authority rang hollow in its preparations for the treaties. Leaders from the three southern states would select the individual treaty commissioners to represent the United States. Commissioners were to consult with Creeks and Cherokees about their boundaries but in such a way that would not infringe on states' rights. Yet these commissioners could not demand a land cession from Native diplomats, and Congress expected states to share equally the treaty's expense of $10,000. Congress also ordered the commissioners to negotiate for the return of all escaped enslaved people in the Creek and Cherokee Nations, including many who had been adopted by Native families or made to labor for their Indigenous captors.[11] In other words, federal officials assumed that commissioners appointed by state governments could negotiate with Native leaders about their national boundaries without violating states' claimed sovereignty over Cherokee and Creek land or asking Native diplomats for territorial cessions, all while expecting state governments to foot the bill.

With the most to lose from a new Cherokee treaty, North Carolina legislators were particularly wary of federal overreach. They forbid their treaty commissioner, John Steele, from renegotiating the Cherokee–North Carolina border and declared any treaty that would guarantee hunting territory to any Native nation within the state's chartered limits to be a violation of both the state constitution and the Articles of Confederation. For speculators like William Blount, the treaty conversely offered a means to protect their claims to Native land. Blount advised Steele to reference North Carolina's right of conquest over Cherokee territory in upcoming negotiations and warned him not to agree to any treaty that acknowledged Cherokees' notions of their expansive boundaries. North Carolina legislators may have decided to support the upcoming negotiations, but they refused to sanction any federal treaty that might jeopardize their land claims.[12]

More than North Carolina speculators, white inhabitants of the Tennessee Country disrupted the federal government's growing involvement in Native affairs through violence and political intrigue. In June 1788, Sevier led attacks on nearby Cherokees at Chilhowee, Settico, and Hiwassee as retaliation for recent murders of white settlers. Though many Cherokees fled before the raid, Franklin soldiers tortured and killed around thirty people, including women and children. They repeatedly feigned peaceful intentions to lure Cherokee leaders back to their homes where they could then be executed. Hanging Maw later recounted that Franklin raiders went to Chilhowee, a Cherokee community along the Little Tennessee River in the foothills of the Smoky Mountains, "and hoisted a white Flag, and the Old Tassell & Old Abraham and his Son & the Leech hoisted another and came straight to them. They immediately fell upon them with out speaking a word & killed every one." The attack on the Overhill Towns initially "so raised [Sevier] in the esteem of the people on the frontier, that the people began to flock to his Standard," according to reports from North Carolina officers in the area.[13]

Old Tassel was a beloved man in the Cherokee Nation and had long emphasized peaceful relations between Cherokees and nearby white settlers. His murder prompted Cherokees to retaliate against Tennessee Valley whites. In late June and early July, Cherokee soldiers from across the nation attacked six separate American settlements, killing and wounding fifteen people. They considered these raids to be retaliatory justice for their murdered kin. By November, Cherokees including prominent Chickamaugas Dragging Canoe and John Watts favored peace. Little Turkey (Kenneteag), a beloved man who had recently relocated to new Cherokee communities in northern Georgia, still distrusted white inhabitants of the State of Franklin but insisted that Cherokees welcomed the opportunity to negotiate a new treaty. Peace would allow many Cherokees to return to their homes in the Tennessee Valley after fleeing south from Franklinite raids the previous summer.[14]

Tennessee Country inhabitants had no intention of allowing successful treaty negotiations to take place. In early January 1789, Sevier once again raided nearby Cherokee settlements, capturing twenty-nine Native women and children. The attack was done at the behest of the so-called privy council of the new state of Franklin, a body of settlers living on Cherokee land, and the raid itself reflected these intruders' vision for unchecked expansion. According to Anthony Foreman, a trader living among the Cherokees, Sevier informed the assembly upon his return that

North Carolina had now thrown the people of this country from under their protection, and that they had no other way now but to stand in their own defense. . . . You all well know, that the Cherokees have Refused selling their lands to us from time to time, and we have no other way now but to take it by the sword. By going into their nation, killing, and taking their women and children, destroying their Provisions, and by these means we will Compell them to give up their lands to us.

Settlers cheered Sevier's recipe for genocidal conquest. They passed resolves calling for further raids against Chickamauga communities and voiced their determination to prevent treaty negotiations. Settlers could abide no agreement that would recognize Native sovereignty and thereby limit their access to the Tennessee Valley's valuable territory.[15] Cherokees may have experienced settlers' attacks directly, but the violence also signified whites' opposition to federal intervention in the Tennessee Country.

No more attacks took place, but Sevier and his party of white intruders found other means to disrupt preparations for the federal treaty. They initially tried to coerce Cherokee leaders to cede land by using the imprisoned women and children as leverage. Later in the spring, however, Sevier transported the prisoners back to the Cherokee Nation under the supervision of Bennet Ballew. This was no innocent show of mercy. Ballew was a tool of Sevier, employed to disrupt the treaty proceedings. Six months before, Sevier had ordered Ballew to negotiate with Chickasaw leaders for a lease of their national land on behalf of unspecified "good men of The Country." One newspaper editor rightly described it as "a very deep scheme, to possess . . . land belonging to the Chickasaw nation." Ballew later declared himself the "Agent plenipotentiary from the chiefs & Head warrior of Cherokee Nation" in a communication with George Washington and claimed that Cherokees living in the upper Tennessee Valley wanted to "be incorporated with the white people and become subjects of the united States." Because no Cherokee leader had ever before proposed anything of the sort, Washington questioned Ballew's motives. In a subsequent communication with the federal government, Bloody Fellow (Nentooyah), a Chickamauga war leader, criticized Ballew as "not a good interpreter." "We do not approve of Mr. Ballue, frequenting this Land," echoed Dragging Canoe's brother The Badger (Ocunna) to U.S. officials.[16]

Ballew's duplicity, along with Cherokees' fears of further attacks, destroyed any possibility that the federal government could check white expansion in the Tennessee Valley through a new treaty. North Carolina legislators had ordered negotiations to take place in the early summer along the French Broad River near its confluence with the Swannanoa. Hanging Maw, Little Turkey, and Dragging Canoe—the three together representing a cross-section of Cherokee regional power—deemed the French Broad "too near to those who have injured us." All were invested in the treaty's success and proposed to negotiate again at Seneca or Keowee, the location of the 1785 Hopewell negotiations. Confident that Cherokees nevertheless would meet them along the French Broad River, American commissioners arrived at the treaty grounds in late May 1789. With no word from Native ambassadors after twelve days, the commissioners from Georgia and South Carolina left to commence separate negotiations with the Creeks, though Steele remained at the French Broad site for a few more days. King Fisher, Hanging Maw, Kittagusta (Prince of Chota), Tuskegatahee, and Beloved Woman Nancy Ward, along with five hundred other Cherokees, eventually arrived at the French Broad on June 18, but, because Congress dictated that formal treaties required the participation of multiple commissioners, Steele and the assembled Cherokees could agree only to a temporary peace.[17]

The Cherokees' delayed arrival was the result of confusion caused by Ballew. A trader swore that Ballew claimed he was appointed by Congress to purchase Cherokee land on behalf of North Carolina. Congress, however, had no relationship with Ballew, whom Steele described to assembled Cherokees as a person "of bad character" with "no authority from government." The Cherokees' uncertainty regarding the federal government's intentions for the treaty likely encouraged their participation at an international conference with the Creek Nation in early May. There, they decried ongoing white encroachment and Franklinite raids and contacted British officials about military support.[18] Cherokee diplomats' decision to prioritize the Creek conference as more important than their negotiations with American officials revealed how the incessant settler attacks and political intrigue threatened any successful negotiation with the United States.

The disruption of the 1789 treaty attempt marked a new era in the history of the Tennessee Country. For nearly two decades, white settlers had railed against Indigenous sovereignty. They had settled on Native land and attacked nearby Cherokee towns. They had even created breakaway governments, like the ruined State of Franklin, to secure their property rights. Yet the federal government's growing involvement in the region meant that settlers' commitment to unchecked expansion directly conflicted with the Washington administration's emphasis on order and stability in U.S. diplomacy with Native nations. Cherokees and Chickasaws recognized that a powerful federal government could help protect their sovereignty, whereas many local whites saw the United States as yet another obstacle to overcome in their creation of an expansive settler empire.

The Southwest Territory

As much as Tennessee Valley settlers hated the federal government's meddling, white inhabitants of the Cumberland Valley clamored for greater protection from Cherokee and Creek attacks. North Carolina had abandoned them, cried residents of Sumner and Davidson Counties, "without any other dependence than their own strength and determined resolution to support their little growing Settlement." Many believed that Spanish rule might be preferable to the current situation. Speculators and their western land agents even organized the Cumberland settlements into the Mero District, named for Spain's New Orleans governor, Esteban Miró. "All the encouragement I can give the people," explained a Mero District militia officer, "is that I have no doubt but the next Assembly will cede us to Congress." White inhabitants of the Cumberland Valley had high hopes in 1789 that they would benefit from the centralized power of the United States.[19]

Federal governance required North Carolina's consent. Despite their representatives' participation in the Constitutional Convention of 1787, North Carolinians rejected the U.S. Constitution in a 1788 state convention, believing that it threatened individual and state rights. In November 1789, North Carolina delegates once again met in convention, but this time, with overwhelming support, particularly from Tennessee Country representatives, the body agreed on ratification. North Carolina's cession of its western land claims proceeded along similar lines. Only two days after ratifying the Constitution, Robert Ewing of Davidson County introduced a new bill in the state house of commons for ceding North Carolina's western land to the United States. Legislators approved the cession with only minor amendments. Westerners overwhelmingly supported it in the general assembly, and land speculators from eastern North Carolina also were essential to the act's passage. They believed that U.S. governance could bring stability and order to the Tennessee Country. The presence of federal troops, according to Hugh Williamson, a speculator ally of the Blount family, would "equally curb the White and Red Savages [and] naturally raise the Value of Lands." Authors of North Carolina's Cession Act ensured that all existing land claims would remain valid in the ceded territory and that grantees could make new locations if necessary. Notably, the act prohibited the federal government from interfering with the institution of slavery.[20]

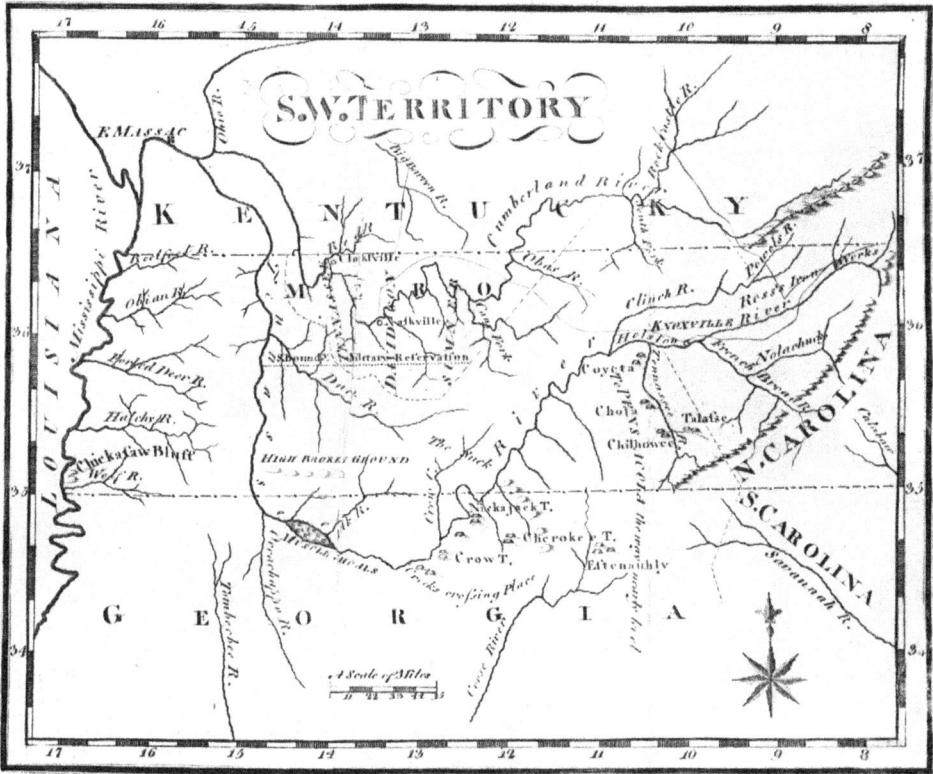

S. W. Territory, 1795. Tennessee State Library and Archives. This map shows the boundaries of the Southwest Territory, organized by the United States in 1790 to govern the Tennessee Country directly. It also includes locations of Cherokee towns in the Tennessee Valley and identifies Chickasaw Bluff along the Mississippi River.

For nearly a decade, national leaders had called on state governments to cede their western lands to the federal government. Not only would the sale of this vast territory eliminate the national debt, but state cessions might also curb states' competing financial interests in the West and bind the nation together. The organization of the Northwest Territory in 1787 represented what one historian terms Americans' "vision for imperial expansion" across the continent. Unlike the former situation under British rule, distant territories could transition into states on equal footing with the original thirteen colonies, so long as they surpassed required population thresholds and proceeded through several phases of government. Congress therefore readily accepted North Carolina's cession of its western land to the United States in April 1790 and organized the Territory South of the River Ohio, colloquially known as the Southwest Territory, to provide direct federal governance of the Tennessee Country. The only notable difference between the Northwest Territory and the Southwest Territory appeared to be the legalization of slavery; nevertheless, the operation of national state power and the administration of Indian affairs would challenge slavery as the greatest contrast between the two U.S. territories.[21]

Given the rapid organization of the Southwest Territory alongside corresponding rhetoric of U.S. sovereignty, it is no wonder that historians have overemphasized the role of federal authority in the Tennessee Country. Upon the recommendation of North Carolina congressmen and state leaders, President Washington appointed William Blount the governor of the new territory and the superintendent of Indian affairs for the Southern Department. His combined roles demonstrated federal officials' recognition that successful governance depended on placating Native southerners and administering the territory's American population. Blount was no disinterested public servant committed to virtuous service to the United States. The new governor remained invested in his earlier speculative ventures and believed his joint offices would allow him to boost his commodification of Indigenous territory. "My Western Lands had become so great an object to me," exclaimed Blount upon learning of his appointment, "that it had become absolutely necessary that I should go to the Western Country, to secure them." He was confident that his position would increase his lands' value. He planned to establish the territory's capital somewhere near his family's landholdings to drive up prices there. Washington knew of Blount's interest in western lands, but he may have agreed with a North Carolina congressman that the new governor would be committed to the peace and stability of the Southwest Territory because of his widespread commercial ventures.[22] Successful land speculation required peace and order, which had always been significant in Federalist visions for the trans-Appalachian West.

The Southwest Territory contained only a small quantity of unclaimed public lands, so Indian affairs became the most important dimension of federal governance. Despite the 1785 Hopewell Treaty and the 1789 truce, white settlers continued to invade the Cherokee Nation on the basis of the coerced State of Franklin agreements. By 1791, more than 3,500 American settlers and 163 enslaved people lived in Cherokee territory. Although Native leaders insisted their negotiations with Franklin were invalid, they still demanded that they receive payment for the ceded land. Rumor spread that Cherokees were receiving Indigenous peoples of the Ohio Valley into Nickajack Town, given their increasing dissatisfaction with American expansionists. Chickamaugas even sent two diplomats to London to consult with British officials about strengthening ties with the Cherokee Nation. Chickasaws, too, had grown irritated after Georgia land speculators had tried to pressure them into a land cession. Piominko refused, telling the speculators' agents that the "Villages, the Fields and the Tombs of his Ancestors he will never barter away."[23] Cherokees and Chickasaws cautiously welcomed federal administration of the Southwest Territory, seeing it as a possible check on American expansion.

"The Greatest Difficulty was the Agreeing on the Boundary"

Cherokees and territory officials cemented their new diplomatic relationship in the summer of 1791 when both sides came together near the confluence of the Holston and French Broad Rivers, near present-day Knoxville, to negotiate the 1791 Holston Treaty. Only weeks after Congress had organized the Southwest Territory, Washington pondered whether to evict settlers from Cherokee land in accordance with the previous Hopewell Treaty or to negotiate a new border that could encompass the illegal settlements within the United States. Upon Jefferson's recommendation, the president ultimately decided that a new boundary with the Cherokee Nation would be the most effective means for a permanent peace in the Tennessee Country. Yet the treaty also represented the first opportunity for federal officials to enforce U.S. rule on the white inhabitants of the new Southwest Territory and prevent their ongoing invasion of Native land. The transition from state to federal governance was important to national leaders. Effective administration of the Southwest Territory depended on peaceful relations with Indigenous peoples made possible only by controlling American settlers and speculators.[24]

Treaty negotiations revealed Cherokees' growing national unity regarding their national borders. Although internal political divisions persisted, the leading Native diplomats hailed from across the Cherokee Nation—including Chickamauga leaders Bloody Fellow and John Watts, Upper Town/Overhill officials Nontuaka and Hanging Maw, and Chulcoah (Creek Linguister/The Boot) and Auquotague, there to represent Little Turkey on behalf of displaced Cherokees now in northern Georgia. At least 1,200 other Cherokee men, women, and children also traveled to the treaty ground to witness negotiations and hold their representatives accountable. Moreover, Cherokees began the conference on June 26, 1791, with the "Eagle-tail dance." Although Native diplomats explained that the performance represented their "great sincerity for peace," the dance was known for its connection to war and heroism. Cherokees had not performed it since the Revolutionary War.[25] That the Eagle Tail Dance opened treaty negotiations demonstrated the Cherokees' continued commitment to their own national interests in their first negotiations with the reorganized U.S. government.

"The greatest difficulty" of the treaty negotiations, according to Governor Blount, "was the agreeing on the boundary" separating the Cherokee Nation from United States. Secretary of war Henry Knox authorized Blount to negotiate new cessions that would include settlers living south of the French Broad and Tennessee Rivers, those who claimed property rights based on dubious State of Franklin treaties. If the Cherokees consented, Knox's proposed border would meander east from the Duck River south of Nashville to the Holston River near present-day Knoxville. Blount disagreed. He argued that the Tennessee and Little Tennessee Rivers offered a more obvious border and would encompass nearly all white settlers living on Cherokee land. Such expansive boundaries would boost Blount's speculation of the Tennessee River's Great Bend, a project that had grown stagnant in past years as a result of Native resistance, federal opposition, and Franklin's disintegration. The demand for a new boundary surprised Cherokee delegates. They wanted the United States to evict white intruders from Native land, not facilitate ongoing invasion with expanded boundaries. "Do the white people look on us as the Buffalow and other wild beasts in the woods, and that they have a right to take our property at their pleasure," responded Cherokee diplomats to Blount's appeals for land cessions. "Tho' we are Red we think we was made by the same power and certainly we think we have as much right to enjoy our property as any other human being that inhabit the Earth." Americans' disregard for Cherokees' property rights and treaty agreements exposed their general contempt for Indigenous peoples.[26]

Cherokee intransigence put Blount on the defensive. Not only would he have to convince Native diplomats to accept a new boundary, but Blount would also have to assure them that the United States would now honor its agreements rather than allow white settlers and speculators to violate Cherokee sovereignty perpetually. Blount ironically resorted to a narrative of past U.S. powerlessness. When American commissioners negotiated the Hopewell Treaty in 1785, "the government was weak and things in confusion," he explained. Now, however, the United States had the ability to enforce treaties against white intruders and preserve inviolate the bordered land. Blount projected a future narrative of U.S. state power into the Tennessee Country, assuring Cherokees that the United

States could enforce their sovereignty. This treaty would be different than past agreements, continued Blount. The Hopewell Treaty existed "only on paper," but this time around U.S. officials would "mark [new boundaries] on Trees and rivers." The federal government could prove its commitment to a negotiated boundary by surveying the line on the region's landscape. Surveys were important for Cherokee leaders, but they still refused to consent to any land cessions. Cherokees understood the current negotiation as an existential crisis in the face of an expanding American empire. Accepting further cessions risked sanctioning whites' perpetual encroachment on their land.[27]

As negotiations intensified, Cherokees' traditional region-centric diplomacy replaced the nation's newfound national unity regarding boundary lines. Chulcoah, as Little Turkey's agent, had acted as the Cherokee Nation's primary negotiator for the first five days of the conference. Yet by June 30 his position was in jeopardy. Representing Cherokee communities hundreds of miles away, Chulcoah was willing to make a cession of Tennessee Valley land and was growing frustrated with Native diplomats from surrounding towns. "The red people who were raised here are the men who had disputed for their hunting grounds," he explained. "I could not do any good because these young men" oppose a new border. Chickamauga and Upper Town Cherokees lived, hunted, and farmed in the Tennessee Country and therefore had a greater stake in the negotiations. Chulcoah remained at the treaty ground, but Chickamaugas John Watts and Bloody Fellow and Upper Town leaders Nontuaka and Hanging Maw grew more vocal as Cherokees continued to haggle with Blount over a new boundary.[28]

The official boundary line of the Treaty of Holston was something of a compromise between Cherokee delegates and Governor Blount. Cherokees arrived at the treaty ground with little expectation that a cession would even be a topic of discussion, much less that the United States would pressure them to grant even more land to white settlers. They eventually accepted most of Blount's proposals for the Tennessee Valley portion of the border but argued for a "straight course not along the top of the ridge" dividing the Little River from the Little Tennessee River. The finalized cession boundary in the Cumberland Valley was a ridge that divided the Cumberland River watershed from the Duck River watershed. A new border between the United States and the Cherokee Nation may have been a major goal for the treaty's U.S. organizers, but Cherokees demanded that they would be the ones to control the boundary's survey. John Watts insisted that Cherokee leaders would agree to the treaty only if "the Indians shall go before to mark the line." He even named three Cherokees living in Chota as the nation's surveyors, likely because they were most familiar with the region's terrain.[29] The surveying process would provide a vehicle for Cherokees to further enforce their national sovereignty against white expansion, even as it perpetuated controversies about the process of American empire in the Tennessee Country.

With its land cession of over 4,000 square miles, the Holston Treaty convinced American settlers that the centralized federal government intended to wield its power to accelerate white expansion. The treaty displayed the United States' commitment to order in the Tennessee Country by embracing the illegal settlements of many whites within Cherokee territory and establishing permanent, marked boundaries backed by federal authority. Blount personally received praise for the treaty's confirmation of the national government's authority over Indian affairs, as opposed to the prior meddling of state governments. Southwest Territory militia officers rejoiced that Blount "hath done every thing that a man could do, to restore Peace to the Teritory." Local whites had few reasons to oppose a government that seemingly accepted their visions for an expansionist American empire.[30]

Protesting Holston

Cherokees fumed over the Holston Treaty. Cherokee diplomats later accused Blount of bribing their interpreters at the conference. Through such deception, Native attendees were not aware that the treaty granted Americans free transportation along the Tennessee River, authorized the construction of a road from Nashville to the Tennessee Valley, slashed Cherokees' annuity payment by half, and ceded a larger expanse of Cumberland Valley territory than they had intended. So distressed were Cherokees about the actual results of the Holston Treaty that they organized a diplomatic mission in early 1792 to meet directly with the Washington administration in Philadelphia, believing fairer negotiations could take place away from Blount and territory settlers who coveted their land. With the Chickamauga leader Bloody Fellow at their head, Cherokee delegates successfully convinced Secretary Knox to increase their annuity payment from $1,000 to $1,500, allow Cherokees to select their own interpreters, and appoint a federal agent to live in the Cherokee Nation and act in their best interest in dealings with the United States. Though Knox refused to repudiate the treaty, he promised that the federal government would prohibit illegal settlement in the Cherokee Nation. After the meeting disbanded, Knox penned a letter to Blount and advised the governor to respect Native interpretations of the bordered land when surveying the treaty boundary line.

Knox also ordered Blount to remove whites settled illegally in the Cherokee Nation.[31]

As months went by without the eviction of white intruders, Cherokees grew estranged from the United States, and the nascent political consensus between the Chickamauga and Upper Town leaders became increasingly fraught. In June 1792, Cherokees held a conference at Ustanali, where the Philadelphia delegation informed the nation's leaders of their meeting with Knox. Cherokees wanted to know whether the secretary of war had "altered the lines," and they asked Leonard Shaw, the nation's new federal Indian agent, to read the treaty aloud for them. Native delegates interrupted Shaw's account when he described "the line striking Cumberland, forty miles above Nashville." Cherokees' best hunting land was continually disappearing at the hands of white settlers with the tacit consent of the federal government. Little Turkey criticized the boundary for encroaching on Cherokee land and the shared hunting territory of all Native southerners. The national leader even proposed to trade the spiritually significant Long Island of the Holston in the northeastern reaches of the Southwest Territory for a new boundary that would transfer much of the Cumberland Valley back to the Cherokee Nation.[32]

Tension within the council foreshadowed further resistance. Chickamaugas voiced the harshest criticism of the United States. The "young warriors," who composed most of Chickamauga ranks, relied on hunting "to maintain their families" and resented that the federal government had not renegotiated the Holston boundaries. National edicts meant little if the federal government would not enforce them. "Some of the whites are the cause of the President's wishing to purchase our land," argued Little Nephew of Nickajack Town. They "settle on our land, and improve till he is obliged to purchase." The Chickamauga leader demanded that the United States "remove the people off our land" in accordance with the Holston Treaty. Whites' ongoing invasion of Cherokee territory made Little Nephew doubt whether the president actually had the power to enforce the treaty. He viewed Washington as a pawn of frontier whites. Little Nephew remained for the entirety of the conference, but Dick Justice (Uwenahi) and The Glass (Atawgwatihih), both of Lookout Mountain Town, departed before its conclusion, symbolizing that their town would not be bound by the council's decisions.[33]

Chickamauga leaders John Watts and Bloody Fellow stayed away from Ustanali altogether. Bloody Fellow had led the delegation to Philadelphia, making his absence particularly striking. Yet, when he returned to the Tennessee

Valley later in the summer, he found white settlers "building mills, and picketing forts" on Cherokee land. Bloody Fellow denounced Congress, Washington, and Blount as "Liars" for these blatant violations of the Holston Treaty and likely considered any future diplomacy to be useless. John Watts, for his part, had publicly doubted that American settlers would ever respect federal treaties. Rather than attend the national council, Watts traveled to Pensacola, where he negotiated with Spanish traders to supply Chickamaugas with goods, perhaps thinking that closer ties with Spain would weaken Cherokees' attachment to the United States. Bloody Fellow also met Spanish officials at New Orleans and Natchez in late 1792 and requested that they reestablish a military presence in the region and acknowledge the Cherokee Nation's borders, especially those in the Cumberland Valley. He spoke of creating a pro-Spanish alliance of Native southerners. Cherokees had tried diplomacy with the United States, but federal inaction had encouraged them to cultivate international ties elsewhere.[34]

Rather than negotiate, many Chickamauga Cherokees resorted to military action to enforce their sovereignty in the Tennessee Country. Bloody Fellow had hinted that Cherokees would police their borders should federal officials renege on their promise to remove white intruders from their nation. Even before the Ustanali meeting in June, Cherokee raiders had attacked white settlements near the boundary line along the Clinch and Powell Rivers, and at least one skirmish occurred when Cherokees encountered whites on their hunting land. These border raids increased in frequency in the summer and fall of 1792 after Cherokees received word that an army of Shawnees, Delawares, and Miamis had defeated a force of American soldiers at the Battle of the Wabash in the Northwest Territory. Chickamauga Cherokees, along with their Shawnee and Creek allies, captured or killed around seventy residents of the Mero District between January and November. Captives included an enslaved African American named Eader and at least three others unnamed, whom Native raiders likely intended to trade for goods or keep for their own purposes.[35]

Chickamaugas employed a more formalized military strategy in the year's final months. In September 1792, Upper Town leaders notified territory officials that the Chickamaugas favored war against the United States and were amassing an army of over one thousand Native soldiers for an attack on the region's white settlements. No attack came, at least not initially. Cherokee men had assembled for a raid at Lookout Mountain Town after learning that a militia general in the Mero District planned to retaliate for recent murders along the Cumberland River. The Glass and Bloody Fellow informed Blount several days later that they had diffused the situation, and they implored the governor to prevent similar militancy among white settlers. A force of Chickamaugas and Creeks led by John Watts did, however, attack Buchanan's Station, located four miles south of Nashville, on September 30, though the Southwest Territory militia fought them off. The news prompted Blount to reevaluate Chickamauga overtures for peace. He believed that the communications from two weeks earlier had been written merely as a ruse, though it is much more likely that The Glass and Bloody Fellow had notified the governor prematurely that the Chickamaugas had called off the campaign.[36]

Watts's raid was a powerful display of Cherokee sovereignty. In their previous letters to Blount, Chickamauga leaders had made clear the connection between the federal government's lax enforcement of the Holston Treaty boundary line, Chickamaugas' resort to military action, and the ongoing disputes between the federal government, local whites, and the Cherokee Nation. Bloody Fellow explained that the reason for the Chickamauga soldiers' preparation for war was whites' constant invasion of Cherokee territory. "If you was to consider well, you would see it was more your people's fault than mine," he had told Blount, "by daily encroaching on our lands, and sending threatening talks," despite President Washington's recent promises that intrusions would end. The Glass furthermore ordered that residents of the Southwest Territory travel to the Cherokee Nation only "on public business" and proceed first to Ustanali, where Cherokee leaders could better regulate their behavior.[37] Tennessee Country whites perpetuated conflict by settling on Cherokee land or traveling privately throughout the nation. The United States seemingly lacked the ability to halt the ongoing invasion so the Chickamaugas had little choice but to enforce their nation's borders through direct military action.

Chickasaws closely followed the growing federal involvement in the Tennessee Country. At least thirteen Chickasaw diplomats had attended the Holston Treaty negotiations, and national leaders sent their own message to Congress in late 1791. In a near echo of Cherokee demands, the Chickasaws implored President Washington "that the Carolina people ought not to be appointed to hold talks with the Indians, as they always ask for lands." They wanted the federal government to "make the white people equally quiet and not breed disturbances." The Chickasaws recognized the United States as a possible ally in a potential conflict with the Creeks or their Native enemies west of the Mississippi River. Even as they maintained existing connections with Spain, they, led by Piominko, cultivated closer ties with American officials—like James

Robertson, their temporary federal agent—tying the United States into their nation's growing web of diplomacy.[38]

In the early 1790s, Chickasaws even shaped federal Indian policy to protect their boundaries. At the 1792 Nashville conference that opens this book, Piominko and other leading Chickasaw officials provided a detailed outline of their borders, specifically mentioning that all of the Elk and Duck River valleys and territory upstream from the Muscle Shoals were within their nation. In a proclamation issued on July 21, 1794, Washington echoed Piominko's articulation of the Chickasaws' national boundaries and ordered American citizens "not to commit any injury, trespass or molestation whatever on the persons, Lands, hunting Grounds or other rights or property of the Said [Chickasaw] Indians." The Chickasaws were now officially "under the protection of the United States," a statement that, from a U.S. perspective, both vested Chickasaw sovereignty in the Native nation's relationship with the United States and warned European empires not to meddle in Americans' relations with the Chickasaw Nation. Chickasaws were used to accepting such statements and likely disregarded the proclamation's implicit threat to their sovereignty.[39] For decades, they continued to draw on Washington's proclamation as evidence of their legal title to Tennessee Country land.

Federal Neglect and Disorderly Violence

Even as Chickasaws and U.S. officials strengthened diplomatic relations, much of the Tennessee Country was already a war zone. The powerlessness of the federal government was on full display between 1792 and 1794 as whites and Cherokees warred over their competing geographies of the Tennessee Country. Americans continued to settle illegally on Native land, and Chickamauga Cherokees contested this ongoing colonization with military force. Territory residents called on the federal government to authorize campaigns against Chickamauga towns. Yet Washington, Knox, and even the expansionist Blount, in many cases, prohibited offensive military measures against Native peoples; the territorial militia could be employed for "defensive protection" only. Settlers were left to their own devices to defend themselves. Exasperated militia commanders and local strongmen organized a number of unsanctioned invasions of the Cherokee and Creek Nations, in clear violation of existing treaty agreements. A Mero District militia general offered $100 bounties for each Native scalp taken by American vigilantes. Local whites even captured the federal agent to the Cherokee Nation and nearly executed him, proof of their dissatisfaction with federal Indian policy.[40] U.S. powerlessness made orderly governance impossible in the Southwest Territory.

Federal neglect led Tennessee Country residents to organize several large-scale attacks against the Cherokee Nation in 1793 and 1794. Territory officials knew that any breach of Cherokee sovereignty by white soldiers crossing the Holston Treaty boundary would result in retaliation. Yet Major John Beard of the Southwest Territory militia took little notice of the international border when he led an unauthorized invasion of the Cherokee Nation in June 1793. Beard initially ranged throughout the Tennessee Valley searching for Native raiders who had killed white settlers near the Clinch River. Failing to find them, Beard moved against peaceful Upper Town Cherokees living at Coyatee near the Tellico River. He and his men massacred twelve or thirteen Cherokees and injured even more, including Hanging Maw's wife Betty. They also fired on white inhabitants of the town, who were involved in peaceful diplomacy with Cherokee leaders.[41]

Beard's raid represented more than whites' desire to crush Native resistance; it was an intentional challenge to the federal government's recognition of Cherokee sovereignty. Tennessee Country inhabitants knew that Cherokees, including Chickamaugan John Watts, were about to assemble at Coyatee to organize a new peace conference at Philadelphia. The massacre disrupted such plans. Hanging Maw wrote to President Washington that he and other Cherokees had "thought very well of your talk of restoring peace, and our land being made safe to use; but the white people have spoiled the talk at present." Cherokee leaders no longer had any intention of traveling to Philadelphia and preferred instead to remain in the Tennessee Valley to protect their homes from further invasions. They refused to even consider peace until territory officials punished Beard and his men. Still, many local whites organized their own separate raids on other peaceful Upper Town Cherokees living only a short distance from the Holston Treaty boundary line along the Little Tennessee and Tuckasegee Rivers.[42]

Cherokees initially promised no retaliation for Beard's attack, willing to wait until federal officials punished him. But Beard continued to move freely about the region and even led another campaign against Native towns along the Hiwassee River in July, proving to Cherokee leaders that territory officials possessed neither the authority nor the desire to arrest him. In retaliation, John Watts and his uncle Doublehead (Chuquilatague), who was Old Tassel's brother, led an army of more than a thousand Chickamauga Cherokees and Creeks in an assault on Cavett's Station, located west of Knoxville, in late September 1793.

They killed or captured all of the fort's inhabitants before returning to the Cherokee Nation.[43]

The attack on Cavett's Station convinced territory officials to sanction offensive measures against Cherokees and Creeks without federal authorization. Daniel Smith, serving as acting governor while Blount was away in Philadelphia, ordered John Sevier, the former Franklin governor and current territory militia general, to attack the Native army. Sevier and a six hundred–man force assembled from the surrounding counties chased the Cherokees and Creeks across the Tennessee River to the Coosa River, destroyed several Chickamauga and Creek towns, slaughtered their livestock, and returned to the Southwest Territory by mid-October 1793. Sevier's invasion convinced Tennessee Country whites that territory officials shared their expansionist goals even if the Washington administration refused to mobilize federal troops for their protection.[44]

A Cherokee delegation, led by Nontuaka of the Upper Towns and the Chickamaugan Doublehead, attempted to parlay the violence in the Tennessee Country to their advantage. Meeting once again in Philadelphia in summer 1794, they tried to renegotiate the Holston boundary to include more Cumberland Valley land within the Cherokee Nation. Though Knox and Washington refused to reconsider, they agreed to increase Cherokees' annuity payment to $5,000 and to appoint Silas Dinsmoor as the new federal Cherokee agent. Both sides promised to recommit themselves to peace and enforce the Treaty of Holston. Notably, the new agreement included a stipulation about the need to survey the treaty boundary lines, though negotiators did not insist on a deadline by which the survey had to be completed.[45] Federal officials still believed treaties to be the most effective mechanism for creating order in the trans-Appalachian West despite the growing disorder in the Tennessee Country.

While the Native diplomats were returning to their homes, local white troops conducted one of the most destructive campaigns ever organized against any part of the Cherokee Nation. A recent spate of Chickamauga attacks had incensed territory whites and further alienated them from the United States. While Doublehead "and his sanguinary Brothers are received and caressed at Philadelphia," complained Blount, "we are daily Suffering at the Hands of their Associates." In September, General James Robertson of the Mero District called for a major raid against Chickamauga towns along the Tennessee River. He was careful to couch his order to Major James Ore, the expedition's leader, in defensive terms, basing it on rumors of impending Native attacks. On September 13, Ore's small army of 550 militia troops, including one hundred Kentuckians, razed Nickajack and

Running Water, two Chickamauga towns specifically targeted as sanctuaries for Creek and Chickamauga raiders. White soldiers killed fifty Native individuals in the campaign, and Ore's force marched around twenty prisoners back to Nashville. White inhabitants of the Southwest Territory considered the attack "the most brilliant thing that has happened or could have happened for this Country."[46] Ore's raid crushed any remaining Chickamauga resistance.

Cherokee Unity, Chickasaw Alliances, and Tennessee Statehood

According to historians, Cherokees in 1794 were a "people in crisis," entering a "critical junction in their history" after decades of violent invasions by American expansionists. Ore's raid certainly did force Native leaders to negotiate peace and plan a prisoner exchange with Governor Blount at the newly constructed Tellico Blockhouse on the north bank of the Little Tennessee River near Chota. Rather than a conquered people, however, Hanging Maw, John Watts and the more than four hundred Cherokees in attendance offered a united front for federal officials when the meeting began in early November. Internal disputes over the proper response to American encroachment had divided the Cherokee Nation for the past several decades. Though the 1791 Holston Treaty had been a product of Cherokees' growing centralization, political discord had reached a heightened level of intensity during the previous two years. Hanging Maw explained that the Chickamaugas "were once my people, but not now." Cherokee diplomats, however, used the negotiations to repair their national fractures. Prominent Chickamaugan John Watts made peace with Hanging Maw, whom he recognized as "the head of the nation," and all Native leaders blamed Creeks for recent attacks on American settlements, despite Chickamauga involvement. Bloody Fellow also called for a new diplomatic relationship between the United States and the Cherokee Nation based on easy access to trade goods.[47]

Cherokees' national unity represented a marked contrast to their criticism of U.S. disorder and national disunity. To Blount's embarrassment, the conference devolved into an exposé of federal impotence. Reports were circling that a volunteer army of Kentucky militia was marching against Chickamauga towns. Though Blount had been trying frantically to stop the illegal invasion, he had had little success and pleaded with the assembled Cherokees not to retaliate. No attack materialized, but Cherokees offered even more vocal critiques of the United States at the December prisoner exchange. During negotiations, Blount begged the Cherokee diplomats—including numerous Chickamauga leaders from Wills Town, Running Water, Nickajack, and High Tower—for military support. The governor implored Cherokees to enforce their borders against Creek invasions or defend American settlements along the Cumberland River. "Is it that this Country is not under the Protection of the U.S., or is it that the President is uninformed of the many murders & Thefts committed by the Creeks?" asked a sarcastic Hanging Maw after hearing Blount's appeal for protection. Cherokees had no patience for U.S. officials who could neither defend American settlements from Creek raids nor prevent their own citizens from encroaching on Native land. Direct federal governance of the Southwest Territory had done little to convince Cherokees that the United States possessed coercive national state power.[48]

Chickasaws soon experienced firsthand the federal government's powerlessness in the Tennessee Country. Since the 1780s, they had been on bad terms with their Creek neighbors. Their closer ties with the United States and their claims to hunting territory in the Tennessee River's Great Bend, a region that Creeks also claimed, had generated tension between the two Native nations. In 1793, a party of Creeks attacked Chickasaw hunters, killing one man and desecrating his corpse to show disrespect for the Chickasaw Nation. Existing distrust became open war. Hostilities intensified in early 1795 after Chickasaw raiders commanded by William Colbert (Chooshemataha), the son of a prominent Chickasaw woman and the Scottish trader James Colbert, killed and scalped five Creeks near the Duck River. Chenabee, Piominko, William Colbert, his brother George (Tootemastubbe), and other Chickasaw diplomats insisted that it was mutually beneficial for the United States to join their nation in war. They repeatedly appealed to U.S. officials for assistance against the Creeks as raiding continued into the fall. Nevertheless, fearing conflict with the Creek Nation, the Washington administration prohibited a formal alliance in no uncertain terms because of the United States' existing treaty agreements with the Creeks.[49]

Southwest Territory residents made their own decision to ally with the Chickasaw Nation. Inhabitants of the Cumberland Valley were well aware that they owed a decline in Creek raids to the efforts of William Colbert and other Chickasaw defenders, who had been guarding their region's southern flank since the early months of 1795. In April, around one hundred Mero District militia troops joined Colbert and his Native soldiers in defending Chickasaw communities from Creek incursions. The combined force repulsed Creek attacks on Chickasaw territory in late May, killing or wounding more than twenty raiders. It would take another Chickasaw victory in September to temporarily end hostilities with the Creek Nation. Despite their relationship with the U.S. government, Chickasaws had to rely on informal alliances with nearby white expansionists to neutralize the Creek threat. Federal officials could not be counted upon for military support.[50]

Tennessee Country whites had come to the same conclusions as they grew increasingly alienated from the United States over Indian affairs. For years, American inhabitants of the Tennessee Country had pleaded with U.S. officials to organize military campaigns against Creeks and Chickamauga Cherokees. They wanted to conquer the two peoples and end their decades-long resistance to white settlement and land speculation. By 1795, residents of the Southwest Territory had largely succeeded on their own, with little military support from the United States. Such experiences led them to question whether federal leaders considered them to be citizens, on equal footing with white Americans in other parts of the new nation. "It is a fact not to be denied that the most extreme frontier family, in their poverty, are as much entitled to protection as the most wealthy member of Congress in his ease and luxury," cried George Roulstone, editor of the *Knoxville Gazette*. Roulstone had already concluded that the Southwest Territory should become a state because "the people would then, by their immediate representatives, have a right to vote upon the important questions of peace or war." Over time, federal inaction even convinced Blount to support statehood although it would end his authority as territorial governor. Statehood would guarantee that the federal government could neither overturn the hard-won expansionist victories of Tennessee Country whites nor quash their goal to rid the region of Native sovereignty entirely.[51]

As had been the case with the State of Franklin a decade earlier, American inhabitants of the Tennessee Country believed it better to construct a state government before consulting Congress about its admission to the Union. Fifty-five delegates convened in Knoxville in January 1796 and drafted a constitution for the new state of Tennessee. Convention delegates, most of whom had long chafed under restrictive federal rule, organized the state government in direct opposition to U.S. oversight and Native sovereignty. Not only did the constitution contain a provision that affirmed American intruders' property rights to Cherokee land south of the French Broad and Tennessee Rivers, but it also proclaimed that Tennessee's borders stretched from the high peaks of the Appalachian Mountains in the east to the Mississippi River in the west, a domain that included Cherokee and Chickasaw territory.[52]

Delegate Andrew Jackson, representing Cumberland Valley inhabitants from Davidson County, furthermore made the radical proposal that Tennessee exercised the "right of soil" within these borders. During the 1790s, white

Americans used the phrase "right of soil" to convey notions of land ownership. By offering this phrase for inclusion in the state constitution, Jackson intended that only the state of Tennessee should exercise property rights and administer land within its expansive borders, meaning that Cherokee and Chickasaw property ownership was invalid within the geographic boundaries of the new state. Worrying that Jackson's proposal, unless altered, also jeopardized speculators' North Carolina land claims and settlers' existing homesteads, convention delegates eventually added the necessary caveats that Tennessee exercised its right of soil only in a manner "consistent with the Constitution of the United States" and "the claim or claims of individuals, to any part of the soil which is recognized to them by the aforesaid cession act" of North Carolina. The final draft of Tennessee's 1796 constitution may not have been as militantly opposed to federal jurisdiction within the limits of the state as Jackson hoped. But delegates' decision to include "right of soil" nevertheless demonstrated early Tennesseans' opposition to Native sovereignty.[53] They inscribed settler colonialism into Tennessee's first constitution, and state leaders, including John Sevier, who was elected the state's first governor, would work incessantly to acquire Chickasaw and Cherokee territory over the ensuing decades.

Peace may have come to the Tennessee Country by the mid-1790s, but it was not by means of peaceful, orderly relations with Native nations, as the Washington administration had anticipated. Instead, it was whites' unchecked violence that had destroyed Chickamauga Cherokees' military resistance to American expansion and their unsanctioned alliance with the Chickasaws that had limited Creek attacks. Nevertheless, defeat did not silence Cherokees' sovereignty claims. Chickasaw and Cherokee leaders began to rely solely on diplomatic pressure to convince the United States to protect their national lands by marking the Tennessee Country's Native borders. The federal government's search for order, initiated seven years before at the Constitutional Convention, had failed.

Chapter 4

Creating and Enforcing International Borders in the Tennessee Country

In early October 1792, Charles McClung, John McKee, and David Campbell traveled to the home of Major David Craig, an officer in the Southwest Territory militia. Craig lived in the foothills of the Great Smoky Mountains along Nine Mile Creek, a tributary of the Little Tennessee River, and was on familiar terms with his Cherokee neighbors. His home was only twelve miles from Chota, and he frequently acted as a messenger between territory officials and Upper Town Cherokees. Governor Blount had ordered McClung, McKee, and Campbell to assemble at Craig's home and investigate a segment of the international border between the Cherokee Nation and the United States negotiated at the 1791 Holston Treaty conference. Blount was interested in the region's geography, especially the ridge that divided the Little River and Little Tennessee River, and he wanted to know whether any Americans lived illegally in the Cherokee Nation, a grievance Cherokees often repeated in their numerous communications with the United States.[1]

Over the next several weeks, McClung, McKee, and Campbell explored the border from Chilhowee Mountain to the Clinch River, a distance of around twenty-six miles and the section of the Holston Treaty boundary considered the most contentious. They found that a few whites did reside on Cherokee land but that most already had moved out of the nation. More significantly, the boundary commissioners reported that the geographical features of the landscape did not conform to the negotiated borders. Native leaders at the Holston Treaty conference had insisted that the U.S.-Cherokee border be "a straight course" that would intersect with the junction of the Tennessee River and a ridge dividing the

Little River and Little Tennessee River watersheds. Yet, as McClung would later recount, "there was no ridge answering the discription of the dividing ridge." The commissioners eventually settled on an arbitrary boundary that would locate Coyatee, Talasee, Settico, Chota, and Chilhowee within the United States. The boundary commissioners recommended that the border be revised to include these Native communities in the Cherokee Nation, and they submitted a map of their findings to Governor Blount. The commissioners' "line of experiment"— so called because it did not represent an official border on the landscape—would serve as the basis for Daniel Smith's "Map of the Tennassee Government," published in a 1793 promotional tract to encourage American migration to the Tennessee Country. The Cherokee-U.S. border drawn on Smith's map corresponded with a fictitious rugged mountainous ridge, which was nothing like the region's actual geography. Smith, the secretary of the Southwest Territory, later admitted that his map "was in many respects imperfect." Knowing local whites' disdain for Cherokee sovereignty, subsequent U.S. officials wondered whether Smith's false boundary might have been intentionally deceptive.[2]

Although it would serve as a significant geographical reference, the border identified by Campbell, McClung, and McKee in 1792 would not become the permanent boundary line because no Cherokees had participated in the survey. During the Holston Treaty negotiations in July 1791 and again at a meeting with Secretary Knox in January 1792, Cherokee leaders emphasized that their nation must approve the new border. Even Governor Blount, who coveted Native land, knew that the border would not be legitimate unless Cherokees took part in its survey. Blount had instructed the three boundary commissioners to mark the border if Cherokees met them at Craig's home, but if they did not McClung, McKee, and Campbell were to spend most their time merely investigating the region's geography. Cherokees knew that they possessed the power to legitimize the boundary. Their refusal to participate demonstrated their opposition, a common strategy of resistance among Native peoples who disagreed with imposed treaty borders.[3]

Yet Cherokees *did* want to mark their border with the United States, just not with Blount in charge.[4] The Hopewell Treaties and the 1791 Treaty of Holston included clear descriptions of boundary lines that divided Native land from U.S territory. In these negotiations, Native diplomats and federal representatives agreed that clear borders would create peace and order in the Tennessee Country by separating Cherokees and Chickasaws from white intruders, thereby limiting violent interactions. Yet by the mid-1790s these boundaries existed only

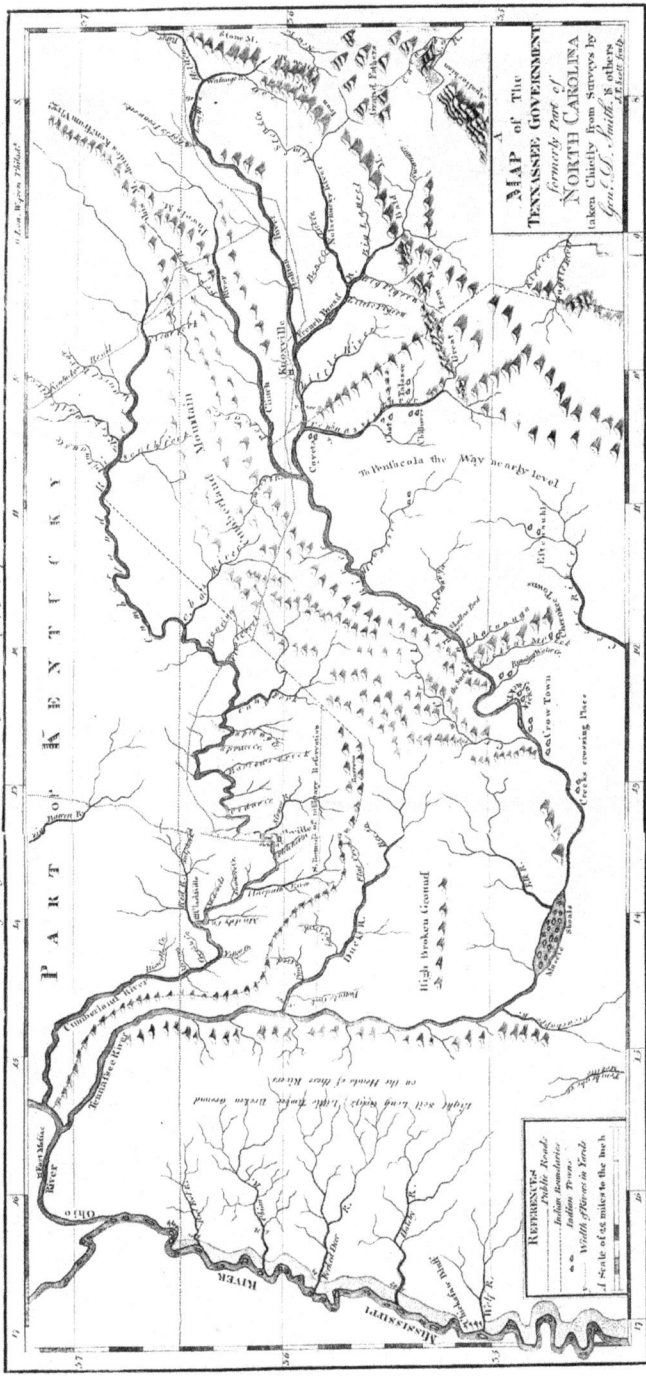

A Map of the Tennassee Government formerly Part of North Carolina, Mathew Carey, 1795. Tennessee State Library and Archives. Originally published in 1793, this map, based on the surveys of Southwest Territory secretary Daniel Smith, perpetuated controversy over the true course of the Holston Treaty border.

as imagined geographical markers; no permanent borders had been surveyed despite previous treaty negotiations. Only after Chickasaw and Cherokee diplomats put increased pressure on federal officials in 1796 did Congress organize a survey party for the Tennessee Country. Months later, Cherokee officials and U.S. boundary commissioners made their way across the region's mountains and valleys to mark a formal border between the Cherokee Nation and the United States.

Clear international borders were no longer solely the imagined projections of European and American settler empires; they had become Indigenous tools to resist colonization as well. During previous decades, Native peoples and white intruders had demonstrated their localized visions of sovereignty and territorial control through cycles of peaceful negotiations and violent attacks. Now, the survey and subsequent enforcement of boundary lines done at the behest of many Chickasaw and Cherokee leaders represented a new direction in the federal government's relationship with Native nations and local whites. The bordered landscape disrupted speculators' ongoing attempts to commodify Native territory, facilitated the identification of illegal white squatters, and enabled federal troops to evict intruders from the Cherokee Nation beginning in 1798.

By demanding that the federal government mark their nation's boundaries in the Tennessee Country, Cherokee and Chickasaw leaders made powerful assertions of Native sovereignty using a strategy that was widespread throughout the eighteenth-century Atlantic World. Leaders of the infant United States understood that their new nation's legitimacy depended on international acceptance by European powers. In treaty agreements with the United States, Native peoples like the Cherokees and Chickasaws sought similar recognition of their national sovereignty, and they were surprisingly successful. Federalist politicians of the 1790s acknowledged Native sovereignty, particularly in the Southeast. Many envisioned a possible "long-term coexistence" between the United States and the region's Indigenous nations.[5] That the federal government spent the time and money to meticulously mark the dividing lines between the United States and the Cherokee and Chickasaw Nations proves that at least some U.S. officials did envision a future where Native peoples and Americans experienced sovereignty within their stable, permanent national limits. White intruders' unending attempts to disrupt the survey of Indigenous borders in the Tennessee Country reveal the very real threat of Cherokee and Chickasaw boundaries to the expansionist geographies of settlers and speculators, a threat realized when U.S. troops evicted white intruders from the Cherokee Nation.

Renewed Interest in the Southwest Territory

Federal officials initially hoped to mark the Holston Treaty boundary within a year of its negotiation, but ongoing violence in the Tennessee Country and the distraction of war in the Northwest Territory precluded any formal survey of the boundary line for several years. American victory over the confederation of Native nations north of the Ohio River in the final months of 1794 finally allowed U.S. leaders to devote more attention to affairs in the Southwest Territory. Whereas the federal government had tacitly ignored periodic military attacks against the Cherokee Nation by white settlers, national officials like new secretary of war Timothy Pickering took a more active role in administering Indian affairs beginning in 1795. Pickering had long despised frontier whites for threatening Federalist visions for orderly governance premised on controlled national expansion and federally regulated land transactions.[6]

Cherokees directly benefitted from Pickering's interest in the Tennessee Country. Pickering recognized that the financial stability of the United States depended on the federal government's enforcement of Native nations' boundary lines. The new secretary of war immediately tried to cut administrative and military expenses in the Southwest Territory, a goal that could be accomplished only by ending the localized violence that plagued the region. He also learned from Silas Dinsmoor, the Cherokees' federal Indian agent, and David Henley, federal paymaster of the Southwest Territory, that Cherokees complained "of old settlers on their lands," whom they wished to "have removed, and the intrusion of new adventurers prevented." Outraged that Southwest Territory whites continued to invade the Cherokee Nation, Pickering demanded that Blount take action. "Tranquility on the frontiers," he lectured, "is not to be expected while we permit our Citizens to encroach on Indian lands." In response, Blount did make several halfhearted attempts enforce the Holston Treaty boundary in 1795, even as he and other territory officials made plans to counter federal authority by organizing the state of Tennessee.[7]

Legislating Federal Authority

As Americans in the Tennessee Country debated the merits of statehood, Congress debated new legislation to strengthen federal authority in the region.

The Constitution granted the federal government sole authority to regulate relations with Native nations. U.S. officials exercised this newfound power not only through numerous treaty agreements but also in a series of legislation known colloquially as the Trade and Intercourse Acts. Congress passed the first of these acts in 1790 and a revised version in 1793, both of which prohibited Americans' invasion of Native lands, controlled the interactions between traders and Native nations, and attempted to punish whites who committed crimes within Native borders. The 1793 act also codified Washington's goal "to promote civilization among the friendly Indian tribes" by encouraging Indigenous peoples to live like white yeoman farmers. Both acts were only temporary, necessitating that Congress reevaluate the parameters of the United States' relationship with Native nations once again in 1795, a time when many federal officials, like Pickering and Washington, were growing increasingly committed to bringing order to the trans-Appalachian West.[8]

Debate on the bill exposed the contested nature of American expansion, with Federalists preferring an orderly, controlled expansion directed by the national government and nascent Democratic-Republicans favoring decentralized governance and fewer restrictions on whites' access to Native land. The initial draft of the 1796 Trade and Intercourse Act broke from previous iterations by describing an international boundary that would separate the United States from Native nations. Stretching from Lake Erie to Spanish Florida, the proposed border conformed to existing treaty agreements with Indigenous peoples living both south and north of the Ohio River. The boundary in the Tennessee Country, for example, duplicated the Holston Treaty border of 1791. Federalists had struggled for years to control frontier whites, whom they blamed for instigating violence and disorder in the trans-Appalachian West. When American "citizens went over the boundary lines," argued Federalist James Crabb of Maryland, "war was the consequence." A clear and firm boundary legislated by Congress and administered by the president would be more effective than disconnected Indian treaties that white intruders often ignored.[9]

Partisan divide over American expansion and property rights exploded onto the floor of the House of Representatives after the bill's reading on April 8, 1796. Federalists and Democratic-Republicans debated the bill's fifth section, which punished anyone who attempted to settle or survey "any lands belonging, or secured, or granted by treaty with the United States, to any Indian tribe" with forfeiture of their land claims, imprisonment of up to a year, and a $1,000 fine.

It authorized the president to use force to remove white invaders from Native territory. Fines and imprisonments were punitive measures of the 1793 Trade and Intercourse Act; even opponents of the 1796 bill generally approved of these tactics. Yet the possibility of forfeiture incensed many representatives because it voided the federal government's contractual obligations. North Carolina's 1789 cession of its western land claims to the United States included the provision, argued Democratic-Republican James Holland of North Carolina, "that the faith of the General Government was explicitly pledged to enable these citizens to survey those lands, and to authorize the Governor to execute the grants." The treaties now in force, however, contradicted this agreement. The federal government, continued Holland, was "bound to extinguish this Indian claim, and put the injured citizens in possession of their realized property, which they had so long been kept out of, and so justly bought." Other opponents of the bill's fifth section further emphasized the hypocrisy of confiscating real property from American citizens as if they were British Loyalists. "Such a penalty," noted western Pennsylvania's Albert Gallatin, "would not have been thought of any where but on the frontier. It was greater than the crime would justify." The threat of forfeiture was further proof of federal discrimination.[10]

By the late eighteenth century, people across the Atlantic World recognized contracts as authentic representations of individual landownership. Governments' enforcement of such "paper property" through the rule of law proved their legitimacy to govern. This was especially pertinent in the European colonization of North America, where speculators claimed, surveyed, and exchanged massive amounts of western territory, a process that historian Jane Kaminsky calls "the transformation of earth into paper." Indeed, scholarly interpretations of the First Party System often stress Federalists' commitment to the stability and permanence of property ownership, especially real estate. When House Federalists such as James Cooper of New York argued that speculators who violated U.S. treaties by ignoring Native sovereignty should lose their land claims, representatives apparently broke from foundational tenets of their political ideology by favoring permanent boundary lines with Native peoples over Americans' access to legitimate forms of property.[11]

Yet Federalist opposition to speculators and settlers of Cherokee and Chickasaw land, individuals who possessed title through North Carolina land grants, was less about property ownership and more about a commitment to centralized governance, a vision that prioritized federal treaty law and control over the continental interior. When pressed by critics of the forfeiture provision, Federalists responded by highlighting the supremacy of U.S. treaties over North Carolina state law. James Hillhouse of Connecticut, the most vocal proponent of restricting speculators' access to Native land, believed that Indians "were justly entitled to the lands which they possessed" because "this right and title . . . had been expressly recognized by the United States in the Treaties they had made." Hillhouse downplayed the nature of North Carolina grants as something less than real property, describing them merely as "the pre-emption right of such people to Indian land, which is not a title, but a right only of becoming, in preference to all others, owners of the land, by some future grant or cession to be made by the Indians." The United States would recognize these North Carolina preemption claims as legitimate land grants only if Indigenous peoples ceded the territory.[12] Chickasaws and Cherokees determined when and where grantees could access their Tennessee Country property, according to Federalist leaders.

Forfeiture was necessary to prevent conflict with Cherokees and Chickasaws. Though many Federalists had supported the expensive war for conquest in the Northwest when their land grants had conflicted with Native peoples' homelands in the Ohio Valley, a war in the South would be of little personal benefit to most national leaders. Moreover, the widespread speculation of Tennessee Country lands meant that the United States could not realize its goal of repaying wartime debts through land sales, as was the case in the Northwest Territory. Defending white intruders' right to Chickasaw and Cherokee land would only complicate matters for the federal government. Theodore Sedgwick of Massachusetts bluntly explained that the forfeiture clause was simply "saying no more to the people than, you shall not go upon this territory to prove war." Federalists nimbly jettisoned their commitment to whites' property rights when speculators' possession of Native land jeopardized peace and threatened effective national governance, a marked contrast to the more localized visions of Democratic-Republicans in the House of Representatives and in the Tennessee Country. Nevertheless, the forfeiture clause passed only because of the support of several Democratic-Republicans from the eastern states, revealing the sectional nature of U.S. land policy, Indian affairs, and American state power.[13] The Trade and Intercourse Act of 1796 expanded federal authority over Indian affairs as never before and authorized the federal government to survey boundary lines in the Tennessee Country. But it would be Cherokee and Chickasaw diplomats who ultimately provided the necessary pressure on the United States to create these borders, first negotiated over a decade earlier with the Hopewell Treaties and once again with the 1791 Treaty of Holston.

Cherokees and Chickasaws Demand a Survey

In the final months of 1796, Native women and men traveled to Philadelphia seeking an audience with President Washington and James McHenry, the newly appointed secretary of war. Members of Washington's cabinet could not have imagined the dramatic show of Native power they were about to encounter. Cherokee, Chickasaw, Choctaw, and Creek representatives arrived together at the capital, where they joined Shawnees, Wyandots, Ojibwes, Miamis, Delawares, Potawatomis, Odawas, and other Indigenous peoples from the Ohio Country, there to renegotiate portions of the Treaty of Greenville. Taking the opportunity to meet in conference and "be all as one people," Indigenous diplomats hinted at a shared opposition to the United States. Red Pole (Painted Pole/Messquakenoe), a Shawnee leader, explained that in a previous treaty negotiation the president had "told me our lands were good and that we should take care of them—the speech spoke for itself—for if our lands were not good, the Americans would not have become so great a Nation as they now are." U.S. greatness depended on the colonization of Native territory. This demonstration of Indigenous unity, especially expressed by Shawnees, known for their ability to organize Native military alliances, must have distressed federal officials, who had worked for decades to foment disunity among North America's Indigenous peoples.[14]

Native southerners' trip to Philadelphia was not solely to build alliances but also to pressure U.S. leaders to survey and enforce treaty boundary lines. Creeks, Chickasaws, Choctaws, and Cherokees all emphasized the massive increase in American migration across the Appalachian Mountains, which threatened both the relative peace that had existed for the past several years and Native nations' sovereignty. Piominko, the leading Chickasaw at the conference, described the population explosion of whites near the Cumberland River, in particular, and worried that they would soon threaten his nation. "Our boundaries are not yet marked," explained Piominko, "and frontier Settlers when they make encroachments on our hunting Ground will readily find an excuse in their ignorance of our limits. We wish therefore that the president will order the line to be run immediately, and so marked, as to put it out of the power of any person to excuse Encroachments on that Ground." The federal government had guaranteed these borders in numerous treaty agreements, and now it was time for the United States to enforce them.[15]

John Watts, a leader of Cherokee Lower Towns, not only echoed Piominko's emphasis on boundary lines but also narrated federal impotence to shame the Washington administration into recognizing Native nations' sovereignty. He reminded McHenry that white perpetrators remained unpunished for the murder of Cherokees during the first months of 1796. His nation's treaty agreements required justice, but federal inaction "greatly weakened his belief in such promises." Watts thought "the laws of Congress . . . very good; but as they have to reach so far they get weak and will be of no use to the Indians unless they can be executed with the same good intention with which they have been made." After directly criticizing the United States, Watts pivoted to the Holston Treaty boundary. From Cherokees' many interactions with Governor Blount and other leaders of the Southwest Territory, they knew that U.S. officials often had a financial interest in Native land. Watts, therefore, demanded that "no person should be appointed by the United States [to mark the Cherokee border] who is a Speculator, or who may be supposed to have any Interest which might prejudice them in favour of the Whites or against the Cherokees." He also reminded McHenry that a group of Cherokee officials would accompany the U.S. boundary commission both to legitimize the border and to provide oversight of the American surveyors. Watts even appointed himself as one of the Cherokee boundary commissioners, along with Will Elders and The Bark (Ohadlokee), who were likely among Watts's closest allies in the Lower Towns.[16]

Both Piominko and Watts got their wishes. McHenry promised the Native diplomats that the federal government would defend their sovereignty from trespassing whites and begin surveying the Cherokee border on April 1. American officials would contact Watts regarding where the Cherokee commissioners should meet them.[17] Chickasaw and Cherokee leaders made their way back to the Tennessee Country in the early months of 1797 cautiously optimistic that the United States was finally committed to surveying boundary lines from previous treaties and would enforce their borders against the region's white residents. They would not be disappointed. During 1797 and 1798, federal commissioners not only located the U.S. boundary with the Cherokee Nation but also forcibly evicted illegal white settlers found within Indigenous territory. Chickasaws would participate in the federal survey of their boundaries in 1800.

Beginning the New Border

Federal officials began preparing for the boundary survey promised with the Hopewell and Holston treaties soon after Native leaders departed from Philadelphia. McHenry had informed Cherokee diplomats that Benjamin Hawkins and Andrew Pickens would be two of the federal government's boundary commissioners. Hawkins had recently replaced William Blount as the superintendent for Indian affairs of the Southern Department, and Silas Dinsmoor had recommended Pickens, who had represented the United States in past negotiations, because of his good reputation among the Cherokees. Despite Watts's insistence that no commissioner have financial interests in Native land, Washington and McHenry selected James Winchester as the third commissioner. Winchester was a prominent Tennessee politician, land speculator, and militia commander. He certainly possessed the necessary local knowledge to survey the Cherokee border, but choosing him was a capitulation to Tennessee Country whites who wanted a Tennessean on the boundary commission. McHenry directed the three commissioners "to ascertain and mark the boundary lines agreeably to treaties between the [southern] Indian Nations and the United States." It was important that Hawkins, Pickens, and Winchester communicate with Native leaders so that they could appoint their own boundary commissioners and together create permanent, visible borders across the American South. Commissioners could even order federal troops to accompany them should they encounter any resistance from local inhabitants.[18] The U.S. border with Native nations had to be marked to last many years and be obvious to anyone who crossed it.

Hawkins and Pickens took to the task of locating the boundary lines with enthusiasm. The two men were familiar with one another and had represented the United States at the Creek Treaty of Colerain, negotiated the previous fall. Though McHenry had ordered the commissioners to locate the U.S. border with the Creek Nation first, Hawkins instead prioritized the Cherokee boundary because of the greater degree of white encroachment in the Tennessee Country. The two federal commissioners' urgency to begin surveying the Cherokee boundary was genuine. In only a month they had recruited two professional surveyors, Joseph Whitner and John Clark Kilpatrick, to join the commission; made preparations for federal soldiers to accompany them in Tennessee; informed Cherokee leaders that the commissioners wished to meet with representatives of their nation; and journeyed across the Appalachian Mountains from South Carolina to the Cherokee Nation, arriving at the fortified Tellico Blockhouse on March 31, 1797.[19]

The boundary commissioners entered a region on edge, with a population ill prepared to welcome agents of the federal government. Six months before, two Tennesseans had murdered two Cherokee hunters in Kentucky near the

Cumberland River. The attack was especially reprehensible because one victim suffered from a physical disability and the other was the prominent Cherokee diplomat Red Bird, who had participated in numerous treaty negotiations over the past decade. The killings were more than another example of frontier violence; they were an assassination, designed to disrupt federal Indian policy. Many white inhabitants of the Tennessee Country had known for years that they lived on Native land, as outlined in prior federal treaties with the Cherokee Nation. Until 1797, these intruders, numbering around five hundred families, had never faced the possibility of eviction. Yet Hawkins and Pickens embodied the very real threat that they might lose their land should the federal boundary commission complete its survey of the Cherokee-U.S. border. Indeed, Red Bird's murderers hailed from Powell Valley, a community where many residents lived on what was unquestionably Cherokee land. War offered Tennesseans a possible alternative to forced removal. According to future French king Louis-Philippe, who toured the Tennessee Country in 1797, many white Tennesseans "would like a war with the Indians so a new treaty can strip them of the coveted lands." The strategy appeared to be working once again in the spring of 1797. Cherokees did retaliate for the murders by killing several white men, one of whom lived in Powell Valley.[20] White settlers and speculators, for the most part, had benefitted from military conflict with their Native neighbors, which often resulted in land cessions, so they wanted to perpetuate violence for their own benefit once again.

The boundary survey would increase local whites' hostility toward the federal government and the Cherokee Nation. For three weeks after their arrival at the Tellico Blockhouse, Hawkins and Pickens made preliminary investigations of the border. Most Tennesseans initially cooperated with the commissioners. Local leaders accompanied Hawkins and Pickens as they scoured the landscape of Blount County, Tennessee, looking for the ridge that divided the Little River from the Little Tennessee River and searching for where it intersected the Tennessee River. Others provided the two federal agents with food and lodging. Yet by mid-April prominent Tennesseans began to disrupt the commissioners' work. The United States had previously capitulated to white expansionists. That federal boundary commissioners were unwilling to do so shocked and enraged many Tennesseans. "The situation rouses great anger against the federal government," noticed Louis-Philippe. "Everyone makes his own sort of threat, and some even talk about pillaging the trading post at Tellico!" White residents of the Tennessee Valley expected Hawkins and Pickens to replicate the 1792 line of experiment or negotiate with Cherokees for a land cession.[21]

John Sevier and William Blount offered especially powerful opposition to the boundary survey. Governor Sevier resented the intrusion of the federal government into what he considered a state matter. Native borders threatened Tennessee's sovereignty over all land within its expansive boundaries. Not only did Sevier try to delay the survey after Hawkins and Pickens arrived in Tennessee, but he also likely influenced Richard Sparks, a commander of federal troops within Tennessee and his future son-in-law, to instruct his soldiers to disobey the commissioners' orders. Blount issued protests directly to the Washington administration from his new position as one of Tennessee's U.S. senators. He took it as a personal affront that U.S. officials would not merely confirm the line of experiment he had organized while governor of the Southwest Territory. According to Blount, Pickens and Hawkins were "strangers in the country," unacquainted with the Tennessee Valley's geography, whereas local officials had identified the line in 1792. Blount's implication was clear: the boundary was a local matter, and the federal government should defer to white Tennesseans. During his ensuing six terms as governor, Sevier would remain a powerful opponent of the federal government's meddling in the Tennessee Country, even as Blount would lose credibility with U.S. officials after his 1797 impeachment for attempting to organize an invasion of Spain's Gulf Coast territory.[22]

Cherokees and the Federal Boundary Commission

Whereas whites worried about the federal boundary commissioners' presence in the Tennessee Country, Cherokees largely welcomed it. Only a week after their arrival, thirteen Cherokee diplomats met with the boundary commission and, according to the group's speaker, Little Woman Holder of Hiwassee Town, "rejoiced at the expectation of having their line closed." The presence of The Bark, whom Watts had chosen as a boundary commissioner in late 1796, was further proof of Cherokees' support for surveying their international border with the United States. Hawkins and Pickens had intended to hold a more formal conference with Cherokee leaders, but Native people feared for their safety in light of the recent killings. Some wondered whether the two commissioners planned to pressure their nation for another land cession. Until Cherokees felt safe to travel to the Tellico Blockhouse, Little Woman Holder recommended that the commissioners investigate the border but make no immediate decisions. Cherokees were particularly anxious that the surveyors "hear both sides and do justice," not merely locate the border to appease white Tennesseans.[23]

Cherokee leaders reiterated this point to Hawkins and Pickens when they met in late April at Tuskegee. Though likely selected for its convenient location adjacent to the Tellico Blockhouse along the Tellico River, the town was also a symbol of Native power. Tuskegee residents lived within sight of Fort Loudoun and even planted their crops around its ruins. British troops had occupied the fort during the Seven Years' War until the force surrendered to Native soldiers in 1760. Cherokee families inhabited the post after their victory. When viewing the site nearly forty years later, Louis-Philippe found only "a little rubble and a few irregularities of terrain to commemorate the fort's existence."[24] As Hawkins and Pickens began negotiating with Cherokees about the Holston boundary, they could not have failed to notice the ruined fort, a historical commemoration of Native power in the Tennessee Country.

The Cherokees' preparation for the boundary survey was a national project. Native diplomats from across the Cherokee Nation attended the Tuskegee conference. According to the American commissioners, "almost every town in the nation has sent 1, 2, or 3" leaders, amounting to 147 "chiefs and warriors," a tabulation that did not include the Cherokee women and children who would have been in attendance, as was common practice. Native negotiators hailed from both the Upper Towns and Lower Towns, the nation's primary centers of political power. They included Dragging Canoe's brother The Badger and Watts, both former Chickamaugas, and Little Turkey, the most prominent Upper Town Cherokee leader. On the first day of the conference, Cherokees appointed four boundary surveyors to accompany Hawkins and Pickens in marking the border. The Bark of the Lower Towns was among these four. More significantly, however, Cherokees emphasized that "we have appointed two old men and two young ones," a reference to the generational divide within Cherokee society between elderly political leaders and younger Cherokees who traditionally led the nation in battle. The regional dimension of the boundary survey was on display the next day, when Native diplomats identified eight other Cherokee boundary commissioners and agreed "to divide the line between them . . . four at a time." Bloody Fellow, Turtle at Home (Selukuki Wohellengh), Doublehead, and Cayilcatee would represent the Lower Town Cherokees during the boundary survey. They would share responsibilities with four Upper Town Cherokees from the community of Cowee.[25] The survey was of national interest and therefore included Cherokees from both across the nation and across several generations.

Cherokee officials concluded the four-day conference with one final attempt to alter the Holston boundary near the Cumberland River, stressing that they had never intended to cede any land there. "From the manner the treaty [of Holston] was made there was great cause of difference of opinion" regarding the boundary line, explained Little Turkey and The Badger in a talk to President Adams. They believed Cherokee diplomats had "never agreed to it." Nevertheless, many Cherokees expressed confidence in Hawkins and Pickens to survey the border properly. Not only did both men have reputations for fair dealings with Native southerners, but Cherokees knew that twelve of their own surveyors would accompany the U.S. commissioners to guarantee that the boundary aligned with national leaders' understanding of the Holston Treaty.[26] The Cherokees' presence within the U.S. boundary commission would give the new international border the necessary legitimacy lacking in the 1792 line of experiment.

Cherokees and Chickasaws Mark Their Borders

The boundary commission left Tellico on April 29 and began its survey of the Cherokee Nation's border with the United States, a task that would last until late October. For a week the party remained near the Holston, Tennessee, and Clinch Rivers, investigating the landscape in and around both Cherokee and white settlements. This work was relatively easy, given that Hawkins and Pickens had spent so much time in the area before the Cherokee conference. The party then traveled over the Cumberland Plateau, arriving at Nashville on May 16. James Winchester, the third U.S. boundary commissioner, met his colleagues on their arrival to the Cumberland Valley in what was likely a tense first interaction. Pickens and Hawkins knew of Winchester's speculation in Native land and suspected that he had intentionally delayed meeting with them to disrupt the boundary survey. Winchester professed his innocence of any ill intention. Yet the fact that white Tennesseans maintained "much confidence in [Winchester] respecting the line" and that state leaders considered him "honest," compared to their vocal disapproval of Hawkins and Pickens, supported the commissioners' suspicions that Winchester was more interested in facilitating American expansion than supporting Native sovereignty and federal treaty law. Nevertheless, Winchester officially joined the boundary commission on May 20 and accompanied the U.S. and Cherokee surveyors as they journeyed south to identify the dividing ridge between the Duck and Cumberland Rivers, in accordance with the Holston and Hopewell Treaties.[27]

Cherokee influence on the survey increased as the body entered the rugged, sparsely populated region south of Nashville. The commissioners had made sure to resupply, replace their horses, and hire new packhorse men, chain carriers, and a doctor from the Cumberland settlements, knowing that they would have few opportunities as the party neared the Duck River. A fellow traveler in 1797 described the region between the Duck and Cumberland Rivers as "a very mountainous and hilly country," in many places too steep for horseback travel, with soil so rocky as to penetrate shoes. The boundary commissioners likewise became "so much in the woods" that Hawkins felt "almost cut off from society." They struggled to navigate the difficult terrain and averaged only nine miles per day, occasionally failing to mark even four miles of the border. Yet Indigenous peoples knew the area well, having hunted and traveled throughout the Tennessee Country for generations; the American commissioners frequently commented on the many roads that crisscrossed the landscape. Bloody Fellow, Turtle at Home, Doublehead, and Cayilcatee provided food and offered information about the landscape when the American guides could not locate the proper boundary line. In some places their familiarity with the region meant that Cherokees were essentially leading the commission. American officials depended on Native knowledge to survey the line properly.[28]

The Cherokee commissioners were well aware of their power and importance to the survey's success and pressured the federal surveyors to draw the boundary in accordance with their nation's wishes. At least three of the four Native commissioners had been leading figures among the Chickamauga Cherokees, and the Lower Town diplomats at Tuskegee likely had appointed them because of their longstanding commitment to Cherokee sovereignty. In several instances, the Cherokees brought the party to a halt over the proper course of the border. As the surveyors searched for the ridge dividing the Tennessee River watershed from that of the Cumberland River, Hawkins, Pickens, and Winchester learned that the accompanying "Indian commissioners were discontendid with their situation." Although their grievances included a lack of necessary supplies and rations, Cherokees' central complaint was "that the course [the survey was] going would deprive them of much more land than the Nation ever had the idea they should loose." The Cherokees were especially concerned about land around Crab Orchard on the Cumberland Plateau—for good reason. According to a contemporary observer, Crab Orchard consisted of a "natural meadow, containing many hundred acres, and covered throughout its whole extent with a tall, rich grass, surrounded on every side by the neighbouring mountains." Springs and salt licks could also be found throughout the area and would have attracted wild game for Native hunters. The Cherokee commissioners were loath to lose the valuable territory and wished to "return to their Nation to consult them, before they proceeded any further" in marking the border.[29]

The U.S. officials understood the importance of Native peoples' consent for the long-term goal of permanent, clearly marked borders and did their best to placate the Cherokee commissioners. Hawkins increased their rations, agreed to share supplies, and replaced their tired horses, even drafting a certificate to articulate this new agreement at Bloody Fellow's behest. Most importantly, the Americans dismissed the Cherokees' concerns about losing valuable hunting territory as unnecessary. "As to the course of the line," promised Hawkins to the Cherokee commissioners, "we could not say where it would go, but we were certain it would never go near the crab orchard." The Native officials assented to the Americans' promises, and the party initially resumed its journey.[30]

But the Cherokees continued to voice their opposition as the commission traced the dividing ridge between the Duck and Cumberland Rivers north toward Kentucky over the next three weeks. On June 18, Hawkins and Pickens agreed that their ongoing survey might be incorrect and halted the group until they could estimate where the new border might terminate. Commissioners wondered whether it would intersect the Cumberland River in Kentucky—as outlined in the Holston Treaty—or miss it entirely. Against Winchester's objections, they decided to survey the border to Walton's Road, a trace through the Cherokee Nation that connected Nashville to the Tennessee Valley, and then return to East Tennessee for supplies before marking other portions of the border in closer proximity to American settlements. When confronted by his fellow commissioners, Winchester tried to delay the remaining survey, likely to provide white intruders in the Cherokee Nation time to harvest their crops. But Hawkins, Pickens, and the Cherokee commissioners, already suspicious of Winchester's motives, decided to continue surveying the border between the Great Smoky Mountains and the Kentucky Trace, believing it essential for peace to finish the survey of this region before the beginning of hunting season. By late June the party had returned to Fort Southwest Point, a federal fort constructed during the year along the Clinch River, and they remained in the area for several weeks. New Cherokee surveyors joined the American officials before the boundary commission began marking the Cherokee-U.S. border northwest of Knoxville.[31]

For parts of the next four months, the boundary commission continued its survey of the international boundary without additional recorded objections from Cherokee officials. The commissioners physically inscribed the boundary on the landscape as they went, marking trees at mile intervals with "C" on one side for the Cherokee Nation and "US" to indicate U.S. territory. In some places the commission even cut a road through the wilderness to facilitate the survey process, a strategy designed as "a double security, against its being passed without a knowledge of it."[32] A clearly marked border was essential because it would indicate the territorial limits of both the United States and the Cherokee Nation to inhabitants of the Tennessee Country.

When the boundary commission completed the survey, Crab Orchard and much of the valuable hunting lands on the Cumberland Plateau remained within the Cherokee Nation, a testament to the Cherokees' influence on the border. The American commissioners all knew that they had to satisfy the Native officials for the border to be legitimate. Indeed, after Hawkins and Pickens left the Tennessee Valley, Turtle at Home, the son of Attakullakulla and himself a leading Cherokee diplomat from the Lower Towns, and other Lower Town Cherokees met with Commissioner Winchester and accompanied him along the nearly 140 miles of the Cherokee-U.S. line from Walton's Road to the Cumberland River in October 1797. This was the portion of the boundary that commissioners had considered so contentious earlier in June. Yet, according to Winchester, "The Turtle at Home and five other of the lower Cherokees . . . appeared well satisfied with the border." It was probably the truth. One of the Native commissioners carved a likeness of himself in a tree near the border's intersection with the Cumberland River to symbolize his nation's approval, and all Cherokees remained with Winchester for the entire survey.[33] Even the Tennessee land speculator had to rely on Native knowledge to complete the proper international border between the United States and the Cherokee Nation.

Winchester experienced a similar situation when marking the Chickasaw Nation's boundary with the United States in late 1800. This survey was much less of a priority than that of the Cherokee Nation because of the distance between Chickasaw territory and American settlements in the Cumberland Valley. Chickasaw leaders George Colbert (Tootemastubbe) and John Brown (Hulltewmarlatha) nevertheless guided the U.S. boundary commission for over 150 miles as it marked the border on the landscape. The survey began at the same tree "marked U.S. : C.I." from the 1797 Cherokee boundary, but instead of traveling northeast toward the Tennessee Valley the Chickasaw and U.S. surveyors marked a line northwest, following the dividing ridge between the Tennessee and Cumberland Rivers to its intersection with the Ohio River in Kentucky. For the first two weeks of the survey, Winchester and accompanying U.S. commissioner Captain Edward Butler stumbled through the dense canebrakes and rugged landscape alongside a detachment of federal troops and at least one enslaved laborer named Neptune. They often had to retrace their steps after realizing errors in the survey. Once Colbert and Brown joined the commission on October 22, however, the process went much more smoothly, with no more major mistakes until the party reached the Ohio River on December 2, 1800.[34] As had been the case three years before with the Cherokees, the successful survey of the Chickasaw-U.S. border depended on Native knowledge of the landscape.

Tennesseans Oppose the Survey

White inhabitants of the Tennessee Country attempted to shape the Cherokee boundary survey to suit their local interests, but they would not be as successful as their Native neighbors. Throughout 1797, the federal commissioners had encountered hostility from white Tennesseans, who had been protesting the Trade and Intercourse Act since its passage a year before and were worried that Hawkins and Pickens would disregard their settlements' locations when surveying the border with the Cherokee Nation. They had tried to intrude on the commissioners' conference with the Cherokee Nation in April, and Hawkins had even heard a rumor that white settlers might attack Cherokee towns to delay the survey. The potential for violence so disturbed Agent Dinsmoor that he felt "more safe in the interior of the Indian country than on the frontiers of our own in the time of disturbance," a statement that must have come as a shock to Secretary McHenry, accustomed as he was to accounts of Native attacks. Yet the boundary commission encountered no direct confrontation with local whites in the early weeks of the survey. In fact, white inhabitants of the Cumberland Valley supported the commission's work because it opened new land for white settlers and speculators.[35]

As boundary commissioners made their way north from Knoxville in July 1797, however, they met militant opposition from local white settlers intent on halting the surveyors' progress. The flashpoint occurred in mid-July, as the federal surveyors crossed the Clinch River north into Powell Valley. Commissioners learned that more than three hundred men had already assembled there to prevent the survey. The community of 1,200 white intruders knew that they lived in Cherokee territory, but they were not squatters with no legitimate justification for inhabiting Indigenous land. Not only had they purchased land claims from speculators before the ratification of the Holston Treaty or the passage of the Trade and Intercourse Acts, but they had also defended their settlements from Native attacks in previous years. "We Bought our Lands paid deer for it Both by the Sword propertity [property] and money," explained militia officer John Hunt. "To be turned off from our Lands and livings like a perceel of heathens will Look very unhuman and I expect will Cause a revelution." Settlers were "to a man determined to stop [the commissioners] from running the line." They succeeded, at least temporarily. The boundary commissioners remained in the area for nearly a week, likely worried that settlers would overpower them if they continued their work. Hawkins wanted U.S. troops to be prepared should Powell Valley inhabitants attack the commission.[36]

Settlers organized a formal conference with the boundary commission to diffuse the situation. Negotiations commenced on July 24 between federal officials and a delegation of ten men that included two justices of the peace, two militia captains, and a road overseer, all significant local political leaders. White settlers began by appealing to the commissioners' sense of justice. They emphasized their loss of property and the personal injury that would result should their families be forced to leave their settlements on land they had purchased from North Carolina. Locals knew that Hawkins, Pickens, and Winchester had "stoped the line to gratify the Indians" and hoped that the commissioners would similarly postpone surveying the portion of the border north of Knoxville. In response, the three U.S. officials made it clear that they had postponed the survey of the boundary west of the Cumberland Plateau only until the line could be investigated further. They also reiterated their duty to run the line as described in the Holston Treaty and as agreed upon with Cherokee leaders, who had demanded the border's survey for the past several years. It was important given "the present situation of our political affairs," continued the commissioners, that the "United States should preserve their faith plighted to the Indians" so that the Cherokees would not form an alliance with European empires. The survey of the U.S.-Cherokee border across a tiny valley in the Tennessee mountains had implications for the entire Atlantic World. Federal commissioners insisted that they press on to mark the boundary.[37]

After a day's recess, the conference continued without tension. The federal commissioners worked with Powell Valley residents to draft a plea to President Adams. Elijah Chisholm, speaking on behalf of Powell Valley intruders, knew that the commissioners intended to continue the survey. There was no way to stop them except by direct force, something that they would not sanction, though Hawkins speculated that locals' commitment to peace had resulted from their knowledge of U.S. troops moving into the region to accompany the federal boundary commission. The conference ended with white intruders and federal commissioners on good terms. Local representatives promised to use their

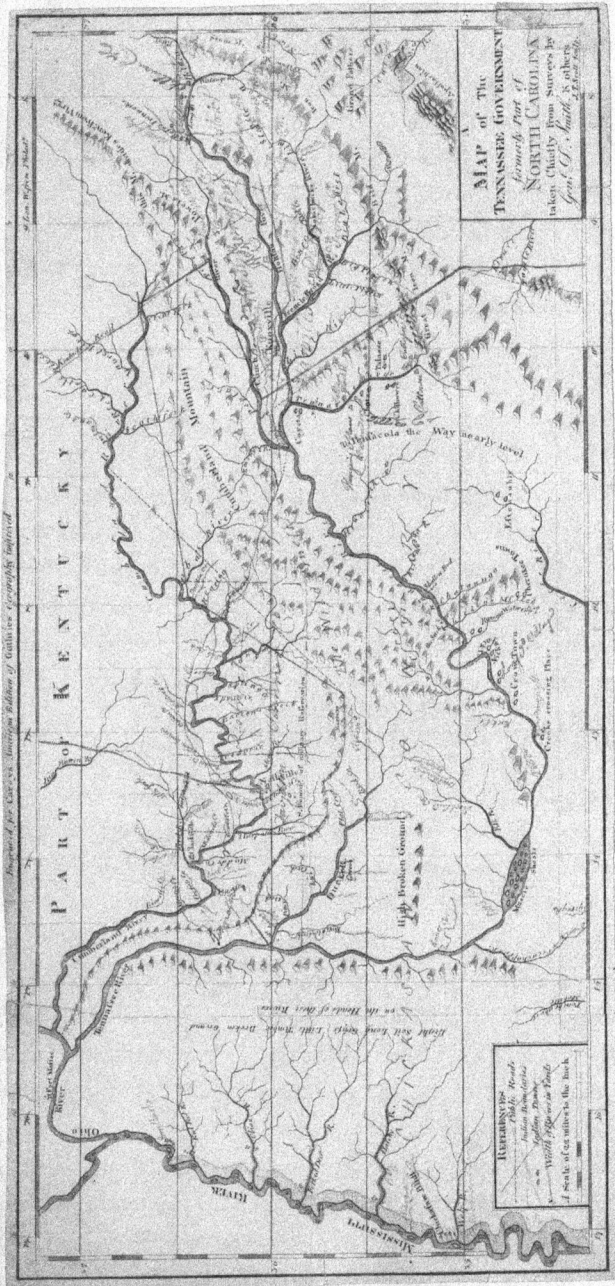

A Map of the Tennassee Government Formerly Part of North Carolina, Mathew Carey, c. 1797. American Philosophical Society. This map includes a revised, hand-drawn U.S–Cherokee border based on the 1797 boundary survey.

influence to prevent any outbreak of violence, and the federal officials agreed to furnish them with a map of the completed boundary. Locals had decided that petitioning the federal government was more effective than violence to guarantee permanent access to their land and homes in the Cherokee Nation. By September, a representative of these "Intruders on the Indian lands" was in Philadelphia advocating on their behalf.[38]

U.S. and Cherokee commissioners resumed marking the border to Kentucky before surveying the boundary from the Clinch River to the Great Smoky Mountains. After Winchester returned to Nashville on August 28, Hawkins, Pickens, and three Cherokee guides surveyed fifty more miles of the border. Along the way, surveyors made note of the "many Intruders on Indian land" and where they lived relative to the new boundary line. Hardly remorseful for violating Cherokee sovereignty, these white squatters possessed no claim to the land and called "intrusion a right." Rugged terrain and dry weather prevented the commissioners' further passage across the mountains. Hawkins decided to return to the Creek Nation and Pickens to his home in South Carolina. Winchester finalized the boundary from Walton's Road to the Cumberland River in October, and Pickens later organized the remaining survey from the Big Pigeon River across the Appalachian Mountains to the South Carolina line. An edited copy of Smith's 1793 Tennessee surveys reflected the region's new bordered landscape.[39]

Cherokee and federal leaders sanctioned the survey of the Holston Treaty boundary in 1791 to demarcate Native land from American territory. For decades, white settlers and speculators had disregarded Indigenous sovereignty, perpetuating violent conflict as Native peoples defended their nations militarily. In previous years, however, local whites could claim ignorance when found hunting, surveying, or clearing land because there were no obvious boundary lines in the Tennessee Country. Even if whites were within the Cherokee Nation, federal officials often took no action to remove them and instead pressured Native leaders for new land cessions to encompass illegal settlements. Cherokees' and Chickasaws' growing support for the survey and enforcement of their international borders alongside the United States' commitment to firm boundaries in the 1796 Trade and Intercourse Act represented a new direction in the federal government's relationship with both Native peoples and white inhabitants of the Tennessee Country.

But the survey's ultimate success depended on the federal government's enforcement of the Cherokee-U.S. border. Indeed, the difficulties for white intruders on Native land were only beginning as the U.S. commissioners departed from Tennessee. Over the ensuing months, soldiers under the command of Colonel Thomas Butler did enforce the Holston Treaty boundary line. They rounded up many white intruders either farming Cherokee land or living in the Cherokee Nation and destroyed their property. Captain Thomas T. Underwood, acting under Butler's orders, explained that he and his men had "had a laborious time this Winter in moving the settlers of[f] the indian lands" near the Hiwassee River in January 1798. Though "the intruders had Timely notice to move of[f,] a number of the settlers were obstinate, at length they were removed, some of there Cabbins burnt. Also there fencing, which ended our Business." Powell Valley intruders similarly encountered the power of the American national state when Butler evicted them and built a fort near their former settlements.[40]

Intruders' social class did not make them immune from forced relocation. In early 1798, Butler's troops arrested David Campbell, a current Tennessee judge and the former surveyor of the 1792 line of experiment, and evicted him and his family from their home near the confluence of the Little Tennessee and Tennessee Rivers. It had been common knowledge that the new border would locate Campbell's property in the Cherokee Nation. The judge had admitted as much to Benjamin Hawkins, explaining that he had lived at his current home for "ten years, knowing himself to be an intruder." Yet Campbell felt justified in violating Cherokee sovereignty. "No erratic nation has a right to claim a whole quarter of the globe, which they cannot occupy or cultivate," he argued, before further defending his property rights on the basis of the United States' right of conquest, the Discovery Doctrine, and his possession of North Carolina land grants, a plea he had been making for months in the pages of the *Knoxville Gazette*. The arrest shocked Campbell, so convinced was he of his right to Native land. He railed against Colonel Butler for confiscating his real and personal property, including at least two enslaved people. He also filed suit against Butler and other federal officers for trespass and false imprisonment, setting his personal damages at $10,000.[41] Campbell's eviction, more than any other forced relocation, further alienated white Tennesseans from the federal government and accelerated their attempts to shape the Tennessee Country to suit their expansionist geographies.

Chapter 5

Native Ferries, National Highways, and the Limits of U.S. State Power in the Cherokee and Chickasaw Nations

"No event has taken place since the epoch of the American Revolution, which involves more important consequences, than the treaty concluded between the Cherokee nation of Indians, known by the name of the treaty of Holston," blustered Judge David Campbell in May 1797. The federal government, in its recognition and enforcement of Native sovereignty, was guilty of "injustice to her own citizens of the state of Tennessee." Other prominent Tennessee politicians shared Campbell's sentiment. Governor Sevier described Colonel Thomas Butler's arrest of Campbell in early 1798 as "despotic and inimical to the liberties of our citizens" and warned President John Adams of Tennesseans' growing hostility toward the federal government in light of such actions. The state's congressional delegation, consisting of Senators Joseph Anderson and Andrew Jackson and Congressman William Claiborne, offered an even more vociferous criticism of "Such Military Tyranny." Butler's arrest of Campbell was an outrage to Tennessee sovereignty and a violation of their constituents' "rights of Civil liberty."[1]

Members of Tennessee's general assembly voiced similar protests in a 1797 remonstrance to U.S. officials. Meeting in Knoxville only weeks after the federal boundary commissioners finished surveying the U.S.-Cherokee border, state legislators defended intruders' right to Cherokee land. The two-year period of relative peace between the region's Indigenous and white inhabitants, they insisted, proved that there was no need to remove white families living in the Cherokee Nation. Tennessee's house of representatives even created its own state commission to determine whether the new border conformed to that agreed upon in the Holston Treaty. After only a week-long investigation, the state commissioners unsurprisingly reported that the team of U.S. and Cherokee officials had marked the border in error. Based on this information, the general assembly considered settlers' eviction "an act of violent oppression, and an undue exercise of the military over the civil authority."[2]

Legislators did not limit their objections to the forced removal of white Tennesseans from Cherokee land. The remonstrance also included resolutions proclaiming state citizens' right to "free and unmolested use of a road from Washington to Mero District and of the navigation of the river Tennessee," as outlined in prior agreements with the Cherokee Nation. Tennessee officials were especially indignant that Benjamin Hawkins, in his capacity as federal Indian agent, had declared that the Clinch River "was *Indian water*" and had allowed the operator of a ferry along the existing road between Knoxville and the Cumberland settlements to set his own ferriage fee in consultation with Cherokee leaders, whose nation owned lands on both sides of the river. "If the Indians or their Agent Mr. Hawkins . . . have a right to demand a price for ferriage," argued state legislators, "they may demand such a price as will amount to a prohibition of the use of the said road." Members of the general assembly passed the remonstrance in the final days of the 1797 session and sent copies to Congress and President Adams.[3]

Considering the charged rhetoric of prominent Tennessee politicians against the 1797 Holston Treaty boundary survey and federal troops' subsequent removal of white settlers from the Cherokee Nation, the legislators' addition of seemingly innocuous minutiae in their petition to the federal government is puzzling. How could the fair cost of ferriage across the Clinch River, whether "one fourth of a dollar" or "one eighth of a dollar," compare to federal troops' eviction of white Tennesseans from Native land? Was the legislators' defense of intruders' property rights commensurate with whether American travelers could circumvent the Clinch Ferry with a nearby ford? White Tennesseans certainly would have agreed that federal troops' arrest of intruders was a more important issue. Indeed, the general assembly's first draft of the remonstrance to Congress did not include the references to ferries, roads, and river travel.[4] Yet Tennesseans' expansionist geographies required not only unchecked access to Native land but also actual physical transformations of the Tennessee Country. Though less conspicuous than the enforcement of Native borders, attempts by U.S. officials and Cherokee leaders to control whites' movement within the state had to be challenged. If Tennessee was going to perpetuate the growing American empire, state officials could not overlook the smallest threat to their sovereignty, even if it meant demanding that a trip across the Clinch River should cost twelve-and-a-half cents rather than a quarter dollar.

Historians have long explored U.S. political leaders' attempts to "bind the republic together" and "conquer space" with transportation projects in the early nineteenth century.[5] Federalists believed that the national government should use its newfound power under the Constitution to improve commerce throughout the nation. Many nascent Jeffersonian Republicans had similar goals but insisted that these internal improvement projects be funded by states, a notion that emerged from their fears of expanding federal power. Debates over the Cumberland, or "National," Road, which linked the Ohio Valley with Atlantic markets, epitomized this partisan dimension of American political economy.[6] Yet before Congress approved the National Road in 1802 or voted on its extension in 1806, U.S. leaders had already authorized transportation projects within Native nations, and they continued to do so for much of the nineteenth century. Recognizing that early Jeffersonians, in particular, favored these internal improvement projects—funded by the federal government but constructed through Indigenous territory—reveals a significant continuity between Federalist and Republican rule. White Americans, regardless of partisan ties, had few scruples about federal power when it facilitated territorial expansion and operated "out of sight" on Native land. Even Jefferson, known for his opposition to centralized national state power, sustained many of the transportation and commercial projects of his Federalist predecessors. The United States could act unencumbered outside of states' borders.[7]

As Tennessee leaders attempted to transform the Tennessee Country to enable their expansionist geographies, Cherokees and Chickasaws shaped Americans' infrastructural and economic development of their Indigenous homelands to suit their own interests. Chickasaws and Cherokees influenced road construction, operated ferries, and generally regulated interstate and international travel. A complete understanding of internal improvements and American state power during the early Republic period requires perspectives that include the trans-Appalachian West and the Native peoples who made the region home.[8] Roads, ferries, and roadside stands would become nearly as contentious as Indigenous borders, for they revealed stakeholders' competing geographies for the Tennessee Country in the first decade of the nineteenth century.

The 1798 Treaty of Tellico
The federal government's forced eviction of white intruders from Native land in 1797 and early 1798 escalated tension between Tennessee Country whites and

the United States. Unlike in previous decades, when inhabitants of the region had little influence at the national level, Tennessee statehood provided white expansionists with representatives in Congress who could influence U.S. Indian policy. From the moment they arrived in Philadelphia, Tennessee's congressional delegates hounded the Adams administration to acquire Cherokee land on behalf of American intruders. With the support of President Adams, Congress ultimately appropriated funds for a new treaty despite initial reservations from Federalist congressmen.[9]

White Tennesseans had high hopes that the upcoming treaty would be a watershed moment in the history of their state. Not only could successful negotiations redraw Cherokee borders to allow evicted intruders to return to their homes, but they might also revolutionize transportation networks within the Tennessee Country. Governor Sevier considered connecting Knoxville and Nashville, separated as they were "by the space of unextinguished hunting grounds of near eighty miles," to be "an object of great importance" for the negotiations. Free access to all roads and waterways within the state would energize Tennessee commerce by improving transportation to distant markets, and it might also suppress the regional polarization of Tennessee politics that resulted from Cherokee territory separating the Cumberland settlements around Nashville from the more populous communities in East Tennessee. Sevier was so adamant that Tennesseans' interests be protected that he appointed three state commissioners to attend treaty negotiations. These men were to pressure Cherokees for a land cession of all territory north of the Tennessee River, including the valuable Muscle Shoals, and coerce Native diplomats to grant access to road and river transportation through the Cherokee Nation. U.S. commissioners had similar, though not as expansive, goals in mind. In addition to a land cession, Secretary McHenry ordered them to press Cherokees to grant American citizens free ferriage across the Clinch River and allow "houses of entertainment" along the Nashville-Knoxville Road. Travelers could find lodgings and refreshment at these roadside stands.[10]

Cherokees rejected a new treaty during negotiations in July 1798 at the Tellico Blockhouse. Before either the U.S. or Tennessee commissioners could make any proposals about boundaries and land cessions, Bloody Fellow stated his nation's refusal to sell territory or allow intruders to return to their homes. Such a brusque rejection of the commissioners' demands at the beginning of a conference was unusual within Native diplomacy. It may have reflected Cherokees' frustration over a lack of punishment for white murderers eighteen months earlier as much as it did a commitment to their national sovereignty. U.S. commissioner Alfred Moore later recounted Bloody Fellow and Doublehead's resentment toward Tennesseans' presence at the treaty grounds. The two former Chickamauga leaders knew of state leaders' speculation in Cherokee land and distrusted their intentions. Before leaving the Tellico Blockhouse, the Cherokees agreed to renew negotiations in the fall, when American officials expected them to be more receptive to a new treaty.[11]

Cherokees did agree to a land cession in early October 1798, though to a much smaller extent than initially favored by both state and federal commissioners. In his initial instructions, Secretary McHenry had ordered the U.S. negotiators to pressure Cherokees for a territorial cession that would stretch east from the Duck River Valley across the Cumberland Plateau to the heights of the Great Smoky Mountains, a range of several million acres that would have included the Cherokee Nation's richest remaining hunting territory. Yet, after three weeks of negotiations at the Tellico Blockhouse, Cherokees agreed to cede only three separate slivers of territory encompassing around 500,000 acres in the northern reaches of their nation. In return, they received a one-time gift of $5,000 in trade goods and an additional $1,000 to their existing annuity, sums that dwarfed the funds received by the nation in the 1791 Holston Treaty in exchange for a much larger land cession. It was a skillful negotiation made by many of the Cherokee Nation's most prominent leaders, including John Watts, Bloody Fellow, Doublehead, Little Turkey, and The Glass. These Native diplomats made sure that Cherokee officials would oversee the survey of their nation's land cessions, as had been the case with the Holston Treaty. Bloody Fellow approved of the initial boundary survey, which took place only days after negotiations ended, and at least five Cherokees accompanied American commissioners when finalizing the border in 1802. Cherokees' land cessions did allow evicted settlers from Powell Valley and Blount County to return to their former homes, now located within the boundaries of the United States.[12]

Although Cherokee diplomats did cede some land, they would not cede control of transportation networks. During treaty negotiations, the team of U.S. and Tennessee commissioners convinced Cherokees to declare a road from Kentucky "open and free" from where it entered their nation at a crossing of the Cumberland River. But this was only a small victory. Cherokee diplomats opposed roadside lodgings and refused to relinquish ownership of the Clinch Ferry. They considered "houses of entertainment" to be "the lurking places of the most disorderly and bad intentioned whites" and likely wanted to prevent conflict between Americans and Cherokees as much as possible. The Clinch Ferry, on the other hand, was an important source of income, and the nation's leaders jealously maintained their control over it and other ferries constructed in subsequent years. The Cherokees' federal agent had the responsibility of leasing the Clinch Ferry to American contractors, who would then recoup their expenses by charging white passengers for transportation and provisions. Although Cherokees and federal troops crossed the Clinch River for free, it was a lucrative business. A year after the Tellico Treaty, the ferry operator charged "12½ ¢ for a horseman and $1 for a loaded wagon" and estimated his daily income to be $20, owing to the growing number of white Americans migrating west. Annual ferry leases ranged from $100 to $600, a sum that Cherokees were loath to surrender. Federal agents distributed lease payments to the Cherokee Nation as part of the regular annuity, and Native leaders were quick to complain of late payments or if the amount paid did not match their estimation of ferries' value. Cherokee diplomats remained committed to regulating whites' transportation through their nation, especially when they could generate income in the process.[13]

Indian Footpaths and International Highways

Tennessee whites could not stomach the persistence of Native sovereignty in the Tennessee Country. Only two months after the 1798 Tellico Treaty, Governor Sevier once again blasted Cherokee control of the territory between Nashville and Knoxville. Not only did Americans' land grants supersede the ownership rights of such "faithless savages," but travel throughout the state also would remain dangerous until Tennessee could police the road. "It is time for this [state] government to assert her just rights & claim of domain of country included in her chartered limits," lectured Sevier to Tennessee legislators. During the 1798 legislative session, Tennessee lawmakers reminded the federal government that their grievances regarding the Clinch Ferry and river transportation had yet to be addressed, and they called on President Adams to secure permission from the Cherokees for a new road between Knoxville and Frankfort, Kentucky. Without waiting for federal officials or Cherokee leaders to react, state legislators began planning internal improvement projects through Native land, confident that the United States would accede to their expansionist demands.[14]

Tennesseans' primary goal was to improve transportation between Knoxville and Nashville. Travelers frequently remarked on the difficult and dangerous passage between the state's two hubs of American settlement. "I have to pass the Wilderness four times in the Year," complained state judge David Campbell, "and sometimes exposed to heavy rains and Snow Storms in the Mountains, and no house to retire to at night." Cherokees had granted Americans free access to a road through Cherokee country with the 1791 Holston Treaty. Such a highway was already in use, but legislators argued that it was not the most direct route and insisted that the Holston Treaty actually allowed the Tennessee government to build a new road. In 1799, lawmakers appropriated funds for a toll road constructed by the state through the Cherokee Nation. The law was itself a challenge to Native sovereignty. State leaders protested that the Cherokees' ferry over the Clinch River, with its fee for American travelers, violated treaty agreements. The new route between Nashville and Knoxville would instead cross the river at a nearby ford, preventing Tennesseans from suffering the indignity of paying the Cherokee Nation for transportation within what white expansionists considered to be their state's sovereign limits.[15]

U.S. officials agreed that the rugged terrain of the Tennessee Country impeded American transportation and communication, but they had different goals than their counterparts in Tennessee. Instead of an intrastate road across the Cumberland Plateau, Timothy Pickering, who had remained secretary of state after President Adams took office, envisioned a highway of national significance that would benefit the entire United States, a fitting goal for Federalists interested in large-scale commercial and transportation projects. Congress had organized the Mississippi Territory in early 1798, but the region remained isolated from the rest of the nation, exposed to potential attacks from Spanish and Native forces. "At present," complained Pickering in late 1798, "a letter is as long in travelling between Philadelphia and the Natchez, as between Philadelphia and Europe." Men from Kentucky and Tennessee regularly exported produce down the Mississippi River to New Orleans. The river's strong current made a return trip up the Mississippi impossible, so traders instead sold their boats with their cargo and relied on overland transportation back to their homes.[16] A new highway would increase national security and generate better trading opportunities for the entire trans-Appalachian West.

The existing road through the Mississippi Territory—known as Mountain Leader's Trace for its connection to the Chickasaw leader Piominko—was notoriously bad, "an Indian footpath very devious and narrow," according to U.S. postmaster general John Habersham. Francis Baily, an English scientist on a grand tour of North America, traveled from Natchez to Nashville in 1797 and described the "rough, broken, and bushy" road in great detail. Upon leaving Grindstone Ford, seventy miles north of Natchez, Baily "bid adieu to all marks

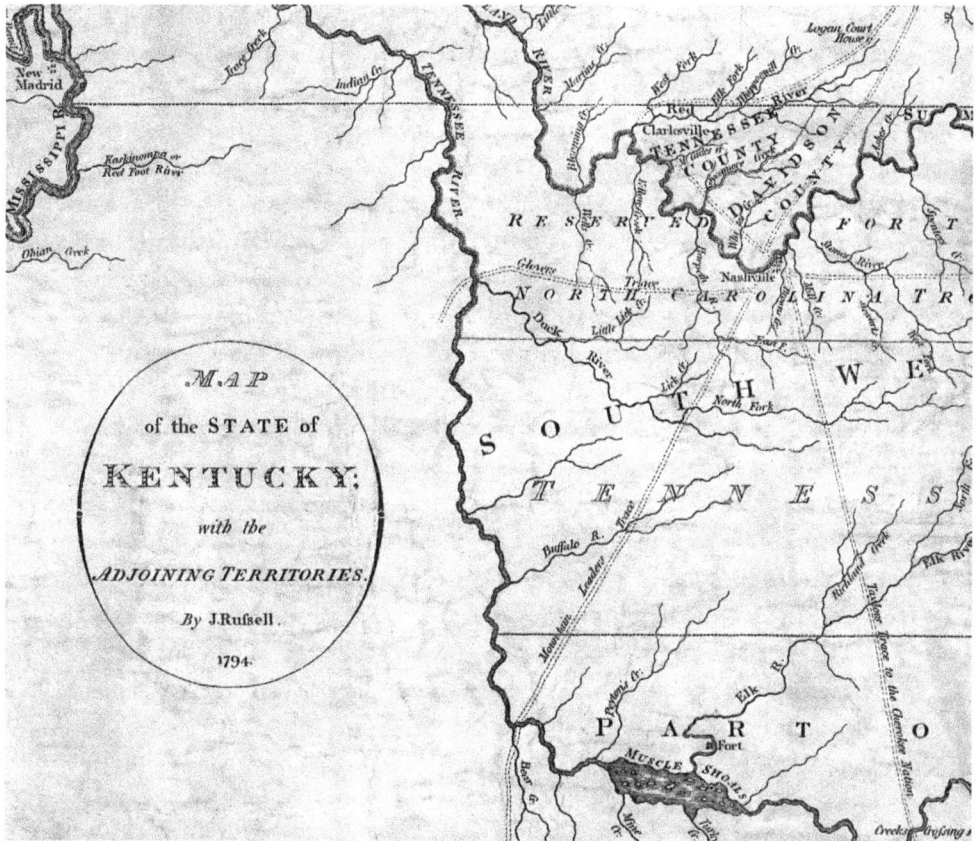

Map of the State of Kentucky, 1794. Tennessee State Library and Archives. Mountain Leader's Trace linked the Chickasaw Nation to American settlements along the Cumberland River.

of civilization." Until he arrived at Nashville three weeks later, Baily and various companions experienced a comically difficult journey. Horses ran away with goods and provisions; flooded creeks and rivers resulted in several mishaps; and Baily endured such horrible swelling from poison ivy that his boots no longer fit his feet, forcing him to trek barefoot on many occasions.[17] Federal officials had high hopes that a new road would eliminate such tortuous travel and benefit the entire United States.

Habersham's comment was not hyperbole. The "Indian footpath" did cross Chickasaw and Choctaw territory, complicating federal goals for a new road. Native sovereignty, according to Pickering, was "a great object to be removed." He proposed a new road from Natchez to Nashville that crossed the Tennessee

River at the Muscle Shoals. Numerous roadside stands would ease the difficult journey for mail carriers and American travelers, who presently relied on Choctaw and Chickasaw hospitality for provisions and lodging. Moreover, Pickering believed that the operation of these roadside taverns by "*industrious* and *trusty* white persons" would contribute to the federal goal of familiarizing Choctaws and Chickasaws with white Americans' cultural norms by providing them with examples to emulate. Indigenous peoples' racial and cultural "improvement" accompanied Americans' wishes for improved transportation and commerce across Native nations.[18] After taking power from Federalists in the election of 1800, Jefferson maintained most aspects of his predecessors' federal Indian policy, including Pickering's goal of a new federal road.

Not satisfied, white Tennesseans successfully lobbied the new administration to attempt a grander plan. Instead of a single highway from Nashville to Natchez, they wanted a transportation network that would revolutionize travel and commerce throughout the American Southeast. Tennessee leaders maintained their pressure on Congress to appropriate funds for a new road from Knoxville to Nashville that would circumvent the Clinch Ferry. They also convinced Jefferson, whom many Tennesseans backed in the election of 1800 because of his support for American expansion, to authorize a possible purchase of Cherokee territory north of the Tennessee River. This would give the state uninhibited control over its internal transportation and allow North Carolina and Tennessee residents to possess their land claims, which remained inaccessible within the Cherokee Nation.[19] Though they would have to rely on federal treaty negotiators, Tennessee expansionists anticipated land cessions and a new state road from Knoxville to Nashville along with the federal road from Nashville to Natchez.

Cementing the Union

The Jefferson administration had grand plans for the upcoming negotiations with Native southerners. The United States proposed to purchase nearly all Cherokee land north of the Tennessee River. Such a cession would include much of the valuable Great Bend region, long coveted by American land speculators, and would eliminate Cherokee control of the Cumberland Plateau, allowing Tennessee leaders to construct their new road over the mountain. Federal officials considered highways to be of greater importance than territorial expansion. If Cherokees refused to consider land cessions, Henry Dearborn, Thomas Jefferson's new secretary of war, instructed U.S. treaty commissioners to acquire "a strip of land from one to five miles in width to include the said road in its whole extent" from Knoxville to Nashville. He hoped Cherokees would at the very least allow "three or four White Families at such points on the road across their lands," likely to manage roadside accommodations. After first meeting with the Cherokees at Southwest Point, Dearborn ordered commissioners to travel to Chickasaw Bluffs on the banks of the Mississippi and then on to the Choctaw Nation, where they would negotiate for the new highway from Nashville to Natchez. These instructions made clear the federal government's desire for a spatial transformation of the American Southeast. As an anonymous correspondent of Jefferson's noted, such roads would "cement & unite the Union" and "destroy that idea that the Eastern & Western States have two separate interests."[20] Geographical barriers would no longer hamper the growing American empire.

Cherokees disrupted Dearborn's plans. A delegation of five officials from across the Cherokee Nation, led by The Glass, the prominent diplomat and former Chickamauga war leader, arrived at the U.S. capital in late June 1801. They were there upon the orders of Little Turkey, who worried that a recent decrease of federal troops in the Tennessee Country might encourage more white settlers to invade Cherokee territory, but their protest expanded into a broader defense of their national lands. The Glass interrogated Dearborn about the rumor "that the United States have authorized a Treaty to be held . . . to deprive us of more of our land." He reminded the secretary of war that it was he, The Glass, who three years before had "mentioned at the [Tellico] Treaty, that we had no desire to part with any more lands." The Cherokees' arguments had an immediate impact on federal goals for the upcoming treaty negotiations. After the meeting, Dearborn revised his orders to U.S. treaty commissioners, instructing them to avoid discussing land cessions or boundary lines and instead prioritize permission for the new road projects. Transportation and communication needs temporarily outweighed the desire for more land. Dearborn continued to plead with the assembled Cherokees to agree to a new highway through their nation. The Native delegates, however, worried that such roads would result in the theft of Cherokees' horses and cattle by white travelers, generating more disorder in the Tennessee Country. Americans already had passage from Fort Southwest Point to Nashville, argued The Glass. More roads through their nation would not be popular among Cherokees.[21]

As U.S. treaty commissioners Benjamin Hawkins, James Wilkinson, and Andrew Pickens arrived in the Tennessee Valley in early August 1801, Cherokee leaders already were preparing their diplomatic strategies. Instead of beginning negotiations immediately, Upper Town leaders convened their own private conference at Ustanali, where they even excluded Charles Hicks, their nation's interpreter, because of his ties to the United States. Not only did the Cherokees discuss American demands for roads and land at the Ustanali meeting, but they also deliberated upon a recent murder of a Cherokee woman, killed along Stock Creek a few miles south of Knoxville. Attendees grew angry that the United States would dare press them for a land cession even as white murderers went unpunished. The Cherokees ultimately agreed to meet with U.S. commissioners, though Little Turkey, the beloved man of the entire nation, declined to attend the treaty negotiations in person, a sure sign of his hostility toward the United States. Needless to say, U.S. commissioners had little hope for the treaty's success.[22]

In a powerful show of national unity, around forty Cherokee diplomats from both the Upper Towns and Lower Towns rejected U.S. appeals for roads and land cessions when negotiations finally began on September 4, 1801. American commissioners repeated the pleas that Dearborn had made only months before. "Your white brethren who live at Natchez, at Nashville, and in South Carolina," outlined James Wilkinson to the assembled Cherokees, "are very far removed from each other and have complained . . . that the roads by which they travel are narrow and obstructed with fallen timber, with rivers and creeks, which prevent them from pursuing their lawful business." The commissioners wanted Cherokees to allow the United States to improve the existing roads and appoint respectable white Americans to operate ferries and roadside stands to ease the difficulties of American travelers. Such improvements, continued Wilkinson, would increase Cherokees' revenue through annual rent "in the manner of your ferry over the Clinch River." He concluded with a meek reference to land cessions, though by this time commissioners were well aware that the Cherokees had no interest in surrendering any territory.[23]

Both Doublehead and Chulio—likely Little Turkey's representative from the Upper Towns—responded to the commissioners on the following day, but it was Doublehead, the former Chickamaugan, who crafted the most vocal defense of Cherokee sovereignty. "The roads you propose we do not wish to have made thru' our Country," he bluntly explained. "Our objection to this road is this—a great many people of all discriptions would pass them, & that would happen which has recently happened & you would labor under the same difficulties you do now." This clear reference to the Cherokee woman's recent murder in East Tennessee exemplified Cherokees' belief that violence would only increase should more Americans travel through their lands. The existing roads through the Cherokee Nation, from Knoxville to Nashville and from Tennessee to Kentucky across the

Cumberland River, should suffice for white travelers. "Before the whites inhabited this land there was nothing but small paths," explained Doublehead, but "they had no trouble finding those when they wanted to take away our land." American encroachment on Cherokee territory had proceeded long before any highways crossed the nation, and it would only accelerate should Native diplomats approve additional roads. In light of such blatant Cherokee opposition to a new treaty, Hawkins, Wilkinson, and Pickens decided to continue on to the Chickasaw Nation. Their conference with Cherokee diplomats ended on bad terms.[24]

Compared to their trying time in the Cherokee Nation, the U.S. commissioners experienced much less difficulty in their October 1801 negotiations with Chickasaw diplomats. Meeting at Chickasaw Bluffs along the Mississippi River, Chickasaws agreed to a new federal road through their nation. Wilkinson explained to the Native leaders that the existing road from Natchez to Nashville "thro' your nation . . . is an uncomfortable one and very inconvenient . . . in its present unimproved condition." The United States hoped to "make it suitable to the accommodation of those who may use it and at the same time beneficial" to the Chickasaw Nation. After only one evening's deliberation, George Colbert, serving as the Chickasaws' speaker, agreed "that a waggon road may be cut thro' their land." In return, Chickasaw negotiators received $700 worth of trade goods and vague promises that the United States would protect Chickasaw territory from white intruders. In December, the three U.S. commissioners convinced diplomats from the Choctaw Nation to agree to similar provisions, making it possible for the United States to realize Pickering's vision and connect Natchez and Nashville with a new highway, which would become known as the Natchez Trace.[25]

The Chickasaws' agreement seems to display their willingness to surrender components of their national sovereignty to the United States, a marked contrast to Cherokees' rejection of new roads through their nation. But it was more complicated. Chickasaws were accustomed to travelers—like Francis Baily—crossing their national lands on trips to and from the Gulf Coast. They likely thought it of little consequence to allow the United States to merely expand the existing path into a highway suitable for wagon transportation. Furthermore, the Chickasaw council would appoint two representatives to oversee the road's construction a year later, allowing national leaders to ensure that the new highway aligned with Chickasaw interpretations of the treaty agreement.[26]

Even as the Chickasaw diplomats agreed to the new road, they retained control over significant dimensions of their nation's transportation network. When pressed by commissioners to allow white Americans to operate lodgings along the new highway, Chickasaws refused. They committed the subject to "future consideration" but insisted that for "the mean time travellers will always find provisions in the nation sufficient to carry . . . them through." The Native diplomats also included a provision in the treaty "that the necessary ferries over the water courses crossed by the said road shall be held and deemed to be the property of the Chickasaw nation."[27] Chickasaws actually stood to gain from the improved highway. More travelers meant increased revenue.

The Natchez Trace and the Tennessee-Georgia Highway

The 1801 Chickasaw treaty reveals how Native peoples continued to shape American transportation even as they allowed the United States to construct new roads through their nations. Control of roadside stands, ownership of ferries, and input on highway routes were all ways in which Chickasaws, as well as their Cherokee neighbors, influenced the competing geographies of the Tennessee Country in first decade of the nineteenth century. The Natchez Trace, in particular, became central to this ongoing dispute over transportation and internal improvements between Native nations and the United States, but Cherokee highways also increased in significance. White inhabitants of the Tennessee Country remained committed to their expansionist vision of American empire, even as Cherokees and Chickasaws insisted that they retained sovereignty within their respective nations.

Construction of the Natchez Trace began soon after American officials concluded their negotiations in the Chickasaw and Choctaw Nations. As was the case in other parts of the trans-Appalachian West, U.S. troops provided the labor for road projects, a symbolic representation of growing federal state power. Local people, however, both Chickasaws and white Tennesseans, had the greatest influence on the road's course. During the winter of 1801–02, two Chickasaws surveyed a "guide line" for the new road through the Chickasaw Nation. Yet, even before the conclusion of treaty negotiations about the Natchez Trace, George Colbert argued that the proposed route over the Tennessee River was "an improper one," given the swampy bottomlands and rugged hill country. He convinced the American diplomats, who all recognized the need to placate the prominent Chickasaw leader, that a better crossing could be found twenty miles to the east where he operated a ferry.[28]

Two years later, Colbert was raking in fees for ferriage over the Tennessee River and for operating roadside lodgings. Colbert certainly accrued personal income through his commercial operations, but it is likely that he distributed portions of his wealth to his Chickasaw neighbors and kin, following the custom of reciprocal leadership among Native southerners. By 1803, numerous Chickasaw families had moved from Long Town, in the nation's interior, to the Tennessee River, where they created a new community near the ferry crossing and sold provisions to American travelers. Colbert had been one of Long Town's most prominent leaders, so the resettlement of Chickasaws near his ferry reflected the draw of his leadership and the possibility that former residents of the town would benefit from his financial success. Chickasaws also generated revenue through a ferry across the Duck River, which they leased to John Gordon, an early American inhabitant of the Mero District who relocated south to manage the ferry crossing.[29]

Gordon was not the only white Tennessean to benefit financially from the construction of the Natchez Trace. Federal troops commanded by Thomas Butler, the same officer who evicted white intruders from the Cherokee Nation in 1797 and negotiated the Tellico Treaty in 1798, began cutting the road between the Tennessee River and Nashville in the summer of 1802. As his command entered Tennessee, Butler feared that the construction of the road would infringe on the state's jurisdiction. Despite knowing of the Chickasaw treaty, Tennessee legislators had taken no action regarding the highway. Governor Archibald Roane, inaugurated the previous fall, put the burden of the road survey on the county courts of Davidson County and Williamson County, both bisected by the Natchez Trace.[30] Given Republicans' fears of federal overreach, it appeared to be the perfect solution: U.S. troops would construct the road within the Chickasaw Nation, and Tennesseans would construct the road within the bounds of their state.

But county authority over the road's course proved more difficult in practice than in theory. The Williamson County court insisted that instead of a direct route from the "Indian boundary line" to Nashville the trace should pass through Franklin, the county seat, where it would increase commerce for the village's American inhabitants. The Franklin course, however, deviated by three or four miles from the "most direct route," as required in the Chickasaw treaty. Governor Roane pleaded with federal officials to allow this alteration. Secretary Dearborn refused. "It ought not to be expected that a great public road made for . . . national purposes should be diverted from the shortest and best route merely to accommodate the Inhabitants of a Single County," he explained to Roane. Federal troops followed their original orders and constructed the Natchez Trace through the rural parts of Williamson County. The county court later constructed its own branch road from Franklin to the federal highway.

Foreshadowing subsequent rhetoric about internal improvement projects, federal officials had prioritized the national benefits of the Natchez Trace over the commercial desires of local Williamson County residents.[31] Chickasaws had a greater influence on the region's expanding transportation network than white Tennesseans.

For much of 1802 and 1803, federal and state officials continued to pester Cherokees for permission to build a highway from Kentucky through Tennessee to Augusta, Georgia, which would cross the Cherokee Nation. The existing route from Georgia to East Tennessee, according to several travelers, consisted of "a narrow path . . . for a long way by an immense precipice of rock," a dangerous road with "mountainous bad areas" that made travel between the two states especially difficult. Despite the risk, it was still well traveled. Between July 1801 and October 1804, 135 white Americans and several enslaved people received passports to cross Cherokee territory between Tennessee and Georgia. Many more likely journeyed illegally, in violation of the U.S. Trade and Intercourse Acts. In April 1802, Secretary Dearborn ordered Return J. Meigs, appointed the year before as the new federal agent for the Cherokee Nation, to inform Cherokee leaders that the United States resented their continuing opposition to transportation projects. The federal government would "not consider the Cherokees as good neighbors unless" they would allow "their best friends . . . to make a road at their own expense through their Country from one settlement to another." Meigs dutifully relayed Dearborn's messages to Native leaders and refused to allow Cherokees to make a trip to Washington until they approved the new road.[32]

In October 1803, Cherokee leaders did agree to the federal road through their nation, which would begin in two branches at Fort Southwest Point and Tellico Blockhouse in Tennessee and terminate near the University of Georgia in Athens. Despite the cost of feeding the two thousand Cherokees in attendance at Southwest Point, there to receive the nation's annuity payment during the negotiations, the treaty was a great victory for American expansionists committed to binding the Union together. Meigs bragged that the expense meant little when compared to "the great advantages which we acquired" by connecting Tennessee, Georgia, and Kentucky.[33]

Cherokees consented to the road because it was highly advantageous to them as well. One scholar of Cherokee history implies that Native leaders accepted the treaty terms because "it was fruitless to oppose the President of the United States" and that Cherokees negotiated from a position of weakness in the fall of 1803. Although it is true that federal and state officials had been increasing their pressure for the Georgia-Tennessee road over the previous eighteen months, this was also a time when many Cherokee leaders were beginning to realize the benefits of transportation projects through their nation. At a conference in April 1803, Turtle at Home, who had surveyed portions of the Cherokee border in 1797, was explicit that Cherokees agreed not to approve a road through their nation. Much of their opposition, he explained, stemmed from the United States' failure to punish white murderers for the recent killing of a Cherokee man near the Little Pigeon River in Tennessee.[34]

Even as the crime went unpunished over the ensuing months, Native diplomats nevertheless softened on the issue of the Georgia-Tennessee road as they generated income from other transportation projects. In May 1803, Cherokee leaders began leasing roadside stands along the Knoxville-Nashville Road to white Americans. According to one contract, for example, Toluntuskee, another former Chickamaugan and likely the uncle of John Watts, possessed "a Grant from his nation to Establish Houses of Entertainment" and arranged with Thomas N. Clark, the former postmaster of Fort Southwest Point, to operate stands at Crab Orchard and at the foot of the Cumberland Plateau for five years. The two men would split all profits equally, and Toluntuskee agreed to reside nearby to keep "good order" between Cherokee and American travelers. The contract explicitly stated that Clark had "no right, title, or claim" to land around the two stands. Such contracts required the consent of the nation's leaders. In July, a group of Lower Town Cherokees agreed to the terms negotiated by Toluntuskee and Clark. At the same meeting, Native leaders granted a stand near the Obed River to Arthur Coody, a former British Loyalist living in the Cherokee Nation. Coody soon made his own contract with Sampson Williams, an officer in the Tennessee militia and longtime land speculator.[35]

These agreements contributed to Cherokees' approval of the Georgia-Tennessee Road in 1803. Before negotiations began, Meigs received word that several Lower Town leaders, including Kategiska and Old Cabin, who lived near the Muscle Shoals, likely would allow the highway between Tennessee and Georgia because they would reap commercial benefits, similar to Toluntuskee's lease of stands along the Nashville-Knoxville Road. The treaty itself further bolstered Cherokees' control of their nation's transportation networks. As Native diplomats approved the new road, they made sure that Agent Meigs acknowledged their right to ferries and roadside stands, as well as the income that came from such enterprises. The treaty granted the ferry at Fort Southwest Point to Doublehead and ordered Meigs to rent two other ferries for the

Cherokees' benefit. The Cherokees also included a passing reference to a future toll, implying that they would control who traveled through their nation and at what price. During negotiations, Native diplomats even agreed to three additional stands along the road between Nashville and Knoxville, which they later rented for $200 annually. With the blessing of the assembled council, Doublehead also negotiated a contract to lease his ferry at the confluence of the Tennessee and Clinch Rivers. In April 1804, Cherokees approved an extension of the Georgia-Tennessee highway from Fort Southwest Point to Kentucky, though they made sure that the nation would control roadside stands along this route as well. The Glass hoped that the agreement would lead to greater federal funding and more commercial benefits for his nation.[36]

Cherokees maintained control of their nation's transportation network even after authorizing the new federal highway. Some individuals, like James Vann and John Lowery, pressured Meigs to survey the road near their homesteads. Not only would better roads ease Vann's transportation of cattle and other trade goods to markets in Knoxville and elsewhere, but he also owned a store and would certainly benefit from travelers' business. Vann even had plans to operate the post route for the United States. Lowery likely had similar intentions. He proposed to move permanently to a site along the Hiwassee River should the road be located nearby. By 1807, Lowery operated a ferry across the river.[37]

As was the case with national boundaries, Native leaders insisted that five Cherokee commissioners accompany American surveyors as they marked the Georgia Road across their nation. When Georgia, Tennessee, and federal commissioners began identifying the proper course to connect the two states in August 1804, they began at Vann's home in the Cherokee Nation, where the prominent Native leader could oversee the project and likely guarantee that it aligned with his personal interests. The Americans were joined by a number of other Cherokees, whom Black Fox (Enola), the nation's new principal chief, had appointed the previous December. These Cherokee commissioners were more than mere diplomats; they were experts in the region's geography. One, Jolly, hailed from Willstown, originally a Chickamauga community located near the Tennessee-Georgia state line. Three other Cherokee commissioners— Dry Scalp, The Big Half Breed, and Keelacheela—lived along river valleys in the mountains of present-day northern Georgia.[38] All four men would have been intimately familiar with the topography along the proposed route and, more importantly, would have been able to encourage American surveyors to identify the most beneficial course for the new highway. Though they may have resisted the Tennessee-Georgia Road for several years, many Cherokee leaders now believed the highway's financial benefit outweighed the potential for violence caused by increased traffic through their nation.

———

Despite Tennesseans' growing impact on the process of U.S. empire in the early nineteenth century, Native people still were able to realize their imagined geographies of the Tennessee Country. Cherokees and Chickasaws influenced road courses through their nations and maintained control over roadside stands and ferries. In 1818, for example, an American traveler relied on Cherokee women and men for lodging and provisions for nearly every day of his ten-day journey between Georgia and Tennessee. Several Tennesseans worried that Native peoples' ownership of these transportation resources actually increased their opposition to U.S. expansion. While pondering the potential for future land cessions, one Tennessee resident believed that "the warriors of several tribes wish to Exchange their lands for lands on the other side of the Mississippi but the chiefs are not willing as they receive an Annual pension for the Roads that leads through their Country." Daniel Smith, the former surveyor and one of Tennessee's sitting U.S. senators, was even more specific. Echoing other American officials, he attributed Chickasaws' opposition to an 1805 land cession to the "pernicious consequences arising from the ferries and stands on the road belonging to indians." George Colbert's ferry across the Tennessee River particularly irritated Smith. Furthermore, in August 1806, Cherokees created the Cherokee Turnpike Company, which charged travelers for use of the 220-mile road from Georgia to Tennessee and used the income to keep the highway in good condition. Later that year, Cherokees in council at Lookout Mountain Town underscored the connection between their nation's commercial gains from transportation networks and their national sovereignty. "If there is aney Bennefit to be got we [ought] to have it of our ow[n]e Land," they declared.[39] Transportation improvements gave Chickasaws and Cherokees additional reasons to persist against the forces of American empire in the first decade of the nineteenth century.

Chapter 6

Shared Territory, Competing Geographies, and Indigenous Law in the Early Nineteenth Century

In the late summer of 1807, Cherokee leaders Black Fox, The Glass, Turtle at Home, Richard Brown, and Totowiltoto met U.S. boundary commissioners Return J. Meigs and James Robertson at the Chickasaw Old Fields along the Tennessee River. Meigs and Robertson had been in the area for several months to mark a new U.S. border with the Chickasaw and Cherokee Nations, agreed upon in several 1805 and 1806 treaties. Robertson and his team of professional surveyors and chain carriers began their survey of the U.S.-Chickasaw boundary line in May near where the Natchez Trace crossed the Duck River. They then slowly meandered southeast, marking the boundary as they went. Cherokees joined the federal officials to supervise the survey of the border's remaining section, stretching northeast from the Tennessee River to the headwaters of the Duck River in what would become Middle Tennessee. Yet, once on the ground, Meigs and Robertson convinced the Cherokee leaders to approve a different border that would locate two hundred American families, settled illegally on Native land, within the limits of the United States. Surveyor Thomas Freeman's map of the new boundaries revealed the proximity of Cherokee and Chickasaw borders.[1]

This cession of Indigenous land infuriated Chickasaw leaders. Chenabee and other leading Chickasaw officials argued that the territory ceded by Cherokees actually belonged to the Chickasaw Nation. Only days after the Cherokee diplomats negotiated the new border, Chickasaws attempted to settle their boundary dispute at a summit in the Creek Nation. Despite Cherokees' attendance, leaders of the two nations failed to come to an agreement. Chickasaw

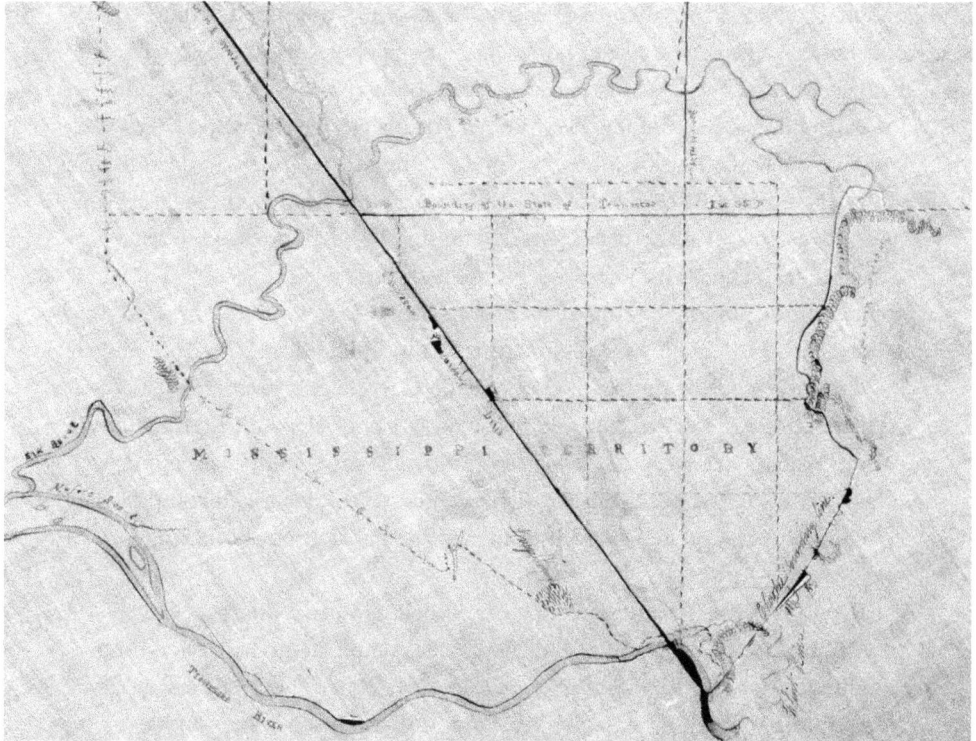

A Map of Indian Boundary Lines and the Southern Boundary of the State of Tennessee, 1807.
Tennessee State Library and Archives. The Chickasaws' boundary line stretched northwest
from the Tennessee River, where it intersected the Cherokee border. The surveyed
territory would be organized a year later as Madison County under the jurisdiction
of the Mississippi Territory.

negotiators demanded that the United States "have the white people removed
off our land, that the Cherokees have sold," or Chickasaws would "move them
off by force." Cherokees never had the authority to cede the land, and therefore
the cession should be invalidated.[2]

The 1807 land cession and accompanying controversy represented only one
flashpoint in the longstanding conflict between Chickasaws and Cherokees
regarding their overlapping boundaries in the Tennessee Country. Beginning
in the late eighteenth century, Cherokees and Chickasaws began to support
clear borders as a way to both identify when white intruders settled illegally in
their territory and guarantee that other Indigenous nations could not cede their
land to settler governments. As the 1807 Cherokee cession suggests, bounding

national territory forced Cherokees and Chickasaws to argue for their particular nation's exclusive right to land that Native peoples had long shared. This
strategy strained relations between the two Indigenous nations beginning in
the early nineteenth century, as white Americans elected national leaders who
could facilitate their vision for empire in the Tennessee Country. To defend their
national land against U.S. expansion, Native leaders crafted intricate legal arguments based on a variety of evidence, including Indigenous peoples' historical
occupation and creation stories, conquest theory, and even U.S. treaty law. Their
compelling arguments during treaty negotiations and in more informal conversations with U.S. and Native diplomats made it difficult for American officials
to wrest land away from the Chickasaws and Cherokees by requiring the cash-
strapped United States to fund numerous treaty councils with representatives
of both nations. In doing so, however, both peoples also were challenging each
other's claims to the region. Their dispute offers a window into a complex diplomatic conversation generated by American expansion but occurring within
Native North America.

Recovering these arguments made by Chickasaws and Cherokees to defend
their Tennessee Country lands adds necessary complexity to historians' understanding of Native sovereignty. Native leaders defended their nations' territory
by combining emerging Atlantic World legal theories with their own existing
Indigenous laws. Indeed, law was much more accessible and diffuse in the early
republic than many scholars have previously realized. Native peoples not only
had their own legal cultures but also were widely familiar with European legal
regimes, and they used both to lay claim to their national lands.[3] Exploring how
Cherokees and Chickasaws defended their Tennessee Country borders well into
the nineteenth century reveals the persistence of Indigenous peoples' legal traditions and their competing geographies in the face of American empire.

Division and Dispossession

In the early months of 1804, Return J. Meigs, the U.S. agent to the Cherokee
Nation, investigated the Tennessee Valley's Great Bend region, where the Tennessee River makes its great swerve north toward its intersection with the Ohio.
His description of the area's rich natural resources and healthy climate would
have made any worthwhile nineteenth-century speculator salivate. "That part
of the Cherokee Country on the South Side of Tennessee River," gushed Meigs,
"is a very desireable & valuable Country," perfect for growing cotton and corn
or raising livestock. His implication was clear: American settlers would benefit

greatly if they could pursue plantation-style agriculture in the region. Yet Native sovereignty hampered Meigs's speculator fantasy. "The Cherokees call this land theirs," explained Meigs. The Chickasaws, Creeks, and Choctaws also "pretend to have a claim there including some of the lands on the southside of the musell Shoals," a shallow area of the Tennessee River known equally for its agricultural riches as for its impediment to riverine transportation. These overlapping land claims meant that federal officials would have to determine which Indigenous nation had the most legitimate ownership of the Tennessee's Great Bend if white Americans were ever going to acquire it.[4]

White Americans had speculated in, traveled through, fought on, and organized several settlement ventures to the Tennessee River's Great Bend, but until the first decade of the 1800s the United States had not formally attempted to negotiate with Indigenous peoples for the territory. Cherokees refused to even consider a cession of the area in 1801. Yet they and their Chickasaw neighbors faced increasing pressure from all fronts in the ensuing years, particularly as the surge of short-staple cotton production in South Carolina and Georgia in the final years of the eighteenth century made land west of the Appalachian Mountains all the more valuable. To acquire the Great Bend, white settlers employed a strategy that had worked in the past: invade Native land, resist removal, and petition for a cession. They were aided by state leaders. In his annual message to the general assembly in 1803, Tennessee governor John Sevier clamored that the state's congressional delegation must convince the United States to acquire all territory north of the Great Bend. Federal officials themselves did favor a major land cession. Without large tracts of land, Cherokees and Chickasaws would be forced to give up hunting and adopt commercial and subsistence agriculture, like surrounding white southerners, and then might agree to cede more land to the United States.[5]

Based on popular pressure and federal policy, Secretary Dearborn appointed Meigs and Daniel Smith, the longtime surveyor and former U.S. senator from Tennessee, to negotiate for a Cherokee cession in 1804. Though joined by Tennessee commissioners, including Governor Sevier, there to add more pressure on Native negotiators, Meigs and Smith could convince Cherokee diplomats only to surrender a small tract of land in the southeastern portion of their nation. They failed in their larger effort to acquire Cherokees' Great Bend territory. Before leaving the treaty ground, however, federal and state commissioners devised a new strategy to coerce the Cherokee Nation to cede more land. Sevier ordered James Robertson, the other Tennessee commissioner, to travel to the Chickasaw

Nation and warn the Chickasaws that the Cherokees might cede the disputed territory. He was to emphasize to that nation's leaders that "it would be well for them to get something for their lands, as to let the Cherokees have it all." Robertson would exaggerate the Cherokee Nation's ownership to pressure Chickasaws to sell, and then the federal government could subsequently acquire Cherokees' claims to the land.[6] Americans fomented division to facilitate dispossession.

Division also existed within the Chickasaw Nation itself. When initially confronted privately by Robertson in Nashville about a cession, George Colbert responded positively. He promised to return to the nation and consult with other leaders on the matter. A number of Chickasaws purportedly owed $50,000 to private traders, and the United States offered to pay their debts if they agreed to cede land. But, upon reflection, Colbert, Chenabee, and two other Chickasaws refused to meet with officers of the United States. The Chickasaw leaders were fully aware of the value of their hunting lands north of the Tennessee River and would never consent to a large-scale cession. If they ever were to sell the territory, Chickasaws would instead "have it surveyed and have so much an acre for it," noted Chenabee, "the same as the white people does to one another with their lands." This threat to commodify national property along the same lines as the United States spoke to Chickasaws' numerous encounters with land agents, who had been surveying North Carolina land grants within the Chickasaw Nation for thirty years. Colbert and Chenabee threatened to use Americans' notions of property to oppose further colonization.[7]

The Chickasaws also took the opportunity to remind American leaders that the United States could not claim Chickasaw land on the basis of prior conquest. Chickasaws had always maintained peaceful relations with the United States, unlike the Creeks and Cherokees, who had been defeated by U.S. forces during the Revolutionary War. Americans had never defeated the Chickasaws, so they had no right to any of their lands. Chenabee, Colbert, and the other assembled leaders articulated their own claims of conquest by referencing the fact that Chickasaws drove Shawnees out of the Tennessee Valley in the eighteenth century. Accustomed to Americans' defense of U.S. land claims in the trans-Appalachian West, Chickasaws repurposed such arguments to support their own sovereignty and property rights in the Tennessee Country. When confronted with Chickasaws' refusal to make a cession, coming even as another delegation of Chickasaw leaders met with the president, federal officials lacked an effective response. A few even agreed that the Chickasaw Nation had the best claim to the Great Bend.[8]

Chickasaw leaders did, however, eventually cede a portion of their nation's most northeastern territory in the Duck River and Elk River watersheds, including portions of the Tennessee Country's Great Bend, in a treaty concluded on July 23, 1805. George Colbert and his brother Levi even signed the agreement, a marked transformation from George's strong opposition to a cession only seven months before. This decision appears to support scholarly interpretations that stress Native peoples' powerlessness to resist American expansion, but it was actually much more complicated. The Colberts, like many Indigenous leaders, were personally indebted to trading companies. Most Native people opposed land cessions and would quickly retaliate against anyone in their nation who ceded land. Although U.S. negotiators awarded $1,000 to George Colbert and agreed that the monies for Chickasaws' Tennessee Country land would go to pay the nation's debts to traders, the presence of 1,500 Chickasaws at the treaty negotiations makes it likely that the treaty met the approval of the entire nation rather than being a cash grab for specific Chickasaw diplomats.[9]

Chickasaws, ironically, sold land when they did in order to protect their national interests. They had known for years that the Cherokee Nation also claimed much of the Tennessee Valley's Great Bend and that the United States was attempting to negotiate cessions with the two nations concurrently. They also recognized the true value of their national territory, given the windfall that the federal government and speculators hoped to gain from a cession, and resented the low price offered by the United States for their land. Cherokees' conflicting claim, however, devalued Chickasaws' property, at least according to white negotiators familiar with American speculators' overlapping land claims. Chickasaw leaders could best maximize their profit by ceding first, when demand for land was at its peak and before a possible Cherokee cession. The Chickasaw Nation received $22,000 from the federal government compared to the Cherokees' eventual $14,000 reimbursement for a subsequent land cession of comparable size.[10]

As Chickasaw leaders negotiated with U.S. treaty commissioners in the spring and summer of 1805, Cherokees were defending their nation's exclusive ownership of the Great Bend region. They had previously insisted that Native southerners collectively owned much of the rich hunting land of the Tennessee Country, but by the first decade of the nineteenth century Cherokees had retooled their opposition to American expansion and Chickasaw claims by combining European and Indigenous notions of sovereignty and property. Chickasaws may have articulated conquest rights to the Great Bend on the basis of military victories over the Shawnees, but Cherokees narrated their own story of conquest over the Chickasaw Nation. Cherokee leaders admitted that Chickasaw troops defeated Shawnee soldiers but insisted that their nation possessed "a prior right, & reconquered [the Great Bend] by driving the Chickasaws" from the area. Cherokees repeatedly mentioned that only their nation had Native settlers, including the prominent Lower Town leader Doublehead, living within the disputed territory at the Muscle Shoals. An American traveler down the Tennessee River in 1801 had noted Doublehead's settlement on the river's south bank, bolstering the Cherokee claim. This was an important piece of evidence given white Americans' belief that occupation and improvement of vacant land constituted legitimate property ownership.[11]

Cherokees even hoped that Creek leaders could vouch for their land claims. In June 1805, thirty Cherokee diplomats traveled south to Tukabatchee in the Creek Nation ostensibly to consult with Creek, Choctaw, and Chickasaw representatives about Native southerners' overlapping claims to the Tennessee Country. Yet no Chickasaws attended. Cherokees instead complained to the Creeks of the pending Chickasaw-U.S. treaty.[12] The Cherokees likely expected Creeks to support their nation's sovereignty and property rights or, at the very least, to agree that the land was shared hunting territory and could not be the sole possession of one Indigenous people.

In this way, Cherokees supported their ownership of the Great Bend with a formula common throughout the Atlantic World. Their defeat of the Chickasaws gave them a right of conquest to the region; Cherokee settlers living within the disputed boundaries legitimized their possession; and recognition of their claims from a foreign power, like the Creek Nation, shared similarities with Americans' attempts to gain international recognition for the United States. Federal officials could not simply ignore the Cherokee arguments, because they themselves were making similar points to defend U.S. possessions in North America.[13] Native peoples reformulated European defenses of colonization for their own purposes.

The 1805 Chickasaw treaty, however, destroyed Cherokee opposition to a land cession. Conflicting Chickasaw land claims had insulated Cherokees from the full force of federal negotiators, enabling them to resist American pressure for a sale, as they relied on Native unity and arguments about their rightful possession of the Tennessee Country. Yet, upon learning that their valuable hunting territory would soon open for white settlement because of the Chickasaw treaty, many Cherokee leaders began to favor a cession of their own. Federal negotiators had threatened as much during a failed treaty conference in July 1805.

Sketch of the Muscle Shoals, James Wilkinson, 1801. American Philosophical Society. Doublehead's settlement can be found on the Tennessee River's south bank.

According to Moravian missionaries living in the Cherokee Nation, U.S. diplomats warned that should Cherokees refuse a cession "the government would turn to the Chickasaws, and the requested land would be possessed by the white people." Doublehead and his neighbors living at the Muscle Shoals subsequently became the nation's greatest advocates for a treaty, and they convinced Black Fox and other Lower Town leaders to call for another Cherokee council.[14]

Like George Colbert of the Chickasaw Nation, Cherokee leaders were motivated to negotiate a cession by potential personal gain and the protection of private property. Doublehead, in particular, owed a significant amount of money to the United States for purchased goods, and he and other Cherokee settlers rightly feared that the Chickasaw cession jeopardized their settlements along the Tennessee River. Still, Cherokee leaders did not cede as much territory in an October 1805 treaty as demanded by federal commissioners. The cession included all of the Cumberland Plateau that had long separated East Tennessee from the Cumberland settlements around Nashville and the remaining Cherokee territory north of the Duck River. The thirty-three Cherokee signatories refused to cede any territory south of the confluence of the Hiwassee and Tennessee Rivers, to the chagrin of U.S. negotiators. No Chickasaw could object to the treaty, since Cherokees only sold land that Chickasaws had previously ceded three months earlier.[15]

Private Property and Political Assassination

A Cherokee land cession in January 1806 reinvigorated conflict with the Chickasaw Nation. Even before the October 1805 treaty negotiations began, Agent Meigs and the most prominent Cherokee leaders, including Black Fox, Doublehead, The Glass, James Vann, Turtle at Home, John Lowery, and The Ridge (Kahmungdaclageh), had organized a Cherokee delegation to visit Washington later in the winter. Cherokee and American leaders hoped that a negotiation would finally create order in the Tennessee Country by resolving the overlapping claims of the two Indigenous nations. After meeting with federal officials at the U.S. capital, the seventeen Native diplomats in attendance, including several who had planned the negotiation, agreed to cede all of their national territory between the Duck River and the Tennessee River, a cession that included nearly all remaining Cherokee land north of the Great Bend.[16]

Cherokee leaders benefitted significantly from the treaty, negotiating it away from public scrutiny outside of the Tennessee Country. They had learned the tenuous nature of shared land claims during the previous summer. Possibly worried that the Colberts, Chenabee, and other Chickasaw diplomats would make a further cession that might once again devalue Cherokee territory, Cherokee delegates ceded their nation's land claims first. In exchange, they received a $3,000 increase to their annuity and a one-time payment of $10,000 from the United States, which they subsequently appropriated to pay their individual debts. Black Fox acquired a $100 annual salary for the rest of his life. U.S. commissioners also included stipulations in the Cherokee treaty that established specific bounded "reserves" that would be owned by Cherokees though located outside of the nation's new border with the United States. The previous year's Chickasaw treaty included a similar one-mile-square tract, but the Cherokee reserves were more controversial because they conflicted with claims of the Chickasaw Nation. One was a strip of 100 square miles along the Tennessee River near the Muscle Shoals that would come to be known colloquially as "Doublehead's Tract." The second included six square miles at a bluff near the confluence of the Elk and Tennessee Rivers, which would be shared by Charles Hicks of the Lower Towns and Moses Melton, a white trader married to a Cherokee woman with close ties to Doublehead. President Jefferson also gave Doublehead $1,000, though this private agreement was not included in the text of the treaty.[17]

Focused on these guarantees of land and money, historians have almost universally emphasized the federal government's bribery as the sole reason Cherokee delegates agreed to the Treaty of Washington.[18] Although it is impossible to separate the treaty from the inducements, especially considering Cherokees' retaliation against these leaders in the ensuing years, Cherokee delegates' decision to cede land was connected to their ongoing contest with the Chickasaw Nation over their overlapping territories. Until the federal government began demanding land cessions, Cherokees had understood the rich lands of the Duck and Elk River watersheds to be the shared domain of all Native southerners and relied on Indigenous unity to resist American entreaties. The Chickasaws' cession in July 1805 disrupted this strategy by incentivizing quick land cessions before Cherokee land could lose its value. Bribes may have been an additional benefit for Cherokee delegates in Washington to agree to a treaty, but their path to the U.S. capital in the winter of 1806 had been much more complex.

Nevertheless, most Cherokees opposed the January 1806 treaty when they learned of its negotiation. Though many objected to the cession itself, their greatest opposition focused on the reserves along the Tennessee River. The response of Chulio, a leader from Turkey Town and a central figure among Upper Town Cherokees, is especially revealing. As a signatory to the recent treaty, Chulio almost certainly agreed that the federal government should recognize Cherokee control of the specified reserves. Yet he, along with two other Upper Town negotiators, Nephew and Kalawaskee, protested that the reserved properties near the Muscle Shoals "shall belong to the whole Nation—and not to individuals." National control of Cherokee land was a central tenet of Cherokee culture and governance, so Doublehead and his allies set a dangerous precedent by claiming the Muscle Shoals as their own personal property. Cherokees knew the difficulty of maintaining national territory against expansion-minded Americans. This task would become nearly impossible should Native individuals be able to dispose of Cherokee land as they saw fit. The land that had been shared for generations by the entire nation could not now become the individual private property of a few Lower Town Cherokees. Public opposition increased as word spread that Doublehead was renting land to white Americans and hiring others to work alongside his enslaved people. Doublehead and his allies responded to their critics, "who talks about our selling land," that "they aught to stop the Chickasaws from selling our land & not blame us."[19] With their long history of contested territorial claims, the Chickasaws were a convenient scapegoat for internal opposition to Cherokee leadership.

In early August 1807, Doublehead's political opponents assassinated him for prioritizing his own personal interests at the expense of the nation as a whole. The murder was a crucial part of what one historian of the Cherokee Nation calls the "revolt of the young chiefs" and marked Upper Town leaders' successful rejection of Lower Town domination of national affairs.[20] Yet Doublehead's death and his nation's accompanying rejection of Black Fox as beloved man were not based solely on a political dispute but also stemmed from conflicting ideas about personal property and the nation's role in administering that property. Cherokees would continue periodically to revisit the connection between property ownership and national sovereignty in the coming decades.

As the Cherokee Nation underwent political upheaval, Chickasaw leaders responded with increased intensity that their nation still exercised sovereignty over much of the Tennessee Country's Great Bend. George Colbert led Chickasaw diplomats to Washington in February 1806, where Secretary Dearborn informed them of the recent Cherokee cession. Although Dearborn insisted that the United States still recognized Chickasaw land claims, the Chickasaws distrusted the Cherokees. Colbert wanted assurances that the federal government would not survey the two reserves along the Tennessee River until the Chickasaws relinquished their claim to the region. The Chickasaws left Washington seemingly confident that their nation's ownership of Great Bend lands remained valid. Yet two years later, twenty-nine prominent Chickasaws, representing a cross-section of their nation, drafted a biting petition to federal officials in which they claimed that Cherokees had gone to Washington in 1806 to sell "part of our Country, laying on the north side of Tennessee river . . . without leting us know any thing and without our approbation." They charged that Cherokee agent Meigs and local land speculators had actively obstructed the efforts of Native southerners to determine their shared borders, implying that unclear boundary lines facilitated dispossession. Over the ensuing years, Chickasaws repeatedly protested that they never agreed to a cession of the Muscle Shoals area. Surveyor Thomas Freeman's 1807 map of the Great Bend supported their arguments, clearly showing the Muscle Shoals to be within the Chickasaw Nation. Federal officials began preparations to identify borders among the Chickasaws, Choctaws, Cherokees, and Creeks in 1811, but war with Great Britain and the Red Stick Creeks interfered. The conflict between Chickasaws and Cherokees over their competing geographies of the Tennessee Country persisted well into the nineteenth century's second decade.[21]

Challenging Claims of Conquest after the War of 1812

The War of 1812 was a war of conquest. The associated Red Stick War, in particular, demonstrates how Americans appropriated the conflicts of the mid-1810s to facilitate ongoing continental expansion. U.S. victory over Britain and its Indigenous allies destroyed much of the remaining Native military power in the eastern half of North America, which resulted in a series of land cessions to the United States at the war's end. In the South, U.S. territorial expansion began with the Treaty of Fort Jackson. The agreement negotiated in August 1814 between Andrew Jackson and Creek leaders allied with the United States decimated the territory of the Creek Nation. Ostensibly compensation for expenses related to the Red Stick War, the treaty was a massive landgrab designed to isolate Native peoples geographically from one another. Jackson coerced Creek allies of the United States to cede 23 million acres in what would become central Alabama and southern Georgia, regions that quickly developed into the American South's slave country. The boundaries of the cession were vague, leaving it unclear where the Creek cession ended and Cherokee and Chickasaw land began.[22]

Richard Brown, a Cherokee veteran of the Red Stick War, and the other Cherokee leaders in attendance at Fort Jackson realized that unclear boundaries could threaten their national territory and wanted the Creeks to define the border with the Cherokee Nation. Creek diplomats insisted that the internal disorder among their people made it impossible to settle the boundaries definitively, though they agreed to draft an informal outline of the border. Yet even this description was unclear with regard to the northern boundary of the Creek cession. It hinged on the specific location of "the old corner boundary" between the Creeks, Cherokees, and Chickasaws, defined by Creek leaders as "the Flat rock" and "known to the Cherokees by the appellation of the long leafed pine." The unclear location of this boundary marker would plague Cherokees and Chickasaws for the next two years. As federal officials made preparations to survey the limits of the Creek cession in 1815, many Cherokees worried that it would encompass their land along the south side of the Tennessee River. U.S. surveyors agreed to postpone marking the new border until after a September meeting at Tukabatchee in the Creek Nation, where Cherokee and Creek representatives could determine their shared boundaries. Negotiations between the two nations failed, though, when Creek leaders objected that the treaty at Fort Jackson was invalid because Jackson had forced them to make the agreement.[23]

Indigenous geographies were critical as Cherokees attempted to prove that their nation owned land in the proposed Creek cession. The few unofficial conversations that Cherokees and Creeks did have before the Tukabatchee conference disbanded centered on Native peoples' traditional understandings of the Tennessee Country. The speaker for the Upper Creeks had previously insisted that the borders of the Creek Nation extended all the way to the Tennessee River, known by Creeks as "Chelokee hatchee," or Cherokee River. Admitting that the Cherokee Nation had settlements south of the river, Creek history taught that these Cherokees had originally been wartime refugees. Creeks' benevolence to receive "all distressed red people into their confederacy" was the only reason Cherokees remained. Cherokee leaders, in response, considered Creek claims to any portion of the Tennessee Country invalid. If Creeks continued to argue for such a boundary, the Cherokees would themselves employ conquest theory and narrate their past military victories over the Creek Nation.[24] After the failed conference, Cherokees continued to combine their Indigenous histories with European concepts of international law to support their ownership over territory south of the Tennessee River.

Cherokee officials organized a delegation of six prominent leaders to discuss the matter further with President Madison in the early months of 1816. Before leaving for Washington, they compiled oral histories from elderly leaders in support of their contested land claims. The Glass, who was around seventy years of age and had occupied a prominent position in the nation for more than thirty years, explained that Cherokees' right to territory south of the Tennessee River stemmed from the 1773 treaty conference at Augusta. There, Cherokees and Creeks had ceded land to the British as payment for debts to Georgia traders. In this eighteenth-century conference, Creek representatives had agreed that the northern Cherokee-Creek border extended only as far as Standing Peachtree, a Creek village along the Chattahoochee River, well south of their current claims to Tennessee Country land. All territory on the Tennessee "to its mouth on *both sides* including the lands on any of its waters" was within the Cherokee Nation. The Creeks and the Chickasaws, continued The Glass, had "no good foundation" for their claims.[25]

Cherokees also relied on fictive kinship conceptions to prove their nation's superior status over both Creeks and Chickasaws. The Glass recounted that the Creeks admitted at the Augusta conference that Cherokees were their "oldest Brothers and the Cherokees always called the Creeks their younger Brothers." Other Cherokees later reported that the Chickasaws and Choctaws similarly considered Cherokees to be their "elder brothers" in numerous diplomatic negotiations. Cherokees, however, knew these peoples as "nephews," a significant metaphor given that maternal uncles held much of the responsibility for child rearing in Cherokee society. Kinship notions were essential components of diplomatic relationships throughout Native America, but in the context of the competing Indigenous land claims they took on a meaning not dissimilar from elements of European international law. By arguing that they were elder brothers or uncles to the three other southern Native peoples, Cherokee leaders believed that their national superiority would give them added credibility during negotiations with the federal government.[26]

Cherokee delegates John Lowery, John Walker, The Ridge, Richard Taylor, Cheucunsenee, and the emerging national leader John Ross (Cooweeskoowee) confronted federal officials with such arguments once they arrived in Washington in February 1816. Soldier pay, spoliation claims, agricultural and manufacturing tools, and American intruders were a few of the remaining issues from the Red Stick War that Cherokees discussed with the Madison administration, but the delegates focused most of their energy on the Treaty of Fort Jackson. Lowery, as the spokesman, emphasized the hostility of Red Stick Creeks to remind Madison of Cherokee allegiance to the United States during the recent war. But his criticism extended to U.S. leaders, too. He told the president that "you have with you, as with us red children, those who make crooked talks, like the serpent, speak with a split tongue. Believe not their talks, for they are false; nor their actions, for they are deceitful. The spirit of gain urges them, the laurel of popularity prompts them, and we, your faithful children of the Cherokee nation, who expected nothing but justice, are to fall a sacrifice to their rapaciousness." Cherokees delivered this biting critique of Jackson's negotiations early in the conference, painting the Fort Jackson Treaty as a betrayal of the Cherokee Nation.[27]

Cherokee delegates extended their indignation to John Coffee, one of Jackson's former soldiers and now a federal surveyor. In early 1816, Coffee had been investigating the limits of the Creek cession in the Tennessee Country and had even met with a few Cherokees in the area, who deferred a final decision on the boundary to their representatives in Washington. Coffee's urgency to mark the border stemmed from Jackson's wish to open land for white settlement before Cherokees or Chickasaws realized what was happening. The strategy backfired on the two speculator-soldiers. Learning of the ongoing survey while they were still in Washington, Cherokee delegates emphasized Coffee's actions as further proof of U.S. injustice to their nation. The newly inaugurated James Monroe quickly agreed to Cherokees' ownership of Great Bend territory south of the Tennessee River in a new treaty signed on March 22. He then ordered U.S. boundary commissioners to delay marking the Creek cession until Cherokee surveyors could accompany them. Cherokee arguments based in oral tradition, right of conquest, and kinship hierarchy succeeded in convincing President Madison and President Monroe that the Cherokee Nation possessed the superior title to the Tennessee Country's Great Bend.[28]

Chickasaws also objected to the boundary of the Creek cession and mounted their own campaign against the Treaty of Fort Jackson. For decades Chickasaws had insisted that they possessed title over the Great Bend in various disputes with the Cherokees. Now, with the backing of Andrew Jackson, Creeks were contending that the entire region had been within their nation until 1814 and that the border between Creek and Chickasaw land intersected at a point along "the Tennessee below the muscle shoals." Such arguments fit with Coffee's broad interpretations of the Creek cession, and he began surveying the proposed Chickasaw border from the Tennessee River south to Cotton Gin Port along the Tombigbee River after completing the Cherokee boundary. Throughout the survey, Chickasaws insulted Coffee and threatened to forcibly prevent him from running the line. The Chickasaw council also sent a delegation to Cotton Gin Port to negotiate directly with Coffee about their national boundaries, but he left before their arrival, which only increased Chickasaws' suspicions of the border.[29]

The Chickasaws grew increasingly angry over Coffee's survey as white intruders flooded into their national territory. Like the Cherokees, they organized a national council and gathered oral histories from the nation's elderly residents. The collected evidence, including oral tradition, U.S. treaties, and George Washington's 1794 proclamation that described Chickasaw national lands, all supported their claim to the Great Bend's Muscle Shoals. The Black Warrior River was the historic border between the Chickasaw and Creek Nations, and the international boundary extended north to a point on the Tennessee River above the Shoals, meaning that the valuable territory had always been within the Chickasaw Nation. A delegation led by William Colbert did go to Washington in early summer 1816 to consult with U.S. leaders, but the Chickasaws had primarily gathered the evidence of their land claims in preparation for a meeting of Native southerners in late May at Turkey Town in the Cherokee Nation.[30]

Richard Brown and Pathkiller (Nunna-tihi), the nation's principal chief, organized the council because they wanted news from the Cherokee delegation to Washington. They knew that the information would have ramifications for Choctaws, Chickasaws, and Creeks and intended the meeting to solve the issue of overlapping Native boundaries. Federal officials were aware of the significance of such a council. Accustomed to perpetuating division among Indigenous peoples, they worried about the potential for Native unity. Cherokees and Creeks decided that from now on they would "make a joint stock of their lands," allowing members of either nation to settle where they wished. Creeks and Choctaws easily agreed to maintain their existing border. Chickasaws and Cherokees, however, still articulated competing geographies of the Tennessee Country. Their two-day dispute once again centered on the Great Bend. Chickasaw delegates introduced their accumulated evidence as proof of their claims. Cherokees responded that the territory was theirs because Cherokee settlers lived on land south of the Tennessee River. They preferred that the issue between the two nations be postponed to a more "proper time" and that the "the lines between the red and white people to [be] finished first." But the Chickasaws refused Cherokee appeals. For thirty years Chickasaws had deemed clear borders to be the most effective protection of their sovereignty and property rights, and the two sides left the conference without coming to an effective agreement.[31] Their disputes at Turkey Town were so tense because Cherokees and Chickasaws were once again under pressure to cede land to the United States, a testament to the two peoples' successes in challenging the limits of the Creek cession.

Investigating Indigenous Geographies at the Chickasaw Council House

Southern whites erupted in anger upon learning that the federal government had accepted Cherokee interpretations of their national boundaries in the March 1816 treaty. Many, such as William Russell living along Bear Creek near the Muscle Shoals, were veterans of the Red Stick War and had occupied land in the Creek cession before the boundaries could be surveyed as their just reward for victory. Russell and those like him felt betrayed when hearing that "the president and secretary at war have settled the southwestern boundary of the cherokee nation so as to leave our improvements within their Territory." Andrew Jackson fumed that "the cherokees has been tampering with the creeks to filch the U States out of the land which they well knew had been ceded by the creek treaty" at Fort Jackson. Petitioners and politicians barked at federal officials to open the land so that they could transform Indians' "pathless wilderness into peaceful habitations of freemen, yielding individual wealth and natural prosperity." It took little time for U.S. officials to succumb to public pressure. Monroe's secretary of war, William Crawford, quickly organized another round of conferences.[32]

Crawford couched future negotiations as opportunities for finalizing the borders between the United States and Native nations, but he really intended to acquire more land for American settlers. White Tennesseans had long clamored for access to all land north of the Tennessee River, a region not included in anyone's interpretation of the Fort Jackson Treaty. Crawford believed Cherokees and Chickasaws would be willing to negotiate since only a few Cherokees lived in the area and it was of little value to Native hunters. Yet Chickasaws and Cherokees initially resisted such appeals. Hearing of the planned treaty, the Chickasaw council declared that their nation had no intention of selling any lands. Cherokees likewise refused. In a July meeting, Meigs and two negotiators from Tennessee, including the state's governor, Joseph McMinn, demanded a cession of all Cherokee territory north of the Tennessee River. Meigs and McMinn tried to sow division once again. The American commissioners lectured the assembled Cherokees that the Creeks and Chickasaws were "combining to deprive you of the land on the So. Side of the Tennessee river. . . . they allow you to have the precedence in the rank of nations: but while they acknowledge this they are trying to invalidate your rights." Cherokees, continued the commissioners, should cede all their claims south *and* north of the river before a Chickasaw cession of the same land would devalue Cherokee claims.[33] The assembled council possibly found such arguments compelling, remembering that Chickasaws had sold Tennessee Country territory to the federal government in 1805.

Nevertheless, Cherokees resisted the commissioners' pleas. Some of the nation's wealthiest families, including the Lowerys and Browns, lived north of the Tennessee River, and Cherokee leaders thought that the commissioners' offer of $20,000 was nowhere close to the real value of their plantations. Beginning with the Washington administration, federal officials had assumed that individual property ownership would facilitate the acquisition of Native land. In the Cherokees' case, it guaranteed their opposition. Cherokee leaders did, however, appoint a delegation to attend treaty negotiations in the Chickasaw Nation and empowered the negotiators to make decisions regarding their nation's land claims in the Great Bend.[34]

Cherokees and Chickasaws hoped that the upcoming treaty council, organized for September 1816 at the Chickasaw Council House near George Colbert's home in the Chickasaw Nation, would settle forever the dispute over their competing geographies of the Tennessee Country. To represent the United States, Crawford appointed Andrew Jackson, David Meriwether, and Jesse Franklin, who all hailed from states with a financial interest in acquiring more Native land. Jackson saw the negotiations as little more than a formality. He was confident that the commission would "regain by tribute, what I fairly . . . purchased with the sword." Once negotiations began on September 8, the American commissioners, led by Jackson, invited the Native delegates to present evidence of their land claims. Tishominko, speaker for the Chickasaws, began by introducing Washington's 1794 proclamation and a packet of oral histories collected during the previous spring. The negotiations soon took on the semblance of legal proceedings. Chickasaws called on witnesses to vouch for their interpretations of the boundary, and Cherokees and American commissioners cross-examined them. Chickasaw deponents focused much of their testimony on past military campaigns and negotiations, their memories reaching as far back as the 1780s.[35]

Several Chickasaw diplomats used Indigenous notions of "ancient times" to challenge Cherokee land claims. Major William Glover (Hullteropory) and John Brown had been taught that Cherokees had originally lived along the Atlantic coast before moving west. Chickasaws, argued Brown, "have occupied the present lands long before either his recollection, or of that of any of the nations living." Mattahameeko was even more specific in his testimony.

After coming from the west, he explained that Chickasaws "settled first at what is called the Chickasaw old Fields . . . to collect a great quantity of Flint on the Tennessee & then called the Tennessee the river where they gathered flint. That from the Chickasaw old Fields they removed to the field in this vicinity & there formed the land of life." According to such arguments, Cherokees were relatively recent immigrants, whereas Chickasaws had lived in the Tennessee Country before recorded memory. Their indigeneity proved their sovereignty. Cherokees recognized the power of such arguments and were unable to counter them. Their speaker, Toochalar of the Lower Towns, freely admitted that Cherokee delegates "were not prepared . . . that they had no witnesses with them, their old People & Traders having been left in the nation." They did, once again, insist that Doublehead's settlement along the Tennessee River proved Cherokee ownership of the region, but Chickasaws countered that Cherokees lived there only with the permission of their nation.[36]

Jackson and the other federal commissioners were prepared, however, and matched the Chickasaws' arguments with their own evidence. Their goal was to prove that the region south of the Tennessee River had been within the national boundaries of the Creek Nation until 1814, making it U.S. territory after the cession at Fort Jackson. Thus Andrew Jackson, the very embodiment of American expansion, set about making the case for Creek sovereignty in Native terms. Oral histories, witness testimony, and reports from federal surveyors were all included in the commissioners' case for the Creeks' claim. Unlike the Chickasaws, who relied on the knowledge of their elderly leaders, all of Jackson's witnesses were former officers under his command in the Red Stick War. The affidavits presented by Jackson included oral histories from white inhabitants of Tennessee and the Mississippi Territory, settlers with a vested interest in acquiring as much Native land as possible. The only Indigenous knowledge offered by the American commissioners was a June 1816 statement made by Creek leaders that merely outlined their national boundaries. Even this document reeked of Jackson's interference; it was delivered in the presence of his speculator ally John Coffee two years after the land cession, a time when Creek leaders had little incentive to oppose the wishes of U.S. officials. The assembled Chickasaws and Cherokees must have been little surprised, therefore, when the federal commissioners declared that they favored the Creeks' land claims, based, of course, on evidence provided by American expansionists.[37]

The U.S. commissioners then pressured leaders of both nations to cede land on the north and south sides of the Tennessee River. They uttered the standard refrain that smaller national limits would facilitate Native peoples' transformation from savage hunters to civilized planters, but they also acknowledged that Americans were presently living in the Creek cession and could not be evicted. Cherokees and Chickasaws were already deluged by incoming white intruders. Hearing that the United States might never remove them must have come as quite a shock, especially for the Cherokees, who six months earlier had been promised that their borders would be enforced by the United States. Cherokees were first to relent. On September 14, they agreed to a provisional cession, approved later by a national council, of all their land south of the Tennessee River included in the Creek cession in exchange for a ten-year annuity of $6,000 and a one-time payment of $5,000, though they refused to sell any other Tennessee Country territory. Chickasaws held out for several more days, possibly while some of the Native leaders negotiated for separate cash payments or guarantees that they could keep their personal plantations within the ceded territory. Then, on September 20, they too agreed to a massive cession. They sold their remaining land in the Tennessee River's Great Bend and all their territory south of the river that had been within the Creek cession for a ten-year annuity of $12,000 and a separate payment of $4,500. The treaty also recognized the individual property rights of George Colbert, Levi Colbert, John McLeish, and Apassantubby to specified parcels of land within the ceded territory that would now be under Tennessee jurisdiction.[38]

———

The two treaties crafted at the Chickasaw Council House ended the contest between Chickasaws and Cherokees over their competing geographies of the Tennessee Country, though to the detriment of both nations. Richard Brown, the frequent Cherokee diplomat living near the Tennessee River, described the 1816 treaty as "one of the crookadist line that Ever was Run in this countrey," since white speculators had convinced Creek leaders "to say there is more land belonging to them." It is tempting for historians to share Brown's sentiment and focus solely on Americans' deception in opening Native land for white settlement. Yet such a perspective overlooks the ways Native peoples resisted U.S. empire by adapting their Indigenous geographies into complex and convincing legal arguments. These "hidden transcripts," as one historian calls them, were powerful diplomatic tools in negotiations with both American officials and leaders of other Native nations.[39]

Epilogue

Ancient Lines, Enduring Geographies

Toochalar, a prominent Cherokee diplomat from the Lower Towns, dictated two messages to U.S. Cherokee agent Return J. Meigs in late August 1816. In the first, he and three other Lower Towns leaders complained about the actions of Issac McMeans, a white man living in the Cherokee Nation near Willstown. McMeans, they reported, had been stealing hogs and burning fences. Toochalar and the other Cherokees demanded that Meigs evict McMeans from their national lands. In the second message, written the same day as the first, Toochalar began by notifying Meigs that he would be attending the upcoming negotiations in the Chickasaw Nation, but he then pivoted from events in the present to events in the past. "It is a long time ago that the white people . . . first asked us for land," he explained. "They first began at Wataugee with the treatys & we have sold along till we have but a small tract of country left."[1] Toochalar was interpreting the long history of Native dispossession in the Tennessee Country, which according to his understanding began in the early 1770s with white intruders' creation of the Watauga Association in the upper Tennessee Valley. It was no coincidence that Toochalar reflected on this history of land loss as he prepared to travel to the Chickasaw Council House, where he knew he would face pressure for yet another territorial cession. But it is likely that Toochalar's thinking about McMeans also sparked his narrative of past dispossession. Cherokees and Chickasaws had been defending their property from men like McMeans for a generation by reimagining their Tennessee Country territory. Persisting against the forces of American empire, however, whether in the form of U.S. treaty negotiators or white intruders like Isaac McMeans, would become increasingly difficult in the second decade of the nineteenth century.

Ongoing Dispossession

Despite their reluctant decision to cede Tennessee Country territory during negotiations at the Chickasaw Council House, Chickasaws continued to face incessant demands on their national lands. In early 1818, members of James Monroe's cabinet began pressuring them to exchange their territory east of the Mississippi River for lands to the west. At the time, Chickasaws were still waiting to receive the regular annuity payments and financial compensation for previous land cessions and insisted that they would make no additional agreements until the federal government fulfilled its existing obligations. U.S. treaty commissioners Andrew Jackson and Isaac Shelby, the aging former Kentucky governor, used these payments and veiled threats of white settlers' ongoing invasion to convince Chickasaws to assemble once again at the Chickasaw Council House in October. There, Jackson and Shelby distributed the funds and insisted that Chickasaw diplomats cede their existing national lands for territory across the Mississippi. Refusing to abandon the entirety of their homelands, Chickasaws eventually agreed to cede all of their land between the Tennessee and Mississippi Rivers in present-day Kentucky and Tennessee. In return, Jackson and Shelby promised the Chickasaw Nation a fifteen-year annuity of $20,000 and offered payments to several individual Chickasaw negotiators. The only remaining Chickasaw land in the Tennessee Country included a valuable salt lick along the Big Sandy River, which Levi Colbert and James Brown could lease for the benefit of the nation, and a few small individual reserves secured in earlier treaties. The salt lick and the reserves reflected the ongoing emergence of some Chickasaws' interest in individual land ownership. The federal government's recognition of these property rights allowed specified Native diplomats to maintain land outside of their nation's borders, a strategy that hundreds of Cherokees would soon employ as well. Nevertheless, white Americans would acquire even these Chickasaw properties in the coming years. Residents of Nashville honored Jackson and Shelby with a celebratory ball after learning of the 1818 treaty. They were thrilled that the Chickasaw cession opened 10,700 square miles for settlers and land speculators.[2]

White Americans sought a similar victory over Cherokee sovereignty. Cherokees had ceded land in the southwestern portions of their nation with their 1816 treaty, but mere months later North Carolina legislators demanded that they surrender all of their remaining territory within North Carolina's borders, a region almost entirely located within the Tennessee River watershed. The Cherokee Nation's national council rejected their appeals. Sickatowee, speaking on behalf of his Valley Town neighbors living along the headwaters of the Hiwassee River, was especially direct. "The white people are now all around us," he explained to Agent Meigs. "We are just like an island. We want the ancient lines yet to stand." Sickatowee insisted that Cherokee borders remain unchanged. Surprised that American officials would even propose a new treaty, Pathkiller speculated that the pressure for a land cession was the result of a "collusion of Designing men of our white brothers on the frontier, and our Idle people wishing to go over the Mississippi."[3] That white Americans wanted Cherokee land was nothing new. Pathkiller's admission that some Cherokees favored a cession, however, reflected internal disagreement within the nation about Cherokees' future in the Tennessee Country.

As early as the 1780s, Cherokees had been migrating west in search of new territory away from white intruders. Scholars estimate that roughly five thousand Cherokees had created new lives in the trans-Mississippi West by the 1820s, first settling along the St. Francis River and then moving farther west in subsequent years. "It was not a national movement," explained one Cherokee leader remaining in the east, "but that of persons indulging themselves in their natural liberty, in going to the place where they thought they could pass through life more pleasantly than in their own country." Federal officials began encouraging such emigration in the first decades of the nineteenth century. To persuade Cherokees to make a cession of their Tennessee Country lands in early 1809, for example, Thomas Jefferson promised that the United States would allow prospective emigrants to explore the Arkansas and White River watersheds for a suitable tract of land and then guarantee their right to this new territory. Migrating Cherokees knew, though, that the promised land west of the Mississippi was not empty but home to the Osage people. Osages responded to Cherokees' infringement on their sovereignty and their valuable hunting territory by attacking the region's new Native inhabitants. Cherokees retaliated and organized a military alliance among the Osages' traditional enemies. This conflict simmered for years until Osages recognized Cherokee rights to Arkansas Valley territory in 1822, showing how the effects of American empire could generate violence among Indigenous peoples. War with the Osage Nation led the Western Cherokees, as this group of Cherokee emigrants became known, to appeal to the United States for a bordered land of their own that would be acknowledged by white Americans and Native peoples alike.[4]

Normally deaf to Native peoples' wishes in their ongoing effort to wrest land from Cherokees still living in the Tennessee Country, federal officials underscored the Western Cherokees' perilous situation. In June 1817, U.S. commissioners arrived in the Cherokee Nation to coerce Cherokee diplomats to surrender their Tennessee Country territory. In exchange, the federal government would guarantee Cherokee sovereignty over a tract of land in the Arkansas Valley that would include the Western Cherokees' existing settlements. Acting secretary of war George Graham recognized that some Cherokees, particularly those who owned a significant amount of property, would resist emigrating west, so he allowed federal commissioners to issue 640-acre reserves to heads of these families. Graham saw no future for the Cherokee Nation in the Tennessee Country. Cherokees could either leave and maintain a communal land base in Arkansas or remain and exercise individual property rights under state jurisdiction.[5]

After days of negotiation, Cherokee diplomats would not relent to a complete exchange of lands. They did cede more than 400 square miles in Tennessee's Sequatchie Valley and roughly 600 square miles along Georgia's Chattahoochee River, territory that supposedly would compensate for a bordered land of proportional size for the Western Cherokees. The 1817 treaty also included vague details about Cherokees' further emigration to Arkansas and outlined provisions that would allow the heads of Cherokee families living on ceded land to apply for individual reserves of 640 acres. Negotiations were tense. Richard Brown later accused Western Cherokees of forging his name on treaty documents. Some Native diplomats simply left the treaty ground before the meeting concluded.[6]

Such disorder continued for much of 1818. Parties of Cherokee emigrants began leaving the Tennessee Country for Arkansas, with emigration opponents resorting to political pressure and even violence to prevent their movement west. Cherokees remaining in the east wanted to limit the population of Western Cherokees. They knew that the federal government might expect additional Tennessee Country land cessions and would provide Western Cherokees with a greater portion of the nation's annuity payment as the number of Cherokees living in the Arkansas Valley increased. In a July meeting, the National Council raised the stakes by ruling that any Cherokee ceding land without proper authorization faced execution. A separate council of Cherokee women took the opportunity to register their own protests to emigration. They unanimously passed a resolution to "hold our country in common as hitherto," refusing the federal government's attempt to force Cherokees either to remain in the east and take land individually or to leave for Arkansas.[7]

Members of the National Council appointed yet another Cherokee delegation to negotiate directly with federal officials in Washington during the winter months and clarify all remaining uncertainty from the 1817 treaty. The twelve Cherokee diplomats, including Charles Hicks, John Ross, and George Lowery (Agili), arrived at the U.S. capital in early February 1819. They met with secretary of war John C. Calhoun, who repeated U.S. officials' earlier remarks that Cherokees must either "hold your land separate among yourselves, as your white neighbors" or "emigrate." Cherokee diplomats would not capitulate to Calhoun's demands. They eventually agreed to relinquish more Tennessee Country territory to compensate for the federal government's guarantee of land for the Western Cherokees, but they dictated the cession boundaries. Charles Hicks, speaking on behalf of the Cherokee delegation, offered to cede a crescent of territory that stretched from Madison County, Alabama, northeast to the watersheds of the Hiwassee and Little Tennessee Rivers and then southeast across the Great Smoky Mountains into North Carolina and northern Georgia. Federal officials accepted the Cherokees' boundary proposals in a treaty signed on February 27.[8]

The 1819 treaty ended the federal government's formal pressure for western emigration, albeit temporarily, and represented the final Cherokee cession of Tennessee Country territory until the infamous Treaty of New Echota sixteen years later. The inclusion of individual reserves of 640 acres in the treaty was especially significant for both Native and U.S. negotiators. "This cession," admitted Hicks, "will disturb a large portion of Our Citizens but we confide in the Liberality of the Government in providing for them by Reservations & compensation for their improvements." Hicks knew that Cherokees lived on these ceded lands, but he demanded that the federal government acknowledge their property rights. Three years earlier, members of the National Council had ruled that Cherokee leaders had "no right to dispossess any Cherokee whatever of his improvements without his consent." Thus, the 1819 treaty's recognition of Native individuals' personal property rights aligned with Cherokee notions of individual land ownership in the second decade of the nineteenth century. By possessing a reserve within the ceded territory, a Cherokee would be able to "live on such an estate," continued Hicks, "or move elsewhere and lease it for his benefit as he should think proper."[9] The 1819 treaty, along with the previous 1817 agreement that it clarified, sparked a new era of Native border making in the Tennessee Country by allowing Cherokees to exercise individual property rights outside of their nation's boundaries.

Cherokee Reserves in History and Memory

One scholar of Cherokee history insists that the story of reservees, those individuals securing 640-acre reserves under the 1817 and 1819 treaties, represents a failed "experiment in Cherokee citizenship." Almost all reservees lost their property over the course of the 1820s as states sold the ceded lands to white buyers without acknowledging Cherokees' rights and as white intruders drove Native families back into the nation itself.[10] Yet assuming that Native individuals hoped to become American citizens and anticipating reservees' so-called failure discounts the fact that Cherokees took reserves to maintain their property. Generations of Native inhabitants of the Tennessee Country had been bounding their national territories. It should come as little surprise that some Cherokees sought to create a border around their individual lands in territory ceded to the United States.

Cherokees began securing their individual property in the immediate aftermath of the 1819 treaty. In June, for example, Eight Killer traveled to the Cherokee Agency along the Hiwassee River. There, he submitted an application for a reserve "on a place that he settled" along Fire Gizzard Creek, a branch of Battle Creek that flowed south into the Tennessee River. Eight Killer was not alone; numerous Cherokees applied in person or submitted written declarations about their wish for a reserve. Overall, nearly 350 Cherokees received reserves under the terms of the 1817 and 1819 treaties. Most held their property as a "life estate" that they would possess for the rest of their lives, becoming the property of their heirs at the time of their death. Owners of life estate reserves risked their land reverting to the United States if they did not reside on it permanently. The 1819 treaty, however, specified thirty-one Cherokee men and women who could apply for "fee simple" reserves, meaning that they could live on the property or sell it without any restrictions.[11] Though an important distinction, Cherokees taking fee simple and life estate reserves both did so as a way to preserve their property in the aftermath of major land cessions.

Among the recipients of a fee simple reserve was Elizabeth Pack. Pack was the daughter of Elizabeth Shorey and John Lowery, a prominent Cherokee leader living north of the Tennessee River. She eventually married William Shorey Pack, though he was likely deceased by 1819. Kinship ties were certainly important for Pack's acquisition of a reserve. Her uncle, George Lowery, had represented the Cherokee Nation at the 1819 negotiations and possibly encouraged the delegates to recognize Pack's property rights in the ceded territory. As required by the treaty, Pack dutifully informed Agent Meigs that she wished to secure ownership of her property. "It is my intention," she wrote Meigs in June 1819, "to continue to reside permanently on the land reserved to me in said Treaty." Seven months later, a team of American surveyors arrived at Pack's home and marked her reserve on the Tennessee Country landscape in accordance with their instructions.[12]

The neatly drawn plat that identified the borders of Elizabeth Pack's property does little to reveal the complex history of the reserve and its connection to broader themes of American empire, Native dispossession, and ongoing settler erasure. In the second decade of the nineteenth century, Pack was a business partner of the longtime Lower Town Cherokee leader Turtle at Home, working with him at his property in the Sequatchie Valley until his death. Pack's reserve included much of Turtle at Home's land. A visitor to Turtle at Home's residence in 1816 mentioned a "transparent fountain" nearby, "which gushing out from the earth forms at once a pretty running stream." Surveyors of Pack's reserve identified a similar spring directly west of her home. Not only was Pack's property valuable because it was well watered, but the main highway from Georgia to Nashville also bisected it, meaning that Pack could sell supplies and provisions to travelers along the road, as she had done in previous years as an innkeeper. The land's value did not go unnoticed. Only weeks after the survey of her reserve, Pack asked members of the National Council for permission to move back within the boundaries of the Cherokee Nation and occupy property on the south side of the Tennessee River near Nickajack Town where she might operate a ferry. Pack "could not stand to live among some of the bad white people in her neighborhood." These settlers had recently moved into the Cherokee territory ceded a year earlier and were harassing Cherokee reservees, like Pack and Eight Killer, living near Battle Creek.[13]

The council approved her request, but Pack had little success establishing a new residence at Nickajack. As she began transferring her personal effects and enslaved people across the Tennessee River, Pack encountered opposition from John H. Jeffrey, a white man married to Alcey Wilson, the daughter of Thomas Wilson, a Cherokee who possessed a fee simple reserve in the Alabama Territory. Jeffrey, a suspected embezzler, was known to already live at Nickajack. He had been hired to occupy the area for another white man named Underwood, who wished to farm the property. Underwood employed Jeffrey because his marriage

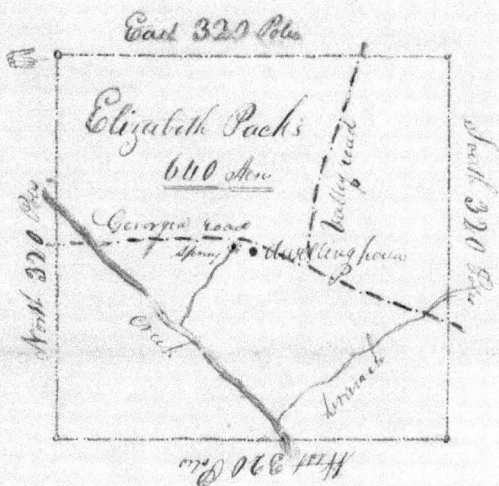

C 2-9-11

East 320 Poles

Elizabeth Pack's
640 Acre

Georgia road
Spring • dwelling house
valley road

North 320 Poles

South 320 Poles

road

branch

West 320 Poles

State of Tennessee

The undersigned Commissioner and Surveyor (duly authorised) have agreeably to the terms of the late Cherokee Treaty concluded at the city of Washington on the twenty seventh day of February one thousand eight hundred and nineteen, surveyed and laid off to Elizabeth Pack six hundred and forty acres of land on the North side of Tennessee River. Beginning at a Sweet gum sapling, and a bunch of White oaks: (about twenty poles on the East side of a large spring) thence East three hundred and twenty poles, to a double white oak: (crossing the valley road at two hundred and forty eight poles) thence South three hundred and twenty poles to a small hickory: (crossing the branch at one hundred

---

Survey of Elizabeth Pack Reserve, January 28, 1820, Tennessee State Library and Archives. Pack's reserve was made especially valuable because of its location along the Georgia Road, its proximity to the Tennessee River, and its inclusion of a spring.

143

to Alcey Wilson supposedly gave him a right to live in the Cherokee Nation. When Jeffrey learned that Pack was trying to move onto the Nickajack property, "he came running with a company of fellows," complained Pack, "with clubs dirks and gathering of stones putting on every appearance they possibly could to scare me and my hands off trying to make believe they would beat us." The National Committee, a group of Cherokee officials charged with governing the nation between meetings of the National Council, quickly sent a force of their own to drive Jeffrey from Pack's property and enforce their jurisdiction over the nation's lands, but Pack was not able to make a permanent home at Nickajack. By the 1830s, she was living in the southwestern region of the Cherokee Nation near Big Wills Creek in present-day northeast Alabama.[14]

But what of Pack's original 1819 reserve? Visitors to Jasper, Tennessee, can find an answer on a historical marker erected in 1954 by the Tennessee Historical Commission on the grounds of the Marion County courthouse. The marker mentions that Pack provided the land that became the town of Jasper in 1820. A journalist for the *Chattanooga News* explained the details of the donation in 1936, reporting that Jasper's twentieth-century residents owed their town's location to "the canny financial sense of an Indian." Pack gave forty acres so that Marion County's seat of government would be moved ten miles down the Sequatchie Valley from its original location at Whitwell, Tennessee. Marion County records seemingly support Pack's beneficence. On July 1, 1821, she sold forty acres to commissioners of Marion County for $1.00 for the establishment of Jasper, though town commissioners had organized the sale of town plots five months earlier. Pack already had made plans to lease other portions of her reserve, and soon after she arranged to move south to Nickajack. For decades, Native peoples of the Tennessee Country had shaped how white Americans moved through their lands in order to increase their personal income.[15] Pack may have had similar intentions in mind, particularly considering that she and Turtle at Home had previously operated their own business along the highway to Nashville.

Marion County's white residents soon turned against their early benefactor. When Pack was sued over a dispute involving a fraudulent contract in 1823, her attorney, Nathan Green, appealed to the Tennessee legislature for a change in venue. "The reservation made for her under" the 1819 treaty, noted Green, had "excited a strong prejudice in the minds of many of the people who have settled the territory acquired by the treaty." Although by this time Pack had sold all of her land in Marion County and lived once again in the Cherokee Nation, Green insisted that "this prejudice still prevails against her & that she has been very much harassed by pretended claims set up against her."[16] The outcome of her lawsuit is unclear, but the fact that Pack worried about Marion County residents' impartiality is revealing. Despite her apparent generosity in establishing the town of Jasper in 1821, two years later Pack believed that she would not receive a fair trial among the community's white residents because she had been the owner of a fee simple reserve, the very same piece of property she had donated to these Jasper inhabitants.

Elizabeth Pack's memory survives in Jasper today. In addition to the historical marker, the town's central north-south thoroughfare is known as Betsy Pack Drive, an example of what historian Andrew Denson terms a monument to absence. Such public commemorations of Cherokee history recognize that certain places were once significant to Cherokee people even as they also "confirm the familiar narrative of Indian disappearance."[17] Elizabeth Pack's decision to acquire a reserve under the 1819 treaty was another way that Cherokees reimagined their space and territory in the Tennessee Country to maintain their property in the face of American expansion. Yet nostalgic odes and perfunctory public commemorations relegate Native peoples to the past, ignoring the process of dispossession that resulted in their removal and their contemporary ties to their traditional homelands. However, members of the Eastern Band of Cherokee Indians are creating their own public commemorations, persisting against the forces of settler empire in the present-day Tennessee Country.

Competing Geographies, Past and Present

Mount Collins, one of the highest peaks in the Great Smoky Mountains, is an impressive sight. Thousands of visitors climb it annually because of its location along the Appalachian Trail, the most iconic footpath in the United States. Rising to an elevation of 6,188 feet, the mountain offers commanding views of Tennessee to the west and North Carolina to the east. The peak's crest serves as the border between the two states. Water from Mount Collins's western slope forms the Little River, a small tributary that flows through Blount County, Tennessee, before emptying into the main channel of the Tennessee River south of Knoxville. Runoff from the mountain's eastern slope finds its way into the Tuckasegee River, which intersects the Little Tennessee River in western North Carolina. The Little Tennessee carves a deep valley before meeting the Tennessee River near Lenoir City, Tennessee. Despite its position along a state border, Mount Collins is entirely within the Tennessee Country, the watery geography that continues to connect today's inhabitants of western North Carolina and East Tennessee.

As important as the peak remains for twenty-first-century residents of the Tennessee Country, Mount Collins was a site of international significance for two decades at the beginning of the nineteenth century. In August 1802, a party of Cherokee and American officials summited the mountain and identified the peak as the "top" of the Great Iron Mountains, the original name for the Great Smoky Mountains. The exact location was important, for the tallest summit in the range as selected by the surveying party was to signify the beginning of a new border between the Cherokee Nation and the United States, negotiated four years earlier at the 1798 Treaty of Tellico. According to one account of the event, the Americans and Cherokees "erected a Post of spruce pine 15 inches in diameter Six feet high Pointed at top drawing a line from top to Bottom to designate our course & marked on the North side U.S. 1802. R. J. Meigs, A.W. & T. Freeman USS & on the South side C.N. U & E Cherokee Chiefs. & erected a mound of Stone around the post of about 2 Tons of Stone . . . from that moment we commenced our line between the Cherokees & North Carolina." The six-foot post surrounded by two tons of rock would be difficult to miss for inhabitants of the Tennessee Country. Leading members of the surveying team inscribed their names deep into the pine post to further demonstrate the marker's legitimacy as the dividing line between the United States to the north and the Cherokee Nation to the south. The marker included the names of Return J. Meigs, U.S. agent for the Cherokee Nation, and Thomas Freeman, a professional surveyor frequently employed by the United States to identify boundaries throughout the American Southeast. The initials of the two "Cherokee Chiefs" likely abbreviated the names of William Elders, a longtime Native diplomat of Cherokee towns along the Tennessee River in the southwestern portion of the nation, and either Unokola or Ukaloukee, two Cherokees working as guides for the surveying party. Until the early twentieth century, Mount Collins was known colloquially as Meigs Post, a recognition of the 1802 boundary marker's significance. The original wood post has long disintegrated, but an inconspicuous pylon, constructed in the 1950s, marks its original location only feet from the Appalachian Trail. Most hikers traversing the busy footpath likely pay no mind to the stubby moss-covered structure of concrete and rebar. Yet it serves as a lasting symbol of American empire, Native sovereignty, and the bordered land of the Tennessee Country.[18]

The area around the site of the 1802 Meigs Post continues to be especially important for Cherokee people. Roughly three miles southwest of Mount Collins is the highest point in the Great Smoky Mountains National Park, a peak

This short concrete pylon replaced the original wooden post that identified the border between the United States and the Cherokee Nation, negotiated in 1798 and surveyed in 1802. The marker can be found along the Appalachian Trail near its intersection with Sugarland Mountain Trail in the Great Smoky Mountains National Park. Photograph by Emma J. Kelley.

known as Kuwohi (ᎫᏫᎯ), which translates to "mulberry place" in the Cherokee language. Annually, hundreds of thousands of visitors take in the 360-degree view atop the mountain's observation tower, which is accessible by automobile. Until recently, these tourists would have referred to the peak as Clingman's Dome, a name that it had held since the mid-nineteenth century after the forced relocation of most Cherokee people to Indian Territory. The new designation of Kuwohi, which officially took effect on September 18, 2024, was the result of a resolution by the Eastern Band of Cherokee Indians, whose leaders called on the U.S. Board on Geographic Names to restore the peak's original, Indigenous name. Lavita Hill and Mary "Missy" Crowe, the authors of the resolution, argued that Kuwohi was much more appropriate than Clingman's Dome. Not only does the mountain hold historical and spiritual significance for Cherokee people, but Thomas Clingman, the peak's eponym, was also "an avowed racist" who opposed emancipation and later fought to preserve slavery as a general in the Confederate Army. "From time immemorial, the landscape, including the mountains and streams, has shaped our history as Cherokee people," noted Hill and Crowe. Their successful restoration of Kuwohi as the peak's name is a contemporary acknowledgment of this history. Indigenous notions of space and territory defined the landscape of the Tennessee Country long before white expansionists drove Cherokees and Chickasaws from their national lands. Cherokee efforts to recover the region's Indigenous nomenclature demonstrate how Native peoples' geographical understandings continue to impact the Tennessee Country in the present day, as was the case in the eighteenth and nineteenth centuries.[19]

Notes

Abbreviations

ADAH	Alabama Department of Archives and History, Montgomery
ASP:IA	*American State Papers: Documents, Legislative and Executive, of the United States*, Class II: Indian Affairs, ed. Walter Lowrie and Walter S. Franklin, 2 vols. Washington, DC: Gales and Seaton, 1834
BIA-M15	Records from the Office of the Secretary of War, Letters Sent by the Office of the Secretary of War Relating to Indian Affairs, 1800–1823, Record Group 75, Microcopy 15, Bureau of Indian Affairs, NA
BIA-M208	Records of the Cherokee Indian Agency in Tennessee, 1801–1835, Record Group 75, Microcopy 208, Bureau of Indian Affairs, NA
BIA-M271	Records from the Office of the Secretary of War, Letters Received by the Secretary of War Relating to Indian Affairs, 1800–1823, Record Group 75, Microcopy 271, Bureau of Indian Affairs, NA
BIA-T494	Documents Relating to the Negotiation of Ratified and Unratified Treaties with Various Tribes of Indians, 1801–69, Record Group 75, Microcopy T494, Bureau of Indian Affairs, NA
CSRNC	*The Colonial Records of North Carolina*, 10 vols., ed. William L. Saunders; and *The State Records of North Carolina*, 16 vols., ed. Walter Clark. Raleigh, 1886–1907
CVSP	*Calendar of Virginia State Papers and Other Manuscripts*, ed. William P. Palmer et al., 11 vols. Richmond, 1875–1893
DRAPER	Lyman Draper Manuscripts, microfilm, State Historical Society of Wisconsin, Madison
EAID	*Early American Indian Documents: Treaties and Laws, 1607–1789*, ed. Alden T. Vaughan. Bethesda, MD: University Publications of America, 1979–
FHS	Filson Historical Society, Louisville, Kentucky
GASR	General Assembly Session Records, SANC
JGB	*The John Gray Blount Papers*, ed. Alice Barnwell Keith, William H. Masterson, and David T. Morgan, 4 vols. Raleigh, NC: State Department of Archives and History, 1952–1982

LBH	*Letters, Journals, and Writings of Benjamin Hawkins*, ed. C.L. Grant, 2 vols. Savannah, GA: Beehive Press, 1980
LC	Library of Congress, Washington, DC
MHS	Massachusetts Historical Society, Boston
NA	National Archives and Records Administration, Washington, DC
NL	Newberry Library, Chicago, Illinois
PAJ	*The Papers of Andrew Jackson*, ed. Sam B. Smith et al., 11 vols. Knoxville: University of Tennessee Press, 1980–
PGW	*The Papers of George Washington: Presidential Series*, ed. Dorothy Twohig et al., 21 vols. Charlottesville: University Press of Virginia, 1987–2020
PICKENS	Journal of the Proceedings of the Commissioners Appointed to Ascertain & Mark the Boundary Lines Agreeably to the Treaties Between the Indian Nations & the United States, vol. 1, Andrew Pickens Papers, South Caroliniana Library, University of South Carolina
PTJ	*The Papers of Thomas Jefferson*, ed. Julian P. Boyd et al., 45 vols. Princeton, NJ: Princeton University Press, 1950–
RL	Rubenstein Rare Book and Manuscript Library, Duke University, Durham, NC
SANC	State Archives of North Carolina, Raleigh
SHC	Southern Historical Collection, Wilson Library, University of North Carolina at Chapel Hill
TPUS	*The Territorial Papers of the United States*, ed. Clarence Edwin Carter, 28 vols. Washington, DC: Government Printing Office, 1934–1962
TSLA	Tennessee State Library and Archives, Nashville
UGA	Hargrett Rare Book and Manuscript Library, University of Georgia Libraries, Athens
UTK	Betsey B. Creekmore Special Collections and University Archives, University of Tennessee at Knoxville
WINCHESTER	Surveyor's Notebook—Winchester, James, 1787–1800, box 4, folder 16, Winchester, James (1752–1826) Papers, 1787–1923, TSLA

Introduction

1. *ASP:IA*, 1:284–285; Commission of Governor Blount, June 8, 1790, Henry Knox to William Blount, March 31, 1792, Henry Knox to William Blount, April 22, 1792, and William Blount to Henry Knox, July 4, 1792, all in *TPUS*, 4:24, 131–132, 137–143, 157–158; Henry Knox to Chiefs and Warriors of the Choctaw Nation, February 17, 1792, Henry Knox to Piomin[k]o and Other Chickasaw Leaders, February 17, 1792, Henry Knox to Andrew Pickens, April 21, 1792, and William Blount to Piomin[k]o, April 27, 1792, all in

ASP:IA, 1:248–249, 251, 266; Henry Knox, Report to President Washington, January 17, 1792, *PGW*, 9:449–452; O'Brien, *Choctaws in a Revolutionary Age*, 94; Andrew, *Life and Times of General Andrew Pickens*, 237–239. On St. Clair's defeat, see Calloway, *Victory with No Name*. Wolf's Friend is identified as Mooleshawskek in the conference minutes, but most sources use Ugulayacabe. See Atkinson, *Splendid Land, Splendid People*, 274–275n15; and Weeks, "Of Rattlesnakes, Wolves, and Tigers," 487–488n2. Historians have traditionally referred to Piominko as "Piomingo," but I use Piominko in accordance with a recent decision of the Chickasaw Nation. His personal and war names remain unknown; Piominko translates to "prophet leader." Chickasaw Nation, "Native History: Chickasaw Nation Corrects Names of Famed Leaders, *Indian Country Today*, September 13, 2018, https://ictnews.org/archive/native-history-chickasaw-nation-corrects-names-of-famed -leaders, accessed May 3, 2024. See also, Cowger and Caver, *Piominko*.

2. *ASP:IA*, 1:286; Treaty of Natchez, May 14, 1792, in Weeks, *Paths to a Middle Ground*, 201–202, see also 77–80. Descriptions of treaty negotiations were most often made by European or American observers, leading some scholars to rightly question whether the Native ideas presented in these sources actually were their own or merely European ideas embedded in Indigenous voices, a concept described by Andrew Fitz-maurice as "ethnological ventriloquism." Fitzmaurice agrees that scholars should approach such sources critically but insists that these Indigenous arguments must be taken seriously or risk overlooking Native perspectives entirely. See Fitzmaurice, "Powhatan Legal Claims," 86–87. For treaty negotiations as colonialism, see Jones, *License for Empire*. Throughout this work, I maintain the spelling and verbiage of the original sources unless otherwise noted.

3. *ASP:IA*, 1:204, 273, 286. For Nontuaka's home, see John McKee to William Blount, March 28, 1793, *ASP:IA*, 1:444.

4. *ASP:IA*, 1:286–287.

5. *ASP:IA*, 1:285–286. On the region's significance as a crossroads for Native peoples, see Ray, "Understanding the Tennessee Corridor."

6. For my understanding of sovereignty, see Onuf, "Sovereignty," 429–433; Ford, *Settler Sovereignty*; and Barr, "Geographies of Power."

7. *Knoxville Gazette*, March 6, 1797. Arguments about the Tennessee Country's vacant or empty lands reflected longstanding notions of international law based on Lockean concepts of occupancy and improvement. Because Chickasaws and Cherokees used much of the region for hunting, many white Americans claimed that Native peoples' property ownership was illegitimate. See Banner, *How the Indians Lost Their Land*, 150–190; MacMillan, *Sovereignty and Possession in the English New World*; Pagden, "Law, Colonization, Legitimation, and the European Background," 21–22; Greer, "Commons and Enclosure in the Colonization of North America"; Greer, *Property and Dispossession*, 243–254; Erbig, *Where Caciques and Mapmakers Met*, 43–44; and Witgen, "Nation of Settlers." Lauren Benton complicates scholars' emphasis on occupation as the driving force behind colonization by highlighting the significance of the legal concept of possession. Benton, "Possessing Empire." On Americans' intentional overemphasis of Native peoples' reliance on hunting to denigrate their property rights, see Usner, "Iroquois Livelihood and Jeffersonian Agrarianism."

8. Guyatt, "Imperialism and the American Imagination"; Onuf, *Jefferson's Empire*; Onuf, "'Empire for Liberty'"; Onuf, "Imperialism and Nationalism in the Early American Republic"; Ostler, "Native Americans against Empire and Colonial Rule"; Conroy-Krutz,

"Empire and the Early Republic"; Bjork, *Prairie Imperialists*; Dahl, *Empire of the People*; Steele and Onuf, "South in the Revolutionary Era and Early Republic," 75–79. On the imagined nature of the British, Spanish, and French North American empires that preceded the United States, see Mapp, *Elusive West and the Contest for Empire*; and Edelson, *New Map of Empire*. Mapp's analysis is especially useful for demonstrating how architects of European empires based their imagined imperial visions on Indigenous peoples' geographies. For the utility of imperial frameworks and a historiographical overview of American empire, see Kramer, "Power and Connection"; and Blaakman and Conroy-Krutz, introduction to *Early Imperial Republic*.

9. Rothman, *Slave Country*; Johnson, *River of Dark Dreams*; Shire, *Threshold of Manifest Destiny*; Taylor, "War of 1812 and the Struggle for a Continent." Scholarship on the American colonization north of the Ohio River is vast. For analyses of the many ways the federal government created a continental empire in this region, see Cayton, "'Separate Interests' and the Nation-State"; Hinderaker, *Elusive Empires*; Griffin, *American Leviathan*; Clark, "Ohio Country in the Political Economy of Nation Building"; Van Atta, *Securing the West*; Bergmann, *American National State and the Early West*; Saler, *Settlers' Empire*; Bowes, *Land Too Good for Indians*; and Daggar, "Mission Complex." For standard interpretations of U.S. land policies within the public domain, see Gates, *History of Public Land Law Development*; and Rohrbough, *Land Office Business*. For an excellent overview of the evolution of U.S. land policy, see Huston, "Land Conflict and Land Policy in the United States." On U.S. state power in the Northwest Territory, see Pasley, "Midget on Horseback"; Griffin, *American Leviathan*; Clark, "Ohio Country in the Political Economy of Nation Building"; Van Atta, *Securing the West*; Bergmann, *American National State and the Early West*; Saler, *Settlers' Empire*; and Daggar, "Mission Complex." Michael Blaakman employs a more expansive definition of state power that includes an analysis of state governments. Blaakman, *Speculation Nation*. Rachel St. John argues that the U.S. state was present but just not powerful in the American West. St. John, "State Power in the West in the Early American Republic." Rob Harper offers a provocative analysis that posits that Ohio Valley violence stemmed from efforts of state building rather than from a lack of state power. Harper, *Unsettling the West*. On U.S. Indian policy as a vehicle for American state power, see Rockwell, *Indian Affairs and the Administrative State in the Nineteenth Century*.

10. Shankman, "Toward a Social History of Federalism"; Roney, "1776, Viewed from the West" (for "bottom-up, settler-driven," 659); Hammond, *Slavery, Freedom, and Expansion in the Early American West*; Hammond, "Slavery, Settlement, and Empire." Historian Andrew Cayton has explored this difference in federal policy north and south of the Ohio River and argues that U.S leaders cared more about the Northwest Territory because of their personal speculation in northwest land. Cayton, "'Separate Interests' and the Nation-State." See also Holton, *Forced Founders*. Historian and legal scholar Gregory Ablavsky argues against a clear distinction between events in the Northwest and Southwest Territories. Instead, he contends that the federal government gained authority throughout the trans-Appalachian West by resolving the competing land claims to the region and attempting to control violence between Native peoples and white Americans. Ablavsky, *Federal Ground*.

11. Barr and Countryman, "Maps and Spaces, Paths to Connect, and Lines to Divide," 22–23; Merrell, "Some Thoughts on Colonial Historians and American Indians"; Merrell, "Second Thoughts on Colonial Historians and American Indians";

Johnson and Graybill, "Borders and Their Historians in North America," 2; Hoxie, "Retrieving the Red Continent"; Witgen, "Rethinking Colonial History as Continental History"; Witgen, "A Nation of Settlers." Chad Anderson contends that British cartographers acknowledged the presence of Native settlements on colonial maps to facilitate the incorporation of Indigenous peoples within the British empire. Anderson, "Rediscovering Native North America." For recent studies that emphasize Native agency, see Merrell, *Indians' New World*; White, *Middle Ground*; Richter, *Ordeal of the Longhouse*; Calloway, *One Vast Winter Count*; DuVal, *Native Ground*; Taylor, *Divided Ground*; Barr, *Peace Came in the Form of a Woman*; Hämäläinen, *Comanche Empire*; Fenn, *Encounters at the Heart of the World*; McDonnell, *Masters of Empire*; Hämäläinen, *Lakota America*; Lakomäki, *Gathering Together*; Witgen, *Infinity of Nations*; Greene, *Their Determination to Remain*; and Bauer, *Becoming Catawba*. For a few works that focus on Native peoples' ongoing commitment to their sovereignty, see Miller, *Forgotten Tribes*; Cattelino, *High Stakes*; Osburn, *Choctaw Resurgence in Mississippi*; and Lowery, *Lumbee Indians*. For the need to think of Native persistence as a form of anti-imperialism, see Ostler, "Native Americans against Empire and Colonial Rule." On contemporary settler erasure, see Shire and Knetsch, "Ambivalence of the Settler Colonial Present."

12. Adelman and Aron, "From Borderlands to Borders," esp. 816. For critiques of Adelman and Aron alongside useful overviews of borderlands methodology and terminology, see Hämäläinen and Truett, "On Borderlands"; Frank and Crothers, introduction to *Borderland Narratives*; Rivaya-Martínez, "Problematizing Indigenous Borderlands." The essays included in both *Borderland Narratives* and *Indigenous Borderlands* are excellent examples of the diversity of borderlands scholarship. For the persistence of Native borderlands amid the creation of imperial and nation-state borders, see Hogue, *Metis and the Medicine Line*; and Hall, *Beneath the Backbone of the World*.

13. Historian Juliana Barr makes a similar appeal about the importance of borders in her analysis of Indigenous boundaries in the Southwest. See Barr, "Geographies of Power"; and Barr, "Borders and Borderlands." The few studies of Native borders include Braund, "'Like a Stone Wall Never to Be Broke'"; Lakomäki, "'Our Line'"; West, "'They Have Exercised Every Art'"; Seeley, *Race, Removal, and the Right to Remain*; and Taylor, *Plain Paths and Dividing Lines*. For how several scholars have explored Indigenous peoples' conceptions of space, see Basso, *Wisdom Sits in Places*; Brooks, *Common Pot*; Mack, "Chickasaws' Place-World"; Hudson, *Creek Paths and Federal Roads*; Chambers, "Movement of Great Tellico"; Erbig, *Where Caciques and Mapmakers Met*; Fenn, *Encounters at the Heart of the World*; and the collected essays in Barr and Countryman, *Contested Spaces of Early America*.

14. Rothman, *Slave Country*, 9–70. On enslaved and free African Americans in Tennessee and North Carolina, see England, "Free Negro in Ante-Bellum Tennessee"; Mooney, *Slavery in Tennessee*; Franklin, *Free Negro in North Carolina*; Ray, *Middle Tennessee*, 69–74; Ford, *Deliver Us from Evil*; and Kelley, "Like a Herd of Cattle Terrified by the Scream of a Panther." For the connection between slavery and Native dispossession, see Leroy, "Black History in Occupied Territory"; Smallwood, "Reflections on Settler Colonialism, the Hemispheric Americas, and Chattel Slavery"; Miles, "Beyond a Boundary"; Stremlau, Lowery, and Reed, "Interconnected Histories of Enslavement and Settler Colonialism"; and Seeley, *Race, Removal, and the Right to Remain*. Jessica Taylor explores African American challenges to the legitimacy of boundaries in Taylor, *Plain Paths and Dividing Lines*, 12–13. For race and slavery in Native societies, see

Perdue, *Slavery and the Evolution of Cherokee Society*; Perdue, *"Mixed Blood" Indians*; Shoemaker, *Strange Likeness*; Shoemaker, "How Indians Got to Be Red"; Frank, *Creeks and Southerners*; Miles, *Ties That Bind*; Saunt, *Black, White, and Indian*; Yarborough, *Race and the Cherokee Nation*; Cumfer, *Separate Peoples, One Land*; Snyder, *Slavery in Indian Country*; Snyder, *Great Crossings*; and Roberts, *I've Been Here All the While*.

15. Grasso and Wulf, "Nothing Says 'Democracy' Like a Visit from the Queen," 780; Furstenberg, "Significance of the Trans-Appalachian Frontier in Atlantic History." Jace Weaver demonstrates Native peoples' wide-ranging impact on the broader Atlantic World in *Red Atlantic*.

16. Roberts, *Founding of Alabama*, 34–35; *Course of the River Mississippi, from the Balise to Fort Chartres; Taken on an Expedition to the Illinois, in the Latter End of the Year 1765*, Lieut Ross and Robert Sayer, 1772, LC, www.loc.gov/resource/g4042m.ar078000, accessed May 24, 2024; *A Map of the American Indian Nations, Adjoining to the Mississippi, West & East Florida, Georgia, S. & N. Carolina, Virginia, &c*, John Lodge and James Adair, 1775, North Carolina Maps, University of North Carolina at Chapel Hill, https://dc.lib.unc.edu/cdm/ref/collection/ncmaps/id/2074, accessed May 24, 2024. For the location of Tenasi, see Smith, "Distribution of Eighteenth-Century Cherokee Settlements," 48–50, 56–57. On Native peoples' general influence on Tennessee geography, see Keith, "Tennessee's Indigenous Geography." Gregory Smithers visualizes the cultural, spiritual, and epistemological significance of waterways for Cherokee people in the digital humanities project Cherokee Riverkeepers, www.cherokeeriverkeepers.org. For the history of Indigenous peoples other than the Cherokees and Chickasaws in the Tennessee Country, see Satz, *Tennessee's Indian Peoples*; Worth, "Enigmatic Origins"; Ethridge, "European Invasion and the Transformation of the Indians of Tennessee"; and Bowes, "Shawnee Geography and the Tennessee Corridor in the Seventeenth and Eighteenth Centuries."

17. Barr, "Red Continent and the Cant of Coastline," 523; Lakomäki, *Gathering Together*, 6–11; DuVal, *Native Nations*, xxviii–xxix; Ablavsky, "'With the Indian Tribes.'" Ablavsky's article is especially useful for understanding the historical terminology's relevance for issues of contemporary U.S. Indian law.

18. For an example, see Boulware, *Deconstructing the Cherokee Nation*, 47–48.

19. Perdue, *"Mixed Blood" Indians*, 91–93. For a list of the multiple names of prominent Cherokees, see Cumfer, *Separate Peoples, One Land*, xi–xii; and Smithers, *Cherokee Diaspora*, 267–268. I also draw on treaty documents and other assorted primary and secondary sources for Native individuals' names.

20. On this point and for conceptions of race more generally in early America, see Shoemaker, *Strange Likeness*, 125–140.

21. Fitzmaurice, *Sovereignty, Property and Empire*, 22. See also Dahl, *Empire of the People*, 13.

Chapter 1. Straight Paths and Bordered Lands in the Eighteenth-Century Tennessee Country

1. Talk of Sallowie to the North Carolina Commissioners, June 13, 1767, *EAID*, 14:258; Order Book for William Tryon's Expedition to Meet with the Cherokee Nation Concerning the Boundary between North Carolina and Cherokee Land, May 19–June 13, 1767, *CSRNC*, 7:991–1008; Hudson, *Creek Paths and Federal Roads*, 12; Calloway, *Pen and Ink Witchcraft*, 22–23; Paulett, *Empire of Small Places*, 116–118. On

Ostenaco, see Fullagar, *Warrior, the Voyager, and the Artist*, 12–43, 104–126; and Evans, "Ostenaco."

2. Talk of Sallowie to the North Carolina Commissioners, June 13, 1767, *EAID*, 14:258–259; Cherokees' Reply to Governor Tryon, June 2, 1767, *EAID*, 14:254; Talk of Jud's Friend [Ostenaco] to the North Carolina Commissioners, June 13, 1763, *EAID*, 14:257; Agreement between Governor Tryon and the Indians in Regard to the Western Boundary, June 13, 1767, *EAID*, 14:254–256; Cherokee Cession of Land at Fort Prince George Conference, October 19, 1765, *EAID*, 14:232–233; Journal of the Congress at Augusta with the Indians, October 1–November 21, 1763, *EAID*, 5:263–303; Kittagusta Talk, May 8, 1766, in John Stuart to William Bull, Jr., [1766], *EAID*, 14:239–240; Alexander Cameron to John Stuart, May 10, 1766, *EAID*, 14:240–244; North Carolina Commissioners' Answer to Jud's Friend's Talk, June [13], 1767, *EAID*, 14:257–258; De Vorsey, *Indian Boundary in the Southern Colonies*, 93–107, 126–133; Fullagar, *Warrior, the Voyager, and the Artist*, 115–117. For "crisis of cosmology," see Carson, "Ethnogeography and the Native American Past," 769. For a fascinating analysis about how this 1767 boundary survey, specifically, and Governor Tryon's Indian policy, in general, contributed to the North Carolina regular movement, see Marshall, "Facing East from Tryon Mountain."

3. Holton, *Forced Founders*; Curtis, *Jefferson's Freeholders*, esp. 1–94. On the continental scope of the American Revolution, see Taylor, *American Revolutions*; Saunt, *West of the Revolution*; Narrett, *Adventurism and Empire*; DuVal, *Independence Lost*; and Roney, "1776, Viewed from the West." For the revolution's specific significance for Native peoples, see Calloway, *American Revolution in Indian Country*.

4. For the concept of the "shatter zone," see Ethridge, "Introduction: Mapping the Mississippian Shatter Zone." *Mapping the Mississippian Shatter Zone* is an edited collection of essays that all apply Ethridge's shatter zone thesis to a variety of Native polities. Also on the shattering and general coalescence of Native polities in the American South, see Hudson, *Southeastern Indians*, 77–119; Ethridge and Hudson, "Early Historic Transformation of the Southeastern Indians"; and Smithers, *Native Southerners*, esp. 59–66, 87–104. On Chickasaws and Cherokees, in particular, during this era, see Ethridge, *From Chicaza to Chickasaw*; Rodning, "Reconstructing the Coalescence of Cherokee Communities in Southern Appalachia"; Perdue, *Cherokee Women*, 8–9; Boulware, *Deconstructing the Cherokee Nation*, 4–6, 10–12; and Kelton, *Cherokee Medicine, Colonial Germs*, 1–101.

5. This overview of Cherokee and Chickasaw history before 1763 is based on Gibson, *Chickasaws*, 31–57; Atkinson, *Splendid Land, Splendid People*, 1–87; Cashin, *Guardians of the Valley*; Cegielski and Lieb, "'Hina' Falaa, 'The Long Path'"; Kelton, "British and Indian War"; Tortora, *Carolina in Crisis*; Calloway, *Indian World of George Washington*, 124–174; O'Brien, "Quieting the Ghosts"; Wallace, "More Than 'Strangers to Each Others Persons & Manners'"; Boulware, *Deconstructing the Cherokee Nation*, 75–129; Ray, *Cherokee Power*; and Fullagar, *Warrior, the Voyager, and the Artist*, 104–111. For Cherokee-French relations during the eighteenth century, see Ray, "Cherokees and the Franco-British Confrontation in the Tennessee Corridor"; and Boulware, *Deconstructing the Cherokee Nation*, 75–93. On the British government's goal for the Proclamation Line, see Edelson, *New Map of Empire*, 141–159; and Calloway, *Indian World of George Washington*, 177–185. Kristofer Ray argues that the Quebec Act similarly reflected British administrators' wish to centralize governance of North America's continental interior. Ray, "'Our Concerns with Indians Are Now Greatly Extended.'"

6. John Stuart to the Board of Trade about the Congress at Augusta, December 1, 1763, *EAID*, 5:306; Attakullakulla Talk, November 8, 1763, *EAID*, 5:288; *Map of the Southern Indian District*, 1764, Archives and Special Collections, University of Pittsburgh Library System, http://https://digital.library.pitt.edu/islandora/object/pitt:DAR MAP0398, accessed October 16, 2024; Edelson, *New Map of Empire*, 164–167; Boulware, "'It Seems Like Coming into Our Houses.'" For the Augusta conference, see *EAID*, 2:263–302; Edelson, *New Map of Empire*, 159–168; and Fullagar, *Warrior, the Voyager, and the Artist*, 111–113. Cherokees had begun the process of outlining their national borders with South Carolina in 1761, two years before the Proclamation Line. On this point, see Ray, *Cherokee Power*, 115. On Attakullakulla's diplomatic role among Cherokee people in the decades before the Seven Years' War, see Ray, *Cherokee Power*, 77–79.

7. Alexander Cameron to John Stuart, May 10, 1766, *EAID*, 14:241; Memorial of the House of Burgesses about Western Land Boundaries, December 13, 1769, *EAID*, 5:348; Governor Dunmore to the Earl of Hillsborough, March 1772, *EAID*, 14:320–321; Journal of the Proceedings at the Treaty of Hard Labo[u]r, October 8–October 21, 1768, *EAID*, 14:272–285; Journal of Proceedings at Treaty of Lochaber, October 18–October 22, 1770, *EAID*, 5:360–371; De Vorsey, *Indian Boundary in the Southern Colonies*, 64–92; Calloway, *Indian World of George Washington*, 183–193; Edelson, *New Map of Empire*, 178–182.

8. Ramsey, *Annals of Tennessee*, 103, 109; Abernethy, *From Frontier to Plantation in Tennessee*, 1–18; Barksdale, *Lost State of Franklin*, 18–35; Finger, *Tennessee Frontiers*, 41–52; Roney, "1776, Viewed from the West," 674–680.

9. Petition from Jacob Brown to Halifax Congress, 1776, *CSRNC*, 10:885–887; Talk by Raven of Chota to Henry Stuart, May 2, 1776, *CSRNC*, 22:995; Finger, *Tennessee Frontiers*, 45–46; Cumfer, *Separate Peoples, One Land*, 28.

10. Indenture between Oconostota et al. and Charles Robertson, March 19, 1775, and Indenture between Oconostota et al. and Jacob Brown, March 25, 1775, both in Ramsey, *Annals of Tennessee*, 119–121 (quotation 121); Deposition of James Robertson, April 16, 1777, *CVSP*, 1:287; Abernethy, *From Frontier to Plantation in Tennessee*, 9; Roney, "1776, Viewed from the West," 675. On Indian land deeds elsewhere in British North America, see Taylor, *Liberty Men and Great Proprietors*, 12–14; Muldoon, "Discovery, Grant, Charter, Conquest, or Purchase"; Saxine, *Properties of Empire*; and Pagden, "Law, Colonization, Legitimation, and the European Background," 25.

11. Ray, *Cherokee Power*, 4–6; Boulware, *Deconstructing the Cherokee Nation*, 19–31, 130–131, 177.

12. Oconostota et al. to John Stuart, July 29, 1769, *EAID*, 14:288; Altahkullahkullah [Attakullakulla] Talk, October 19, 1770, in Journal of the Proceedings at Treaty of Lochaber," *EAID*, 5:365; Oconostota et al. to John Stuart, September 25, 1769, *EAID*, 14:288; [Old] Tassel Talk, November 29, 1785, *ASP:IA*, 1:43; Governor Earl of Dunmore to the Earl of Hillsborough, March 1772, *EAID*, 14:320–321; King, "Long Island of the Holston"; De Vorsey, *Indian Boundary in the Southern Colonies*, 76–92; Finger, *Tennessee Frontiers*, 43–44. On the title of "the Raven" as a Cherokee military leader, see Calloway, *American Revolution in Indian Country*, 190n36.

13. Talk by Raven of Chota [Savanukeh] to Henry Stuart, May 2, 1776, *CSRNC*, 22:995; [Old] Tassel Talk, November 26, 1785, *ASP:IA*, 1:42; Ramsey, *Annals of Tennessee*, 117–118. On the Treaty of Sycamore Shoals, see Abernethy, *Western Lands and the American Revolution*, 124–135, 162–166; Aron, *How the West Was Lost*, 59–64; Abernethy, *From Frontier to Plantation in Tennessee*, 23–27, 50; and Finger, *Tennessee Frontiers*, 50–51.

14. Deposition of Isaac Shelby, December 3, 1777, in *CVSP*, 1:297; Hatley, *Dividing Paths*, 210; Calloway, *American Revolution in Indian Country*, 189; Gildrie, "Tennessee in the American Revolution," 118.

15. Oconostota et al. to John Stuart, September 25, 1769, *EAID*, 14:288; Oconostota Talk, October 19, 1770, Journal of Proceedings at Treaty of Lochaber, October 18–October 22, 1770, *EAID*, 5:363; Mize, "Sons of Selu"; Perdue, *Cherokee Women*, 85; Sheidley, "Hunting and the Politics of Masculinity in Cherokee Treaty-Making." On Cherokee leaders' strategic diplomatic rhetoric about uncontrollable "young men," see Boulware, "'Our Mad Young Men.'"

16. Deposition of Samuel Wilson, April 15, 1777, and Deposition of James Robinson [Robertson], April 16, 1777, both in *CVSP*, 1:283, 285–286; Henry Stuart to John Stuart, August 25, 1776, *CSRNC*, 10:763–785; Calloway, *American Revolution in Indian Country*, 190–191; Boulware, *Deconstructing the Cherokee Nation*, 152–155. On "warrior-diplomats" and the significance of masculinity for Chickamauga Cherokees, see Mize, "'To Conclude a General Union.'" For Dragging Canoe's identity and sobriquet, see Calloway, "Declaring Independence and Rebuilding a Nation," 185–186.

17. John Murray, Earl of Dunmore to the Earl of Dartmouth, May 6, 1774, quoted in Roney, "1776, Viewed from the West," 676; John Stuart to Josiah Martin, February 22, 1774, and Minutes of the North Carolina Governor's Council, April 23, 1774, both in *CSRNC*, 9:825–826, 982–983; Alexander Cameron to John Stuart, March 1, 1774, and Alexander Cameron to John Stuart, June 2, 1774, both in *EAID*, 14:353, 357.

18. John Carter et al. to the Honorable Provincial Council of North Carolina, [1776], in Ramsey, *Annals of Tennessee*, 134–138; Petition from Jacob Brown to Halifax Congress, 1776, *CSRNC*, 10:885–887.

19. Minutes of the North Carolina Council of Safety, July 22, 1776, and Minutes of the Provincial Congress of North Carolina, November 19, 1776, both in *CSRNC*, 10:682, 926; Dixon, *Wataugans*, 69; Finger, *Tennessee Frontiers*, 58.

20. Finger, *Tennessee Frontiers*, 59–66, 89–95, 100–101 (quotation 63); Parkinson, *Common Cause*, 243–244, 272–276; Barksdale, *Lost State of Franklin*, 98–99; Hatley, *Dividing Paths*, 191–200; Boulware, *Deconstructing the Cherokee Nation*, 158–160; Rindfleisch, "Journal of William Dells"; Ray, *Middle Tennessee*, 1–17. In 1791, for example, counties in the Tennessee Valley contained a population of 28,649 compared to 7,042 inhabitants of the Cumberland settlements. Census Report, September 19, 1791, in *TPUS*, 4:81. On the expanding population in the Cumberland Valley, see Ray, *Middle Tennessee*, 60, 86–91.

21. Roney, "1776, Viewed from the West," 678.

22. Richard Caswell to Waightstill Avery et al., June 12, 1777, and Patrick Henry to William Christian, William Preston, and Evan Shelby, undated, both in Henderson, "Treaty of Long Island of Holston," 61, 58–59; Powell, *North Carolina through Four Centuries*, 187. For Virginia's negotiations with the Cherokee Nation in spring 1776, see *EAID*, 18:215–218.

23. Proceedings with the Overhill Cherokees at Fort Patrick Henry, Near Long Island on the Holston River, July 14, 1777, and Treaty of Dewitt's Corner, May 20, 1777, both in *EAID*, 18:227–230, 218–220; Oconostota Talk, July 15, 1777, *EAID*, 18:230; Cumfer, *Separate Peoples, One Land*, 29–30. The treaty minutes record Cherokee leaders from the Overhill Towns of Chota, Notchy Creek, Toqua, Chilhoe [Chilhowee], Tellico, Hiwassee, the Island Town, Settico, and Taskeegee [Tuskegee]. Proceedings with the Overhill

Cherokees at Fort Patrick Henry, Near Long Island on the Holston River, July 14, 1777, *EAID*, 18:227, 233. For the locations of these towns, see Smith, "Distribution of Eighteenth-Century Cherokee Settlements." Similar to the Valley Town representative at the Long Island Treaty, the Overhill Cherokees sent their own representative, Oosknah (Old Abram), to observe the treaty with South Carolina and Georgia. See *EAID*, 18:583n75.

24. Proceedings with the Overhill Cherokees at Fort Patrick Henry, Near Long Island on the Holston River, and Treaty of Long Island on the Holston, July 20, 1777, both in *EAID*, 18:233–234, 236–237, 239, 243–244, 251–255; Treaty of July 20, 1777, in Hagy and Folmsbee, "Lost Archives of the Cherokee Nation," 92–95.

25. Proceedings with the Overhill Cherokees at Fort Patrick Henry, Near Long Island on the Holston River, *EAID*, 18:238; Treaty of July 20, 1777, in Hagy and Folmsbee, "Lost Archives of the Cherokee Nation," 94; Treaty of Long Island of the Holston, *EAID*, 18:252; The Raven [Savanukeh] to Richard Caswell, April 14, 1778, *CSRNC*, 13:90; Constitution of North Carolina, December 18, 1776, Avalon Project, Yale Law School, https://avalon.law.yale.edu/18th_century/nc07.asp, accessed May 24, 2024; William Sharpe and Waightstill Avery to Richard Caswell, August 7, 1777, *CSRNC*, 11:566; Proclamation by Richard Caswell, May 5, 1778, *CSRNC*, 13:115–116; An Act to Amend an Act, Intitled An Act for Establishing Offices for Receiving Entries of Claims for Lands in the Several Counties within this State, for Ascertaining the Method of Obtaining Titles to the Same, and for Other Purposes Therein Mentioned, 1778, *CSRNC*, 24:159–161.

26. Arthur Campbell to Thomas Jefferson, January 15, 1781, DRAPER, 9DD24; Arthur Campbell, John Sevier, and Joseph Martin to the Indian Chiefs, January 4, 1781, and The Tassel Talk, July 31, 1781, Treaty of Long Island of the Holston, both in *EAID*, 18:264, 266; Deposition of William Springston, January 19, 1791, box 2, folder 1, Arthur Campbell to Thomas Jefferson, January 16, 1781, box 1, folder 1, Arthur Campbell to Thomas Jefferson, March 12, 1781, box 1, folder 1, and Arthur Campbell to Benjamin Harrison, August 26, 1782, box 1, folder 1, all in Penelope Johnson Allen Cherokee Collection, TSLA; Cumfer, "Nan-ye-hi (Nancy Ward)"; Perdue, *Cherokee Women*, 54, 87, 38–39; Finger, *Tennessee Frontiers*, 71–74; Hatley, *Dividing Paths*, 218, 222–227; Boulware, *Deconstructing the Cherokee Nation*, 161–163.

27. Nathanael Greene to William Christian et al., February 26, 1781, DRAPER, 1XX30; Report of Proceedings of a Commission Appointed by General Nathanael Greene on 26 February 1781 to Conduct Talks with the Cherokees, box 5, Nathanael Greene Papers, LC. Excerpts from these negotiations have been published in vol. 18 of *EAID* based on the originals in the Draper Collection. When they are legible, I cite from the complete report in the Greene Papers.

28. Oconostota Talk, Treaty of Long Island of the Holston, *EAID*, 18:266; Au-koo Talk and Talk from "the [Chic]kamogge Young Warriors," both in box 5, Nathanael Greene Papers, LC; Treaty of Long Island of the Holston, *EAID*, 18:266. For Native peoples' conception of hunting territory as their property, see Smalley, "'They Steal Our Deer and Land.'"

29. Talk of the "Women of the Cherokee Nation," box 5, Nathanael Greene Papers, LC. Theda Perdue and Cynthia Cumfer agree that historical context makes it almost certain that Nancy Ward led the women's delegation. See Perdue, *Cherokee Women*, 101; Cumfer, "Nan-ye-hi (Nancy Ward)," 9–10; and Cumfer, *Separate Peoples, One Land*, 36–38. Furthermore, Perdue argues that "women did not completely acquiesce to a new

order shaped by a European presence in their country and European attitudes toward women. They found ways to retain traditional prerogatives, preserve corporate values, and maintain the fundamental structures of Cherokee society on which their status rested." Perdue, *Cherokee Women*, 63. On Cherokee kinship and family structures, see Stremlau, *Sustaining the Cherokee Family*, esp. 21–25.

30. William Christian Talk, Greene commission (a more legible version is in *EAID*, 18:269–270), and Arthur Campbell to Nathanael Greene, undated, both in box 5, Nathanael Greene Papers, LC; Arthur Campbell to unknown, July 10, 1781, folder 3, Revolutionary War Papers #2194-z, SHC; William Christian, Joseph Martin, and Evan Shelby to Nathanael Greene, July 31, 1781, box 4, Nathanael Greene Papers, LC. For general information on the 1781 treaty proceedings, see box 5 of the Nathanael Greene Papers.

31. Alexander Martin to Charles McDowell, John Sevier, and Waightstill Avery, September 20, 1782, Alexander Martin to Benjamin Harrison, November 20, 1782, Alexander Martin to Jean-Baptiste-Donatien de Vimeur, Comte de Rochambeau, June 19, 1782, and Alexander Martin to Charles McDowell, July 23, 1782, all in *CSRNC*, 16:710, 460–462, 692, 697–698; Treaty of Long Island of the Holston, *EAID*, 18:269; Arthur Campbell to George Washington, October 26, 1781, reel 81, Series 4, General Correspondence, 1697–1799, George Washington Papers, LC; Andrew, *Life and Times of General Andrew Pickens*, 157–162; Finger, *Tennessee Frontiers*, 94–97; Boulware, *Deconstructing the Cherokee Nation*, 162–163; Calloway, *American Revolution in Indian Country*, 205–207. For a map of the Catawba reservation, see Merrell, *Indians' New World*, 199.

32. Mingo Homaw [Houma], Paymaw Tauhaw [Payamataha], and Tuskau Pautapau to Congress, May 22, 1779, *EAID*, 18:262–263; DuVal, *Native Ground*, 153–158; Duval, *Independence Lost*, 238–243; Calloway, *American Revolution in Indian Country*, 221–234; Atkinson, *Splendid Land, Splendid People*, 102–110.

33. Poymau Tauhaw [Payamataha] et al. to the Commanders of Every Different Station Between this Nation and the Falls of the Ohio, July 9, 1782, and Benjamin Harrison to Joseph Martin, John Donelson, and Isaac Shelby, January 11, 1783, both in *EAID*, 18:270, 364–365; John Bowman to Benjamin Harrison, August 30, 1782, Benjamin Logan to Benjamin Harrison, August 31, 1782, John Donelson to Benjamin Harrison, September 1, 1782, and "To the Chickasaw Chiefs," September 10, 1782, all in *CVSP*, 3:280–284, 277, 297; Nichols, "Enterprise of War"; Benjamin Harrison to Joseph Martin, January 6, 1783, DRAPER, 1XX54; Cotterill, "Virginia-Chickasaw Treaty of 1783," 488. Shelby did not attend the negotiations because of the death of his brother. See Joseph Martin to Benjamin Harrison, September 27, 1783, miscellaneous reel 2978, Executive Papers of Governor Benjamin Harrison, 1781–1784, Library of Virginia, Richmond.

34. Benjamin Harrison to Alexander Martin, October 22, 1782, *EAID*, 18:274; Alexander Martin to Benjamin Harrison, November 20, 1782, *CSRNC*, 16:460–462; Prucha, *Great Father*, 1:36–39.

35. Benjamin Harrison to Joseph Martin, John Donelson, and Isaac Shelby, January 11, 1783, and Benjamin Harrison to Alexander Martin, October 22, 1782, both in *EAID*, 18:365, 275; Miller et al., *Discovering Indigenous Lands*, 2; Pommersheim, *Broken Landscape*, 21–22; Miller, "Doctrine of Discovery, Manifest Destiny, and American Indians."

36. Mingo Houma et al. to the Great Chiefs of the Americans, and the Chiefs and Warriors of the Virginians in Particular, July 28, 1783, miscellaneous reel 2978, Executive Papers of Governor Benjamin Harrison, 1781–1784, Library of Virginia, Richmond;

Mingo Houma et al. to His Excellency the President of the Honorable Congress of the United American States," July 28, 1783, *CVSP*, 3:515–517; Arthur Campbell et al. to the Chickasaw Nation, March 22, 1781, Item 6583, Thomas Addis Emmett Collection, 1483–1876, New York Public Library, New York; Council with the Chickasaws, October 25, 1782, *EAID*, 18:275–277.

37. Treaty of French Lick between Virginia and the Chickasaws, [November 5–6, 1783], *EAID*, 18:375–376; John Donelson and Joseph Martin to Benjamin Harrison, December 16, 1783, *CVSP*, 3:548; DRAPER, 1XX55.

38. Talk of Jud's Friend [Ostenaco] to the North Carolina Commissioners, June 13, 1763, *EAID*, 14:257.

39. Agreement between Governor Tryon and the Indians in Regard to the Western Boundary, June 13, 1767, *EAID*, 14:255.

Chapter 2. Land Speculators, White Intruders, and the Beginnings of a "Great American Empire"

1. Mingo Houma et al. to His Excellency the President of the Honorable Congress of the United American States, July 28, 1783, *CVSP*, 3:515–517; James Colbert to Benjamin Harrison, July 25, 1783, and Mingo Houma et al. to the Great Chiefs of the Americans, and the Chiefs and Warriors of the Virginians in Particular, July 28, 1783, both in miscellaneous reel 2978, Executive Papers of Governor Benjamin Harrison, 1781–1784, Library of Virginia, Richmond.

2. Dahl, *Empire of the People*, 9. Generations of U.S. historians overlooked the State of Franklin, with the only book-length study being Williams, *History of the Lost State of Franklin*. This changed with Barksdale, *Lost State of Franklin*, which sparked a renewed interested in the breakaway government. On the complexity of Franklin inhabitants' loyalty to the United States, see Ray, "Leadership, Loyalty, and Sovereignty in the Revolutionary American Southwest."

3. Greer, *Property and Dispossession*, 405–408; Banner, *How the Indians Lost Their Land*, 17–22, 121–131; Ablavsky, "Savage Constitution," 1013–1016; Calloway, *Pen and Ink Witchcraft*, 100–105; MacMillan, *Sovereignty and Possession in the English New World*, 7–10; Pagden, "Law, Colonization, Legitimation, and the European Background," 4–15.

4. Prucha, *American Indian Policy in the Formative Years*; Cayton, "Radicals in the 'Western World'"; Nichols, *Red Gentlemen and White Savages*; Sadosky, *Revolutionary Negotiations*, 148–175; Kokomoor, "Creeks, Federalists, and the Idea of Coexistence in the Early Republic"; Banner, *How the Indians Lost Their Land*, 135–139, 160–168.

5. Henry Knox quoted in Banner, *How Indians Lost Their Land*, 131; Cayton, *Frontier Republic*, 12–50; Nichols, *Red Gentlemen and White Savages*; Kokomoor, "Creeks, Federalists, and the Idea of Coexistence in the Early Republic." On the transition of U.S. Indian policy from notions of conquest to negotiated treaties, see Horsman, "Indian Policy of an 'Empire for Liberty'"; and Merrell, "Declarations of Independence."

6. Minutes of the North Carolina House of Commons, May 12, 1783, *CSRNC*, 19:340; Minutes of the North Carolina Senate, May 12, 1783, *CSRNC*, 19:220; An Act for Opening the Land Office for the Redemption of Specie and Other Certificates, and Discharging the Arrears Due to the Army, Acts of the North Carolina General Assembly, 1783, *CSRNC*, 24:478–482; Arthur Campbell to Samuel Purviance, November 18, 1784, folder 4a, Arthur Campbell Papers, 1752–1811, FHS; Cherokee Nation to Baron de Caronde-

let, April 5, 1793, *PTJ*, 26:316–317; Abernethy, *From Frontier to Plantation in Tennessee*, 48–50; Ablavsky, "Empire States," 1826–1827; Ablavsky, "Savage Constitution," 1009–1013; Blackhawk, "Federal Indian Law as Paradigm within Public Law," 1807; Calloway, *Indian World of George Washington*, 301; Cumfer, *Separate Peoples, One Land*, 46–47.

7. Arthur Campbell to Samuel Purviance, November 18, 1784, folder 4a, Arthur Campbell Papers, 1752–1811, FHS; Richard Caswell to William Caswell, May 4, 1783, and Alexander Martin to Benjamin Hawkins, Hugh Williamson, and Richard Dobbs Spaight, December 8, 1783, both in *CSRNC*, 16:958–960, 919–920; Resolution Closing the Land Office, North Carolina House of Commons, May 25, 1784, box 2, folder 5, April 1784–June 1784, GASR; Abernethy, *Western Lands and the American Revolution*, 261; Abernethy, *From Frontier to Plantation in Tennessee*, 58.

8. Alexander Martin to All the Warriors of the Friendly Towns of the Cherokee Nation, August 4, 1783, *CSRNC*, 16:855–856; An Act for Opening the Land Office for the Redemption of Specie and Other Certificates, and Discharging the Arrears due to the Army, in Acts of the North Carolina General Assembly, 1783, *CSRNC*, 24:479; Alexander Martin to the Chiefs and Warriors of All the Friendly Towns of the Cherokee Nation, May 25, 1783, *CSRNC*, 16:810; An Act for Appointing an Agent and Holding a Treaty with the Cherokee Indians, and for Other Purposes, Acts of the North Carolina General Assembly, 1783, *CSRNC*, 24:509–510; Alexander Martin to Joseph Martin, August 4, 1783, *CSRNC*, 16:856–857.

9. Whitaker, "Muscle Shoals Speculation," 365–366; Finger, *Tennessee Frontiers*, 107.

10. William Blount to John Donelson, Joseph Martin, and John Sevier, May 31, 1784, and John Donelson to William Blount, September 24, 1783, both in *JGB Papers*, 1:169, 111–112; Joseph Martin to Benjamin Harrison, February 16, 1784, *CVSP*, 3:560–561; William Blount to Joseph Martin, October 26, 1783, DRAPER, 4XX17; Richard Caswell to John Sevier, June 18, 1785, in the Richard Caswell Papers #145-z, SHC; William Blount to John Donelson, March 9, 1784, DRAPER, 1XX72. For a general, though uncritical, overview of the Blount family's land dealings, see Masterson, *William Blount*.

11. Joseph Martin to Patrick Henry, May 21, 1783, in Henry, *Patrick Henry*, 3:244; William Blount to Joseph Martin, October 26, 1783, DRAPER, 4XX17; Joseph Martin to Benjamin Harrison, July 20, 1783, *CVSP*, 3:511–512; Benjamin Logan to Benjamin Harrison, August 11, 1783, miscellaneous reel 2978, Executive Papers of Governor Benjamin Harrison, 1781–1784, Library of Virginia, Richmond; William Blount to John Gray Blount, August 21, 1783, and John Donelson to William Blount, September 24, 1783, both in *JGB Papers*, 1:86–89, 111–112; Abernethy, *Western Lands and the American Revolution*, 260–261; De Vorsey, *Georgia-South Carolina Boundary*, 23–50. Tennessee Company officials did not identify the Cherokee delegates in attendance at the Long Island, but it is likely that they consisted of Overhill representatives because Cherokees from other regions were negotiating with Georgia at Augusta. Treaty of Augusta with the Cherokees, May 31, 1783, *EAID*, 18:368–369.

12. Extract of Minutes, House of Assembly of Georgia, February 20–21, 1784, and Petition of William Blount and Associates to the Assembly of Georgia for Grant of Land, February 7, 1784, both in *JGB Papers*, 1:535–537; Stephen Heard to Samuel Elbert, April 13, 1785, in "Creek Indian Letters, Talks, and Treaties, 1705–1839," bound transcripts, WPA Project No. 665-34-3-224, comp. Hays, vol. 1, 71; William Blount to John Sevier, John Donelson, and Joseph Martin, December 4, 1784, DRAPER, 4XX18; Ramsey, *Annals of Tennessee*, 377.

13. An Act Ceding to the Congress of the United States Certain Western Lands Therein Described, and Authorizing the Delegates from this State in Congress to Execute a Deed or Deeds for the Same, in Acts of the North Carolina General Assembly, 1784, *CSRNC*, 24:561–563; Benjamin Hawkins and Hugh Williamson to Alexander Martin, September 26, 1783, *CSRNC*, 16:882–889; Minutes of the North Carolina House of Commons, June 2, 1784, *CSRNC*, 19:711–714; Onuf, *Origins of the Federal Republic*, 3–46; Abernethy, *From Frontier to Plantation in Tennessee*, 67; Finger, *Tennessee Frontiers*, 109.

14. John Sevier to Arthur Campbell, February 16, 1782, folder 2, and David Campbell to Arthur Campbell, December 27, 1784, folder 3, both in Arthur Campbell Papers, 1752–1811, FHS; William Cocke to Benjamin Franklin, June 15, 1786, Part 8: Letters to Benjamin Franklin, 1784–1786, Benjamin Franklin Papers, Mss.B.F85, American Philosophical Society, Philadelphia, PA; Barksdale, "State of Franklin," 158–159; Barksdale, *Lost State of Franklin*, 56–60; Finger, *Tennessee Frontiers*, 111–113.

15. Plan of Association presented by William Cocke and Joseph Hardin, September 16, 1784, quoted in Barksdale, *Lost State of Franklin*, 59; David Campbell to Arthur Campbell, December 27, 1784, folder 3, Arthur Campbell Papers, 1752–1811, FHS; Committee Report on Franklin Independence, December 17, 1784, GP14, Governor Richard Caswell (Second Administration), 1785–1787, n.d., Governors' Papers, SANC.

16. Corn Tassel [Old Tassel] to Alexander Martin, October 10, 1784, *CSRNC*, 17:175–176; Proclamation of Alexander Martin, November 26, 1784, GLB7, Governor Richard Caswell (Second Administration), 1785–1787, n.d., Governors' Papers, SANC.

17. Manifesto of Alexander Martin, April 25, 1785, GLB7, Governor Richard Caswell (Second Administration), 1785–1787, n.d., Governors' Papers, SANC; Alexander Martin to John Gray Blount, February 26, 1785, *JGB Papers*, 1:191.

18. Treaty of Dumplin Creek, June 10, 1785, GP11, Joseph Martin to Richard Caswell, September 19, 1785, GP 11, and Old Tassel to Richard Caswell, September 19, 1785, GLB 8, all in Governor Richard Caswell (Second Administration), 1785–1787, n.d., Governors' Papers, SANC; Deposition of David Craig, June 7, 1789, GP17, Governor Samuel Johnston, 1787–1789, n.d., Governors' Papers, SANC; Joseph Martin to William Russell, August 1, 1785, DRAPER, 2XX5; Barksdale, *Lost State of Franklin*, 103–104.

19. A Declaration of Rights, Also the Constitution or Form of Government; State of Franklin, 1786, Tennessee Virtual Archive, TLSA, https://teva.contentdm.oclc.org/digital/collection/tfd/id/639, accessed May 23, 2024; Constitution of North Carolina: December 18, 1776, Avalon Project, Yale Law School, https://avalon.law.yale.edu/18th_century/nc07.asp, accessed May 23, 2024; Opal, *Avenging the People*, 56–59; Barksdale, *Lost State of Franklin*, 68–71.

20. Thomas Jefferson, quoted in DuVal, *Independence Lost*, 315; Barksdale, *Lost State of Franklin*, 66–67.

21. Resolution of Congress, March 15, 1785, GLB7, Governor Richard Caswell (Second Administration), 1785–1787, n.d., Governors' Papers, SANC; Benjamin Hawkins to Samuel Elbert, June 12, 1785, Benjamin Hawkins Letter, 1785, MS.2042, UTK.

22. *ASP:IA*, 1:41; Talk of War Woman of Chota [Nancy Ward], November 23, 1785, and Benjamin Hawkins et al. to Henry Lee, December 2, 1785, both in *ASP:IA*, 1:41, 38–39; Tuskegetchee [Tuskegatahee] Talk, June 12, 1787, *CVSP*, 4:307; Boulware, *Deconstructing the Cherokee Nation*, 161–164; Kelton, *Cherokee Medicine, Colonial Germs*, 165–173. On Native southerners' wish to observe treaty negotiations, see Hudson, *Creek Paths and Federal Roads*, 33.

23. Treaty with the Chickasaw, June 22–23, 1784, in Deloria and Demallie, *Documents of American Indian Diplomacy*, 1:125; Calloway, *American Revolution in Indian Country*, 235; Atkinson, *Splendid Land, Splendid People*, 124–127; DuVal, *Independence Lost*, 304–306. For the identity of Taski Etoka, see *EAID*, 18:598n66.

24. Hopewell Negotiations, *ASP:IA*, 1:41, 52; Benjamin Hawkins and Andrew Pickens to Charles Thompson, December 30, 1785, *ASP:IA*, 1:49. For how livestock facilitated European and American colonization, see Anderson, *Creatures of Empire*.

25. Hopewell Negotiations, *ASP:IA*:1, 40–43; Treaty with the Cherokee, 1785, in Kappler, *Indian Treaties*, 8–11; Benjamin Hawkins et al. to Henry Lee, December 2, 1785, *ASP:IA*, 1:38–39; Boulware, *Deconstructing the Cherokee Nation*, 121. On Tuskegatahee, see Cumfer, "Nan-ye-hi (Nancy Ward)." For European powers' use of maps to buttress their imperial claims, see Paulett, *Empire of Small Places*, 12–48; Edelson, *New Map of Empire*; and Erbig, *Where Caciques and Mapmakers Met*.

26. Hopewell Negotiations, *ASP:IA*, 1:51–52; DuVal, *Independence Lost*, 306.

27. Hopewell Negotiations, *ASP:IA*, 1:43; Treaty with the Chickasaw, 1786, in Kappler, *Indian Treaties*, 14–16; Benjamin Hawkins, Andrew Pickens, and Joseph Martin to [John Hancock], January 14, 1786, *ASP:IA*, 1:50.

28. William Blount to Joseph Martin, December 23, 1785, DRAPER, 2XX8; Richard Caswell to William Blount, September 3, 1785, folder 87, GP11, William Blount to Benjamin Hawkins, Joseph Martin, and Andrew Pickens, January 10, 1786, GLB8, Richard Caswell to William Blount, June 21, 1786, GLB 6, William Blount to Benjamin Hawkins et al., November 22, 1785, GLB8, William Blount to Benjamin Hawkins et al., November 28, 1785, GLB8, William Blount to Richard Caswell, March 1, 1786, GLB8, William Blount, Protest to the Cherokee Treaty, November 28, 1785, GLB8, and William Blount, Protest to the Chickasaw Treaty, January 10, 1786, GLB8, all in Governor Richard Caswell (Second Administration), 1785–1787, n.d., Governors' Papers, SANC; Thomas Polk to William Blount, July 5, 1783, *JGB Papers*, 1:67–68; Stockley Donelson to William Polk, May 15, 1790, folder 4, in the Polk and Yeatman Family Papers #606, SHC; Richard Caswell to John Sevier, July 12, 1786, DRAPER, 4XX18; North Carolina Senate Resolution, November 29, 1788, in William Blount Papers, 1783–1823, LC; Sellers, *James K. Polk*, 18–19.

29. Hill, *Journals of the Continental Congress*, 34:478; Committee Report on Indian Treaties and Indian Affairs, January 6, 1787, North Carolina House of Commons, box 1, folder 17, November 1786–January 1787, GASR; Hugh Williamson to Samuel Johnston, September 6, 1788, GLB9, Governor Samuel Johnston, 1787–1789, n.d., Governors' Papers, SANC.

30. Owld Tossell [Old Tassel] to Edward Telfair, February 24, 1786, box 77, folder 3, Telamon Cuyler Collection, UGA; John Sevier to Richard Caswell, October 28, 1786, GP14, Governor Richard Caswell (Second Administration), 1785–1787, n.d., Governors' Papers, SANC; Richard Caswell to John Sevier, July 12, 1786, DRAPER, 4XX18.

31. John Sevier to Edward Telfair, May 14, 1786, box 40A, folder 16, Telamon Cuyler Collection, UGA; Corn Tassle [Old Tassel] to Richard Caswell, April 22, 1786, Joseph Martin to Richard Caswell, May 11, 1786, Anthony Bledsoe to Richard Caswell, May 12, 1786, and Joseph Martin to Richard Caswell, May 15, 1786, all in GLB7, Governor Richard Caswell (Second Administration), 1785–1787, n.d., Governors' Papers, SANC; Barksdale, *Lost State of Franklin*, 108–109.

32. A Treaty held between the Officers of the State of Franklin and the Cherokee Indian Chiefs, July 31 and August 3, 1786, GP12, Governor Richard Caswell (Second Administration), 1785–1787, n.d., Governors' Papers, SANC; Deposition of David Craig, June 7, 1789, GP17, Governor Samuel Johnston, 1787–1789, n.d., Governors' Papers, SANC.

33. Alexander Outlaw to Richard Caswell, October 8, 1786, GP13, and David Campbell to Richard Caswell, November 30, 1786, both in GP13, Governor Richard Caswell (Second Administration), 1785–1787, n.d., Governors' Papers, SANC.

34. Joseph Martin to Richard Caswell, March 25, 1787, GP13, David Campbell to Richard Caswell, March 18, 1787, GP13, Evan Shelby to Richard Caswell, March 21, 1787, GP13, Thomas Hutchings to Richard Caswell, April 1, 1787, GP14, Evan Shelby to Caswell, May 4, 1787, GP14, and Anthony Bledsoe to Richard Caswell, May 4, 1787, GP14, all in Governor Richard Caswell (Second Administration), 1785–1787, n.d., Governors' Papers, SANC.

35. Thomas Hutchings to Richard Caswell, April 1, 1787, GP14, and Evan Shelby to Richard Caswell, May 4, 1787, GP13, both in Governor Richard Caswell (Second Administration), 1785–1787, n.d., Governors' Papers, SANC; Barksdale, *Lost State of Franklin*, 128.

36. Corn Tassell [Old Tassel] and Hanging Maw to Richard Caswell, September 15, 1786, GP13, Hanging Maw to Joseph Martin, March 24, 1787, GP13, and Corn Tassell [Old Tassel] to Joseph Martin, March 25, 1787, GP13, Richard Caswell to Thomas Hutchings, February 27, 1787, GP 13, Richard Caswell to John Sevier, February 23, 1787, GP13, Evan Shelby to Richard Caswell, March 21, 1787, GP13, and Thomas Hutchings to Richard Caswell, April 1, 1787, GP14, all in Governor Richard Caswell (Second Administration), 1785–1787, n.d., Governors' Papers, SANC; Richard Caswell to John Sevier, February 27, 1787, John Sevier Papers, 1778–1812, RL.

37. Mountain Leader [Piominko] to unknown, July 7, 1787, box 1, folder 3, November 1787–December 1787, GASR; Piominko to Joseph Martin, February 15, 1787, GP13 Governor Richard Caswell (Second Administration), 1785–1787, n.d., Governors' Papers, SANC; Hair Lip King [Taski Etoka] et al. to unknown, September 6, 1787, box 1, folder 3, November 1787–December 1787, GASR; Arthur Campbell to Edmund Randolph, April 15, 1797, box 1, folder 1, Penelope Johnson Allen Cherokee Collection, TSLA; Atkinson, *Splendid Land, Splendid People*, 125, 137.

Chapter 3. The Federal Government's Failings in the Tennessee Country

1. Joseph Martin to Richard Caswell, November 26, 1787, GP14, Governor Richard Caswell (Second Administration), 1785–1787, n.d., Governors' Papers, SANC; Alexander McGillivray to Esteban Miró, June 20, 1787, in Corbitt and Corbitt, "Papers from the Spanish Archives relating to Tennessee and the Old Southwest, 1783–1800: III, 1787," 82–84; Joseph Martin to Edmund Randolph, June 28, 1787, *CVSP*, 4:302–304; Chickasaw Chiefs to John Sevier, September 20, 1787, box 1, folder 21, Miscellaneous Collections: Subjects, Manuscripts and Archives Division, New York Public Library, New York; A Generall meting of the King Chiefs and Warriors of the Chickasaw Nation in Answer to a Talk they Recd from William Davenport, [May 1787], and William Davenport to George Mathews, May 27, 1787, both in box 78, folder 12, Telamon Cuyler Collection, UGA; Tolentuskee [Toluntuskee] et al. to James Robertson, box 1, folder 3, Novem-

ber 1787–December 1787, GASR; Andrew Pickens to Thomas Pinckney, October 15, 1787, Andrew Pickens Papers, 1782–1804, microfiche 51–121, South Carolina Historical Society, Charleston; McLoughlin, *Cherokee Renascence*, 58–59; Boulware, *Deconstructing the Cherokee Nation*, 152–165, 177. On the confederacy of Native peoples of the Ohio Valley, see Dowd, *Spirited Resistance*. For wampum's diplomatic significance, see Shoemaker, *Strange Likeness*, 65–68. By 1800, a Moravian missionary remarked that Ustanali "belongs to the Upper Cherokees." See Journal Entry, September 30, 1800, Report of the Brethren Abraham Steiner and Friedrich von Schweinitz concerning Their Second Visit to the Cherokees from 25 August to 2 November 1800, trans. Roy Ledbetter, in Crews and Starbuck, *Records of the Moravians among the Cherokees*, 1:207. Ustanali's location is evident in *Map of the Former Territorial Limits of the Cherokee Nation of Indians*, Charles C. Royce, 1884, North Carolina Maps, University of North Carolina at Chapel Hill, https://dc .lib.unc.edu/cdm/ref/collection/ncmaps/id/1059, accessed October 18, 2024.

2. Chickasaw Chiefs to John Sevier, September 20, 1787, box 1, folder 21, Miscellaneous Collections: Subjects, Manuscripts and Archives Division, New York Public Library, New York; Hair Lip King [Taski Etoka] et al. to unknown, September 6, 1787, and Anthony Bledsoe et al. to the General Assembly of North Carolina, [1787], both in box 1, folder 3, November 1787–December 1787, GASR; Tuskegetchee [Tuskegatahee] to Edmund Randolph, June 12, 1787, King Fisher to Joseph Martin, June 8, 1787, and [Old] Tassel to Edmund Randolph, June 12, 1787, all in *CVSP*, 4:304–307. On Long Town's location, see Cegielski and Lieb, "*Hina' Falaa*, 'The Long Path.'"

3. James Robertson to John Sevier, August 1, 1787, in "Creek Indian Letters, Talks, and Treaties, 1705–1839," bound transcripts, WPA Project No. 665-34-3-224, comp. Hays, vol. 1, 157; Anthony Bledsoe to John Sevier, August 5, 1787, box 78, folder 13, James Robertson to George Mathews, October 3, 1787, Mathews Letters, box 40A, and John Sevier to George Mathews, August 30, 1787, box 81, folder 21, all in Telamon Cuyler Collection, UGA; Anthony Bledsoe et al. to the General Assembly of North Carolina, [1787], box 1, folder 3, November 1787–December 1787, GASR; Arthur Campbell to David Campbell, August 14, 1787, folder 4, Arthur Campbell Papers, 1752–1811, FHS.

4. William Blount to Richard Caswell, July 19, 1787, *JGB Papers*, 1:323; William Blount to Richard Caswell, August 20, 1787, *CSRNC*, 20:764–765. On founders' goals for government centralization, see Ablavsky, "Savage Constitution"; Cayton, "Radicals in the 'Western World,'" 84–86; Sadosky, *Revolutionary Negotiations*, 127–140; and Edling, *Revolution in Favor of Government*.

5. Griffin, *American Leviathan*; Clark, "Ohio Country in the Political Economy of Nation Building," 146–165; Rockwell, *Indian Affairs and the Administrative State in the Nineteenth Century*; Van Atta, *Securing the West*; Bergmann, *American National State and the Early West*; Saler, *Settlers' Empire*; Balough, *Government out of Sight*; Frymer, "'A Rush and a Push and the Land Is Ours'"; Flanagan, "Revolution for Empire"; Onuf, *Statehood and Union*.

6. Prucha, *American Indian Policy in the Formative Years*; Horsman, "Indian Policy of an 'Empire for Liberty'"; Kokomoor, "Creeks, Federalists, and the Idea of Coexistence in the Early Republic"; Onuf, *Jefferson and the Virginians*, 117–154; Calloway, *Indian World of George Washington*, 321–345; Nichols, *Red Gentlemen and White Savages*; Cayton, "Radicals in the 'Western World.'" Gregory Ablavsky articulates a complex understanding of expanding U.S. governance of the trans-Appalachian West, though I

disagree with his conclusions regarding the success of federal authority in the Southwest Territory. See Ablavsky, *Federal Ground.*

7. George Washington to Henry Knox, August 5, 1792, *PGW*, 10:614; Calloway, *Indian World of George Washington*, 356; *ASP:IA*, 1:38, 39, 48.

8. John Sevier to Benjamin Franklin, November 2, 1787, John Sevier to Benjamin Franklin, April 9, 1787, and John Sevier to Benjamin Franklin, September 12, 1787, all in Part 9: Letters to Benjamin Franklin, 1787–1790, n.d., Benjamin Franklin Papers, Mss.B.F85, American Philosophical Society, Philadelphia, PA; Benjamin Franklin to John Sevier, June 30, 1787, *The Papers of Benjamin Franklin*, Digital Edition, American Philosophical Society and Yale University, http://franklinpapers.org/framedVolumes.jsp?vol =45&page=080, accessed May 23, 2024; Benjamin Franklin to John Sevier, December 16, 1787, *The Papers of Benjamin Franklin*, Digital Edition, American Philosophical Society and Yale University,, http://franklinpapers.org/framedVolumes.jsp?vol=45&page=318, accessed May 23, 2024.

9. Alexander Hamilton, *The Federalist Papers: No. 6*, Avalon Project, Yale Law School, https://avalon.law.yale.edu/18th_century/fed06.asp; Barksdale, *Lost State of Franklin*, 82–83, 130–144.

10. *The Committee Consisting of Mr. Kearney, Mr. Carrington, Mr. Bingham, Mr. Smith, and Mr. Dane, to Whom was Referred the Report of the Secretary at War, and Sundry Papers Relative to Indian Affairs in the Southern Department; and also a Motion of the Delegates from the State of Georgia, Report,* [August 3,] 1787, United States Continental Congress and Continental Congress Broadside Collection, LC; "Philadelphia, June 20," *Freeman's Journal; or, The North American Intelligencer* (Philadelphia, PA), June 20, 1787; *Pennsylvania Packet and Daily Advertiser* (Philadelphia, PA), June 15, 1787; "Philadelphia, July 28," *Georgia State Gazette or Independent Register* (Augusta, GA), September 8, 1787; Benjamin Franklin to John Sevier, June 30, 1787, *The Papers of Benjamin Franklin*, Digital Edition, American Philosophical Society and Yale University, http://franklinpapers.org/framedVolumes.jsp?vol=45&page=080, accessed May 23, 2024; William Blount to Richard Caswell, July 19, 1787, *JGB Papers*, 1:321–323; Hill, *Journals of the Continental Congress*, 33:311–312, 353, 455–463; Henry Knox, Report of the Secretary of War on the Southern Indians, July 18, 1787, *EAID*, 18:449–451; Articles of Confederation, art. 9; Calloway, *Indian World of George Washington*, 300–304; Sadosky, *Revolutionary Negotiations*, 127–138.

11. Hill, *Journals of the Continental Congress*, 33:707–711, 34:423–425; Charles Thompson to Samuel Johnston, October 27, 1787, and John Steele to Samuel Johnston, April 8, 1789, both in GLB9, Governor Samuel Johnston, 1787–1789, n.d., Governors' Papers, SANC; Perdue, *Slavery and the Evolution of Cherokee Society*, 36–49.

12. Minutes of the North Carolina Senate, November 3–December 6, 1788, *CSRNC*, 20:562, 551, 568, 582–583; William Blount to John Steele, January 17, 1789, and William Blount to John Steele, May 5, 1789, in Wagstaff, *Papers of John Steele*, 1:39, 29.

13. The Hanging Maw to Andrew Pickens, June 25, 1788, George Maxwell to Joseph Martin, July 9, 1788, Jam, the Prince of Notoly to Samuel Johnston, June 5, 1788, Jobber's Son to Andrew Pickens, June 20, 1788, Hanging Maw, John Watts, and Black Dog to Andrew Pickens, June 25, 1788, Jobber's Son to Andrew Pickens, June 30, 1788, Joseph Martin to Henry Knox, July 10, 1788, and Thomas Hutchings to Joseph Martin, July 11, 1788, all in GP16, Governor Samuel Johnston, 1787–1789, n.d., Governors' Papers, SANC; Richard Winn to Henry Knox, August 5, 1788, and Joseph Martin to Henry

Knox, February 2, 1789, both in *ASP:IA*, 1:28, 48; Depositions from Greene County, October 25, 1788, box 1, folder 7, November 1788–December 1788, GASR.

14. James Carey to Samuel Johnston, February 16, 1789, GP17, Jobber's Son to Andrew Pickens, June 30, 1788, GP16, Thomas Hutchings to Joseph Martin, July 11, 1788, GP16, Thomas Hutchings to John Donelson, July 12, 1788, GP 16, and Joseph Martin to Samuel Johnston, February 5, 1789, GLB9, all in Governor Samuel Johnston, 1787–1789, n.d., Governors' Papers, SANC; Talk of Little Turkey, November 20, 1788, and A Talk from the Head-men and Warriors of the Cherokees to Joseph Martin, November 1, 1788, both in *ASP:IA*, 1:46–47. On Little Turkey's status as a beloved man, see A Talk from the Head-men and Warriors of Several Cherokee Towns met at Ustinali, June 20, 1788, GP16, Governor Samuel Johnston, 1787–1789, n.d., Governors' Papers, SANC; and Boulware, *Deconstructing the Cherokee Nation*, 162. For retaliatory justice, what Cherokees termed "crying blood," see Strickland, *Fire and the Spirits*, 54–55; and McLoughlin, *Cherokee Renascence*, 12–13.

15. *Maryland Gazette* (Annapolis, MD), April 2, 1789; Information of Anthony Foreman, January 26, 1789, box 1, folder 15, November 1789–December 1789, GASR; John Sevier to Privy Council of the New State of Franklin, January 12, 1789, in Williams, *History of the Lost State of Franklin*, 218–219; Minutes of a Meeting of Inhabitants of the North Carolina Frontier, January 12–January 13, 1789, *CSRNC*, 22:722–725; Joseph Martin to Samuel Johnston, February 2, 1789, GLB9, Governor Samuel Johnston, 1787–1789, n.d., Governors' Papers, SANC; Joseph Martin to Henry Knox, January 15, 1789, and Joseph Martin to Henry Knox, February 2,1789, both in *ASP:IA*, 1:46–48; Faulkner, *Life and Times of Reverend Stephen Foreman*, 1–2. Sevier exaggerated the attack's success in his letter to the privy council, likely as a way to increase popular support for the newly organized government. Compare Sevier's January 12, 1789, letter with Joseph Martin's reports to Samuel Johnston and Henry Knox. For a further discussion, see Ostler, *Surviving Genocide*, 113, 423n52.

16. John Sevier to Chanuby [Chenabee], December 15, 1788, GP17, Governor Samuel Johnston, 1787–1789, n.d., Governors' Papers, SANC; "Winchester, July 8," *Independent Gazetteer or the Chronicle of Freedom* (Philadelphia, PA), July 16, 1789; Bennet Ballew to George Washington, August 22, 1789, in *PGW*, 3:516–519; Bloody Fellow Talk, January 7, 1792, *ASP:IA*, 1:203; The Badger to Richard Winn and Andrew Pickens, April 15, 1789, Andrew Pickens Papers, 1782–1804, microfiche 51–121, South Carolina Historical Society, Charleston; Joseph Martin to Henry Knox, February 2, 1789, *ASP:IA*, 1:48; Charles McDowell to Samuel Johnston, April 17, 1789, Alexander Dromgoole to Samuel Johnston, October 16, 1789, John Sevier to Hardy Perry, December 15, 1788, John Sevier to Piomin[k]o, December 15, 1788, John Sevier to Robert Thompson, December 15, 1788, John Sevier to John Turnbull, December 15, 1788, and John Sevier to William Glover, December 15, 1788, all in GP17, Governor Samuel Johnston, 1787–1789, n.d., Governors' Papers, SANC; Andrew Pickens to Richard Winn, April 16, 1789, and Andrew Pickens to Little Turkey, June 15, 1789, both in Andrew Pickens Papers, 1782–1804, microfiche 51–121, South Carolina Historical Society, Charleston; John Sevier to Bennet Ballew, March 10, 1789, and John Sevier to the Warriors and Chiefs of the Cherokees, May 17, 1789, both in *Pennsylvania Packet and Daily Advertiser* (Philadelphia, PA), August 18, 1789; Robert Hays to Daniel Smith, June 8–18, 1789, DRAPER, 4XX6; John Steele to James Carey, June 8, 1789, in Wagstaff, *Papers of John Steele*, 1:51–52; Joseph Martin to Patrick Henry, July 2, 1789, DRAPER, 2XX30; George Washington, Instructions to

the U.S. Commissioners for Treating with the Southern Indians, August 29, 1789, *EAID*, 28:544. Ballew even traveled to New York to deliver his message to Washington in person and likely carried with him a talk purportedly from a May 1789 Cherokee council held at Chota. Yet the council took place while the most prominent Overhill leaders remained refugees in Ustanali and other distant towns and could not have been authorized by the nation as a whole. See Tickagiska King to George Washington, May 19, 1789, in *PGW*, 2:325–326; Maclay, *Journal of William Maclay*, 128–129; and *Pennsylvania Packet and Daily Advertiser* (Philadelphia), August 25, 1789. Ballew later joined with Sevier in speculating in Native land. Joseph Martin to Patrick Henry, January 18, 1791, DRAPER, 2XX37. On the origins of Bloody Fellow's sobriquet, see Norton, *Journal of Major John Norton*, 154–155.

17. Little Turkey, Hanging Maw, and Dragging Canoe to Samuel Johnston, March 10, 1789, GLB9, Governor Samuel Johnston, 1787–1789, n.d., Governors' Papers, SANC; The Badger to Richard Winn and Andrew Pickens, April 15, 1789, Andrew Pickens to Richard Winn, May 16, 1789, and Andrew Pickens to Little Turkey, June 15, 1789, all in Andrew Pickens Papers, 1782–1804, microfiche 51-121, South Carolina Historical Society, Charleston; Talk by the Cherokee Leaders to Samuel Johnson, February 16, 1789, *CSRNC*, 22:788–789; Andrew Pickens, John Steele, and Henry Osborne to the Headman Chief and Warriors of the Cherokees, June 7, 1789, and John Steele to James Carey, June 8, 1789, in Wagstaff, *Papers of John Steele*, 1:50–52; Robert Hays to Daniel Smith, June 8–18, 1789, DRAPER, 4XX6; *Pennsylvania Gazette* (Philadelphia, PA), August 12, 1789; *Pennsylvania Packet and Daily Advertiser* (Philadelphia, PA), August 25, 1789.

18. John Steele Talk, *Pennsylvania Packet and Daily Advertiser* (Philadelphia, PA), August 25, 1789; Deposition of Anthony For[e]man, June 15, 1789, in Wagstaff, *Papers of John Steele*, 1:53; Address from Cherokee Kings and Chiefs to George III, May 6, 1789, C.O. 42/68 Original Correspondence, Sec. of State, Quebec: 1790, in Cherokee Documents in Foreign Archives Collection, Hunter Library Special Collections, Western Carolina University, Cullowhee, NC.

19. Citizens of Mero District, North Carolina, to George Washington, November 30, 1789, in *PGW*, 4:345–347; James Robertson to Daniel Smith, July 7, 1789, and James Robertson to Samuel Johnston, September 2, 1789, both in *CSRNC*, 22:790–792; Daniel Smith to Samuel Johnston, July 24, 1789, GLB9, Governor Samuel Johnston, 1787–1789, n.d., Governors' Papers, SANC; Finger, *Tennessee Frontiers*, 126; Barksdale, *Lost State of Franklin*, 145–161.

20. Hugh Williamson to John Gray Blount, August 8, 1789, *JGB Papers*, 1:500; Minutes of the North Carolina Constitutional Convention at Fayetteville, *CSRNC*, 22:36–39, 48–49; Minutes of the North Carolina House of Commons, November 2, 1789–December 22, 1789, *CSRNC*, 21:257, 270, 311, 345–346; Minutes of the North Carolina Senate, November 5, 1789–December 22, 1789, *CSRNC*, 21:626, 663–664, 679; Bill for the Purpose of Ceding to the U.S.A. Certain Western Lands Therein Described, November 26, [1789], box 4, folder 32, November 1789–December 1789, GASR; An Act for the Purpose of Ceding to the United States of America, Certain Western Lands Therein Described, *CSRNC*, 25:4–6; Abernethy, *From Frontier to Plantation in Tennessee*, 106–114; Cavanagh, *Decision at Fayetteville*.

21. Rao, "New Historiography of the Early Federal Government," 105; An Ordinance for the Government of the Territory of the United States Northwest of the River

Ohio, July 13, 1787, Avalon Project, Yale Law School, https://avalon.law.yale.edu/18th
_century/nworder.asp, accessed May 29, 2024; An Act to Accept the North Carolina
Cession, April 2, 1790, and An Act for the Government of the Territory South of the
River Ohio, May 26, 1790, both in *TPUS*, 4:13–19.

22. William Blount to John Steele, July 10, 1790, in Wagstaff, *Papers of John Steele*,
1:67–68, Hugh Williamson to George Washington, May 28, 1790, Timothy Bloodworth
to George Washington, June 5, 1790, John B. Ashe to George Washington, June 5, 1790,
and George Washington, Commission of Governor Blount, June 8, 1790, all in *TPUS*,
4:19–23, 24; William Blount to John Gray Blount, April 17, 1790, William Blount to John
Gray Blount, June 26, 1790, and William Blount to John Gray Blount, November 10,
1790, all in *JGB Papers*, 2:40–44, 67–72, 136–137.

23. Arthur Campbell to Henry Knox, August 19, 1790, DRAPER, 9DD63–64; Census Report, July 1791, *TPUS*, 4:81; John Watts to John Sevier, October 17, 1789, DRAPER,
11DD84a; Wright, *William Augustus Bowles*, 38–58; Sturtevant, "Cherokee Frontiers,
the French Revolution, and William Augustus Bowles." On public lands in the Southwest Territory, see Thomas Jefferson, Report of the Secretary of State to the President,
November 8, 1791, *TPUS*, 4:85–100; and Toomey, "Prelude to Statehood."

24. George Washington to Congress, August 11, 1790, *ASP:IA*, 1:83; Thomas Jefferson to Henry Knox, August 26, 1790, *TPUS*, 4:34–35; Henry Knox to William Blount,
August 27, 1790, box 1, folder 36, Northwest Territory Collection, 1721–1825, Indiana Historical Society, Indianapolis, Indiana; Benjamin Hawkins to William Blount,
March 10, 1791, William Blount Papers, 1783–1823, LC.

25. DRAPER, 15U7; John Whitney to William Lytle and Absalom Tatum, June 28,
1791, folder 3, William Lytle Papers #445-z, SHC; Ramsey, *Annals of Tennessee*, 555;
Cumfer, *Separate Peoples, One Land*, 58. For a list of Cherokee signatories to the treaty,
see *TPUS*, 4:65–66.

26. William Blount to Henry Knox, July 2, 1791, extract, *ASP:IA*, 1:628; DRAPER,
15U35–36; *ASP:IA*, 1:204; Henry Knox to William Blount, August 27, 1790, box 1, folder
36, Northwest Territory Collection, 1721–1825, Indiana Historical Society, Indianapolis,
Indiana; Benjamin Hawkins to William Blount, March 10, 1791, William Blount Papers,
1783–1823, LC; Alexander McGillivray to Joseph Martin, April 15, 1788, box 1, folder 14,
Penelope Johnson Allen Cherokee Collection, TSLA; Cherokee Headmen of Hiwassee
to William Blount, January 28, 1791, box 6, folder 20, Keith M. Read Collection, ms921,
UGA; Whitaker, "Muscle Shoals Speculation," 376–386.

27. DRAPER, 15U8–9, 15U11, 15U37–38.

28. DRAPER, 15U14, 15U17.

29. DRAPER, 15U18; Treaty of Holston, *TPUS*, 4:60–67.

30. Memorial from the Civil and Military Officers of Mero District, August 1, 1791,
TPUS, 4:72; Benjamin Hawkins, Senate Committee Report, November 9, 1791, *ASP:IA*,
1:135; Benjamin Hawkins to William Blount, November 14, 1791, William Blount
Papers, 1783–1823, LC; William Blount to Isaac Shelby, December 21, 1791, DRAPER,
11DD48; McLoughlin, *Cherokee Renascence*, 26.

31. Timothy Pickering notes, [1793], 14, reel 59, Timothy Pickering Papers, MHS;
Journal Extract about George Welbank's Information, August 13, 1793, enclosed in Bev-
erly Randolph to George Washington, September 30, 1793, *PGW*, 14:143–152; George
Welbank to Alexander McKee, January 16, 1793, in Hamer, "British in Canada and the
Southern Indians," 115–118; Cherokee Nation to Baron de Carondelet, April 5, 1793,

PTJ, 26:316–317; *ASP:IA*, 1:203–205; Henry Knox, Report to President Washington, January 17, 1792, *PGW*, 9:449–452; Henry Knox to William Blount, January 31, 1792, *TPUS*, 4:115–117.

32. *ASP:IA*, 1:272–273; DRAPER, 15U10, 15U25.

33. *ASP:IA*, 1:272.

34. Lindley, Moore, and Paxson, "Expedition to Detroit, 1793," 611–612; Journal Extract about George Welbank's Information, August 13, 1793, in *PGW*, 14:147–152; *ASP:IA*, 1:271, 204; William Blount to Henry Knox, July 4, 1792, *TPUS*, 4:157–159; William Blount to Isaac Shelby, September 11, 1792, box 2, Shelby Family Papers, LC; Information of Red Bird, September 15, 1792, Information by Richard Finnelson, November 1, 1792, and Information by James Carey, November 3, 1792, all in *ASP:IA*, 1:282, 288–291, 327–329; Baron de Carondelet to Don Luis de Las Casas, November 20, 1792, in Kinnaird, *Spain in the Mississippi Valley*, 4:96–98; Manuel Gayoso de Lemos to the Baron de Carondelet, January 8, 1793, in Weeks, *Paths to a Middle Ground*, 203–206; Carondelet's Speech to the Cherokee Nation, November 24, 1792, and Cherokee Nation to Baron de Carondelet, April 5, 1793, both in *PTJ*, 26:120, 316–317.

35. *ASP:IA*, 1:206; William Blount to Hugh Williamson, April 14, 1792, *JGB Papers*, 2:194–196; *Knoxville Gazette*, March 24, 1792; *Knoxville Gazette*, April 21, 1792; *Knoxville Gazette*, May 5, 1792; Richard Justice and Thomas Glass to William Blount, March 5, 1792, David Campbell to William Blount, May 16, 1792, William Blount to Henry Knox, March 20, 1792, A Return of Persons Killed, Wounded, and Taken Prisoners from Miro District, n.d., all in *ASP:IA*, 1:263–264, 266, 329–330; Andrew Pickens to William Blount, September 12, 1792, William Blount Papers, 1783–1823, LC; Calloway, *Victory with No Name*. On the importance of interpreting Native attacks as border patrols, see Haynes, *Patrolling the Border*.

36. Little Turkey to William Blount, September 2, 1792, The Boots to William Blount, September 2, 1792, John Thompson to William Blount, September 2, 1792, James Carey to William Blount, September 7, 1792, John Sevier to William Blount, September 13, 1792, Bloody Fellow to William Blount, September 10, 1792, The Glass to William Blount, September 10, 1792, Information by Richard Finnelson, November 1, 1792, and Report of James Carey, November 5, 1792, all in *ASP:IA*, 1:276–277, 280, 288–291, 329; William Blount to Isaac Shelby, September 11, 1792, and Ebenezer Brooks to Isaac Shelby, September 17, 1792, both in box 2, Shelby Family Papers, LC; James Robertson to Isaac Shelby, October 7, 1792, DRAPER, 4XX14; William Blount to Henry Knox, October 10, 1792, *TPUS*, 4:195–197; William Blount to James Robertson, October 17, 1792, box 1, folder 7, James Robertson Papers, TSLA.

37. Bloody Fellow to William Blount, September 10, 1792, and The Glass to William Blount, September 10, 1792, both in *ASP:IA*, 1:280; George Washington, Proclamation of the Treaty of Holston, November 11, 1791, *TPUS*, 4:68.

38. Chickasaws Talk, *ASP:IA*, 1:205; John Whitney to William Lytle and Absalom Tatum, June 28, 1791, folder 3, William Lytle Papers #445-z, SHC; Henry Knox to William Blount, April 22, 1792, *TPUS*, 4:137–143; James Colbert to William Blount, February 10, 1792, William Blount Papers, 1783–1823, LC; William Blount to James Robertson, May 16, 1792, box 1, folder 7, James Robertson Papers, TSLA; Manuel Gayoso de Lemos to Baron de Carondelet, December 6, 1793, folder 41, and Baron de Carondelet to unknown, January 24, 1794, folder 42, both in Diego de Gardoqui Papers, Tulane University Special Collections, New Orleans, LA.

39. Proclamation of George Washington, July 21, 1794, box 4, folder 14, James Robertson Papers, TSLA; Nashville Conference, *ASP:IA*, 1:286; Daniel Smith to William Dickson, [1804], DRAPER 4XX59; DuVal, *Independence Lost*, 305.

40. Henry Knox to William Blount, April 31, 1792, George Washington communication to Congress, December 7, 1792, and William Blount Proclamation, January 28, 1793, all in *ASP:IA*, 1:250, 325, 435; William Blount to James Robertson, October 27, 1792, box 1, folder 7, James Robertson Papers, TSLA; James Robertson to William Blount, October 12, 1792, *TPUS*, 4:198; Tanner Williams to William Blount, November 25, 1792, William Blount Papers, 1783–1823, LC.

41. William Blount to James Robertson, January 8, 1793, William Blount to James Robertson, February 13, 1793, William Blount to James Robertson April 18, 1793, and William Blount to James Robertson, April 28, 1793, all in box 1, folder 8, James Robertson Papers, TSLA; William Blount to Henry Knox, May 28, 1793, *TPUS*, 4:264; Robert King and Daniel Carmichael to Daniel Smith, June 12, 1793, and Daniel Smith to Henry Knox, June 13, 1793, both in *ASP:IA*, 1:459; John Chisholm to John Sevier, June 13, 1793, in Ramsey, *Annals of Tennessee*, 577; Arthur Campbell to Henry Lee, June 24, 1793, *CVSP*, 6:409–410; Ablavsky, *Federal Ground*, 169.

42. Hanging Maw to George Washington, June 15, 1793, Doublehead to Daniel Smith, June 15, 1793, John McKee to William Blount, June 3, 1793, John Watts et al. to William Blount, February 2, 1792, and Henry Knox to William Blount, February 7, 1792, all in *ASP:IA*, 1:459–460, 457, 447–448, 429; William Blount to John Sevier, June 2, 1793, DRAPER, 4XX31; *Knoxville Gazette*, June 15, 1793; James Ore to Isaac Shelby, June 26, 1793, DRAPER, 11DD50; Arthur Campbell, undated draft, folder 10, Arthur Campbell Papers, 1752–1811, FHS; Arthur Campbell to Henry Lee, June 24, 1793, and Arthur Campbell to Henry Lee, July 6, 1793, both in *CVSP*, 6:409–410, 435–436; Daniel Smith to Henry Knox, July 19, 1793, and Daniel Smith to Henry Knox, August 31, 1793, both in *TPUS*, 4:280–283, 305–307; *Knoxville Gazette*, July 27, 1793; John McKee to William Blount, October 26, 1793, in the John McKee Papers #1194-z, SHC; Ramsey, *Annals of Tennessee*, 578–579. On the support for peace among Upper Town Cherokees, see Boulware, *Deconstructing the Cherokee Nation*, 168–169.

43. John Thompson to Daniel Smith, June 18, 1793, Bold Hunter, Tickekisky, and Others to Daniel Smith, June 18, 1793, and Daniel Smith to Chiefs of the Cherokees, June 20, 1793, all in *ASP:IA*, 1:462–463; *Knoxville Gazette*, July 23, 1793; Faulkner, *Massacre at Cavett's Station*, 49–60; 76–81; Ramsey, *Annals of Tennessee*, 579–583; Finger, *Tennessee Frontiers*, 144. For Doublehead's relationship to Old Tassel and John Watts, see Brown, *Old Frontiers*, 278, 353.

44. Daniel Smith to John Sevier, September 30, 1793, William Blount to Henry Knox, October 12, 1793, John Sevier to William Blount, October 25, 1793, and William Blount to Henry Knox, October 28, 1793, all in *ASP:IA*, 458, 469–470; John Sevier to Daniel Smith, September 27, 1793, DRAPER, 11DD107; John Sevier to Daniel Kennedy, September 16, 1793, John Sevier Letters, MS.368, UTK; William Blount to Henry Knox, October 18, 1793, *TPUS*, 4:308; William Blount to James Robertson, October 29, 1793, box 1, folder 8, James Robertson Papers, TSLA; George Welbank to Alexander McKee, April 12, 1794, in Hamer, "British in Canada and the Southern Indians," 129–133; William Blount to John Gray Blount, October 22, 1793, *JGB Papers*, 2:325; Ray, *Middle Tennessee*, 28.

45. Conference with Certain Chiefs and Warriors of the Cherokee Nation at Philadelphia in June 1794, box 7, folder 15–16, John Howard Payne Papers, 1794–1841,

1814–1841, Edward E. Ayer Manuscript Collection, NL; Silas Dinsmoor, undated, letter draft, box 4, folder 1, Dinsmoor Family Papers, MS-40, Rauner Special Collections Library, Dartmouth University, Hanover, NH; William Blount to James Robertson, April 15, 1794, and Treaty with the Cherokee Nation, June 26, 1794, both in *TPUS*, 4: 340–341, 346–348; George Washington to Cherokee Chiefs and Warriors, June 14, 1794, in *PGW*, 16:222–224.

46. William Blount to John Gray Blount, July 29, 1794, and Abishai C. Thomas to John Gray Blount, October 26, 1794, both in *JGB Papers*, 2:421, 448; William Blount to James Robertson, June 14, 1794, *TPUS*, 4:345–346; *Knoxville Gazette*, July 3, 1794; *Knoxville Gazette*, July 17, 1794; James Robertson to James Ore, September 9, 1794, James Robertson to John Watts, September 20, 1794, James Ore to William Blount, September 24, 1794, and James Robertson to William Blount, October 8, 1794, all in *ASP:IA*, 1:530–531, 632–633; William Blount to James Robertson, July 21, 1794, box 1, folder 9, and James Robertson to [Timothy Pickering], October 6, 1795, box 3, folder 20, both in James Robertson Papers, TSLA; William Blount to Henry Knox, September 22, 1794, *TPUS*, 4:356; *Knoxville Gazette*, September 26, 1794; Norton, *Journal of Major John Norton*, 37–38; Addington, "Chief Benge's Last Raid," 24–33.

47. Calloway, *Indian World of George Washington*, 462; McLoughlin, *Cherokee Renascence*, 25; Hanging Maw Talk, November 7, 1794, John Watts Talk, November 7, 1794, Doublehead to William Blount, October 20, 1794, John McKee to William Blount, October 28, 1794, John McKee to William Blount, November 4, 1794, William Blount to Double-head and other Chiefs and Warriors, November 1, 1794, and A Conference Held on the 7th and 8th of November, 1794, at Tellico Block House, all in *ASP:IA*, 1:532, 534, 536–538; Conference at Tellico Block House, box 2, folder 16, James Robertson Papers, TSLA. On the blockhouse's location and construction, see John McKee to William Blount, undated, folder 12, John McKee Papers, circa 1792–1825, LC.

48. Hanging Maw Talk, January 3, 1795, Bloody Fellow Talk, December 30, 1794, William Blount Talk, January 2, 1795, and William Blount Talk, January 3, 1795, all in Conference at Tellico Block House, box 2, folder 16, James Robertson Papers, TSLA; William Blount to John McKee, November 1, 1794, William Blount to Double-head and other Chiefs and Warriors, November 1, 1794, William Blount to James Robertson, November 1, 1794, William Blount to William Whitley, November 1, 1794, William Blount Talk, November 8, 1794, and William Blount to Benjamin Logan, November 1, 1794, all in *ASP:IA*, 1:533–534, 537.

49. William Blount to Henry Knox, March 23, 1793, and Timothy Pickering to William Blount, March 23, 1795, both in *TPUS*, 4:247–248, 386–393; James Robertson to William Blount, January 13, 1795, *ASP:IA*, 1:556; Chenubee King, et al. to James Robertson, February 13, 1795, box 2, folder 17, George Colbert to James Robertson, March 5, 1795, box 1, folder 11, and George Washington to William Colbert et al., August 22, 1795, box 4, folder 14, all in James Robertson Papers, TSLA; Willie Blount to John Haywood, September 15, 1795, folder 13, box 1, in the Ernest Haywood Collection of Haywood Family Papers #1290, SHC; Anthony Foster to [Robert] Hays, October 25, 1795, Letters from Timothy Pickering, Oliver Wolcott and Others to David Henley, Calvin M. McClung Historical Collection, Knox County Public Library, Knoxville, TN; Timothy Pickering to David Campbell, August 28, 1795, and Timothy Pickering to David Henley, July 22, 1795, both in Timothy Pickering Letters, 1795–1807, Edward E. Ayer Manuscript Collection, NL; Timothy Pickering to David

Henley, March 11, 1795, David Henley Papers, RL; Gibson, *Chickasaws*, 82–88; Atkinson, *Splendid Land, Splendid People*, 132–138, 155–159; St. Jean, "How the Chickasaws Saved the Cumberland Settlement," 4–8. Ronald Eugene Craig is particularly successful in exploring how the Colberts' political power stemmed from their maternal kinship relations. Craig, "Colberts in Chickasaw History."

50. William Blount to James Robertson, January 20, 1795, *ASP:IA*, 1:557; William Blount to James Robertson, January 22, 1795, box 1, folder 11, and James Robertson to William Blount, April 20, 1795, box 3, folder 20, both in James Robertson Papers, TSLA; *Knoxville Gazette*, January 23, 1795; Piomin[k]o to James Robertson, October 24, 1795, David Henley Papers, TSLA; St. Jean, "How the Chickasaws Saved the Cumberland Settlement," 13–14; Atkinson, *Splendid Land*, 174–177.

51. *Knoxville Gazette*, December 13, 1794; *Knoxville Gazette*, August 25, 1794; William Blount to James Robertson, November 22, 1794, box 1, folder 10, James Robertson Papers, TSLA; Masterson, *William Blount*, 275–277; Ray, *Middle Tennessee*, 28–31.

52. Article 11, Sections 31–32, Tennessee State Constitution (1796). For a list of the convention delegates, see *Journal of the Proceedings of a Convention Began and Held at Knoxville, January 11, 1796*, 30–31.

53. *Journal . . . of a Convention . . . Held at Knoxville, January 11, 1796*, 8; Article 11, Section 32, Tennessee State Constitution (1796); Opal, *Avenging the People*, 103; Barnhart, "Tennessee Constitution of 1796," 544.

Chapter 4. Creating and Enforcing International Borders in the Tennessee Country

1. William Blount to Henry Knox, March 20, 1792, *TPUS*, 4:129–130; Report of David Craig to William Blount, March 15, 1792, and William Blount to David Campbell, Charles McClung, and John McKee, October 7, 1792, both in *ASP:IA*, 1:264–265, 630; William Blount to James McHenry, June 6, 1797, 59–61, in PICKENS.

2. DRAPER, 15UU18; A Narrative of Major Charles McClung, July 1797, 64–67, in Surveyor's Notebook—Winchester, James, 1787–1800, box 4, folder 16, Winchester, James (1752–1826) Papers, 1787–1923, WINCHESTER; William Blount to James McHenry, June 6, 1797, 59–61, PICKENS; Micheaux, *Travels to the West of the Alleghany Mountains*, 3:255; David Campbell, Charles McClung, and John McKee to William Blount, November 30, 1792, and William Blount to Henry Knox, December 16, 1792, both in *ASP:IA*, 1:630–631; Treaty of Holston, *TPUS*, 4:61; *Knoxville Gazette*, June 5, 1797; *A Short Description of the Tennassee Government, or the Territory of the United States South of the River Ohio, to Accompany and Explain a Map of that Country* (Philadelphia: Mathew Carey, 1793); Benjamin Hawkins and Andrew Pickens to James McHenry, July 12, 1797, 61–64, PICKENS. Until the late nineteenth century, residents of the Tennessee Valley referred to the present-day Little Tennessee River as the Tennessee River and everything between the confluence of the French Broad and Holston Rivers, near Knoxville, and the mouth of the Little Tennessee River as the Holston River. I use modern designations throughout for the sake of clarity. On this point, see Montgomery, "Nomenclature of the Upper Tennessee River."

3. DRAPER, 15U18; *ASP:IA*, 1:205; Henry Knox to William Blount, April 22, 1792, and William Blount to David Campbell, Charles McClung, and John McKee, October 7, 1792, both in *ASP:IA*, 1:252, 630; Hudson, *Creek Paths and Federal Roads*, 44.

4. For Cherokees' opposition to Blount, see McLoughlin, *Cherokee Renascence*, 40–41; and Report of James Carey to Governor Blount, March 19, 1793, *ASP:IA*, 1:437.

5. Kokomoor, "Creeks, Federalists, and the Idea of Coexistence in the Early Republic," 805. On white Americans' attempts to gain international recognition for the United States, see Gould, *Among the Powers of the Earth*. For more on Indigenous peoples' appropriation of colonial powers' conceptions of international law for their own benefit, see the collected essays in Belmessous, *Native Claims*.

6. Timothy Pickering, Report to the House of Representatives, January 26, 1795, *ASP:IA*, 1:547; Timothy Pickering to David Henley, March 23, 1795, Timothy Pickering Letters, 1795–1798, Edward E. Ayer Manuscript Collection, NL; Nichols, *Red Gentlemen and White Savages*, 132.

7. Timothy Pickering to William Blount, March 23, 1795, *TPUS*, 4:391–392; Silas Dinsmoor to David Henley, July 8, 1795, Silas Dinsmore [Dinsmoor] Papers, 1794–1796, Edward E. Ayer Manuscript Collection, NL; William Blount to Timothy Pickering, January 10, 1795, *ASP:IA*, 1:556; Timothy Pickering to David Henley, March 23, 1795, David Henley Papers, RL; William Blount to James Robertson, April 24, 1795, box 1, folder 11, and William Blount to James Robertson, October 25, 1795, box 1, folder 12, both in James Robertson Papers, TSLA; William Blount to Thomas Mitchell, June 11, 1795, William Blount Papers, 1794–1796, Edward E. Ayer Manuscript Collection, NL; William Blount to Alexander Kelley and Littlepage Sims, December 1, 1795, *TPUS*, 4:408–410; Valentine Sevier to John Sevier, December 31, 1795, DRAPER, 11DD128.

8. An Act to Regulate Trade and Intercourse with the Indian Tribes (1793), section 9, Avalon Project, Yale Law School, http://avalon.law.yale.edu/18th_century/na025 .asp, accessed May 22, 2024; George Washington, Seventh Annual Message to Congress, December 8, 1795, The American Presidency Project, UC Santa Barbara, 2024, www .presidency.ucsb.edu/documents/seventh-annual-address-congress, accessed May 22, 2024; Prucha, *American Indian Policy in the Formative Years*, 45; Ablavsky, *Federal Ground*, 114–116; Nichols, *Red Gentlemen and White Savages*, 77–127. For a brief overview of these laws, see Prucha, *American Indian Policy in the Formative Years*, 45–49. On the federal government's so-called civilization plan in the Native South, see Washburn, "'Labor in the Field Is Much Changed.'"

9. Proceedings of Saturday April 9, and Tuesday February 2, *Annals of the Congress*, 4th Cong., 1st sess., 897, 287; Cayton, *Frontier Republic*, 12–50; Cayton, "Radicals in the 'Western World'"; Murrin, "Jeffersonian Triumph and American Exceptionalism"; Onuf, *Jefferson's Empire*, 41–46; Van Atta, *Securing the West*, 37–51. For how this boundary line perpetuated a vision of centralized imperial administration of Indian affairs begun by British officials with the Proclamation Line of 1763, see Lee, "Indian Boundary Line and the Imperialization of U.S.-Indian Affairs."

10. Trade and Intercourse Act (1796); Proceedings of Saturday April 9, *Annals of the Congress*, 4th Cong., 1st sess., 903–904; *Journal of the House of Representatives of the United States, 1795*, 506, 508; Trade and Intercourse Act (1793). On North Carolinians' claims, see Petition of Thomas Person et al., December 21, 1793, box 3, folder 4, December 1793–January 1794, Petition of James Glasgow, J[ohn] G[ray] Blount, and [illegible], [1796], box 3, folder 4, November 1796–December 1796, Memorial of the Trustees of the University of North Carolina, December 23, 1791, box 3, folder 4, December 1791–January 1792, William R. Davie, Committee Report on the Petition of Thomas Person and Others, December 26, 1793, December 1793–January 1794, box 2, folder 6,

and Petition of the Trustees of the University of North Carolina, December 21, 1793, box 3, folder 4, December 1793–January 1794, all in GASR.

11. Opal, *Avenging the People*, 3–4; Kaminsky, *Exchange Artist*, 14–48 (quotation 35); Blaakman, *Speculation Nation*; Huston, "Land Conflict and Land Policy in the United States," 328–329; Proceedings of Saturday April 9, *Annals of the Congress*, 4th Cong., 1st sess., 897–899.

12. Proceedings of Saturday April 9, *Annals of the Congress*, 4th Cong., 1st sess., 898–899; Claims on the Lands Ceded by North Carolina, March 10, 1796, in Lowrie, *American State Papers* 1:27. On the significance of preemption land claims, see Blaakman, *Speculation Nation*, 215–250.

13. Proceedings of Saturday April 9, *Annals of the Congress*, 4th Cong., 1st sess., 901, 905; *Journal of the House of Representatives of the United States, 1795*, 508–509; Roney, "1776, Viewed from the West," 694; Opal, *Avenging the People*, 69; Cayton, "Radicals in the Western World," 79–80; Cayton, "'Separate Interests' and the Nation State"; Ray, *Middle Tennessee*, 26; Blaakman, *Speculation Nation*, 9. William Barry Grove of North Carolina and Josiah Parker of Virginia were the only Federalists to oppose forfeiture. Grove possessed at least one warrant for 1,500 acres of land along the Big Hatchie River in the Chickasaw Nation, so unlike many of his political allies he had a financial incentive to favor speculators' unchecked access to Native land. Early Tennessee/North Carolina Land Records, 1783–1927, 247, Book C, Roll 5, Record Group 50, TSLA.

14. Red Pole Talk, December 2, 1796, 42, 47–48, Letterbook Copy, John Adams Papers, MHS; James McHenry to George Washington, July 12, 1796, reel 109, Series 4, General Correspondence, 1797–1799, George Washington Papers, LC; George Washington to James McHenry, July 18, 1796, box 5, James McHenry Papers, LC; David Henley to John Chisholm, October 29, 1796, David Henley Papers, TSLA; John Adams to Abigail Adams, December 4, 1796, in Hogan et al., *Adams Family Correspondence*, 11:430–432; Calloway, *Indian World of George Washington*, 459; Calloway, *Shawnees and the War for America*.

15. Piomin[k]o Talk, November 24, 1796, 51, Letterbook Copy, John Adams Papers, MHS; James McHenry Notes, December 9, 1796, box 2, James McHenry Papers, William L. Clements Library, University of Michigan, Ann Arbor.

16. John Watts Talk, December 22, 1796, 58, Letterbook Copy, John Adams Papers, MHS. Will Elders had been a Chickamauga chief and represented the Lower Towns in subsequent negotiations. The Bark was a signatory to later Cherokee treaties where Lower Town leaders were prominent. See Cumfer, *Separate Peoples, One Land*, 56; and McLoughlin, *Cherokee Renascence*, 210–211. On white settlers' murder of Cherokee hunters in 1796, see John Sevier to the Chiefs and Warriors of the Cherokee Nation, April 2, 1796, box 1, folder 2, James D. Puckett et al. to John Sevier, April 27, 1796, Oversize Letterbook, and Doublehead to John Sevier, May 18, 1796, box 2, folder 1, all in GP-2, John Sevier Papers, TSLA.

17. Talk of the Secretary of War to the Chiefs and Warriors of the Chickasaw Nation, December 19, 1796, and Talk of the Secretary of War to John Watts and the Other Chiefs and Warriors of the Cherokee Nation, December 21, 1796, both 54, 58–60, Letterbook Copy, John Adams Papers, MHS; William Blount to John Sevier, January 4, 1797, William Blount Letters to John Sevier, MssCol 7455, Manuscripts and Archives Division, New York Public Library, New York; John Sevier to William Blount, January 29, 1797, box 1, folder 3, GP-2, John Sevier Papers, TSLA.

18. James McHenry to Benjamin Hawkins, Andrew Pickens, and James Winchester, February 2, 1797, and James McHenry to Richard Sparks, January 27, 1797, 38–39, 133, Letterbook Copy, John Adams Papers, MHS; James McHenry to George Washington, July 12, 1796, Series 4, General Correspondence, 1797–1799, reel 109, George Washington Papers, LC; George Washington to the Cherokee Nation, August 29, 1796, Founders Online, NA, https://founders.archives.gov/documents/Washington/05-20-02-0388, accessed May 22, 2024; Timothy Pickering to George Washington, August 29, 1796, Founders Online, NA, https://founders.archives.gov/documents/Washington/05-20-02-0391, accessed May 22, 2024; William Blount to John Sevier, January 4, 1797, William Blount Letters to John Sevier, New York Public Library, New York; George Washington to the Senate, January 19, 1797, Founders Online, NA, https://founders.archives.gov/documents/Washington/05-21-02-0236, accessed May 22, 2024; James Winchester to John Sevier, March 31, 1797, Sevier's letterbook, GP-2, John Sevier Papers, TSLA. On Winchester's speculation interests, see William Blount to John Gray Blount, March 28, 1795, *JGB Papers*, 2:520–523.

19. Benjamin Hawkins to James McHenry, March 1, 1797, *LBH*, 1:86; James McHenry to George Washington, February 25, 1797, box 2, James McHenry Papers, William L. Clements Library, University of Michigan, Ann Arbor. For commissioners' preparations, see Hawkins's letters and journal entries in *LBH*, 1:52–59, 69–72.

20. Louis-Philippe, *Diary of My Travels in America*, 74–75; James McHenry to George Washington, February 25, 1797, box 2, James McHenry Papers, William L. Clements Library, University of Michigan, Ann Arbor; Sampson Williams to Andrew Jackson, [1796–1797], Sampson Williams Letter, MS.1959, UTK; Silas Dinsmoor to John Sevier, March 8, 1797, box 2, folder 2, and John Sevier to William Blount, February 14, 1797, box 1, folder 3, both in GP-2, John Sevier Papers, TLSA; James Robertson to David Henley, February 2, 1797, box 2, folder 11, Stanley Horn Collection, TSLA; Owens, "'Between Two Fires,'" 38–46. Silas Dinsmoor created a relatively formal census of "all persons residing in the Cherokee country not natives of the land" in March 1797. Silas Dinsmoor to John Sevier, March 11, 1797, box 5, folder 9, GP-2, John Sevier Papers, TSLA.

21. Louis-Philippe, *Diary of My Travels in America*, 98–99; Hawkins Journal Entries, April 1–April 11, April 15, 1797, *LBH*, 1:59–61, 72–76; David Campbell to John McKee, November 13, 1800, folder 2, John McKee Papers, circa 1792–1825, LC; Benjamin Hawkins to James McHenry, April 11, 1797, *LBH*, 1:100; Benjamin Hawkins to David Henley, April 8, 1797, David Henley Papers, RL; David Henley to George Washington, June 11, 1797, folder 3, David Henley Papers, TSLA.

22. William Blount to James McHenry, June 6, 1797, 59–61, PICKENS; John Sevier to Benjamin Hawkins and Andrew Pickens, April 19, 1797, box 1, folder 3, GP-2, John Sevier Papers, TSLA; John Sevier to Silas Dinsmoor, January 12, 1797, John Sevier Correspondence, LC; George Strother to Benjamin Hawkins, n.d., *LBH*, 1:101n1; John Sevier to Andrew Jackson, May 11, 1797, *PAJ*, 1:142; Hawkins Journal Entry, April 12, 1797, *LBH*, 1:76; James McHenry to Benjamin Hawkins and Andrew Pickens, June 18, 1797, Papers of the War Department, 1784–1800, Roy Rosenzweig Center for History and New Media, George Mason University, https://wardepartmentpapers.org/s/home/item/57844, accessed May 28, 2024; Andrew, *Life and Times of General Andrew Pickens*, 264; Melton, *First Impeachment*; Cayton, "'When Shall We Cease to Have Judases?'"

23. Hawkins Journal Entries, April 7, 1797, April 5, 1797, April 18, 1797, and April 19, 1797, all in *LBH*, 1:73–74, 78–79; Benjamin Hawkins to David Henley, April 11, 1797, David Henley Papers, RL.

24. Louis-Philippe, *Diary of My Travels in America*, 83; Hawkins Journal Entries, March 31, 1797, and April 25, 1797, *LBH*, 1:58, 80; Kelley, *Historic Fort Loudoun*; Tortora, *Carolina in Crisis*, 117–138; Boulware, *Deconstructing the Cherokee Nation*, 120–124.

25. Benjamin Hawkins and Andrew Pickens to James McHenry, April 24, 1797, *LBH*, 1:106–107; Hawkins Journal Entries, April 25–27, 1797, *LBH*, 1:80–81; Entry April 27, 1797, n.p., PICKENS; Persico, "Early Nineteenth-Century Cherokee Political Organization," 92–98. The Pickens journal manuscript is more useful for identifying the names of individual Cherokees than the published *Letters of Benjamin Hawkins*, which contains some transcription errors.

26. Keanotah [Little Turkey] and Ocunna [The Badger] to John Adams, April 28, 1797, *LBH*, 1:82–83; Hawkins Journal Entries, April 26–27, 1797, *LBH*, 1:80–81; Benjamin Hawkins to David Henley, April 29, 1797, David Henley Papers, RL.

27. John Sevier to James McHenry, June 8, 1797, box 1, folder 3, GP-2, John Sevier Papers, TSLA; William Blount notes on the Tennessee Legislature's Report of the Commissioners Appointed to Trace the Line Lately Designated by the Commissioners of the United States, [1797], PC 193.28, John Gray Blount Papers, SANC; Benjamin Hawkins to Silas Dinsmoor, April 6, 1797, Benjamin Hawkins and Andrew Pickens to James McHenry, April 24, 1797, and Benjamin Hawkins to James McHenry, May 4, 1797, all in *LBH*, 1:98, 106–107, 110; Hawkins Journal Entries, April 15, 1797, April 24, 1797, April 29, 1797, April 30, 1797, and May 6, 1797, all in *LBH*, 1:77, 84–85; Benjamin Hawkins to David Henley, April 29, 1797, and Benjamin Hawkins to David Henley, May 8, 1797, both in David Henley Papers, RL; Entries May 1–May 14, 1797, n.p., Pickens Journal; May 16, 1797, WINCHESTER, 1; James Winchester to John Sevier, March 31, 1797, Oversize Letterbook, GP-2, John Sevier Papers, TSLA; James Winchester to Silas Dinsmoor, March 31, 1797, *LBH*, 1:73–74; William Blount to James McHenry, June 6, 1797, 59–61, Pickens Journal; May 20, 1797, WINCHESTER, 1.

28. Baily, *Journal of a Tour in Unsettled Parts of North America*, 404; Benjamin Hawkins to James McHenry, June 4, 1797, *LBH*, 1:114; Benjamin Hawkins to John Overton, June 6, 1797, box 4, folder 14, Murdock Collection of John Overton Papers, 1780–[1797–1820]–1908, TSLA; May 21–June 2, 1797, WINCHESTER, 2–4, 9, 14–29. For commissioners' comments on the many existing roads they encountered during the survey, see WINCHESTER, October 24–October 25, 1797, 83–84.

29. May 27, 1797, WINCHESTER, 15–19; Baily, *Journal of a Tour in Unsettled Parts of North America*, 432–433; James Winchester to John Sevier, July 16, 1797, box 2, folder 1, Winchester, James (1752–1826) Papers, 1787–1923, TSLA; Entry June 29, 1797, 54, Pickens Journal.

30. May 27, 1797, WINCHESTER, 17–19; Benjamin Hawkins to David Henley, June 4, 1797, David Henley Papers, RL; Benjamin Hawkins to John Overton, June 6, 1797, box 4, folder 14, Murdock Collection of John Overton Papers, TSLA; Benjamin Hawkins to Keanetuh, the [Little] Turkey and Ocunna, the Badger, June 10, 1797, *LBH*, 1:115.

31. June 18, 1797, WINCHESTER, 52–53; James Winchester to John Sevier, July 16, 1797, box 2, folder 1, Winchester, James (1752–1826) Papers, 1787–1923, TSLA; Report of the Commissioners, n.d., James Winchester to Hawkins and Pickens, June 24, [1797],

Hawkins and Pickens to James Winchester, June 24, [1797], and Benjamin Hawkins, Order for Payment to Cherokee Commissioners from the Cumberland River to the Clinch River, June 25, 1797, all in WINCHESTER, 57–58, 62; Benjamin Hawkins to James McHenry, extract, July 5, 1797, 64–65, Pickens Journal; Benjamin Hawkins to David Henley, June 28, 1797, David Henley Papers, RL; Entries June 23–July 5, 1797, 53–55, Pickens Journal. On Fort Southwest Point, see Smith, *Fort Southwest Point Archaeological Site*, 20–36.

32. June 8, 1797, WINCHESTER, 37–38.

33. James Winchester to James Robertson, November 8, 1797, box 4, folder 19, James Robertson Papers, TSLA; October 12–October 30, 1797, WINCHESTER, 70–91, 125. On Turtle at Home, see Norton, *Journal of Major John Norton*, 32, 40–41.

34. September 19–December 11, 1800, WINCHESTER, 92–124; Journal Entry, September 7, 1800, Report of the Brethren Abraham Steiner and Friedrich von Schweinitz Concerning Their Second Visit to the Cherokees from 25 August to 2 November 1800, trans. Roy Ledbetter, in Crews and Starbuck, *Records of the Moravians among the Cherokees*, 1:196; James Winchester and Edward Butler to Head Men and Bearers of the Chickasaw Nation, n.d., in *Tennessee Gazette* (Nashville), October 22, 1800; *Boundary Line Running on Tennessee Ridge between the United States and the Chickasaw Nation of Indians*, James Winchester, February 5, 1801, Map 466, Map Collection, TSLA.

35. Silas Dinsmoor to James McHenry, June 4, 1797, box 2, and James McHenry to David Henley, April 20, 1797, box 15, both in James McHenry Papers, LC; *Journal of the House of Representatives of the State of Tennessee, Begun and Held at Knoxville, on Saturday, the Thirtieth Day of July, One Thousand Seven Hundred and Ninety Six*, 20–22; Hawkins Journal Entries, April 15, 1797, and April 28, 1797, both in *LBH*, 1:77, 83–84; William Charles Cole Claiborne to Andrew Jackson, July 20, 1797, *PAJ*, 1:146; William Blount to John Gray Blount, November 7, 1797, *JGB Papers*, 3:174–186.

36. John Hunt to John Sevier, July 17, 1797, Oversize Letterbook, and Residents of Powells Valley to John Sevier, [undated], 1797, box 2, folder 2, both in GP-2, John Sevier Papers, TSLA; Entry July 19, 1797, 55, PICKENS; Benjamin Hawkins to David Henley, July 20, 1797, Benjamin Hawkins Letters, 1797–1812, Edward E. Ayer Manuscript Collection, NL; John Sevier to Andrew Jackson, November 26, 1797, *PAJ*, 1:154–156; Elijah Chisum and Isaac Lane to John Adams, August 21, 1797, Founders Online, NA, https://founders.archives.gov/documents/Adams/99-02-02-2101, accessed May 22, 2024; Journal of the Proceedings of Governor Blount in the Territory South of the River Ohio, 1790–1796, November 3, 1790, *TPUS*, 4:437; Andrew Rights Editorial, February 17, 1797, in *Knoxville Gazette*, January 30, 1797. Either the editorial or the newspaper issue is misdated.

37. Silas Dinsmoor, Conference Notes, July 24, 1797, enclosure in Benjamin Hawkins to David Henley, July 25, 1797, David Henley Papers, RL; Works Progress Administration, *Grainger County, Tennessee, Court Minutes*, vol. 1, 1796–1802; Grainger County Court Minutes, June 13, 1796, Grainger County Clerk Loose Records, TSLA.

38. James McHenry to Thomas Butler, September 17, 1797, box 2, James McHenry Papers, William L. Clements Library, University of Michigan, Ann Arbor; Silas Dinsmoor, Conference Notes, July 25, 1797, enclosure in Benjamin Hawkins to David Henley, July 25, 1797, and Benjamin Hawkins to David Henley, July 28, 1797, both in David Henley Papers, RL; Benjamin Hawkins to James McHenry, July 5, 1797, *LBH*, 1:117–118;

Elijah Chisum [Chisholm] and Isaac Lane to John Adams, August 21, 1797, Founders Online, NA, https://founders.archives.gov/documents/Adams/99-02-02-2101, accessed May 22, 2024.

39. Comments of Joseph Whitner and John Clark Kilpatrick on *Re-Survey of Indian Boundary Line of 1791 Commencing at South-West Point and Terminating at Tuckaleechee Cove*, Joseph Whitner and John Clark Kilpatrick, [1797], Map 1363, Map Collection, TSLA; Benjamin Hawkins to David Henley, July 25, 1797, Benjamin Hawkins to David Henley, July 28, 1797, and Benjamin Hawkins to David Henley, August 28, 1797, all in David Henley Papers, RL; Benjamin Hawkins to Silas Dinsmoor, September 20, 1797, and Benjamin Hawkins to James Winchester, November 9, 1797, both in *LBH*, 1:130–131, 151; Benjamin Hawkins and Andrew Pickens to John Sevier, September 9, 1797, Oversize Letterbook, GP-2, John Sevier Papers, TSLA; WINCHESTER, 68–92; Andrew Pickens to Abraham Nott, January 1, 1800, in Lowrie, *American State Papers* 1:93; *Map of the Tennessee Government Formerly Part of North Carolina, taken Chiefly from Surveys by Gen'l. D. Smith & Others*, Mathew Carey, [ca. 1797], Individually Catalogued Manuscript Maps, Map 21a, Realms of Gold, American Philosophical Society, Philadelphia.

40. DRAPER, 16U143–144; Arthur Campbell to Timothy Pickering, February 5, 1798, 23–24, reel 22, Timothy Pickering Papers, MHS; Willie Blount to John Gray Blount, February 6, 1798, *JGB Papers*, 3:204–205; Thomas Butler to Samuel Hodgdon, February 18, 1798, in Papers of the War Department, 1784–1800, Roy Rosenzweig Center for History and New Media, George Mason University, https://wardepartmentpapers .org/s/home/item/61227, accessed May 22, 2024; DRAPER, 11DD140; Benjamin Hawkins to Andrew Pickens, November 19, 1797, *LBH*, 1:160–161; John Sevier to the People Lately Removed from Powel[l]'s Valley, April 12, 1798, and John Sevier to Thomas Butler, February 15, 1798, both in box 1, folder 5, GP-2, John Sevier Papers, TSLA; *Hall's Wilmington Gazette* (Wilmington, NC), February 22, 1798; Ray, *Middle Tennessee*, 169n90.

41. Benjamin Hawkins to Thomas Butler, November 9, 1797, and Benjamin Hawkins to Andrew Pickens, November 19, 1797, both in *LBH*, 1:148, 160–161; David Campbell to Benjamin Hawkins, August 13, 1797, box 10, folder 1, Penelope Johnson Allen Papers, Chattanooga Public Library, Chattanooga, TN; John Sevier to John Adams, February 6, 1798, box 1, folder 5, Joseph Anderson, Andrew Jackson, and William Claiborne to John Adams, March 5, 1798, box 2, folder 3, and David Campbell to John Sevier, April 4, 1797, Oversize Letterbook, all in GP-2, John Sevier Papers, TSLA; Louis-Philippe, *Diary of My Travels in America*, 98–99; David Campbell, "To the Citizens of the State of Tennessee who are About to be Alienated and Dismembered by the Acts and Proceedings of the Federal Government," *Knoxville Gazette*, March 13, 1797; David Campbell, "For the *Knoxville Gazette*," March 17, 1797, in *Knoxville Gazette*, April 3, 1797; David Campbell to Benjamin Hawkins, Andrew Pickens, and James Winchester, May 1, 1797, *Knoxville Gazette*, May 29, 1797; David Campbell, "For the *Knoxville Gazette*," May 10, 1797, *Knoxville Gazette*, June 12, 1797; David Campbell to Andrew Jackson, Joseph Anderson, and William Charles Cole Claiborne, January 16, 1798, *Knoxville Gazette*, February 2, 1798; Dockett 377 and 386, March 1798, Hamilton Superior Court Records, Knox County Archives, Knoxville, TN. On Campbell as the author of anonymous essays in the *Knoxville Gazette*, see John Sevier to John Adams, April 5, 1798, box 1, folder 5, GP-2, John Sevier Papers, TSLA.

Chapter 5. Native Ferries, National Highways, and the Limits of U.S. State Power in the Cherokee and Chickasaw Nations

1. David Campbell, "For the Knoxville Gazette," May 10, 1797, *Knoxville Gazette*, June 12, 1797; David Campbell to Benjamin Hawkins, Andrew Pickens, and James Winchester, May 1, 1797, *Knoxville Gazette*, May 29, 1797; John Sevier to John Adams, February 6, 1798, box 1, folder 5, and Joseph Anderson, Andrew Jackson, and William Charles Cole Claiborne to John Adams, March 5, 1798, box 2, folder 3, both in GP-2, John Sevier Papers, TSLA.

2. *Journals of the Senate and House . . . of Tennessee Held at Knoxville: First Session: Monday, September 18, 1797; Second Session: Monday, December 3, 1798*, 174, 199–201, (quotation 202), 249–255.

3. *Journals of the Senate and House . . . December 3, 1798*, 208, 251–252, 255 (emphasis in original); *ASP:IA*, 1:628.

4. *Journals of the Senate and House . . . December 3, 1798*, 208, 251–252.

5. John C. Calhoun, Speech on the Bill . . . for the Construction of Roads and Canals, February 4, 1817, in Crallé, *Speeches of John C. Calhoun*, 190. Foundational works on internal improvement include Sellers, *Market Revolution*; Larson, *Internal Improvement*; and Howe, *What Hath God Wrought*.

6. Cayton, "'Radicals in the 'Western World'"; Larson, "'Wisdom Enough to Improve Them'"; Raitz, *National Road*; Sellers, *Market Revolution*, 34–69.

7. Saler, *Settlers' Empire*, 32–34; Nichols, *Red Gentlemen and White Savages*, 193–199; Onuf, *Jefferson and the Virginians*, 129, 133–145; Wallace, *Jefferson and the Indians*, 218–226; Southerland and Brown, *Federal Road*. On the early national state operating on the margins, see Balogh, *Government out of Sight*; and Novak, "Myth of the 'Weak' American State," 766–768. For Jefferson and internal improvements, see Harrison, "Thomas Jefferson and Internal Improvement." John William Nelson makes the compelling point that white Americans' attempt to transform North America's physical geography facilitated Native dispossession in the borderlands. Nelson, *Muddy Waters*.

8. Hudson, *Creek Paths and Federal Roads*; Wainwright, "Both Native South and Deep South"; Washburn, "Directing Their Own Change." Scholars have begun to view national state power and political development from the perspective of western stakeholders. For examples, see Bergmann, *American National State and the Early West*; Van Atta, *Securing the West*; and Saler, *Settlers' Empire*. For a summary of internal improvement projects in the Cumberland Valley, see Ray, *Middle Tennessee*, 75–78. Recent historiographical overviews of American state power include "Taking Stock of the State in Nineteenth-Century America," a forum in *Journal of the Early Republic* 38, no. 1 (Spring 2018): 61–118; and Rao, "New Historiography of the Early Federal Government."

9. John Adams to the Senate and House of Representatives, January 17, 1798, in *Journal of the House of Representatives of the United States, 1797*, 136; *Annals of the Congress*, House of Representatives, 5th Cong., 2nd sess., 842–845, 919, 1058–1060; John Adams to Joseph Anderson, Andrew Jackson, and William Charles Cole Claiborne, December 1, 1797, Andrew Jackson to James Robertson, January 11, 1798, Andrew Jackson to Robert Hays, January 25, 1798, and Andrew Jackson to Robert Hays, March 2, 1798, all in *PAJ*, 1:156–157, 165, 172–173, 184–185; An Act Appropriating a Certain Sum of Money to Defray the Expense of Holding a Treaty or Treaties with the Indians, Chap. XIV, February 27, 1798, in *Acts of the Fifth Congress of the United States*, 539–540; Andrew Jackson

to David Campbell, January 11, 1798, Campbell Family Papers, RL. On the overlooked influence of John Adams on U.S. Indian policy, see Usner, "John Adams and the Paradoxical Origins of Federal Indian Policy."

10. John Sevier to James Robertson, James Stuart, and Lachlan McIntosh, July 4, 1798, box 1, folder 6, John Sevier to George Walton and John Steele, May 20, 1798, box 1, folder 5, John Sevier Proclamation, June 23, 1798, box 1, folder 5, John Sevier to James Ore, May 12, 1798, box 1, folder 5, all in GP-2, John Sevier Papers, TSLA; James McHenry to Alfred Moore, George Walton, and John Steel[e], March 30, 1798, *ASP:IA*, 1:639–640; Journal Entry, November 7, 1799, in Fries, "Report of the Brethren Abraham Steiner and Friedrich Christian von Schweinitz," 337; Hudson, *Creek Paths and Federal Roads*, 76. On the political disputes between East Tennessee and the Cumberland settlements, see Abernethy, *From Frontier to Plantation in Tennessee*, 164–181.

11. John Sevier to William C. C. Claiborne and Joseph Anderson, July 15, 1798, box 1, folder 6, GP-2, John Sevier Papers, TSLA; Silas Dinsmoor to John Sevier, July 18, 1798, in Sevier and Madden, *Sevier Family History, with the Collected Letters of Gen. John Sevier, First Governor of Tennessee*, 143–144; Alfred Moore to James McHenry, June 30, 1799, box 7, James McHenry Papers, LC; Ramsey, *Annals of Tennessee*, 695.

12. James McHenry to Alfred Moore, George Walton, and John Steel[e], March 30, 1798, *ASP:IA*, 1:639–640; Thomas Butler to Benjamin Lockwood, September 6, 1798, and Thomas Butler to Benjamin Lockwood, October 3, 1798, both in Thomas Butler Letters, 1798, Miscellaneous Papers, FHS; Treaty with the Cherokee, 1798, in Kappler, *Indian Treaties*, 51–55; Benjamin Hawkins to David Henley, October 25, 1798, Benjamin Hawkins Letters, 1797–1812, Edward E. Ayer Manuscript Collection, NL; Return J. Meigs to Henry Dearborn, October 20, 1802, and Return J. Meigs to Henry Dearborn, October 22, 1802, both in reel 1, BIA-M208; Royce, "Cherokee Nation of Indians," 181; Benjamin Hawkins to William Panton, November 22, 1798, *LBH*, 1:225–226; Usner, "John Adams and the Paradoxical Origins of Federal Indian Policy," 631. The Cherokee surveyors were Whiteman Killer, William Elders, Bighters, Saukuney, Lusun, and Big Bear. See the receipts for the 1802 survey at the end of reel 1, BIA-M208.

13. Treaty with the Cherokee, 1798, in Kappler, *Indian Treaties*, 53; James McHenry to George Walton and Thomas Butler, August 27, 1798, *ASP:IA*, 1:640; Journal Entry, November 20, 1799, in Fries, "Report of the Brethren Abraham Steiner and Friedrich Christian von Schweinitz," 362; Benjamin Hawkins to David Henley, August 28, 1797, *LBH*, 1:128; Nicholas Byers et al., Report on the Clinch River Ferry, [1809], reel 3, BIA-M208; Thomas Butler to James McHenry, March 5, 1800, 303, reel 13, Timothy Pickering Papers, MHS; Silas Dinsmoor to Return J. Meigs, January 27, 1803, reel 2, BIA-M208; Chulio to Return J. Meigs, April 25, 1806, reel 3, BIA-M208.

14. John Sevier, Legislative Message, December 18, 1798, in White, *Messages of the Governors of the State of Tennessee*, 1:89; *Journals of the Senate and House . . . December 3, 1798*, 388; William Blount, Memorial to Congress on Behalf of the State Legislature, [1799], petition 43, session 2, reel 1, Tennessee Legislative Petitions, 1799–1850, TSLA; An Act Respecting the Road as Stipulated for by the Treaty of Holston, October 26, 1799, Chapter X, in *Acts Passed at the First Session of the Third General Assembly of the State of Tennessee . . . One Thousand Seven Hundred and Ninety Nine*, 33.

15. David Campbell to Thomas Jefferson, June 12, 1801, *PTJ*, 34:315–316; Treaty with the Cherokee, 1791, in Kappler, *Indian Treaties*, 30; *Journals of the Senate and House . . . December 3, 1798*, 341; An Act Respecting the Road as Stipulated for by the Treaty of

Holston, October 26, 1799, Chapter X, in *Acts Passed at the First Session of the Third General Assembly of the State of Tennessee . . . One Thousand Seven Hundred and Ninety Nine*, 32–36; John Sevier to William Cocke, Joseph Anderson and William Claiborne, December 9, 1799, box 1, folder 7, and John Sevier to William Cocke, Joseph Anderson and William Claiborne, December 8, 1800, box 1, folder 8, both in GP-2, John Sevier Papers, TSLA.

16. Timothy Pickering to Winthrop Sargent, December 10, 1798, An Act for the Government of the Mississippi Territory, April 7, 1798, and John Habersham to Henry Dearborn, March 12, 1801, all in *TPUS*, 5:54, 18–22, 118–119; Winthrop Sargent to Timothy Pickering, April 20, 1799, Mississippi (Territory) Governor Correspondence, 1798–1819, Government Records Collections, ADAH; Anonymous to Thomas Jefferson, June 1801, signed "Kentucky Citizen," Thomas Jefferson Papers, Series 1: General Correspondence, 1651–1827, LC, www.loc.gov/item/mtjbib010234, accessed May 22, 2024.

17. John Habersham to Henry Dearborn, March 12, 1801, *TPUS*, 5:118; Baily, *Journal of a Tour in Unsettled Parts of North America*, 350–411; Gideon Granger to Thomas Jefferson, August 4, 1806, *TPUS*, 5:472–476; *Map of the State of Kentucky: With the Adjoining Territories*, 1794, Map Collection, TSLA, https://teva.contentdm.oclc.org/digital /collection/p15138c01123/id/10389, accessed June 24, 2024.

18. Timothy Pickering to Winthrop Sargent, May 20, 1799, *TPUS*, 5:56–60 (emphasis in original); John Habersham to Henry Dearborn, March 12, 1801, *TPUS*, 5:118–119; Baily, *Journal of a Tour in Unsettled Parts of North America*, 364–372. On this connection between race and culture, see Shire, *Threshold of Manifest Destiny*; and Pierce, *Making the White Man's West*.

19. Thomas Butler to James McHenry, March 5, 1800, 303–304, reel 13, Timothy Pickering Papers, MHS; John Sevier to Daniel Smith, June 2, 1800, and John Sevier to William Cocke, Joseph Anderson, and William Claiborne, December 8, 1800, both in box 1, folder 8, GP-2, John Sevier Papers, TSLA; Joseph Anderson and William Cocke to Thomas Jefferson, February 26, 1801, and March 5, 1801, both in *PTJ*, 33:69–70, 174–175; Notes on a Cabinet Meeting, May 17, 1801, and Thomas Jefferson to Henry Dearborn, June 26, 1801, both in *PTJ*, 34:129–131, 458; Henry Dearborn to William R. Davie, James Wilkinson, and Benjamin Hawkins, June 24, 1801, reel 1, BIA-M15; Archibald Roane to David Campbell, October 19, 1800, Campbell Family Papers, RL.

20. Henry Dearborn to William R. Davie, James Wilkinson, and Benjamin Hawkins, June 24, 1801, reel 1, BIA-M15; Anonymous to Thomas Jefferson, June 1801, signed "Kentucky Citizen," Thomas Jefferson Papers, Series 1: General Correspondence, 1651– 1827, LC, www.loc.gov/item/mtjbib010234, accessed May 22, 2024.

21. Minutes of a Conference holden at the War Office in the City of Washington between the Secretary of the Department of War on behalf of the United States and a Deputation from the Cherokee Nation of Indians on behalf of the Said Nation, June 30, 1801, and July 3, 1801, reel 1, BIA-M15; Henry Dearborn, Passport for Cherokee Chiefs, July 9, 1801, reel 1, BIA-M15; Diary Entry, May 22, 1801, Diary of Brn. Abraham Steiner and Gottlieb Byhan in the Cherokee Land from the End of April to Toward the End of September 1801, trans. Roy Ledbetter, in Crews and Starbuck, *Records of the Moravians among the Cherokees*, 1:265; Henry Dearborn to William R. Davie, James Wilkinson, and Benjamin Hawkins, July 3, 1801, *ASP:IA*, 1:650; Heads of Answer to Speech of the Glass, [June 30–July 3, 1801], in *PTJ*, 34:508–510; Cumfer, *Separate Peoples, One Land*, 55, 105. The other named members of the Cherokee delegation were Chulio, Sour Mush, and the

Big Halfbreed, all from the Upper Towns. Diary Entries, May 22, 1801, and July 30, 1801, in Crews and Starbuck, *Records of the Moravians among the Cherokees*, 1:265, 288.

22. Diary Entries, July 30–31, 1801, August 20, 1801, and September 3, 1801, in Crews and Starbuck, *Records of the Moravians among the Cherokees*, 1:288–289, 295, 300; Abraham Steiner to Christian Lewis Benzien, August 18, 1801, trans. Elizabeth Marx, in Crews and Starbuck, *Records of the Moravians among the Cherokees*, 1:251–256; The Glass to Benjamin Hawkins, Andrew Pickens, and James Wilkinson, August 19, 1801, James Wilkinson and Benjamin Hawkins to Henry Dearborn, September 1, 1801, Benjamin Hawkins, Andrew Pickens, and James Wilkinson to Henry Dearborn, September 6, 1801, and Benjamin Hawkins to Henry Dearborn, September 6, 1801, all in *LBH*, 1:367, 377–381; Owens, "'Between Two Fires,'" 48–49; Benjamin Hawkins to John Sevier, August 16, 1801, in Journal Entry, August 16, 1801, and Journal Entries, August 10–31, 1801, all in Journal of the Commissioners of the United States, Appointed to Hold Conferences with the Several Nations of Indians South of the Ohio, Edward E. Ayer Manuscript Collection, NL. Extracts of this journal can be found in *ASP:IA*, 1:656–657; and Grant, *Letters, Journals, and Writings of Benjamin Hawkins*. I rely on the manuscript journal because it includes the most complete description of the treaty negotiations. Instead of Pickens, Dearborn and Jefferson originally had selected William R. Davie of North Carolina to the commission, but he declined. Thomas Jefferson to Abraham Baldwin, July 13, 1801, in *PTJ*, 34:558–560; and Journal Entry, August 10, 1801, Journal of the Commissioners . . . Indians South of the Ohio, NL.

23. Journal Entry, September 4, 1801, Journal of the Commissioners . . . Indians South of the Ohio, NL; Diary Entry, September 4, 1801, in Crews and Starbuck, *Records of the Moravians among the Cherokees*, 1:302–303.

24. Journal Entry, September 5, 1801, Journal of the Commissioners . . . Indians South of the Ohio, NL; Diary Entry, September 5, 1801, in Crews and Starbuck, *Records of the Moravians among the Cherokees*, 1:304–305. For Chulio's (often mistaken) identity, see Miles, *Ties That Bind*, 216; and McLoughlin, *Cherokee Renascence*, 114.

25. Journal Entries, October 21–22, 1801, Journal of the Commissioners . . . Indians South of the Ohio, NL; Benjamin Hawkins to Henry Dearborn, October 28, 1801, *LBH*, 1:387; Treaty with the Chickasaw, 1801, October 24, 1801, and Treaty with the Choctaw, 1801, December 17, 1801, both in Kappler, *Indian Treaties*, 55–58; *ASP:IA*, 1:652. For the Choctaw conference, see Journal Entries, December 12–18, 1801, in Journal of the Commissioners . . . Indians South of the Ohio, NL.

26. James Wilkinson, Benjamin Hawkins, and Andrew Pickens to Henry Dearborn, October 25, 1801, *LBH*, 1:384–385.

27. Journal Entry, October 22, 1801, Journal of the Commissioners . . . Indians South of the Ohio, NL; Treaty with the Chickasaw, 1801, October 24, 1801, in Kappler, *Indian Treaties*, 55–56; James Wilkinson, Benjamin Hawkins, and Andrew Pickens to Henry Dearborn, October 25, 1801, *LBH*, 1:384–385.

28. James Wilkinson to Henry Dearborn, October 27, 1801, *ASP:IA*, 1:653; Samuel Mitchell to Return J. Meigs, April 2, 1802, reel 1, BIA-M208; Atkinson, *Splendid Land, Splendid People*, 190–191. On federal soldiers' construction of transportation networks, see Bergmann, *American National State and the Early West*; and Hudson, *Creek Paths and Federal Roads*.

29. Samuel Mitchell to William C. C. Claiborne, January 23, 1803, document 138, series 488, Mississippi Territory Administration Papers, 1769, 1788–1817, Digital

Archives, Mississippi Department of Archives and History, Jackson; Henry Dearborn to Samuel Mitchell, July 9, 1803, reel 1, BIA-M15; Leach, "John Gordon of Gordon's Ferry," 191, 197; Washburn, "Directing Their Own Change," 99. For a description of Colbert's ferry, see George Colbert and Levi Colbert to James Robertson and Return J. Meigs, June 24, 1806, reel 3, BIA-M208.

30. Jamie Kingou to Archibald Roane, March 5, 1802, Thomas Butler to Archibald Roane, March 20, 1802, and Thomas Butler to Archibald Roane, May 16, 1802, all in box 1, folder 5, and Archibald Roane to John Overton, March 31, 1802, and Archibald Roane to Henry Dearborn, June 18, 1802, both in box 1, folder 2, of GP-3, Archibald Roane Papers, TSLA.

31. Archibald Roane to Henry Dearborn, June 16, 1802, box 1, folder 2, John Overton to Archibald Roane, June 11, 1802, box 1, folder 5, Henry Dearborn to Archibald Roane, July 9, 1802, box 1, folder 6, all in GP-3, Archibald Roane Papers, TSLA; Marshall, "True Route of the Natchez Trace," 175–176. On Americans' later notions of internal improvement projects, see Watson, *Liberty and Power*, 135–139; Larson, *Laid Waste!*, 123–150; and Larson, *Internal Improvement*.

32. Journal Entry, November 19, 1799, in Fries, "Report of the Brethren Abraham Steiner and Friedrich Christian von Schweinitz," 360; Journal Entry, August 19, 1803, Report of Brn. Abr. Steiner and Jac. Wohlfarth of Their Doings in the Land of the Cherokees and of Their Dealings with the Chiefs and Council of the Cherokee Nation, etc., from 20 July to 1 Sept. 1803 Along with a Letter from Br. Steiner to Col. Return J. Meigs, Dated Springplace 2 Sept. 1803, in Crews and Starbuck, *Records of the Moravians among the Cherokees*, 2:639; Henry Dearborn to Return J. Meigs, February 19, 1803, Henry Dearborn to Return J. Meigs, March 16, 1803, and Eustinali [Ustanali] Conference Notes, April 20–April 23, 1803, all in reel 2, BIA-M208; John Breckenridge et al. to Thomas Jefferson, February 10, 1803, and Joseph Anderson, William Cocke, and William Dickson to Thomas Jefferson, February 19, 1803, both in box 13, folder 3, Daniel Parker Papers (Collection 466), Historical Society of Pennsylvania, Philadelphia; Henry Dearborn to Return J. Meigs, April 7, 1802, reel 1, BIA-M208; Henry Dearborn to Return J. Meigs, March 24, 1801, BIA-M15; Cherokee Agency Pass Book, Return J. Meigs, 1801–1804, reel 13, BIA-M208. On passports, see Prucha, *Indian Policy in the Formative Years*, 145; and Hudson, *Creek Paths and Federal Roads*, 53–55. For a biographical overview of Meigs, see Henry T. Malone, "Return Jonathan Meigs."

33. Return J. Meigs to Henry Dearborn, October 25, 1803, reel 2, BIA-M208; Extract from Articles of Agreement Between the United States and the Cherokee Nation for Opening a Road from the State of Tennessee to the State of Georgia through the Cherokee Nation, October 20, 1803, box 1, folder 1, GP-4, John Sevier Papers, TSLA; Jacob Wohlfahrt to Christian Lewis Benzien, October 9, 1803, trans. Elizabeth Marx, in Crews and Starbuck, *Records of the Moravians among the Cherokees*, 2:667–669.

34. McLoughlin, *Cherokee Renascence*, 86–89 (quotation 87); Turtle at Home Talk, April 22–23, 1803, in Eustinali [Ustanali] Conference Notes, April 20–April 23, 1803, and Return J. Meigs to Henry Dearborn, May 4, 1803, both in reel 2, BIA-M208. For details of the murder, see Return J. Meigs to Henry Dearborn, October 5, 1802, reel 2, BIA-M208; Entry for July–November, 1802, Journal of Occurrences, Meigs Family Papers, 1772–1862, Microfilm 17,052-1N-1P, LC; and Owens, "'Between Two Fires,'" 50.

35. Memorandum of an Agreement between Toluntuskee and Thomas N. Clark, May 11, 1803, Regulating Houses of Entertainment on Cumberland Road, July 22, 1803,

Return J. Meigs to Sampson Williams, July 29, 1803, Sampson Williams to Return J. Meigs, August 2, 1803, John Overton to Return J. Meigs, October 14, 1803, and Arthur Coody to Return J. Meigs, February 21, 1804, all in reel 2, BIA-M208; Sampson Williams to David Henley, January 27, 1800, Sampson Williams Letter to Colonel David Henley, AC-1069, Appalachian State University Special Collections, Boone, NC; McLoughlin, *Cherokee Renascence*, 20. On Clark as the postmaster, see Entry December 2, 1802, Account of U.S. with R. Meigs in 1802, reel 11, BIA-M208; Jacob Wohlfahrt to Charles G. Reichel, July 22, 1803, trans. C. Daniel Crews, in Crews and Starbuck, *Records of the Moravians among the Cherokees*, 2:604–606; and Information by Richard Finnelson, November 1, 1792, *ASP:IA*, 1:288–291.

36. Daniel Ross to Return J. Meigs, October 10, 1803, Return J. Meigs to Henry Dearborn, October 25, 1803, Minutes of the Cherokee National Council at Eustinalee [Ustanali], April 4–10, 1804, Contract Between Doublehead and William Sharpe, October 20, 1803, and The Glass, Speech to Henry Dearborn, October 21, 1803, all in reel 2, BIA-M208; Extract from Articles of Agreement Between the United States and the Cherokee Nation for Opening a Road from the State of Tennessee to the State of Georgia through the Cherokee Nation, October 20, 1803, box 1, folder 1, GP-4, John Sevier Papers, TSLA; Return J. Meigs to Henry Dearborn, January 15, 1805, reel 3, BIA-M208; Handwritten Copy of Document of National Council of the Cherokees, April 9, 1804, folder 3, Cherokee Papers Manuscript Collection, Gilcrease Museum, Tulsa, OK, https://collections.gilcrease.org/object/482628-0, accessed May 22, 2024. For the toll rates Cherokees charged travelers, see Malone, *Cherokees of the Old South*, 147–148. Many of the most vocal proponents of national highways, ferries, and roadside stands were former Chickamauga Cherokees, who had opposed American expansion with force until the mid-1790s. Historian Nathaniel J. Sheidley explains this apparent irony—Chickamaugas' transition from militant opposition to the United States to peaceful negotiation and even personal benefit from transportation projects—by emphasizing how many Chickamauga leaders acquired horses and cattle, along with numbers of enslaved people, through raids against white settlers. Such growing wealth, speculates Sheidley, reoriented many Chickamaugas' masculine ideal from hunting to farming and ranching and gave them a material incentive to support commercial improvements within the Cherokee Nation. Sheidley, "Unruly Men," 238–242.

37. James Vann to Return J. Meigs, March 26, 1803, Return J. Meigs to Henry Dearborn, October 25, 1803, William Lovely to Return J. Meigs, November 4, 1803, and William Lovely to Return J. Meigs, December 17, 1803, all in reel 2, BIA-M208; John Lowery to Sam[uel] Ryley [Riley], March 27, 1807, reel 3, BIA-M208; Diary Entry, August 23, 1801, in Crews and Starbuck, *Records of the Moravians among the Cherokees*, 1:297–298; Miles, *House on Diamond Hill*, 60–61.

38. Extract from Articles of Agreement Between the United States and the Cherokee Nation for Opening a Road from the State of Tennessee to the State of Georgia through the Cherokee Nation, October 20, 1803, and John Sevier to Joseph McMinn, Samuel Wear, and John Cowan, August 9, 1804, both in box 1, folder 1, GP-4, John Sevier Papers, TSLA; William Barnett and Buckner Harris to John Sevier, July 6, 1804, and John Sevier to William Barnett and Buckner Harris, July 19, 1804, both in box 81, folder 20, Telamon Cuyler Collection, UGA; Return J. Meigs to Buckner Harris and William Barnett, August 9, 1804, Charles Hicks to Return J. Meigs, December 20, 1803, and Return J. Meigs to Henry Dearborn, October 1, 1804, all in reel 2, BIA-M208; Diary Entries, August 13–16,

1804, Diary of Our Brethren and Sisters in Springplace from 1 September to 31 Decemb. 1803, in Crews and Starbuck, *Records of the Moravians among the Cherokees*, 2:751–752. Black Fox became the principal chief of the Cherokee Nation in August 1802 after the death of Little Turkey earlier in March. See Return J. Meigs, Journal of Occurrences in the Cherokee Nation in 1802, enclosed in Return J. Meigs to Henry Dearborn, January 1, 1803, reel 2, BIA-M208.

39. George Hulme to William Lenoir, August 14, 1804, box 1, Thomas Lenoir Papers, RL; Daniel Smith to Return J. Meigs, August 9, 1805, reel 3, BIA-M208; The Glass et al. to Return J. Meigs, November 25, 1806, box 1, folder 36, Penelope Allen Collection, UTK; Ebenezer Newton Diary, ms515, UGA; James Robertson and Silas Dinsmoor to Henry Dearborne [Dearborn], July 23, 1805, 65–70, Journal of Commissioners to Treaty with Choctaw and Chickasaw Indians, 1805, reel 1, BIA-T494; Charles Hicks to Return J. Meigs, August 19, 1806, reel 3, BIA-M208; Return J. Meigs to William Eustis, December 1, 1809, reel 4, BIA-M208; David McNair et al., [Charter of the Cherokee Turnpike Company], August 18, 1806, Tennessee Documentary History, University of Tennessee Libraries, https://digital.lib.utk.edu/collections/islandora/object/tdh%3A1605, accessed May 22, 2024.

Chapter 6. Shared Territory, Competing Geographies, and Indigenous Law in the Early Nineteenth Century

1. Entry for September 9, 1807, Journal of Occurrences, Meigs Family Papers, 1772–1862, Microfilm 17,052-1N-1P, LC; Elucidation of a Convention with the Cherokee Nation, September 11, 1807, in Kappler, *Indian Treaties*, 91–92; Henry Dearborn to James Robertson, April 1, 1807, box 4, folder 10, and Return J. Meigs to James Robertson, May 5, 1807, box 3, folder 8, both in James Robertson Papers, TSLA; James Robertson to Return J. Meigs, May 13, 1807, and Henry Dearborn to Return J. Meigs, April 1, 1807, both in reel 3, BIA-M208; An Account of Expenses for Surveying Convention Line, undated, reel 11, BIA-M208; Return J. Meigs to Henry Dearborn, September 28, 1807, *ASP:IA*, 1:249; Receipt for 2000$ Paid the Cherokee Nation, November 1, 1807, box 1, folder 2, Penelope Allen Collection, UTK; *A Map of Indian Boundary Lines and the Southern Boundary of the State of Tennessee*, Thomas Freeman, 1807, Map 1407, Map Collection, TSLA, https://teva.contentdm.oclc.org/digital/collection/p15138c01123/id/9064/rec/5, accessed May 29, 2024; Thomas Freeman to Henry Dearborn, June 15, 1807, *TPUS*, 5:553–554.

2. Chinnubbee King et al. to Henry Dearborn, August 25, 1808, reel 4, BIA-M208; Chinubbee Mingo et al. to James Robertson, April 19, 1809, box 2, folder 17, James Robertson Papers, TSLA; Benjamin Hawkins to Henry Dearborn, September 16, 1807, *LBH*, 2:524–526; Thomas Freeman to Albert Gallatin, March 4, 1809, *TPUS*, 5:721.

3. Edwards, "Sarah Allingham's Sheet and Other Lessons from Legal History." For recent scholars' emphasis on the significance of Indigenous land claims in early America, see Ablavsky, "Species of Sovereignty"; Saxine, *Properties of Empire*; Greer, *Property and Dispossession*; Belmessous, "Problem of Indigenous Claim Making in Colonial History"; Fitzmaurice, "Powhatan Legal Claims"; Shoemaker, *Strange Likeness*, 13–34; and Lewandoski, "Empire of Indian Titles." On earlier tension between Cherokees and members of the Haudenosaunee Confederacy over their overlapping boundaries, see Ray, *Cherokee Power*, 119–121.

4. All quotations are from an incomplete draft of the report, Return J. Meigs to Henry Dearborn, undated, reel 1, BIA-M208. For the complete first draft, see Return J. Meigs to Henry Dearborn, January 17, 1804, box 1, folder 28, Penelope Allen Collection, UTK.

5. The Glass to Return J. Meigs, March 10, 1804, Return J. Meigs to John Ballinger, July 15, 1804, and Henry Dearborn to Return J. Meigs, April 23, 1804, all in reel 2, BIA-M208; John Sevier to Inhabitants and People Said to be Settled on the Indian Lands, April 1, 1804, box 1, folder 1, GP-4, John Sevier Papers, TSLA; John Sevier Legislative Message, October 7, 1803, in White, *Messages of the Governors of the State of Tennessee*, 138; Return J. Meigs to Benjamin Hawkins, February 13, 1805, reel 3, BIA-M208. On the interconnected nature of Native dispossession, cotton production, and slave labor in early Alabama, the state that ultimately would exercise jurisdiction over the Tennessee River's Great Bend, see Dupre, *Alabama's Frontiers and the Rise of the Old South*.

6. John Sevier to James Robertson, November 7, 1804, John Sevier to James Robertson, August 23, 1804, and John Sevier to James Robertson, September 26, 1804, all in box 4, folder 2, James Robertson Papers, TSLA; Henry Dearborn to Daniel Smith and Return J. Meigs, April 4, 1804, reel 2, BIA-M208; John Sevier to Daniel Smith and Return J. Meigs, August 20, 1804, box 1, folder 1, GP-4, John Sevier Papers, TSLA; Toluntuskee to [Return J. Meigs and Daniel Smith], October 19, 1804, and Daniel Smith to Henry Dearborn, October 31, 1804, both in BIA-T494; Treaty with the Cherokee, 1804, in Kappler, *Indian Treaties*, 73–74; Return J. Meigs to James Robertson, December 21, 1804, box 3, folder 8, James Robertson Papers, TSLA; McLoughlin, *Cherokee Renascence*, 91. It would be twenty years before the United States paid the Cherokee Nation for this minor land cession in accordance with the treaty agreement. For context, see Morgan, "'Fraught with Disastrous Consequences for Our Country,'" 7–10, 30–44.

7. Chennebee et al. to James Robertson, January 25, 1805, and Return J. Meigs to Henry Dearborn, January 23, 1805, both in reel 3, BIA-M208; Daniel Smith to William Dickson, [1804], DRAPER, 4XX59; Thomas Jefferson to Chickasaw Nation, March 7, 1805, reel 32, Series 1: General Correspondence, Thomas Jefferson Papers, LC, http://hdl.loc.gov/loc.mss/mtj.mtjbib014449, accessed May 29, 2024; Atkinson, *Splendid Land, Splendid People*, 195.

8. Chennebee et al. to James Robertson, January 25, 1805, and Return J. Meigs to Henry Dearborn, January 25, 1805, both in reel 3, BIA-M208; Thomas Jefferson to Chickasaw Nation, March 7, 1805, reel 32, Series 1: General Correspondence, Thomas Jefferson Papers, LC, http://hdl.loc.gov/loc.mss/mtj.mtjbib014449, accessed May 29, 2024.

9. Treaty with the Chickasaw, 1805, in Kappler, *Indian Treaties*, 79–80; Return J. Meigs to Daniel Smith, March 7, 1805, reel 3, BIA-M208; Journal Entry, July 20, 1805, 52, Journal of Commissioners to Treaty with Choctaw and Chickasaw Indians, 1805, reel 1, BIA-T494.

10. James Robertson to Henry Dearborn, August 8, 1805, box 3, folder 20, James Robertson Papers, TSLA; Journal of Commissioners to Treaty with Choctaw and Chickasaw Indians, 1805, 65–70, reel 1, BIA-T494; Treaty with the Chickasaw, 1805, and Treaty with the Cherokee, 1805, both in Kappler, *Indian Treaties*, 79–80, 82–83. For examples of how overlapping claims affected land prices in various locales, see Aron, *How the West Was Lost*, 82–123; and Ablavsky, *Federal Ground*, 31–50.

11. Return J. Meigs to James Robertson, May 5, 1805, reel 3, BIA-M208; James Robertson to James Vann, August 26, 1805, box 4, folder 20, James Robertson Papers, TSLA;

Return J. Meigs to Henry Dearborn, January 23, 1805, Return J. Meigs to Daniel Smith, February 1, 1805, and James Robertson to James Vann, April 22, 1805, all in reel 3, BIA-M208; Sketch of the Muscle Shoals, James Wilkinson, 1801, Individually Catalogued Manuscript Maps, Map 66, Realms of Gold, American Philosophical Society, Philadelphia, PA. Saliha Belmessous points out that Indigenous and European arguments about both sovereignty and property rights frequently overlapped and are difficult to differentiate. Belmessous, "Problem of Indigenous Claim Making in Colonial History," 11–13. On how theories of occupation contributed to European colonization of Indigenous land, see Banner, *How the Indians Lost Their Land*, 150–190; Fitzmaurice, *Sovereignty, Property and Empire, 1500–2000*; Greer, "Commons and Enclosure in the Colonization of North America"; and Witgen, "A Nation of Settlers."

12. Benjamin Hawkins to Return J. Meigs, June 12, 1805, and Return J. Meigs to James Robertson, May 27, 1805, both in reel 3, BIA-M208; Benjamin Hawkins to Henry Dearborn, June 14, 1805, *LBH*, 2:493; Daniel Smith to James Robertson, box 4, folder 4, James Robertson Papers, TSLA.

13. Gould, *Among the Powers of the Earth*.

14. Journal Entry, July 21, 1805, in McClinton, *Moravian Springplace Mission to the Cherokees*, 1:60; Doublehead et al. to Black Fox et al., August 9, 1805, and Return J. Meigs to Daniel Smith, August 19, 1805, both in reel 3, BIA-M208.

15. Nicholas Byers to Return J. Meigs, August 4, 1805, Nicholas Byers to Return J. Meigs, August 16, 1804, Return J. Meigs to Daniel Smith, August 19, 1805, and Doublehead et al. to Black Fox et al., August 9, 1805, all in reel 3, BIA-M208; Treaty with the Cherokee, 1805, in Kappler, *Indian Treaties*, 82–83.

16. Black Fox et al. to Return J. Meigs, September 16, 1805, Return J. Meigs to Daniel Smith, September 21, 1805, and Return J. Meigs to Henry Dearborn, September 22, 1805, all in reel 3, BIA-M208; Henry Dearborn to Return J. Meigs, October 8, 1805, and Henry Dearborn, Passport for Chiefs of the Cherokee Nation of Indians, October 8, 1805, both in reel 2, BIA-M15; Treaty with the Cherokee, 1806, in Kappler, *Indian Treaties*, 90–91.

17. Doublehead et al. to Return J. Meigs, January 4, 1806, reel 3, BIA-M208; Treaty with the Cherokee, 1806, and Treaty with the Chickasaw, 1805, both in Kappler, *Indian Treaties*, 90–91, 79; The Black Fox's Receipt for His Annuity for 1808, October 29, 1808, reel 11, BIA-M208; Moses Melton to Return J. Meigs, June 30, 1815, reel 6, BIA-M208; Charles Hicks to Return J. Meigs, January 15, 1817, reel 7, BIA-M208; Henry Dearborn to Return J. Meigs, January 8, 1806, reel 2, BIA-M15.

18. Perdue and Green, *Cherokee Nation and the Trail of Tears*, 36–37; Cumfer, *Separate Peoples, One Land*, 118–119; Finger, *Tennessee Frontiers*, 220–221; McLoughlin, *Cherokee Renascence*, 104–108.

19. Address of the Chiefs in Council at Oostanuala, April 25, 1806, reel 3, BIA-M208; Address of the C[herokee] Chiefs to Their Nation in the Different Parts, Doublehead et al., 1806, box 1, folder 37, Penelope Allen Collection, UTK; Charles Hicks to Return J. Meigs, August 19, 1806, Black Fox et al. to Return J. Meigs, September 19, 1806, Hutson Alford and Newit Drew to John Chisholm, January 12, 1807, John Chisholm to Return J. Meigs, January 25, 1807, and Return J. Meigs to Daniel Smith, February 12, 1807, all in reel 3, BIA-M208; Return J. Meigs to Jesse Arnold, September 9, 1820, reel 8, BIA-M208; John Walker to Henry Dearborn, October 4, 1806, reel 1, BIA-M271. On the enslaved people living on and around Doublehead's reserve, see John Nevin to Doublehead, August 13, 1802, reel 1, BIA-M208; Samuel Mitchell to Return J. Meigs,

September 7, 1802, Doublehead to Samuel Miller, February 21, 1803, and William L. Cooper to Doublehead, March 23, 1803, all in reel 2, BIA-M208; Negro Paul [Paul Smith] to Return J. Meigs, July 29, 1805, reel 3, BIA-M208; and Paul Smith to Henry Dearborn, August 18, 1805, reel 1, BIA-M271. For an overview of early nineteenth-century Lower Town and Upper Town leaders, including the important role of women in each group, see Cumfer, *Separate Peoples, One Land*, 117–118; McLoughlin, *Cherokee Renascence*, 110–111.

20. McLoughlin, *Cherokee Renascence*, 109–127 (quotation 109); Cumfer, *Separate Peoples, One Land*, 118–123. For descriptions of the assassination, see Journal Entry, August 12, 1807, in McClinton, *Springplace Mission to the Cherokees*, 1:206; and *Knoxville Gazette*, August 5, 1807.

21. Chinnubbee King et al. to Henry Dearborn, August 25, 1808, and Chinubbee et al. to William Eustis, June 27, 1809, both in reel 4, BIA-M208; Malcolm McGee and George Colbert to Henry Dearborn, February 21, 1806, and Henry Dearborn to George Colbert, February 21, 1806, both in reel 2, BIA-M15; William Eustis to Return J. Meigs, May 8, 1811, reel 5, BIA-M208; *A Map of Indian Boundary Lines and the Southern Boundary of the State of Tennessee*, Thomas Freeman, 1807, Map Collection, TSLA, https://teva .contentdm.oclc.org/digital/collection/p15138c01123/id/9064/rec/5, accessed May 29, 2024. This is the map that opens this chapter.

22. Andrew Jackson to William Crawford, August 10, 1814, *ASP:IA*, 1:838; Treaty with the Creeks, 1814, in Kappler, *Indian Treaties*, 108; Benjamin Hawkins to John Armstrong, August 16, 1814, *LBH*, 2:693; Green, *Politics of Indian Removal*, 43, 45–46; Waselkov, *Conquering Spirit*; Braund, *Tohopeka*; Ray, *Middle Tennessee*, 113–115; Opal, *Avenging the People*, 156; Rothman, *Slave Country*, 168. On negotiations at Fort Jackson, see Benjamin Hawkins to George Graham, August 1, 1815, *LBH*, 2:743–746. For how white Tennesseans' public memory of eighteenth-century conflicts with Native peoples influenced their interpretations of the Red Stick War, see Kanon, "Kidnapping of Martha Crawley and Settler-Indian Relations prior to the War of 1812."

23. Notes of a Convention between the Creeks and Cherokees, August 9, 1814, Return J. Meigs to Andrew Jackson, August 8, 1815, and Return J. Meigs to William Crawford, August 20, 1815, all in reel 6, BIA-M208; George Graham to Return J. Meigs, August 5, 1815, reel 3, BIA-M15; Benjamin Hawkins to George Graham, August 11, 1815, Journal of Occurrences at the Convention of the Creeks at Tookaubatche, September 21, 1815, and Benjamin Hawkins to George Graham, September 22, 1815, all in *LBH*, 2:747–748, 755, 763; McLoughlin, *Cherokee Renascence*, 191–192. For an overview of Cherokees' contributions to the Red Stick War, see Abram, *Forging a Cherokee-American Alliance in the Creek War*.

24. Benjamin Hawkins to Return J. Meigs, September 18, 1815, *LBH*, 2:762; Return J. Meigs to Andrew Jackson, August 8, 1815, reel 6, BIA-M208; Statement of Chinabee or the "Natchez Warrior," January 22, 1816, and Return J. Meigs to Benjamin Hawkins, September 19, 1815, both in reel 1, BIA-M271.

25. Affidavit of The Glass, December 21, 1815, reel 6, BIA-M208; Return J. Meigs to William Crawford, November 4, 1815, reel 6, BIA-M208; William Crawford to Return J. Meigs, November 22, 1815, reel 3, BIA-M15; Nanohetahee to John Lowery et al., January 10, 1816, in Moulton, *Papers of John Ross*, 1:22–24. On the 1773 Treaty of Augusta and the overlapping land claims between the Creeks and Cherokees, see Juricek, *Endgame for Empire*, 147–184.

26. Affidavit of The Glass, December 21, 1815, and Charles Hicks to Return J. Meigs, July 4, 1816, both in reel 6, BIA-M208; Perdue, *Cherokee Women*, 45–46. On kinship diplomacy, see Jennings, *Ambiguous Iroquois Empire*; Richter and Merrell, *Beyond the Covenant Chain*; White, "Fictions of Patriarchy"; and Cumfer, *Separate Peoples, One Land*, 23–49.

27. John Lowery address to James Madison, quoted in Wilkins, *Cherokee Tragedy*, 90; Nanohetahee (Pathkiller) to John Lowery et al., January 10, 1816, and John Lowery et al. to George Graham, March 4, 1816, both in Moulton, *Papers of John Ross*, 1:22–26; John Lowery to James Madison, February 16, 1816, reel 7, BIA-M208; Record of Conversation between John Lowery and President James Madison, February 22, 1816, John Ross Papers, Gilcrease Museum, Tulsa, Oklahoma, https://collections.gilcrease.org/object/402617, accessed May 21, 2024; Address to the President of the United States, Richard Brown et al., [1816], reel 6, BIA-M208.

28. George Graham to Edmund Gains, October 24, 1815, box 1, folder 1, and John Coffee, Diary and Memorandum Book, entries February 8 and February 9, 1816, box 3, folder 4, both in John Coffee Papers, ADAH; Edmund Gaines to John Coffee, November 28, 1815, John Coffee to Benjamin Hawkins, Edmund Gains, and William Barnett, February 17, 1816, John Coffee to Edmund Gaines, January 17, 1816, and Article of Agreement between John Coffee and Chiefs and Headmen of the Cherokee Nation, February 8, 1816, all in reel 1, BIA-M271; John Coffee to Andrew Jackson, February 8, 1816, Andrew Jackson Papers, Series 1: General Correspondence and Related Items, 1775–1885, LC, www.loc.gov/item/maj006348, accessed May 21, 2024; Charles Hicks to Return J. Meigs, April 30, 1816, Path Killer's Message, delivered by Chulio, July 22, 1816, and Richard Riley to the Cherokee Delegation, February 10, 1816, all in reel 7, BIA-M208; Andrew Jackson to John Coffee, February 2, 1816, and Andrew Jackson to John Coffee, February 13, 1816, both in *PAJ*, 5:6–7, 11–12; John Lowery et al. to William Crawford, March 12, 1816, in Moulton, *Papers of John Ross*, 1:26–27; Treaty with the Cherokee, 1816, in Kappler, *Indian Treaties*, 125–126; William H. Crawford to William Barnett, Benjamin Hawkins, and Edward P. Gaines, March 14, 1816, William H. Crawford to John Coffee, March 14, 1816, and William H. Crawford to William Barnett, Benjamin Hawkins, and Edward P. Gaines, April 16, 1816, all in reel 3, BIA-M15.

29. Charles Cassidy and John Hutchings Affidavit, January 23, 1816, John Coffee to William Cocke, February 22, 1816, and John Coffee to Edmund Gains and William Barnett, March 13, 1816, all in reel 1, BIA-M271; John Coffee to Andrew Jackson, February 18, 1816, Andrew Jackson Papers, Series 1: General Correspondence and Related Items, 1775–1885, LC, www.loc.gov/item/maj006370, accessed May 21, 2024; John Coffee, Diary and Memorandum Book, February 25–March 2, 1816, box 3, folder 4, and William Cocke to John Coffee, March 7, 1816, box 1, folder 2, both in John Coffee Papers, ADAH; Andrew Jackson to George Colbert, February 13, 1816, *PAJ*, 4:13–14; George Colbert to Andrew Jackson, March 1, 1816, Andrew Jackson Papers, Series 1: General Correspondence and Related Items, 1775–1885, LC, www.loc.gov/item/maj006385, accessed May 21, 2024.

30. Affidavit of George Maxwell Jr., April 25, 1816, Affidavit of Robert G. McKnight, April 29, 1816, William Cocke to unknown, May 12, 1815, Affidavit of Malcolm McGee, May 8, 1816, Affidavit of William James, May 10, 1816, Affidavit of James Gunn, May 10, 1816, Affidavit of Hardey Perry, May 7, 1816, Affidavit of John Hillgrees, May 10, 1816, and Affidavit of James Love, May 10, 1816, all in reel 1, BIA-M271; William H. Craw-

ford to William Cocke, April 16, 1816, reel 3, BIA-M15; *Nashville Whig*, April 30, 1816; "Chickasaw Indians," *Raleigh Register and North-Carolina Gazette*, June 21, 1816; William H. Crawford to William Cocke, March 19, 1816, and William H. Crawford, Talk to the Chickasaw Nation of Indians, June 6, 1816, both in reel 3, BIA-M15; Joseph McMinn to Andrew Jackson, May 27, 1816, box 1, folder 1, GP-6, Joseph McMinn Papers, TSLA.

31. William Barnett to John Coffee, June 7, 1816, box 1, folder 2, John Coffee Papers, ADAH; Path Killer and Richard Brown to Return J. Meigs, April 23, 1816, and Charles Hicks to Return J. Meigs, July 4, 1816, both in reel 7, BIA-M208; Thomas Johnson to Joseph McMinn, June 2, 1816, box 1, folder 2, GP-6, Joseph McMinn Papers, TSLA; "The Indians," *Nashville Whig*, June 18, 1816; McLoughlin, *Cherokee Renascence*, 190.

32. William Russell to John Coffee, May 8, 1816, box 1, folder 2, John Coffee Papers, ADAH; Andrew Jackson to William Crawford, June 16, 1816, *PAJ*, 4:46; Memorial to the President of the United States, Jenkin Whitesides [Whiteside] et al., 1816, Andrew Jackson to William Crawford, June 10, 1816, and William Crawford to John McKee, May 20, 1816, all in *ASP:IA*, 2:89–91, 110–111, 118; William H. Crawford to Return J. Meigs, May 27, 1816, and William H. Crawford to Andrew Jackson, David Meriwether, and Jesse Franklin, June 15, 1816, both in reel 3, BIA-M15; Andrew Jackson to William Crawford, June 4, 1816, *PAJ*, 4:36–39; Joseph McMinn to Andrew Jackson, May 27, 1816, box 1, folder 1, GP-6, Joseph McMinn Papers, TSLA; William Crawford to Return J. Meigs, June 15, 1816, reel 7, BIA-M208; William Crawford to David Meriwether, June 4, 1816, *TPUS*, 6:691; McLoughlin, *Cherokee Renascence*, 201–203. For the location of Bear Creek, see *Map of the State of Kentucky: With the Adjoining Territories*, 1794, Map Collection, TSLA, https://teva.contentdm.oclc.org/digital/collection/p15138c01123/id /10389, accessed May 21, 2024. Historian Evan Nooe argues that veterans of the Red Stick War and other white southerners commemorated the conflict in order to justify Native dispossession. Nooe, *Aggression and Sufferings*, 79–90.

33. William Crawford to Return J. Meigs, June 15, 1816, and Notes of Addresses to Cherokees, [July–August, 1816], both in reel 7, BIA-M208; William Crawford to Andrew Jackson, June 19, 1816, and William H. Crawford to Andrew Jackson, David Meriwether, and Jesse Franklin, September 12, 1816, both in reel 3, BIA-M15; G. W. Campbell et al. to James Madison, April 17, 1816, William Crawford to Return J. Meigs, May 27, 1816, William Crawford to Andrew Jackson, David Meriwether, and Jesse Franklin, July 5, 1816, and James Colbert to Andrew Jackson, July 17, 1816, all in *ASP:IA*, 2:99, 110, 102–103.

34. Return J. Meigs to Andrew Jackson, August 6, 1816, Return J. Meigs to William Crawford, August 10, 1816, and Toochalar to Return J. Meigs, August 24, 1816, all in reel 7, BIA-M208; Return J. Meigs to Andrew Jackson, August 19, 1816, *PAJ*, 4:58–59.

35. Andrew Jackson to Rachel Jackson, September 18, 1816, *PAJ*, 4:62; William Crawford to Andrew Jackson, David Meriwether, and Jesse Franklin, July 5, [3,] 1816, *ASP:IA*, 2:100–102; Journal of the Proceedings of General Andrew Jackson, General David Meriwether, and Jesse Franklin Esq. Commissioners appointed by the President of the United States of America to Hold Conferences & Settle a Treaty with the Chickasaw & Cherokee Tribes or Nations of Indians, 9–18, in the Jesse Franklin Indian Treaty Papers #3656-z, SHC. On the location of the Chickasaw Council House near present-day Tupelo, Mississippi, see Atkinson, *Splendid Land, Splendid People*, 205; and Washburn, "'Labor in the Field Is Much Changed,'" 199. Tishominko, or *Tisho Minko*, was a title that referred to the assistant leader. The speaker at the 1816 conference presumably would have had another personal and war name, but, according to officials from the Chickasaw Nation,

they remain unknown. Like Piominko, historians traditionally referred to Tishominko as "Tishomingo." See Chickasaw Nation, "Native History: Chickasaw Nation Corrects Names of Famed Leaders," *Indian Country Today*, September 13, 2018, https://ictnews .org/archive/native-history-chickasaw-nation-corrects-names-of-famed-leaders, accessed May 3, 2024; and Craig, "Colberts in Chickasaw History," 55–57.

36. Journal of the Proceedings of General Andrew Jackson . . . with the Chickasaw & Cherokee Tribes or Nations of Indians, 16–21, in the Jesse Franklin Indian Treaty Papers #3656-z, SHC. On Toochalar, see McLoughlin, *Cherokee Renascence*, 139, 144, 157.

37. Journal of the Proceedings of General Andrew Jackson . . . with the Chickasaw & Cherokee Tribes or Nations of Indians, 26–37, in the Jesse Franklin Indian Treaty Papers #3656-z, SHC. Jackson's witnesses were Captain John Gordon, Colonel Newton Cannon, Captain John Hutchings (Jackson's nephew), and a Mr. Potter, Jackson's quartermaster.

38. Andrew Jackson to John Coffee, September 19, 1816, and Andrew Jackson, David Meriwether, and Jesse Franklin to William Crawford, September 20, 1816, both in *PAJ*, 4:63, 65–68; Journal of the Proceedings of General Andrew Jackson . . . with the Chickasaw & Cherokee Tribes or Nations of Indians, 38–39, 43–44, in the Jesse Franklin Indian Treaty Papers #3656-z, SHC; Treaty with the Cherokee, 1816, and Treaty with the Chickasaw, 1816, both in Kappler, *Indian Treaties*, 133–137; Atkinson, *Splendid Land, Splendid People*, 206–207.

39. Richard Brown to Charles Hicks, December 12, 1816, reel 1, BIA-M271; Ivison, "Normative Force of the Past," 249.

Epilogue

1. Toochalar to Return J. Meigs, August 24, 1816, and Toochalar et al. to Return J. Meigs, August 24, both in reel 7, BIA-M208; Treaty with the Cherokee, 1816, in Kappler, *Indian Treaties*, 133–134.

2. John C. Calhoun to Isaac Shelby and Andrew Jackson, May 2, 1818, and Andrew Jackson to John C. Calhoun, August 18, 1818, both in *ASP:IA*, 2:173–174, 179; James Colbert to Andrew Jackson, July 17, 1818, reel 2, BIA-M271; Andrew Jackson to John C. Calhoun, July 31, 1818, in Hemphill, *Papers of John C. Calhoun*, 2:446–447; Robert Butler to John C. Calhoun, October 2, 1818, in Hemphill, *Papers of John C. Calhoun*, 3:182; Andrew Jackson to Isaac Shelby, July 7, 1818, and Andrew Jackson to James Colbert, July 24, 1818, both in *PAJ*, 4:219–220, 228–229; Treaty with the Chickasaw, 1818, in Kappler, *Indian Treaties*, 174–177; "Secret" Journal on Negotiations of the Chickasaw Treaty of 1818, Avalon Project, Yale Law School, https://avalon.law.yale.edu/19th _century/nt005.asp, accessed July 24, 2023; *Nashville Whig and Tennessee Advertiser*, November 21, 1818; Barnett, *Mississippi's American Indians*, 178–180; Craig, "Colberts in Chickasaw History," 378–380; Atkinson, *Splendid Land, Splendid People*, 209–212; Finger, *Tennessee Frontiers*, 240.

3. Sickatowee to Return J. Meigs, December 18, 1816, Pathkiller to Return J. Meigs, February 18, 1817, Resolution of the House of Commons and of the Senate of North Carolina, November 22, 1816, George Graham to Return J. Meigs, December 9, 1816, and Return J. Meigs to George Graham, January 27, 1817, all in reel 7, BIA-M208.

4. Norton, *Journal of Major John Norton*, 61, 146; Thomas Jefferson to Cherokees of the Upper and Lower Towns, January 9, 1809, *ASP:IA*, 2:125; Smithers, *Cherokee*

Diaspora, 47–54; DuVal, *Native Ground*, 196–228; West, "'They Have Exercised Every Art'"; Stewart, "Wielding the Power of Mapping"; McLoughlin, *Cherokee Renascence*, 128–130, 152–153.

5. George Graham to Andrew Jackson, May 14, 1817, and George Graham to Andrew Jackson, May 16, 1817, both in *ASP:IA*, 2:141–142.

6. Treaty with the Cherokee, 1817, in Kappler, *Indian Treaties*, 140–144; George Graham to Andrew Jackson, Joseph McMinn, and David Meriwether, August 1, 1817, *ASP:IA*, 2:143; Pathkiller to Return J. Meigs, August 6, 1817, reel 7, BIA-M208; David Meriwether to George Graham, September 15, 1817, reel 2, BIA-M271.

7. Address of Cherokee Women's Council, June 30, 1818, enclosed in Ard Hoyt et al. to Samuel Worcester, July 25, 1818, frame #330, reel 737, Cherokee Mission, Papers of the American Board of Commissioners for Foreign Missions, Houghton Library, Harvard University; John C. Calhoun to Joseph McMinn, July 29, 1818, and Joseph McMinn to John C. Calhoun, June 8, 1818, both in *ASP:IA*, 2:479–481; McLoughlin, *Cherokee Renascence*, 238–246.

8. John C. Calhoun to Cherokee Delegation, February 11, 1819, *ASP:IA*, 2:190; Pathkiller, Instructions to Cherokee Diplomats, December 14, 1818, reel 7, BIA-M208; Charles Hicks to John C. Calhoun, February 8, 1819, and Charles Hicks to John C. Calhoun, February 19, 1819, both in reel 2, BIA-M271; Treaty with the Cherokee, 1819, in Kappler, *Indian Treaties*, 177–181; McLoughlin, *Cherokee Renascence*, 255–256.

9. Charles Hicks to John C. Calhoun, February 12, 1819, and Charles Hicks to John C. Calhoun, February 22, 1819, both in reel 2, BIA-M271; Toochalar, Sour Mush, and Boots to William Crawford, July 31, 1816, reel 7, BIA-M208.

10. McLoughlin, *Cherokee Renascence*, 271–276 (quotation 276); McLoughlin, "Experiment in Cherokee Citizenship." William Jurgelski traces the longer history of Cherokee reservees' experiences in North Carolina and their battle with the state to acknowledge their property ownership. Jurgelski, "New Plow in Old Ground." For Cherokees' perspective on the dispossession of reservees' property rights, see John Ross et al. to Andrew Jackson, March 17, 1834, and Cherokee Petition to the Senate and House of Representatives, February 13, 1835, both in Moulton, *Papers of John Ross*, 1:280–282, 319–320.

11. Eight Killer's Application for Land on the Fire Gizzard, June 23, 1819, Applications for Cherokee Reservations, 1819–1919, Records of the Bureau of Indian Affairs, Record Group 75, NA; Treaty with the Cherokee, 1817, and Treaty with the Cherokee, 1819, both in Kappler, *Indian Treaties*, 140–144, 177–181; John Ross et al. to John C. Calhoun, January 13, 1824, in Moulton, *Papers of Chief John Ross*, 1:56–57. Applications for reserves can be found in Applications for Cherokee Reservations, 1819–1919, Records of the Bureau of Indian Affairs, Record Group 75, NA. For a comprehensive list, see Hampton, *Cherokee Reservees*, 1–13.

12. Elizabeth Pack to Return J. Meigs, June 21, 1819, Applications for Cherokee Reservations, 1819–1919, Records of the Bureau of Indian Affairs, Record Group 75, NA; Petition of Nathan Green for Elizabeth Pack, Marion County, 1823, petition 41, Tennessee Legislative Petitions, TLSA; Treaty with the Cherokee, 1819, in Kappler, *Indian Treaties*, 177–181; Robert Houston and Robert Armstrong, Survey of Elizabeth Pack Reserve, January 28, 1820, folder 9, box 2, Penelope Johnson Allen Cherokee Collection, TSLA; Robert Houston to John C. Calhoun, February 19, 1820, reel 3, BIA-M271; John C. Calhoun to Robert Houston, March 12, 1819, reel 8, BIA-M208; Penelope Johnson Allen,

"Leaves from the Family Tree," *Chattanooga Sunday Times*, May 10, 1936. On the relationship between John and George Lowery, see Return J. Meigs to William Crawford, August 19, 1816, *ASP:IA*, 2:113–114. Pack's mother Elizabeth Lowery also received a fee simple reserve. I am indebted to Stuart Marshall for alerting me to Pack's legislative petition.

13. Norton, *Journal of Major John Norton*, 37; Charles Hicks to Return J. Meigs, March 20, 1820, Statement of Widow Price, May 24, 1818, and Charles Hicks to Return J. Meigs, April 30, 1820, all in reel 8, BIA-M208; Robert Houston and Robert Armstrong, Survey of Elizabeth Pack Reserve, January 28, 1820, folder 9, box 2, Penelope Johnson Allen Cherokee Collection, TSLA; *Holland v. Elizabeth Pack*, 7 Tenn. 151 (1823); Charles Hicks to Return J. Meigs, February 19, 1821, reel 9, BIA-M208; Hugh Montgomery to James Barbour, August 1, 1825, reel 71, microcopy 234, Letters Received by the Office of Indian Affairs, 1824–1880, Records of the Bureau of Indian Affairs, Record Group 75, NA; John Ross to Hugh Montgomery, June 20, 1828, Tennessee Documentary History, University of Tennessee Libraries, https://digital.lib.utk.edu/collections/islandora/object/tdh%3A714, accessed May 28, 2024.

14. Elizabeth Pack to Charles Hicks, March 28, 1820, and Charles Hicks to Return J. Meigs, April 30, 1820, both in reel 8, BIA-M208; "Caution," *Knoxville Register*, February 1, 1820; Order of the National Committee, John Ross, April 22, 1820, folder 4, box 3, Penelope Johnson Allen Cherokee Collection, TSLA; *An Accurate Map of the State of Alabama and West Florida*, John LaTourrette, 1837, Alabama Maps and Architectural Drawings Collection, ADAH, https://digital.archives.alabama.gov/digital/collection/maps/id/1541, accessed November 5, 2023; Penelope Johnson Allen, "Leaves from the Family Tree," *Chattanooga Sunday Times*, May 10, 1936. The 1835 Cherokee census listed Pack as the head of a household that included twenty-nine enslaved people. See *Typewritten Copy of Census of 1835 of Cherokee Indians*, 60, in Indian Archives Division, Oklahoma Historical Society, www.okhistory.org/research/digital/foremantrans/foreman.sup14.pdf, accessed September 15, 2023. On white men's marriages to Native women for financial gain, see Perdue, *"Mixed Blood" Indians*, 29–31.

15. John Ford, "In Old Days, Sequatchie Valley Was Scene of Hectic Politics," *Chattanooga News*, April 11, 1936; "Indian Squaw Gave Land for Site of Jasper," *Chattanooga News*, July 30, 1936; R. D. Beasley to Campbell H. Brown, August 25, 1954, folder titled "Betsy Pack, Marion County," Tennessee Historical Commission, Historical Marker Files, 1950–1993, Record Group 85, TSLA; "Notice. The Lots in the Town of Jasper," *Knoxville Register*, December 12, 1820; Elizabeth Pack Power of Attorney, June 13, 1820, and Elizabeth Pack Deed 40 Acres, July 1, 1821, both in Works Progress Administration, *Tennessee, Records of Marion County, Deed Book Volume A of A & B*, 8, 104–105. Pack's father, John Lowery, for example, had encouraged U.S. officials to survey a road near his land north of the Tennessee River in order to conduct business with travelers. See John Lowery to Sam[uel] Ryley [Riley], March 27, 1807, reel 3, BIA-M208.

16. Petition of Nathan Green for Elizabeth Pack, Marion County, 1823, petition 41, Tennessee Legislative Petitions, TLSA; John Ross et al. to John C. Calhoun, January 19, 1824, in Moulton, *Papers of John Ross*, 1:57–58.

17. Denson, *Monuments to Absence* (quotation 17). See also O'Brien, *Firsting and Lasting*. For other examples of white southerners' public commemorations of a Cherokee past, see Denson, "Remembering Cherokee Removal in Civil-Rights Era Georgia"; Miles, "'Showplace of the Cherokee Nation'"; and Holly, "'Living Memorials to the Past.'"

18. Entry of August 17, 1802, Freeman Survey Notes of 1802, Receipt to Will Elders, October 2, 1802, and entry of August 15, 1802, Freeman Survey Notes of 1802, all in reel 1, BIA-M208; Treaty with the Cherokee, 1798, in Kappler, *Indian Treaties*, 51–55; Carson Brewer, "This Is Your Community," July 6, 1975, *Knoxville News-Sentinel*. Freeman also would survey the United States' contentious border with the Cherokee Nation and the Chickasaw Nation in 1807. On the complicated history of the post's location and the nomenclature of the Great Smoky Mountains and Mount Collins, see Robert Bunnelle, "Post Marking Indian Boundary Line Still Standing in Smokies," *Asheville Times*, April 21, 1929; "Mason Seeking to Change Name of Mt. Kephart," *Knoxville News-Sentinel*, July 31, 1930; and Frome, *Strangers in High Places*.

19. A Resolution by the Tribal Council of the Eastern Band of Cherokee Indians to Support the Exploration of the Process of Petitioning the Federal Government to Restore the Name Kuwahi ᏊᎦᎭ to the Mountain Presently Known as Clingman's Dome, Resolution No. 343 (2022), July 14, 2022, https://easternband.legistar.com/View.ashx?M=F&ID =12300739&GUID=DEF12E79-2D1C-41C8-9135-12A7B7317076, accessed July 24, 2024; Scott McKie, "Cherokee Women Seeking Name Change for Clingman's Dome, *Cherokee One Feather* (Cherokee, NC), June 16, 2022, https://theonefeather.com/2022/06/16 /cherokee-women-seeking-name-change-for-clingmans-dome, accessed July 24, 2024; Scott McKie, "Council Supports Clingman's Dome Name Change," *Cherokee One Feather* (Cherokee, NC), July 14, 2022, https://theonefeather.com/2022/07/14/council-supports -clingmans-dome-name-change, accessed July 24, 2024; Tyler Whetstone, "'History Is Complicated as Hell': Cherokee Will Ask to Restore Native Name for Clingmans Dome," *Knoxville News-Sentinel*, October 31, 2022; A Resolution by the Tribal Council of the Eastern Band of Cherokee Indians to Authorize the Submission of an Application to the U.S. Board on Geographic Names to Restore the Name Kuwohi in the Great Smoky Mountains National Park, Item 21 1.4.24, January 4, 2024, https://easternband.legistar.com/View .ashx?M=F&ID=12538804&GUID=413BD4EA-67F7-4791-8651-23872206B14E, accessed July 24, 2024; "Change Clingmans Dome to Kuwohi," United States Board on Geographic Names, Quarterly Review List 455, April 15, 2024, https://d9-wret.s3.us-west-2.amazonaws .com/assets/palladium/production/s3fs-public/media/files/Review%20List%20455.pdf, accessed July 24, 2024; Scott McKie, "Effort to Restore Kuwohi Name Moving Forward," *Cherokee One Feather* (Cherokee, NC), January 5, 2024, https://theonefeather.com/2024/01 /05/effort-to-restore-kuwohi-name-moving-forward, accessed July 24, 2024; Office of the Principal Chief, "Official Proposal Submitted for Kuwohi Name Change," *Cherokee One Feather* (Cherokee, NC), February 12, 2024, https://theonefeather.com/2024/02/12/official -proposal-submitted-for-kuwohi-name-change, accessed July 24, 2024; Scott McKie, "Kuwohi Name Restored as BGN Approves Application," *Cherokee One Feather* (Cherokee, NC), September 18, 2024, https://https://theonefeather.com/2024/09/18/kuwohi-name -restored-as-bgn-approves-application, accessed September 25, 2024; Frome, *Strangers in High Places*, 102. Clingman also worked to remove Cherokees from the North Carolina mountains to Indian Territory during his time in Congress. See Finger, *Eastern Band of Cherokees*, 58. In 2022 alone, roughly 777,000 people made recreational visits to Clingmans Dome. Melissa Greene, "Great Smoky Mountains National Park Remains Nation's 'Most Visited' as Fee Changes Begin," WATE, February 27, 2023, www.wate.com/news /smoky-mountains/great-smoky-mountains-national-park-remains-nations-most-visited, accessed May 22, 2024. On the cultural importance of mulberries, including earlier examples of Cherokee communities named after mulberries, see Hill, *Weaving New Worlds*, 8–9.

Bibliography

Manuscript Collections

Alabama Department of Archives and History, Montgomery
    John Coffee Papers
    Mississippi (Territory) Governor Correspondence, 1798–1819

American Philosophical Society, Philadelphia
    Benjamin Franklin Papers
    Individually Catalogued Manuscript Maps, Realms of Gold

Appalachian State University Special Collections, Boone, NC
    Sampson Williams Letter to Colonel David Henley

Betsey B. Creekmore Special Collections and University Archives, University of Tennessee at Knoxville
    Benjamin Hawkins Letter, 1785, MS-2042
    John Sevier Letters, MS-0368
    Penelope Allen Collection, MS-2033
    Sampson Williams Letter, MS-1959
    Tennessee Documentary History, Digital Collection

Calvin M. McClung Historical Collection of the Knox County Public Library, Knoxville, TN
    Letters from Timothy Pickering, Oliver Wolcott, and Others to David Henley

Chattanooga Public Library—Downtown Branch, Chattanooga, TN
    Penelope Allen Papers

Edward E. Ayer Manuscript Collection, Newberry Library, Chicago
    Benjamin Hawkins Letters, 1797–1812
    John Howard Payne Papers, 1794–1841, 1814–1841
    Journal of the Commissioners of the United States, appointed to hold conferences with the several Nations of Indians South of the Ohio
    Silas Dinsmore Papers, 1794–1796
    Timothy Pickering Letters, 1795–1798
    William Blount Papers, 1794–1796

Filson Historical Society, Louisville, KY
    Arthur Campbell Papers, 1752–1811

Miscellaneous Papers
Thomas Butler Letters, 1798

Georgia Archives, Morrow
"Creek Indian Letters, Talks, and Treaties, 1705–1839." Bound transcripts. WPA
Project No. 665-34-3-224, compiled by Louise F. Hays. Vol 1. 1939

Gilcrease Museum, Tulsa, OK
Cherokee Papers Manuscript Collection
John Ross Papers

Hargrett Rare Book and Manuscript Library, University of Georgia Libraries, Athens
Ebenezer Newton Diary
Keith M. Read Collection
Telamon Cuyler Collection

Historical Society of Pennsylvania, Philadelphia
Daniel Parker Papers

Houghton Library, Harvard University, Cambridge, MA
Papers of the American Board of Commissioners for Foreign Missions

Hunter Library Special Collections, Western Carolina University, Cullowhee, NC
Cherokee Documents in Foreign Archives Collection

Indiana Historical Society, Indianapolis
Northwest Territory Collection, 1721–1825

Knox County Archives, Knoxville, TN
Hamilton Superior Court Records

Library of Congress, Washington, DC
Andrew Jackson Papers, Series 1: General Correspondence and Related Items,
1775–1885
George Washington Papers, General Correspondence, 1697–1799
James McHenry Papers
John McKee Papers, circa 1792–1825
John Sevier Correspondence
Meigs Family Papers, 1772–1862
Nathanael Greene Papers
Shelby Family Papers
Thomas Jefferson Papers, Series 1: General Correspondence, 1651–1827
United States Continental Congress and Continental Congress Broadside Collection
William Blount Papers, 1783–1823

Library of Virginia, Richmond
Executive Papers of Governor Benjamin Harrison, 1781–1784 (microfilm edition)

Massachusetts Historical Society, Boston
John Adams Papers
Timothy Pickering Papers

Mississippi Department of Archives and History, Digital Archives, Jackson
Mississippi Territory Administration Papers, 1769, 1788–1817

National Archives and Records Administration, Washington, DC
  Bureau of Indian Affairs, Applications for Cherokee Reservations, 1819–1919, Record Group 75
  Bureau of Indian Affairs, Letters Received by the Office of Indian Affairs, 1824–1880, Record Group 75, Microcopy 234
  Bureau of Indian Affairs, Letters Received by the Secretary of War Relating to Indian Affairs, 1800–1823, Record Group 75, Microcopy 271
  Bureau of Indian Affairs, Records of the Cherokee Indian Agency in Tennessee, 1801–1835, Record Group 75, Microcopy 208
  Bureau of Indian Affairs, Documents Relating to the Negotiation of Ratified and Unratified Treaties with Various Tribes of Indians, 1801–69, Record Group 75, Microcopy T-494
  Records of the Office of the Secretary of War, Letters Sent, Indian Affairs, Microcopy 15

New York Public Library, New York, NY
  Miscellaneous Collections
  Thomas Addis Emmett Collection, 1483–1875
  William Blount Letters to John Sevier

Rauner Special Collections Library, Dartmouth University, Hanover, NH
  Dinsmoor Family Papers

Rubenstein Rare Book and Manuscript Library, Duke University, Durham, NC
  Campbell Family Papers
  David Henley Papers
  John Sevier Papers, 1778–1812
  Thomas Lenoir Papers

South Carolina Historical Society, Charleston
  Andrew Pickens Papers, 1782–1804

South Caroliniana Library, University of South Carolina, Columbia
  Andrew Pickens Papers

Southern Historical Collection, Wilson Library, University of North Carolina at Chapel Hill
  Ernest Haywood Collection of Haywood Family Papers #1290
  Jesse Franklin Indian Treaty Papers #3656-z
  John McKee Papers #1194-z
  Polk and Yeatman Family Papers #606
  Revolutionary War Papers #2194-z
  Richard Caswell Papers #145-z
  William Lytle Papers #445-z

State Historical Society of Wisconsin, Madison
  Lyman Draper Manuscripts (microfilm edition)

Tennessee State Library and Archives, Nashville
  David Henley Papers
  Early Tennessee/North Carolina Land Records, 1783–1927
  Grainger County Clerk Loose Records

GP-2, John Sevier Papers
GP-3, Archibald Roane Papers
GP-4, John Sevier Papers
GP-6, Joseph McMinn Papers
James Robertson Papers
Murdock Collection of John Overton Papers, 1780–[1797–1820]–1908
Penelope Johnson Allen Cherokee Collection
Stanley Horn Collection
Tennessee Historical Commission, Historical Marker Files, 1950–1993
Tennessee Legislative Petitions, 1799–1850
Winchester, James (1752–1826) Papers, 1787–1923

Tulane University Special Collections, New Orleans, LA
Diego de Gardoqui Papers

William L. Clements Library, University of Michigan, Ann Arbor
James McHenry Papers

Newspapers and Periodicals

Asheville Times
Chattanooga News
Chattanooga Sunday Times
Cherokee One Feather (Cherokee, NC)
Freeman's Journal; or, The North American Intelligencer (Philadelphia, PA)
Georgia State Gazette or Independent Register (Augusta, GA)
Hall's Wilmington Gazette (Wilmington, NC)
Independent Gazetteer or the Chronicle of Freedom (Philadelphia, PA)
Knoxville Gazette
Knoxville News-Sentinel
Knoxville Register
Maryland Gazette (Annapolis, MD)
Nashville Whig
Pennsylvania Gazette (Philadelphia, PA)
Pennsylvania Packet (Philadelphia, PA)
Raleigh Register and North-Carolina Gazette
Tennessee Gazette (Nashville, TN)

Maps

An Accurate Map of the State of Alabama and West Florida. John LaTourrette. 1837. Alabama Maps and Architectural Drawings Collection. Alabama Department of Archives and History. https://digital.archives.alabama.gov/digital/collection/maps /id/1541.

Boundary Line Running on Tennessee Ridge between the United States and the Chickasaw Nation of Indians. James Winchester. February 5, 1801. Map 466. Map Collection. Tennessee State Library and Archives.

Course of the River Mississippi, from the Balise to Fort Chartres; Taken on an Expedition to the Illinois, in the Latter End of the Year 1765. Lieut. Ross and Robert Sayer. 1772. Library of Congress. www.loc.gov/resource/g4042m.ar078000.

A Map of the American Indian Nations, Adjoining to the Mississippi, West & East Florida, Georgia, S. & N. Carolina, Virginia, &c. John Lodge and James Adair. 1775. North Carolina Maps. University of North Carolina at Chapel Hill. https://dc.lib.unc.edu/cdm/ref/collection/ncmaps/id/2074.

Map of the Former Territorial Limits of the Cherokee Nation of Indians. Charles C. Royce. 1884. North Carolina Maps. University of North Carolina at Chapel Hill. https://dc.lib.unc.edu/cdm/ref/collection/ncmaps/id/1059.

A Map of Indian Boundary Lines and the Southern Boundary of the State of Tennessee. Thomas Freeman. 1807. Map 1407. Map Collection. Tennessee State Library and Archives. https://teva.contentdm.oclc.org/digital/collection/p15138c01123/id/9064/rec/5.

Map of the Southern Indian District. 1764. Archives and Special Collections. University of Pittsburgh Library System. http://https://digital.library.pitt.edu/islandora/object/pitt:DARMAP0398.

Map of the State of Kentucky: With the Adjoining Territories. 1794. Map Collection. Tennessee State Library and Archives. https://teva.contentdm.oclc.org/digital/collection/p15138c01123/id/10389.

Map of the Tennassee Government formerly Part of North Carolina taken Chiefly from Surveys by Gen'l. D. Smith & Others. Mathew Carey. [1795]. Individually Catalogued Manuscript Maps. Map 21. Realms of Gold. American Philosophical Society.

Map of the Tennassee Government formerly Part of North Carolina taken Chiefly from Surveys by Gen'l. D. Smith & Others. Mathew Carey. [ca. 1797]. Individually Catalogued Manuscript Maps. Map 21a. Realms of Gold. American Philosophical Society.

Parts of Tennessee and Alabama (Showing Chickasaw Treaty Cessions). A. Hoen & Co. 1897. Tennessee State Library and Archives. https://teva.contentdm.oclc.org/digital/collection/p15138c01123/id/9053/rec/18.

Re-Survey of Indian Boundary Line of 1791 Commencing at South-West Point and Terminating at Tuckaleechee Cove. Joseph Whitner and John Clark Kilpatrick. [1797]. Map 1363. Map Collection. Tennessee State Library and Archives.

S. W. Territory. Joseph Scott 1795. Grille Books. Tennessee State Library and Archives. https://teva.contentdm.oclc.org/digital/collection/p15138c01123/id/9096.

Sketch of the Muscle Shoals. James Wilkinson. 1801. Individually Catalogued Manuscript Maps. Map 66. Realms of Gold. American Philosophical Society.

Published Sources

Abernethy, Thomas Perkins. *From Frontier to Plantation in Tennessee: A Study in Frontier Democracy.* Chapel Hill: University of North Carolina Press, 1932.

———. *Western Lands and the American Revolution.* 1937. Reprint, New York: Russell and Russell, 1959.

Ablavsky, Gregory. "Empire States: The Coming of Dual Federalism." *Yale Law Journal* 128, no. 7 (May 2019): 1792–1868.

———. *Federal Ground: Governing Property and Violence in the First U.S. Territories.* New York: Oxford University Press, 2021.

———. "The Savage Constitution." *Duke Law Journal* 63, no. 5 (Feb. 2014): 999–1090.

———. "Species of Sovereignty: Native Nationhood, the United States, and International Law, 1783–1795." *Journal of American History* 106, no. 3 (Dec. 2019): 591–613.

———. "'With the Indian Tribes': Race, Citizenship, and Original Constitutional Meanings." *Stanford Law Review* 70, no. 4 (Apr. 2018): 1025–1076.

Abram, Susan M. *Forging a Cherokee-American Alliance in the Creek War: From Creation to Betrayal.* Tuscaloosa: University of Alabama Press, 2015.

Acts Passed at the First Session of the Third General Assembly of the State of Tennessee, Begun and Held at Knoxville, on Monday the Sixteenth Day of September, One Thousand Seven Hundred and Ninety-Nine. Knoxville: Roulstone and Wilson, 1799.

Addington, Luther F. "Chief Benge's Last Raid." *Historical Sketches of Southwest Virginia* 2 (1966): 24–33.

Adelman, Jeremy, and Stephen Aron. "From Borderlands to Borders: Empires, Nation-States, and the Peoples in between North American History." *American Historical Review* 104, no. 3 (June 1999): 814–841.

Anderson, Chad. "Rediscovering Native North America: Settlements, Maps, and Empires in the Eastern Woodlands." *Early American Studies* 14, no. 3 (Summer 2016): 478–505.

Anderson, Virginia DeJohn. *Creatures of Empire: How Domestic Animals Transformed Early America.* New York: Oxford University Press, 2004.

Andrew, Rod, Jr. *The Life and Times of General Andrew Pickens: Revolutionary War Hero, American Founder.* Chapel Hill: University of North Carolina Press, 2017.

Aron, Stephen. *How the West Was Lost: The Transformation of Kentucky from Daniel Boone to Henry Clay.* Baltimore: Johns Hopkins University Press, 1996.

Atkinson, James R. *Splendid Land, Splendid People: The Chickasaw Indians to Removal.* Tuscaloosa: University of Alabama Press, 2004.

Baily, Francis. *Journal of a Tour in Unsettled Parts of North America in 1796 & 1797.* London: Baily Brothers, 1856.

Balogh, Brian. *A Government out of Sight: The Mystery of National Authority in Nineteenth-Century America.* Cambridge: Cambridge University Press, 2009.

Banner, Stuart. *How the Indians Lost Their Land: Law and Power on the Frontier.* Cambridge, MA: Belknap Press of Harvard University Press, 2005.

Barksdale, Kevin T. *The Lost State of Franklin: America's First Secession.* Lexington: University Press of Kentucky, 2009.

———. "The State of Franklin: Separatism, Competition, and the Legacy of Tennessee's First State, 1783–1789." In *Before the Volunteer State: New Thoughts on Early Tennessee, 1540–1800,* edited by Kristofer Ray, 155–184. Knoxville: University of Tennessee Press, 2014.

Barnett, James F. *Mississippi's American Indians.* Jackson: University Press of Mississippi, 2012.

Barnhart, John D. "The Tennessee Constitution of 1796: A Product of the Old West." *Journal of Southern History* 9, no. 4 (Nov. 1943): 532–548.

Barr, Juliana. "Borders and Borderlands." In *Why You Can't Teach United States History without American Indians,* edited by Susan Sleeper-Smith, Juliana Barr, Jean M. O'Brien, Nancy Shoemaker, and Scott Manning Stevens, 9–25. Chapel Hill: University of North Carolina Press, 2015.

———. "Geographies of Power: Mapping Indian Borders in the 'Borderlands' of the Early Southwest." *William and Mary Quarterly* 68, no. 1 (Jan. 2011): 5–46.

———. *Peace Came in the Form of a Woman: Indians and Spaniards in the Texas Borderlands*. Chapel Hill: University of North Carolina Press, 2007.

———. "The Red Continent and the Cant of Coastline." *William and Mary Quarterly* 69, no. 3 (July 2012): 521–526.

Barr, Juliana, and Edward Countryman, eds. *Contested Spaces of Early America*. Philadelphia: University of Pennsylvania Press, 2014.

———. "Maps and Spaces, Paths to Connect, and Lines to Divide." Introduction to *Contested Spaces of Early America*, edited by Juliana Barr and Edward Countryman, 1–28. Philadelphia: University of Pennsylvania Press, 2014.

Basso, Keith. *Wisdom Sits in Places: Landscape and Language among the Western Apache*. Albuquerque: University of New Mexico Press, 1996.

Bauer, Brooke M. *Becoming Catawba: Catawba Indian Women and Nation-Building, 1540–1840*. Tuscaloosa: University of Alabama Press, 2023.

Belmessous, Saliha, ed., *Native Claims: Indigenous Law against Empire, 1500–1920*. New York: Oxford University Press, 2012.

———. "The Problem of Indigenous Claim Making in Colonial History." Introduction to *Native Claims: Indigenous Law against Empire, 1500–1920*, edited by Saliha Belmessous, 3–18. New York: Oxford University Press, 2012.

Benton, Lauren. "Possessing Empire: Iberian Claims and Interpolity Law." In *Native Claims: Indigenous Law against Empire, 1500–1920*, edited by Saliha Belmessous, 19–40. New York: Oxford University Press, 2011.

Bergmann, William H. *The American National State and the Early West*. New York: Cambridge University Press, 2012.

Bjork, Katherine. *Prairie Imperialists: The Indian Country Origins of American Empire*. Philadelphia: University of Pennsylvania Press, 2019.

Blaakman, Michael A. *Speculation Nation: Land Mania in the Revolutionary American Republic*. Philadelphia: University of Pennsylvania Press, 2023.

Blaakman, Michael A., and Emily Conroy-Krutz. Introduction to *The Early Imperial Republic: From the American Revolution to the U.S.-Mexican War*, edited by Michael A. Blaakman, Emily Conroy-Krutz, and Noelani Arista, 1–24. Philadelphia: University of Pennsylvania Press, 2023.

Blackhawk, Maggie. "Federal Indian Law as Paradigm within Public Law." *Harvard Law Review* 132, no. 7 (May 2019): 1787–1877.

Boulware, Tyler. *Deconstructing the Cherokee Nation: Town, Region, and Nation among Eighteenth-Century Cherokees*. Gainesville: University Press of Florida, 2011.

———. "'It Seems like Coming into Our Houses': Challenges to Cherokee Hunting Grounds, 1750–1775." In *Before the Volunteer State: New Thoughts on Early Tennessee, 1540–1800*, edited by Kristofer Ray, 65–81. Knoxville: University of Tennessee Press, 2014.

———. "'Our Mad Young Men': Authority and Violence in Cherokee Country." In *Blood in the Hills: A History of Violence in Appalachia*, edited by Bruce E. Stewart, 80–98. Lexington: University Press of Kentucky, 2012.

Bowes, John P. *Land Too Good for Indians: Northern Indian Removal*. Norman: University of Oklahoma Press, 2016.

———. "Shawnee Geography and the Tennessee Corridor in the Seventeenth and Eighteenth Centuries." In *Before the Volunteer State: New Thoughts on Early Tennessee,*

1540–1800, edited by Kristofer Ray, 83–105. Knoxville: University of Tennessee Press, 2014.

Boyd, Julian P., Charles T. Cullen, John Catanzariti, Barbara B. Oberg, and James P. McClure, eds. *The Papers of Thomas Jefferson*. 45 vols. Princeton, NJ: Princeton University Press, 1950–.

Braund, Kathryn E. Holland. "'Like a Stone Wall Never to Be Broke': The British-Indian Boundary Line with the Creek Indians, 1763–1773." In *Britain and the American South: From Colonialism to Rock and Roll*, edited by Joseph P. Ward, 53–80. Jackson: University Press of Mississippi, 2003.

——, ed. *Tohopeka: Rethinking the Creek War and the War of 1812*. Tuscaloosa: University of Alabama Press, 2012.

Brooks, Lisa. *The Common Pot: The Recovery of Native Space in the Northeast*. Minneapolis: University of Minnesota Press, 2008.

Brown, John P. *Old Frontiers: The Story of the Cherokee Indians from Earliest Times to the Date of Their Removal to the West, 1838*. Kingsport, TN: Southern Publishers, 1938.

Calloway, Colin G. *The American Revolution in Indian Country: Crisis and Diversity in Native American Communities*. Cambridge: Cambridge University Press, 1995.

——. "Declaring Independence and Rebuilding a Nation: Dragging Canoe and the Chickamauga Revolution." In *Revolutionary Founders: Rebels, Radicals, and Reformers in the Making of the Nation*, edited by Alfred F. Young, Gary B. Nash, and Ray Raphael, 185–198. New York: Knopf, 2011.

——. *The Indian World of George Washington: The First President, the First Americans, and the Birth of the Nation*. New York: Oxford University Press, 2018.

——. *One Vast Winter Count: The Native American West before Lewis and Clark*. Lincoln: University of Nebraska Press, 2003.

——. *Pen and Ink Witchcraft: Treaties and Treaty Making in American Indian History*. New York: Oxford University Press, 2014.

——. *The Shawnees and the War for America*. New York: Viking, 2007.

——. *The Victory with No Name: The Native American Defeat of the First American Army*. New York: Oxford University Press, 2015.

Carson, James Taylor. "Ethnogeography and the Native American Past." *Ethnohistory* 49, no. 4 (Fall 2002): 769–788.

Carter, Clarence Edwin, ed. *The Territorial Papers of the United States*. 28 vols. Washington, D.C.: Government Printing Office, 1934–1962.

Cashin, Edward J. *Guardians of the Valley: Chickasaws in Colonial South Carolina and Georgia*. Columbia: University of South Carolina Press, 2009.

Cattelino, Jessica. *High Stakes: Florida Seminole Gaming and Sovereignty*. Durham, NC: Duke University Press, 2008.

Cavanagh, John C. *Decision at Fayetteville: The North Carolina Ratification Convention and General Assembly of 1789*. Raleigh: North Carolina Department of Cultural Resources, 1989.

Cayton, Andrew R. L. *The Frontier Republic: Ideology and Politics in the Ohio Country, 1780–1825*. Kent, OH: Kent State University Press, 1986.

——. "Radicals in the 'Western World': The Federalist Conquest of Trans-Appalachian North America." In *Federalists Reconsidered*, edited by Doron Ben-Atar and Barbara B. Oberg, 77–96. Charlottesville: University Press of Virginia, 1998.

———. "'Separate Interests' and the Nation-State: The Washington Administration and the Origins of Regionalism in the Trans-Appalachian West." *Journal of American History* 79, no. 1 (June 1992): 39–67.

———. "'When Shall We Cease to Have Judases?': The Blount Conspiracy and the Limits of the Extended Republic." In *Launching the "Extended Republic": The Federalist Era*, edited by Ronald Hoffman and Peter J. Albert, 156–189. Charlottesville: University Press of Virginia, 1996.

Cegielski, Wendy, and Brad R. Lieb. "*Hina' Falaa*, 'The Long Path': An Analysis of Chickasaw Settlement Using GIS in Northeast Mississippi, 1650–1840." *Native South* 4 (2011): 24–54.

Chambers, Ian. "The Movement of Great Tellico: The Role of Town and Clan in Cherokee Spatial Understanding." *Native South* 3 (2010): 89–102.

Clark, Christopher. "The Ohio Country in the Political Economy of Nation Building." In *Center of a Great Empire: The Ohio Country in the Early Republic*, edited by Andrew R. L. Cayton and Stuart D. Hobbs, 146–165. Athens: Ohio University Press, 2005.

Clark, Walter, ed. *The State Records of North Carolina*. 16 vols. Raleigh: [North Carolina General Assembly], 1895–1907.

Conroy-Krutz, Emily. "Empire and the Early Republic." *H-Diplo*. Essay 133. September 10, 2015. https://networks.h-net.org/system/files/contributed-files/e133.pdf.

Corbitt, D. C., and Roberta Corbitt, eds. "Papers from the Spanish Archives relating to Tennessee and the Old Southwest, 1783–1800: III, 1787." *East Tennessee Historical Society's Publications* 11 (1939): 62–92.

Cowger, Thomas W., and Mitch Caver. *Piominko: Chickasaw Leader*. Ada, OK: Chickasaw Press, 2017.

Cotterill, Robert S. "The Virginia-Chickasaw Treaty of 1783." *Journal of Southern History* 8, no. 4 (Nov. 1942): 483–496.

Craig, Ronald Eugene. "The Colberts in Chickasaw History, 1783–1818: A Study in Internal Tribal Dynamics." PhD diss., University of New Mexico, 1998.

Crallé, Richard K. *Speeches of John C. Calhoun, Delivered in the House of Representatives, and in the Senate of the United States*. New York: D. Appleton, 1853.

Crews, C. Daniel, and Richard W. Starbuck, eds. *Records of the Moravians among the Cherokees*. Vol. 1, *Early Contact and the Establishment of the First Mission, 1752–1802*. Tahlequah, OK: Cherokee National Press, 2010.

Crews, C. Daniel, and Richard W. Starbuck, eds. *Records of the Moravians among the Cherokees*. Vol. 2, *Beginnings of the Mission and Establishment of the School, 1802–1805*. Tahlequah, OK: Cherokee National Press, 2010.

Cumfer, Cynthia. "Nan-ye-hi (Nancy Ward): Diplomatic Mother." In *Tennessee Women: Their Lives and Times*, edited by Sarah Wilkerson Freeman and Beverly Bond, 1–22. Athens: University of Georgia Press, 2009.

———. *Separate Peoples, One Land: The Minds of Cherokees, Blacks, and Whites on the Tennessee Frontier*. Chapel Hill: University of North Carolina Press 2007.

Curtis, Christopher Michael. *Jefferson's Freeholders and the Politics of Ownership in the Old Dominion*. Cambridge: Cambridge University Press, 2012.

Daggar, Lori J. "The Mission Complex: Economic Development, 'Civilization,' and Empire in the Early Republic." *Journal of the Early Republic* 36, no. 3 (Fall 2016): 467–491.

Dahl, Adam. *Empire of the People: Settler Colonialism and the Foundations of Modern Democratic Thought*. Lawrence: University Press of Kansas, 2018.

Delaney, David. *Territory: A Short Introduction*. Malden, MA: Blackwell, 2005.

Deloria, Vine J., Jr., and Raymond J. Demallie, eds. *Documents of American Indian Diplomacy: Treaties, Agreements and Conventions, 1775–1979*. Vol. 1. Norman: University of Oklahoma Press, 1999.

Denson, Andrew. *Monuments to Absence: Cherokee Removal and the Contest over Southern Memory*. Chapel Hill: University of North Carolina Press, 2017.

———. "Remembering Cherokee Removal in Civil-Rights Era Georgia." *Southern Cultures* 14 (Winter 2008): 85–101.

De Vorsey, Louis, Jr., *The Georgia-South Carolina Boundary: A Problem in Historical Geography*. Athens: University of Georgia Press, 1982.

———. *The Indian Boundary in the Southern Colonies, 1763–1775*. Chapel Hill: University of North Carolina Press, 1961.

Dixon, Matt. *The Wataugans*. Tennessee in the Eighteenth Century: A Bicentennial Series, edited by James C. Kelly and Dan E. Pomeroy. Nashville: Tennessee American Revolution Bicentennial Commission, 1976.

Dowd, Gregory Evans. *A Spirited Resistance: The North American Indian Struggle for Unity, 1745–1815*. Baltimore: Johns Hopkins University Press, 1992.

Dupre, Daniel S. *Alabama's Frontiers and the Rise of the Old South*. Bloomington: Indiana University Press, 2018.

DuVal, Kathleen. *Independence Lost: Lives on the Edge of the American Revolution*. New York: Random House, 2015.

———. *The Native Ground: Indians and Colonists in the Heart of the Continent*. Philadelphia: University of Pennsylvania Press, 2006.

———. *Native Nations: A Millennium in North America*. New York: Random House, 2024.

Edelson, S. Max. *The New Map of Empire: How Britain Imagined America before Independence*. Cambridge, MA: Harvard University Press, 2017.

Edling, Max M. *A Revolution in Favor of Government: Origins of the U.S. Constitution and the Making of the American State*. New York: Oxford University Press, 2003.

Edwards, Laura F. "Sarah Allingham's Sheet and Other Lessons from Legal History." *Journal of the Early Republic* 38, no. 1 (Spring 2018): 121–147.

England, J. Merton. "The Free Negro in Ante-Bellum Tennessee." *Journal of Southern History* 9, no. 1 (Feb. 1943): 37–58.

Erbig, Jeffrey Alan, Jr. *Where Caciques and Mapmakers Met: Border Making in Eighteenth-Century South America*. Chapel Hill: University of North Carolina Press, 2020.

Ethridge, Robbie. "European Invasion and the Transformation of the Indians of Tennessee, 1540–1715." In *Before the Volunteer State: New Thoughts on Early Tennessee, 1540–1800*, edited by Kristofer Ray, 3–34. Knoxville: University of Tennessee Press, 2014.

———. *From Chicaza to Chickasaw: The European Invasion and the Transformation of the Mississippian World, 1540–1715*. Chapel Hill: University of North Carolina Press, 2010.

———. "Introduction: Mapping the Mississippian Shatter Zone." In *Mapping the Mississippian Shatter Zone: The Colonial Indian Slave Trade and Regional Instability in the American South*, edited by Robbie Ethridge and Sheri M. Shuck-Hall, 1–62. Lincoln: University of Nebraska Press, 2009.

Ethridge, Robbie, and Charles Hudson. "The Early Historic Transformation of the Southeastern Indians." In *Cultural Diversity in the U.S. South: Anthropological Con-*

tributions to a Region in Transition, edited by Carole E. Hill and Patricia D. Beaver, 34–50. Athens: University of Georgia Press, 1998.

Ethridge, Robbie, and Sheri M. Shuck-Hall, eds. *Mapping the Mississippian Shatter Zone: The Colonial Indian Slave Trade and Regional Instability in the American South.* Lincoln: University of Nebraska Press, 2009.

Evans, E. Raymond. "Notable Persons in Cherokee History: Ostenaco." *Journal of Cherokee Studies* 1, no. 1 (Summer 1976): 41–54.

Faulkner, Charles H. *Massacre at Cavett's Station: Frontier Tennessee during the Cherokee Wars.* Knoxville: University of Tennessee Press, 2013.

Faulkner, Cooleela. *The Life and Times of Reverend Stephen Foreman.* Tahlequah, OK: Cherokee Heritage Press, 2006.

Fenn, Elizabeth A. *Encounters at the Heart of the World: A History of the Mandan People.* New York: Hill and Wang, 2014.

Finger, John R. *Cherokee Americans: The Eastern Band of Cherokees in the Twentieth Century.* Lincoln: University of Nebraska Press, 1991.

———. *The Eastern Band of Cherokees, 1819–1900.* Knoxville: University of Tennessee Press, 1984.

———. *Tennessee Frontiers: Three Regions in Transition.* Bloomington: Indiana University Press, 2001.

Fitzmaurice, Andrew. "Powhatan Legal Claims." In *Native Claims: Indigenous Law against Empire, 1500–1920*, edited by Saliha Belmessous, 85–106. New York: Oxford University Press, 2011.

———. *Sovereignty, Property and Empire, 1500–2000.* Cambridge: Cambridge University Press, 2014.

Flanagan, Christopher. "A Revolution for Empire: Ideas of Empire and the Making of the Constitution, 1787–8." *Journal of Early American History* 8 (2018): 153–177.

Ford, Lacy K. *Deliver Us from Evil: The Slavery Question in the Old South.* New York: Oxford University Press, 2009.

Ford, Lisa. *Settler Sovereignty: Jurisdiction and Indigenous People in America and Australia, 1788–1836.* Cambridge, MA: Harvard University Press, 2010.

Frank, Andrew K. *Creeks and Southerners: Biculturalism on the Early American Frontier.* Lincoln: University of Nebraska Press, 2005.

Frank, Andrew K., and A. Glenn Crothers. Introduction to *Borderland Narratives: Negotiation and Accommodation in North America's Contested Spaces, 1500–1850*, edited by Andrew K. Frank and A. Glenn Crothers, 1–17. Gainesville: University Press of Florida, 2017.

Franklin, John Hope. *The Free Negro in North Carolina.* Chapel Hill: University of North Carolina Press, 1943.

Fries, Adelaide L., ed. "Report of the Brethren Abraham Steiner and Friedrich Christian von Schweinitz of Their Journey to the Cherokee Nation and in the Cumberland Settlements in the State of Tennessee from 28th October to 28th December, 1799." *North Carolina Historical Review* 21, no. 4 (Oct. 1944): 330–375.

Frome, Michael. *Strangers in High Places: The Story of the Great Smoky Mountains.* Rev. ed. Knoxville: University of Tennessee Press, 1980.

Frymer, Paul. "'A Rush and a Push and the Land Is Ours': Territorial Expansion, Land Policy, and U.S. State Formation." *Perspectives on Politics* 12, no. 1 (March 2014): 119–144.

Fullagar, Kate. *The Warrior, the Voyager, and the Artist: Three Lives in an Age of Empire.* New Haven, CT: Yale University Press, 2020.

Furstenberg, François. "The Significance of the Trans-Appalachian Frontier in Atlantic History." *American Historical Review* 113, no. 3 (June 2008): 647–677.

Gates, Paul Wallace. *History of Public Land Law Development.* Washington, DC: Government Printing Office, 1968.

Gibson, Arrell M. *The Chickasaws.* Norman: University of Oklahoma Press, 1971.

Gildrie, Richard. "Tennessee in the American Revolution: A Reconsideration." In *Before the Volunteer State: New Thoughts on Early Tennessee, 1540–1800*, edited by Kristofer Ray, 109–129. Knoxville: University of Tennessee Press, 2014.

Gould, Eliga H. *Among the Powers of the Earth: The American Revolution and the Making of a New World Empire.* Cambridge, MA: Harvard University Press, 2012.

Grant, C. L., ed. *Letters, Journals, and Writings of Benjamin Hawkins.* 2 vols. Savannah, GA: Beehive Press, 1980.

Grasso, Christopher, and Karin Wulf. "Nothing Says 'Democracy' Like a Visit from the Queen: Reflections on Empire and Nation in Early American Histories." *Journal of American History* 95, no. 3 (Dec. 2008): 764–781.

Green, Michael D. *The Politics of Indian Removal: Creek Government and Society in Crisis.* Lincoln: University of Nebraska Press, 1982.

Greene, Lance. *Their Determination to Remain: A Cherokee Community's Resistance to the Trail of Tears in North Carolina.* Tuscaloosa: University of Alabama Press, 2022.

Greer, Allan. "Commons and Enclosure in the Colonization of North America." *American Historical Review* 117, no. 2 (Apr. 2012): 365–386.

———. *Property and Dispossession: Natives, Empires, and Land in Early Modern North America.* Cambridge: Cambridge University Press, 2018.

Griffin, Patrick. *American Leviathan: Empire, Nation, and Revolutionary Frontier.* New York: Hill and Wang, 2007.

Guyatt, Nicholas. "Imperialism and the American Imagination." In *The Early Imperial Republic: From the American Revolution to the U.S.-Mexican War*, edited by Michael A. Blaakman, Emily Conroy-Krutz, and Noelani Arista, 227–247. Philadelphia: University of Pennsylvania Press, 2023.

Hagy, James William, and Stanley J. Folmsbee. "Lost Archives of the Cherokee Nation." *East Tennessee Historical Society's Publications* 45 (1973): 88–98.

Hall, Ryan. *Beneath the Backbone of the World: Blackfoot People and the North American Borderlands, 1720–1877.* Chapel Hill: University of North Carolina Press, 2020.

Hämäläinen, Pekka. *The Comanche Empire.* New Haven, CT: Yale University Press, 2008.

———. *Lakota America: A New History of Indigenous Power.* New Haven, CT: Yale University Press, 2019.

Hämäläinen, Pekka, and Samuel Truett. "On Borderlands." *Journal of American History* 98, no. 2 (Sept. 2011): 338–361.

Hamer, Philip M. "The British in Canada and the Southern Indians, 1790–1794." *East Tennessee Historical Society's Publications* 2 (1930): 107–134.

Hammond, John Craig. *Slavery, Freedom, and Expansion in the Early American West.* Charlottesville: University of Virginia Press, 2007.

———. "Slavery, Settlement, and Empire: The Expansion and Growth of Slavery in the Interior of the North American Continent, 1770–1820." *Journal of the Early Republic* 32, no. 2 (Spring 2012): 175–206.

Hampton, David Keith. *Cherokee Reservees*. Oklahoma City: Baker, 1979.

Harper, Rob. *Unsettling the West: Violence and State Building in the Ohio Valley*. Philadelphia: University of Pennsylvania Press, 2018.

Harrison, Joseph H., Jr. "'Sic et Non': Thomas Jefferson and Internal Improvement." *Journal of the Early Republic* 7, no. 4 (Winter 1987): 335–349.

Hatley, Thomas. *The Dividing Paths: Cherokees and South Carolinians through the Era of Revolution*. New York: Oxford University Press, 1993.

Haynes, Joshua H. *Patrolling the Border: Theft and Violence on the Creek-Georgia Frontier, 1770–1796*. Athens: University of Georgia Press, 2018.

Hemphill, W. Edwin., ed. *The Papers of John C. Calhoun*. Vol. 2, 1817–1818. Columbia: University of South Carolina Press, 1963.

———, ed. *The Papers of John C. Calhoun*. Vol. 3, 1818–1819. Columbia: University of South Carolina Press, 1967.

Henderson, Archibald. "The Treaty of Long Island of Holston, July, 1777." *North Carolina Historical Review* 8, no. 1 (Jan. 1931): 55–116.

Henry, William Wirt., ed. *Patrick Henry: Life, Correspondence and Speeches*. Vol. 3. New York: Charles Scribner's Sons, 1891.

Hill, Roscoe R., ed. *Journals of the Continental Congress, 1774–1789*. Vols. 32–34. Washington, DC: Government Printing Office, 1936–1937.

Hill, Sarah H. *Weaving New Worlds: Southeastern Cherokee Women and Their Basketry*. Chapel Hill: University of North Carolina Press, 1997.

Hinderaker, Eric. *Elusive Empires: Constructing Colonialism in the Ohio Valley, 1670–1800*. Cambridge: Cambridge University Press, 1997.

Hixson, Walter S. *American Settler Colonialism: A History*. New York: Palgrave Macmillan, 2013.

Hogan, Margaret A., C. James Taylor, Sara Martin, Neal E. Millikan, Hobson Woodward, Sara B. Sikes, and Gregg L. Lint, eds. *Adams Family Correspondence*. Vol. 11, July 1795–February 1797. Cambridge, MA: Harvard University Press, 2013.

Hogue, Michel. *Metis and the Medicine Line: Creating a Border and Dividing a People*. Chapel Hill: University of North Carolina Press, 2015.

Holly, Nathaniel F. "'Living Memorials to the Past': The Preservation of Nikwasi and the 'Disappearance' of North Carolina's Cherokees." *North Carolina Historical Review* 92, no. 3 (July 2015): 312–337.

Holton, Woody. *Forced Founders: Indians, Debtors, Slaves, and the Making of the American Revolution in Virginia*. Chapel Hill: University of North Carolina Press, 1999.

Horsman, Reginald. "The Indian Policy of an 'Empire for Liberty.'" In *Native Americans and the Early Republic*, edited by Frederick E. Hoxie, Ronald Hoffman, and Peter J. Albert, 37–61. Charlottesville: University Press of Virginia, 1999.

Howe, Daniel Walker. *What Hath God Wrought: The Transformation of America, 1815–1848*. New York: Oxford University Press, 2007.

Hoxie, Frederick E. "Retrieving the Red Continent: Settler Colonialism and the History of American Indians in the US." *Ethnic and Racial Studies* 31, no. 6 (Sept. 2008): 1153–1167.

Hudson, Angela Pulley. *Creek Paths and Federal Roads: Indians, Settlers, and Slaves and the Making of the American South*. Chapel Hill: University of North Carolina Press, 2010.

Hudson, Charles. *The Southeastern Indians*. Knoxville: University of Tennessee Press, 1976.

Huston, Reeve. "Land Conflict and Land Policy in the United States, 1785–1841." In *The World of the Revolutionary American Republic: Land, Labor, and the Conflict for a Continent*, edited by Andrew Shankman, 324–345. New York: Routledge, 2014.

Ivison, Duncan. "The Normative Force of the Past." Afterword to *Native Claims: Indigenous Law against Empire, 1500–1920*, edited by Saliha Belmessous, 248–258. New York: Oxford University Press, 2011.

Jennings, Francis. *The Ambiguous Iroquois Empire: The Covenant Chain Confederation of Indian Tribes with English Colonies from Its Beginning to the Lancaster Treaty of 1744*. New York: Norton, 1984.

Johnson, Benjamin H., and Andrew R. Graybill. "Borders and Their Historians in North America." Introduction to *Bridging National Borders in North America: Transnational and Comparative Histories*, edited by Benjamin H. Johnson and Andrew R. Graybill, 1–29. Durham, NC: Duke University Press, 2010.

Johnson, Walter. *River of Dark Dreams: Slavery and Empire in the Cotton Kingdom*. Cambridge, MA: Belknap Press of Harvard University Press, 2013.

Jones, Dorothy V. *License for Empire: Colonialism by Treaty in Early America*. Chicago: University of Chicago Press, 1982.

Journal of the House of Representatives of the State of Tennessee, Begun and Held at Knoxville, on Saturday, the Thirtieth Day of July, One Thousand Seven Hundred and Ninety Six. 1796. Reprint, Nashville: McKennie and Brown, 1852.

Journal of the Proceedings of a Convention Began and Held at Knoxville, January 11, 1796. 1796. Reprint, Nashville: McKennie and Brown, 1852.

Journals of the Senate and House of the General Assembly of the State of Tennessee Held at Knoxville: First Session: Monday, September 18, 1797; Second Session: Monday, December 3, 1798. Kingsport, TN: Southern Publishers, 1933.

Jurgelski, William Martin. "A New Plow in Old Ground: Cherokees, Whites, and Land in Western North Carolina, 1819–1829." PhD diss., University of Georgia, 2004.

Juricek, John T. *Endgame for Empire: British-Creek Relations in Georgia and Vicinity, 1763–1776*. Gainesville: University Press of Florida, 2015.

Kaminsky, Jane. *The Exchange Artist: A Tale of High-Flying Speculation and America's First Banking Collapse*. New York: Viking, 2008.

Kanon, Tom. "The Kidnapping of Martha Crawley and Settler-Indian Relations prior to the War of 1812." *Tennessee Historical Quarterly* 64, no. 1 (Spring 2005): 2–23.

Kappler, Charles, ed. *Indian Treaties, 1778–1883*. 1904. Reprint, Mattituck, NY: Amereon House, 1972.

Keith, Alice Barnwell., ed. *The John Gray Blount Papers*. Vol. 1, 1764–1789. Raleigh, NC: State Department of Archives and History, 1952.

———. *The John Gray Blount Papers*. Vol. 2, 1790–1795. Raleigh, NC: State Department of Archives and History, 1959.

Keith, Zachary. "Tennessee's Indigenous Geography." MA thesis, Middle Tennessee State University, 2020.

Kelley, Lucas P. "Like a Herd of Cattle Terrified by the Scream of a Panther: White Panic, Phantom Uprisings, and the Disfranchisement of Free Men of Color in Antebellum North Carolina." *North Carolina Historical Review* 99, no. 2 (Apr. 2022): 162–191.

Kelley, Paul L. *Historic Fort Loudoun*. Vonore, TN: Fort Loudoun Association, 1958.

Kelton, Paul. "The British and Indian War: Cherokee Power and the Fate of Empire in North America." *William and Mary Quarterly* 69, no. 4 (Oct. 2012): 763–792.

——. *Cherokee Medicine, Colonial Germs: An Indigenous Nation's Fight against Smallpox, 1518–1824*. Norman: University of Oklahoma Press, 2015.

King, Duane H. "Long Island of the Holston: Sacred Cherokee Ground." *Journal of Cherokee Studies* 1 (Fall 1976): 113–127.

Kinnaird, Lawrence, ed. *Spain in the Mississippi Valley*. Vol. 4. Washington, DC: Government Printing Office, 1946.

Kokomoor, Kevin. "Creeks, Federalists, and the Idea of Coexistence in the Early Republic." *Journal of Southern History* 81, no. 4 (Nov. 2015): 803–842.

Kramer, Paul A. "Power and Connection: Imperial Histories of the United States in the World." *American Historical Review* 116, no. 5 (Dec. 2011): 1348–1391.

Lakomäki, Sami. *Gathering Together: The Shawnee People through Diaspora and Nationhood, 1600–1870*. New Haven, CT: Yale University Press, 2014.

——. "'Our Line': The Shawnees, the United States, and Competing Borders on the Great Lakes 'Borderlands,' 1795–1832." *Journal of the Early Republic* 34, no. 4 (Winter 2014): 597–624.

Larson, John Lauritz. *Internal Improvement: National Public Works and the Promise of Popular Government in the Early United States*. Chapel Hill: University of North Carolina Press, 2001.

——. *Laid Waste! The Culture of Exploitation in Early America*. Philadelphia: University of Pennsylvania Press, 2020.

——. "'Wisdom Enough to Improve Them': Government, Liberty, and Inland Waterways in the Rising American Empire." In *Launching the "Extended Republic": The Federalist Era*, edited by Ronald Hoffman and Peter J. Albert, 223–248. Charlottesville: University Press of Virginia, 1996.

Leach, Douglas Edward. "John Gordon of Gordon's Ferry." *Tennessee Historical Quarterly* 18, no. 4 (Dec. 1959): 322–344.

Lee, Robert. "The Indian Boundary Line and the Imperialization of U.S.-Indian Affairs." In *The Early Imperial Republic: From the American Revolution to the U.S.-Mexican War*, edited by Michael A. Blaakman, Emily Conroy-Krutz, and Noelani Arista, 27–44. Philadelphia: University of Pennsylvania Press, 2023.

Leroy, Justin. "Black History in Occupied Territory: On the Entanglements of Slavery and Settler Colonialism." *Theory and Event* 19, no. 4 (2016).

Lewandoski, Julia. "An Empire of Indian Titles: Private Land Claims in Early American Louisiana, 1803–40." In *The Early Imperial Republic: From the American Revolution to the U.S.-Mexican War*, edited by Michael A. Blaakman, Emily Conroy-Krutz, and Noelani Arista, 100–117. Philadelphia: University of Pennsylvania Press, 2023.

Lindley, Jacob, Joseph Moore, and Oliver Paxson. "Expedition to Detroit, 1793." In *Historical Collections: Collections and Researches Made by the Michigan Pioneer and Historical Society, including Reports of Officers and Papers Read at the Annual Meeting of 1890*. Vol. 17, edited by M. Agnes Burton, 565–671. Lansing, MI: Wynkoop Hallenbeck Crawford, 1910.

Louis-Philippe. *Diary of My Travels in America*. Translated by Stephen Becker. New York: Delacorte Press, 1977.

Lowery, Malinda Maynor. *The Lumbee Indians: An American Struggle*. Chapel Hill: University of North Carolina Press, 2018.

Lowrie, Walter, ed. *American State Papers: Documents, Legislative and Executive, of the United States, in Relation to the Public Lands*. 2 vols. Washington, DC: Gales and Seaton, 1834.

Lowrie, Walter, and Walter S. Franklin, eds. *American State Papers: Documents, Legislative and Executive, of the United States*. Class II: Indian Affairs. 2 vols. Washington, DC: Gales and Seaton, 1834.

Mack, Dustin J. "Chickasaws' Place-World: The Mississippi River in Chickasaw History and Geography." *Native South* 11 (2018): 1–28.

Maclay, William. *Journal of William Maclay: United States Senator from Pennsylvania, 1789–1791*. Edited by Edgar S. Maclay. New York: D. Appleton, 1898.

MacMillan, Ken. *Sovereignty and Possession in the English New World: The Legal Foundations of Empire, 1576–1640*. Cambridge: Cambridge University Press, 2006.

Malone, Henry Thomas. *Cherokees of the Old South: A People in Transition*. Athens: University of Georgia Press, 1956.

———. "Return Jonathan Meigs: Indian Agent Extraordinary." *East Tennessee Historical Society's Publications* 28, (1956): 3–22.

Marshall, Paul. "The True Route of the Natchez Trace: The Rectification of a Topographical Error." *Tennessee Historical Magazine* 1, no. 3 (Sept. 1915): 173–182.

Marshall, Stuart H. "Facing East from Tryon Mountain: New Vantages on the 'Great Wolf,' Rogues, and Regulators." *North Carolina Historical Review* 99, no. 1 (Jan. 2022): 1–35.

Masterson, William H., ed. *The John Gray Blount Papers*. Vol. 3, 1796–1802. Raleigh, NC: State Department of Archives and History, 1965.

———. *William Blount*. Baton Rouge: Louisiana State University Press, 1954.

Mapp, Paul W. *The Elusive West and the Contest for Empire, 1713–1763*. Chapel Hill: University of North Carolina Press, 2011.

McClinton, Rowena, ed. *The Moravian Springplace Mission to the Cherokees*. Vol. 1. Lincoln: University of Nebraska Press, 2007.

McDonnell, Michael A. *Masters of Empire: Great Lakes Indians and the Making of America*. New York: Hill and Wang, 2015.

McLoughlin, William G. *Cherokee Renascence in the New Republic*. Princeton, NJ: Princeton University Press, 1986.

———. "Experiment in Cherokee Citizenship, 1817–1829." *American Quarterly* 33, no. 1 (Spring 1981): 3–25.

McRae, Sherwin, ed. *Calendar of Virginia State Papers and Other Manuscripts*. Vol. 6. Richmond, 1886.

Melton, Buckner F., Jr. *The First Impeachment: The Constitution's Framers and the Case of Senator William Blount*. Macon, GA: Mercer University Press, 1998.

Merrell, James H. "Declarations of Independence: Indian-White Relations in the New Nation." In *The American Revolution: Its Character and Limits*, edited by Jack P. Greene, 197–223. New York: New York University Press, 1987.

———. *The Indians' New World: Catawbas and Their Neighbors from European Contact through the Era of Removal*. New York: Norton, 1991.

———. "Second Thoughts on Colonial Historians and American Indians." *William and Mary Quarterly* 69, no. 3 (July 2012): 451–512.

———. "Some Thoughts on Colonial Historians and American Indians." *William and Mary Quarterly* 46, no. 1 (Jan. 1989): 94–119.

Micheaux, F. A. *Travels to the West of the Alleghany Mountains . . . in the Year 1802*. In *Early Western Travels, 1748–1846*. Vol 3, edited by Reuben Gold Thwaites, 107–306. Cleveland: Arthur H. Clark, 1904.

Miles, Tiya. "Beyond a Boundary: Black Lives and the Settler-Native Divide." *William and Mary Quarterly* 76, no. 3 (July 2019): 417–426.

———. *The House on Diamond Hill: A Cherokee Plantation Story*. Chapel Hill: University of North Carolina Press, 2010.

———. "'Showplace of the Cherokee Nation': Race and the Making of a Southern House Museum." *Public Historian* 33, no. 4 (Nov. 2011): 11–34.

———. *Ties That Bind: The Story of an Afro-Cherokee Family in Slavery and Freedom*. Berkeley: University of California Press, 2005.

Miller, Mark Edwin. *Forgotten Tribes: Unrecognized Indians and the Federal Acknowledgement Process*. Lincoln: University of Nebraska Press, 2004.

Miller, Robert J. "The Doctrine of Discovery, Manifest Destiny, and American Indians." In *Why You Can't Teach United States History without American Indians*, edited by Susan Sleeper-Smith, Juliana Barr, Jean M. O'Brien, Nancy Shoemaker, and Scott Manning Stevens, 87–100. Chapel Hill: University of North Carolina Press, 2015.

Miller, Robert J., Jacinta Ruru, Larissa Behrendt, and Tracey Lindberg. *Discovering Indigenous Lands: The Doctrine of Discovery in the English Colonies*. New York: Oxford University Press, 2010.

Mize, Jamie Myers. "Sons of Selu: Masculinity and Gendered Power in Cherokee Society, 1775–1846." PhD diss., University of North Carolina at Greensboro, 2017.

———. "'To Conclude a General Union': Masculinity, the Chickamauga, and Pan-Indian Alliances in the Revolutionary Era." *Ethnohistory* 68, no. 3 (July 2021): 429–448.

Montgomery, James R. "The Nomenclature of the Upper Tennessee River." *East Tennessee Historical Society's Publications* 28 (1956): 46–57.

Mooney, Chase C. *Slavery in Tennessee*. Bloomington: Indiana University Press, 1957.

Morgan, Nancy. "'Fraught with Disastrous Consequences for Our Country': Cherokee Sovereignty, Nullification, and the Sectional Crisis." PhD diss., Temple University, 2015.

Moulton, Gary E., ed. *The Papers of Chief John Ross*. Vol. 1, 1807–1839. Norman: University of Oklahoma Press, 1985.

Muldoon, James. "Discovery, Grant, Charter, Conquest, or Purchase: John Adams on the Legal Basis for English Possession of North America." In *The Many Legalities of Early America*, edited by Christopher Tomlins and Bruce H. Mann, 25–46. Chapel Hill: University of North Carolina Press, 2001.

Murrin, John M. "The Jeffersonian Triumph and American Exceptionalism." *Journal of the Early Republic* 20, no. 1 (Spring 2000): 1–25.

Narrett, David. *Adventurism and Empire: The Struggle for Mastery in the Louisiana-Florida Borderlands, 1762–1803*. Chapel Hill: University of North Carolina Press, 2015.

Nelson, John William. *Muddy Waters: Native Peoples, Chicago's Portage, and the Transformation of a Continent*. Chapel Hill: University of North Carolina Press, 2023.

Nichols, David A. "The Enterprise of War: The Military Economy of the Chickasaw Indians, 1715–1815." *The Native South: New Histories and Enduring Legacies*, edited by Tim Alan Garrison and Greg O'Brien, 33–46. Lincoln: University of Nebraska Press, 2017.

———. *Red Gentlemen and White Savages: Indians, Federalists, and the Search for Order on the American Frontier.* Charlottesville: University of Virginia Press, 2008.

Nooe, F. Evan. *Aggression and Sufferings: Settler Violence, Native Resistance, and the Coalescence of the Old South.* Tuscaloosa: University of Alabama Press, 2024.

Norton, John. *The Journal of Major John Norton, 1816.* Edited by Carl F. Klinck, James J. Talman, and Carl Benn. 1970. Reprint, Toronto: Champlain Society, 2011.

Novak, William J. "The Myth of the 'Weak' American State." *American Historical Review* 113, no. 3 (June 2008): 752–772.

O'Brien, Greg. *Choctaws in a Revolutionary Age, 1750–1830.* Lincoln: University of Nebraska Press, 2002.

———. "Quieting the Ghosts: How the Choctaws and Chickasaws Stopped Fighting." In *The Native South: New Histories and Enduring Legacies,* edited by Tim Alan Garrison and Greg O'Brien, 47–69. Lincoln: University of Nebraska Press, 2017.

O'Brien, Jean M. *Firsting and Lasting: Writing Indians Out of Existence in New England.* Minneapolis: University of Minnesota Press, 2010.

Onuf, Nicholas Greenwood. "Sovereignty: Outline of a Conceptual History." *Alternatives: Global, Local, Political* 16, no. 4 (Oct. 1991): 425–446.

Onuf, Peter S. "'Empire for Liberty': Center and Peripheries in Postcolonial America." In *Negotiated Empires: Centers and Peripheries in the Americas, 1500–1820,* edited by Christine Daniels and Michael V. Kennedy, 301–317. New York: Routledge, 2002.

———. "Imperialism and Nationalism in the Early American Republic." In *Empire's Twin: U.S. Anti-imperialism from the Founding Era to the Age of Terrorism,* edited by Ian Tyrrell and Jay Sexton, 21–40. Ithaca, NY: Cornell University Press, 2015.

———. *Jefferson's Empire: The Language of American Nationhood.* Charlottesville: University Press of Virginia, 2000.

———. *Jefferson and the Virginians: Democracy, Constitutions, and Empire.* Baton Rouge: Louisiana State University Press, 2018.

———. *The Origins of the Federal Republic: Jurisdictional Controversies in the United States, 1775–1787.* Philadelphia: University of Pennsylvania Press, 1983.

———. *Statehood and Union: A History of the Northwest Ordinance,* 2nd ed. [1987] Notre Dame, IN: Notre Dame Press, 2019.

Opal, J. M. *Avenging the People: Andrew Jackson, the Rule of Law, and the American Nation.* New York: Oxford University Press, 2017.

Osburn, Katherine M. B. *Choctaw Resurgence in Mississippi: Race, Class, and Nation Building in the Jim Crow South, 1830–1977.* Lincoln: University of Nebraska Press, 2014.

Ostler, Jeffrey. "Native Americans against Empire and Colonial Rule." In *Empire's Twin: U.S. Anti-imperialism from the Founding Era to the Age of Terrorism,* edited by Ian Tyrrell and Jay Sexton, 41–58. Ithaca, NY: Cornell University Press, 2015.

———. *Surviving Genocide: Native Nations and the United States from the American Revolution to Bleeding Kansas.* New Haven, CT: Yale University Press, 2019.

Owens, Robert M. "'Between Two Fires': Elusive Justice on the Cherokee-Tennessee Frontier, 1796–1814." *American Indian Quarterly* 40, no. 1 (Winter 2016): 38–67.

Pagden, Anthony. "Law, Colonization, Legitimation, and the European Background." In *Cambridge History of Law in America.* Vol. 1, *Early America (1580–1815),* edited by Michael Grossberg and Christopher Tomlins, 1–31. Cambridge: Cambridge University Press, 2008.

Palmer, William P., ed. *Calendar of Virginia State Papers and Other Manuscripts.* Vols. 1, 3, and 4. Richmond, 1875–1884.

The Papers of Benjamin Franklin. Digital Edition. The American Philosophical Society and Yale University. https://franklinpapers.org.

Papers of the War Department, 1784 to 1800. Roy Rosenzweig Center for History and New Media. George Mason University. http://wardepartmentpapers.org.

Parkinson, Robert G. *The Common Cause: Creating Race and Nation in the American Revolution.* Chapel Hill: University of North Carolina Press, 2016.

Pasley, Jeffrey J. "Midget on Horseback: American Indians and the History of the American State." *Commonplace: Journal of Early American Life* 9, no. 1 (Oct. 2008), http://commonplace.online/article/midget-on-horseback.

Paulett, Robert. *An Empire of Small Places: Mapping the Southeastern Anglo-Indian Trade, 1732–1795.* Athens: University of Georgia Press, 2012.

Perdue, Theda. *Cherokee Women: Gender and Culture Change, 1700–1835.* Lincoln: University of Nebraska Press, 1998.

———. *"Mixed Blood" Indians: Racial Construction in the Early South.* Mercer University Lamar Memorial Lectures, no. 45. Athens: University of Georgia Press, 2003.

———. *Slavery and the Evolution of Cherokee Society, 1540–1866.* Knoxville: University of Tennessee Press, 1979.

Perdue, Theda, and Michael D. Green. *The Cherokee Nation and the Trail of Tears.* New York: Viking, 2007.

Persico, V. Richard, Jr. "Early Nineteenth-Century Cherokee Political Organization." In *The Cherokee Indian Nation: A Troubled History*, edited by Duane H. King, 92–109. Knoxville: University of Tennessee Press, 1979.

Pierce, Jason E. *Making the White Man's West: Whiteness and the Creation of the American West.* Boulder: University Press of Colorado, 2016.

Pommersheim, Frank. *Broken Landscape: Indians, Indian Tribes, and the Constitution.* New York: Oxford University Press, 2009.

Powell, William S. *North Carolina through Four Centuries.* Chapel Hill: University of North Carolina Press 1989.

Prucha, Francis Paul. *American Indian Policy in the Formative Years: The Indian Trade and Intercourse Acts, 1780–1834.* Cambridge, MA: Harvard University Press, 1962.

———. *The Great Father: The United States Government and the American Indians.* 2 vols. Lincoln: University of Nebraska Press, 1984.

Raitz, Karl, ed., *The National Road.* Baltimore: Johns Hopkins University Press, 1996.

Ramsey, J. G. M. *The Annals of Tennessee to the End of the Eighteenth Century.* 1853. Reprint, Johnson City, TN: Overmountain Press, 1999.

Rao, Gautham. "The New Historiography of the Early Federal Government: Institutions, Contexts, and the Imperial State." *William and Mary Quarterly* 77, no. 1 (Jan. 2020): 97–128.

Ray, Kristofer. *Cherokee Power: Imperial and Indigenous Geopolitics in the Trans-Appalachian West, 1670–1774.* Norman: University of Oklahoma Press, 2023.

———. "Cherokees and the Franco-British Confrontation in the Tennessee Corridor, 1730–1760." *Native South* 7, no. 1 (2014): 33–67.

———. "Leadership, Loyalty, and Sovereignty in the Revolutionary American Southwest: The State of Franklin as a Test Case." *North Carolina Historical Review* 92, no. 2 (Apr. 2015): 123–144.

———. *Middle Tennessee, 1775–1825: Progress and Popular Democracy on the Southwestern Frontier.* Knoxville: University of Tennessee Press, 2007.

———. "'Our Concerns with Indians Are Now Greatly Extended': Cherokees, Westward Indians, and Interpreting the Quebec Act from the Ohio Valley, 1763–1774." In *Entangling the Quebec Act: Transnational Contexts, Meanings, and Legacies in North America and the British Empire*, edited by Ollivier Hubert and François Furstenberg, 304–334. Montreal: McGill-Queen's University Press, 2020.

———. "Understanding the Tennessee Corridor." Introduction to *Before the Volunteer State: New Thoughts on Early Tennessee, 1540–1800*, edited by Kristofer Ray, ix–xxii. Knoxville: University of Tennessee Press, 2014.

Richter, Daniel K. *The Ordeal of the Longhouse: The Peoples of the Iroquois League in the Era of European Colonization.* Chapel Hill: University of North Carolina Press, 1992.

Richter, Daniel K., and James H. Merrell, eds. *Beyond the Covenant Chain: The Iroquois and Their Neighbors in Indian North America, 1600–1800.* Syracuse, NY: Syracuse University Press, 1987.

Rindfleisch, Bryan C. "The Journal of William Dells: The Many Violences of the Cherokee Expedition of 1776." *Ohio Valley History* 19, no. 4 (Winter 2019): 88–92.

Rivaya-Martínez, Joaquín. "Problematizing Indigenous Borderlands." Introduction to *Indigenous Borderlands: Native Agency, Resilience, and Power in the Americas*, edited by Joaquín Rivaya-Martínez, 1–12. Norman: University of Oklahoma Press, 2023.

Roberts. Alaina E. *I've Been Here All the While: Black Freedom on Native Land.* Philadelphia: University of Pennsylvania Press, 2021.

Roberts, Frances Cabaniss. *The Founding of Alabama: Background and Formative Period in the Great Bend and Madison County.* Edited by Thomas Reidy. Tuscaloosa: University of Alabama Press, 2019.

Rockwell, Stephen J. *Indian Affairs and the Administrative State in the Nineteenth Century.* Cambridge: Cambridge University Press, 2010.

Rodning, Christopher B. "Reconstructing the Coalescence of Cherokee Communities in Southern Appalachia." In *The Transformation of Southeastern Indians, 1540–1760*, edited by Robbie Ethridge and Charles Hudson, 155–175. Jackson: University Press of Mississippi, 2002.

Rohrbough, Malcolm J. *The Land Office Business: The Settlement and Administration of American Public Lands, 1789–1837.* New York: Oxford University Press, 1968.

Roney, Jessica Choppin. "1776, Viewed from the West." *Journal of the Early Republic* 37, no. 4 (Winter 2017): 656–700.

Rothman, Adam. *Slave Country: American Expansion and the Origins of the Deep South.* Cambridge, MA: Harvard University Press, 2005.

Royce, Charles C. "The Cherokee Nation of Indians." In *Fifth Annual Report of the Bureau of American Ethnology*, edited by J. W. Powell, 129–382. Washington, DC: Government Printing Office, 1887.

Sadosky, Leonard J. *Revolutionary Negotiations: Indians, Empires, and Diplomats in the Founding of America.* Charlottesville: University of Virginia Press, 2009.

Saler, Bethel. *The Settlers' Empire: Colonialism and State Formation in America's Old Northwest.* Philadelphia: University of Pennsylvania Press, 2015.

Satz, Ronald N. *Tennessee's Indian Peoples: From White Contact to Removal, 1540–1840.* Knoxville: University of Tennessee Press, 1979.

Saunders, William L., ed. *The Colonial Records of North Carolina.* 10 vols. Raleigh, 1886–1890.

Saunt, Claudio. *Black, White, and Indian: Race and the Unmaking of an American Family.* New York: Oxford University Press, 2005.

———. *Unworthy Republic: The Dispossession of Native Americans and the Road to Indian Territory.* New York: Norton, 2020.

———. *West of the Revolution: An Uncommon History of 1776.* New York: Norton, 2014.

Saxine, Ian. *Properties of Empire: Indians, Colonists, and Land Speculators on the New England Frontier.* New York: New York University Press, 2019.

Sellers, Charles. *James K. Polk.* Vol. 1, *Jacksonian, 1795–1843.* Princeton, NJ: Princeton University Press, 1957.

———. *The Market Revolution: Jacksonian America, 1815–1846.* New York: Oxford University Press, 1991.

Seeley, Samantha. *Race, Removal, and the Right to Remain: Migration and the Making of the United States.* Chapel Hill: University of North Carolina Press, 2021.

Sevier, Cora Bales, and Nancy S. Madden, eds. *Sevier Family History, with the Collected Letters of Gen. John Sevier, First Governor of Tennessee.* Washington, DC: n.p., 1961.

Shankman, Andrew. "Toward a Social History of Federalism: The State and Capitalism to and from the American Revolution." *Journal of the Early Republic* 37, no. 4 (Winter 2017): 615–654.

Sheidley, Nathaniel J. "Hunting and the Politics of Masculinity in Cherokee Treaty-Making, 1763–75." In *Empire and Others: British Encounters with Indigenous Peoples, 1600–1850,* edited by Martin Daunton and Rick Halpern, 167–185. Philadelphia: University of Pennsylvania Press, 1999.

———. "Unruly Men: Indians, Settlers, and the Ethos of Frontier Patriarchy in the Upper Tennessee Watershed, 1763–1815." PhD diss., Princeton University, 1999.

Shire, Laurel Clark. *The Threshold of Manifest Destiny: Gender and National Expansion in Florida.* Philadelphia: University of Pennsylvania Press, 2016.

Shire, Laurel Clark, and Joe Knetsch. "Ambivalence of the Settler Colonial Present: The Legacies of Jacksonian Expansion." *Tennessee Historical Quarterly* 76, no. 3 (Fall 2017): 258–275.

Shoemaker, Nancy. *A Strange Likeness: Becoming Red and White in Eighteenth-Century North America.* New York: Oxford University Press, 2004.

———. "How Indians Got to Be Red." *American Historical Review* (June 1997): 625–644.

A Short Description of the Tennessee Government, or the Territory of the United States South of the River Ohio, to Accompany and Explain a Map of that Country. Philadelphia: Mathew Carey, 1793.

Smalley, Andrea L. "'They Steal Our Deer and Land': Contested Hunting Grounds in the Trans-Appalachian West." *Register of the Kentucky Historical Society* 114, nos. 3/4 (Summer/Autumn 2016): 303–339.

Smallwood, Stephanie. "Reflections on Settler Colonialism, the Hemispheric Americas, and Chattel Slavery." *William and Mary Quarterly* 76, no. 3 (July 2019): 407–416.

Smith, Betty Anderson. "Distribution of Eighteenth-Century Cherokee Settlements." In *The Cherokee Indian Nation: A Troubled History,* edited by Duane H. King, 46–60. Knoxville: University of Tennessee Press, 1979.

Smith, Sam B., Harriet Chappell Owsley, Harold D. Moser, Sharon Macpherson, David R. Hoth, George H. Hoemann, Daniel Feller, Laura-Eve Moss, Thomas Coens, and Erik B. Alexander, eds. *The Papers of Andrew Jackson.* 11 vols. Knoxville: University of Tennessee Press, 1980–.

Smith, Samuel D., ed. *Fort Southwest Point Archaeological Site, Kingston, Tennessee: A Multidisciplinary Interpretation*. Tennessee Department of Environment and Conservation, Division of Archaeology, Research Series No. 9. Nashville: Tennessee Division of Archaeology, 1993.

Smithers, Gregory D. *The Cherokee Diaspora: An Indigenous History of Migration, Resettlement, and Identity*. New Haven, CT: Yale University Press, 2015.

———. *Native Southerners: Indigenous History from Origins to Removal*. Norman: University of Oklahoma Press, 2019.

Snyder, Christina. *Great Crossings: Indians, Settlers, and Slaves in the Age of Jackson*. New York: Oxford University Press, 2017.

———. *Slavery in Indian Country: The Changing Face of Captivity in Early America*. Cambridge, MA: Harvard University Press, 2010.

Southerland, Henry deLeon, Jr., and Jerry Elijah Brown. *The Federal Road through Georgia, the Creek Nation, and Alabama, 1806–1836*. Tuscaloosa: University of Alabama Press, 1989.

Steele, Brian, and Peter S. Onuf. "The South in the Revolutionary Era and Early Republic." In *Reinterpreting Southern Histories: Essays in Historiography*, edited by Craig Thompson Friend and Lorri Glover, 72–98. Baton Route: Louisiana State University Press, 2020.

St. Jean, Wendy. "How the Chickasaws Saved the Cumberland Settlement in the 1790s." *Tennessee Historical Quarterly* 68, no. 1 (Spring 2009): 2–19.

St. John, Rachel. "State Power in the West in the Early American Republic." *Journal of the Early Republic* 38, no. 1 (Spring 2018): 87–94.

Stewart, Austin. "Wielding the Power of Mapping: Cherokee Territoriality, Anglo-American Surveying, and the Creation of Borders in the Early Nineteenth-Century West." *Transactions of the American Philosophical Society* 100, part 4 (2021): 71–92.

Stremlau, Rose. *Sustaining the Cherokee Family: Kinship and Allotment of an Indigenous Nation*. Chapel Hill: University of North Carolina Press, 2011.

Stremlau, Rose, Malinda Lowery, and Julie L. Reed. "Interconnected Histories of Enslavement and Settler Colonialism." *American Historical Review* 127, no. 4 (Dec. 2022): 1799–1805.

Strickland, Rennard. *Fire and the Spirits: Cherokee Law from Clan to Court*. Norman: University of Oklahoma Press, 1975.

Sturtevant, William C. "The Cherokee Frontiers, the French Revolution, and William Augustus Bowles." In *The Cherokee Indian Nation: A Troubled History*, edited by Duane H. King, 61–91. Knoxville: University of Tennessee Press, 1979.

Taylor, Alan. *American Revolutions: A Continental History, 1750–1804*. New York: Norton, 2016.

———. *The Divided Ground: Indians, Settlers, and the Northern Borderland of the American Revolution*. New York: Knopf, 2006.

———. *Liberty Men and Great Proprietors: The Revolutionary Settlement on the Maine Frontier*. Chapel Hill: University of North Carolina Press, 1990.

———. "The War of 1812 and the Struggle for a Continent." In *The World of the Revolutionary American Republic: Land, Labor, and the Conflict for a Continent*, edited by Andrew Shankman, 246–267. New York: Routledge, 2014.

Taylor, Jessica Lauren. *Plain Paths and Dividing Lines: Navigating Native Land and Water in the Seventeenth-Century Chesapeake*. Charlottesville: University of Virginia Press, 2023.

Toomey, Michael. "Prelude to Statehood: The Southwest Territory, 1790–1796." PhD diss., University of Tennessee at Knoxville, 1991.

Tortora, Daniel J. *Carolina in Crisis: Cherokees, Colonists, and Slaves in the American Southeast, 1756–1763*. Chapel Hill: University of North Carolina Press, 2015.

Twohig, Dorothy, Mark A. Mastromarino, Jack D. Warren, Robert F. Haggard, Christine S. Patrick, John C. Pinheiro, David R. Hoth, Carol S. Ebel, William M. Ferraro, and Adrina Garbooshian-Huggins, eds. *The Papers of George Washington: Presidential Series*. 21 vols. Charlottesville: University Press of Virginia, 1987–2020.

Usner, Daniel H. "Iroquois Livelihood and Jeffersonian Agrarianism: Reaching Behind the Models and Metaphors." In *Native Americans and the Early Republic*, edited by Frederick E. Hoxie, Ronald Hoffman, and Peter J. Albert, 200–225. Charlottesville: University Press of Virginia, 1999.

———. "'A Savage Feast They Made of It': John Adams and the Paradoxical Origins of Federal Indian Policy." *Journal of the Early Republic* 33, no. 4 (Winter 2013): 607–641.

US Congress. *Annals of the Congress*. 4th Cong., 1st sess.

———. *Annals of the Congress*, 5th Cong., 2nd sess.

———. *Acts of the Fifth Congress of the United States*.

———. *Journal of the House of Representatives of the United States, Being the First Session of the Fourth Congress: Begun and Held at the City of Philadelphia, December 7, 1795*. Washington: D.C.: Gales and Seaton, 1826.

———. *Journal of the House of Representatives of the United States, Being the First Session of the Fifth Congress: Begun and Held at the City of Philadelphia, May 15, 1797*. Washington: D.C.: Gales and Seaton, 1826.

Van Atta, John R. *Securing the West: Politics, Public Lands, and the Fate of the Old Republic, 1785–1850*. Baltimore: Johns Hopkins University Press, 2014.

Vaughan, Alden T., ed. *Early American Indian Documents: Treaties and Laws, 1607–1789*. Vol. 5, *Virginia Treaties, 1723–1775*, edited by W. Stitt Robinson. Bethesda, MD: University Publications of America, 1983.

———, ed. *Early American Indian Documents: Treaties and Laws, 1607–1789*. Vol. 14, *North and South Carolina Treaties, 1756–1775*, edited by W. Stitt Robinson. Bethesda, MD: University Publications of America, 2003.

———, ed. *Early American Indian Documents: Treaties and Laws, 1607–1789*. Vol. 18, *Revolution and Confederation*, edited by Colin G. Calloway. Bethesda, MD: University Publications of America, 1994.

Wagstaff, H. M., ed. *The Papers of John Steele*. Vol. 1. Raleigh, NC: Edwards and Broughton, 1924.

Wainwright, James Eyre. "Both Native South and Deep South: The Native Transformation of the Gulf South Borderlands, 1770–1835." PhD diss., Rice University, 2013.

Wallace, Anthony F. C. *Jefferson and the Indians: The Tragic Fate of the First Americans*. Cambridge, MA: Belknap Press of Harvard University Press, 1999.

Wallace, Jessica Lynn. "More than 'Strangers to Each Others Persons & Manners': Overhill Cherokees and Fort Loudoun." *Native South* 12 (2020): 120–157.

Waselkov, Gregory A. *A Conquering Spirit: Fort Mims and the Redstick War of 1813–1814*. Tuscaloosa: University of Alabama Press, 2006.

Washburn, Jeffrey. "Directing Their Own Change: Chickasaw Economic Transformation and the Civilization Plan, 1750s–1830s." *Native South* 13 (2020), 94–119.

———. "'Labor in the Field Is Much Changed': The Chickasaws and the Civilization Plan, 1790–1837." PhD diss., University of Mississippi, 2020.

Watson, Harry L. *Liberty and Power: The Politics of Jacksonian America*, 2nd ed. New York: Hill and Wang, 2006.

Weeks, Charles A. "Of Rattlesnakes, Wolves, and Tigers: A Harangue at the Chickasaw Bluffs." *William and Mary Quarterly* 67, no. 3 (July 2010): 487–518.

———. *Paths to a Middle Ground: The Diplomacy of Natchez, Boukfouka, Nogales, and San Fernando de Las Barrancas, 1791–1795*. Tuscaloosa: University of Alabama Press, 2005.

Weaver, Jace. *The Red Atlantic: American Indigenes and the Making of the Modern World, 1000–1927*. Chapel Hill: University of North Carolina Press, 2014.

West, Cane. "'They Have Exercised Every Art': Ecological Rhetoric, a War of Maps, and Cherokee Sovereignty in the Arkansas Valley, 1812–1828." *Journal of the Early Republic* 40, no. 2 (Summer 2020): 297–327.

Whitaker, A. P. "The Muscle Shoals Speculation, 1783–1789." *Mississippi Valley Historical Review* 13, no. 3 (Dec. 1926): 365–386.

White, Richard. "The Fictions of Patriarchy: Indians and Whites in the Early Republic." In *Native Americans and the Early Republic*, edited by Frederick E. Hoxie, Ronald Hoffman, and Peter J. Albert, 62–84. Charlottesville: University Press of Virginia, 1999.

———. *The Middle Ground: Indians, Empires, and Republics in the Great Lakes Region, 1650–1815*. Cambridge: Cambridge University Press, 1991.

White, Robert H., ed. *Messages of the Governors of the State of Tennessee*. Vol 1. Nashville: Tennessee Historical Commission, 1952.

Wilkins, Thurman. *Cherokee Tragedy: The Ridge Family and the Decimation of a People*, 2nd ed. Norman: University of Oklahoma Press, 1989.

Williams, Samuel C. *History of the Lost State of Franklin*. Johnson City, TN: Watauga Press, 1924.

Witgen, Michael. *An Infinity of Nations: How the Native New World Shaped Early North America*. Philadelphia: University of Pennsylvania Press, 2012.

———. "A Nation of Settlers: The Early American Republic and the Colonization of the Northwest Territory." *William and Mary Quarterly* 76, no. 3 (July 2019): 391–398.

———. "Rethinking Colonial History as Continental History." *William and Mary Quarterly* 69, no. 3 (July 2012): 527–530.

Works Progress Administration. *Grainger County, Tennessee, Court Minutes*. Vol. 1, 1796–1802. Nashville: Historical Records Survey, 1937.

———. *Tennessee, Records of Marion County, Deed Book Volume A of A & B, 1819–1830*. [1938] Signal Mountain, TN: Mountain Press, n.d.

Worth, John E. "Enigmatic Origins: On the Yuchi of the Contact Era." In *Yuchi Indian Histories before the Removal Era*, edited by Jason Baird Jackson, 33–41. Lincoln: University of Nebraska Press, 2012.

Wright, J. Leitch, Jr., *William Augustus Bowles: Director General of the Creek Nation*. Athens: University of Georgia Press, 1967.

Yarborough, Fay A. *Race and the Cherokee Nation: Sovereignty in the Nineteenth Century*. Philadelphia: University of Pennsylvania Press, 2008.

Index

Italicized page numbers refer to illustrations.

The manufacturer's authorized representative in the EU for
product safety is Mare Nostrum Group B.V., Mauritskade 21D,
1091 GC Amsterdam, The Netherlands
email: gpsr@mare-nostrum.co.uk

THE VIRTUOUS WEHRMACHT

THE VIRTUOUS WEHRMACHT

CRAFTING THE MYTH OF THE GERMAN SOLDIER ON THE EASTERN FRONT, 1941–1944

DAVID A. HARRISVILLE

CORNELL UNIVERSITY PRESS
Ithaca and London

First published 2020 by Cornell University Press

Library of Congress Cataloging-in-Publication Data

Names: Harrisville, David A., author.
Title: The virtuous Wehrmacht : crafting the myth of the German soldier on the Eastern Front, 1941–1944 / by David A. Harrisville.
Description: Ithaca [New York] : Cornell University Press, 2021. | Series: Battlegrounds: Cornell studies in military history | Includes bibliographical references and index.
Identifiers: LCCN 2021008205 (print) | LCCN 2021008206 (ebook) | ISBN 9781501760044 (hardcover) | ISBN 9781501760051 (pdf) | ISBN 9781501760068 (epub)
Subjects: LCSH: World War, 1939–1945—Moral and ethical aspects—Germany. | World War, 1939–1945—Atrocities—Moral and ethical aspects—Germany. | Justification (Ethics) | World War, 1939–1945—Campaigns—Eastern Front. | World War, 1939–1945—Campaigns—Soviet Union.
Classification: LCC D744.5.G3 H37 2021 (print) | LCC D744.5.G3 (ebook) | DDC 940.54/217—dc23
LC record available at https://lccn.loc.gov/2021008205
LC ebook record available at https://lccn.loc.gov/2021008206

For my father and my grandfather

In the battle against devilry and malice, against hate and the villainy of the world, we know that we are the champions of a just and moral undertaking.

—"Soldat und Religion," *Mitteilungen für die Truppe*, Nr. 254, January 1945, Bundesarchiv-Militärarchiv RW 4/1176

Contents

ACKNOWLEDGMENTS

This project has received generous support from many sources. A seminar in 2012, under the auspices of the German Historical Institute, introduced me to archival holdings in Germany and the delicate art of deciphering handwriting. A travel grant from the University of Wisconsin–Madison History Department allowed me to conduct preliminary research at the Bundesarchiv-Militärarchiv in Freiburg. This stay was followed by a fellowship at the Hebrew University in Jerusalem, made possible by the George L. Mosse Program in History. During that stay, I was able to gather materials from the Yad Vashem Archives and lay the foundations for the project. Thanks to a 2012–2013 fellowship with the Berlin Program for Advanced German and European Studies, led by Karin Goihl, I was able to undertake extensive archival research in Berlin and Freiburg. I then had the opportunity to attend a Mandel Center for Advanced Holocaust Studies workshop at the United States Holocaust Memorial Museum, chaired by Waitman Beorn, Wendy Lower, and Stephen Tyas. This experience broadened my understanding of Holocaust historiography and introduced me to the museum's extensive collections. After returning to Madison, I began writing this book with support from the UW–Madison History Department, a Mellon-Wisconsin summer fellowship, and a fellowship from the Council for European Studies and the Mellon Foundation. The latter was also made possible by the Graduate School and the Office of the Vice Chancellor for Research and Graduate Education at UW–Madison with funding from the Wisconsin Alumni Research Foundation. A seminar at the German Historical Institute gave me the chance, in 2016, to receive extensive feedback from colleagues. Helpful comments on a revised version were provided by the Society for Military History's Edward M. Coffman Award committee, chaired by Samuel Watson, by whom an earlier manuscript of this book was recognized with an honorable mention in 2017.

Along the way, I have enjoyed the advice and support of numerous fellow scholars. With keen insight and words of encouragement at the right moments, Rudy Koshar helped to nurture this project from its inception, looked over drafts, and offered guidance when I altered my initial plans. Lou Roberts, Laird Boswell, John Hall, and Bill Reese also offered helpful commentary and mentorship. Members of the Digital Humanities Research Network at UW–Madison introduced me to new ways of incorporating digital methods into my work. Waitman Beorn, Gilad Natan, Mark Hornburg, and Nina Janz graciously introduced me to new sources at various points during the project. Everywhere I traveled, I encountered patient archivists, including Gunnar Goehle at the Museumsstiftung Post und Telekommunikation, who took an interest in the project and helped me locate critical materials. Conversations and correspondence with scholars in the United States and Europe have greatly enhanced the quality of my work. Among many others, Dan Diner, Steven Aschheim, Norbert Frei, Thomas Kühne, André Mineau, Oliver Janz, Adam Seipp, Konrad Jarausch, Jeff Rutherford, and David Wildermuth have provided thoughtful feedback and challenged my thinking. Skye Doney graciously looked over the manuscript and provided comments. Special thanks also go to the late Diethelm Prowe who, along with many other wonderful teachers, nurtured my intellectual curiosity and sparked my interest in European history.

I have been fortunate to enjoy the encouragement of friends in Madison and beyond, including Nina Janz, Rachel Gross, Skye Doney, Jessica Plummer, Abby Lewis, and Matt Yokell. My family has also been very supportive throughout the process. My grandfather has always been a model for me of the life of the mind and spent hours correcting my German when I was first learning. My parents—Roy and Mary—and my sister, Kendra, have lent a sympathetic ear during the struggles and triumphs of writing, and my father, himself a long-time scholar from whom I learned the art of writing, provided comments on the final draft.

Finally, I would like to thank Cornell University Press, in particular my editor, Emily Andrew, who took an early interest in the manuscript and provided invaluable advice as she shepherded it through the publication process. I also benefited from the commentary of series editor David Silbey. Alexis Siemon helped me assemble the images and answered my formatting questions. My thanks also go to the three anonymous readers for Cornell who took the time to read through the manuscript and made valuable suggestions.

Animated maps displaying the locations over time of the soldiers studied in this book, which I generated using ArcGIS, will appear on my website: https://www.davidharrisville.com/.

Terms and Abbreviations

AK	Armeekorps: army corps
AOK	Armeeoberkommando: army headquarters
Art.	Artillerie: Artillery
DBO	Divisionsbetreuungsoffizier: officer in charge of ideological indoctrination and recreation
Div.	Division
Feldgend.	Feldgendarmerie: field police
Gen. St.	Generalstab: general staff
GFP	Geheime Feldpolizei: secret military police
Gren.	Grenadier
Hiwi	Hilfswillige: non-German volunteer
Inf.	Infanterie: Infantry
Kp.	Kompanie: Company
Nachr.	Nachrichten: Communications
OKH	Oberkommando des Heeres: High Command of the Army
OKW	Oberkommando der Wehrmacht: High Command of the Wehrmacht
Ortskommandantur	military office in charge of administering a specific area behind the lines
Pi.	Pioniere Engineers
PK	Propagandakompanie: propaganda company
Pz.	Panzer: armored
Pz.Jg.	Panzerjäger: anti-tank
Rgt.	Regiment
San.	Sanitäts: medical
WGO	Wehrmachtgräberoffizier: graves officer, in charge of constructing cemeteries
WPr.	Wehrmacht Propaganda Abteilung: Wehrmacht propaganda department
WVW	Wehrmacht Verlustwesen: casualty reporting

Abbreviations for the Administrative Sections (Abteilungen, Abbreviated Abt.) within Each Unit

Ia	Führungsabteilung: operational leadership
Ib	Qu./OQu Quartiermeister/Oberquartiermeister: quartermaster
Ic	Feindnachrichtenabteilung: intelligence, recreation, ideological indoctrination (till 1942)
Ic/A.O.	Feindnachrichtenwesen u. Abwehroffizier: intelligence and counterintelligence
IIa	Adjutant: personnel officer (for officers)
IIb	Adjutant: personnel officer (for enlisted men)
III	Gericht: military justice
IVa	Intendant: administrative officer
IVb	Arzt: medical
IVc	Vetrinär: vetrinarian
IVd(e)	Geistlicher, evangelisch: Protestant chaplain
IVd(k)	Geistlicher, katholisch: Catholic chaplain
V	Kraftfahroffizier: officer in charge of vehicles and transportation
VI	Nationalsozialistische Führungsoffizier: Nazi leadership officer, in charge of ideological indoctrination (established at the end of 1943)
VII	Chef der Zivilverwaltung: head of civilian administration

THE VIRTUOUS WEHRMACHT

Introduction

Toward a Moral History of the Wehrmacht
in the War of Extermination

On June 22, 1941, more than three million troops of the Wehrmacht—the German military—flooded into the Soviet Union in the largest military operation in modern history.[1] Over the next four years, the war they waged would claim more than twenty-six million Soviet lives and ultimately seal the fate of Adolf Hitler's Third Reich.[2] The conflict on the Eastern Front differed from other modern wars not only in its vast scope but also in the genocidal intentions that propelled it. As Nazi officials and military leaders informed their troops, the purpose of the invasion—code-named "Operation Barbarossa"—was to exterminate "Jewish-Bolshevism" and secure *Lebensraum*, or living space, for the German people, who would rule over what remained of the "subhuman" Slavic population.

The ordinary men who carried out this mission reacted to their participation in diverse ways. Among them was Heinz Sartorio.[3] A twenty-seven-year-old insurance salesman from Berlin, Sartorio operated just behind the lines as a private in a bridge-building unit in the center of the front. An avid reader of Joseph Goebbels' newspaper *Das Reich* and, like most soldiers, an admirer of the Führer, Sartorio found himself in harmony with most aspects of the Nazi creed. He largely agreed with Goebbels' assertion that his Red opponents were "animals."[4] He displayed a distrust of Soviet civilians, paired with a hatred for partisans, whom he portrayed as criminals and "vermin."[5] In a chilling expression of approval for the Final Solution, he wrote his sister Elly that "in order

1

to finally bring the world calm and peace, hundreds of thousands of Jews have been executed" in the Soviet Union.[6]

In contrast to Sartorio, the twenty-two-year-old Eugen Altrogge, a Catholic from the Rhineland who had entered the Wehrmacht after taking his university entrance exam, shied away from ideological justifications for the war. Transferred to the Eastern Front in early 1942, he found himself deep in the Ukraine with Army Group South as a lieutenant and platoon leader in the 190th Infantry Division. In his correspondence with Hans Albring, a friend and fellow soldier, Altrogge adopted a much more sympathetic posture toward the population, whom he considered in many ways more pious and authentic than the invading Germans. He occasionally questioned the methods and intentions of Germany's Nazi leaders but rationalized his participation by asserting that the war would free the peoples of Eastern Europe from communist tyranny and save them from the moral vacuum of atheism.

Although their conceptions of the war differed, Sartorio and Altrogge viewed themselves in a similar light—as decent men who belonged to an honorable institution that was ultimately making the world a better place. Sartorio considered himself an involved family man doing a job that needed to be done in order to secure a shining future for the German *Volk*. While he approved of the ruthless treatment of "racial enemies" like partisans and Jews, he insisted that the Wehrmacht did its best to spare the non-Jewish civilian population and described its treatment of POWs as nothing short of generous. "The whole cultured world has closed ranks in the fight against tyranny and oppression and the final victory can only be on our side, we who fight for freedom and justice," he wrote Elly in 1942, adding that the Germans were "clean angels" in comparison to the Allies.[7] While Sartorio's identity and understanding of the war were heavily colored by his adherence to the Nazi worldview, Altrogge's self-concept revolved around his Christian faith. He prided himself on his ability to cultivate friendly ties with the locals he encountered and envisioned the Wehrmacht as a force for good that would make life better for Eastern Europeans and restore Christianity's place in European culture.

The letters of Sartorio and Altrogge numbered among the forty billion conveyed through the German military's postal service during the war, of which roughly a quarter were written by soldiers.[8] They reveal the differing strategies each man employed to reconcile himself to participation in a war of unprecedented criminality: one centered on adherence to racial ideology, the other grounded in a more traditional, humanistic conception of morality. Their writings provide insight into how *Ostkämpfer* (German soldiers on the Eastern Front) viewed themselves and their institution. They also provoke questions regarding how they portrayed the criminal campaign to their readers, including millions of recipients on the home front.

Despite spectacular early victories, the campaign ultimately spelled disaster for the invaders and the Third Reich as a whole. Yet, following the conflict's end, the Wehrmacht enjoyed a surprisingly positive reputation among the German public. In contrast to organizations like the Gestapo and SS, the regular army was remembered as an institution that had conducted itself chivalrously, avoided participation in Nazi crimes, and kept a healthy distance from the Hitler regime. Its men were viewed as decent fellows and faithful Christians who had made enormous sacrifices in the battle against an unworthy foe. This view, which has come to be known as the myth of the Wehrmacht's "clean hands," quickly came to dominate German memory of the Second World War and the men who fought it.[9] According to most historians, the myth began in the final moments of the Third Reich when Grand Admiral Karl Dönitz, who had assumed command of Germany's armed forces, declared that although they were compelled to lay down their arms, the country's troops could take comfort in the fact that they fought "honorably."[10] Due to a legal technicality, the International Military Tribunal refrained from designating the army a criminal organization during the 1945–1946 Nuremberg Trials, in contrast to the Gestapo and SS, a development that contributed to the perception that the army had largely retained its innocence. A handful of top commanders were convicted in the main trial and eleven others were found guilty of war crimes during the follow-on "High Command Trial" of 1948–1949. Besides these, few military personnel were ever investigated for wartime atrocities by the Allies or the West German judicial system.[11]

A whitewashed image of the Wehrmacht would remain entrenched in the public imagination over the following decades, centered on memories of the Eastern Front where the majority of soldiers had served. Veterans and veterans' associations rarely admitted wrongdoing.[12] Popular and political culture in East and West Germany depicted the Wehrmacht soldier as a long-suffering victim, either of fascism or totalitarianism. In the West, the figure of the veteran became a critical locus of Cold War politics as the new democratic government devoted itself to the re-integration of former POWs held in Soviet captivity and with American support rebuilt its armed forces to serve as a bulwark against communism. To facilitate these projects, politicians—most notably the country's first chancellor, Konrad Adenauer—worked to sanitize the Wehrmacht's image, a move that was actively supported by a vocal group of former generals eager to clear their names. Beyond political considerations, there was little desire among the public to delve into a critical investigation of the army's past that might uncover unpleasant truths about the country's fathers, brothers, and sons. Moreover, with fully half of Germany's male population having served at one point in the Wehrmacht, condemnation of their wartime actions would have amounted to a condemnation of German society as a whole. The written record, meanwhile, was distorted by the fact that in their widely-read memoirs, prominent Wehrmacht generals omitted any mention of crimes and laid blame for the army's defeats on Hitler's mismanagement. Their claims were reinforced by early histories of the war on both sides of the Atlantic that portrayed the army as a conventional, "apolitical" fighting force whose personnel had never truly embraced Nazism.[13]

It was not until the late 1960s that the first cracks began to appear in the myth. Meticulous research on the part of historians like Manfred Messerschmidt indicated that the army had been much more sympathetic to the regime than previously supposed.[14] In 1978, by revealing that the army had deliberately starved to death over three million Soviet POWs, Christian Streit demonstrated that the Wehrmacht had willingly put the Nazis' racial policy into practice.[15] Over the next decades, scholars made the case that the army's leaders had agreed with the basic outlines of Hitler's murderous agenda.[16] They also showed that the Wehrmacht had helped to lay the groundwork for the genocide of Eastern European Jews and willingly cooperated with the SS to this end.[17] In the meantime, Omer Bartov, Stephen Fritz, and others reexamined the motivations of the rank and file in a series of "bottom-up" histories.[18] Bartov put forth the influential thesis that soldiers had been held together not by social ties but by a shared commitment to the Nazi worldview, the product of relentless indoctrination.

Today, historians recognize the Wehrmacht's campaign in the East as a *Vernichtungskrieg*, or war of extermination, waged by officers and men steeped in Nazi thinking who aggressively carried out Hitler's vision to re-draw the racial map of Europe. Earlier distinctions between the Wehrmacht and the SS have blurred as researchers paint a portrait of an army that played an important supporting role in the Holocaust, committed frequent war crimes in its battles with the Red Army, and pursued a terroristic occupation policy that resulted in the deaths of over fifteen million Soviet civilians.[19] A 1995 traveling exhibition titled "The German Army and Genocide" brought these findings to the German public. Featuring photographs and written records documenting the Wehrmacht's murderous conduct, it became the most-visited and longest-running exhibition in the history of the Federal Republic of Germany. Sparking intense discussions of the country's past and the older generation's entanglement with Nazism, it had a major impact on German public memory, helping to turn the tide against the Wehrmacht myth.[20]

Although there is now overwhelming evidence that the campaign the German army waged in the Soviet Union was criminal, even genocidal, a close examination of their wartime writings suggests that the men in its ranks did not, in fact, consider themselves criminals.[21] Like Sartorio and Altrogge, *Ostkämpfer* typically harbored a much different understanding of themselves, their institution, and the war they were waging. It may seem impossible in hindsight, but many saw themselves as nothing less than upstanding men pursing noble goals. "And now the Germans are here and the people can always see for themselves that the Germans are decent, nice guys," private Wilhelm Moldenhauser told his wife as his unit rolled through Ukraine in the fall of 1941.[22] "Let all of our previous wars be as they may, just or unjust, let them be the machinations of diplomats, one thing however is certain[:] this war against the criminal work of Bolshevism is the battle for a righteous cause," penned Private Franz Siebeler two months later.[23] "We must win, because we fight for the more righteous cause," opined then-captain Willy Hagemann in a 1944 letter home.[24] Such views were not developed in isolation. Wehrmacht commanders, staff officers, and propagandists consistently encouraged their men to view themselves as honorable warriors and tenaciously defended the army's image. On the home front, too, journalists, church leaders, and Nazi officials painted a portrait of the Wehrmacht as a virtuous institution that embodied long-held German values.

The yawning gap between our current understanding of the Wehrmacht's war in the East and the self-perceptions of those who fought it gives rise to the central question of this book: how did men who participated in perhaps the most murderous campaign of the twentieth century maintain this apparent conviction that they were decent, honorable men fighting for a righteous cause against a morally bankrupt enemy? Why didn't they express remorse for their actions, whether during the conflict or in the years afterward? In more pedestrian terms, how did the "bad guys" of the Second World War convince themselves they were the "good guys" and continue to sleep soundly at night?

In order to answer this question, it is first necessary to understand the ideas regarding right and wrong on which soldiers relied as they evaluated their participation. This leads to the second issue that will be examined here: what moral values and value systems were embedded in the Wehrmacht's wartime culture, and how did they shape its institutional discourse, self-image, and behavior? How did these value systems interact with the racial ideology of the Nazi regime, which exercised a powerful influence throughout the Third Reich?

In seeking to understand the self-conception of the German soldier and the nature of his institution through the lens of moral history, this book approaches the story of the Wehrmacht on the Eastern Front from a novel angle. Rather than addressing why soldiers fought or what crimes they committed—important questions that have already been the subject of much scholarly attention—it examines how value systems within the German Army came to be deployed to hinder or advance Nazi goals and what the men who participated in the *Vernichtungskrieg* thought about who they were and what they were doing.[25] Such an approach helps to explain how committed Nazis and non-Nazis alike came to willingly accept their part in the crimes of the Third Reich, now that these have been extensively uncovered.

This issue is of particular importance because wars are fought on a moral plane as well as a physical one, and soldiers who believe themselves to be in the right are much more effective at carrying out their orders than those who struggle with the burdens of conscience. It is of course true that in modern military history each side in a conflict has often claimed the moral high ground and soldiers have frequently been convinced that they fought for a righteous cause.[26] What makes the Wehrmacht such a compelling subject for the study of morality and violence, however, is the fact that its men accomplished this feat while taking part in a campaign of unprecedented savagery that defied all contemporary ethical standards, including their institution's own traditional code of honor. Furthermore, they did so during the Second World War, a conflict in which—perhaps more so than for any other contest in the twentieth century—victory depended on rallying soldiers and civilians alike behind a cause perceived as morally worthy.[27]

In addition to shedding light on the mentalities and identities of ordinary German soldiers, examining the moral history of the war on the Eastern Front adds to our understanding of the nature and behavior of the Wehrmacht as an institution. In particular, it helps to explain why an army that generally adhered to Hitler's vision sometimes strayed from Nazi orthodoxy. Along the way, this approach offers insight into aspects of the Wehrmacht's experience that have been largely overlooked, such as the interplay between the front and the home front—including the extent to which the latter were aware of the army's crimes—religious life, everyday encounters between soldiers and civilians, and practices surrounding death and burial. Beyond the Wehrmacht itself, this book illuminates the relationship between ideology, morality, and identity in the Third Reich, providing insight into how the Nazi state appropriated existing value systems and how Germans oriented their preexisting beliefs toward Nazi goals.[28] Finally, it introduces a new interpretation of the origins of the Wehrmacht myth that proved so influential in shaping the country's collective memory and serves as a useful case study in how perpetrators violate moral boundaries.

Because of their centrality to this study, it is necessary to first explain what is meant by the terms *ideology* and *morality*. Ideology is defined here as a framework for understanding the world with an accompanying program for social and political action. For instance, Nazi ideology—a diffuse combination of Social Darwinist thought, *völkisch* "blood and soil" traditions, extreme nationalism, and hypermasculine ideals—centered on the belief that life was an existential struggle among distinct, and unequal, races. In practice, Nazism sought to form Germans into an insular racial community, win them land and resources, and promote their biological purity. It also called for the suppression of all threats to the "Aryan" master race. These included the competing ideologies of communism, liberalism, and capitalism, as well as "inferior" races, among whom the Jews were considered the most dangerous. Morality may be described as a set of beliefs held by an individual or community prescribing how one should live one's life by delineating between acceptable ("right") and unacceptable ("wrong") conduct and endorsing a set of values—specific principles to live by—to which one should aspire.[29] Traditional morality, considered here through the context of this book, is defined as the set of ideas about right and wrong that were commonly held among Germans in the first half of the twentieth century. These were never sharply defined but were grounded in Judeo-Christian traditions and Enlightenment humanism and codified in German law and international agreements leading up to Nazi rule. Traditional morality stressed the worth of all human life and the inviolability of property; promoted values like justice, compassion, and selflessness; and condemned actions that caused harm to other human beings.[30]

The subjects of morality and ideology have recently come to the fore in Third Reich scholarship. In contrast to their academic predecessors, many of today's historians regard Nazi Germany as a "racial state" in which the regime's ideology permeated every facet of society.[31] Ordinary Germans, so Peter Fritzsche has argued, willingly formed themselves into a *Volksgemeinschaft* ("people's community") that took care of its own and lashed out at racial outsiders.[32] Ideological motives are now frequently cited to explain the behavior of Third Reich perpetrators.[33]

As scholars have delved into the role of racial ideology in the Third Reich, there has also been growing interest in the moral dimensions of Nazism. Many historians now argue that the Nazis were not "amoral" or self-consciously evil. Instead, they constructed their own self-contained ethical system that diverged sharply from Judeo-Christian morality.[34] "Nazi morality," as Claudia Koonz has termed it, was grounded in the belief that since the Aryan race was biologically superior to its counterparts, any action that helped the Aryans in their struggle for existence was good, while anything that hindered them was evil.[35] In order to win the race war, Germans would need to embrace a "re-valuation of all values" by directing kindness toward fellow members of their racial community, pledging loyalty to Adolf Hitler as the leader of this community, and eliminating all feelings of mercy as they annihilated racial enemies. These enemies were defined primarily by their biological essence rather than their actions.

The scholarship on Nazi morality may be divided into two basic approaches. The first, pioneered by Claudia Koonz, has been to study how the Nazis disseminated their ethic to the population—in her view, with great success.[36] Another interpretation, put forward by Raphael Gross, highlights the ways in which the Nazis also redefined, modified, and appropriated existing value systems.[37] Both approaches build from the assumption that Nazism was ultimately incompatible with most other value systems and generally portray the reception of Nazi ideas as a top-down process by which the regime imposed its will on the populace.

When it comes to the question of moral values within the Wehrmacht, many scholars now stress that Nazi ideology came to exercise enormous influence not only over how the army operated in the field but how personnel at all levels of the military hierarchy evaluated the legitimacy of their actions. According to this interpretation, other more traditional sources of moral meaning were largely expunged from the army's culture and replaced with the principles of Nazi morality, whether before or during Barbarossa.[38] Some historians have cautioned that ideology was not all-pervasive and that other moral reference points, including nationalism and martial virtues, still lived on in some form.[39] Others have pointed out that the army's actions were also influenced by pragmatic concerns, as officers sometimes set aside ideological purity for the sake of strategic advantage or—in rarer cases—out of an attachment to older principles of soldierly honor.[40] While these authors have fruitfully uncovered evidence of the persistent influence of such alternative values in the Wehrmacht, they have typically failed to examine these systematically or to clarify their relationship to Nazism, which is still generally recognized as the single most influential value system within the Wehrmacht.[41]

Only one scholar, André Mineau, has put forward a comprehensive theory addressing both the role of traditional morality and that of its Nazi counterpart in the context of the Wehrmacht. In many ways, he argues, the former ended up reinforcing the latter and it was their confluence that produced the necessary conditions for the war of extermination. In his words, "Traditional morality and the notions attached to it contributed to major Nazi undertakings—especially to Barbarossa. . . . Ethics as traditional morality ingrained in German culture was supple enough to accept reorientation from, and provide support to ideology." Although he has provided an indispensable framework for understanding the morality–ideology relationship, Mineau has focused his attention primarily on leadership elements in the Wehrmacht rather than the rank and file, who will be the central objects of this book.[42]

To the extent that they have grappled with the question of how Wehrmacht personnel came to accept their involvement in a criminal enterprise while avoiding any sense of guilt, some researchers have emphasized the role of situational factors, including group dynamics, the compartmentalization of roles, and the pressures of the army's disciplinary system.[43] All of these lessened any sense of personal responsibility and insulated soldiers from cognitive dissonance—the discomfort experienced when one's actions contradict one's values.[44] More often, however, scholars have emphasized the critical role played by Nazi ideology in permitting and affirming barbaric conduct in the Wehrmacht. According to this interpretation, popularized by Omer Bartov, many personnel adopted the Nazi worldview—and the precepts of Nazi morality—to the point where they considered the murder of Jews and Slavs a positive good.[45] As evidence, scholars have pointed to soldiers' battlefield conduct and excerpts from their wartime writings as well as the extensive indoctrination to which they were subject in the Third Reich, including within the Wehrmacht itself. An alternate theory, put forward by Hannes Heer, is that a combination of ideology and wartime experiences created a situation in which soldiers became "amoral," embracing the belief that their actions fell beyond the realm of good and evil.[46] Whether they concern the moral fabric of the Wehrmacht as a whole or the self-conception of individual soldiers, what ties most of the aforementioned lines of inquiry together is the assumption that in order to commit mass atrocities, it was first necessary to abandon the basic moral precepts that had guided German society for centuries.

The impact of racial ideology at all levels of the military hierarchy should not be understated. Embraced by the Wehrmacht's senior leadership and disseminated through an extensive indoctrination program, Nazism enjoyed pride of place as the doctrine around which all servicemen were encouraged to model their thoughts and behavior. Indeed, without ideology Barbarossa—a campaign conceived to destroy Germany's "racial enemies"—would have been unthinkable. In contrast to those studies that portray the Wehrmacht of 1941–1944 as an institution in which the Nazi worldview had achieved monopoly status, however, this book argues that a broad array of more traditional value systems still played a major role in its discourse and actions on the Eastern Front. The relationship between Nazi morality and these value systems was complex. In some cases, they hindered the achievement of the regime's goals. More often, this work ultimately finds, their continued presence would prove more a boon than a detriment to the Nazi cause.

The influence of traditional value systems surfaced in numerous ways. Officers and propagandists emphasized traditional morality in addition to ideology in their wartime rhetoric, including by encouraging their men to view themselves as upstanding warriors, depicting the Soviets as ethically bankrupt, and attempting to convince the enemy population of the invader's honorable intentions. From time to time, decision-makers took tangible steps that reflected the continued impact of older systems of right and wrong, including by adopting conciliatory occupation policies or devoting resources to religious care within the army's ranks. In doing so, the Wehrmacht sometimes deviated from the ideological principles it otherwise followed, but by promoting and instrumentalizing a wide variety of value systems, officers up and down the military hierarchy recognized they could better motivate their men, preserve the army's reputation, and—most importantly, from their point of view—gain a strategic edge. Thus, the continued presence of moral values became a major element in the Wehrmacht's persistent efforts to demonstrate "moral superiority" over its Soviet enemies throughout the conflict. These efforts form a key theme of this book, one that has received little scholarly attention to date.

Although they did little to lessen the brutality of the *Vernichtungskrieg*, the Wehrmacht's efforts to secure the moral high ground had a variety of important effects. They helped to sanitize the army's wartime image. They generated confusion among the army's enemies, who could never be certain if they would be met with terror or civility. Even more importantly, they helped secure the compliance of a broad and diverse body of soldiers: rather than being forced to accept Nazi ideology as the sole legitimate rationale for the invasion and the Wehrmacht's conduct, army personnel were provided with a wide range of officially sanctioned moral options from which to choose as they made sense of their participation. In the end, traditional value systems not only remained influential in the Wehrmacht alongside ideology; their persistence also made the army an even more terrifying and effective fighting force than it might have been had it insisted on total ideological purity, one capable of masking its intentions, pursuing flexible policies, and fostering the conditions in which its men were able to comfortably continue their willing participation.

As their institution strove to win the moral contest as well as the physical one, soldiers developed their own understanding of the conflict's moral dimensions and the role they played in it. Like the organization in which they served, they absorbed elements of Nazi ideology to a high degree. Some even fully completed the transition to the new racial morality, finding in it all the justification they required. However, the rank and file did not so easily cast aside all the lessons of an upbringing that had included strong elements of the Judeo-Christian moral tradition the moment they donned the uniform. Many still remained attached to earlier value systems, including traditional nationalism, military virtues, Christian principles, and middle-class norms. Further, although the trauma of their wartime experiences did have a numbing effect, their writings indicate that they typically still recognized when their conduct fell beyond the pale of civilization and did not simply abandon all notions of right and wrong.

To return to the central question of this book, how did the agents of the *Vernichtungskrieg* hold on to the conviction that they remained upright men championing a just cause? How did they make peace with their role in a war that shocked the civilized world and continue to insist on their innocence even into the postwar period? It will be argued here that it was by relying not only on the framework of Nazi morality but a wide range of traditional moral value systems that troops of all backgrounds and beliefs maintained their sense of personal integrity and continued their willing participation while avoiding feelings of remorse. They relied on these value systems to cultivate and project identities as dutiful family men, selfless comrades, faithful Christians, virtuous heroes, and, ultimately, victims. This "decent" self-image became part of a larger constellation of self-affirming autobiographical narratives they generated through their wartime writings. Through these narratives, soldiers safeguarded the army's reputation, justified the Wehrmacht's crimes, branded the campaign as a worthy mission, and vilified their Soviet opponents. In limited fashion, troops lent an aura of credibility to this self-image on a performative level by putting their words into action—for instance, by handing out candy to children or reopening churches the Soviet regime had shuttered in the effort to demonstrate that they had come as liberators or pious crusaders.

Soldiers' efforts to maintain a sense of moral legitimacy were bolstered by the work of officers and propagandists who did what they could to ensure that as many troops as possible remained comfortable with their wartime roles. As noted above, these employed the language of traditional morality alongside that of Nazism to present soldiers with a wide variety of officially sanctioned justifications for the war, depictions of the enemy, and self-definitions from which to choose. Recognizing that not all soldiers and citizens would be moved by purely ideological arguments, even Hitler and his top officials sometimes followed a similar course by mixing the rhetoric of Nazi morality with appeals to time-honored values. In the face of such ambiguous messaging from their superiors, soldiers were able to work within both Nazi and alternate value systems to freely choose whatever rationalizations or narratives they personally found most compelling.

Whether they constructed their self-image by adopting officially sanctioned ideas or by devising their own, troops' ability to find some sense of moral legitimacy had at least two important ramifications. First, while servicemen who preferred ideological justifications naturally encountered little difficulty in making sense of their participation in the campaign, by relying on more traditional concepts even those who were less attached to Nazism were able to embrace their own role wholeheartedly when they might otherwise have struggled to do so. Second, believing themselves to be upright warriors pursuing noble goals made the Third Reich's uniformed men more effective and more prolific killers, convinced not only of the righteousness of their cause but the horrifying means employed to achieve it.

Efforts to claim the moral high ground, whether by soldiers or the Wehrmacht as a whole, did not merely affect the army's institutional workings or the inner psychology of the men in its ranks, however. They would also have a profound and lasting influence beyond the battlefields of the Eastern Front, and no more so than on public perceptions in the German homeland. This observation leads to the third and final question of this book: where, and how, did the Wehrmacht myth originate?

The approach taken here offers a new answer, one that provides additional insight into the reasons for the myth's popularity and lasting influence in German society. The myth, so this book will prove, was not the postwar creation of generals, politicians, and veterans' associations, as historians have almost universally assumed.[47] Nor did it constitute a retroactive attempt at "whitewashing" in the sense that its advocates were presenting the German public with a new and unfamiliar interpretation of the army's history. Instead, the Wehrmacht myth was first developed and popularized during the war itself. Its chief authors were ordinary soldiers who huddled in bunkers or paused along the march to compose letters to their family and friends in the homeland—some ten billion in all. Through this medium, more powerful than any weapon of the modern battlefield, they fed the public a distorted and self-serving account of their experiences that reflected their own quest for a sense of moral legitimacy. They portrayed themselves as honorable warriors, accused their enemies of irredeemable evil, insisted on the justice of their cause, depicted their institution as a bastion of civilized norms, and rationalized their side's criminal conduct. As prospects for victory faded, they transformed themselves from aggressors into victims. The Wehrmacht's propaganda apparatus contributed to this image by consistently portraying the army in the best possible light in its wartime messaging. So too did officers who took steps to protect their institution's threatened reputation. Whatever their rank, military personnel were not following any deliberate, well-coordinated strategy aimed at producing a legend that might be useful after the war ended; rather, the narratives they crafted represented the sum of countless individual decisions to present audiences in the homeland with a positive image of "their" men and the organization to which they belonged.

Attempts to salvage the army's image were not always successful, especially as the war lengthened and the Wehrmacht became ever more deeply implicated in atrocities on an enormous scale. Still, soldiers' writings had a profound impact on the way the German home front viewed the war and the men who fought it. Already predisposed to trust the accounts of their loved ones more than any other source, members of the public readily accepted the version of events that reached them from the front lines. By the time the conflict ended, the foundations of the Wehrmacht myth had already been laid. Indeed, they were set so deeply that competing narratives put forward by the Allied powers or critical historians had little chance of altering this image—with one notable exception: the denial of any connection between the army and the Nazi regime. The following decades would see only minor embellishments to the myth's core themes.

Although details of prewar and postwar history will also be discussed, the Wehrmacht's experience on the Eastern Front from the start of the invasion in June 1941 to its retreat from Soviet soil in 1944 is the primary object of focus here.[48] The army's honorable image may in fact have dated back even further in time, but it was on the battlefields of the USSR that the bulk of the Third Reich's warriors served, and as a result the Eastern Front became the chief focal point for German postwar memory. This was also where the reputation of the Wehrmacht was most threatened and required the most strident defense. The year 1941 will be given particular emphasis, largely because this was when soldiers formed their first impressions of the conflict and tended to discuss pertinent questions, such as their views of the civilian population, in the most detail.

Methodologically, this book combines the relative strengths of the "top-down" and "bottom-up" schools of Wehrmacht historiography while offering the chance to draw broader conclusions about the nature of the Wehrmacht than would be possible with a case study focusing on a single unit. The project centers on a core sample of letters, as well as several diaries, written by Wehrmacht troops in the lower ranks who served in a variety of capacities across every sector of the Eastern Front, primarily front-line infantry divisions. Soldiers' wartime writings have the advantage of revealing their authors' reactions to their experiences at the time they occurred, in contrast to postwar recollections. The latter also suffer from the defects of memory and a tendency to leave out any incriminating details.

Whereas many bottom-up studies of life at the front rely exclusively on sources from the soldiers themselves, this analysis supplements personal accounts with a wide range of institutional documents at various levels of the army hierarchy, with particular emphasis on the units to which the men in this sample belonged.[49] These include orders and regulations; the reports of chaplains, intelligence officers, and quartermasters; and propaganda materials, such as newspapers and pamphlets. Such documents provide context for the letters by illuminating such factors as the strategic and tactical situation, the policies different formations pursued, and the mood of the local population as interpreted by the occupiers. They also highlight the army's efforts to safeguard its reputation and win the moral war against its Soviet enemies.

A third set of sources derives from the German home front. Most histories of the Wehrmacht—and most military histories in general—treat the army in isolation. This book considers it as one participant in a larger wartime discourse that involved the Nazi regime, the press, a variety of institutions, and the German public. A diverse set of materials has been used to tell this side of the story. Among them are the records of the Nazi Party and the Propaganda Ministry, books and newspaper articles, and church records. These documents help to explain how Germans outside the Wehrmacht perceived the nation's soldiers and influenced their behavior.

Most of the letters and diaries in this book derive from the *Museumsstiftung Post und Telekommunikation*, a foundation of the *Museum für Kommunikation* in Berlin. This collection, begun in 1995, now houses nearly 100,000 letters sent to or from soldiers from the eighteenth through the twentieth centuries, along with biographical details about their authors. Many of these were donated by families across Germany since the early 2000s and have not yet been examined by scholars. This book also makes use of letters housed at the *Bundesarchiv-Militärarchiv* in Freiburg im Breisgau, as well as several published correspondences. Aside from the novelty of many of the letters used here, what sets them apart from those often cited by previous scholars is that they were accessible in series, rather than in excerpted form or as single letters.[50] For each soldier in this book, between one hundred and five hundred letters were typically available. Examining multiple letters by a single individual allows for a much deeper understanding of his personality, background, worldview, and how his views evolved throughout the war.

The core sample consists of 2,018 letters written by thirty Wehrmacht soldiers from 1941 to 1944. Within the limitations of the available archival record, the men in question were chosen based on several criteria intended to capture the diversity of experiences of those who fought in the Soviet Union. Preference was given to low-ranking soldiers who served in front-line units across all areas of the front, including as infantrymen, artillerymen, and panzer troops. This book also encompasses some men in support capacities—who were numerous in the Wehrmacht—as well as a small number of low-ranking officers. Because their perspective includes critical first impressions of the campaign, troopers who were present at the outset of Barbarossa are highly represented.

In demographic terms, the chosen sample comprises a wide range of social, educational, religious, and geographic backgrounds that accords well with the findings of previous research on the makeup of Wehrmacht divisions.[51] The majority (twenty-two) were young men in their twenties when the invasion started. Five were in their thirties and three in their forties. Most (eighteen) were unmarried. Roughly two-thirds identified as Protestant and one-third as Catholic. They hailed from all corners of Germany, from large cities to backwater villages. The majority had at least some high school education, although only seven attended university. At least nine had prior Nazi affiliations, such as Party or SA membership.[52] They worked in a wide variety of professions, including as salesmen, agricultural workers, apprentices, bankers, and artists. Most could be termed members of the lower-middle class, and few had any substantial wealth. Only eleven would live to see the end of the war, a testament to the mass slaughter that characterized the Eastern Front.[53]

Since letters from the home front to the front were only extant in a few cases, this book concentrates primarily on messages from the soldiers themselves, while keeping in mind the importance of audience.[54] The diaries of four of the letter-writers were also examined, as well as the diaries of three men whose letters were not available.[55] Their inclusion provides a means to verify whether soldiers' private writings harmonized with the statements in their correspondence.[56] Due to the sheer size of the Wehrmacht and the number of letters written during the war, this book makes no claim to capture the thoughts and feelings of all German soldiers; instead, it provides a survey of the narrative strategies available to them and the ideas that were prevalent in their ranks. It should also be kept in mind that the vast majority of letters were dominated by mundane topics, such as food and cigarettes, the weather, or family affairs. Still, soldiers did sometimes discuss the subjects of interest here and by aggregating their individual accounts and comparing these findings to other studies of Wehrmacht correspondence it is possible to begin to understand the moral world in which they lived.[57]

A heavy dose of caution is required when dealing with such sources, however. While they are sometimes interpreted as direct windows into precisely what soldiers experienced, thought, or felt, such an uncritical approach runs the risk of overlooking the many factors that call into question the completeness and factual accuracy of troops' reports. To begin with, all letters from the Eastern Front were subject to official censorship by army officers. Censors were charged with detecting violations of military secrecy, defeatist sentiments, and criticism of Germany's leaders.[58] In practice, their impact was limited by several factors. Due to their relatively small numbers, censors managed to survey only a bare fraction of the billions of letters in question. Further, as many scholars have noted, troops habitually ignored censorship rules.[59] Of greater relevance to the present work is the fact that none of the subjects explored here, such as moral values, religion, and even Wehrmacht atrocities, were explicitly subject to censorship. Even so, knowing that their letters could be intercepted by the censors certainly had an impact on how soldiers wrote. Troops tended not to provide detailed descriptions of military operations and shied away from direct criticism of the regime, for instance.

Avoiding topics that might have caught the censors' attention was one form of what historians have characterized as "self-censorship," but there were many other ways in which soldiers deliberately withheld or altered certain details of their experiences. In general, servicemen avoided offending their readers in any way, projected an improbably optimistic outlook, downplayed the dangers of the front, and sidestepped direct accounts of traumatic experiences, among other topics. They did so partly in response to military propaganda that insisted that letters should raise morale in the homeland and also to avoid upsetting their readers or for the sake of their own emotional well-being. When trying to piece together soldiers' experiences from wartime correspondence, historians must be acutely aware of such distortions.

Building on the interpretive framework of Klaus Latzel, who has studied Wehrmacht correspondence extensively, this book approaches letters not as collections of "facts" about what really happened on the Eastern Front but as subjective documents that provide insight into how soldiers constructed their identities and how they presented their experiences to their readers.[60] Letter writing is an act of self-reflection as well as a narrative form—a means by which people tell stories about themselves. Whether these stories are accurate or not, they become part of our biographies, shaping future thoughts and actions.[61] In this way, identity formation on the Eastern Front became bound up with epistolary narration.

Letters are not merely reflections of selfhood, however. While the majority of studies of soldiers' letters overlook the presence of the homeland readership in favor of events at the front, the present inquiry builds on Latzel's "conversational model" by interpreting letters not only as a marker of identity but also a medium through which soldiers filtered their experiences and projected a particular image of themselves and their institution to their readers. Again, this image may not always have corresponded directly with reality, but it profoundly shaped the way millions of German readers at home viewed the war and the men who fought it.

Since the specific topics that will be discussed here were not prohibited by the censors, and because soldiers gave little heed to the censors overall, official censorship does not constitute a major hindrance in the present case. Further, since this book is concerned with questions of perception and presentation—how soldiers whitewashed their image and curated certain aspects of their identities, rather than who they "really" were or what they "really" did—the phenomenon of self-censorship is treated not as a liability but as an opportunity to understand the formation of the Wehrmacht myth. Institutional sources, diaries, and cross-referencing between letters have been used to evaluate the credibility of an individual soldier's claims when this becomes necessary.

This book treats soldiers as moral agents who still retained space to make their own choices although they operated within the constraints of an institution that demanded obedience and conformity. Advances in the field of social psychology have provided the framework employed for understanding how individuals violate their own moral boundaries without experiencing cognitive dissonance.[62] Of particular relevance is Claude Steele's theory of "self-affirmation." This posits that individuals are capable of acting against their values as long as they retain a positive moral self-image overall, such as by committing occasional redemptive acts that confirm the self's fundamental goodness.[63] For insight into questions of morality and warfare, the works of Michael Walzer and others in the field of ethics and legal history have been consulted.[64]

This book is organized into five thematic chapters, each of which explores a different aspect of soldierly self-perceptions that served as a building block of the Wehrmacht myth. The first provides an overview of the Wehrmacht's moral value systems, including both Nazi morality and more traditional values. It examines how the Wehrmacht deployed these values in orders, propaganda, and letters to cast its enemies as both morally and racially unworthy while presenting itself as an honorable institution populated by decent men.

This virtuous image was frequently called into question by the Wehrmacht's own criminal conduct in the USSR. The second chapter explores how German soldiers wrote about atrocities they witnessed or in which they personally took part. It argues that soldiers frequently turned to a series of moral rationalizations, rather than ideology alone, to justify their actions and defend their image to their readers. Together with their superiors, they simultaneously accused their enemies of flagrant breaches of international law.

The role of religion in the Wehrmacht is the subject of the third chapter. It describes how soldiers clad themselves in the mantle of religious piety and, with the backing of the churches and the tacit support of Nazi leaders, framed the war as a crusade against "godless" communism. Soldiers and chaplains paired this rhetoric with a number of dramatic gestures, including the reopening of Soviet churches, which allowed them to imagine themselves as saviors returning religious freedom to a persecuted populace. This endeavor was undermined, however, by ongoing tensions with the Nazi regime and its ideology.

Chapter 4 explores the relationship between the Wehrmacht and the Soviet population. It argues that, even as they enforced a brutal occupation, servicemen cast themselves in the role of liberators who had come to free an oppressed citizenry from the "Bolshevik yoke." This narrative was reinforced by military propaganda, as well as large- and small-scale actions such as opening prisons, handing out food, and providing medical assistance to civilians. The liberation charade provided a sense of noble mission and challenged some aspects of Nazism while legitimating imperialist goals.

The book concludes with a chapter detailing the Wehrmacht's efforts to present itself as a civilized institution through its treatment of the men who fell on the battlefield, in deliberate contrast to enemies it held in contempt for their alleged lack of respect for life and death. Years into the war, however, the narrative of heroic sacrifice was subverted by an emerging focus on victimhood that helped soldiers evade responsibility for their actions.

Neither Sartorio nor Altrogge would survive the war. Like millions of their countrymen, they found their last rest thousands of miles from home. During their years in uniform, the letters they wrote served as their primary connection to the world outside the Eastern Front, a record not only of their experiences in combat but how each man reconciled himself to his part in a war of unprecedented criminality. In death, as in life, their writings would shape the image of the Wehrmacht in Germany and around the world for decades to come.

MAP 1   The Soviet Union, showing the front line as of June 22, 1941.

CHAPTER 1

Honorable Self and Villainous Other

Value Systems in the Wehrmacht

"[There is] a real difference between the regular German soldier and officer and Hitler and his criminal group," General Dwight D. Eisenhower told reporters as he prepared to board a flight at the Frankfurt airport in 1951. "I have come to know that difference. For my part, I do not believe the German soldier, as such, lost his honor. The fact that certain individuals committed, in war, certain dishonorable and despicable acts reflects on the individuals concerned, and not on the great majority of German soldiers and officers."[1] Eisenhower, who had long been critical of the Wehrmacht, made this statement in response to pressure from West German chancellor Konrad Adenauer and a group of former Wehrmacht generals. These men insisted that in order for West Germany to successfully establish a new military that would bolster the NATO alliance—a development long sought by the United States—it was necessary to ensure that the Wehrmacht enjoyed an untarnished public image. A few months later, Adenauer himself declared before the Bundestag—the West German parliament—that the mass of Wehrmacht personnel had retained their honorable status.[2]

The statements by Eisenhower and Adenauer both reflected and strengthened a set of popular assumptions regarding the character of the German soldier and the nature of the institution in which he served that was emerging as a core component of the Wehrmacht myth. Although he had been led astray by Germany's political leadership, so the belief went, the average bearer of the uniform had been a decent fellow at heart, guided not by malice or Nazi ideology but a set of long-established admirable principles. His institution was not a criminal organization but a conventional military firmly committed to its traditional code of honor. This essential portrait of the Wehrmacht and its personnel would be repeated in many different forms over the postwar decades. But where did it originate? If the answer is largely to be found within the wartime writings of Wehrmacht personnel, as this book argues, how did soldiers assess their moral character in their correspondence with the homeland? How did this self-image compare to the postwar myth? What values and value systems did they draw from as they explained to their readers who they were and what their institution stood for? Finally, what was the nature of the relationship between Nazi morality and rival ethical systems in the Wehrmacht, including older traditions of soldierly honor, if the latter indeed continued to exercise an influence in the army's ranks as Eisenhower suggested?

To investigate these questions, this chapter provides an in-depth analysis of the Wehrmacht's value systems, including both older moral traditions and Nazi innovations. It offers a new perspective by focusing not only on their significance for soldiers' motivations but also how ethical principles were deployed on both the institutional and individual levels to construct an "honorable" self-image that eased complicity in the *Vernichtungskrieg* and influenced how the army was viewed by the German public. On the bottom rungs of the army hierarchy, servicemen relied not only on Nazi values but also traditional moral norms to cultivate identities as "decent" men who belonged to a respectable institution.[3] Whether they truly believed these constructs cannot be known for certain, but through the billions of letters they sent home they profoundly shaped how their readers would come to view the men who fought on the Reich's frontiers. The military's upper echelons played a supporting role in this process. By continuing to deploy the language of the army's traditional honor code alongside the new vocabulary of Nazi morality, generals and propagandists from the divisional level to the Supreme Command of the Wehrmacht (*Oberkommando der Wehrmacht*, or OKW) kept up a veneer of legality, cocooned murderous pronouncements in traditional moral argumentation, and encouraged their men to see themselves as upstanding warriors in terms that appealed to a broad range of servicemen including those less devoted to Nazism.[4] As they pursued a variety of rhetorical strategies to emphasize their own decency and preserve the army's reputation, personnel of all ranks continually pointed out the ethical shortcomings of their enemies, who served as a convenient foil for the invader's self-conceptions.

Thanks to the enormous volume of correspondence from the front to the home front, as well as the long reach of the military's propaganda apparatus, the army's wartime rhetoric would successfully establish one of the key narrative building blocks for the Wehrmacht's image in the German public mind—the belief that both the soldier and his institution had retained their honorable and dignified character. There would be only one major alteration to this essential portrait in the postwar period—namely, references to Nazi value systems were quietly expunged from the record, leaving only the memory of the brave and decent soldier.

As it charts the rhetorical construction of decency, this chapter devotes particular attention to exploring the wide range of value systems in the Wehrmacht and their relationship to Nazi morality. It challenges the notion that the military had completely discarded all reference to pre-Nazi norms before or during Barbarossa and demonstrates instead that traditional beliefs about right and wrong continued to impact the army's rhetoric and actions even as the influence of Nazi ideology intensified. Old and new value systems sometimes found themselves in tension, as when officers issued strict orders for soldiers to conduct themselves in upright fashion vis-à-vis non-Aryan civilians, or when some of their men preferred to see themselves as fighting for the German nation rather than the Führer. At least as often, however, traditional morality, in the myriad forms it took, became a stepping stone by which troops came to adopt Nazi morality or at least to accept Nazi aims.[5] As this book argues more generally, it was precisely the military's ability to maintain at least the trappings of legality, to give lip service to older virtues like honor and upright conduct, and to insist on the moral righteousness of its cause even apart from ideology—in short, to give soldiers and their relatives a reason to believe in their own decency, by whatever standards they defined it—that continued to inspire men of all backgrounds to pursue Nazi goals, goals that seemed all the more appealing when translated into the familiar language of good and evil.[6]

The value systems that exercised a significant influence within the Wehrmacht derived from several principal sources. First and foremost was a cluster of martial virtues that had long enjoyed pride of place not only within the military but German society as a whole.[7] These included love of nation, obedience and loyalty to military superiors and national leaders, duty, bravery, comradeship, and sacrifice. They helped to define what it meant to be a morally worthy soldier and a good man—for the two concepts were deeply intertwined. Military values were enshrined in an honor code that had its roots in the traditions of the Prussian officer corps. Along with the virtues listed above, this code emphasized fairness, self-control, and upright conduct both on and off the battlefield, especially toward noncombatants. It also involved a measure of respect for international agreements, at least those to which Germany was a party.

Along with these, troops who marched into the USSR carried with them a more diffuse set of values that can be categorized under the heading of "bourgeois ethics," since they are strongly associated with the German middle class.[8] These values were bound up with the concepts of civilization, *Bildung*, and *Kultur*—the latter of which had achieved particular prominence in German thought.[9] Among them numbered cleanliness, order, family, hard work, and self-cultivation, alongside dedication to the nation. They can be considered moral values in so far as they acted as prescriptions for "the good life" and counted as markers of individual worth.

A third set of values that exercised a strong influence in the Wehrmacht, particularly among the officer corps, revolved around what Isabel Hull has termed the principle of "military necessity."[10] Integrated into the army's standard operating procedure during the late nineteenth century, this concept held that the armed forces needed to do everything in their power to achieve victory, even if some deviation from the honor code or international norms was required. In the long run, so theorists contended, an ends-justify-the-means mentality would shorten wars and save military and civilian lives. Arguments based on military necessity would frequently be deployed to justify criminal actions during the war, but they could also be used to champion more moderate policies if these seemed to promise a surer road to victory.

National Socialist ethics constituted the most recent influence on the Wehrmacht's moral fabric. Rather than recognizing all life as inherently valuable, the Nazis posited a hierarchy of races in existential competition with each other and the Jewish "anti-race." Good conduct was redefined as any action that promoted the health of superior races or secured their dominance over the others.[11] Proponents of Nazi morality embraced some principles drawn from traditional value systems, but only when these were oriented within a racial framework, such as when Germans were enjoined to courageously battle inferior races or raise loving families in order to propagate Aryan bloodlines.[12] Religion, another important source of moral thought in the Wehrmacht, will be discussed in chapter 3.

Values in the German Army before Barbarossa

Previously considered the exclusive province of the aristocratic professional elite that led the armies of the German states in early modern times, martial values became democratized as Prussia instituted universal conscription during the Wars of Liberation—the campaign to end Napoleon's domination of Europe in the early nineteenth century. Popular literature helped to redefine the traits of the ideal warrior and linked them to emerging notions of national citizenship, middle-class sensibilities, and masculine identity. Among these traits were valor, patriotism, sacrifice, honor, and Christian piety, all of which contrasted with the immorality and femininity German writers attributed to their French foes. It was now the duty of every male member of the national community, and indeed the measure of his worth as a man, to protect his *Heimat* ("homeland"), his family, and his freedom while cultivating a strong emotional bond with the fighters who marched at his side.[13] Military virtues continued to be highly prized in Germany over the following decades as an element of what scholars characterize as a militaristic culture in which the soldier was valued over the civilian and the symbols associated with the army enjoyed wide appeal.[14]

During the 1870 Franco-Prussian War, the army deviated from its honorable ideals by conducting harsh reprisals against local communities in response to ambushes carried out by French civilians. This response, justified on the grounds that the resisters were violating the laws of war, reflected the growing influence of "military necessity" as a core value within the German military. After the victory over France, the reputation of the armed forces soared to new heights in the German public imagination, bolstered by the fact that they had played an instrumental role in the creation of the Empire. Over the following years, Germany became a signatory of the Hague Conventions and other international treaties delineating acceptable practices in warfare. Despite this official commitment to chivalric principles, however, the army's leaders fostered a culture in which total control and total victory were prized over conformity with international law.[15]

The German Army's performance in the First World War produced a mixed record when it came to upholding the traditional honor code. In 1914, it reacted with extreme violence to exaggerated reports of civilian snipers in Belgium, although it later moderated its policies.[16] Over the conflict's next years, the army of the *Kaiserreich* alternated between relatively decent conduct and violations of international convention. Its leaders proved especially willing to cast off moral restraints in cases where these seemed to impede strategic progress, such as when they announced unrestricted submarine warfare in a desperate bid to tip the scales.[17] Throughout the war, military leaders joined public intellectuals in insisting that their men were honorably defending the ideals of German *Kultur*.[18]

Upon Hitler's assumption of the chancellorship in 1933, the army's value system underwent a series of seismic changes. Several prominent generals, including Defense Minister Werner von Blomberg and Walter von Reichenau, actively promoted alignment with Nazi norms. Their task was made easier by the officer corps' longstanding traditions of antisemitism, anti-communism, and right-wing authoritarian leanings, as well as its desire to preserve the military's clout within the new state. Partly in gratitude to Hitler for the purge that thwarted the ambitions of its SA rivals in 1934, the army voluntarily adopted an oath of loyalty to the Führer. It instituted a wide-ranging mandatory indoctrination program, including classroom instruction on ideological topics and a barrage of propaganda materials reflecting the worldview of its new masters.[19] As defined in a 1940 manual for new recruits, the "Duties of the German Soldier" now centered on protecting "the German Reich and Fatherland, the people united in National Socialism, and their living space."[20] The qualities of the ideal soldier still included obedience, bravery, sacrifice, comradeship, and loyalty, all of which had long been part of the military code but would be increasingly re-directed in service of the Nazi movement.

The integration of Nazi morality and the military code was made easier by the fact that the two already had much in common.[21] Bravery, toughness, obedience, love of nation, and heroic sacrifice had been highly prized by Party leaders since the movement's inception. Such values could easily be adapted to Nazi purposes within the Wehrmacht. The rank and file, for instance, were now told to be loyal and obedient to the Führer and to direct their bravery toward annihilating the enemies of the racial community. Further, the fact that the army had long been gravitating toward an obsession with "total" solutions and had a history of selectively ignoring international law made Germany's armed forces readily adaptable to the Nazi outlook.

There were still differences, however, between the Wehrmacht's preferred conception of the soldier and the "new man" of Nazism. The ideal warrior as the army defined him in the lead-up to the USSR campaign carried out his job with ruthless efficiency but in principle still operated within established codes of conduct, avoided excessive brutality, and acted chivalrously toward noncombatants. The 1940 training manual cited above, for instance, declared that the soldier was to remain "upright," "modest," "God-fearing," and "incorruptible."[22] Likewise, it explained that "honor is the highest good of the soldier. . . . It must be clear to each soldier that moral values determine his worth and the worth of the Wehrmacht. The best guardian of honor is unimpeachable conduct."[23] Prisoners were to be "treated humanely," the noncombatant status of medics was to be respected, and soldiers were instructed that "war is not waged against the peaceful civilian population." Plunder, violence, and the destruction of local property were condemned, except in cases of armed resistance.[24] Such regulations, still informed by the army's longstanding honor code, contrasted with the portrait of the ideal Nazi fighter, a man who recognized no limits, adopted an attitude of unfeeling toughness, and showed no mercy in his dealings with lesser races.[25]

Overall then, the relationship between traditional values and Nazi innovations in the Wehrmacht before Operation Barbarossa was rife with ambiguities. In some cases, the two norm systems coexisted uneasily. More and more they appeared to be working together to the Nazis' benefit, however, as age-old military virtues were repurposed in the service of the new regime. Nevertheless, soldiers less keen on the Nazi revolution still had reason to believe that their institution continued to uphold its time-honored codes of conduct leading up to the conflict.[26]

The ongoing divide between Nazism and what remained of military chivalry was still evident during Germany's 1939 invasion of Poland and the subsequent campaign in western Europe. As recent scholarship has demonstrated, the Wehrmacht was directly involved in the murder of Polish intellectuals and clerics, and assisted in the roundup and execution of Jews on a limited scale. A number of senior officers, however, expressed shock at the brutality of the SS and refused to allow their own troops to take part in what they considered conduct unworthy of the German soldier.[27] In 1940, Wehrmacht soldiers massacred thousands of captured black African troops serving in the French Army.[28] Despite this, the Wehrmacht would enjoy a relatively positive reputation among local populations in Western Europe, at least during the war's early stages.[29] By the eve of Barbarossa, then, the Wehrmacht had shown itself to be receptive to many elements of Nazi morality, although it had not yet entirely jettisoned its ties to traditional value systems.

Setting the Moral Stage for the War of Extermination

The extent to which the Nazi "revaluation of all values" had successfully altered the Wehrmacht's moral fabric by 1941 is starkly illustrated by a series of instructions the High Command of the German Army (*Oberkommando des Heeres*, or OKH) issued in preparation for the USSR campaign. One of these, the "Guidelines for the Conduct of the Troops," set the tone for the invasion by informing personnel that the conflict represented a battle of two worldviews that necessitated the ruthless treatment of communists, Jews, and hostile civilians. Next to it, the "Barbarossa Decree" sanctioned the execution of hostages in response to any partisan activity and declared that soldiers would not be prosecuted for crimes against Soviet noncombatants. Finally, the "Commissar Order" instructed Wehrmacht formations to execute communist political functionaries, such as those embedded with Soviet forces. All three were widely if not universally distributed, reaching most soldiers shortly before the invasion began. Taken as a whole, the pronouncements—now collectively known as the Criminal Orders—framed the invasion of the Soviet Union as an existential racial conflict in which the dictates of ordinary morality and military custom would no longer hold. They reflected both the deep influence of Nazi ideology and the mantra of victory at all costs that had crept into the army's institutional culture.[30]

In the opening months of the attack, top-ranking generals broadcast their own variations on the themes of the Criminal Orders in language that indicated their alignment with the Nazi worldview. Reichenau, now a field marshal in command of the Sixth Army, defined the campaign as a battle to destroy the "Jewish-Bolshevik system," punish "Jewish sub-humanity," and exterminate "Asian influence" in Europe. Combatants on the Eastern front, he argued, should think of themselves not as ordinary warriors who fought according to traditional rules, but bearers of the Nazis' "racial idea."[31] Several months later, General Hoth reminded his men that *"sympathy and softness toward the population* is completely out of place" and called for "hard measures" against Jews and other perceived enemies.[32] General Manstein rejected the use of "European rules of war." Instead, he insisted that his men embrace the need for "harshness" and warned against displays of mercy toward prisoners and civilians, especially Jews.[33]

Although they have often been interpreted as a sign that the Wehrmacht had thoroughly embraced the Nazi worldview, the pronouncements of OKH and its generals early in the campaign were in fact a snapshot of an army still in the process of transitioning from its older honor code to a radically different value system. In the series of orders that defined the invasion, traces of that older system surfaced in two important ways. First, instead of citing racism as a singular, self-sufficient rationale for revoking the laws of war, the authors of these decrees typically paired racial language with traditional moral argumentation in order to justify criminality.[34] The Commissar Order, for instance, was primarily justified by the assertion that political functionaries were the ring leaders of an enemy force that could be expected to ignore "the foundations of humanity" and "international law," including by mistreating German prisoners.[35] Regulations for soldierly conduct rested on the assumption that Soviet combatants would employ "insidious fighting methods."[36] Even Hitler's own explanation of the conflict to his generals focused primarily on the supposedly criminal nature of the USSR and its representatives, rather than its ethnic composition.[37] By combining racism with ethical argumentation, the Criminal Orders and related commands served to translate Nazi morality into a more familiar vocabulary of good and evil that would be readily accepted by Wehrmacht servicemen of all persuasions.[38]

Second, the Criminal Orders harbored traces of the army's older honor code in the form of overt references to traditional virtues along with stipulations that conjured up the illusion of conformity with international law.[39] The orders that impeded the prosecution of servicemen for crimes against civilians still allowed for the arrest and punishment of men whose actions were deemed particularly extreme.[40] Manstein's instructions emphasized the need for the troops to preserve their "soldierly honor" and called for the "just treatment of all non-Bolshevik sections of the population."[41] The same Guidelines for the Conduct of the Troops that incited personnel to show no mercy toward Jews, communists, and resisters and to exploit the country's resources to the fullest also told the men to expect a friendly welcome from some civilians and warned of "the harshest punishments" for soldiers who plundered.[42] OKH was particularly insistent on this final point. Troops were required to pay for any property taken from civilians and to issue credit slips for goods costing over 1,000 RM.[43] On the surface, this regulation satisfied the provisions of international law.[44] In reality, it was little more than a license for theft by another name, since few Soviet civilians valued hard currency and the army set exchange rates that were extremely favorable to Germany.[45] This rule became part of a cloud of protocols, procedures, and guidelines that lent the army's activities a veneer of legality.[46] "Plundering" was forbidden, but requisitions with the correct paperwork were fully condoned. Outright brutality was discouraged, but troops could mete out collective punishments if the proper authorities gave their approval.

While this mitigating language bore a family resemblance to the honor codes of the army's past, it likely stemmed largely from commanders' overriding obsession with military necessity rather than humanitarian impulses. The Barbarossa Decree prohibiting the prosecution of soldiers for crimes against civilians made exceptions for cases in which the "maintenance of discipline or the security of the troops" was at stake.[47] Prohibitions against theft or wanton violence likewise served to maintain the levels of discipline necessary for the army to accomplish its mission and effectively police new territories. Sympathy for the population or respect for international law always remained at best secondary concerns. Above all, Wehrmacht leaders sought to ensure that the army could carry out its work with maximum efficiency, even if this sometimes meant reigning in ideological excesses.[48]

As these initial orders indicate, the army that launched Operation Barbarossa in 1941 had largely adopted Nazi principles into its institutional culture but nevertheless retained some of the trappings of its past commitments to honor and chivalry, if only out of a utilitarian interest in ensuring battlefield success. This state of affairs may have caused concern among some members of the Nazi administration.[49] Ultimately, though, it helped to ensure that as many soldiers as possible continued to see their institution in a positive moral light as the campaign got underway. Troops who judged its worthiness by the yardstick of Nazi morality could find ample validation in the ideological language of the Criminal Orders and related instructions. Those less inclined toward Hitler's worldview could still cling to the illusion that they were part of an organization that upheld honorable standards and followed rational rules according to the dictates of more conventional value systems.[50]

Values among the Rank and File

The invasion commenced on June 22, 1941, as Wehrmacht troops jumped off from their staging areas in occupied Poland and East Prussia. They were organized into three Army Groups: North, Center, and South. Army Group North advanced through the Baltic states with the goal of capturing Leningrad. Army Group Center struck out toward the Soviet capital of Moscow. It fell to Army Group South to occupy the Ukraine, with its vital agricultural resources. Out in front of the German forces, Panzer (armored) formations advanced rapidly under cover from the air force, seeking to trap large swaths of Soviet troops in vast encirclements as the less mobile infantry mopped up behind them. Although the defenders put up tenacious resistance, progress was swift. The Wehrmacht advanced hundreds of miles within a matter of weeks, capturing hundreds of thousands of prisoners in the process. To many observers, another German victory appeared already in sight, but the Wehrmacht's sojourn in the USSR was in fact just beginning.[51]

As they stormed into the Soviet Union, soldiers brought with them a rich assortment of ethical norms informed not only by the initial orders they received but also by military traditions, Nazi ideology, and the assumptions of German society as a whole regarding the traits of the ideal man. These helped to provide meaning to their experiences and enabled them to make moral judgments about themselves and the nature of their enemy. By emphasizing their sense of duty, pride, courage, selflessness, and loyalty, as well as their commitment to the nation, the bonds of comradeship, and familial obligation, *Ostkämpfer* developed and—through their letters—projected identities as decent, honorable men committed to their homeland's most cherished ideals, often along fairly traditional lines. However, these same principles often acted as a bridge toward acceptance of Nazi conceptions of masculinity and racial superiority. All the while, troops drew a sharp rhetorical contrast between themselves and enemies they depicted as not only racially but morally degenerate.

Private Johannes Hagemann and his brother Willy, also a private, exemplified the ways in which German soldiers constructed identities as principled men committed to noble ideals during the opening phase of the *Vernichtungskrieg*. Hailing from a Schleswig-Holstein farm family, both served in the 290th Infantry Division, which steadily advanced toward Lake Ilmen with Army Group North. Like so many of their comrades, they expressed deep reverence for the German nation, but it was only after witnessing the contrast with the USSR, Johannes wrote Willy, that one truly came to appreciate "how much one loves his Heimat and how grudgingly one parts from it."[52] The twenty-two-year-old Willy, who was more carefree than his older brother and initially saw the war as a grand adventure, pledged that "we will all do our duty" and insisted that the army was fighting for the future of Germany's children.[53] Both brothers expressed pride, not only in the accomplishments of their units but in one another's bravery and their family's long military heritage. As their unit secured the southern shore of Lake Ilmen in August, Johannes looked forward to the moment of victory when their parents would "be proud of your boys."[54] When Willy was evacuated to a hospital in Germany after being lightly wounded in the head and shoulder on August 15, Johannes assured their parents that Willy "fought bravely for his Fatherland" and was eager to rejoin his comrades.[55] Johannes expressed pride in being able to walk in the footsteps of their father who had fought in the First World War.[56] He expected the family's military tradition to continue after the war concluded. "When you are big, you will also be a brave soldier," he wrote their younger brother Otto, who had turned ten in 1941.[57]

The emphasis on manly bravery and pride in the army's victories became a common refrain in soldiers' letters throughout 1941. Joseph Reinke, who fought with the 35th Infantry Division in Army Group Center and would not survive the war's first year, frequently recounted his battlefield triumphs to Hedwig, a female acquaintance. At the invasion's outset, he declared that "there is nothing above the German army."[58] As one comrade after another fell in pitched battles, Joseph lauded their bravery, told Hedwig that she would be able to read about his unit's victories in the newspaper, and expressed satisfaction in "how much we have accomplished."[59] Statements like these helped signal to homeland readers that soldiers embodied the bravery and self-confidence that was expected of every German man.

The desire to prove one's masculine worth through battlefield deeds even inspired soldiers who initially had difficulty adjusting to army life. The twenty-two-year-old Harald Hoffmann from Berlin struggled with the physical exertions of soldierly service. To his chagrin, he was unable to keep up on the march and had to recuperate in an aid station two weeks after the invasion started. Hoffmann explained to his father that he did not enjoy the war experience, but "yet I am here, not only because I must be, rather, because in such a time every upstanding and healthy man belongs for a time in danger and travail, so I believe and experience."[60] Hoffmann was among a substantial number of troops who saw the war not only in political or ideological terms but as a test of manly character. Another of these was twenty-nine-year-old Hans Roth, a former graphic artist from Frankfurt, now serving as a staff sergeant with the 299th Infantry Division in Army Group South, which faced the strongest initial resistance as it struggled toward Kiev and the Crimea.[61] Holding the line near Voronezh during the first winter, he would describe this test in a combination of moral and ideological terms. "And we are up to the test a hundredfold," he declared in his diary, "a degree of duty and devotion which can truly only be appreciated by the direct leadership and the Führer himself."[62]

The test, it turned out, would only become more strenuous with time. But no matter how fierce the fighting became or how deeply they yearned to return home, Wehrmacht troops evoked the all-important virtue of duty to explain to themselves and their relatives why they were engaged in combat thousands of miles from home. Wilhelm Moldenhauser, a shopkeeper who sold colonial wares near Hannover and now acted as a radio man for the 60th Infantry Division, wrote his wife from the Rostov-on-Don region that "I regard it as our holiest duty to now bear in mind our great collective goal, that we defeat the Russian . . . as soon as possible."[63] In an earlier letter he reassured her of his conviction that the war years were "not a lost time. With proud feelings we should be happy that we have not stood aside. Rather every one of us in his place has done his duty."[64] Their generation, Moldenhauser and others believed, had been given the great task of securing Germany's future, and both they and their loved ones at home had to play their part, no matter the cost. Kurt Niemeyer, a villager from Thuringia who had worked at a sawmill and now served in a transport battalion, explained that he had never felt such affection for his wife and child as he did now, "since I do my duty for the Fatherland so far into enemy territory."[65] Whatever form it took, the language of duty allowed soldiers both to dampen their sense of personal responsibility and to indicate to their readers that they had selflessly set aside their own personal desires in order to pursue what Hans Roth dubbed, "the greater purpose of the war."[66]

Servicemen defined this purpose in various ways. Sometimes they viewed it in purely negative terms, as the destruction of communism or the Jewish enemy. Just as often, however, they defined the invasion's goal as the attainment of noble ideals.[67] The Hagemann brothers focused on the preservation of the German nation and its future, a future they, like so many of their comrades, believed was threatened by a Soviet plot to invade Germany.[68] Others saw their mission in even more expansive terms, as an effort to save all the traditions and values of Western civilization.[69] They projected a vision of a more just European order under German leadership that would replace the oppressive peace established after the First World War, a vision some, but not all, saw through an ideological prism. Lieutenant Hans Wilhelm Sauer, for instance, noted that one could regard the war "from different sides," as a battle to wipe out Jewish influence, win territory, or bring culture to the East, and he speculated that the war might unite Europe while also benefiting Germany.[70]

Troops' sense of duty, along with other traditional military virtues such as loyalty and obedience, often took as its focal point not only the nation but the person of the Führer, to whom they credited Germany's many military successes.[71] Moldenhauser gave voice to this conviction when he remarked that, "our Führer is a man whom no one in this world surpasses. He alone is to thank for the fact that we again can live in peaceful and orderly conditions. Every soldier of the front will be a good follower of our Führer. Of that I am convinced!"[72] "So far," Johannes Hagemann agreed, "our Führer has succeeded in everything, and he will definitely also continue to make things right."[73] It was not, he and others believed, the place of the simple soldier to question the nation's decision makers, only to carry out their will as, in Moldenhauser's words, "small cogs in the great work of our beloved Führer."[74] By expressing this commitment in their letters, personnel depicted themselves as faithful patriots and loyal supporters of the regime. In reality, their newfound allegiance represented an abrogation of their own moral agency: for Moldenhauser and others, Hitler now effectively represented the conscience of the nation, bearing sole responsibility for the actions of his army.[75] Expressions of faith in the Führer, however, did not necessarily indicate full-throated acceptance of Nazi ideology in its entirety.[76] The men studied here typically appropriated a blend of Nazi and pre-Nazi values into the worldviews they expressed in their writings.

Comradeship, a virtue extolled by the Nazis and long prized in Germany's military tradition, took on great importance from the start of the Soviet campaign. The circle of comrades functioned as an insular moral community within which soldiers displayed love, kindness, and softness, traits they resolved never to show their enemies.[77] The bonds between comrades on the Eastern Front were constantly nurtured not only through the shared experience of combat but also social interaction, including the celebration of birthdays and promotions, as well as "comradeship evenings" organized by officers. With mothers, fathers, wives, and siblings thousands of miles away, the front community took on the qualities of family and home, although with a distinctly masculine twist.[78] During pauses in the fighting around Lake Ilmen, south of Leningrad, Johannes Hagemann and his comrades gathered around the table with a bottle of vodka. "For some hours then the cares and the terrors of the war are forgotten," he wrote his sister. "Then we sing our beautiful Heimat songs, we northern Germans. . . . Then come the men from Cologne and Vienna and everyone sings their best songs[;] and every once in a while one has the feeling that one is in the Heimat."[79] Membership in this brotherhood was not guaranteed, however. Harald Hoffmann only gained the respect of his comrades after winning the Iron Cross Second Class by rescuing a wounded soldier during battle.[80]

Once one's masculine credentials had been proven, soldiers described a selfless community of men who looked after each other in difficult times and did not hesitate to sacrifice everything for those at their side. "I could give hundreds of gut-wrenching examples and incidents of . . . selfless comradeship among us *frontschweine*," Hans Roth confided to his diary. He and his comrades, he wrote, were committed to "the unwritten law of brotherhood."[81] In late September, Hans Simon, whose 12th Infantry Division operated south of Lake Ilmen—not far from the Hagemann brothers—complained to his mother that supplies were scarce, to the point that his diet consisted mainly of potatoes. But he appreciated the fact that the rank and file looked after each other: "one . . . learns to share the last with comrades," he penned.[82] Curiously, none of the men ever employed the Nazi term *Volksgemeinschaft* in the writings examined here, though in practice their attitudes and actions overlapped strongly with the National Socialist conception of community, especially in that non-Germans and those deemed cowards or nonconformists found no place in it. Whether or not they understood it in explicitly ideological terms, this community provided a space for combatants to play out roles as decent, virtuous men, even as they lashed out savagely against those they perceived as a threat to the group. By emphasizing the importance of comradeship in their writings, they presented themselves to their readers as altruistic members of an organization that honorably cared for its own.

As they became more familiar with the landscape and peoples of the land they now occupied, German soldiers depicted the Soviet Union as the antithesis of all of the values embodied by the German man-at-arms and the supposedly advanced society he represented. The invaders associated culture with cleanliness, order, hard work, and educational attainment. These qualities had long carried strong moral connotations in German society, particularly among the middle classes, but appeared to the men of the Wehrmacht entirely absent in the Soviet Union with its one-room huts, muddy villages, and ragged clothing. In their letters home, they asserted overlapping claims to cultural, racial, and moral superiority as they highlighted their commitment to such virtues against the backdrop of their enemies' alleged ethical shortcomings.[83]

To his parents and sisters, Hans Wilhelm Sauer described the Soviet Union in typical fashion as a land of *"non-culture. . . . Indeed,"* he wrote, "the meanest German soldier seems a high-class, artful, costly, irreplaceable, gracefully-built entity next to these simple people, who are just as nature made them, the German soldier with his schooling, breeding, and education."[84] According to Sauer, the Soviet peoples required leadership and the imposition of order from the culturally-advanced Germans. Wilhelm Moldenhauser, who traveled through the Ukraine and western Russia in 1941 and 1942, remarked upon the poor living conditions he encountered, including streets that reminded him of a pigsty, the "shoddy" construction projects of the communist regime, and "dirty" children in crowded huts.[85] Like many of his comrades, Moldenhauser concluded that what he witnessed was at least partly the result of flaws in the Slavic character—a flagging work ethic and a lack of self-respect that contrasted starkly with the Wehrmacht's commitment to efficiency and hard work. In one area, he commented that "enough civilians run around here, who otherwise have nothing to do."[86] A month later, he quartered with a family whom he dismissed as "dirty and impudent and lazy."[87] Throughout his correspondence he expressed his belief that the invaders would have to teach their subjects a healthy respect for labor and praised the "Prussian order" they brought to the chaotic East.[88]

Although his impressions of the locals often overlapped with Nazi conceptions of non-Aryans, Moldenhauser admitted that some of the people he met were clean and hardworking, and he generally attributed their situation to individual moral choices rather than biology.[89] As they expressed fantasies of cultural and moral superiority, however, it took only a short leap for some men in uniform to envision the entire enemy population as racially degenerate in terms that reflected the tenets of Nazi morality. Franz Siebeler, a member of 14th Panzer Division, which had recently passed through Ssolonenjkoje during the autumn of 1941, noted that in many places the harvest had yet to be brought in.[90] This was in fact the result of the war's devastations, but Siebeler ascribed his observation to his belief that "the Russian is . . . a lazy guy. Whatever suffices for his own life, that is enough for him. A typical Slav! They . . . still must learn order."[91] When they came across *Volksdeutsch* ("ethnic German") settlements, Wehrmacht troops invariably characterized the occupants as cleaner and more productive than civilians of other ethnicities. "From the build of the houses, above all also the *inside*, one can recognize that German people have lived here," wrote Moldenhauser, who visited several *Volks-*

deutsch settlements in the Donets Basin.[92] Without fail, soldiers described themselves in their letters as orderly, hardworking, and committed to cleanliness at least in principle, all in contrast to the Soviet residents they encountered. Siebeler, for instance, portrayed himself and his comrades as tireless professionals who worked and fought throughout the day and often into the night, in his case as a motorcycle courier.[93]

As they drove deeper into Soviet territory, Germany's warriors began to style their self-conceptions around not only their assessments of civilians but what they perceived to be the vast gulf separating them and their counterparts in the Red Army. Again, so their writings suggested, these differences exposed the Soviet fighter's moral and racial shortcomings and illustrated the superior character of the Wehrmacht trooper. After only a few weeks of battle, many German soldiers began to regard their enemy as devious, unscrupulous, and totally lacking in honor, a view that combined personal observations from the battlefield with Nazi stereotypes regarding the nature of "Asiatic races." "What Bolshevism throws into the field is completely opposite to any concept of true soldierly spirit," Hans Roth wrote in his diary. "It is inhumane cruelty to the highest degree."[94] Hans-Peter Eckener agreed. "One stands opposite an enemy that fights entirely without chivalrous rules," he told his sister.[95] Non-commissioned officer Walter Neuser, a Nazi Party member who managed supplies for an artillery regiment, referred several times to the "vulgar tactics" of Red soldiers who sniped from a distance, fought small engagements, and refused to surrender.[96] He and other Wehrmacht soldiers continually accused their enemies of violating international norms by mutilating prisoners, firing on medics, and disguising themselves in civilian clothes or German uniforms.[97]

Stories like these became a common refrain for Wehrmacht propagandists. Most worked in the *Propaganda Kompanien* ("Propaganda Companies," or PK) that closely followed the line of advance. The PK answered directly to OKW but collaborated with Goebbels's Propaganda Ministry. They would generate over 80,000 press releases and 3 million photographs over the course of the Second World War for consumption by the front and the home front.[98] Soviet troops, so one journalist reported, hid in trees to shoot German soldiers in the back long after the battle had ended and even mutilated their corpses, "against every human right and every soldierly law."[99] The army's reporters directed special ire at the commissars, whom they accused of all manner of atrocities, and at Soviet political leaders who supposedly threw away their people's lives for false ideals.[100] Propagandists joined the rank and file in admitting that the Soviets were tough opponents, but together they predicted that Germans would be victorious since they fought out of "free obedience, for a high battle-goal, for an idea, following an inner command," as PK reporter Peter Weber put it. Soviet combatants, they claimed, were only motivated by fear of the commissars or tricked into compliance by devious rulers.[101]

Wehrmacht personnel frequently explained the alleged unchivalrous behavior of the enemy as well as his bravery as the product of the animal instincts of an inferior race. Walter Neuser, for instance, informed his sister that "the Russian is a dangerous opponent. Because he is incited to hatred with the most pernicious horror stories and kept in check from behind, he keeps resisting till his own death. Especially repulsive to us were the many races and the devious and underhanded tactics."[102] Propagandists, who often adopted the vocabulary of Nazism, likewise defined Red soldiers as "beasts" who fought with "animal-like doggedness."[103] One writer sarcastically suggested that to the enemy, "the appalling atrocities also constitute virtue, [and] virtue the murders with which the Bolshevik sub-humans burden their black consciences even more."[104] The army's journalists agreed that victory would never come to such a despicable foe, but to the army that displayed moral worthiness.[105] In sum, both the Wehrmacht's propaganda apparatus and regular servicemen insisted that they faced an enemy that combined moral bankruptcy with racial inferiority.

When they discussed their own battlefield conduct in their letters home, German soldiers painted a picture of an honorable Wehrmacht whose value systems and methods of fighting were diametrically opposed to those of the Red Army. They credited their early successes to superior fighting skills, better training, dogged bravery, and direct confrontation with the enemy, as when Wilhelm Altmann described to his relatives how his unit stormed forty-five Russian bunkers in succession during a single engagement, an action that won him personal recognition in his regiment's order of the day.[106] Although they rarely gave a precise account of their actions during combat—most likely to avoid causing readers to fear for their safety—servicemen implied in their letters that if the Red Army's methods of fighting were "devious" or wantonly destructive, their own battlefield conduct conformed to civilized standards. For instance, they emphasized that Red troops went gladly into captivity and insisted that the Germans usually treated them well. Hermann Henning noted that Soviet soldiers frequently went over to the German side. For one Uzbek prisoner of war, he explained, "Everything was . . . a delightful revelation, the treatment by our soldiers, the good German cigarettes, the shelter with light and oven and coziness."[107] Fritz Feierabend insisted to his wife that "the prisoners receive from us what food is left over. If they have to work, they are definitely nourished."[108] Such statements created the impression that the Wehrmacht remained committed to international norms, even though in reality the Soviet POWs of 1941 faced murderous conditions.[109] In more general terms, German soldiers described themselves as motivated by personal conviction and high ideals, as well as a selfless commitment to their comrades, in contrast to opponents who supposedly fought without honor and for all the wrong reasons.[110]

As they painted this picture, troops again had a powerful ally in the army's propaganda apparatus, which lauded their moral character both on and off the battlefield. "The cultured world knows that the German soldier at every time and in every place fights openly and honestly. Defamations . . . cannot dissuade him from the decency of his way of fighting," declared one front newspaper.[111] Wehrmacht reporters emphasized time and again that German troops respected the lives, property, and culture of conquered peoples and safeguarded the well-being of Soviet prisoners of war. Several of their articles detailed how, while the Red Army killed German prisoners, Wehrmacht medical personnel went out of their way to tend to the Soviet wounded. War reporter Fred Gressenbauer explained that Red officers left their own injured to their fate. The Germans would be justified in shooting the "sub-human" officers in the face upon capture, he opined, "But we don't do it. We let the wounded Bolsheviks be bandaged by our medics and let the officers keep their faces. We Germans are humans!" he exclaimed.[112] According to the *Mitteilungen für die Truppe*, a widely distributed propaganda bulletin emanating from OKW that typically parroted the Nazi line, the ordinary Wehrmacht trooper took what he needed but never plundered and appreciated the cultural treasures of foreign lands. He did what had to be done to win the war, yet "avoid[ed] further hardships, that only harm innocent people" and did "not wage war against women and children."[113] Such depictions of soldierly character and conduct sometimes came at the expense of ideological purity, especially when they extolled the chivalrous treatment of men and women the Nazi regime considered subhuman. As their authors clearly recognized, however, emphasizing good deeds and upstanding character in conventional moral terms from time to time helped to buoy morale and gave soldiers a further reason to believe in their own worthiness. Further, while propagandists praised the German fighting man as a chivalrous fellow, they simultaneously cast him as a model for the "National Socialist community-ideal" that every German was to strive for, further blending elements of the Nazi value system into the matrix of traditional military virtues.[114]

Shades of a Fading Honor Code

Propaganda materials and soldiers' writings were not the only means by which the Wehrmacht constructed and projected a virtuous image for itself during

1941. Even as they oversaw the implementation of the Criminal Orders, established draconian policies to control the newly occupied lands, and sanctioned terroristic responses to any resistance activity, Wehrmacht commanders from the division level to OKW frequently issued orders that employed the language of the army's traditional code of honor. These called on troops to refrain from disproportionate violence against POWs and noncombatants, to exhibit virtuous behavior, and to exercise fairness toward the population. Such comparatively mild regulations represented the exception rather than the rule and had little real impact on the Wehrmacht's conduct, but they made a critical contribution to the self-image that soldiers and propagandists had already begun to establish: they shielded the army's reputation and provided a veneer of moral and legal legitimacy to its activities in the USSR. In the process, they eased the consciences of any troops who may have had doubts about their participation in the *Vernichtungskrieg* by strengthening their conviction that they remained decent men led by honorable superiors.

During the first months of the invasion, officers up and down the Wehrmacht hierarchy disseminated orders calling for good behavior and a degree of restraint on the part of soldiers who in many cases had seemingly abandoned all sense of military discipline as they mistreated the civilian population and murdered POWs.[115] "Events of the last days," intelligence officers of Third Panzer Army reported, "give occasion for renewed reminder that the troops should act correctly vis-à-vis the civilian population. . . . The population's trust in the German Wehrmacht and their happiness at being freed from the Soviet regime should not be reversed by improper or inept behavior on the part of the troops or the detachments associated with the army." Their statement was coupled, however, with a call for the harsh treatment of "Jewish or communist elements," who were assumed to have hostile intentions.[116] This selective deployment of the honor code was also at work in the dictates of other formations that called on combatants to treat nonhostile elements in a dignified manner. Condemning a spate of "wild requisitions" of civilian property that had caused "bad blood" with Ukrainian inhabitants, the 46th Infantry Division joined many of its counterparts by reiterating that plundering was a punishable offense and that troops were required to pay for confiscated property. In an unlikely twist on Nazi terminology, it even went so far as to urge its troops to recognize the Ukraine as the *"living space of a friendly people."*[117] A few months later, the 10th Panzer Division ordered that troops were to "avoid anything that could lead to unpleasantness" with the population. Only in exceptional cases were soldiers allowed to drive civilians from their homes. Requisitions were to be carried out only per regulations and locals to be compensated for any services they rendered.[118]

Although high-ranking officers sanctioned violence toward all perceived enemies, whether uniformed or civilian, and reserved the right to take hostages and carry out collective punishments, they also issued orders that put limits on such practices. Army Group Center, for example, demanded a halt to indiscriminate violence against civilians in response to isolated partisan attacks *"unless it is perfectly proven that these are the culprits or in connection with them."*[119] Likewise, OKH chief General Walter von Brauchitsch declared that the Wehrmacht was not to undertake "retaliatory measures" (*Vergeltungsmaßnahmen*), including executions, in response to reports of Soviet violations of international law, since doing so would merely play into the hands of enemy propagandists and was unlikely to change the Red Army's behavior.[120] OKH also passed along a reminder to all units, as well as the SS, that, "attention should be paid to a good and just treatment of the loyal population," who were not to be held responsible for occasional acts of sabotage by communists, snipers, and Jews behind the lines.[121] OKW's *Mitteilungen für die Truppe* spread a similar message by calling on troops to adopt a "strict" and "sober" attitude toward the locals.[122] Its authors added that they were to avoid "excessive hardships, arbitrary requisitions and above all every type of open display of contempt vis-à-vis the population."[123] Like the Wehrmacht's generals, propagandists recognized that in some cases a degree of restraint fulfilled the dictates of military necessity better than a total commitment to the principles of Nazi morality.

Indeed, commanders typically justified such relatively mild stipulations on strategic grounds rather than out of concern for the lives and well-being of Soviet men and women who found themselves at the invaders' mercy: a more lenient treatment of civilians and POWs, they believed, could ultimately help to advance the war effort. As the leaders of Second Panzer Army explained in a circular for officers, maintaining the population's trust and avoiding any actions that might turn them against the Wehrmacht would provide the German side with "a meaningful advantage" and counter enemy propaganda.[124] A few generals also cited the need to safeguard the Wehrmacht's public image. The commander of the 167th Infantry Division, Lieutenant General Schönhärl, admonished his troops for conducting requisitions without following officially sanctioned procedures. "Such behavior generates the impression that the German soldier has something to hide. Behavior of this kind is unsoldierly and damages the reputation of the Wehrmacht," he wrote, warning that he would consider banning all requisitions unless his regulations were followed.[125] In an order of the day instructing troops to refrain from plundering or even adopting an "arrogant attitude" toward the locals, the commander of XXXIV Corps cited the need to "preserve the reputation of the German army" and the "dignity of the German soldier," while maintaining discipline and securing the population's support.[126] According to many Wehrmacht leaders, proper conduct also meant keeping a distance from Soviet women.[127] Here, traditional moral norms overlapped directly with ideological goals, since Nazi officials feared the comingling of subhuman blood with the best of Germany's male youth.[128]

Whatever the motives behind such relatively mild decrees, there is little evidence they tangibly diminished criminality in practice. Atrocities against civilians and POWs remained a daily occurrence across the front. Further, the records of the Wehrmacht's Secret Field Police (*Geheime Feldpolizei*, or GFP), who were tasked with monitoring the conduct of the troops and carrying out counter-espionage and occupation duties, indicate that soldiers were seldom prosecuted for crimes against civilians—just as OKH had instructed.[129]

The more moderate orders commanders issued in 1941 reflected the language of the army's traditional honor code as well as a concern for the value of military necessity. In some cases, these may have mitigated Nazi extremism. However, they frequently ended up furthering Nazi goals in the long run. By casting itself as a rational, law-abiding actor, the Wehrmacht provided its men with moral license to annihilate any and all enemies who refused to meet its supposedly reasonable demands. For even as they broke from ideological orthodoxy by encouraging some forms of chivalrous behavior, commanders still condoned criminal violence, merely channeling it toward "proper" targets—Bolsheviks, Jews, partisans, and civilians deemed suspicious or hostile—precisely those groups Nazi leaders had slated for destruction. They also salved the consciences of scrupulous soldiers by quieting any doubts they may have had about the moral integrity of their institution, adding yet another strand to the web of self-delusion the Wehrmacht would weave for itself throughout the war.

Indeed, even if they were rarely enforced, orders calling for lenience and restraint became an important refrain in the narrative ordinary troops spun to their readers, since they served as tangible "proof" that Germany's uniformed men belonged to an organization that upheld time-honored rules of war. In a July 1941 letter, Wilhelm Moldenhauser explained to his wife that, "from the little people [Soviet civilians] one is not allowed . . . to steal the poultry, since [our leadership] would like to win them over for Germany."[130] A month later, he related to her the story of how he and a comrade were berated by an officer who mistakenly believed the pair was stealing from a local bookstore during the advance.[131] "It is strictly forbidden for us to steal anything, even a potato," Hermann Henning emphasized to his parents. "Everything must be paid for."[132] Willy Reese similarly noted that plundering could incur harsh penalties in his unit.[133] Many troops explicitly mentioned to their readers that they paid for goods and services, as when Willy Hagemann informed his parents that he had purchased gloves and a vest in Pskov.[134] The accounts they sent back to the home front rhetorically signaled that they respected civilized norms and had not strayed from an honor code their organization supposedly continued to uphold, however much this image differed from the reality.

Holding On: Soldierly Value Systems in 1942–1943

The year 1941 did not end the way most soldiers expected. Despite spectacular victories at Smolensk and Kiev, the advance was plagued by numerous difficulties that prevented the Wehrmacht from achieving the campaign's most important strategic goal: the swift and total destruction of the Red Army. Even though they were poorly organized and supplied, Soviet forces put up a tenacious defense, slowing the invaders as the Stalin regime hastily mobilized millions of new recruits behind the lines. German losses in men and equipment, already far higher than in any previous campaign, could not be so readily replaced. Within weeks, most of the Wehrmacht's Panzers were out of action. Overstretched supply lines and autumn rains that turned the country's dirt roads into quagmires contributed to a logistical crisis of epic proportions. In the north, Leningrad still held on, besieged by German forces. Army Group South reached Rostov-on-Don only to abandon the city to a Soviet counterattack. Meanwhile, the advance of Army Group Center ground to a halt outside Moscow in the face of extreme winter weather—for which the Wehrmacht was woefully unprepared—and a seemingly endless stream of Soviet reinforcements.[135]

The situation would only become more desperate over the following months. Taking advantage of its manpower and experience in winter warfare, the Red Army launched a series of counterattacks on a wide front that took the invaders by surprise. Army Group Center was forced to make a disastrous retreat from the gates of Moscow. Elsewhere, German troops held on to fortified locations as Soviet forces—sometimes equipped with skis—perforated the thinly held front line. Only the poor coordination of the attacks, brilliant defensive maneuvering on the part of German commanders, and a desperate "stand fast" order from the Führer staved off total collapse.[136] The spring thaw would bring some respite to the Wehrmacht's exhausted ranks and an opportunity to prepare for Case Blue, Hitler's plan to regain the initiative on the southern front by capturing the strategically important oil fields of the Caucasus, and with them the city of Stalingrad.[137]

The letters of Hans Simon, a native of Mecklenburg who had studied law at university and one day hoped to teach secondary school, exemplify the way in which many of the Wehrmacht's soldiers remained grounded in the principles of traditional bourgeois ethics and military virtues, alongside Nazi morality, as a new year dawned and the prospect of a quick victory faded. With reference to these values, including a sustained emphasis on duty, strength, the importance of the nation, and masculine honor, they continued to perform and project identities as decent men who upheld the highest ideals of their society even as the Wehrmacht's military fortunes waned and its personnel descended ever deeper into criminality. After spending several months on leave to pursue studies at Rostock University, Simon had returned to the area south of Lake Ilmen. Many of his comrades were surrounded in the Demyansk Pocket during the Soviet Winter Offensive, but the situation stabilized and he returned to his 12th Infantry Division at the end of April 1942 to lead an anti-tank gun team.[138] The twenty-one-year-old Simon tried to maintain an optimistic attitude and took pride in his accomplishments, including the five medals of which he boasted to his sister.[139] As time went on, however, he spoke less of heroic ideals and more of endurance in the face of ever-worsening conditions. He explained to his father that even though it was "sometimes not easy" he would continue to do his duty.[140]

For Simon, duty was not only a form of patriotism; it was also bound up with his own sense of self-worth as a man and his value within the front community. "I do my duty," he explained to his mother, "so that I can stand before my conscience and my comrades, and try to do it happily for myself. That makes everything much easier."[141] Like many other soldiers, he continued to believe that his generation had been called upon to make great sacrifices. It was difficult, he admitted, to see his comrades fall in battle, but he took comfort in the thought that "one dies for a better and more beautiful Germany," which constituted "in some respects a fulfillment of [a soldier's] life."[142]

As he pledged himself to a higher national ideal, Simon expressed his desire to fight for the friends manning the trenches next to him. "How nice it is for one to save the life of another through his sacrifice," he wrote his parents.[143] Simon's value system, like that of many of his comrades, centered on traditional nationalism, but at the close of 1942 he indicated to his father that he had come to accept most of the Nazi worldview, although he rarely employed ideological language in his writings.[144] Several weeks later he expressed his agreement with Hermann Göring's declaration that Germans would have to become "hard and harder" in order to achieve victory.[145] Despite what he described in July 1943 as the "crazy sacrifices that we are making in Russia," and growing feelings of indifference, he opined that both he and his family at home would have to remain strong.[146] Even after his unit was pushed back 125 miles during heavy fighting over the course of 1942 and 1943, Simon still kept his faith in a victory he had come to believe, in step with both Nazi leaders and military authorities, had to be achieved "no matter the cost."[147] Throughout these difficult days, he continued to view the war as a noble and necessary undertaking—if an unpleasant one—and styled himself an upright specimen of German manhood.

Wilhelm Altmann, a courier who had been promoted to private first class with the 227th Infantry Division, spent the duration of 1942 and 1943 roughly 150 miles north of Simon's unit, on the southern shore of Lake Ladoga as part of the force encircling Leningrad. Like Simon, he remained committed to doing his duty.[148] However, Altmann's letters indicate that he relied primarily on the tenets of Nazi morality to craft his affirmative self-image, rather than the more traditional value systems to which Simon often referred. Altmann rarely spoke of the importance of the nation, preferring instead to stress his personal devotion to the Führer. He eagerly looked forward to the "final victory" envisioned by the Third Reich's leadership. In April 1942, as his unit held the line against intermittent Soviet attacks, he listened to one of Hitler's speeches and reported to his father and sister that, "like our Führer said yesterday, we will yet hunt and strike all enemies till the great final victory[.] Above all he again praised the German infantry, who in the previous winter, in a cold the likes of which had not been seen in 140 years, held out here so bravely[,] and so among us the watchword is always still, 'Führer command, we follow you!'"[149] Altmann's devotion to the Führer found further expression when he attended a Hitler Youth (HJ) meeting at the front two months later.[150] Unlike his younger brother, whom Altmann considered unsuited to a soldier's life, Altmann put a high premium on strength and bravery.[151] He proudly described the ceremony during which his commanding officer awarded him the Iron Cross First Class in September 1942 for destroying an entire Soviet company with the support of two comrades.[152] Altmann also subscribed to a brand of masculine toughness that went beyond traditional conceptions of bravery to include a merciless outlook toward what he termed the Russian "beasts."[153] When four Russian forced laborers ran away and were caught, Altmann approved of the death by firing squad he predicted would be their fate. "They don't understand at all how good they have it with us and the German is all in all too humane," he remarked.[154]

Altmann's fear that what he considered the Germans' innate chivalrous qualities would harm the Wehrmacht's war effort was shared by other soldiers. Motorcycle courier Gustav Böker lamented that "we are much too good toward the [civilian] inhabitants," especially given his belief that the Red Army had planned to lay waste to Germany.[155] Wilhelm Moldenhauser, frustrated by his difficulties in dealing with Soviet mayors as he traveled with his radio equipment as part of Army Group South in early 1942, complained that "the people are invariably treated much too well by the Germans." The new colonial masters, following the English example, would need to be "severe" toward their subjects.[156]

In a similar vein, numerous formations issued dire warnings that their troops were too trusting of civilians and allowed partisan couriers through their checkpoints in spite of orders.[157] Army newspapers reported that the Germans suffered needless casualties because they respected the laws of war, including the white flag of surrender, which Soviet soldiers had begun to abuse.[158] This critique of the "good-naturedness" of the German soldier reached the home front through a widely distributed edited collection of letters assembled for propaganda purposes.[159] Such statements echoed Hitler's own viewpoint that the Germans would have to adopt a pitiless attitude whenever the latent moral scruples of the Aryan race threatened to interfere with the task at hand.[160] By stressing the need to overcome their instinctive goodness, Wehrmacht personnel reinforced for their loved ones an image of an honorable army that was, if anything, too softhearted and too attached to old-fashioned notions of chivalry.

Few of Altmann's old comrades were left alive after his unit broke out of encirclement during a Soviet offensive to relieve Leningrad in January 1943. Still, he continued to express trust in the Führer and the determination that, "we will . . . continue to do our duty and hope that the year 1943 brings the great final victory. . . . You guys know that nothing can so easily shake me."[161] He proudly reported in September 1943 that his division had been honored with the title of "East Division."[162] When his best friend and many other comrades fell the next month, he lamented their loss but, in an affirmation of Nazi values, explained that "one must be hard, and forget everything quickly."[163]

Although he faced his share of struggles on the northern front, Altmann could count himself lucky that he did not take part in the catastrophe that had engulfed the Wehrmacht's southern flank. After advancing across the Don steppe and into the Caucasus in their renewed 1942 summer offensive, German forces became locked into a costly effort to capture the city of Stalingrad. Capitalizing on this situation, Marshall Zhukov launched a two-pronged assault in late November 1942 that led to the encirclement and destruction of the Sixth Army, costing Germany and her allies nearly a million casualties. Further Soviet operations pushed the Wehrmacht back into the Ukraine by early 1943. From this point forward, it would find itself increasingly on the defensive, unable to replenish its enormous losses in men and material in the face of a Red Army that grew more numerous and capable by the day.[164]

Following the catastrophic defeat at Stalingrad, the value of comradeship became ever more important for maintaining social cohesion and providing a space where troops who had often not seen home for a year or more could experience warmth and kindness.[165] Writing about the loving, selfless community they formed became another way to indicate to their readers that their institution remained firmly grounded in the values prized by German society. In the 290th Infantry Division, which had held the line around Lake Ladoga and Leningrad before pulling back in mid-1943 toward Nevel, Willy and Johannes Hagemann prized the feelings of togetherness that had developed after months of combat. While Willy recuperated in a hospital in Holland, Johannes, who took care of the unit's horses, had endured heavy fighting and a lack of supplies during the first winter.[166] Still, he wrote fondly of the strong friendships he formed. He especially enjoyed playing cards and took pleasure in handing out the mail to his fellow soldiers. "In action, in battle we have become good comrades and, as it should be, everything is divided in thirds," he told his parents.[167]

On Christmas Eve of 1942, Johannes helped decorate his bunker, arranged the presents, and helped a comrade prepare a lavish dinner. They listened to music, sang, and went from bunker to bunker spreading Christmas cheer.[168] According to its intelligence officers, the division even gave out "games of all types," along with Christmas tree ornaments to enhance the holiday atmosphere.[169] Willy recovered from his wounds in late 1942 and returned to the division after training as an officer. During a brief rest period behind the lines, he reported to their parents that the company he now helped lead was playing a series of soccer games against other units.[170] On a warm Pentecost Sunday in 1943, he and his men took part in a game and the regimental band came to lift the soldiers' spirits as they enjoyed a handout of "alcohol and tobacco," which ensured that "the proper mood was not missing."[171] He made an effort to get to know his men by visiting their bunkers and took part in social gatherings for officers, including a memorable ride through the countryside on horseback.[172] The two brothers were able to spend time together on several occasions, such as when they took turns observing Soviet positions with a telescope, "an experience," Willy wrote, "that both of us brothers will truly never forget."[173] These encounters helped to nurture a special brand of comradeship and solidify the family's proud martial tradition, a message their readers were eager to hear.

The self-contained community so treasured by Wehrmacht soldiers also extended to their loved ones in the homeland. When troops recognized that their deployment in Russia would not be over by the winter of 1941, connections to home became ever more important. Like those among the front community, these relationships were marked by generosity, warmth, and all of the softness the *Landser* ("German soldiers") denied their enemies. One man who cultivated particularly strong ties to the homeland was Kurt Niemeyer, who had worked at a lumber mill in a Thuringian village and now, in his mid-thirties, traveled extensively through the East on transport and guard duty with a *Landeschützen* Battalion. Although he was proud of how he looked with a rifle and uniform, Niemeyer, who was older than most, considered himself more a family man than a professional soldier.[174] When his duties prevented him from coming home for Christmas in 1941, he sent his wife money to buy a present for their young daughter, Lieselotte.[175] He reminded Lieselotte to listen to her mother and remember her prayers, else the *Weihnachtsmann* would not come.[176] Over the next two years, as he crisscrossed Poland and Belarus, he assured his wife that his every thought was with home.[177] He sent home his wages, gave his wife advice on running the family farm, mailed chocolate to Lieselotte, and composed poems for their enjoyment.[178] In contrast to some, he viewed his time in the Wehrmacht not as an opportunity for glory but an unpleasant job that had to be done before he could return.

Although he may have been more intensely preoccupied with family life than most, Niemeyer was far from the only soldier who cultivated robust ties with home and continued to perform his peacetime roles as best he could. Soldiers sent home Christmas, Mother's Day, anniversary, and birthday cards, sometimes decorated with flowers or hand-made illustrations.[179] When conditions permitted, they shipped treats to their children and sent extra food, cigarettes, and portions of their paycheck to family members.[180] Adolf Dick, who could not be physically present for the birth of his second child, sent flowers, a letter, and money to his father-in-law to hand to his wife on his behalf. Dick later sent her three pieces of a fox so that she could have it made into a collar, and sent lotion, toothpaste, toothbrushes, and a hairbrush to her and the children.[181] Despite the deprivations of life at the front, Walter Neuser happily announced to his parents that he and his comrades had started a collection for the *Winterhilfswerk* ("Winter Relief Fund"), an annual Nazi-administered charity drive.[182]

When viewed in isolation such gestures may seem inconsequential, but in aggregate they played a critical role in nurturing a virtuous self-image and projecting this image to the homeland. They helped soldiers assure themselves and their loved ones that even in the face of vast distances and the horrors of the Eastern Front they remained loving fathers, devoted husbands, and obedient sons who exemplified the most deeply held values of German society. Whether they embraced their identities as warriors wholeheartedly or, like Niemeyer, considered them temporary constructs, they used their epistolary connections to home to salvage what they could of their peacetime selves and prove to their readers that they had not turned into monsters.

As they cultivated their ties with the homeland, troops also strove to bring the middle-class values of hard work, education, order, cleanliness, and domesticity directly to the land of *"Unkultur,"* with the institutional support provided by officers and the propaganda corps. Still defending their positions around Leningrad in the spring of 1943, Willy Hagemann and his comrades took it upon themselves to renovate the Russian dwelling in which they were staying so that it conformed to German standards. "In the simple Russian house we have set ourselves up in homely fashion," he wrote his parents. "The big room was divided up into bedroom, living room and kitchen. In front of the window stand flowers, and as we hung up curtains and laid a cover on the table in addition, the Russian occupants could not suppress a joyful astonishment."[183] Wilhelm Altmann recounted refurbishing Russian houses to make them "somewhat cozy."[184] Kurt Niemeyer described to his wife how he and his fellow soldiers had planted a garden, a sign, he explained, that "where[ever] the German *Landser* is, culture arises."[185] Such attempts to domesticate their environment were not only a means for soldiers to cultivate a familiar, comfortable atmosphere.[186] They also represented an attempt to introduce German culture and middle-class sensibilities to the Soviet Union, an effort for which, so Willy believed, the population owed them a debt of gratitude.[187]

Often subscribing to the stereotype of the "lazy" Eastern European, soldiers also regularly forced residents to clean their vehicles and wash their clothing. Kurt Niemeyer, who frequently oversaw civilian forced laborers, explained that Russians were made to clean the former Jewish school where he and his comrades were staying. "I, however, don't get a single finger dirty," he assured his wife.[188] On a grander scale, Wehrmacht units constructed toilets and saunas, and forcibly introduced new hygienic practices, such as delousing, to the local population.[189] In the eyes of the invaders, such measures formed part of a larger effort to bring civilization, with its attendant moral virtues, to the "wild East."

The army itself also became a site for the maintenance of culture. Willy and Johannes Hagemann's 290th Infantry Division made hundreds of books available to its men, helped organize a group of artists from among its ranks, and arranged visits by famous writers and artists.[190] Other units followed suit, often working in tandem with propaganda troops to organize cultural events such as a variety show Wilhelm Moldenhauser attended in March 1942 featuring a Ukrainian theater troupe.[191] Soldiers also kept up artistic and intellectual pursuits on their own time. Willy Hagemann asked Kressen, the sister of a fallen friend with whom he frequently corresponded, to send him a book by Tolstoy or Dostoevsky and mailed her a collection of poems he enjoyed.[192] Many peppered their letters with philosophical reflections alongside accounts of daily life. Hans Albring, for example, found the time to read works by St. Augustine, among other classic authors, mused over theological questions, and nursed his artistic talents by sketching the faces of locals he encountered.[193] Such intellectual and cultural activities were, above all, a pastime that staved off boredom between operations. However, they presented soldiers with a further opportunity to remind themselves and their readers that they remained committed to the values of beauty and self-cultivation as they journeyed through what most considered a cultural wasteland.

Keeping Up Appearances: The Honor Code in 1942–1943

While their men nurtured their sense of personal integrity in their writings, Wehrmacht commanders continued to draw from the language of traditional morality in their own proclamations. Recognizing that civilian cooperation was critical for the army's food and labor requirements in what was proving to be a drawn-out conflict and troubled by the growing partisan threat, they renewed their calls for troops to exercise restraint and conduct themselves in an upright manner.[194] As in 1941, such orders often simultaneously called for unrelenting brutality toward any active resisters—especially communists and Jews. Still, directives issued in the following years continued to prop up the Wehrmacht's moral image and made it easier for soldiers of all backgrounds and beliefs to claim identities as noble warriors whose organization played by the rules, all the while affording the army what commanders hoped would be a strategic edge in the battle to pacify the occupied territories.

In May 1942, OKH circulated a new code of conduct for German soldiers. Each man was to be "received as lord in the East," it insisted, but "lordship may never degenerate into contempt toward defenseless conquered [peoples]." Instead, German troops were to behave like enlightened rulers who treated the population "strictly but fairly," cultivating an image that was bound to win the locals' trust, even though civilians who displayed hostility would be shown no mercy.[195] One month later, von Salmuth, the commander of Fourth Army, which operated in the center of the front, issued a new set of regulations for his troops in their dealings with noncombatants. He emphasized that the Germans required the support of local civilians and could not afford to provoke them into joining the partisans. "The honor of the German soldier," he proclaimed, "demands a respectable appearance vis-à-vis the population in the occupied areas. . . . The population of the areas that have been cleared again of the Bolsheviks must feelingly recognize the difference between the behavior of the Bolsheviks and of the German soldiers, based on the good conduct of each individual German soldier." Von Salmuth instructed his officers to "appeal to the decency and orderly disposition of the mass of our soldiers," although, perhaps cognizant of the failure of previous regulations, he also warned of severe punishments for any transgressors. Following in the footsteps of other generals, he condemned plundering as a criminal act, but nevertheless described the USSR as "German economic land" and fully condoned the use of mass requisitions as long as they conformed to proper bureaucratic procedures.[196]

This attempt to maintain a respectable image in the midst of the *Vernichtungskrieg* extended to frontline commanders on all rungs of the Wehrmacht hierarchy. Intelligence officers of the 290th Infantry Division, to which Johannes and Willy Hagemann belonged, concluded in mid-1942 that "the best propaganda . . . consists of a good (in no way soft) treatment and sufficient supply of the population and of the prisoners."[197] Recognizing that brutality toward the population was fueling the partisan movement, the Third Panzer Army issued extensive ground rules for its troops' conduct in the spring of 1943. "Strict order, but justice, decency, and consideration of the foreign national character" were to be exercised, as well as "care of those who willingly cooperate, as far as is possible," although hostile elements could expect no mild treatment. Civilians pressed into service by the Wehrmacht were to be viewed as "helpers in the fight against the world-enemy" rather than forced laborers, and not subjected to corporal punishment. Only the proper authorities were allowed to confiscate local property. Following these guidelines, Army leaders stated, would raise the image of the Wehrmacht in the eyes of the culturally inferior Soviets and help the invaders exploit the land to the fullest.[198] As in the case of the more moderate sets of instructions sometimes issued in 1941, these later directives appear to have had little tangible effect on troops' actions or the attitude of the population, with few exceptions.[199] Still, they indicate that Wehrmacht leaders had not yet given up on the hope of salvaging the army's reputation by selectively deploying the language of traditional morality, lending further support to the narrative of decency their men continued to promote.

A Threatened Identity: Values in 1943–1944

After the battering it had sustained in the winter of 1942–1943, the Wehrmacht was no longer the formidable offensive force it had once been. In a final gamble to win back the initiative, however, Hitler and his generals launched Operation

Citadel in July 1943, a massive two-pronged strike aimed at severing Soviet forces in the Kursk salient, a bulge in the line between Orel and Kharkov that had resulted from the winter battles. Despite throwing 2,600 armored vehicles and 1,800 aircraft into the assault, the Wehrmacht ultimately gained little ground in the teeth of deeply layered Soviet defenses and soon pulled back on Hitler's orders.[200] This was the last major offensive the Germans would undertake on the Eastern Front. Over the next months, German personnel found themselves on the retreat against the overwhelming might of the Red Army. By the spring of 1944, Soviet armies had reached the prewar borders of Poland and were poised to cut off German forces in the Baltic.[201]

As the strategic situation crumbled, the image German warriors projected as virtuous, civilized men showed signs of cracking under the strain of constant defensive combat and the weight of the army's crimes. Mounting casualties threatened the selfless community to which the rank and file aspired. The sense of moral superiority afforded by a commitment to cleanliness and culture similarly crumbled as they accustomed themselves to a way of life more modest than that of the lowliest Soviet peasant. Most disturbing of all, many soldiers began to report a growing distance from their peacetime civilian personas that brought with it the fear that their participation in the *Vernichtungskrieg* was eroding the sense of personal decency they had guarded for so long. Even amid these creeping doubts, however, many continued to insist to their readers that they still possessed exemplary moral character, especially when they compared themselves to their enemies.

Willy Hagemann, who returned in 1943 to his old division as a lieutenant, and by 1944 was leading a company, attempted to hold on to his soldierly ideals even as disaster closed in. He extolled the bravery of his men, actively promoted ties among comrades, spoke of the need to endure in the face of great sacrifices, and kept his faith in the goodness of the German cause.[202] After he helped capture a group of Red soldiers on patrol, he concluded that the enemy was cowardly and still no match for "German organization and precision-work."[203] Still, like many of his fellow men in uniform, he no longer dwelt on the hope of a shining future; instead, he now recognized the war's purpose in the singular need to keep the Soviets out of the Reich. "We must and will win," he told Kressen, "because we fight for the more righteous cause. What would the enemy do with our homeland?"[204] As his 18th Panzer Division prepared for the final throw of the dice at the Battle of Kursk, Heinz Sartorio directed his contempt toward the British and American pilots who bombed German cities behind the lines. "In comparison we really are the clean angels," he wrote his sister. "We all hope that they soon get their punishment."[205]

Over time, the value of comradeship so highly prized by German troops became more and more difficult to maintain. Willy's company was beaten back through Latvia in 1944 with massive casualties. "Again we stood in hard operations that demanded great sacrifices. Oh, my brave men, I have lost almost all of them," he lamented. "I would like to remain with them always, they were the true German comrades. With whom should I speak about our deeds when everything is over?" A new sense of soldierly community would arise, he believed, but it would never be the same.[206] In January 1943, Wilhelm Altmann reported that he was the only long-serving veteran left in his group.[207] "So death rips wide gaps and it is often the best who depart from us," commented Hans Simon in 1944 after reading in the paper of the death of yet another comrade.[208] The front community, on which soldiers relied not only for strength but also opportunities to demonstrate their selfless decency, was starting to disintegrate.[209]

Years of war began to alter soldierly self-conceptions in more fundamental ways as well. Even as he kept up a brave, optimistic outlook in his letters to his parents, Willy Hagemann confessed to Kressen that he was "almost at the end of my strength." His commander told him that he and the other officers barely recognized Willy after one particularly fierce battle.[210] While he maintained a regular correspondence with his parents and sent them a heartfelt greeting on their anniversary to thank them for "such a beautiful and carefree childhood," he felt his connection to his former life slipping away.[211] In the heat of battle, he tried to forget about his family and friends at home, "so that it is more bearable for me." He also worried that he would never be able to learn a normal job when the war ended. Above all, however, he feared the loss of his own humanity. "My spirit has become numb and immovable in the monotony of the trench warfare," he told Kressen. "I saw death so often and have become hard." He still expressed pride that he had been recommended for the Knight's Cross, pending the approval of the Führer himself, whom Willy continued to respect and admire. But at the same time, he recognized that the war had permanently changed him: "Despite my youth I will not be able to be so boisterous, cheerful, and gay. The impressions of the war cannot be so easily forgotten and continually stand, admonishing, before my eyes."[212]

In spite of their many efforts to demonstrate to loved ones that they remained decent men, ready to rejoin their families at a moment's notice, many soldiers shared with Willy the fear that the war experience was severing them from their own humanity.[213] As they witnessed and took part in the Wehrmacht's pattern of criminality, along with all the other horrors of the Eastern Front, troops often recognized that they were losing the ability to empathize with their fellow human beings. For some this happened already in the war's first weeks; for others it was a slow, terrifying process by which they began to shed aspects of their civilian identities. Even Kurt Niemeyer, who continued to send chocolate to his daughter and cried when a *Volksdeutsch* family reminded him of home, explained to his wife that "through the war and everything I have seen I have become completely coldblooded."[214] Already in 1941, Niemeyer had explained that he no longer felt sympathy for Soviet POWs. "First I was soft, but now I have become cold," he wrote.[215] After mentioning that killing prisoners had become common practice, Heinz Rahe told his wife that the war had a "numbing" effect, and that "one gradually becomes indifferent or harder."[216] Going a step further, the especially reflective Harald Hoffmann wrote his aunt that, "one ceases to emphasize morality[;] above all one gets to know oneself as 'sub-human.'"[217] Hoffmann did not explain what he meant by this statement, although many of his letters expressed feelings of guilt at his and his comrades' participation in crimes against civilians.[218]

The transition from struggling to preserve one's own sense of decency to experiencing a profound feeling of indifference or even embracing the inhumanity of war was perhaps most powerfully encapsulated in the writings of Willy Reese, a member of the 95th Infantry Division that fought primarily in central Russia. An aspiring writer who had reluctantly answered his country's call, he kept a meticulous diary he intended to publish to document his reactions to the war. Reese described how the endless suffering he endured, his place at the bottom of the military hierarchy, the seeming triviality of human life in the face of mass death, and his own deeds that often went against his deeply held convictions made him feel disconnected from home and foreign to himself. "I strayed along the frontier," he wrote, "wiped out my memories of sea, music, and poetry, almost forgot my own name, and gave myself over to the shadows, the spectral existence of my mask, the mask of the laughing soldier."[219] Up until his death in 1944, Reese struggled to adopt an attitude of "heroic nihilism" to affirm the necessity of his own actions and salvage a sense of meaning from a war he ultimately recognized as a "suicide of the soul."[220] The feeling of personal decency he and other soldiers had tried so hard to maintain did not survive unscathed in a war in which right and wrong seemed increasingly difficult to distinguish.

The attempt to assert moral superiority over the enemy in the cultural realm also began to break down as the war went on. Troops who had emphasized the importance of order, cleanliness, education, and all the normative principles they associated with civilization found themselves living lives more suited to cavemen than members of a refined master race. Wilhelm Altmann, who had previously reminded his father and sister of his love of cleanliness, lamented that his bunker was filled with lice and bugs when he returned from a short home leave in August 1943.[221] During combat, he often went long periods without being able to wash or shave and spent much of his time underground.[222] Willy Hagemann, who complained about the lack of "clean and orderly" conditions in the East, detailed his and his comrades' efforts to make their bunker as comfortable as possible in the winter of 1943. Despite cold showers each morning, however, they could not rid themselves of the "little house pets" (insects) that lived with them.[223] After the company he now led took part in particularly difficult battles a few months later, Willy told Kressen that "if you saw me, you would not be able to recognize me. Ragged and torn to shreds, dirty and unshaven, we live our lives in burrows in the ground. I myself don't know how I look[.] I don't have a mirror."[224] It was in precisely such terms that the men of the Wehrmacht had described the Soviet population as they entered the country in 1941. After a seeming eternity in foxholes, trenches, and earthen bunkers, even the humble Soviet dwellings often seemed like a paradise. "It is cozy and warm here," Willy commented of a house he stayed in at the start of 1944, "if one overlooks the dirt and filth."[225]

Attempts to maintain the hallmarks of culture and civilization also broke down at the institutional level. Units found it more and more difficult to arrange cultural and artistic events as the fighting intensified. In 1942, Willy's 290th Infantry Division had to cancel its plans for sporting events and experienced difficulty distributing newspapers and reading material.[226] In early 1943, its mobile film projector could no longer be employed on the frontlines since every man was needed for combat.[227] Shortages of books and radios also became a problem for some units, few of which were in any case able to dedicate many resources to anything but combat activities as the Red Army pressed inexorably toward Berlin.[228]

Studying the values that Wehrmacht personnel and their commanding officers claimed to espouse from the start of Barbarossa to their disastrous retreat from the Soviet Union in 1943–1944 reveals a complex picture. The new moral code promoted by the Nazi regime had made great inroads in the army's culture, as exemplified by the Criminal Orders and reflected in soldiers' writings. At the same time, however, traditional ethical systems still remained influential, including the army's longstanding honor code with its emphasis on "upright" conduct, an array of middle-class norms, and the utilitarian calculus of military necessity. These value systems sometimes existed in tension with Nazi morality, but they could just as easily serve as a bridge toward the acceptance of ideology and willing participation in the *Vernichtungskrieg*. They supplied the moral vocabulary from which officers and men drew as they molded the Wehrmacht's public image.

With reference to this vocabulary, men in uniform constructed identities as "decent" men while painting their enemies as both racially inferior and morally corrupt. Some preferred to emphasize their commitment to values not dissimilar from those their fathers had championed in the First World War. Others judged their own character by a new moral yardstick, proudly declaring their allegiance to the Nazi worldview and adopting an uncompromising attitude toward their "subhuman" enemies. Still others combined elements of each. Whether they truly believed in their own goodness or whether this was simply an outward-facing mask may never be known for certain with the sources at hand. What is clear is that soldiers used the power of the pen to insist to their readers that they had not turned into bloodthirsty monsters but remained fundamentally decent men—selfless fathers, sons, and brothers-in-arms—who exemplified their nation's highest ideals however they defined them. To the extent they were able, they also attempted to perform these identities, whether this meant showing kindness toward comrades or sending gifts to their loved ones back home.

Soldiers' writings were buttressed by a steady stream of orders and propaganda that often combined the language of Nazi morality with old-fashioned notions of chivalry. Whether these instructed the men to wholeheartedly embrace their role as merciless racial warriors or to conduct themselves with restraint was often determined by the all-important principle of military necessity—the quest to gain a strategic advantage in the ever-changing context of battle—as well as officers' interest in preserving the army's reputation. The schizophrenic messaging that resulted may well have caused confusion among the rank and file, but it also reinforced the narrative of decency that soldiers were crafting about themselves and their institution, whatever their ideological outlook. Avid Nazi supporters could rest assured that their officers stood behind them. Men with little taste for Nazism could still take solace in the Wehrmacht's ostensible commitment to international law and "upright" conduct.

Troops' honorable self-perceptions showed signs of fracture as the campaign lengthened and their belief in their cultural and moral superiority ran up against the grimy realities of life at the front. Despite these setbacks, the army on the whole was remarkably successful in laying the rhetorical groundwork for the core assumption that would undergird the Wehrmacht myth—the notion that, on balance, the ordinary soldier had been a man of upstanding character within an honorable organization. This narrative was not the consequence of any intentional strategy on the part of officers and men but rather the collective product of the statements they made to themselves and to their sympathetic readership back home. There was, of course, one major modification to this picture in the postwar years: references to Nazi values, such as loyalty to the Führer and the racial community, would be scrubbed from the record, leaving an image that was politically acceptable in the aftermath of the Third Reich.[229] It would not be enough, however, for the men and their institution to simply insist on their own virtue. They would also have to defend their reputation in the face of the "dishonorable and despicable acts," as Eisenhower termed them, that constituted the defining feature of their conduct on the Eastern Front.

CHAPTER 2

Rationalizing Atrocities

Self-Exoneration in Soldiers' Letters

Harald Hoffmann was among the first men to cross the Soviet border on June 22, 1941. Born in Berlin in 1919, Hoffmann was better educated than most soldiers, having studied German literature, philosophy, and mathematics at the University of Berlin. He participated in the Hitler Youth, joined the Nazi Student Association, and volunteered for the Reich Labor Service (Reichsarbeitsdienst, or RAD), a national program that provided employment and instilled Nazi values. When war broke out in 1939, he joined the Wehrmacht as a member of a building battalion before returning to the University of Berlin to continue his studies and work as a research assistant. The spring of 1941 found Hoffmann once more in the army as a private first class with the 23rd Infantry Division, operating in Army Group Center. An astute observer and prolific writer, he strove to provide his parents and his sister Marion—as well as his future self—with a record of his experiences that did not gloss over the war's horrors: "In contrast to other comrades I try not to conceal or sugar-coat anything, even at the risk of creating more worries for you than if I withheld much," he told them in a 1941 letter.[1]

It was not long before Hoffmann began regularly recounting atrocities he witnessed or heard about, whether committed by the Soviet side or his own. Barely a week after the invasion's start, he stated that his unit was no longer taking prisoners, a decision he portrayed as an "appropriate" reaction to nefarious Soviet tactics and the behavior of "Kyrgyzs, Bashkirs, and other Asians who raged bestially in the Polish villages and toward German prisoners."[2] As winter set in, Hoffmann expressed strong reservations regarding his own side's brutal treatment of the Soviet population but attempted to make the men's behavior comprehensible to his family. In mid-November, for example, he described the tragic scene that transpired when he and his comrades entered a hut and stole the last potatoes from a woman and her children. The officer in charge took solace in offering her money in compensation. Another soldier blamed Stalin for neglecting his people. Hoffmann agonized over his own participation in the theft but cited his unit's massive food shortage as justification: "It was really terrible, but we also had to eat, had to at least have potatoes with the three teaspoons of dark sauce with two pieces of meat that we received as goulash from the [field] kitchen," he explained.[3] Until his death one month later, Hoffmann would continue to struggle with feelings of remorse but consistently managed to provide what he considered strong justifications for his actions.

In the decades following the war, tales of criminal violence like those Hoffmann described became central to the Wehrmacht myth largely due to their conspicuous absence. Memoirists up and down the ranks, journalists, politicians, and leaders of the new West German army loudly insisted that the Wehrmacht had played no part in the crimes of the Third Reich. If they admitted that the war in the East had been a particularly brutal affair, they laid most of the blame at the feet of the Red Army, which they painted as a savage institution with a litany of atrocities to its name—a narrative German civilians readily believed, especially in the wake of the Soviet invasion of Germany. Only a handful of officers and men were ever investigated for war crimes in West Germany. Any attempts to reverse this state of affairs were met with political opposition or public outcry. In East Germany, although superficial admissions of past guilt were an important element in the integration of former Wehrmacht officers into the country's political project, it was generally assumed that low-ranking (and lower-class) soldiers bore no responsibility for Nazi crimes. The question of the army's past crimes would remain largely dormant until the 1995 Wehrmacht Exhibition brought it to the fore of public discourse in the newly reunified nation.[4]

As the myth has crumbled in the face of overwhelming evidence over the past several decades, it has become clear that Hoffmann's experiences were far from unique. From the moment it began, the war on the Eastern Front witnessed a level of criminal violence unmatched by any previous campaign.[5] Wehrmacht personnel executed prisoners, burned villages to the ground, terrorized the civilian population through mass shootings and forced evacuations, and provided critical logistical support for the murder of Soviet Jews. Army leaders declared at the outset that the rules of war would no longer be followed and that the enemy represented an existential racial threat. In a related decision, high-ranking generals collaborated with regime officials to develop the Hunger Plan, which called for foodstuffs to be extracted from the USSR to feed the army and the German homeland. Tens of millions of Soviet citizens were expected to starve to death as a direct result, creating space for future German colonists.[6] All of this was in service to Adolf Hitler's vision of an East cleansed of Jews and other undesirables, in which any survivors would serve German overlords as agricultural laborers.

Although they did not come close to matching the invaders' genocidal intentions, Soviet troops were not models of innocence themselves. They often ignored the stipulations of international law, executed German prisoners, and conducted their own scorched-earth campaigns, and at the war's end, they wreaked a terrible revenge on the citizens of eastern Germany, all providing ample material for Wehrmacht propaganda. The harshness of the environment added fuel to the fire, as did the desperation of each side and the emergence of a partisan movement behind the front that blurred the line between civilian and combatant.

If the Wehrmacht's campaign on the Eastern Front was fought on a moral plane as well as a physical battlefield in the minds of soldiers and their homeland correspondents, atrocities and the narratives that surrounded them were among the most potent weapons, albeit weapons that could cut both ways. Tales of Soviet acts of barbarism served as proof that the enemy was beneath contempt. The crimes Wehrmacht troops themselves committed, however, had the potential to sow doubts about the invaders' moral character in the eyes of the German public and even cause servicemen to second-guess their own actions. Indeed, given the fact that unrestrained criminal violence was the distinguishing feature of the campaign, the Wehrmacht's atrocities constituted perhaps the single greatest threat to the decent self-image servicemen endeavored to project to the homeland, as well as their army's quest to demonstrate moral superiority over the Soviet enemy. How did soldiers write about violations of international law, whether committed by themselves or their foes, and what impressions did their accounts convey to their readers? How did men like Hoffmann retain their belief in their own goodness and continue to cultivate an honorable self-understanding in the face of overwhelming evidence? What accounts for the pervasive postwar assumption that the army had never crossed moral boundaries, in contrast to the Red Army?

It is only possible to answer these queries if the men in question were actually willing to record some of their most traumatic experiences at the front. Generally speaking, soldiers sought to spare their relatives from anxiety. But although they had many reasons to keep silent, German fighters in fact opted to inform their relatives about atrocities they witnessed—even those committed by their own side—far more frequently than scholars have recognized. They did so with a variety of motives, including the impulse to report new or "interesting" events, out of a conviction to provide an accurate account of their experiences, or in some cases to express their full-throated approval of extreme violence.

Another reason troops wrote about crimes was to provide themselves an outlet through which to grapple with troubled consciences and find ways to justify their conduct. Even though they became inured to violence over time, many expressed qualms about their side's behavior or at least recognized that their readers might find it questionable, a fact that by itself suggests they had not completely abandoned all ties to traditional morality. No doubt there was much they held back; indeed, certain subjects, such as rape, were only mentioned in passing or avoided altogether.[7] Nor should we expect that their descriptions of atrocities represented accurate or unbiased views. Nevertheless, accounts of criminal actions can be an invaluable source for understanding how soldiers curated their experiences in an effort to influence readers' perceptions and reinforce their own preferred self-image.

Regardless of whether they were willing to pen such accounts in the first place, it is sometimes assumed that the Wehrmacht's official censorship apparatus forbade troops from discussing criminal violence.[8] In actuality, censors were tasked with preserving military secrets and weeding out defeatism or resistance activity. Repressing accounts of atrocities was not part of their mandate.[9] This was, after all, an army that actively encouraged crimes and had declared that soldiers would not be prosecuted for committing them. The many examples of Ostkämpfer writing relatively openly about their own cruelties, and the fact that they routinely ignored wartime mail regulations, further indicate that external censorship did little to inhibit them from broaching the subject.[10]

This chapter examines how soldiers wrote about crimes they attributed to their enemies and violations committed by their own side, with an emphasis on the year 1941, when these subjects were most strongly present in their writings. In tandem with propaganda, troops' correspondence on this subject profoundly shaped the narrative of the Wehrmacht's activities in the USSR in the eyes of writers and recipients alike. By drawing from the language and principles of both Nazi morality and traditional moral norms, combatants developed a wide range of justifications for their actions that helped them assuage their consciences and defend their self-image as virtuous men who filled the ranks of an honorable organization. When they recorded enemy crimes, troops cast their opponents—particularly members of the Red Army, Jews, and communists—as both racially degenerate and morally bankrupt. While discussing their own participation in the *Vernichtungskrieg*, however, soldiers tended to prefer more traditional arguments about survival, justice, and necessity.[11] As the first popularizers of the Wehrmacht myth, they exploited their near-monopoly on information, their credibility as firsthand witnesses, and the formidable narrative platform that some ten billion items of correspondence afforded to transmute accounts of their crimes into opportunities for self-justification.[12] While they became desensitized to these occurrences as the war went on, their efforts appear to have been largely successful in preemptively shutting down any serious dialogue about the darkest aspects of the army's past even into the postwar era. Studying how German soldiers depicted their own atrocities thus provides us with a better understanding of the relationship between front and home front, above all how men in the field wielded the power of the pen to alter the interpretive framework within which recipients viewed the war, even at the point where their self-image was most vulnerable. In addition, it helps address the question of how much the German public knew of the Holocaust and the Wehrmacht's murderous activities in the East, a subject that has long been of interest to historians.[13]

Recounting Soviet Atrocities

As they stormed Soviet defenses in the war's opening phase, servicemen and propagandists joined Harald Hoffmann in making it clear that, in their eyes, it was the Red Army and not the Wehrmacht that committed the first acts of barbarism across the Eastern Front. Their frequent denunciations of what they perceived to be the Soviets' unfair fighting methods, mistreatment of wounded or captured comrades, and other breaches of international law painted a picture of an enemy that had tossed aside all respect for civilized norms.[14] When it came to explaining alleged Soviet atrocities, personnel often combined the racialized language of Nazi morality with an image of their enemies as evil men who, in contrast to themselves, made no effort to obey the laws of war. Whether they made reference to older or newer ethical systems, accounts of Soviet wrongdoing served an important dual purpose from the perspective of German servicemen and their readers in the homeland: they opened up moral distance between the Wehrmacht and the Red Army while simultaneously providing a convenient justification for the invaders' own barbarous conduct.

Advancing through woods and swamps toward the area of Cholm in the face of relentless counterattacks, Hans Simon, who manned an anti-tank cannon in the 12th Infantry Division, quickly joined the chorus of soldiers who told their correspondents grisly stories of Soviet cruelty. During the second month of the invasion, he explained to his father that when Red troops captured their German counterparts, "they put out their eyes and break their legs (like with [our comrade] Dwinger). He was on watch at night and he paid for it with his life."[15] Two weeks earlier, Simon had reported that the Soviets had fired poison gas near his battalion, a very improbable claim, but one that demonstrates how readily Wehrmacht personnel were willing to ascribe war crimes to the Red Army.[16] Writing to his mother from Demyansk—roughly halfway between Moscow and Leningrad—at the end of September, Simon attributed the "toughness" of his opponents to the nefarious influence of communism, the terror of the commissars who drove Red soldiers into battle, and the "cruelty that is part of the Asian character," hinting that racial differences played a part in their conduct.[17]

Non-commissioned officer Walter Neuser adopted a similar tone during the invasion's first months. A Nazi Party member who managed supplies for the 59th Artillery Regiment, attached to Harald Hoffmann's 23rd Infantry Division in Army Group Center, Neuser referred several times to the "vulgar tactics" of Russian fighters.[18] "They show white flags, one approaches, and then they shoot," he complained to his parents. "Many soldiers have already lost their lives here this way."[19] Like Simon, he ascribed at least some of the Red Army's behavior to its racial composition. "The Russian is a dangerous opponent," he informed his sister. "Because he is incited to hatred with the most pernicious horror stories and kept in check from behind, he keeps resisting till his own death. Especially repulsive to us were the many races and the devious and underhanded tactics."[20] Descriptions like these, which surfaced regularly in Wehrmacht correspondence as troops made first contact with the enemy, blended longstanding notions of honor and dishonor grounded in the army's traditional code with racist assumptions about the enemy's biological characteristics. The two went hand in hand: the barbarous methods attributed to the Red Army served as proof of the Soviets' racial inferiority. Not all troops suggested this link, however. To take one example, Hermann Henning, a machine-gunner in the 123rd Infantry Division, wrote several times about atrocities committed by the other side as his unit marched toward Demyansk but never resorted to racial terminology to explain them.[21]

Servicemen's views were shaped in part by Wehrmacht propagandists, who consistently portrayed the Soviet enemy as both racially degenerate and guilty of serious moral violations. Scores of articles in army newspapers, sporting titles like "Bolsheviks Disregard Red Cross," "Bolshevik Murder of Defenseless Prisoners," and "Bolsheviks Camouflaged as German Soldiers" illustrated the crimes of the Red Army and its commissars in graphic detail.[22] Soviet troops were described as "beasts" or "animalistic," "dehumanized," and an "Asian horde" incited by Jews to destroy European civilization.[23] The Germans were fighting an enemy, wrote war reporter K. G. von Stackelberg, for whom "any means is just, who breaks with all laws of humanity and . . . fights, one can truly say, with animalistic doggedness."[24] Reporter Gert Sachs described the "mean tactics" developed by the "Russian leaders of the Mongolians and other races," who disguised themselves in civilian clothing and hid in cornfields to shoot Wehrmacht troopers in the back.[25] The OKW publication *Mitteilungen für die Truppe* cited Soviet atrocities as proof that Germany faced a "stampede of sub-humanity."[26] Through such messaging, soldiers were encouraged to view the enemy through the lens of Nazi morality, as well as older ideas regarding proper and improper conduct.

The practice of combining Nazi values and traditional moral norms was also at play in the most far-reaching allegation leveled by Wehrmacht personnel at their Soviet enemies: that the Red Army had been secretly planning to launch its own invasion of Germany, and perhaps all of Europe besides.[27] Surfacing in Hitler's public declarations and communications to the troops and amplified by the Third Reich's propaganda machine, this fictional assertion was repeated by roughly half of the men examined here. The day before the invasion, Franz Siebeler told his parents and siblings that despite the 1939 nonaggression pact between the two nations, "there was never going to be any long-term friendship with the Russians. They would simply have waited for the most favorable opportunity to pounce on us."[28] During the attack's opening hours, Hans Roth penned in his diary: "How wonderful it is that we are able to exterminate these murderous beasts. How good it is that we have preempted them; for in the coming weeks these bloodhounds might have been standing on German soil. It is inconceivable what would have happened then!"[29] As Roth's statement reflects, the preemptive strike myth conjured up a racial nightmare filled with hordes of subhuman Slavs storming into the European heartlands. It also built on the concept of the "just war"—waged to protect the innocent from an aggressor—that had been deployed by European intellectuals and political leaders for centuries.[30] Whether a soldier preferred to view the claim in this light or, like Roth, in ideological terms, the notion that Barbarossa represented an effort to save Europe from a devastating Soviet assault served as a powerful source of legitimation. To lend the myth credibility, Wehrmacht propagandists published a slew of articles purporting to detail captured Soviet invasion plans or mischaracterizing the USSR's recent military buildup along their western border as a sign of aggression.[31]

As German formations continued their lightning advance in the summer and fall of 1941, Stalin implemented a desperate "scorched-earth" policy to destroy anything that could be useful to the invaders as the Red Army continued its haphazard retreat.[32] This was soon seized on by both German troops and propagandists alike as yet another sign of Soviet degeneracy. Drawing a comparison with Russian tactics in 1812, gunner Hans Simon wrote that the enemy demolished bridges and "set villages on fire" along the Wehrmacht's path in an effort to ensure that food stores would not fall into German hands.[33] Fritz Feierabend informed his wife the same month that "the Russian burns down all the bigger cities and towns alike before he leaves, without consideration for women and children."[34] Propagandists eagerly exploited the issue as evidence that the enemy was committed to a policy of senseless destruction. One Wehrmacht newspaper reported on the special units tasked with fulfilling Stalin's order:

> They are equipped with flamethrowers for incinerating grain and with explosives to destroy the farmhouses. They exterminate the cattle, without forgetting the chickens, which are poisoned so that the flesh is not edible. . . . This insane work of destruction by the Moscow mercenaries is directed in its entire effect against the Ukrainian population, which is deliberately abandoned to hunger and suffering.[35]

Another newspaper accused the Soviets of "hand[ing] over hundreds of thousands to starvation" through scorched-earth tactics. "These are Soviet methods[;] these are methods that only a sub-humanity can conceive of," it concluded.[36] By emphasizing the impact of Stalin's directive, the Wehrmacht would find a convenient scapegoat for the wartime hardships borne by the population and an excuse not to assume responsibility for their well-being.[37]

Perhaps the most shocking evidence of Soviet criminality the Germans publicized was the mass execution of prisoners by the Soviet secret state police (NKVD) in cities across occupied Poland and the western Soviet Union in the summer and fall of 1941. In the absence of sufficient transportation, some NKVD officials had decided to execute inmates rather than allow them to fall into German hands.[38] In his diary, private Wilhelm Moldenhauser, whose 60th Infantry Division had just reached the Polish city of Żółkiew, described watching the recovery of the bodies of men, women, and children who had been tortured and shot by Soviet authorities. "It is the Jews again," he wrote, "who had their hand in these terrible goings-on. The Bolsheviks have committed this terrible murder in every city."[39] Moldenhauser snapped several colored photos of the victims and asked his wife to have them developed.[40]

Other *Ostkämpfer* reported similar massacres, murders, kidnappings, and acts of sabotage committed by the retreating Soviets. Hermann Henning told his parents that Soviet officials had abducted a portion of Riga's male population as they fled the city.[41] Far to the south, Hans Roth described how Kiev was wracked by bombs left behind by Soviet operatives.[42] Besides these high-visibility events, soldiers and army reporters referred to countless other instances of brutality committed by the Soviet regime, ranging from the deportation of *Volksdeutsch* to the persecution of political dissidents and brutal requisitions in the countryside.[43] All such descriptions fed into a larger conception of the Soviet Union as an evil state that presided over a socially and economically unjust system in which human life held no value.

This mentality was strongly encouraged by the army's publications, which carried one story after another of the discovery of mass graves and mountains of corpses left behind by Soviet officials. Like the crimes of the Red Army, these were portrayed with moral indignation as acts that the honorable Germans simply could not comprehend. War reporter Siegfried Pistorius announced that the NKVD had slaughtered 528 Ukrainians in the city of Dubno before they left: "The women and men, the mothers and fathers, the childless children, the German soldiers, the Ukrainian people, the whole civilized world," he wrote, "denounces the Jewish-Bolshevik murderers, the organized sub-humanity of Moscow, denounces a regime that organizes murder and criminality."[44] Such stories attracted the attention of the Propaganda Ministry and the German press, both of which themselves regularly emphasized Soviet atrocities.[45] Joseph Goebbels even dispatched a team of propagandists to Lvov (modern-day Lviv), the site of the most notorious massacre of the Soviet retreat.[46] The story featured in the *Wochenschau*—a weekly newsreel that played in German cinemas—and according to Goebbels' diary garnered high praise from Hitler.[47] The Wehrmacht, however, demonstrated little interest in thoroughly investigating these cases; instead, they were used to legitimate massacres of Jews, who were invariably blamed for Soviet crimes.[48]

German combatants continued to recount tales of their enemy's moral degeneracy as their initial advance ground to a halt and they were forced onto the defensive in the winter and spring of 1941–1942. Hermann Henning, whose unit tried to stem the tide of Soviet counterattacks around Demyansk, wrote his brother Hansl in what would be his last letter that Red Army soldiers sometimes wore German uniforms and that they frequently attacked the wounded as they were being transported. "Often," he explained, "they removed the clothing of the wounded and mutilated them beyond recognition."[49] In May, as the lines stabilized, non-commissioned officer Hans Albring, who carried out communications duties for the Sixth Army Corps in the town of Velizh, told his comrade Eugen Altrogge that in one area the Germans recaptured: "the dehumanized hordes . . . commenced a huge crime and murdered helpless wounded, who couldn't be brought out."[50]

As resistance on the part of the civilian population increased in response to harsh occupation policies, soldiers railed against what they viewed as illegitimate attacks by civilians or partisans, whom Kurt Niemeyer described as "dastardly brothers" and Hans-Peter Eckener as a "plague."[51] The latter explained to his parents in November 1942 that partisans had attacked a village in his sector, stolen thirty horses, and beaten eight troopers to death.[52] As his unit struggled to contain a powerful partisan movement in his area at the end of 1941, Hermann Henning dubbed their tactics "perfidious [hinterhältig] murder" and claimed that they targeted ambulances along with the army's sled caravans.[53] "There are always women in play, too, who convey news and spy around," he added, reflecting a widespread obsession with the threat posed by female partisans.[54] Soldiers also accused resistance groups of terrorizing local villages that refused to support them. "There are gangs in the woods and swamps," wrote Hans-Peter Eckener to his mother. "They often come into the villages and shake down the farmers for food."[55] Likewise, Wehrmacht newspapers continued to highlight examples of Soviet brutality in the war's second year, although to a lesser degree than they had previously.[56]

Tales of Soviet misconduct still attracted the attention of higher authorities in the army. Even as it consciously abandoned the stipulations of international law in its own operations, the Wehrmacht went out of its way to collect evidence of its opponent's misconduct. The Wehrmacht Investigation Office for Violations of International Law (WUSt), founded in 1939 to investigate war crimes against German soldiers, assembled copious amounts of material, including photographs and witness statements, to document a litany of Red Army violations.[57] For instance, in January 1942, the WUSt recorded the testimony under oath of a sergeant who claimed to have discovered the bodies of 27 Wehrmacht troops beaten to death in Red Army captivity, and it collected copies of captured Soviet documents suggesting the practice was fairly widespread.[58] Wehrmacht units also attempted to uncover evidence of Soviet crimes against German prisoners during routine interrogations of POWs and deserters.[59] Back in Berlin, the SS and SD developed propaganda materials encouraging German combatants to expect barbaric treatment upon capture by the Red Army.[60]

After 1942, Soviet atrocities rarely appeared in soldiers' letters or in Wehrmacht publications, perhaps simply because the topic had lost its novelty, but they remained an important element in the regime's propaganda efforts.[61] These reached another high point in 1943 when the Propaganda Ministry publicized the Katyń massacre, which the Wehrmacht investigated.[62] The incident provided further proof of the enemy's unscrupulous conduct and what could be expected if the Red Army ever reached German soil, a theme Goebbels would forcefully hammer home till the end of the war.[63]

Although accusations of real or imagined Soviet atrocities lost their prominence within the Wehrmacht as the war went on, their impact on the army's moral discourse and soldierly self-understanding was far-reaching. They served to vividly confirm the racial inferiority of the Soviets as well as the belief that they could always be expected to behave with a savage cruelty devoid of all civilized impulses. Years after the war, as the Wehrmacht myth crystalized, veterans and civilians alike would continue to propagate the notion that only German arms and honor had kept at bay the barbarous Red hordes intent on laying waste to European civilization. Further, the enemy's perceived misdeeds were often viewed as ample justification for a response in kind—a phenomenon not unique to the Eastern Front or the Second World War.[64] If the Soviets would not follow the example of the "upright" Germans by honoring the Wehrmacht's preferred rules, this line of reasoning went, then the latter were themselves no longer bound to follow them.

Rationalizing German Crimes

Even as they continually censured their enemy for violating the laws of war, German soldiers found themselves having to grapple with the ever-growing catalogue of their own side's transgressions—transgressions with the potential to put at serious risk the decent image they so deeply cherished. Many admitted they felt troubled by conduct that overstepped ethical boundaries, but on the whole personnel were remarkably successful in devising a vast array of rationalizations to overcome any pangs of conscience. They provided their readers with a version of events in which they emerged not as criminals but as reasonable men who from time to time were forced to take harsh measures. Although they had frequently incorporated racial ideology into their explanations of the Red Army's crimes, the men of the Wehrmacht rarely resorted to the new framework of Nazi morality when they felt the need to explain their own misdeeds. Especially when discussing atrocities against civilians, they typically favored justifications grounded in more traditional moral value systems, perhaps because they sensed these would find broad acceptance among their correspondents. Aside from casting acts of brutality as a necessary response to Soviet crimes, these justifications included downplaying the harm they inflicted, reframing atrocities as acts of justice or as beneficial to the victims, making legalistic distinctions, and stressing their own need to survive.[65]

Many of the first crimes German men in uniform confessed to their relatives during the invasion's first weeks involved the mistreatment or summary execution of Red Army soldiers and commissars, a phenomenon historians have documented as a regular occurrence in the Wehrmacht.[66] Troops typically explained such actions as legitimate responses to what they depicted as the unconscionable tactics of the Soviet armed forces. One of the men who advanced this moral argument was Hans Albring, a staunch Catholic from the Rhineland with a penchant for theological reflection. Although it did not operate on the front lines, his unit, a communication section of Sixth Army Corps, encountered occasional resistance from Red soldiers who had been bypassed during the advance. Writing from a barn outside the modern-day city of Velizh to his longtime friend Eugen Altrogge, himself a Wehrmacht lieutenant in France, Albring related that Soviet sharpshooters were active in a nearby woods.[67] He then revealed the gruesome fate that awaited them upon capture: they would be led to a ditch and shot one by one in the back of the head, a procedure Albring said he had personally witnessed twice before. He admitted his initial astonishment at the casual way the killings were carried out but insisted that "this is a . . . just end, when one knows the events that led up to it, however much one can argue about the methods, which bear the signa temporis [signs of the times]."[68] Albring did not elaborate on the events that preceded the executions, but his phrasing implied that the Germans had found the gunmen's actions so reprehensible that their deaths were well-deserved. Albring, who personally had little taste for Nazism, gave no hint that the murders were racially motivated; instead, he depicted them as a harsh but understandable brand of justice.

Far to the south with the 13th Panzer Division, lieutenant Heinz Rahe, a former Protestant pastor, described Russian soldiers as "fanatical fighters" who systematically massacred captured German troops, refused to surrender even when wounded, and prepared dastardly ambushes behind the lines. "Today I saw how [German soldiers] let a prisoner run for a while and then killed him," Rahe confided to his wife in early July. "This is how both sides deal with their prisoners," he added.[69] Like Albring, Rahe presented this decision to ignore the rules of war as a legitimate reaction to objectionable fighting methods on the part of the Red Army, a simple balancing of the moral scales. In some cases, Ostkämpfer blended this mode of argumentation with racial stereotypes, as Harald Hoffmann had done when he asserted that "Asian" combatants were prone to committing atrocities against German POWs and Polish civilians, prompting the need for retaliation.[70]

In the same vein, troops tended to describe the Commissar Order as a defensive measure in the face of the commissars' alleged barbaric activities. Fritz Feierabend, on the road to Smolensk with the 7th Panzer Division in July 1941, revealed to his wife that he and his comrades shot every political functionary they captured. The rationale he gave was that Soviet officials lived well while their population suffered, and he added that they regularly assaulted German troops after pretending to surrender.[71] These observations, in Feierabend's mind, were sufficient to make such brutality comprehensible to his loved ones. Heinz Rahe recounted to his wife that he had spent time with a general who informed him that "every functionary who is taken prisoner is shot." The reason, Rahe related, was that "the Soviets supposedly killed many Ukrainians, like in 1919."[72] In each case, Feierabend and Rahe explained the killings as acts of justice rather than what they actually were: ideologically motivated mass murders. Even Walter Neuser, a Party member who often espoused Nazi views, revealed no hint of ideological motives when he told his mother in October 1941 that his unit shot commissars out of hand. The reason he gave was simply that the commissars strengthened the enemy's will to fight.[73] In general, troops espoused the belief that most commissars were Jews and fanatical representatives of a regime that would have to be eliminated.[74] However, when it came to justifying their murder at the hands of the Wehrmacht, they seem to have taken a different rhetorical tack, either because they were not aware of the order's ideological origins or because they believed that rationalizations based on more familiar moral principles—in this case, justice— would be more readily accepted by their readers.

In the wake of the major battles of encirclement that unfolded in the summer of 1941, the number of Soviet prisoners in Wehrmacht captivity quickly climbed into the millions. Those who escaped a swift execution found themselves subjected to endless marches, forced labor, and for many—more than three million over the war's course—death from starvation or exposure in overcrowded camps.[75] Since most of the men in this book fought in front-line units, their contact with prisoners tended to be limited. On occasion, however, they did signal that they had firsthand knowledge of the Wehrmacht's criminal treatment of POWs and conveyed information to their families about the state of the prisoners' health and their use as forced laborers. In their letters home, soldiers typically rationalized these abuses through a combination of racist stereotypes and assumptions regarding their victims' moral character.

As his 23rd Infantry Division continued its drive toward Moscow in the fall of 1941, Harald Hoffmann bore witness to the condition of the seemingly endless legions of POWs captured by Army Group Center. He described in frightening detail how POWs, many of them wounded, were forced to haul ammunition boxes for the invaders and slept through "horrific nights without a roof, without fire in the snow, lying over each other." He also revealed to his family that a comrade had told him the prisoners were given only "1 bread per week and some water soup with potatoes." Hoffmann fretted over this brutal treatment but in the end concluded that they deserved their fate on account of the Red Army's reprehensible conduct: "these prisoners are treated in accordance with their misdeeds," he wrote.[76] In other letters, Hoffmann described how he and his comrades stole whatever food and clothing they could from the prisoners. He did not dwell on the morality of his actions but implied that he and his comrades sorely needed the supplies, that the victors had the right to take whatever they wished, and that the prisoners' condition was not a great deal worse than that of Wehrmacht soldiers, observations that helped to ease his often-troubled conscience and make his actions morally comprehensible to his parents and sister at home. Like many others, Hoffmann also portrayed newly captured POWs as more satisfied in German captivity than in Red Army service, implying that the invaders were practically doing them a favor.[77]

Prisoners were transported by rail or forced to march to massive enclosures where starvation rations, disease, and the total absence of shelter from the piercing cold of the advancing winter began to take their toll. Kurt Niemeyer, whose work in a Security (*Landeschützen*) Division required him to travel extensively throughout Poland and the USSR, had more opportunities than most to observe the POWs' fate. In a letter he addressed to his wife and daughter in September 1941 he mentioned the catastrophic death rate in a camp in Siedlice.[78] In subsequent letters, he described how thousands of prisoners were loaded "like cattle" into open boxcars for transport. Niemeyer admitted that he had been "soft" at first but had come to realize that sympathy was out of place. Employing Nazi diction, he dubbed the captives a lice-ridden "horde" and explained that they easily became "impudent." Beatings and shootings, he stated, were the only way to keep them in line.[79] Several months later, Walter Neuser, in action outside Moscow, observed a train carrying roughly a thousand POWs. "One does not easily forget these impressions," he wrote his parents. "All types are represented, but thoroughly exhausted to the point of collapsing; a miserable image. One may not have sympathy for them, however. What would have happened if their intention to stab us in the back had been successful?"[80] Here again, pity was ruled out and the language of race merged with an emphasis on the victims' nefarious intentions. Dr. Konrad Jarausch, a kitchen supervisor at a large POW camp, had a much more intimate knowledge of the horrific fate that ultimately lay in store for such men. After relating to his wife how he watched prisoners perish from starvation, disease, and exposure on a daily basis, Jarausch, a committed nationalist, began to question the righteousness of his side and took small steps to improve the POWs' condition.[81] However, he was an exception in an army whose rank and file had become adept at rationalizing the criminal treatment of their captives, whether with reference to racial ideology or assumptions about their enemies' ethical shortcomings.

As Red Army prisoners suffered and died in German captivity, specially designated SS and Order Police units began the systematic persecution, ghettoization, and extermination of Soviet Jews in newly occupied lands. The army played an important role in identifying Jews, providing logistical support, and in some cases directly taking part in the killings, especially in rear areas under the guise of anti-partisan operations. It had also spent years portraying Jews as an existential threat through its indoctrination program and in countless orders issued throughout the campaign.[82]

The fate of the Jews of Eastern Europe rarely appeared as a sustained topic of discussion in soldiers' writings, but it was not entirely absent.[83] From the core sample, twelve men wrote about Jewish ghettos they observed as they marched through Polish and Soviet cities, described how the Wehrmacht forcibly put Jews to work or expelled them from their homes, and, much more rarely, depicted mass shootings or individual acts of violence. Most of these were passing references devoid of any commentary, however, and it is evident that many soldiers felt uncomfortable telling their loved ones about any acts of genocide they may have observed. Hans Albring, for instance, wrote his comrade Eugen with no further context that "the bodies, that one earlier randomly threw on a pile, were already, as well as it goes, sorted out and one had already thrown lime over the half-thousand executed Jews. What in detail occurred here—to write about that, it is not the proper place."[84] None of the men reported personally taking part in the killing of Jews, but a few did mention massacres by either the army or SS. Along with their discussions of the abuse of Soviet prisoners, soldiers' accounts of anti-Jewish violence stand out among their descriptions of Wehrmacht crimes as instances in which the language of Nazi morality suffused the justifications they offered.[85]

Writing in May 1942, Heinz Sartorio informed his sister that the bodies of 20,000 Jews and 40,000 Russians filled mass graves outside an unnamed city—likely Orel (modern-day Oryol)—and that "hundreds of thousands of Jews" had been executed in the East. Sartorio was a lance corporal in a bridge-building unit with Army Group Center, whose views rarely deviated from Nazi orthodoxy. When he discussed the fate of what he termed the "foreign Jew-vermin," he expressed his clear approval. He noted that the killings were shocking "at first, but when one thinks about the big idea, then one must say to oneself that it was necessary." For Sartorio, it appears that racial ideology alone was sufficient justification for the massacre, even as he hastened to add that the SS bore sole responsibility.[86]

Other soldiers blended racial prejudice with moral arguments when they attempted to provide some explanation for acts of genocide, often asserting that the victims had deserved their fate because they had supposedly committed crimes against the occupiers. Anton Böhrer made a cryptic reference to imaginary Jewish violence against Germans when he told his sister and parents in December 1941, that 24,000 Jews had been expelled from an unnamed city and many had died in the process.[87] Böhrer expressed satisfaction, since he considered them a "wretched, lice-ridden and dirty riff-raff" who refused to work, bore responsibility for starting the war, and were "guilty of much mischief after the occupation."[88] Kurt Niemeyer told his wife in March 1942 that he had seen Jewish mass graves "by the hundreds and hundreds" outside the Warsaw Ghetto. He declined to provide the full story of what had transpired, but like Böhrer he attempted to explain what had happened as an understandable reaction to the Jews' supposed criminal activity: "They did not deserve any better," he wrote, "since they murdered the Germans by the thousands."[89] In their diaries, Hans Roth and Wilhelm Moldenhauser depicted massacres of Jews in Tarnopol (modern-day Ternopil), Lutsk, and Kiev as fully justified responses to acts of sabotage and the murder of Ukrainian prisoners by the NKVD as the Soviets retreated.[90] Both soldiers paired these rationalizations with the language of racial prejudice and emphasized the role of the SS and local Ukrainians, although Roth did not hesitate to state, approvingly, that his Wehrmacht comrades had committed the murders in Lutsk. When it came to justifying crimes against Jews, then, race-centered explanations often appeared in tandem with the moralistic language of deserving, worthiness, good, and evil. This combination had long been present in Nazi propaganda.[91] However, it in fact deviated from the core of Nazi morality, which measured human worth on the basis of racial essence rather than personal behavior.[92]

Having been instructed to act as "lords in the East" and increasingly cognizant that their commanders did little to restrain them, soldiers began to abuse the position of power they enjoyed over the Soviet Union's non-Jewish population as well. Theft, the imposition of forced labor, rape, murder, and wholesale destruction became commonplace, whether committed by individuals on their own initiative or under orders.[93] If soldiers were relatively reticent when it came to describing the killing of POWs, commissars, and Jews, they were much more prolix as they narrated the widespread abuse of Slavic civilians, and much more willing to admit personal culpability. As in their writings about crimes against Jews and the Red Army, soldiers filtered their experiences to convey a one-sided narrative of the army's activities, project a whitewashed image of their own identities, and absolve themselves from any sense of guilt. However, the justifications they offered for violence against non-Jewish civilians were rarely couched in racial terms; instead, Wehrmacht servicemen typically fell back on the more familiar language of traditional morality when they explained their involvement to their readers.

During the war's opening months, *Ostkämpfer* obscured the terror that frequently characterized their relationship with the population by depicting themselves as welcome guests and recipients of civilian generosity rather than agents of violence and exploitation. According to soldiers' letters, civilians voluntarily performed chores for the invaders, served meals, and shared supplies in a spontaneous show of appreciation at being "liberated" by German arms.[94] In October, Harald Hoffmann wrote his parents and sister that in the last home in which he quartered, "the matka [mother] . . . cooked us potatoes with milk daily." In his current quarters, he continued, "the people . . . are really nice, also cook potatoes for us and would cook even more for us if they had anything, but chickens and eggs have already fallen victim to our predecessors."[95] In other words, Hoffmann admitted that some German soldiers committed theft, but suggested that in his own case the supplies had been freely given. Wilhelm Moldenhauser similarly portrayed the relationship between occupier and occupied in Ukraine in a relatively positive light. "Since two days ago," he told his wife, "we have been in a village at the house of a small farmer where we were treated for the first time very hospitably. . . . We received butter and eggs and smoked meat with boiled potatoes."[96]

Accounts of civilian hospitality accorded well with *Wochenschau* newsreels of cheering crowds and army newspapers that described the invaders as the honored guests of a grateful population.[97] While some elements of the population did in fact express support for the invaders at least early on, civilians ultimately had little choice in the matter of handing over food or providing shelter, knowing that any refusal could meet with instant and deadly retribution. As Moldenhauser admitted to his wife in 1942, "When we want something, we must beg for it from the Russians or during the advance we must forcibly pilfer it."[98] Further, it was not long before troops began to see themselves as entitled to any resources they came across, whether or not they were freely offered.[99] Still, by frequently portraying themselves as the recipients of locals' generosity, soldiers transmuted exploitation into its opposite, giving their readers in the homeland the impression of a benign, even friendly relationship between conquerors and conquered that papered over the realities of the occupation.

In cases where civilians took measures to defend against the encroachments of the invaders, soldiers cited the population's hostility as justification for the employment of unrestrained violence, including the collective punishments—mass executions of local citizens—that quickly became the Wehrmacht's standard operating procedure in response to any signs of resistance.[100] Having just reached the Bug River on the invasion's third day, Franz Siebeler explained to his parents why a group of civilians was killed, apparently by members of his unit: "The civil population has taken part in the battles and ambushes. 20 people, among them 2 women, were summarily executed. That is also more than just, because there is scarcely anything so vile," he penned.[101] In a similar vein, Kurt Lang insisted to his mother a year into the invasion that his unit had been fully justified in employing mass terror in response to acts of sabotage by partisans who had evaded capture: "In consequence, 3 villages, in which the partisans have resided, were completely burned down by us and the male population shot dead. That is the necessary, inexorable revenge, under which of course the innocent must suffer with the guilty."[102] Here again, Wehrmacht members reversed the victim–perpetrator binary by portraying their actions as morally defensible responses to alleged Soviet crimes and signaled their agreement with the army's habitual policy of punishing the slightest infraction with indiscriminate force.

Even though it did not always involve such overt displays of violence, the widespread theft of civilian property, which became a permanent feature of the Wehrmacht's occupation, was even more devastating in the long run for a population that had barely lived above subsistence level even in the best of times. The loss of a cow or a single bag of potatoes was nothing short of a death sentence for many of the citizens in the army's path. They would soon suffer the consequences of the decision by OKW and regime officials that the bulk of the country's foodstuffs would be allocated to the German home front and armed forces. Some troops made a point of emphasizing to their readers that stealing was strictly punished in their units, a claim that implied that it was a relatively rare occurrence and further reinforced the perception of the Wehrmacht as an institution that adhered to civilized norms.[103] Still, their letters indicate soldiers routinely admitted that enormous amounts of civilian property ended up in Wehrmacht hands, and even on occasion expressed sympathy for the victims as well as flashes of moral self-doubt.

Soldiers often justified their actions to themselves and their readers by highlighting the distinction-without-a-difference between "stealing" and legitimate requisitions that Wehrmacht commanders had established in order to provide legal cover for the regime's hunger strategy.[104] As he informed his parents and sister of the disturbing scene that transpired when he and his comrades entered a house and took the last potatoes from a Russian woman and her children outside Moscow in November 1941, Harald Hoffmann recounted that the officer who accompanied them insisted that she would be paid for each kilo, as regulations called for.[105] Although the woman clearly would not consent, the lieutenant forced her to accept the money. "The lieutenant is satisfied again and has eaten," Hoffmann commented.[106] In the officer's mind, offering payment not only satisfied army rules but transformed an act of theft into a legitimate transaction. Much later in the war, as his unit retreated from the Caucasus, Heinz Rahe wrote to his wife describing a major who also exemplified the culture of following rules and regulations for their own sake, with little regard for the implications. "On the subject of the treatment of the Russians," wrote Rahe, "he's very exact. He pays for every chicken or egg and in this [manner] very consciously wants to differentiate himself from the Romanians. Whether the Russians now have to heat the fire in 8 days with the money or not is all the same to him—consciously correct."[107]

Only a few soldiers openly admitted the truth—that the practice of offering monetary payment was little more than a charade since money was essentially worthless to most Soviet families.[108] Still, this does not appear to have stopped them from continuing the practice, whether for legal appearances or to quiet troubled consciences. Hermann Henning described to his relatives in late September 1941 how soldiers acquired food from the area around Demyansk. "It's strictly forbidden for us to steal anything, even a single potato," he wrote. "Everything must be paid for. . . . Often, however," Henning confessed, "it happens that one must really force the money on the people, since they can't do anything with it."[109] In an ironic twist, the act of paying that was supposed to demonstrate the civilized quality of the invading army and its correct treatment of the population frequently took the form of an act of violence as soldiers imposed unwanted transactions. Henning further explained in a separate letter to his parents a few days later that "we can once in a while buy some milk or also honey," an action he still differentiated from theft, which he again noted was not allowed.[110] Whether Henning found solace in the empty gesture of offering payment is unclear. He also implied that in any case the Soviet regime, not the invaders, bore responsibility for the population's hardships and explained that his unit's supplies were sorely lacking.[111]

Another strategy that helped Ostkämpfer come to terms with their actions was depicting exchanges with civilians not as a form of theft but as mutually desired trades. Heinz Rahe, who had taken issue with his "consciously correct" fellow officer, made sure to point out to his wife in late 1941 that it was standard practice in his unit to pay for food with tobacco products and sometimes "a mark or two."[112] One of these interactions even resulted in a delicious goose dinner for him and his fellow officers.[113] Similarly, Wilhelm Moldenhauser told his wife that he and his comrades offered soap and sugar to pay civilians back for the milk, eggs, and honey they had generously supplied.[114] Such descriptions, which often left out the fact that not all such exchanges were conducted willingly on the Soviet side, further encouraged family members to believe that their husbands and sons acted honorably and followed the rules of war.

As the days grew colder and the German advance stalled before the gates of Moscow in the winter of 1941, soldiers turned more and more to rationalizations centered on survival and personal need in order to explain to family members why they ransacked villages, stole equipment from POWs, and occupied Soviet homes, sometimes turning their owners out into the deadly cold. At times, their livelihoods were indeed precarious due to a total lack of planning for a winter campaign, logistical weaknesses, and the determination by Nazi and Wehrmacht leaders that the army would "live off the land" to ease the burden on German stomachs at home.[115] Hans Simon described chronic supply problems in his 12th Infantry Division during the muddy autumn and the solutions to which he and his comrades turned. "No provisions came for 6 days," he wrote in early September to his mother after his unit crossed through a forest in rainy weather near the Valdai Hills between Moscow and Leningrad.[116] Their solution was to forage in the surrounding area: "We had to slaughter something for ourselves. . . . Now we have an abundance of food and—everyone has an upset stomach."[117] Despite this momentary reprieve, Simon wrote over the next months of constant hunger and learning to dig up potatoes on days when no bread was available, a story that was repeated in the letters of many other servicemen.[118]

Walter Neuser, whose 23rd Infantry Division inched forward toward Moscow in late fall of 1941, often performed supply-related duties. He described to his parents how men of his artillery regiment, which had not yet received any winter equipment in mid-October 1941, pilfered fur and cloth wherever they could find it and took gloves from Soviet POWs. "Whoever has not done that yet has to reckon with frozen bones," he explained, since the first snowfalls had already started on October 6.[119] Neuser himself, who benefitted from an extensive network of relatives and friends, was already prepared. He had asked his mother weeks earlier to send him leather gloves and other winter clothing.[120] Despite the lack of proper gear, Neuser reported that his artillery regiment received sufficient food supplies.[121]

In the same division but closer to the front with the infantry, Harald Hoffmann described alternating periods of deprivation and plenty. After joining a recon patrol to procure food from a ruined village, he slaughtered a chicken for the first time in his life and fried onions, tomatoes, and other ingredients to supplement his rations, but wrote that "despite this I still am constantly hungry."[122] Toward the start of their renewed push toward Moscow, Hoffmann's company used up the last of its bread supply, and as winter arrived in full force he observed that the troops' clothing was essentially unchanged from what they had worn in the summer, a situation that even blankets and straw did not assuage during the frigid nights.[123] The Protestant chaplain of Neuser and Hoffmann's division found himself facing difficult questions from the soldiers, who had taken up defensive positions for the winter after their offensive ground to a halt: "When do reinforcements come[;] when winter clothing[;] why do we have no antitank weapons?"[124] In dire straits, Hoffmann and his fellow combatants stole whatever food and warm clothing they could from the villagers they encountered, as well as from the POWs their unit helped capture in October. "The *Landser* takes everything, honey, chickens, pots, milk as if it had simply been waiting for him. . . . And so gradually this great land begins to render up its riches to us," Hoffmann commented.[125] He repeatedly lamented the suffering of the army's victims but implied in his letters that such brutality was unavoidable given the situation. Readers in the homeland, who tended to value their men's well-being above all other considerations, readily accepted such rationales.[126]

Just as hunger justified economic exploitation, the need for shelter from the cold became an argument for the brutal treatment of the country's inhabitants. Thousands of troops ended up quartering in Soviet homes for extended periods. Hoffmann described the scenes that resulted:

> The quarters get worse almost daily, often 30 men in a room, lying on the floor. . . . And then the farmers themselves must be driven out of these quarters, with a flock of little children shivering from the cold not knowing where to go, they always storm inside again onto the oven, the children cry, the old people cry too, since all their chickens have been slaughtered. At night they lie on the oven if the *Landser* haven't surged there themselves.[127]

Although he had reservations about expelling civilians from their homes, Hoffmann, like many others, seems to have accepted the argument that theft, forced labor, and eviction were the only means for him and his comrades to make it through the Russian winter. Not far from Hoffmann, Walter Neuser described to his mother how he and his comrades turned civilians out into the cold after they refused to move to another house. He rationalized this action on the basis of the survival imperative and the victims' resistance, while adding a touch of sympathy: "I didn't do this gladly, but what else can one do. We can't sleep outside. I have never seen such impertinent behavior."[128] Of all the moral arguments soldiers advanced as they explained the Wehrmacht's crimes to their relatives, the claim of self-preservation was undoubtedly the strongest. It cannot be doubted that the deliberate choices of the regime and military authorities, as well as environmental conditions, sometimes conspired to put them in a seemingly impossible position. However, it is often unclear to what extent their actual physical survival was at stake, and exploitation continued even when troops had adequate supplies.

To add to soldiers' troubles, the Wehrmacht was now reeling from the impact of the Soviet Winter Offensive. Germany's men in uniform found themselves spread thin—outgunned and outnumbered by a Red Army that grew in strength every day despite staggering losses. In this atmosphere, *Ostkämpfer* took up the language of "military necessity" invoked by higher Wehrmacht authorities to justify the use of ever more extreme forms of violence as they retreated, including forced evacuations and the implementation of scorched-earth measures.[129] They depicted these actions as the only way to maintain order, reduce perceived threats to the army's security, and advance the war effort, especially as the strategic situation grew more desperate.

Harald Hoffmann's 23rd Infantry Division had been momentarily forced to adopt a defensive posture in September 1941 as it tried to fend off Soviet attempts to slow the advance on Moscow.[130] The unit turned to a policy that was becoming standard practice in the Wehrmacht—ejecting civilians from their homes into the unforgiving winter and burning their villages to the ground to deprive the enemy of shelter and supplies. Hoffmann described his own role in one of these operations in a letter to his parents and sister:

> We had to cover the action of the engineers, who had to burn down a village in front of our positions. At one in the morning the village had to be rapidly cleared of the pitiable inhabitants, and, while cattle and pigs bellowed and the women hauled away their meager belongings, we went ahead . . . from farmhouse to farmhouse[;] the engineers threw the smoke candles and smoke grenades that burn at a high temperature into the 60 to 70 houses or shot flares into the straw roofs. In a few minutes the buildings blazed up, the night was suddenly blood red. . . . Crouched, watching inquisitively, we went back, while between us and the Russians the sea of flames undulated.[131]

Although his relatively sympathetic portrayal of the victims suggests that he was troubled by the experience, Hoffmann appears to have accepted the logic that the army was doing what it had to do in order to thwart the Red Army's advance.[132] Such thinking did not, however, dispel the feelings of guilt and despair that would dominate his writings until his death outside Moscow at the end of the year.[133]

As scorched-earth operations became a ubiquitous feature of the Wehrmacht's strategy, other soldiers remarked upon the ever-higher number of forced laborers the army employed, including women and children, but defended the practice on the grounds that the additional manpower was sorely needed. As the commander of an engineering battalion within Army Group South, Dr. Wilhelm Bacher had frequent contact with civilians, and his unit routinely employed forced laborers to construct bridges and carry out other building projects. In his diary he described the use of civilian labor as a strategic necessity as his unit prepared to defend a town from Soviet attack but depicted the relationship as one of cooperation, rather than coercion:

> We need the civilians urgently for work purposes. The pro-German attitude of the inhabitants continues to amaze me, they all gladly and very willingly perform all tasks, from the oldest down to the smallest boy, who—even though they can already scarcely stand—tirelessly saw wood or travel with the horses into the woods in order to fetch brushwood.[134]

Combatants also portrayed the use of violence against civilians as an essential means to ensure the Wehrmacht's security and keep the occupation from sliding into chaos. In his diary, Hans Roth, also with Army Group South, recorded his unit's encounter with partisans in the town of Lebedyn, northwest of Kharkov: "During the afternoon, ten hostages were shot dead. We are now acting with an iron fist; the gallows in the town square is always busy. Executions are the daily norm. It has to be this way." When his unit captured several teenage girls and a boy who confessed to having been pressed into the partisans' service, Roth wrote that he and his comrades felt deep sympathy, but he agreed with their commander's decision to execute them by firing squad: "I can see how difficult it is for him to give this order," Roth commented, "but this is how it has to be!"[135] Following Roth's logic, to respond with anything less than stone-cold brutality would have invited further attacks and weakened the Germans' position. The laws of war took precedence over sentiment. Writing to his sister and father from Kharkov, Anton Böhrer also made the case that only public hangings of suspected partisans would drive home the occupiers' message to the population: "It is a radical way, but it definitely has the biggest impact on the Russians, when they see their fellows swinging from the rope," he rationalized.[136] Whether confronted with executions, theft, or scorched-earth tactics, soldiers relied less on ideology and more on traditional moral ideas—such as the need to balance the scales of justice, the desire to maintain order, or the imperatives of physical survival—as they explained such instances of violence against noncombatants to their correspondents back home.

Rhetorical Moral Strategies

Alongside specific moral justifications, German personnel employed a wide range of rhetorical devices to obscure the details of their side's crimes and reassure their readers of their own commitment to decency. One strategy was to employ a host of euphemisms that conveniently masked countless acts of brutality and exploitation against civilians and other victims.[137] Food was "organized," "procured" (*"besorgt"*), or "requisitioned." Partisans—frequently described as "bandits" in both official and non-official parlance—and Red soldiers were "bumped off" (*"umgelegt"*). Although readers at home were thoroughly aware of the meaning of these terms, soldiers' use of them circumvented any need to provide a more complete description. They also served to normalize the army's misconduct and disrupt the workings of conscience. Moreover, servicemen avoided unpleasant terms that might have alerted readers to the realities of the occupation.[138] Walter Neuser, for instance, informed his mother on the road to Leningrad in August 1941, that "the inhabitants here are required by us to do the harvest work."[139] Such careful phrasing tiptoed around the realities of forced labor and violent requisition, obscuring the suffering and death that often accompanied them.

A further tactic, deployed by commanders and infantrymen alike, was to blur distinctions between enemy combatants and noncombatants. Both in letters and the army's official documentation, civilian and partisan became interchangeable, as did partisan and Jew.[140] It was also common to record the benefits of criminality rather than the crimes themselves. For instance, soldiers told their readers that they had "found" certain items or cited a sudden improvement in their dietary outlook that almost certainly resulted from theft— without providing any further explanation. "From today on we are feeding ourselves," wrote Walter Neuser to his mother, in an offhanded reference to the Wehrmacht's devastating policy of living off the land. He made no attempt to explain where the food would come from or what effect this would have on local inhabitants.[141] Harald Hoffmann announced to his family that he had "found" twenty chickens after taking part in a fierce battle during the Moscow advance, but like Neuser he left his readers in the dark regarding the circumstances.[142]

While relatives may have wondered how exactly their men had suddenly come into the possession of a chicken, a sack of potatoes, or a pair of boots, few took the time to inquire into the details. Indeed, it appears that most correspondents on the home front approved of and sometimes even encouraged any measures that might make their men more comfortable, whatever the cost to the civilian population.[143] In fact, a major reason some soldiers mentioned thefts in the first place was to reassure loved ones that they were well-fed, well-clothed, and warmly sheltered. "You don't need to worry that your papa has to suffer hunger," wrote Kurt Niemeyer to his wife and daughter in October 1941, as his unit headed to Russia from Siedlice, Poland, to conduct support operations. "We organize so much that we always have something to eat; we live the life of a count."[144] Through constant expressions of concern for their men's health and livelihoods, families wrote their husbands, fathers, and brothers the moral equivalent of a blank check. Some even went so far as to ask their men to send fur coats and other forms of plunder. One father, a First World War veteran and enthusiastic Nazi supporter, wondered in a letter if his soldier son Helmut could send his family cooking oils, in spite of the Soviet Union's desperate economic conditions.[145] Such messages from the homeland encouraged soldiers to put their own well-being first, even if doing so jeopardized the lives of Soviet civilians.

One of the most striking features of the language *Ostkämpfer* employed when describing their side's crimes is the frequency with which their authors went out of their way to express sympathy for the victims, especially civilians. This practice highlighted the authors' humane qualities and signaled to readers that they were not perpetrators at heart. Troops' accounts are replete with condemnations of the suffering caused by the war and descriptions of the impossible situation of Soviet noncombatants. Such statements were made by men who personally behaved in a dignified manner toward civilians as well as convinced Nazis and troops who displayed no qualms about taking advantage of their monopoly on force. Harald Hoffmann spoke of the "suffering of the prisoners" and his "sympathy and commiseration for the distress of the population."[146] He frequently deplored his comrades' treatment of civilians, elaborating to his family at the end of October that "the Russians . . . are to be pitied, they must carry their household utensils into stall and barn, . . . have to cook and work the whole day in order to improve the state of our crappy clothing. For this they have to exchange their poor food for German 10-cent pieces. And how one treats them!" Despite these feelings, Hoffmann reported that his own platoon, with the help of a Russian-speaking Sudeten German, always managed to get the best quarters and had the best chances "to employ the population."[147] Wilhelm Moldenhauser confided to his wife, Erika, earlier in the same month that he sympathized with the situation of the women with whom he quartered:

> Often it occurred to me that women tried to bury their pain. . . . They
> will often only serve us with reluctance and inner willpower. Then
> when suddenly eight men move into a small hut, this brings a great

adjustment for the housewife. If one puts oneself in the shoes of these women, all of this is entirely apprehensible. Almost every woman has her husband and almost every girl her beloved engaged in the fight against the men to whom they suddenly are supposed to be friendly.[148]

In another letter, Moldenhauser speculated that the women he met wondered to themselves if their husbands had been killed by the very Germans they interacted with.[149] Other soldiers were less interested in the emotional lives of their reluctant hosts but still peppered their letters with passing remarks in which they bemoaned the dismal situation of civilians and deplored the war's horrors. They seem to have been particularly moved when they encountered families with children who reminded them of home.[150] Showing sympathy for the enemy—even women and children—was strongly discouraged by army leaders, who reminded their troops again and again that "soft" emotions were out of place in the war for Germany's existence.[151] Nevertheless, their expressions of concern allowed soldiers like Hoffmann and Moldenhauser to maintain their sense of humanity, assert the continued presence of their prewar identities, and reassure relatives who may have worried about the effect the war was having on their sons and husbands.[152] Alongside their use of euphemisms, expressing concern for the Wehrmacht's victims also helped suppress the fear that they themselves could be counted among the criminals. In very rare instances, soldiers' feelings of compassion led them to question the righteousness of the German cause or attempt to mitigate the suffering around them.[153] For most, however, such feelings took the form of passing moments of private self-reflection and did not translate into altered convictions or tangible actions. Furthermore, troops extended these feelings primarily toward Slavic civilians. In their minds, Jews, POWs, and Soviet officials were far less worthy of empathy, as were the men and women who took up arms against German rule.

The Partisan War

As the war entered its second year, more and more soldiers informed their relatives of the Wehrmacht's increasingly vicious campaign against a partisan movement that was gaining momentum after relatively modest beginnings.[154] They documented the army's brutal reprisals, which often took the form of collective punishments against entire communities or the execution of any civilian suspected of partisan activity, a designation that often meant simply being in the wrong place at the wrong time.[155] Just as they had rationalized the killing of Jews and prisoners as an act of justice, soldiers represented reprisal operations to their readers as legitimate responses to partisan atrocities or what they perceived as an illegal form of warfare waged behind German lines.[156] Indeed, following their superiors' lead, most portrayed Soviet insurgents as little more than common criminals—"bandits" who threatened not only the army's security but that of the entire region.[157]

The judgments made by Wehrmacht personnel regarding the moral status of civilian resistance fighters were heavily influenced by their institution's history and culture. Shocked and outraged at the emergence of a guerilla movement during the Franco-Prussian War of 1870, the Prusso-German army had conducted swift reprisals, including hostage-taking, summary executions, and the destruction of entire villages. Despite Germany's signing of the Hague Convention and other international agreements limiting many of these practices, German officers and military theorists regarded unconventional tactics—particularly by civilians—as a dishonorable practice and defended their right to take sweeping retaliatory measures. Following the same logic, German troops executed several thousand civilians in response to real or imagined partisan activity in the opening years of the First World War.[158] Continuing this tradition, commanders and propagandists frequently warned their troops to expect resistance from the outset of Operation Barbarossa and to respond in merciless fashion toward partisans, suspected partisans, and anyone accused of offering them support.[159]

Hans-Peter Eckener exemplified common attitudes toward partisans in one of his first letters from the USSR, where he was newly stationed in 1942. He noted that "we always have our carbines loaded—due to the partisans, who aren't just talked about a lot but actually exist. This evening here in town fifteen of them were shot at the marketplace—and this was due to the fact that one did not have enough rope to hang them."[160] Replying a few weeks later, his father suggested that many of the partisans were Jews and encouraged his son to "shoot first and don't miss" if he had to face them.[161] Suspected partisans were sometimes hanged with signs around their necks describing their alleged crimes, a further indication of the bandit–partisan conflation.[162] Eckener and others seem to have taken the legitimacy of the Wehrmacht's draconian policies for granted; except in a handful of cases, they never expressed doubts regarding whether executed civilians had actually been partisans in the first place.[163] While a few admitted that revenge was also a factor, soldiers generally depicted punishments and executions as nothing short of justice. Walter Neuser, writing to his parents in late 1941, stated directly that the partisans in his area deserved retribution, although he did not explain precisely how they were handled. "There are always still some [partisans] around, who feel the urge to wage gang warfare [*"Bandenkrieg"*]. . . . [Who]ever is captured definitely does not escape just punishment," he stated ominously.[164] Eckener was considerably more expressive regarding the army's methods in November 1942: "While combing through the land in pursuit of such gangs entire villages are torched and all women and children completely wiped out—a sentence," he added, "that is easily spoken; but one can imagine what is concealed behind such austere words."[165] Here was the true nature of the Wehrmacht's "antipartisan operations" described in plain terms to relatives in the homeland. Such operations figured from Eckener's point of view as necessary responses to dangerous partisan incursions, including the killing of eight soldiers in a village two days earlier.[166] A week later, Eckener related to his father that his unit had captured 300 partisans and burned down four villages in the process, a tactic he implied had been necessary to secure the hinterland from the "bandits."[167] Even if troops asserted that these actions were justified, however, they rarely admitted personal culpability. Instead, they employed the passive voice or stated that they were describing only the actions of their comrades, members of other units, or unit-wide policies.[168] This practice generated moral distance between the men and decisions they may have approved of or participated in but sometimes still recognized as questionable. After all, they did not want their parents to think that their sons had become murderers.

Crimes after 1941

By the conflict's later stages, descriptions of criminality appeared far less frequently in front correspondence.[169] When they did, they often figured as events that had become so routine they no longer required detailed explanation.[170] Near Amvrosiivka, preparing for the advance toward Stalingrad in the spring of 1942, Wilhelm Moldenhauser informed his wife that the men of his unit typically obtained food by visiting the Slovakian field kitchen or "with a measure of luck and five minutes of fear 'organize' something as is the infantryman's way. I am not reluctant to do so anymore," he told her, since, "I have already done things like this. . . . One does it for the comrades. And an infantryman is always hungry," he added.[171] Since the new replacements in Hans Simon's unit had no skill at cooking, he informed his mother in June 1943, "I go once in a while to the next village and procure for myself potatoes and milk and so forth," he wrote, without expending ink to describe what this entailed.[172] Portraying such actions as routine, however, was in itself a kind of moral strategy: it minimized the harm done to the Wehrmacht's victims and circumvented any need for soldiers to explain their actions. Atrocities had become a background feature of the war, rather than extraordinary events that could call their convictions into question. Relatedly, troops sometimes opined that because the Soviet peoples were inured to violence after years of war, only the most extreme policies could have any effect on their behavior.[173] As soldiers accepted the ubiquity of Eastern Front atrocities, their writings contributed to a larger process in which violence became normalized both on the front and in the homeland, desensitizing the men and their correspondents to the war's horrors.

Still, some men continued to offer explanations for their most questionable actions or found a way to paint them in a positive light. Just as they had emphasized the population's "hospitality" earlier in the campaign, for example, many still took pains to describe the Wehrmacht–civilian relationship as one of cooperation even during the later years of the war. As his unit constructed bunkers to defend against Soviet attacks around Vitebsk in October 1942, Hans-Peter Eckener informed his parents that the locals were forced to bring in the harvest for the Germans. "The population, as far as they are still here, must now work for us, must deliver milk that we make into butter and cheese in our own 'creamery'; potatoes, hay, oats and so forth were partly requisitioned by us. By the way, the people are not at all badly treated by us," he made sure to add. He described how Russian girls giggled and sang as they left the village to work, and noted that "they don't work too much."[174] All of this suggested that the occupation did not place undue burdens on a populace that labored gladly for the invaders. Rolf Dietrich, who worked in a baking company and like Eckener had recently arrived at the Eastern Front, wrote to his acquaintance, Hilde, of the harvest preparations in the fall of 1942 from the center of the front:

> Now all the hay that [the civilians] made for the Wehrmacht is brought together into big piles. The fields are ploughed, the horses are made available by us, everywhere there is already building going on. The Compulsory Labor Office [*Arbeitsdienst*], that lies in the next village, works on the village street [and] keeps the cottages in good repair[;] we will already bake our bread again[;] everybody has a role.[175]

Like Eckener, Dietrich depicted the civilian–Wehrmacht relationship more in terms of mutual aid than exploitation; both also implicitly upheld Germany's supposed right to colonize Soviet territory. Dietrich would continue to describe the German occupation in a similar light as more and more civilians were pressed into Wehrmacht service. In one city, he noted in 1943, "one sees much suffering, but everywhere one sees on the other hand our ordering hand[;] many inhabitants are in the service of the Wehrmacht or accomplish other work for us."[176] Through such paternalist language, soldiers transfigured the brutality of the occupation into an orderly project of reconstruction that benefited both invader and occupied, in the process representing themselves as a force for positive change.[177]

One soldier who painted a more lucid picture of the civilian–soldier relationship toward the end of the war was Lieutenant Heinz Rahe. His 13th Panzer Division had taken part in the invasion of the Caucasus and by early 1943 was retreating toward Kuban. Rahe reflected on the decisions he had made regarding the population and wondered if they aligned with the biblical principles he cherished as a former pastor. "Does the war actually have its own law?" he asked. He tried to provide an answer in a letter to his wife:

> An old man just came to me[;] someone has taken his pig. Now he wants at least to have something for it. In any case the animal is gone. Of course it is for our kitchen, but it is hard for the one who is affected. Should I now allow less for the lives of my men, in order to protect the civilian population? Or am I duty-bound to take care of my men, so that they live as well as possible? In general one says to oneself that the war has its own law. With that the case is closed.

Next to his stated conviction that "war brings not only a re-valuation, but also a revolution in the moral field," a stance long promoted by the High Command, Rahe rationalized such acts of theft by explaining the dire situation in which his unit had found itself. He admitted that as they fled the town of Baksan, he had "tolerated" and "perhaps even encouraged" his men to take what they could. "Back then we were in such a predatory mood," he wrote. "This was certainly something the retreat brought with it." A soft-hearted fellow officer, Rahe reported, told him that memories of the soldiers' brutality would haunt him for the rest of his life. Rahe, however, took solace in his observation that "we soldiers can also be very generous."[178] He described in several letters how he had personally treated civilians well, including by giving sugar to a civilian woman with whom he quartered and protecting another from having her pig slaughtered by one of his men.[179] By cycling among rationalizations like these, Rahe appears to have found a way to live with his choices and explain them to his wife. Ultimately, though, he could never shake the unnerving feeling that "in many connections . . . the conscience of our people is largely deadened."[180]

While Rahe asserted that ordinary morality no longer applied to the war in the East and insisted on his own goodness, other soldiers generated moral distance between themselves and the horrors wrought by the institution to which they belonged by depicting the violence that surrounded them as the product of cosmic forces that transcended human volition. Even though the conflict had been initiated through the deliberate choices of Germany's leaders and only continued with the willing affirmation of both generals and the rank and file alike, many men characterized the war as an event that shared all the features of a natural calamity. Like an earthquake, it caused destruction in random fashion; no single individual or collective could be blamed for the horrors that resulted. "Let us hope that this war with its horrifying murder finds its end soon," wrote Hans Simon to his parents in August 1941.[181] And a year later: "Everywhere, the war demands its bloody toll."[182] Wilhelm Moldenhauser, after witnessing the tearful reunion of a Russian couple, commented to his wife that "in this moment I became truly conscious of what great suffering, how much pain this war brings with it."[183] In his distinctive poetic language, Willy Reese dubbed the war "an elemental planetary occurrence."[184] Adhering to this viewpoint made it possible for soldiers to lament the war's terrors while obscuring any feelings of personal responsibility. Instead, those who inflicted suffering on a daily basis often cast themselves in the role of tourists or audience members watching the tragic reels of history's horror show.

The manner in which Wehrmacht personnel narrated atrocities reveals not only the details of the crimes and the circumstances surrounding them but how troops reflected on their conduct and found ways to vindicate even the grossest violations of international law. With the aid of propagandists, they employed a series of moral rationalizations and rhetorical sleight of hand to make their transgressions comprehensible to themselves and their loved ones. In so doing, they acted as the first line of defense for the Wehrmacht's reputation, effectively preserving the illusion that they remained honorable warriors battling a despicable foe even when it was their own actions that had called this reputation into question in the first place.

The stories soldiers told about atrocities on the Eastern Front played a critical role in the wartime production of the ideas that would coalesce into the clean Wehrmacht myth. To begin with, they painted a portrait of the Soviet enemy as not only racially inferior but morally repugnant, a barbaric threat to all the values of European civilization that had to be annihilated at any cost. This image would remain a constant in West German public memory over the following decades, neatly overlapping with the anti-communist rhetoric of the Cold War. It even emerged as a major axis of the *Historikerstreit* of the 1980s—a wide-ranging debate about the country's Nazi past—as historians weighed the relative sins of the Nazi and Soviet regimes and whether the *Ostkämpfer* deserved sympathy for their battle against the Red Army.[185] The preemptive strike myth proved equally long-lived.[186]

In stark contrast to this lasting obsession with Soviet misconduct, the subject of crimes committed by the Wehrmacht was denied or avoided by veterans and their families alike well into the 1990s. Instead, German memory was dominated by the image of a Wehrmacht that had struggled against a criminal Red Army without itself crossing the boundaries of international law—except, perhaps, in the most extreme circumstances. This chapter, however, reinforces what many scholars have long argued—that a high proportion of soldiers were well aware that their side committed crimes on a regular basis. It also demonstrates that the silence that dominated the postwar era did not necessarily prevail during the war itself, as is often assumed. Of the core sample of thirty men, at least twenty-three discussed the murder or mistreatment of POWs, commissars, and Jews, or—more commonly—crimes against non-Jewish civilians, and they did so with surprising frequency especially during the first year of the war.[187] Further, the manner in which they wrote about atrocities suggests that combatants still recognized when common moral boundaries were being crossed, a point some scholars have disputed.[188] As the examples presented here suggest, soldiers frequently wrestled with their personal participation and felt the need to explain their actions. They may have become numb to human suffering as the war went on, but they had not abandoned morality in its entirety.

The observation that German warriors frequently included accounts of their own side's crimes in their letters also implies that relatives and friends on the home front were much better informed of the realities of the *Vernichtungskrieg*, at least in its basic outlines, than previously supposed. Even if such themes only surfaced in a small fraction of the roughly ten billion letters soldiers sent during the war, these numbers still add up to tens of millions of items of correspondence. This suggests that the truth of their army's conduct was not a secret among the German public during the war that was only "exposed" decades later, as has commonly been assumed.[189] While later generations may certainly have been shocked by the evidence presented at the Wehrmacht Exhibition, in light of the contents of soldiers' letters it is difficult to imagine that the war generation itself—servicemen and civilians alike—had been similarly ignorant of wartime atrocities, including the murder of Soviet Jews.[190]

What, then, explains the gap between these contemporary accounts and the Wehrmacht myth in its postwar form, with its almost total silence on the subject of German atrocities? Certainly, fear of censure or imprisonment played a significant role in the choice of most veterans not to discuss their most reprehensible deeds once they rejoined the civilian world. Nor was there much interest among the German public in dwelling on the Nazi past, especially when it involved their loved ones. However, there may have been another reason why the topic was rarely broached: the image of the *Vernichtungskrieg* that reached the German homeland had already been preemptively filtered, not only by the censors but also by soldiers intent on making sure their actions were viewed in a sympathetic light. Tales of the Wehrmacht's crimes had indeed been widely circulated but presented as fully justified or as not constituting crimes at all, a claim the home front appears to have taken at face value. Together with propagandists, *Ostkämpfer* successfully depicted themselves as upright warriors who generally played by the rules while battling an enemy whose misdeeds revealed both racial inferiority and malevolence. Thus, the postwar insistence on the Wehrmacht's "clean" track record in fact represented an extension of a narrative begun by the men in the foxholes. These men had judged their own case, pronounced themselves innocent, and worked over the next decades to ensure that the wider public continued to accept their verdict.

To explain their own crimes and clear their consciences, German troops turned to a combination of ideological justifications and rationalizations that relied on traditional moral argumentation. When discussing the treatment of Red prisoners, Soviet officials, and Jews, soldiers often depicted their victims as both dishonorable criminals who deserved no mercy and subhumans whose lives meant nothing. Here, traditional morality and Nazi morality were mutually reinforcing, but they could also be relied upon separately. When it came to crimes against civilians, however, servicemen rarely explained their behavior on the basis of race, preferring instead to develop rationalizations that revolved around pre-Nazi conceptions of justice and injustice, good and evil, survival, and "military necessity."[191] Significantly, only one soldier ever used the excuse of "following orders" that enjoyed widespread currency among veterans after the war.[192] Nor did any soldier explain his actions as the result of sadistic impulses; all insisted that there were valid reasons for their behavior.[193]

The fact that troops did not consistently refer to Nazi racial ideology in their descriptions and that racial explanations often appeared in tandem with traditional moral argumentation should by no means be taken as an indication that ideology was not the primary impulse behind the army's crimes in a general sense, or that soldiers did not exhibit strong racist tendencies that contributed to atrocities. However, many seem to have frequently found the vocabulary of traditional morality preferable to that of Nazism when they broached this subject. This may indicate that soldiers did not find biological essentialism alone to be sufficient justification for their actions. Or perhaps they believed that more pedestrian moral arguments had a better chance of being accepted by their readers. Either possibility is what might be expected of a society and a military that had not yet fully completed its transition to the Nazi value system.

Regardless of whether servicemen preferred to explain their deeds through racial ideology or longstanding concepts of right and wrong, when they wrote about crimes they were doing more than simply conducting a public relations exercise to manipulate opinion back home. Their letters were part of a deeply personal process of "coming to terms" with their actions—of absolving themselves of any feelings of guilt or responsibility with reference to whatever value systems they preferred.[194] This phenomenon is certainly not unique to the Wehrmacht—throughout history soldiers have often endeavored to justify morally questionable conduct. But what is remarkable was the ability of men who ostensibly prided themselves on their commitment to civilized norms to do so even as they participated in atrocities on a scale never before seen in modern military history. Their seemingly boundless capacity to rationalize their side's misdeeds made them more effective agents of the *Vernichtungsrieg*, able to circumvent the workings of conscience and willfully carry out the regime's darkest desires.

Generating and defending their self-styled image of decency was not the only means by which *Ostkämpfer* made moral sense of their participation, however. They would also go a step further by finding ways to recast a genocidal conflict as nothing less than a righteous cause.

CHAPTER 3

The "Crusaders"

Religious Justifications for Barbarossa

In August 1941, private first class Hans Albring, a radio operator for the Sixth Army Corps, witnessed an unusual event as his unit continued its advance deep into Soviet territory in the Vitebsk region. In a small church along the Daugava River, he and his comrades took part in a worship service led by a Wehrmacht chaplain. Also crowded into the small sanctuary were Russian civilians, who looked on reverently as the chaplain preached and the soldiers sang hymns. When the service ended, the civilians rushed toward the altar to kiss the holy images. Although one of the men became annoyed at the sobbing of two women who stood next to them, most of the servicemen, Albring reported, were moved by what they saw:

> They [women and children] fell to the ground, as is the custom in this land, and though every extreme situation evokes the mockery of the *Landser* . . . here everyone recognized what this simple Wehrmacht worship service meant to each Russian after 24 years of deprivation. The presence of God . . . was truly made manifest and I have never experienced such a feeling of being touched from above, and others said the same to me.[1]

The experience resonated deeply with Albring. A committed Catholic from Gelsenkirchen-Buer in the Rhineland, he had entered the Wehrmacht in 1939 after passing his *Abitur* (university entrance) exam. With deep connections to the church and a strong interest in theology, he actively sought out worship opportunities, befriended fellow Christian soldiers, and kept abreast of religious affairs at home. Although he worried that Germany was becoming increasingly secularized, he never abandoned the conviction that he and his comrades represented an army—and a nation—that still upheld the traditions of European Christianity.

Albring was not ignorant of the wanton brutality with which the Wehrmacht conducted the campaign. In his letters to his friend Lt. Eugen Altrogge, he recounted atrocities against civilians and POWs, including a massacre of several hundred Jews, sometimes expressing his unease at the army's behavior but always confident of the need to crush the power of a state he associated with atheism and immorality.[2] He displayed little interest in the racial ideology that animated the invasion and usually got along well with Soviet civilians, especially fellow Christians, who took him on tours of churches and indulged his fascination with Orthodox artwork. Later in the war, he would reveal to Altrogge his intense hostility to a Nazi Party he believed was undermining the church at home. Despite these misgivings, Albring still considered himself a decent Christian man, fighting for a cause he could believe in. He would continue to support the war until his death in early 1944.

Although he was more devout than most, Albring's self-understanding was not so different from that of his comrades, many of whom saw themselves as members of an army that upheld the values of European Christendom. Like Albring, many also justified the war as a religious crusade, a conflict between the godless Soviets and a Wehrmacht determined to oust the country's atheist rulers and restore the religious traditions many considered the cornerstone of all moral values. This conviction persisted through the end of the war, even as the army's involvement in atrocities deepened and Germany's own leaders proved time and again that they harbored little love for Christianity.

Visions of the war as a crusade would fade during the postwar decades, but religion nevertheless came to occupy a prominent place in the Wehrmacht myth. Veterans were often depicted—especially in West Germany—as good Christian men who had been led astray by the Nazi regime but had repented of any past sins and rediscovered their religious roots during long years in Soviet captivity. With the help of increasingly influential church communities, the veterans could now fulfill an important role in the country's reconstruction. The so-called Stalingrad Madonna, a charcoal drawing made by pastor-soldier Kurt Reuber in 1942, became a focal point for German memory, linking the front experience with notions of Christian suffering and redemption. Placed in the Kaiser Wilhelm Memorial Church in 1983, it helped to cement a lasting view of servicemen as martyrs who had striven with an atheist power even as their own regime persecuted the churches behind their backs.[3]

Where did these concepts of a Christian Wehrmacht and a holy mission originate, and how pervasive were they within the army's ranks? How did the Wehrmacht and its men preserve them over time, especially in the face of Nazi interference and the army's pattern of routinely violating Christian principles? More broadly, what role did religion play in the Wehrmacht and how did it relate to the army's efforts to cultivate an image of decency?

While the subject of religion and the German military up to the end of the First World War has received considerable attention, historians have largely ignored its place in the Wehrmacht's story during the Second World War. Along with the assumption that Nazi ideology constituted the primary spiritual touchstone in the Wehrmacht, historians' persistent focus on Europe's transition toward a more secular society in the first half of the twentieth century has led many to presume that religion no longer played a significant role in the lives of the Third Reich's uniformed men.[4] Emblematic of this interpretation, Hans Joachim Schröder has concluded in his study of postwar interviews that religion held only "minor importance" among ordinary troops.[5] It is generally acknowledged that the Nazi regime's propagandists styled the war with the Soviet Union as a "crusade" against communism, but historians have emphasized that this crusade was conceived of purely in ideological, rather than religious terms.[6] The few scholars who have investigated the Wehrmacht's religious life have largely confined themselves to the study of small, well-defined groups, such as chaplains or Jesuits.[7] Their work has often centered on the question of whether religion ultimately reinforced or undermined the Nazi agenda on the Eastern Front.[8]

This chapter adopts a more wholistic approach to the history of religion in the Wehrmacht during the USSR campaign, one that takes account of the attitudes of soldiers of both confessions; the impressions of chaplains, propagandists, and military commanders; and the influence of German church leaders and the Nazi ruling class. It demonstrates that religion, in fact, played a major role in the experience of ordinary combatants and became an important element in the army's efforts to employ traditional values to cast itself as a morally worthy organization pursuing a noble goal. This image had roots that preceded the war itself and was nurtured by the words and actions of a variety of actors within the Wehrmacht and German society as a whole, including Nazi officials, church leaders, chaplains, propagandists, officers, and the rank and file themselves. Together, they painted a portrait of the Wehrmacht as a faithful Christian army on crusade against godless enemies, working to restore religion to its rightful place in Eastern Europe.

Efforts to define the Wehrmacht as a devout institution would run into many complications. Christian conceptions of the invasion, stressing both anti-Bolshevism and the need to bring religious freedom to Soviet fellow believers, came into conflict with Nazi racial orthodoxy. Battlefield conditions undermined formal religious life, as did the increasingly harsh restrictions issued by the Nazi regime. Ultimately, however, the image of a "Christian" Wehrmacht on crusade served as a powerful justification for the invasion and deflected attention from the army's many moral failings.

Religious Traditions in the Wehrmacht

Religion, politics, and military affairs had been entwined in Germany long before the invasion of the Soviet Union. Prussia's Hohenzollern monarchy established a standing chaplaincy at the turn of the eighteenth century, guided by the belief that religion would improve military discipline.[9] Guards posted outside the chapel doors made sure that delinquent soldiers could not escape from mandatory worship services.[10] German theologians expanded upon centuries-old "just war" doctrines that upheld the right of the state to use force against its neighbors under certain circumstances.[11] The alliance between throne, altar, and sword continued unabated throughout the nineteenth century, propelled by opportunistic political leaders, patriotic preachers, and the chaplains who accompanied the men onto the field.[12] Into the early twentieth century, religion was seen by many Germans as the foundation of morality and an important element in German *Kultur*, which stood in opposition to Western Europe's heartless *Zivilization* and the *Unkultur* of the wild East.[13]

For Germany, the First World War represented a high-water mark in the relationship between religion and the state.[14] Kaiser Wilhelm II confidently petitioned God to bless the weapons of soldiers whose belt buckles sported the motto "God is with us" (*Gott mit uns*). Religious officials declared that Germany was pursuing a divinely sanctioned cause and welcomed the heightened religiosity the conflict engendered. However, the churches' initial hurrah-patriotism gave way to a focus on suffering and mourning as the conflict lengthened.[15] Religion would remain influential in the lives of German citizens and soldiers, but worship attendance steadily decreased in the interwar period.[16]

The Russian Revolution added a further complication to Germany's religious landscape, striking fear into the hearts of clergy who had long dreaded the social and spiritual implications of a movement that openly embraced atheism. Throughout the 1920s and 1930s, the German churches joined with international aid organizations to publicize the plight of the USSR's Christians and support their communities in the face of systematic and often deadly persecution.[17] Fatefully, religious leaders on both sides of the confessional aisle considered communism, rather than fascism, to be Germany's greatest internal threat. Their unwavering anti-Bolshevik message made its way to parishioners through sermons, publications, and Christian youth organizations.[18]

When Hitler came to power in 1933, he enjoyed broad support among Christians in Germany, particularly Protestants, a fact that owed not a little to his strong anti-communist stance.[19] Despite misgivings about Nazi intentions, the churches for the most part accommodated themselves to the new regime.[20] Some Christians, including members of the German Christian movement—a new Protestant denomination that was initially fostered by Nazi officials— actively combatted Jewish theological influences and embraced a militarized, hyper-masculine "positive Christianity" that overlapped with Nazi gender ideals.[21] When German troops stormed the Polish border in 1939, the heads of the German Protestant and Catholic Churches assured the state that they could be counted on to aid the war effort. A raft of religious publications, including pastoral letters from bishops and chaplains, encouraged troops to see themselves as selfless defenders of the Fatherland.[22] Enthusiasm for the war among church circles, however, never reached First World War heights, partly because by this time both churches were suffering increasing encroachments by the Nazi state.

Within the Wehrmacht, Nazi officials occasionally strove to co-opt religion for their own ends. For example, at the Party's insistence, the army's official Protestant and Catholic songbooks were redesigned to incorporate prayers for Hitler alongside a mix of nationalistic and religious hymns stripped of Jewish references.[23] More often, however, the Nazis worked to push religion to the sidelines so they could establish their own monopoly on spiritual and ideological influence over the country's uniformed young men. Regime officials made attendance at worship voluntary and allowed servicemen to identify as belonging to neither Christian confession.[24] After the war's outbreak, they increasingly restricted the distribution of religious literature in the army.[25] This escalated in 1941 when the Propaganda Ministry used the occasion of a paper shortage to halt the printing of nearly all religious publications for the troops.[26]

High-ranking officers generally accommodated Nazi wishes. However, they did not go so far as to fully dismantle religious life. In their view, spiritual care was still an irreplaceable means to lift morale. As a result, the chaplaincy survived but fielded a grossly inadequate nine hundred clergy during the war.[27] Regulations made clear that the chaplain's primary job was to bolster the fighting power of the men, not spread the Gospel, a revision that reflected both the Nazi fear of competition for hearts and minds and the military's utilitarian focus on battlefield effectiveness.[28] Still, *Gott mit uns* remained the Wehrmacht's official motto. Training manuals continued to bear the mark of its religious traditions. For instance, among the "duties of the German soldier" that every member of the Wehrmacht was required to memorize was the injunction that he be a "God-fearing" example to his people.[29] And, as chaplains would attest throughout the conflict, numerous officers remained supportive of Christianity.[30]

At the launch of Barbarossa in June 1941, the most prominent Nazi officials remained united in their contempt for Christianity. However, in order to mobilize Christian support for a war that proved deeply unpopular with the German public, they settled on the characteristically cynical policy of appropriating religious rhetoric while continuing to undermine Christianity in the Wehrmacht in practice.[31] This tactical shift was signaled by a slew of pronouncements that described the invasion as "Europe's crusade against Bolshevism."[32] The Foreign Office's formal explanation for the invasion, which used this precise phrasing, went on to describe the communist system as "organized godlessness" and insisted that "the churchly communities also sense . . . that their interests are being defended on the enormous front in the East."[33] Despite personal misgivings, Joseph Goebbels quickly made the European crusade theme a propaganda centerpiece.[34] In his editorials, he depicted the invasion in pseudo-religious terms as a "war of moral humanity against spiritual rottenness."[35] Hitler himself chose a codename for the campaign—Barbarossa—that recalled one of German history's most famous crusaders.[36] He laced his notices to troops and his speeches to the public with appeals for divine aid, a continuation of his habitual practice of portraying himself as a pious leader.[37] Nor did he shy away from directly referring to the war as a "European crusade" in public addresses.[38] It is well-established that top Nazis viewed this "crusade" in ideological, rather than religious terms.[39] However, by giving lip service to a vaguely defined notion of spiritual conflict, regime officials opened up discursive space for religious interpretations of the invasion.

When the war with the Soviet Union began, both mainstream churches expressed their full support. They did so not only out of nationalist sentiment but because they recognized an opportunity to strike a blow against the heart of European communism, return religion to what had once been a Christian nation, and revitalize Christianity at home.[40] When news of the invasion broke, leaders of the mainstream Protestant Church thanked Hitler for "calling our people and the peoples of Europe to the decisive confrontation with the mortal enemy of all order and all western Christianity."[41] The Confessing Church followed suit in spite of its usual opposition to Nazi policies.[42] The Catholic

Church displayed initial reserve but soon assured the regime of its solidarity against the Bolshevik enemy.[43] Clergy of both churches stopped short of officially declaring the campaign a crusade and remained embroiled in disputes with Nazi authorities, but over the next few years they would continue to offer rhetorical and moral support for the conflict.

Marching under Cross and Swastika

Although church attendance had been steadily decreasing in Germany for decades, the soldiers who marched into the Soviet Union retained strong ties to organized religion. They hailed from a nation where 95 percent of the population still identified as either Catholic or Protestant.[44] All had grown up in a culture deeply influenced by Christian traditions and Christian conceptions of right and wrong. Chaplains consistently reported that their men expressed strong interest in religious matters even though many were less attached to formal church organizations than their Great War counterparts.[45]

Religious outlooks among Ostkämpfer who identified as Christian came in innumerable guises and gradations. Some maintained a strong connection to their faith, both spiritually and institutionally. Among them was Hans Albring, who sprinkled his letters with theological reflections, expressed a deep interest in religious artwork, and took an active role in the army's religious life. Albring had been raised in a Catholic household in the Rhineland, where he became friends with Eugen Altrogge, an active member of the Catholic youth movement and later Wehrmacht lieutenant with whom he kept up a correspondence during the war. Albring and Altrogge shared a similar outlook, including a basic attachment to German national identity but also a sense of Christian universalism and a nagging fear that Nazism was eroding religious belief.[46]

A much larger group of soldiers could be termed cultural Christians. Their connection to the institutional church was much more tenuous, and they displayed little interest in theology. The former accountant Walter Neuser, for instance, grew up in a Protestant household and later joined the Nazi Party. During his time as a non-commissioned officer he attended at least a handful of worship services, celebrated Christian holidays, and occasionally called on God's aid but otherwise had little to say of religious matters.[47] Other men went a step further and left the church entirely, although this did not necessarily mean they had lost all interest in religion.

Theological opinions among the Reich's Christian servicemen regarding the meaning of their military service were just as diverse as the spectrum of religiosity in the Wehrmacht, but several patterns emerged. Many, perhaps a majority, subscribed to a form of religious nationalism with deep roots in German history. This outlook linked Christian identity with service to the nation, a divinely ordained community governed by a state that ultimately derived its authority from above. Lt. Hans Wilhelm Sauer exemplified this attitude. Born in Braunschweig in 1915, he went to Gymnasium at Colburg and served in the Wehrmacht throughout the 1930s, during which time he also began a degree in Protestant theology at Tübingen. The war cut Sauer's studies short, but he embraced his role as both Christian and warrior. In a letter sent shortly after the invasion of the USSR, he told his parents and sisters of his deep desire to wield both "sword and Bible," following in the footsteps of two ordained comrades who had fallen in France.[48]

Another exemplar of the Christian–nationalist tradition, Hans Simon, was the son of a Protestant minister. Simon ended many of his letters with the slogan *"Gott mit uns "* and believed he had a duty to defend the Fatherland.[49] The much older Konrad Jarausch subscribed to a similar worldview. Born into a middle-class Protestant family in Berlin, Jarausch had studied history, with a theology minor, and received his PhD in 1925. He went on to teach secondary school in Brandenburg and published on questions of theological pedagogy. Having rejected both liberalism and communism, Jarausch hoped for an organic national revival, dreamed of a German empire, and enjoyed the comradeship of the military community after being drafted in 1939. However, he ultimately valued religion above nation and expressed discomfort with the militarization of religion he witnessed in the Wehrmacht.[50]

Catholic soldiers were swept up by the nationalistic impulse as well, although their relationship to the state was more complex than in the Protestant case. The memory of the *Kulturkampf* in the late nineteenth century—an attempt by the government to bring the Catholic Church to heel—and their minority status had made Catholics wary of the state and uncertain of their place in German society. They felt an affinity toward the international Catholic Church and cultivated a distinct Catholic identity, but at the same time considered themselves to be thoroughly German, a sentiment they were eager to prove.[51] Catholic private Franz Siebeler, an unwavering nationalist with Nazi sympathies, spoke of protecting "our beautiful Germany" from the "Asian hordes."[52] Hans Albring was much more ambivalent. At times he appeared to embrace the notion of patriotic sacrifice, but he also questioned whether, as he wrote to his friend Eugen Altrogge, "our Heimat [is] so holy, that for it 'not one person too many has fallen.'"[53]

While they rarely dwelt at length on the relationship between Christianity and Nazism, their letters indicate that early in the invasion few soldiers of either denomination fundamentally questioned the regime's legitimacy or even recognized it as a threat to their beliefs. Protestants in particular seem to have accepted the Nazis as Germany's legitimate rulers and often shared at least some elements of the Nazi worldview. Hans Wilhelm Sauer, for example, enjoyed reading both Luther's sermons and the Nazi publication *Völkischer Beobachter*.[54] Konrad Jarausch recognized Nazi authority and welcomed its antimodern tendencies, although he hoped that Nazi radicalism might be tempered by Christian influence. Catholics also expressed support for Hitler in his capacity as Germany's leader. In November 1941, after asking for the blessings of the Christ child for his family, Franz Siebeler expressed his wish that Christ's "mercy will illuminate the Führer of the Volk, so that in the next year Christmas will again be a festival of peace."[55] It was only over time that many Catholic soldiers, and to a lesser extent Protestants, would grow increasingly concerned about the impact of Nazism on the Christian faith in the army and the homeland.

In the days and weeks before the campaign, as Siebeler, Jarausch, and their comrades in uniform stood poised on the Soviet border, chaplains held special worship services to make sure the troops were spiritually prepared for combat. Typical of the Wehrmacht's peacetime religious ceremonies, these were relatively large and formal affairs, with officers and sometimes entire units in attendance, often accompanied by a band or orchestra. Hans Simon attended a ceremony a week before the assault. "Yesterday we had a field prayer service," he wrote his mother. "Under high birches a table with a white cover and the battle flag on top."[56] These services—often specially requested by unit commanders who wanted to make sure their men were mentally ready for combat—cleared soldiers' consciences and set the stage for the showdown with the "godless" enemy.[57]

As the attack commenced, combatants were bombarded by messages that encouraged them to view themselves as righteous Christian warriors battling a hellish regime, part of a pragmatic effort by army propagandists to secure the enthusiastic participation of men from all backgrounds. Army newspapers carried speeches by Nazi leaders that repeated the crusade theme, amplified by the statements of public intellectuals, church officials, and the Wehrmacht's reporters. Along with quotes from the Führer explaining that God was on Germany's side, the front newspaper *Der Durchbruch* carried articles from Swedish scientist Sven Hedin declaring that all civilized Christian nations had a holy duty to "exterminate" the communist menace and rescue the oppressed Russian people.[58] *Der Kampf* insisted that a "spiritual watershed" separated the Wehrmacht soldier from his Soviet counterpart. While the former exhibited "reverence . . . for God," which was the bedrock of civilization, the latter represented "the powers of destruction and of the underworld."[59] In one of many articles that promoted German Christian–style theology, OKW's *Mitteilungen für die Truppe* proclaimed that "Adolf Hitler is an instrument of Providence" who would effect Europe's "salvation from Bolshevism." It reminded soldiers that for Germans, "faith in God" was "the beginning of all wisdom" and would have to be defended at all costs against the atheist enemy.[60] Still other outlets reassured them that the Christian churches in Germany and around the world fully condoned the invasion.[61] Propagandists offered many other justifications for the war—including explanations grounded in racial ideology—but they hoped that such messages would resonate deeply with the large proportion of troops who still harbored a reverence for Christian traditions.

Although they did not always see eye-to-eye with the Nazi regime, chaplains also insisted on the war's deep religious meaning. Field Bishop Franz Justus Rarkowski, who headed the Catholic chaplaincy, proclaimed in a pastoral message to the troops that the operation constituted a "European crusade" against a "demonic regime of barbarism."[62] The Protestant chaplaincy promoted similar themes. Preaching before the staff of the 18th Infantry Division after four weeks on the march, one Protestant chaplain explained that years of communist rule had destroyed Russia's religious heritage and corrupted the souls of its people. The Soviets, he contended, were a threat to the fundamental values of Western civilization.[63] His like-minded colleagues of both confessions, including non-chaplain clergymen serving in the Wehrmacht, referred to their Russian opponents in demonic terms and a number cited a strong anti-communist impulse as their primary motivation for serving.[64]

As German troops advanced into the endless expanse of Soviet Russia, whether inspired by the Nazis' pseudo-religious propaganda, the anti-communist stance of the churches, their own personal backgrounds, or simply out of sheer curiosity, they began to take an active interest in the fate of religion in the USSR. Had the atheist government stamped it out entirely, they wondered, or were there still remnants to be found? One of the first things Wehrmacht servicemen remarked upon was the ubiquity of churches in the villages, towns, and cities they passed through on the march. "Already on the way here," wrote Konrad Jarausch in August, "I had kept my eyes open for signs of churches and crucifixes."[65] He spotted church towers in destroyed Polish villages, and as his unit crossed into the USSR he identified "a number of . . . churches here in the East, some with old paintings."[66] Other soldiers made similar observations, and the onion-domed buildings that prominently dotted the landscape quickly became a mainstay in their photo albums.[67] So ubiquitous were they that one front newspaper made a church the centerpiece of a cut-out Ukrainian village it printed for the men to play with.[68]

Despite the fact that many houses of worship appeared intact, however, servicemen expressed skepticism regarding whether religious practice had survived two decades of communism. In Minsk, Jarausch remarked that Russian civilians appeared to be interested in a local church, but he was unsure what conclusion to draw. "Were they expressing some kind of religious sentiment?" he wondered.[69] Like Jarausch, Hans Simon noticed that "the churches still stand," but he was not convinced that they were actually in use.[70] Still in France, the deeply Catholic Lt. Eugen Altrogge asked his friend Hans Albring to send him a Russian icon if possible, but predicted that "after twenty years of Bolshevism this will be highly doubtful."[71]

Albring did manage to send a treasured icon, but he also confirmed Altrogge's fears regarding the impact of communist rule on Soviet spiritual life. In July 1941, he shared a sobering revelation. In contrast to Poland and Lithuania, "things look different here with the churches," he explained. Some had been "converted into warehouses." Others were "in a state of terrible disrepair, and one has removed statues and crosses from them. It pains one to see how so many splendid buildings are decaying."[72] As his communications unit came within 250 miles of Moscow in September, he discovered another church that had been turned into a grain storehouse. The Soviet government "had sent all the priests to Siberia in 1929," he lamented. "In this city," he went on, "all the churches have been converted and the most beautiful ones burned down."[73] Not far from where Albring was stationed, Walter Neuser encountered a church near a small village in mid-July as his artillery regiment neared Smolensk. "It looked terrible inside," he told his mother. "It had been used as a warehouse."[74] Over the following months he recorded similar sights in other areas.[75]

The observations made by Albring and Neuser were repeated many times in soldiers' writings as they advanced across the western Soviet Union in the summer of 1941. Everywhere they marched, from the smallest village to the most sprawling metropolis, troops found that if they had not been simply torn down, most Christian houses of worship had been repurposed for profane uses by the nation's communist rulers. They now served as warehouses, theaters, dance halls, factories, or—most offensive of all in the invaders' eyes— "museums of atheism" intended to expose religion as the "opiate of the masses." As Franz Siebeler observed of one church, altars and paintings had been stripped away and crosses replaced with Soviet stars. "It looks sad!" he declared.[76] Even the familiar German religious soundscape was absent: in the Soviet Union, the clang of church bells never reached soldiers' ears.[77]

Those servicemen who did not have time to inspect former churches for themselves could read about the impact of Soviet religious policies in Wehrmacht publications. In the Russian city of Velikiye Luki, one front newspaper reported that the churches still stood but "it has been a long time since worship services have been held inside. They serve as storage sheds, granaries, or cinemas."[78] The same paper also carried the story of a *Volksdeutsch* pastor who returned to Vilnius only to find that the Soviets had used his church as "a Jew-club and for the red transportation workers' association. In the spot where the altar stood for 400 years, there hung the red star of the Bolshevik world-revolution [and] below them pictures of the butchers Lenin and Stalin. . . . Everything that was holy to generations of German men is defiled, ridiculed, profaned."[79] Another paper announced the discovery in Kaunas of the bodies of 1,100 priests who had been tortured, imprisoned, and finally executed.[80] If they had not destroyed them already, army reporters added, the USSR's rulers made sure churches were set ablaze as the Red Army retreated.[81] Back in Germany, journalists related the tragic story of Christianity in the Soviet Union—its leadership arrested, its priests relocated or killed, its communities heavily taxed, and its buildings desecrated by the state.[82]

Spurred on by their firsthand observations and encouraged by opportunistic propagandists, many soldiers concluded that their enemies had strayed far beyond the pale of Christian civilization. Franz Siebeler had already made up his mind on this subject the day before the attack. "I would not like to wage war against anyone," he wrote his parents and siblings in Nordhausen, "but these murderers and God-deniers must receive their just punishment."[83] The more intellectually minded Eugen Altrogge obtained a copy of Lenin's complete works. His reading confirmed what he had already known—that the Bolshevik founder had been an inveterate enemy of Christianity.[84] It was not only pious church-goers who reacted with dismay at the communist stance on religion. Less theologically oriented *Ostkämpfer*, like Hans Roth, displayed profound shock and did not hesitate to condemn their "godless" adversary. Roth constantly referred to Soviet fighters as "red devils," opined that communism had destroyed the soul of the Russian people, and declared that his enemies "h[e]ld nothing sacred in this world."[85]

Although participation in faith institutions had long been on the wane in Germany, many troops still considered religion the bedrock of civilization, culture, and morality. The absence of religion in the USSR thus soon came to serve as an explanation for what soldiers saw as the country's complete economic and social decay.[86] In Russia, so Albring penned, "we see and let ourselves be taught in what direction a people is pushed [when they] deify labor and work and do not lift up the throne of God above [earthly] achievements and machines."[87] Throughout his service, Albring constantly worried that Russia had been taken over by satanic forces, which was particularly troubling because "without religion no culture seems to be able to grow or [even] exist."[88] Albring was not alone in his reaction. The Protestant chaplain for the Ninth Army, in which Albring served, took note of the troops' "recognition of the connection between godlessness and Soviet conditions."[89] Other chaplains made similar remarks.[90] For Germans in uniform, the USSR came to represent the catastrophe in store for any society that turned its back on the Almighty. Its treatment of religion ensured that God would grant victory to the Wehrmacht.

Even as they condemned Soviet godlessness, personnel faced mounting difficulties as they attempted to maintain their self-styled image as a Christian army during the breakneck advance. The Protestant chaplain of Franz Siebeler's 14th Panzer Division explained that it was impossible to assemble any group larger than half a battalion for worship, since there were few buildings available and Soviet aircraft posed a constant threat. Typical of most chaplains, he also had to travel enormous distances to reach the dispersed elements of his division.[91] As a result of these problems, which exacerbated the army's perpetual shortage of chaplains, many troops informed their relatives that the accustomed patterns of religious life had already begun to break down. "Yesterday was Sunday," Walter Neuser told his mother in late August, "and as in all the past Sundays we had to march again."[92] Two days earlier, fellow Protestant Wilhelm Moldenhauer complained that on the drive through Ukraine, "one often scarcely notices or does not know at all when it is Sunday."[93] Despite the disruptions of combat and marching, chaplains still managed to hold smaller, ad hoc services whether on the front or behind the lines.[94]

Religious life in the Wehrmacht soon settled into a familiar pattern. For the most part it became a personal affair or a topic discussed among small groups of comrades or with a visiting chaplain. As institutional frameworks and formal ceremony fell away, many of the Wehrmacht's more religious soldiers began to cultivate their faith in more private forms. Frustrated by the lack of worship services, Franz Siebeler tried to mark the significance of Sundays by washing and shaving.[95] Heinz Rahe, former Protestant pastor and lieutenant in the 13th Panzer Division, which raced ahead of Siebeler's across the Ukraine, conducted solitary church services or devotions on his own time.[96] Others went into battle with crosses and rosaries, and in quiet moments they read the Bible, Wehrmacht hymnals, and the few religious texts that were still available.[97]

Christian soldiers often identified like-minded comrades with whom they could discuss spiritual matters. After being transferred to Russia in 1942, Hans Wilhelm Sauer conversed with chaplains as often as he could and made the acquaintance of several fellow theologians in his unit.[98] Worship services and Bible studies brought together men from a wide a variety of backgrounds and helped engender a sense of group solidarity in the face of an enemy supposedly bereft of all values. As the Second Army's Catholic chaplain put it, "In many units, officers and soldiers create an exemplary community by taking part in the worship service and by taking the sacrament."[99] Feelings of religious togetherness also encompassed the homeland. When they had the rare opportunity for formal worship in the field, the rank and file eagerly informed their loved ones and found in the familiar rituals a connection to home, a "piece of the homeland," as the Eleventh Army's Catholic chaplain put it.[100]

Chaplains and soldiers alike recognized religion as a source of strength, whether this was conceived of in spiritual, emotional, or physical terms. The exceedingly nationalistic chaplain of the 8th Jäger Division opined that "a healthy religious life of faith gives the soldierly bearing the requisite inner strength and drives [the men] toward the fulfillment of duty up to the point of sacrificial death, and to endurance through all the failure of the nerves."[101] Hans Wilhelm Sauer, Hans Simon, and others would ask God many times for strength during the conflict. They had few doubts that the Wehrmacht enjoyed God's favor; indeed, many believed that the Almighty was the source of Germany's spectacular initial victories. Just as Sauer had speculated in 1940 that the victory over France should be credited not just to Germany's Nazi leadership but divine support, Wilhelm Moldenhauer told his wife that "if one has witnessed [the successes against Poland and Russia] one must often say to oneself [that] this is a miracle, or this is a higher power that grants the victory to justice and reason."[102] As they mused about the invasions' religious dimensions or mentioned their participation in spiritual activities, troops sent a clear message to their homeland audience: unlike their enemies, they remained deeply devoted to their nation's Christian traditions.

Religious Encounters and the Discourse of "Crusade"

The simplistic binary between the Reich's self-styled Christian warriors and the forces of atheism so long cultivated by the churches, the Nazi regime, and Germany's armed forces ran into a significant complication as soon as Wehrmacht troops made contact with Soviet civilians. The more they familiarized themselves with local culture, the more soldiers came to realize that the land of Lenin and Marx was not as godless as scenes of dilapidated churches had initially suggested.[103] In July, a week after breaking through the Stalin Line in northwestern Russia, Hans Simon commented to his father that "at the vanguard action that we were undertaking it was not uncommon for me to see women praying [and] crossing themselves, who kissed their crosses that they wear around their necks like uncle Ernst does."[104] Hans Albring discovered that locals had buried their icons to keep them hidden from Soviet authorities.[105] His deep fascination with Russian iconography brought him into contact with many inhabitants of the city of Velizh who had held on to Christian traditions, including a couple who introduced him to Orthodox church music.[106] As he spent time in Russian homes, he found that many families maintained "God-corners": small shrines that featured icons, crucifixes, and other Christian symbols.[107] Albring's observations were shared by many others. While he deplored what the nation's leaders had done to the churches, Franz Siebeler noted that in every farmhouse "holy images still hang there in the corner . . . after the style of the famous Russian icon. Faith still sits deep in the heart."[108] Although it was too early to ascertain precisely how much damage the Soviets had wrought, many troops and chaplains began to view the Soviet Union as living proof that no amount of persecution could extinguish Christian belief.

The persistence of religious convictions among ordinary Soviets did not escape the notice of army propagandists. War reporter Bernd Poiess wrote of the mysterious religiosity of "holy Russia," whose people possessed a "childlike trust in God" and had secretly awaited the day of religious revival: "Now since the Germans have come, they dig their holy implements and the kitschy icons again out of the fields and set them up in their rooms." Poiess even reported that pious women murmured blessings as Wehrmacht soldiers passed.[109] To underscore this news, the same army paper published a picture a week later of a Russian woman praying before an icon. The caption announced that "the liberation from Bolshevism has again awakened the deeply-rooted faith of the Russian people."[110] Through such accounts, propagandists accentuated the moral distinction between the country's previous leadership and the new rulers, who would once again allow civilians to openly practice their faith.

Wehrmacht authorities were also quick to recognize religion's continued importance for the Soviet people. Intelligence officials spoke with surviving leaders of the Russian Orthodox Church and worked to ascertain the extent to which the populace still held to religious traditions, with an eye toward exploiting the situation for the occupiers' advantage.[111] As intelligence operatives of the Second Army wrote, "Also here, propaganda has a rich field of activity, especially now, where the bishops of England and America pray for Soviet Russia, while the National Socialist Wehrmacht gives the Russian church its old freedom back."[112] With such considerations in mind, many Wehrmacht commanders began to favor a policy of religious toleration for the occupied areas.

While high-ranking officers considered how to exploit the situation, Wehrmacht troops pondered the invasion's spiritual meaning. Having witnessed firsthand not only the results of religious persecution but also the fact that many civilians held fast to their Christian faith, a substantial number of servicemen began to nurse an understanding of Barbarossa in which religious justifications played a major role. Some, like Siebeler, focused on the need to destroy a regime they saw as a threat to the religious underpinnings of European civilization.[113] Others favored a more positive interpretation of the invasion as a quest to bring back religion to a forlorn land. One of the latter was Heinz Rahe, who recounted to his wife how he and several comrades, including a chaplain, had discussed the purpose of the invasion in its early weeks. Rahe largely dismissed the notion that Germans needed to sacrifice to destroy the "mostly-Jewish commissars," as one comrade had opined. He found economic justifications somewhat plausible but was most interested in the conflict's religious implications. Disagreeing with the chaplain's stance that Germany was God's instrument in a divine plan to eliminate the Soviets, Rahe focused less on the need to destroy atheist enemies in a holy crusade than on the opportunity to restore religion to the USSR. "As we then were walking by [a] former church," he wrote his wife, "the hope grew again in me that in a free Ukraine perhaps also Christian preaching would be possible again. This wish is also a goal for me, for which it is worth fighting."[114]

Other soldiers followed suit by embracing the invasion as something akin to a missionary enterprise. As soon as he was told by a translator in Kharkov that Russian civilians still took an active interest in religion, Konrad Jarausch wrote to the Martin Luther Association asking for Bibles and religious brochures in Russian that he planned to distribute.[115] He openly wondered whether "a new Christian spirit [could] rise up from the rubble," and he feared for Russia's future in the event this did not come to pass.[116] Eugen Altrogge, like Rahe, explicitly downplayed "political or ideological" rationales. Instead, he found meaning in the war as a chance to "straighten out" a land he believed had been infected by satanic forces.[117] The desire to return the Soviet Union to the fold of Christian nations proved an especially powerful motivation for Wehrmacht chaplains of both confessions.[118] Whether expressed in terms of hatred for the "godless enemy" or a sense of missionary optimism, religious justifications for the war found purchase with soldiers from a range of backgrounds, including some who regarded ideological arguments as less compelling.

Troops and chaplains alike soon got the chance to put this sense of Christian mission into action. During the first months of Barbarossa, from the Baltic and Bessarabia to the Ukraine and Russia itself, thousands of troops, under the supervision of chaplains of both confessions, worked to refurbish former churches and restore them to Christian use.[119] Although there were many local variations, these events generally followed a common sequence. When German units reached a settlement for the first time, soldiers set to work clearing out the interiors of abandoned or converted churches. In this task, they were frequently joined by crowds of enthusiastic civilians, many of whom had strongly opposed the Soviet government's religious policies and who now, having as yet little clear understanding of the invaders' full intentions, hoped the Wehrmacht's arrival would bring a new era of religious freedom and better economic prospects.[120]

Taking direction from chaplains, soldiers and civilians hauled boxes from churches that had been serving as warehouses, removed machinery from sanctuaries-turned-factories, and emptied "museums of atheism" of their antireligious propaganda. Once the interiors had been emptied, they repaired structural damage, scrubbed floors, and restored altars, crosses, and other religious implements, many of which had been brought out of hiding by pious civilians. One *Ostkämpfer* described such a scene to Catholic leaders in Freiburg: "In the city where I am now, there was a church that was made into a godless museum. We threw out all the exhibit materials and burned them in a public place. The population took part vigorously; old people trampled on the pictures of Lenin and Stalin."[121] These events were both physical and symbolic cleansings that provided an opportunity for civilians to distance themselves from the Stalin regime, on the one hand, and for the invaders to portray themselves as pious Christian warriors who had come to the rescue of their fellow believers.

Once a church building had been restored, chaplains held re-dedication services, such as the one Hans Albring attended along the Daugava. Despite linguistic and cultural barriers, the services tied soldiers and civilians together in shared ritual and imbued the invasion with religious significance. In his memoirs, Catholic chaplain Ernst Tewes described their emotional impact and the enthusiastic participation of the population. After dismantling a museum of atheism in Bila Tserkva with the help of Russian POWs, he invited servicemen and locals to worship. The Germans ringed a makeshift altar as a crowd of Ukrainian men and women stood behind them. The civilians "could no longer control their joy and emotion," Tewes recalled. "They cried. And at the end of the Mass . . . they all fell in and sang their Ukrainian songs."[122] Whether the population took part from a distance or mingled with German servicemen, the reopenings provided an opportunity for mutual expressions of faith and animosity toward the Soviet state. The work of refurbishing and re-consecrating churches took time away from an advance in which every minute counted. Troops considered them no mere sideshows, however. They were a chance, as Franz Siebeler put it, "to completely turn the population away from communism," a moral blow aimed at the heart of the Soviet system whose significance rivaled that of any battlefield victory.[123]

To further underscore the message that the Wehrmacht was returning religion to the land of atheism, chaplains also held worship in physical spaces that had been associated with communist rule. In July, the Catholic chaplain of the Second Army conducted worship for members of that formation's general staff at the former Red Party house in Minsk.[124] In Velizh, Hans Albring attended a service "between the beheaded monuments of Lenin and Stalin," together with a crowd of Russian civilians.[125] Far to the south, in Kiev, chaplain Hans Leidl could not pass up the chance to turn a former commissar gathering room into a makeshift chapel. "This meeting room of the godless," Leidl proclaimed, "has become a worship room. The men felt this," he added.[126]

Along with worship services, clergymen in uniform performed enormous numbers of baptisms throughout the western USSR. These were often initiated by civilians who thronged around German chaplains the moment their presence was recognized. Alfons Mende, Catholic chaplain of the 16th Panzergrenadier Division, reflected on his experiences in the Ukraine:

> There we were greeted enthusiastically by the people. And when the people heard that there was a pastor among the soldiers, things really got going. . . . I baptized en masse with a bathtub, really en masse. And the soldiers and doctors, they all helped busily, regularly carried along the people in order to be their baptismal sponsors and gave them the most diverse sorts of gifts.[127]

Similarly, the Protestant chaplain of XXIX Corps held services that drew *Volksdeutsch* civilians "from neighboring villages over 5 kilometers away."[128] Clergymen also found themselves conducting marriages for couples who, on account of Soviet policies, had never received the blessing of a priest.[129]

Although they were for the most part spontaneous events initiated by chaplains and troops on the ground, reopenings and related events were generally sanctioned and sometimes actively encouraged by the Wehrmacht's leadership, more for their propaganda value than their religious implications. The commander of Infantry Regiment 413 composed a glowing report to his superiors in which he described how the initial uneasiness and hostility among the population of one settlement turned to "immense trust" after a squad of German engineers attempted to repair a former church and the troops of his unit worshiped inside.[130] Since many of the regulations regarding the religious interaction of chaplains, civilians, and soldiers had been fairly ambiguous at the start of the campaign, units established diverse policies as they awaited further instructions from OKW.[131] In a few cases, officers directly ordered reopening services or religious care for civilians, especially *Volksdeutsch*.[132] More often, they gave the events their tacit approval as a means to enhance the army's image, but they also feared the strategic and ideological implications of fraternization between Soviet inhabitants and Germans in uniform.[133] Displaying no such reservations, Wehrmacht propagandists publicized the events in glowing terms.[134] The cover of the September 1941 issue of *Signal* magazine, the army's only international publication, sported a picture of a Wehrmacht priest–soldier baptizing Soviet children.[135] The reopenings also received coverage in the wider German press, where they were interpreted as a sign that Germany was tangibly advancing the cause of Christianity, while England supported the forces of the devil.[136]

Church officials in the homeland, who continued to support the war effort through both word and deed, particularly welcomed this news. In his pastoral letter of September 14, 1941, Bishop Graf von Galen praised the reestablishment of churches as a sign that Germany's leaders were committed to destroying Bolshevism and effecting the "liberation of the Russian people."[137] The sole remaining nationally distributed Catholic periodical followed suit and carried firsthand accounts from participants.[138] Inquiries to the Vatican confirmed that priests in the Wehrmacht were indeed allowed to perform Christian rites for Orthodox civilians, although only in emergencies, a development that lent further credence to the crusade theme.[139]

The German Protestant Church also appears to have given its blessing to religious ministrations for Soviet civilians.[140] Protestant leaders collected accounts by *Volksdeutsch* Protestants who had been "liberated" by the Wehrmacht and took up collections for religious communities in lands seized from the Soviets.[141] The Protestant Church's director of foreign affairs even authored a book describing how the communists had persecuted religion that included a glowing account of the reopenings.[142] On both sides of the confessional divide, leaders hoped the events were an indication that the Nazi regime was softening its policies toward religion, a hope that would continue to go unfulfilled despite the churches' continued support for the war.

The reopening of Christian sanctuaries across the western Soviet Union represented a high-water mark for crusading sentiments in the Wehrmacht and the German homeland. They appeared to offer incontrovertible proof that Germany's warriors stood on the side of Christianity and placed the Soviets' anti-religious policies into sharp relief for the world to see. This not only legitimized the invasion as a whole, but cast troops and chaplains in the role of righteous saviors returning religion to a grateful population. The reopening of churches also reinforced colonial stereotypes by portraying the populace as unable to care for their own spiritual well-being and reinforced the notion that the Soviets had to be utterly destroyed. At the same time, however, they subverted Nazi racial hierarchies by emphasizing shared religious outlooks and experiences between the invaders and the population.

The events would not last long. When news of them reached the Führer's ear at the beginning of August, OKW swiftly handed down a *Führer-Erlass* (decree) that "members of the Wehrmacht must unconditionally keep their distance" from the population's religious activities, which were to be "neither promoted nor hindered." The order also forcefully stated that chaplains were forbidden from ministering to anyone outside the Wehrmacht.[143] In the middle of September, Hitler issued several clarifications, including that Wehrmacht worship services could not be performed in Soviet churches and that "the participation of the civil population (including *Volksdeutsch*) in field worship services of the Wehrmacht is forbidden." In an indication of how seriously the Führer took the matter, every chaplain was required to acknowledge the order in writing.[144] Army units received news of these decisions slowly and in piecemeal fashion, but by at least October 1941 the reopening phenomenon had effectively come to an end.[145]

The heads of the Protestant and Catholic chaplaincies, other high-ranking chaplains, and the highest-ranking officers of Army Group Center all protested the orders with arguments centered on military necessity and the significance of religion, but their pleas fell on deaf ears.[146] The decrees came as a shock not only to chaplains but also many enlisted men, who regarded them as a profound betrayal of the ideals for which they had claimed to be fighting. They brought into sharp focus the previously unrecognized chasm between a Nazi worldview that stressed irreconcilable racial differences and a sense of Christian universalism that cast Soviet civilians as fellow believers, if less culturally advanced and in need of German leadership. "The ban on the use of former Russian churches for Wehrmacht services is a great concern," the Catholic chaplain of the Second Army wrote his superiors. "The agitation among the troops, among officers and men, was equally great." He paraphrased their response: "'We're supposed to be fighting for a Christian Europe. . . . Why this prohibition?'"[147] The Catholic chaplain of the Eleventh Army made a similar observation in a report on the spiritual health of the troops:

> News from the homeland regarding certain actions vis-à-vis the civil church, as well as both decrees of OKW that forbid any spiritual activity for the civilian population have effected confusion and a certain undermining

of trust among the soldiers. The disappointment regarding the denial of spiritual help for the civil population has hurt the German image, since the civil population had also expected liberation in religious matters from the person of the Führer.[148]

The presumptive image of Hitler as a good Christian leader at the forefront of a crusading mission was beginning to lose its luster.

The prohibition on the use of Soviet churches not only dampened missionary sentiments but also significantly handicapped the ability of Wehrmacht clergymen to conduct worship services since few other structures could be found that were large enough to accommodate formal religious gatherings. This was especially true as the months grew colder and outdoor services became increasingly impractical. Even in the face of these setbacks, however, the men of the Wehrmacht kept up an active religious life during the remainder of 1941. Religion remained an especially important cornerstone in the army's construction of an insular moral community. This community encompassed the immediate circle of comrades and also bound the front to the home front in the knowledge of shared beliefs and traditions that—Wehrmacht personnel continued to insist—set them apart from their "godless" enemies.

Nowhere was this pious image more pronounced than during Christmas, a festival Germans had long treasured above all others.[149] For some combatants, the Christmas of 1941 was their first "war Christmas," a concept that had taken on special national significance during the First World War.[150] Despite temperatures as cold as −40°C and the shock of the Soviet Winter Offensive that would spark months of desperate defensive battles, soldiers came together to celebrate the holiday. Braving blizzard conditions, chaplains did their best to reach as many men as possible. They held small services in bunkers, barns, or whatever spaces were available. Troops listened to the Christmas gospel, sang songs they had known since childhood, opened presents from home, and recalled past Christmases they had spent with their families. "Yesterday evening we celebrated the festival of love and of togetherness," Johannes Hagemann told his parents. After listening to an officer's speech about the holiday's meaning, he opened gifts from home and enjoyed a meal of ham and potatoes with comrades just behind the front lines.[151] In celebrating Christmas, personnel solidified their spiritual connection to the homeland, where they knew relatives would be hearing the same words and singing the same melodies. "Christmas songs, and such songs that tell of yearning for something beloved ring in my ear," wrote Willy Nagel to an acquaintance. "Forgotten for hours are the rough customs of war, replaced by a soft childlike mood."[152] Through their descriptions of the holiday, soldiers presented themselves as the caretakers of Christian and German values like hope, love, warmth, and coziness—values they claimed their Soviet enemies could not understand. Even if it evoked memories of home, however, Christmas on the front had its own unique flavor. Gone were the towering cathedrals, the pomp and the circumstance; as many troops recognized, religion was returning to its primitive roots, where content trumped form and the space between God and man collapsed.

As they celebrated one of the most important Christian holidays in unfamiliar circumstances, soldiers made sure to emphasize how foreign these customs were to the Soviets. In 1941, Hans Roth pointed out that as men of his unit celebrated reverently on Christmas Eve, the Red Army launched an attack.[153] Wilhelm Altmann recounted to his family a Christmas speech made by his commander, who emphasized that if the Soviets had reached Germany, "there would be no more Christmas."[154] During the Christmas of 1943, Willy Hagemann would inform the sister of a fallen comrade that the enemy continued to fire on his men's position even during their holiday celebrations. "The Bolsheviks do not want love, no, they hate it," he declared.[155] In his next letter to his parents, he continued: "the Russians do not know and do not want Christmas."[156]

A Changing Religious Culture

As the year 1942 dawned and the army worked to stabilize the lines against constant Soviet aggression, the combination of significant military setbacks and the unforgiving environment fostered a more somber mood. Many men continued to nurture identities as decent Christian warriors, and religious life in the Wehrmacht remained strong—even as it began to enter a new phase, one in which prayers for endurance replaced prayers for a quick victory. At the end of their strength after months of combat, many Christians in uniform were coming to view the war as a kind of spiritual test—a test of their loyalty to their comrades and to the homeland, a test of their own will and of their faith in a God they still firmly believed was on their side. As the writings of troops and chaplains attest, interest in religion was heightened by nearness to death and the terrors of combat, but it still remained to be seen whether the war experience was generating an authentic religious awakening within the ranks.

Like most soldiers, Hans Simon had expected to be home by Christmas. He was fortunate enough to have been granted several months of leave during the winter, but the experience of never-ending trench warfare between Leningrad and Moscow began to take its toll after he returned in June. His confident assertions of *"Gott mit uns "* began to give way to simple gratitude that God had allowed him to survive, and he resolved to make the most of whatever time he had left. He told his parents in September 1942 that the war had become an "emotional strain," but he asked them to pray that God would "give me the strength to stand through these hours as a man. Not my will, rather His will be done."[157] Despite the increasing pressure of a war Simon felt was robbing him of his youth, he continued to ask God for victory.[158] As one comrade after another fell, he prayed that they had not died in vain.[159] Hans Simon's religious world extended primarily to himself and his correspondents; he did not record attending a single worship service in 1942. This was perhaps unsurprising, given the observation of the Protestant chaplain of his 12th Infantry Division that few suitable locations could be found and that "in winter 1941 / 42 it was almost impossible to hold worship and devotions, since every man was needed during the difficult defensive battles."[160]

Formal rituals and religious connections to the homeland and other soldiers played a much more prominent role in Franz Siebeler's experience. After being frustrated by the lack of opportunities for Catholic worship in 1941, Siebeler was able to consistently attend Mass in the spring of 1942 as his unit prepared to move on Stalingrad. He remarked that the services, conducted by the Catholic division chaplain, were usually very well attended. Of the service for the second Sunday in Pentecost, which drew 250 visitors, he wrote that "it was really a glorious day. The theatre . . . was full to the last seat. Everyone was there, also many officers. Also Red Cross nurses were there. About half of everyone went to Holy Communion." During the service, Siebeler experienced a strong sense of connection to home: "my thoughts were very, very often with you loved ones in the beautiful German Heimat. . . . The Holy Mass reminded [me] of so many music-Masses of the cathedral choir [at home]."[161] Indeed, Siebeler always tried to keep himself informed of developments in his home church.[162] He inquired as to how his relatives were celebrating religious holidays and made sure to ask for their prayers.[163] He also cultivated a sense of religious community in his unit by attending Mass with comrades and spending time with the division chaplain.[164] Still, he expressed concern that religious needs were being ignored by the Wehrmacht's leadership.[165]

The experiences of Simon and Siebeler raise the question of to what extent the rank and file had begun to turn even more to religion during the war. Already in the summer of 1941, scores of chaplains reported that their time in combat had led troops toward a more serious engagement with religious questions. The Catholic chaplain of the 20th Panzer Division, for example, explained that his unit "remained largely intact spiritually and religiously" after months of constant fighting. He recorded an 80 percent Communion participation rate and observed a strong desire for Mass and the sacraments among Catholic soldiers.[166] At the end of 1941, the Protestant chaplain of the Sixteenth Army reported that "the inner concern of the comrades in this work of the chaplain was truly clearly stronger than in the previous time," and quoted one soldier as saying that "'the difficult war here has led many nearer again to [the] Lord God.'"[167]

According to chaplains' accounts, these trends continued into the campaign's second year. The Protestant chaplain of Hans Simons's 12th Infantry Division reported that despite many difficulties he was able to lead a total of 119 worship services in "stalls[,] . . . barns, . . . bunkers and houses" from December 1941 to February 1943 that drew 200 officers and 3,900 men. Like most of his colleagues, he often heard requests for return visits and reported that "field song books and New Testaments" were "more asked for than could be given out."[168] Based on his own experience and conversations with troop leaders, the Protestant chaplain of the 11th Infantry Division commented that "the length of the war, the difficulty of the fight and the severity of the deprivations have led the soldiers in general to a more serious view of life and caused religious feeling to grow in them."[169] He and other chaplains continued to consider it their duty to give the men strength in the midst of mounting difficulties on the battlefield.[170]

Chaplains' reports cannot always be taken at face value, since their authors tended to interact with the most religiously engaged soldiers and often equated attendance at rituals with inner faith. Still, the writings of troops themselves give some credence to the notion that the war experience had ushered in a more earnest attitude toward religion. Hans Simon quickly recognized that "this campaign . . . has deepened and turned inward so many comrades" whom he had initially considered superficial.[171] After watching a movie in Demyansk when his unit was temporarily pulled off the line in November 1941, he struggled to explain how the war had changed his and others' spiritual outlook. "One sees everything with other eyes and one perhaps also finds a little more faith in the ideals that every person fosters within himself," he remarked.[172] After a month of bitter fighting as the Soviets besieged the city of Velizh in February 1942, Hans Albring found that prayer had taken on increased significance in his life and for the first time he began to notice the importance of religion for others in his unit.[173] Experiences differed considerably, however. Heinz Rahe, who had held devotions for himself in 1941, now feared that he had become indifferent about practicing his religion.[174] Other soldiers displayed little religious interest to begin with, a predilection that war did not change.

Even the habitually optimistic chaplains worried that the religious revival they detected was only skin deep. A few reported lackluster worship attendance in their units, although this appears to have been the exception rather than the rule.[175] Some noticed that although attendance spiked before battle, it tended to level out during pauses in the fighting.[176] Chaplains also described encounters with soldiers, officers, and doctors who exhibited hostility toward the churches, which they considered weak or old-fashioned. These men may have been adherents of the Nazi movement, although chaplains rarely identified them as such.[177] Further, chaplains found themselves engaged in a constant battle to reinvigorate the faith of the large mass of "indifferent, lukewarm, wavering, fair-weather friends" who had lost their "rel[igious] antennae," as the Catholic chaplain of 123rd Infantry Division colorfully put it.[178]

As chaplains did their best to nurture religious interest among their flock, propagandists continued even after the *Erlass* to pay lip service to the notion that the Wehrmacht was a Christian army that held to the "God-connected teaching of German faith" against the "soulless" enemy, as one publication asserted.[179] They even occasionally printed prayers for the troops to recite.[180] Religion also served as the trump card of the army's propaganda to the civilian population. After much deliberation, the Wehrmacht, the German civilian administrations in the occupied territories, and Hitler himself settled on a policy of tacit toleration: Soviet civilians would be allowed to worship, although religious organizations were subject to surveillance and, with few exceptions, did not enjoy direct support from the occupiers. The policy proved to be one of the few genuine successes of Germany's imperial rule in the east, enjoying widespread support from the occupied population.[181] Although Nazi administrators still fretted about the possibility of a church-centered revolt, many Orthodox leaders expressed gratitude toward the invaders for restoring freedom of worship.[182] Army propagandists made sure to inform the men that thanks to their efforts religion was once again enjoying a renaissance in the occupied lands.[183]

The *Erlass* may have put an end to the Wehrmacht's active support of local churches, but religious contact between the Wehrmacht and Soviet inhabitants persisted. Curious soldiers attended local worship services, explored the world of Orthodox religious art, and continued to encounter signs of piety among the population. Although they did not always understand Orthodox customs, many servicemen came to recognize Soviet civilians as fellow Christians, a view that undercut the Nazi insistence on strict racial boundaries.

In 1941 and 1942, Hans Albring attended at least two Orthodox worship services—including a three-hour service in Velizh.[184] In his description of the latter, he noted the striking figure of the priest, the "very solemn and serious" polyphonic voices of the choir, and the fascinating rituals that punctuated the liturgy. Albring also visited other churches and made the acquaintance of several local priests.[185] In his free time, he attempted to buy or barter for icons that had survived Soviet rule—which he discovered were in every Russian house—and frequently interacted on friendly terms with devout civilians.[186] During his stay in Velizh, he was delighted when his host family asked him to sing German church music for them.[187] On several occasions, he recounted how locals expressed animosity toward the Soviet regime for its suppression of religious practice.[188]

Similarly, Dr. Wilhelm Bacher attended an Orthodox worship service in early 1943 and, like Albring, continually noted the ubiquity of icons and the piety of the population.[189] He recorded in his diary in January 1942, that the woman in whose home he was quartering prayed out loud for hours over a Bible after her neighbor had been killed by shelling. Her neighbor's surviving ten-year-old daughter crossed herself and bowed as she listened.[190] Others continued to emphasize religious similarities that transcended cultural and ideological boundaries. Franz Siebeler told his relatives that "Bolshevism is only a matter of a few [people]," a conclusion he drew after observing the ubiquity of icons in Soviet farmhouses.[191] Likewise, Rudolf Dietrich commented in a letter that the Russians put on their best clothes for Easter and Pentecost and went into the churches, just as, he noted, Germans did at home.[192]

As they recognized similarities between their own faith and that of ordinary Soviets, Ostkämpfer sometimes even came to wonder whether the local inhabitants in fact possessed a closer connection to the divine than the Westerners who claimed to be bringing them religion. Albring's friend, Eugen Altrogge, spoke of the "reverence" that was part of the Russian character and expressed his fear that the invaders viewed the populace with blind arrogance. Germans and western Europeans, with their concern for "gardens and culture, wooden floors and culture, clean fingernails and culture . . . usually have no idea of the strong primitiveness, spiritual simplicity, simple-minded strength and terrible force of this people," he wrote.[193] Like many other soldiers and not a few propagandists, he drew a distinction between the diabolic communist regime and Russia's long-held religious traditions.[194] Albring took a more ambivalent view. "There is in the true faces of the Russians a daemonie [sic] . . . that frightens us," he wrote, "but also then again a holiness, a sign from above and from the light that . . . terrifies us, when we think about the largely corrupt and . . . in religious matters largely degenerate West."[195] Elsewhere, Albring remarked that their proximity to nature gave the Russians a nearness to God, although they lacked the sophisticated theology and humanism of the West. He worried that the Russian preoccupation with icons could morph into "primitive image-worship" but also detected "much true worship" among them.[196]

On the other hand, the strange rituals and esoteric practices of the Orthodox creed occasionally evoked outright condemnation from men who dismissed local religiosity as little more than superstition or its practitioners as subhuman barbarians. Wilhelm Moldenhauser disparagingly recounted to his wife how Soviets celebrated "so-called worship services" in their homes and frequently crossed themselves. "This condition is really an old tradition," he explained, "to which also the younger generations adhere. The people have been stultified by the Bolshevik state and made submissive by it. They have fear and reverence for the superhuman power that we call God or fate. I'd like to know sometime if they give it any thought at all."[197] Moldenhauser also remarked that between the icons villagers hung on their walls one could sometimes see nail holes from the pictures of Stalin and Lenin they had taken down when the Germans came.[198] Still, even Moldenhauser acknowledged many similarities between Soviet and German practice, particularly on holidays like Christmas and Easter.[199] In contrast, Walter Neuser, a more critical Nazi Party member, told his parents about a burial that civilians conducted in the village where he was staying in April 1942. He called the event "a sensation for the village" that "one can only describe with the term 'horde' or 'gang of rascals.'"[200]

The Wehrmacht's continuing encounter with Russian religiosity had a multiplicity of effects. It allowed soldiers to perform identities as faithful Christians, in contradistinction to a Soviet army and regime they still dismissed as thoroughly atheist. At the same time, it closed the distance between occupiers and occupied, in subversion of Nazi wishes, and in some cases caused the invaders to question whether their side was the true representative of Christianity. Even so, religious interactions with local civilians reinforced the delusion that the invasion served the legitimate purpose of restoring religion to the USSR and cast the population as primitives who required the aid of the more advanced Germans to realize their spiritual potential.

Religion under Fire

By 1943, the Wehrmacht's already-strained religious fabric had begun to fray. Chaplain numbers, paltry when the conflict began, dwindled due to sickness and enemy action. Troops found themselves spread across vast distances and engaged in nonstop combat for months at a time. Regularly scheduled formal worship services were little more than a distant memory. For men who had counted on a decisive, divinely sanctioned victory over communist atheism, the devastating loss of the Sixth Army at Stalingrad in the winter of 1942–1943 came as a profound shock. Many troops continued to expect God's help in a war they still ultimately believed Germany would win, but their religious outlooks shifted once again, turning increasingly toward the subjects of overcoming suffering and enduring what was proving to be a much harder test than any had anticipated. As in the First World War, Germany's path had become not so much a "crusade" as a "way of the cross."[201] This transition was symbolically captured by the Stalingrad Madonna, a charcoal drawing by Lieutenant Kurt Reuber, a Protestant pastor serving as a staff doctor. Flown out on the last plane to escape the battlefield, it depicted a robed Virgin Mary cradling the Christ child in a warm embrace ringed by the words "Christmas in the cauldron [Kessel]," "light, life, love," and "Fortress Stalingrad."[202] Like Reuber, the Wehrmacht's Christian warriors yearned for an end to their ordeal, all the while clinging to their faith in a God they still believed would set things right.

Himself an ordained Protestant minister, First Lieutenant Heinz Rahe nurtured his faith by conducting several worship services when his division's Protestant chaplain was on leave in the spring of 1943. Rahe relished the opportunity, despite the lack of field song books and an interruption by Soviet combat aircraft. He noted that the men "seemed to me to be really paying attention."[203] The suffering he experienced during his unit's 1943 retreat from the Caucasus following the Battle of Stalingrad led him toward a new spiritual interpretation of the war. When his brother-in-law fell in battle, Rahe saw the event as a sign of God's punishment. "But we should not only think on foreign sins," he wrote his wife. "At once we are collectively guilty as members of the whole and deserve such wrath[;] in addition we Christians have deserved God's wrath in great quantities."[204]

Hans Simon continued to pray for an end to the war, which he still believed Germany had to win "no matter the cost."[205] As his family endured Allied bombing raids in the city of Malchow, he asked God to grant them strength.[206] When he heard of the disastrous news from Stalingrad, he praised Sixth Army General Paulus' final message of loyalty to Hitler as a sign of heroism that Germany's youth needed to emulate.[207] Like Rahe, he became acutely aware of the suffering he and his compatriots endured. Aside from asking for God's protection and resigning himself to the fact that "our fate lies in God's hand," Simon turned to reading poetry for spiritual inspiration as his unit held on between Leningrad and Moscow.[208] "In these hours, where it looks gloomy outside, one must draw strength and believe in our mission," he wrote. "It's crazy, the sacrifices that we must make in Russia."[209] Kurt Niemeyer could only echo this sentiment after he and a handful of comrades escaped death during a massive Soviet assault on the city of Orel. "I must really thank God that I came out of that hell," he told his wife in August 1943.[210] Like Rahe and Simon, he continued to tell his family to trust in God despite the crumbling strategic situation.[211] The somber mood at the front was echoed by clergy in the homeland who came under criticism from Nazi authorities for their increased focus on the themes of suffering and mourning in worship services across the country.[212]

As formal religious practice in the Wehrmacht continued to deteriorate, soldiers' faith that God remained steadfastly on Germany's side was shaken by the impact of ever-stricter Nazi policies. The year 1942 saw a new stipulation that fallen chaplains would no longer be replaced, one of a spate of new restrictions.[213] The lack of chaplains was partly made up for by priests and pastors in uniform who conducted religious activities unofficially, but regulations restricted their activity as well.[214] Religious literature remained forbidden, despite the repeated protests of chaplains, enlisted men, and church officials.[215] Anti-Christian propaganda appeared in its stead.[216] Zealous Nazi officers interfered with Christian practice by altering holiday ceremonies and refusing to notify troops of upcoming worship services. Already in 1941, Hans Albring lamented that there was no Christmas service for his unit. "The authorities even debated whether it was appropriate to allow the singing of 'Silent Night' at the Christmas celebration," he added. "Isn't it too Christian?—that's what one asks here." The men sang it anyway, he noted proudly.[217] Franz Siebeler complained to his family the same Christmas that there was supposed to be a worship service but military authorities never announced it. "It's already happened enough [times] that one hears about [a service] after the event," he lamented. "For the leaders it is also not exactly something important. Every sh[itty] regulation is read aloud a hundred times[;] religious things are simply withheld," he went on, in an apparent reference to restrictions on Christian reading material. "As in the Reich, so also in the military."[218] He was finally able to attend a small Christmas ceremony held by a Protestant pastor–soldier and was happy to find that the man was "definitely not a 'German Christian'!"[219] Siebeler, who would not live to see the Christmas of 1942, continued to deplore the fact that "our leaders have no interest in religion" and snuck away from his unit to attend services in May and June 1942 that the army had again failed to publicize.[220]

Like Siebeler, Hans Albring and other devout Christians increasingly worried not only that the army was becoming too atheist but also that the influence of religion back home was on the decline. Some blamed Nazi policies for what they saw as a weakening of religious institutions. In September 1941, Albring spoke of the Nazi persecution of the churches after one of his comrades received a copy of a sermon by the bishop in Überwasser. Albring especially deplored the hypocrisy of reopening churches in Russia while the churches in Germany came under attack:

This underhandedness and cowardice, even more the satanic double-grimace: here one films the field Masses: see, we are giving the Russians their churches back!—and at home! . . . We see *here* [in Russia] . . . how it will look in the future in the West, in our homeland. . . . Do not such news reports out of the homeland offend you, this betrayal of us soldiers, behind whose back one so secretly destroys a whole world, a piece of the most significant of those things which signify to us the Fatherland, the Reich. . . . It is not just against the church, rather it is aimed against the spirit of Christianity and of German history and culture itself, what these barbarians want to destroy.[221]

No doubt with the censors in mind, Albring did not explicitly state that the "barbarians" in question were Germany's Nazi leadership, but this is clearly what he implied. His fears were shared by other Christian soldiers. The Protestant Jarausch described tensions in his unit between the older men and the "national socialist' generation" when his commanding officer insisted on a communal recitation of the Lord's Prayer during Christmas 1941.[222] Military censors also picked up on widespread criticism of the regime's anti-church policies by the rank and file. In October 1941 the Second Army's censors had already reported that "the religious question has repeatedly given occasion for unrest and discussion in the letters and therefore also among the troops." In particular, they cited a rumor that Nazi officials were planning to have all crucifixes removed from schoolrooms in Bavaria.[223] All in all, religious soldiers found themselves in a difficult situation. Most remained staunch nationalists who yearned for German victory and reflexively assumed that God was on their side, but as time passed it appeared to some that the Wehrmacht and the country at large were becoming more and more like the atheist enemy they had pledged to defeat.

Even so, their criticism of Nazi religious policies should not necessarily be interpreted as an indication that Christians in uniform rejected Nazism wholesale. Franz Siebeler's dismissal of German Christian theology came just a month after he offered a prayer for Hitler in one of his letters.[224] Many, particularly Protestants, never voiced complaints about Nazi practices. Some, including the relatively devout Hans Simon, even appeared to warm up to Nazism as the war progressed. In December 1942, Simon wrote his father that after long discussions with his comrades, "I can say 'yes' to all things, to the new movement, except for a few points. . . . I am happy that I can affirm the new *Weltanschauung* ['worldview'] and revolution more and more, in areas where I did not come along before, [about which I] had reservations."[225] Few seemed to recognize the Nazi movement as an absolute enemy of Christianity.

Throughout the war, Christian soldiers often became eyewitnesses to the atrocities that were the hallmark of the *Vernichtungskrieg*. Konrad Jarausch, who managed the kitchen for a POW camp, came face-to-face with the Wehrmacht's policy of deliberate starvation that resulted in over three million deaths. Having originally assumed the goodness of the German cause, he began to realize that the Wehrmacht's activities ran directly counter to the Christian principles in which he believed and began to question the purpose of the war. Jarausch ended up befriending several POWs and did his best to improve their conditions.[226] Several other Christian servicemen, as well as chaplains, expressed dismay at the routine mistreatment of civilians and prisoners. However, few appear to have taken action to prevent such behavior and many turned to the same rationalizations that others employed.[227] After all, in a war some styled as a crusade to annihilate communism, any methods that might bring victory might have seemed preferable to allowing the atheist enemy to continue to plague humanity.

Relatively few of the Christian soldiers in the core sample mentioned the Wehrmacht's treatment of the USSR's Jewish community. When they mentioned Jews, they typically expressed varying degrees of antisemitism or indifference, although the former was almost never couched in explicitly religious terms. Franz Siebeler subscribed to the common assumption that all Jews were communists.[228] Hans Albring and his comrades made Jewish women peel potatoes for them after attending a reopening service in July 1941 and he alluded to a massacre of five hundred Jews without providing further detail.[229] Heinz Rahe, whose unit also employed Jewish forced labor, mentioned to his wife that he heard the pistol shots as German soldiers killed a Jewish man in Lvov after he walked away from the scene without intervening.[230] There were a few detractors, although it is unclear whether their objections were religiously grounded. In a shocking admission, Eugen Altrogge confided to Hans Albring that "one must feel ashamed to be German" and "doubt the purpose of our fight" after discussing the fate of the Jews with his comrades. He believed the Germans had moved beyond "anti-Semitism" into the realm of "inhumanity." However, he reasoned that there was nothing he could do. "What remains to us?" he wrote. "Shut up and keep serving."[231]

Soviet efforts to counteract German crusade propaganda added to the confusion over whether the USSR could indeed be considered a "godless" adversary and whether the Wehrmacht truly represented Christian civilization. Moscow's leaders recognized early on that their hostility toward religion was proving a major liability in their efforts to maintain the loyalty of subjects now under German occupation and to win the support of the skeptical Western Allies. Slowly but surely, Soviet officials lifted restrictions on religious practice and scaled back persecution. Within weeks of the invasion, cathedrals in Moscow began holding worship services to ask for God's aid against the German onslaught. In a surprising move, Stalin allowed the election of a new Patriarch, Sergius, in 1943 to head the Russian Orthodox Church, filling a longstanding vacancy.[232] A year previously, Sergius had coauthored a book with other church officials in which he denied that Soviet Christians needed any kind of liberation and asserted that it was the church's duty to lend its support to the fight against fascism.[233]

As might be expected, the Wehrmacht and the wider German press responded with a propaganda broadside excoriating the USSR's sudden displays of piety. One of the Wehrmacht's many cartoons on the subject depicted the Soviet leader pretending to pray next to the skulls of murdered priests.[234] Journalists particularly relished the opportunity to lambast the Church of England for its alliance with the land of atheism. One Wehrmacht newspaper reported that the English were observing a day of prayer for the Soviet Union at the king's behest in the very same churches where its priests had formerly railed against communism.[235] Another derided the pious English puritans who had made common cause with the enemies of Christianity in "the nastiest spectacles of mendacious hypocrisy."[236] Hitler himself made much of the Church of England's rapid about-face.[237]

German troops picked up on these themes and uniformly rejected any claim that the communist regime had changed its course. "Today I read about the English worship service in which the Internationale is also supposed to be played," wrote Heinz Rahe in early September 1941. "Although I am sure the English High Church commits much blasphemy, this is something I really can't imagine," he declared.[238] In an apparent reference to English support for the USSR, Hans Roth described Jews and Red Army soldiers as "ascend[ing] to the heavens of 'the English High Church'" when they were murdered by his comrades near Lutsk.[239] Throughout the war, the assumption that the Western Allies were guilty by association with the Soviet Union remained a staple of German servicemen's worldviews, even as their own side's religious credentials came increasingly into question.

Waiting for a Miracle

As the Red Army surged across the Ukraine in 1944, *Ostkämpfer* continued to turn to religion for inner strength and yearned for an act of divine intervention that would save Germany from destruction. Hans Simon, who by 1944 had largely ceased signing his letters with *"Gott mit uns,"* began to realize just how little chance Germany had left. He reflected on the deaths of so many comrades and, as usual, resolved to adopt an attitude of "knightly joyfulness" in appreciation of the time he still had left.[240] His prayers for victory took a different turn, however: "Never break down or give anything up," he wrote his family. "That we may not do! God always helps . . . where our human understanding fails. One must often hope for a miracle." Simon also repeated a sentiment that formed the bedrock of Hitler's own religious outlook: "God helps the brave and the strong."[241] In the minds of many soldiers, their extreme suffering and the fact that they still held out against seemingly insurmountable odds guaranteed divine favor, an attitude that sometimes lent itself to a self-image of Christian martyrdom in the final years.[242]

The Protestant Willy Hagemann also recognized the severity of the Wehrmacht's situation but believed that God was watching over him. He was promoted to *Oberleutnant* in early 1944.[243] The two-hundred-man unit he commanded was almost entirely destroyed during defensive fighting in Lithuania and then reformed in the fall. After countless near-death experiences, he told his love interest, "I ask the dear Lord why he has always spared me. Already for a long time it is impossible to understand."[244] In September he announced to his grandmother that he had won the Knight's Cross and marveled that he was still alive after thirty close-combat engagements. "The constant luck that stood by my side I can only understand as a miracle," he confided.[245] He also managed to attend a worship service and make the acquaintance of a chaplain—both rare occurrences in the Wehrmacht of 1944.[246]

The year 1944 also witnessed intensified competition from Nazism for hearts and minds, as well as increased blending of Christianity and ideology in the Wehrmacht. In December 1943, a new type of official—the National Socialist Leadership Officer (NSFO)—was introduced to the army. Tasked with overseeing the "spiritual" and ideological health of the soldiers, the NSFO functioned as a kind of Nazi replacement for the chaplain, preaching the doctrines of the Party instead of traditional religious values.[247] Further, the sweeping censorship reports Hitler ordered after the 1944 July Plot indicate that many combatants began to combine Christian terminology with a Nazi outlook. They professed faith in God, the Führer, and the final victory; hoped for a miracle—often in the form of the regime's promised "miracle weapons"; and awaited the coming apocalypse, through which Germany would either achieve national salvation or be annihilated and transformed into a communist hell. Ninth Army censors quoted one soldier as writing, "How will all this take another turn? No matter, it is all the same. Our Führer will make everything right, and Providence has sustained him for us!" Another insisted, "It will change everything when our new weapons are put into action. We just don't

want to lose courage and believe strongly in our Führer and in Germany."[248]
The previous year, the censors of the Second Panzer Army had recorded numerous uses of apocalyptic language, including a soldier's statement that "we . . . always want to be great in faith. I believe in a German victory. I believe in our Führer. At the end of our battle the sun will rise over us and we will march into a new Age."[249] In what perhaps represented a last-ditch effort to mobilize religious sentiments to strengthen the war effort and merge them with Nazi ideology, the Führer approved a propaganda booklet for soldiers that stressed the godlessness of the Soviet enemy and insisted that the Nazi movement was not anti-religious but "rooted in [the] reverent recognition of God."[250] Remarkably, the Propaganda Ministry even contemplated enlisting a Protestant pastor to officially declare the war a religious crusade but never put the idea into action.[251] In the end, whether they looked to God, the Führer, or both for salvation, soldiers still held out hope for the intervention of a higher power to end their suffering and restore the nation to greatness as they retreated toward the Reich's borders.

Religion played a much greater role in the Wehrmacht than scholars have assumed, especially among ordinary servicemen. It influenced how troops constructed their identities, how they behaved, how they understood their enemy, and, for some, how they conceptualized the war itself. It also became a key element in the Wehrmacht's efforts to assert moral superiority over the Soviets and to whitewash its image. At the campaign's outset, German churchmen joined army chaplains and pragmatic Nazi officials to frame the war as a crusade against a godless enemy intent on destroying religion in Europe, and with it the foundation of all morality. Many religious soldiers embraced this justification, and together with chaplains they worked to reopen Soviet houses of worship. When this drew the ire of Nazi leaders who feared racial intermixing, crusading sentiments lessened. The combination of practical difficulties and Nazi animosity toward religion undermined formal religious practice over the next years, but religion survived in a more personal, less ritualized form and remained an important element in how soldiers viewed themselves and their enemy.

In some ways, religion represented a very real threat to the Nazi project on the Eastern Front. Christian soldiers often recognized Soviet civilians as fellow believers and hoped the invasion would bring them spiritual freedom—a goal that diverged sharply from the genocidal aims of the *Vernichtungskrieg*. Rather than shunning the population as subhuman, many troops displayed a willingness to worship together and learn more about Orthodox practices, to the horror of Nazi leaders. Their religious convictions also led some to question

Nazi policies in the Wehrmacht and the homeland that they feared would undermine centuries of Christian tradition.

On the other hand, however, certain religious interpretations cast the local population as primitive and superstitious, rather than authentically spiritual. Even chaplains and men who harbored the best of intentions tended to assume that the more theologically and culturally advanced Germans would need to bring religious freedom and enlightenment to a benighted population, a view that overlapped strongly with an imperialist outlook. Further, the more Christian soldiers depicted their enemy as a satanic threat to the religious foundations of Europe, the easier it became to agree with the merciless treatment of Soviet officials, Red fighters, and POWs. Thus, while it posed a serious challenge to the Nazi worldview, religion too often ended up being used as an instrument for legitimizing Hitler's *Vernichtungskrieg* by reframing it as a righteous quest to advance the interests of Christendom and rescue the peoples of the USSR from communist atheism.

Although religious discourse often worked to the Nazis' benefit during the war, it would also become an important element in veterans' postwar efforts to distance themselves from the regime. During the conflict, German soldiers had portrayed themselves as long-suffering Christian warriors fighting the good fight against a godless enemy, even as the Nazis worked to dismantle religion in Germany behind their backs. With little alternation, this image would become another key building block of the Wehrmacht myth over the next decades. After the war, many veterans claimed to have rediscovered religion and repented of their sins. Their narrative was eagerly accepted by the public, particularly in West Germany, where memory of the army often coalesced around the figure of the devout Christian warrior who had experienced more than his fair share of hardship and now had an important role to play in the task of national reconstruction. The result was an uncritical reading of the Wehrmacht's past, one that overlooked the extent to which Christianity had been employed as a justification for war and encouraged the assumption that Germany's uniformed men had been far too pious to commit atrocities or support the Nazi regime.[252] Tales of the reopening of Soviet churches or friendly relations with Christian civilians also furthered the legitimating narrative that the Wehrmacht had come to free Soviet peoples from an oppressive regime—the subject of the next chapter.

FIGURE 1. Self-Portrait of Private First Class Hans Albring. Drawn July 31, 1942, in Russia. Museumsstiftung Post und Telekommunikation 3.2002.0211.

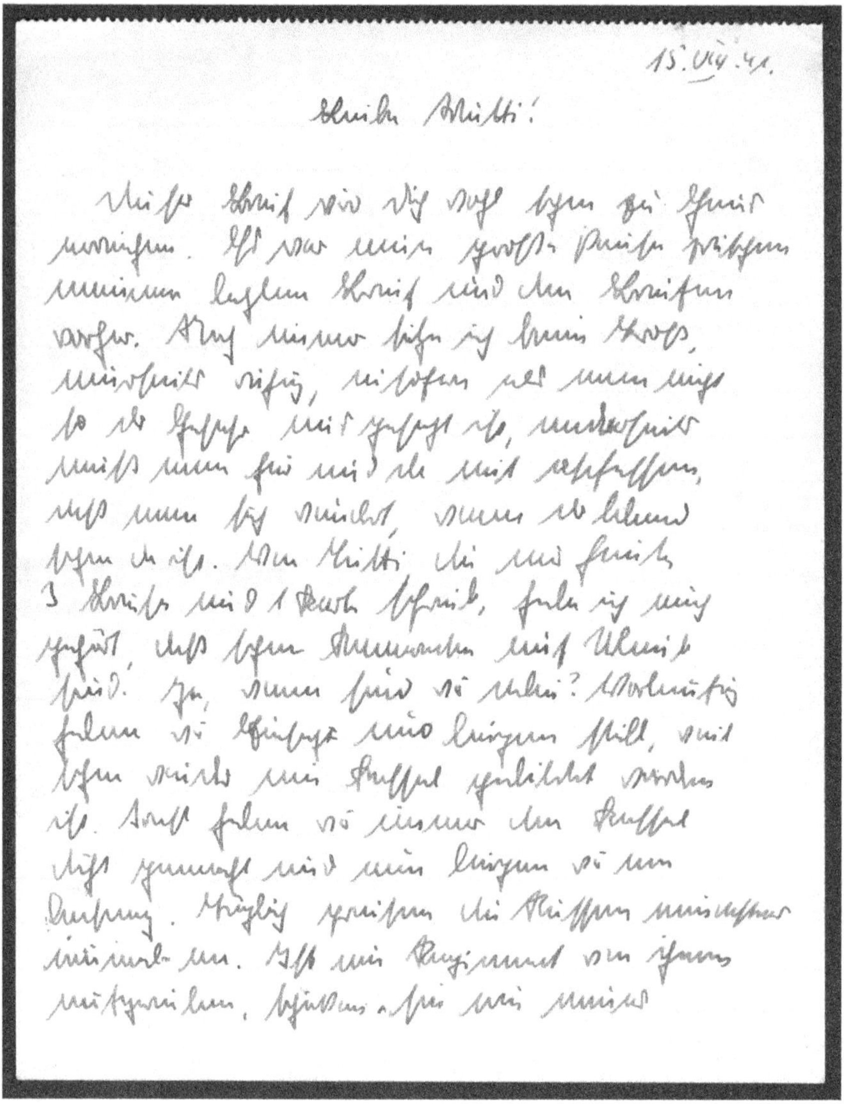
15.VIII.41.

Liebe Mutti!

FIGURE 2. Letter by non-commissioned officer Hans Simon to his mother. August 15, 1941. Museumsstiftung Post und Telekommunikation 3.2002.1288.

FIGURE 3. A Wehrmacht soldier kicks the corpse of a man hanged as a suspected partisan. The sign reads, "Worked against the German Wehrmacht as a partisan." After October 1941. United States Holocaust Memorial Museum 42881, courtesy of Claranne Bechtler.

FIGURE 4. A Wehrmacht firing squad executes suspected partisans. Circa July 1942. Bundesarchiv Bild 101I-212-0221-07.

FIGURE 5. Civilians and soldiers side by side at a Wehrmacht worship service in Witebsk. Circa August 4, 1941. PK reporter Wundshammer. Bundesarchiv Bild 146-2018-0001.

FIGURE 6. Photo of officer Wilhelm Brunner (seated) next to a peasant family. The text on the back reads, "First quarters east of the Dnieper." 1941. Such photos helped create the illusion of an amicable relationship between occupier and occupied. Museumsstiftung Post und Telekommunikation 3.2002.1376.

FIGURE 7. Soviet civilians tear down a statue of Lenin in the courtyard of the Branicki Palace in Bialystok as German troops look on. Circa July 1941. PK reporter Röder. Bundesarchiv Bild 101I-348-1113-18.

FIGURE 8. In this propaganda photo printed in a Wehrmacht newspaper, a German military doctor is pictured caring for a Soviet child. Images like these reinforced the fiction that the army had come as a liberating force. Original caption: "Mothers with children are the perpetual patients of our helpful military doctors." PK reporter v. d. Becke (photographer) and PK reporter Gert Sachs. "Die kleine Kapelle von Topolewo: Väterchen Doktor hilft der Landbevölkerung. In *Feldzeitung von der Maas bis an die Memel*. October 25, 1941. Bundesarchiv-Militärarchiv RH 20-16/2078 (formerly RHD 69/76).

Figure 9. Burial of a Panzer Regiment commander killed at Stalingrad. The chaplain can be recognized by the cross around his neck. Southern USSR. August 1942. PK reporter Dieck. Bundesarchiv Bild 101I-217-0498-26.

Caption within image: Ehrenfriedhof Borissow 18. 9. 1943

FIGURE 10. Wehrmacht cemetery in Borisov (modern-day Barysaw, Belarus). September 18, 1943. Bundesarchiv-Militärarchiv RH 45/149 (formerly RH 13/68).

CHAPTER 4

The "Liberators"

Barbarossa as an Emancipatory Act

Presenting themselves as noble Christian warriors on crusade was one way in which soldiers justified the war of extermination. Another was by developing a grossly misleading narrative of the relationship between the army and the Soviet Union's vast population, one in which the invaders emerged as a humanitarian force bringing freedom and a better life to men and women who had known only servitude. Among those who propagated this version of events was Wilhelm Moldenhauser, a father of two who owned a retail store for colonial imports in a village near Hannover. He had joined the SA in 1937, partly to enhance his business opportunities, before being conscripted into the Wehrmacht in 1940. One year later, Moldenhauser found himself working as a mobile radio operator with the 60th Infantry Division as it surged into Ukraine with Army Group South.

It was not long before Moldenhauser came into contact with Soviet civilians, who quickly became a favorite subject for his reflection. A few days into the invasion, his unit reached a small Ukrainian village. He recorded that the inhabitants were "very German-friendly," "trusting," and eager to converse with the invaders in their broken German.[1] As they continued on toward Mariupol in September, he wrote his wife, Erika, that "the Ukrainians have already reckoned that one day the Germans would come and liberate them from the yoke of Bolshevism and Jewry."[2] A week later, he quartered in the home of a Ukrainian woman who offered him and his comrades milk and bacon.

They spent the evening around the table with her, her husband, and their two children, passing around pictures, telling stories, and finishing off a bottle of vodka before the family retired to sleep on the oven.[3] "They feel only affection and sympathy towards us Germans," he told Erika. "And now the Germans are here and the people can always see for themselves that the Germans are decent, nice guys," he proudly reported.[4] Although his views of the population would frequently oscillate between sympathy, racism, and imperialist fantasies, over the next years Moldenhauser consistently portrayed his personal dealings with them in an amicable light and insisted that Wehrmacht occupation authorities had brought security and a better life to inhabitants who had suffered under communist rule.[5] His sentiments were not an aberration; they were repeated many times in the writings of his comrades. They also became a mainstay of Wehrmacht propaganda—both to Soviet civilians and German soldiers alike—and sometimes found expression in the policies set by Wehrmacht commanders in the field.

Moldenhauser's depiction of cordial relations between occupier and occupied was wildly incongruent with the realities of a *Vernichtungskrieg* that took the lives of more than fifteen million Soviet civilian men and women, among them 2.4 million Jews.[6] Nevertheless, his writings provide insight into how servicemen, propagandists, and military leaders portrayed the Wehrmacht's relationship with Soviet civilians and raise questions regarding the nature of the occupation. What steps did personnel take to convince themselves, readers in the homeland, and Soviet civilians that they were, as Moldenhauser put it, "nice guys" who would improve life in the USSR, even as the army enacted Hitler's genocidal vision? As an institution, how did the Wehrmacht generate a narrative of the occupation that furthered its larger project of asserting moral superiority over its enemies? Finally, how did these efforts manifest themselves in the postwar memory of the campaign?

Although the notion that the invasion had constituted a humanitarian project became difficult to maintain after the war ended, the sentiments expressed by Moldenhauser and his comrades regarding the occupation would nevertheless have an important impact on public remembrance of the conflict. The belief remained widespread in West Germany that Wehrmacht personnel had generally conducted themselves with respect toward a civilian population that had suffered immeasurably under the Stalinist regime. At the very least, so this thinking went, Eastern Europeans would have been better off under German rule than behind the Iron Curtain.[7]

Grounded in evidence from soldiers' letters, the Wehrmacht's institutional records, and a variety of home front sources, this chapter offers a close examination of the relationship between the army and the Soviet population. It traces how through word and deed, the Wehrmacht as an institution, its propaganda apparatus, and ordinary servicemen reimagined the war as a battle to destroy an illegitimate and tyrannical regime and bring order, peace, and prosperity to a grateful population. Although it would eventually break down under the weight of the army's crimes, this chapter argues, the liberation fantasy constituted a critical element in the Wehrmacht's larger attempt to imbue the war with moral legitimacy and safeguard its reputation. *Ostkämpfer*, including Nazis and non-Nazis alike, took solace in self-styled identities as heralds of freedom rather than agents of annihilation. Officers and propagandists found in this narrative a powerful tool to bolster morale and secure the moral high ground against their enemies. The rhetoric of emancipation and actions that gave it a semblance of credibility also colored how the German public understood the war and how Soviet civilians responded to the occupation. Although partly enabled by the opaque rhetoric of Nazi leaders—as had been the case for the "crusade" trope—this discourse deviated from Nazi orthodoxy, in large part because it drew from a host of traditional moral values, including respect for all human life and the obligation to oppose injustice and help those in need. Like the crusade line, however, it would ultimately help enable troops to reconcile themselves to their participation in acts of criminal violence.

Germans, Nazis, and the East before 1941

The Wehrmacht's view of the Soviet Union and its peoples was in many ways a radicalization of a much older nexus of ideas that Vejas Liulevicius has termed the "myth of the East."[8] Although nineteenth-century German liberals supported Polish national aspirations and intellectuals praised Russia for its artistic achievements, negative stereotypes of Eastern Europe had long enjoyed wide popularity among the German public. Eastern dirtiness, poverty, and lack of initiative were contrasted with German industriousness, cleanliness, and self-cultivation, summed up in the twin concepts of *Kultur* ("culture") and *Arbeit* ("work"). Germans both feared the "primitive," rapidly reproducing peoples on their eastern border and nursed the fantasy of a reinvigorated Teutonic empire that would bring scattered German-speakers who had relocated to Eastern Europe once more under the Reich's protective wings. These images coalesced into the notion of a German "Drive to the East" (*Drang nach Osten*) that seemed to present the country with colonial possibilities it had been denied elsewhere. Eastern expansion meant a chance to demonstrate the advantages German culture could bring to "noble savages" and bolster Germany's standing on the world stage.[9]

The First World War presented an opportunity to play out these imperialist fantasies. When Russian armies invaded East Prussia in 1914, their brief occupation revived long-held stereotypes and fears of "ethnic invasion" by eastern barbarians.[10] After the Russian defeat at Tannenberg and the signing of the Brest-Litovsk Treaty, Germany found itself in possession of vast swathes of Russian territory. German military rule there was characterized by the brutal imposition of "total security" alongside attempts to introduce "culture" to an ethnically diverse land that soldiers found both frightening and fascinating. The army founded schools, introduced modern hygiene, and improved local infrastructure. At the same time, it instituted harsh regulations that severely restricted local autonomy and focused most of its efforts on exploiting the region's economic potential for Germany's benefit. Servicemen tended to view the population as primitive and unclean but relatively benign. Instances of wanton violence against civilians were not unknown but constituted the exception rather than the rule.[11]

Germany's eastern empire vanished into thin air with the signing of the Treaty of Versailles in 1918, but the notion of a German future in the East lived on in increasingly radical form.[12] The experience of *Freikorps* troopers and the shock of the Russian Revolution, coupled with fears of a communist takeover at home, seemed to confirm that the eastern threat was more potent than ever.[13] As their movement took shape, the Nazis melded older aspirations for an eastern empire with fierce anti-communism, racial antisemitism, and Social Darwinist theory. According to the Nazi worldview, the Soviet Union, which was populated by subhuman Slavs infected with "Jewish-Bolshevik" ideology, simultaneously represented an existential threat to the German *Volk* and an opportunity to secure the *Lebensraum* it needed to survive.[14] Unlike earlier proponents of empire, however, Nazi leaders explicitly rejected any attempt to "civilize" or "Germanize" the peoples of the USSR, since they believed that racial deficiencies could never be corrected. As Hitler flatly declared, "Anyone who talks about cherishing the local inhabitant and civilizing him, goes straight off to a concentration camp!"[15] Armed with this outlook, the Nazi regime sketched out plans for the occupation that envisioned mass starvation for civilians and POWs and the immediate execution of Jews, Bolsheviks, and other so-called racial enemies.

While they railed against Bolshevism and Jewry, Nazi officials adopted a more ambiguous rhetorical stance toward the non-Jewish peoples of the Soviet Union. On the one hand, the Nazi-controlled press typically portrayed Slavs as subhuman. Nazi officials avoided all talk of a "civilizing mission" and refused to allow national autonomy in former Soviet lands. However, in their wartime appeals both to the public and to the army, Third Reich leaders directed most of their wrath against the country's "Jewish-Bolshevik" leaders and often depicted the peoples of the USSR in milder terms, sometimes as victims of Soviet rule or even potential allies.[16]

In part, this rhetorical softening constituted an effort to secure the support of those members of the German public who would be more inclined to support the war if it were framed as a humanitarian mission rather than an act of ethnic cleansing, and it had the added benefit of misrepresenting the invaders' true intentions in the arena of world opinion. It was also a strategic move aimed at dampening unrest in the newly occupied regions. Recognizing that a sharp anti-Slavic message might spark widespread resistance against the German occupation, Joseph Goebbels deliberately toned down such rhetoric in favor of messaging that focused on the evils of Bolshevism and its representatives.[17] In his editorials, he portrayed Soviet troops as the dupes of a manipulative regime fighting with animal fierceness and the population as dull slaves victimized by oppressive rulers.[18] Over the war's course, he and several other prominent Nazis, including Alfred Rosenberg, argued for a more conciliatory policy toward Eastern Europeans in the near term, largely on the pragmatic grounds that winning local cooperation would help the German cause.[19]

The Führer himself took an uncompromising anti-Slavic line.[20] But even he occasionally dabbled in more ambiguous rhetoric. He insisted in his widely publicized message to his soldiers at the start of the invasion that his quarrel was with the Soviet rulers, not their people.[21] In 1942, he ordered the Wehrmacht to treat the population in a "strict but correct" manner.[22] In his *Winterhilfswerk* speech of the same year, he declared that the population had been "released from the pressures of a Bolshevik power" and praised their assistance in the war effort.[23] Overall then, and despite the regime's genocidal plans for Eastern Europe, the image of non-Jewish Soviet civilians in the Third Reich's public discourse was not a uniform one. It vacillated between a vicious brand of racism and the portrayal of Slavs as hapless, victims, or even potential helpers against the true "Jewish Bolshevik" enemy. Just as opaque statements regarding a "crusading" mission gave Wehrmacht personnel permission to cultivate religious interpretations of the invasion, this ambiguity at the top would open up space for generals and soldiers alike to develop views and policies toward the Soviet population that deviated from the racist conception of Eastern Europeans that remained a core component of Nazi ideology.

Wehrmacht Views of the Soviet Union

In the years leading up to Barbarossa, the army's image of the East came to closely align with that of the Nazi regime.[24] Antisemitism and anti-communism were widespread among those in uniform, and the army had already displayed a decades-long penchant for extreme violence against civilians. Like most Germans, the army's leaders considered Slavs inferior. Still, their views were complex and frequently contradictory. Older notions of a "civilizing mission" in the East did not wholly disappear. Some of the Wehrmacht's top generals advocated a liberation-centered strategy when the invasion of the USSR was being formulated.[25] OKW's initial instructions to the troops encouraged them to recognize that "a great portion" of the Russian population rejected Bolshevism.[26] Further, wartime anti-Slavic propaganda in the Wehrmacht never reached the levels of extremity that characterized portrayals of Jews and communist officials.[27]

When the invasion commenced, army leaders issued numerous orders that corresponded closely with the Nazi vision of racial domination. Here, too, however, ambiguities arose. Many commanders also handed down instructions that called on troops to treat civilians well, sometimes explicitly drawing on the notion that the Wehrmacht had come as a liberating force or needed to be seen as such. The 46th Infantry Division, for instance, passed along the guideline that "special attention must be paid to a good and just handling of the loyal population," since these "welcomed their liberation."[28] Such messaging may have been an extension of the "civilizing" discourse of the First World War, but it also contained a heavy dose of pragmatism: if the army could convince the population its intentions were benign, the prospects for violent resistance would be lessened. When the invasion began, then, the Wehrmacht may have been united behind its Führer and determined to crush "Jewish Bolshevism," but its institutional discourse regarding the treatment of non-Jewish civilians spanned a broad spectrum.[29] The rhetoric of emancipation and a positive cultural mission coexisted with extreme racism and the seeds of genocide.

On the eve of the invasion, views among the rank and file about the USSR and her neighbors integrated elements of the Nazi worldview, older imperialist notions about Germany's "civilizing mission" in the East, orientalism, the USSR's own rhetoric, and a profound ignorance of the realities of Soviet life.[30] Conditioned by their time in the HJ, SA, Reich Labor Service, and other Nazi organizations as well as years-long exposure to the regime's propaganda apparatus, many troops were predisposed toward a view of Eastern Europeans, above all Jews, as a "sub-human" threat. A minority—primarily members of the working class—initially harbored a favorable view of the USSR.[31] But during the political upheaval of the interwar years, many more had learned to view communism as a disease that had to be eradicated. Others clung to a more romanticized vision of Russia as a land of oriental mystery. Such an outlook, which drew on diverse variations of the German "myth of the East," overlapped with racist sentiments but also acknowledged a certain degree of humanity in Germany's eastern neighbors. The Soviet Union's own propaganda acted as a final influence on soldiers' views: during the 1930s, the Soviets had insisted that their land had been transformed into a "paradise for workers and farmers." Experience would soon put each of these images to the test.

As they marched along dusty roads under the hot sun during the invasion's opening weeks, the Reich's warriors took time during brief lulls in the advance to provide their friends and families with their first impressions of the country they now occupied. Their most common reaction was one of shock at the conditions they encountered. Entering the Ukraine with the 60th Infantry Division, Wilhelm Moldenhauser commented to his wife that "the people here is very poor. . . . The land is not at all comparable to our beautiful Germany."[32] He described "primitive" houses and little in the way of economic development.[33] "A sad picture, when one goes through Russia," gunner Hans Simon told his father at the end of July from several hundred miles farther north. "I did not imagine that this land would be so poor. The houses usually [have] slanted walls, supported by planks. The roofs [are] decked with straw, leaky if not to say in tatters. . . . To see this and remain a communist is impossible."[34] Johannes Hagemann echoed these observations when he wrote his sister, "Here in Russia, everything is filthy and lice-ridden. The houses [are] thrown together out of boards, [there are] newspapers for carpets, chickens and pigs live placidly with the humans. The people is poor, the roads are bad."[35]

As they surveyed the state of the country, soldiers often singled out the Soviet regime as the primary culprit. Further investigation of their surroundings and conversations with local civilians—amounting to a kind of moral research project—seemed to confirm this conclusion. Wilhelm Moldenhauser spoke to villagers about the difficulties of life on the collective farms.[36] Fritz Feierabend composed long letters detailing to his wife how terribly the population had suffered under state requisitions and crushing poverty while communist leaders led "carefree" lives.[37] Others sent home reports on the State Political Administration of the NKVD's (GPU's) terror, mass deportations, requisitions, and high prices coupled with pitiful wages that conspired to make even the most basic goods unaffordable in the USSR.[38] With these impressions in mind, many soldiers began to conclude that the Soviet system was morally degenerate and the invasion fully justified, especially if they already believed the myth that the Red Army had planned to invade Germany.

The revelation that social and economic conditions in the USSR were far below German standards was quickly incorporated into the moral case against the Soviet Union being constructed by the Reich Propaganda Ministry and the Wehrmacht's propaganda corps. Both were eager to prove that the USSR's rulers had forfeited their right to govern and that only German arms could rectify the situation. After hearing the initial reports from the front, Goebbels decided to make conditions in the USSR a linchpin of his strategy for mobilizing public support.[39] He and his propagandists declared that what had once been a charming backwater was now a hellish world of oppression, state-sponsored violence, abject poverty, and social injustice. The promised equality had never materialized; instead, the nation's Jewish overlords had exploited the simple populace and squandered the land's resources on a vast armament program intended to threaten European security.[40] Newspapers throughout the country carried shocking exposés on life behind what Goebbels termed "the veil."[41] The *Wochenschau* conveyed image after image of dilapidated houses, muddy streets, and miserable people.[42] The dire situation of the *Volksdeutsch* also became a common propaganda refrain.[43] All of these efforts recast the war as an act of humanitarian intervention rather than the genocidal project it actually was.

In perhaps its most grandiose attempt to convince the European public of the necessity of the war, the Propaganda Ministry organized a massive 1942 exhibition titled "the Soviet Paradise."[44] Attracting millions of visitors, it featured charts of Jewish overrepresentation in government along with artifacts collected by the Wehrmacht to illustrate the USSR's oppressive conditions. Low wages, inflated prices, thankless labor, and the destruction of family life served as proof that the communist regime "has degraded the masses of millions of peoples of the East to lawless and starving work-slaves" and would do the same throughout Europe, its curators claimed. The exhibition created the impression that the only way to save the peoples of the Soviet Union was through the complete destruction of the Soviet system, followed by German rule. Casting Slavic civilians in the role of victims in need of assistance was a surprising strategy, given that it undermined the racial essentialism at the heart of Nazi morality, but the exhibition's planners appear to have believed it was an effective means of convincing the public to support the invasion.

Propagandists in the Wehrmacht advanced a similar argument regarding the communist government's unworthiness, the victimhood of the region's inhabitants, and the need for salvation at German hands. Early in the campaign, troop newspapers were awash with stories of oppressive Soviet rule. "The misery in the villages . . . of this much-lauded Soviet state," explained war reporter Drobig, "is unimaginable. . . . Many of the emaciated people say that it is better to die than to live in this hardship."[45] A Second Army journalist wrote of the USSR's "enslavement of humanity, suppression of the freedom

of the peoples and de-nationalization for the benefit of an unrestrained des-
potism."[46] Another dubbed it the "poorest, most primitive, most backward and
squalid zone of Europe."[47] These and countless other observations in the Wehrmacht press added up to the conclusion that the Soviet Union was not a
paradise but a living hell where millions of people suffered the consequences
of the Bolshevik experiment. This was all the more tragic because the Soviet
regime had squandered the natural riches of a land that, under proper leadership, could easily feed all of Europe.

The army's portrayals of Soviet rule invariably railed against the "Jewish-
Bolsheviks" in Moscow and linked the country's economic state with the supposed biological inferiority of its many ethnic groups, as Nazi ideology dictated.
At the same time, however, they often made a distinction between the "two
Russias"—the Russia of Stalin and the land of the simple worker and farmer
who suffered under the "Soviet yoke." They described Red troops alternately
as ravenous beasts or simple and naïve men forced to fight and die for a cause
in which they did not truly believe.[48] Even the *Mitteilungen für die Truppe*, among
the Wehrmacht's most stridently Nazi publications, portrayed locals as victims,
if also racial and cultural inferiors.[49] This relative softness when it came to the
Slavic population can be traced to the Wehrmacht's pragmatic interest in upholding its soldiers' morale by furthering the notion that they were committing a good deed. It also—so propagandists hoped—would prevent bad blood
between the population and the new occupiers at a moment when undiluted
racial hatred could be counterproductive.

A Savior's Welcome: Popular Reactions through Wehrmacht Eyes

If troops were shocked to learn that the USSR was much less prosperous than
they had expected, they were even more astonished at the reception they often experienced in their first encounters with civilians. Not only across eastern Poland, the Baltic States, and former Romanian and Finnish provinces, but
also throughout the Ukraine, Belarus, and even Russia proper, Wehrmacht soldiers often found themselves greeted not with hostility but with flowers,
glasses of fresh milk, and even the occasional kiss from civilians who had suffered under the communist system and yearned for a better life.[50] As he advanced through the Ukraine, Wilhelm Moldenhauser informed his sister that
"in the little villages I have . . . the impression that the people [are] happy to
be free of the Russians."[51] He described how women gave him cherries from
their orchard.[52] Like other combatants, he mentioned that statues of Soviet

leaders had been toppled or defaced, whether by the invaders or the locals.[53] In July, Heinz Rahe registered his surprise at being greeted with flowers by civilians lining the highway. He also observed that "some of the prisoners . . . saluted [us] with the Hitler greeting!"[54] In a private conversation, his division's general confirmed to Rahe that the Ukrainian population was giving the invaders a "flower-rich reception." Rahe expressed disappointment that he himself had only seen one triumphal arch set up to welcome the Wehrmacht but predicted to his wife that "when we've pushed farther that will definitely increase."[55] Motorcycle courier Gustav Böker informed his parents that as his Infantry Division passed through rural Ukraine "some [people] put flowers on our vehicles [and] others gave us buttermilk, sour milk, or white bread. Yes, the Ukrainians are in fact German-friendly," he wrote. "I definitely didn't anticipate this."[56] Others had less dramatic tales to tell of their first encounters with Soviet civilians but, like Böker, they often remarked upon the surprisingly welcoming attitude that reigned in newly occupied areas across the USSR.[57] They also quickly recognized that most civilians were not in fact hardened communists. As Hermann Henning put it from his observations in northwestern Russia, "Bolshevism mostly passed by the rural population without a trace."[58] In their initial reports on their reception by the population, troops gave their homeland readers the impression that they were entering the Soviet Union not as conquerors but saviors, a trope that lent further credibility to the narrative that they belonged to an honorable institution pursuing a worthy cause.

Wehrmacht formations also detected a welcoming mood among the population in many areas. Intelligence officers for the Third Panzer Group, for example, reported that although they had anticipated hostility after crossing the former Soviet–Polish border, they found that in Belarus, as in the Baltic, "here also, particularly in rural areas, the population perceived the arrival of the German troops as [a] liberation from the Bolshevik yoke that had brought to the farmer, along with the system of forced collectivization in agriculture, the hardest toil and scarcely sufficient food supplies."[59] Other units recorded a similar welcome across the western USSR, including in Russia itself, noting that civilians frequently offered supplies to German soldiers and appeared ready to cooperate with Wehrmacht authorities.[60] Unaware of the invaders' true intentions, many Soviet civilians—at least those who were not immediately targeted for violent treatment—hoped that the Germans would bring with them a chance for economic renewal and a measure of political autonomy after two decades under a Stalinist regime that had been deeply unpopular in many areas, particularly the countryside. It also seemed preferable to get on the invaders' good side at a time when victory for the Reich appeared likely.[61]

Always eager to bolster morale by encouraging German troops to see themselves as righteous warriors, the army's Propaganda Companies jumped on the opportunity to circulate stories of the population's jubilant welcome. In doing so, they added momentum to a narrative of liberation that was steadily gaining traction within the army and among the German public. During the first months of the invasion, Wehrmacht publications were awash with triumphant headlines proclaiming that the army had saved the peoples of the USSR from the "Soviet yoke."[62] With captions like the "Ukrainian population welcomes the German soldiers with grateful happiness," army newspapers displayed photographs of smiling civilians handing food and flowers to the invaders or Wehrmacht columns passing underneath triumphal arches the locals had hastily erected.[63] War reporter Erich Pecher described extraordinary scenes that unfolded with the Wehrmacht's arrival in Bialystok:

> The inhabitants . . . , mainly Belarusians, stood in the streets and threw flowers into the dust-covered vehicles of the German soldiers. In their faces the happiness at the final disappearance of the Bolshevik rulers was plain to see. Now, since German soldiers were marching into the city, they, who had gotten to know the decent behavior of the Feldgrauen, knew that they were safe.[64]

Pecher went on to explain that the citizens, who had already gleefully toppled statues of Lenin and Stalin, awaited a "just future" guaranteed by the Wehrmacht.[65] "There is no doubt," declared another reporter, "that the Ukrainian population considers the Germans as liberators. In the cities one has put up inscriptions with 'Heil Hitler' or 'We greet our Hitler.' One sees swastikas everywhere."[66] Several army papers reprinted thank-you speeches by local politicians.[67] Journalists conducted interviews with civilians who highlighted the horrors of Soviet rule and the population's relief at being "freed."[68] Through such reports, propagandists aimed to convince soldiers that the Wehrmacht was undertaking a humanitarian intervention and that Germany had a moral right to rule the East. Over the next months, they would set their sights on providing evidence that the army was committed to rebuilding the country and providing a fairer system to replace the evils of Bolshevism.

It mattered little to the army's journalists whether they exaggerated accounts of the Wehrmacht's reception, which appears to have often been the case, or that they wildly misrepresented German intentions by implying that the new rulers had the best interests of the population at heart.[69] Nor did they appear to mind that the liberation message to some extent undermined Nazi orthodoxy by depicting the non-Jewish population as fellow human beings who deserved German aid rather than a collection of racial pests to be exploited and eventually destroyed. Styling the war as a battle for freedom lent the invasion an air of moral legitimacy that helped to motivate servicemen of all persuasions.

The reframing of the invasion as an emancipatory act also found its way to the home front. *Wochenschau* newsreels filled the screens of Germany's theaters with images of cheering crowds as the army "liberated" city after city.[70] The German press eagerly reported that Soviet citizens had been waiting all along for Germany to save them from Bolshevik terror.[71] Emblematic of this emergent discourse was the 1943 book *Klinzy: Portrait of a Russian City after its Liberation from Bolshevism.*[72] In it, author Walter Engelhardt, who had visited Klinzy (Klintsy) with the Wehrmacht, made the case for German occupation. Engelhardt painted a picture of the horrific conditions workers and farmers—above all, the *Volksdeutsch*—had endured under a nightmarish trifecta of Jews, commissars, and communists who profited off their labor. He explained how the new German-run administration, in concert with the Wehrmacht, put industry back in motion, promoted employment, paid workers fairly, distributed ration cards, reopened churches, improved schools, and allowed some private land ownership. While he reserved only hatred for Jews and communists, Engelhardt depicted the population as indigent and uncultivated but also hardworking, good-willed, and full of hope for a better future. He expressed satisfaction that German soldiers "differentiate what is Russian from what is Jewish-Bolshevik and from this recognition meet the Russian people with justice."[73]

Unsurprisingly, the Wehrmacht quickly exploited the liberation theme in its propaganda to the Soviet population.[74] Two months into the invasion, OKW instructed its propagandists that "it must . . . always be emphasized, that the German soldier does not come to destroy socialism, rather to make an end of Bolshevik enslavement and create social justice."[75] Throughout the war, a never-ending stream of radio broadcasts, films, newspapers printed in local languages, vehicles armed with megaphones, and specially trained speakers would remind the population that they owed their freedom to German arms.[76] The army employed similar messaging in its efforts to convince Red troops to desert to the Germans or to recruit local collaborators.[77] German soldiers seem to have been aware of these propaganda campaigns. Johannes Lohr, for instance, recorded in his diary that his unit put up a placard in Russian proclaiming that "we come as liberators and everyone is guaranteed his property."[78]

In a sign that some of them took this rhetoric quite seriously, Wehrmacht personnel carried out several dramatic feats that caught the attention of military authorities. In the chaotic early weeks of the attack, German troops began to spontaneously open prisons as they advanced.[79] The 20th Infantry

Division's intelligence section reported in early July that combatants released Soviet political prisoners in the city of Brest—at least 5,000 by the count of Wehrmacht reporter Gustav Schenk, who roundly approved the action.[80] In the Latvian city of Liepāja (German: Libau), another army newspaper reported, soldiers rushed to rescue survivors of a GPU prison.[81] Evidently, many assumed that captives of the Soviet state had been wrongfully held and deserved their freedom. Releasing them was a tangible way of demonstrating goodwill toward the population and announcing the invaders' intention to replace communism with a more just system. This phenomenon occurred only during the war with the USSR, an indication that many soldiers subscribed to the liberation fantasy from the outset and associated it exclusively with the Soviet lands.

The freeing of captives, however, proved to be an area where propaganda and the attitude of the rank and file clashed with Nazi ideology and the army's desire for security. In their enthusiasm to "liberate" the areas under Soviet control, troops had gone too far. The army had no wish to allow potential criminals to roam the streets of newly occupied cities, and the Nazi regime feared the consequences of releasing anyone with a record of political activism—especially "subhuman" Slavs. The 20th Division immediately ordered a halt to further prison breaks.[82] Other units, including the Second Army and Army Group Center, issued similar instructions.[83] Army officials did, however, end up releasing a large number of POWs.[84] *Volksdeutsch* were freed first, followed by members of other ethnicities after screening by the Einsatzgruppen.[85] Thousands of servicemen also spontaneously joined with chaplains to reopen churches across the western USSR, a move that further positioned the invaders as a liberating force until Hitler himself intervened to stop the practice.[86]

Conquerors and Conquered: Views of the Population and Emancipatory Gestures

Dramatic encounters in the opening weeks of the invasion soon gave way to more sustained contact that allowed soldiers to form lasting impressions of the population. During the summer, troops had typically slept in tents or the open air, but as the weather grew colder, many spent weeks or months quartering in Soviet houses.[87] Although the majority expressed varying degrees of racism ranging from the older, cultural variety to biological essentialism, their writings indicate that they developed a varied and complex understanding of the USSR's non-Jewish population.[88] Over the next years, soldiers' interactions with civilians also occupied a wide spectrum, running the gamut from racially inspired violence to more honorable conduct. Although the occupation was characterized above all by the former, and although many troops admitted that theft, collective punishments, and scorched-earth measures had become commonplace in the Wehrmacht's dealings with civilians, many troops used their letters to present a narrative of benign occupation marked by friendly relations and generosity on the part of the invaders. Particularly in 1941 and 1942, when the war's outcome was in doubt and the population's hopes for positive change still lingered, soldiers reported befriending locals; handing out food, cigarettes, and candy; and performing chores. These gestures paled in comparison to the overall horrors of the occupation. They also violated military policy regarding fraternization with the enemy and transgressed the strict racial boundaries that underpinned the Nazi worldview.[89] Even so, the image of amicable relations that Wehrmacht personnel projected would help to ease the invaders' consciences and justify a criminal campaign by reimagining the horrors of German rule as a "friendly" arrangement that benefited the victims.

Wilhelm Moldenhauser's experience illustrates the complexity of soldiers' views toward the non-Jewish population, as well as the attempt to cast the occupation in a positive light. Influenced by his SA background along with Wehrmacht propaganda, Moldenhauser adhered to a typical mixture of antisemitism and anti-communism and absorbed common prejudices toward Eastern Europeans. His perspective on civilians, however, deviated in important respects from the Nazi creed. As he drove through the Ukraine in the summer of 1941, his views vacillated between racially tinged stereotypes and imperialist fantasies, on one hand, and on the other an apparently genuine sympathy for the numerous civilians he met. During the initial advance, he was pleasantly surprised by the hospitality he and his comrades experienced. Farm families with whom he quartered generously provided milk and foodstuffs.[90] One Ukrainian woman handed him flowers.[91] Everywhere he turned, he remarked to his wife, the attitude was "German-friendly" and the people were "very nice."[92] Moldenhauser, like many of his comrades, did his share of "organizing," although he habitually claimed to respect his division's ban on theft. He conducted numerous purchases and trades, such as exchanging cigarettes for eggs.[93] On several occasions, he and his comrades pressed civilians into service doing laundry or collecting food.[94] At the same time, he made sure to tell his wife that they repaid civilian hospitality by handing out soap or sugar to the families with whom they quartered.[95]

Moldenhauser painted her an unflattering portrait of life in the Soviet Union. He was especially repulsed by the dirtiness of the streets and houses. The population, whom he sometimes dubbed "the little people," appeared to him lazy and "dumb." He blamed their situation not only on Soviet misrule but also their own lack of enterprise and ignorance of hygiene.[96] Although his views partly overlapped with Nazi conceptions of the "sub-human," Moldenhauser thought less in racial–biological terms and instead emphasized the role of individual choice. As he put it, "It is always up to the people themselves, whether they live as pigs or as civilized people."[97] Anxious about his family's food supply in Germany, Moldenhauser imagined that the Ukraine and the borderlands of Russia would become German colonies, a belief that accorded well with Nazi ideology.[98] He even worried that the Wehrmacht was being too lenient. The Germans would have to be harsh, like the English, if they were to be successful rulers, he told his wife. He illustrated this point with a tale about how he had resorted to violence to get a civilian to help him transport supplies. He gave a more compliant man tobacco in thanks, a gesture emblematic of his belief that the occupiers could be generous—as long as the population obeyed.[99]

As summer turned to fall, Moldenhauser spent more time quartering in civilian homes, primarily in the countryside. His curiosity about the USSR and its people grew as he armed himself with a dictionary and engaged in halting conversations with his hosts, confirming that they were happy to be rid of Soviet rule.[100] He met more and more locals who appeared to him "clean" and "orderly," in contrast to their typical depiction in Nazi propaganda, and his relations with these were especially friendly.[101] Several times he was delighted to encounter *Volksdeutsch*, whom he invariably described as particularly clean.[102] He voiced sympathy for Russian and Ukrainian women who treated the men who invaded their homes with untiring politeness despite knowing that the same men might have already killed their husbands on the front.[103] Moldenhauser and his friends, he informed his wife in September 1941, endeavored to demonstrate that German soldiers were "decent, nice guys" who would do no harm to a population that was happy to be rid of "Soviet and Jewish rule." He bolstered this claim in the same letter with an anecdote about how he had reassured a frightened woman that she was safe and gave candy to her son.[104] In other villages, he and his comrades shared vodka and cigarettes with their hosts.[105] From time to time, he shared pictures of his children with Soviet mothers, whose families reminded him of his own, although he considered their children "dirty" by comparison.[106] With residents with whom he quartered for extended periods, Moldenhauser sometimes forged lasting friendships. In the town of Marfinka in the Donetsk region of Ukraine where he spent the early months of 1942, he proudly reported that "his Lieschen"—a woman in whose home he stayed—called him a "good comrade" in front of her neighbors and gifted him two eggs.[107] Her attitude may have stemmed in part from the material benefits his unit provided. Moldenhauser was told by one woman that without the firewood and coal the soldiers supplied, the locals would have frozen to death in the winter. He also noted that German medics took them on as patients.[108] While he approved of imperial expansion, he claimed that the Wehrmacht had brought security and order and would make sure the population had what it needed.[109] Taken together, Moldenhauser's letters of 1941 and 1942 (he would be reported Missing in Action in January 1943) illustrate both his contradictory views of the population and his efforts to prove to his wife that he and the men of his unit treated the population with a measure of dignity, at least more than they had enjoyed under Moscow's Soviet leaders.

Other men conveyed similarly complex outlooks and experiences regarding the population in their writings. Hans Albring, the deeply Catholic communications specialist who had little affinity for Nazism, described uniformly cordial relations with Soviet civilians, and, like many other *Landser*, reported that few of the people they met had anything but hatred for communism.[110] Albring expressed boundless fascination for Russian history and religion, a view that reflected longstanding orientalist notions of the East as a mysterious land of hidden riches. He also praised various aspects of the Russian character, but like Moldenhauser considered Russians a childlike people beneath the European level.[111] During an assignment that spanned the end of 1941 and most of 1942 in the city of Velizh, he befriended many of the locals, attended a dance with Russians in a private residence, joined his comrades to collect firewood for the mother of a civilian acquaintance so she could survive the winter, and gifted one of his hostesses a pig.[112] In the spring of 1942 he described saving the life of an old man after several other soldiers mistook him for a threat.[113] Albring did note that some of his comrades were less respectful toward the population, but on the whole he insisted that in the Wehrmacht, "many people know how to behave well toward the locals."[114]

Many other *Ostkämpfer*, even ones who sometimes expelled civilians from their homes, stole their last scraps of food, or had prior Nazi associations, reported friendly relationships with some of their hosts, especially those they considered particularly "clean."[115] Harald Hoffmann's narrative of the 1941 campaign, which is punctuated by violent requisitions and scorched-earth measures, also includes his account of making music and playing soccer with friendly Polish civilians and sharing candy and vodka with a "clean" Russian family.[116] Hoffmann, a former member of the National Socialist Student Association, preferred the Poles to the "uncultured" Russians.[117] Still, he reportedly managed to get along well with some hosts, while others—particularly those who forcefully defended their food supplies—suffered his and his comrades' wrath.[118]

Major Dr. Wilhelm Bacher, a Nazi Party member since 1934, frequently oversaw civilian slave labor, directed requisitions, and carried out orders for the engineers under his command to incinerate villages in the winter of 1941–1942. Bacher, however, took an interest in the culture of the Ukrainians, whom he described as pro-German. He lamented their sufferings and went out of his way to transport a refugee family in his car during a retreat in early 1943.[119] Bacher snapped photos of himself and other soldiers posing side-by-side with smiling civilians, a practice that was very widespread in the Wehrmacht.[120] Gustav Böker, who spent most of the war with the 111th Infantry Division in Ukraine, reported that he and his fellow men in uniform helped thresh sunflower seeds for the family with whom he quartered.[121] Whether in epistolary or photographic form, all of these images evoked the impression of a cordial relationship between occupier and occupied that papered over the terroristic realities of the Wehrmacht's rule.

So, too, did tales of mutual merry-making. Hans Simon, Johannes Lohr, and Willy Nagel were among those servicemen who described spontaneous dances between civilians and servicemen, although the latter was careful to assure his love interest that he was simply testing his legs, not chasing after Russian women.[122] Others tried their best to learn Russian, and a few succeeded.[123] Many were careful to point out that they made what they apparently considered equitable trades with civilians for food, instead of adhering to the army's superficial payment system or simply seizing whatever they wanted as ideology prescribed.[124] Rolf Dietrich, whose experiences were colored by his position in a field kitchen behind the lines, wrote in his diary in 1942 and 1943 that wherever he was stationed, his kitchen distributed food supplies to the local inhabitants. Several times when his unit was ordered to relocate, he noted that residents were sad to see him go.[125] As his unit conducted operations in the forests around Priluki (Pryluky) in September 1941, Hans Roth also recorded that his unit's field kitchen regularly served civilians. Even a hardened veteran like Roth, who railed against the "Jewish-Bolsheviks" and described his unit's pitiless treatment of captured partisans, was effusive in his expressions of sympathy. "These poor starved people!" he exclaimed. "It is always the same; a piece of dry bread makes them happy."[126] Dr. Konrad Jarausch, supervising a POW camp kitchen, wrote his wife about his efforts to ameliorate conditions for the starving inmates.[127] Gestures like these fulfilled two redemptive moral functions of critical importance: they reassured soldiers of their own inherent goodness and demonstrated to the homeland that the occupation was nothing like the bloodbath depicted in enemy propaganda.

Outside the kitchens, men of a variety of ideological leanings spoke of sharing food from time to time with their hosts or the many impoverished civilians they encountered, a practice the High Command expressly forbade.[128] Hans Albring's friend, Eugen Altrogge, described giving bread from his breakfast to a grateful Russian beggar.[129] Willy Nagel, who had lost his appetite after becoming sick, shared his lunch with the Russian family he stayed with.[130] On other occasions, Nagel listened enthusiastically to the Führer's speeches and dubbed Red fighters "beasts in human form."[131] Despite his small act of kindness, he continually used civilians as forced laborers and took their generosity for granted.[132] Heinz Sartorio, who described the Russians as "unpleasant" and "stupid," and had also approved the killing of Jews, offered his sister a colorful description of the locals with whom he quartered.[133] He considered them primitive but enjoyed cooking with them and shared leftover rations with the man of the house.[134] Even Willy Reese, whose diary described a litany of crimes he and his comrades committed against civilians, shared captured food with two women he stayed with. He also took the time to write out a death certificate for a baby whose father was illiterate.[135]

The spontaneous provision of food for civilians on the part of Wehrmacht troops was widespread enough to catch the attention and spark the ire of army authorities. Months after the High Command issued orders for troops not to feed starving civilians, a military police (*Geheime Feldpolizei*, or GFP) unit of the Third Panzer Army warned that in its area, "although it is strictly forbidden, many soldiers share their rations with the destitute population."[136] The *Mitteilungen für die Truppe* issued reminders not to act on any feelings of compassion for desperate civilians. One of its articles explained that even though he might be moved by the sight of "starving women and children," the Wehrmacht serviceman needed to understand that "every piece of bread that he gives up out of sympathy is for all intents and purposes taken away from the Wehrmacht and the German people." The military would do what it could for them, the author asserted, but their welfare was at best a peripheral concern.[137] Army newspapers followed suit by admonishing the rank and file not to share their provisions with hungry locals, even though the same publications had initially praised the occupiers' supposed generosity.[138] Although the army's stance on this subject was unambiguous, the very persistence of such appeals suggests that many troops habitually ignored them—just as they also ignored injunctions not to violate civilian property.

Besides offering food, servicemen gifted candy to children and tobacco to Russian men, who greatly prized German cigarettes.[139] Willy Hagemann, who in the spring of 1943 was temporarily stationed behind the front lines, wrote his parents that "the Russians receive tobacco, cigarettes and candy from us and with that they are content."[140] Shortly after his arrival in the USSR, Hans-Peter Eckener reported handing candy to the child in the house where he quartered. He also gave tobacco to an old man.[141] A few months later, he wrote that German soldiers in the village of Krasnoje gave children candy in exchange for various chores.[142] Such tiny gestures naturally did little to counteract the desolation the army inflicted on the country, but troops were all too ready to write home about their supposed generosity. Doing so helped to confirm to the invaders that they were still decent men who retained the moral high ground in a war against a regime that had abandoned its people to poverty and despair. In the coming years, chocolate and cigarettes would become the world-renowned symbols of the American soldier's liberation of western and southern Europe, but on the Eastern Front they served, for brief moments at least, as potent weapons in the Wehrmacht's moral arsenal.[143]

Overall, soldiers' views of the Soviet population and their reports home regarding the nature of the occupation were fraught with contradictions. Feelings of sympathy, curiosity, racial animus, and cultural superiority existed side-by-side, often expressed by the same individual. While they frequently admitted to the army's exploitation and abuse of Soviet civilians, Germany's warriors also took pride in telling loved ones about their chivalrous gestures toward the population, in the process generating an occupation narrative that diverged sharply from reality.

With the possible exception of the reopening of churches and prisons, most of these actions did not amount to a concerted, conscious effort to "liberate" the Soviet Union on the part of the rank and file. More often, they involved spontaneous acts of sympathy undertaken on individual initiative. However, the concept of a humanitarian mission to free the USSR from Soviet tyranny, ever-present in Wehrmacht propaganda, would enjoy relatively widespread currency among the men, with some even going a step further by citing it as their primary justification for the campaign.

Eugen Altrogge was one soldier who preferred to understand the war on the Eastern Front in terms of a German mission to bring liberty to oppressed peoples. On the day of the invasion, while still in France, he speculated to his friend Hans Albring about what the war might bring. "Far from all political and military considerations," he wrote, "I want to hope [that] many people would really like to experience . . . freedom from the Bolshevist yoke[.] I'm especially thinking of the Ukraine."[144] Altrogge's unit was transferred to Russia in March 1942. After witnessing conditions in the USSR for himself, he continued to see meaning in the war as a conflict that had the potential to bring positive change to uncultured eastern lands. "Let us hope," he wrote after describing how he had given bread to a Russian beggar, "that we can help to straighten out the savage features to [give Russia] a peaceful appearance. Our sacrifices should have a profound effect in this sense, too," he remarked.[145]

Heinz Rahe went so far as to compose a poem to his wife about the evils of communism and how German arms would return freedom to the Ukraine.[146] "Hopefully a just order comes here," he added several months later. "May God help this country!"[147] Hans Wilhelm Sauer argued that Soviet soldiers gladly went into German captivity because they were able to experience the benefits of civilization. Like many others, Sauer was enamored with the endless possibilities the East and its "uncultured" people seemed to offer. Parroting the common stereotype of easterners as children, he mused that they looked forward to "good leadership," although this entailed a great "responsibility" on the part of the invaders. After noting that Göring had justified the war as necessary for preventing Jewish world domination, Sauer commented, "At the same time occupation and liberation of the culture-less East and its development for culture also gives the battle a meaning. . . . Who knows which is the most meaningful consequence of our fight?"[148] Although such ideas were laced with imperialist assumptions about the German right to rule in the East, seeing themselves as liberators bringing a better life to a victimized people was a particularly potent means by which combatants imbued their actions with moral meaning and reframed the war as a worthy endeavor.

Bolstering the Liberation Charade: Institutional Actions

As contact between the rank and file and Soviet civilians intensified and fantasies of liberation crept into soldiers' writings, high-ranking officers set to work formulating unit-level policies regarding the treatment of the conquered population. Following the outlines for the *Vernichtungskrieg* established by OKW and the Führer himself at the invasion's outset, and continuing institutional precedents from prior conflicts, they swiftly established a system of rule that allowed little room for mercy toward the USSR's inhabitants. Jews, communists, and partisans were targeted for execution or handed over to the SS. Other civilians faced strict curfews, surveillance, travel restrictions, forced evacuations, mass requisitions, and compulsory labor. Failure to follow even the smallest regulation usually meant a death sentence, as did any hint of resistance activity. Many commanders quickly instituted a system of collective punishments, whereby an entire community or at least its male population would be wiped out in response to any partisan attacks. Such was the reality of the Wehrmacht's rule, a reality that would only become more brutal over time.[149]

As historians have begun to recognize, however, variations emerged in the occupation policies established by individual formations, a state of affairs that reflected the wide latitude officers were afforded to act on their own initiative in pursuit of the army's larger strategic goals. Some began to recognize that naked terror by itself was not always the most efficient means of establishing control over their sectors. As a result, even though they generally adhered to the Nazi vision, officers occasionally adopted policies that could be described as mild, or even conciliatory. These varied widely on account of local conditions, commanders' attitudes, and the course of military operations. For units that attempted it, a "mixed" occupation strategy involved frequent reminders to the men to avoid excessive violence and treat the population fairly. More concretely, it included undertakings such as the reconstruction of local economies, the establishment of a security apparatus to protect the loyal non-Jewish population, medical care for civilians, the organization of holiday events, support for the *Volksdeutsch*, and even the preservation of art and architecture.[150]

Many of these practices were more symbolic than tangible. All paled in comparison to the nightmarish character of the military occupation as a whole. However, they constituted a marked departure from Nazi plans and a sharp deviation from the ideological orthodoxy the army had attempted to instill in its ranks since 1933. They also contradicted many of OKW's own directives. Such policies were typically animated not by humanitarian concerns or resistance to Nazi ideology, however, but the desire of pragmatic Wehrmacht officers to lessen the chance of armed resistance, enhance local cooperation, and more fully exploit the local economy—goals that reflected the army's long-standing obsession with "military necessity." Officers also hoped to salvage the army's reputation abroad and at home by reinforcing the illusion that its honor remained untarnished.

The 12th Infantry Division, to which Hans Simon belonged, was among those formations that began to incorporate relatively mild measures aimed at winning over the population into its occupation strategy. Like most divisions, the 12th issued strict orders that included the establishment of curfews, surveillance, identification cards, forced labor, travel restrictions, and sometimes the forcible removal of civilians from the front area. Anyone who violated the curfew was to be shot, as were those who aided partisans, possessed weapons, lacked proper identification, or were deemed suspicious for any reason.[151] However, division leaders quickly recognized that the vast majority of the population in their area—the Novgorod region of northwestern Russia—were well-disposed toward the Wehrmacht. To capitalize on this situation, the division and its parent II Corps courted the locals with liberation propaganda and encouraged troops to support the effort. As the chief of the Corps' general staff announced in November, officers and the rank and file alike were "under all circumstances to preserve and promote the favorable disposition of the inhabitants toward us, but to avoid all activities that are likely to drive the inhabitants into the arms of the partisans."[152] According to the division's records from 1941 and 1942, it took an active role in rebuilding the local economy, left the population enough horses for the harvest, paid civilian drivers for their services, and worked to ensure that the locals were able to feed themselves.[153] Hans Simon took note of this, writing to his parents in June 1942 that "we are making horses available to [the population] for the cultivation of the fields," and speculating that this was one reason local civilians struck him as "very German-friendly."[154] The division's policy of at least marginally supporting the population paid dividends in the winter of 1941–1942 when it was trapped in the Demyansk Pocket south of Lake Ilmen. Its intelligence section stated that the inhabitants remained actively loyal to the Wehrmacht even while it was surrounded by Soviet armies, and the division took steps to mitigate their hardship.[155] At the same time, it continued to conduct requisitions, execute suspected Soviet agents, and employ forced labor.[156] By 1943, the division was relying heavily on civilian volunteers and *Hiwis* (local men recruited as auxiliaries) in its anti-partisan campaigns. It simultaneously stepped up its propaganda, including by organizing a festival for civilians to celebrate the anniversary of the invasion and opening a school in Ossinowka.[157]

Although both OKW and Nazi leaders expressly forbade the rebuilding of the local economy beyond providing surpluses for the Wehrmacht and the German people, various frontline units followed a strategy similar to that of the 12th Infantry.[158] They took measures to revive agriculture and industry and in the process provided at least a marginal improvement in the food situation for Soviet residents. Wehrmacht formations put collective farms, mills, and factories back in action; provided horses, seeds, and German manpower for the harvest; released prisoners for work; distributed food to civilians; issued and sometimes actually enforced orders against theft by soldiers; made sure native workers received payment in kind; and, later in the war, aided in the partial transition to private property.[159] For instance, in response to supply problems in Army Group Center, the 167th Infantry Division set up a system for overseeing the former collective farms with the cooperation of village elders.[160] Division staff instructed personnel "to make the food supply of the population independent of German help" by putting local bakeries and mills back in action and ensuring that food was available for local residents in the hardest-hit areas. They also earmarked some of the unit's own precious fuel supply for tractors to help with the harvest.[161] The 8th Infantry Division, in a nearby sector of Army Group Center's front, reopened three mills for the exclusive use of the population and provided captured tools for civilians to rebuild their war-torn villages.[162] Other units loosened private property restrictions without waiting for higher orders on the subject.[163]

Such efforts to restart the local economy did not go unnoticed by the troops. Johannes Lohr recorded in his diary that his 1st Panzer Division distributed horses among the local farmers at the town hall in Borki and even snapped a photograph of the event.[164] Rolf Dietrich informed his female friend that his division followed the same policy, and he insisted that it worked cooperatively with civilians in the economic sphere.[165] In a gesture apparently meant as much as a reward for helping German wounded as a means to combat the inhabitants' economic woes, Dr. Wilhelm Bacher wrote that his engineering battalion was ordered to transfer one cow from their current village to a neighboring one. He also noted in a subsequent diary entry that his unit was responsible for feeding the Soviet workers it had been assigned.[166] Armed with such examples—exceptional though they were—soldiers found it easier to report to their homeland correspondents that they were part of an army that still displayed concern for innocent lives.

Army propagandists loudly trumpeted such efforts at restoring or improving local economic conditions, hailing them as a sign that German "order" was replacing eastern backwardness and that the occupied territories were supplying Germany with their agricultural bounty just as the Führer had envisioned. Army newspapers praised soldiers' efforts to put out fires and repair damage caused by Soviet saboteurs.[167] The same publications described in word and image how the invaders distributed food and clothing, implemented rationing, and put local infrastructure back in operation.[168] During the harvest season, journalists exhibited photographs of German combatants working side-by-side with smiling civilians in the fields.[169] When it was unveiled in early 1942, propagandists greeted the *Agrarordnung*—a new policy allowing limited forms of private property—as a concrete sign that the Germans were replacing decades of ruinous Soviet policies with a fairer system.[170] For their part, civilians were said to be overjoyed at the "'opportunity" the army gave them to work in Germany.[171] Overall, army reporters insisted that the Wehrmacht was an important player in the mission to establish a new, more just economic order in the East.

Contrary to the claims of propagandists, the primary motive of Wehrmacht authorities in reviving local economies in areas near the front was utilitarian rather than humanitarian: to ensure that food supplies and labor would be available to the army when needed. As the records of the 167th Infantry Division show, for instance, its decision to reopen mills and bakeries was intended not solely to sustain the population; it was also taken in order to make sure the division could "exploit the recovered enterprises as quickly as possible."[172] Economic improvements also reinforced the racist and imperialist conception of Eastern Europeans as uncultured sloths in desperate need of German leadership. Still, the economic activities of frontline units appear to have occasionally improved local civilians' prospects for survival, sometimes even at the expense of the army's own rations and fighting power.[173] And despite ulterior motives, some commanders may have taken a genuine interest in civilian welfare, perhaps out of a lingering attachment to the military's traditional honor code. Whatever the intentions behind them, all of these efforts directly contradicted Nazi intentions to keep Slavic civilians in a perpetual state of hunger and slavery, as well as policies set by the High Command.

Just as they claimed it was reviving the region economically, many representatives of the Wehrmacht presented their institution as a defender of order, a fair administrator on whom civilians could rely for justice, security, and the restoration of some semblance of normal life. Chief among these were army propagandists. War reporter Bernd Poiess, for instance, wrote that the Reich would "be a good father of the peoples of the East" on whose protection the simple Russian farmer could rely.[174] In November 1941, army journalists laid special emphasis on the creation of the Ministry for the Occupied Eastern Territories as a symbol of the new order.[175] This refrain was also taken up by the rank and file. Wilhelm Moldenhauser wrote to his wife in September 1941 that "the Prussians have already established all kinds of order. The Russian population is protected by our police agencies."[176] Rolf Dietrich spoke with satisfaction of the Germans' "ordering hand."[177]

Such claims bore little relation to the reality of the occupation, but Wehrmacht units sometimes did take concrete measures that gave them at least a hint of credibility. Behind the lines, units appointed new mayors and local officials. Where resources permitted, they established schools and set public life in motion, at least in limited fashion.[178] They also established some semblance of a security apparatus, even though in reality it was just as likely to terrorize the population as protect it.[179] They claimed to shield civilians—at least those who cooperated with the Germans—from partisans.[180] The Hagemann brothers' Second Corps, for instance, ordered its men to "protect the civilian population from all hostile elements" in late 1942.[181] In limited cases, GFP units attempted to enforce commanders' orders against the plundering and abuse of civilians by their own soldiers.[182] Modest though they were, these efforts at restoring security and public life contributed to the fiction that, as one army newspaper put it, "German willingness to rebuild, German hard work and German thoroughness have triumphed here over the senseless destructive wrath of the Bolsheviks."[183]

Medical treatment was another area in which the Wehrmacht, in limited fashion, tried to don the liberator's mantle. Early in the war, army newspapers carried stories about the generosity of German medics and other health workers who purportedly went out of their way to care for the population. War reporter E. A. Klockenbring praised Wehrmacht doctors for treating injured civilians. "Here again," he concluded, "is a great example of the helpful attitude of the German soldier in enemy territory, who only wages war against armed enemies, but not against the harmless population."[184] Another front paper carried a story about medics arranging care for crippled children, and, a week later, about a tireless German staff doctor who set up shop in a former chapel in the village of Topolewo (possibly modern-day Topolevo) to treat a steady stream of ailing civilians.[185]

Such articles greatly exaggerated the Wehrmacht's supposed altruism—while neglecting to mention that the invasion itself had caused a massive health crisis—but the army did in fact implement care for civilians in some cases, a policy that had precedents in the First World War.[186] Practices differed from unit to unit. In Kiev and the surrounding area, the Second Corps' head doctor worked to improve health conditions in POW camps, which he noted were in terrible condition. He inspected civilian hospitals and ordered that civilian clinics be reopened. At the same time, however, he expelled the occupants of a civilian hospital to make room for military use and ordered that blankets be taken from civilians to make up for army shortages.[187] Other units, such as the 14th Infantry Division and Hans-Peter Eckener's 205th Infantry Division, conducted delousing operations for civilians, set up quarantine houses for any who contracted infectious diseases, and established new civilian hospitals.[188] After the war, medical personnel often claimed to have regularly extended help to civilians.[189]

Their assertions are given some credence by the letters of their contemporaries in uniform. Wilhelm Moldenhauser commented that the widow with whom he was housing during the war's first winter called the local German medic "doctor," indicating a high level of familiarity. He wrote his wife that "Russian women and men come once in a while and have him treat them."[190] After moving into new, overcrowded quarters in a village in the winter of 1942–1943 as both he and Moldenhauser took part in the Battle of Stalingrad, Heinz Sartorio told his sister that one of the hut's occupants, a Russian baby, had taken ill. Its mother received advice from a German military physician.[191] While advancing into the city of Voronezh in the same campaign, Hans Roth noted that his unit administered ad hoc first aid to civilian refugees injured by Soviet bombing.[192]

Just as was the case for economic relief, however, the narrative of an army that cared for civilian health, whether expressed in soldiers' writings or military newspapers, was more mythical than real. While individual doctors may have acted from altruistic motives, the Wehrmacht as an institution, when it did supply medical aid to civilians, typically did so out of a utilitarian desire to safeguard the health of its own men or preserve its workforce. When civilians received care, its quality was invariably far below army standards.[193] Moreover, it was often reserved only for civilians who worked for the Wehrmacht in some capacity.[194] Resources were scarce and, as even propagandists admitted, German lives always took priority.[195]

Further, even as they were presented as evidence that Germany was improving life in the East, the actions of medical personnel helped to reinforce imperialist, paternalist, and racist conceptions of Slavs, who were assumed to be thoroughly ignorant of civilized hygiene and too primitive to care for themselves. Reporter Gert Sachs described the "almost childlike helplessness" of the adults who came to the staff doctor in Topolewo and how the children looked up to him "like a saint."[196] Still, the army's sanitary measures provided at least some tangible benefits to the population, in the process violating the core tenets of Nazi morality—as well as the operation's guiding directives— in the service of both military necessity and the opportunity to claim moral high ground for the German side.

The treatment of ethnic Germans in the occupied USSR was another area in which the Wehrmacht bolstered the liberation fantasy on an institutional level.[197] Its propagandists received instructions from Berlin early on that the *Volksdeutsch* were to be supported at every turn.[198] When it was recognized that *Volksdeutsch* had been conscripted into the Red Army, units set them free from POW camps.[199] The "liberation" of the *Volksdeutsch*, a topic dear to Nazi leaders, soon became a familiar refrain in the narrative the army's propagandists constructed as German troops swept across the western Soviet Union. When soldiers made contact with German-speaking villages, war reporters rushed to document their stories of suffering under communist rule and their joy at being freed by German arms. Troops spoke with pride of entering *Volksdeutsch* villages and conversing with the populace.[200] Writing from the house of *Volksdeutsch* farmers in the Black Sea region who had been deported by the Soviet regime, Franz Siebeler predicted to his relatives, "For these our brothers the hour of liberation will come."[201] Many *Volksdeutsch* ended up serving the Wehrmacht in various capacities, especially as translators.[202] They were also singled out for favorable treatment under military occupation.[203] When resources permitted, Wehrmacht units established special schools for them behind the lines.[204] Such relief efforts were also aided by public institutions in Germany, including the German Protestant Church, which collected heartfelt thank-you letters from *Volksdeutsch* communities.[205] Together with the

SD and SS, the army financed and facilitated mass evacuations in which thousands of *Volksdeutsch* families were transported out of frontline areas.[206] Although the army ran into difficulties in determining who exactly counted as "*Volksdeutsch*," its emphasis on extending a helping hand to these racial brethren, even at the cost of military resources, played a small but important part in the liberation charade.[207]

In addition to taking part in the "rescue" of *Volksdeutsch*, Wehrmacht units organized holiday festivities in an effort to win the goodwill of the population, particularly during the war's later years.[208] On these special occasions, they expended considerable resources to arrange church services, work recesses, medical checkups, food handouts, and even games with prizes. The army especially sought to establish June 22 as a new holiday to commemorate the invasion. It likewise transformed the first of May—International Workers' Day—into a celebration of "liberation" from communism and also encouraged the population to celebrate the harvest days. The Ninth Army Corps was among the formations that adopted this policy, which its officers described in a 1943 report:

> The celebration of the Russian Easter festival and the 1st of May were specially configured for propaganda purposes. . . . In almost all towns, May festivals were organized. . . . In the center of the celebrations stood the gathering of the population around the maypole and the announcement of the new social measures; song and dance, film screenings, [and] small athletic competitions supplemented the festivities.[209]

The Second Panzer Army staged a major Christmas event for schoolchildren, parents, and soldiers during the first winter in Russia.[210] Not to be outdone, the 6th Infantry Division gave residents the day off for Easter celebrations in 1942 and arranged for them to attend church services "as a sign of liberation from Bolshevism."[211] As usual, the Wehrmacht's motives were anything but magnanimous. Such efforts represented a naked attempt to win popular support, drum up hatred against the Soviets, and increase the region's economic output for the army's benefit, particularly after 1942 when military leaders feared that the population—and the tides of war—were turning against them.

By all accounts from the German side, however, the holiday events were a success. The 8th Infantry Division reported that 1,650 civilians attended the four celebrations it held in 1943 on the invasion's anniversary. The church services were particularly popular.[212] Such ceremonies also made a great impression on German troops. In his diary, Dr. Wilhelm Bacher recorded in 1943 how soldiers and civilians alike celebrated the invasion's anniversary. "In Dubowizy, like everywhere else where there are still civilians, there's a big public festival," he wrote. He described how civilians and the occasional soldier took to the dance floor to the alternating accompaniment of military and local orchestras. Bacher kept three photographs of the event.[213] Rolf Dietrich described to his soon-to-be love interest, Hilde, how he had taken part in a harvest festival organized by the Wehrmacht and local villagers in October 1942. On the appointed day there was a small procession. Dietrich's unit set up several field kitchens to make sure that "on the fairground there was something to eat for each Russian." A confectioner by trade, Dietrich was particularly pleased to see children eating sweets they had never tasted before. The meal was followed by folk dances and a visit from the general. German soldiers sang, followed by a choir of Cossacks in the army's service as *Hiwis*. In the evening, "everyone received bread, sausage, [and] honey."[214] Dietrich sent Hilde photographs of the overjoyed children.[215] Shortly after he was promoted to company commander in the spring of 1944, Willy Hagemann told his wife that he and his comrades had "celebrated the Easter holiday together with the Russian population" the previous year.[216] Gatherings like these flagrantly violated all the precepts of the Nazi worldview but provided an opportunity for the Wehrmacht to enhance its public image in the face of growing civilian hostility—hostility that was fueled by the army's own brutality. They also allowed men in uniform to reprise their role as liberators and tell their readers how grateful the population were to their German rulers.

In one of its most bizarre attempts to signal its good intentions, the Wehrmacht also went out of its way to prevent damage to Soviet artistic treasures. This effort hearkened back to the army's *Kultur* program of the First World War.[217] It also reflected Germany's centuries-old self-image as an exemplary custodian of culture and history.[218] After the invasion, the Wehrmacht assembled a team to carry out art preservation in the USSR. This team was part of a larger organization, the Wehrmacht *Kunstschutz*, whose activities were intended to highlight the Wehrmacht's ostensible commitment to safeguarding artistic and cultural treasures in occupied lands, even beyond stipulations called for in the Hague Conventions.[219] According to the 1944 report of its leading delegate, the *Kunstschutz'* work was not just a duty but "an urgent propagandistic necessity to prove by deed that the German Reich did not wage war against culture and art, . . . [and] was determined to protect the cultural record in exemplary manner in the occupied lands."[220]

Army newspapers featured accounts of the organization's work in the USSR, including its efforts to assemble and protect icons, paintings, and historical manuscripts, and publicized other art preservation measures by military authorities.[221] In the East, its mission was soon taken over by Rosenberg's *Reichsministerium für die besetzten Ostgebiete*, which continued to collect "cultural goods" with Wehrmacht assistance.[222] In parallel with these efforts, the

Wehrmacht Propaganda Department and its "Cultural Group" (*Gruppe Kultur*) took steps to preserve some of the country's most notable architectural and artistic treasures and to "save" items from Soviet museums by transporting them to Germany.[223]

Even Hitler himself played a part in the army's façade of cultural preservation. In 1942, he ordered that all local artists in Wehrmacht service were to be given rations equal to those of German soldiers.[224] Later in the war, the army still sometimes went out of its way to demonstrate its alleged artistic commitments. In August 1943, men from an army signals regiment were tasked with taking down five chandeliers and salvaging sacred objects from the St. Sophia cathedral in Novgorod, which the Wehrmacht had designated a protected building subsequent to its service as a "godless museum" under the Soviets. Participating officers reported that the experience was one their men would never forget.[225] Whatever form they took, measures like these helped bolster the Wehrmacht's claim that as a representative of a culture-loving nation it cared for aesthetic objects in its area of occupation. Any men who took part were able to view themselves as saviors of art and culture, even though the army's "cultural preservation" initiatives were in reality little more than a thin smokescreen for imperialist designs, organized theft, the elimination of Jewish influence, and heavy-handed censorship.[226]

The End of "Liberation"

In spite of propagandists' claims and the army's efforts to appear as a liberating force, relations between invaders and civilians spiraled downward over the course of the war. As partisan activity escalated and the strategic situation became more desperate, the Wehrmacht employed ever-greater levels of terror. Draconian policies such as collective punishments and scorched-earth tactics, combined with massive, deliberate food shortages and mounting expectations of the Red Army's return convinced many civilians that the Germans were not the saviors they had been promised.[227] Across Army Group Center, for instance, propaganda officers reported already in June 1942 that lack of food, requisitions in the countryside, the failure to fully restore private property, and the forcible removal of laborers to Germany led many to conclude that the new rulers were no better than the last. As they played, children were even overheard singing, "Adolf Hitler, the Führer of the German Volk, liberates us from bacon, meat, and bread."[228] This hostility went both ways. Obsessed with the partisan threat, the Wehrmacht constantly warned its troops that every civilian was a potential enemy.[229] The men appear to have gotten the message. They wrote their families about partisan attacks and described plummeting levels of trust for a population they had previously regarded as relatively harmless.[230]

Relations did not deteriorate all at once, however. In 1942–1943, the army experimented with "softer" occupation strategies, particularly in the Caucasus.[231] There, propagandists went so far as to compose a prayer for Muslim residents—seen as a potential source of support—to thank Hitler for freeing them from the Bolsheviks.[232] A surprising number of frontline units reported in 1943 and 1944 that civilians remained "German-friendly" in many areas, an observation officers sometimes attributed to their use of relatively mild occupation strategies.[233] Soldiers themselves also continued to report instances of amicable relations, even though no one could be sure exactly what civilians thought of the Wehrmacht after years of ruinous occupation.[234] Heinz Sartorio put it this way during a retreat in December 1943: "The population is friendly and fulfills our every wish. Whether that is now out of fear or from other grounds . . . I do not know. It's all the same to me."[235]

As the tides of war turned against the Wehrmacht and the mood of the civilian population grew more hostile, the army and its soldiers pointed increasingly to the recruitment of native auxiliary troops (*Hiwis*) as a sign that Germany was still cooperating in a mutually beneficial way with Soviet peoples. Hitler grudgingly approved their use in 1942.[236] In 1944 he authorized the creation of the "liberation army," led by General Vlassov, whose ranks were filled with Soviet volunteers.[237] Aware that his unit was turning to local civilians for labor and frontline manpower, Heinz Sartorio commented to his sister, "A comical war it is, in which the enemies of yesterday are today's allies."[238] In 1943, as waves of Red troops crashed against his unit's defenses, he noted that Russian POWs "have the possibility to be employed for the Wehrmacht as *Hilfswillige*. They are then treated like German soldiers and fed and are then very satisfied and loyal helpers for us."[239] Although they did not always trust their new comrades, German troops voiced their appreciation that Soviet citizens were joining the cause by taking up arms against Stalin, in the process supposedly contributing to their own liberation.[240]

By the time German units were retreating across Belarus and into Poland, the liberation fantasy had largely dissipated in the press and the minds of soldiers, who were now focused on mere survival as local residents turned openly hostile around them.[241] However, propagandists still made a last-ditch attempt to salvage the narrative by highlighting the military's evacuation efforts. One reporter interviewed Soviet refugees and explained how grateful they were to be able to flee under the protection of German arms.[242] Wehrmacht units had long conducted evacuations in various forms and occasionally worked to make them as painless as possible.[243] For the most part, though, "evacuation" was simply a euphemism for expelling civilians from their homes and thereby stripping them of all means of subsistence.[244]

During the USSR campaign, the Wehrmacht and its men developed a narrative of the occupation that sharply diverged from the daily reality of terror and exploitation that historians have uncovered. In private writings, propaganda, and official pronouncements, the invaders often portrayed their relationship with the population as one of mutual cooperation, even friendship, and reimagined the invasion as a morally praiseworthy struggle to liberate oppressed Eastern Europeans from Bolshevism. Like the army's other efforts to whitewash its image, this narrative vastly distorted the actual experience of the *Vernichtungskrieg*. However, just as the reopening of churches had given the "crusade" mantra a veneer of plausibility, Wehrmacht personnel could point to a variety of concrete actions—running the gauntlet from moments of generosity on the part of individual soldiers to unit-wide occupation strategies that incorporated conciliatory policies—as "proof" that their side was bringing a better life to the USSR's inhabitants.[245]

The rhetoric of liberation and the actions that lent it a modicum of credibility were grounded in traditional, universalist moral principles, such as the value of all human life, the importance of freedom for all peoples, and the imperative to help those in need. Efforts by officers and men to at least appear to honor these notions sharply contradicted the racial ideology that animated the invasion and that the military itself had emphasized in its own prewar indoctrination program, an ideology that called for domination, not emancipation, and emphatically denied the humanity of Eastern Europeans. However, they fulfilled critical functions within the Wehrmacht at both the individual and institutional levels, even though each nurtured the fantasy for different reasons.

Soldiers' motivations for adopting and propagating the liberation narrative were complex and varied. Mixed messages from Nazi and military authorities, ingrained racism, the assumptions of culture and class, longstanding imperialist tropes, curiosity about foreign peoples, and direct personal encounters engendered a complicated relationship between the ordinary *Landser* and the population that could include feelings of sympathy as well as criminal violence. By imagining that they had come to rescue Soviet peoples from tyranny and occasionally pairing this notion with small redemptive gestures, men in uniform found yet another powerful means to maintain their self-image as decent men, confirm their belief that they bore no resemblance to their wicked opponents, and transform a genocidal occupation into an altruistic mission. This illusion was particularly comforting for *Ostkämpfer* seeking non-ideological justifications for the invasion and was sometimes even taken up by men with strong Nazi leanings. The sentiments they expressed and the stories they told about their interactions with Soviet civilians became part of the larger moral narrative they conveyed to their homeland recipients about the worthiness of their conduct and the righteousness of their cause.

Given the deep influence of Nazi ideology within the Wehrmacht and its pattern of extreme brutality on the Eastern Front, the fact that the leadership of some units defied the very spirit of the *Vernichtungskrieg* by occasionally using the carrot as well as the stick or promoting the "liberation" line to their own men requires explanation. Several factors were at play. The first was the institution's history, which combined a penchant for viewing civilians as expendable and an outlook that devalued the lives of Jews, communists, and Slavs, on the one hand, with First World War–era fantasies of a "civilizing mission" and the lingering impact of the military's code of honor on the other. Humanitarian considerations may also have been a factor, at least for a small minority of officers. Much more decisive, however, was officers' obsession with the value of "military necessity." This value sometimes conflicted with Nazi ideology, as when milder treatment of the population seemed to promise greater security or more abundant food supplies. Their occasional willingness to adopt such policies should in no way be interpreted as an act of resistance against Germany's political leaders on the part of Wehrmacht officials, however. Some military leaders simply found that in order to meet the regime's goals—goals that enjoyed wide appeal among the higher ranks—a flexible approach to occupation proved more effective. Put differently, in the long run officers hoped to achieve the total domination of the country along Nazi lines, but in the short term they sometimes found that, in a reversal of the infamous Vietnam War mantra, it was necessary to save the village in order to destroy it. Finally, the army's propagandists, who adopted a markedly utilitarian stance toward their work, recognized that the rhetoric of emancipation could win over civilians and provide soldiers with a sense of righteous mission even if it was inconsistent with the ideology the Wehrmacht had emphasized in its training program for almost a decade. Thus, on an institutional level, the liberation fantasy functioned as a means to lessen resistance among the population, maintain the Wehrmacht's image in the eyes of its own men as well as the German public, and prop up morale. In pursuit of these goals, the army proved sometimes willing to sacrifice ideological purity.

Whatever the intentions behind it, however, the liberation fantasy may in many ways have intensified rather than mitigated the worst features of the *Vernichtungskrieg*. Liberation discourse may have accorded more respect to Slavic civilians than Nazi leaders would have liked, but it still perpetuated stereotypes of Eastern Europeans as inferior—whether culturally or biologically—and may have acted as an engine for further violence against the population, particularly when they did not display the proper amount of gratitude or submission. Purportedly quoting a Belarusian farmer, *Das Reich* gave voice to this twisted logic: "The Germans are our liberators and therefore we belong to them."[246] More than this, the liberation narrative helped to camouflage the invaders' true intentions, generating confusion and in some cases a certain level of trust among non-Jewish Soviet civilians, a state of affairs that ultimately made them all the more vulnerable as ever-broader segments were targeted for exploitation and violence. Thus, studying the army's efforts to disguise itself as an agent of salvation helps to explain why not all Soviet citizens displayed instant hostility toward their new rulers and why some even proved willing to cooperate with the invaders.

The liberation fantasy resonated widely both within the institutional Wehrmacht, among ordinary soldiers, and on the home front, particularly early in the war. It not only eased consciences on the German side; it also, for a time, helped to secure the loyalty of many civilians who had yet to apprehend Nazi intentions. By the end of the war, the fantasy was no longer credible, either for German men in uniform or a Soviet population that had experienced the full force of Hitler's racist vision. Having torn the country apart over the course of four years, the Wehrmacht could no longer maintain the charade that it had improved the lives of Soviet citizens. But the influence of liberation discourse lived on as an important aspect of a Wehrmacht myth that insisted that the army had treated the population fairly and fought against an economically and morally bankrupt Soviet system.

CHAPTER 5

Death and Victimhood
Cultivating Moral Superiority through Burial Practices

In 1939, two years before Wehrmacht personnel began to propagate the narratives of liberation and religious crusade to justify the USSR campaign, political and military leaders unveiled their vision for honoring the country's war dead—one they hoped would not only further ideological goals but help to cement the army's self-styled image as an enlightened institution. In an official communication issued shortly after the victory over Poland, OKW asserted that "the Wehrmacht sees in the care of the graves of its dead a self-evident comradely duty." It also expressed agreement with the Führer's decision to let the dead lie in the countries where they fell and laid plans to fulfill his intention to construct "honor-cemeteries with . . . memorials [that] should form a protective wall around the German living-space and bear witness to later generations about the battles for this space." The army's leaders confidently predicted that the graves of its fallen heroes would be honored and cared for in the centuries to come.[1]

Throughout the war, officers and men alike would work to actualize this vision. They devoted considerable resources in the effort to provide a dignified burial for each of the army's fallen, a practice that signaled adherence to civilized norms while framing death on the battlefield as a morally laudable act of self-sacrifice. In the face of escalating losses and innumerable hardships, however, this narrative—like the army's burial system itself—would gradually erode, replaced by feelings of shared victimhood that insulated Wehrmacht soldiers from any meaningful sense of guilt.

In popular memory, the image of the German serviceman as victim—whether of fate, war, the Third Reich's criminal leaders, or communist oppression—would go on to form yet another pillar of the Wehrmacht myth, shielding the front generation from any criticism of their wartime conduct.[2] In West Germany, the hardships of Wehrmacht POWs—over three million of whom still languished in Soviet captivity—were the subject of intense public attention and political action in the late 1940s and early 1950s.[3] A resurgent German film industry depicted the man of the Eastern Front as an honorable figure who had suffered, and often died, in a cataclysm that was not of his own making.[4] The popularity of the "Stalingrad Madonna" connected the suffering of Germany's fallen warriors and POWs with Christian martyrdom.[5] Memorial ceremonies commemorated the nation's fallen soldiers alongside victims of the Holocaust and German civilian dead—especially the 400,000 who had perished under Allied bombs.[6] The East German regime was more willing to admonish the German people for their complicity in the Nazi project, but in keeping with Marxist doctrine, as well as the mood of the population, it rarely stressed the guilt of the Wehrmacht rank and file. Instead, it lumped them together with other "victims of fascism" while condemning the army's leaders.[7]

Despite their vast differences, these two interpretations of the soldier's death—the notion of heroic sacrifice espoused by Germany's wartime leadership and the postwar trope of victimhood—each carried important moral connotations. In the wartime case, they presented the army as an honorable institution that cared for its dead in a civilized manner and sanctioned troops' sacrifices as morally and ideologically necessary. In postwar conceits, soldiers appeared as pawns of forces beyond their control lacking any meaningful moral agency. How did the discourse on death and sacrifice championed by Nazi and Wehrmacht leaders give way to a postwar narrative that cast the ordinary soldier as a tortured victim? What role did practices surrounding death and burial play in the Wehrmacht's larger project of asserting moral superiority over its Soviet enemies, and how did encounters with death and privation shape the self-understanding of the rank and file during the war?

By and large, scholars have viewed the narrative of victimhood surrounding Wehrmacht troops—as they have other elements of the Wehrmacht myth—as a postwar construction, the product of politics, culture, and public ritual. In contrast, little attention has been paid to the formation of victim discourses within the army during the war itself, how burial practices contributed to a larger wartime narrative of moral superiority, and how these twin developments helped to lay the foundations for postwar understandings of the Wehrmacht. This chapter examines practices and attitudes toward death in the Wehrmacht during the Soviet campaign. It analyzes their contribution to the army's attempts to present itself as a morally worthy organization and traces how the experience of death and day-to-day suffering contributed to a growing emphasis on victimhood in soldiers' writings that would go on to shape public memory. The first half of this chapter argues that, just as it had cast itself as a force for religious renewal or freedom from communist tyranny, the Wehrmacht also laid claim to the status of a civilized institution by using burial and memorial practices to demonstrate reverence for life and death. Haunted by its inability to care for Germany's fallen of the First World War, the army devoted substantial resources to provide an individual grave for each soldier and notify the bereaved, while honoring the fallen with funerals, memorial ceremonies, and worthy cemeteries. These actions highlighted the Wehrmacht's stated commitment to civilized conduct, given the widespread belief that, as one army propagandist put it, "the culture of the living is shown in the reverence before the dead."[8] They also imbued soldiers' deaths with positive moral meaning, framing them as glorious acts of self-sacrifice for a higher ideal, whether this ideal was understood in nationalist, religious, or National Socialist terms, or some combination of the three. The emphasis that officers and enlisted men placed on the care of the dead formed a deliberate contrast with the practices of the Red Army, which, unlike the Wehrmacht, possessed no official burial system at the war's outbreak and—so the Germans claimed—squandered the lives of its men in nihilistic fashion.

The second half of this chapter demonstrates that most of the elements of the victimhood narrative scholars have identified as a primary feature of the Wehrmacht myth in the post-1945 period already permeated soldiers' writings by the later years of the war. In the wake of mounting casualties that overwhelmed the army's burial system—casting doubt on its status as a civilized institution—as well as the deprivations and strains they experienced on a daily basis, Wehrmacht personnel began to nurse a self-image in which notions of victimhood played a prominent role. This identity deviated from both Nazi and institutional expectations but made it easier for troops to reconcile themselves to their continued participation in the *Vernichtungskrieg* by eroding sympathy for the POWs and civilians who bore the brunt of the army's terror and diminishing any sense of moral agency on the part of the perpetrators.[9]

Military Commemoration before 1941

Germany's traditions surrounding the memorialization of fallen warriors stretched back centuries before the advent of the Second World War. By the time of the War of Liberation against Napoleon, death on the battlefield had become strongly associated in the public imagination with patriotic sentiments and Christian conceptions of sacrifice. These manifested themselves in poetry and song as well as monuments that marked the resting places of men who would come to be seen as national heroes.[10]

It was the First World War, however, that introduced Germans to mass death on a scale that dwarfed all previous experiences. The Imperial German Army made an effort to bury each soldier in his own grave, but the unanticipated scale of the slaughter made this task well-nigh impossible.[11] Since most of the fighting occurred outside German territory, the majority of the nation's dead would find their rest in cemeteries throughout Belgium and France.[12] To the army's eternal shame, political complications prevented it from caring for the graves of its fallen that remained on foreign soil after the conflict ended. Instead, the newly formed civilian organization *Volksbund Deutsche Kriegsgräberfürsorge* took over this role.[13] Back home in Germany, the bereaved constructed cemeteries for those veterans who later died of their wounds. Almost every town and village erected a memorial to its dead, often in the guise of a grieving mother. As Jay Winter has shown, many Germans turned to traditional mourning practices centered on church and family as they dealt with the trauma of loss.[14]

Commemoration of the dead was a source of constant tension in the interwar years. The Weimar government sought to distance itself from the *Kaiserreich*'s militaristic past while also according respect to the nation's veterans. One product of this balancing act was *Volkstrauertag*, the "People's Day of Mourning," which memorialized the dead of the First World War in relatively muted fashion. Pacifists, such as Erich Maria Remarque, argued that the ceremony still went too far in promoting militarism. Members of right-wing nationalist parties such as the Nazis took a sharply different view. They raised the sacrifices of the First World War's "front community" to mythical heights and established a new pantheon of ultranationalist martyrs such as SA leader Horst Wessel and the fallen insurgents of the 1923 Beer Hall Putsch. At the same time, they accused the Weimar government of betraying the country's war dead by signing the Versailles Treaty and abandoning the nation's military traditions. A year after Hitler became chancellor, the new government replaced *Volkstrauertag* with *Heldengedenktag*, a day on which Germans were to celebrate, rather than mourn, the country's uniformed heroes. The Führer made frequent appearances at the monuments and memorials of the First World War to demonstrate his reverence for the dead and promote a culture of resurgent armed strength.[15]

At the outset of the Second World War, responsibility for military burials and the care of graves in German-occupied territory outside the Reich once again passed to the Wehrmacht.[16] The army welcomed this development as a chance to redeem its lost honor. Following the 1939 invasion of Poland, it established a graves registration service, the *Wehrmachtgräberfürsorge*, led by *Wehrmachtgräberoffiziere* (Wehrmacht Graves Officers, or WGO), at least one of whom was assigned to each large unit. After the dead had been buried by their comrades on the front lines, the WGOs were responsible for registering their graves and constructing more permanent cemeteries to which the bodies would be transferred. In a series of extensive regulations, OKW placed special care on the appearance of these resting places for the army's dead. They would feature pleasant landscaping, well-maintained foliage, and an orderly appearance. Each soldier was to receive an individual grave and, in deliberate contrast to First World War practices, an individual grave marker. This often took the form of a wooden cross or slab, which regulations stated was to be adorned with the traditional German military symbol of the Iron Cross. Care for these cemeteries also fell to the WGOs.[17] Funerals for Christian soldiers would be conducted by the army's chaplains, many of whom also acted as graves officers during the war.[18] Troop leaders or doctors would notify surviving relatives of a soldier's death, and the unit in question would mail them his personal belongings.[19] Backed by OKW, Hitler decreed that at least during the war Germany's fallen would remain on the battlefields where they fell. The transfer of bodies into the Reich was strictly prohibited, a decision that caused some controversy among the German public.[20] The dead, Hitler insisted, belonged to the nation and could not be separated from the comrades who had fought beside them.

Despite this emphasis on honoring the fallen, the work of burying and registering bodies was plagued by unforeseen difficulties during the war's opening campaigns. In Poland, partly due to confusion regarding burial practices and the WGOs' distance from the front lines during the quick advance, roughly 10 percent of the German dead could not be identified.[21] After the fall of France, the WGOs found that their job was "frequently made the object of ridicule" by troops who "do not see it as a self-evident honor-duty to care adequately for the graves of our fallen comrades." Some officers stated that they had received no orders to do so, and the tendency of Wehrmacht units to look after the graves of their own dead while ignoring those of neighboring units also created problems. Other formations, so the WGO reported, conducted themselves more honorably, but there was clearly room for improvement.[22]

In the months leading up to the invasion of the Soviet Union, the Wehrmacht vowed to rectify past embarrassments by redoubling its commitment to ensuring proper burials for its fallen. "The condition of a warrior-grave is the mirror image of the inner bearing of a military and a people," one report on the status and future of the army's graves registration service stated. "It is unbearable for the honor and the appearance of the German Wehrmacht not only that there is a German warrior-grave in bad condition, but also, as is often reported, that the French graves are carefully tended and decorated with flowers."[23] To prevent a repeat of this situation, OKW directed the three Army Groups that would take part in Barbarossa to recognize that "the care of the graves of the fallen in the current war is the honor-duty of *all* members of the army" and that each unit was not simply responsible for its own dead.[24] In anticipation of difficult conditions in Russia, OKW allowed for more flexibility in burial practices but kept the same institutional model in place.[25]

Given his interest in architecture, the Third Reich's historical legacy, and German feats of arms, it was only a matter of time before Hitler himself took a personal interest in how the nation's heroes would be laid to rest. In March 1941 he ordered the creation of the *Generalbaurat* ("General Building Council"), an organization that would design massive permanent cemeteries after the war, subject to his final approval.[26] Each would become "for all time a pilgrimage site of the entire Volk" that marked the location of an important battle, "beautiful in terms of landscape, easy to access with transportation, and artistically exemplary in its conception and arrangement," OKW burial regulations decreed.[27]

All of the army's plans, from the establishment of the WGO to the preparations for worthy resting places for every soldier, were aimed at demonstrating to the homeland and the world "the care with which the Wehrmacht looks after its fallen."[28] Having experienced difficulties with its ability to provide this care in the past, the army now pledged itself to making proper burial a central commitment. By taking on this task, the army positioned itself as an honorable institution that understood the value of human life and accorded dignity to the dead in a manner that other armies—and other nations—could respect and admire.

Surprisingly, the Wehrmacht's dedication to providing what it considered civilized treatment of the fallen also extended to enemy combatants, at least on paper. Three weeks before the invasion, even though it was already busily promulgating orders that trivialized the lives of Red Army soldiers, OKW handed down a set of guidelines that instructed the WGOs to care for the graves of its foes. "As a matter of principle," OKW stipulated, "the graves of fallen enemies, regardless of nationality, will be treated and honored in the same manner as the German ones." Their resting places would be registered through the same procedure used for Wehrmacht casualties.[29] As further regulations made clear, the army also pledged to undertake the burial of enemy troops, including Soviets, in accordance with the guidelines laid out in international agreements.[30] These commitments to show respect to its Red Army adversaries—in death, if not in life—flew in the face of Hitler's own pronouncement that the communist soldier was not to be accorded the dignity of "soldierly comradeship."[31] However, it fit with the Wehrmacht's general pattern of claiming to uphold its honor code and conform to international law even as it made preparations to wage a criminal war.

OKW commanders appear to have been motivated by more than altruism, however. They planned to make the burial of enemy combatants into a propaganda opportunity for the Wehrmacht. According to OKW's instructions for the registration of enemy dead, "When a successful registration occurs, then the grave is to be marked through the affixing of a . . . label with the inscription: 'registered by the German Wehrmacht.' The mounting of the label is important," OKW's staff emphasized, "in order to prevent incorrect duplications and to make it obvious to the enemy population that the German Wehrmacht also honors the fallen enemies in a caring manner." Local residents would be expected to take some responsibility for tending these graves, but in any event the army would do its part to make sure they enjoyed worthy resting places.[32] The burial of enemy soldiers thus took its place among the many attempts to impress upon the Soviet people that the Wehrmacht was an organization of high moral standing.

OKW's pledge is all the more striking given the fact that at the war's outset the Red Army possessed no burial system, a fact of which Wehrmacht planners were cognizant. As one WGO report put it, "The Russian knows no graves registration service," since he considered death to be final.[33] In effect, then, the army had committed itself to honoring fighters of an opposing force that it anticipated would not do the same for its own men. These circumstances appeared to offer a golden opportunity for the Wehrmacht to publicly assert moral superiority over its Soviet foe through its burial practices. However, it remained to be seen if the army would follow through on these seemingly chivalrous designs.

Mortuary Rituals and Rhetoric in the Invasion's Opening Stages

During the advance into the USSR in the summer of 1941, and even as they suffered setbacks over the following year, the men and officers of the Wehrmacht largely fulfilled and in many ways exceeded the vision laid out by OKW regarding practices surrounding death and burial when it came to their own fallen. Units did their best to locate the dead and provide them with individual graves, as long as conditions permitted. The living went out of their way to offer surviving relatives photographs and accounts of the final moments of their lost comrades. Chaplains and unit leaders conducted funerals and elaborate memorial ceremonies, while WGOs made sure the dead were registered and relocated to beautified cemeteries. In its treatment of the dead, the Wehrmacht hoped to strengthen the bonds of comradeship, honor the wishes of grieving family members, and reinforce the conviction that Hitler's army remained committed to civilized practices, in contrast to its Soviet enemy.

As his 299th Infantry Division pressed forward into Ukraine in the summer of 1941 against stiff resistance, Hans Roth and his comrades buried their dead whenever they were able. After one particularly murderous battle in a village near Zhitomir, braving "the stench of decay" and the "horrific images," they dug individual graves for twenty-one comrades, although they had difficulty separating their own dead from the village's Soviet defenders, fifty-eight of whom they buried in a mass grave.[34] Several days later, Roth's unit took part in the battle of Kiev. As they suffered casualties under relentless artillery fire outside the city, Roth noted in his diary that "groups [of soldiers] are sitting together in holes and carve crosses."[35] After they were temporarily forced to retreat, Roth volunteered to carry a makeshift wooden cross through a minefield into no-man's land to mark the resting place of a beloved lieutenant, in what everyone recognized as a suicide mission. He managed to reach the spot. "With my hands trembling, I push the cross into the ground," he narrated. "I then pay him my respects, my one and only comrade, our lieutenant, at his final place of rest, and then start to cry like a child."[36] To Roth, the act of honoring a fallen brother-in-arms was worth the personal risk; allowing his friend to remain in an unmarked grave was simply unthinkable.

The men of other units followed suit by doing everything they could to ensure that each fallen serviceman received an individual grave. Rudi Haller, who served primarily behind the lines in the 227th Infantry Division near Leningrad, reported burying a young comrade in September 1942.[37] A few months later his corporal fell to enemy fire. "The sad thing is that we cannot dig him a grave," he confided to his brother Hans, "since there where he fell on the retreat the Russian [now] sits."[38] A messenger on the front lines in the same division, Wilhelm Altmann, described to his father and sister how after battle he and his comrades quickly searched the field to make sure their dead were buried, since their unit rarely stayed in the same place for long.[39] Several months later, after the first winter, Altmann received a letter from Frau L., the mother of a fallen soldier. She asked for details about her son's death and expressed gratitude that his unit planned to photograph his grave.[40]

Altmann's reply is not extant, but it was only one of hundreds of thousands of letters written by Wehrmacht personnel to relatives of the fallen. Whether a soldier was killed or missing, the army made a concerted effort to inform his family members in personalized letters that demonstrated how much his comrades and superiors had valued his service and sacrifice. Per regulations, the initial notice was typically sent by the commanding officer, who in times of heavy fighting often worked late into the night composing what Major Dr. Wilhelm Bacher termed "the painful letters of mourning."[41] First Lieutenant Hans Wilhelm Sauer explained that answering "urgent casualty mail" was one of his responsibilities as an officer.[42] A year later, a fellow officer would inform Sauer's family of his own death. The officer's letter stressed that Sauer had done his duty well, won the respect of his comrades, and died bravely— and instantly—in the face of enemy fire, themes that appear again and again in Wehrmacht death notices. He also explained that Sauer had been a faithful comrade and a "good son" who had never forgotten his family.[43]

Like Altmann, many troops took it upon themselves to offer their condolences upon the loss of a comrade or to answer relatives' queries about the circumstances of his death. Before he himself became an officer, Willy Hagemann carried on a regular correspondence with Kressen, the widow of a fellow soldier, Hans-Jochen, who had marched with him into Russia. He conveyed his memories of their friendship and Hans-Jochen's stories of home, and told Kressen she would have to be strong for her grieving parents.[44] Although new sets of regulations restricted their ability to converse with the bereaved, chaplains also found themselves composing letters to explain how a soldier had died and reassure relatives that he had done so with the comfort of religious faith.[45] The Protestant chaplain of the First Panzer Army, for example, reported that he and his subordinate pastors wrote nine hundred letters to relatives of the dead and wounded over the course of three months in 1942.[46] Chaplains were joined in this task by doctors, nurses, and priest-soldiers who were often present for a soldier's final moments.[47] Above all, their letters conveyed the message that a family's father, husband, or son had remained true to the soldierly virtues and would not be forgotten.[48]

Ten days after Altmann received Frau L.'s letter, his commander gave him photographic film and sent him to a city in the same area—most likely Staraya Ladoga—to snap pictures of the graves at the division's cemetery. "The family members all want to have a little picture," Altmann explained.[49] He mailed the photos to his younger brother, Ernst, and asked him to make duplicates.[50] Altmann's was not the only unit to take pictures of individual graves and send them to grieving relatives. This became a standard practice across the Eastern Front among soldiers, chaplains, and grave officers, and was encouraged, although not required, by regulations, a ritual that reflected the Wehrmacht's larger emphasis on honoring the dead.[51] Hans Wilhelm Sauer visited his regiment's cemetery in the area of Voronezh for the first time in October 1942. "I thought about the same sites in Belgium and France that I first saw in 1940," he wrote. "Just now the pictures of the fallen are being made for our relatives."[52] In one of his activity reports, the Protestant chaplain of Hans-Peter Eckener's 205th Infantry Division recorded having sent 390 photographs of graves to surviving relatives over a four-month period.[53] The Grave Officer of the 223rd Infantry Division made arrangements with a photography firm in Dresden to ensure that "the relatives of all the fallen are given *a picture of the grave* as quickly as possible."[54] The Catholic chaplain of the 297th Infantry Division explained the significance of the photographs in a 1941 report. "Already from my activity in the Polish campaign I knew how thankful the relatives are for pictures of the graves," he wrote. "Therefore I have regularly photographed the grave of each comrade I have buried, more often also the funeral parade and in the meantime already usually sent the relatives and the unit of the fallen pictures of the grave. How very much such an image helps with comforting is proven by the letters of the surviving relatives."[55] The photographs he sent not only collapsed space and time, providing a tangible connection between loved ones and their fallen friends and family members thousands of miles away; they also demonstrated that the Wehrmacht was doing all it could to make sure every soldier's name stayed alive to be honored in the nation's collective memory.

While most burials at the front were undertaken in haste by the fighting troops, the Wehrmacht conducted funerals whenever conditions permitted. These typically took place near hospitals or large cemeteries behind the lines to which graves officers systematically transferred the scattered bodies of the fallen. There was a great deal of variation depending on local circumstances. Sometimes, a funeral took the form of a short blessing from a chaplain or a few words from an officer as comrades stood around the grave. In other cases, dozens or hundreds of soldiers gathered at the resting places of their unit's dead, listening to formal speeches and sermons as they paid their final respects. During a pause in his unit's advance with Army Group Center, Harald Hoffmann described how his captain assembled the troops and held a "short, but deep and heartfelt address" to honor the fallen men of the battalion, which had already lost half its strength after only two months of fighting. The captain reminded his men of their accomplishments and "blood sacrifices" that would "stand elevated in the history of Germany."[56] Walter Neuser, with the artillery in the same 23rd Infantry Division, explained that he and his comrades marked All-Saints Day in 1941 by visiting the graves near their lines.[57] He also described the funerals they held at the start of 1942, including one for an officer whose grave Neuser and his comrades later decorated with wreaths.[58] "All the fallen were buried at the appointed division cemeteries," reported the Protestant chaplain of 5th Jäger Division. He recorded 209 funerals for 1,279 fallen, attended by 5,015 soldiers over the course of one year between 1942 and 1943, a testament to the emphasis the Wehrmacht laid on honoring its dead. "The ceremonies are always conducted in worthy fashion with all military honors," he explained.[59] In the absence of precise regulations on mortuary liturgies, most chaplains improvised or relied on templates from church officials in the homeland.[60] The Catholic chaplain of the 18th Infantry Division described how he organized funerals: "With very few exceptions the burials took place in very worthy form. Military honors were always paid. The ritual was taken from the booklet [titled] 'The Church at the Grave' in the Mass kit. Each time, a eulogy was given and an Our Father and Ave Maria was prayed."[61]

The Wehrmacht's most elaborate rituals took place on *Heldengedenktag*. With as much pageantry as it could muster, the army celebrated the accomplishments of its dead in the field while the Party organized memorial events in the homeland on this official day of remembrance for fallen heroes.[62] On March 13, 1942, Dr. Wilhelm Bacher, who commanded an engineer company and would later be promoted to major, visited the cemetery in Karfagen in eastern Ukraine where several members of his company were buried.[63] On a cold and windy morning two days later his men assembled before the graves for an official *Heldengedenktag* ceremony. "I speak to the company and recall the men who have marched, fought, and endured together with us," Bacher recorded in his diary. "At the end I announce promotions."[64] On the same day, roughly 550 miles to the north, the Protestant chaplain of Hoffmann and Neuser's 23rd Infantry Division sent a long letter to the relatives of the unit's fallen comrades. He praised the heroism of the dead and called on their families to put their trust in God and look forward to Easter.[65] Hans Simon described his and his comrades' much more informal way of marking the occasion in 1944: "We veterans sat together and many of those who are no longer among us surfaced in the conversations. But it was a happy evening. We had our own way of thinking about the dead," he told his mother.[66]

The sites where most funerals and memorial ceremonies took place were the cemeteries carefully planned and constructed by the army's graves officers. Following regulations, they sought out idyllic locations, such as hilltops and groves, where the dead of a regiment or division rested together as comrades. Graves were registered and arranged in neat rows with birch crosses or wooden markers crowned with the Iron Cross, sometimes organized around a central memorial.[67] When possible, units planted flowers or laid wreaths for decoration, some of which were sent by relatives in the homeland.[68] The reactions of officers and men alike suggest that the army achieved its aim of creating worthy resting places for the dead during the first phases of the war. The Catholic chaplain of one military hospital described the location of its nearby "heroes-cemetery" as "a very elegant and aesthetically pleasing *Schmuckkästchen* [literally: "jewelry box"] and in the best sense of the word a worthy place of honor and a solemn resting place of our dead comrades."[69] When he passed through Warsaw on his way to Russia in early 1942, Kurt Niemeyer visited a soldier-cemetery with three thousand graves from the Polish and Soviet campaigns. "Each one has his grave with a wooden cross and the name on it; the cemetery is laid out beautifully," he wrote. He compared it to the city's Jewish cemetery with its hundreds of unmarked mass graves.[70] The contrast was deliberate and laden with moral meaning. While the names of Germany's enemies would soon be forgotten, each of its own heroic soldiers would enjoy the eternal recognition of the Fatherland. As graves officers labored to construct midsize cemeteries, the planners of the *Generalbaurat* worked with OKW and high-ranking generals to identify picturesque locations near the sites of major battles for the massive cemeteries that would house the army's dead after the conflict ended.[71]

Ostkämpfer who were unable to attend such ceremonies or personally visit the cemeteries behind their lines could read about them in the Wehrmacht's news reports. Several army publications detailed the extensive steps taken to ensure proper resting places and emphasized the care that was spent in crafting their worthy appearance.[72] "A fresh grave, covered with pale Michaelmas daisies, with the deep yellow umbels of the sunflowers. Gray helmets faintly clang in the wind against the white, bright birch cross," so a Wehrmacht reporter described the last resting place of two anti-tank troopers in characteristically reverent tones.[73] Indeed, the army's propaganda apparatus was at its most eloquent when it came to the subject of fallen heroes. Its newspapers were speckled with poems, most prominently those of the famous First World

War writer Walter Flex, that called up the tranquil image of crosses adorning the hilltops and woods of Russia. Such writings connected the recently fallen with romanticized images from the German army's past and its honorable traditions.[74] Reverent poems appeared alongside accounts of *Heldengedenktag* celebrations, often complete with excerpts from Hitler's annual speech for the occasion.[75] Soldiers could also read about memorial rituals for General Reichenau and other fallen leaders whose sacrificial example, they were told, inspired the living to continue the fight.[76]

Army journalists also did their part to reassure servicemen that in the event of their deaths their families would receive all the care befitting the relatives of fallen heroes. The Reich Finance Ministry, they reported, would provide a stipend for a soldier's widow and each of their children.[77] To make sure his lineage would not die with him, the Interior Ministry granted the fiancée of a fallen soldier the right to adopt his last name and use the prefix "Mrs."[78] Wehrmacht troops could further count on the fact that the state would defend their honor even in death: any German civilian who besmirched their good name could expect time in prison.[79] An army policy of pulling from the front lines the last surviving son of families that had already suffered "particularly high blood sacrifices" served to further honor the nation's dead.[80] Front newspapers also publicized the generosity of surviving comrades toward the families of the fallen. In one company, reported *Der Durchbruch*, non-commissioned officers banded together to take on the role of godparents for the children of two of their number who had lost their lives on the Eastern Front. Following German tradition, they each pledged a small portion of their salary for the children's upbringing.[81] Reports like these eased soldiers' fears that their deaths would ruin the livelihoods of their families and provided tangible proof that state and army would care for their personal honor, as well as their legacy. Even in death, their masculine role as providers and heads of the household would remain intact.

Taken together, all of these actions, whether by the army or the state—providing a resting place for each fallen soldier, notifying relatives, photographing grave sites, conducting funerals, laying out cemeteries, staging memorial rituals, and caring for the bereaved—represented a significant investment of resources, especially in the midst of the largest military operation in German history. Indeed, few nations matched this commitment, which continued to contrast starkly with the Soviet Union's relative inattention to questions of burial, just as Wehrmacht planners had intended. The quality and comprehensiveness of the army's system for honoring the dead served as a powerful claim to civilized status and an affirmation of the individual worth of every German soldier.

Attitudes in the homeland suggest that the Wehrmacht largely succeeded in cementing this claim, at least during the war's early years. The written statements and photographs sent by soldiers, chaplains, and graves officers providing details of a comrade's last moments and burial were met with an outpouring of gratitude from relatives in the homeland who found a measure of peace in the knowledge that their men had been laid to rest in worthy fashion and received the ministrations of military clergy. Frau L. sent Wilhelm Altmann a letter thanking him for his plans to photograph her son's grave and for not forgetting his fallen comrade.[82] Many chaplains kept records of the hundreds of letters they received from relatives whose men they had buried. "Now we know that our son was buried in an honor-cemetery in your presence," wrote one family member to a Catholic chaplain. "For us it is a good comfort in the pain that has stricken us."[83] The Protestant chaplain of Harald Hoffmann and Walter Neuser's 23rd Infantry Division recorded the words of another mother who informed him, "I find it an especial comfort that you . . . were able to bestow on [my son] the last honor and love at his grave."[84] During the war, then, the homeland seems to have accepted—and appreciated—the image of a Wehrmacht that treated its dead in humane fashion.

Soviet Burial Practices through German Eyes

For the men of the Wehrmacht, practices surrounding death and burial were not simply a way of cementing their own institution's commitment to civilization; they also became a powerful means to assert moral superiority over their Soviet opponents. From the very first days of the campaign, enlisted men, officers, and propagandists alike depicted their enemy as utterly devoid of respect for human life and similarly lacking in any sense of honor when it came to the treatment of the dead. Building on stereotypes regarding the communist emphasis on material over spiritual matters and the accusation that the Red Army lacked all moral principles, the Wehrmacht and its propaganda machine cast the enemy army as a faceless mass in which the individual faded into the background and life had no meaning—especially for the callous leaders who urged their men forward, often with insufficient training and weaponry.

Starting in the first days of the invasion, Germany's warriors expressed astonishment at what they saw as the Soviet regime's propensity to throw thousands of ill-equipped recruits against Wehrmacht lines in suicidal counterattacks. Witnessing such desperate assaults as he advanced with Army Group Center, Walter Neuser explained that "the Russian spares no one. He always drives new troops into the fire."[85] Typical of many German soldiers, Neuser also observed several times to his loved ones at home that the men of the Red Army preferred death to surrender, even when they were encircled.[86] On an almost daily basis, servicemen described battles in which staggering numbers of Soviets fell, while the German side sustained only a handful of casualties. Karl Müller, a member of the 36th Infantry Division, reported two German dead and fifteen wounded compared to twelve hundred enemy casualties in one early battle in the Ukraine.[87]

Like Neuser, Hans Roth was astounded by the losses the Soviets were willing to sustain. "Many times," he noted in his diary, "we ask ourselves during the . . . hours between the attacks: did the dead awaken again?"[88] He also documented how Red commissars mowed down their own troops whenever they attempted to retreat.[89] For both German servicemen and propagandists, the commissars became the ultimate symbol of the Red Army's cruel disregard for the lives of its own men.[90] One propagandist captured their sentiment when he wrote that "the political commissars think nothing of sacrificing their human material, allowing regiments and divisions to bleed, simply in order to pointlessly prolong the resistance." Despite the knowledge that their cause was hopeless, "they throw forward ever more men as cannon fodder and themselves build [a] merciless front in the back of the Soviet soldiers, who fight between two fronts."[91]

To explain this gruesome state of affairs, troops and propagandists at the front and reporters in the homeland depicted the USSR as a nation steeped in Marxist materialism and a nihilistic outlook led by a regime that stood ready to sacrifice everyone and everything to serve its own ambitions. Its followers—whether out of ignorance, years of oppression, or racial degeneracy—did not even value their own lives. The Red Army, summed up Hans Roth, resembled a "dull, indifferent, soulless machine of destruction and death."[92] A lieutenant interviewed by a PK reporter described the differences between the two armies in equally stark terms: "The seeming courage of these people is nothing other than a vast indifference toward life and death," the officer explained. "What is human life to these Bolsheviks? A cheap commodity: that is why they pay so little heed to it."[93] Goebbels advanced a similar interpretation in his public pronouncements.[94] In his private diary he went even further, writing that to the Russians, life was "worth less than a glass of lemonade."[95]

Not only did they attach little importance to life, Wehrmacht servicemen contended in their letters, but Soviet troops also committed the ultimate sin by desecrating the bodies and resting places of German dead. Herman Henning reported to his relatives from the battles south of Lake Ilmen in September 1941 that Russian combatants frequently stole whatever property they could from deceased German soldiers, including a fallen comrade who was found "completely ransacked and undressed."[96] This phenomenon was cited by many other Wehrmacht personnel, including the 15th Infantry Division's graves officer.[97] Not far from Henning's position, Wilhelm Altmann told his father and sister a month later that a German patrol had discovered the bodies of fallen comrades who had been mutilated by Red troops.[98] Even more alarming were the many cases in which dog tags and identification papers had been taken from the dead, effectively negating any possibility for the personalized remembrance so prized by the German side.[99]

Whether or not they were accurate, such reports constantly circulated throughout the German lines. The most shocking examples often wound up in Wehrmacht newspapers. One carried the story of how a group of Soviet defenders used their own cemetery—a rarity in an army that, the author insisted, usually did not bury its dead—to hide their cannons as they ambushed the advancing Germans. "Even the grave crosses and the names of the fallen were not sacred to them, [they merely acted] as camouflage," its author wrote.[100] Worse still, units and propagandists sometimes reported that the enemy desecrated captured German cemeteries whenever the Wehrmacht lost ground.[101] Convinced that this fate would befall his division's burial ground, one chaplain and graves officer had the crosses dismantled to conceal the site's significance, a practice Heinz Rahe's division also followed on its retreat from the Caucasus.[102]

Wehrmacht reporters seized on the differences between the Wehrmacht's treatment of the dead and that of the Soviets to illustrate what they described as a vast moral chasm separating the two sides. "Have you seen," asked one of the army's reporters in the 1942 *Heldengedenktag* issue of a front newspaper,

> any other Russian soldier-graves on the highways of your advance than these pitiful mounds, on which no helmet lay or bayonet was planted? And even these were usually constructed on our orders. For those who raised up inanimate machines to divine levels, the dead mean nothing. They bury them the way they push their broken tractors together in a pile. So the graves are the things that show us most palpably the difference between us and our opponents. We are the defenders, the Bolsheviks the undertakers of European culture.[103]

Reports like these conjured up the image of an enemy that operated outside the most basic tenets of enlightened society, whose moral failings were even more obvious against the backdrop of the Germans' honorable practices.

It was not only propagandists who drew this distinction; ordinary soldiers and officers placed themselves on the moral witness stand and found the enemy wanting. "In the front most line, often in enemy artillery fire, efforts are made to arrange the [funeral] ceremonies in as worthy a fashion as possible," the Protestant chaplain of Sixteenth Army reported in late 1941. "The comrades of the fallen themselves attach the greatest value to this and go out of their way to ensure their dead receive the last honors," he claimed, "in complete contrast to the manner in which the Russian handles his dead."[104] Willy Nagel described to his love interest an experience he saw as emblematic of the two armies' contrasting attitudes toward the dead. Near Gagarin, in the center of the front, his 20th Panzer Division reached a chapel overlooking a lake. "Our chief had us dismount from the tanks and had the bell rung, that by chance still hung in the steeple," Nagel wrote. "After this he commemorated the dead and wounded of our company in a short address. However, the Russian has little understanding for such ceremonies. He directed his artillery fire so well that we were forced to seek shelter from shrapnel in the tanks."[105] In Nagel's view, which was widely shared on the German side, the Soviets, whom he had referred to as "beasts" a few months earlier, were simply too racially degenerate and uncivilized to appreciate any ritual that displayed respect toward human life.[106] The Germans, who took time out from fighting to observe funeral solemnities, held themselves to a higher standard.

Wehrmacht personnel sometimes mentioned that Russian soldiers buried their dead, and even on occasion that they buried fallen German soldiers.[107] For the most part, however, they gave their readers the impression that their enemies left the deceased where they fell, with nothing resembling the dignified ceremony Nagel described.[108] Hans-Karl, an infantryman who saw many graves as his unit advanced almost 1,250 miles in the first month of the campaign, expressed relief that while Soviet corpses lay in the open air all day long before he and his comrades interred them—evidently in mass graves—German soldiers received a much more timely and more honorable burial.[109] "Thank God it is different with our dead," he wrote in mid-July 1941. "Each one has his identification tag, they get a real grave." The same day, Hans-Karl related to his family his conversation with a fatally wounded officer. The officer took comfort in his conviction that "he did not go under into a nothingness, like our Red opponents," since "his relatives, his mother would be informed." Hans-Karl explained that fallen Soviets, many of whom he had personally buried, remained "eternally missing" since, he claimed, the Red Army did not notify their surviving relatives.[110] His words encapsulated the pervasive sense among Wehrmacht personnel that while their side recognized and carried out a moral duty to honor their fallen in all possible ways, their opponents fell far short of civilized standards.

From time to time, other German combatants joined Hans-Karl in reporting that their side buried fallen enemies, as Wehrmacht regulations had called for. In early 1942, Wilhelm Altmann wrote home to mention that he had been appointed to supervise a group of Russians—most likely POWs or civilians—to bury the bodies of hundreds of Soviets who had fallen in the winter before the German lines and were now surfacing as the snow melted.[111] When the Wehrmacht buried Soviet dead, these often ended up in mass graves, as Dr. Wilhelm Bacher noted in his diary, in stark contrast to their German counterparts who received individualized and ceremonious treatment.[112]

Bacher's writings, however, give the impression that the Wehrmacht did not often go out of its way to lay the bodies of its opponents to rest as OKW had ordered. In fact, for the most part it appears that they were simply ignored. "In the fields and along the roads there always still lie [the] bodies of Russians," Bacher commented in August 1941.[113] Others reported time and again that hundreds of enemy corpses littered the ground in front of the Germans' positions, while making no mention of any attempt on the Wehrmacht's part to bury them.[114] It does not appear that chaplains regularly concerned themselves with the burial of Soviet soldiers, either.[115] There are many possible explanations for troops' lack of action: the sheer number of dead, a shortage of manpower on the German side, and, not least, animosity toward an enemy many Wehrmacht servicemen considered racially or morally unworthy. Whatever the reason, this deviation from the army's plans represented a retreat from the chivalrous codes of conduct the army had promulgated at the war's outset.

Three Interpretations of Death in the Wehrmacht

Although Germany's officers and fighting men unanimously rejected their enemy's attitudes and practices surrounding death, the Wehrmacht itself never achieved a coherent, unified understanding of what the deaths of its own soldiers signified. Instead, it played host to several interpretations—one centered on traditional nationalism, another on Christian theology, and a third on Nazi ideology—that sometimes overlapped and sometimes conflicted. These would manifest themselves in the army's rhetoric, its rituals, and its institutional workings, and had an important impact on how ordinary soldiers came to terms with the sacrifices they made and how they imbued these sacrifices with moral meaning.

What was perhaps the most pervasive interpretation of death in the Wehrmacht derived from the army's long nationalist–militarist tradition, as well as the "front myth" of the Great War.[116] This held that fallen soldiers sacrificed their lives for *Volk* and Fatherland—for the security and the greatness of Germany. Their loss was indeed a sad blow to the loved ones they left behind, but their lives and deaths exemplified the values of bravery, comradeship, and duty that every soldier and every man was to embody. Above all, the fallen were to be honored for their willingness to subordinate their own desires to the needs of the nation.

The language that officers employed in their notices to families often drew heavily from this tradition. "I have the duty to give you the sad news that your son, the non-commissioned officer Walter Neuser has given his life for his Fatherland, true to his oath," wrote Neuser's commanding officer in typical fashion on the event of Neuser's death in 1942.[117] Hermann Henning's sister was similarly informed that her brother had died "in courageous action for the greatness and security of our Fatherland."[118] The Wehrmacht also relied on a rich history of traditional nationalistic symbols and artistic forms in its commemoration of the dead throughout the war. The Iron Cross marked all permanent Wehrmacht graves.[119] Poems and songs about soldierly death—links in a chain dating to the nineteenth century—formed an important element of funeral ceremonies and propaganda literature. The most famous of these, *"Ich hatt' einen Kameraden"* ("I Had a Comrade"), was frequently sung at the grave by survivors, evoking both the value of comradeship and the fallen soldier's connection to national heroes who had gone before.

The Nazi conception of death was in many ways a radicalization of this older tradition, with the infusion of a more forceful brand of masculinity and the re-definition of German identity along biological lines.[120] In the eyes of Nazi observers, fallen soldiers were heroes of the national racial community who had remained loyal to the Führer. A "hero's death"—the Nazis' preferred term—represented the ultimate fulfillment of a warrior's life. He had expended his strength in the battle against Germany's racial enemies, earning him an equal place among his fallen comrades as an eternal guardian of the nation's *Lebensraum*, made immortal in his race's collective memory. With its emphasis on struggle as the central fact of human existence, Nazism rejected the language of mourning in favor of the celebration of a fallen hero's bravery and martial accomplishments. The dead served as a powerful call to arms that inspired their racial comrades to continue the fight and take revenge on the nation's enemies. In its purest form, this ideology had little place for more traditional practices surrounding death, particularly Christian rituals, which contained too much softness and lacked the celebratory quality the Nazis sought. In practice, however, Hitler and his followers pragmatically adopted many of the forms and symbols of older modes of remembrance while attempting to ensure that the Party had the final say in how the nation mourned its dead.

The Nazi vision of death manifested itself in many ways in the Wehrmacht. *Heldengedenktag* ceremonies typically followed the Nazi formula of adopting a celebratory attitude toward the dead.[121] The army's "honor cemeteries" frequently featured swastikas and were deliberately designed to inspire pride in the army's battlefield accomplishments while marking out the boundary between Aryans and barbarians. Propagandists extolled the heroes who died fulfilling their oath to the Führer and explained why this sacrifice had been necessary for the *Volksgemeinschaft*.[122] In the homeland, the death notices written by unit commanders were delivered in person by Party officials in order to underscore the movement's concern for the bereaved.[123]

Religion—in the form of Christianity—acted as the third major influence on Wehrmacht burial discourse.[124] Since the French Revolution, religious interpretations of death on the battlefield had increasingly become intertwined with nationalist discourses through a series of analogies that linked soldierly qualities with ideal Christian traits.[125] A soldier's sense of duty and selfless concern for comrades and a nation many Germans considered a Christian community came to be seen as an expression of the other-directed life that Christ preached. His death was considered akin to Christ's sacrifice on the cross. However, Christian views on death diverged from nationalist and Nazi interpretations in their focus on the power of God and an otherworldly afterlife, their universalistic understanding of the value of human life, their yearning for peace, and their veneration of suffering. As a result, although the Nazi-supported German Christian movement attempted to inject a tougher, more masculine tone into Christian theology, the churches remained much more accepting of expressions of sadness and mourning, and took a less celebratory view of the soldier's profession than nationalist or ideological interpretations called for.[126]

Despite Nazi efforts to limit its reach in the Wehrmacht, the Christian tradition still exercised a powerful influence on burial and mourning practices, particularly through the work of the army's chaplains.[127] Although few examples survive, the sermons they preached at the side of the grave appear to have run the gauntlet from traditional Christian messages that would not have been out of place in a peacetime civilian context to much more militaristic and nationalistic orations. Liturgical materials assembled by the Protestant chaplain of the Sixteenth Army included sample funeral orations, one of which read: "In sorrow we remember our dead comrades . . . who were taken from us and shed their blood for the fatherland. With selfless dedication they have served their *Volk* and put their lives on the line for the German homeland."[128]

The sermon and eulogy templates mailed to chaplains by the Catholic war-time welfare organization, *Kirchliches Kriegeshilfe*, typically contained purely Christian themes, or a mix of Christianity and nationalism.[129] Some clergy took a more militant tone. One Catholic chaplain, for instance, preached in April 1944 that, in an unlikely twist on the theme of the Good Shepherd, "now the time has come when it no longer suffices to simply be little sheep, rather where the sheep must become lions who take up the battle against the wolves."[130] The minority of Protestant chaplains who were heavily influenced by German Christian theology went a step further by emphasizing the Nazi regime as an object worthy of sacrifice.[131]

Along with funeral rituals, the symbolism of death in the Wehrmacht remained strongly influenced by Christian practices throughout the war, as evidenced by the ubiquitous use of wooden crosses to mark graves. The letters between chaplains and family members in the homeland frequently reflected the latter's concern that their sons and husbands had lived by Christian principles and received a Christian burial. They also exhibited a broad acceptance of nationalist tropes.[132] Much more rarely, chaplains encountered resistance from relatives steeped in Nazi ideology who preferred the cult of manly toughness over notions of sin and repentance. Frau Anneliese T., for instance, replied angrily to a chaplain's letter of comfort that her husband had not fought "timidly" out of Christian anti-Bolshevik convictions. It was instead, she wrote, the "feeling of standing for the Führer and our beloved Germany in battle that made him strong."[133] Chaplains' letters also caused consternation in the Propaganda Ministry for their frequent deviations from Nazi conceptions of death, including an acceptance of mourning and an emphasis on religious over national or ideological concerns.[134]

Indeed, although they sometimes saw value in appropriating Christian forms, high-ranking officers who adhered to the Nazi worldview did all they could to dampen the influence of Christianity when it came to the commemoration of the army's dead. Chaplains were forbidden from writing to relatives of the fallen unless they or the soldier expressly wished it.[135] Nazi leaders at home worked to reign in what they saw as the sorrowful, morale-depleting worship services held by churches to memorialize the nation's fallen warriors. Instead, they sought to make Party ceremonies the locus of public remembrance.[136] They also criticized the Wehrmacht's forms of commemoration for their use of Christian hymns and speeches that contained too many elements of "earlier times."[137] These efforts met with only limited success on both fronts.[138] The regime found itself forced to make concessions to a public that very often, as it had during the First World War, clung to religious traditions in what one propaganda official fearfully predicted could precipitate a "'falling-back' into the bosom of the church."[139]

There were certainly stark differences among these three competing visions of death, particularly between a Christian tradition that allowed for much more open displays of grief and the Nazi celebration of heroic brutality. However, each ultimately fulfilled a similar function in the Wehrmacht at the institutional level by fostering the shared conviction that a German soldier's death was never in vain but rather contained positive meaning. Self-sacrifice—whether for the Aryan race, the Führer, the nation, German political interests, for comrades, fellow Christians, or in the name of God—appeared as an unmitigated virtue that elevated the fallen combatant to a status worthy of eternal honor. His death was something noble, to be lauded and respected as the fulfillment of his existence, whether as a racial warrior, a defender of the *Heimat*, or a dutiful Christian.

Although they rarely reflected at length on the subject, the ordinary men of the Wehrmacht expressed views about death that often featured one or more elements of these wider discourses.[140] Hans Wilhelm Sauer reported that as he stood by the graves of his comrades he was reminded of "the duty that the Fatherland requires," and ultimately of the power of God. Sauer felt the presence of the dead around him as both a symbol of comradeship unbroken even in death and as a warning to stay on his guard.[141] Wilhelm Altmann was similarly reminded of the need for every Wehrmacht soldier to "do his duty to the last breath" after his sister sent him a newspaper story about a soldier who had been posthumously decorated with the Knight's Cross.[142] Like most of their fellows, Sauer and Altmann were convinced that their sacrifices were necessary, whether to secure the nation's future, to preserve European civilization, or to ensure the survival of the Aryan race.[143] Invariably, they praised the virtuous qualities of the men who fell around them, often describing them as "the best of us" or "a good comrade," although they rarely approached the nationalist enthusiasm of the official death notices from unit leaders that lauded the fallen as heroes who had sacrificed for "*Volk*, Führer, and Fatherland."[144]

Some soldiers also interpreted the deaths of their comrades in a religious sense, as an expression of the will of a benevolent God and the fulfillment of a pious life. "Nothing happens without God's will," Wilhelm Altmann stated to his relatives after describing the death of a thirty-year-old comrade who had left behind a wife and child.[145] Hans Albring and Hans Wilhelm Sauer reflected on the deaths of Christian comrades, whom they saw as models of faith and a "*lived* Christian attitude," as Albring put it.[146] When his brother-in-law, Peter, was reported as fallen, Heinz Rahe, a Protestant pastor in peacetime, comforted his wife with the thought that Peter had already fulfilled God's plans for his life.

He encouraged her to think of the blessings the Almighty had given them through him, as well as the eternal life God would grant him.[147]

Conceptions of death favored by the Nazis were less present in their writings, but they still influenced troops' views. Willy Nagel spoke of being inspired to revenge against the Red Army for the losses incurred by his unit, a sentiment strongly encouraged by Nazi ideology.[148] Hans Roth directed similar feelings against Jewish civilians, whom he blamed for acts of sabotage that caused Wehrmacht casualties in Kiev.[149] Following Nazi parlance the army had also adopted at the institutional level, they sometimes referred to burial grounds as "hero cemeteries," although they rarely, if ever, used the term "hero's death" so often employed by Nazi officials.

In another deviation from Nazi orthodoxy, the rank and file expressed grief at the loss of friends rather than simply celebrating their heroism. Harald Hoffmann, for instance, took delight in receiving his first military decoration after battle but also explained that he was "sad about the fallen comrades."[150] Eugen Altrogge wrote of the "bitter pain" he felt when one of his friends fell in late 1942.[151] Other soldiers admitted similar feelings of grief when comrades were torn from their ranks and expressed sympathy for the loved ones they left behind, although they rarely dwelt long on the subject.[152] In their writings, they portrayed the men their units buried not only as brothers-in-arms but as friends whose deaths contained meaning that was not just of national but also personal significance.[153] The letters they wrote to the bereaved sometimes raised alarm bells with Nazi and Wehrmacht officials for containing accounts of a comrade's last moments that revealed the realities of battlefield suffering alongside praise for his heroism.[154]

In the war's first years, soldiers generally continued to interpret death on the battlefield as a form of meaningful sacrifice, whether they drew from it Christian lessons, the confirmation of nationalistic convictions, or inspiration to take revenge on the Reich's racial enemies. However, their writings on the subject never matched the triumphalist tenor called for by National Socialism or the patriotic bombast that had characterized many religious forms of commemoration in previous wars. Troops' relative ambivalence on the subject of the army's losses would open the door to attitudes that strayed even further from the regime's vision.

From Heroism to Victimhood

During 1943 and 1944, the Wehrmacht's attempts to assign moral and ideological meaning to battlefield death and to demonstrate to the world that it followed civilized burial practices were increasingly undermined by the realities of a war of attrition that made life a living hell for the millions who manned the bunkers on the Eastern Front. The war's seemingly endless cost in blood was one contributing factor to a growing narrative in the Wehrmacht that became more and more pronounced among the rank and file during the war's final years. This narrative, which undermined the emphasis on glorious heroism envisioned by Nazi officials and military leaders, recast the invaders in the role of suffering victims. Its roots reached back early in the war, and it was fed not only by the bourgeoning number of casualties but also the myriad physical and psychological tribulations that soldiers daily endured.

There was no shortage of experiences that lent this self-image a degree of plausibility. As they braved a hostile environment that alternated between blistering heat and arctic cold and took part in ferocious battles thousands of miles from families many did not see for years at a time, the men of the Wehrmacht regularly came up against the boundaries of human endurance. The narrative of victimhood troops began to construct in their letters would become an integral part of their wartime identities. Whereas the discourses adopted by the army and its men in the first years had depicted death on the battlefield as the result of the conscious moral choices of individuals who glimpsed in the war a higher purpose, the victimhood trope would have the opposite effect, transforming German soldiers into playthings of fate who could not be considered morally responsible for their actions. Dwelling on their physical and psychological hardship also became a vehicle for self-exoneration ultimately fueling the fires of the *Vernichtungskrieg* by erasing what vestiges of empathy remained for those on the receiving end of the Wehrmacht's violence. In the longer term, it would become a cornerstone of the Wehrmacht myth.

At the close of August 1941, the Wehrmacht's casualties in the USSR stood at 84,354 dead, 292,690 wounded, and 18,921 missing—higher than the totals for all of its previous campaigns combined.[155] The figures were released by the German press after Goebbels persuaded Hitler that doing so would undermine Soviet propaganda and alert the German public to the seriousness of the conflict.[156] By July 1942, the reported figure had jumped to 271,612 dead.[157] The next year of fighting, including the Stalingrad disaster, brought with it roughly a million and a half additional casualties.[158] These losses, however, were dwarfed by the absolute slaughter visited upon the Wehrmacht in the final two years of the war. During the Red Army's final push through Belarus and the Ukraine in 1944, the Wehrmacht's fighting strength was reduced by a million men in the space of 150 days.[159] By the war's end, Nazi Germany's armed forces had suffered over five million deaths across all fronts, substantially more than the number it had deployed at the start of Barbarossa.[160]

Behind these staggering figures lay the daily experience of mass death in the Wehrmacht, a subject that became more and more present in front correspondence as the war dragged on, fueling the growing sense of victimhood. Typical of many soldiers, Walter Neuser reported his unit's losses to his family as he made his way through central Russia during the war's first year. He read the newspapers of his hometown, not only to keep up on current events but to scan the obituary section where the names of fallen friends began to appear with disturbing frequency. "I am shocked over the many death notices," he told his mother in late August 1941. "The newspapers bring them, and you guys constantly report new ones."[161] He and his family tried to keep track of the friends and acquaintances who died in the fighting, but this became increasingly difficult. By early 1942, his unit's losses were so high that the men turned to gallows humor describing how quickly losses were filled by new replacements. "Each day different people!" became the watchword, Neuser reported. In the same letter, he listed the latest group of fallen acquaintances in the obituaries: "I could hardly believe the notice of the death of Fritz P. The young Page, Anders' son, fallen[;] R.'s son missing. . . . Now Father W. also dead. . . . . What should one say about the fate of the young R.[?] It is the fate of countless soldiers, who have to share this lot."[162]

The longer servicemen survived, the fewer comrades they recognized around them. Although he avoided the slaughter of the first winter while recuperating in a hospital from wounds he suffered early in the invasion, Willy Hagemann received a constant stream of letters from his comrades informing him of mounting casualties, including the death of one of his best friends, Hans-Jochen. Over the space of six days in mid-1942, a comrade told him, the company leader, another officer, seven non-commissioned officers, and eighteen men lost their lives to a Soviet attack.[163] By 1944, Hagemann was leading a company of his own, but in early August it was wiped out during Army Group North's retreat. "Oh, my brave men, I have lost almost all of them," he wrote to Kressen, Hans-Jochen's widow. "I cannot believe it. Of my old friends, after the commander [died] also the last one is gone. I would like to remain with them forever, they were the true German comrades. With whom should I speak about our deeds, when everything is over?"[164] His company was rebuilt and continued to fight in Latvia, but he was haunted by his experiences. "I have to think of my lost men every day," he confided.[165] By war's end, many reported that they were the only members of their original unit left alive, or numbered among a bare handful of "old fighters" surrounded by younger replacements.[166]

Even in the face of mass slaughter, few men renounced their support for the war or questioned Germany's highest leadership. Still, their constant proximity to death took a heavy psychological toll, prompting some to question whether they were making a meaningful sacrifice after all and whether the death of so many comrades was truly necessary.[167] In poetic language, Hans Albring reflected on these questions in August 1942 to his friend Eugen: "One can not only see the death dances, rather [one can] often also hear their music translated into numbers and dressed up. . . . It is often haunting—in the nights! Does not the blood cry to heaven? Is our Heimat so holy, that for it 'not one person too many has fallen'?"[168] Hans-Peter Eckener was also not so sure. "One says," he confided to his sister in 1943, "this great sacrifice that we are making cannot be in vain," but, he pointed out, "I believe that the Russians bring the same argument for themselves into the field, since no one has made greater sacrifices than they." Rather than accepting the celebratory attitude toward death held up by the Nazis, Eckener welcomed it as a "mercy gift" that would put to rest the endless pain of life on the Eastern Front.[169] Others began to adopt a more fatalistic outlook in which battlefield death appeared less a meaningful, divinely or nationally ordained occurrence and more the result of random chance, with no more rhyme or reason than a lightning strike.[170]

The discursive construction of victimhood that emerged among the Wehrmacht's rank and file was fueled not only by the disappearance of the men who stood beside them but the seemingly limitless experience of physical and psychological suffering that began in the invasion's first weeks and appeared more and more to be the central hallmark of the Soviet campaign as time went on. In their letters and diaries, soldiers not only documented their pain but increasingly viewed it as an integral part of their identities as *Ostkämpfer*. As an officer in an engineering unit, Dr. Wilhelm Bacher was more acquainted than most with the logistical difficulties Barbarossa presented, as well as the frightening effects they had on him and his men. Making their way through the heart of Ukraine in 1941 to construct bridges for the advancing 94th Infantry Division, his engineers quickly experienced massive shortages in supplies. Even on days when no food was available, Bacher described endless marches in the scorching heat and riders who fell asleep on their horses from exhaustion.[171] Fall rains added to their misery. Near Kramatorskaja, Bacher wrote of a harrowing night march: "The suffering is indescribable. . . . Dozens of vehicles remain stuck. The people look deserving of God's pity. Ripped pants, no clean clothes, no food, nothing to smoke, only rain, mud, strong wind and darkness. The swamp is knee deep." Bacher spotted a soldier with only one boot and on the other foot a torn sock covered by a rubber overshoe. "I want to howl and despair," Bacher commented.[172] The next month he felt the onset of a nervous breakdown after his unit was ordered to launch an attack along bad roads in stormy weather despite the fact that supplies were barely getting through and no food was to be found in the area.[173] Their losses increased over the winter, when his engineers were forced to take part in heavy defensive fighting. In 1942, Bacher recorded a joke making the rounds that in 1962 a ragged band sporting Wehrmacht medals were discovered in China, having forgotten their native language. It turned out, so the joke went, that they were elements of the 94th Infantry Division whom German leaders had simply forgotten.[174]

The joke, which surfaced in several variations in the letters of other soldiers, expressed a widespread sentiment. Willy Reese put it into words in his diary when he wrote that, "I felt abandoned by God and His angels, left out in a vast cosmos, swinging in the void between distant stars."[175] More poetically than most of his brothers-in-arms, Reese gave voice to the psychological torment that attended their time in the USSR. Alongside endless marching, hunger, disease, and battlefield wounds, the artistically minded Reese recorded his profound sense of disillusionment as the noble ideals in which he had believed, such as "freedom, poesy, and song," were drowned by the realities of the war experience, and as he compromised his sense of moral integrity "for a piece of bread."[176] At first, Reese tried to make sense of the death he saw around him through the familiar lens of duty and heroism, but ultimately he could find no meaning in the war or the sacrifices he and his comrades made. "We were moved by dreams of Crusades," he wrote, "and we decorated ourselves with roses for battle and dying. The roses withered; in the end there was only death."[177]

While the most agonizing accounts are more often found in diaries, even their letters home, in which they often tried to adopt a more optimistic attitude, could not conceal the immensity of the suffering Germany's warriors experienced. The unforgiving environment, exacerbated by the Wehrmacht's total lack of preparation for Soviet winters, led many soldiers to conclude that they were also at war with nature itself. In February 1942, specialist Rudi Haller, who generally insisted to his relatives that he managed to stay warm, described how he and his comrades spent three days doing construction work on the front line in $-40\,^{\circ}$C temperatures. Two men of his unit, he reported, were hospitalized for frozen feet, "and I hardly believe they will become well again soon."[178] Hunger, malnutrition, and a lack of hygiene and medical aid took their toll. During the first winter, Johannes Hagemann found himself reduced to eating the horses it had been his job to care for.[179] Hermann Henning asked his parents for vitamins and candy in December 1941 because, he explained, "the one-sided provisions already leaves behind its unhealthy manifestations (teeth falling out, etc.)."[180] Many other soldiers experienced dental problems or fell sick with dysentery, typhus, and other deadly diseases. Günther Schmidt, for instance, fell so seriously ill toward the end of 1941 that he had to be transported to a hospital in Germany.[181] He was lucky. Limited resources meant that such ailments were frequently left untreated.[182] Living conditions, whether in bunkers, foxholes, or Soviet huts condemned the Wehrmacht's millions to "a life . . . that in some ways is situated below the level of the stone age," as Hans-Peter Eckener put it in the spring of 1942.[183]

Injuries incurred in constant combat, both physical and psychological, added another strain. Harald Hoffmann, who provided his family with a shockingly honest account of the deprivations of life on the Eastern Front, described not only biting cold, gnawing hunger, and constant sickness but also the psychological effects of combat and exhaustion. "How we all suffer!" he wrote during the first winter. "In the night, when I can't sleep because of pains and bites [from bugs and lice], I often observed in what tortured fashion [my comrades] groan in their sleep, whimper, [and] with a sudden cry abruptly start up and then collapse again."[184] Hoffmann tried to keep his spirits up, but by Christmas he was already on the verge of despair. "This will be my Christmas letter for you," he informed his family, "written out of the deepest bitterness of a life that has become appalling." He lamented, "Not only these years that we lose here, rather . . . we are also robbed of the future, enfeebled, pushed to the limit, and apathetic."[185]

Hoffmann would not survive the winter, but his remarks encapsulated the common sentiment among Wehrmacht soldiers that their time in the USSR amounted to "lost years," a rift in the natural course of their lives.[186] Many had not yet embarked upon careers and worried that there would be no place for them in society when they returned. What should have been the golden years of their youth had been replaced by a violent, premature entry into adulthood. "One becomes damned older in this war. And then still no job, no livelihood," wrote Hans Simon to his mother in September 1942.[187] Like Simon, who was twenty-one when the war began, the even younger Willy Hagemann also feared that "I still have so much to learn and here I can learn little for my career."[188] Willy considered himself lucky for being granted the chance to visit his family roughly once a year. Franz Siebeler, in contrast, did not see home from the day the march began till he fell at Stalingrad more than two years later, although at least fifty of his letters registered his hopes on the subject. During their time at the front, combatants missed the births of their children, the funerals of grandparents, and all the rituals of young adulthood. Taken together, all of these experiences—from the death of comrades, to the harshness of the environment, to the sense that their young lives were being cut short—contributed to the deep-seated feelings of victimhood that would only intensify as the strategic situation deteriorated further.

This sense of victimhood only rarely brought with it a wholesale rejection of their own institutions, however.[189] A few criticized particularly brutal or incompetent officers.[190] Germany's generals were not always objects of reverence in their writings, especially as the army lost ground in the war's final years. Some, like Harald Hoffmann, openly admitted their difficulty fitting into an organization that demanded so much from them physically and emotionally. Trust in the Führer, however, remained strong among the rank and file till the end.[191] The discourse of victimhood they constructed during the war was focused primarily on the harsh climate, the deprivations of day-to-day life, and the enemy who lay across from them, rather than their own leadership.

As casualties mounted, civilians in the German homeland also moved away from Nazi visions of heroism and toward a greater recognition of the enormous suffering of their men that furthered the victimhood narrative.[192] According to Nazi officials, Catholic pastors habitually read the names of the fallen from the pulpit and brought women in their congregations to tears by preaching about the travails of the men in the East.[193] Both the army and the Party recognized by 1942 that wives' letters to the front were often more pessimistic than mail going in the opposite direction.[194] The loss at Stalingrad created an even more worrisome mood, as surviving relatives sought to contact their men whose fates often remained unknown.[195] Letters written by friends and family members of the soldiers examined here also evince constant worry for the men on the front and a growing recognition of the massive sacrifices demanded by what one correspondent called the "terrible awful war."[196] There was still room for pride in their men's accomplishments and willingness to sacrifice, but space had opened for the tropes of victimization that would dominate postwar memory.[197]

Victimhood not only figured as an element in soldierly identity or of perceptions in the homeland; it also had important implications for troops' behavior, as well as their ability to shield themselves from any sense of moral responsibility for the crimes in which they took part. The constant emphasis on their own struggles with lice, hunger, sickness, and a dozen other personal trials helped to immunize the men of the Wehrmacht from any natural tendencies toward sympathy for their victims. When they mentioned thefts, for example, they often devoted more time to explaining their own deprivation and need than that of the Soviet inhabitants whose homes they ransacked. By placing their own suffering at the center of the stories they told, German troops obscured the harm done to the civilians, Red soldiers, and POWs on the receiving end of the Wehrmacht's brutality.

The greater their own sense of victimhood, the more *Ostkämpfer* also felt license to employ violence against those who, in their minds, had not suffered as they had. Even Harald Hoffmann, who frequently expressed pity for the population, informed his family that he understood why German troops took advantage of local civilians, especially those who showed hostility, since the invaders were "exhausted, hungry" and "our nerves [were] at the breaking point."[198] As he described the population's woes, he consistently noted that the men of the Wehrmacht endured the same, or worse. "The suffering of . . . [Soviet] prisoners is the only thing that exceeds our own suffering," he opined.[199] In his diary, Willy Reese was even more blunt on the connection between victimhood and violence: "We pulled the boots off the old men and women on the street if ours were wanting," he wrote. "The torture of the marches embittered us to the point that we became impervious to the sufferings of others."[200] Taking advantage of civilians or POWs became a way for the men to alleviate their own afflictions, after self-pity had eroded their capacity for empathy.

Further, feelings of victimhood undermined soldiers' sense of personal agency, as they portrayed themselves as caught up in—and oppressed by—forces beyond their control. "We were the playthings of history and probabilities," Reese penned.[201] Many spoke of the vicissitudes of fate, including Rudi Haller, who admitted to his brother Hans that "my nerves are no longer the best" after the death of a member of his company and constant Russian attacks caused him to wonder if his luck would continue to hold.[202] Under such circumstances, soldiers tended not to dwell on the suffering of the men and women who lived under the army's terror.

The Breakdown of the Burial System

The transition from fantasies of heroic sacrifice to a preoccupation with victimhood was accelerated by an accompanying decline in the army's ability to make good on its promise to maintain the most civilized standards when it came to honoring the fallen. This was particularly true by 1943, when the number of dead rose sharply. Difficulties had emerged already in 1941, however. During the war's first months, units sometimes found themselves moving so quickly and so often that there was not enough time to locate and identify bodies. The Protestant chaplain and WGO of the 223rd Infantry Division reported that due to its frequent repositioning during its battles in northern Russia, "a constant maintenance of grave sites was not possible."[203] Chaplain Westphal, WGO for the 15th Infantry Division, had to inform the relative of a fallen soldier that it was impossible to send pictures of his resting place, since the division had moved away from the cemetery where he lay.[204] Westphal also encountered difficulty procuring the supplies necessary for his small burial detail to complete its work. Months of appeals were unable to produce the proper tools for cutting the birch trees needed to construct crosses.[205] A shortage of black paint—a symptom of the army's larger logistical problems—also meant that his group had to resort to writing burial inscriptions in pencil for a period of several weeks in 1942.[206]

Much worse was the fact that due to the severity of Russian winters, Westphal found it difficult if not impossible to conduct reburials at centralized cemeteries.[207] As another chaplain explained during the first winter, "Bodies of fallen comrades can only be buried with the greatest difficulties, because the ground is frozen too hard."[208] During the spring thaw, the men of Westphal's division constantly discovered bodies that had lain unburied beneath the snow.[209] Far to the south, Hans Roth and his comrades in the 299th Infantry Division resorted to using dynamite to blast holes in the frozen ground to allow for burial.[210] By 1944 this practice was sanctioned in official regulations—an illustration of how far the army's standards had fallen.[211] Blizzards and constantly shifting snow disrupted the appearance of the army's meticulously planned cemeteries.[212] Both Roth's and Westphal's divisions began using "comrade graves" (mass graves) that held the bodies of up to ten German soldiers, a practice the Wehrmacht had explicitly rejected at the outset of the campaign, but which appears to have been employed by an increasing number of formations.[213] Logistical challenges and environmental conditions were not the only sources of difficulty. Enemy units sometimes overran Wehrmacht cemeteries, a fate that befell the large 223rd Infantry Division burial ground west of Kharkov in 1943, the construction of which had already been hampered by military operations.[214] In other cases, enemy action interrupted funerals or simply made it impossible to reach the dead.[215]

Worse still, according to some chaplains, burials and the care of grave sites became less of a priority for Wehrmacht troops as time passed. In his "soul-care" report for the final quarter of 1942, the Catholic chaplain of the Sixteenth Army summarized the statements of his subordinate priests regarding death and burial with the remark: "with the lengthening of the war a certain lethargy vis-à-vis the dead seems to have taken hold." He cited one chaplain's alarming statement that men smoked and lounged about with hands in their pockets at funerals.[216] Georg Werthmann, the second-ranking figure in the Catholic chaplaincy, recorded shortly after the war that "from many quarters moving complaints were made that the reverence for fallen comrades, especially in the course of the Eastern campaign, had been falling sharply."[217] In his postwar notes he explained that after so many hard-fought battles, "the chaplain had to remind and to force" soldiers to respect the "majesty of death."[218] Although many troops still insisted in their letters that they displayed the proper attitude toward the dead throughout the war, a number did remark that after losing so many comrades, indifference began to replace reverence. During the second winter, Willy Reese gave voice to such feelings when he confided to his diary that "we counted the fallen in front of our lines and picked out our dead and wounded, named names whose bearers were no longer alive. Almost unmoved, without regret, like mere statistical data, from which we passed on to the duties of the day."[219]

Over time, the sheer number of dead began to simply overwhelm the Wehrmacht's burial system. With so many fallen soldiers and so few ministers, explained the Catholic chaplain of the Second Army in 1944, "many soldiers before and in battle must go without pastoral care[;] many wounded can find no spiritual assistance, and also many fallen have to be buried without a priest." This situation, he noted, depressed the morale of the troops and caused agitation among their family members back home.[220] The deficit was partly— but never fully—ameliorated by the actions of Catholic priest-soldiers, many of whom served in medical companies, as well as the thousands of Protestant pastors who served on the front lines.[221] Care for the endless legions of dead also sapped the emotional strength of the personnel involved. One Protestant chaplain encountered a colleague who had suffered a nervous breakdown after burying fifteen hundred men.[222] Generous alcohol rations helped personnel assigned to burial details to cope with the psychological strain, but manpower was increasingly in short supply.[223] As a result, a substantial number, if not the majority, of the Wehrmacht's fallen would end up being buried by groups of Soviet POWs or civilian laborers forced into this role under German supervision.[224] Indeed, perhaps nothing better illustrates the ultimate failure of the Wehrmacht's efforts to portray itself as a high-minded institution that respected the dead more clearly than the fact that by 1944 its very process of conferring dignity to its fallen constituted a war crime under contemporary international law.[225]

The Wehrmacht entered the war with the Soviet Union hoping to honor its dead in a manner that would correct past failings and illustrate to the world that the German armed forces held themselves to a high moral standard. This standard, so it was planned, would even extend to the nation's enemies, offering the chance to reveal a stark contrast between a "civilized" Wehrmacht and a Soviet regime accused of having strayed from the most fundamental human norms. Although its care for the enemy dead quickly lagged behind the vision set out by its planners, the Wehrmacht was broadly successful in emphasizing the worthy burial and commemoration of its own fallen during the war's initial years. Pageantry that blended Christian, nationalist, and Nazi systems of meaning helped to undergird the sense among the army's personnel that their dead comrades had made commendable sacrifices. It also provided the desired contrast with a Red Army most soldiers continued to view as bereft of all respect for the lives of its own men.

Over the following years, the army's designs unraveled in the midst of logistical hurdles, a lack of manpower, and a growing feeling of indifference toward the ever-rising number of dead. In the end, despite the Wehrmacht's emphasis on honoring its fallen and in violation of Nazi visions of racial purity, the Third Reich's Aryan so-called heroes were frequently laid to rest not by their own comrades but by men they considered subhuman, under conditions that army personnel would have considered barbaric a few years earlier.

Many of the factors that endangered the Wehrmacht's reputation for according proper dignity to its fallen, such as the unforgiving environment, hunger, sickness, and the enormity of the army's casualties, also led soldiers to stray from the more heroic interpretations of battlefield death that ideology favored. German combatants began to question whether the death that enveloped them contained any positive meaning at all, and to construct and project identities not as heroes who made the conscious choice to continue the fight but long-suffering victims who ultimately possessed no moral responsibility for their actions. Their feelings of victimhood provided license for the barbaric treatment of noncombatants and simultaneously deflected attention away from the sufferings they endured at the Wehrmacht's hands.

By the time the guns fell silent, yet another foundational piece of the Wehrmacht myth had fallen into place. Men who entered the USSR as triumphant invaders and agents of a criminal war had successfully rebranded themselves with an image that was more likely to evoke pity than moral outrage. The postwar memoirs, novels, films, commemoration ceremonies, and pronouncements by veterans and public figures casting German soldiers in the role of sympathetic victims simply continued a trend that millions of servicemen had already begun during the conflict itself. There was at least one minor adjustment, however: veterans would now name the Hitler regime itself as one of the prime sources of their wartime sufferings.[226]

Conclusion

A Myth Is Born

The force that retreated from Soviet borders in the summer of 1944 was no more than a shadow of the one that had won victory after victory against the Red Army in 1941. The men who filled its ranks were "ordinary" by any standard definition. They hailed from all walks of life and from every corner of a modern nation that prided itself on its cultural accomplishments and deeply held traditions. Although they had spent a significant portion of their young lives as citizens of the Third Reich, their worldviews had been shaped by traditional moral values in addition to Nazi propaganda. Yet, during their time in the Soviet Union, they became complicit in Nazi crimes as members of an institution that proved a willing instrument in Hitler's plans to annihilate Eastern Europe's Jews and to kill or enslave the remaining population.

This book has approached the history of the Wehrmacht on the Eastern Front by engaging with questions of morality and self-perception. How did ordinary servicemen of all backgrounds come to willingly accept their participation in Hitler's *Vernichtungskrieg* while holding on to the conviction that they remained morally decent? Did Nazi ideology constitute the only source of moral legitimacy in the organization in which they served, and if not, what impact did other ethical systems have on the army's self-image, discourse, and behavior? Finally, where did the myth of the Wehrmacht's "clean hands" come from, and how did it become so firmly embedded in German memory?

The Institution

This investigation confirms that the Nazi value system had come to exert a powerful influence on the Wehrmacht's institutional culture. Orders up and down the chain of command, regulations for troop conduct, and official propaganda strongly reflected the worldview of the Nazi regime. As numerous other scholars have documented, the Wehrmacht pursued a terroristic course on the Eastern Front that included the implementation of the Criminal Orders, scorched-earth tactics, a brutal occupation policy involving the wholesale exploitation and mass murder of "racial and ideological enemies," and complicity in the Holocaust, just as called for in Hitler's vision. All of this built on the foundations the Wehrmacht had established since the 1930s through an extensive and ongoing program of ideological indoctrination.[1]

Although it had clearly made great strides toward embracing the principles of Nazi morality, this work has argued that the Wehrmacht never fully completed its transition to the new value system. A sprawling, complex organization with embedded historical traditions, it proved large enough and flexible enough to continue to accommodate multiple value systems, even contradictory ones. Nazi morality was certainly in the ascendant, but a wide variety of more traditional concepts of right and wrong still shaped the army's institutional culture. These included the military's centuries-old code of honor, nationalist virtues, middle-class norms, Christian ethics, and a powerful attachment to the principle of military necessity.

The relationship between more traditional moral norms and the values of Nazism was a complex one. In some cases they overlapped to a significant degree. The military honor code, for instance, stressed the importance of bravery and comradeship, just as Nazism celebrated the use of violence and the centrality of the *Volksgemeinschaft*. When applied to conquered populations, middle-class standards of cleanliness easily blended with attributions of biological inferiority. In such respects, traditional morality had the potential to become a stepping stone toward acceptance of ideology.[2] In other cases, Nazi morality and alternative value systems proved less compatible. For instance, while Nazism recognized only Nordic lives as valuable, Christian traditions emphasized a common humanity that transcended national and racial boundaries.

The influence of these other value systems surfaced in numerous ways in the army's institutional fabric. Even as they consistently sanctioned terror against suspected enemies, generals up and down the Wehrmacht hierarchy issued orders relying on traditional moral argumentation, reminded their men to comport themselves in an upstanding manner, and insisted on legalistic procedures such as paying for stolen goods. Propagandists emphasized the justice of the German cause and the malevolent nature of the enemy. Taking advantage of the wide latitude they enjoyed in their decision making, units occasionally implemented policies that starkly contravened ideological prescriptions. These included providing food and medical care to the local population, sanctioning the reopening of churches, and aiding in the reconstruction of local economies. They also took steps to burnish their side's image, including through the memorialization of fallen soldiers.

Rhetorical gestures and actions that reflected the continued influence of traditional value systems were rarely the product of altruistic sentiments on the part of army officials. Nor were they motivated by the desire to consciously undermine the Hitler regime, even though they sometimes ran afoul of the core principles of Nazi morality. Rather, commanders and propagandists who employed them aimed to enhance morale, preserve the Wehrmacht's reputation, and seize the moral high ground by proving that the invaders were not only racially but ethically superior to their Soviet counterparts. Most of all, they endeavored to fulfill the dictates of military necessity by winning the population over to the German side or convincing Red Army fighters to lay down their arms. In pursuit of these goals, men in positions of authority in the army demonstrated their situational readiness to follow a different path than the one set out by the Nazi regime.

Although they amounted to little more than window dressing against the backdrop of the unmitigated reign of terror unleashed in the East, the fact that its vocabulary and actions continued to reflect the influence of traditional moral systems indicates that the Wehrmacht was more than an instrument of naked ideological terror. Instead of openly broadcasting its murderous intentions at every turn, it displayed the chameleon-like capacity to disguise itself as a conventional army that played by civilized rules even as it fulfilled a critical role in enacting the Nazis' genocidal vision. Sometimes it adopted the mantle of the liberator. At other times, it took up the robe of the pious crusader. It showed itself capable of respecting civilians and prisoners of war, if only when this suited its strategic purposes. Such behavior generated confusion among Soviet civilians and members of the Red Army by masking the invaders' true aims, making them more vulnerable to the army's brutality and dampening their efforts to successfully resist.

The army's ability to selectively emphasize traditional ideas of right and wrong had important consequences for the men in its own ranks. By promoting a wide range of moral arguments and value systems and providing these with what appeared to be official sanction, high-ranking officers and propagandists made it psychologically easier for men of all backgrounds to feel secure in their moral self-image and justified in their participation in the

Vernichtungskrieg regardless of their ideological views. If Wehrmacht leaders had insisted that Nazi morality was the only legitimate source of martial identity and the singular rationale for the war, some troops may have struggled to make sense of their participation—even more than they already did. But despite the fact that the army had spent a decade trying to mold its men into ideological warriors, propagandists and commanders from the division level upwards appear to have recognized that not all soldiers had fully committed themselves to the new moral orientation. By casting a wide rhetorical net and even occasionally instituting conciliatory policies, they buoyed morale and helped provide men of all persuasions a reason to believe in their own decency, the integrity of their institution, and the righteousness of their cause.

In sum, the Wehrmacht proved willing in many instances to deviate from ideological purity in its quest to win strategic advantages, weaken enemy resolve, and encourage its personnel to view themselves as members of a "civilized" organization that still, at least on paper, upheld honorable codes of conduct. The Wehrmacht played the role of Hitler's hatchet man, leaving the corpses of millions of innocent Soviet men, women, and children in its wake, but it shied away from fully embracing the bloodthirsty image of ideological fanaticism that attended this role, often preferring to wrap itself in a cloak—transparent though it was—of civility and moral decency. The Wehrmacht was an even more dangerous entity than scholars have recognized, one with the chilling capacity not only to burn down villages but to hand out candy first. While its willingness to incorporate other value systems into its institutional workings sometimes undermined Nazi plans in the short term, in the long run doing so made it easier to secure the broad support of its members and make the Führer's vision for Eastern Europe a reality.

The Men

Within an army that still housed a variety of value systems, individual soldiers crafted their identities, worldviews, and understandings of the campaign not only with reference to ideology but traditional ethical precepts. As it did for the Wehrmacht as a whole, the Nazi worldview played a key role in the lives of Germany's warriors. Men-at-arms frequently voiced their allegiance to the Führer, pledged to annihilate "Jewish-Bolshevism," exhibited racist attitudes toward Eastern Europeans, and took a merciless stance toward all perceived enemies. During their time in the Soviet Union, they employed forced labor, executed POWs and civilian hostages, razed towns, and played their part in the persecution of Jews, whether acting under orders or on their own initiative. In so doing, they displayed a high degree of loyalty to the regime and a willingness to carry out the bloody work of the racial war of extermination with ruthless efficiency. Some adopted the new moral system wholesale and found in it sufficient validation for all of their actions.

As was the case for the organization to which they belonged, however, a close examination of their writings suggests that the self-image of many German soldiers was still heavily informed by value systems that predated Nazism. These included a traditional nationalistic outlook and a military code of honor that emphasized comradeship, courage, and chivalrous conduct. The rank and file were also influenced by a constellation of values associated with middle-class status, domestic life, and civilization, such as a concern for cleanliness, order, hard work, and warm familial relations. Religion remained central to the lives of many troops. To a lesser extent, they also imbibed the principle of military necessity that was so influential for the army's conduct at the institutional level.

Even as they carried out Hitler's murderous vision, soldiers often relied on such moral concepts to cultivate identities not as fanatical ideologues or agents of genocide but as "decent," virtuous men fighting to preserve a host of worthy ideals, men who conducted themselves as honorably as circumstances allowed. In their letters and diaries, they depicted themselves as the very embodiment of all the virtues prized in German society: good husbands, brave comrades, devout Christians, selfless patriots, and upright individuals who did not enjoy war but did what had to be done for the greater good. Whenever this identity was threatened—especially by their own side's reprehensible conduct—they frequently turned to common moral rationalizations rather than ideology to explain that their deeds had been necessary, unavoidable, or fully justified. Throughout the conflict, they generated self-affirming autobiographical narratives in which they figured as liberators, crusaders, and finally victims, rather than unscrupulous killers. They portrayed their institution not as a genocidal instrument of destruction but a civilized fighting force, one that retained its commitments to tradition and honor even if its opponents did not.

It was not simply a case of *Ostkämpfer* making a binary choice between Nazi morality and traditional morality, however. Many seem to have adopted specific aspects of different value systems without necessarily reflecting on the question of their fundamental compatibility. Men who agreed with much of the Nazi worldview sometimes stressed their sympathetic stance toward local civilians. Troops who prided themselves on their commitment to the military's honor code harbored racist views toward Jews and POWs. Many Christian soldiers, even those who were critical of some aspects of Nazism, held Hitler in high regard and found themselves agreeing with the general outlines of Barbarossa.

The Wehrmacht's warriors did not operate in a vacuum as they discursively constructed "decent" identities; they also followed in the footsteps of commanders and propagandists by employing the language of traditional morality to draw favorable comparisons with their enemies. In their writings, troops portrayed commissars and other members of the Red Army as both biological inferiors and dishonorable fighters who ignored the laws of war. They railed against a "godless" Soviet regime that they accused of abandoning its people to extreme poverty while carrying out a program of systematic oppression. Any who resisted were labeled "bandits" deserving of a swift execution. By using their enemies as a foil, troops helped to establish the moral superiority of their side while directing attention away from their own misdeeds.

It was also often with reference to traditional moral concepts that soldiers asserted the justice of their cause. Men like the Hagemann brothers repeated the preemptive strike myth that cast the invasion as a just war to forestall a nightmarish Soviet assault. Men like Hans Albring and Eugen Altrogge, whose lives revolved around their religious faith, found solace in the belief that the invasion constituted a crusade to destroy godless communism and restore religion to a populace they recognized as fellow believers. Revisiting an argument that had been advanced during the First World War, still others preferred to insist that they had come to bring civilization to the East and rid the continent of an oppressive regime, a view favored by Wilhelm Moldenhauser.

Soldiers did not confine themselves to rhetoric alone as they fashioned narratives about themselves and their enemies. Even as they participated in a criminal enterprise, they frequently took actions that seemed to confirm the "decent" self-image to which so many of them clung. They reopened churches, released inmates from Soviet prisons, handed out food to needy civilians, demonstrated generosity toward comrades and relatives, and strove to provide dignified burials for their dead. Some of these actions ran afoul of Nazi plans and even threatened the very bedrock of Nazi ideology itself, especially when they blurred racial boundaries. Yet, just as certain policies on the institutional level "proved" that the Wehrmacht remained committed to its honor code, small gestures like these could serve as tangible evidence that a soldier had remained decent even if his other actions on the battlefield sometimes called this identity into question. They may have amounted to little in the grand scheme of the *Vernichtungskrieg*, but they were a psychologically important means of finding some measure of moral redemption, a way to re-affirm, in word and deed, one's standing as a good man and the respectability of one's side.[3]

The fact that soldiers felt comfortable crafting identities and projecting a self-image that drew from whatever moral systems they personally found most compelling was due in part to the pragmatic stance of Wehrmacht officers and journalists. These constantly reminded troops of their inherent goodness and sanctioned a wide range of moral justifications from which they could choose. In some cases, even Hitler, Goebbels, and other Nazi leaders themselves promoted the notion of a Christian crusade, deployed traditional moral argumentation, or encouraged servicemen to view themselves as a liberating force. Within this environment, men like Heinz Sartorio, who had largely adopted the moral logic of the Nazi regime, had only to look to the Criminal Orders, the racialized discourse of Wehrmacht propaganda, and the army's terroristic practices for affirmation. Yet even men who expressed reservations about the Wehrmacht's conduct or gravitated toward non-ideological explanations for the campaign—such as Harald Hoffmann or Hans Albring—could still find ways to come to terms with their participation without sensing that their views made them outcasts.[4]

There were limits to how far commanders, propagandists, and the regime would go to allow soldiers flexibility in their quest for moral legitimacy. When the reopening of churches and prisons or the provisioning of food to starving civilians threatened racial hierarchies and military discipline, for instance, these were quickly shut down by higher authorities. Still, had the army insisted on absolute ideological purity and openly proclaimed the extermination of millions of men, women, and children of Jewish and Slavic decent as the campaign's sole purpose, troops may not have enthusiastically complied. Contrary to the views of some historians, it was not so much the army's complete adoption of the Nazi worldview to the exclusion of all others as its ability to find room for a wide variety of value systems that secured the compliance of the broad range of ordinary men who filled its ranks, including those who were less comfortable with Nazi thinking.

The process by which soldiers developed their moral self-image has an important bearing on the central question of this analysis: how did German men in uniform manage to avoid any sense of guilt as they took part in the *Vernichtungskrieg*, and why did they refuse to admit culpability even decades afterward? Some have answered these questions by arguing that *Ostkämpfer* derived their sense of moral legitimation from Nazi ideology. According to this interpretation, soldiers quickly and comfortably took on the role of enthusiastic killers and evaluated the war, their enemies, and their own identities through a distinctly ideological lens. Others have contended that owing to years of uninterrupted combat, Germany's warriors had come to reject the very concept of morality altogether.

Without discounting the significant role ideology played in shaping soldiers' worldviews as well as the psychological numbing they experienced at the front, the present work favors a different explanation. It was their ability to develop and maintain identities as "decent" men, to rationalize their crimes, and to create and perform self-affirming narratives with reference to a wide array of traditional moral systems—alongside or sometimes in contradiction to Nazi morality—that allowed men of all walks of life and all ideological leanings to make peace with their participation in violations of international law. A substantial number of men expressed unease regarding their side's criminal practices, particularly during the early stages of the war. However, through the processes enumerated above, the vast majority found ways to maintain a positive self-image and sleep soundly at night. Whenever this image was threatened, their autobiographical writings and small redemptive acts helped to salve troubled consciences.

Along with factors historians have studied elsewhere, such as a strict disciplinary system and the diffusion of responsibility within the group, soldiers' remarkable powers of self-deception and self-exoneration had important implications for the Wehrmacht's battlefield effectiveness and staying power. It can be speculated that those troops who believed in their moral legitimacy proved more effective fighters and were less prone to desertion and more dedicated to victory.[5] Their rationalizations went a long way toward helping them mentally cope with their actions and repeat them the next day.

Perhaps the most troubling finding of this book is that while Nazi morality certainly constituted a source of legitimacy for some soldiers, adherence to the regime's preferred ethical system was far from a necessary prerequisite for willing participation in the campaign. By drawing from traditional moral values and argumentation, even men with little taste for ideology or outright opponents of Nazism proved able to reconcile themselves to their role while avoiding cognitive dissonance. For Nazi leaders and military authorities, a dedicated National Socialist soldier may well have been the ideal, but a non-Nazi convinced of the righteousness of his cause could be just as effective. At the end of the day, whether he saw himself as a crusader bringing religion to a needy population or as a chivalrous warrior who obeyed the laws of war, by his very presence on the Eastern Front the *Ostkämpfer* advanced the goals of the Nazi regime and created the preconditions for its genocidal policies. Further, the transmutation of the war of extermination into a righteous enterprise may well have led to even more brutal conduct by promoting an ends-justify-the-means mentality. In their desire to annihilate a regime they had become convinced was irredeemably evil, troops may have reasoned that innocent deaths were a price worth paying, especially if they also believed in their opponents' racial inferiority.

What emerges is a portrait of an army whose members strove in any way they could to hold on to a positive sense of self and find legitimation for the many atrocities their side routinely committed, whether they embraced Nazi morality or remained anchored in traditional value systems. The Wehrmacht's project of self-justification was never fully complete, however. The basic fact of its barbaric modus operandi constantly undermined the self-righteous image enlisted men and their superiors attempted to maintain. The gap between traditional morality and Nazi morality was another source of tension. Although servicemen were surprisingly successful at rationalizing crimes and insisting on their own fundamental goodness, by the end of the war many felt their youthful innocence and their sense of their own humanity slipping away. Men who emphasized their religiosity as a source of moral superiority over the Soviets were continually disappointed as the Nazis limited Christian influences in the Wehrmacht. The liberation fantasy, another promising means for soldiers to prove their virtue, was soon eclipsed by the daily reality of mass executions and indiscriminate terror. Even the practice of burying and honoring the dead, a self-understood marker of civilization, began to break down in the face of weather conditions, logistical problems, and growing indifference. In spite of these setbacks, however, troops appear to have still found sufficient justification, whether through traditional morality or ideology, to continue the fight and rarely abandoned the conviction that theirs was a righteous cause.

The Myth

In hindsight, the most profound and enduring effect of the Wehrmacht's efforts to sanitize its image and demonstrate moral legitimacy was their impact on perceptions among the German public. The myth that the Wehrmacht's hands had remained "clean" would find near universal appeal in both West and East Germany well into the 1990s. Scholars have typically located its origins in the postwar era and identify former military leaders or political figures such as Konrad Adenauer as its first proponents. In fact, the primary pillars of the myth were firmly in place long before the last shots were fired. Its original authors were not politicians or high-ranking veterans but ordinary soldiers recounting wartime events to their loved ones from bunkers and foxholes across the front.

Officers and propagandists certainly played their part in the shaping of wartime public opinion. In cinemas across the country, audiences could see *Wochenschau* footage of their men being welcomed with flowers in the Baltic and Ukraine. PK journalists delivered over 80,000 press reports for distribution in the German media that emphasized the decency of the *Landser* and the savagery of his Soviet counterparts.[6] When a soldier fell, officers and chaplains reassured his family that he had stayed true to the highest soldierly principles and sacrificed his life for a worthy cause.

Far more influential in establishing the first draft of the Wehrmacht myth, however, were the letters that flooded the army's postal routes—some ten billion of which made their way from the front to the home front. With the authority of firsthand witnesses writing to a sympathetic audience, soldiers described their experiences and presented an image of themselves and their institution that papered over the harsh realities of the *Vernichtungskrieg*. Rather than describing the campaign in terms of criminal violence or genocidal intentions, servicemen emphasized their enemies' degeneracy, their own admirable qualities, and the dignity of their institution while offering their readers an array of arguments about the worthiness of their cause. When they did disclose misdeeds by their side, they managed to explain these as not just ideologically but morally necessary.

The myth would undergo several alterations after 1945, shaped by postwar trials, the dynamics of occupation, and the politics of the Cold War. All references to the Wehrmacht's deep attachment to the Nazi regime and its ideology were stripped away. The army's crimes, an open secret during the war, were likewise scrubbed from the record. Yet the basic story remained substantially the same: the ordinary Wehrmacht trooper had been a man of unimpeachable moral character who fought for a just cause against an evil enemy and was far more a victim than a perpetrator. Later changes generally amounted to variations on this core theme.

Reconceptualizing the origins of the Wehrmacht myth helps to explain the depth and longevity of its influence. For years on end, the German public had been fed a steady diet of news from the front that provided a grossly distorted picture of the army's conduct. The men and women who remained in the homeland were only too eager to accept what they read or were told, and the ties of kinship and friendship lent their sources a further air of credibility. By the time the Allied occupiers attempted to introduce a different version of events, the narratives spun by Wehrmacht personnel were already deeply embedded within German society. When veterans discussed their wartime service or politicians passed laws protecting former war criminals, they were simply confirming what the German public already "knew": that "their" men had held themselves to a high moral standard, even if others had not. Seen in this light, the myth appears less as a desperate attempt to retroactively whitewash the past than a continuation of a long-accepted story with deep psychological roots.

Beyond the Wehrmacht

Although it has highlighted the men who fought on the Eastern Front, the present investigation has important ramifications for our understanding of the Third Reich more generally. First, it indicates that much can be learned by recognizing the deep connection between the front and the home front in wartime Germany. These are typically studied in isolation but were in fact in constant contact, and each had important effects on the other.[7] Soldiers were influenced by the statements of public figures in the homeland, as well as the opinions of friends and family. Conversely, their writings strongly shaped how the latter viewed the conflict, likely even more than official propaganda sources. In terms of this relationship, one of the most significant findings is that Germany's wartime public may have been much better informed of the Wehrmacht's criminal activities than is commonly assumed, including the genocide of Eastern European Jews.

Second, this project challenges the common assumption that in order for Nazism to triumph in Germany society it was first necessary for other value systems to be extinguished or replaced. The Third Reich's leadership certainly worked toward this outcome, but in the short term the continued presence of alternative conceptions of right and wrong proved less of an obstacle to the Nazi agenda than might be expected. This was partly due to the fact that there was significant overlap between Nazism and other value systems, particularly the militaristic virtues many Germans had long held in high regard. Like the Wehrmacht, the Nazi regime also proved adept at pragmatically appropriating elements of these value systems to secure a broader base of support.

The transition from traditional morality to Nazi morality was not solely a top-down process in which the regime imposed its ideology on the German public, however. Closely examining the personal stories of Third Reich citizens reveals a complex process that differed greatly from individual to individual. Some embraced the biological ethic with ease. Others remained grounded in more traditional ways of thinking. Still others selectively adopted certain elements of the Nazi worldview while rejecting others. Whatever path they took, the road to barbarism was paved not only by ideology or social pressures but by the ability of ordinary Germans to continue to convince themselves of their own personal integrity and the moral acceptability—or even necessity—of their conduct.

Appendix

Biographical Details on the Core Sample of Soldiers

Biographical Details on the Core Sample of Soldiers

	NAME OF SOLDIER	SOURCE	SOURCE TYPE	LETTERS SENT	LETTERS RECEIVED
1	Adolf Dick	MSPT 3.2002.7565	letters	26	0
2	Anton Böhrer	MSPT 3.2002.0889	letters and diary	20	0
3	Dr. Konrad H. Jarausch	*Reluctant Accomplice*	letters	73	0
4	Eugen Altrogge	MSPT 3.2002.0210	letters	26	52
5	Franz Siebeler	MSPT 3.2002.1285	letters	184	0
6	Fritz Feierabend	BA-MA MSG 2/4048	letters	28	2
7	Günther Schmidt	MSPT 3.2002.0989	letters	51	0
8	Gustav Böker	MSPT 3.2002.0966	letters and diary	109	0
9	Hans Albring	MSPT 3.2002.0211	letters	52	26
10	Hans Roth	*Eastern Inferno*	diary	0	0
11	Hans Simon	MSPT 3.2002.1288	letters	196	3
12	Hans Wilhelm Sauer	MSPT 3.2002.1271	letters	67	0
13	Hans-Peter Eckener	MSPT 3.2002.0307	letters	83	41
14	Harald Hoffmann	MSPT 3.2002.0382	letters	65	0
15	Heinz Rahe	MSPT 3.2002.0985	letters	27	0
16	Heinz Sartorio	MSPT 3.2002.0827	letters	23	0
17	Helmut Nick	MSPT 3.2002.0274	letters	55	0
18	Hermann Henning	MSPT 3.2002.7217	letters	56	0
19	Johannes Hagemann	MSPT 3.2002.7234	letters	151	3
20	Johannes Lohr	MSPT 3.2010.1156	diary	0	0
21	Kurt Niemeyer	MSPT 3.2002.1750	letters	103	23
22	Rudi Haller	MSPT 3.2002.0368	letters	48	1

23	Rudolf Dietrich	MSPT 3.2002.7236	letters	56	0
24	Walter Neuser	MSPT 3.2002.0947	letters	106	0
25	Wilhelm Altmann	MSPT 3.2002.0201	letters	134	5
26	Wilhelm Bacher	MSPT 3.2002.1376	diary	0	0
27	Wilhelm Moldenhauser	*Im Funkwagen der Wehrmacht*	letters and diary	91	0
28	Willy Hagemann	MSPT 3.2002.7169	letters	133	26
29	Willy Nagel	MSPT 3.2002.0326	letters	55	16
30	Willy Reese	*A Stranger to Myself*	diary	0	0
	Summary/Totals			2,018	198

NAME OF SOLDIER	DATE RANGE EXAMINED	RECIPIENT(S)	BIRTH YEAR	AGE IN 1941
Adolf Dick	12.6.1941–1.1.1945	wife, child, father-in-law	1909	32
Anton Böhrer	4.1.1941–31.8.1943	parents, sisters	1915	26
Dr. Konrad H. Jarausch	12.8.1941–13.1.1942	wife, relatives, friends	1900	41
Eugen Altrogge	22.6.1941–29.12.1942	friend (Hans Albring)	1919	22
Franz Siebeler	12.1.1941–18.11.1942	parents, siblings	1919	22
Fritz Feierabend	8.7.1941–4.9.1943	wife	unknown	unknown
Günther Schmidt	11.4.1941–20.8.1942	parents	1920	21
Gustav Böker	21.6.1941–11.7.1943	family	1920	21
Hans Albring	5.7.1941–1.9.1942	friend (Eugen Altrogge)	1918	23
Hans Roth	12.6.1941–6.5.1943	N/A	1912	29
Hans Simon	17.6.1941–31.5.1944	parents, sister	1920	21
Hans Wilhelm Sauer	1.3.1941–17.1.1943	parents, sisters, grandmother	1915	26
Hans-Peter Eckener	23.1.1942–10.2.1944	parents	1910	31

(continued)

(continued)

NAME OF SOLDIER	DATE RANGE EXAMINED	RECIPIENT(S)	BIRTH YEAR	AGE IN 1941
Harald Hoffmann	15.6.1941–21.12.1941	parents and sister, grandmother, aunt	1919	22
Heinz Rahe	23.6.1941–6.7.1944	wife	1912	29
Heinz Sartorio	28.3.1942–11.3.1944	sister	1914	27
Helmut Nick	24.6.1941–21.4.1943	wife and son	1910	31
Hermann Henning	6.10.1940–2.2.1942	parents, relatives	1921	20
Johannes Hagemann	15.5.1941–4.1.1945	parents, siblings, friends	1919	22
Johannes Lohr	21.6.1941–15.7.1944	N/A	1897	44
Kurt Niemeyer	9.1.1941–7.1.1944	wife, daughter	1907	34
Rudi Haller	25.6.1941–19.10.1944	brother, sister-in-law, parents	1913	28
Rudolf Dietrich	15.8.1942–7.2.1944	wife, children	1912	29
Walter Neuser	12.6.1941–7.5.1942	parents and siblings	1915	26
Wilhelm Altmann	15.6.1941–13.3.1944	father and sister, brother	1919	22
Wilhelm Bacher	7.6.1941–24.10.1943	N/A	1899	42
Wilhelm Moldenhauser	1.4.1941–4.1.1943	wife	1906	35
Willy Hagemann	8.3.1941–28.9.1944	parents, siblings, friends, comrade's widow	1921	20
Willy Nagel	5.5.1941–23.12.1942	female friend	1921	20
Willy Reese	1941–12.1.1944	N/A	1921	20
Summary/Totals			Average: 1914	Average: 27

NAME OF SOLDIER	BIRTHPLACE	HOME/RECIPIENT ADDRESS	MARITAL STATUS (THROUGH 1945)	RELIGIOUS AFFILIATION
Adolf Dick	Hannover	Hannover	married	Protestant
Anton Böhrer	Höpfingen (Nordbaden)	Höpfingen (Nordbaden)	single	Roman Catholic
Dr. Konrad H. Jarausch	Berlin	Berlin	married	Protestant
Eugen Altrogge	Gelsenkirchen-Buer	Wehrmacht	single	Roman Catholic
Franz Siebeler	unknown	Nordhausen (Harz)	single	Roman Catholic
Fritz Feierabend	unknown	unknown	married	unknown
Günther Schmidt	Bischleben (district in Erfurt)	Berlin	single	Protestant
Gustav Böker	Oberg	Oberg	single	Roman Catholic
Hans Albring	Gelsenkirchen-Buer	Wehrmacht	single	Roman Catholic
Hans Roth	unknown	Frankfurt am Main	married	unknown
Hans Simon	Rostock	Malchow (Meckl.)	single	Protestant
Hans Wilhelm Sauer	Braunschweig	Coburg	single	Protestant
Hans-Peter Eckener	Stuttgart	Stuttgart	single	unknown
Harald Hoffmann	Berlin	Eberswalde	single	unknown
Heinz Rahe	Heiligendorf	Hamburg	married	Protestant
Heinz Sartorio	Berlin	Berlin	single	Protestant
Helmut Nick	Langenberg	unknown	married	Protestant
Hermann Henning	Trochtelfingen	Trochtelfingen	single	unknown
Johannes Hagemann	Fleckeby	Fleckeby	single	Protestant
Johannes Lohr	Berlin-Lichtenberg	unknown	married	Protestant
Kurt Niemeyer	Serba (Thür.)	Serba (Thür.)	married	Protestant

(continued)

(continued)

NAME OF SOLDIER	BIRTHPLACE	HOME/RECIPIENT ADDRESS	MARITAL STATUS (THROUGH 1945)	RELIGIOUS AFFILIATION
Rudi Haller	Hattingen	Hattingen	married	Roman Catholic
Rudolf Dietrich	Dortmund	Dortmund	married	Roman Catholic
Walter Neuser	Beeskow	Beeskow (Brandenbg.)	single	Protestant
Wilhelm Altmann	Valbert (Westfalen)	Valbert (Westfalen)	single	Protestant
Wilhelm Bacher	Siersleben	Pirna	married	Protestant
Wilhelm Moldenhauser	Nordstemmen	Nordstemmen	married	Protestant
Willy Hagemann	Fleckeby	Fleckeby	single	Protestant
Willy Nagel	Bayern	Bayern	single	Roman Catholic
Willy Reese	Duisburg	Duisburg	single	unknown
Summary/Totals			12 married, 18 single	16 Protestant, 8 Catholic, 6 unknown

NAME OF SOLDIER	HAS CHILDREN? (TO 1945)	EDUCATION	NAZI AFFILIATIONS
Adolf Dick	yes	Realgymnasium[1]	unknown
Anton Böhrer	no	unknown	unknown
Dr. Konrad H. Jarausch	yes	University, PhD (German literature, history, theology)	unknown
Eugen Altrogge	no	Abitur[2]	none
Franz Siebeler	no	Realschule (similar to Gymnasium)	unknown
Fritz Feierabend	unknown	unknown	unknown
Günther Schmidt	no	Abitur	unknown
Gustav Böker	no	Mittlere Reife (Abitur equivalent)	unknown
Hans Albring	no	Abitur	none
Hans Roth	yes	unknown	unknown

Name		Education	Nazi affiliation
Hans Simon	no	Abitur, Hochschulstudium[3] (law)	RAD
Hans Wilhelm Sauer	no	Abitur, university studies (theology)	unknown
Hans-Peter Eckener	no	Abitur, Hochschulstudium (architecture)	none
Harald Hoffmann	no	Abitur, Hochschulstudium (philosophy, German), doctoral study	HJ, N.S.Dt.St.B, RAD
Heinz Rahe	yes	Abitur, university studies (theology)	SA
Heinz Sartorio	no	unknown	unknown
Helmut Nick	unknown	Volksschule[4]	NSDAP
Hermann Henning	no	Abitur	none
Johannes Hagemann	no	Volksschule	yes (unspecified)
Johannes Lohr	yes	Gemeindeschule	unknown
Kurt Niemeyer	yes	Volksschule	unknown
Rudi Haller	yes	Volksschule	unknown
Rudolf Dietrich	no	Mittlere Reife (Abitur equivalent)	unknown
Walter Neuser	no	unknown	NSDAP
Wilhelm Altmann	no	Volksschule	HJ
Wilhelm Bacher	yes	Abitur, Hochschulstudium, doctoral studies (law)	NSDAP (1934 only)
Wilhelm Moldenhauser	yes	Gymnasium	SA (1937 on)
Willy Hagemann	no	Staatliche Aufbauschule, Abitur	unknown
Willy Nagel	no	Gymnasium	unknown
Willy Reese	no	Abitur (1939)	none
Summary/Totals	9 yes, 19 no, 2 unknown	Highest Educational Level: 6 elementary or equivalent, 4 high school, 9 university entrance exam, 4 university, 3 doctoral study	9 with known Nazi affiliations. The true number is likely higher.

(continued)

(continued)

NAME OF SOLDIER	JOB TRAINING/CAREER BEFORE WAR'S OUTBREAK	DATE CONSCRIPTED/VOLUNTEERED
Adolf Dick	clerk (auditor)	August 28, 1939
Anton Böhrer	gardener	January 1941
Dr. Konrad H. Jarausch	secondary school teacher	1939
Eugen Altrogge	active in Catholic youth movement	1937
Franz Siebeler	banker	October 3, 1940
Fritz Feierabend	unknown	unknown
Günther Schmidt	commercial apprenticeship (industrial clerk)	October 1940
Gustav Böker	commercial apprenticeship (savings bank)	August 21, 1939
Hans Albring	unknown	1939
Hans Roth	graphic design	mid-1930s
Hans Simon	Reichsarbeitsdienst (1938)	1938
Hans Wilhelm Sauer	unknown	September 1, 1939
Hans-Peter Eckener	graphic designer/illustrator	December 4, 1940
Harald Hoffmann	Reichsarbeitsdienst, research associate at Berlin University	unknown
Heinz Rahe	military service, seminarian, assistant pastor	September 1939
Heinz Sartorio	insurance salesman	around 1942
Helmut Nick	bank official	around 1939
Hermann Henning	unknown	October 1940
Johannes Hagemann	agriculture (food retail)	October 3, 1940
Johannes Lohr	salesman, post office clerk	August, 1930
Kurt Niemeyer	coachman (lumber mill)	unknown
Rudi Haller	assistant painter	October 1939
Rudolf Dietrich	confectioner's apprentice, master confectioner	unknown
Walter Neuser	banking apprenticeship, accountant	1938

Wilhelm Altmann	baker's apprentice, baker	1939
Wilhelm Bacher	engineer in WWI, legal assistant, assistant mayor, mayor, legal work	September 1939
Wilhelm Moldenhauser	small business owner (colonial wares shop)	1940
Willy Hagemann	none	October 1, 1940 (volunteer)
Willy Nagel	unknown	October, 1939 (volunteer)
Willy Reese	banking apprenticeship, writer	February 1941
Summary/Totals		

NAME OF SOLDIER	UNIT WHEN BARBAROSSA BEGINS	UNIT 2 (IF APPLICABLE)	UNIT 3 (IF APPLICABLE)
Adolf Dick	96th Inf.Div., Pz.Jg.Abt.196		
Anton Böhrer	221th Inf.Div., Art.Rgt.221 (till 25.8.1942)	294th Inf.Div., Art.Rgt.294 (25.8.1942–17.8.1944)	387th Inf.Div., San.Kp.387 (from 17.8.1944)
Dr. Konrad H. Jarausch	286th Sich.Div., Dulag 203		
Eugen Altrogge	327th Inf.Div., Inf.Rgt.597	190th Inf.Div., Inf.Rgt.591	323rd Inf.Div., Inf.Rgt.591 (from 10/1942)
Franz Siebeler	14th Pz.Div., Art.Rgt.4		
Fritz Feierabend	unknown, possibly 7th Pz.Div. or 17th Pz.Div.		
Günther Schmidt	76th Inf.Div., Inf.Rgt.203		
Gustav Böker	111th Inf.Div., Pz.Jg.Abt.111, schw.Heeres-Pz.Jg.Abt. 661		
Hans Albring	VI A.K., Korps-Nachr.-Abt.46 (until May 1942)	Inf.Rgt. 199 or 689	
Hans Roth	229th Inf. Div., Pz.Jg.Abt. 299		
Hans Simon	12th Inf.Div., Inf.Rgt.27		
Hans Wilhelm Sauer	340th Inf.Div., Stab III of Gren.Rgt.694		
Hans-Peter Eckener	205th Inf.Div., Art.Rgt.205		
Harald Hoffmann	23rd Inf.Div., Inf.Rgt.67		
Heinz Rahe	13th Pz.Div., Pz.Gren.Rgt.66 (1941–1942)	Krad-Schtz.Btl.43[5] (1942, possibly 1943)	Sich.Rgt.197 (1943)

(continued)

(continued)

NAME OF SOLDIER	UNIT WHEN BARBAROSSA BEGINS	UNIT 2 (IF APPLICABLE)	UNIT 3 (IF APPLICABLE)
Heinz Sartorio	2nd Pz.Armee, Br.Kol.98[6]		
Helmut Nick	43rd A.K., Korps-Nachr.Abt.443		
Hermann Henning	123rd Inf.Div., Inf.Rgt.415		
Johannes Hagemann	290th Inf.Div., Art.Rgt.		
Johannes Lohr	Feldpostamt 900		
Kurt Niemeyer	Divz.b.V.409, Ld.Schtz.Btl.643[7]		
Rudi Haller	227th Inf.Div., Inf.Div.Nachr.Abt.227		
Rudolf Dietrich	34th Inf.Div., Bäck-Kp.34[8]	34th Inf.Div., Verw.-Kp.34[9]	
Walter Neuser	Art.Rgt.59 (Heerestruppe)		
Wilhelm Altmann	227th Inf.Div., Gren.Rgt.412		
Wilhelm Bacher	94th Inf.Div., Pi.Btl. 194 (1939–1942)	30th Inf.Div., Pi.Btl. 30 (1942–1943)	Pi.Rgt. 519
Wilhelm Moldenhauser	60th Inf.Div.		
Willy Hagemann	290th Inf.Div., Inf.Rgt.503	290th Inf.Div., Inf.Rgt.501	
Willy Nagel	20th Pz.Div., Pz.Rgt.21		
Willy Reese	95th Inf.Div., 279.Rgt., 14.Kompanie		
Summary/Totals			

NAME OF SOLDIER	LAST KNOWN RANK	EQUIVALENT RANK IN U.S. ARMY	SPECIFIC DUTIES
Adolf Dick	Hauptfeldwebel	master sergeant	anti-tank gun crew
Anton Böhrer	Hauptwachtmeister	master sergeant	company sergeant major ("Spiess")
Dr. Konrad H. Jarausch	Feldwebel	staff sergeant	POW camp kitchen overseer
Eugen Altrogge	Leutnant	2nd Lieutenant	platoon leader

Name	Rank	Duties
Franz Siebeler	Gefreiter	private first class	motorcycle courier, headquarters work
Fritz Feierabend	unknown	unknown	unknown
Günther Schmidt	Gefreiter	private first class	unknown
Gustav Böker	Gefreiter	private first class	motorcycle courier, bookkeeper
Hans Albring	Gefreiter	private first class	radioman
Hans Roth	Feldwebel	staff sergeant	anti-tank recon, cartographer
Hans Simon	Unteroffizier	noncommissioned officer	gunner, gun leader (June, 1942–February, 1943)
Hans Wilhelm Sauer	Oberleutnant	1st Lieutenant	leader of a company, battalion leader
Hans-Peter Eckener	unknown	unknown	radio man, illustrator, artilleryman
Harald Hoffmann	Gefreiter	private first class	unknown
Heinz Rahe	Oberleutnant	1st Lieutenant	adjutant
Heinz Sartorio	Obergefreiter	private first class	engineering and transport work
Helmut Nick	Hauptfeldwebel	master sergeant	company sergeant major ("Spiess")
Hermann Henning	Obersoldat	private first class	machine gunner
Johannes Hagemann	Obergefreiter	private first class	takes care of horses, in regiment staff
Johannes Lohr	Leutnant	2nd Lieutenant	army post office
Kurt Niemeyer	Schütz	private	transport and supply work
Rudi Haller	unknown	unknown	communications, aid to staff sergeant (May 1942)
Rudolf Dietrich	Stabsgefreiter	private first class	baker
Walter Neuser	Unteroffizier	corporal	artilleryman, supply duties
Wilhelm Altmann	Feldwebel	staff sergeant	courier (1941)
Wilhelm Bacher	Major d. R.	Major	regiment commander
Wilhelm Moldenhauser	Gefreiter	private first class	mobile radio
Willy Hagemann	Hauptmann	Captain	courier (1941), leader of a company (1943)
Willy Nagel	unknown	unknown	tank radioman
Willy Reese	unknown	unknown	field gun crew
Summary/Totals		24 enlisted men or noncommissioned officers; 6 commissioned officers[10]	

(continued)

(continued)

NAME OF SOLDIER	PROXIMITY TO FRONT	FATE
Adolf Dick	on the front	returned home, American captivity till 21.5.1945
Anton Böhrer	behind the lines	missing after 17.8.1944
Dr. Konrad H. Jarausch	behind the lines	fell 27.1.1942
Eugen Altrogge	on the front	missing 1/1943
Franz Siebeler	occasionally on the front	fell 12.6.1942
Fritz Feierabend	on the front	returned home 1945
Günther Schmidt	on the front	fell 4.9.1942
Gustav Böker	on the front	fell 22.7.1943
Hans Albring	typically behind the lines	fell 1/1944
Hans Roth	on the front	missing (25.61944), later declared dead
Hans Simon	on the front	missing 1944
Hans Wilhelm Sauer	on the front	fell 8.2.1943
Hans-Peter Eckener	intermittently on the front	fell 4.12.1944
Harald Hoffmann	on the front	fell 12/1941
Heinz Rahe	typically on the front	returned home, American captivity till 18.6.1946
Heinz Sartorio	behind the lines	missing around 1944
Helmut Nick	on the front	returned home
Hermann Henning	on the front	fell 9.2.1942
Johannes Hagemann	occasionally on the front	returned home, Russian captivity 9.5.1945–1953/54
Johannes Lohr	behind the lines	returned home, American captivity 4/1945–6/1945
Kurt Niemeyer	behind the lines	returned home
Rudi Haller	typically behind the lines	returned home 1949
Rudolf Dietrich	behind the lines	returned home, American captivity 1945–1947

Walter Neuser	behind the lines	fell 10.5.1942
Wilhelm Altmann	frequently on the front	Russian captivity, returned home 1946
Wilhelm Bacher	behind the lines	fell 22.4.1944
Wilhelm Moldenhauser	behind the lines	missing after 4.1.1943
Willy Hagemann	on the front	returned home
Willy Nagel	on the front	fell 24.12.1942
Willy Reese	on the front	fell 6/1944
Summary/Totals		19 dead or missing; 11 returned home

Sources: Museumstiftung Post und Telekommunikation; Bundesarchiv-Militärarchiv; published primary works (see bibliography); Lexikon der Wehrmacht (http://www.lexikon-der-wehrmacht.de/).

1. Gymnasium: high school.
2. Abitur: university entrance exam.
3. Hochschulstudium: university studies.
4. Volksschule: elementary/grammar school.
5. Krad-Schtz.Btl. (Krad-Schützen Bataillone): light motorized infantry battalion.
6. Br.Kol. (Brückenbau Kolonne): bridge-building column.
7. l.d.Schtz.Btl. (Landesschützen Bataillone): security/occupation battalion.
8. Bäck.-Kp. (Bäckereikompanie): bakery company.
9. Verw.-Kp. (Verwaltungsdienste Kompanie): administrative services company.
10. Among the officers, one (Willy Hagemann) began as a private.

NOTES

Introduction

1. Although "Wehrmacht" properly refers to all branches of the Third Reich's military, it will be used throughout this work to denote the ground forces of the German Army, since they played by far the largest role in the campaign.

2. See Christian Hartmann, *Wehrmacht im Ostkrieg: Front und militärisches Hinterland 1941/42* (München: R. Oldenbourg Verlag, 2009), 789. As Hartmann notes, by 1945 roughly 70,000 villages and 1,710 towns and cities had been reduced to rubble and 26.6 million Soviet citizens lay dead, including 3 million POWs and 2.4 million Jews.

3. To comply with German law and archival regulations, pseudonymous or abbreviated last names have been adopted in some cases.

4. Heinz Sartorio to Elly (sister), 4.8.1942, Museumsstiftung Post und Telekommunikation (hereafter: MSPT) 3.2002.0827. The German dating system (dd. mm.yyyy) will be employed for German sources.

5. Heinz Sartorio to Elly, 28.3.1942, MSPT 3.2002.0827.

6. Heinz Sartorio to Elly, 26.5.1942, MSPT 3.2002.0827.

7. Heinz Sartorio to sister, 26.4.1942, MSPT 3.2002.0827.

8. See Ortwin Buchbender and Reinhold Sterz, eds., *Das Andere Gesicht des Krieges: Deutsche Feldpostbriefe 1939–1945* (München: Verlag C. H. Beck, 1982), 13–16; Stephen Fritz, *Frontsoldaten: The German Soldier in World War II* (University Press of Kentucky, 1995). The remaining thirty billion were sent from the home front to the front.

9. On the development of the Wehrmacht myth, see especially Wolfram Wette, *The Wehrmacht: History, Myth, Reality*, trans. Deborah Lucas Schneider (Cambridge, MA: Harvard University Press, 2006), 195–291; Klaus Naumann, "The 'Unblemished' Wehrmacht: The Social History of a Myth," in *War of Extermination: The German Military in World War II 1941–1944*, ed. Hannes Heer and Klaus Naumann, trans. Roy Shelton (New York: Klaus Naumann, 2000), 417–29; Hannes Heer et al., eds., *The Discursive Construction of History: Remembering the Wehrmacht's War of Annihilation* (Basingstoke: Palgrave Macmillan, 2008); Kurt Pätzold, *Ihr waret die besten Soldaten: Ursprung und Geschichte einer Legende* (Leipzig: Militzk Verlag, 2000).

10. Quotation from Wette, *The Wehrmacht*, 205.

11. On the war crimes issue, see especially Norbert Frei, *Adenauer's Germany and the Nazi Past: The Politics of Amnesty and Integration*, trans. Joel Golb (New York: Columbia University Press, 2002), 93–234.

12. See, especially, Christina Morina, "Legacies of Stalingrad: The Eastern Front War and the Politics of Memory in Divided Germany, 1943–1989" (PhD diss., College Park, University of Maryland, 2007), 329–55.

13. See, for example, Basil Liddell Hart, *The Other Side of the Hill: Germany's Generals. Their Rise and Fall, with Their Own Account of Military Events 1939–1945*, revised ed. (London: Cassell, 1951); Gordon A. Craig, *The Politics of the Prussian Army 1640–1945* (Oxford: Clarendon Press, 1964); Robert J. O'Neill, *The German Army and the Nazi Party, 1933–1939* (London: Cassell, 1966). On the myth's influence on American popular memory, see Ronald Smelser and Edward Davies, *The Myth of the Eastern Front: The Nazi-Soviet War in American Popular Culture* (New York: Cambridge University Press, 2008).

14. See, especially, Manfred Messerschmidt, *Die Wehrmacht im NS-Staat: Zeit der Indoktrination* (Hamburg: R. v. Decker's Verlag, 1969); Klaus-Jürgen Müller, *Das Heer und Hitler: Armee und nationalsozialistisches Regime, 1933–1940* (Stuttgart: Deutsche Verlags-Anstalt, 1969).

15. Christian Streit, *Keine Kameraden: Die Wehrmacht und die sowjetischen Kriegsgefangenen 1941–1945* (Stuttgart: Deutsche Verlags-Anstalt, 1978).

16. See, for instance, Jürgen Förster, "The German Army and the Ideological War against the Soviet Union," in *The Policies of Genocide: Jews and Soviet Prisoners of War in Nazi Germany*, ed. Gerhard Hirschfeld (Boston: The German Historical Institute, 1986).

17. See Helmut Krausnick, *Die Truppe des Weltanschauungskrieges: Die Einsatzgruppen der Sicherheitspolizei und des SD 1938–1942* (Stuttgart: Deutsche Verlags-Anstalt, 1981).

18. Omer Bartov, *The Eastern Front, 1941–45, German Troops and the Barbarisation of Warfare* (Hong Kong: MacMillan, 1985); Omer Bartov, *Hitler's Army: Soldiers, Nazis, and War in the Third Reich* (New York: Oxford University Press, 1991); Fritz, *Frontsoldaten*.

19. For an overview of this historiographical shift, see Ben Shepherd, "The Clean Wehrmacht, the War of Extermination, and Beyond," *The Historical Journal* 52 (2009): 455–73.

20. See Hamburger Institut für Sozialforschung, *Verbrechen der Wehrmacht: Dimensionen des Vernichtungskrieges 1941–1944* (Hamburg: Hamburger Edition, 2002); Hannes Heer and Jane Caplan, "The Difficulty of Ending a War: Reactions to the Exhibition 'War of Extermination: Crimes of the Wehrmacht 1941 to 1944,'" *History Workshop Journal*, no. 46 (1998): 182–203.

21. In support of this point, see Fritz, *Frontsoldaten*, 241; Sönke Neitzel and Harald Welzer, *Soldaten: Protokolle vom Kämpfen, Töten und Sterben* (Frankfurt am Main: S. Fischer, 2011), 201. More recently, Nicholas Stargardt has demonstrated that both civilians and soldiers alike believed they were waging a just war. See Nicholas Stargardt, *The German War: A Nation Under Arms, 1939–1945; Citizens and Soldiers* (New York: Basic Books, 2017).

22. Wilhelm Moldenhauser to Erika (wife), 17.9.1941, *Im Funkwagen der Wehrmacht*.

23. Franz Siebeler to parents and siblings, 23.11.1941, MSPT 3.2002.1285.

24. Willy Hagemann to Kressen, 3.9.1944, MSPT 3.2002.7169.

25. The importance of this question has been highlighted by Timothy Schroer in his study of SS camp guards. See Timothy L. Schroer, "Civilization, Barbarism, and the Ethos of Self-Control among the Perpetrators," *German Studies Review* 35, no. 1 (February 2012): 33–54.

26. See Michael Walzer, *Just and Unjust Wars: A Moral Argument with Historical Illustrations* (Allen Lane, 1978), 127.

27. See Richard Overy, *Why the Allies Won* (London: Jonathan Cape, 1995); Michael Burleigh, *Moral Combat: Good and Evil in World War II* (New York: HarperCollins, 2011); Peter Haas, "Militärische Ethik im Totalen Krieg," in *Ideologie und Moral im Nationalsozialismus*, ed. Wolfgang Bialas and Lothar Fritze (Göttingen: Vandenhoeck & Ruprecht, 2014), 177–92.

28. Regarding the first point, this book relies on advances made by Raphael Gross. See Raphael Gross, *Anständig geblieben: Nationalsozialistische Moral* (Frankfurt am Main: S. Fischer, 2010).

29. Although they are sometimes considered separate concepts, "morality" and "ethics" will be used here interchangeably for the sake of simplicity.

30. On the definitions of these terms, see André Mineau, *Operation Barbarossa: Ideology and Ethics against Human Dignity* (Amsterdam: Rodopi, 2004), 8–10; Wolfgang Bialas, "Nationalsozialistische Ethik und Moral: Konzepte, Probleme, offene Fragen," in Bialas and Fritze, *Ideologie und Moral*, 32.

31. See Michael Burleigh and Wolfgang Wippermann, *The Racial State: Germany 1933–1945* (Cambridge: Cambridge University Press, 1993). For a critical analysis of this paradigm, see Devin Pendas, Mark Roseman, and Richard Wetzell, eds., *Beyond the Racial State: Rethinking Nazi Germany* (Cambridge: Cambridge University Press, 2017).

32. See Peter Fritzsche, *Life and Death in the Third Reich* (Cambridge, MA: Belknap Press, 2008); Götz Aly, *Hitler's Beneficiaries: Plunder, Racial War, and the Nazi Welfare State*, trans. Jefferson Chase (NY: Metropolitan Books, 2006).

33. For example, see Edward Westermann, *Hitler's Police Battalions: Enforcing Racial War in the East* (Lawrence: University Press of Kansas, 2005); David Cesarani, *Becoming Eichmann: Rethinking the Life, Crimes, and Trial of a "Desk Murderer"* (Cambridge, MA: Da Capo Press, 2006).

34. See Claudia Koonz, *The Nazi Conscience* (Cambridge, MA: Harvard University Press, 2003); Wolfgang Bialas, *Moralische Ordnungen des Nationalsozialismus* (Göttingen: Vandenhoeck & Ruprecht, 2014); Richard Weikart, *Hitler's Ethic: The Nazi Pursuit of Evolutionary Progress* (New York: Palgrave MacMillan, 2009); Gross, *Anständig geblieben*.

35. Koonz, *Nazi Conscience*.

36. Koonz, *Nazi Conscience*.

37. Gross, *Anständig geblieben*. Bialas' interpretation falls between these two poles, acknowledging both the newness of the Nazi biological ethic and its partial reliance on older values. See Bialas, "Nationalsozialistische Ethik und Moral."

38. See, especially, Walter Manoschek, ed., *Die Wehrmacht Im Rassenkrieg: Der Vernichtungskrieg Hinter Der Front* (Vienna: Picus, 1996); Bartov, *Hitler's Army*; Jürgen Förster, *Die Wehrmacht im NS-Staat: Eine strukturgeschichtliche Analyse* (Munich: Oldenbourg Wissenschaftsverlag, 2007); Bryce Sait, *The Indoctrination of the Wehrmacht:*

Nazi Ideology and the War Crimes of the German Military (New York: Berghahn Books, 2019).

39. See, especially, Neitzel and Welzer, *Soldaten*, 298–99; Hartmann, *Wehrmacht im Ostkrieg*, 471; Felix Römer, *Kameraden: Die Wehrmacht von Innen* (München: Piper, 2012), 111–57.

40. See Ben Shepherd, *War in the Wild East: The German Army and Soviet Partisans* (Cambridge, MA: Harvard University Press, 2004); David W. Wildermuth, "Widening the Circle: General Weikersthal and the War of Annihilation, 1941–42," *Central European History* 45 (2012): 306–24; Hartmann, *Wehrmacht im Ostkrieg*; Jeff Rutherford, *Combat and Genocide on the Eastern Front: The German Infantry's War, 1941–1944* (Cambridge, MA: Cambridge University Press, 2014).

41. A partial exception here is Thomas Kühne, *Kameradschaft: Die Soldaten des nationalsozialistischen Krieges und das 20. Jahrhundert* (Göttingen: Vandenhoeck & Ruprecht, 2006). Kühne explains how traditional ideas of comradeship evolved toward the *Volksgemeinschaft* envisioned by the Nazis and how the creation of an inward-looking community became an engine for violence against outsiders.

42. Mineau, *Operation Barbarossa*, 11.

43. See, especially, Waitman Beorn, *Marching into Darkness: The Wehrmacht and the Holocaust in Belarus* (Cambridge, MA: Harvard University Press, 2014); Robert Loeffel, "Soldiers and Terror: Re-Evaluating the Complicity of the Wehrmacht in Nazi Germany," *German History* 27, no. 4 (2009): 514–30. Also influential in this discussion is Christopher Browning, *Ordinary Men: Reserve Police Battalion 101 and the Final Solution in Poland* (New York: HarperCollins, 1992).

44. See Joel Cooper, *Cognitive Dissonance: Fifty Years of a Classic Theory* (London: Sage Publications, 2013).

45. See Bartov, *The Eastern Front*, 6; Haas, "Militärische Ethik im Totalen Krieg"; Koonz, *Nazi Conscience*, 221–52; Sait, *The Indoctrination of the Wehrmacht*, 169; Walter Manoscheck, *"Serbien Ist Judenfrei": Militärische Besatzungspolitik Und Judenvernichtung in Serbien 1941/42* (Munich: Oldenbourg, 1993).

46. Hannes Heer, "How Amorality Became Normality: Reflections on the Mentality of German Soldiers on the Eastern Front," in *War of Extermination: The German Military in World War II 1941–1944*, ed. Hannes Heer and Klaus Naumann, trans. Roy Shelton (New York: Berghahn Books, 2000), 329–44.

47. See, especially, Wette, *The Wehrmacht*, 195–250; Morina, "Legacies of Stalingrad"; Heer and Caplan, "The Difficulty of Ending a War," 189; Naumann, "The 'Unblemished' Wehrmacht"; Pätzold, *Ihr waret die besten Soldaten*. Pätzold has speculated that the myth began during the war, but he nevertheless begins his account of its history with Germany's surrender.

48. Another reason for ending in 1944 is the fact that many men in the core sample did not survive into 1945.

49. Along with documents from the army's highest levels of leadership, selected sources from sixty-four infantry or artillery divisions, twelve panzer divisions, twenty corps, and fifteen armies were consulted.

50. Many edited volumes contain small excerpts or individual letters from hundreds of different soldiers. See, for example, Buchbender and Sterz, eds., *Das Andere Gesicht des Krieges*; Walter Bähr and Hans W. Bähr, eds., *Kriegsbriefe gefallene Studenten, 1939–1945* (Tübingen: Rainer Wunderlich Verlag, 1952); Franz Schneider and Charles

Gullans, trans., *Last Letters from Stalingrad* (New York: William Morrow, 1962). Volumes like these have been consulted here to confirm general patterns in soldiers' letters but were not extensively used.

51. See Christoph Rass, *"Menschenmaterial": Deutsche Soldaten an der Ostfront. Innenansichten einer Infanteriedivision 1939–1945* (Paderborn: Ferdinand Schöningh, 2003), 88–134.

52. Precise information for the others was unavailable, but their ages suggest that a fair number likely had served in the Reich Labour Service or been Hitler Youth members. See Sait, *The Indoctrination of the Wehrmacht*, 47.

53. For more precise demographic data on the book's sample, see the appendix.

54. The most likely explanation is that soldiers were simply unable to carry with them all the letters they received throughout the war, or that such letters were frequently lost to enemy action or upon a soldier's death.

55. Among the latter, the diary of Willy Reese was explicitly intended for publication, however, which makes it in some respects more akin to a series of public-facing letters.

56. Generally speaking, diaries tend to describe day-to-day happenings in more detail, contain additional moments of introspection, and provide fuller accounts of combat activities than letters.

57. Those most frequently consulted were Klaus Latzel, *Deutsche Soldaten— nationalsozialistsicher Krieg? Kriegserlebnis—Kriegserfahrung 1939–1945* (Paderborn: Ferdinand Schöningh, 1998); Martin Humburg, *Das Gesicht des Krieges: Feldpostbriefe von Wehrmachtssoldaten aus der Sowjetunion 1941–1944* (Opladen/Wiesbaden: Westdeutscher Verlag, 1998); Kühne, *Kameradschaft*; Fritz, *Frontsoldaten*.

58. See PzAOK3 Ic/AO (Abw III) Nr. 647/43 geh., Betr.: Feldpostprüfung, Bundesarchiv-Militärarchiv (hereafter BA-MA) RH 21-3 470. On censorship see Latzel, *Deutsche Soldaten*, 25–30; Humburg, *Gesicht des Krieges*, 17–18; Buchbender and Sterz, *Andere Gesicht*, 1982, 13–24.

59. See Stephen Fritz, "'We Are Trying . . . to Change the Face of the World'— Ideology and Motivation in the Wehrmacht on the Eastern Front: The View from Below," *The Journal of Military History* 60, no. 4 (October 1996): 686; Sait, *The Indoctrination of the Wehrmacht*, 160–61.

60. Latzel, *Deutsche Soldaten*, 130. For further insight on the interpretation of letters, see Klaus Latzel, "Vom Kriegserlebnis zur Kriegserfahrung: Theoretische und Methodische Überlegungen zur Erfahrungsgeschichtlichen Untersuchung von Feldpostbriefen," *Militärgeschichtliche Mitteilungen* 56, no. 1 (1997): 1–30; Ebert Veit and Thomas Jander, eds., *Schreiben im Krieg—Schreiben vom Krieg: Feldpost im Zeitalter der Weltkriege* (Essen: Klartext Verlag, 2011).

61. See Michael Bamberg, "Narrative Discourse and Identities," in *Narratologia: Narratology Beyond Literary Criticism: Mediality, Disciplinarity*, ed. Jan Christoph Meister, Tom Kindt, and Wilhelm Schernus (Walter de Gruyter, 2005), 213–37.

62. See, especially, Albert Bandura and Claudio Barbaranelli, "Mechanisms of Moral Disengagement in the Exercise of Moral Agency," *Journal of Personality and Social Psychology* 71, no. 2 (1996): 364–74; Jo-Ann Tsang, "Moral Rationalization and the Integration of Situational Factors and Psychological Processes in Immoral Behavior," *Review of General Psychology* 6, no. 1 (2002): 25–50.

63. Claude Steele, "The Psychology of Self-Affirmation: Sustaining the Integrity of the Self," *Advances in Experimental Social Psychology* 21 (1988): 261–302.

64. See Walzer, *Just and Unjust Wars*; Barrie Paskins and Michael Dockrill, *The Ethics of War* (Minneapolis: University of Minnesota Press, 1979); Steven P. Lee, *Ethics and War: An Introduction* (New York: Cambridge University Press, 2012); David Rodin and Henry Shue, eds., *Just and Unjust Warriors: The Moral and Legal Status of Soldiers* (New York: Oxford University Press, 2008), among many others.

1. Honorable Self and Villainous Other

1. Howard Kennedy, "Eisenhower Gives View on German Soldiers," *Stars and Stripes*, January 24, 1951.

2. Wolfram Wette, *The Wehrmacht: History, Myth, Reality*, trans. Deborah Lucas Schneider (Cambridge, MA: Harvard University Press, 2006), 236–37; Ronald Smelser and Edward Davies, *The Myth of the Eastern Front: The Nazi-Soviet War in American Popular Culture* (New York: Cambridge University Press, 2008), 72–73.

3. Here, they endeavored to satisfy what social psychologists have identified as a near-universal human desire to be seen as a "good" person. See Claude Steele, "The Psychology of Self-Affirmation: Sustaining the Integrity of the Self," *Advances in Experimental Social Psychology* 21 (1988): 261–302.

4. See André Mineau, *Operation Barbarossa: Ideology and Ethics against Human Dignity* (Amsterdam: Rodopi, 2004), 95–106.

5. See Felix Römer, *Kameraden: Die Wehrmacht von Innen* (München: Piper, 2012), 71; Mineau, *Operation Barbarossa*, 10–11.

6. Here, this book offers empirical support for the theories put forth by Mineau, *Operation Barbarossa*, 95.

7. See Felix Römer, *Kameraden*, 114–15; Klaus Latzel, *Deutsche Soldaten—nationalsozialitsicher Krieg? Kriegserlebnis—Kriegserfahrung 1939–1945* (Paderborn: Ferdinand Schöningh, 1998), 284–310; Peter Haas, "Militärische Ethik im Totalen Krieg," in *Ideologie und Moral im Nationalsozialismus*, ed. Wolfgang Bialas and Lothar Fritze (Göttingen: Vandenhoeck & Ruprecht, 2014), 177. Haas defines this code as a set of ideas governing "correct behavior" for military professionals that stressed concepts like "chivalry" and "gallantry."

8. See George E. Mosse, *Nationalism and Sexuality: Respectability and Abnormal Sexuality in Modern Europe* (New York: Howard Fertig, 1985); Wolfgang Bialas, "Nationalsozialistische Ethik und Moral: Konzepte, Probleme, offene Fragen," in Bialas and Fritze, *Ideologie und Moral*, 32; Manuel Frey, *Der reinliche Bürger: Entstehung und Verbreitung bürgerlicher Tugenden in Deutschland, 1760–1860* (Göttingen: Vandenhoeck & Ruprecht, 1997).

9. *"Bildung,"* sometimes translated as "education," describes a life of self-cultivation—a norm that came to be highly prized by the German middle class. On the meaning of *"Kultur,"* which denoted a people's artistic, intellectual, and cultural depth, see Vejas Gabriel Liulevicius, *The German Myth of the East: 1800 to the Present* (New York: Oxford University Press, 2009), 47–48.

10. Isabel Hull, *Absolute Destruction: Military Culture and the Practices of War in Imperial Germany* (Ithaca, NY: Cornell University Press, 2005). Also see Jeff Rutherford, *Combat and Genocide on the Eastern Front: The German Infantry's War, 1941–1944* (Cambridge, MA: Cambridge University Press, 2014), 7–10.

11. See Introduction.

12. See Richard Weikart, *Hitler's Ethic: The Nazi Pursuit of Evolutionary Progress* (New York: Palgrave Macmillan, 2009), 18; Wolfgang Bialas, *Moralische Ordnungen des National-sozialismus* (Göttingen: Vandenhoeck & Ruprecht, 2014), 233–72.

13. Karen Hagemann, "Of 'Manly Valor' and 'German Honor': Nation, War, and Masculinity in the Age of the Prussian Uprising against Napoleon," *Central European History*, 30, no. 2 (1997): 187–220.

14. Römer, *Kameraden*, 114–15; Wolfram Wette, *Militarismus in Deutschland: Geschichte einer kriegerischen Kultur* (Darmstadt: Wissenschaftliche Buchgesellschaft, 2008).

15. On these developments see Hull, *Absolute Destruction*, especially 19–29 and 117–29.

16. See John Horne and Alan Kramer, *German Atrocities, 1914: A History of Denial* (New Haven, CT: Yale University Press, 2001).

17. See Dennis Showalter, "Comrades, Enemies, Victims: The Prussian/German Army and the Ostvölker," in *The Germans and the East*, ed. Charles Ingrao and Franz A. J. Szabo (West Lafayette, IN: Purdue University Press, 2008), 209–25. On German submarine policy, see Michael Walzer, *Just and Unjust Wars: A Moral Argument with Historical Illustrations* (Allen Lane, 1978), 147–50.

18. See, especially, Jürgen von Ungern-Sternberg and Wolfgang von Ungern-Sternberg, *Der Aufruf "An die Kulturwelt!" Das Manifest der 93 und die Anfänge der Kriegspropaganda im Ersten Weltkrieg* (Stuttgart: Steiner, 1996).

19. For a recent overview of this process, see Bryce Sait, *The Indoctrination of the Wehrmacht: Nazi Ideology and the War Crimes of the German Military* (New York: Berghahn Books, 2019).

20. Reibert, *Der Dienstunterricht im Heer: Ausgabe für den Kanonier der bespannten Batterie* (Berlin: E. S. Mittler & Sohn, 1940), 31.

21. See Manfred Messerschmidt, *Die Wehrmacht im NS-Staat: Zeit der Indoktrination* (Hamburg: R.v. Decker's Verlag, 1969), 5; Römer, *Kameraden*, 70.

22. Reibert, *Der Dienstunterricht im Heer*, 31.

23. Ibid., 33.

24. Ibid., quotations from 48 and 49.

25. On Nazi conceptions of heroic masculinity, see René Schilling, *"Kriegshelden": Deutungsmuster Heroischer Männlichkeit in Deutschland 1813–1945* (Paderborn: Schöningh, 2002), 321–41; Mosse, *Nationalism and Sexuality*, 153–80; Christina Jarvis, *The Male Body at War: American Masculinity during World War II* (DeKalb: Northern Illinois University Press, 2004), 44–48.

26. See Mineau, *Operation Barbarossa*, 95; Messerschmidt, *Die Wehrmacht im NS-Staat*, 30–31.

27. See Alexander Rossino, *Hitler Strikes Poland: Blitzkrieg, Ideology, and Atrocity* (Lawrence: University Press of Kansas, 2003); Michael Burleigh, *Moral Combat: Good and Evil in World War II* (New York: HarperCollins, 2011), 132–33 and 227.

28. See Raffael Scheck, "The Killing of Black Soldiers from the French Army by the 'Wehrmacht' in 1940: The Question of Authorization," *German Studies Review* 28, no. 3 (2005): 595–606.

29. See, for example, Jennifer Foray, "The 'Clean Wehrmacht' in the German-Occupied Netherlands, 1940–5," *Journal of Contemporary History* 45, no. 4 (2010): 773–74;

Philippe Burrin, *France under the Germans: Collaboration and Compromise* (New York: The New Press, 1996), 21–22.

30. The text of the Criminal Orders and related instructions are reprinted in Gerd R. Ueberschär and Wolfram Wette, eds., *"Unternehmen Barbarossa": Der deutsche Überfall auf die Sowjetunion 1941* (Paderborn: Schöningh, 1984), 302–14. For detailed analysis, see Felix Römer, *Der Kommissarbefehl: Wehrmacht und NS-Verbrechen an der Ostfront 1941/42* (Paderborn: Schöningh, 2008); Ben Shepherd, *Hitler's Soldiers: The German Army in the Third Reich* (New Haven, CT: Yale University Press, 2017), 126–30.

31. Generalfeldmarschall von Reichenau, AOK6, Abt. Ia-Az. 7, Betr.: Verhalten der Truppe im Ostraum, 10.10.1941, reprinted in Gerd R. Ueberschär and Wolfram Wette, *"Unternehmen Barbarossa."*

32. Generaloberst Hoth, AOK17, Ia Nr. 0973/41 geh., Verhalten der deutschen Soldaten im Ostraum, 17.11.1941, reprinted in Ueberschär and Wette. Emphasis in original.

33. Generaloberst von Manstein, AOK11, Abt. Ic/AO, Nr. 2379/41 geh., 20.11.1941, reprinted in Ueberschär and Wette, 344. Other commanders followed suit, and few expressed any principled reservations. See Shepherd, *Hitler's Soldiers*, 127–29.

34. See Mineau, *Operation Barbarossa*, 100–106.

35. Anlage zu OKW/WFSt/Abt. L IV/Qu Nr. 44822/41 g. K.Chefs., Richtlinien für die Behandlung politischer Kommissare, reprinted ibid., 313.

36. Anlage 3 zu OKW/WFSt/Abt. L. IV/Qu Nr. 44560/41 g. K Chefs. 19. Ausf., *Richtlinien für das Verhalten der Truppe in Rußland*, reprinted ibid., 312.

37. See notes of Generaloberst Halder, 30.3.1941, reprinted ibid., 303.

38. See Mineau, *Operation Barbarossa*, 65.

39. See ibid., 100–106.

40. See Erlaß über die Ausübung der Kriegsgerichtsbarkeit im Gebiet "Barbarossa" und über besondere Maßnahmen der Truppe, 13.5.1941 and Brauchitsch's addendums on the same, reprinted in Ueberschär and Wette, 306–8.

41. Generaloberst von Manstein, AOK11, Abt. Ic/AO Nr. 2379/41 geh., 20.11.1941, reprinted ibid., 344.

42. Anlage 3 zu OKW/WFst/Abt. L. IV/Qu Nr. 44560/41 g. K. Chefs. 19 Ausf., *Richtlinien für das Verhalten der Truppe in Russland*, reprinted ibid., 312.

43. RM: "Reichsmarks," the currency of Nazi Germany. A copy of this 26.5.1941 order can be found in 14th Inf. Div., Anlage 4 to Qu Ib Nr. 190/41 geh., 16.6.1941, Bundesarchiv-Militärarchiv (hereafter BA-MA) RH 26-14/78. The army followed a similar policy in the First World War. See Hull, *Absolute Destruction*, 245.

44. See Hamburger Institut für Sozialforschung, *Verbrechen der Wehrmacht: Dimensionen des Vernichtungskrieges 1941–1944: Ausstellungskatalog* (Hamburg: Hamburger edition, 2002), 15–36.

45. On this practice, see Götz Aly, *Hitler's Beneficiaries: Plunder, Racial War, and the Nazi Welfare State*, trans. Jefferson Chase (New York: Metropolitan Books, 2006).

46. The erection of a legal façade was typical for the Third Reich as a whole. See Peter Haas, *Morality after Auschwitz: The Radical Challenge of the Nazi Ethic* (Philadelphia, PA: Fortress Press, 1988), 70; Koonz, *Nazi Conscience*, esp. chap. 8.

47. Erlaß über die Ausübung der Kriegsgerichtsbarkeit im Gebiet "Barbarossa" und über besondere Maßnahmen der Truppe, 13.5.1941 and Brauchitsch's addendum, reprinted in Ueberschär and Wette, 306–8.

48. See Shepherd, *Hitler's Soldiers*, 128–30; Burleigh, *Moral Combat*, 228. Tellingly, Hitler's generals would even successfully lobby for the suspension of the Commissar Order in 1942 on the grounds that it harmed the war effort by encouraging fiercer resistance. See Christian Hartmann, *Wehrmacht im Ostkrieg: Front und militärisches Hinterland 1941/42* (München: R. Oldenbourg Verlag, 2009), 491–92.

49. For example, Hitler himself had decided two years earlier to place the SS, rather than the Wehrmacht, in charge of the Polish occupation out of fear that the latter was still too wedded to traditional codes of conduct. See Burleigh, *Moral Combat*, 133.

50. See Mineau, *Operation Barbarossa*, 11.

51. Shepherd, *Hitler's Soldiers*, 119–20 and 134–83.

52. Johannes Hagemann to Willy Hagemann, 2.11.1941, MSPT 3.2002.7234.

53. Willy Hagemann to parents, 12.8.1941, and to Kressen, 17.2.1942, MSPT 3.2002.7169.

54. Johannes Hagemann to parents, 16.8.1941, MSPT 3.2002.7234.

55. Johannes Hagemann to parents, 30.10.1941, MSPT 3.2002.7234.

56. Johannes Hagemann to parents, 16.6.1944, MSPT 3.2002.7234.

57. Johannes Hagemann to Otto, 3.10.1941, MSPT 3.2002.7234.

58. Joseph Reinke to Hedwig F., 24.6.1941, MSPT 3.2002.7275.

59. Joseph Reinke to Hedwig F., 4.8.1941 and 17.8.1941, MSPT 3.2002.7275.

60. Harald Hoffmann to parents and Marion (sister), 16.9.1941, MSPT 3.2002.0382.

61. See Shepherd, *Hitler's Soldiers*, 138.

62. Hans Roth, diary entry of 24–28.2.1942, in Hans Roth, *Eastern Inferno: The Journals of a German Panzerjäger on the Eastern Front, 1941–1943*, ed. Christine Alexander and Mason Kunze (Philadelphia: Casemate, 2010).

63. Wilhelm Moldenhauser to Erika (wife), 25.11.1941, *Im Funkwagen der Wehrmacht durch Europa: Balkan, Ukraine, Stalingrad: Feldpostbriefe des Gefreiten Wilhelm Moldenhauser 1940–1943*, ed. Jens Ebert (Berlin: Trafo, 2008).

64. Wilhelm Moldenhauser to Erika, 8.8.1941, *Im Funkwagen der Wehrmacht*.

65. Kurt Niemeyer to Johanna "Hanni" (wife) and Lieselotte (daughter), 10.10.1941, MSPT 3.2008.1750.

66. Hans Roth, diary entry of 24–28.2.1942, *Eastern Inferno*.

67. On this phenomenon, see Stephen Fritz, "'We Are Trying . . . to Change the Face of the World'—Ideology and Motivation in the Wehrmacht on the Eastern Front: The View from Below," *The Journal of Military History* 60, no. 4 (October 1996): 683–710.

68. On this "preemptive strike" myth, see chapter 2.

69. For example, see Heinz Sartorio to Elly (sister) and Fred, 28.3.1942, MSPT 3.2002.0827.

70. Hans Wilhelm Sauer to parents and sisters, 8.10.1942, MSPT 3.2002.1271. Specific efforts to recast the invasion as a righteous cause are discussed in detail in subsequent chapters.

71. See Latzel, *Deutsche Soldaten*, 295–300 on Führer devotion among Wehrmacht troops.

72. Wilhelm Moldenhauser to Erika (wife), 6.7.1941, *Im Funkwagen der Wehrmacht*.

73. Johannes Hagemann to parents, May 1941, MSPT 3.2002.7234.

74. Wilhelm Moldenhauser to Erika, 25.11.1941, *Im Funkwagen der Wehrmacht*.

75. See Raphael Gross, "'Loyalty' in National Socialism: A Contribution to the Moral History of the National Socialist Period," *History of European Ideas* 33 (2007): 488–503.

76. See Ian Kershaw, *The "Hitler Myth": Image and Reality in the Third Reich* (New York: Oxford University Press, 2001).

77. See especially Thomas Kühne, *Kameradschaft: Die Soldaten des nationalsozialistischen Krieges und das 20. Jahrhundert* (Göttingen: Vandenhoeck & Ruprecht, 2006); Fritz, *Frontsoldaten*, 156–86.

78. See Kühne, *Kameradschaft*, 153–65.

79. Johannes Hagemann to Lisa, 8.11.1941, MSPT 3.2002.7234.

80. Harald Hoffmann to parents and Marion, 23.7.1941, MSPT 3.2002.0382. Two Russian POWs helped him accomplish this task.

81. Hans Roth, diary entry of 24–28.2.1942, *Eastern Inferno*.

82. Hans Simon to mother, 27.9.1941, MSPT 3.2002.1288.

83. On the important theme of cleanliness and dirtiness in soldiers' letters, see especially Michaela Kipp, *"Großreinemachen im Osten": Feindbilder in deutschen Feldpostbriefen im Zweiten Weltkrieg* (Frankfurt am Main: Campus Verlag, 2014).

84. Hans Wilhelm Sauer to parents and sisters, 8.10.1942, MSPT 3.2002.1271.

85. Quotations from Wilhelm Moldenhauer to Erika, 16.7.1941 and 6.9.1941, *Im Funkwagen der Wehrmacht*.

86. Wilhelm Moldenhauer to Erika, 22.4.1942, *Im Funkwagen der Wehrmacht*.

87. Wilhelm Moldenhauer to Erika, 11.5.1942, *Im Funkwagen der Wehrmacht*.

88. Quotation from Wilhelm Moldenhauer to Erika, 5.7.1942, *Im Funkwagen der Wehrmacht*.

89. See Wilhelm Moldenhauer to Erika, 4.4.1942, 25.3.2942, and 3.6.1942, *Im Funkwagen der Wehrmacht*.

90. See 14th Pz. Div., Abt. Ib, Kriegstagebuch Nr. 2, 1.6-15.12.1941, BA-MA RH 27-14/22.

91. Franz Siebeler to parents and siblings, 16.7.1941 and 19.9.1941, MSPT 3.2002.1285.

92. Wilhelm Moldenhauer to Erika, 2.11.1941, *Im Funkwagen der Wehrmacht*.

93. See, for example, Franz Siebeler to parents and siblings, 30.8.1941, MSPT 3.2002.1285.

94. Hans Roth, diary entry of 24–28.2.1942, *Eastern Inferno*.

95. Hans-Peter Eckener to Heidi (sister), 13.4.1943, MSPT 3.2002.0307.

96. See Walter Neuser to mother, 4.7.1941 and to Leni (sister), 9.7.1941, MSPT 3.2002.0947.

97. Chapter 2 discusses such accusations in more detail.

98. On the PK, see Daniel Uziel, *The Propaganda Warriors: The Wehrmacht and the Consolidation of the German Home Front* (New York: Peter Lang, 2008), 243–335.

99. "Wir klagen an! Vor den Gräbern gemarterter Kameraden," *Ost-Front*, 8.7.1941, BA-MA RHD 53/20.

100. See, for instance, "Sowjetsoldaten zwischen zwei Fronten: Kommissare hetzen zur brutalen und feigen Kriegsführung," *Ost-Front*, 27.8.1941, BA-MA RHD 53/20.

101. Quote from Peter Weber, "Freier Männergehorsam," *Feldzeitung von der Maas bis an die Memel*, BA-MA RHD 69/76.

102. Walter Neuser to Leni (sister), 8.8.1941, MSPT 3.2002.0947. See also Hans Albring to Eugen Altrogge, Hoher Pfingsttag 1942, MSPT 3.2002.0211, describing Soviet soldiers as "dehumanized hordes" who "murdered helpless wounded."

103. Quotations from "Rote Bestien," *Der Kampf*, Nr. 21, 22.8.1941, BA-MA RHD 69/41; K.G. von Stackelberg, "Wie kämpft der Sowjet-Soldat?" *Der deutsche Kamerad*, 27.7.1941, BA-MA RHD 69/30.

104. "Christliche Stunde," *Der deutsche Kamerad*, 14.9.1941, BA-MA RHD 69/30.

105. See, for example, "Der russische und der deutsche Soldat," *Der Kampf*, Nr. 28, 30.8.1941, BA-MA RHD 69/41.

106. Willy Altmann to unspecified recipient(s) (most likely parents), 8.1.1942, MSPT 3.2002.0201.

107. See Hermann Henning to parents and sisters, 8.10.1942, MSPT 3.2002.7217.

108. Fritz Feierabend to wife, 19.7.1941, BA-MA MSG 2/4048.

109. See Christian Streit, *Keine Kameraden: Die Wehrmacht und die sowjetischen Kriegsgefangenen 1941–1945* (Stuttgart: Deutsche Verlags-Anstalt, 1978).

110. See, for example, Hans Simon to parents, 12.10.1942, MSPT 3.2002.1288; Joseph Reinke to Hedwig F., 19.8.1941, MSPT 3.2002.7275.

111. "Der deutsche Soldat kämpft ritterlich," *Ost-Front*, 10.7.1941, BA-MA RHD 53/20.

112. Fred Gressenbauer, "Ein bolschewistischer Offizier: Was gilt ihm das Leben eines Rotgardisten?" *Ost-Front*, 6.8.1941, BA-MA RHD 53/20. Propaganda reporters were given instructions from Berlin to emphasize the supposed contrast between the Soviet and German treatment of prisoners. See PK 612, Kriegstagebuch, April–August 1941, entry of 4.7.1941, BA-MA RH 45/6.

113. "Der rauhe Krieger als Kulturträger," *Mitteilungen für die Truppe*, Nr. 126, August 1941, BA-MA RW 4/357.

114. Quotation from "Das grosse nationalsozialistische Gemeinschaftsideal," ibid., Nr. 138, September 1941, BA-MA RW 4/357.

115. See chapter 2.

116. PzAOK3, Abt. Ic, Feindnachrichtenblatt Nr. 13, 11.7.1941, BA-MA RH 26-20/84.

117. 46th Inf. Div., Abt. Ic, Betr.: Verhalten der Truppe gegenüber der ukrainsichen Bevölkerung, 18.7.1941 (Anlage 28 to Ic Report for 12.6-30.10.1941), BA-MA RH 26-46/49. Emphasis in original.

118. 10th Pz. Div., Abt. Ib, Bes. Anordnungen f.d. Versorgung und die Versorgungstruppen Nr. 101, 24.12.1941, BA-MA 27-10/101.

119. Heeresgruppe Mitte, Abt.Ic/AO Nr. 103/41 g Kdos (AO III), Betr.: Kollektive Gewaltmassnahmen, 7.8.1941, BA-MA RH 20-2/1091. Emphasis in original.

120. OKH to AOK6, Betr.: Völkerrechtswidrige Behandlung deutscher Soldaten in Sowjetrussicher Kriegsgefangenschaft, 9.7.1941, BA-MA RH 20-2/1091.

121. Its instructions are paraphrased in 46th Inf. Div., Abt. Ic, Auszug aus dem Armeetagesbefehl Nr. 22, 29.7.1941 (Anlage 37 to Ic Report for 12.6-30.10.1941), BA-MA RH 26-46/49.

122. "Der Soldat im besetzten Gebiet als Vertreter von Volk und Reich," *Mitteilungen für die Truppe*, Nr. 179, February 1942, BA-MA RW 4/357.

123. "Pflichten und Aufgaben des deutschen Soldaten im besetzten Osten," *Mitteilungen für die Truppe*, Nr. 192, April 1942, BA-MA RW 4/357.

124. PzAOK2, Merkblatt für Offiziere, Zur dauernden Unterrichtung aller Wehrmachtangehörigen, Betr.: Feindbevölkerung, 3.12.1942, BA-MA RH 21-2/713.

125. 167th Inf. Div. Kommandeur, Befehl, 7.7.1941, BA-MA RH 26-167/42.

126. XXXIVAK, Tagesbefehl, 3.8.1941, Yad Vashem JM5322.

127. See Shepherd, *Hitler's Soldiers*, 285.

128. See Regina Mühlhäuser, *Eroberungen: Sexuelle Gewalttaten und intime Beziehungen deutscher Soldaten in der Sowjetunion 1941–1945* (Hamburg: HIS Verlag, 2010).

129. There were exceptions to this rule. For example, see GFP 703, Tagebuch Nr. 172/42 geh., Betr.: Report for June 1942, BA-MA RH 21-3/447; GFP Gruppe 580, Tagebuch Nr. 363/41 geh., Activity Report for October 1941, Yad Vashem, M29.114.

130. Wilhelm Moldenhauser to Erika (wife), 16.7.1941, *Im Funkwagen der Wehrmacht*.

131. Wilhelm Moldenhauser to Erika (wife), 14.9.1941, *Im Funkwagen der Wehrmacht*.

132. Hermann Henning to relatives, 25.9.1941, MSPT 3.2002.7217.

133. See Willy Reese, *A Stranger to Myself: The Inhumanity of War: Russia, 1941–1944*, ed. Stefan Schmitz, trans. Michael Hofmann (New York: Farrar, Straus and Giroux, 2003), 53.

134. Willy Hagemann to parents, 19.1.1943, MSPT 3.2002.7169.

135. See Shepherd, *Hitler's Soldiers*, 176–86.

136. Shepherd, 203–11.

137. Shepherd, 242–43.

138. *"Geschütz-Führer,"* in a *Jäger* (anti-tank) company. See Hans Simon to mother, 11.3.1943, MSPT 3.2002.1288; 12th Inf. Div., reports of the division commander for 1941 and 1942, BA-MA RH 26-12/164.

139. Hans Simon to Tutti (sister), 25.8.1942, MSPT 3.2002.1288.

140. Hans Simon to father, 20.12.1942), MSPT 3.20021288.

141. Hans Simon to mother, 12.10.1942, MSPT 3.2002.1288.

142. Hans Simon to Tutti, 21.11.1942, MSPT 3.2002.1288.

143. Hans Simon to parents, 20.4.1942, MSPT 3.2002.1288.

144. Hans Simon to father, 9.12.1942, MSPT 3.2002.1288.

145. Hans Simon to mother, 31.1.1943, MSPT 3.2002.1288.

146. Hans Simon to mother, 10.7.1943 and 22.11.1942, and to parents, 10.9.1943, MSPT 3.2002.1288.

147. Hans Simon to mother, 29.8.1943, MSPT 3.2002.1288; 12th Inf. Div., Abt. IVd(e), Activity Report, 1.3–30.6.1943, BA-MA RH 26-12/145.

148. See Wilhelm Altmann to father and sister, 9.3.1942, MSPT 3.2002.0201.

149. Wilhelm Altmann to father and sister, 28.4.1942, MSPT 3.2002.0201.

150. Wilhelm Altmann to father and sister, 13.6.1942, MSPT 3.2002.0201.

151. Wilhelm Altmann to father and sister, 20.6.1942, MSPT 3.2002.0201.

152. Wilhelm Altmann to father and sister, 24.9.1942 and 26.9.1942, MSPT 3.2002.0201.

153. See Wilhelm Altmann to father and sister, 28.12.1941, MSPT 3.2002.0201.

154. Wilhelm Altmann to father and sister, 10.8.1942, MSPT 3.2002.0201.

155. Gustav Böker to parents, 7.8.1941, MSPT 3.2002.0966.

156. Wilhelm Moldenhauser to Erika, 20.3.1942, *Im Funkwagen der Wehrmacht*.

157. See for example 8th Inf. Div., Abt. Ic, Report for June 1942, BA-MA RH 26-8/74; AOK9, OQu/VII/Ic/AO, Betr.: Ausgabe von Ausweisen an die Zivilbevölkerung, 15.11.1942, BA-MA RH 20-9/642.

158. See "Sowjetkriegsführung arbeitet mit Gangstermethoden: Missbrauch der weißen Flagge—Immer neue Völkerrechtsverletzungen," 11.7.1941, *"Wacht im Osten,"* BA-MA RHD 69/84.

159. The book is *Deutsche Soldaten sehen die Sowjet-Union: Feldpostbriefe aus dem Osten,* ed. Wolfgang Diewerge (Berlin: Wilhelm Limbert Verlag, 1941). On its development, see Bundesarchiv Berlin-Lichterfelde (hereafter BArch) R 55/1308, NS 18/648, and NS 18/652.

160. See Weikart, *Hitler's Ethic,* 85–100.

161. Wilhelm Altmann to father and sister, 14.5.1943 and 29.1.1943, MSPT 3.2002.0201. Quotation from the latter.

162. Wilhelm Altmann to father and sister, 21.9.1943, MSPT 3.2002.0201.

163. Wilhelm Altmann to father and sister, 17.10.1943, MSPT 3.2002.0201.

164. Shepherd, *Hitler's Soldiers,* 242–73 and 317–20; Antony Beevor, *Stalingrad: The Fateful Siege: 1942–1943* (Penguin Books, 1999).

165. See Kühne, *Kameradschaft.*

166. Johannes Hagemann to parents, 12.2.1942, MSPT 3.2002.7234.

167. Johannes to parents, 29.5.1942, MSPT 3.2002.7234.

168. Johannes to parents, Christmas 1942, MSPT 3.2002.7234.

169. 290th Inf. Div., Abt. Ic, Report for 1.7-31.12.1942, National Archives and Records Administration (hereafter NARA) T315, reel 1896.

170. See, for instance, Willy Hagemann to parents, 7.5.1943, MSPT 3.2002.7169.

171. Willy Hagemann to mother, 14.6.1943, MSPT 3.2002.7169.

172. Willy Hagemann to Kressen, 12.9.1943, and to parents, 28.10.1943, MSPT 3.2002.7169.

173. Willy Hagemann to Kressen, 5.10.1943, MSPT 3.2002.7169.

174. Kurt Niemeyer to Johanna and Lieselotte, 8.10.1941, MSPT 3.2008.1750.

175. Kurt Niemeyer to Johanna and Lieselotte, 2.12.1941, MSPT 3.2008.1750.

176. Kurt Niemeyer to Johanna and Lieselotte, 3.12.1941, MSPT 3.2008.1750.

177. Kurt Niemeyer to Johanna and Lieselotte, 12.3.1942, MSPT 3.2008.1750.

178. For example, see Kurt Niemeyer to Johanna and Lieselotte, 10.7.1942, MSPT 3.2008.1750.

179. See, for example, Hans Wilhelm Sauer to family, 1.9.1942, MSPT 3.2002.1271.

180. See Johannes Hagemann to parents, 19.9.1943, MSPT 3.2002.7234.

181. Adolf Dick to Ernst, 22.8.1941 and to Marieluise, 1.12.1942 and 27.11.1942, MSPT 3.2002.7565.

182. Walter Neuser to parents, 3.3.1942, MSPT 3.2002.0947.

183. Willy Hagemann to parents, 1.4.1943, MSPT 3.2002.7169.

184. Wilhelm Altmann to father and sister, 5.5.1943, MSPT 3.2002.0201.

185. Kurt Niemeyer to Johanna, 26.5.1942, MSPT 3.2008.1750.

186. See Kühne, *Kameradschaft,* 153–65.

187. The actions of Wehrmacht soldiers in these cases were not dissimilar from the efforts of female volunteers from the NS-Frauenschaft and a variety of other civilian agencies attempting to transform the "chaotic" landscape of the East through German order, domesticity, cleanliness, and culture. See Elizabeth Harvey, *Women and the Nazi East: Agents and Witnesses of Germanization* (New Haven, CT: Yale University Press, 2003).

188. Kurt Niemeyer to Johanna, 16.4.1942, MSPT 3.2008.1750.

189. See, for instance, 205th Inf. Div., IVb, Activity Report, 1.7–15.7.1943, BA-MA RH 26-205/78.

190. 290th Inf. Div., Abt. Ic, Activity Report, 1.7–31.12.1942, NARA T315, reel 1896.

191. Wilhelm Moldenhauser to Erika, 5.3.1942, *Im Funkwagen der Wehrmacht.*

192. Willy Hagemann to Kressen, 7.9.1943 and 30.8.1943, MSPT 3.2002.7169.

193. See Hans Albring to Eugen Altrogge, Allerseelen, 1941 and 28.10.1941, MSPT 3.2002.0211.

194. See Shepherd, *Hitler's Soldiers*, 274–84.

195. OKH, Nr. II 3033/42 geh., Richtlinien für die Behandlung der einheimischen Bevölkerung im Osten, 10.5.1942, BA-MA RH 26-285/44.

196. AOK4 Oberbefehlshaber, Abschrift, Abt. Ic/AO (Abw III), Tgb Nr. 1870/42 geh., 22.6.1942, Betr.: Befriedung des besetzten Gebiets- Aufrechterhaltung der Manneszucht, and AOK4, Anlage zu AOK4 Ic/AO (AbwIII) Tgb Nr. 1870/42 geh., 22.6.42, BA-MA RH 26-10/73. Quotations from the former.

197. 290th Inf. Div., Abt. Ic, Activity Report for 16.12.1941–30.6.1942, NARA, T315, roll 1892.

198. PzAOK3, Abt. Ic/AO (Abw.III), Nr.1000/43 geh., 1.4.1943, BA-MA RH 21-3/470.

199. Some units did report that such instructions led to more exemplary behavior on the part of their men. For example, see GFP 703, Tagebuch Nr. 253/43 geh., 27.6.1943, Report for June 1943, BA-MA RH 21-3/470.

200. Shepherd, *Hitler's Soldiers*, 327–33.

201. Ibid., 356–75.

202. See Willy Hagemann to Kressen, 7.7.1944 and 22.8.1944, and to parents, 30.5.1944 and 26.8.1944, MSPT 3.2002.7169.

203. See Willy Hagemann to Kressen, 4.6.1944 and to parents, 22.6.1944, MSPT 3.2002.7169. Quotation from the former.

204. Willy Hagemann to Kressen, 3.9.1944, MSPT 3.2002.7169.

205. Heinz Sartorio to Elly (sister), 30.6.1943, MSPT 3.2002.0827.

206. Willy Hagemann to Kressen, 9.8.1944, MSPT 3.2002.7169.

207. Wilhelm Altmann to father and sister, 23.1.1943, MSPT 3.2002.0201.

208. Hans Simon to sister, 7.3.1944, MSPT 3.2002.

209. See Omer Bartov, *Hitler's Army: Soldiers, Nazis, and War in the Third Reich* (New York: Oxford University Press, 1991), 29–58.

210. Willy Hagemann to Kressen, 3.9.1944, MSPT 3.2002.7169.

211. See Willy Hagemann to parents, 12.6.1944, MSPT 3.2002.7169.

212. Quotations from Willy Hagemann to Kressen, 3.9.1944, MSPT 3.2002.7169.

213. On this subject see Hannes Heer, "How Amorality Became Normality: Reflections on the Mentality of German Soldiers on the Eastern Front," in *War of Extermination*, 329–44.

214. Kurt Niemeyer to Johanna and Lieselotte 12.8.1942, 6.6.1942, and 15.11.1942, MSPT 3.2008.1750. Quotation from the latter.

215. Kurt Niemeyer to Johanna and Lieselotte, 19.10.1941, MSPT 3.2008.1750.

216. Heinz Rahe to Ursula (wife), 2.7.1941, MSPT 3.2002.0985.

217. Harald Hoffmann to Hertha, 27.8.1941, MSPT 3.2002.0382.

218. See chapter 2.

219. Reese, *Stranger to Myself*, 137.

220. Ibid., quotations from 26 and 56, respectively.

221. Wilhelm Altmann to father and sister, 24.8.1943, MSPT 3.2002.0201.

222. See Wilhelm Altmann to father and sister, 14.10.1943 and 19.10.1941, MSPT 3.2002.0201.

223. Quotations from Willy Hagemann to parents, 30.11.1942 and to Kressen, 26.1.1943, MSPT 3.2002.7169, respectively.

224. Willy Hagemann to Kressen, 7.11.1943, MSPT 3.2002.7169.

225. Willy Hagemann to parents, 9.1.1944, MSPT 3.2002.7169.

226. 290th Inf. Div., Abt. Ic, Report for 1.7-31.12.42, NARA T315, reel 1896.

227. 290th Inf. Div., Abt. Ic, Report for 1.1-31.5.1943, NARA T315, reel 1899.

228. See, for example, 12th Inf. Div., Abt. Ic, Activity Report for 1.6.1941–15.12.1941, BA-MA RH 26-12/82.

229. See Wette, *The Wehrmacht*, 198–250.

2. Rationalizing Atrocities

1. Harald Hoffmann to parents and Marion, 14.8.1941, MSPT 3.2002.0382.

2. Harald Hoffmann to parents and Marion, 30.6.1941, MSPT 3.2002.0382.

3. Harald Hoffmann to parents and Marion, 15.11.1941, MSPT 3.2002.0382.

4. See especially Wolfram Wette, *The Wehrmacht: History, Myth, Reality*, trans. Deborah Lucas Schneider (Cambridge, MA: Harvard University Press, 2006), 195–274; Norbert Frei, *Adenauer's Germany and the Nazi Past: The Politics of Amnesty and Integration*, trans. Joel Golb (New York: Columbia University Press, 2002), 93–234; Christina Morina, "Legacies of Stalingrad: The Eastern Front War and the Politics of Memory in Divided Germany, 1943–1989" (PhD diss., College Park, University of Maryland, 2007).

5. "Crime" is defined here based on the international standards of the time, including the Hague Convention and other agreements to which Germany was a party, as well as German law, accepted international conventions, and the legal judgments at Nuremburg, which took the above factors into consideration. See US Military Tribunal Nuremberg, Judgment of 27 October 1948, in *Trials of War Criminals Before the Nuremberg Military Tribunals under Control Council Law No. 10*, vol. 11, (Washington, DC: United States Government Printing Office, 1950); Hamburger Institut für Sozialforschung, *Verbrechen der Wehrmacht: Dimensionen des Vernichtungskrieges 1941–1944* (Hamburg: Hamburger Edition, 2002), 15–36. Mistreatment of prisoners, uncompensated requisitions, and the summary execution and abuse of civilians were explicitly forbidden, for example, and occupying powers were to look after the welfare and security of the populace.

6. See especially Ben Shepherd, *Hitler's Soldiers: The German Army in the Third Reich* (New Haven, CT: Yale University Press, 2017), 110–30.

7. On soldiers' reticence to discuss sexual violence and sex in general, see Martin Humburg, *Das Gesicht des Krieges: Feldpostbriefe von Wehrmachtssoldaten aus der Sowjetunion 1941–1944* (Opladen/Wiesbaden: Westdeutscher Verlag, 1998), 110–17.

8. See Omer Bartov, *Hitler's Army: Soldiers, Nazis, and War in the Third Reich* (New York: Oxford University Press, 1991), 164; Peter Longerich, *"Davon haben wir nichts gewusst!" Die Deutschen und die Judenverfolgung 1933–1945* (München: Siedler Verlag, 2006), 224–25; Humburg, *Gesicht des Krieges*, 196.

9. For the protocols the censors followed, see PzAOK3 Ic/AO (Abw III) Nr. 647/43 geh., Betr: Feldpostprüfung, BA-MA RH 21-3 470. For more on official censorship,

see Klaus Latzel, *Deutsche Soldaten—nationalsozialistsicher Krieg? Kriegserlebnis—Kriegserfahrung 1939–1945* (Paderborn: Ferdinand Schöningh, 1998), 25–30; Humburg, *Gesicht des Krieges*, 17–18; Fritz, *Frontsoldaten*, 8–9; Ortwin Buchbender and Reinhold Sterz, eds., *Das Andere Gesicht des Krieges: Deutsche Feldpostbriefe 1939–1945* (München: Verlag C. H. Beck, 1982), 13–24.

10. See Bryce Sait, *The Indoctrination of the Wehrmacht: Nazi Ideology and the War Crimes of the German Military* (New York: Berghahn Books, 2019), 159–63.

11. On the psychology of moral rationalization, see especially Jo-Ann Tsang, "Moral Rationalization and the Integration of Situational Factors and Psychological Processes in Immoral Behavior," *Review of General Psychology* 6, no. 1 (2002): 25–50; Albert Bandura and Claudio Barbaranelli, "Mechanisms of Moral Disengagement in the Exercise of Moral Agency," *Journal of Personality and Social Psychology* 71, no. 2 (1996): 364–74.

12. See Buchbender and Sterz, *Andere Gesicht*, 13–16.

13. See especially Saul Friedländer, "The Wehrmacht, German Society, and the Knowledge of the Mass Extermination of the Jews," in *Crimes of War: Guilt and Denial in the Twentieth Century*, ed. Omer Bartov, Atina Grossmann, and Mary Nolan (New York: New Press, 2002), 17–30; Walter Manoschek, *Es gibt nur eines für das Judentum: Vernichtung: Das Judenbild in deutschen Soldatenbriefen 1939–1944* (Hamburg, 1996); Nicholas Stargardt, *The German War: A Nation Under Arms, 1939–1945; Citizens and Soldiers* (New York: Basic Books, 2017).

14. On soldiers' views of the Red Army, including its crimes, see Fritz, *Frontsoldaten*, 60–61; Latzel, *Deutsche Soldaten*, 206–11 and 219–26; Humburg, *Gesicht des Krieges*, 193–97; Christian Hartmann, *Wehrmacht im Ostkrieg: Front und militärisches Hinterland 1941/42* (München: R. Oldenbourg Verlag, 2009), 537–42.

15. Hans Simon to unknown recipient, most likely father or mother, 15.8.1941, MSPT 3.2002.1288. For context, see 12th Inf. Div. Befehlshaber, report for 6.7-28.7.1941 and 29.7 to 30.8.1941, BA-MA RH 26-12/164. Reports of Second Corps, its parent formation, confirm that Russian troops in the area sometimes executed prisoners. See Generalkommando II AK, Abt. Ic to AOK16 Abt. Ic, 25.8.1941, BA-MA 26–12/242.

16. Hans Simon to father, 28.7.1941, MSPT 3.2002.1288.

17. Hans Simon to mother, 27.9.1941, MSPT 3.2002.1288. Simon's unit reported very early on that Red snipers (Heckenschützen) repeatedly attacked field hospitals and medical companies. See 12th Inf. Div., IVb, Beitrag zur Tagesmeldung der 12 Infanterie Division for 25.6.1941, BA-MA RH 26–12/130.

18. Walter Neuser to mother, 4.7.1941 MSPT 3.2002.0947, quotation from the former.

19. Walter Neuser to parents, 3.7.1941, MSPT 3.2002.0947.

20. Walter Neuser to Leni (sister), 8.8.1941, MSPT 3.2002.0947. See also Walter Neuser to mother, 4.7.1941, mentioning "Mongolian types" in the Red Army and asserting that "the Russian deserves the rope."

21. See for example Hermann Henning to parents, 28.9.1941, MSPT 3.2002.7217. There was a measure of truth to the claims that the Red Army frequently violated international law. However, practices condemned by the German side, such as adopting guerilla-style tactics and refusing to surrender, were partly a consequence of the lightning speed of the Wehrmacht's advance: thousands of Red soldiers found themselves surrounded behind the lines but continued to fight desperately out of fear they

would be executed if they gave themselves up—either by the Germans or their own superiors.

22. *Ost-Front*, 9.7.1941, BA-MA RHD 53/20; *Blücher*, 18.8.1941, BA-MA RHD 69/34; *Feldzeitung von der Maas bis an die Memel*, 6.11.1941, BA-MA RHD 69/76. See Hartmann, *Wehrmacht im Ostkrieg*, 501–11 for perceptions of the commissars in the Wehrmacht, which were tinged with both racism and moral condemnation.

23. See, for example "So hausten mongolische Horden," *Der deutsche Kamerad*, 20.7.1941, BA-MA RHD 69/30.

24. K. G. von Stackelberg, "Wie kämpft der Sowjet-Soldat?" *Der Deutsche Kamerad*, 27.7.1941, BA-MA RHD 69/30.

25. Gert Sachs, "Verschlagene Mongolen als Kornfeldbriganten: Von der heimtückischen Kampfesweise der Roten Armee—Dum-Dum-Geschosse—Missachtung des Roten Kreuzes," *Feldzeitung von der Maas bis an die Memel*, 25.6.1941, BA-MA RHD 69/15.

26. "Die Rettung Deutschlands vor dem Ansturm des Untermenschentums," *Mitteilungen für die Truppe*, July 1941, Nr. 118, BA-MA RW 4/357.

27. See especially Bianka Pietrow-Ennker, ed., *Präventiv-krieg? Der deutsche Angriff auf die Sowjetunion* (Frankfurt am Main: Fischer Taschenbuch Verlag, 2011); Erich F. Sommer, *Das Memorandum: Wie Der Sowjetunion Der Krieg Erklärt Wurde* (Frankfurt am Main: Verlag Ullstein, 1991); Wolfram Wette, "Die propagandistische Begleitmusik zum deutschen Überfall auf die Sowjet-union am 22. Juni 1941," in *"Unternehmen Barbarossa": Der deutsche Überfall auf die Sowjetunion 1941*, ed. Gerd R. Ueberschär and Wolfram Wette (Paderborn: Schöningh, 1984), 111–30.

28. Franz Siebeler to parents and siblings, 21.6.1941, MSPT 3.2002.01285.

29. Hans Roth, diary entry of 22.6.1941, in Hans Roth, *Eastern Inferno: The Journals of a German Panzerjäger on the Eastern Front, 1941–1943*, ed. Christine Alexander and Mason Kunze (Philadelphia, PA: Casemate, 2010).

30. See Michael Walzer, *Just and Unjust Wars: A Moral Argument with Historical Illustrations* (Allen Lane, 1978), esp. 74–85; John A. Moses, "Dietrich Bonhoeffer's Repudiation of Protestant German War Theology," *The Journal of Religious History* 30, no. 3 (2006): 354–70.

31. For example, see "Beweise für Moskaus Angriffspläne: Kartenmaterial und wertvolle Aufzeichnungen erbeutet," *Ost-Front*, 7.7.1941, BA-MA RHD 53/20. In reality, Soviet forces had been mobilized to protect the country from a potential German assault. See Shepherd, *Hitler's Soldiers*, 135–36.

32. On this order and its consequences, see Karel Berkhoff, *Harvest of Despair: Life and Death in Ukraine Under Nazi Rule* (Cambridge, MA: Belknap Press, 2004), 17–24.

33. Hans Simon to father, 28.7.1941, MSPT 3.2002.1288.

34. Fritz Feierabend to wife, 19.7.1941, BA-MA MSG2/4048.

35. "Moskaus Söldner als Mordbrenner: Wahnsinnig Zerstörungswut tobt sich in der Ukraine aus," *Ost-Front*, 8.7.1941, BA-MA RHD 53/20.

36. "Gemeine Kampfmethoden," *Blücher*, 31.8.1941, BA-MA RHD 69/34. The article also detailed how the Soviets booby-trapped bottles of vodka to explode when opened by German soldiers.

37. See Jay W. Baird, *The Mythical World of Nazi War Propaganda, 1939–1945* (Minneapolis: University of Minnesota Press, 1974), 159, discussing Brauchitsch's directive of November 1, 1941, that any hunger-related deaths among the urban population were to be blamed on Soviet policies.

38. See Berkhoff, *Harvest of Despair*, 13–17; Dieter Pohl, *Die Herrschaft der Wehrmacht: Deutsche Militärbesatzung und einheimische Bevölkerung in der Sowjetunion 1941–1944* (München: R. Oldenbourg Verlag, 2008), 129 and 137. Pohl cites estimates of between 25,000 and 50,000 victims.

39. Wilhelm Moldenhauser, diary entry of 29.6.1941, *Im Funkwagen der Wehrmacht durch Europa: Balkan, Ukraine, Stalingrad: Feldpostbriefe des Gefreiten Wilhelm Moldenhauser 1940–1943*, ed. Jens Ebert (Berlin: Trafo, 2008).

40. Wilhelm Moldenhauser to Erika (wife) 26.10.1941 and 8.12.1941, *Im Funkwagen der Wehrmacht.*

41. See Hermann Henning to parents, 3.9.1941, MSPT 3.2002.7217.

42. Hans Roth, diary entries of 23–26.9.1941, *Eastern Inferno.* These events, which were used by the Germans as justification for arrests and killings of Jews, are described in more detail in Berkhoff, *Harvest of Despair*, 29–34.

43. For example, see Martin Rebhan, PK (mot) 666, "Ein Dorf soll sterben," 10.12.1941, BA-MA RH 45/41.

44. Siegfried Pistorius, "Im Schreckenshaus von Dubno. 528 unschuldige Opfer von GPU-Agenten gemordet—Die Ukraine trauert," *Feldzeitung von der Maas bis an die Memel*, 10.7.1941, BA-MA RHD 69/15.

45. See, for instance, entries of July 11 and 25, 1941, in *Die Tagebücher von Joseph Goebbels: Teil II: Diktate 1941–1945*, Band 1 Juli–September 1941, ed. Elke Fröhlich (K. G. Sauer, München, 1996); Lorna Waddington, *Hitler's Crusade: Bolshevism, the Jews and the Myth of Conspiracy* (New York: I. B. Tauris, 2009), 187–95.

46. Entries of July 6, 7, and 8, 1941, in *Die Tagebücher von Joseph Goebbels: Teil I: Aufzeichnungen 1923–1941*, Band 9, ed. Elke Fröhlich (München: K. G. Saur, 1998).

47. Deutsche Wochenschau GmbH, *Die Deutsche Wochenschau*, Nr. 566, 9.7.1941, Bundesarchiv-Filmarchiv DW (566/1941); Goebbels, diary entry of 10.7.1941 in *Die Tagebücher von Joseph Goebbels: Teil II: Diktate 1941–1945*, Band 1, Juli–September 1941, 40.

48. See Pohl, *Herrschaft*, 136–37.

49. Hermann Henning to Hansl (brother), 2.2.1942, MSPT 3.2002.7217.

50. Hans Albring to Eugen Altrogge (comrade), hoher Pfingsttag 1942, MSPT 3.2002.0211.

51. See Kurt Niemeyer to Johanna (wife), 26.8.1942, MSPT 3.2008.1750 and Hans-Peter Eckener to father, 20.6.1942, 3.2002.0307.

52. Hans-Peter Eckener to parents, 21.11.1942, MSPT 3.2002.0307.

53. Hermann Henning to Hansl (brother), 29.12.1941, and to unspecified relatives, 5.12.1941, MSPT 3.2002.7217. See entry of 6.12.1941, 123rd Inf. Div., Abt. Ic, Tätigkeitsbericht for 15.5.-15.12.1941, BA-MA RH 26-123/143 for records of his unit's encounter with partisans at this time.

54. Hermann Henning to parents, 28.9.1941, MSPT 3.2002.7217.

55. Hans-Peter Eckener to mother, 9.3.1942, MSPT 3.2002.0307. As a rule, however, Wehrmacht soldiers do not seem to have often dwelt on the issue of partisan violence against local civilians. They directed most of their ire against attacks against German troops.

56. Examples include Hauptmann Dr. v. Lölhöffel, "Menschenopfer," *Der Durchbruch*, 4.2.1942, BA-MA RHD 69/19; "Hinterhältige Kampfmethoden der Bolschewisten," *Blücher*, 5.5.1942, BA-MA RHD 69/34.

57. WUSt investigated roughly 8,000 cases throughout the war. Alfred de Zayas was able to corroborate the authenticity of much of its work, which he believed proved that the Wehrmacht had still committed itself to the principles of international law. Christoph Rass, however, has convincingly argued that even though its work may have been legitimate, the office typically ended up serving the purposes of Nazi propaganda. See Alfred de Zayas, *Die Wehrmacht-Untersuchungsstelle: Deutsche Ermittlungen über alliierte Völkerrechtsverletzungen im Zweiten Weltkrieg* (München: Verlag Universitas Langen-Müller, 1979); Christoph Rass, "Die 'Wehrmacht-Untersuchungsstelle für Verletzungen des Völkerrechts' war nicht viel mehr als eine Hilfstruppe der NS-Propaganda," *Die Zeit*, November 16, 2009. For Soviet investigations of German crimes, see, for example, United States Holocaust Memorial Museum (hereafter USHMM) RG-22.014M, esp. Reels 2–6, 17, and 19.

58. OKW/WR Kriegsverbrechen der russsichen Wehrmacht, OKW (WR) Wehrmacht-Untersuchungsstelle für Verletzungen des Völkerrechts, Anlagen zu der Denkschrift: "Kriegsverbrechen der russischen Wehrmacht," BA-MA RW 2/268.

59. See, for example, Div Befehl Nr. 24, 14.8.1941 (Anlage 12 to 102nd Inf. Div., Ic, report of 1.8.1941–3.9.1941), BA-MA RH 26-102/61.

60. This was to counter rumors that the soldiers were actually well treated, or at least allowed to live. See Der Chef der Sicherheitspolizei und des SD to Reichsführer-SS, z.Zt. Feld-Kommandostelle, Betr.: Stimmung unter den Angehörigen vermisster Soldaten, 22.10.1943, BArch NS 19/2444; Reichsführer-SS Chef des SS-Hauptamtes to Reichsführer SS and Reichsminister des Innern, Betr.: Schrift gegen die bolschewistische Propaganda mit deutschen Kriegsgefangenen, 20.11.1943, BArch, NS 19/2445.

61. See Pohl, *Herrschaft*, 137.

62. See Waddington, *Hitler's Crusade*, 195; Baird, *The Mythical World of Nazi War Propaganda*, 197; Daniel Uziel, *The Propaganda Warriors: The Wehrmacht and the Consolidation of the German Home Front* (New York: Peter Lang, 2008), 311; Paul Allen, *Katyń: The Untold Story of Stalin's Polish Massacre* (New York: C. Scribner's Sons, 1991).

63. Waddington, *Hitler's Crusade*, 194–95.

64. For an insightful discussion of divergent cultures of war in another context, see Wayne Lee, *Barbarians and Brothers: Anglo-American Warfare, 1500–1865* (New York: Oxford University Press, 2011).

65. Regarding this phenomenon, see Tsang, "Moral Rationalization."

66. See Christian Streit, *Keine Kameraden: Die Wehrmacht und die sowjetischen Kriegsgefangenen 1941–1945* (Stuttgart: Deutsche Verlags-Anstalt, 1978); Alfred Streim, *Sowjetische Gefangene in Hitlers Vernichtungskrieg: Berichte und Dokumente 1941–1945* (Heidelberg: Müller, 1982).

67. *Heckenschützen*: a term soldiers frequently used to refer to Red soldiers or partisans who resisted the invaders behind the front lines.

68. Hans Albring to Eugen Altrogge (friend and fellow soldier), 30–31.8.1941, MSPT 3.2002.0211.

69. Heinz Rahe to Ursula (wife), 2.7.1941, MSPT 3.2002.0985.

70. See above.

71. Fritz Feierabend to wife, 19.7.1941, BA-MA MSG 2/4048.

72. Heinz Rahe to Ursula, 29.9.1941, MSPT 3.2002.0985.

73. Walter Neuser to mother, 12.10.1941, MSPT 3.2002.0947.

74. Hartmann, *Wehrmacht im Ostkrieg*, 501–511.

75. See especially Streit, *Keine Kameraden*. POW labor was technically allowed under international law, but it could not be in war-related work and the prisoners were to receive adequate wages, as well as food and basic supplies. None of these conditions were met. See Hamburger Institut für Sozialforschung, *Verbrechen der Wehrmacht*, 217–46.

76. Both quotations from Harald Hoffmann to unspecified recipients (most likely parents and sister), 18.10.1941, MSPT 3.2002.0382.

77. See Harald Hoffmann to unspecified recipients (most likely parents and sister), 9.10.1941 and 12.10.1941, MSPT 3.2002.0382.

78. Kurt Niemeyer to Johanna and Lieselotte (daughter), 4.9.1941, MSPT 3.2008.1750.

79. Kurt Niemeyer to Johanna and Lieselotte, 14.10.1941 and 19.10.1941, MSPT 3.2008.1750.

80. Walter Neuser to parents, 18.4.1942, MSPT 3.2002.0947. "Types" [*Typen*] was a common synonym for "races."

81. See, for instance, Dr. Konrad Jarausch to wife, 25.10.1941, in *Reluctant Accomplice: A Wehrmacht Soldier's Letters from the Eastern Front*, ed. Konrad H. Jarausch (Princeton, NJ: Princeton University Press, 2011), 310–11.

82. Key works on the Wehrmacht and the Final Solution in the Soviet Union include Helmut Krausnick, *Die Truppe des Weltanschauungskrieges: Die Einsatzgruppen der Sicherheitspolizei und des SD 1938–1942* (Stuttgart: Deutsche Verlags-Anstalt, 1981); Arno J. Mayer, *Der Krieg als Kreuzzug: Das Deutsche Reich, Hitlers Wehrmacht und die "Endlösung,"* trans. Karl Siber (Hamburg: Rowohlt, 1988); Omer Bartov, *Germany's War and the Holocaust: Disputed Histories* (Ithaca, NY: Cornell University Press, 2003); Waitman Beorn, *Marching into Darkness: The Wehrmacht and the Holocaust in Belarus* (Cambridge, MA: Harvard University Press, 2014).

83. The question of how much soldiers knew about the Holocaust in all its dimensions has still not been fully resolved, although it is well-established that many harbored antisemitic sentiments. It is also clear that many witnessed the persecution and killing of Jews and in some cases participated, whether on their own initiative or acting under orders. On the issue of to what extent soldiers wrote about the Holocaust, see especially Manoschek, *Es gibt nur eines für das Judentum*; Longerich, "*Davon haben wir nichts gewusst!*" 224–26; Latzel, *Deutsche Soldaten*, 201–4; Humburg, *Gesicht des Krieges*, 197–205. In Latzel's study, the topic of "Jews and Jewish persecution" appeared only fifteen times in 2,609 letters (.53 percent) and appeared in the writings of five of twenty-two soldiers (Latzel, 120). In Humburg's investigation, fifteen of 739 letters (2 percent) mentioned Jews or their persecution (Humburg, 197–98). In this book, at least nineteen letters mentioned the persecution of Jews (.94 percent).

84. Hans Albring to Eugen Altrogge, 21.3.1942, MSPT 3.2002.0211.

85. Humburg, who has also found several instances of antisemitic remarks including approval of the Final Solution, cautions, however, that it is not always clear to what extent soldiers embraced the Nazis' eliminationist brand of racism and to what extent they leaned on older stereotypes. See Humburg, *Gesicht des Krieges*, 203–4.

86. All quotations from Heinz Sartorio to Elly (sister), 20.5.1942, MSPT 3.2002.0827. Sartorio's explicit attempt to lay responsibility at the foot of the SS foreshadowed the postwar myth that the SS alone had been culpable in the East. In some cases, troops

also identified local residents as the authors of anti-Jewish or anti-communist violence, rather than the Wehrmacht.

87. This may have been Kharkov, where Böhrer was stationed around this time.

88. Anton Böhrer to sister, 21.12.1941 and to sister and parents, 25.12.1941, MSPT 3.2002.0889. Quotations from the former.

89. Kurt Niemeyer to Johanna, 10.3.1942, MSPT 3.2008.1750.

90. Wilhelm Moldenhauser, diary entry of 2–3.7.1941, *Im Funkwagen der Wehrmacht*; Hans Roth, diary entries of 26.6.1941 and 23.9.194, *Eastern Inferno*.

91. See especially Raphael Gross, *Anständig geblieben: Nationalsozialistische Moral* (Frankfurt am Main: S. Fischer, 2010). This method of propagating antisemitism may have been more readily accepted by the German public, particularly among those who found racial arguments less appealing.

92. See Richard Weikart, *Hitler's Ethic: The Nazi Pursuit of Evolutionary Progress* (New York: Palgrave Macmillan, 2009), 87–88.

93. On sexual violence, see especially Regina Mühlhäuser, *Eroberungen: Sexuelle Gewalttaten und intime Beziehungen deutscher Soldaten in der Sowjetunion 1941–1945* (Hamburg: HIS Verlag, 2010).

94. For an in-depth exploration of the liberation narrative, see chapter 4.

95. Harald Hoffmann to parents and Marion (sister), 28.10.1941, MSPT 3.2002.0382. This account is corroborated by the files of Hoffmann's neighboring 68th Infantry Regiment, which recorded in October and November 1941 that the civilians it encountered were friendly to the Germans. See Feldtagebuch von Ltn. S., BA-MA RH 37/1907.

96. Wilhelm Moldenhauser to Erika, 2.8.1941, *Im Funkwagen der Wehrmacht*.

97. See chapter 4.

98. Wilhelm Moldenhauser to Erika, 22.4.1942, *Im Funkwagen der Wehrmacht*. See also Harald Hoffmann to parents and sister, 24.7.1941, MSPT 3.2002.0382.

99. See Willy Reese, *A Stranger to Myself: The Inhumanity of War: Russia, 1941–1944*, ed. Stefan Schmitz, trans. Michael Hofmann (New York: Farrar, Straus and Giroux, 2003), 37: "We were oblivious to the way we were often given food when we set foot in a hut, to the peasants giving us their makhorka to smoke, a woman freely offering us a couple of eggs, or a girl sharing her milk with us. . . . Our commands kept telling us that we were the lords of the universe, in a conquered country."

100. See especially Shepherd, *Hitler's Soldiers*, 168–69.

101. Franz Siebeler to parents, 24.6.1941, MSPT 3.2002.1285.

102. Kurt Lang to mother, 26.6.1942, MSPT 3.2002.0885. See also Harald Hoffmann to parents and Marion, 24.7.1941, MSPT 3.2002.0382.

103. See chapter 1.

104. See chapter 1 on the army's rules against "plundering" and insistence that soldiers pay for all requisitioned goods at exchange rates extremely favorable to the German side.

105. Harald Hoffmann to parents and Marion, 15.11.41, MSPT 3.2002.0382.

106. See the beginning of this chapter.

107. Heinz Rahe to Ursula, 18.2.1943, MSPT 3.2002.0985. Rahe refers here to Romanian troops who fought in his area as allies of Germany.

108. The invaders recognized this fact early on. See for example 167th Infantry Division, Abt. Ib, 3.8.1941, BA-MA 26-167/64. It was the product of economic cir-

cumstances in the USSR, especially in rural areas where there were no consumer goods to buy, and also resulted from the fact that the Germans had massively devalued the ruble. See Götz Aly, *Hitler's Beneficiaries: Plunder, Racial War, and the Nazi Welfare State*, trans. Jefferson Chase (New York: Metropolitan Books, 2006), 156–82; Berkhoff, *Harvest of Despair*, 114–63.

109. Hermann Henning to relatives, 25.9.1941, MSPT 3.2002.7217.

110. Hermann Henning to parents, 28.9.1941, MSPT 3.2002.7217.

111. See Hermann Henning to parents, 3.11.1941 and 7.11.1941, MSPT 3.2002.7217.

112. Heinz Rahe to Ursula, 18.2.1943, MSPT 3.2002.0985.

113. Heinz Rahe to Ursula, 28.10.1941, MSPT 3.2002.0985.

114. Wilhelm Moldenhauer to parents, 24.8.1941, *Im Funkwagen der Wehrmacht*.

115. On supply problems and food shortages from the perspective of ordinary soldiers, see Bartov, *Hitler's Army*, 12–28; Humburg, *Gesicht des Krieges*, 161–64; Latzel, *Deutsche Soldaten*, 140–45.

116. See the report of 12th Inf. Div. commander von Seydlitz, 22.12.1941, BA-MA RH 26-12/164.

117. Both quotations from Hans Simon to mother, 8.9.1941, MSPT 3.2002.1288. Simon and many other soldiers turned in desperation to their relatives to provide them with food and supplies through the mail. In the letters surveyed here, this practice appears to have been so pervasive that it could be speculated that such deliveries were a decisive factor in the Wehrmacht's ability to stay in the fight.

118. See Hans Simon to sister, 28.9.1941, and to parents, 3.11.1941, MSPT 3.2002.1288.

119. Walter Neuser to parents, 15.10.1941, MSPT 3.2002.0947.

120. Walter Neuser to mother, 24.9.1941, MSPT 3.2002.0947.

121. Walter Neuser to mother, 21.9.1941, MSPT 3.2002.0947.

122. Harald Hoffmann to grandmother and aunt Hertha, 25.9.1941, MSPT 3.2002.0382.

123. Harald Hoffmann to parents and Marion, 6.10,1941, 30.9.1941 and 19.9.1941, MSPT 3.2002.0382.

124. 23rd Inf. Div., Abt. IVd(e), Activity Report for 8.8.1941–24.1.1942, BA-MA RH 26-23/76.

125. Harald Hoffmann to unspecified recipient(s), 9.10.1941, MSPT 3.2002.0382.

126. For example, see the letters of his father to Hans-Peter Eckener in MSPT 3.2002.0307.

127. Harald Hoffmann to parents and Marion, 21.10.1941, MSPT 3.2002.0382.

128. Walter Neuser to mother, 24.11.1941, 3.2002.0947.

129. See Fritz, *Frontsoldaten*, 49–50; Hartmann, *Wehrmacht im Ostkrieg*, 765–88; Ben Shepherd, "Hawks, Doves and Tote Zonen: A Wehrmacht Security Division in Central Russia, 1943," *Journal of Contemporary History* 37, no. 3 (2002): 349–69.

130. See 23rd Inf. Div., Abt. IVd(k), Activity Report for 28.8.1941–1.1.1942, BA-MA RH 26-23/76.

131. Harald Hoffmann to parents and Marion, 5.9.1941, MSPT 3.2002.0382.

132. For other examples of soldiers using the logic of "military necessity" to explain scorched-earth tactics and forced evacuations, see Johannes Hagemann to Willy (brother), 4.1.1942, MSPT 3.2002.7234 and Rolf Dietrich to Hilde, 6.8.1943, MSPT 3.2002.7236.

133. Hoffmann's last letter home was on December 21, 1941.

134. Dr. Wilhelm Bacher, diary entry of 7.11.1942, MSPT 3.2002.1376.

135. Both citations from Hans Roth, diary entry of 18.11.1941, in *Eastern Inferno*.

136. Anton Böhrer to sister and father, 2.12.1941, MSPT 3.2002.0889.

137. See Latzel, *Deutsche Soldaten*, 144.

138. For instance, words and phrases such as "forced labor," "murder," "plunder," and "theft" appear very rarely.

139. Walter Neuser to mother, 21–22.8.1941, MSPT 3.2002.0947.

140. See discussion of partisans below.

141. Walter Neuser to mother, 21–22.8.41, MSPT 3.2002.0947.

142. Harald Hoffmann to parents and Marion, 30.9.1941, MSPT 3.2002.0382.

143. See especially Aly, *Hitler's Beneficiaries*, 94–110.

144. Kurt Niemeyer to Johanna and Lieselotte, 12.10.1941, MSPT 3.2008.1750.

145. Father to Helmut, 24.7.1941, MSPT 3.2002.7595. See also Aly, *Hitler's Beneficiaries*, 94–110; Humburg, *Gesicht des Krieges*, 167.

146. Quotations from Harald Hoffmann to parents and Marion, 14.10.1941, 24.7.1941, MSPT 3.2002.0382, respectively.

147. Harald Hoffmann to unknown recipient (most likely parents and sister), 31.10.1941, MSPT 3.2002.0382.

148. Wilhelm Moldenhauer to Erika, 12.10.1941, *Im Funkwagen der Wehrmacht*.

149. Wilhelm Moldenhauer to Erika, 6.9.1941, *Im Funkwagen der Wehrmacht*.

150. See for example Kurt Niemeyer to Johanna, 6.6.1942, MSPT 3.2008.1750.

151. See Generalobserst Hoth, AOK 17 Ia Nr. 0973/41 geh.,17.11.1941, Verhalten der deutschen Soldaten im Ostraum, in Ueberschär and Wette, "*Unternehmen Barbarossa*," 341–43; "*Nicht weich werden!*" *Mitteilungen für die Truppe*, Nr. 157, respectively, November 1941, BA-MA RW 4/357.

152. See chapter 1 on the dehumanizing impact many soldiers feared the war was having on their personalities.

153. See for example Jarausch, *Reluctant Accomplice*; Eugen Altrogge to Hans Albring, 24.3.1942, MSPT 3.2002.0210.

154. On the Wehrmacht and the partisan movement, see Ben Shepherd, *War in the Wild East: The German Army and Soviet Partisans* (Cambridge, MA: Harvard University Press, 2004); Kenneth Slepyan, *Stalin's Guerillas: Soviet Partisans in World War II* (Lawrence: University Press of Kansas, 2006); Ben Shepherd and Juliette Pattinson, *War in a Twilight World: Partisan and Anti-Partisan Warfare in Eastern Europe, 1939–45* (New York: Palgrave Macmillan, 2010). As historians have documented, the Wehrmacht murdered countless Jews and other innocent civilians under the guise of "anti-partisan" operations. This followed the general calculus conflating Jews, communists, and partisans promoted by the Wehrmacht and Nazi authorities, who saw the partisan war as a convenient way to eliminate various categories of "undesirables."

155. See especially Hannes Heer, "The Logic of the War of Extermination: The Wehrmacht and the Anti-Partisan War," in *War of Extermination: The German Military in World War II 1941–1944*, edited by Hannes Heer and Klaus Naumann, translated by Roy Shelton, 92–126.

156. Guerilla fighters were in fact not recognized in contemporary international law as legitimate combatants and could be lawfully killed upon capture. In addition, reprisals on a small scale were not technically illegal. However, the Wehrmacht's policies on

the Eastern Front far exceeded the legal and moral boundaries of the time. See Hamburger Institut für Sozialforschung, *Verbrechen der Wehrmacht*, 15–36.

157. See Latzel, *Deutsche Soldaten*, 183–96. On soldiers' use of this rationalization in southern Europe, see Mark Mazower, "Military Violence and National Socialist Values: The Wehrmacht in Greece 1941–1944," *Past & Present*, no. 134 (1992): 137–38.

158. See Isabel Hull, *Absolute Destruction: Military Culture and the Practices of War in Imperial Germany* (Ithaca, NY: Cornell University Press, 2005), 117–26 and 207–15.

159. For example see AOI9 Ic/AO/O.Qu Nr. 238/41 geh., 2.9.1941, Yad Vashem M29 Fr, 114.

160. Hans-Peter Eckener to parents, 1.3.1942, MSPT 3.2002.0307. Eckener's 205th Infantry Division indeed reported partisan activity in their sector during this time, and instituted curfews and surveillance of the population. See for instance Gruppe-Feldgendarmerie 205, Betr.: Kriegstagebuch 1, 11.5.1942, BA-MA RH 26-205/63.

161. Father to Hans-Peter Eckener, 31.3.1942, MPST 3.2002.0307.

162. See Fritz, *Frontsoldaten*, 51.

163. For one exception, see Fritz, *Frontsoldaten*, 50–51. Fritz quotes a private H. M. whose letter of 17.11.1943 regarding the killing of forty men in a village in the wake of a partisan attack makes it clear he believed that many of the victims were not in fact partisans: "Naturally there were a number of innocent people who had to give up their lives. . . . One didn't waste a lot of time on this and just shot the ones who happened to be around." (51)

164. Walter Neuser to parents, 30.10.1941, MSPT 3.2002.0947.

165. Hans-Peter Eckener to parents, 21.11.1942, MSPT 3.2002.0307.

166. Ibid.

167. Hans-Peter Eckener to father, 27.11.1942, MSPT 3.2002.0307.

168. See for example Johannes Hagemann to parents, 2.12.1941, MSPT 3.2002.7234, on his unit's policy of killing civilians after a forced evacuation.

169. See Humburg, *Gesicht des Krieges*, 204.

170. On the routinization of criminality in the East, see Fritz, *Frontsoldaten*, 50 and 58–59; Christopher Browning, *Ordinary Men: Reserve Police Battalion 101 and the Final Solution in Poland* (New York: HarperCollins, 1992), xix; Hannes Heer, "How Amorality Became Normality: Reflections on the Mentality of German Soldiers on the Eastern Front," in Heer and Naumann, *War of Extermination*, 329–44.

171. Wilhelm Moldenhauser to Erika, 22.4.1942, *Im Funkwagen der Wehrmacht*.

172. Hans Simon to mother, 6.6.1943, MSPT 3.2002.1288.

173. See, for example, Heinz Sartorio to father, 6.4.1942, MSPT 3.2002.0827.

174. Hans-Peter Eckener to parents, 21.10.1942, MSPT 3.2002.0307. For his unit's situation during this time, see BA-MA RH 26–205/71.

175. Rolf Dietrich to Hilde, 2.9.1942, MSPT 3.2002.7236.

176. Rolf Dietrich to Hilde, 24.1.1943, MSPT 3.2002.7236. The city was likely Orel. See also Wilhelm Moldenhauser to Erika, 2.8.1941 and 5.7.1942, *Im Funkwagen der Wehrmacht*.

177. See chapter 4 for a more extensive discussion of the rhetoric of occupation.

178. Quotations from Heinz Rahe to Ursula, 29.1.1943, MSPT 3.2002.0985.

179. See ibid. and Heinz Rahe to Ursula, 29.1.1943, MSPT 3.2002.0985. It is possible that both letters referred to the same woman, but this is unlikely given how frequently Rahe's unit changed locations at this time.

180. Heinz Rahe to Ursula, 18.2.1943, MSPT 3.2002.0985.

181. Hans Simon to parents, 15.7.1941, MSPT 3.2002.1288.

182. Hans Simon to mother, 17.8.1943, MSPT 3.2002.1288.

183. Wilhelm Moldenhauser to Erika, 3.10.1941, *Im Funkwagen der Wehrmacht*.

184. Reese, *A Stranger to Myself*, 155.

185. See Wette, *The Wehrmacht*, 195–250; Omer Bartov, "Historians on the Eastern Front. Andreas Hillgruber and Germany's Tragedy," *Tel Aviver Jahrbuch für deutsche Geschichte* 16 (1987): 325–45; Klaus Naumann, "The 'Unblemished' Wehrmacht: The Social History of a Myth," in Heer and Naumann, *War of Extermination*, 417–29.

186. See Teddy Uldricks, "The Icebreaker Controversy: Did Stalin Plan to Attack Hitler?," *Slavic Review* 58, no. 3 (1999): 626–43.

187. The findings here accord fairly well with those found in Latzel, *Deutsche Soldaten*. In his study of twenty-two soldiers, sixteen mentioned stealing, eight mentioned assorted war crimes, and five mentioned Jews and their persecution. These numbers would likely have been even higher had he focused exclusively on letters from the Soviet Union.

188. See especially Heer, "How Amorality Became Normality."

189. See, for instance, Hannes Heer and Jane Caplan, "The Difficulty of Ending a War: Reactions to the Exhibition 'War of Extermination: Crimes of the Wehrmacht 1941 to 1944,'" *History Workshop Journal*, no. 46 (1998): 182–203, quotation from 190.

190. Further evidence for this conclusion can be found in Stargardt, *The German War*.

191. Those discussed here closely resemble what social psychologists have identified as common moral rationalizations employed to obviate cognitive dissonance. See Bandura and Barbaranelli, "Mechanisms of Moral Disengagement"; Tsang, "Moral Rationalization."

192. Rolf Dietrich to Hilde, 22.2.1944, MSPT 3.2002.7236 regarding his unit's forced evacuation of civilians. For a discussion of the "orders" defense in the context of the Nuremberg Trials, see Barrie Paskins and Michael Dockrill, *The Ethics of War* (Minneapolis: University of Minnesota Press, 1979), 272–74.

193. This accords with the findings of social psychologists, who have typically argued that few perpetrators commit violence purely because they enjoy it, and that even fewer would admit to such a motive. See Arthur G. Miller, ed., *The Social Psychology of Good and Evil* (New York: Guilford Press, 2004) esp. "Four Roots of Evil" by Roy Baumeister and Kathleen Vohs (85–101).

194. This phrase is taken from Bartov, *Hitler's Army*, 107.

3. The "Crusaders"

1. Hans Albring to Eugen Altrogge, August 1941, MSPT 3.2002.0211. Since only the second half of the letter survives, it is unclear what events led up to the service.

2. See chapter 2.

3. See Joseph Perry, "The Madonna of Stalingrad: Mastering the (Christmas) Past and West German National Identity after World War II," *Radical History Review*, no. 83 (Spring 2002): 6–27; Frank Biess, *Homecomings: Returning POWs and the Legacies of Defeat in Postwar Germany* (Princeton, NJ: Princeton University Press, 2006).

4. On the phenomenon of secularization, see especially Charles Taylor, *A Secular Age* (Cambridge, MA: Harvard University Press, 2007).

5. Hans Joachim Schröder, *Die gestohlenen Jahre: Erzählungsgeschichten und Geschicht-serzählung im Interview: der Zweite Weltkrieg aus der Sicht ehemaliger Mannschaftssoldaten*, vols. 1 and 2 (Tübingen: Max Niemeyer Verlag, 1992), 889. A notable exception to this trend is Thomas Kühne, who takes account of the attitudes of devout soldiers and the formation of a Christian subcommunity within the Wehrmacht. See Thomas Kühne, *Kameradschaft: Die Soldaten des nationalsozialistischen Krieges und das 20. Jahrhundert* (Göttingen: Vandenhoeck & Ruprecht, 2006).

6. See Arno J. Mayer, *Der Krieg als Kreuzzug: Das Deutsche Reich, Hitlers Wehrmacht und die "Endlösung,"* trans. Karl Siber (Hamburg: Rowohlt, 1988); Lorna Waddington, *Hitler's Crusade: Bolshevism, the Jews and the Myth of Conspiracy* (New York: I. B. Tauris, 2009).

7. See, for example, Dieter Beese, *Seelsorger in Uniform: Evangelische Militärseelsorge im Zweiten Weltkrieg. Aufgabe, Leitung, Predigt* (Hannover: Lutherisches Verlagshaus, 1995); Antonia Leugers, *Jesuiten in Hitlers Wehrmacht: Kriegslegitimation und Kriegserfahrung* (Paderborn: Ferdinand Schöningh, 2009).

8. For two competing interpretations, see Doris Bergen, "German Military Chaplains in the Second World War and the Dilemmas of Legitimacy," in *The Sword of the Lord: Military Chaplains from the First to the Twenty-First Century*, ed. Doris Bergen (Notre Dame, IN: University of Notre Dame Press, 2004), 165–86; Lauren Faulkner Rossi, *Wehrmacht Priests: Catholicism and the Nazi War of Annihilation* (Cambridge, MA: Harvard University Press, 2015). Here, historians have followed in the footsteps of Manfred Messerschmidt, who portrayed the army as an important battleground for the competing visions of church and Nazi leaders. See Manfred Messerschmidt, "Zur Militärseelsorgepolitik im Zweiten Weltkrieg," *Militärgeschichtliche Mitteilungen* 1 (1969): 37–85.

9. See Hartmut Lehmann, "In the Service of Two Kings: Protestant Prussian Military Chaplains, 1713–1918," in Bergen, *The Sword of the Lord*, 125–40.

10. See *New Regulations for the Prussian Infantry* (London, 1757).

11. See Arnold Angenendt, *Toleranz und Gewalt: Das Christentum zwischen Bibel und Schwert* (Münster, 2012); John A. Moses, "The Rise and Decline of Christian Militarism in Prussia-Germany from Hegel to Bonhoeffer: The End Effect of the Fallacy of Sacred Violence," *War & Society* 23, no. 1 (May 2005): 21–40.

12. Gerd Krumeich, "'Gott mit uns'? Der Erste Weltkrieg als Religionskrieg," in *"Gott mit uns": Nation, Religion und Gewalt im 19. und frühen 20. Jahrhundert*, ed. Gerd Krumeich and Hartmut Lehmann (Göttingen: Vandenhoeck & Ruprecht, 2000), 278; Lehmann, "In the Service of Two Kings," 129–32.

13. See George L. Mosse, *Nationalism and Sexuality: Respectability and Abnormal Sexuality in Modern Europe* (New York: Howard Fertig, 1985), 4–6; Vejas Gabriel Liulevicius, *The German Myth of the East: 1800 to the Present* (New York: Oxford University Press, 2009).

14. See Wolfgang Mommsen, "Die nationalgeschichtliche Umdeutung der christlichen Botschaft im Ersten Weltkrieg," in Krumeich and Lehmann, *"Gott mit uns,"* 249–61.

15. See Mommsen, "Die nationalgeschichtliche Umdeutung," 260–61; Krumeich, "Gott mit uns?," 280–83; Jay Winter, *Sites of Memory, Sites of Mourning: The Great War in European Cultural History* (Cambridge: Cambridge University Press, 1995).

16. See Hugh McLeod and Werner Ustorf, eds., *The Decline of Christendom in Western Europe, 1750–2000* (Cambridge: Cambridge University Press, 2003).

17. See, for instance, Evangelisches Zentralarchiv (hereafter EZA) 5/1129, as well as EZA 5/209, 5/210 and 5/211.

18. See Giuliana Chamedes, "The Vatican and the Reshaping of the European International Order after the First World War," *The Historical Journal* 56, no. 4 (2013): 955–76; Gordon Zahn, *German Catholics and Hitler's Wars* (New York: Sheed and Ward, 1962); Kurt Meier, "Sowjetrußland im Urteil der evangelischen Kirche (1917–1945)," in *Das Rußlandbild im Dritten Reich*, ed. Hans-Erich Volkmann (Köln: Böhlau Verlag, 1994), 285–321.

19. See Thomas Childers, *The Nazi Voter: The Social Foundations of Fascism in Germany, 1919–1933* (Chapel Hill: University of North Carolina Press, 1983).

20. See Robert Ericksen and Susannah Heschel, "The German Churches Face Hitler: An Assessment of the Historiography," *Tel Aviver Jahrbuch für deutsche Geschichte* 23 (1994): 433–59; Kevin Spicer, *Hitler's Priests: Catholic Clergy and National Socialism* (DeKalb: Illinois University Press, 2008); Guenter Lewy, *The Catholic Church and Nazi Germany* (Boston: Da Capo Press, 2000).

21. See Doris Bergen, *Twisted Cross: The German Christian Movement in the Third Reich* (Chapel Hill: University of North Carolina Press, 1996); Susannah Heschel, *The Aryan Jesus: Christian Theologians and the Bible in Nazi Germany* (Princeton, NJ: Princeton University Press, 2008).

22. See, for example, *Der Neue Wille: Wochenzeitschrift für Katholische Deutsche* (Frankfurt am Main: Carolus-Verlag, 1939–1941); Mitteilungen and Verordnungsblätter of the Protestant Field Bishop, Archiv des Katholischen Militärbischofsamtes (hereafter KMBA) WmS 86; Kirchliche Kriegshilfe Sendungen, 1941, EAF B2-35/83.

23. *Evangelisches Feldgesangbuch* (Berlin: Verlag E. S. Mittler & Sohn, 1939); *Katholisches Feldgesangbuch* (Berlin: Verlag E. S. Mittler & Sohn, 1939).

24. Messerschmidt, "Zur Militärseelsorgepolitik," 41–64; Bergen, "German Military Chaplains," 173–175. Although done in the name of religious freedom, this move was largely aimed at weakening church influence.

25. See EZA 1-3235, passim.; Chef der Heeresrüstung und Befehlshaber des Ersatzheeres to Ev. and Kat. Kriegsbischöfe, Betr.: Anforderung religiösen Schrifttums, 30.9.1941, BA-MA RH 20-16/1096.

26. See Messerschmidt, "Zur Militärseelsorgepolitik," 61.

27. Typically, this meant two (one Protestant and one Catholic) for each military formation from the division level up and for each major hospital. On the Protestant chaplaincy during the Second World War, see especially Beese, *Seelsorger in Uniform*; Bergen, "German Military Chaplains." For the Catholic chaplaincy and priest–soldiers, see Heinrich Missalla, *Für Gott, Führer und Vaterland: Die Verstrickung der katholischen Seelsorge in Hitlers Krieg* (München: Kösel, 1999); Faulkner Rossi, *Wehrmacht Priests*; Dagmar Pöpping, *Kriegspfarrer an der Ostfront: Evangelische und katholische Wehrmachtseelsorge im Vernichtungskrieg 1941–1945* (Göttingen: Vandenhoeck & Ruprecht, 2017).

28. See "Merkblatt über die Feldseelsorge," 12.8.1941, BA-MA RH 15/281 and KMBA SW 5; OKW, "Richtlinien für die Ausübung der Feldseelsorge," 24.5.1942, KMBA SW 5.

29. Reibert, "Wortlaut der Pflichten des deutschen Soldaten," in *Der Dienstunterricht im Heer*, 31.

30. See Messerschmidt, "Zur Militärseelsorgepolitik," 61.

31. See Hans Mommsen, "Der Krieg gegen die Sowjetunion und die deutsche Gesellschaft," in *Präventiv-krieg? Der deutsche Angriff auf die Sowjetunion*, ed. Bianka Pietrow-Ennker (Frankfurt am Main: Fischer Taschenbuch Verlag, 2011), 59–68.

32. See Wolfram Wette, "Die propagandistische Begleitmusik zum deutschen Überfall auf die Sowjet-union am 22. Juni 1941," in *"Unternehmen Barbarossa": Der deutsche Überfall auf die Sowjetunion 1941*, ed. Gerd R. Ueberschär and Wolfram Wette (Paderborn: Schöningh, 1984), 122–23; Waddington, *Hitler's Crusade*, 188–89.

33. "Erklärung der 'Deutschen diplomatisch-politischen Information' vom 27.6.1941 über den Krieg gegen die Sowjetunion," *Völkischer Beobachter*, Berliner Ausgabe, Nr. 179 vom 28 Juni 1941, reprinted in Ueberschär and Wette, *"Unternehmen Barbarossa,"* 323–324.

34. Joseph Goebbels, diary entries of 23.6.1941 and 24.6.1941, *Die Tagebücher von Joseph Goebbels: Teil I: Aufzeichnungen 1923–1941*, Band 9, ed. Elke Fröhlich (K. G. Sauer, München, 1998) 398–399 and diary entry of 16.7.1941, *Die Tagebücher von Joseph Goebbels: Teil II: Diktate 1941–1945*, Band 1, Juli–September 1941, ed. Elke Fröhlich (K. G. Sauer, München, 1996), 74. Goebbels confided to his diary that the crusade line was useful but that it was preferable to avoid any talk of a crusade for "Christendom" specifically, since that would be "simply too cynical" (398).

35. Joseph Goebbels, "Der Schleier Fällt," *Das Reich*, July 6, 1941, reprinted in *Die Zeit ohne Beispiel* (München: Zentralverlag der NSDAP, 1941).

36. Perhaps fittingly, the emperor Hitler referenced, Frederick I, died in the attempt. See Wette, "Die propagandistische Begleitmusik," 123.

37. See Hitlers Aufruf an die "Soldaten der Ostfront" vom 22.6.1941, reprinted in Ueberschär and Wette, *"Unternehmen Barbarossa,"* 323.

38. See Adolf Hitler, speech at the opening of the Winter Relief Fund, 30.9.1942, reprinted in Max Domarus, ed., *Hitler: Speeches and Proclamations 1932–1945 and Commentary by a Contemporary: The Chronicles of a Dictatorship*, vol. 4 (1941–1945) (Wauconda, IL: Bolchazy-Carducci Publishers, 2004), 2678.

39. This point is demonstrated most clearly in Waddington, *Hitler's Crusade*.

40. See especially Hartmut Lenhard, "'. . . keine Zweifel an der Richtigkeit dieses Krieges': Christen und Kirchen im Krieg gegen die Sowjetunion," in *Frieden mit der Sowjetunion—eine unerledigte Aufgabe*, ed. Dietrich Goldschmidt (Gütersloher: Gütersloher Verlagshaus G. Mohn, 1989), 237–62.

41. Der Vorsitzende des Geistlichen Vertrauensrats der Deutschen Evangeslichen Kirche an den Führer, Telegram, 1.7.1941, EZA 1/2420.

42. See Victoria Barnett, *For the Soul of the People: Protestant Protest against Hitler* (New York: Oxford University Press, 1998), 155–94.

43. See Adolf Kardinal Bertram, *Hirtenbriefe und Hirtenworte*, ed. Werner Marschall (Köln: Böhlau Verlag, 2000), esp. 809, 818, and 829; Bischof Clemens August Graf von Galen, *Akten, Briefe und Predigten 1933–1946*, vol. 2 (1939–1946), ed. Peter Löffler (Mainz: Matthias-Grünewald Verlag, 1988), 901–8 and 944.

44. Richard J. Evans, *The Third Reich at War 1939–1945* (New York: Penguin Books, 2010), 546.

45. On this shift, see 131st Inf. Div., Abt. IVd(e), Activity Report, 7.4.1941, BA-MA RH 26-131/35; AOK6, Abt. IVd(k), Seelsorgebericht for July–September 1941, KMBA WmS 7.

46. Their letters are housed under MSPT 3.2002.0211 and 3.2002.0210, respectively.

47. See MSPT 3.2002.0947.

48. Hans Wilhelm Sauer to parents and sisters, 7.9.1941, MSPT 3.2002.1271.

49. See, for example, Hans Simon to father, 28.7.1941, MSPT 3.2002.1288.

50. Konrad Jarausch, *Reluctant Accomplice: A Wehrmacht Soldier's Letters from the Eastern Front*, ed. Konrad H. Jarausch (Princeton, NJ: Princeton University Press, 2011), 1–31.

51. See Helmut Walser Smith, *German Nationalism and Religious Conflict: Culture, Ideology, Politics, 1870–1914* (Princeton, NJ: Princeton University Press, 1995).

52. Franz Siebeler to parents and siblings, 23.11.1941, MSPT 3.2002.1285.

53. Hans Albring to Eugen Altrogge, 15.8.1942, MSPT 3.2002.0211.

54. See Hans Wilhelm Sauer to parents, sisters, and grandmother, 24.9.1942, MSPT 3.2002.1271.

55. See Franz Siebeler to parents and siblings, 23.11.1941, MSPT 3.2002.1285.

56. Hans Simon to mother, 17.6.1941, MSPT 3.2002.1288.

57. See, for example, 131st Inf. Div., Abt. IVd(k), Seelsorgebericht, undated, KMBA WmS 8.

58. See Dr. Sven Hedin, "Kreuzzug gegen den Kommunismus," *Der Durchbruch*, 16.11.1941, BA-MA RHD 69/19; "Dein Brief, Kamerad . . . ," *Der Durchbruch*, 16.9.1941, ibid.

59. "Die geistige Wasserscheide," *Der Kampf*, Nr. 26, 28.8.1941, BA-MA RHD 69/41.

60. "Welche besonderen Pflichten erwachsen jetzt den im Osten nicht eingesetzten Soldaten?" *Mitteilungen für die Truppe*, Nr. 116, July, 1941, BA-MA RW 4-357. Between 1941 and 1945, the *Mitteilungen* carried no fewer than 25 religiously themed articles.

61. See, for instance, "Vatikan und Bolschewismus: Die Haltung zum antibolschewistischen Krieg," *Feldzeitung von der Maas bis an die Memel*, 2.8.1941, BA-MA RHD 69/15.

62. Franz Justus Rarkowski, "Hirtenwort an die katholischen Wehrmachtsangehörigen zu dem großen Entscheidungskampf im Osten," 29.7.1941, in Heinrich Missalla, *Wie der Krieg zur Schule Gottes wurde: Hitlers Feldbischof Rarkowski: Eine notwendige Erinnerung* (Taschenbuch, 1997), 57–58.

63. 18th Inf. Div., Abt. IVd(e), Feldpredigt, 16.8.1941, BA-MA RH 26-18/100.

64. See David Harrisville, "Shepherds of Wolves: Wehrmacht Chaplains, the Second World War, German Colonialism, and Nazi Ideology" (master's thesis, University of Wisconsin–Madison, 2012).

65. Konrad Jarausch to wife, 14.8.1941, *Reluctant Accomplice*, 250.

66. Ibid.

67. Dr. Wilhelm Bacher, for instance, snapped two photos of a Staraja Russa cathedral for his diary. See Bacher, diary entry for 22.3.1943 with pictures, MSPT 3.2002.1376.

68. Willi Groß, "'Das ukrainische Dorf.' Eine Spielzeugbastelei für jeden Landser," *Ostkurier*, 1.9.1943, BA-MA RHD 69/5.

69. Konrad Jarausch to wife, 14.8.1941, *Reluctant Accomplice*, 251.

70. Hans Simon to father, 21.7.1941, MSPT 3.2002.1288.

71. Eugen Altrogge to Hans Albring, 3.7.1941, MSPT 3.2002.0210.

72. Hans Albring to Eugen Altrogge, 25.7.1941, MSPT 3.2002.0211.

73. Hans Albring to Eugen Altrogge, undated, MSPT 3.2002.0211.

74. Walter Neuser to mother, 17.7.1941, MSPT 3.2002.0947.

75. Walter Neuser to parents, 15.10.1941 and to mother, 11.11.1941, MSPT 3.2002.0947.

76. Franz Siebeler to parents and siblings, 10.7.1941, 15.7.1941 and 24.8.1941, MSPT 3.2002.1285, quote from 15.7.1941.

77. See Willy Nagel to Wandelgard, 1.1.1942, MSPT 3.2002.0326.

78. L. Henninger, "Das Gesicht einer Sowjet-Stadt," *Der Durchbruch*, 4.9.1941, BA-MA RHD 69/19. Also see "Kirchen als Pferdeställe," *Feldzeitung von der Maas bis an die Memel*, 30.8.1941, BA-MA RHD 69/76.

79. Hans Dähn, "Ein Wiedersehen in Wilna," *Der Durchbruch*, 8.7.1941, BA-MA RHD 69/19.

80. "1100 Geistliche in Kauen ermordet: Kreuze im Oberkörper und Arm einge-brannt," *Feldzeitung von der Maas bis an die Memel*, 13.7.1941, BA-MA RHD 69/15.

81. See Elle, "An der Wolgaquelle," *Feldzeitung von der Maas bis an die Memel*, 6.11.1941, BA-MA RHD 69/76.

82. See Dr. Werner Haugg, "Die Religion in der Sowjet-Union, " *Deutsche Allgemeine Zeitung*, October 19, 1941; "Kirchen Ohne Kreuz," *Frankfurter Zeitung*, September 28, 1941.

83. Franz Siebeler to parents and siblings, 21.6.1941, MSPT 3.2002.1285.

84. Eugen Altrogge to Hans Albring, 13.4.1942, MSPT 3.2002.0210.

85. See Hans Roth, diary entries of 14.7.1941, 29.9.1941, and 24.12.1941, in Hans Roth, *Eastern Inferno: The Journals of a German Panzerjäger on the Eastern Front, 1941–1943*, ed. Christine Alexander and Mason Kunze (Philadelphia, PA: Casemate, 2010).

86. See chapter 4 for more on soldiers' opinions regarding conditions in the Soviet Union.

87. Hans Albring to Eugen Altrogge, 28.7.1941, MSPT 3.2002.0211.

88. Hans Albring to Eugen Altrogge, undated, MSPT 3.2002.0211.

89. AOK9, Abt. IVd(e) Activity Report for 23.7–14.9.1941, BA-MA RH 20-9/323.

90. Examples include 11th Inf. Div., Abt. IVd(k) Activity Report for 18.8.1941–31.3.1942, BA-MA RH 26-11/91; PzAOK3, Abt. IVd(k), Activity Report, 15.3.1942, BA-MA RH 27-3/226.

91. 14th Pz. Div., Abt. IVd(e), Monthly Report for August 1941, BA-MA RH 27-14/24.

92. Walter Neuser to mother, 25.8.1941, MSPT 3.2002.0947.

93. Wilhelm Moldenhauser to Erika (wife), 23.8.1941, *Im Funkwagen der Wehrmacht durch Europa: Balkan, Ukraine, Stalingrad: Feldpostbriefe des Gefreiten Wilhelm Molden-hauser 1940–1943*, ed. Jens Ebert (Berlin: Trafo, 2008).

94. Examples abound. See AOK2, Abt. IVd(k), Activity Report for 1.10–31.12.1941, BA-MA RH 20-2/1606.

95. See, for example, Franz Siebeler to parents and siblings, 28.9.1941, MSPT 3.20002.1285.

96. Heinz Rahe to Ursula (wife), 29.9.1941 and 23.11.1941, MSPT 3.2002.0985.

97. See, for instance, 8th Jäger Div., Abt. IVd(k), Activity Report for 16.3.1942-10.7.1942, 10.7.1942, BA-MA RH 26-8/74.

98. See, for example, Hans Wilhelm Sauer to unspecified recipient(s), 27.7.1942, and to parents and Christa, 2.11.1942, MSPT 3.2002.1271; Kühne, *Kameradschaft*, 166.

99. AOK2, Abt. IVd(k), Seelsorgebericht for 1.7–30.9.1944, BA-MA N 338/3.

100. AOK11, Abt. IVd(k), Activity Report for 1.1–31.3.1942, BA-MA RH 20-11/414. See also Hans-Wilhelm Sauer to parents, sisters, and grandmother, 3.2002.1271.

101. 8th Jäger Div., Abt. IVd(k), Seelsorgebericht, 1.7–15.7.1941, KMBA WmS 8.

102. Hans Wilhelm Sauer to parents and sisters, 14.6.1940, MSPT 3.2002.1271; Wilhelm Moldenhauser to Erika (wife), 6.7.1941, *Im Funkwagen der Wehrmacht*.

103. On popular piety in the region during the invasion, see Karel Berkhoff, *Harvest of Despair: Life and Death in Ukraine Under Nazi Rule* (Cambridge, MA: Belknap Press, 2004), 232–52.

104. Hans Simon to his father, 21.7.41, MSPT 3.2002.1288.

105. See Hans Albring to Eugen Altrogge, undated, MSPT 3.2002.0211.

106. Hans Albring to Eugen Altrogge, Michaelstag, 1941, MSPT 3.2002.0211.

107. See Hans Albring to Eugen Altrogge 30–31.8.1941, MSPT 3.2002.0211.

108. Franz Siebeler to parents and siblings, 15.7.1941, MSPT 3.2002.1285.

109. Kriegsberichter Bernd Poiess, "Das Rätsel der russischen Seele," 2.10.1941, *Feldzeitung von der Maas bis an die Memel*, BA-MA RHD 69/76.

110. *Feldzeitung von der Maas bis an die Memel*, 7.10.1941, BA-MA RHD 69/76. See also "Am Rande der Straße ein kleines Dorf: 'Seid Ihr deutsche oder bolschewistische Soldaten?'—Erlebnis mit der Zivilbevölkerung," 23.8.1941, ibid., BA-MA RHD 69/15.

111. For example, see AOK2, Abt. Ic/VAA, Bericht Nr. 8, 1.8.1941, BA-MA RH 20-2/1091.

112. AOK2, Abt. Ic/VAA, Bericht Nr. 21, 24.9.1941, BA-MA RH 20-2/1093.

113. See Franz Siebeler to parents and siblings, 21.6.1941, MSPT 3.2002.1285.

114. Heinz Rahe to Ursula (wife), 18–20.07.41, MSPT 3.2002.0985.

115. Konrad Jarausch to wife, 28.8.1941, *Reluctant Accomplice*, 271–72; ibid., 1.9.1941, *Reluctant Accomplice*, 274. Quotation from the latter.

116. Konrad Jarausch to wife, 14.8.1941, *Reluctant Accomplice*, 251; ibid., 1.9.1941, *Reluctant Accomplice*, 274. Quotation from the former.

117. Eugen Altrogge to Hans Albring, 18.7.1942, MSPT 3.2002.0210.

118. See Harrisville, "Shepherds of Wolves."

119. On these events, see David Harrisville, "Unholy Crusaders: The Wehrmacht and the Re-Establishment of Soviet Churches during Operation Barbarossa," *Central European History* 52, no. 4 (2019): 620–49; Alexander Dallin, *German Rule in Russia, 1941–1945: A Study of Occupation Politics* (London: Macmillan, 1957), 477–78; Berkhoff, *Harvest of Despair*, 233–34 and 239–42.

120. On the religious outlook of the populace, see Berkhoff, *Harvest of Despair*, 239–43.

121. "Mitteilungen aus dem kirchlichen Leben," 1.9.1941, EAF B2-43-26.

122. Ernst Tewes, *Seelsorger bei den Soldaten: Erinnerungen an die Zeit von 1940 bis 1945* (München: Don Bosco Verlag, 1995), 20–21.

123. Quotation from Franz Siebeler to parents and siblings, 10.12.1941, MSPT 3.2002.1285.

124. AOK2, Abt. IVd(k), Activity Report for 23.6–1.10.1941, BA-MA RH 20-2/1604.

125. Hans Albring to Eugen Altrogge, 5.10.1041, MSPT 3.2002.0211.

126. Wilhelm Schabel, ed., *Herr, in Deine Hände* (Stuttgart: Alfred Scherz Verlag, 1963), 92.

127. Katholischen Militärbischofsamt, *Mensch, was wollt ihr denen sagen? Katholische Feldseelsorge im Zweiten Weltkrieg* (Augsburg: Pattloch Verlag, 1991), 86–87. The civilians in question were likely *Volksdeutsch*.

128. XXIX AK, Abt. IVd(e) Activity Report, 30.4–26.7.1941, BA-MA RH 24-29/100.

129. See, for example, Pfarramt Achdorf to Erz. Ordinariat Freiburg, "Bericht des Geistl. Rates Pieger-Bukarest über die religiöse Lage der katholischen deutschen Gemeinden in der West-Ukraine," 12.12.41, EAF B2-43-26.

130. Infantry Regiment 413 to 206th Division, Betr.: Verhalten der Zivilbevölkerung zum deutschen Militär, 21.9.1941, in BA-MA RH 20–9/323. The engineers were halted by civilians who insisted on doing the work themselves.

131. On the prior regulations, see Ev. Feldbischof to Oberbefehlshaber des Heeres, 6.10.1941, KMBA SW/111 and OKH, "Bestimmungen für besondere Dienstverhältnisse der Kriegspfarrer beim Feldheer," 18.6.1941, KMBA SW/5.

132. See, for instance, 14th Pz. Div., Abt. IVd(e) monthly report, September 1941, BA-MA RH 27-14/24; XXIX AK, Abt. IVd(e), Activity Report for April–July, 1941, BA-MA RH 24-29/100.

133. To cite one example, Army Group Center allowed reopenings due to their propaganda value but stated that the religious intermixing of soldiers and civilians was "not desired." See Katholischer Armeepfarrer AOK2 to Katholische Kriegspfarrer im Dienstbereich, 15.8.1941, BA-MA RH 20-2/1604. Further discussions between the Armeepfarrer and the Army Group led to the clarification that baptisms of Catholic children were allowed upon the family's request, and Orthodox children could be baptized in emergencies.

134. See, for example, "Nach 23 Jahren öffnet sich die Tür . . . Soldaten erleben die Öffnung einer russischen Kirche," *Feldzeitung von der Maas bis an die Memel*, 31.8.1941, BA-MA RHD 69/76.

135. *Signal*, Nr. 18, 2.9.1941. Also see Signal Heft 23, December 1941. Evidently, the editors either ignored or did not know about Hitler's August *Erlass* prohibiting such activity (see below).

136. See "Kirchen Ohne Kreuz," *Frankfurter Zeitung*, September 28, 1941; "Der erste Gottesdienst nach 20 Jahren," *Liebenwerdär Kreisblatt*, Nr. 139, 19.8.1941, copied in EZA 5/211.

137. Hirtenbrief of Clemens August Bishop of Münster, 14.9.1941, KMBA SW 1059.

138. See "Mitteilungen aus dem kirchlichen Leben," 1.10.1941, EAF B2/43/26.

139. "Verordnungsblatt des Katholischen Feldbischofs der Wehrmacht," Nr. 3, 15.3.1942, KMBA SW 1046; ibid., Nr. 5, 1941, reprinted in "Amtsblatt des Bischöflichen Ordinariats Berlin," Katholisches Erzbistum Archiv Berlin (KEAB), W 320.

140. This applied at least to the *Volksdeutsch*. See EZA 50/572, Bl. 1f.

141. See EZA 5/211, EZA 1/2421 and "Mitteilungen des Kirchlichen Aussenamtes," 2.9.1941, EZA 1/3230.

142. Dr. Th. Heckel, *Der Bolschewismus im Kampf gegen Gott 1917–1942* (manuscript, June 1943), EZA 5/211.

143. "Weisung an militärische Dienststellen über Verhalten in der Religionsfrage," 3.8.1941, BA-MA RW 4/578. Three days later, OKW issued its army groups and rear army areas a directive based on the *Erlass*: Az 31vAWA/J (Ia) Nr. 4798/41, 6.8.1941, KMBA SW 111.

144. OKW Az. 31 v AWA/J (Ia) Nr. 4798/41 II.Ang., 10.9.1941, KMBA SW 111. See KMBA SW 111 for further clarifications issued by OKW in an exchange with the field bishops.

145. There were exceptions, as some chaplains and troops ignored Hitler's order and continued to offer religious care for civilians. For one example, see Dietrich Baedeker, *Das Volk, das im finstern wandelt: Stationen eines Militärpfarrers 1938–1946*, edited by Evang. Kirchenamt für d. Bundeswehr Bonn. (Hanover: Lutherisches Verlagshaus, 1987), 58.

146. Ev. Feldbischof to Oberbefehlshaber des Heeres, 6.10.41, and Kat. Feldbischof to Oberbefehlshaber des Heeres, 7.10.41, KMBA SW 111; Wehrmacht Deacons Thomann and Bemann to all subordinate chaplains, 7.10.41, KMBA SW 8; Wehrmacht Deacon Thomann to Rarkowski, 17.10.41, KMBA SW 81.

147. AOK2, Abt. IVd(kat), Report for July–September, 1941, KMBA WmS 8.

148. AOK11 Abt. IVd(kat) Seelsorgebericht, July–September, 1941, KMBA WmS 7.

149. See Joe Perry, *Christmas in Germany: A Cultural History* (Chapel Hill: University of North Carolina Press, 2010).

150. Ibid., 93–138.

151. Johannes Hagemann to parents, 25.12.1941, MSPT 3.2002. 7234.

152. Willy Nagel to Wanda, 24.12.1941, MSPT 3.2002.0326.

153. See Hans Roth, diary of 24.12.1941, *Eastern Inferno*.

154. Wilhelm Altmann to father and sister, Christmas Day 1941, MSPT 3.2002.0201.

155. Willy Hagemann to Kressen, 24.12.1943, MSPT 3.2002.7169.

156. Willy Hagemann to parents, 26.12.1943, MSPT 3.2002.7169.

157. Quotations from Hans Simon to mother, 9.9.1942, MSPT 3.2002.1288 and Hans Simon to parents, 20.4.1942, MSPT 3.2002.1288, respectively.

158. See Hans Simon to mother, 9.9.1942, MSPT 3.2002.1288.

159. Hans Simon to sister, 21.11.1942, MSPT 3.2002.1288.

160. 12th Inf. Div., Abt. IVd(e) Activity Report for 16.12.1941–28.2.1943, BA-MA RH 26-12/144.

161. Franz Siebeler to parents and siblings, 2 Pfingstag, 1942, MSPT 3.2002.1285.

162. See Franz Siebeler to parents and siblings, 26.2.1942, MSPT 3.2002.1285.

163. See Franz Siebeler to parents and siblings, Oster Sonntag, 1942, MSPT 3.2002.1285; Franz Siebeler to parents and siblings, 18.11.1942, MSPT 3.2002.1285.

164. See Franz Siebeler to parents and siblings, 2 Pfingstag, 1942, 8.6.1942.

165. See Franz Siebeler to parents and siblings, 4.10.1942, MSPT 3.2002.1285, and below.

166. 20th Pz. Div., Abt. IVd(k), Seelsorgebericht, 1.7-30.9.1941, KMBA WmS 6.

167. AOK16, Abt. IVd(e), Activity Report, 8.8-15.10.1941, BA-MA RH 20-16/1095.

168. 12th Inf. Div., Abt. IVd(e), Activity Report, 16.12.1941-28.2.1943, BA-MA RH 26/12 144.

169. 11th Inf. Div., Abt. IVd(e), Activity Report, 1.10-31.12.1942, BA-MA RH 20-11/413.

170. See, for instance, 297th Inf. Div., Abt. IVd(k), Activity Report, 15.5–22.11.1941, KMBA WmS 9.

171. Hans Simon to unspecified recipient(s), 16.8.1941, MSPT 3.2002.1288.

172. Hans Simon to mother, 4.11.1941, MSPT 3.2002.1288.

173. See Hans Albring to Eugen Altrogge, 1.3.1942, MSPT 3.2002.0211; Hans Albring to Eugen Altrogge, 29.4.1942, MSPT 3.2002.0211.

174. Heinz Rahe to Ursula (wife), 21.1.1943, MSPT 3.2002.0985.

175. See AOK2, Abt. IVd(e), Activity Report, 1.10–31.12.1942, BA-MA RH 20-9/386, which mentions "variable" attendance at services and a 5–25 percent participation rate in Communion in the subordinate 86th Infantry Division.

176. See 56th Inf. Div., Abt. IVd(k) Seelsorgebericht, 1.6–5.10.1941, KMBA WmS 7.

177. See 268th Inf. Div., Abt. IVd(k), Seelsorgebericht, July–September, 1941, KMBA WmS 6.

178. 123rd Inf. Div., Abt. IVd(k), Seelsorgebericht for 1.7–31.12.1942, KMBA WmS 10.

179. "Eine bestialische Lehre," *Mitteilungen für die Truppe*, Nr. 187, March 1942, BA-MA RW 4/357.

180. For example, see "Soldatengebet," *Blücher* 9.10.1941, BA-MA RHD 69/33.

181. See Dallin, *German Rule*, 474–80; Dieter Pohl, *Die Herrschaft der Wehrmacht: Deutsche Militärbesatzung und einheimische Bevölkerung in der Sowjetunion 1941–1944* (München: R. Oldenbourg Verlag, 2008), 139–41; Berkhoff, *Harvest of Despair*, 232–52; Harvey Fireside, *Icon and Swastika: The Russian Orthodox Church under Nazi and Soviet Control* (Cambridge, MA: Harvard University Press, 1971).

182. See Weisung an militärische Dienststellen über Verhalten in der Religions-frage, Berlin, 3.8.1941, BArch R 6/177 expressing such fears. For Orthodox attitudes in the occupied lands, see Oberpriester K. to the Metropoliten S., Berlin, in KMBA SW II-1 599; USHMM, RG-22.014M, Reel 6, Nr. 57 (475–485).

183. See, for example, "Eigenständige Kirche der Ukraine," 17.2.1942, *Soldaten-zeitung der Ukraine*, BA-MA RHD 69/9.

184. Hans Albring to Eugen Altrogge, 8.7.1941 and Allerseelen, 1941, MSPT 3.2002.0211.

185. Hans Albring to Eugen Altrogge, 8.7.1941, 5.10.1941, Allerseelen, 1941, and Fronleichnamstag, 1942, MSPT 3.2002.0211.

186. See Hans Albring to Eugen Altrogge, 30–31.8.1941, 14.9.1941, 5.10.41, and Allerseelen, 1941, MSPT 3.2002.0211.

187. Hans Albring to Eugen Altrogge, Michaelstag 1941 and 5.10.1941, MSPT 3.2002.0211.

188. See Hans Albring to Eugen Altrogge, Fronleichnamstag, 1942, MSPT 3.2002.0211.

189. Dr. Wilhelm Bacher, diary entries of 22.3.1943 and 23.9.1941, MSPT 3.2002.1376.

190. Dr. Wilhelm Bacher, diary entry of 14.1.1942, MSPT 3.2002.1376.

191. Franz Siebeler to parents and siblings, 15.7.1941, MSPT 3.2002.1285.

192. Rudolf ("Rolf") Dietrich to Hilde, 26.4.43, MSPT 3.2002.7236.

193. Eugen Altrogge to Hans Albring, 28.10.1942, MSPT 3.2002.0210.

194. See Eugen Altrogge to Hans Albring, 18.7.1942, MSPT 3.2002.0210.

195. Hans Albring to Eugen Altrogge, 30–31.8.1941, MSPT 3.2002.0211.

196. Hans Albring to Eugen Altrogge, 4.9.1941, MSPT 3.2002.0211.

197. Wilhelm Moldenhauer to Erika, 7.1.1942, *Im Funkwagen der Wehrmacht*.

198. Wilhelm Moldenhauer to Erika, 2.8.1941, *Im Funkwagen der Wehrmacht*.

199. See Wilhelm Moldenhauer to Erika, 4.4.1942 and 7.1.1942, *Im Funkwagen der Wehrmacht*.

200. Walter Neuser to parents, 22.4.1942, MSPT 3.2002.0947.

201. Krumeich, "Gott mit uns?," 280.

202. See Joseph Perry, "The Madonna of Stalingrad." "Cauldron" was a common term for an area encircled by military forces.

203. Heinz Rahe to Ursula (wife), 23.4.1943, MSPT 3.2002.0985.

204. Heinz Rahe to Ursula, 23.1.1943, MSPT 3.2002.0985.

205. Hans Simon to mother, 29.8.1943, MSPT 3.2002.1288.

206. Hans Simon to mother, 26.9.1943, MSPT 3.2002.1288.

207. Hans Simon to mother, 6–7.2.1943, MSPT 3.2002.1288.

208. See Hans Simon to mother, 30.1.1943 and 2.2.1943, MSPT 3.2002.1288. Quotation from the latter.

209. Hans Simon to mother, 10.7.1943, MSPT 3.2002.1288.

210. Kurt Niemeyer to Johanna (wife), 10.8.1943 and 16.8.1943, MSPT 3.2008.1750. Quotation from the former.

211. Kurt Niemeyer to Johanna, 5.8.1943, MSPT 3.2008.1750.

212. See, for example, Gauleitung Köln-Aachen to Reichspropagandaleitung der NSDAP, Betr.: Veröffentlichung von Gefallenen durch die Kirche, 19.3.1942, BArch NS 18/474.

213. See Bergen, "German Military Chaplains," 173–75.

214. See Faulkner Rossi, *Wehrmacht Priests*, Introduction.

215. See soldiers' letters in KMBA SW 1024; Bartsch to the Kirchenkanzlei der Deutschen Evangl Kirche, 8.11.1943, EZA 1/3235; Erzbischof of Breslau to Reichsminister for Church Affairs, 26.11.1942, EAF B2-47-46

216. See Commissariat Fuldaer Bischofskonferenz to the Erzbischof of Freiburg, 11.12.1943, EAF B2-47-46.

217. Hans Albring to Eugen Altrogge, Christmas 1941, MSPT 3.2002.0211.

218. Franz Siebeler to parents and siblings, Christmas, 1941, MSPT 3.2002.1285.

219. Franz Siebeler to parents and siblings, 27.12.1941, MSPT 3.2002.1285.

220. Franz Siebeler to parents and siblings, 27.12.1941 and 4.10.1942, MSPT 3.2002.1285. Quotation from the former.

221. Hans Albring to Eugen Altrogge, 14.9.1941, MSPT 3.2002.0211.

222. See Konrad Jarausch to wife, 29.12.1941, *Reluctant Accomplice*, 351.

223. AOK2, Feldpostprüfstelle Report for October 1941, BA-MA RH 20-2/1094.

224. Franz Siebeler to parents and siblings, 23.11.1941, MSPT 3.2002.1285.

225. Hans Simon to father, 9.12.1942, MSPT 3.2002.1288.

226. *Reluctant Accomplice*, 273–366.

227. See chapter 2.

228. Franz Siebeler to parents and siblings, 15.7.1941, MSPT 3.2002.1285.

229. Hans Albring to Eugen Altrogge, 8.7.1941 and 21.3.1942, respectively, MSPT 3.2002.0211.

230. Heinz Rahe to Ursula (wife), 7.9.1941 and 26.6.1941, MSPT 3.2002.0985. Rahe appears to have known about the mass murder of Jews, but his personal reaction is unclear. See Rahe to Ursula, 18.2.1943, MSPT 3.2002.0985.

231. Eugen Altrogge to Hans Albring, 24.3.1942, MSPT 3.2002.0210.

232. See Steven Miner, *Stalin's Holy War: Religion, Nationalism, and Alliance Politics, 1941–1945* (Chapel Hill: University of North Carolina Press, 2003).

233. Moskauer Patriarchat, *Die Wahrheit über die Religion in Russland* (1942), translated from Russian, BArch R6/177.

234. "Das Moskauer Schau-Beten!" *Der Kampf*, 12.7.1941, BA-MA RHD 69/41.

235. "Englische Gebete für die Sowjetunion: Praktische Beweise für die britisch-sowjetische Einheitsfront," *Feldzeitung von der Maas bis an die Memel*, 10.9.41, BA-MA RHD 69/76.

236. "Puritaner und Bolschewisten: Die English-sowjetischen Beziehungen nun durch einen Pakt gekrönt," *Feldzeitung von der Maas bis an die Memel*, 16.7.1941, BA-MA RHD 69/15.

237. Adolf Hitler, speech of 30.9.1942, reprinted in Domarus, *Hitler*, 2677.

238. Heinz Rahe to Ursula, 7.9.1941, MSPT 3.2002.0985.

239. Hans Roth, diary entry of 26.6.1941, *Eastern Inferno*.

240. Hans Simon to parents and sister, 13.3.1944, MSPT 3.2002.1288.

241. Hans Simon to mother, 20.1.1944, MSPT 3.2002.1288. On Hitler's view of God as a judge in the struggle among the races—unconnected to any organized religion—see Richard Weikart, *Hitler's Ethic: The Nazi Pursuit of Evolutionary Progress* (New York: Palgrave Macmillan, 2009)., 39–41.

242. See Monica Ann Black, "On Death in Germany: Perceptions of Death among Wehrmacht Soldiers, 1939–1945" (master's thesis, University of Virginia, 2002).

243. First Lieutenant.

244. Willy Hagemann to Kressen, 25.8.1944, MSPT 3.2002.7169.

245. Willy Hagemann to grandmother, 28.9.1944, MSPT 3.2002.7169.

246. Willy Hagemann to parents, 4.2.1944 and to Kressen, 22.8.1944, MSPT 3.2002.7169.

247. See Arne W. G. Zoepf, *Wehrmacht zwischen Tradition und Ideologie: Der NS-Führungsoffizier im Zweiten Weltkrieg* (Frankfurt am Main: Peter Lang, 1988); Pöpping, "Die Wehrmachtseelsorge," 263 and 271.

248. Feldpostprüfstelle AOK9, Activity Report for September, 1944, 1.10.1944, BA-MA RH 13/49.

249. Letter of Obgefr. W., 1.4.1943, in PzAOK2, Feldpostprüfstelle, March 1943, BA-MA RH 21-2/732. On the blending of Nazi and Christian tropes by soldiers, see Black, "On Death in Germany."

250. Personal-Amt des Heeres, *Wofür Kämpfen Wir?* (Berlin: Ashelmdruck, 1944), 21–27 and 109–110. Quotation on 109.

251. See "Dr. theol. B., Propagandavorschlag Proklamierung des Krieges als Kreuzzug," 1943–44, BArch R 55/1339.

252. See especially Biess, *Homecomings*; Frank Biess, "Survivors of Totalitarianism: Returning POWs and the Reconstruction of Masculine Citizenship in West Germany, 1945–1955," in *The Miracle Years: A Cultural History of West Germany, 1949–1968*, ed. Hanna Schissler (Princeton, NJ: Princeton University Press, 2001); Perry, "Madonna of Stalingrad."

4. The "Liberators"

1. Wilhelm Moldenhauser, diary entry of 28.6.1941, *Im Funkwagen der Wehrmacht durch Europa: Balkan, Ukraine, Stalingrad: Feldpostbriefe des Gefreiten Wilhelm Moldenhauser 1940–1943*, ed. Jens Ebert (Berlin: Trafo, 2008).

2. Wilhelm Moldenhauser to Erika, 6.9.1941, *Im Funkwagen der Wehrmacht*.

3. Soviet families traditionally slept on the oven during the winter, for extra warmth.

4. Wilhelm Moldenhauser to Erika, 17.9.1941, *Im Funkwagen der Wehrmacht*.

5. See, for example, Wilhelm Moldenhauser to Erika and children, 5.7.1942, *Im Funkwagen der Wehrmacht*.

6. Christian Hartmann, *Wehrmacht im Ostkrieg: Front und militärisches Hinterland 1941/42* (München: R. Oldenbourg Verlag, 2009), 789.

7. See Kurt Pätzold, *Ihr waret die besten Soldaten. Ursprung und Geschichte einer Legende* (Leizig: Militzk Verlag, 2000).

8. Vejas Gabriel Liulevicius, *The German Myth of the East: 1800 to the Present* (New York: Oxford University Press, 2009).

9. See Liulevicius, *German Myth of the East*; Charles Ingrao and Franz A. J. Szabo, eds., *The Germans and the East* (West Lafayette, IN: Purdue University Press, 2008); Shelley Baranowski, *Nazi Empire: German Colonialism and Imperialism from Bismarck to Hitler* (New York: Cambridge University Press, 2011), 9–66.

10. Liulevicius, *German Myth of the East*, 133.

11. See Vejas Gabriel Liulevicius, *War Land on the Eastern Front: Culture, National Identity, and German Occupation in World War I* (New York: Cambridge University Press, 2000), 89–150; Dennis Showalter, "Comrades, Enemies, Victims: The Prussian/German Army and the Ostvölker," in Ingrao and Szabo, *Germans and the East*, 209–25; Dieter Pohl, *Die Herrschaft der Wehrmacht: Deutsche Militärbesatzung und einheimische Bevölkerung in der Sowjetunion 1941–1944* (München: R. Oldenbourg Verlag, 2008), 25–34.

12. See, especially, Florian Krobb and Elaine Martin, eds., *Weimar Colonialism: Discourses and Legacies of Post-Imperialism in Germany after 1918* (Bielefeld: Aisthesis Verlag, 2014); Liulevicius, *War Land*, 227–72; Pohl, *Herrschaft*, 34–62; John Connelly, "Nazis and Slavs: From Racial Theory to Racist Practice," *Central European History* 32, no. 1 (1999): 1–33.

13. The *Freikorps* were right-wing paramilitary organizations that operated during the interwar years.

14. On Nazi views of the Soviet Union, see Manfred Weißbecker, "'Wenn hier Deutsche wohnten . . .' Beharrung und Veränderung im Rußlandbild Hitlers und der NSDAP," in *Das Rußlandbild im Dritten Reich*, ed. Hans-Erich Volkmann (Köln: Böhlau Verlag, 1994), 9–54.

15. Quoted in Liulevicius, *German Myth of the East*, 197.

16. See Lorna Waddington, *Hitler's Crusade: Bolshevism, the Jews and the Myth of Conspiracy* (New York: I. B. Tauris, 2009), 187–95; Jay W. Baird, *The Mythical World of Nazi War Propaganda, 1939–1945* (Minneapolis: University of Minnesota Press, 1974), 155–65; Wolfram Wette, "Das Rußlandbild in der NS-Propaganda: Ein Problemaufriß," in Volkmann, *Das Rußlandbild im Dritten Reich*, 55–78. Even in Nazi publications, liberation discourse would make inroads to a limited extent. For example, see Bruno Brehm, "Zeitenwende," *Völkischer Beobachter*, 26.6.1941.

17. See Baird, *Nazi War Propaganda*, 160–64. Joseph Goebbels, diary entries of 12.7.1941, 29.7.1941, and 30.7.1941, in Elke Fröhlich, ed., *Die Tagebücher von Joseph Goebbels: Teil II: Diktate 1941–1945*, Band 1, Juli–September 1941 (München K.G. Sauer, 1996).

18. See Joseph Goebbels, "Der Schleier fällt," *Das Reich*, 6.7.1941, reprinted in *Die Zeit ohne Beispiel* (München: Zentralverlag der NSDAP, 1941), 521; ibid., "Die sogenannte russische Seele," in *Das eherne Herz*, 19.7.1942 (München: Zentralverlag der NSDAP, 1943), 398–405.

19. See Alexander Dallin, *German Rule in Russia, 1941–1945: A Study of Occupation Politics* (London: Macmillan, 1957), 7–19; Weißbecker, "'Wenn hier Deutsche wohnten . . . ,'" 42–45.

20. See Weißbecker, "'Wenn hier Deutsche wohnten . . .'" This extended even to refusing the requests of military commanders to recruit local auxiliaries. See Dallin, *German Rule*, esp. 663–64.

21. See Hitlers Aufruf an die "Soldaten der Ostfront" vom 22.6.1941, reprinted in Gerd R. Ueberschär and Wolfram Wette, eds., *"Unternehmen Barbarossa": Der deutsche Überfall auf die Sowjetunion 1941* (Paderborn: Schöningh, 1984), 323.

22. Weisung Nr. 46, Richtlinien für die verstärkte Bekämpfung des Bandenunwesens im Osten, 18.8.1942, in Walther Hubatsch, ed., *Hitlers Weisungen für die Kriegführung 1939–1945. Dokumente des Oberkommandos der Wehrmacht* (Koblenz: Bernard & Graefe Verlag, 1983), 201–205.

23. Adolf Hitler, speech of 30.9.1942, reprinted in Max Domarus, ed., *Hitler: Speeches and Proclamations 1932–1945 and Commentary by a Contemporary, The Chronicle of a Dictatorship*, vol. 4 (1941–1945) (Wauconda, IL: Bolchazy-Carducci Publishers, 1987), 2677.

24. See Wolfram Wette, *The Wehrmacht: History, Myth, Reality*, trans. Deborah Lucas Schneider (Cambridge, MA: Harvard University Press, 2006), 17–24; Wolfram Wette, "Juden, Bolschewisten, Slawen: Rassenideologische Rußland-Feindbilder Hitlers und der Wehrmachtgeneräle," in *Präventiv-krieg? Der deutsche Angriff auf die Sowjetunion*, ed. Bianka Pietrow-Ennker (Frankfurt am Main: Fischer Taschenbuch Verlag, 2011), 40–58; Jürgen Förster, "Zum Rußland-Bild der Militärs 1941–1945," in Volkmann, *Das Rußlandbild im Dritten Reich*, 141–64.

25. See Pohl, *Herrschaft*, 136.

26. OKW, Richtlinien für das Verhalten der Truppe im Feindesland, 19.5.1941, in Ueberschär and Wette, *"Unternehmen Barbarossa,"* 312.

27. See Jürgen Kilian, *Wehrmacht und Besatzungsherrschaft im russischen Nordwesten 1941–1944: Praxis und Alltag im Militärverwaltungsgebiet der Heeresgruppe Nord* (Paderborn: Ferdinand Schöningh, 2012), 193–95 and 233–40. See also OKW to all propaganda troops, Auszug aus den Tagesweisungen Nr. 165–167 for the military Zensur, 3.9.1942, BA-MA RW 4/191.

28. 46th Inf. Div., Abt. Ic, Auszug aus dem Armeetagesbefehl Nr. 22, 29.7.1941, BA-MA RH 26/46. Also see Kilian, *Wehrmacht und Besatzungsherrschaft*, 187–97.

29. On the range of opinion among military leaders regarding the USSR throughout the war, see Förster, "Zum Rußland-Bild der Militärs 1941–1945."

30. See Förster, "Zum Rußland-Bild der Militärs 1941–1945"; Pohl, *Herrschaft*, 127–29; Kilian, *Wehrmacht und Besatzungsherrschaft*, 187–88.

31. These often changed their minds once they experienced conditions in the country, however. See Omer Bartov, "The Missing Years: German Workers, German Soldiers," in *Nazism and German Society 1933–1945*, ed. David Crew (London: Routledge, 1994).

32. Wilhelm Moldenhauer to Erika, 16.7.1941, *Im Funkwagen der Wehrmacht*.

33. Wilhelm Moldenhauer to Erika, 2.8.1941, *Im Funkwagen der Wehrmacht*.

34. Hans Simon to father, 28.7.1941, MSPT 3.2002.1288.

35. Johannes Hagemann to Lisa (sister), 1.8.1941, MSPT 3.2002.7234. Also see AOK2, Feldpostprüfstelle, report for June 1941, 1.8.1941, BA-MA RH 20-2/1091. On conditions in the USSR at this time, see Sheila Fitzpatrick, *Everyday Stalinism: Ordinary Life in Extraordinary Times: Soviet Russia in the 1930s* (Oxford University Press, 2000). While communist rulers had managed to build up the USSR's industrial capacity, it remained largely impoverished, lacking in consumer goods, and wracked by famine.

36. Wilhelm Moldenhauser to Erika, 12.8.1941, *Im Funkwagen der Wehrmacht.*

37. See Fritz Feierabend to wife, 19.7.1941, BA-MA MSG2/4048.

38. See, for example, Harald Hoffmann to parents, 6.7.1941 and to parents and Marion (sister), 5.9.1941, MSPT 3.2002.0382. For their part, the locals appeared eager to tell the Germans what they wanted to hear, including that Jews had authored many of the regime's policies.

39. See Joseph Goebbels, diary entry of 6 July1941 in *Die Tagebücher von Joseph Goebbels: Teil I*, Band 9, 428 and ibid., diary entries of July 14, 28, and 31, in *Die Tagebücher von Joseph Goebbels: Teil II*, Band 1, 65–69, 136–37, and 149–51.

40. See Joseph Goebbels, "Der Schleier fällt," in *Das Reich*, 6.7.1941, reprinted in *Die Zeit ohne Beispiel* (München: Zentralverlag der NSDAP, 1941), 521.

41. See, for example, Kriegsberichter Herbert Neumann, "Hammer, Sichel, Tod," *Allgemeine Zeitung*, 82. Jahrgang, 8.4.a Nr. 168 and "Das verlorene Paradies," *Illustrierter Beobachter*, 28.5.1942, EZA 686/8582.

42. See, for example, Deutsche Wochenschau GmbH, *Die Deutsche Wochenschau*, Nr. 584, 26.11.1941 and Nr. 586, 11.12.1941, Bundesarchiv-Filmarchiv DW (584/1941) and (586/1941).

43. See Goebbels, diary entries of 9.9.1941 and 10.9.1941, in *Die Tagebücher von Joseph Goebbels: Teil II*, Band 1, 384 and 388–89.

44. *Das Sowjetparadies: Ausstellung der Reichspropagandaleitung der NSDAP: ein Bericht in Wort und Bild* (Berlin: Zentralverlag der NSDAP, Franz Eher Nachf. GmbH, 1942), quote on 47; Waddington, *Hitler's Crusade*, 129; Baird, *Nazi War Propaganda*, 155–65.

45. Kriegsberichter Drobig, "Unvorstellbares Elend in den Sowjetstaaten," *Blücher*, Nr. 21, 17.7.1941, BA-MA RHD 69/33.

46. "Moskaus Blutweg: 24 Jahre Sowjetverbrechen in allen Erdteilen," in *Der Kampf*, Nr. 3, 19.7.1941, BA-MA RHD 69/41.

47. Kriegsberichter Heinz-Dieter Pilgram, "Auf Wacht im Sowjetland. Rätselhaftes, feindliches und trostloses Land—Die Heimat denkt an uns," *Feldzeitung von der Maas bis an die Memel*, BA-MA RHD 69/76.

48. For this two-sided portrayal, see especially Kriegsberichter Bernd Poiess, "Das Rätsel der russischen Seele," *Feldzeitung von der Maas bis an die Memel*, 2.10.1941, BA-MA RHD 69/76.

49. See, for example, "Die Rettung Deutschlands vor dem Ansturm des Untermenschentums," Nr. 136, September 1941.

50. See Pohl, *Herrschaft*, 135–36; Kilian, *Wehrmacht und Besatzungsherrschaft*, 191 and 197–98; Karel Berkhoff, *Harvest of Despair: Life and Death in Ukraine Under Nazi Rule* (Cambridge, MA: Belknap Press, 2004), 20–21.

51. Wilhelm Moldenhauser to Erika (wife), 16.7.1941, *Im Funkwagen der Wehrmacht.*

52. Wilhelm Moldenhauser to Erika, 28.7.1941, *Im Funkwagen der Wehrmacht.*

53. See Wilhelm Moldenhauser to Erika, 14.9.1941, *Im Funkwagen der Wehrmacht.*

54. Heinz Rahe to Ursula (wife), 9–10.7.1941, MSPT 3.2002.0985.

55. Heinz Rahe to Ursula, 29.9.1941, MSPT 3.2002.0985.

56. Gustav Böker to parents, 27.6.1941, MSPT 3.2002.0966.

57. See, for instance, Hans Simon to mother, 27.9.1941, MSPT 3.2002.1288; Hermann Henning to parents, 3.9.1941, MSPT 3.2002.7217.

58. Hermann Henning to Georg and parents, 3.12.1941, MSPT 3.2002.7217.

59. Panzer Group 3, Ic, report Nr. 2, January–July 1941, BA-MA RH 23–3/432.

60. Examples abound. See Auszüge aus dem Bericht der 6 Inf.Div, Abt. Ic, 3.7.1941, BA-MA RH 26-6/63; AOK2, Ic/VAA, Bericht Nr. 8, 1.8.1941 and Heeresgruppe Mitte, Ic/AO, Nr. 103/41 g Kdos (AO III), Betr.: Kollektive Gewaltmaßnahmen, 7.8.1941, BA-MA RH 20–2/1091.

61. On the population's view of the invaders, see Wendy Lower, *Nazi Empire-Building and the Holocaust in Ukraine* (Chapel Hill: University of North Carolina Press, 2005), 36–38; Berkhoff, *Harvest of Despair*, chap. 1, esp. 20–21.

62. This quickly became a stock phrase in Wehrmacht propaganda. See, for instance, "Der Soldat in besetzten Gebiet als Vertreter von Volk und Reich," *Mitteilungen für die Truppe*, Nr. 179, February 1942, BA-MA RW 4/357.

63. Quotation from *Der Deutsche Kamerad*, 20.7.1941, BA-MA RHD 69/30. Also see photographs in *Blücher*, 14.8.1941 and 9.9.1941, BA-MA RHD 69/33.

64. *Feldgrauen:* "Field gray," a reference to the German uniform.

65. Kriegsberichter Erich Pecher, "Bialystock in deutscher Hand: Weissruthenen begrüssen die deutschen Soldaten," *Ost-Front*, 5.7.1941, BA-MA RHD 53-20. For civilians toppling Soviet statues, see PK, "Wie ein Lenin aus Gips umgelegt wurde: Das bolschewistische Denkmal von Lubaszow fällt der Volkswut zum Opfer," *Wacht im Osten*, 8.7.1941, BA-MA RHD 69/84.

66. "Deutsche in der Ukraine als Befreier begrüsst: 'Stockholms Tidningen' über die sowjetische Gewaltherrschaft," *Feldzeitung von der Maas bis an die Memel*, 8.7.1941, BA-MA RHD 69/15. For photographs of civilians waving Nazi flags, see Hauptreferat Bildpresse, "Kiew: Ein Sonderbericht. Aufnahmen: Kriegsberichter Mittelstädt," BA-MA RW 4/1175.

67. See "Weißruthenische Botschaft an deutsche Truppen," *Feldzeitung von der Maas bis an die Memel*, 31.7.1941, BA-MA RHD 69/15.

68. See, for instance, "'Wir grüssen die zurückgekehrte Freiheit': Russische Frauen schreiben—Erlebnis am Rande der Schlachten," *Feldzeitung von der Maas bis an die Memel*, 23.7.1941, BA-MA RHD 69/15.

69. Some units registered a much more reserved attitude on the part of the population as they made initial contact. See, for example, 27th Pz. Div., report on the village of Wassikowo, 27.9.1941, BA-MA RH 27-5/131; Anlage 2g to 6th ID Activity Report for 22.6-31.7.1941, Betr.: Stimmung und Verhalten der Weißrussischen Bevölkerung, 25.7.1941, BA-MA RH 26-6/63.

70. See, for example, Deutsche Wochenschau GmbH, *Die Deutsche Wochenschau*, Nr. 566, 9.7.1941, Bundesarchiv-Filmarchiv DW (566/1941).

71. For example, see Sonderberichter Oberstleutnant Soldan, "'Sieg im Osten:' Anmerkungen zum neuen Bewegungskrieg" and Bruno Brehm, "Tagebuchblätter aus dem Osten," *Das Reich*, 17.8.1941 and 28.9.1941, EZA 686/8524.

72. Walter Engelhardt, *Klinzy: Bildnis einer Russischen Stadt nach ihrer Befreiung vom Bolschewismus* (Berlin: Nibelungen Verlag, 1943).

73. Ibid., 104.

74. See Pohl, *Herrschaft*, 138.

75. OKW Nr. 486/41 g.K. WFSt/WPr (Ia), 21.8.1941, BA-MA RH 26-12/244.

76. See Joseph Goebbels, diary entries of 28–31.7.1941 and 3.8.1941, *Die Tagebücher von Joseph Goebbels: Teil II*, Band I, 136–51 and 168; OKW to OKH and others, Ergänzende Weisungen für die Handhabung der Propaganda gegen die Sowjetunion, 21.8.1941, BA-MA RW 4/578; report on the Einsatz des Rednertrupps des

Ostpro-Zuges mit dem Redner W. im Bereich der 35 Infanterie Division, 23.4.1943, Yad Vashem JM5288. For copies of propaganda posters and others appeals to the population, see USHMM RG-22.014M, reel 7, no. 75, 392–503, and reel 18, nos. 171 and 175.

77. For example, see 20 Inf. Div. (mot), Abt. Ic, 5, copy of flier to Red soldiers, 5.7.1941, BA-MA RH 26-20/84.

78. Johannes Lohr, diary entry of 20.8.1941, MSPT 3.2010.1156.

79. See Pohl, *Herrschaft*, 137–38.

80. 20th Inf. Div., Abt. Ic, Nr. 760/41 geh., Feindnachrichtenblatt Nr. 11, 6.7.1941, BA-MA RH 26-20/84; Kriegsberichter Gustav Schenk, "Nach der Einnahme von Brest-Litowsk: Straßenkämpfe mit Heckenschützen—Volksdeutsche aus Gefängnis befreit," *Ost-Front*, 1.7.1941, BA-MA RHD 53-20, Bd. 1.

81. Kriegsberichter W. Hartmann, "'Herr Leutnant, befreien sie uns'! Grauenhafte Morde der GPU-Entsetzlicher Fund in Libau," *Feldzeitung von der Maas bis an die Memel*, 5.7.1941, BA-MA RHD 69/15.

82. 20th Inf. Div., Abt. Ic, Nr. 760/41 geh., Feindnachrichtenblatt Nr. 11, 6.7.1941, BA-MA RH 26-20/84.

83. Anlage 2 to 102nd Inf. Div., Abt. Ia, Nr. 13, 9.7.1941; AOK2, Ic/AO/Abw III, Besprechungspunkte für Ic-Besprechung am 6.7.1941, Yad Vashem M 29 FR 154.

84. See Lower, *Nazi Empire-Building*, 47.

85. See Pohl, *Herrschaft*, 137–38.

86. See chapter 3.

87. See Kilian, *Wehrmacht und Besatzungsherrschaft*, 198. The majority of soldiers in this book quartered with civilians on multiple occasions.

88. See Kilian, *Wehrmacht und Besatzungsherrschaft*,195–97 and 593; Omer Bartov, *Hitler's Army: Soldiers, Nazis, and War in the Third Reich* (New York: Oxford University Press, 1991), 106–78; Klaus Latzel, *Deutsche Soldaten—nationalsozialistsicher Krieg? Kriegserlebnis—Kriegserfahrung 1939–1945* (Paderborn: Ferdinand Schöningh, 1998), 145–56. Kilian finds little evidence of Nazi-inspired biological racism against Slavs, although he detects strong anti-Bolshevism and antisemitism and a general belief in Slavic inferiority. Bartov, in contrast, argues that soldiers were uniformly steeped in Nazi-inspired racism toward the population. Latzel has taken an intermediate position.

89. Military authorities tried their best to keep contact between soldiers and civilians to a minimum, but they were rarely successful. See Kilian, *Wehrmacht und Besatzungsherrschaft*, 198–99.

90. For a few examples, see Wilhelm Moldenhauser, diary entries of 2.8.1941, 23.8.1941, and 17.9.1941, *Im Funkwagen der Wehrmacht*.

91. Wilhelm Moldenhauser diary entry of 10.8.1941, *Im Funkwagen der Wehrmacht*.

92. Wilhelm Moldenhauser diary entry of 16.9.1941 and 28.6.1941, to Erika, 17.9.1941, *Im Funkwagen der Wehrmacht*.

93. Wilhelm Moldenhauser to Erika, 6.9.1941, 2.8.1941, and 3.6.1942, *Im Funkwagen der Wehrmacht*.

94. See, for example, Wilhelm Moldenhauser to Erika, 12.7.1941, *Im Funkwagen der Wehrmacht*.

95. Wilhelm Moldenhauser to parents, 24.8.1941, *Im Funkwagen der Wehrmacht*.

96. Both quotations from Wilhelm Moldenhauser to Erika, 16.7.1941 and 2.11.1941, *Im Funkwagen der Wehrmacht*, respectively.

97. Wilhelm Moldenhauser to Erika and children, First and Second Pfingsttag, *Im Funkwagen der Wehrmacht.*

98. Wilhelm Moldenhauser to Erika, 8.8.1941, to parents, 24.8.1941, *Im Funkwagen der Wehrmacht.*

99. Wilhelm Moldenhauser to Erika, 30.3.1942, *Im Funkwagen der Wehrmacht.*

100. Wilhelm Moldenhauser to Erika, 10.9.1941 and 12.8.1941, *Im Funkwagen der Wehrmacht.*

101. See, for instance, Wilhelm Moldenhauser to Erika, 17.9.1941 and 26.9.1941, *Im Funkwagen der Wehrmacht.* On cleanliness as a moral value highly prized by the invaders, see chapter 1.

102. Wilhelm Moldenhauser to Erika, 13.10.1941, *Im Funkwagen der Wehrmacht.*

103. See Wilhelm Moldenhauser to Erika, 6.9.1941 and 23.12.1941, *Im Funkwagen der Wehrmacht.*

104. See Wilhelm Moldenhauser to Erika, 17.9.1941 and 26.9.1941, *Im Funkwagen der Wehrmacht.* Quotations from the former.

105. Wilhelm Moldenhauser to Erika, 17.9.1941 and 23.12.1941, *Im Funkwagen der Wehrmacht.*

106. Wilhelm Moldenhauser to Erika, 6.9.1941, *Im Funkwagen der Wehrmacht.*

107. Wilhelm Moldenhauser to Erika, 31.1.1942 and 4.4.1942, *Im Funkwagen der Wehrmacht.*

108. Wilhelm Moldenhauser to Erika, 7.1.1942 and 31.1.1942, *Im Funkwagen der Wehrmacht.*

109. Wilhelm Moldenhauser to Erika and children, 5.7.1942, *Im Funkwagen der Wehrmacht.* He was, however, aware of the mass starvation in Soviet cities.

110. See Hans Albring to Eugen Altrogge, Fronleichnamstag 1942, MSPT 3.2002.0211.

111. See Hans Albring to Eugen Altrogge, 28.7.1941, 30–31.8.1941, 4.9.1941 and Allerseelen, 1941, MSPT 3.2002.0211.

112. See Hans Albring to Eugen Altrogge, 10.1.1942, October 1942, 15.1.1942, 6.11.1941, and 16.11.1941, MSPT 3.2002.0211. The family named the pig in Albring's honor.

113. Hans Albring to Eugen Altrogge, 15.5.1942, MSPT 3.2002.0211.

114. Hans Albring to Eugen Altrogge, 25.1.1942, MSPT 3.2002.0211.

115. Indeed, much of the racism expressed by soldiers toward the population was couched in terms of middle-class standards of hygiene and decorum rather than "biological" characteristics, but it is often difficult to tell where one began and the other ended. See Liulevicius, *German Myth of the East,* 8; Latzel, *Deutsche Soldaten,* 145–56 and 171–82.

116. Harald Hoffmann to parents and Marion (sister), 8.7.1941 and 12.11.1941, MSPT 3.2002.0382.

117. See Harald Hoffmann to parents and Marion, 5.9.1941 and to unspecified recipient(s), 17.7.1941, MSPT 3.2002.0382.

118. For example, see Harald Hoffmann to parents 6.7.1941, to parents and Marion 8.7.1941, and to parents and Marion, 24.7.1941 and 21.10.1941, MSPT 3.2002.0382.

119. See Dr. Wilhelm Bacher, diary entries of 23.9.1941, October 1942, 22.6.1943, 9.7.1941, 10.7.1941, 3.8.1941, 7.11.1942, and 18.2.1943, and photographs on pages 100, 116, 191, 357, and 379, MSPT 3.2002.1376.

120. For example, see Dr. Wilhelm Bacher, diary pages 100 and 190, MSPT 3.2002.1376.

121. Gustav Böker to parents, 22.1.1941, MSPT 3.2002.0966.

122. Hans Simon to parents, 3.6.1942; Johannes Lohr, diary entry of 27.12.1941, MSPT 3.2010.1156; Willy Nagel to Wandelgard ("Wanda"), 8.8.1942, MSPT 3.2002.0326.

123. See Konrad Jarausch to wife, 3.10.1941, *Reluctant Accomplice*, 299; Hans Simon to mother, 9.6.1943, MSPT 3.20021288.

124. See, for example, Johannes Hagemann to parents, 193.1943, MSPT 3.2002.7234.

125. Rolf Dietrich, diary entries of 22.3.1943, 7.5.1943, and 3.11.1942, MSPT 3.2002.1376.

126. Hans Roth, diary entry of 30.9.1941, Hans Roth, *Eastern Inferno: The Journals of a German Panzerjäger on the Eastern Front, 1941–1943*, ed. Christine Alexander and Mason Kunze (Philadelphia, PA: Casemate, 2010), 113.

127. Konrad H. Jarausch, ed., *Reluctant Accomplice*, esp. 237–311.

128. See Baird, *Nazi War Propaganda*, 159.

129. Eugen Altrogge to Hans Albring, 18.7.1942, MSPT 3.2002.0210.

130. Willy Nagel to Wandelgard, 25.11.1942, MSPT 3.2002.0326.

131. Quotation from Willy Nagel to Wandelgard, 27.3.1942, MSPT 3.2002.0326.

132. See Willy Nagel to Wandelgard, 4.7.1941, 1.1.1942, and 22.10.1942, MSPT 3.2002.0326.

133. Quotation from Heinz Sartorio to Elly and Fred, 28.3.1942, MSPT 3.2002.0287.

134. Heinz Sartorio to Elly, 11.11.1942, MSPT 3.2002.0827.

135. Reese, *Stranger to Myself*, 44 and 37–38.

136. Cru. Geheime Feldpolizei 703, Tagebuch Nr. 143/42 geh., Activity Report for May 1942, 25.5.1942, BA-MA RH 21-3/447. The GFP officers did not record any arrests of German soldiers for this offense. In addition, they stated that in their area, "in general it can be observed that the German soldiers live in good understanding with the Russian population."

137. See "Grausame Folgen bolschewistischer Zerstörungen für die sowjetische Bevölkerung," *Mitteilungen für die Truppe*, Nr. 152, November 1941, BA-MA RW 4/357. See also "Nicht weich werden!" (Nr. 157, November 1941).

138. See, for example, "Brot!" *Das Neuste für den Soldaten*, 21.11.1941, BA-MA RHD 69/14.

139. See Kilian, *Wehrmacht und Besatzungsherrschaft*, 197–98 on soldiers in Army Group North distributing candy during the first months of the invasion. This greatly alarmed Soviet authorities.

140. Willy Hagemann to parents, 9.5.1943, MSPT 3.2002.7169.

141. Hans-Peter Eckener to mother, 9.3.1942, MSPT 3.2002.0307.

142. Hans-Peter Eckener to unknown recipient, 12.7.1942, MSPT 3.2002.0307.

143. See Mary Louise Roberts, *What Soldiers Do: Sex and the American GI in World War II France* (Chicago: The University of Chicago Press, 2013), 15–55.

144. Eugen Altrogge to Hans Albring, 22.6.1941, MSPT 3.2002.0210

145. Eugen Altrogge to Hans Albring, 18.7.1942, MSPT 3.2002.0210.

146. Heinz Rahe to Ursula (wife), 18–20.7.1941, MSPT 3.2002.0985.

147. Heinz Rahe to Ursula, 29.9.1941, MSPT 3.2002.0985.

148. Hans Wilhelm Sauer to parents and sisters, 8.10.1942, MSPT 3.2002.1271. His attitude is surprising given the fact that he displayed a strong affinity for Nazism.

149. See chapter 2.

150. For scholarship that has identified such "mixed" policies toward civilians by Wehrmacht units, see Jeff Rutherford, *Combat and Genocide on the Eastern Front: The German Infantry's War, 1941–1944* (Cambridge, MA: Cambridge University Press, 2014); Ben Shepherd, *War in the Wild East: The German Army and Soviet Partisans* (Cambridge, MA: Harvard University Press, 2004); David W. Wildermuth, "Widening the Circle: General Weikersthal and the War of Annihilation, 1941–42," *Central European History* 45 (2012): 306–24; Pohl, *Herrschaft*; Kilian, *Wehrmacht und Besatzungsherrschaft*.

151. See 12th Inf. Div., Abt. Ic, Activity Report for 1.6.1941–15.12.1941 and Anlage 3 to the same, Betr.: Sicherung der Truppe gegen Partisanen und Sabotage, BA-MA RH 26-12/82.

152. See IIAK, Abt. Ic, 2.11.1941, Betr.: Partisanenbekämpfung and IIAK, Abt. Ic, Aufrufe an die Bevölkerung, 7.11.1941, BA-MA RH 26-12/244.

153. IIAK, Abt. Ic, 2.11.1941, Betr.: Partisanenbekämpfung, BA-MA RH 26-12/244; 12th Inf. Div., Abt. Ib/IV Wi, 7.4.1942, Betr.: Pferde-Erfassung; Ortskommandantur Borok to 12th Inf. Div., 31.3.1942, Betr.: Panje-Pferde, BA-MA RH 26-12/292.

154. Hams Simon to parents, 3.6.1942, MSPT 3.2002.1288.

155. See 12th Inf. Div., Abt. Ic, Activity Report for 16.12.1941–28.2.1943, BA-MA RH 26-12/83. Rutherford has uncovered a similar combination of harsh and conciliatory treatment by the 123rd Infantry, also trapped in the Demyansk Pocket. See Rutherford, "Life and Death in the Demiansk Pocket."

156. See 12th Inf. Div., Abt. Ic, Activity Report for 16.12.1941–28.2.1943, BA-MA RH 26-12/83.

157. See 12th Inf. Div., Abt. Ic, Activity Report for 1.3–30.6.1943, BA-MA RH 26-12/86.

158. See especially Jeff Rutherford, "'One Senses Danger from All Sides, Especially from Fanatical Civilians': The 121st Infantry Division and Partisan War, June 1941–April 1942," in *War in a Twilight World: Partisan and Anti-Partisan Warfare in Eastern Europe, 1939–45*, ed. Ben Shepherd and Juliette Pattinson (New York: Palgrave Macmillan, 2010), 70.

159. Examples are too numerous to list here in detail, but a survey of the institutional sources from this book alone reveals at least eighteen units, including armies, corps, and divisions that followed such policies at some point in the war.

160. Following higher orders, Wehrmacht units, as well as the civilian administration, kept the collective system essentially intact for purposes of economic efficiency, although they somewhat modified its workings. See Anlage zu OKW/Nr. 486/41 g.K. WFSt/WPr (Ia) Richtlinien zur Behandlung der Kollektivfragen, [1941], BA-MA RW 4/578. This would change with the 1942 *Agrarordnung* (see below).

161. Both quotes from 167th Inf. Div., Abt. Ib, 3.8.1941, BA-MA 26-167/64.

162. 8th Inf. Div., Offizier für Landwirtschaft to the Kreislandwirt Herrn B., 19.9.1941, BA-MA RH 26-8/73.

163. See, for example, 6th Inf. Div., Abt. Ic, Betr.: Zuteilung des Hoflandes und Frühjahrsbestellung, 13.3.1942, BA-MA RH 26/6/64.

164. Johannes Lohr, diary entry of 10.9.1941, MSPT 3.2010.1156.

165. Rolf Dietrich to Hilde, 2.9.1942, MSPT 3.2002.7236.

166. Dr. Wilhelm Bacher, diary entries of 7.11.1942 and 2.3.1943, MSPT 3.2002.1376.

167. See, for example, "Zerstörung: Was die Roten verwüsteten . . ." and "Aufbau . . . wird hier wieder aufgebaut," *Der Deutsche Kamerad*, 31.8.1941, BA-MA RHD 69/30; PK photo series from Kiev, RW 4/1175.

168. See "Verlorenes Paradies?" (photo) by PK Hauptmann Werner Schneider, and "Väterchen Babuschkin wird Starosta: An Stelle der Dorfsowjets treten wieder Bürgermeister," *Blücher*, 5.8.1941, 6.8.1941, and 8.9.1941 (respectively), BA-MA RHD 69/33.

169. See, for example, "Deutsche Soldaten helfen bei der Ernte" (photograph with caption), *Der deutsche Kamerad*, 24.8.1941, BA-MA RHD 69/30.

170. See, for instance, "Neue Agrarordnung für die besetzten Gebiete," *Das Neuste für den Soldaten*, 1.3.1942, BA-MA RHD 69/14.

171. See "Arbeiter für das Reich," *Soldatenzeitung der Ukraine*, Year 2, Nr. 30, 12.3.1942, BA-MA RHD 69/9. On the horrific realities of what was in fact a slave labor program, see Ulrich Herbert, *Fremdarbeiter. Politik und Praxis des "Ausländer-Einsatzes" in der Kriegswirtschaft des Dritten Reiches* (Bonn: Verlag Dietz, 1999).

172. 167th Inf. Div., Abt. Ib, 3.8.1941, BA-MA 26-167/64.

173. See for example 205th Inf. Div., IVa, Activity Report for 1–16.10.1942, 16.10.1942, BA-MA RH 26-205/71 on reducing soldiers' rations to increase food supplies for civilians.

174. Kriegsberichter Bernd Poiess, "Das Rätsel der russischen Seele," 2.10.1941, *Feldzeitung von der Maas bis an die Memel*, BA-MA RHD 69/76.

175. For example, see "Zivilverwaltung für befreite Ostgebiete: Alfred Rosenberg Reichsminister—Dr. Meyer Stellverterter—Lohse und Koch Reichskommissare," 18.11.1941, *Feldzeitung von der Maas bis an die Memel*, BA-MA RHD 69/76.

176. Wilhelm Moldenhauser to Erika, 17.9.1941, *Im Funkwagen der Wehrmacht*.

177. Rolf Dietrich to Hilde, 24.1.1943, MSPT 3.2002.7236.

178. See Chef der Militärverwaltung beim Okdo der Heeresgruppe Mitte, Erfahrungsbericht der Militärverwaltung beim Okdo der Heeresgruppe Mitte, 22.6.1941–August 1944, BA-MA RH 19/II 334; Lower, *Nazi Empire-Building*, 44–68; Pohl, *Herrschaft*, 144–46; Kilian, *Wehrmacht und Besatzungsherrschaft*, 101–86.

179. See 102nd Inf. Div., Abt. Ia, Division Order Nr. 27 (Anlage 30 to Ic report for 1.8-3.9.1941), BA-MA RH 26-102/61 61; 205th Inf. Div., Abt. Ib/IVa, Befehl über die Sicherstellung der Ernte im Operationsgebiet der Division, 16.8.1942, BA-MA RH 26-205/65.

180. See Generalkommando IIAK, Abt. Ic, Aufrufe an die Bevölkerung, 7.11.1941, BA-MA RH 26-12/244; 8th Inf. Div., Abt. Ic, "Aufruf!" 12.9.1941, BA-MA RH 26-8/73. See also Erich Haberer, "The German Gendarmerie and Partisans in Belorussia, 1941–4," in Shepherd and Pattinson, *War in a Twilight World*, 102–25.

181. 290th Inf. Div., Abt. Ic, 21.9.1942, Befehl für die Überwachung der Zivilbevölkerung, National Archives and Records Administration (hereafter NARA) T315, reel 1896.

182. See, for example, GFP Gruppe 580, Tagebuch Nr. 363/41 geh., Activity Report for October 1941, 31.10.1941, Yad Vashem M 29, 114.

183. PK, "Von der 'Proletarischen Wahrheit' zur 'Ost-Front': Eine Frontzeitung entsteht im Sowjet-Paradies," *Ost-Front*, 30.10.1941, BA-MA RHD 53/20.

184. "Ein Feldlazarett," *Der Durchbruch*, 5.8.1941, BA-MA RHD 69/19.

185. "Im Krüppelasyl zu Ashewa: 'Sozialhygiene im Sowjetparadies,'" *Feldzeitung von der Maas bis an die Memel*, 11.8.1941, BA-MA RHD 69/15; Kriegsberichter Gert Sachs, "Die kleine Kapelle von Topolewo: Väterchen Doktor hilft der Landbevölkerung," *Feldzeitung von der Maas bis an die Memel*, 25.10.1941, BA-MA RHD 69/76.

186. These had included introducing the population to soap (sometimes forcibly) and taking various measures to prevent disease as part of the "civilizing" project. See Vegas and Dennis Showalter, "Comrades, Enemies, Victims: The Prussian/German Army and the Ostvölker," in Ingrao and Szabo, *Germans and the East*, 217–18; Liulevicius, *War Land on the Eastern Front*, 105–6.

187. XXIXAK Korpsarzt, Activity Report for 22.6–31.12.1941 and short Activity Report for 22.6–31.12.1941, BA-MA RH 24-29/125.

188. See 14th Inf. Div., Sanitäts Einheiten, Activity Report for 1.5–31.5.1942 (within Qu Abt. Activity Report for 5.3–19.10.1942), BA-MA RH 26-14/80; 205th Inf. Div., IVb, Activity Report for 16.4–30.4.1943, BA-MA RH 26-205/74. Civilians, of course, had no choice in these matters, especially in the case of quarantine and delousing.

189. See Katholisches Militärbischofsamt and Hans Jürgen Brant, eds., *Priester in Uniform: Seelsorger, Ordensleute und Theologen als Soldaten im Zweiten Weltkrieg* (Augsburg: Pattloch Verlag, 1994), 39, 87, 103, and 200.

190. Wilhelm Moldenhauser to Erika, 31.1.1942, *Im Funkwagen der Wehrmacht*, 195. Moldenhauser also implied that people brought the doctor eggs and milk in payment and noted that he mostly just provided them with instructions.

191. Heinz Sartorio to Elly (sister), 11.11.1942, MSPT 3.2002.0827.

192. Hans Roth, diary entry of 16.9.1942, *Eastern Inferno*, 195.

193. For example, the division doctor noted that the civilian hospital established in Kersch "experienced significant difficulties" in "the supply of medicine and bandage materials." 46th Inf. Div., Abt. IVb, Activity Report for 20.11–2.1.1942, BA-MA RH 26-46/81.

194. See OKH Gen St DH/Gen qu/IVa (III, 3), Betr.: Versorgung der für Zweck der Wehrmacht eingesetzten Landeseinwohner aus den besetzten Ostgebieten und ihrer Hinterbliebenen," 20.8.1942, Yad Vashem, JM5283.

195. See "Vor den Deutschen haben wir keine Angst," *Der Durchbruch*, 6.10.1941, BA-MA RHD 69/19.

196. Gert Sachs, "Die kleine Kapelle von Topolewo: Väterchen Doktor hilft der Landbevölkerung," *Feldzeitung von der Maas bis an die Memel*, 25.10.1941, BA-MA RHD 69/76.

197. See Pohl, *Herrschaft*, 146–47.

198. Reichsministerium für Volksaufklärung und Propaganda to Herrn Major Krause im Oberkommando der Wehrmacht, Betr.: Weisungen für die Propaganda-Abteilungen im Ostraum (draft), 2.8.1941, Yad Vashem M 29 Fr 84.

199. See 102nd Inf. Div., Order Nr. 24, 14.8.1941, BA-MA RH 26-102/61; Lower, *Nazi Empire-Building*, 47.

200. See, for instance, Dr. Wilhelm Bacher, diary entry of 10.7.1941, MSPT 3.2002.1376; Kurt Niemeyer to Johanna, 6.6.1942, MSPT 3.2008.1750.

201. Franz Siebeler to parents and siblings, 13.1.1941, MSPT 3.2002.1285.

202. See the commanding general of the Sicherungstruppen and Befehlshaber im Heeresgebiet Nord to Oberkommando H Gr Nord, 24.11.1943, BA-MA RH 19-III/660.

203. See, for instance, OKW, Abt. Ausl/Abw/Abt. Abw III, Nr. 2123/5.41 g (III C 5), 15.7.1941, Betr.: Behandlung von Volksdeutschen, BA-MA RH 24-42/239.

204. PzAOK2, Abt. Ic, BA-MA RH 21-2/902, passim.

205. See Verband für evangelische Auswandererfürsorge EV, Tgb. Nr. 1621/41, 20.10.1941, EZA 5/210; Evangelisches Landeskirchliches Archiv in Berlin (ELAB) 29/224, passim.

206. See Oberkommando der Heeresgruppe Nord, OQu/VII/13 101/43 geh., to AOK16 and AOK18, 4.10.1943, Betr.: Rückführung der Volksdeutschen, and passim, BA-MA RH 19-III/660.

207. On these difficulties, see OKW, Abt. Ausl/Abw/Abt. Abw III, Nr. 2123/5.41 g (III C 5), 15.7.1941, Betr.: Behandlung von Volksdeutschen and Oberbefehlshaber Krim, Abt. VII, 22.9.1942, Betr.: Behandlung von Volksdeutschen, BA-MA RH 24-42/239.

208. See Pohl, *Herrschaft*, 138; Wildermuth, "Widening the Circle," 316.

209. IX Armeekorps, situation report to AOK4, 24.5.1943, Yad Vashem JM5288. See also IX Armee Korps, Qu, Besondere Anordnungen für die Gebietsverwaltung, 21.4.1943 and IX Armeekorps, Nr. 092.43 geh., 27.4.1943, Yad Vashem JM5287.

210. PzAOK2, Abt. Ic, Report for 15–30.11.1942, BA-MA RH 21-2/902. Likewise, the 79th Infantry Division celebrated Christmas together with local civilians in Belgorod. See *Freizeit und Feier: Divisions-Blatt für die Geistige Betreuung*, Nr. 9, Christmas 1942, 4–5, in MSPT 3.2002.7171.

211. 6th Inf. Div., Abt. Ic, Report for 1–31.3.1942, 31.3.1942, and Anlage 11 to the same, Betr.: Förderung russischer Osterfeiern, BA-MA RH 26-6/64.

212. 8th Inf. Div., Abt. Ic to AOK16, 23.6.1943, Betr.: Propagand. Gestaltung des 22.6.1943, BA-MA RH 26-8/79. See also 6th Inf. Div, Abt. Ic, report for 1–31.3.1942, 31.3.1942, BA-MA RH 26-6/64.

213. Dr. Wilhelm Bacher, diary entry of 22.6.1943, MSPT 3.2002.1376.

214. Rolf Dietrich to Hilde, 10.10.1942, MSPT 3.2002.7236.

215. He admitted, however, that on most days they went hungry and begged at his field kitchen. Rolf Dietrich to Hilde, 3.11.1942, MSPT 3.2002.7236.

216. Willy Hagemann to parents, 1.4.1944, MSPT 3.2002.7169.

217. See Liulevicius, *War Land*, 129–131.

218. On the uniquely German obsession with culture, see Wolf Lepenies, *The Seduction of Culture in German History* (Princeton, NJ: Princeton University Press, 2014). For the strong preservationist tradition in German history and its relation to German identities, see Rudy Koshar, *Germany's Transient Pasts: Preservation and National Memory in the Twentieth Century* (Chapel Hill: The University of North Carolina Press, 1998).

219. Ironically, the Wehrmacht *Kunstschutz'* mandate was explicitly grounded in the same Hague regulations regarding the inviolability of private property that the army otherwise habitually ignored.

220. Kunstschutzbeauftragten beim OKH, Abschließender Bericht über die Arbeit des Kunstschutzbeauftragten in der Zeit von Mai 1940–September 1944, BA-MA RH 3/154.

221. See, for instance, "Deutsche Soldaten retten Kulturgüter," *Feldzeitung von der Maas bis an die Memel*, 25.8.1941, BA-MA RHD 69/76.

222. See BArch R 6/170, passim.

223. See, for instance, Wehrmachtführungsstab (Heeresgruppe Mitte) Abteilung für Wehrmacht Propaganda, Situation and Activity Report, 1.11.1941 and Der Befehlshaber

für das rückwärtige Heeresgebiet Mitte Prop. Abteilung W, Propaganda and Activity Report for 16–30.11.1941, 30.11.1941, BA-MA RW 4/236.

224. Adjutantur der Wehrmacht beim Führer to Chef des Oberkommandos der Wehrmacht and Reichsminister für die Besetzten Ostgebiete, 20.7.1942 Führerhauptquartier, BArch R 55/1288. Perhaps this order stemmed from his own experience as a "starving artist."

225. Obgefr. G., Nachrichten-Regiment 501, 2.9.1943, Bericht über die Bergung von Kronleuchtern und anderem Kirchengerät aus der Sophienkathedrale im Kreml von Nowgorod, BA-MA RH 44/384. The chandeliers had been made by German craftsmen in the Middle Ages; the other objects were presumably Russian in origin.

226. See Reichsministerium für Volksaufklärung und Propaganda to Major K. im Oberkommando der Wehrmacht, 2.8.1941, Betr.: Weisungen für die Propaganda-Abteilungen im Ostraum, Yad Vashem M.29.FR/84; BArch R 6/170, passim.

227. See, for example, Kilian, *Wehrmacht und Besatzungsherrschaft*, 313–73 on the mood of the population in the rear area of Army Group North, which tended to rise and fall based on German conduct and the course of military operations, taking a sharp turn for the worse by 1943.

228. Prop. Abt. W, Stimmungsbericht Monat Juni 1942, 4.7.1942, Yad Vashem M 29 FR 82.

229. See, for example, "Achtung, Partisanen!" and "Das sind Partisanen!" 16.11.1941 and 19.9.1941, *Das Neuste für den Soldaten*, BA-MA RHD 69/14l; "'Andere Länder, andere Sitten,'" Nr. 203, June 1942, *Mitteilungen für die Truppe*, BA-MA RW 4/357.

230. See Kurt Niemeyer to unspecified recipient(s), 8.5.1942, MSPT 3.2008.1750; Heinz Sartorio to Elly and Fred, 28.3.1942, MSPT 3.2002.0827.

231. See Pohl, *Herrschaft*, 339–40.

232. Leiter Ost to Herrn Reichsminister, 9.11.1942, Betr.: Kaukasisches Gebet für den Führer, BArch, R 55-1288.

233. For example see 12th Inf. Div., Abt. Ic, Activity Report for 1.3–30.6.1943, BA-MA RH 26-12/86; PzAOK1, Gruppe Geh. Feldpolizei 626, Lage und Stimmung der Bevölkerung in den besetzten Gebieten, 25.6.1944, BA-MA RH 21-1/184. What lends these reports credibility is the fact that Wehrmacht formations had habitually exaggerated civilian hostility throughout the conflict.

234. Rolf Dietrich to Hilde, 4.9.1943, MSPT 3.2002.7236; Willy Hagemann to parents, 5.4.1943, MSPT 3.2002.7169; Heinz Rahe to Ursula, 11.3.1943, MSPT 3.2002.0985.

235. Heinz Sartorio to sister, 3.12.1943, MSPT 3.2002.0827.

236. See Kilian, *Wehrmacht und Besatzungsherrschaft*, 182–83.

237. See Rolf-Dieter Müller, *The Unknown Eastern Front: The Wehrmacht and Hitler's Foreign Soldiers* (London: I. B. Tauris, 2012), 213–36.

238. Heinz Sartorio to Elly (sister), 4.8.1942, MSPT 3.2002.0827.

239. Heinz Sartorio to Elly, 21.6.1943, MSPT 3.2002.0827.

240. See "Freiwillige und Hilfswillige im Osten," Nr. 241, 9.1.1943, *Mitteilungen für die Truppe*, BA-MA RW 4/357.

241. See especially Erfahrungsbericht der Militärverwaltung beim Oberkommando der Heeresgruppe Mitte, 22.6-1941-8.1944, BA-MA RH 19-II/334, a remarkable document that assessed three years of occupation and concluded that the Germans had ultimately failed to offer Soviet civilians any positive political ideas in place of Bolshevism.

242. See Kriegsberichter Hermann-Josef Haentemann, PK (mot) 670, "Vier Menschen—vier Schicksals. Bilder aus dem großen Zug—'Unser Vertrauen zu Deutschland ist unerschütterlich!'" 12.10.1943, BA-MA RW 4/803. See also Daniel Uziel, *The Propaganda Warriors: The Wehrmacht and the Consolidation of the German Home Front* (New York: Peter Lang, 2008), 312.

243. See for example 205th Inf. Div., Feldgend. Trupp A, Activity Report for 11.9–20.9.1943, 20.9.1943, BA-MA RH 26-205/78; 12th Inf. Div., Abt. Ic, Activity Report for 1.3–30.6.1943, BA-MA RH 26-12/86.

244. See Ben Shepherd, "Hawks, Doves and Tote Zonen: A Wehrmacht Security Division in Central Russia, 1943," *Journal of Contemporary History* 37, no. 3 (2002): 349–69.

245. This book alone has identified four armies, five corps, twelve infantry divisions, and one panzer division that incorporated conciliatory policies into its strategy at least to some extent. For context, the invasion commenced with 184 divisions. See Wildermuth, "Widening the Circle," 307.

246. Sonderberichter Oberstleutnant Soldan, "'Sieg im Osten,' Anmerkungen zum neuen Bewegungskrieg," *Das Reich*, 17.8.1941, EZA 686/8524.

5. Death and Victimhood

1. OKW, Nr. 2240/39 W Allg. (II), to Reichsministerium des Innern, 15.11.1939, Betr.: Gräberfürsorge und Überführungen, BArch NS 18/1054.

2. For a general overview of German postwar memory, see Alon Confino, "Remembering the Second World War, 1945–1965: Narratives of Victimhood and Genocide," *Cultural Analysis* 4 (2005): 46–75; Gilad Margalit, *Guilt, Suffering, and Memory: Germany Remembers Its Dead of World War II*, trans. Haim Watzman (Bloomington: Indiana University Press, 2010); Jeffrey Herf, *Divided Memory: The Nazi Past in the Two Germanys* (Cambridge, MA: Harvard University Press, 1997).

3. Robert G. Moeller, *War Stories: The Search for a Usable Past in the Federal Republic of Germany* (Berkeley: University of California Press, 2003); Norman Naimark, *Fires of Hatred: Ethnic Cleansing in Twentieth-Century Europe* (Cambridge, MA: Harvard University Press, 2001), chap. 4; Frank Biess, *Homecomings: Returning POWs and the Legacies of Defeat in Postwar Germany* (Princeton, NJ: Princeton University Press, 2006); Frank Biess, "Survivors of Totalitarianism: Returning POWs and the Reconstruction of Masculine Citizenship in West Germany, 1945–1955," in *The Miracle Years: A Cultural History of West Germany, 1949–1968*, ed. Hanna Schissler (Princeton, NJ: Princeton University Press, 2001).

4. See Helen Wolfenden, "The Representation of *Wehrmacht* Soldiers as Victims in Post-War German Film: *Hunde, wollt ihr ewig leben?* and *Der Arzt von Stalingrad*," in Helmut Schmitz, ed., *A Nation of Victims? Representations of German Wartime Suffering from 1945 to the Present* (New York: Rodopi B. V., 2007), 71–86; Paul Cooke and Marc Silberman, eds., *Screening War: Perspectives on German Suffering* (Rochester, NY: Camden House, 2010).

5. Joseph Perry, "The Madonna of Stalingrad: Mastering the (Christmas) Past and West German National Identity After World War II," *Radical History Review*, no. 83 (Spring 2002): 6–27.

6. Margalit, *Guilt, Suffering, and Memory*, 119–85; W. G. Sebald, *Luftkrieg und Literatur* (München: Carl Hanser Verlag, 1999).

7. See Margalit, *Guilt, Suffering, and Memory*, esp. 79–93.

8. "Die hölzernen Kreuze," *Das Neuste für den Soldaten*, 15.3.1942, BA-MA RHD 69/14.

9. Support for these claims can be found in the work of social psychologists. See Julia Chaitin and Shoshana Steinberg, "You Should Know Better: Expressions of Empathy and Disregard among Victims of Massive Social Trauma," *Journal of Aggression, Maltreatment & Trauma* 17 (2008): 197–226.

10. See Klaus Latzel, *Vom Sterben im Krieg: Wandlungen in der Einstellung zum Soldatentod vom Siebenjährigen Krieg bis zum II. Weltkrieg* (Warendorf: Verlag Fahlbusch, 1988), 20–54.

11. According to Jay Winter, only about half the war's dead could be identified, and burial in mass graves became a common practice. See Jay Winter, *Sites of Memory, Sites of Mourning: The Great War in European Cultural History* (Cambridge: Cambridge University Press, 1995), 36.

12. Klaus Latzel, *Vom Sterben im Krieg*, 77–78; Wehrmachtgräberfürsorge: Stand, Wünsche und Künftige Planung, undated, BA-MA RH 13/20.

13. Rüdiger Overmans, *Deutsche militärische Verluste im Zweiten Weltkrieg* (München: Oldenbourg, 2004), 94.

14. Jay Winter, *Sites of Memory, Sites of Mourning: The Great War in European Cultural History* (Cambridge: Cambridge University Press, 1995); Latzel, *Vom Sterben im Krieg*, 77–83; George L. Mosse, *Fallen Soldiers: Reshaping the Memory of the World Wars* (New York: Oxford University Press, 1990), chap. 2–7; Monica Black, *Death in Berlin: From Weimar to Divided Germany* (Cambridge: Cambridge University Press, 2013), 19–67.

15. Latzel, *Vom Sterben im Krieg*, 80–85; Black, *Death in Berlin*, 69–110; Mosse, *Fallen Soldiers*; Jay Baird, *To Die for Germany: Heroes in the Nazi Pantheon* (Bloomington: Indiana University Press, 1990); Sabine Behrenbeck, *Der Kult um die toten Helden: Nationalsozialistische Mythen, Riten und Symbole 1923–1945* (Vierow bei Greifswald: SH-Verlag, 2011).

16. See Verordnung über die Gräberfürsorge der Wehrmacht des Großdeutschen Reichs, *Reichsgesetzblatt*, Teil I, v.12.4.40, Seite 621, 2.4.1940, BA-MA RH 13/16.

17. See Wehrmachtgräberfürsorge, undated, Verordnung über die Gräberfürsorge der Wehrmacht des Großdeutschen Reichs, Reichsgesetzblatt, Teil I, v.12.4.40, Seite 621, 2.4.1940, and OKW, IVa, Merkblatt über die Wehrmacht-Gräberfürsorge, 2.9.1940, in BA-MA RH 13/16; Forderungen des Heeres für die Gestaltung von Kriegerfriedhöfen und Ehrenmalen, undated, BA-MA RH 13/21.

18. See undated regulations, KMBA SW 140; notes of Georg Werthmann, 30.5.1943 and OKH 31 v AHA/Ag/S (IV), 29.12.1941, KMBA SW 141. This sometimes interfered with chaplains' ability to conduct their primary work. OKH changed its policy after 1942 to no longer allow chaplains to be appointed graves officers. It appears, however, that those already appointed usually kept their positions. See Ag EH 31 v Gr S (II) 1655/42 to H/S L, June 1942, KMBA SW 141.

19. See Merkblatt für die Truppe, Betr.: Beerdigung gefallener Kameraden, April 1943, Nr. 31, BA-MA RH 13/18.

20. See Chief of Staff of the German Red Cross to Herrn Generalmajor Reinicke, OKW, 12.2.1940, and Frau L. to Generalbaurat Herrn Professor Dr. Kreis, 12.5.1941, and passim., BA-MA RW 6/525.

21. OKW, Allgemeine Abteilung, Richtlinien für die Wehrmacht Gräberoffiziere im Bewegungskrieg, 26.3.1940, BA-MA RH 13/16.

22. Wehrmachtgräberfürsorge: Stand, Wünsche und Künftige Planung, undated, BA-MA RH 13/20.

23. Ibid.

24. OKW to various subordinate formations, 11.9.1940, BA-MA RH 13/20. Emphasis in original.

25. See OKW, Betr.: Grabkreuze, 5.2.1942, BA-MA RH 13/16.

26. See Führer Erlass über die Gestaltung deutscher Kriegerfriedhöfe, 16.3.1941, BA-MA RH 13/20.

27. OKW, IVa, Merkblatt über die Wehrmacht-Gräberfürsorge, 2.9.1940, BA-MA RH 13/16.

28. Wehrmachtgräberfürsorge, undated, BA-MA RH 13/16.

29. OKW, Dienstanweisung für die Wehrmacht-Gräberoffiziere, 1.6.1941, BA-MA 13/16.

30. See Sonderabdruck Nr. 145 aus dem Ministerialblatt des Reichs- und Preußischen Ministeriums des Innern 1943 Nr. 49, BA-MA RW 6/523; OKW AWA/W Allg/IId, 950/44 geh., Betr.: Beisetzung gefallener oder verstorbener feindlicher Wehrmachtangehöriger, 13.8.1944, BA-MA RW 6/454; OKW, Bestimmungen und Richtlinien für den Wehrmacht-Gräberdienst bei der Truppe, 18.10.1944, RW 6-182. The first set of instructions cited here added, in apparent contradiction to the 1941 orders, that burials for Soviet soldiers were to be done in the simplest possible form. The second set denied military honors at the burial of "terror-fliers" (i.e., Allied bomber crewmen).

31. See Generaloberst Halder's notes on Hitler's talk of 30.3.1941, reprinted in Gerd R. Ueberschär and Wolfram Wette, eds., *"Unternehmen Barbarossa": Der deutsche Überfall auf die Sowjetunion 1941* (Paderborn: Schöningh, 1984), 303.

32. Both quotations from OKW, Dienstanweisung für Wehrmacht Gräber-Offiziere, 1.6.1941, BA-MA RH 13/16.

33. Wehrmachtgräberfürsorge: Stand, Wünsche und Künftige Planung, undated, BA-MA RH 13/20. This was an apparent reference to Marxist materialism, which the Wehrmacht hoped to contrast with its own religious piety. Later reports within the Wehrmacht suggest that the Red Army did possess burial details, and its frontline soldiers usually buried their dead when possible. See Vernehmung eines Überläufers, 6.7.1942, BA-MA RW 6/522.

34. Hans Roth, diary entry of 22.7.1941, in Hans Roth, *Eastern Inferno: The Journals of a German Panzerjäger on the Eastern Front, 1941–1943*, ed. Christine Alexander and Mason Kunze (Philadelphia, PA: Casemate, 2010).

35. Hans Roth, diary entry of 9.8.1941, *Eastern Inferno*.

36. Hans Roth, diary entry of 11.8.1941, *Eastern Inferno*.

37. Rudi Haller to Hans (brother), 4.9.1942, MSPT 3.2002.0368.

38. Rudi Haller to Hans, 20.1.1943, MSPT 3.2002.0368.

39. Wilhelm Altmann to father and sister, 13.11.1941, MSPT 3.2002.0201.

40. Frau L. to Wilhelm Altmann, 3.5.1942, MSPT 3.2002.0201.

41. Dr. Wilhelm Bacher, diary entry of 16.8.1941, MSPT 3.2002.1376.

42. Hans Wilhelm Sauer to parents and sisters, 4.10.1942, MSPT 3.2002.1271.

43. Oberleutnant R. to family of Hans Wilhelm Sauer, 19.3.1943, MSPT 3.2002.1271.

44. Willy Hagemann to Kressen, 17.2.1942, MSPT 3.2002.7169.

45. See H Dv 22/I Pol.Handbuch Teil I, 1.4.1943, excerpted in KMBA SW 140, with subsequent addendums. By 1943, chaplains could only write at the express wish of a soldier or his family, at least ten days after the commanding officer or doctor's initial letter.

46. PzAOK1, Abt. IVd(e), Bericht über den Stand der Feldseelsorge, 1.1-31.3.1942, BA-MA RH 21-1/485.

47. See, especially, Hans Jürgen Brandt and the Katholisches Militärbischofsamt, eds., *Priester in Uniform: Seelsorger, Ordensleute und Theologen als Soldaten im Zweiten Weltkrieg* (Augsburg: Pattloch, 1994).

48. On these virtues see chapter 1.

49. Wilhelm Altmann to father and sister, 13.5.1942, MSPT 3.2002.0201.

50. Wilhelm Altmann to Ernst, 17.6.1942, MSPT 3.2002.0201.

51. See Bestimmungen und Richtlinien für den Wehrmacht-Gräberdienst bei der Truppe, 18.10.1944, BA-MA RW 6/182. To this author's knowledge, no other military attempted formally or informally to make such a commitment during the Second World War.

52. Hans Wilhelm Sauer to parents and sisters, 5.10.1942, MSPT 3.2002.1271.

53. 205th Inf. Div., Abt. IVd(e), Activity Report, 1.9-31.12.1943, BA-MA RH 26-205/78.

54. 223rd Inf. Div., WGO, Report for 1941-30.6.1942, BA-MA RH 26-223/72. Emphasis in original.

55. 297th Inf. Div., Abt. IVd(k), Activity Report, 15.5-22.1.1941, KMBA WmS 9.

56. Harald Hoffmann to parents and Marion (sister), 10.8.1941, MSPT 3.2002.0382.

57. Walter Neuser to mother, 24.11.1941, MSPT 3.2002.0947.

58. Walter Neuser to Fräulein W., 6.1.1942, to parents, 24.3.1942, and to mother, 6.5.1942, MSPT 3.2002.0947.

59. 5th Jäger Div., Abt. IVd(e), Activity Report, 16.7.1942–15.7.1943, BA-MA RH 26-5/50.

60. See AOK2, Abt. IVd(k), Seelsorgebericht, 1.7-30.9.1941, KMBA WmS 6.

61. 18th Inf. Div. (mot), Abt. IVd(k), Seelsorgebericht, KMBA WmS 8.

62. See Black, *Death in Berlin*, 69–110; Nina Janz, "Der Heldengedenktag in der Wehrmacht" (master's thesis, Hagen, FernUniversität Hagen, 2013).

63. Dr. Wilhelm Bacher, diary entry of 13.3.1942, MSPT 3.2002.1376.

64. Dr. Wilhelm Bacher, diary entry of 15.3.1942, MSPT 3.2002.1376.

65. Lic. D., Ostergruss to the Angehörigen der Gefallenen der 23 Division, Heldengedenktag, 1942, BA-MA RH 26-23/76.

66. Hans Simon to family, 13.3.1944, MSPT 3.2002.1288.

67. See, for instance, sketches and photographs of the *Heldenfriedhof* in Andrejewka, BA-MA MSG 2/5916; 25. Inf. Div., Ib/Gräberoffz., Erläuterungen zur Anlage des Heldenfriedhofes der 25. J. D. (mot) in Deschinko, 24.6.1942, BA-MA 26-25/100.

68. For example, see Walter Neuser to mother, 6.5.1942, MSPT 3.2002.0947.

69. Kr. Laz. Abt. 609, Abt. IVd(k), Seelsorgebericht, 1.7.1941–30.9.1941, KMBA WmS 8.

70. Kurt Niemeyer to wife, 10.3.1942, MSPT 3.2008.1750.

71. See BA-MA RH 13/35.

72. See, for example, Oberleutnant Nerger, "Bei unseren Gefallenen," *Der Kampf*, 24.8.1941, BA-MA RHD 69/41.

73. "Sieger geblieben—auch im Tode!" *Blücher*, 22.10.1941, BA-MA RHD 69/33.

74. See, for instance, Ottomar von Wedel-Parlom, "Soldatentod," *Feldzeitung von der Maas bis an die Memel*, 31.8.1941, BA-MA RHD 69/76.

75. For example, see "Wir werden die Sowjets vernichten," *Soldatenzeitung der Ukraine*, 17.3.1942, BA-MA RHD 69/9.

76. See "Am Grab des Generals von Briesen: Nachruf Generalfeldmarschalls von Rundstedt," *Der Durchbruch*, 25.11.1941, BA-MA RHD 69/85.

77. See "Sorge für unsere Kinder: Kinderbeihilfen bei Gefallenen, Vermissten und Verschollenen," *Soldatenzeitung der Ukraine*, 18.10.1942, BA-MA RHD 69/9.

78. "Die Braut des Gefallenen wird 'Frau': Erweitertes Recht auf den Namen des Bräutigams," *Ost-Front*, 6/7.7.1941, BA-MA RHD 53/20.

79. See "Erweiterter Ehrenschutz für Gefallene," *Der Ostkämpfer*, 24.11.1942, BA-MA 69/48.

80. See 95th Inf. Div., Abt. IIa/IIb, Report on 1941, BA-MA RH 26-258/95. The need for manpower appears to have put a damper on this program by 1942, however.

81. "Soldaten als Paten von Kindern gefallener Kameraden," *Der Durchbruch*, 11.11.1941, BA-MA RHD 69/85.

82. Frau L. to Wilhelm Altmann, 28.5.1942, MSPT 3.2002.0201.

83. Unnamed mother to a Catholic chaplain, 24.1.1943, KMBA SW 140.

84. Frau K. to Chaplain D., undated, BA-MA RH 26-23/76.

85. Walter Neuser to mother, 25.8.1941, MSPT 3.2002.0947.

86. See, for instance, Walter Neuser to mother, 6.8.1941 and to sister, 8.8.1941, MSPT 3.2002.0947. The Red Army's behavior was the result of several factors, including Soviet propaganda to the effect that all Red soldiers would be executed if captured, the USSR's massive reserves of manpower, and a deliberate strategy on the part of Soviet generals to slow German progress with thousands of localized counterattacks. See especially John Erickson, *The Road to Stalingrad: Stalin's War with Germany* (London: Weidenfeld and Nicolson, 1975).

87. See Karl Müller to parents and sister, 7.8.1941, MSPT 3.2002.0209.

88. Hans Roth, diary entry of 7.2.1943, *Eastern Inferno*.

89. See Hans Roth, diary entry of 23.8.1941, *Eastern Inferno*; Franz Siebeler to parents and siblings, 24.6.1941, MSPT 3.2002.1285.

90. See Christian Hartmann, *Wehrmacht im Ostkrieg: Front und militärisches Hinterland 1941/42* (München: R. Oldenbourg Verlag, 2009), 501–11.

91. "Sowjetsoldaten zwischen zwei Fronten: Kommissare hetzen zur brutalen und feigen Kriegsführung," *Ost-Front*, 27.8.1941, BA-MA RHD 53/20.

92. Hans Roth, diary entries of 18.7.1941 and 8-14.2.1942, *Eastern Inferno*.

93. "Ein Gespräch zwischen den Schlachten: Was ist Mut? Bolschewistischer Gleichgültigkeit und deutscher Einsatzwille stehen sich im Kampfe gegenüber," *von der Maas bis an die Memel*, 22.7.1941, BA-MA RHD 69/15.

94. See, for example, Joseph Goebbels, "Die sogenannte russische Seele," 19.7.1942, reprinted in *Das eherne Herz* (Munich: Zentralverlag der NSDAP, 1943), 398–405.

95. See Joseph Goebbels, diary entry of 11.8.1941, in Elke Fröhlich, ed., *Die Tagebücher von Joseph Goebbels: Teil II: Diktate 1941–1945*, Band I Juli–September 1941 (München: K. G. Sauer, 1996).

96. Hermann Henning to parents, 28.9.1941, MSPT 3.2002.7217.

97. See 15th Inf. Div. GO to WGO 61 beim PzAOK1, Betr.: Gefallene, die nicht geborgen werden konnten, 12.5.1943, BA-MA RH 26-15/101; Hans Roth, diary entry of 22.2.1942, *Eastern Inferno.*

98. Wilhelm Altmann to father and sister, 19.10.1941, MSPT 3.2002.0201.

99. For example, see 15th Inf. Div. WGO, to WGO 61 beim PzAOK1, Betr.: Gefallene, die nicht geborgen werden konnten, 12.5.1943, BA-MA RH 26-15/101.

100. "Sowjetkanonen unter Grabkreuzen," *Feldzeitung von der Maas bis an die Memel,* 28.8.1941, BA-MA RHD 69–76.

101. For example, see 131st Inf. Div., Abt. IVd(k), Activity Report, 22.6–31.7.1941, KMBA WmS 8; "Eine wahre Hölle: Pressvertreter besichtigen die Stadt Reval," *Feldzeitung von der Maas bis an die Memel,* 12.9.1941, BA-MA RHD 69/76.

102. See Wilhelm Schabel, ed., *Herr in deine Hände* (Stuttgart: Alfred Scherz Verlag, 1963), 103–4; Heinz Rahe to wife, 21.1.1943, MSPT 3.2002.0985.

103. "Die hölzernen Kreuze," *Das Neuste für den Soldaten,* 15.3.1942, BA-MA RHD 69/14.

104. AOK16, Abt. IVd(e), Activity Report, 16.10–21.12.1941, BA-MA RH 20-16/1095.

105. Willy Nagel to Wandelgard, 7.1.1942, MSPT 3.2002.0236.

106. Willy Nagel to Wandelgard, 27.3.1942, MSPT 3.2002.0236.

107. For example, see 15th Inf. Div., GO, to WGO 46 of AOK4, Betr.: Schreiben vom 7.11.1941, 10.11.1941, BA-MA RH 26-15/99.

108. There was a grain of truth to this assertion. Due to its lack of an official graves registration service and the desperate situation in which the Red Army found itself in the first years of the war, systematic burial was fairly uncommon on the Soviet side. This was also—a fact German commentators never mentioned—the consequence of a swift Wehrmacht advance that often prevented Red soldiers from reaching the bodies of their dead in the first place. See Erickson, *The Road to Stalingrad.*

109. See Hans-Karl to parents and Enge, 2.7.1941 and 5.7.1941, BA-MA MSG 2/14466.

110. Hans-Karl to parents and Enge, 15.7.1941, BA-MA MSG 2/14466.

111. Wilhelm Altmann to father and sister, 28.4.1942, MSPT 3.2002.0201.

112. Dr. Wilhelm Bacher, diary entry of 9.7.1941, MSPT 3.2002.1376.

113. Dr. Wilhelm Bacher, diary entry of 16.8.1941, MSPT 3.2002.1376.

114. For example, see Hans Simon to parents, 24.5.1942, MSPT 3.2002.1288; Wilhelm Moldenhauser to Erika, 29.10.1942, *Im Funkwagen der Wehrmacht durch Europa: Balkan, Ukraine, Stalingrad: Feldpostbriefe des Gefreiten Wilhelm Moldenhauser 1940–1943,* ed. Jens Ebert (Berlin: Trafo, 2008).

115. For exceptions, see AOK2 Abt. IVd(k) to all Catholic chaplains in the service area, 10.10.1941, BA-MA RH 20-2/1606; Wilhelm Schabel, ed., *Herr in deine Hände,* 83; 293rd Inf. Div., Abt. IVd(k), Activity Report, July–August 1941, KMBA WmS 8.

116. Klaus Latzel, *Vom Sterben im Krieg,* 80–95.

117. Commander of Feldposteinheit 25144 B to the father of Walter Neuser, 10.5.1942, MSPT 3.2002.0947.

118. Gerhard P. to Marie R., undated, MSPT 3.2002.7217.

119. See OKW to all Wehrmachtgräberoffiziere, 13.8.1940, in BA-MA RH 13/16.

120. See Latzel, *Vom Sterben im Krieg,* 84–85, 91–92 and 101; Mosse, *Fallen Soldiers;* Baird, *To Die for Germany;* Behrenbeck, *Der Kult um die toten Helden;* Black, *Death in Berlin,* 6–110.

121. See "Unser Bekenntnis zur Tat: Heldengedenkfeier am Sitz des Wehrmacht-befehlshaber Ukraine," *Soldatenzeitung der Ukraine*, 24.3.1942, BA-MA RHD 69/9; Janz, "Der Heldengedenktag in der Wehrmacht."

122. See, for instance, "Sieger geblieben—auch im Tode!" *Blücher*, 22.10.1941, BA-MA RHD 69/33.

123. See Baird, *To Die for Germany*, 221.

124. See, especially, Monica Ann Black, "On Death in Germany: Perceptions of Death among Wehrmacht Soldiers, 1939–1945" (master's thesis, University of Virginia, 2002).

125. See Latzel, *Vom Sterben im Krieg*, 98–99.

126. On Christian views of war and soldiering, see Arnold Angenendt, *Toleranz und Gewalt: Das Christentum zwischen Bibel und Schwert* (Münster, 2012). On the German Christian movement, see chapter 3.

127. See Manfred Messerschmidt, "Zur Militärseelsorgepolitik im Zweiten Welt-krieg," *Militärgeschichtliche Mitteilungen* 1 (1969): 37–85.

128. Schriftlesungen, Gebete und Gedichte zur Gestaltung von Totenfeiern im Felde, für die H. Kriegspfarrer zusammengestellt, AOK16, BA-MA RH 20-16/1096.

129. See, for example, Kirchliches Kriegshilfe, Predigtskizzen, Reihe XIX, un-dated, KMBA WmS 54.

130. Sermon of Kriegspfarrer a.K. G., 23.4.1944, KMBA SW 135.

131. For one example, see 18th Inf. Div. (mot), Abt. IVd(e), Feldpredigt, 16.8.1941, BA-MA RH 26-18/100.

132. Extensive collections of correspondence between chaplains and surviving relatives, as well as relatives and a soldier's still-living comrades, can be found in KMBA SW 140; 23rd Inf. Div., Abt. IVd(e), Activity Report, 8.8.1941–24.1.1942, BA-MA RH 26-23/76; Archiv des Erzbistums München und Freising (hereafter AEMF) Priesterseminar Freising 145 (1–62).

133. Anneliese T. to (chaplain) Herr S., 18.1.1942, KMBA SW 140.

134. See Baird, *To Die for Germany*, 222.

135. See H Dv 22/I Pol.Handbuch Teil I, 1.4.1943, excerpted in KMBA SW 140, with subsequent addendums.

136. See, for instance, Gaupropaganda, Gauleitung Köln-Aachen to Reichspropa-gandaleitung der NSDAP, Betr.: Veröffentlichung von Gefallenen durch die Kirche, 19.3.1942, and Vorlage, Betr.: Heldenehrungen und Gefallenengedenkfeiern der Kirchen, 11.12.1942, BArch NS 18/474; Baird, *To Die for Germany*, 225–42.

137. See Pg. T. to Leiter des Hauptkulturamtes in der Reichspropagandaleitung, 26.1.1942, Betr.: Trauermusik bei von Partei und Wehrmacht gemeinsam durchge-führten Beerdigungen, and "Feiergestaltung," undated, BArch NS 18/1056.

138. As Klaus Latzel puts it, "In the ideological battle over the meanings of the soldier's death the traditional church ceremonies ultimately retained the upper hand." See Latzel, *Vom Sterben im Krieg*, 101; Ian Kershaw, *The Nazi Dictatorship: Problems and Perspectives of Interpretation*, 3rd ed. (New York: E. Arnold, 1993), 145; Baird, *To Die for Germany*, 223. For a contrasting interpretation, see Black, *Death in Berlin*, 84–88.

139. Reichspropagandaleitung, Chef des Propagandastabes to Pg. S., 21.8.1942, BArch, NS 18/276.

140. See Latzel, *Deutsche Soldaten*, 227–283; Latzel, *Vom Sterben im Krieg*, 93–95.

141. Hans Wilhelm Sauer to parents and Christa, 11.10.1942, MSPT 3.2002.1271.

142. Wilhelm Altmann to father and sister, 12.7.1942, MSPT 3.2002.0201.

143. See chapter 1.

144. See Willy Nagel to Wandelgard, 27.3.1942, MSPT 3.2002.0326 and Helmut Nick to Ilse (wife) 7.1.1941, MSPT 3.2002.0274.

145. Wilhelm Altmann to father and sister, 17.6.1942, MSPT 3.2002.0201.

146. Hans Albring to Eugen Altrogge, 17.6.1942, MSPT 3.2002.0211; Hans Wilhelm Sauer, 7.9.1941, MSPT 3.2002.1271. Quotation from the former.

147. Heinz Rahe to Ursula, 21.1.1943, MSPT 3.2002.0985.

148. See Willy Nagel to Wandelgard, 27.3.1942, MSPT 3.2002.0326.

149. Hans Roth, diary entry of 26.9.1941, *Eastern Inferno*.

150. See Harald Hoffmann to parents and Marion, 23.7.1941, MSPT 3.2002.0382.

151. Eugen Altrogge to Hans Albring, 11.11.1942, MSPT 3.2002.0210.

152. This may be partly due to the fact that German society associated mourning with femininity. See Thomas Kühne, *Kameradschaft: Die Soldaten des nationalsozialistischen Krieges und das 20. Jahrhundert* (Göttingen: Vandenhoeck & Ruprecht, 2006), 169. Avoiding reflection about death was also a way to insulate oneself from battlefield dangers.

153. See, for example, Hans Wilhelm Sauer, 7.9.1941, MSPT 3.2002.1271.

154. See Baird, *To Die for Germany*, 221–22; "Der Brief des Kameraden," *Ost-Front*, 3.1.1942, BA-MA RH 52/20.

155. See "85,896 Gefallene," *Mitteilungen für die Truppe*, Nr. 138, September 1941, BA-MA RW 4/357.

156. See Joseph Goebbels, diary entry of 22.8.1941, Elke Fröhlich, ed., *Die Tagebücher von Joseph Goebbels: Teil II,* Band I; Daniel Uziel, *The Propaganda Warriors: The Wehrmacht and the Consolidation of the German Home Front* (New York: Peter Lang, 2008), chap. 6.

157. "271,612 Gefallene," *Mitteilungen für die Truppe*, Nr. 209, July 1942, BA-MA RW 4/357.

158. See Omer Bartov, *Hitler's Army: Soldiers, Nazis, and War in the Third Reich* (New York: Oxford University Press, 1991), 44.

159. Ian Kershaw, *The End: Hitler's Germany 1944–45* (Allen Lane, 2011), 92.

160. See Overmans, *Deutsche militärische Verluste im Zweiten Weltkrieg*, 228–32.

161. Walter Neuser to mother, 21–22.8.1941, MSPT 3.2002.0947.

162. Walter Neuser to parents, 18.4.1942, MSPT 3.2002.0947.

163. Uffz. Heinz B. to Willy Hagemann, 24.6.1942, MSPT 3.2002.7169.

164. Willy Hagemann to Kressen, 9.8.1944, MSPT 3.2002.7169.

165. Willy Hagemann to Kressen, 22.8.1944, MSPT 3.2002.7169.

166. For example, see Wilhelm Altmann to father and sister, 23.1.1943, MSPT 3.2002.0201.

167. On this phenomenon, which André Mineau describes as a "limit situation" in which ideology begins to break down in the face of reality, see Mineau, *Operation Barbarossa: Ideology and Ethics against Human Dignity* (Amsterdam: Rodopi, 2004), 121–23. Also see Latzel, *Deutsche Soldaten*, 362–67.

168. Hans Albring to Eugen Altrogge, 3.8.1942, MSPT 3.2002.0211.

169. Hans-Peter Eckener to sister, 13.4.1943, MSPT 3.2002.0307.

170. For example, see Rudi Haller to Hans, 4.9.1942, MSPT 3.2002.0368.

171. See Dr. Wilhelm Bacher, diary entry of 1.8.1941, MSPT 3.2002.1376.

172. Dr. Wilhelm Bacher, diary entry of 29.10.1941, MSPT 3.2002.1376.

173. Dr. Wilhelm Bacher, diary entries of 11.11.1941 and 19.11.1941, MSPT 3.2002.1376.

174. Dr. Wilhelm Bacher, diary entry of 3.4.1942, MSPT 3.2002.1376.

175. Willy Reese, *A Stranger to Myself: The Inhumanity of War: Russia, 1941–1944*, ed. Stefan Schmitz, trans. Michael Hofmann (New York: Farrar, Straus and Giroux: 2003), 105.

176. Ibid., quotations from 155 and 36, respectively.

177. Ibid., 70–71, also 138.

178. Rudi Haller to Hans, 14.2.1942, MSPT 3.2002.0368.

179. Johannes Hagemann to parents, 12.2.1942, MSPT 3.2002.7234.

180. Hermann Henning to family, 9.12.1941, MSPT 3.2002.7217.

181. Günther Schmidt to parents, 27.10.1941, MSPT 3.2002.0989.

182. See, for example, XXIX AK, Korpsarzt, Erfahrungsbericht zum Activity Report, 22.6–31.12.1941.

183. Hans-Peter Eckener to relatives, 1.4.1942, MSPT 3.2002.0307.

184. Harald Hoffmann to parents and Marion, 28.10.1941, MSPT 3.2002.0382.

185. Harald Hoffmann to parents and Marion, 1.12.1941, MSPT 3.2002.0382.

186. On this sentiment among veterans after the war, see Stephen Fritz, *Frontsoldaten: The German Soldier in World War II* (Lexington: University Press of Kentucky, 1995), 219–32.

187. Hans Simon to mother, 3.9.1942, MSPT 3.2002.1288.

188. Willy Hagemann to Kressen, 9.10.1943, MSPT 3.2002.7169.

189. See Latzel, *Deutsche Soldaten*, 352–62.

190. See Heinz Sartorio to Elly (sister), 6.6.1942, MSPT 3.2002.0827 complaining about his superiors and the pettiness of military life.

191. See, especially, Chief of the General Staff, Feldpostprüfungsberichte, September 1944, BA-MA RH 13/49; Kershaw, *The End*.

192. See Biess, *Homecomings*, 42.

193. Gaupropaganda, Gauleitung Köln-Aachen to Reichspropagandaleitung der NSDAP, 19.3.1942, BArch NS 18/474.

194. See WPr to z.b.V. Chef OKW (Verbindung Partei-Kanzlei), BArch NS 18/790.

195. See Stimmung unter den Angehörigen vermisster Soldaten, 21.10.1943, BArch NS 19/2444.

196. Mother R. to Hedwig F., 4.1.1943, MSPT 3.2002.2725. See also Wanda G.'s grandmother to Wanda, 6.2.1943, MSPT 3.2002.0326.

197. On this sense of pride, see Black, *Death in Berlin*, 105.

198. Harald Hoffmann to parents and Marion, 24.7.1941, MSPT 3.2002.0382.

199. Harald Hoffmann to parents and Marion, 18.10.1941, MSPT 3.2002.0382.

200. Reese, *Stranger to Myself*, 37.

201. Ibid., 98.

202. Rudi Haller to Hans, 4.9.1942, MSPT 3.2002.0368.

203. 223rd Inf. Div., Abschluss-Bericht des Divisionsgräberoffiziers der 223 ID for 10.11.1941–15.9.1943, BA-MA RH 26-223/77.

204. Chaplain Westphal to Frau M., 16.3.1943, BA-MA RH 26-15/101.

205. See 15th Inf. Div. Gräberoffizier to 15th Inf. Div. Abt. Ib W&G, Betr.: Bestattungsgerät, 8.4.1942, BA-MA RH 26-15/101.

206. See Wehrmachtgräber Offz. 46 b AOK4 to 15th Inf. Div. Gräberoffizier, Betr.: Anforderung von schwarzer Farbe zur Beschriftung von Grabkreuzen, 8.3.1942, BA-MA RH 26-15/101.

207. See, for example, 15th Inf. Div. Gräberoffizier to Wehrmachtgräberoffizier beim AOK4, Betr.: Ehrenfriedhof, 22.3.1942, BA-MA RH 26-15/101.

208. 126th Inf. Div., Abt. IVd(e), Activity Report, 22.6-31.12.1941, BA-MA RH 26-126/140.

209. GO of 15th Inf. Div. to Wehrmachtgräberoffizier 46 beim AOK4, Betr.: Auffindung Gefallener, BA-MA RH 26-15/101.

210. Hans Roth, diary entry of 17.1.1942, *Eastern Inferno*.

211. See Wehrmachtverlustwesen (II M), Merkblatt für Truppen-Gräberoffiziere, 19.1.1944, BA-MA RH 13/18.

212. See 25th Inf. Div. (mot), Ib/Gräberoffz., Erläuterungen zur Anlage des Heldenfriedhofes der 25 J.D. (mot) in Deschkino, 24.6.1942, BA-MA RH 26-25/100.

213. See Hans Roth, diary entry of 22.2.1942, *Eastern Inferno*; 15th Inf. Div. Gräberoffizier, 22.3.1942, Betr.: Ehrenfriedhof in Ssuschewo, BA-MA RH 26-15/101.

214. 223rd Inf. Div., Abschluss-Bericht des Divisionsgräberoffiziers der 223. Inf. Div. for 10.11.1941–15.9.1943, BA-MA RH 26-223/77.

215. See, for example, Rudi Haller to Hans, 20.1.1943, MSPT 3.2002.0368.

216. AOK 16, Abt. IVd(k), Seelsorgebericht, 1.10–31.12.1942, KMBA WmS 10.

217. Notes of Georg Werthmann, 30.6.1943, KMBA SW 140.

218. Notes of Georg Werthmann, 15.7.1945, KMBA SW 140.

219. Reese, *Stranger to Myself*, 93.

220. AOK2, Abt. IVd(k), Activity Report, 1.7-30.9.1944, BA-MA N 338/3.

221. See, especially, Brandt and the Katholisches Militärbischofsamt, *Priester in Uniform*.

222. Hans Leonhard, *Wieviel Leid erträgt ein Mensch? Aufzeichnungen eines Kriegspfarrers über die Jahre 1939 bis 1945*, ed. Hans-Walter Leonhard (Amberg: Buch & Kunstverlag Oberpfalz, 1994), 30.

223. See OKW, IVa, Merkblatt über die Wehrmacht-Gräberfürsorge, 2.9.1940, BA-MA RH 13/16.

224. Examples are numerous. See AOK2, Abt. IVd(k), Activity Report, 1.1–31.3.1942, BA-MA RH 20-2/1606; 297th Inf. Div., Abt. IVd(k), Activity Report, 15.5-22.11.1941, KMBA WmS 9.

225. Civilian and POW labor was allowed by international law under certain circumstances, but never without adequate compensation and the achievement of minimum standards of care, which the Wehrmacht did not meet. See Hamburger Institut für Sozialforschung, *Verbrechen der Wehrmacht. Dimensionen des Vernichtungskrieges 1941–1944* (2002), 11, 18–20, and 28.

226. On postwar victimhood narratives, see especially Helmut Schmitz, ed., *A Nation of Victims? Representations of German Wartime Suffering from 1945 to the Present* (New York: Rodopi B. V., 2007); Margalit, *Guilt, Suffering, and Memory*; Confino, "Remembering the Second World War, 1945–1965: Narratives of Victimhood and Genocide."

Conclusion

1. On the breadth of this program, see especially Bryce Sait, *The Indoctrination of the Wehrmacht: Nazi Ideology and the War Crimes of the German Military* (New York: Berghahn Books, 2019).

2. See Klaus Latzel, *Deutsche Soldaten—nationalsozialistsicher Krieg? Kriegserlebnis—Kriegserfahrung 1939–1945* (Paderborn: Ferdinand Schöningh, 1998), 284–310; Felix Römer, *Kameraden: Die Wehrmacht von Innen* (München: Piper, 2012), 70; Thomas Kühne, *Kameradschaft: Die Soldaten des nationalsozialistischen Krieges und das 20. Jahrhundert* (Göttingen: Vandenhoeck & Ruprecht, 2006); André Mineau, *Operation Barbarossa: Ideology and Ethics against Human Dignity* (Amsterdam: Rodopi, 2004), 95.

3. On this phenomenon see especially Claude Steele, "The Psychology of Self-Affirmation: Sustaining the Integrity of the Self," *Advances in Experimental Social Psychology* 21 (1988): 261–302.

4. Here, this work confirms the views expressed in Mineau, *Operation Barbarossa*, 11.

5. See Peter Haas, "Militärische Ethik im Totalen Krieg," in *Ideologie und Moral im Nationalsozialismus*, ed. Wolfgang Bialas and Lothar Fritze (Göttingen: Vandenhoeck & Ruprecht, 2014), 181.

6. Daniel Uziel, *The Propaganda Warriors: The Wehrmacht and the Consolidation of the German Home Front* (New York: Peter Lang, 2008), 245.

7. Here, this book reinforces the findings of Nicholas Stargardt, *The German War: A Nation Under Arms, 1939–1945: Citizens and Soldiers* (New York: Basic Books, 2017).

BIBLIOGRAPHY

Guide to Archival Abbreviations

AEMF	Archiv des Erzbistums München und Freising
BA-MA	Bundesarchiv-Militärarchiv
BArch	Bundesarchiv Berlin-Lichterfelde
EAF	Erzbischöfliches Archiv Freiburg
ELAB	Evangesliches Landeskirchliches Archiv in Berlin
EZA	Evangelisches Zentralarchiv
KEAB	Katholisches Erzbistum Archiv Berlin
KMBA	Archiv des Katholischen Militärbischofsamtes
MSPT	Museumsstiftung Post und Telekommunikation
NARA	National Archives and Records Administration
USHMM	United States Holocaust Memorial Museum

Published Primary Sources

AWA, Abt. Inland. *Die Sowjetunion: Gegebenheiten und Möglichkeiten des Ostraumes: Tornisterschrift des Oberkommandos der Wehrmacht*, Heft 72. Berlin: O. Stollberg, 1943.

Baedeker, Dietrich. *Das Volk, das im finstern wandelt: Stationen eines Militarpfarrers 1938–1946*. Edited by Evang. Kirchenamt für d. Bundeswehr Bonn. Hanover: Lutherisches Verlagshaus, 1987.

Bähr, Walter, and Hans W. Bähr, eds. *Kriegsbriefe gefallene Studenten, 1939–1945*. Tübingen: Rainer Wunderlich Verlag, 1952.

Baumeister, Roy, and Kathleen Vohs. "Four Roots of Evil." In *The Social Psychology of Good and Evil*, edited by Arthur G. Miller, 85–101. New York: Guilford Press, 2004.

Bertram, Adolf Kardinal. *Hirtenbriefe und Hirtenworte*. Edited by Werner Marschall. Köln: Böhlau Verlag, 2000.

Brandt, Hans Jürgen, and Katholisches Militärbischofsamt, eds. *Priester in Uniform: Seelsorger, Ordensleute und Theologen als Soldaten im Zweiten Weltkrieg*. Augsburg: Pattloch Verlag, 1994.

Buchbender, Ortwin, and Reinhold Sterz, eds. *Das Andere Gesicht des Krieges: Deutsche Feldpostbriefe 1939–1945*. München: Verlag C. H. Beck, 1982.

Das Sowjetparadies: Ausstellung der Reichspropagandaleitung der NSDAP: ein Bericht in Wort und Bild. Berlin: Zentralverlag der NSDAP, Franz Eher Nachf. GmbH, 1942.

Der Neue Wille: Wochenzeitschrift für Katholische Deutsche. Frankfurt am Main: Carolus-Verlag, 1939–1941.

Didier, Friedrich, ed. *Ich sah den Bolschewismus: Dokumente der Wahrheit gegen die bolschewistische Lüge*. Weimar, 1942.

Die Berichte des Oberkommandos der Wehrmacht 1939–1945, Bd. 2: 1. Januar 1941 bis 31. Dezember 1941. München: Verlag für Wehrwissenschaften, 1983.

Domarus, Max, ed. *Hitler: Speeches and Proclamations 1932–1945 and Commentary by a Contemporary: The Chronicles of a Dictatorship*. Vol. 4 (1941–1945). Wauconda, IL: Bolchazy-Carducci Publishers, 2004.

Engelhardt, Walter. *Klinzy: Bildnis einer Russischen Stadt nach ihrer Befreiung vom Bolschewismus*. Berlin: Nibelungen Verlag, 1943.

Europas Soldaten berichten über die Sowjet-Union. Berlin: Erasmusdruckerei, 1942.

Evangelisches Feldgesangbuch. Berlin: Verlag E. S. Mittler & Sohn, 1939.

Goebbels, Joseph. "Der Schleier fällt," *Das Reich*, July 7, 1941, reprinted in *Die Zeit ohne Beispiel*. München: Zentralverlag der NSDAP, 1941, 521.

———. "Die sogenannte russische Seele," reprinted in *Das eherne Herz*. München: Zentralverlag der NSDAP, 1943, 398–405.

———. *Die Tagebücher von Joseph Goebbels: Teil I: Aufzeichnungen 1923–1941*, Band 9, edited by Elke Fröhlich. München: K. G. Saur, 1998.

———. *Die Tagebücher von Joseph Goebbels: Teil II: Diktate 1941–1945*, Band 1, Juli–September 1941, edited by Elke Fröhlich. München: K. G. Saur, 1998.

Gorlitz, Walter. ed., *The Memoirs of Field-Marshal Wilhelm Keitel, Chief of the German High Command, 1938–1945*, translated by David Irving. Cooper Square Press, 2000.

Graf von Galen, Clemens August. *Akten, Briefe und Predigten 1933–1946*. Vol. 2 (1939–1946). Edited by Peter Löffler. Mainz: Matthias-Grünewald Verlag, 1988.

Kennedy, Howard. "Eisenhower Gives View on German Soldiers." *Stars and Stripes*, January 24, 1951.

Hubatsch, Walther, ed. *Hitlers Weisungen für die Kriegführung 1939–1945: Dokumente des Oberkommandos der Wehrmacht*. Koblenz: Bernard & Graefe Verlag, 1983.

Jarausch, Konrad. *Reluctant Accomplice: A Wehrmacht Soldier's Letters from the Eastern Front*, edited by Konrad H. Jarausch. Princeton, NJ: Princeton University Press, 2011.

Katholisches Feldgesangbuch. Berlin: Verlag E. S. Mittler & Sohn, 1939.

Katholisches Militärbischofsamt, ed. *Mensch, was wollt ihr denen sagen? Katholische Feldseelsorge im Zweiten Weltkrieg*. Augsburg: Pattloch Verlag, 1991.

Klemperer, Victor. *The Language of the Third Reich: LTI, lingua tertii imperii: a Philologist's Notebook*, translated by Martin Brady. New York: Continuum, 2002.

Koschorrek, Günter K. *Blood Red Snow: The Memoirs of a German Soldier on the Eastern Front*, translated by Olav R. Crome-Aamot. Minneapolis: Zenith Press, 2005.

Laros, M. *Krieg und Christentum*. Duelmen: Verlag Laumann, 1940.

Leonhard, Hans. *Wieviel Leid erträgt ein Mensch? Aufzeichnungen eines Kriegspfarrers über die Jahre 1939 bis 1945*, edited by Hans-Walter Leonhard. Amberg: Buch & Kunstverlag Oberpfalz, 1994.

Moldenhauser, Wilhelm. *Im Funkwagen der Wehrmacht durch Europa: Balkan, Ukraine, Stalingrad: Feldpostbriefe des Gefreiten Wilhelm Moldenhauser 1940–1943*, edited by Jens Ebert. Berlin: Trafo, 2008.

Personal-Amt des Heeres, *Wofür Kämpfen Wir?* Berlin: Ashelmdruck, 1944.

Reese, Willy. *A Stranger to Myself: The Inhumanity of War: Russia, 1941–1944*, edited by Stefan Schmitz, translated by Michael Hofmann. New York: Farrar, Straus and Giroux, 2003.

Reibert, *Der Dienstunterricht im Heer: Ausgabe für den Kanonier der bespannten Batterie.* Berlin: E. S. Mittler & Sohn, 1940.

Roth, Hans. *Eastern Inferno: The Journals of a German Panzerjäger on the Eastern Front, 1941–1943*, edited by Christine Alexander and Mason Kunze. Philadelphia, PA: Casemate, 2010.

Schabel, Wilhelm, ed. *Herr, in Deine Hände.* Stuttgart: Alfred Scherz Verlag, 1963.

Schneider, Franz, and Gullans, Charles, trans. *Last Letters from Stalingrad.* New York: William Morrow, 1962.

Tewes, Ernst. *Seelsorger bei den Soldaten: Erinnerungen an die Zeit von 1940 bis 1945.* München: Don Bosco Verlag, 1995.

The General Board, United States Forces, European Theater, *Report on The Army Chaplain in the European Theater*, Appendix 11: Chaplains and Clergymen in the Wehrmacht. 1946.

Trials of War Criminals before the Nuremberg Military Tribunals under Control Council Law No. 10. Vol. 11. Washington, DC: United States Government Printing Office, 1950.

Ungern-Sternberg, Jürgen von, and Wolfgang von Ungern-Sternberg. *Der Aufruf "An die Kulturwelt!" Das Manifest der 93 und die Anfänge der Kriegspropaganda im Ersten Weltkrieg.* Stuttgart: Steiner, 1996.

Weber, Max. *The Protestant Ethic and the Spirit of Capitalism.* New York: Routledge, 2005.

Weitenhagen, Holger, ed. *"Wie ein böser Traum . . .": Briefe rheinischer und thüringischer evangelischer Theologen im Zweiten Weltkrieg aus dem Feld.* Bonn: Verlag Dr. Rudolf Habelt GmbH, 2006.

Wolfgang Diewerge, ed. *Deutsche Soldaten sehen die Sowjet-Union: Feldpostbriefe aus dem Osten.* Berlin: Wilhelm Limbert Verlag, 1941.

Secondary Sources

Allen, Paul. *Katyń: The Untold Story of Stalin's Polish Massacre.* New York: C. Scribner's Sons, 1991.

Aly, Götz. *Hitler's Beneficiaries: Plunder, Racial War, and the Nazi Welfare State.* Translated by Jefferson Chase. New York: Metropolitan Books, 2006.

Angenendt, Arnold. *Toleranz und Gewalt: Das Christentum zwischen Bibel und Schwert.* Münster, 2012.

Baird, Jay. *To Die for Germany: Heroes in the Nazi Pantheon.* Bloomington: Indiana University Press, 1990.

Baird, Jay W. *The Mythical World of Nazi War Propaganda, 1939–1945.* Minneapolis: University of Minnesota Press, 1974.

Bamberg, Michael. "Narrative Discourse and Identities." In *Narratologia: Narratology Beyond Literary Criticism: Mediality, Disciplinarity*, edited by Jan Christoph

Meister, Tom Kindt, and Wilhelm Schernus, 213–37. Walter de Gruyter, 2005.

Bandura, Albert, and Claudio Barbaranelli. "Mechanisms of Moral Disengagement in the Exercise of Moral Agency." *Journal of Personality and Social Psychology* 71, no. 2 (1996): 364–74.

Baranowski, Shelley. *Nazi Empire: German Colonialism and Imperialism from Bismarck to Hitler.* New York: Cambridge University Press, 2011.

Barnett, Victoria. *For the Soul of the People: Protestant Protest against Hitler.* New York: Oxford University Press, 1998.

Bartov, Omer. *Germany's War and the Holocaust: Disputed Histories.* Ithaca, NY: Cornell University Press, 2003.

——. "Historians on the Eastern Front: Andreas Hillgruber and Germany's Tragedy." *Tel Aviver Jahrbuch für deutsche Geschichte* 16 (1987): 325–45.

——. *Hitler's Army: Soldiers, Nazis, and War in the Third Reich.* New York: Oxford University Press, 1991.

——. *The Eastern Front, 1941–45, German Troops and the Barbarisation of Warfare.* Hong Kong: MacMillan, 1985.

——. "The Missing Years: German Workers, German Soldiers." In *Nazism and German Society 1933–1945*, edited by David Crew. London: Routledge, 1994.

Beese, Dieter. *Seelsorger in Uniform: Evangelische Militärseelsorge im Zweiten Weltkrieg. Aufgabe, Leitung, Predigt.* Hannover: Lutherisches Verlagshaus, 1995.

Beevor, Antony. *Stalingrad: The Fateful Siege: 1942–1943.* Penguin Books, 1999.

Behrenbeck, Sabine. *Der Kult um die toten Helden: Nationalsozialistische Mythen, Riten und Symbole 1923–1945.* Vierow bei Greifswald: SH-Verlag, 2011.

Beorn, Waitman. *Marching into Darkness: The Wehrmacht and the Holocaust in Belarus.* Cambridge, MA: Harvard University Press, 2014.

Bergen, Doris. "German Military Chaplains in the Second World War and the Dilemmas of Legitimacy." In *The Sword of the Lord: Military Chaplains from the First to the Twenty- First Century*, edited by Doris Bergen, 165–86. Notre Dame, IN: University of Notre Dame Press, 2004.

——. *Twisted Cross: The German Christian Movement in the Third Reich.* Chapel Hill: University of North Carolina Press, 1996.

Berkhoff, Karel. *Harvest of Despair: Life and Death in Ukraine Under Nazi Rule.* Cambridge, MA: Belknap Press, 2004.

Bialas, Wolfgang. *Moralische Ordnungen des Nationalsozialismus.* Göttingen: Vandenhoeck & Ruprecht, 2014.

——. "Nationalsozialistische Ethik und Moral: Konzepte, Probleme, offene Fragen." In *Ideologie und Moral im Nationalsozialismus*, edited by Wolfgang Bialas and Lothar Fritze, 23–63. Göttingen: Vandenhoeck & Ruprecht, 2014.

Biess, Frank. *Homecomings: Returning POWs and the Legacies of Defeat in Postwar Germany.* Princeton, NJ: Princeton University Press, 2006.

——. "Survivors of Totalitarianism: Returning POWs and the Reconstruction of Masculine Citizenship in West Germany, 1945–1955." In *The Miracle Years: A Cultural History of West Germany, 1949–1968*, edited by Hanna Schissler. Princeton, NJ: Princeton University Press, 2001.

Black, Monica. *Death in Berlin: From Weimar to Divided Germany.* Cambridge: Cambridge University Press, 2013.

Black, Monica Ann. "On Death in Germany: Perceptions of Death among Wehrmacht Soldiers, 1939–1945." Master's thesis, University of Virginia, 2002.

Browning, Christopher. *Ordinary Men: Reserve Police Battalion 101 and the Final Solution in Poland.* New York: HarperCollins, 1992.

Burleigh, Michael. *Moral Combat: Good and Evil in World War II.* New York: HarperCollins, 2011.

Burleigh, Michael, and Wolfgang Wippermann. *The Racial State: Germany 1933–1945.* Cambridge: Cambridge University Press, 1993.

Burrin, Philippe. *France under the Germans: Collaboration and Compromise.* New York: The New Press, 1996.

Cesarani, David. *Becoming Eichmann: Rethinking the Life, Crimes, and Trial of a "Desk Murderer."* Cambridge, MA: Da Capo Press, 2006.

Chaitin, Julia, and Shoshana Steinberg. "You Should Know Better: Expressions of Empathy and Disregard among Victims of Massive Social Trauma." *Journal of Aggression, Maltreatment & Trauma* 17 (2008): 197–226.

Chamedes, Giuliana. "The Vatican and the Reshaping of the European International Order after the First World War." *Historical Journal* 56, no. 4 (2013): 955–76.

Childers, Thomas. *The Nazi Voter: The Social Foundations of Fascism in Germany, 1919–1933.* Chapel Hill: University of North Carolina Press, 1983.

Confino, Alon. "Remembering the Second World War, 1945–1965: Narratives of Victimhood and Genocide." *Cultural Analysis* 4 (2005): 46–75.

Connelly, John. "Nazis and Slavs: From Racial Theory to Racist Practice." *Central European History* 32, no. 1 (1999): 1–33.

Cooke, Paul, and Marc Silberman, eds. *Screening War: Perspectives on German Suffering.* Rochester, NY: Camden House, 2010.

Cooper, Joel. *Cognitive Dissonance: Fifty Years of a Classic Theory.* London: Sage Publications, 2013.

Craig, Gordon A. *The Politics of the Prussian Army 1640–1945.* Oxford: Clarendon Press, 1964.

Dallin, Alexander. *German Rule in Russia, 1941–1945: A Study of Occupation Politics.* London: Macmillan, 1957.

Ericksen, Robert, and Susannah Heschel. "The German Churches Face Hitler: An Assessment of the Historiography." *Tel Aviver Jahrbuch für deutsche Geschichte* 23 (1994): 433–59.

Erickson, John. *The Road to Stalingrad: Stalin's War with Germany.* London: Weidenfeld and Nicolson, 1975.

Evans, Richard J. *The Third Reich at War 1939–1945.* New York: Penguin Books, 2010.

Faulkner Rossi, Lauren. *Wehrmacht Priests: Catholicism and the Nazi War of Annihilation.* Cambridge, MA: Harvard University Press, 2015.

Fireside, Harvey. *Icon and Swastika: The Russian Orthodox Church under Nazi and Soviet Control.* Cambridge, MA: Harvard University Press, 1971.

Fitzpatrick, Sheila. *Everyday Stalinism: Ordinary Life in Extraordinary Times: Soviet Russia in the 1930s.* Oxford University Press, 2000.

Foray, Jennifer. "The 'Clean Wehrmacht' in the German-Occupied Netherlands, 1940–5." *Journal of Contemporary History* 45, no. 4 (2010): 768–87.

Frei, Norbert. *Adenauer's Germany and the Nazi Past: The Politics of Amnesty and Integration*. Translated by Joel Golb. New York: Columbia University Press, 2002.

Frey, Manuel. *Der reinliche Bürger: Entstehung und Verbreitung bürgerlicher Tugenden in Deutschland, 1760–1860*. Göttingen: Vandenhoeck & Ruprecht, 1997.

Friedländer, Saul. "The Wehrmacht, German Society, and the Knowledge of the Mass Extermination of the Jews." In *Crimes of War: Guilt and Denial in the Twentieth Century*, edited by Omer Bartov, Atina Grossmann, and Mary Nolan, 17–30. New York: New Press, 2002.

Fritz, Stephen. *Frontsoldaten: The German Soldier in World War II*. Lexington: University Press of Kentucky, 1995.

———. "'We Are Trying . . . to Change the Face of the World'—Ideology and Motivation in the Wehrmacht on the Eastern Front: The View from Below." *Journal of Military History* 60, no. 4 (October 1996): 683–710.

Fritzsche, Peter. *Life and Death in the Third Reich*. Cambridge, MA: Belknap Press, 2008.

Förster, Jürgen. *Die Wehrmacht im NS-Staat: Eine strukturgeschichtliche Analyse*. Munich: Oldenbourg Wissenschaftsverlag, 2007.

———. "The German Army and the Ideological War against the Soviet Union." In *The Policies of Genocide: Jews and Soviet Prisoners of War in Nazi Germany*, edited by Gerhard Hirschfeld. Boston: The German Historical Institute, 1986.

———. "Zum Rußland-Bild der Militärs 1941–1945." In *Das Rußlandbild im Dritten Reich*, edited by Hans-Erich Volkmann, 141–64. Köln: Böhlau Verlag, 1994.

Gross, Raphael. *Anständig geblieben: Nationalsozialistische Moral*. Frankfurt am Main: S. Fischer, 2010.

———. "'Loyalty' in National Socialism: A Contribution to the Moral History of the National Socialist Period." *History of European Ideas* 33 (2007): 488–503.

Haas, Peter. "Militärische Ethik im Totalen Krieg." In *Ideologie und Moral im Nationalsozialismus*, edited by Wolfgang Bialas and Lothar Fritze, 177–92. Göttingen: Vandenhoeck & Ruprecht, 2014.

———. *Morality after Auschwitz: The Radical Challenge of the Nazi Ethic*. Philadelphia, PA: Fortress Press, 1988.

Hagemann, Karen. "Of 'Manly Valor' and 'German Honor': Nation, War, and Masculinity in the Age of the Prussian Uprising against Napoleon." *Central European History* 30, no. 2 (1997): 187–220.

Hamburger Institut für Sozialforschung. *Verbrechen der Wehrmacht: Dimensionen des Vernichtungskrieges 1941–1944*. Hamburg: Hamburger Edition, 2002.

Harrisville, David. "Shepherds of Wolves: Wehrmacht Chaplains, the Second World War, German Colonialism, and Nazi Ideology." Master's thesis, University of Wisconsin—Madison, 2012.

———. "Unholy Crusaders: The Wehrmacht and the Re-Establishment of Soviet Churches during Operation Barbarossa." *Central European History* 52, no. 4 (2019): 620–49.

Hart, Basil Liddell. *The Other Side of the Hill: Germany's Generals. Their Rise and Fall, with Their Own Account of Military Events 1939–1945*. Revised edition. London: Cassell, 1951.

Hartmann, Christian. *Wehrmacht im Ostkrieg: Front und militärisches Hinterland 1941/42*. München: R. Oldenbourg Verlag, 2009.

Harvey, Elizabeth. *Women and the Nazi East: Agents and Witnesses of Germanization*. New Haven, CT: Yale University Press, 2003.

Heer, Hannes. "How Amorality Became Normality: Reflections on the Mentality of German Soldiers on the Eastern Front." In *War of Extermination: The German Military in World War II 1941–1944*, edited by Hannes Heer and Klaus Naumann, translated by Roy Shelton, 329–44. New York: Berghahn Books, 2000.

———. "The Logic of the War of Extermination: The Wehrmacht and the Anti-Partisan War." In *War of Extermination: The German Military in World War II 1941–1944*, edited by Hannes Heer and Klaus Naumann, translated by Roy Shelton, 92–126. New York: Berghahn Books, 2000.

Heer, Hannes, and Jane Caplan. "The Difficulty of Ending a War: Reactions to the Exhibition 'War of Extermination: Crimes of the Wehrmacht 1941 to 1944.'" *History Workshop Journal*, no. 46 (1998): 182–203.

Heer, Hannes, Walter Manoschek, Alexander Pollak, and Ruth Wodak, eds. *The Discursive Construction of History: Remembering the Wehrmacht's War of Annihilation*. Basingstoke: Palgrave Macmillan, 2008.

Herf, Jeffrey. *Divided Memory: The Nazi Past in the Two Germanys*. Cambridge, MA: Harvard University Press, 1997.

Heschel, Susannah. *The Aryan Jesus: Christian Theologians and the Bible in Nazi Germany*. Princeton, NJ: Princeton University Press, 2008.

Horne, John, and Alan Kramer. *German Atrocities, 1914: A History of Denial*. New Haven, CT: Yale University Press, 2001.

Hull, Isabel. *Absolute Destruction: Military Culture and the Practices of War in Imperial Germany*. Ithaca, NY: Cornell University Press, 2005.

Humburg, Martin. *Das Gesicht des Krieges: Feldpostbriefe von Wehrmachtssoldaten aus der Sowjetunion 1941–1944*. Opladen/Wiesbaden: Westdeutscher Verlag, 1998.

Ingrao, Charles, and Franz A. J. Szabo, eds. *The Germans and the East*. West Lafayette, IN: Purdue University Press, 2008.

Janz, Nina. "Der Heldengedenktag in der Wehrmacht." Master's thesis, FernUniversität Hagen, 2013.

Jarvis, Christina. *The Male Body at War: American Masculinity during World War II*. Dekalb: Northern Illinois University Press, 2004.

Kershaw, Ian. *The End: Hitler's Germany 1944–45*. Allen Lane, 2011.

———. *The "Hitler Myth": Image and Reality in the Third Reich*. New York: Oxford University Press, 2001.

———. *The Nazi Dictatorship: Problems and Perspectives of Interpretation*. Third. New York: E. Arnold, 1993.

Kilian, Jürgen. *Wehrmacht und Besatzungsherrschaft im russischen Nordwesten 1941–1944: Praxis und Alltag im Militärverwaltungsgebiet der Heeresgruppe Nord*. Paderborn: Ferdinand Schöningh, 2012.

Kipp, Michaela. *"Großreinemachen im Osten": Feindbilder in deutschen Feldpostbriefen im Zweiten Weltkrieg*. Frankfurt am Main: Campus Verlag, 2014.

Koonz, Claudia. *The Nazi Conscience*. Cambridge, MA: Harvard University Press, 2003.

Koshar, Rudy. *Germany's Transient Pasts: Preservation and National Memory in the Twentieth Century.* Chapel Hill: The University of North Carolina Press, 1998.

Krausnick, Helmut. *Die Truppe des Weltanschauungskrieges: Die Einsatzgruppen der Sicherheitspolizei und des SD 1938–1942.* Stuttgart: Deutsche Verlags-Anstalt, 1981.

Krobb, Florian, and Elaine Martin, eds. *Weimar Colonialism: Discourses and Legacies of Post- Imperialism in Germany after 1918.* Bielefeld: Aisthesis Verlag, 2014.

Krumeich, Gerd. "'Gott mit uns'? Der Erste Weltkrieg als Religionskrieg." In *"Gott mit uns": Nation, Religion und Gewalt im 19. und frühen 20. Jahrhundert,* edited by Gerd Krumeich and Hartmut Lehmann, 273–83. Göttingen: Vandenhoeck & Ruprecht, 2000.

Kühne, Thomas. *Kameradschaft: Die Soldaten des nationalsozialistischen Krieges und das 20. Jahrhundert.* Göttingen: Vandenhoeck & Ruprecht, 2006.

Latzel, Klaus. *Deutsche Soldaten—nationalsozialistsicher Krieg? Kriegserlebnis— Kriegserfahrung 1939–1945.* Paderborn: Ferdinand Schöningh, 1998.

———. "Vom Kriegserlebnis zur Kriegserfahrung: Theoretische und Methodische Überlegungen zur Erfahrungsgeschichtlichen Untersuchung von Feldpostbriefen." *Militärgeschichtliche Mitteilungen* 56, no. 1 (1997): 1–30.

———. *Vom Sterben im Krieg: Wandlungen in der Einstellung zum Soldatentod vom Siebenjährigen Krieg bis zum II. Weltkrieg.* Warendorf: Verlag Fahlbusch, 1988.

Lee, Steven P. *Ethics and War: An Introduction.* New York: Cambridge University Press, 2012.

Lee, Wayne. *Barbarians and Brothers: Anglo-American Warfare, 1500–1865.* New York: Oxford University Press, 2011.

Lehmann, Hartmut. "In the Service of Two Kings: Protestant Prussian Military Chaplains, 1713–1918." In *The Sword of the Lord: Military Chaplains from the First to the Twenty-First Century,* edited by Doris Bergen, 125–40. Notre Dame, IN: University of Notre Dame Press, 2004.

Lenhard, Hartmut. "'. . . keine Zweifel an der Richtigkeit dieses Krieges': Christen und Kirchen im Krieg gegen die Sowjetunion." In *Frieden mit der Sowjetunion— eine unerledigte Aufgabe,* edited by Dietrich Goldschmidt, 237–62. Gütersloher: Gütersloher Verlagshaus G. Mohn, 1989.

Lepenies, Wolf. *The Seduction of Culture in German History.* Princeton, NJ: Princeton University Press, 2014.

Leugers, Antonia. *Jesuiten in Hitlers Wehrmacht: Kriegslegitimation und Kriegserfahrung.* Paderborn: Ferdinand Schöningh, 2009.

Lewy, Guenter. *The Catholic Church and Nazi Germany.* Boston: Da Capo Press, 2000.

Liulevicius, Vejas Gabriel. *The German Myth of the East: 1800 to the Present.* New York: Oxford University Press, 2009.

———. *War Land on the Eastern Front: Culture, National Identity, and German Occupation in World War I.* New York: Cambridge University Press, 2000.

Loeffel, Robert. "Soldiers and Terror: Re-Evaluating the Complicity of the Wehrmacht in Nazi Germany." *German History* 27, no. 4 (2009): 514–30.

Longerich, Peter. *"Davon haben wir nichts gewusst!" Die Deutschen und die Judenverfolgung 1933–1945.* München: Siedler Verlag, 2006.

Lower, Wendy. *Nazi Empire-Building and the Holocaust in Ukraine.* Chapel Hill: University of North Carolina Press, 2005.

Manoscheck, Walter. *"Serbien Ist Judenfrei": Militärische Besatzungspolitik und Judenvernichtung in Serbien 1941/42.* Munich: Oldenbourg, 1993.

Manoschek, Walter, ed. *Die Wehrmacht im Rassenkrieg: Der Vernichtungskrieg hinter der Front.* Vienna: Picus, 1996.

———. *Es gibt nur eines für das Judentum: Vernichtung: Das Judenbild in deutschen Soldatenbriefen 1939–1944.* Hamburg, 1996.

Margalit, Gilad. *Guilt, Suffering, and Memory: Germany Remembers Its Dead of World War II.* Translated by Haim Watzman. Bloomington: Indiana University Press, 2010.

Mayer, Arno J. *Der Krieg als Kreuzzug: Das Deutsche Reich, Hitlers Wehrmacht und die "Endlösung."* Translated by Karl Siber. Hamburg: Rowohlt, 1988.

Mazower, Mark. "Military Violence and National Socialist Values: The Wehrmacht in Greece 1941–1944." *Past & Present*, no. 134 (1992): 129–58.

McLeod, Hugh, and Werner Ustorf, eds. *The Decline of Christendom in Western Europe, 1750–2000.* Cambridge: Cambridge University Press, 2003.

Meier, Kurt. "Sowjetrußland im Urteil der evangelischen Kirche (1917–1945)." In *Das Rußlandbild im Dritten Reich*, edited by Hans-Erich Volkmann, 285–321. Köln: Böhlau Verlag, 1994.

Messerschmidt, Manfred. *Die Wehrmacht im NS-Staat: Zeit der Indoktrination.* Hamburg: R.v. Decker's Verlag, 1969.

———. "Zur Militärseelsorgepolitik im Zweiten Weltkrieg." *Militärgeschichtliche Mitteilungen* 1 (1969): 37–85.

Miller, Arthur G., ed. *The Social Psychology of Good and Evil.* New York: Guilford Press, 2004.

Mineau, André. *Operation Barbarossa: Ideology and Ethics against Human Dignity.* Amsterdam: Rodopi, 2004.

Miner, Steven. *Stalin's Holy War: Religion, Nationalism, and Alliance Politics, 1941–1945.* Chapel Hill: University of North Carolina Press, 2003.

Missalla, Heinrich. *Für Gott, Führer und Vaterland: Die Verstrickung der katholischen Seelsorge in Hitlers Krieg.* München: Kösel, 1999.

———. *Wie der Krieg zur Schule Gottes wurde: Hitlers Feldbischof Rarkowski. Eine notwendige Erinnerung.* Taschenbuch, 1997.

Moeller, Robert G. *War Stories: The Search for a Usable Past in the Federal Republic of Germany.* Berkeley: University of California Press, 2003.

Mommsen, Hans. "Der Krieg gegen die Sowjetunion und die deutsche Gesellschaft." In *Präventiv-krieg? Der deutsche Angriff auf die Sowjetunion*, edited by Bianka Pietrow- Ennker, 59–68. Frankfurt am Main: Fischer Taschenbuch Verlag, 2011.

Mommsen, Wolfgang. "Die nationalgeschichtliche Umdeutung der christlichen Botschaft im Ersten Weltkrieg." In *"Gott mit uns": Nation, Religion und Gewalt im 19. und frühen 20. Jahrhundert*, edited by Gerd Krumeich and Hartmut Lehmann, 249–61. Göttingen: Vandenhoeck & Ruprecht, 2000.

Morina, Christina. "Legacies of Stalingrad: The Eastern Front War and the Politics of Memory in Divided Germany, 1943–1989." PhD diss., University of Maryland, 2007.

Moses, John A. "Dietrich Bonhoeffer's Repudiation of Protestant German War Theology." *Journal of Religious History* 30, no. 3 (2006): 354–70.

———. "The Rise and Decline of Christian Militarism in Prussia-Germany from Hegel to Bonhoeffer: The End Effect of the Fallacy of Sacred Violence." *War & Society* 23, no. 1 (May 2005): 21–40.

Mosse, George L. *Fallen Soldiers: Reshaping the Memory of the World Wars.* New York: Oxford University Press, 1990.

———. *Nationalism and Sexuality: Respectability and Abnormal Sexuality in Modern Europe.* New York: Howard Fertig, 1985.

Mühlhäuser, Regina. *Eroberungen: Sexuelle Gewalttaten und intime Beziehungen deutscher Soldaten in der Sowjetunion 1941–1945.* Hamburg: HIS Verlag, 2010.

Müller, Klaus-Jürgen. *Das Heer und Hitler: Armee und nationalsozialistisches Regime, 1933–1940.* Stuttgart: Deutsche Verlags-Anstalt, 1969.

Müller, Rolf-Dieter. *The Unknown Eastern Front: The Wehrmacht and Hitler's Foreign Soldiers.* London: I. B. Tauris, 2012.

Naimark, Norman. *Fires of Hatred: Ethnic Cleansing in Twentieth-Century Europe.* Cambridge, MA: Harvard University Press, 2001.

Naumann, Klaus. "The 'Unblemished' Wehrmacht: The Social History of a Myth." In *War of Extermination: The German Military in World War II 1941–1944*, edited by Hannes Heer and Klaus Naumann, translated by Roy Shelton, 417–29. New York: Klaus Naumann, 2000.

Neitzel, Sönke, and Harald Welzer. *Soldaten. Protokolle vom Kämpfen, Töten und Sterben.* Frankfurt am.Main.: S. Fischer, 2011.

O'Neill, Robert J. *The German Army and the Nazi Party, 1933–1939.* London: Cassell, 1966.

Overmans, Rüdiger. *Deutsche militärische Verluste im Zweiten Weltkrieg.* München: Oldenbourg, 2004.

Overy, Richard. *Why the Allies Won.* London: Jonathan Cape, 1995.

Paskins, Barrie, and Michael Dockrill. *The Ethics of War.* Minneapolis: University of Minnesota Press, 1979.

Pätzold, Kurt. *Ihr waret die besten Soldaten: Ursprung und Geschichte einer Legende.* Leipzig: Militzk Verlag, 2000.

Pendas, Devin, Mark Roseman, and Richard Wetzell, eds. *Beyond the Racial State: Rethinking Nazi Germany.* Cambridge: Cambridge University Press, 2017.

Perry, Joe. *Christmas in Germany: A Cultural History.* Chapel Hill: University of North Carolina Press, 2010.

Perry, Joseph. "The Madonna of Stalingrad: Mastering the (Christmas) Past and West German National Identity after World War II." *Radical History Review,* no. 83 (Spring 2002): 6–27.

Pietrow-Ennker, Bianka, ed. *Präventiv-krieg? Der deutsche Angriff auf die Sowjetunion.* Frankfurt am Main: Fischer Taschenbuch Verlag, 2011.

Pohl, Dieter. *Die Herrschaft der Wehrmacht: Deutsche Militärbesatzung und einheimische Bevölkerung in der Sowjetunion 1941–1944.* München: R. Oldenbourg Verlag, 2008.

Pöpping, Dagmar. *Kriegspfarrer an der Ostfront: Evangelische und katholische Wehrmachtseelsorge im Vernichtungskrieg 1941–1945.* Göttingen: Vandenhoeck & Ruprecht, 2017.

Rass, Christoph. "Die 'Wehrmacht-Untersuchungsstelle für Verletzungen des Völkerrechts' war nicht viel mehr als eine Hilfstruppe der NS-Propaganda." *Die Zeit,* November 16, 2009.

——. *"Menschenmaterial": Deutsche Soldaten an der Ostfront: Innenansichten einer Infanteriedivision 1939–1945*. Paderborn: Ferdinand Schöningh, 2003.

Roberts, Mary Louise. *What Soldiers Do: Sex and the American GI in World War II France*. Chicago: The University of Chicago Press, 2013.

Rodin, David, and Henry Shue, eds. *Just and Unjust Warriors: The Moral and Legal Status of Soldiers*. New York: Oxford University Press, 2008.

Römer, Felix. *Kameraden: Die Wehrmacht von Innen*. München: Piper, 2012.

——. *Der Kommissarbefehl: Wehrmacht und NS-Verbrechen an der Ostfront 1941/42*. Paderborn: Schöningh, 2008.

Rossino, Alexander. *Hitler Strikes Poland: Blitzkrieg, Ideology, and Atrocity*. Lawrence: University Press of Kansas, 2003.

Rutherford, Jeff. *Combat and Genocide on the Eastern Front: The German Infantry's War, 1941–1944*. Cambridge, MA: Cambridge University Press, 2014.

——. "'One Senses Danger from All Sides, Especially from Fanatical Civilians': The 121st Infantry Division and Partisan War, June 1941–April 1942." In *War in a Twilight World: Partisan and Anti-Partisan Warfare in Eastern Europe, 1939–45*, edited by Ben Shepherd and Juliette Pattinson, 58–79. New York: Palgrave Macmillan, 2010.

Sait, Bryce. *The Indoctrination of the Wehrmacht: Nazi Ideology and the War Crimes of the German Military*. New York: Berghahn Books, 2019.

Scheck, Raffael. "The Killing of Black Soldiers from the French Army by the 'Wehrmacht' in 1940: The Question of Authorization." *German Studies Review* 28, no. 3 (2005): 595–606.

Schilling, René. *"Kriegshelden": Deutungsmuster Heroischer Männlichkeit in Deutschland 1813–1945*. Paderborn: Schöningh, 2002.

Schmitz, Helmut, ed. *A Nation of Victims? Representations of German Wartime Suffering from 1945 to the Present*. New York: Rodopi B. V., 2007.

Schröder, Hans Joachim. *Die gestohlenen Jahre: Erzählungsgeschichten und Geschichtser-zählung im Interview: der Zweite Weltkrieg aus der Sicht ehemaliger Mannschaftssol-daten*. Vols. 1 and 2. Tübingen: Max Niemeyer Verlag, 1992.

Schroer, Timothy L. "Civilization, Barbarism, and the Ethos of Self-Control among the Perpetrators." *German Studies Review* 35, no. 1 (February 2012): 33–54.

Sebald, W. G. *Luftkrieg und Literatur*. München: Carl Hanser Verlag, 1999.

Shepherd, Ben. "Hawks, Doves and Tote Zonen: A Wehrmacht Security Division in Central Russia, 1943." *Journal of Contemporary History* 37, no. 3 (2002): 349–69.

——. *Hitler's Soldiers: The German Army in the Third Reich*. New Haven, CT: Yale University Press, 2017.

——. "The Clean Wehrmacht, the War of Extermination, and Beyond." *Historical Journal* 52 (2009): 455–73.

——. *War in the Wild East: The German Army and Soviet Partisans*. Cambridge, MA: Harvard University Press, 2004.

Shepherd, Ben, and Juliette Pattinson. *War in a Twilight World: Partisan and Anti-Partisan Warfare in Eastern Europe, 1939–45*. New York: Palgrave Macmillan, 2010.

Showalter, Dennis. "Comrades, Enemies, Victims: The Prussian/German Army and the Ostvölker." In *The Germans and the East*, edited by Charles Ingrao and Franz A. J. Szabo, 209–25. West Lafayette, IN: Purdue University Press, 2008.

Slepyan, Kenneth. *Stalin's Guerillas: Soviet Partisans in World War II.* Lawrence, KS: University Press of Kansas, 2006.

Smelser, Ronald, and Edward Davies. *The Myth of the Eastern Front: The Nazi-Soviet War in American Popular Culture.* New York: Cambridge University Press, 2008.

Smith, Helmut Walser. *German Nationalism and Religious Conflict: Culture, Ideology, Politics, 1870–1914.* Princeton, NJ: Princeton University Press, 1995.

Sommer, Erich F. *Das Memorandum: Wie Der Sowjetunion Der Krieg Erklärt Wurde.* Frankfurt am Main: Verlag Ullstein, 1991.

Spicer, Kevin. *Hitler's Priests: Catholic Clergy and National Socialism.* DeKalb: Illinois University Press, 2008.

Stargardt, Nicholas. *The German War: A Nation Under Arms, 1939–1945: Citizens and Soldiers.* New York: Basic Books, 2017.

Steele, Claude. "The Psychology of Self-Affirmation: Sustaining the Integrity of the Self." *Advances in Experimental Social Psychology* 21 (1988): 261–302.

Streim, Alfred. *Sowjetische Gefangene in Hitlers Vernichtungskrieg: Berichte und Dokumente 1941–1945.* Heidelberg: Müller, 1982.

Streit, Christian. *Keine Kameraden: Die Wehrmacht und die sowjetischen Kriegsgefangenen 1941–1945.* Stuttgart: Deutsche Verlags-Anstalt, 1978.

Taylor, Charles. *A Secular Age.* Cambridge, MA: Harvard University Press, 2007.

Tsang, Jo-Ann. "Moral Rationalization and the Integration of Situational Factors and Psychological Processes in Immoral Behavior." *Review of General Psychology* 6, no. 1 (2002): 25–50.

Ueberschär, Gerd R., and Wolfram Wette, eds. *"Unternehmen Barbarossa": Der deutsche Überfall auf die Sowjetunion 1941.* Paderborn: Schöningh, 1984.

Uldricks, Teddy. "The Icebreaker Controversy: Did Stalin Plan to Attack Hitler?" *Slavic Review* 58, no. 3 (1999): 626–43.

Uziel, Daniel. *The Propaganda Warriors: The Wehrmacht and the Consolidation of the German Home Front.* New York: Peter Lang, 2008.

Veit, Ebert, and Thomas Jander, eds. *Schreiben im Krieg—Schreiben vom Krieg: Feldpost im Zeitalter der Weltkriege.* Essen: Klartext Verlag, 2011.

Waddington, Lorna. *Hitler's Crusade: Bolshevism, the Jews and the Myth of Conspiracy.* New York: I. B. Tauris, 2009.

Walzer, Michael. *Just and Unjust Wars: A Moral Argument with Historical Illustrations.* Allen Lane, 1978.

Weikart, Richard. *Hitler's Ethic: The Nazi Pursuit of Evolutionary Progress.* New York: Palgrave Macmillan, 2009.

Weißbecker, Manfred. "'Wenn hier Deutsche wohnten . . .' Beharrung und Veränderung im Rußlandbild Hitlers und der NSDAP." In *Das Rußlandbild im Dritten Reich,* edited by Hans-Erich Volkmann, 9–54. Köln: Böhlau Verlag, 1994.

Westermann, Edward. *Hitler's Police Battalions: Enforcing Racial War in the East.* Lawrence: University Press of Kansas, 2005.

Wette, Wolfram. "Das Rußlandbild in der NS-Propaganda: Ein Problemaufriß." In *Das Rußlandbild im Dritten Reich,* edited by Hans-Erich Volkmann, 55–78. Köln: Böhlau Verlag, 1994.

——. "Die propagandistische Begleitmusik zum deutschen Überfall auf die Sowjetunion am 22. Juni 1941." In *"Unternehmen Barbarossa": Der deutsche Überfall auf die Sowjetunion 1941*, edited by Gerd R. Ueberschär and Wolfram Wette, 111–30. Paderborn: Schöningh, 1984.

———. "Juden, Bolschewisten, Slawen: Rassenideologische Rußland-Feindbilder Hitlers und der Wehrmachtgeneräle." In *Präventiv-krieg? Der deutsche Angriff auf die Sowjetunion*, edited by Bianka Pietrow-Ennker, 40–58. Frankfurt am Main: Fischer Taschenbuch Verlag, 2011.

———. *Militarismus in Deutschland: Geschichte einer kriegerischen Kultur*. Darmstadt: Wissenschaftliche Buchgesellschaft, 2008.

———. *The Wehrmacht: History, Myth, Reality*. Translated by Deborah Lucas Schneider. Cambridge, MA: Harvard University Press, 2006.

Wildermuth, David W. "Widening the Circle: General Weikersthal and the War of Annihilation, 1941–42." *Central European History* 45 (2012): 306–24.

Winter, Jay. *Sites of Memory, Sites of Mourning: The Great War in European Cultural History*. Cambridge: Cambridge University Press, 1995.

Wolfenden, Helen. "The Representation of *Wehrmacht* Soldiers as Victims in Post-War German Film: *Hunde, wollt ihr ewig leben?* and *Der Arzt von Stalingrad*." In *A Nation of Victims? Representations of German Wartime Suffering from 1945 to the Present*, edited by Helmut Schmitz, 71–86. New York: Rodopi B. V., 2007.

Zahn, Gordon. *German Catholics and Hitler's Wars*. New York: Sheed and Ward, 1962.

Zayas, Alfred de. *Die Wehrmacht-Untersuchungsstelle: Deutsche Ermittlungen über alliierte Völkerrechtsverletzungen im Zweiten Weltkrieg*. München: Verlag Universitas Langen- Müller, 1979.

Zoepf, Arne W. G. *Wehrmacht zwischen Tradition und Ideologie: Der NS-Führungsoffizier im Zweiten Weltkrieg*. Frankfurt am Main: Peter Lang, 1988.

INDEX

Page numbers in italics denote figures.

የብሔርተኝነት ፖለቲካዊ ኤኮኖሚ

የብሔርተኝነት ፖለቲካዊ ኤኮኖሚ

ዶ/ር ሲሞን ሔሊሶ ኩካ

θ ሐ ይ

አሳታሚና አከፋፋይ ድርጅት

ፀሐይ

አሳታሚና አከፋፋይ ድርጅት

የብሔርተኝነት ፖለቲካዊ ኢኮኖሚ
ዶ/ር ሲሞን ሐሊሶ ኩካ © ሚያዝያ ወር 2016 ዓ.ም
የደራሲው እና የአሳታሚው መብት በሕግ የተጠበቀ ነው።

የመጀመሪያው እትም ሚያዝያ ወር 2016 ዓ.ም በሎስ አንጀለስ ከተማ ታተመ።

የመጽሐፉ ዓለማቀፍ መለያ ቁጥር (መዓመቀ)
[ISBN]:- 978-1-59907-320-0 (ስስ ሽፋን)
978-1-59907-321-7 (ጠንካራ ሽፋን)

አሳታሚ ኤልያስ ወንድሙ
የመጽሐፍ ቅንብር ዮሴፍ ገዛኸኝ
የሽፋን ቅንብር ብሩክ መላኩ
ረዳት አቀናባሪ አቤል ተስፋዬ

ይህንን ወይም ሌሎች የፀሐይ አሳታሚ ድርጅት መጻሕፍትን ለመግዛት፤ ድርሰትዎን ለማሳተም፤
ሊያማክሩን ከፈለጉ በሚከተሉት እድራሻዎቻችን መልዕክትዎን ይላኩልን፤

ፀሐይ አሳታሚ ድርጅት
TSEHAI Publishers
www.tsehaipublishers.com
info@tsehaipublishers.com

ካለአሳታሚው ሕጋዊ ፍቃድ በስተቀር፤ ይህንን መጽሐፍ ማባዛት፤ መቅዳት፤
መተርጎምም ሆነ በማንኛውም አይነት ዘዴ ማሰራጨት በሕግ የተከለከለ ነው።

የዚህ መጽሐፍ የእትመት ምዝገባ መረጃ በወመዘክር የኢትዮጵያ ብሔራዊ ቤተመጻሕፍት፤
በአሜሪካ የኮንግረስ ቤተመጻሕፍት እና በብሪቲሽ ቤተመጻሕፍት ተመዝግቦ ይገኛል።

ይህ መጽሐፍ ከአሲድ ነፃ በሆነ ወረቀት በአሜሪካን ሀገር ታተመ።

፩ ፪ ፫ ፬ ፭ ፮ ፯ ፰ ፱ ፲

ማውጫ

ማውጫ

አበርክቶት
የዘር መድልዎ ለሚጸየፉ

መግቢያ

"ጴው ለምድር፤ ብርሃኑ ለዓለም"

ጌታችን መድኃኒታችን ኢየሱስ ክርስቶስ፤ "እኔ የዓለም ብርሃን ነኝ"[1] ማለቱ ሳያንስ፤ የእርሱን እውነተኛ ደቀ መዛሙርት፤ "እናንተ የዓለም ጨው ናችሁ፤ እናንተ የዓለም ብርሃን ናችሁ"[2] ሲል ማንነታቸውን አብሥሮአል። ይህ ቃል የሚያስደስተውን ያህል ተጠያቂነትንም እንደሚጠቅስ ልብ ይሏል። ይኸውም የክርስቶስ እውነተኛ ደቀ መዛሙርት የጽድቅ ሕይወት ባለቤት መሆናቸውን አመልካች ብቻ ሳይሆን፤ ለሌሎች አብነታዊ የሆነ ሕይወት መኖር እንደሚችሉ፤ እንደሚጠበቅባቸውም የሚያሳስብ ነው።

ጨው ምግብ እንዳይበላሽ ከመከላከሉ በላይ፤ ለምግብ ጣዕም ይሰጣል። በጥንቱ ዓለም መበስበሱን ከማስቄሙም ባሻገር፤ ለምግብ ጣዕምና የሚሰጥ እንደ ጨው ያለ የለም ይባላል። በዚህ አንጻር ኢየሱስ በወቅቱ የነበረውን፤ የመጨረሻውን ትልቅ ምሳሌ ተጠቅሞአል ማለት እንችላለን። ብርሃን፤ ጨለማን መጋፈጡ ብቻ ሳይሆን፤ ሰዎች ነገሮችን በትክክል እንዲመለከቱ ያደርጋል። ክርስቲያኖች በሚኖሩበትና በሚገኙበት ጊዜና ቦታ ሁሉ፤ ጨው ናቸው፤ ብርሃን ናቸው። ይህ ምሳሌነታቸው ብቻ ሳይሆን ሥራታቸው ነው። ጥሪአቸው ነው፤ ሕይወታቸው ነው። የሕይወት ግባቸው አልፋና ያሜጋ ነው።

ከክርስቶስና ከክርስቲያኖች ውጪ ዓለም ጥንብ ናት፤ ዓለም ጨለማ ናት። የዓለም ለዛዋና ብርሃኗ፤ የመሲሑ እንደ ራሴዎች ብቻ ናቸው። ጨው ናችሁ፤ ብርሃን ናችሁ፤ የሚለው ጉዳይ የሰውን መላ ሕይወት እንዲሁም የወስተሳሰብ አድማስ ቀንብብ እንደሚይዝ እሙን ነው።

ይህ ሐቅ ቢሆንም የኢትዮጵያ ክርስቲያኖች በአገራቱ ማኅበራዊ ሕይወት ውስጥ ያላቸው ተጽዕኖ እምብዛም ነው። በተለይም፤ በኤኮኖሚና በፖለቲካው ውስጥ የዳር ተመልካች ሆነዋ ኖረዋል። ቤተ ክርስቲያንም ሆኑ ክርስቲያኖች፤ በብዙ በጉ

[1] "እኔ ውእቱ ብርሃኑ ለዓለም" (ዮሐ 8÷12)።

[2] "አንትሙ ውእቱ ጴው ለምድር"፤ "አንትሙ ውእቱ ብርሃኑ ለዓለም" (ማቴዎስ 5÷13-14)።

አድራጎት *ሥራዎች* ውስጥ ተሳታፊ ቢሆኑም፤ ለኢትዮጵያ ፖለቲካ እጅግ ሲበዛ ባይተዋር ናቸው ቢባል እብለትም ግነትም አይሆንም። ጨውና ብርሃን መሆናቸውን ማረጋገጥ አልቻሉምና።

ለዚህ ብዙ ምክንያት ሊኖር ቢችልም፤ "እባብ ያየ በልጥ በረየ" ዐይነት ጠባይ እንዳለው መገመት አያዳግትም። የአገራችን ፖለቲካ በኢ-አማኒነት ፍልስፍና የተሞላ፤ በዘርና በአድር ባይነት ክፉኛ የተበላሸ ነው። ጨው ናቸው፤ ብርሃን ናቸው ካልን ዘንዳ ግን፤ የክርስቲያኖችን ጨውነትና ብርሃንነት የሚገድብ አንዳችም የሕይወት ክፍል የለም። እንዲያውም እግዚአብሔርን የሚፈሩ ሰዎች በዐይን አፋርነት ከዳር ከቤው፤ ጎፍረት ዐለባዎቹ ዋልጌዎች፤ ተሰጥያ ዐለባ በሆነ እጅ ያጨማልቁታል።

በየዋህነቱ አምላክ የመስከረለት ሙሴም ሆነ፤ ልብ አምላክ የተባለው ዳዊት፤ የአገር *መሪዎች* ነበሩ። በዘመኑ አነጋገር ፖለተከዎች ነበሩ ማለት ነው። በቀላል ቋንቋ እንግለጸው ካልን፤ ፖለቲካ ማለት መንግሥት ሕዝብን የሚያስተዳድርበት ሥርዐትና ሕግ ነው። በአገራችን ግን አንድ ሰው ፖለቲከኛ ነው ማለት ቀኑጭ በሉ (ጤሮጠ ቀጥል) ነው። ወሬ እንጂ ምግባር የማያውቅ፤ ሰዎችን የሚያፋጅ፤ ለኹዱ ያደረ ማለት ነው። ሕዝቡ ይህ ዐይነት አመለካከት የያዘው ከመሬት ተነሥቶ አይደለም። የፖለቲከኞቻችንን ማንነት በውል ገምግሞ እንጂ፤ ስለዚህ ሕዝባችንን በአንድ ጀንበር አቋምሁን ቀይር ልንለው አንችልም። ፖለቲካ ሳይንስ ነው። ፍልስፍና ነው ...ወዘተ ብንለው፤ ሞኝሁን ፈልግ ነው የሚልህ፤ ሙያው በክፉዎች እጅ ገብቶ ክፉኛ እንደ ተበላሸ ሕዝቡ የዐይን እማኝ ነው።

ቤተ ክርስቲያን ግብረ ሥናይ ምግባሮች ላይ በመሳተፍ ትልቅ ስም እንዳላት ይታወቃል። ሆስፒታሎችን ብቻ እንኳ አንድ ነቀኍጥ ቴንትረን እንመልከት ብንል ብዙ እንማራለን። የሚከተሉት ዕውቅ ሆስፒታሎች በቤተ ክርስቲያን የታነጹ ናቸው፦— ቅዱስ ጻውሎስ ሆስፒታል፤ ዘውዲቱ ሆስፒታል፤ አለርት (ዘነበ ወረቅ) ሆስፒታል፤ ወሊሶ የሚገኘው ቅዱስ ሉቃስ ሆስፒታል፤ ሐረር የሚገኘው ሕይወት ፋና ሆስፒታል፤ ሶዶ ክርስቲያን ሆስፒታል፤ ጊንቢ አድቬንቲስት ሆስፒታል፤እንዲሁ ሌሎች።

ሞትና ሕመም የሚወገደው፤ ሆስፒታል በመሥራት ብቻ አይደለም። የፖለቲካውን አካሄድ በመቀየር የምንታደጋቸው ሰዎች ቁጥር ሆስፒታል ከሚታደጋቸው ሰዎች ይበልጣል። በሰሜኑ የአገራችን ክፍል፤ ለሁለት ዓመት የተካሄደው ጦርነት፤ የጦርነቱ *መሪዎች* ራሳቸው እንደሚያወሩት ከሆነ፤ ወደ አንድ ሚሊዮን ሰው፤ በትሪሊዮን የሚቆጠር ሀብትና ንብረት ጨርሶአል። በዓል አመራርና ጥሩ ፖለቲካ ቢኖር ኖሮ፤ ይህ ሁሉ የሀብት ውድመትና የሰው ዕልቂት እንዴት ሊከሠት ይችላል?

ሰላምን የምናሰፍነው ግብረ ሥናይ ድርጅቶችን በማነጽ ብቻ አይደለም። ወላጅ ዐልባ ልጆችን በማሳደግ ብቻ አይደለም። ጠዋሪ ቀባሪ ያጡ አረጋውያንን በመርዳት

ብቻም አይደለም። ነገር ግን ልጆች ወላጅ ዐልባ እንዲሆኑ ምክንያት የሆነውን፤ አረጋውያን ጠዋሪ ቀባሪ እንዲያጡ ያደረገውን የፖለቲካና የምጣኔ ሀብት ፍልስፍናና ፖሊሲ በመቀየር እንጂ።

እኔ በነገረ መለኮትና በፍልስፍናው ዙሪያ የምጽፍ ብሆንም፤ የፖለቲካውን ዓለም እንዳላያ ነው የማልፈው። ይህ የእኔ ብቻ ሳይሆን የብዙ ክርስቲያኖች ቅኝት ነው። በቅርቡ በአገራችን በኢትዮጵያ ትልቅ የፖለቲካ መነቃቃት ተከሥቶ የነበረ ይመስለኛል። ይህን መነቃቃት እንዴት ልንደግፈው እንችላለን? በተለይ የተማርንበት የሙያ ዘርፍ እንዴት ለውጡን ሊደግፍ ይችላል የሚለው ጉዳይ ብዙዎቻችንን እያወያየ ነበር።

በተለያየ የሙያ ዘርፍ የተማሩ ወገኖችን አስተባብሬ ሁሉም በሙያው ዘርፍ ለአገር ይጠቅማል የሚለውን እንዲያወጣ ለባልንጀሮቼ ዐሳብ አቀረብሁ። ዶክተር ሲሞን ሔሊሶን ጨምሮ ወደ ሃያ የሚደርሱ ምሁራንን ለማሰባሰብ ሞከርሁ። እነዚህ ወገኖች፤ በምጣኔ ሀብት፤ በፍልስፍና፤ በሃይማኖት፤ በፖለቲካ፤ በታሪክ፤ በሥነ ጽሑፍ ... ወዘተ ዕውቅ ከሚባሉ የትምህርት ተቋማት ትምህርታቸውን የተከታተሉና በሙያቸው አገርንና ሕዝብን በማገልገል ላይ የሚገኙ ናቸው።

ሁሉም ልጽፍበት እፈልጋለሁ ያለውን ርእስ ጉዳይ በማዘጋጀቱ ተጠምዶ ሳለ፤ የዶክተር ሲሞን ሔሊሶ በምጣኔ ሀብትና በተወሰነ መጠን በፖለቲካ ላይ ያዘጋጀው መጽሐፍ ዳብሮ ወጣ። ጥራዙ ከፍ ከማለቱ የተነሣ ከሌሎቻችን ጽሑፍ ጋር ተቀላቅሎ መውጣት እንደማይችል ተረዳን። እነሆ ዛሬ እርሱም የሚያነብቡት መጽሐፍ የዚህ ጥረት ውጤት ነው።

እኔም ይህን መቅድም እንድጽፍ ምክንያት የሆነው፤ ለመጀመሪ ምክንያት ሆነህልና መቅድሙን ልትጽፍ ትችላለህ የሚል ዕድል ስለተሰጠኝ ነው።

ሰሚ ከተገኘ፤ ይህ ጽሑፍ ብዙ በረከት እንደሚያመጣ ከልብ አምናለሁ። አምላካችን እግዚአብሔር ይህን ጥረት ይባርክ። ወንድሜ ሲሞንንም ጌታ አትረፍርፎ ይባርክ።

ተስፋዬ ሮበሌ (ዶክተር)

ከተስፋ ዐቃብያን ክርስትና ማኅበር

ከታላላቆች የዘመናዊ ኤኮኖሚክስ አባቶች የሚመደበው፣ ጆን ሜይናርድ ኪንስ፣ ቶማስ ካርላይልን ተከትሎ ኤኮኖሚክስ "አደገኛ ሳይንስ"[11] ነው ያለው።

ስሚዝ፣ ማርክስ፣ እና ኪንስ የዘመናዊውን ኤኮኖሚክስ ሦስት ዋና ዋና አምዶች መሠረቶች ናቸው። አዳም ስሚዝ የገበያ መር "ስውር እጅ"[12] ኤኮኖሚክስ አባት ሲሆን፣ ካርል ማርክስ የወዛደር መር "አብዮተኛ እጅ" ኤኮኖሚክስ፣ እንዲሁም ጆን ሜይናርድ ኪንስ የመንግሥት መር "ጣልቃ ገብ እጅ" ኤኮኖሚክስ አባቶች ናቸው። ሌላው ሁሉ ጥፍራ ነው።

በእርግጥ፣ ጥቂት በስም ሊጠቀሱ የሚችሉ አፈንጋጮች አሉ። የኤኮኖሚ እንቅስቃሴ የተቃሚያት ጥንካሬ እና የባሕል ለውጥ ጉዳይ[13] እንደሆነ አሜሪካዊው የኤኮኖሚ ሊቅ ቶርስተን ቨብሌን (1857–1929)[14] ከመጀመሪያው የዓላም ጦርነት ፍጻሜ በኋላ አንሥቶ ነበር። ምክንያቱም፣ በእርሱ ዕይታ፣ በተለይ ትልልቆቹ የኤኮኖሚ ተዋንያን ትኩረታቸው ገንዘብ ማከማቸት እንጂ ምርትን ማሳደግ አይደለም። ምን ገደቸው? ምርት ሲያሽቆለቆል ዋጋ ያሻቅብና የተሻለ ገንዘብ ይከማቻል።

በዚህ መልክ ሲታይ የቨብሌን ዐሳብ ጥቂት ሐቅ አለው። ነገር ግን ምርትን ማምረት ሃብት ከማከማቸት ውጭ ሌላም ፋይዳ ስላለው ብዙ አልተገፋበትም። ስለዚህ፣ እንዳንድ አመለካከቶችን ከማረቅ ውጭ ከላይ የተጠቀሱ ሦስቱን በሚተካ ደረጃ አልሰፋም። ይልቅ፣ የኦስትሪያ ኤኮኖሚክስ ትምህርት ቤት ተብሎ የሚጠራው አመለካከት፣ አንጋፋም፣ የተሻለ ስፋትም አለው። ተሰሚነቱም የጎላው ዘመናዊውን ኤኮኖሚክስ ስለሚተች ነው። ለዘመናዊው ኤኮኖሚክስም አስተዋጽኦ አድርጓል።

---

11 በእርግጥ ጆን ሜይናርድ ኪንስ የኤኮኖሚክስን አደገኝነት ከዚህ ሰፋ አድርጎ ያየዋል። ሳይንሱ ጠንካራ የትንታኔ ዐቅም ከመፍጠሩ ጋራ "ብልጉ ሰዎች የራሳቸውን ካፒታል ለማድለብ ያገኙትን አጋጣሚ ሁሉ በዕውቀት ጥምም እንዲጠቀሙ የሚከላከላቸው የለም" ብሎ ስለሚያምን የመንግሥት ጣልቃ ገብነት ንድፈ ዐብሱን ለመደገፍ ተጠቅሞበታል። Keyenes, J. M. (1935). The General Theory of Employment, Interest and Money. International Relations and Security Network; Primary Soruces. https://www.files. ethz.ch/isn/125515/1366_KeynesTheoryofEmployment.pdf

12 "ስውር እጅ" ወይም በተለምዶ "The Invisible Hand" የተባለው ዐንጾ ዐሳብ ኤኮኖሚው ያለ ማንም ጣልቃ ገብነት በሰዎች ኤኮኖሚ ሕዋሳት ፍላጎትና ነጻ ውድድር ላይ ብቻ በመመሥረት፣ ማለትም በገበያ በመመራት ብቻ፣ ለሁሉ በሚበጅ አካሄድ ሊንቀሳቀስ ይችላል ብሎ ያስተምራል። "ጣልቃ ገብ እጅ" የሚለው "Government Intervention" መንግሥት በኤኮኖሚው ጣልቃ መግባት አለበት ይላል። ገበያ መር ኤኮኖሚ የመረጃ ፍሰትና የእኩልነት ችግር ስላለበትና፣ ነጻ ውድድር ማስፈን ከባድ ስለሆነ፣ በጥሪት አመዳደብና ሃብት ከፍፍል ላይ አድልዎን ስለሚያስከትል መንግሥት ይግራውን የሚል ነው። "አብዮተኛ እጅ" ተብሎ የተገለጠው የወዛደሩ አብዮት ፖለቲካውንም፣ ኤኮኖሚውንም፣ መሪራት ብቻ ሳይሆን መምራት አለበት ከሚል አስተሳሰብ ተነሥቶ በማዕከላዊ ጥላን "Central Planning" የሚመራውን የዕዝ ኤኮኖሚ ለማመልከት ነው።

13 Vablen, T. (1899). The Theory of Leisurly Class. http://moglen.law.columbia.edu/LCS/theoryleisureclass.pdf

14 Pierce, Francis S. (2022). "Thorstein Veblen". *Encyclopedia Britannica*, 30 Jul. 2022, https://www.britannica.com/biography/Thorstein-Veblen. Accessed 3 February 2023.

የቀድሞ አስትሪያ፤ በዛሬዋ ፖላንድ የተወለደው ካርል መንገር (1840–1921)[15] እና እንግሊዛዊው ዊሊያም ስታንሴይ ጀቮንስ (1835–1882)[16] አንጋፋ ፈላስፎች ነበሩ። በእንሱ ዕይታ የኤኮኖሚ እንቅስቃሴ የሚወሰነው ሃብትና የሰው ጎይል ሲዋሄዱ በሚሰጡት ዕሴት ላይ ሳይሆን፤ ያ ዕሴት ለሰዎች በሚሰጠው እርካታ አንጻር ሰዎች በሚሰጡት ዋጋ ላይ ነው። ለምሳሌ፤ በውሃ ጥም እጅግ ተጠቅቶ ወደ ሞት አፋፍ ለቀረበ ሰው አንድ ብርጭቆ ውሃ ከአንድ ዘለሳ የወርቅ ወይም አልማዝ ጥምዝ ይበልጥበታል።

እንዲሁም "ሲበዛ ማርም ይመራል" እንደሚባለው የአገራችን ብሂል፤ ከክምችት የሚገኘው ደስታ እየቀነሰ ይሄዳል። የአንድ ነገር ዋጋ የሚለካውም፤ ምንም ደስታ በማይሰጥበት ጊዜ ሰዎች በሚወስኑት አንጻራዊ ምዘና ላይ ነው። ይህ አስተሳሰብ ዘመናዊውን ኤኮኖሚክስ ጭምር ያረቀ ነው። አስትሪያዊው ሊቅ ሉድዊግ ቮን ማይዘስ (1881–1973)[17] እና በእሳቸው ስም የሚጠራው የማይዘስ ኢንስቲትዩት ይህን ዐሳብ እስከ ዛሬ ድረስ በስፋት ያራምዱታል።

ማይዘስና የአስትሪያው ትምህርት ቤት የኤኮኖሚ አመራርን በተመለከተ በትንትና ደረጃ ይለዩ እንጂ የጸ ምርጫ፤ ጎ ውድድር ደጋፊዎች ናቸው። ስለዚህ ከመናዊውን ለየት ያሉ ናቸው ለማለት፤ በተለይም የዘረፉ ሊቅ ላልሆኑት ይከብዳል። ወጣ ያለ ዐሳብ በማራመድ ከቅርብ ጊዜ ወዲህ ዕይታን የሳበው ግን የባሕርይ ኤኮኖሚክስ ተብሎ የሚጠራው ነው። ሰው በባሕርይው ጎ አይደለም ባዮች ናቸው። የሰው ምርጫ በራስ ፍላጎት ብቻ ሳይሆን፤ በቤተሰብ፤ በማኅበረሰብ፤ በተቋማትና በሚኖርበት አካባቢ ወይም ፖሊሲ ይወሰናል።

አሜሪካዊው የሥነ ባሕርይ (ሳይኮሎጂ)፤ ሒሳብ፤ እና ስታትስቲክስ ሊቅ ሄርበርት ሳይሞን (1916–2001)[18] በባሕርይ ጥናት ዘርፍ በ1976 የኖቤል ሽልማት ሲያገኝ የባሕርይ ኤኮኖሚክስ ተወለደ ቢባልም ጥንሱሱ ከ1940ዎቹ ጀምሮ እንደነበር የሚከራከሩ አሉ። [19] እሥራኤላዊው ዳንኤል ካነማን[20] በ2002 እና ሪቻርድ ታለር[21] በ2017 የኤኮኖሚክሱን ዘርፍ ሽልማት ስለወሰዱ የባሕርይ ኤኮኖሚክስ ራሱን ያደላደለ ይመስላል።

15 Menger, C. (1871). Principles of Economics. https://cdn.mises.org/principles_of_economics.pdf

16 Jevons, S. W. (1871). *The Theory of Political Economy*, first edition, London and New York: MacMillan and Co. https://socialsciences.mcmaster.ca/econ/ugcm/3ll3/jevons/TheoryPoliticalEconomy.pdf

17 Mises Institute. (2023). Ludwig Heinrich Edler von Mises (1881–1973). https://mises.org/profile/ludwig-von-mises?page=29

18 Britannica, The Editors of Encyclopaedia. "Herbert A. Simon". *Encyclopedia Britannica*, 30 Jun. 2022, https://www.britannica.com/biography/Herbert-A-Simon

19 Frantz, R. (2020). The Beginings of Behavioral Economics: Katona, Simon, and Leibenstein's X-efficiency theory. London.

20 Britannica, The Editors of Encyclopaedia. "Daniel Kahneman". *Encyclopedia Britannica*, 11 Jan. 2023, https://www.britannica.com/biography/Daniel-Kahneman

21 Duignan, Brian. "Richard Thaler". *Encyclopedia Britannica*, 8 Sep. 2022, https://www.britannica.com/biography/Richard-Thaler

የዚህ ዕሳቤ አቀንቃኞች ኤኮኖሚክስን ሰው፣ ሰው እንዲሸት ያደረጉ በመባል ይወደሳሉ። ይሁን እንጂ ዘመናዊው ኤኮኖሚክስ ገና እጅ አልሰጠም። አብዛኛው የግለሰብ፣ ቤተሰብ፣ የአገርም ሆነ የዓለም ኤኮኖሚ እንቅስቃሴ በተለይም አዲሱ ዘመናዊ (ኒዮ ክላሲካል) በሚባለው አመለካከት ጫና ስር ነው። ግፋ ቢል ከእርሱ ጋር ሌሎችን እያጣመሩ ይተገብሩታል። የነጻ ገበያ እና ነጻ ምርጫ ዕሳቤ ያልተካተተበት የኤኮኖሚ ፖሊሲ ለማግኘት አስቸጋሪ ነው። የመንግሥት ጣልቃ ገብነትን የሚያደፋፍሩ እንኳን የገበያን የዕላይነት ያከብራሉ።

ኤኮኖሚ እና ፖለቲካ ደግሞ ቁርኝታቸው አይጣል ነው። መለያየት እስከማይቻሩ ድረስ ይዋደዳሉ፤ ይቀዋወማሉም። እንዲያውም ከላይ የተጠቀሱት የዘመናዊ ኤኮኖሚክስ ንድፈ ዐሳብ አበዚች ፖለቲካዊ ኤኮኖሚስት ይባሉ ነበር። ምክንያቱም ኤኮኖሚው በፖለቲካው ላይ ከባድ ተጽዕኖ ያሳድራልና። ፖለቲካ ኤኮኖሚውን ያለ ልክ ከሚረብሹት፣ ይበልጥ ከሚጠቅሙት ነገሮች መኃል አንዱ ነው። አንድ የፖለቲካ ውሳኔ ምን ኤኮኖሚያዊ ተጽዕኖ ያደርስ ይሆን የሚለውን ሳያመዛዝን የወሰነ መሪ አበሳው ብዙ ነው።

በዘመናዊ ፖለቲካ አስተሳሰብ የብዙኃን አመለካከት ጎሽ ነው። ብዙኃኑ የሚደግፈውን ያልተካተለ የፖለቲካ መሪ ለውድቀት አሥር ጉዳይ ላይ ነው። ካናዳዊው የኤኮኖሚ ሊቅ ጆን ኬኔት ጋልብሬዝ (1908–2006)[22] እንዳለው ከሆነ ደግሞ፣ ብዙኃኑ ብዙውን ጊዜ ስገተት ነው።[23] በዚህ ዐይነት ፖለቲካና ኤኮኖሚክስ ፌት ለፌት ሊጋጩ ነው።

ኤኮኖሚስቶች ግን ከቅርብ ጊዜ ወዲህ የፖለቲካዊ ኤኮኖሚ ጥናት ራሱን ችሎ ከኤኮኖሚክስ ዘርፎች አንዱ ሆኖ እንዲወጣ ጥረዋል። የተወሰነ የፖለቲካ ንድፈ ዐሳብ ስለሚከተል ፍረጃ ቢቀናውም፣ ለሌሎች የኤኮኖሚክስ ዘርፎች የዋሉትን የጥናት መንገዶችን እንዲጠቀም አስማምተውለታል። ማለትም ፖለቲካው በኤኮኖሚው ላይ የሚያሳድረውን ጫና አመክንዖዊ በሆነ መልክ ይመረምራሉ።

የተለያዩ የፖለቲካ አመለካከቶች ኤኮኖሚውን ሲመሩ፣ ውጤታቸው ሊለያይ ይችላል። ሳይንሱ ውጤትን ለማሻሻል መወሰድ ስለሚገባቸው እርምጃዎች ብይን እንዲሰጥ ይጠበቃል። እንዲሁም፣ ኤኮኖሚው ደግሞ በተራው በፖለቲካው ላይ እንዴትና ምን ተፅዕኖ እንደሚያደርግ ፍንጭ እንዲሰጥ ከመጣር ጋር የኤኮኖሚክስ ጥናት ግምቶችንና መሣሪያዎችን በመጠቀም ፖለቲካውን ለመረዳት ስፌ መከራዎች ይደረጋሉ።

---

22 Britannica, The Editors of Encyclopaedia. "John Kenneth Galbraith". Encyclopedia Britannica, 11 Oct. 2021, https://www.britannica.com/biography/John-Kenneth-Galbraith

23 ጋልብሬዝ ይህንን የተናገረው፣ የአሜሪካ ፖለቲካ ወደ ወገ አጥባቂዎች አዘንብለ ተሰሎ በተገመተበት ዘመን፣ የወገ አጥባቂዎችም ሆነ ዴሞክራቶች ፖለቲካ፣ በአብዛኛው በሃብታሞችና ልዕለ ሃያል ኮርፖሬት ቡድኖች የሚዘወር መሆኑን ሰው ሁሉ ባለማስተዋሉ ነበር። Dunn, S. P. & Pressman, S. (2005). The Economic Contributions of John, K. Galbraith. *Review of Political Economy,* Volume 17, Number 2; 160 – 209. https://www.researchgate.net/publication/24088369_The_Economic_Contributions_of_John_Kenneth_Galbraith

በኢትዮጵያ ፖለቲካዊ ኤኮኖሚን የሚዳስሱ ጽሑፎች ከአሁን በፊት በጥቂቱም ቢሆን ለአንባቢያን ቀርበዋል። አብዛኞቹ ጽሑፍት የሚያተኩሩት የመንግሥት ፖለቲካዊ ውሳኔዎች በኤኮኖሚያችን ላይ ምን ዐይነት ጫና እንዳሳደሩ ጠቆሚ የሆኑ ነገሮችን በማንሣት ነው። በዚህ ረገድ፣ ይህም መጽሐፍ ወፍ በረር ዳሰሳ ለማድረግ ይጥራል።

ይሁን እንጂ ከዚህ በፊት ከተጻፉት፣ በተለይ ደግሞ፣ የዛሬውን የአገሪቱ ፖለቲካ አቅጣጫ ለመረዳት ይበልጥ ትኩረት ስጥቷል። ኢትዮጵያውያን የኤኮኖሚ ጠብብቶች በአገሪቱ ፖለቲካ መኃል ሜዳ ውስጥ በብዛት ይገኛሉ። የብሔር ፖለቲካ ያዋዛው የፖሊሲ ብያኔ ከዋናዎቹ የኤኮኖሚ ንድፈ ዐሳቦች አንጻር እንዴት ይታያል? ይህ ጽሑፍ፣ በፖለቲካው ክርክርና እንካ ሰላንቲያው መኃል ጥቂት አመክንዮአዊ ዐሳቦች ለማንሳት ያህል የተሰነዘረ ጨኸት ነው። መሰል ወይም ጠለቅ ያለ ጥያቄዎችን ቢጋብዝ ግቡን መተቷል።

ሲሞን ሔሊሶ ኩካ (ዶክተር)

አዲስ አበባ

ዘርና ዘረኝነት

"በእጃችን ላይ የታሰረው ሠንሰለት ወድቋል፤
በአዕምሮችን ውስጥ ያለው ግን እንደ ጠፈረን ነው።"

ዶ/ር አሪካና ቺሆምቦሪ

ሐኪምና ዲፕሎማት፤ በአሜሪካ የአፍሪካ ኅብረት አምባሳደር የነበሩ (ዚምባብዌት)

ሁለት መላጦች

"ተመልከቲቸው፤ ሲያስቀኑ።"

አጠገባቸው ሆነው በአንድም በሌላም የታዘቧቸው ሰዎች የሚናገሩት ንግግር ነበር። በአንድ ወቅት። አብዱልቃዲር እና መሐመድ ከተለያየ የኢትዮጵያ ክፍሎች ወደ አዲስ አበባ የመጡ የግንብ ሥራ ባለሙያዎች ናቸው። የእንጅራ ነገር አዲስ አበባ፤ ቦሌ ቡልቡላ አካባቢ አገናኝቷቸዋል።

በአካባቢው ቤት በሚያሰሩ ባለ ሀብቶች እና መሐንዲሶች የሚወደደው አብዱልቃዲር ብርቱ ሠራተኛ ነው። እዚህም እዚያም ይፈልጉታል። 'ሥራው አንጀት ያርሳል' ይላሉ። እናም ብዙዎች ሥራ ይሰጡታል። እርሱም የመጣ ሥራ እምቢ አይልም። አይንቅም።

ታዲያ ይህንንም፤ ያንንም "እሺ" ሲል፤ ሥራ በዛበት፤ ስለዚህም፤ አንዳንድ ጊዜ ዐብሮት የሚሠራውን መሐመድ የተባለ ታታሪ ሠራተኛ አጋዥ ሊያደርገው አሰበ በመጀመሪያ በቋሚ ረዳትነት ዐብሮት እንዲሠራ አግባባው። መሐመድም ጥሩ አጣማጅ ሆነለት። ለሁለቱም የሚበጅ ወዳጅነት ፈካ።

አብዱልቃዲር ብዙዎች የመስከሩለት ጥሩ ሰው ነው። እያደር አንዳንዶችን ሥራዎች መሐመድ በራሱ ስም በኃላፊነት እንዲወስድ ፈቀደለት። መሐመድም ተፈልጎ

የታጣውን ታማኝነት አሳየው፤ አይፈራሩም፤ ጥርጣሬ በውስጣቸው የለም። "አብዲ፤ ሙሔ" ሲባባሉ ወንድማማች እንጂ ከተለያየ የአገሪቱ ጫፍ የመጡ፤ እንጅራ ያገናኛቸው ፈጽሞ አይመስሉም ነበር። እናም፤ "ያስቀናሉ" አሉ።

ከዚህ ሌላ፤ መሐመድ ፈጣን ተማሪ ነበር። በሥራውም ጥንቁቅ፤ አብዲ ወጣ ቢል እንኳ በሥራው አያሳፍረውም። እንዲያውም በአንዳንዶች ዘንድ ከአብዲ ይልቅ እየተወደደ፤ የሥራ ኮንትራቶችንም በራሱ ስም፤ በብዛት እያገኘ ሄደ። ውጤቱንም በፍቅር ይካፈሉታል።

ታዲያ እያደር፤ ይህን የጋራ የሥራ ውጤት ልክ እንደ ቀድሞው በጋራ ቢካፈሉም፤ አብዲ ከንግግሩና ከአሠራሩ መንፈሳዊ ቅንዓት እንዳደረበት ያስታውቅ ጀመር፤ መሐመድ ከአንዴም ሁለቴ ስቆ ቢያልፍም፤ የጓላ ጓላ ጥርጣሬ መወለዱ አልቀረም፤ ተወለደ።

እናም በነገር ነቤር፤ በምላስ ጉሽም መደራረግ ተጀመረ። እንኳ ሰላንቲያው እየበረታ፤ ሆድ ሻከር፤ ነገር ከረር ሲል የተመለከቱ በአቅራቢያቸው ያሉት ሰዎች ከአንዴም ሁለቴ ገስፀዋቸው ነበር።

"ተዉ እናንተ፤ ደግ አይደለም" እያሉ ቸው።

ፍቅር ለሚያገኙት ብቻ ሳይሆን፤ ለሚያዩትም እኩ ይጥማል። እናም የነበራቸውን ግንኙነት እያስታወሱ ቸው። "ተዉ፤ በምላስ መጐነታተል ይቅርባችሁ" ይሉ ጀመር።

በዚያውም "አይ የገንዘብ ነገር፤ እነ አብዲም ተጣሉ?" ከሚል ጥያቄ አዘል ትዝብት ጋር።

"ገንዘብ ብቻ አጣልቷቸው ብለህ ነው?" ይላል አንድ የበለጠ የተመራመረ የመሠለው።

"ታዲያ ምን?"

የዘር ዕሳቤ

ትርጉም

ስለ ዘር፤ ብሔር፤ ጐሣ ወይም ነገድ ሰዎች ያላቸውን መረዳት ለማወቅ ጐሣ ላይ ወጥተን ብንጠይቅ እያንዳንዱ ሰው ምን ይል ይሆን? ከዚያስ ተነስተን ስለ ዘረኝነት ወይም ብሔርተኝነት ብናጠና ምን መረዳት እናገኝ ይሆን? ዘር፤ ብሔር፤ ነገድ ወይም ጐሣ ምን ያመለክታሉ?

ስለ ዘርና ብሔር ሰው ሁሉ ያወራል። ሲያወራም፤ "እኔም ተነክቼ፤ ተጐድቼ አውቃለሁ" ከሚል ማጉረምረም ጋር ነው። ስለ ዘር ሲነሣ ሰው ሁሉ ዘልሎ ወደ ጉዳቱ

የሚመለከተው ነገር እንዴት ነው? ይህ ጉዳይ ተገልጦ፣ ተፈርጥሮ፣ እና ከተለያዩ ጉዳዮች አንጻር ሰፊ የዐሳብ መለዋወጥ ተደርጎበት ይሆን? አይመስልም።

ይልቁን፣ ዘር ፖለቲካዊ ነው ሲባል ብቻ እናደምጣለን፣ አብዛኞቻችን ደግሞ ፖለቲካን እንፈራለን። ግልፅ ያልሆነውስ፣ ንግግር ስለ ተፈራ ይሆን? ይህ መጽሐፍ ስለ ፖለቲካዊ ኤኮኖሚ ከማንሣቱ በፊት ስለ ዘር ያለንን መረዳት በመጠኑም ቢሆን ማጥራት ይኖርበታል። የዘር ፖለቲካችን ኤኮኖሚውን ጠቀም ወይስ ጉዳ የሚለውን ለማስጨበጥ፣ የዘር ፖለቲካውን አመጣጥ በዋል ልንረዳ ያስፈልጋልና።

የዘር ፅንስ ዐሳብ ብዙ ክርክር ያለበት ነው። ደርሶ ከብሔርተኝነት ጋር ሲላተም ይበልጥ ያደናግራል። ሁለቱ ፈጽሞ አይገናኙም የሚሉ እንዳሉ ሁሉ፣ እጅግ የተቄራኙ ዐሳቦች ናቸው ብለው በድፍረት የሚናገሩም ሞልተዋል። እንዲሁም ብዝኀ ብሔርና ብሔርተኝነትን ለመረዳት በቅድሚያ ስለ ሰው ዘር እና ዘረኝነት መረዳት ይጠቅመን ይሆናል።

ዘረኝነትና ብሔርተኝነት ምን ያገናኛቸዋል? ተመሳሳይ ወይስ እጅግ የተለያዩ ፅንስ ዐሳቦች? አንድ ከሆኑ፣ አንድነታቸውን? የተለያዩ ከሆኑስ መገለጫው ምንድን ነው?

አብዛኛው የአገራችን ሰው ኀይማኖተኛ ስለሆነ ፈጣሪ፣ የፍጥረት ዓለሙ ጌታ የሆነ፣ አንድ አምላክ እንዳለ ያምናል። ስለዚህ ጉዳና ላይ ወጥተን 'ሰው ከየት መጣ?' ብለን ብንጠይቅ አምላክ እግዚአብሔር ፈጠረው ለማለት አያወላዳም። ስለዚህ፣ የሰው ዘር የሚባል በፍጥረት አንድ ብቻ አለ ብሎ ማስረዳትም ከባድ አይሆንም። በእርግጥ፣ በአንድ ጽሑፍ ሁሉን ኀይማኖት ወክሎ መናገር ከባድ ቢሆንም ፈጣሪ፣ ሆነ ብሎ፣ ሰውን አበላልጦ ፈጠረ የሚል ብዙ አይሆንም።

ስለ ሰው ዘር አንድነት ኀይማኖት የሚነግረንን ብቻ፣ ያለ ምንም ጥያቄ፣ እንቀበል ካልን፣ ይህ ጽሑፍ እዚህ ላይ ይገታል። ሰው የማወቅ ፍላጎቱን ሳያረካ፣ በኀይማኖት ብቻ ከታሠረ ዕውቀት ባለው ግልጠት አንዳች የመኘዝ ተስፋው የመነመነ ነው። በዚህ ጽሑፍ ግን የክርስትና እምነት ጥላ ያጠላበት ብቻ ሳይሆን፣ ክርስቲያናዊ አስተምህሮ እንደ መሠረትም ተወስዷል።

መጽሐፍ ቅዱስ ስለ ጥብብ የሚቀዳበት ታላቅ መጽሐፍ ነው። ስለዚህ ባስፈለገ መጠን ጥቅም ላይ ውዪል። ይህ ታላቅ መጽሐፍ ገና በዘፍጥረት የመጀመሪያው ምዕራፍ እግዚአብሔር ሰውን በራሱ መልክና አምሳል አንዳበጀው፣ ወንድና ቤት አድርጎ እንደ ፈጠረም ይናገራል (ዘፍጥረት 1÷27)። [24]

ሰው ሲባል ወንድና ቤት መሆናቸውን ማስተዋል ያሻል። ቤቶችም፣ ወንዶችም ሰዎች ናቸው። በመጽሐፍ ቅዱስ ዐይታ፣ አምላክ ሰውን በራሱ አምሳል አዘጋጅ፣

---

[24] የኢትዮጵያ መጽሐፍ ቅዱስ ማኀበር (1954)። መጽሐፍ ቅዱስ፣ የብሉይና የሐዲስ ኪዳን መጽሐፍት። ብርሃንና ሰላም ማተሚያ ቤት፣ 1954 ዓ.ም እንደ ኢትዮጵያ አቆጣጠር። በዚህ መጽሐፍ ያሉ የመጽሐፍ ቅዱስ ጥቅሶች ሁሉ ካልተጠቀሰ በቀር የተሰወዱት ከ1954 ዕትም ነው።

እንግዲህ ሰው ፈጣሪውን በአካል ስላሳየ፤ በአጠገቡ ያለውን ሰው በማየት ጥቂት ስለ እግዚአብሔር ይረዳል። ደግሞም የፈጣሪ አምሳል ከሆነ፤ የሰው ተፈጥሮ ክቡር፤ የተፈራ፤ እንዲሁም ልዩ መሆኑ ይገባናል።

በዚህ አመለካከት መሠረት ተፈጥሮ የዘርና ወገን ልዩነት አላደረገችብንም። አምላክ ሲፈጥር አንድ ነጭ፤ ሌላ ጥቁር፤ አንድ ዐጭር፤ ሌላ ረዥም፤ አንድ ወፍራም፤ ሌላ ቀጭን፤ እያለ ጊዜ አላፈጀም፤ ብዙ ዐይነት ሰው አልሠራም። አንድ ወንድ፤ አንዲት ሴት ብቻ። ሁላችን ከእነዚያ መጣን፤ ሰው ከፍጥረቱ አንድ ነው።

ብዙ ተባዙ (ዘፍጥረት 1÷28) ብሏልና ዐጭርና ረዥም ተጋብተው ልጅ ቢወልዱ ሕጻኑ ሰው ነው። ነጭ ቆዳ ያለው ፈረንጅና ጥቁር ቆዳ ያለው አፍሪካዊ ቢጣመሩ ከአብራካቸው የሚፈጠረው ፍጹም ሰው ነው። ሴትም ትሁን ወንድ፤ ሰው፤ ሰው ነው።

እና በሰው ዘር መኳል ምንም ልዩነት የለም? ዳግመኛ ጉዳና ላይ ወጥተን 'በሰው ዘር መካከል ልዩነት አለ ወይስ የለም?' ብለን ብንጠይቅ፤ ምን መልስ እናገኝ ይሆን? በእርግጠኝነት፤ በጥቂቱም ቢሆን የሚያቅማማ አይጠፋም። ምክንያቱም በሰዎች መካከል የሚታይ ልዩነት አለ። ግልጥ ልዩነት።

ሃብታምና ድኻ፤ ረዥምና ዐጭር፤ ጥቁርና ነጭ፤ ብልጌና የዋህ፤ ቀጭንና ወፍራም፤ ክፉ 'ጭራቅና' ደግ 'መሬት' የሆነ ሰው፤ ሌላም ሌላም፤ ታዲያ ይህ ከየት መጣ? እግዚአብሔር ሲፈጥር፤ የአርባ ቀን ዕድል ወስኖልን ይሆን?

ሰዎች እየበዙ ሲሄዱ፤ እየተበተኑም፤ አንድ ላይም ሲኖሩ፤ ልዩነት መፈጠሩ አልቀረም። ለምሳሌ፦ ሃብታምና ድኻ የሚባል የማኅበራዊ ኑሮ ልዩነት። በአብዛኛው፤ የድኻ ልጅ ድኻ ነው። ከድኽነት ለመውጣት ዕድል፤ ጥረትና አምላክ ካልታከሉ በቀር፤ የሃብታሙ ልጅ ግን ይህ ጣጣ የለበትም። ያው ሃብትንና ድኽነትን በገንዘብ ወይም በጥሪት መጠን ከለካን ማለት ነው።

ጥሪት ኖሮት አዕምሮ የጎደለውንም "ሃብታም" እንበለው? ልዩነታችን ማኅበራዊ ብቻ ነው ለማለት አያመችም። ነጭና ጥቁር የሚያደርገውስ ማኅበራዊ ነው? ነጮች ሲባል በሙሉ በሚባል ደረጃ አገራቸው እንዲያ አድጉ ስናይ ምን ይሰማናል? እነርሱ ሌሎችን ሲረዱ ጥቆሮች የተባሉ በሙሉ በሚባል ደረጃ ድኻ ለምን ሆኑ? ጥቁርና ሲፈጥር ረግሞ፤ ነጩን በልዩ ባርኮት ይሆን ፈጣሪ? ጥቁር ቆዳስ፤ ከጥቁር አዕምሮ ጋር ቁርኝት ይኖረው ይሆን?

ይህን ጥያቄ ለመሸሽ ምናልባት ልዩነቱ መልክዐ ምድራዊ ሳይሆን አይቀርም የሚሉ አሉ። የሰው ዘር በምድር እየበዛ ሲሄድ፤ እና ሲበተን ከወደ አፍሪካ የቀፉ ቀንርና ሐሩር ፈታቸውን አከሰለ። ነጮች በበርድ ሲታፈኑ ነጭ ሆኑ። ወደ እስያ ያሉትም ሙቀትም ቢሆን ውሃ ገብ ስለሆነ ቀይ ሆኑ የሚሉ አሉ።

ከእንዚህ አመለካከቶች የትኛውም ምሉዕ ትርጉም አይሰጠንም። የዘር ዕሳቤ ማኅበራዊም፣ መልክዐ ምድራዊም፣ ፖለቲካዊ እና መዋቅራዊም ገጽታ አለው። ይህን ስንል ግን ተፈጥሯዊ ነገሮች የሉበትም ማለትም አይደለም። ምክንያቱም ማኅበራዊ ኑር የሚጀምረው ከተሰብ ነው። ቤተሰብ ደግሞ የደም ትስስር አለው። ተፈጥሮ የሚያስብለው ይህ ነው።

በምድር ላይ ሣርና ቡቃያ ዘር አለው። በወገኑ ይለያል። ዛሬ ያለው ለነገ ዘርን የሚሰጥ፣ ሲሰጥም እርሱን ዐይነት ብቻ የሚሰጥ ተደርጎ የተሠራ ነው። ሣርና ቡቃያ ከሆነ፣ ያው ሣርና ቡቃያ ነው። ዐንጨት ወይም ዛፍ ከሆነ ዛፍ፣ አውሬ ከሆነ አውሬ። እንደ ወገኑ የሆነ ዘር፣ ዘሩም በውስጡ ያለበትን ፍሬ የሚሰጥ ነው።

እንደ ወገኑ ይለያያል እንጂ ያለ ወገን አይዳቀልም። ተክል እንስሳት አይሆንለትም። እንስሳም ሣር አይሆንም። ሳይንሱ አድጎ ማዳቀልን አስተዋውቆናል። ነገር ግን፣ ቢያንስ እስከ ዛሬ፣ ቅጠል ያወጣ ጥንቸል፣ ወይም አንጀት ያለው ባሕር ዛፍ አላየንም። እንስሳ ሞቶ፣ ወደ አፈር ተለውጦ ሣር ቢበቅልበት እንጂ፣ ምን ቢሉት ተክል አይሆንም።

የሰው ዘርስ? የሰው ዘርም የሰው ነው። ከሣር ጋር አይዋኻድም፣ ሞላ፣ ጎላ ያለ ዛፍ ተጠግቶ አዛምድኝ ቢል አይሆንለትም። በምድር ላይ የተፈጠረ ነገር ሁሉ ወገኑን ብቻ ይሰጣል። እንጂ ሌላ ዘር የለውም። የሰው ዘርም? የሰው ነው፣ የአትክልት አይደለም። ሲወልድ፣ ሲዋለድ፣ ሲራባ፣ ዘሩን ሳይለቅ፣ ወገኑን ሳይክድ እስከ ዛሬ አለ።

እንዲህ ከሆነ፣ ዘረኝነትና እንዲሁም ብሔርተኝነት ከየት መጡ? ሰውን አንዱን ትልቅ፣ ሌላውን ትንሽ፣ አንዱ ምርጥ፣ ሌላው መናኛ፣ አድርገው የሚያዩ፣ ልዩነትን ከፍጥረት ላይ ካልሆነ መሠረቱን ከየት አገኙት? አንድ ከሆነንስ ለምን ተባላን?

ግልባጩንም እንጠይቅ። ሰው ሁሉ ሰው ነው? ሰው፣ እንደ ሰው ዘር፣ ፈጽሞ አንድ ነው ወይስ ሁለትም፣ ሦስትም የሰው ዘር ዐይነት አለ? የቆዳ ቀለም፣ የቁንቁ፣ የባሕል፣ የአካባቢ፣ እንዲሁም ሌሎች አካላዊ፣ አዕምሮአዊና፣ መንፈሳዊ ልዩነቶች የሰውን ዘር ከፍፍለን እንድናይ ያደርጋሉ ወይስ የውብት መለኪያ ብቻ ናቸው?

ስለ ሰው ዘርና የዘር ዕሳቤ ሲነሣ 'ዘር ተፈጥሯዊ፣ ማኅበራዊ ምናባዊ' እየተባለ ቢያንስ አምስት የተለያዩ ምልከታዎች አሉ ትላለች ናዖሚ ዛክ።[25] እያንዳንዳችን ከአምስቱ አንዱን? አለያም ሌላውን ዐሳብ እንከተላለን። እንዚህ የተለያዩ ዕሳቤዎች ብሔርተኝነትንም የሚመለከቱ ይሆን? ትክክል የሆነው ግን የትኛው ነው?

ሀ) ዘር ተፈጥሮ ነው

በዚህ አመለካከት መሠረት፣ ዘራችን በተፈጥሮ የምናገኘው ወይም ሥነ ሕይወታዊ ውርስ ሲሆን ሁሉም ነገር በዚህ ይወሰናል። ስለዚህ ሰውን በዘሩ መለየት ይቻላል።

25   Zack, N. (2018). The Philsophy of Race. *Palgrave Philsophy Today*. McMillan.

ዘር የሰዎችን አንድነትና ልዩነት ለማወቅ አካላዊ፣ ባሕላዊ፣ እና የግብረ ገብ ባሕርያትን በተጨባጭ የምንለካበት ነው። ዘር ውርስ ስለሆነ በሰዎች ዘንድ የሚታየው ልዩነትም ከዘር የተወረሰ ነው። ማለትም፣ ዘር ተፈጥሮ ስለሆነ በቀላሉ አንቀይረውም።

እንዲህ ዐይነት ዐሳቤ ጥንታዊ ቢሆንም፣ ዛሬም ይዘወተራል። ጄኒፈር ዋግነር እና ጓደኞቿ በቅርቡ ባካሄዱት ጥናት መሠረት የሥነ ሕይወት (ባዮሎጂ) ጥናት እና ሥነ ሰብ (አንትሮፖሎጂ) ጥናት ዘርፎች ዘንድ የተንሰራፋ አመለካከት ነው። [26] እናም፣ ለዘረኝነት መስፋፋት መንገድ እንዳይከፍቱ በብርቱ አስጠንቅቀዋል።

ድኽነትና ሃብት፣ ጭካኔና ጀግንነት፣ ጥበብና ሞኝነት ልክ እንደ ቁንመት፣ የጸጉር ቀለም፣ ወይም የፊት ቆዳ ከዘር የሚወረሱ ናቸው። በተፈጥሮ ለመግዛት የተፈጠሩ፣ በተፈጥሮ ደግሞ ለመገዛት (ለባርነት) የተወሰነላቸው አሉ። በተፈጥሮ ርጉም፣ ቡሩክ የሆኑ ዘሮች አሉን ማለት ነው። ይህን መካድም፣ ለመቀየር መሞከርም ዋጋ ያስከፍላል። ልክ እንደ ማይክል ጃክሰን ሙሉ ቆዳ ቢቀይሩም ቀለም ብቻ እንጂ ጥቁሮች ወደ ፈረንጅነት አይለወጡም።

ለ) ዘር ተፈጥሯዊ ቢሆንም አካላዊ ልዩነቶችን ብቻ የምንለካበት ነው።

በዚህ አመለካከት መሠረት ዘር የሁሉም ነገር መለኪያ ተደርጎ መታየቱ ስንተት ነው። ዘራችን በተፈጥሮ የምንወርሰው ቢሆንም፣ አካላዊ ማንነታችን ብቻ የሚገልጽና የሚወስን ነው። ለምሳሌ:- የቆዳ ቀለም፣ የዐይን አቀማመጥ፣ ጸጉር ወዘተ። ባሕርይ ግን የሚቀረጽ እንጂ የሚወረስ አይሆንም።

ስለዚህ ተቀያያሪ ነገሮች ተፈጥሮ ልንላቸው አንችልም። መልካምም፣ መጥፎም መሆን፣ ጀግናና ደፋር ሆኖ ማደግ፣ ጥበብን ዐውቀት፣ የመሳሰሉት ተፈጥሮ አይደሉም። ሔሎችም በሰዎች መካከል ያሉ ልዩነቶች ተፈጥሯዊ ያልሆኑ ሞልተዋል። መቀየር የሚችሉ ነገሮች ናቸውና፣ አይወረሱምም። ጀግናም ፈሪ ይወለዳል። ብርቱም ደካማን ይፀንሳል።

ካሾን ስፔንሰር የተባሉ የተፈጥሮ ተመራማሪ[27] ሥነ ፍጥረት ባያለያየን ኖሮ እንዲህ በቁመት፣ በመልክ፣ የፊትና የሰውነት ገጽታ ዝብርቅርቅ አንሆንም ነበር ይላሉ። በቆዳ ወይም በጸጉር ቀለም ተመሥርተን ዘርን መመደብ እንችላለን፣ ነውርም የለውም ብለው ያስተምራሉ። ከረገጒሹም እናትና አባት ረገጒሹም ልጆች የመውለድ ዕድል ከፍተኛ ነው።

---

26 Wagner, J. K., Yu, J., Ifekwunigwe, J. O., Harrell, T. M., Bamshad, M. J. & Royal, C. D. (2017). Anthropologists' views on race, ancestry, and genetics. *American Journal of Physical Anthropology.* 2017 Feb; 162(2): 318–327. https://www.ncbi.nlm.nih.gov/pmc/articles/PMC5299519/

27 Spencer, Q. (2019). How to be a Bilogocal Realist; in What is Race; Glasgow, et al. OUP.

አካላዊ የተፈጥሮ ልዩነት ግን የማኅበራዊ ተዋረድን ወይም ደረጃን አያመለክትም ሲሉ ስፔንሰር ይከራከራሉ። ረጃጅሞች ጥሩ ሰብዕናና ከፍተኛ ቦታ ይሰጣቸው ማለት ልክ አይሆንም። ወይም ጥምዝምዝ ያለ ፀጉር የታደሉትን ከባለ ቀጥተኛዎቹ ጋር በማወዳደር አንዳቸውን አስበልጦ፤ ሌላውን አምላክ ፈርዶባቸው፤ አላያም ሊያሳንስ ወድዶ አልፈጠረም።

በእርግጥ ጥቁር ሆነ ሀብታም መሆን ይቻላል። ይህ በመሆኑ ግን የስፔንሰር አመለካከት ልዩነትን በትክክል አላስረዳንም። ጥቁር ሀብታም ሆነ በነጮች መናቅን ማስወገድ ያልተቻለው ለምንድነው? የምን ነጮች ብቻ? ኢትዮጵያውያንም፤ በተለይም ከእንደዋ የተነሣ ከሌሎች ጥቁር ሕዝቦች ይልቅ ራሳችንን ከፍ የማድረግ ሥነ ልቦና እንዳለን እንታማ የለ? ታዲያ በአካላዊ ልዩነት የሰውን ዘር ማለያየት አይቻልም ከተባለ፤ ልዩነቱ እንዴት መጣ? እንዴትስ ሊዘልቅ ቻለ?

ሐ) ዘር የይስሙላ ልዩነት ነው

በዚህ አመለካከት መሠረት ደግሞ፤ ተፈጥሮ የቸረችን ውጫዊ ምስል ማንነትን አያሰረዳም። የሰው ማንነቱ ከቆዳ በላይ ነው። ወይንም በተፈጥሮ ብቻ ተመሥርቶ የዘር ልዩነት አለ ብሎ መፈረጅ ስንተት ነው። እንዲያውም፤ የዘር ልዩነት ለይስሙላ ብቻ የፈጠርነው ነገር ነው።

የዚህ ዕሳቤ አራማጆች ዋና ክርክራቸው በሰዎች መካከል የዘር ልዩነት የሚባል ነገር የለም፤ መነሣት እንኳን የለበትም የሚል ነው። ነገር ግን የዘር ልዩነት የሚባለው ዕሳቤ በተለይ የቆዳ ልዩነትን ለማመልከት በዚያውም ምርጥና ምራጭ ዘር ብሎ ከፍፍልን ለመፍጠር የተፀነሰ ክፉ ዕሳብ ነው ይላሉ። እንዲያ ከሆነ ደግሞ ዘር ማንነትን የምንለካበት ነገር አይደለም።

ለምሳሌ ቻይክ ጀፈርስ[28] የተባሉ የማኅበራዊ ጥናት ባለሙያ ዘር ተፈጥሯዊ ነው የሚለውን አመለካከት አጥብቀው ይቃወማሉ። ዘር ማኅበራዊ ልዩነት፤ በተለይም የባሕል መንጸባረቅ ብቻ ነው ብለው ያምናሉ። በእርሳቸው እምነት፤ ዘር ባሕል ያደራጀው የሕዝቦች ስብስብ ነው። ቀደም ሲል የነበሩ የዘር ልዩነቶችን ስናጤንና ሆነ ለወደፊቱ የሰው ዘር ግንኙነት ስንናገር ባሕልን ብቻ እንደ ዋነኛ የልዩነት ምንጭ አድርገን ልንወስድ ይገባል።

ለጀፈርስ፤ አንድ ሰው ዘሩ እንዲህ ነው ብለን ብንፈርጅ ስንኳ ፍጹም የይስሙላ ይሆናል። ኢትዮጵያ ተወልዶ እንግሊዝ አገር ከነሙሉ ጥቅሙ ጋር ያደገ ልጅ፤ ያደገበትን አገር ባሕል ስለሚይዝ ከትውልድ ሥፍራው መራቀኝ አይቀርም። የምን ዘር ብለን እንጥራው? ባሕል ራሱ ይቀየራል፤ ያድጋል፤ ይሞታል፤ ዘርስ ዐብሮ ይሞታል ልንል ነው? ዘር በባሕል የምንገልጸው የይስሙላ ልዩነት የሚሆነው ለዚህ ነው።

---

28 Jeffers, C. (2019). Cultural Constructionism: in What is Race; Glasgow, et al. OUP.

ነገር ግን፣ አንዳንድ ጊዜ ግን ባሕል ራሱ የይስሙላ አልሆን ብሎ ያስቸግራል። ከባህሉ ወይም ከቋንቋው የተነሣ ሰው ራሱን ይወስናል። እዚህ ነኝ ብሎ ጉራ ይይዛል። ሥፍራውን ለቆ እንኳን ሲሄድ ሰው ከባህሉ የተነሣ ከብጤው ጋር የመሳሳብ ኃይል አለው። ይህ እንዴት ለይስሙላ ብቻ ይሆናል?

መ) ዘር ተፈጥሯዊ ቢሆንም ምናባዊ የባሕል መለያየትም ነው

የባዮሎጂ ጥናት ባልደረጀበት ወቅት የኖሩ ቀደምት ጸሐፍት፣ ከኦባሬ በመነሣት፣ የዘር ልዩነት እንዳለ ያምኑ ነበር። 29 ስለዚህ ዘር የይስሙላ ብቻ ሳይነ ምናባዊ (ዐሳባዊ ዕይታ፣ በዘፈቀደ፣ ሳይንሳዊ ያልሆነ) ነው። ነገር ግን ጠጣር መስፈርቶችን ያዘለ ምናብ ነው ይላሉ። ከእነዚህ ጠጣር መስፈርቶች ጥቂቶቹን የግድ ከተፈጥሮም ቢሆን እናገኛለን ብለው ያምናሉ።

ጠጣር የተባለበትም ምክንያት፣ እነዚህ ልዩነቶች በቀላሉ የሚጠፉ ስላይደለ ነው። ለምሳሌ፦- ዘር ባሕርይን ባይወስንም፣ በተፈጥሮ ላይ የተመሠረቱ የባሕል ቅርሶች መለያየትን ያመጣል። ይህ ባሕላዊ ልዩነት ግን ሳይንሳዊ ሳሆን፣ በአብዛኛው በክፋት ላይ ተመሥርቶ፣ አንዱን ለማራቅ፣ ሌላውን ለማቅረብ የተፈጠረ ዐሳባዊ መለያየት ነው። ምናብም ይፈርጃል።

በዚህ አመለካከት መሠረት እንግዲህ ዘር ማንነት ነው። ነገር ግን ማንነታችን በተለያዩ ቡድኖች ዕይታ ይወሰናል። ይህ ደግሞ አንጻራዊ ምልከታ ይሆናል ማለት ነው። እኔ ነኝ ያልሁትን፣ ሌላው አያይለሁም ማለት ይችላል። ጠጣር ልዩነቶች ቢታዩም ምናባዊ የሚሆኑት ለዚያ ነው። ኢትዮጵያዊ 'ጥቁር ነህ' ሲባል 'አይደለሁም ቀይ ነኝ አለ' ተብሎ እንደሚወራው።

በሳሊ ሃዝላንገር30 አባባል፣ ዘር የባሕል ነጸብራቅ ቢሆንም፣ በአመዛኙ ፖለቲካዊ ክፍፍል ነው። ፖለቲካዊነቱ ደግሞ የሚመነጨው ተፈጥሯዊ ልዩነታችንን ከመሳሰሉ ነገሮች ለጋለቲካ የሚበጀውን በመመንተፍ ነው። ፖለቲካው የሚመቸውን ልዩነት እስከሚያገኝ ድረስ ይንዛል። ምናባዊ የሚያሰኘው ደግሞ ይህ ነው። ልዩነትን ሆነ ብሎ ፈልጎ የማግኘት አባዜ።

ለምሳሌ፦- የነጭ አሜሪካውያንን የበላይነትን የሚያቀነቅንትን እንመልከት። የፖለቲካ ሜዳውን ለማጥበብ ሲከጅሉ፣ ነጭ ወንድ የተሻለ አሜሪካዊ ተደርጎ እንዲወሰድ ይዳክራሉ። ከጥቁሮች፣ ከላቲኖዎች፣ ወይም ከሌሎች ብቻ ሳይሆን ነጭም

29 Bonnoil, J., Edward-Grossi, E. & Wang, S. (2021). Introduction to *Race and Biology*. https://journals.openedition.org/alterites/338

30 Haslanger, S. (2019). Tracing the Sociopolitical Reality of Race; in What is Race; Glasgow, et al. OUP.

ቢሆኑ ከሴቶች ይልቅ ነጭ ወንድ ሠፍራ ይሰጠዋል። ይህ ዕይታ በሁሉም ቦታና ፈርጅ ዐቅም እንዲገኝ ይጥራሉ።

በእርግጥም ይህ ዕሳቤ አገሪቱን ገዝቶ ኖሯል። ፖለቲካው ከአሜሪካዊነት ባሕል ልቆ ስለሚታይ፤ እስከ 1920 ዓ.ም. ድረስ ነጭ እንኳ ቢሆኑ፤ ሴቶች መምረጥ አይችሉም ነበር። እንዲሁም፤ ነባር አሜሪካውያን ሴት ዜጎች እስከ 1924 ዓ.ም.፤ ቻይናዊ ዝርያ ያላቸው ሴቶች እስከ 1943 ዓ. ም.፤ የመምረጥ መብት አላገኙም ነበር። ጥቁሮችና ላቲኖዎች (ከደቡብ አሜሪካ የፈለሱ) ግን እስከ 1962 ዓ.ም. ድረስ መምረጥ አይችሉም ነበር። [31]

ይህም ማለት፤ ተፈጥሮንም ሆነ ባሕልን ለመለያየት ተጠቀሙበት እንጂ፤ የዘር ዕሳቤ ቀድሞውኑ የተሰደረው ለፖለቲካ ፍጆታ ብቻ ነው ማለት ነው። ያልተለያየውን አለያይተው፤ ወይንም ጥቂት ቀዳዶችን አስፍተው፤ ፖለቲካ ይሠሩበታል። ፖለቲካዊ እፐተጠናከረ ሲሄድ ልዩነቶችም ጠጥር እየሆኑ መጡ። ነገር ግን፤ ፖለቲካዊ ያልሆኑ ልዩነቶችም በተለያዩ ማኅበረሰቦች መካከል ይታያሉ። ለምሳሌ፦ አንዳንድ ባሕል ልጅ ያልናቸውን አንድ ሲያደርግ፤ በተመሳሳዮችም መካከል ልዩነት ይከሠታል።

ሠ) ዘር ማኅበራዊ ዕሳቤ ነው

እስካሁን ከተጠቀሱት ሁሉ የሚለየውና ከቅርብ ጊዜ ወዲህ እየጠነከረ የመጣው ዕሳቤ፤ ዘር ከተፈጥሮ ጋር ምንም ግንኙነት የሌለው፤ ነገር ግን ማኅበራዊ ትርጉምና ፋይዳ ያለው ጠንካራ ዕሳቤ እንደሆነ የሚያተተው ነው። ለምሳሌ እንደ ሜሊዛ ስቴይን[32] ገለጻ፤ ሰው በተፈጥሮ አይለያይም፤ ነገር ግን በግልፅ የምንመለከተው ቀጣይነት ያላቸውን ማኅበራዊ ልዩነቶች የሙጥኝ ማለታችን ነው።

በስቴይን ዕይታ፤ የዘር ዕሳቤ በሃይለኛና ደካማ (በጨቋኝና ተጨቋኝ) ቤተሰቦ (ጐሣዎች፤ ሕዝብ፤ ወይም አገራት) መካከል ያለ የታሪክ፤ የፖለቲካ፤ እና የማኅበራዊ ግንኙነት ነጸብራቅ ነው። ዘር ካልተጠቀሰ እንዚህን ልዩነቶች ማስጠበቅ አዳጋች ነው። ወይንም በዘር ዕሳቤ ጠፍር ካልሆን "የእኛ" የምንላቸውን ነገሮች የመመበቅ እና የማስጠበቅ ዐቅም ገና አላዳበርንም።

በዘር ጄጠራ ተጠቃሚ የሆኑ አሉ። እንርሱም፤ በሰዎች መካከል አሉ የተባሉ ልዩነቶች እንዲሰፉ እንጂ እንዳይጠብ ይጋደላሉ። ልዩነቱን ለማጥበብ ብንፈልግም በቀላሉ የማይጠብበው ለዚህ ነው። ይሁን እንጂ፤ ሜሊዛ ስቴይን በትክክል

31 Bloch, E, and Wong, R. (2020). When Did Women Get the Right to Vote in the United States? A Timeline. *Teen Vogue*; August 17, 2020. Accessed from https://www.teenvogue.com/story/when-women-got-right-to-vote-united-states

32 Stein, M. M. (2015). *Measuring Manhood: Race and the Science of Masculinity, 1830–1934.* Minneapolis, Minnesota, University of Minnesota Press, 2015

እንዳስተዋለችው "የበላይነትን ለማስጠበቅ 'ዘር ተፈጥሮ ነው' ብለው ባከረሩ መጠን፤ የእኩልነት መብታቸውን ለማስከበር የሚጥሩ ወገኖችን ይበልጥ ወኔ አጠነከሩ።"

ከወዴት ወደቅን?

እንዚህን አመለካከቶች እያተመላለስን የምንንዳስስ ይሆናል። ለጊዜው ግን አንድ ጥያቄ:- ብሔርን በሚመለከት የአብዛኛው ኢትዮጵያዊ አመለካከት ከእነዚህ ወደ የትኛው ያደላል? አንዳንዶች አክራሪ ነገር ሲካሰት ውሑድ መረዳት አላቸው። ምናልባት እኛም ከእያንዳንዱ ቀንጪጭበን እንረዳ ይሆን? በተለይም የፖለቲካና መሰል ጥቅም ያለው ጉዳይ ሲሆን የትኛው ዐሳብ ያይልብናል?

ሌላ ጥያቄ:- ብሔርስ ተፈጥሯዊ፤ ወይስ ማኅበራዊ፤ ወይስ ምንባዊ? ስለ ብሔር እና ብሔርተኝነት ያለንን አመለካከት እንዴት እንፈተሻለን? እግዚአብሔር የፈጠረው ልዩነት ነው? ወይስ ማኅበራዊ ብቻ? "ጥያቄውንም አንጠይቅ፤ ምን ያስፈልጋል?" የሚሉስ አይኖሩም? ወይስ፤ የብሔር ልዩነት ዝም ብሎ ባዶ ቅዠት ነው?

ዘር ወይም ብሔር ተፈጥሯዊ፤ ማኅበራዊና ምንባዊ መሆኑ በሕዝብ መካከል ያለውን ግንኙነት ያዛብራርቃል። ስለ ብሔር እንመለስበታለን፤ ዘርን በተመለከተ ግን የዘረኝነት ዕሳቤ የሚመነጨው "የራሳችን ወይም ሌላ" ለምንለው ዘር ካለን አመለካከት የተነሳ እንደሆን አለ አይባልም።

ለምሳሌ:- የነጩ ሰው ዘር ከጥቁሩ ሰው ዘር የማይለይ ሆኖ ሳለ 'ነጭ ነኝ' ብሎ መመጻደቅ፤ 'ጥቁር ነኝ' ብሎም ራስን ዝቅ አድርጎ ማየት ይስተዋላል። ይህን ታዲያ ልዩነት ብለው የሚያራግቡ፤ በዚህ ልዩነት መሠረት አላግባብ የሚያገኙ፤ ወይም አላግባብ ድርሻቸውን ከፍ ለማድረግ የሚፈልጉ እጅግ ብዙ ናቸው። እነዚህን "ዘረኛ" ብሎ መጥራት ይቻላል? ዘረኛ ማን ነው? ማለት ምን ዐይነት መስፈርት የሚያሟላ 'ዘረኛ' ተብሎ ይጠራ?

የዌብስቴር መዝገበ ቃላት[33] "ዘረኛ" ለሚለው ቃል ትርጉም ሲሰጥ፤ በሰዎች መካከል የሚታየው ልዩነት ከተፈጥሮ የመነጨ ነው ብሎ ማመን፤ በዚህም ምክንያት በተለይም አናሳ ቁጥር ያላቸውን ማኅበረሰቦች ማግለል፤ መገፋት፤ እና እኩል ሥፍራ አለመስጠት ነው ይላል። በአግላይ ሥርዓት የሚማቅቁ፤ በቀጥር አናሳ የሆኑ ብቻ ስላይደለ፤ ይህን ትርጉም ማስፋት ሳይኖርብን አይቀርም።

የዘር ልዩነት አለ ብለው የሚያምኑ ከተፈጥሮ በተጨማሪ በርካታ መሠረቶችን ይጠቅሳሉ። በምንም መሠረት ይሁን ልዩነት አለ ብሎ የሚነሣ ሰው፤ ከዚህም የተነሣ

33 Merriam Webster. (2021), Definition of Racism. https://www.merriam-webster.com/dictionary/racism

"ሌላ" ያላቸውን ማግለል፣ መግፋት፣ እና መጨቆን ትክክል ነው ብሎ የሚያምንና የሚያደርግ ዘረኛ መባል አለበት።

እኛም የሰውን ዘርና ማንነት ከተፈጥሮ፣ ከማኅበራዊና ምንባዊ ምልከታዎች የተነሣ ልዩ ልዩ መረዳት ይኖረናል። ነገር ግን ሰከን ብሎ ለማሰብ፣ አመክኞአዊና ምንባዊ ብያኔዎችን በትክክል መረዳትና ማጤን ያስፈልጋል። ይህን በሚቀጥለው ክፍል ለመዳሰስ ተሞክሯል። እስከዚያው ግን፣ በዚህ መጽሐፍ የሚከተለው ዕሳቤ ተንጸባርቋል።

የሰው ዘር የፍጥረት ልዩነት የለውም፣ አንድ ብቻ ነው። በሰዎች መካከል የሚታዩት ልዩነቶች ማኅበራዊ፣ ፖለቲካዊና ምንባዊ ናቸው። በማናቸውም መልክ የሚከሰቱ ልዩነቶችን ግን በመመርኮዝ አንድን የማኅበረሰብ ክፍል ወይም አባል፣ በዚያ ልዩነት መሠረት ማግለል፣ ማሸማቀቅ፣ "እኛና እንርሱ" የሚባል ሰው ሠራሽ ድንበር መፍጠር፣ ወይም መግፋት 'ዘረኝነት' ይባላል። በተለምዶ "እኔ ከዚህ ዘር ነኝ ወይም እገሊት ዘር እንዲህ ነው" ማለትም አይጠቅምም። የሰው ዘር አንድ ነውና።

ሰዎች በምድር ላይ እየበዙ ሲሄዱ ግን በተለያዩ ምክንያቶች ልዩነቶች ተፈጠሩ። የቋንቋ፣ የባሕል፣ የእኑኑር፣ የሕይወት ገጠመኝ፣ ... ወዘተ። የተለያያ የሥነ ልቦና፣ የዓላማ፣ የዝምድና ትስስር፣ ... ወዘተ አንድነትም ሆነ ልዩነት በሰዎች መካከል ግንኙነቶችን ማጉልበት ወይም ማሻከር ይችላል። የሰው ዘር መሀናቸውን ግን ሊሸር አይችልም።

በእንዲህ ዐይነት ልዩነት ምክንያት ግን ማንኛውንም ሰው መጥላት፣ ማክፋፋት፣ መናቅ፣ መለየት፣ ወይም ማጥላላት ግን ዘረኝነት ነው። ሌላ ስም የለውም። የዘር ልዩነት መኖሩን ብንምንም፣ በናምንም ዘረኝነት ክፉ እንደሆነ መረዳት አዳጎች አይሆንብንም።

በታሪክም ሆነ በሌሎች ዘርፎች፣ ጠበብት በሰዎች መካከል ያለውን ልዩነትና ብዝኃነት ለማጥናት ላይ ታች ብለዋል። አንዳንድ ልዩነት ለመረዳት ቀላል ነው። ሌላው ደግሞ ምስጢራዊ ነው። ሰዎችን ከዕድሜ ያታ በተጨማሪ፣ በሚኖሩበት ሥፍራ (ገጠር፣ ከተማ ወይም ቆለኛ፣ ደጋኛ) ብሎ መለየት ይቻላል። በባሕርይ፣ በአካላዊውም ሆነ የአዕምሮ ዕድገት ደረጃ፣ እና ከላይ በተጠቀሱት በሌሎች አንጻር ብዙዎች ሰዎችን ከፋፍለው ለማጥናት ምክርዋል።[34] ይህ እጅግም አያጣላንም።

ምክንያቱም፣ በባሕል (ቋንቋና ኃይማኖትን ጨምሮ) እጅግ ሰፊ ልዩነት አለ፣ እጅግም አንድነት አለ። ይህ ለምን እንደሆን በጥናት ይደረስበታል። በቤተሰብ የዘር ሐረግ፣ በአካላዊ ሁኔታ ልክ፣ ቁመና፣ የቆዳ ወይም የጸጉር ቀለም፣ የዐይንና አፍንጫ አቀማመጥ፣ ወዘተ ለዪተን ብናጠና ክፉት የለውም።

---

34   Glasgow, J., Haslanger, S., Jeffers, C. & Spencer, Q. (2019). *What is Race: Four Philosophical Views.* Oxford University Press.

ነገር ግን ይህ ልዩነት ባሕርይንና ማንነትን በማንጸባረቅ ወደ አካላዊ ድንበር ከወሰደን ችግር ያስከትላል። ልዩነትን አካል አልብሶ፣ በዘር አመካኘቶ፣ የአቋም ድንበር ማበጀት፣ በታሪክ እንዲ ክፉ ነገሮችን ለመሥራት ክፍተት ሲፈጥር ታይቷል። ማንነት ከዘር ነው ለሚለው ከማኅበራዊና ፖለቲካዊ ትንተና በቀር ሁሉን በሚያረካ መንገድ በብቃት መልስ መስጠት አይቻልም። ይልቁንም የዘር ልዩነት የሰው ማንነት ነው የሚሉ፣ በዘር አመካኝተው የበላይነት ለማስጠበቅ የሚጥሩ ናቸው።

ጆሽዋ ግላስጐው[35] የተባሉ ጸሐፊ የዘር ዕሳቤ እንዲኖር፣ የግድ የአንድን ማኅበረሰብ ማንነት የሚወስኑ ነገሮች ከሴላው በለጥ ብለው በዚያ ማኅበር ውስጥ መገኘት አለባቸው ይላል፣ እነዚህን ነገሮች ግን ማጣኔት አዳጋች ነው። በተጨባጭ አንድን ማኅበረሰብ ከሴላው የሚለዩ ነገሮች፣ በአትኩሮት የተመለከትናቸው እንደሆን አይረጉም።

ባሕርያትን፣ ከሥነ ፍጥረትም ሆነ ባሕላዊ መሠረቶች በማነሣት ማጉላት ካስፈለገን፣ በግላስጐው አመለካከት ዘር የሚባል የለም። ወይም የዘር ልዩነት የሚባል ነገር በሰዎች መካከል የለም። በሴላ አነጋገር፣ ጫን ጨከን ብለን ካልፈለግን በስተቀር አይኖሩም። አሉ ተብለው የሚነሡ ልዩነቶች ሁሉም ሆነ ብለን ካላጎላናቸው በስተቀር በራሳቸው መቆም አይችሉም።

ነገር ግን በሰዎች መካከል የሚታዩን ማኅበራዊም ሆነ የተፈጥሮ ልዩነቶች እንዳሉ፣ በለሆሳስ ለጥናት ያህል ብቻ የምንጠቀም ከሆነ የዘር ሳይሆን፣ የለምድም ልዩነት እውነታ እንዳለ ልንቀበል እንችላለን። ልዩነቶች የሚያለያዩን ሳይሆን የተለያየ መልክና ዘርፍ እንዳለን የሚገልጹ ቢሆን ይህን ልዩነት ብለን ብንጠራውም ባንጠራውም ለመልካም ውጤን ልንጠቀምበት እንችላለን።

የዘረኝነት ታሪካዊ ዳራ

የዘረኝነት ዕሳቤ ግን "ለሆሳስ" አያውቅም። ከላይ የተጠቀሱት አምስት የተለያዩ የዕሳቤ ምድቦች መነሻ አላቸው። ይህን ለመረዳት፣ የዘርና ዘረኝነት ዕሳቤ በታሪክና በተለይም በፖለቲካዊ ፍልስፍናና ዘርፍ እንዴት ይታይ እንደ ነበር ዳሰሳ ማድረግ ያስፈልጋል። ይህ የተመረጠው፣ ስለ ዘረኝነት ስናጠና ስለ ብሔርተኝነትም በዚያው አስተምሮን ሊያልፍ ይችላል በሚል እምነት ነው።

ስለ ሰዎች ማንነት የተለያዩ ምልክታዎች የተቃኙበትን አመክንዮአዊና ምናባዊ ብያኔ ከተረዳን በአገራችን ያለውን የብሔር፣ ብሔረሰብ ፖለቲካ ምንጭ እናስተውላለን። በእግር መንገድ፣ የዚህ ጽሑፍ ትኩረት የሆነውን የብሔርተኝነት ፖለቲካዊ ኤኮኖሚ በተሻለ መልክ ልንረዳው እንችላለን።

---

35 Glasgow, J. (2019). Is Race an Illusion of a (very) Basic Reality? in What is Race; Glasgow, et al. OUP.

የዘረኝነት አመለካከት በታሪክ ውስጥ እና በዘመን መካከል እየተቀያየረ መምጣቱን መገመት ይቻላል። ምንም እንኳ ጥልቅ ጥናት ባናደርግም፣ በሦስት ክፍሎች ከፍለን እናየዋለን (ጥንታዊ፣ ዘመናዊ፣ እና ዘመን ቀደማዊ) ብለን። ዘረኝነት ፖለቲካዊ ፍልስፍናና ስለሆነ እንዴት ዘመንን ይዞ እንደ ተጓዘና እንደ ተለወጠም ማወቅ እጅግ የሚያስፈልገን ነው።

በዚህ ዐጭር ዳሰሳ የፍልስፍናን ሊቆችን የሕይወት ዘመን ሥራ ፍተሐዊ ሆኖ ማቅረብ አይቻልም። እንዲሁም ይህ ጽሑፍ በተጻለ መጠን በሁሉ ዘንድ ተነባቢ እንዲሆን ስለ ተፈለገ ጥልቅ ወደ ሆነ አካዳሚያዊ ትንተና ውስጥ አልተገባም። በአጭሩ ዋና ዋና ዐሳቦችን ብቻ እንዳስሳለን።

በዚህ ዳሰሳ የተጠቀሱት የዘመን ክፍፍሎችም ለግንዛቤ ይረዱን ዘንድ ብቻ የተደረጉ ናቸው። ጥንታዊ የተባለው፣ እስከ 13ኛው ክፍል ዘመን ድረስ የነበረስ ጊዜ ነው። ይህ ዘመን በአብዛኛው በብዙዎቻችን ዘንድ የታወቁ ፈላስፎች የተነሡበት ጊዜ ነው። የዘር ልዩነት ፅንስ ዐሳብ ገና በእንሩ ጊዜም እንደ ነበረ እናያለን።

ይህ ብቻ ሳይሆን የዘር ዐሳቢ፣ ከጥንት ጀምሮ በዘመኑ የነበረውን የጉብረተሰብን የኑሮ ፍልስፍናና ተግባር የቃኘ ወይም የተከተለ ሆነ እናገኘዋለን። ይህ ደግሞ ፍተሐዊነትን ያዛባል፣ አዛብቶታልም። የዘር ልዩነት ከጹሕ ፍልስፍና ማለትም (አሜክንዮአዊ ንድፈ ዐሳብ) ይልቅ ወደ ፖለቲካነት ያደላ ያልንበትን ምክንያያ እናጤናለን።

እንዲያውም አንዳንድ ፈላስፎች ከአገር አስተዳደርና መሪዎች ጋር ጥብቅ ቁርኝት ነበራቸው። የግል ፍላጎትና የሳይንሱ አስገዳጅነት ምን ያህል እንደ ተሳሰቡ እንመለከታለን። በአብዛኛው ግን፣ ፈላስፋም ሆነው፣ ዐሳባቸው አንድም የአስተዳደሩን ምናብ የሚወክል አለያም ለዚያ መነሻ ሆነ እናገኘዋለን።

ዘመናዊ ያልናቸው ዐሳቢዎች በተለይም ከእንግሊዙ የኢንዱስትሪ አብዮት፣ ከፈረንሳይ የወዛደር አብዮትና ተመሳሳይ ክስተቶች መዳረሻ አካባቢ አንሥቶ ያሉትን ጊዜያት ነው። ከክስተቶቹ የተነሣ የመጣውን የዓለም የፖለቲካ፣ ማህበራዊ እና ኤኮኖሚያዊ ለውጦችን የታከኩ ዐሳቦች። ጥልቅ የመነቃቃት እና ሕዳሴ ዘመን ስለ ነበር ብዙ ዐሳቦች የፈለቁበት ዘመን ነበር።

ይህ "አዲስ" ዘመን የሰው ልጆች መሠረታዊ እኩልነት፣ እንዲሁም የመብት ጥያቄዎች በአብዮት መልክ ገንፍለው የወጡበት ነበር። የአመለካከት ልዩነቶችም እንዲሁ ጎልተው እንዲታዩ አድርጓል። ዐውቀትም የተተረፈፈፈበት ዘመን ስለነበር የሕዳሴው ዘመን ይባላል።

በዚህ ዘመን የነበረውን ሁሉ ዐሳብ አጠቃላሎ ማቅረብ አይቻልም። ለዚህ ጽሑፍ ግብዓት ይሆን ዘንድ ግን የዘር ልዩነትን በሰው ልጆች መካከል ያለ ልዩነት ነባራዊ ነጽብራቅ አድርገው በሚመለከቱት ላይ ብቻ ትኩረት አድርገን ዳሰሳ እናደርጋለን።

"ዘመን ቀደም"[36] ባልነው ክፍል ጊዜም በእንደዚህ ዐይነት ዐሳቦች ላይ ዋንኛ ትኩረት እናደርጋለን። ይህ የጊዜ ክፍል ያለንበትን ዘመን የሚያመለክት ሲሆን የድህረ መነቃቃት ጊዜን ያመለክታል። በዘመናችን የኖሩ ውጥንቅጥ ዐሳቢዎች ለዘረኝነትና ብሔርተኝነት ያበረከቱት አስተዋጽኦ አለ። ዛሬ ያለንበት ይህ ዘመን ዐውቀትም፣ የባሕልና ተግባር መወራረስም እየበዛ የመጣበት ነው።

ጊዜአችን ውጥንቅጥ ነው። ግለኝነት፣ የእውነትና የእምነት አንጻራዊነት፣ የታሪክና መርህ ሕይወት ቁንጽልነትና፣ መደዴነት የሚያይልበት ዘመን ነው። አንዳንድ ጊዜ ወጥ ናቸው ብለን ስንከተለ ዝብርቅርቅ የሆነ አመለካከቶች ይሆኑብናል። በተለይም፣ "እኔ ያልሁት ካልሆነ" ከሚለ ጽንፈኝነት አንሥቶ፣ "የእኔም የአንተም ልክ ነው" የሚል "አካታችነት" የታጫቀበት ስለሆነ ውል ይጠፋል።

ስለዚህ፣ በዚህ ባለንበት ዘመን እንደ ብሔርና ብሔርተኝነት የመሰሳሉ ዐሳቢዎችን በሰከነ መንገድ ካላየናቸው ለብዙ ንትርክና እንግልት ሊዳርጉን ይችላሉ። ዘመን ደግሞ ለዘመን የሚናገረው አለው። አንዳንድ ዐሳቦች ዘመናትንም የዘለቁ መሆናቸውን ማጤን ያሻል። የወደራ ገንዘብ እንደ ማለት ነው። ከጊዜ ሂደት ጋር አስተሳሰቦች ያድጉም፣ ይስፋሙም፣ ይጣሉም ነበርና።

ጥንታዊ

የዘር ቀመር እንዲህ እያነታረክ በዘር ልዩነት የተሠራ ፖለቲካም ሆነ ማኅበራዊውን ሕይወት ለመምራት መወሰን የመጣው ጥንታዊ ሊባል ከሚችሉ የተለያዩ የፍልስፍና አመለካከቶች ነው። የዘረኝነት ፍልስፍናን ሳያስበው የጀመረው፣ የፈላስፎች አባት ተብሎ የሚታወቀው ግሪካዊው ጠቢብ ፕላቶ[37] (428–328 ዓመተ ዓለም)[38] እንደሆነ ይታመናል።

ፕላቶ ማኅበረሰብ ልክ እንደ ግለሰብ ነው ብሎ ያምናል። አንድን ግለሰብ በዐሳብ ልዕልና ቁንጮውን ይዞ የሚመራው ጭንቅላቱ ነው፣ ልብና አዕምሮ። እንደ ፕላቶ ዐሳብ፣ ማኅበረሰብ የሚባለው ነገርም ልብና አዕምሮ አለው። መሪ፣ ወይም የመሪዎች ስብስብ የማኅበረሰብ ልብ ነው።

አዕምሮ ሲያዝ፣ ሌላው አካል ሁሉ ይንቀሳቀሳል። እጅ አድርግ የተባለውን ያደርጋል፣ እግርም ወደ ታዘዘበት ይንዛል፣ ዐይንም እንደዚሁ። ማኅበረሰብም ልክ እንደ

---

36 "ዘመን ቀደምነት" የተባለው "ድህረ ዘመናዊነት" የሚለውን ለመተካት ሲሆን የዚህ ዐሳቤ ምንጭት ሲምን ሐሊሶ ኮካ (2019) "ዘመን ቀደምነትና የዛሬይቱ ቤተ ክርስቲያን" በሚለው መጽሐፍ በሰፊው ተመልክቷል። ይህም ክፍል ከዚያ መጽሐፍ ተቀንጭቦ የተወሰደ ነው።

37 Meinwald, C. C. (2021). Plato: Greek Philospher. *Encyclopedia Britanica.* https://www. britannica.com/biography/Plato

38 በዚህ ጽሑፍ "ዓመተ ዓለም የሚለው ከተጨመረ ከክርስቶስ ልደት በፊት የነበረን ጊዜ ለማመልከት ነው።

ሰውነት በትክክል እንዲሠራ ከተፈለገ መሪ ያስፈልገዋል። መሪዎች ያዝዛሉ፤ ሌሎች የሰውነት አካላት ትዕዛዝን ይፈጽማሉ።

ለዚህም፣ እንደ ፕሌቶ አባባል፣ ከማኅበረሰቡ ውስጥ በአካልና በአዕምሮ የዳበሩትን መርጦ እንዲያስቡና የማኅበሩ አዕምሮ እንዲሆኑ መርዳትና ማለማመድ ያስፈልጋል። በዚያውም 'እጅ፣ እጅን፣ እግር፣ እግርን፣ እንዲሁም አዕምሮ አዕምሮን እየወለደ እንዲኖር በተደጋጋሚ ይነገረዋል። ይበረታታልም፤ አዕምሮ ታዲያ ይከበራልም።[39]

በጭራ ቃል፣ የፈላስፎች አባት ፕሌቶ፣ በምናቡ የአዛኙና ታዛኙ ስምሪት፣ የዘር ክፍፍል ወይም ምደባ ፈጣሪ ማለት ነው። ናፖሚ ዛክ እንደ ጻፈችው ፕሌቶ የመጀመሪያውም፣ ከሁሉም በተሻለ መልክ ዘረኝነቱን ያልደበቀ (ምናልባት ዘረኝነትም ሆነ ትርጉሙ ገና የዳበረ ስላልነበረ) የሰው ዘር ልዩነትና የዘረኝነት ፍልስፍና ፅንሰ ዐሳብ መሥራች ነው።

ከእርሱ ቀጥሎ ያሉት ፈላስፎች በሙሉ ይህን ወይ በማዳበር፣ አለያም በማኮሰስ የጸፉ ናቸው። ፍልስፍና ለነገሥታታት ቅርብ ስለ ነበረ፣ የእነዚህ ሰዎች ዐሳብ ፖለቲካንና አስተዳደርን ይገዛ እንደ ነበረ ማስተዋል ያሻል። ስለዚህ በድንገት ይጀምረው እንጂ በቀላሉ አይጠፋም፣ አልጠፋምም።

ነገር ግን የፕሌቶ ተከታይና ተማሪ የሆነው አርስቶትል (384–322 ዓመተ ዓለም)[40] ይህን አስታከኮ የቀመረው የዘር ፍልስፍና እስከ ዛሬ ድረስ ተዛኚሯ ለቀሪው የሰው ዘር ልዩነት ፅንሰ ዐሳብ መነሻ ነው ማለት ይቻላል። ማለትም:- የሰው ዘር ልዩነት ዕሳቤ መሥረቱ የተንሻፈፈ ነው። ምክንያቱም የአርስቶትል ፍልስፍና የሳይንስትና መነሻውን ረስቷታና።

የፍልስፍና መሥረታዊ አመክንዮ እንድ ነው። ይህም፣ የወደፊቱን የማኅበረሰብ ዕድገት ባለመ መንገድ አመክንዮን ተከትሎ፣ በአብዛኛው ለመረዳት አስቸጋራ ለሆኑ ነገሮች መልስ መስጠት ነው። የአርስቶትል የዘር ልዩነት ዕሳቤ የማኅበረሰብ ዕድገትን ያለመ አመክንዮ ይዞ አልተነሳም።

ይልቁንም:- በጊዜው የዳበረ የአስተዳደር መዋቅርና የግንኙነት ተዋረድ ነበረው የግሪክ ሥልጣኔ መነሻው ነበር፤ 'ምን ይበጃል?' ከሚለው የአድማስ ባሻገር ጥያቄ ይልቅ የግሪክን አስተዳደርና መዋቅር መተንተን መርጦ ነበር። ኑባሬን ተንትኖ፣ ነገን መወሰን መፈለጥ ፍልስፍናውን መሥረቱን የሳተ ያደርገዋል።

ለግሪኮችም ሆነ ለሌሎች አገራት፣ ነገ የተሻለ ሥልጣኔ እንዴት ሊመጣ ይችላል የሚለውን መሥረታዊ ፍልስፍና ጥያቄ ትቶ፣ ግሪኮች እንዴት ስለጠኑ ለሚለው ጥያቄ <u>መልስ ለመስጠት</u> ወሰነ። ከዚህም መልስ በመነሣት፣ ነገም እንዲህ ይሆናል በማለት

39 Zack, N. (2018). The Philsophy of Race. *Palgrave Philsophy Today.* McMillan.

40 Kenny, A. J. P. (2021). Aristotle: Greek Philospher. *Encyclopedia Britanica.* https://www. britannica.com/biography/Aristotle

ገደበው፤ ታሪክ የፍልስፍና መሠረት ሆነ ማለት ነው። ይባስ ብሎ፤ ትንተናውን ያካሄደው፤ የግሪክን ሥልጣኔ በጋርዮሽ ዘመን አስተዳደር ከሚኖሩ ሕዝብና ቡድኖች አሥራ ጋር በማስተያየት ነበር።

ከዚህ ስሁት አካሄድ በመነሣትም፤ ግሪኮች የተሻለ የአስተዳደር ሥርዓት መፍጠር የቻሉ ምጡቅ ሕዝቦች ናቸው ወደሚል ለጥናት ከመነሣቱ በፊት ወደ ደረሰበት መደምደሚያ ደረሰ። ስለዚህ፤ በአርስቶትል እምነት የተሻለ የሚባለው ራስን ከማስተዳደር አልፎ፤ ሌላውን በዕውቀትና ጉልበት በሌሎ በመገኘት መግዛት ወይም ማስገበር መቻል ነው።

ለአርስቶትል የማኅበረሰብ መሠረት ወንድና ሴት ሲጣሙሩ የሚፈጥሩት ቤተሰብ ነው። ቤተሰቡ ልጅ ይወልዳል፤ ኑሮውን ለማሸነፍ ይፍጨረጨራል። ቤተሰቡ፤ በሃብትም፤ በጉልበትም ሲበረታ ባርያዎችን ለራሱ ያደርጋል። ያደገ ማኅበረሰብም እንዲሁ።

እንደ አርስቶትል አስተሳሰብ፤ የቤተሰብ ግንኙነትም የዕድገት ውጤት ነው። ቤተሰብም ሆነ ማኅበረሰብ ሲያድግ፤ ለአባላቱ ሥፍራና ተወረድ ይወስናል። ልጅና ባርያ ይለያል። የቤተሰብ ኃላፊ ልጅና ባርያን፤ ወንድ ባርያና ሴትና ባርያን ለይቶ የማስተዳደር ዐቅም ከሌለው 'ያለ ማደግ ምልክት ነው' ብሎ ያምናል።

እጅግ ያደጉ ቤተሰቦች ይህን የማኅበረሰብ ተወረደ እስከ መንግሥት በሚደርስ ጽኑዕ ልግድ ወይንም ሕግ ጠንቅቀው ይይዛሉ። ሴት፤ ልጅ፤ እና ባርያ ሥፍራቸውን አውቀው ሊኖሩ ይገባል፤ ሥርዓት የሚባለውም ይህ ነው። በተለይም:- በአርስቶትል እምነት፤ ባርያ ለራሱ አያስብም። እንዲያስብም አይፈለግም። ይህን የመሰለ ከቡር አገልግሎት ከጌቶቹ ስለሚያገኝ በደስታ የጉልበት ሥራ እያከናወን፤ ግፉ ቢል ባርያ እየወለደ ሊኖር ይችላል። [41]

አርስቶትል ግሪካዊ ነው። የግሪክን ኑሮና ሕዝብ መውደዱ ችግር የለውም። የግሪክ ሥልጣኔን በመመልከት የቀነጨበውን የሰው ዘር "ፍልስፍና" ግን መልክ ምድራዊ ለማድረግ መጣሩ ችግር ነው። በዚህም አላቆመም፤ በእርሱ እምነት መልክ ምድርም ማንነትን ይገልጣል።

ለምሳሌ:- አውሮፓውያን በሙሉ ብርድ በሚበዛበት ሥፍራ ስለሚኖሩ ዐሳባዊነት ያጠቃቸዋል። አርቆ አሳቢ ናቸው። ጥበብና ብልኃት ግን የላቸውም። በተለይ የእጅ ጥበብ ያጥራቸዋል። ጉ ዱሎ ናቸው። በአንጻሩ ግን የእስያ አሕጉር ሰዎች እጅግ ሞቃት አካባቢ ስለሚኖሩ በተፈጥሮ የእጅ ጥበብ የሚቀናቸው ብልኖች ናቸው። ሙቀት ግን ለአዕምሮ ሥራ አመቺ አይደለም። ስለዚህ የእስያ ሰዎች አርቆ ማሰብ አይሆንላቸውም፤ ይህም ሌላ ጉድለት።

41 Zack, N. (2018). The Philsophy of Race. *Palgrave Philsophy Today*. McMillan.

ጉድለት ካለባቸው ደግሞ፤ ገ� ለመሆን አንዳች ይጉድላቸዋል፤ ሙሉ አያደርጋቸውም። ለአርስቶትል፤ ግሪኮች ሙቀትም፤ ብርድም በልክም ደረጃ ባለበት አገር ስለሚኖሩ የታደሉ ናቸው። ሁለቱን ያዋኸዱ፤ አርቆ ዐሳቢም፤ ጠቢብም፤ ብልኅም መሆን የሚችሉ፤ ደግሞም ሁኔታቸው ሲታያ በእርግጥም የቻሉ፤ ዓለምንም የገዙ።

ስለዚህ፤ በአርስቶትል ዕይታ ግሪኮች ራስን ከማስተዳደር አልፈ ሌላውን ለመግዛት ተፈጥሮም ጭምር ያደላቸው ናቸው። ይህ እንግዲህ ግሪኮች በዚያን ጊዜ በተጨባጭ እያደረጉት የነበረው ነገር ነው። ከዚህ የተነሣ አርስቶትል ልዩ ሕዝቦች ናቸው ሲል አተተ።

የአርስቶትል የዘር ፍልስፍና ዘርንና መልክዐ ምድርን ከኩነት ተነስቶ ያጣመረ እንጂ ለዕድገት ሲባል ተጠብቦ የወጣ አመክንዮ አለ መሆኑ ግልፅ ነው። ሳይንሳዊ አይደለም የምንለው ለዚህ ነው፤ ኩነትን ገለጸ እንጂ ሁለንታናዊ ዕይታ አልነበረም። ይሁን እንጂ ጥንታውያን ፈላስፎች፤ ከእንርሱም አብዛኞቹ ግሪኮች ነበሩና፤ በገፍ ተከተሉት።

ጥንታውያን ፈላስፎች፤ በሰዎች መካከል በተፈጥሮ ፈጽሞ የሌለን ልዩነት፤ በጉልበትም፤ በብልጠትም ለመጫን ታተሩ። እስከ መንግሥት መዋቀር ድረስ ይህን ዐሳብ በማስረጽ የዘር ልዩነት አለ ብለው አስተማሩ። የሰው ዘር ልዩነት ዕሳቤና ዘረኝነት የተወለደው በዚያን ጊዜ ነው። ዘረኝነትም እየከፋና እየተራቀቀ ሄደ።

ተከታታይ ፈላስፎችም የዘር ልዩነት መኖሩን ብቻ ሳይሆን፤ በጥንቃቄ በሚደረግ ቀመር መፍጠርም እንደሚቻል አስተማሩ። ይህም ለዕድገት አመቺ እንደሆነ ያለ ጎፍረት ጸፉ። የሰው ዘር ልዩነት ሆን ተብሎ የተወለደ ፖለቲካዊ ፅንስ ዐሳብ ነው የሚባለው ከዚህ የተነሳ ነው። ችግሩ፤ ይህ ዐሳብ እስከ ዛሬ የተፈራረቁ የፖለቲካ አስተዳደር መዋቅሮችን የቀፈደደና በቀላሉ የማይላቀቅ በሽታ መሆኑ ነው።

በሽታው ግን ፈላጊ አያጣም። መርዘኑን ለመጠጣት የሚቻክል ብዙ ነው። በበለጠ መራቀቅ፤ በበለጠ ጉልበትም ይተገበራል። ጥንት የዘረኝነት ፍልስፍናና አስተዳደር በተግባር ይገለጥ የነበረው በባርያ አሳዳሪነት ሥርዓት ነው። ጥንታዊ ዘረኝነት መግዛትና መገዛትን በከንቱ አያዋውም። ባርያና ንብረት ተመሳሳይ ደረጃ አላቸው። የሰውና የአገር ትልቅነትም በባርያ ብዛት ይወሰናል።

የቀድሞ የካርቴጅ፤ የጢሮስ፤ የሮማ፤ የባቢሎንና በቅርብ የምናውቀው የግብፅ ሥልጣኔ መሠረቱ የባርያ ጉልበት ነበር።[42] ዘረኝነት ትርፍ ባይኖርበትማ ለምን አጥብቀው ይሹታል? እስከ ዛሬ ድረስ በሰዎች መካከል ልዩነት እንዳለ የሚያራግቡ ከዚህ ትርክት የሚጨልፉት ነገር ባይኖር ለምን ያጠብቁታል? ሲጠብቅ ደግሞ እንዳይነቃነቅ፤ መዋቅራዊና ተቋማዊ እንዲሆን ይደረጋል።

<hr>

42 Raymer, A. J. (1940). Slavery-The Graeco-Roman Defence. *Greece & Rome*; Vol. 10; No. 28 (Oct. 1940; pp. 17 – 21)

በተለይም በግሪክና ሮማ የሥልጣኔ ዘመን በሕግ፣ እንዳይለወጥ በጥንቅ ተደንግጎ እናገኘዋለን። ሕጋዊ ሲሆን በትክክል ተተግብሮ ይታያል፤ ያልተገበረው ካለ ይቀጣል። ስለዚህ ባርነት በጊዜው በሕግ ተደንግጎ፣ ተስፋፉ። ባርያ ዘመድ የለውም። የባርያ ዘር ከሰው ዘር ጋር አይዳበልም። አይቆጠርም። የመውለድም ሆነ የማግባት መብትና ጾታነት የለውም። ቢወልድ ልጅ የለውም። ለአሳዳሪው ተጨማሪ ባርያ አስገኘለት እንጂ፣ ካደገ።

ባርያ ስሙን እንኳ የሚያገኘው አሳዳሪው ሲሰጠው ብቻ ነው። ደረጃው ንብረትነት፣ እንደ እንስሳም መሆኑ ብቻ ነው። አሳዳሪው ቢፈልግ ይሸጠዋል። ለሚወደው ያወርሳል፣ ያውሳል፣ ቢፈልግ መግደልም መብቱ ነው። [43]

በአንጻሩ ግን ባርያ ባይኖር አሳዳሪዎች ቅንጡ ሕይወት መምራት አይችሉም። ስለዚህ ባርያ ለመሰብሰብ እጅግ ብዙ ወታደራዊ ዘመቻዎች እና ጦርነቶች ይካሄዱ ነበር። ባሮች ባርያ የነበሩ ሕዝቦች ሳይሆኑ የጦርነቱ ውጤት የወሰናቸው ናቸው። ይህ ተፈጥሯዊ ሳይሆን ማኅበራዊ መስተጋብር የፈጠረው ክስተት ነው። በቀድም ውሱንነት ወይም በብልጠት ማነስ ተሸናፊ የሆኑ አገራትና ሕዝቦች በሙሉ ወደ ባርነት ይወድቃሉ። [44]

እንድገመው፣ በታሪክ እንዳየነው በጦርነት ወይም በጉልበት የተሸነፉ ሰዎች ባሮች ይሆናሉ እንጂ ባርያ ሆኖ የተፈጠረ የሰው ዘር የለም። የጥንት ፈላስፎች ግን ባርነትን የዘር ልዩነት ነው ከማለት አልፈው፣ መልክዐ ምድራዊ ነው ብለው፣ ራሳቸውንና ሌላውንም አሳመኑ። ባርያ የሆኑ "ሰዎች" ያሉባቸው አካባቢዎችም ተከለሱ።

የባርያ አስተዳደር ሥርዓት ዋነኛው በሰው ልጆች መካከል ልዩነት እንዲፈጠር ያደረገ የፍልስፍና ውሉድ ፖለቲካና አስተዳደር ነው። ሥርዓቱ በሕግ ከተገረሰሰ ብዙ ዘመን ቢሆንውም ተጋባሩም፣ ውጤቱም እስከ ዛሬ ድረስ ዘልቋል። ባርነትን እስካላጠፋነው ድረስ ለልጆቻችንም፣ ገና ለብዙ መጪው ትውልድም ይደርሳል።

አጥፍተነው የለ እንዳትሉኝ፣ መልኩን ቀይሮ በየሠፈራችን ሞልቷል። ሰው የማይፈልገውን እንዲያደርግ፣ ለሌላው መሰል ሰው እንዲያጐብድድ ካደረግነው ባርነት እሹሩፉ እያልነው ነው። በጉልበትና በሹፍት ሰውን፣ በተለያም ሕጻናትና ሴቶችን ከቀያቸው ማሸሽን ስንታገሠው ባርነትን እንዲጐለብት ዕድል እየሰጠን ነው። በባርነት ላይ ቁጣችን እንደሚገባ ስላልተገለጸ፣ ወጣቶችን እስከ መሸጥ የሚደርስ ሹፍት እስከ ዛሬ ይሠራል።

ሕግ ወጥ የሰዎች ዝውውር፣ በተለይም ሴት እንቶቻችን ላይ የሚደርሰው በደል ባርነት አይደለም ካልን ራስን ማታለል ነው። ያለ አቅማቸው ሥራ የተጫነባቸው ጨቅላዎች ምናልባት በየቤቶቻችን አሉ። እንደ ሁላችን ልጆች ትምህርት ቤት ቢሄዱ፣

43 Wiedemann, T. (1981). *Greek and Roman Slavery*; Routlege; London, New York.
44 Cartwrght, M. (2013). Slavery in the Roman World. *World History Encyclopedia*. https://www.worldhistory.org/article/629/slavery-in-the-roman-world/

ሮጠው የልጅነት ጊዜአቸውን ቢቀጨ አይጠሉም። ገንዘብ ስላለን እንደ ባርያ እቤት ውስጥ እንዲቀሩ ገዘናቸው እንጂ።

በአንዳንድ ሥፍራዎች ብድር ሰጥቶ፣ ክፍያው በጉልበት ሥራ መልክ እንዲመለስ ሲደረግ ይስተዋላል። ወይም ልጅ ለአበዳሪው ሥራ እንዲሠራ ይሰማራል፣ ከብት ጠባቂ ወይም እርሻ ውስጥ። የተቸገረ ቤተሰብ ካለም፣ ልጅ በሃብታም ቤት ሥራ እንዲሠራ ይደረግና ለወላጅ ገንዘብ ወይም መሠል ጥቅም ይላካል፣ ወይም ተልኳል ይባላል።

የፍትህ መንደል ካላንገበገበን፣ ከአቅም በላይ የሆነ ሥራ ተሸክሞ በሚውተረተረው ሕጻን ላይ የሚደርሰው አካላዊና ሞራላዊ ግፍ ካላበሳጨን፣ ባርነትን ታቅፈነዋል። ግፍ ያዘለ ሥራ በፍላጎትም ቢሆን ባርነት ቀመስ ነው። እንዲሁም፣ ልጆቻቸውን ያለ ዕድሜአቸው፣ በጨቅላነት ዘመን ሳሉ ጋብቻ እንዲመሠርቱ የሚያስገድዱ ወላጆች ለባርነት ሸጠዋቸዋል።

የቀደሙት የሁሉም ታላላቅ ኅይማኖቶች መሪዎችም፣ በዚያ ዘመን የኖሩ በመሆናቸው የዘረኝነት ፍልስፍና ሰለባ ነበሩ። የጥንት መንፈሳዊ አባቶች፣ ምንልባትም ከእምነቱ አስተምህሮ ውጭ በመውጣት ጥምር፣ ከጊዜው የተስማማ አካኼድን ለመምረጥ ተገደዋል። ለዘመኑ ጉልበተኛ ያጎበደደ እንጂ፣ ጊዜውን የዋጀ አካኼድ እንዳልነበረ እናያለን። በዚህ ጽሑፍ ለአብነት ያህል ጥቂት የክርስቲያን የሥነ መለኮት ምሁራንና አስተማሪዎችን እናነሳለን።

ለምሳሌ:- ቅዱስ አጉስቲን (354–428)[45] ታላቅ የቤተ ክርስቲያን መሪና የሥነ መለኮት ሊቅ ነበር። ሲናገርም:- 'እግዚአብሔር ሰውን ሲፈጥር ባርያ አትሆንም አላለም' ያለው ለነበረው ሥርዓት አጎብብጅ የሆነ የሥነ መለኮት አጥኚዎች ዋና መደበቂያ ነበር። [46] የባርያ አሳዳሪነት በአምላክ ፈቃድ የተገኘ ሥርዓት እንደሆነ ተቆጠረ።

የቅዱስ አጉስቲን የአንድ ጊዜ ንግግር እስከ 19ኛው መቶ ክፍለ ዘመን ድረስ በሁሉም የክርስቲያን ማኅበረሰብ አንቱታን ያገኘ እንደሆን እናውቃለን። ስለዚህ ይህ ዕሳቤው በቤተ ክርስቲያን ላይ ምን ያህል ጫና ሊያሳድር እንደ ቻለ መገመት አያዳግትም። [47] የባርያ አሳዳሪነትን በግልፅ መጽየፍ ያለባት ቤተ ክርስቲያን ነበረች። ከአስተምህሮዋ ጋር በቀጥታ የሚጻረር ነውና። ቤተ ክርስቲያን ላይ ከጥንት ጀምሮ የባርያ አሳዳሪ ሥርዓትን አልተቃወመችም የሚል ወቀሳ የሚነሳው ከዚህ ነው።

ከቅዱስ አጉስቲን የባሱ መምህራንና ቀሳውስትም ነበሩ። ሐዋርያት እንኳ ባሮችን 'ተገዙ' ብለው አስተምረዋል ሲሉ ሸንጣቸውን ገትረው የሚከራከሩ አልታጡም።

---

45 በቅንጽ በዚህ መልክ የተቀመጡ ዓመታት በሙሉ እንደ አውሮፓ አቆጣጠር የተገለጡና ዓ.ም የሚያመለክቱ ናቸው።

46 Zack, N. (2018). The Philsophy of Race. *Palgrave Philsophy Today*. McMillan.

47 Tornau, C. (2019). "Saint Augustine", *The Stanford Encyclopedia of Philosophy* (Summer 2020 Edition), Edward N. Zalta (ed.), https://plato.stanford.edu/archives/sum2020/entries/augustine/

በጥቂቱም ቢሆን እነዚህም ከቅዱስ አገስቲን ወጥ እየጨለፉ ነው። መጽሐፍ ቅዱሳቸውን በትክክል አላዩትም። ቅዱስ ጳውሎስ ስለ ባሮች መገዛት በተናገረበት ሥፍራ 'ነጻ መውጣት የሚችሉ ነጻ ይውጡ' (1ኛ ቆሮ. 7፥21) ያለውን ዘልለውታል። ወይም በፍጹም መጥቀስ አይፈልጉም።

በቅዱስ ጳውሎስ አስተምህሮ ባርነት በጉልበት በሰው ልጅ ላይ የተጫነ አሣር እንጂ ከዘር የመጣ እንዳይደለ ይህ ክፍል ማረጋገጫ ነበር። አናሲሞስ የተባለ ከአሳዳሪው ከፊልሞና ኮብልሎ ቅዱስ ጳውሎስን ባገኘው ጊዜ፤ ወደ ክርስትና ከመለሰው በኋላ የጻፈው ደብዳቤ (ፊልሞና 1) ሐዋርያው ስለ ባርነት ያለውን አመለካከት ቁልጭ አድርጎ ያሳያል።

ፊልሞና የአናሲሞስ አሳዳሪ ነበር። "እንደ ወንድም እንድትቀበለው ማዘዝ እችል ነበር" ይለዋል። የሐዋርያነት ሥልጣኑን በመጠቀም፤ ወንድምነቱን ማስረገጥ አንደሚችል አሳየው። ነገር ግን ስለ ትሕትና "እለምንሃለው" አለው። አናሲሞስ ወንድም እንጂ ባርያ አይሆንም። የሰው ልጅ አንዱ ለሌላው ፈጽሞ እንደ ንብረት መገዛት የለበትም፤ ልዩነት የለምና። መጽሐፍ ቅዱስንም ሆነ ሐዋርያው ጳውሎስን የባርነት ደጋፊ አድርገው፤ እንደ አስረጅ ሊጠቀሙ የሚፈልጉ ስተዋል።

ታዲያ፦ እጅግ የተሻሉ የሚባሉ የጥንት ሥነ መለኮት አስተማሪዎች ስንኳ "ባርያ በመንፈሱ ነጻ ነው" ከማለት አያልፉም። ነጻ አመለካከት፤ የመንፈስ ነጻነት፤ በአጠቃላይ የሰው ልጆችን ነጻነት በስፋት የሚያስተምሩ ጥንታዊ ስቶይኮች እንኳ ሳይቀሩ የባርነት አስፈላጊነትና መፃቅሩን አይቃወሙም ነበር፤ ወይንም ተቀብለውታል። አለያም ፈርተው፤ ቸልተኝነትን መርጠዋል።

ይልቁንም ይህ የፈሪ ግልጠታቸው በባርነት ለሚቸገሩ ተስፋ አስቆራጭ መልዕክት የሚያቀብል ነበር። አንዳንድ ችግሮችን ልንጋፈጣቸው እንጂ ልናናፍጫቸው አንችልም የሚለው ደግም ከዋና ዋና አስተምህሮአቸው ውስጥ ይካተታል።[48] መውደቅ ላይቀር አትፍጨርጨሩ ዓይነት መልዕክት፤ የተሻለ ብለው እንኳን ሲያስቡ፤ መፍትሔአቸው አንቅሮ መትፋትን አያበረታታም። ተቻለህ ኑር የሚል እንድምታ አለው። ነገር ማበላሸት ነው ይላሉ፤ የተንሰራፉ መፃቅር መቃናቀን ይፈራል።

የሚከተለውን እውነተኛ ታሪክ ይመስላል። ከጥቂት ዓመታት በፊት የስፔኑ ባርሴሎና እግር ኳስ ቡድን ተጫዋች የሆነ ዳኒ አልቪስ የተባለ ጥቁር ወጣት ነበር። በጨዋታ ወቅት የማዕዘን ምት ለመምታት እየተዘጋጀ ሳለ፤ ዘረኞች እንደ ዝንጀሮ እየጮኹ ያውኩት ጀመር። ወዲያውም፤ ወደ እርሱ አቅጣጫ የበሰለ ሙዝ ተወረወረ። 'ዝንጀሮ ነህ' ማለታቸው ነው። አልቪስ፤ ዓይኑን ከኳሱ ላይ ሳይነቅል፤ የወረወሩትን ሙዝ አንሥቶ በላ። ሕዝቡም ሳቀ፤ ጨዋታውም ቀጠለ።

48   Baltzly, Dirk, "Stoicism", The Stanford Encyclopedia of Philosophy (Spring 2019 Edition), Edward N. Zalta (ed.), https://plato.stanford.edu/archives/spr2019/entries/stoicism/

የሕዝቡ መፍስ 'ለዘረኝነት ግፉ ቢል ከዚህ በላይ መፍትሔ አይፈለግም' የሚል ዐይነት ነበር። በእርግጥ ዘረኝነትን ንቀን መተው ብቻውን መፍትሔ ይሆናል? የልጁ ልብ ሙሉነት ቢደገፍም በጊዜው የባርሴሎና እግር ኳስ ቡድን ተቀናቃኝ የነበረው የቪላ ሬይል ቡድን የወሰደው እርምጃ የተሻለ መፍትሔ ነው። ሙዝ የወረወረውን የቡድኑ ደጋፊ ለዐድሜ ልክ ከደጋፊነት አገዱት፤ አስወገዱት።

ስለዚህ ዘረኝነትን መታገሥ፤ ከጥንታዊ ክርስቲያን ስቶይኮች 'ባርነትን በጸጋ ተቀበሉ' የሚል ዐይነት አስተምህሮ ጋር ይመሳሰላል። የዛሬ ዘመን ስቶይኮችም ስለ ዘረኝነት ምን ትላላችሁ ቢባሉ፤ የማናመልጠው ዕዳ ስለሆነ መውጫ እናብጅ ይላሉ እንጂ መፍትሔው የጋራ ጥረት እንደሆነ አያስቀምጡም። ለዚህም ዕሳቤያቸው፤ እነ ኔልሰን ማንዴላን፤ እነ ጋንዲን፤ እነ ማርቲን ሉተርን እማኝ ይጠራሉ። ዘረኝነትን በተጸየፉ ጊዜ እንቢተኝነትን መረጡ እንጂ አጋዥ አልጠበቁም ይላሉ። 49

ነገሩ እውነትነት ቢኖረውም፤ አስፈላጊ እንጂ በቂ ምላሽ አይሆንም። በመወቅርና ተቋማት የተጠናከረን አሠራር በመወቅርና ተቋማት የተጐዱ ብቻ ታግለው አይጥሉትም። በልብ ሙሉነት ተነስተው ቢታገሉት እንኳን ረጅም ጊዜ ይወስዳል።

በአንጻሩ ግን የአይሁድ ፈላስፎች አይሁድ ሆኑ ወንድሞችን ባርነት እንደማይደግፉ በጥልቀት ይታወቅ ነበር። ክርስቲያን የሥነ መለኮት ሊቆች ይህን ችላ ብለው፤ በአንድ ኅብረተሰብ መካከል የነበረውን ባርነት ለመቃወም ዐቅም አጡ። የበረታው ደካማውን ባርያ እንደሚያደርገው እያዩ ዝም አሉ። ባርነትን ሲታገሱት፤ ሌላላ አገር በመውረር ወይም በማሸነፍ ባርያ ማፈስ ብቻ ሳይሆን አንዱ ተነሥቶ ጐረቤቱን ባርያ አድርጐ ሊገዛና ሊይዝ እንደሚችልም ፈቅደውለታል ማለት ነው።

ጥንታውያን የጐይማኖት መምህራን፤ የባርያ አሳዳሪ ሥርዓት እስከ ዛሬ ጸንቶ እንዲቆይ በማድረግ፤ ሰፊ አበርክቶት ነበራቸው። 50 የዚህ ጽሑፍ ዓላማ የዘረኝነት ዕንስ ዐሳብ ፖለቲካውን፤ ባህሉን፤ አመራሩን፤ መንፈሳዊ የምንለውንም ምንኛ ጠፍሮ እንደያዘ ማመልከት እንጂ በስም የተጠቀሱ የጐይማኖት አባቶችን ለማሳጣት አይደለም። በቀላል የሚላቀቀንም ነገር አንዳይደለ፤ በዘረኝነት የተገፉ ብቻ ሳይሆን ኅብረተሰቡ በሞላ ተነሥቶ ሊቃወመው እንደሚገባ ማሳየት ነው።

ከቀደሙት አባቶች ውስጥ በጣም ታዋቂ የሥነ መለኮት ሰው ኢጣሊያዊው ቶማስ አኩዊናስም (1224–1274) ለውጥ ባረገዘው የ13ኛው ክፍለ ዘመን ጭምር የአርስቶትልን ዐይነት እምነት ያራምድ ነበር። 51 በእርሱ ትምህርት መሠረት፤ ባል

49 Thermitus, F. (2021). A Stoic Approach to Racism. Philosphy Now: *A Magazine of Ideas.* Volume 144, June/July 2021

50 Kirchschlaeger, P. G. (2016). Slavery And Early Christianity – A Reflection from a Human Rights Perspective. *Acta Theologica* 2016 Suppl 23: 66-93

51 Chenu, M. (2021). St. Thomas Aquinas: Italian Christian theologian and philosopher. *Encyclopedia Beritanninca.* https://www.britannica.com/biography/Saint-Thomas-Aquinas

ከሚስት ይበልጣል፤ አባትም ከልጅ። አኩዊናስ ይህን ያስተማረበት ጊዜ የካቶሊክ ቤተ ክርስቲያንም ሆነ አውሮፓ በአጠቃላይ የለውጥ ሽታ ውስጥ ያሉበት ጊዜ ስለ ነበር የበለጠ ያሳጣል።

የእሥራኤል ሕዝብ በግብፅ ምድር ባርያ በነበሩበት 430 ዓመታት ውስጥ ይደርስባቸው የነበረ መከራ ለዚህ አስረጂ ነው። ጥንታዊት ግብፅም ኃያማኖት ነበራት። ከእሥራኤል ሴቶች የሚወለዱ ወንድ ልጆች ግን በአዋላጆቻቸው እንዲገደሉ መንግሥታዊ አዋጅ ከማውጣት አልተቆጠቡም (ዘፀአት 1 እና 2)። ግፍን የሚቆጥር አምላክ እግዚአብሔር ታደገው እንጂ፣ የእሥራኤል ነጻነት መሪ የነበረው ሙሴም እንደማንኛውም አይሁዳዊ ሕጻን ከጭቃ ጋር ይረገጥ ነበር።

ቶማስ አኩዊናስ "ተራማጅ" ከሚባሉት ሊቃውንት ይመደባል። በለውጥ ዘመን እንደ መጣ የሥነ መለኮት ሊቅ አዲስ ዐሳብ ይጠበቅበት ነበር። ግና ለአኩዊናስ ባርያና ጌታውን "ሰው" ብሎ እኩል ማስቀመጥ ቀርቶ ማዳዳር እንኳን አይቻልም። እርሱም እንደ ስቶይኮች ማንኛውም ሰው፣ ባርያም ቢሆን የማምለክ ነጻነት ቢኖረው ከመደገፍ፣ ቢቻል የመብላት፣ የመጠጣት፣ የማግባትና የመውለድም ነጻነት ቢሰጠው እንደማይጠላ ከመጻፍ አልዘለለም። ባርነትን የመቃወም ዐቅም አልነበረውምና።[52]

ዘመናይ

የባርያ አሳዳሪነት ሥርዓት ከባርያ አሳዳሪነት ዘመን አልፎ እስክ ዛሬ ድረስ ያስችገረ የልዩነት መፈልፈያ ነው። የሰው ልጅ በወገኑ ላይ ምን ያህል መጨከን እንደሚችል አስረጂ ነው። በተለይ በቅኝ አገዛዝ ወቅት የባርያ ጉልበት መጠቀም አማራጭ እንደሌለው ሆኖ ተወስዷል። በጉልታዊ (የመሬት ከበርቴ) ሥርዓትም ሆነ በኢንዱስትሪ አብዮት ወቅት እንዲጠፋ ፈለገ አልነበረም።

እና ከላይ እንዳየነው፤ የኃይማኖት ሊቃውንትም ሳይቀሩ እንደ ቶማስ አኩዊናስ 'እጅግ የተሻሉ' የተባሉትም ጭምር ባርነትን ፈት ለፈት አልተቃወሙም። ከዚህ ይልቅ 'ይህ ባይሆን ይመረጥ ነበር' በማለት ተገድበዋል። ይሁን እንጂ፣ ከጥንታውያን ፈላስፎች ወደ ዘመናይ ዕሳቤዎች ለመሻገት መንደርደሪያ የሆኑትም ክርስቲያን ሊቃውንት ናቸው የሚያሳኝ ብዙ ምክንያት አለ።

ምሳሌ:- ከዘመናይ አስተሳሰብ ውስጥ ቀዳሚውን ያነሣው እንግሊዛዊው ክርስቲያናዊ ፈላስፋ ጆን ሎክ (1632–1704) ነው። ይህ ሰው የነጻነት ዐሳቤ አባት እንደሆን ይነገራል። ከጊዜው ቀደም ያለ አስተሳሰብ ያራምድ ነበር። አንድ ነጋ መንግሥት የአገሩ ሕዝቦች ለመተዳደር ፈቃደኛ እስክ ሆኑ ድረስ ነጻነትን ከገደበ ራሱ ነጻ አይደለም ይል ነበር።

---

52 Cornish, P. J. (2011). Marriage, Slavery, and Natural Rights in the Political Thought of Aquinas. *The Review of Politics*; Vol. 60; No. 3; pp. 545-56

በሎክ አስተሳሰብ ነጻነት ፍፁማዊ መብት ሲሆን ሦስት መሠረታዊ መብቶችን ያጠቃልላል፤ በሕይወት የመኖር፣ በነጻነት የመንቀሳቀስና የመናገር፣ እንዲሁም ርስት የማግኘት። ይህን መሰል ነጻነት የሚፈልግና ያለው ሰው እነዚህን መብቶች በሚገድብ መንግሥትም ሆነ ሌላ አካል ላይ ቢያምፅ ፍትሐዊ ዓመፅ ይሆናል። ፍጹም፣ ከፍጥረታችን ጋር የሚያያዙ መብቶች ናቸው ብሎ ያምናል።

ከዚህ ዕሳቤው የተነሣ "በአገር ልጅ ባሮች" ላይ የሚደርሰው ግፍ ይህን የ17ኛው ክፍለ ዘመን ፈላስፋ እጅግ ያስቆጣውና ያሳዝነው ነበር። ይህ ሰው ሁለት ዐይነት የባርያ አሳዳሪነት አለ ብሎ ያምናል። አንዱ ሕጋዊና ከዚህ የተነሣ የሚደገፍ ሲሆን ሌላው ሕገ ወጥ ነው።

ሕጋዊ የሆነው የባርያ አሳዳሪነት፣ በተለይ በጦርነት ተሸንፈው የተያዙ ወይም የተጋዙ ሰዎችን እንደ ባርያ፣ እንደ እንስሳም ቢሆን ማሳደር ነው፣ ይህ ሕጋዊ ነው፣ ተዋግተው ተሸንፈዋል። ሕገ ወጥ የባርያ አሳዳሪነት በአገሩ ሕግ ለመተዳደር ፈቃደኛ የሆኑትን በተመሳሳይ መልክ መያዝ ነው።

በሎክ ዕይታ የአንድ አገር ሰዎች በተለያየ ምክንያት ዐቅም ሲያጡ፣ ጉልበታቸውን በመሸጥ ለብዝበዛ ሊዳረጉ ይችላሉ። የአገሬው ሰው ግን መበዝበዣቸው ባይቀር እንኳ ነጻነታቸው መገፈፍ እንደ ሌለበት ይናገር ነበር። ጉልበት መሸጥ ችግር የለውም፣ በባላቤቱ ፍላጎት፣ የአገሩን ሰዎች ፍላጎት ተጭኖ፣ ነጻነት ነስቶ፣ ልክ እንደ ተማረኩ ባሮች መግዛት ግን ፈጽሞ ልክ አይደለም። [53]

ሎክ፣ የባርያ አሳዳሪነት ሥርዓት ክፋቱ በተገለጠ መጠን ለመቃወም ዐቅም ያጣውም ያለ ምክንያት አልነበረም። ጊዜው ከአፍሪካና ከሌሎችም አገራት እጅግ ብዙ ሰዎች በባርያ ፍንገላና ንግድ አማካይነት የሚሸጡበት ነበር። የባርያ ንግድ ታላቅና አስፈሪ ጉልበት ያለው "ሥራ" ነበር። ይህን ንግድ መቃወም ተራራን የመግፋት ያህል ነው።

ይህ ብቻ አይደለም፣ ባሮች ተሸጠው የሚሰማሩት በአዲሱ ክፍለ ዓለም በተለይም በሰሜንና ደቡብ አሜሪካ እርሻዎች ነበር። ናታን ናን እንደጻፈው፦ ከአፍሪካ የተጋዙ እስከ 15 ሚሊዮን የሚደርሱ ጥቁሮች[54] አፍሪካ እንድትራቆት ምክንያት ሲሆኑ፣ አሜሪካንንና አውሮፓን ዛሬ ለደረሱበት የዕድገት ደረጃ አብቅተዋቸዋል። ሎክ ደግሞ የባርያ ንግድ ከሚያካሄዱ ኩባንያዎች በአንዱ የአክስዮን ድርሻ ነበረው። "ሕጋዊ" ያለው ባርነት ለእርሱም የሀብት ምንጭ ኖሯል።

---

53 Uzgalis, W. (2017). John Locke, Racism, Slavery, and Indian Lands. *The Oxford Handbook of Philosophy and Race* (ed. Naomi Zack), Oxford,

54 Nunn, N. (2008). The Long-Term Effects of Africa's Slave Trades. *The Quarterly Journal of Economics*. February 2008. https://scholar.harvard.edu/files/nunn/files/empirical_slavery.pdf

አፍሪካውያን የተጋዙት ግን በሙሉ በጦርነት ተሸንፈው አልነበረም። ከጦርነት ጋር በብዙ ተንኰልና የማታለል ስልት፣ በፍንገላ ... ወዘተ የተሰበሰቡ ናቸው። በጦርነት ተገዝተውም ቢሆን ድንበር አቋርጠው ከተጓዙ በኋላ ወደ አገራቸው የመመለስ ዕድል አልነበራቸውም። በተሸጡበት አገር ሕግ መገዛት የውዴታ ግዴታቸው ነበር።

የጆን ሎክ አስተምህሮት ስነመለከት የባርያ አሳዳሪ ሥርዓት በባርነት ስንኪ የሚያዳዳ መሆኑን እንገነዘባለን። በጦርነት የተጋዙ እንደ እንስሳ ይታዩ፣ የአገር ውስጥ ባሮች ጥቂቱ ነጻነት ይኑራቸው የሚል ነበር። ከማኅበራዊ ኑሮ ዕገገት ጋር የሰውም አስተሳሰብ እየተቀየረ ሲሄድ ቀላል ይመስላል። በጊዜው ግን ባርያ ሰው ሳይሆን እንስሳ ነው የሚለው አመለካከት አገር የሚተዳደርበት አስተሳሰብ ነበር።

ያም ሆኖ ሎክ ተራማጅ ተብሏል። የግሉ ነገር ቢጎተትተውም አንድ ሰው ሌላ መሰል ወንድሙን ባርያ ማድረግ ተጠያቂነት እንዳለው አስተውሏል። ሁለቱ እየተምታታበት ቢሆን ባሮች እንደ ነጻ ሰው እንኪ ባይሆን የመብላት፣ የመጠጣት፣ የማገባት፣ ልጆችንም የማፍራት ነጻነት ሊያገኙ ይገባል ሲል በጽኑ ተከራክሯል።

ባርኔትን ፈጽሞ ባያወግዘውም፣ ሎክ የዘረኝነትን ዕሳቤ ሆነ ብሎ ያስተናገደ አይመስልም። ሳያስበው ፈጥሮት እንዳይሆን የሚሉ ግን አሉ። ምክንያቱም፣ አንድም ለባሮች ነጻነት ይከራከር የነበረው እነዚህ ሰዎች ከሚደርስባቸው መከራ የተነሣ አንድ ቀን ተነስተው ያመሩ እንደሆን አለቀልን ሲል ይደፍ ስለነበር ነው። ተባብረው መብታቸውን መጠየቅ ከጀመሩ ፖለቲካ መሆኑ አይደል? ሎክ በእርግጥ ፈርቶ ነበር።

ሕጋዊ ከሆነ ፍርጓትን ምን አመጣው? ይህ የክፍፍል ምልክታ ውስጡ እንዳለ ያመላክታል። "እኛ" እና "እንሱ" በማለት ሲከፍል ልቡ ምን ብላው ይሆን? በባርያ አሳዳሪ ነጮች፣ በአብዛኛው እንግሊዛውያንና በባሮች፣ በአብዛኛው ጥቁር አፍሪካውያንና አሜሪካዊ ህንዶች መካከል ልዩነት እንዳለ በሰውር ተናግሮ እንዳይሆን የሚሉም አሉ። [55]

ያም ሆነ ይህ፣ ሎክ የዘመናይ አመለካከት ፈር ቀዳጅ ከሚባሉት ውስጥ እንደሚካተት ይታመናል። የእርሱ ሁለት ዐይነት ባርነት በሕዳሴው ዘመን የተሥነዘሩ የዘር ፍልስፍናዎችን ሁሉ የቃኘ አመለካከት ሆነ። በዚያን ጊዜ የተነሡ ፈላስፎችም የባርነት ሕልውና የተቀበሉ እንጂ ከእንርሱ ውስጥ ባርነት ባይኖር ብሎ የሚጽፍ፣ የሚያስተምር አልተገኘም።

ይልቅ የጆን ሎክ አመለካከት ለቀኝ ገዥነትም ፈር ቀዳጅ አመለካከት ነው ማለት ይቻላል። አውሮፓ በዚያን ጊዜ ከባርያ ማጋዝ ወደ ቅኝ አገዛዝ እያዘነበለች ነበር። አውሮፓውያን ቅኝ ለመግዛት በሚሄዱበት አገር፣ ሰዎችን እንደ ባርያ ሳይሆን እንደ ተገገር፣ ግን መጠኛ ነጻነት ያላቸው አድርጎ መያዝ እንደሚገባ ፍንጭ የሰጠ ዕሳቤ ነውና። "ሕጋዊ" ነው ብሎት የለ?

55   Zack, N. (2018). The Philsophy of Race. Palgrave Philsophy Today. McMillan.

አመለካከቱ ፈርጀ ብዙ ነበር፤ በዚህ ብቻ አላበቃም። ከሎጂክ በኋላ ሕጋዊ ባርነትን አስታክሎ ሰዎችን ሁሉ በፍጥረት፤ ሁለት መልክ ሊይዙ እንደሚችሉ በሰፈው መጽፍ ተጀመረ። ከእርሱ ተነሥተው እጅግ ተሰሚነት ያላቸው ጉምቱ የሕዳሴ ዘመን ፈላስፎች እነ ሄግል፤ ካንት፤ ሚልና ኒቼ የዘር ልዩነት ዕሳቤን በማይነቃነቅ መሠረት አቆሙት።[56]

በሀገረ ብሪታኒያ ታዋቂ ከሆኑት ታላላቅ ፈላስፎች ውስጥ የሚመደበው ዴቪድ ሂዩም (1711–1776) የተወለደው ከእንድ ሃብታም የስኮትላንድ ቤተሰብ ነበር።[57] ሃብትና ድኽነትም በሰዎች ውስጥ የዘር ልዩነት መንሥኤ ሊሆን? እንዴታ! ለሂዩም ድኽነት የሥነ ምግባር መላሸቅ ውጤት ነው። ሥነ ምግባር ደግሞ ዘርን ይቆራኛል።

እንደ ሂዩም እምነት፤ በኔጭሮችና በጥቁሮች ወይም በህንዶች መካከል ያለው ልዩነት የመልክና ቁመና ብቻ አይደለም። ከነጮች በበለጠ በጥቁርና ህንድ "ዘሮች" ውስጥ ሲወርድ ሲዋረድ የመጣ የሥነ ምግባር ብልሽት አለ። 'ሲወርድ ሲዋረድ' ማለት በዘር ይተላለፋል ማለት ነው።

ሂዩም በዚህ አያቆምም። በእርሱ አመለካከት መሠረት፤ ምግባረ ብልሹዎችን ሥርዓት ማስያዝ የሌሎች ኃላፊነት ነው። ሥነ ምግባር ዐልባውን ረግጦ መግዛት፤ አገራቸውንም "ማቅናት፤" እና ማሰልጠን ፍትሐዊ ነው።[58] ፍትሐዊ የሆነ ደግሞ አይደገፋል እንጂ።

በሌላ በኩል፤ ጥቁሮች ምክንያታዊነት የማይታይባቸው፤ የኑሮን ጣዕም የማያውቁ ስለሆኑ በእርሱ ላይ የሥነ ሰብዕ (አንትሮፖሎጂ) ጥናት[59] ማድረግ ራሱ ሥራ መፍታት ነው ብሎ የሚያስበው የሥነ ሰብዕ እና የመልክዐ ምድሩ ሊቅ ኢማኑኤል ካንት (1724–1804) ነው። ካንት አንቱ የተባለ ፈላስፋ ነው። በቀድሞ የጀርመን ግዛት፤ (የአሁን ሩሲያ) ውስጥ የተወለደ።

ምናልባትም ግንባር ቀደም አግላይ ፈላስፋ ነው። የዘር ልዩነትን ፍልስፍና ወደ መልክዐ ምድራዊ ዘረኝነት ለመጀመሪያ ጊዜ ያሳደገና የቀረጸ ቢባል ያስኬዳል። ከእርሱ ዕሳቤ ጫና የተነሣ እስከ ዛሬም ድረስ የአፍሪካ አሕጉርና ሕዝቦቿ፤ ምናልባት የዓለም ሥልጣኔ መሠረት ሆነው ሳለ በቂ የሥነ ሰብዕ ጥናት አልተደረገባትም።[60]

---

56 Zack, N. (2018). The Philsophy of Race. Palgrave Philsophy Today. McMillan.

57 Morris, W. E. and Charlotte R. B. (2021), "David Hume", *The Stanford Encyclopedia of Philosophy* (Spring 2021 Edition), Edward N. Zalta (ed.), https://plato.stanford.edu/archives/spr2021/entries/hume/

58 Immerwahr, I. (1992) Hume's Revised Racism. *Journal of the History of Ideas*; Vol. 53; No. 3 (July – Sept 1992).

59 አንትሮፖሎጂ የሚለውን እንዳወልል ነው፤

60 Rohlf, M. (2021). "Immanuel Kant", *The Stanford Encyclopedia of Philosophy* (Fall 2020 Edition), Edward N. Zalta (ed.), https://plato.stanford.edu/archives/fall2020/entries/kant/

ጥቄት በኢትዮጵያ ሰሜናዊ፤ በተለይም በአፋር አካባቢ፤ በታንዛኒያ፤ በደቡብ አፍሪካና በአንዳንድ የምዕራብ አፍሪካ አገራት ከስንት አንዴ ከሚደረጉ የቅሪተ አካል ቁፋሮዎች በቀር የአፍሪካውያን ማኅበራዊ ኑሮ ትሩፋት አልተጠናም። ስለ አፍሪካ ሲታሰብ "ሰው" የሚባለው ነገር ወዲያው ሁለተኛ ደረጃ ይይዛል። መልክዐ ምድሩ፤ ዕጽዋት አራዊቱ፤ ቀዳሚ ትኩረት ይሰጣቸዋል።

ሁሉም ስለ አፍሪካዊው ሰው ሳይሆን ስለ ወንዝ፤ ስለ እንስሳቱና ዕጽዋቱ ማጥናቱ የሚቀናው ከዚህ የካንት አመለካከት ተጽዕኖ የተነሣ ነው። ኢማኑኤል ካንት ከዚህም የተለየ፤ ተጨማሪ ተጽዕኖ የፈጠረ ፈላስፋ ነው። የሰዎች የቆዳ ቀለም ከዘር ልዩነት ጋር ጥብቅ ቁርኝት እንዳለው ያምናል። ምክንያቱም፤ ሰዎችን ነጭ፤ ብጫ፤ መዳብ ቀይ፤ ድቅልና ጥቁር ብሎ በመከፋፈልም ካንት የመጀመሪያው ሰው ነው። [61]

እየባሰ የሄደውን የዘረኝነት አመለካከት እጅግ ጽንፍ ያስያዘው ደግሞ ታላቁ ጀርመናዊ ፈላስፋ ሄግል (1770–1843) ነው። [62] ሄግል ፍልስፍናዊ አመክኒዮው ወደ አርስቶትል ያደላል። በባርያ ንግድና ፍንገላ መከራ የበላውን የአፍሪካ አሕጉር "ታሪክ" ሲጽፍ፤ ሆነ ብሎ፤ የባርያ ንግዱ ሥርዓት ትክክለኛ እና ፍትሐዊ መሆኑን ለማስረዳት ዕስቦ ነበር የጻፈው።

አፍሪካ፤ ሕዝቦቿም፤ ምድሩም ጥቁር፤ ለዓለም ሥልጣኔ ምንም ያላበረከተች ሲል አትታአል። በሄግል አመለካከት፤ አፍሪካውያን የሥነ ፍጥረት ልዩነት በፈጠረው ምክንያት ሕዝቦቿ እንጭጭ ፣ ናቸው። የአፍሪካዊ ዘር ጭሮርቃነት የሥልጣኔና የባሕል ኋላ ቀርነት መሠረት ነው ሲል ስለ ዘር ልዩነት ፍፁማዊነት ያመነበትን አመለካከት ያለ መታከት ያራመደ ፈላስፋ ነው።

እንደ ሄግልና ከእርሱ በኋላ እንደ ተነሱት ሌሎች ጸሐፍት አባባል አፍሪካ በመልክዐ ምድር ከሌላው ዓለም የተገለለች ናት። በዚህ ምክንያት ነዋሪዎቿም ከሰው በታች ሆነው እንዲቀሩ የተገደዱ፤ ማደግ የማይችሉ፤ ጨቅላዎች ናቸው። ስለዚህ እንደዚያው ልንቀጥራቸው ያስፈልጋል የሚል አመለካከት ነበራቸው።

በእርሱ አስተሳሰብ፤ አፍሪካውያን በራሳቸው መሥልጠን አይችሉም። ስለሆነም፤ በተቻለ መጠን ወደ ዕድገት እንዲደርሱ ለማገዝ እየተጋዙ ባርያ ቢሆኑ ይመረጣል። ይህን ደብቀው ሳይሆን ያለ ጎፍረት ይናገሩ። አፍሪካን ገድለው፤ ሕዝቦቿን ካንገላቱ በኋላ፤ ይህ እርምጃ ትክክለኛ እንደሆነ ለማስረዳት 'ቀድሞም ሰው አልነበሩም፤ እንስሳ ነበሩ እንጂ' አሉ።

61 Kleingeld, P. (2019). On Dealing with Kant's Sexism and Racism. *SGIR Review* 2, no. 2, 3-22, 2019

62 Brooks, T. (2021). "Hegel's Social and Political Philosophy", *The Stanford Encyclopedia of Philosophy* (Summer 2021 Edition), Edward N. Zalta (ed.), https://plato.stanford.edu/archives/sum2021/entries/hegel-social-political/

ባርያ አሳዳሪዎችና ቅኝ ገዢዎች እንዲህ ሲሉ አያፍሩም። የዘረኝነት ጎፋረታቸውን
መልካም እንዳደረጉ ይመጻደቁበታል። ቅኝ እገዙ፣ አገር ለማቅናት፣ ሕዝቡንም ለማዘመን
እንደሚመጡ ይናገራሉ። ሄግል ጎፋረት ቢስ ዘረኛ የሚሆነው ለዚህ እያደገ ለመጣው
የዘረኝነት ዕሳቤ የ"ታሪክ" ምሕዳር በማሰቀመጥ ቀዳሚው ሰው በመሆኑ ነው። [63]

ዘረኝነት 'ተራማጅ' የተባሉ ፈላስፎችንም ያንገዳገደ ጉዳይ ነው። ዛሬ እንኳን
የብዙዎችን ክብር ሲሸልት አይታወቅበትም፣ እየተመጻደቁ ይወርዳሉ፣ እየሸፋፈኑም
ይገለጥባቸዋል። ከስኮቲሽ ወላጆቹ ለንደን ተወልዶ ያደገው እንግሊዛዊው ጆን ስቱዋርት
ሚል (1806– 1873)[64] እያከበርናቸው ከሚወርዱብን ፈላስፎች አንዱ እንደሆነ
አሜሪካዊው ፈላስፋና ታሪክ ጸሓፊ ኤድዋርድ ዛልታ ያትታል።

ይህ ሰው፣ ተራማጅ ከሚባሉ ታላላቅ ፈላስፎች መካከል የሚመደብ ነበር።
የዕሳብና የመናገር ነጻነትን በማቀንቀን ቀዳሚና ታዋቂም ነው። እጅግ ዘነጋኝ የሚባሉ
ዕሳቦችን ሳይቀር መታገስ አለብን ባይ ነው። ከዕሳብ ነጻነት በተጨማሪ፣ ስለ ሴቶች
እኩልነትም በማሳሰብ የዘረኝነት ዕሳቤ አላቸው ከተባሉ ፈላስፎች ይልቅ የመጠቀ
የእኩልነት ዕሳብ ያመነጨ ሰው ነው።

ሰው ሁሉ ሌላውን እስካልጎዳ ድረስ ዕሳቡን መናገርና መግለጥ መብቱ ነው ይል
ነበር። ይህ የእርሱ ዕሳብ በዘመናችን የፖለቲካ አስተሳሰብ የነጻ ሥፍራ የያዘ ነው።
"ሰብዓዊ መብት" ከሚባሉት አንደኛውን በትክክል ያቀነበረ ሰው ነው። የጆን ስቲዋርት
ሚል የነጻነት ቅንብር በተባበሩት መንግሥታትና በሌሎችም ዓለም አቀፍ የዕሳብ እና
የጎሊና ነጻነት አቀንቃኝ ድርጅቶች ስፈ ሥፍራ የተሰጠው ነው።

ይሁን እንጂ፣ እጅግ የገዘፈው የዘረኝነት ዕሳቤ ሚልንም ጠልፎ ጣለው። ነጻነትን
አጥብቆ እንዳይ ሳይሆን መብቱ የሚገባቸውን ሲዘረዝር ተንተባተበ። ነጻት የሚገባቸው
በዕሳባቸውና በምግባራቸው ያደጉ ሰዎች ናቸው ሲል። ስለዚህ የራሱን መልካም አቋም
ይዞ መቀጠል አልተቻለውም። ልክ እንደ ሄግል 'ታዳጊ' የሰው ዘር እንዳለ በማውሳቱ
ከዘረኞች ጉራ አሳምሮ ይሰደራል። [65]

ሚል ተራ ሰው አልነበረም። እንደ አባቱ በህንድ አገር የታላቋ ብሪታኒያን የቅኝ
ግዛት ጥቅም አስከባሪ ኩባንያ መሪ ነበር። የቅኝ ግዛት አስተዳዳር፣ የቤተሰብ ታሪክና
የድርጅት መሪነት በልቡ ከተተከለው የሰው ልጆች ነጻነት ፍላጎት ጋር እያታገበት

63 Moellendorf, D. (1992). Racism And Rationality in Hegel's Philosophy of Subjective Spirit.
    History of Political Thought vol. 13, No, 2; Summer 1992.

64 Macleod, C. (2021). "John Stuart Mill", *The Stanford Encyclopedia of Philosophy* (Summer
    2020 Edition), Edward N. Zalta (ed.), https://plato.stanford.edu/archives/sum2020/entries/
    mill/

65 Tunick, M. (2006). Tolerant Imperialism: John Stuart Mill's Defense of British Rule in India.
    The Review of Politics 68 (2006), 1 –26.

የጸፈ ሊቅ ነበር። ምን ያህል እንደ ተጠፈረ ስለሚረዱ ተቺዎች ያዝኑለታል። [66] ሚል፤ ነጻነትን በአፉ ሰበከው፤ በተግባር ገደለው።

የቀደሙት የፖለቲካዊ ፍልስፍና አባቶች ዘረኝነታቸው "የባሰ አታምጣ" ያሰኛል። በእርግጥ የባሰ አለና፦ ጭራሽ ከባሰባቸው መካከል ደግሞ ቤተ ክርስቲያንን የታከኩ መኖራቸው! ለምሳሌ በጀርመን ልፕሲሽ ተወልዶ ያደገው የሉተራዊ ኒቼ (1844–1900)[67] የዘር ፅንሰ ዐሳብ፤ ከሰው ኅብል ፍላጐት ጣጣ ለመገላገል፤ ባርያ ከማሳደር ይልቅ ምርጥ ዘር ማባዛት አለብን የሚል ነበር።

ነጭ፤ አውሮፓዊ፤ ንዱ-ህ፤ ባለ ቢጫና ቀጥተኛ ጸጉር ሰዎችን መርጠን እያባዛን፤ ምድሪቱን መሙላት አለብን ሲል ጽፏል። ራስን ለመቻል (በጉልበት ፍላጐት) መሆኑ ነው። ምንልባትም፤ በልቡ ሌላውን እየጠረስን፤ የሚልም ጭማሪ ኖሮ ይሆን? እርሱ በቀጥታ እንደዚያ ባይልም፤ ከነጭ ውጭ ሌላው እያለቀ ቢሄድ ደንታ እንደማይሰጠው መገንዘብ አያዳግትም።

ከጥቂት ዓመታት በኋላ የተውልድ አገሩ የጀርመን ጀብደኞች፤ ጀርመናዊ ዝርያ የሌላቸውን ሁሉ መጨረስ አለብን የሚል ዕሳቤ አንግበው ተነስተው እንደ ነበር ይታወቃል። ሂትለር ኒቼን ተውሶ እንደሆን የሚያስብል ነገር አለና። በናዚ ዘመን አይሁድና ጂፕሲ ወይም ሮማ የሚባሉ አውሮፓዊ ዘላን ጐሣዎች ከጀርመን ምድር እንዲጠፉ ተፈለገ። አንድ ፍልስፍና ሲወራ ቀላል ነው፤ መዘዙ ግን ብዙ። ወደ ሰው አዕምሮ ሲሠርግ የሚፈጥረውን ምላሽ መቆጣጠር አዳጋች ነው።

ኒቼ ራሱ በአይሁድ ላይ ክፉ ዕሳቤ አልነበረውም። አይሁድን ተመቅኝቶ ስለ መጻፍም አይታወቅም። ነገር ግን፤ የአውሮፓውያን የበላይነት ዕሳቤው፤ ምርጥና ሻለ ያለ የሰው ዘር የመፍጠር ውጥኑ፤ በምድሪቱ ላይ በሰው ዕርዳታም ቢሆን ምርጥ ዘር እያሸነፈ መሄድ እንዳለበት መጻፉ የዘርጓል ቁንጮ ያደርገዋል። በአይሁድ ላይ በናዚ ጀርመን አማካይነት ለነደደው እሳት ቀጥተኛ ተጠያቂ።

በእርግጥ፤ የናዚ መንግሥት ከመምጣቱም በፊት አውሮፓዊ ምርጥና ገናና ዘር የመፍጠር ውጥን ያለ ምንም መሸማቀቅ በአደባባይ ይወጣ ነበር። ኒቼ ከሞተ በኋላ ታናሽ እኅቱ የእርሱን ሥራዎች ሰብስባ በመጽሐፍ መልክ አሳተመች። በመጽሐፉ፦ "የምርጥ ዘር" ዕሳቤው እንዲነጋ ጥራለች። የዘር ምልመላና ጥራት ትኩረት እንዲሰጠው አቀነባብራለች።

66 Hansson, S. O. (2022). John Stuart Mill and the Conflicts of Equality. *Journal of Ethics.* Volume 26, pages 433–453 (2022). https://link.springer.com/article/10.1007/s10892-022-09393-7

67 Anderson, R. Lanier, "Friedrich Nietzsche", *The Stanford Encyclopedia of Philosophy* (Winter 2021 Edition), Edward N. Zalta (ed.), https://plato.stanford.edu/archives/win2021/entries/nietzsche/

ናዚዎችም የአይሁድን ዕልቂት ለመቆመር በብዛት ይጠቅሱ የነበሩት የእርሱን ፍልስፍና እንደ ነበር በሰፊው ይታመናል። [68] በዐሳብ ብቻም አልተውም፤ የፖለቲካቸው አንኳር አደረጉት። በሁለተኛው የዓለም ጦርነት መባቻና ማግሥት ከስድስት ሚሊዮን በላይ አይሁዶች፤ ምናልባትም እስከ ግማሽ ሚሊዮን የሚደርሱ ሮማዎች በዘረኝነት መርዝ ያለ ርህራሄ በመጨፍጨፍ አልቀዋል።

ይህን ክፍል ከመቋጨታችንና ያለንበትን ዘመን ዝብርቅርቅ ዐይታ ከማጋራታችን በፊት በባርያ አሳዳሪነት እና በዘረኝነት ላይ የቤተ ክርስቲያን ሚና ጥቂት እናንሳ፡ ቀደም ሲል የቤተ ክርስቲያን አባቶች ለዘር ፍልስፍና ዕድገት ፈር ቀዳጅ ከሚባሉ ውስጥ እንደ ነበሩ አንስተናል። ይህን ወሰዓ ማለዘብ ይኖርብናል። ምክንያቱም፤ ባርነትንም ሆነ ዘረኝነትን አጥብቀው ከተቃወሙትም ቀዳሚዉን ሥፍራ የሚወስዱት የቤተ ክርስቲያን አባቶች ናቸው።

በ18ኛው መቶ ምዕተ ዓመት አጋማሽ አካባቢ አብዛኛው ክርስቲያን ማኅበረሰብ የባርያ አሳዳሪነትን የሕይወት እውነታ፤ ወይም የኑሮ አካል አድርጎ ተቀብሎ ነበር። በዚህ መካከል ተቃውሞ ማሰማት ዋጋ ያስከፍላል። ቅሬታ ለማሰማት ከበረቱ መካከል ጥቂት የአሜሪካን ቤተ ክርስቲያን መሪዎች ነበሩ፤ ትኩረታቸው ግን በሥርዓቱ ላይ አልነበረም።

ሙግታቸው በባሮች ላይ የሚደረገውን ከልክ ያለፈ የጭከናና አያያዝ በመቃወም ነበር። ምክንያቱም፤ ሥርዓቱ የሚወገድ አልመሰላቸውም ነበር። ስለዚህ ያደርጉት የነበረው፤ በስብከት ወይንም በንግግር አስታክኮ ወንድሞችን መውቀስ ብቻ ነበር። "እኛ ልክ ዮሴፍን ለሚሰፖታሚያ ነጋዴዎች እንደ ሸጡ ወንድማማቾች ነን" የሚል ዐይነት ስብከት።

መጽሐፍ ቅዱስ "ለሁሉም ነገር ጊዜ አለው፤ ከሰማይ በታች ለሚከናነወነው ለማንኛውም ነገር ወቅት አለው" (መክብብ 3÷1) ይላል። አንዳንድ ጊዜ በምድር ላይ በሚከናወኑ ነገሮች ውስጥ ጽዋው የሚሞላበት ጊዜ አለ፤ በቃ የሚባልበት። ማለትም ተፈጥሮ ራስዋን የምታርምበት ወቅት አለ። አንዳንድ ጊዜ መሸከም አልቻልም የምትልበት ቀን አላት። አንድ የተፈጥሮ አካል በሌላው ላይ ደርሶ ግፍና ጭቆና ሲያበዛ ለትዕቢተኛ ማዕበል ገደብ ማበጀትን ትችልበታለች።

ሰውም በወንድሙ ላይ ያሻውን ሲያደርግ፤ ግፍና ጭቆና ከሰው ልብ ዘልቆ ምድርን ሲሞላት፤ ተፈጥሮ ዝም እንድትል ተፈጥሮዋ ራሱ አይፈቅድም። የባርያ አስተዳደርም ሥርዓት ይህ ደረሰበት ማለት ይቻላል። ግፍ ሞልቶ የፈሰሰበት ዘመን ላይ ደርሶ ነበር። ከየአቅጣጫው የሚሰማው ጩኸት ሥርዓቱ መቀጠል እንደማይችል

አመላካች ነበር። ጽዋው ሞላ። በንዳም፣ በአደባባይም ባርነትን እንደ ነበረ ተሸክሞ የሚዘልቅ ጫንቃ እየታጣ መጣ።

ቀስ በቀስ፣ ከንግግር ያለፈ ነገር ይዘው፣ ደፍረው፣ ቀዳሚ ሆነው፣ ብቅ ያሉ የቤተ ክርስቲያን አባቶች ተከሰቱ። በሥርዓቱ ላይ ተቃውሞ የተነሣው ከሥስት አቅጣጫ ነበር። የመጀመሪያው በእርግጥ በባርነት የሚተዳደሩ ሰዎች እምቢ ማለትን መቀጠላቸው ነው። ቀድሞውንም ወድደውት አልተቀበሉትም ነበርና። በራሳቸው፣ በሳዳሪያቸው፣ እና በንብረት ላይ ባለ በሌላ ነገር የምሬት ከንዳቸውን ማንሣትን አበዙ። አብዛኛውን ጊዜ በግል፣ ሲመችም በጋራ።

ቤተ ክርስቲያን ሁለተኛዋ የሥርዓቱ ቀንደኛ ጠላት ሆና ብቅ አለች። ባርያ አሳዳሪነት ከያዘችው የእምነት መጽሐፍ ጋር እየተጋጨ አስቸገረ። ብዙ ባሮችም ክርስትናን ተቀብለው የቤተ ክርስቲያን አባል ሲሆኑ ጥራሽ ነገር ተመስቃቀለ። ክርስቲያኖች 'ወንድሞችም' አይደሉ? ባርያ ወንድም ሊሆን? ጉዳዩ ግልፅ ነበር። ባርነት የፖለቲካ ሥሪት ስለሆነ በአማራጭ ሥሪት መወገድ እንዳለበት ታወቀ።

ስለዚህ ቤተ ክርስቲያንን ተከትሎ መሪዎችና የፖለቲካ ሰዎች በባርነት ላይ ዘመቱ። የቤተ ክርስቲያን አባቶች ሚና ይህን ግንኙነት ማቀጣጠል ነበር። ይህን ሚና ጥቂት ዘርዘር አድርገን እንመልከት። ለዛሬውም ክርስትና ፍሬት አለውና።

የጸረ ባርነት ትግል ጉልት ወጥቶ፣ ቤተ ክርስቲያን ባርነትን አውግዛ አቋም መያዝ የጀመረችው በአሜሪካም ሆነ በእንግሊዝ በተመሳሳይ ወቅት በ19ኛው መቶ አጋማሽ ላይ ነበር። ሁለቱ አገራት ለባርነት መስፋፋት ዋና መሣሪያ ነበሩ። አንዱ አቀባይ፣ ሌላው ተቀባይ፣ ተቃውሞም የተነሣው በሁለቱ።[69] ይሁን እንጂ እንቅስቃሴው በ18ኛው መቶ ክፍለ ዘመንም እያቆጠቆጠ ነበር።

የቤተ ክርስቲያን አባቶች የጸረ ባርነት ትግል በሁለት ዋና ዋና እንቅስቃሴዎች የተመራ ነበር ማለት ይቻላል። የመጀመሪያው የወንጌል ሥርጭት (ሚስዮናዊነት) እንቅስቃሴ ሲሆን ሁለተኛው የቅድስና እንቅስቃሴ ነው። እነዚህ የሰውን ልጅ ደህንነት ያማከሉ እንቅስቃሴዎች በባርያ አሳዳሪ ሥርዓት ላይ ከፍተኛ ጫና ፈጥረዋል።

በ18ኛው ክፍለ ዘመን በፕሮቴስታንቶች መካከል የቅድስና እንቅስቃሴ ተነሣ። ኩዌከርስ (በቀጥታ አማርኛ ትርጉም ተንቀጥቃጭ) የሚባሉ ክርስቲያኖች በግንባር ቀደምትነት። ክርስቲያን ከሆንን መጽሐፍ ቅዱስ የሚያዘንን በሙሉ ሆነን መገኘት

69 Brown, C. L. (2007). Evangelicals and the origins of anti-slavery in England. *Oxford Dictionary of National Biography.* 04 January 2007. https://www.oxforddnb.com/view/10.1093/ref:odnb/9780198614128.001.0001/odnb-9780198614128-e-96075

አለብን አሉ። ቤተ ክርስቲያን መጥፎ ስብከት ከአንድ ሰው ከመስማት ይልቅ መጽሐፉን በዝምታ ማንበብ ይመርጡ ነበር። [70]

መጽሐፉ ሰው ሁሉ በእግዚአብሔር አምሳል የተፈጠረ፤ እኩል ነው እያለ፤ በዘርና በጉማ ማከፋፈል፣ አንዱኑ ገዝቶ፣ ሌላውን አንግሦ መኖር ትክክል አይደለም ሲሉ ተከራከሩ። መጽሐፉን በቀጥታ በማንበብ ልንገባበት እንጂ የሚመቸንን ብቻ መርጦ መታዘዝ ሙሉ አያደርገንም አሉ። ስለዚህ ባርያ ያልናቸውን ሰዎች በሙሉ ነፃ ማውጣት አለብን በማለት መጋገጥ ጀመሩ።

በተለይም ክርስቲያን ሆነው ሌሎች ሰዎችን ባርያ ያደረጉትን ፊት ለፊት መውቀስ ብቻ ሳይሆን በራሳቸው ቤት ባርያ የሆነ ሰው ካለ ሕጉን ሳይፈሩ ነፃ ማውጣት ጀመሩ። ባሮችንም ይመክሯቸው ጀመር። በግልፅ፣ ያሉበት ሁኔታ ሰው ሥራሽ እንደሆነ አሳዩአቸው። በጋራ ሆነው ዓመፅ ጥምር ያራምዱ ዘንድ የደገፉም ነበሩ። ለአምልኮም፣ የሐርሌሚ አበሲኒያውያን መጥምቃዊ (ባፕቲስት) ቤተ ክርስቲያን[71] በ1808 እንዳደረገቸው፣ ተገንጥለው የራሳቸውን አብያተ ክርስቲያናት መሠረቱ።

ልክ በዚህ ጊዜም ሌላው በ18ኛው ክፍለ ዘመን የናኘው የድንበር ተሻጋሪ ሚስዮናዊነት እንቅስቃሴ ተከሰተ። ብዙዎች ወደ አፍሪካ እና ሌሎችም በቅኝ ወደ ተያዙ አገራት ይጉሩፉ ጀመር። ብዙ አልነበሩም እንጂ ሚስዮናውያን ቀድሞም ነበሩ። ባርያ አሳዳሪዎችን ወይም ቅኝ ገዢዎችን ታክከው የመጡ ስለነበሩ እምብዛም አይወደዱም ነበር።

ነጮች መጽሐፍ ቅዱስን ይዘው ወደ አፍሪካ ሲመጡ አምላክን አሳይተው አገርና ነጻነታችንን ቀሙን የሚባለው እውነትነት ነበረው። አዲሱ የፕሮቴስታንት ሚስዮናውያን እንቅስቃሴ ግን ሰዎች ክርስቲያን እንዲሆኑ ብቻ ሳይሆን፣ ወደ ክርስትና ሲመጡ ነጻነታቸውንም ጥምር የተጉናጸፉ መሆናቸውን ይሰብክ ነበር። ባሮን፣ ቅኝ ተገዢዎችን፣ የተረሱትን 'ወንድሞች' አደረጋቸው።

70 Wyatt-Brown, Bertram. "American Abolitionism and Religion." Divining America, TeacherServe®. National Humanities Center. http://nationalhumanitiescenter.org/tserve/nineteen/nkeyinfo/amabrel.html

71 Abyssinian Baptist Church. (2023). History of the Abyssinan Baptist Church. https://abyssinian.org/about-us/history/

አሜሪካውያኑ ጆን ዉልማን (1720–1772)[72]፣ አንቶኒ ቤንዜት (1713–1784)[73]፣ ቤንጃሚን ሌይ (1682–1759)[74] እና ቤንጃሚን ላንዲ (1789–1839)[75] በኩዌከር ጉባዔያት ውስጥ ጸረ ባርነት ጽሑፎችን በማሠራጨት ቀዳሚ ነበሩ። ቤንጃሚን ሌይ ከእንዚህ ይበልጥ ይታወቅ ነበረ። ራሱም ድንክና ጀርባውም የጎበጠ ከመሆኑ የተነሣ በሌሎች ሰዎች መናቅና መገፋት ምን እንደሚመስል ጠንቅቆ ያውቅ ነበርና፣ ባርነትንም ሲጋፈጥ በሙሉ ጉልበቱ ነበር።

ነገር ግን በጆን ዌስሊይ የሚመሩት አዳዲሶቹ የመጥምቃውያን አብይተ ክርስቲያናት እስኪቀላቀሉ ድረስ እምብዛም ጥልቀት ያለው እንቅስቃሴ አልነበረም። ክርስቲያን ጸረ ባርነት ተጋዳዮች በሦስት ዋና ቀና ምክንያቶች ባርነትን ይጠየፉና ይታወሙም ነበር። ሁሉም በእንዚህ ምክንያቶች ባያደርጉ ስንኳ ውጤቱ ተመሳሳይ የሆነ እንቅስቃሴ ያካሂዱ ነበር።[76]

በመጀመሪያ ደረጃ፣ መጽሐፍ ቅዱስ ሰዎች ክርስቲያኖች ሲሆኑ የጌታ ኢየሱስ ክርስቶስ ተከታይ ብቻ ሳይሆን ተወካይ ወይም የመንግሥቱ አምባሳደር ጭምር እንደሚሆኑ ስለሚናገር እንደ ላኪው ፈቃድ መኖር ይገባናል የሚሉ ናቸው። ማለትም ሰዎችን "ልጆቹ" ብሎ የዘላለም ሕይወትን እንዲሁም ከእርሱ ጋር ይነግሡ ዘንድ የሰጠ አምላክ፣ ልጆቹ የሰው ባርያ ይሆኑ ዘንድ አይፈልግም ይላሉ።

ሌሎች ደግሞ በጊዜው የነበሩት ቤተ ክርስቲያን የውስጥ አደረጃጀትና መዋቅር ላይ ያተኮሩ ዐሳቦችን ይዘው ተነሡ። ቤተ ክርስቲያን በአብዛኛው ሰፈውን ሕዝብ በአባልነት ያቀፈች ናት። መሪዎች፣ በተለይም በከፍተኛ ደረጃ የተማሩ ቢኖሩአትም። የቤት ክርስቲያን መሪዎች ክበር የሚወሰነው ለተከታዮቻቸው በሚሰጡት ሥፍራ ስለሆነ በጸረ ባርነት ተጋድሎው ግንባር ቀደም ሆኑ።

በሦስተኛ ደረጃም፣ በተለይም የ19ኛው መቶ ክፍለ ዘመን አጋማሽ እልህ አስጨራሽ ፖለቲካዊ ተቃርኖ የበረታበት ነበር። ክርስትና ደግሞ ጥልቅ ውስጣዊ ለውጥን ስለሚያስከትል ተስፋ ለቆረጡት ሰዎች የነጻነት ትግልን በመደገፍ ረገድ ትርጉም ያለው

---

72 Britannica, The Editors of Encyclopaedia. "John Woolman". Encyclopedia Britannica, 15 Oct. 2021, https://www.britannica.com/biography/John-Woolman.

73 Britannica, The Editors of Encyclopaedia. "Anthony Benezet". Encyclopedia Britannica, 27 Jan. 2022, https://www.britannica.com/biography/Anthony-Benezet.

74 Rediker, M. (2017). Benjamin Lay: The "Quaker Comet" Was the Greatest Abolitionist You've Never Heard of. History; Secrets of American History; Smithonan Magazine. September 2017. https://www.smithsonianmag.com/history/quaker-comet-greatest-abolitionist-never-heard-180964401/

75 Britannica, The Editors of Encyclopaedia. "Benjamin Lundy". Encyclopedia Britannica, 1 Jan. 2022, https://www.britannica.com/biography/Benjamin-Lundy.

76 McInerney, D. J. (1991). "A Faith for Freedom": The Political Gospel of Abolition. Journal of the Early Republic. Vol. 11. No. 3 (Autumn, 1991; pp. 371-393 (23 pages). University of Pennsylvania Press

የሕይወት መርሀ የሚሰጥ ሆኖ ብቅ አለ። ስለዚህ በክርስትናው አመለካከት ላይ ፖለቲካዊ ዓላማም ያነገበ ነበር ማለት ይቻላል።

በአገረ እንግሊዝም ባርነትን ቀድመው ከነፈፋት መካከል የለንደኑ ታላቅ ሰበኪ፣ ዘማሪ፣ እና ጸሐፊ የነበረው ሬቨረንድ ጆን ኒውተን (1725–1807)[77] ይገኝበታል። ኒውተን በባርያ ንግድ ጭምር የተካፈለ እና ሰቆቃውን የሚረዳ ሲሆን ራሱን "የአፍሪካው ዘላፊ" በማለት ይጠራ ነበር። የባርያ ንግድ ሰውንም፣ አምላክንም መዝለፍ ነው የሚል ጥልቅ እምነት ነበረው።

"እንደ እኔ ያለ ጉስቋላ ሰው ያዳነ፣ የሚገርም ጸጋ" ብሎ በ1773 የጻፈው ዝማሬ በእንግሊዝም በአሜሪካም ሰዎች ያለ ዜማ ይደግሙት ነበር። ይህ መዝሙር በ1779 ታትሞ ከወጣበት ጊዜ አንሥቶ ከታላላቅ የቤተ ክርስቲያን ቅኖሶች የሚመደብ ሥራ ሆኗል። ኒውተን በአፍሪካውያን ላይ በባርያ ፈንጋይነትና አስተላላፊነት ያደረሰውን ግፍ እያሰበ በግሉ ንስሃ የገባበት ዝማሬ ነው ተብሎ ይታመናል።

የኒውተን ጓደኛ እና ዕውቀ ፖለቲካ ሰው ዊልያም ዊልበርፎርስ (1759–1833) ግንባር ቀደም ተጠቃሽ የጻፈ ባርነት እንቅስቃሴ መሪ ነበር። በወቅቱ የእንግሊዝ ጠቅላላ ሚንስትር ከኖት ልጅ ዊልያም ፒት (1759–1806)[78] ጋር በካምብሪጅ ዩኒቨርሲቲ ከሚማሩበት ጊዜ ጀምሮ ጥብቅ ጓደኝነት ነበራቸው። ዊልበርፎርስ ከልጅ ዊልያም ፒት ጋር በ1780 የፓርላማ አባል ሆነ።

ልጅ ፒት አባቱም ዊልያም ፒት ጠቅላይ ሚኒስትር የነበረ ሲሆን በእናትም በኩል ከታወቁ የእንግሊዝ መሪዎች ቤተሰብ የተወለደ ነው። ብልሀ ፖለቲከኛ የነበረው ዊልበርፎርስ ይህን ሰው ከልጅነቱ ጀምሮ ይቀርበው ነበር፣ የፓርላማ አባል ለመሆንም በቃ፣ በፈረንሳይ አብዮት ወቅት ካጋጠመው የፖለቲካ ውጥንቅጥ ለማገገም በ1785 ክርስቲያን ሆነ፣ የጠራ የፖለቲካ ትግል ተልዕኮም አገኘ።

ከኒውተን ጋር የነበረው ግንኙነት በወቅቱ ታዋቂ ከሆኑ ሌሎች የፖለቲካና ኢኮኖሚ መሪዎችና እንደ እርሱ ጥብቅ ፕሮቴስታንት አማኞች ከሆኑ ከቶማስ ክላርክሰን፣ ግራንቪል ሻርፕ፣ ሄንሪ ትሮንቶን፣ ቻርለስ ግራንት፣ ኤድዋርድ ኤሊየት፣ ዛካሪ ማካውሌ፣ እና ጄምስ ስቲፈን ጋር አስተዋወቀው። መሪያቸውም ሆነ፣ ዋና የፖለቲካ ዓላማቸው ባርነትን ማጥፋት ነበር። [79]

የዚህ እንቅስቃሴ ግንባር ቀደም አቀንቃኝ የሆነውን የጻፈ ባርነት ማገበር መሠረቱ። በዊልበርፎርስ መሪነት ያለ መታከት በእንግሊዝ ፓርላማ እየተፋለሙ አገሪቱ የባርያ

77 Petruzzello, M. (2021). "John Newton". Encyclopedia Britannica, 17 Dec. 2021, https://www.britannica.com/biography/John-Newton.

78 Aspinall, Arthur C. V. D. "William Pitt, the Younger". *Encyclopedia Britannica*, 19 Jan. 2022, https://www.britannica.com/biography/William-Pitt-the-Younger.

79 Britannica, The Editors of Encyclopaedia. "William Wilberforce". *Encyclopedia Britannica*, 20 Aug. 2021, https://www.britannica.com/biography/William-Wilberforce.

ንግድን በ1806 በሕግ እንድታግድ አደረጉ። [80] ዊልበርፎርስ ከዚያ አስከትሎ ባርነት ጨርሶ እስኪወገድ ድረስ ሃይወቱን ሙሉ ታግሏል። በአሜሪካ እንቅስቃሴው ፖለቲካዊ መልክ የያዘው ከዚህ ስኬት በኋላ ነበር። [81]

ባርነት ሙሉ በመሉ በሕግ እስኪወገድ ግን ተጨማሪ ጊዜ ፈጅቷል። የአሜሪካው እንቅስቃሴ እያደገ ሄዶ በ1865 በአሜሪካ ባርነትን በሙሉ የሚገረስ የሕግ መንግሥት 13ኛው ማሻሻያ[82] ሊጸድቅ ችሏል። [83] እስከዚያው ግን እንቅስቃሴው በ1850ዎቹ ውስጥ ታላላቅ ፖለቲካዊ ክስተቶችን ፈጥሯል። ከዚህም አንዱ የአሜሪካ ሪፑብሊካን ፓርቲ መመሥረት ነው። [84]

የባርያ አሳዳሪ ሥርዓት ለዘረኝነትም ሆነ በሰዎች መካከል በአንድም በሌላ መንገድ ለዕኩይ ዓላማ ልዩነትን ለመፍጠር ለሚፈልጉ ሁሉ መሠረት የሆነ የፖለቲካዊ ኤኮኖሚ መዋቅር ነው። ሥርዓቱ ሕግ ወጥ ተብሎ መታገዱ የግለሰቦች ትግል ውጤት ብቻ ሳይሆን በግል ከመለወጥ ባሻገር የእምነት አባቶችን፤ የፖለቲካ መሪዎችን፤ እና ሌሎች መዋቅሮችን መሥዋዕትነት ጠይቋል።

መታገድ፤ መወገድ አይሆንም። ዘረኝነትንም ሆነ ማናቸውንም ዐይነት አግላይነትና መድልዎ የተጠናወታቸውን አመለካከቶችና ድርጊቶች ለማጥፋት የአንድ ሰው ወይም የግል ጥረት ብቻ በቂ አይሆንም። የተኖጀዎችም ተነሳሽነት ብቻውን አጥጋቢ መልስ አይሰጥም። የእምነት አባቶች፤ አብያተ እምነቶች በመዋቅሮቻቸው፤ የፖለቲካ መሪዎችና ታዋቂ ግለሰቦች በቂ መሥዋዕትነት ሊከፍሉ ይገባል።

ዘመን ቀደማዊ

ዘረኝነት እያደገ ሄዶ በዓለም ሁሉ ፊት ዘገናኝ በነበረው በሁለተኛው የዓለም ጦርነት ወቅት በተከወነው የአይሁድ ዕልቂት ነው። ከዚያ በፊት በአፍሪካ፤ በህንድ፤

80 Wyatt-Brown, Bertram. "American Abolitionism and Religion." Divining America, TeacherServe®. National Humanities Center. http://nationalhumanitiescenter.org/tserve/nineteen/nkeyinfo/amabrel.html

81 Britannica, The Editors of Encyclopaedia. "William Wilberforce". Encyclopedia Britannica, 20 Aug. 2021, https://www.britannica.com/biography/William-Wilberforce.

82 የአሜሪካው 13ኛ የሕግ መንግሥት ማሻሻያ እንዲህ የሚል አንቀጽ ይዟል፦ "በተከከል ከተፈረደበት የወንጀል ቅጣት በስተቀር ማንም ሰው በባርነትም ሆነ ያለፈቃዱ አገልጋይ እንዲሆን በየናይትድ ስቴትስ ግዛት ውስጥ ኣኣወይም በማንኛውም የአገሩቱ የስልጣን ወሰን ስር ሊኖር (ሊያዝ፤ ሊታዳደር) አይችልም"

83 National Archives, (2016). America's Historical Documents: 13th Amendment to the U.S. Constitution: Abolition of Slavery. https://www.archives.gov/historical-docs/13th-amendment#:~:text=Passed%20by%20Congress%20on%20January,within%20the%20United%20States%2C%20or

84 Wyatt-Brown, Bertram. "American Abolitionism and Religion." Divining America, TeacherServe®. National Humanities Center. http://nationalhumanitiescenter.org/tserve/nineteen/nkeyinfo/amabrel.html

በአሜሪካና ሌሎች ሥፍራዎችም በጥቁሮችና በነጭ ሕዝቦች ላይ የተፈጸመው የዘር ማጥፋት ግን በብዙ እጥፍ የሚበልጥ እንደሆነ እሙን ነው። ትኮረትም፤ ክትትልም እምብዛም ነበር እንጂ።

ቢሆንም፤ የዘረኝነት አባዜ እያደገ ሲሄድ ሁሉን የሚበላ መሆኑ በጥቂቱም ቢሆን በአሁኑ ዕልቂት ጊዜ ተስተውሏል። አይሁድስ ከነጭ ወይም አውሮፓዊ ዘር አይደላችሁም ተብለው አለቁ። የጓላኛው የሃያኛው ክፍለ ዘመን ዕልቂት ግን አውሮፓውያንንም በዘር አቢደኖ ያፋጀ፤ ጥቁሮቹንም በጉሃ ከፋፍሎ ያባላ ሆኗል። ዘረኝነትና ጉሥኝነት ተጣመሩ።

በቦስኒያ እና በባልካን ግዛቶች የተከሰተው የዘር ጭፍጨፋ "ነጭ" በሚባሉ መካከል የተከወነ ነው። የነይማኖት ልዩነት ቢጠቀስም ምንጩ ጉሥኝነት ነበር። በአፍሪካም የሩዋንዳው የዘር ጭፍጨፋ ይግነን እንጂ በጉሣዎች መካከል እጅግ ብዙ ዕልቂት ያስከተለ እብደቶች ተኪሂደዋል። ነጭ መጥቶ ሳይሆን እርስ በርስ ተባላን። ባለፉት 50 ያህል ዓመታት የነይማኖት ልዩነት እንኳ ሳይኖረን ተጋደልን።

ታዲያ ዘመናችን፤ ዘረኝነት እጅግ እየተጠላ ሳለ፤ በተገላቢጦሽ ግን እጅግ በፍጥነት እያደገ እንዲሄድ ተጋምራዊ ጎይል ያገኘበት ጊዜ ነው ቢባል ያስሄዳል። ይህ ተቃርኖ ዘመናችንን ልዩ ያደርገዋል። ይህ ዘመን ደግሞ 'አወቅን' ባዮች የበዙበት፤ "ዘመን ቀደምነት" ወይንም "ፖስት ሞዴርኒዝም" እየተባለ የሚጠራው ፍልስፍና የተንሰራፋበት ነው።

"ዘመን ቀደም"[85] ተብሎ የተተረጐመበት ምክንያት የፍልስፍናው አቀንቃኞች ማንኛውንም ዘመን በብዙ ርቀት የቀደሙ መሆናቸውን አበክረው ስለሚናገሩ ነው። ዘመን ቢከተላቸው እንጂ የማይመራቸው እንደሆነ ያወሳሉ። በምጡቅ፤ በለጥ ባለ አስተሳሰብ የተካኑ መሆናቸውን ስለሚናገሩ ዘመኑን የቀደሙ ለማለት ያሀል።

የሚገርመው ግን የዘመን ቀደምነት ዕሳቤ አራማጆች ብቻ አይደሉም ይህ መዘባነን የተጠናወታቸው። እኛም በዚህ ዘመን የተከሰተን የፍልስፍናው ተቋዳሾች ተጋብቶብናል። የጓላውን እየቃረምን ወደ ጎላ መመልከታችንን እንጠየፈዋለን። በዘመናት ውስጥ ከታየው የፍልስፍና፤ የሳይንስና ቴክኖሎጂ ዕድገት የእኛ ንድፈ ዐሳብና ተግባር የሚበልጥ ይመስለናል። ታሪክን ጥልት አደረግን።

የዘመን ቀደምነት ዕሳቤ ያያለበት ይህ ዘመን ውጥንቅጡ የበዛ በመሆኑ በዚህ ጊዜ ስለ ተገለጠው ዘረኝነት ከማውራት በፊት ራሱን ዘመኑን መረዳት ስለሚያስፈልግ ጥቂት እንበል። ዘመን ቀደምነት ለትርጉም አስቸጋሪ ስለሆነ ከመተርጐም ይልቅ በባሕርያቱ

85   ሲምን ሔሊሶ ኩካ (2019). ዘመን ቀደምነትና የዛሬይቱ ቤተ ክርስቲያን. አማዞን

መግለጽ መሞከር ይሻሳል። ይህ ዕሳቤ፣ አንጻራዊነት፣ ቁንጽልነትና መደዴነት ተብለው የሚታወቁ ሦስት አበይት መገለጫዎች አሉት። [86]

አንጻራዊነት

በዘመን ቀደሞች ዕይታ እምነት፣ ዕውቀት፣ እና እውነት አንጻራዊ ናቸው። በተለይም፣ እውነት የሚባል ነገር የለም። ወይም እውነት ሁሉ አንጻራዊ ነው። ዘመን ቀደማች በራሱ ምሉዕ፣ ፍፁማዊ፣ ወይም ዋና የሚባል እውነት የለም ይላሉ። ሁሉን አቀፍ፣ ገዢ፣ ዋና፣ ፈሳጭ ቆራጭ የሚባል እውነት አይገኝም። በተለይም፣ ሳይንሳዊ የማይለወጥ፣ ዘለዓለማዊ፣ ወይም እርግጠኛ የሚባል እውነት ሰዎች የፈጠሩት እንጂ ነባራዊ አይደለም ይላሉ። [87]

ለአምላክ የለሾች ይህ ግንዛቤ አይከብድ ይሆናል። ጎይማኖተኞች ግን እንዴት ይውጡታል? ፍልስፍናው ባላ ጎይማኖት ተከታዮች እጅግ አፍርቲልና፣ የዘመን ቀደሞች ዕሳብ ወዲያው አድማጭ የሚያገኘው ለዚህ ዕይነት ግንዛቤ በሚሰጡት ምሳሌ ነው። አስገዳጅ ምሳሌ። ለምሳሌ ባርነትን፣ ቅኝ ግዛትን፣ የዘር መድልዎንና፣ መሰል ነገሮችን ለሚጠሉ ሰዎች ገሥሪዎች ምን ያህል እውነትን እያዛቡ እንደሚያቀርቡ ያስረዱቻቸዋል።

አንዱ ገገር ሄዶ ሌላው ሲተካ፣ ቀድም እውነት ብለን የተቀበልናቸውን ያጠፋቸዋል። ስለዚህ እውነት ተለዋዋጭ ናት ይላሉ። አሁናዊ የገጽታ ግንባታ የፖለቲካ አካል ነው፣ ያለፈው ይንቋሸሻል፣ ይክለሳል። በጊዜና ቦታም የሚለዋወጥ ሐቅ አለ።

ከሐጻንነት ወደ ጉልማሳነት እያደገ ያለ ሰው ምሳሌ እንውሰድ። ሐጻንም ጉልማሳም ሆኖ ሰው ነው። እውነት አንድ። በልጅነት ዕድሜው ማድረግ የማይችላቸውን ነገሮች አድጎ በወጣትነት ዕድሜው ያቀላጥፈዋል። ሰው በአካል እያደገ ሲሄድ ቀድሞ የማይችለውን ማድረግ መቻሉም እውነት ነው። ዘመን ቀደሞች 'ሰው አንዴ ይሻላል፣ ሌላ ጊዜ አይችልም' ከተባለ አንጻራዊነትን ያመለክታል ይላሉ። ሁሉቱ በጊዜ የተለያዩ ሐቆች እንጂ የእውነትን እንጻራዊነት አያስረዱንም።

በተለይም አንዳንድ ክርስቲያኖች ፍጹም እውነት የለም የሚለውን አባባል ለመቀበል የዬዱበት ፍጥነት ትዝብት ላይ ይጥሳቸዋል። ክርስቶስ ኢየሱስ በምድር ሲመሳለስ "እውነትና መንገድ፣ ሕይወትም እኔ ነኝ" (ዮሐንስ ወንጌል 14፤ 6) አለ። ክርስቶስን የሚከተሉ ከሆነ ለእውነት አንጻራዊነት እንዴት ልባቸውን ሰጡ? እርሱም ተለዋዋጭ ነው ማለታቸው ይሆን?

---

86 Duignan, B. (2020, September 4). *postmodernism. Encyclopedia Britannica.* https://www. britannica.com/topic/postmodernism-philosophy

87 Baudrillard, Jean (1995). *Simulacra and Simulation.* Translated by Sheila Faria Glaser. Ann Arbor: University of Michigan Press.

ዘመን ቀደሞች ለሰው ልጆች መብት ቆመናል ባይ ናቸው። የእውነት አንጻራዊነት ትምህርት ግን ያሳጣቸዋል። እኔን እንደ ባርያ መግዛት የሚፈልግ 'አንተን አምላክ ባርያ እንድትሆነኝ ፈጥሮሃል' ካለኝ ለእርሱ እውነት መሆኑ ነው። እኔም 'አልገዛም፤ እኔና አንተ እኩል ነን' ካልኩት የእኔም ለራሴ እውነት ነው። አንጻራዊነት ለሁለቱም ስለሚሠራ። መግዛትና መገዛትም ትክክል ሊሆን ነው።

አንጻራዊነት ጭቆና አስወጋጅ ሳይሆን ይልቁን መንገድ ጠራጊ እንዳይሆን ያሰጋል። ለእኔ እውነት የሆነ ለአንተ እውነት ባይሆንስ? እውነት ከየራስ አንጻር የሚታይ፤ ብዝጎነት የሚያጠቃው ነውን? አፍሪካ በቅኝ ተገዛሁ አለች፤ አውሮፓ ግን ላሰለጥን፤ አምላክ የለሾችን ከአምላክ ጋር ላስተዋውቅ መጣሁ አለች። የማን ነው ትክክል? አሥለጠኑን ወይስ ገዙን?

ለዘመን ቀደሞች መልሱ ቀላል ነው፤ ሁለቱም ትክክል። ምክንያቱም ሁሉ አቀፍ የሚባል ፍጹም እውነት የለምና። እውነት ሁሌም አንጻራዊ ብቻ ነው ብለው ስለምያምኑ።

ዕውቀት፤ እውነትን ከመፈለጊያ መንገዶች አንዱ እንደሆነ ይታወቃል። በዘመን ቀደሞች ዕሳቤ ግን ዕውቀትም አንጻራዊ ነው፤ ፍለጋውም ከንቱ ነው። እንቁላል መብላት አንዱ ለሰውነት ጠቃሚ ፕሮቲን ይገኝበታል እያልን፤ ቤላ ጊዜ ለኮልስትሮል ያጋጥማል ካልን ዕውቀት ምን ፋይዳ አለው? በራሱ፤ በወሰነው ስለማይቆም።

የዚህ ፍልስፍና መገለጫ፤ ጥናትና ምርምርን፤ በተለይም ሳይንስንና ቴክኖሎጂን መጥላት ነው። ጥናትና ምርምር የተሻለ መብራትና ውሃ ብቻ ሳይሆን የሰጡን የተሻለ ቦንብም፤ ሌሎች ሰዎች የምንጨቀነበትን ስልትና መሣሪያ ያቀበሉን ስለሆኑ ለሰው ልጅ ልዕልና አስፈላጊ አይደሉም እስከ ማለት ይደርሳሉ። ከተጻፈው፤ ያልተጻፈው፤ ከተጠናው ያልተጠናው፤ ከተነገረው ያልተነገረው ስለሚበልጥ ጥናትና ምርምር ምን ፋይዳ አለው ብለው ይጠይቃሉ።

እንዲሁም፤ ምክንያትና አመክንዮ፤ የሰውን የአዕምሮ ውጤት እያጸደቅን የኖርንበት መንገድ ሁሉ ምናባዊ፤ እኛው በእኛው የፈጠርነው ነው። ለምሳሌ፦ ብርሃንን ከአምፑል የሰጠውን ሰው እጅግ በማግዘፋችን ብርሃን ቤላ መንገድ እንዳይገኝ ዘጋን። እንዲሁም አባቶቻችን ጀግኖች ናቸው እያልን የሌላ ሥልጣኔ ከእኛ ጋር እንዳይዳቀል በር መዝጋትን የተሻለ አድርገን ቆጠርን። ቀጥሉ እንግዲህ።

የዘመን ቀደምነት ዕሳቤ እስካሁን ሁለንተናዊ እውነት ብለን የያዝናቸውን ነገሮች ከ ስር ከመሠረቱ ያናጋል። እንዲያውም መሠረትን ካላንጋ፤ ካልረበሽ ዘመን ቀደም የመባል ልዕልና አይሰጠውም። የቴክኖሎጂ ዕድገት ከሆነ ረባሽ መሆን አለበት፤ የገበያ ሥልትም የተለመደውን የሚያናጋ ካልሆነ የበታችና ድኩም ነው። አስተሳሰብም እንደዚያው።

ከዚህ ሌላ ችሎታ፣ ዕውቀት፣ ዝንባሌ ወይም አመክንዮ የተባለ የሰው ልጅ መገለጫዎች ከፍጥረት የሚወረሱ ሳይሆን በትምህርት እና ከአካባቢ የሚመነጩ እንደሆኑ ያምናሉ። ይህም ማለት በድኽነት ውስጥ ያሉ አገራት የድኽነት ቀኖመናቸው ሁሌም ድኽ ሆነው እንዲኖሩ ያስገድዳቸዋል። ለረብሻ ካልሆነ መነካካት አስፈላጊ አይሆንም ወደሚል ድምዳሜ ያመራናል።

በመጨረሻም፣ ለዘመን ቀደሞች እውነታን ከንድፈ ዐሳቦ ተነስቶ ለመግለጥ መሞከር ከጉዱ ብቻ ሳይሆን አደገኛ ነው። 88 ለምርምር ከንድፈ ዐሳብ መነሳት ግን የተለመደ ነው። ይህ የደረጀ ሳይንሳዊ ዘዴ፣ ጥናትም፣ ምርምርም ፋይዳ ቢስ ናቸው። ምክንያቱም ቀድሞ ያወቅነውን መልስ ማፍረስ ስለሆነ ብለው ያስተምራሉ።

ስለዚህ በዘመን ቀድሞች ዐሳብ ዕውቀትም አንጻራዊ ነው። ፍልስፍናዊ መሠረት የሚባል፣ ሰው ሁሉ የሚጋጨራት ጥበብም ሆነ ጠቢብ የለም። ሳይንሳዊ ማስረጃ ማቅረብ አይቻልም። ሳይንሳዊ የሚባለው ነገር ሳይንቲስቶች ራሳቸውን በራሳቸው ለማሞካሸት የፈጠሩት ነው ብለው ያምናሉ። ግሩም የክርክር መድረክ፣ ለምሳሌ፦ ሰው ነህ ወይስ አይደለህም? ተከራክሩህ ልታሳምነኝ አትችልም። ምክንያቱም ማስረጃ የለህም። ሳይንሳዊ ሐቅ የሚባል፣ በጥናትና በአመክንዮ ሊረጋገጥ የሚችል ስላልሆነ።

በቃ 'ሰው ነኝ ብዬ አምናለሁ' ብለህም አታመልጥም። እውነትና ዕውቀት ብቻ ሳይሆን፣ እምነትም አንጻራዊ ነው። እምነት እንዲያውም የጋል ስለሆነ ምንም ዐይነት ትችትም ሆነ አስተያየት አንዱ በሌላው እምነት ላይ መግለጥ አይችልም ይላሉ። ዘመን ቀደሞች በዚህ ረገድ የሚዋኙበት መልካ ምንኛ ጥልቀት ዐልባ እንደሆነ እንኳን አያስተውሉም።

የአንድን ሰው እምነት ማክበር እንዳለብን በዐይነያየ ያስተምራሉ። እምነቱ ሰውዬው ራሱ ስለሆነ እምነትን ለማንቋሸሽ መከጀል ሰውዬውን ማንቋሸሽ ነው ይላሉ በጁ። ማንም ሰው በእምነቱ ምክንያት ልናንቋሽሸው አይገባም። ነገር ግን፣ ችግር ያለበት እምነት ሲኖርሳ?

እምነት ማንንት ስለሆነ የሁሉ ሊከበር ስለሚገባው "ባዕድ" እያልን የምንጠራቸውን ስንኳ መተው አለብን? መልሳቸው ቀጥተኛ ነው። ባዕድ እምነትም መብት ነው። አንጻራዊ ስለሆነ፣ ላንተ ባዕድ፣ ለእኔ ትክክለኛ ሊሆን ይችላል። እንዲህ ዐይነት ገደብ ዐልባ ነጻነት መፈለጋቸው፣ በስፋት ተቀባይነትን አስገኝቶላቸዋል። አንዳንድ ጎይማኖተኞች በዚህ ፍልስፍና ውስጥ ግር ብለው መግባታቸው ግን ያስተዛዝባል።

በእርግጥ እምነት ሁሉ በአንጻራዊነት ትክክል ነው? መበየን የሚችል እምነት ባይኖር ጎሊና የለንም? ለምሳሌ፦ ለእምነታቸው ሥርዓት ማስፈጸሚያ ሲሉ እምቦቃቅላ <u>ቤት ልጆች እየተሰዉ</u> ማምለክ አለብን የሚሉ በአንጻራዊነት ልክ ናቸው ብለን እንለፍ?

88 Foucault, Michel (1970). *The Order of Things: An Archaeology of the Human Sciences*. New York: Pantheon.

ወይንም፤ እንደ ጥንት አምልኮዎች እምነት ማለት የማያቋርጥ ፍትወት ለጣያት ማቅረብ ነው ብለው ልቅ የግብረ ሥጋ ግንኙነት "በቤተ መቅደስ" የሚፈጸሙትም ልክ ናቸው ብለን እንቀበል?

ፈጣሪ፤ ሁሉን ቻይ፤ የሁሉ አባት የምንለው አምላክ ወዴት ሄደ? ግፍ የሚፈጸምባቸው የእርሱ ፍትረት አይደሉም? ወይስ እኛ ልንፋንን ስለከጀልን ትተነው ሄድን? እምነት ቢጠፋ የነሊና ሕግ የሚባል በሰው ዘንድ ሁሉ የለምን?

እንግዲያማ፤ አምላክ ሰውን ለያይቶ ፈጠረ የሚሉም ልክ ናቸው፤ አንዱን ነጭ፤ ብልነ፤ ዕውቀት የተሞላ፤ ኅይል ያለው፤ ... ወዘተ አድርጎ ለገገሪነት፤ ሌላውን ጥቁር፤ ሰውነት ደልዳላ፤ ትናንሽ ዐይን፤ ድኻ፤ ዕውቀት ዐልባ አድርጎ ለተገዥነት፤ አንጸራዊነት ምንኛ አማላይ አስተምህሮ ቢሆንም እንኳን አምላክን ከመሳደብ የሚስተካከል ድፍረት ነው።

ቅንጽልነት

ቅንጽል ማለት፤ የጨርፍታ መረዳት፤ ጥራዝ ነጠቅነት፤ ጥቂት ዕውቀት፤ በቅምሻ መርካት፤ ጠልቆ አለመረዳት፤ ከላይ ከላይ መጋለብ ማለት ነው። ለዘመን ቀደሞች ገዥ ወይም አጠቃላይ ትርክት የሚባሉ ነገሮች አይጥማቸውም። 89 ምክንያቱም ለእንርሱ ትርክት ሁሉ ቅንጽል ነው። አጠቃላይ ትርክትን መጥላታቸው ከተጨቆኑ ሕዝቦች ጉን የወገኑ ያስመስላቸዋል፤ ከዚህ የተነሣ ይህ ዐሳባቸው ቶሎ የመሥረጽ ዕድል አግኝቷል።

ለምሳሌ ቅኝ ገዢዋ እንግሊዝ የምታዘወትረው ጠቅላይ ትርክት "በእንግሊዝ ግዛት ፀሓይ አትጠልቅም" የሚል ነበር። ምሥራቁም ምዕራቡም የእኔ ነው ማለቷ ነው። አገራት ጠቅላይ ትርክት የሚወዱት በራሳቸው ሕዝብ ላይ መነቃቃትን፤ በሰሚው ደግሞ ፍርኃትን ስለሚሰድ ነው።

አጼ ቴዎድሮስም 'የኢትዮጵያ ባል፤ የኢየሩሳሌም እጮኛ' እየተባሉ ይሞካሹ ነበር። የዓድዋ ድል የኢትዮጵያን፤ አልፎም የአፍሪካን ሕዝብ ለማሰባሰብ የሚውል ትርክትን ፈጥሯል። የአሜሪካ ፊልሞች ሁልጊዜ አሜሪካውያን ወይንም ነጮች ሲያሸንፉ ያሳያሉ። እስከ ነጩ ቤተ መንግሥት መመታት ድረስ ልብ አንጠልጣይ ልብ ወለድ ይሠራና በመጨረሻ አንድ ጀግና ወይም ጥበበኛ አሜሪካዊ ዓለምን በሞላ ጉድ ሥርቶ የማታ ማታ አሸናፊ ይሆናል፤ ትርክት ነው።

ዘመን ቀደሞች ይህን መሰል ትርክት ያወግዛሉ፤ ስለሆነም ኢትዮጵያዊ ጀግንነት፤ የአሜሪካ ህልመኝነት፤ የአይሁድ መመረጥ፤ ... ወዘተ የሚባል ነገር የለም። አጠቃላይ ትርክትም ሆነ ተጨባጭ ታሪካዊ እውነታ የሚባል ነገር የለም። የታሪክ እውነታም

89   Jean-François Lyotard, La condition postmoderne: rapport sur le savoir (Paris: Minuit, 1979).

ምናባዊ ብቻ፣ ሰዎች ሲናገሩ፣ ሲጽፉ፣ ሲያጠኑ የራሳቸውን ነገር እየጨመሩ ያዛቡት ነው ብለው ያምናሉ። 90

ያለ አንዳች ማጋነን ይህ ዕሳቤ ይገዳደራል። እንደ ክርስትና ላሉ እምነቶች ግን ሳያላምጡ መቀበል አዳጋች ነው። እግዚአብሔር ሰማይና ምድርን ፈጠረ ከሚለው አንሥቶ፣ ሰውን ወደደ፣ ስለዚህ ልጁን ላክ፣ በልጁ ሞት የሰውን ኃጢአት ዕዳ ከፍሎ ልጁቼ አደረገን፣ ወደ ራሱ ሊወስደን ዳግመኛ ይመጣል፣ ... ወዘተ የሚሉ ግዙፍ ትርክቶችን ዋጋ ቢስ ያደርጋና።

ዘመን ቀደሞች ስለ ሰው እኩልነት አጥብቀው ይከራከሩ እንጂ፣ ቁንጽልነትን ስለሚያቀነቅኑ ክርክራቸውን ያረክስባቸዋል። ሰው እግዚአብሔር የፈጠረው፣ በእግዚአብሔር የተወደደ የሚለው እውነት ይተናቃቸዋል። ሌላው የባርያ ንግድ ፍንገላ እና የመሳሰሉ የታሪክ እውነታዎች በትርክት ላይ መመሥረታቸውን ክደን እንደገና ማጤን አለብን ማለት ነው።

ጥቁሮች ለባርነት ሲ.ጋዙ ወድደው፣ ወደ አዲሱ ክፍለ ዓለም ለመሄድ አስበው፣ የሚያስፈልገውን ኪ.ሣሪ ተምነው፣ ተነስተዋል የሚሉ ትክክል እንደሆነስ? በእርግጥ አንዳንድ ትርክቶች በከንቱ አልመጡም። ታሪካዊ እውነታን የታከኩ ናቸውና። ዘመን ቀደሞች ግን ትርክት ሁሉ ከንቱ ነው፣ ምን ይፈይዳል ይላሉ። አንድን ነገር ከፈለግን ብቻ ግን ተሸካሚ ትርክት መቅረጽ ይሻላል ይላሉ።

መደዴነት

ሌላው አስገራሚ የዘመን ቀደሞች መረዳት ከአንጻራዊነት አስተሳሰብ የመነጨ ነው። አንድ ነገር፣ ከሌሎች ጋር እየተነጻጸረ እንጂ ብቻውን መቆም አይችልም ይላሉ። ተነጻጻሪ ደግሞ ትከሻ ለትከሻ የተነካካ ነው፣ እኩል። ስለዚህ ተዋረድ የሚባል ነገር የለም። የምንናገረው ቋንቋ እንኳ የተመሰረተባቸው ቃላት ለሰሚም፣ ለተናጋሪም ምሉዕ ገላጭ እንዲሆን ተነጻጸሪ ይፈልጋሉ። ለምሳሌ ብርሃንን ጨለማ ባይኖር አናውቀውም ነበር። ስለዚህ፣ በአንክሮ ስናስብ ብርሃንም ጨለማ ነው ይላሉ።

እንዲያውም፣ ከፈረንሳዊው ፈላስፋና የሥነ ጽሑፍ ሊቅ ዣክ ዴሪዳ (1930– 2004) ንድፈ ዕሳብ በመነሣት የነበረተሰብ ዕሴት የምንለው ነገር ቋንቋንም ጨምሮ እውነታን የማይገልጥ ነው ይላሉ። 91 ቋንቋ ራሱን በራሱ የመተርጉም ብቃት ያለው ነገር ስለሆነ ተለዋዋጭ ነው። የአንድ ቃል ትርጉምም አንጻራዊ እንጂ ወጥ አይደለም።

---

90 Hutcheon, L. (1987). The Politics of Postmodernism. Cultural Critique No. 5, Modernity and Modernism Postmodernity and Postmodernism (Winter, 1986-1987), pp. 179-207

91 Derrida, J. (1997). Of Grammatology. Corrected ed. Baltimore: Johns Hopkins University Press

ቆንቆ የባለቤቱን ፅንሰ ዐሳብ የማይገልጥ፣ የተገኘበትን ባሕልና ሕዝብ የማያሳይ ከሆነ አስቸጋሪ ነው። የግብረ ገብ፣ የትውፊት፣ እና የአዕምሮ ዕሴቶችን የማይገልጥ ፊደልና ቃል የምንስድር ከሆነ በእርግጥም ሁሉም እስከ ዛሬ ያዝን የምንላቸው ነገሮች ሁሉ ፈርሰው እንደገና ሊሠሩ ይገባቸዋል።

ለምሳሌ፦ "ስድብ" የምንለው ቃል በጽድቅ ራሱን በራሱ ይተረጉም እንበል። ተመሳሳይና ተቃራኒ ቃላቶችን በመጠቀም ለቋንቋው ተናጋሪዎች "ስደብ" የሚለው ቃል 'ዘለፈ፣ ወረፈ፣ አዋረደ' የሚለውን ይወክላል። ለዘመን ቀደሞች ግን ስድብን ከበረከት ጋር ካላነጻጸርነው ምሉዕ ፍቺ የለውም። በአንድ ጐን የተሰጠው ቁጥጽል ፍቺ ይራባል ይላሉ።

ያለ ምንም ጥርጥር፣ እንደ አንድ ሳንቲም ሁለት ገጽታ ተነጻጻሪ የሆኑ ነገሮች አሉ። ነገር ግን፣ ሁሉን በተነጻጻሪ እንተርጉመው ካልን "ስድብ" የሚለው ቃል እየተዘመደና እየተገፋ ሄዶ "በረከት" የሚለውን ሊወክል እስከሚችል ዐቅም ያገኛል። ቃላት፣ እንዲሁም የቃላቱ ምንጭ ፅንሰ ዐሳቦች ራሳቸውን ችለው መቆም የሚችሉ መሆናቸውን ማስተዋል ያሻል። "ስድብ" እና "በረከት" ግን ራሳቸውን ችለው መቆምም ይችላሉ።

መደዳነት፣ አልገዛዛም ባይነትን የሚደግፍ ስለሚመስል ወዳጁ፣ ብዙ ነው። መንፈሳዊም ሆነ ማኅበራዊ ሕግ፣ አስተዳደር፣ መዋቅር፣ ሥርዐቶችና ደንቦች አሳሪ ናቸው ይላል። ምክንያቱም የእነዚህ ምንጭ አንጻራዊ እምነት፣ ቁንጽል ዕውቀት፣ አንጻራዊ ታሪክና ትርክት ስለሆነ፣ ስለዚህ ቢቻል ታግሎ መጣልን ይደግፋል። የሰውን ልጅ አንቆ የሚይዝ ጭቆናና በደል ካለ ታግሎ መጣል ባልከፋ። ችግሩ የቀደም ነገር ሁሉ ሲጠላ፣ መዋቅር ሲንኳሰስ፣ ሲነቀፍ፣ አባቶችና መሪዎች መለገጫ ሲሆኑ ነው።

አንዳንዶች መተቸትና ሲመችም መበጣበጥ ከሌሎች ላቅ ያለ ሥፍራ ያስሰጠናል ብለው ያምናሉ። ለውጥን፣ በተለይም መልካም ፋይዳ ያለውን ለውጥ ማለም፣ ይህንንም ለማምጣት ሲባል ዕቅል መኖሩ በታወቀ ጊዜ በሰከነ መንገድ መቃወም አስፈላጊ ነው። ለመልካም ውጤትና ሥራ ለውጥ እንዲመጣ የሚተጉ ብዙ ተግዳሮት እንደሚያገኛቸው የታወቀ ነው። ልቅ፣ ልጓም ዐልባ መሆን ግን አያስፈልግም። ለመልካም የተነሡት ደግሞ መደዳነት አይመቻቸውም።

ዘመን ቀደማዊ የዘር ዕሳቤ

ይህ ፍልስፍናና በዘር ልዩነት ዕሳቤና ዘረኝነት ላይ ያሳረፈው ጫናም እንደ ፍልስፍናው ምስትልቅል ነው። ይሁን እንጂ ከምስቅልቅሉ መካከል የሚመዘዝ የዘር ልዩነት ዐሳቦች አይታጡም። በአንድ በኩል፣ ሳያስቡ የሚናገሩት ነገር የዘረኝነትን ምሰሶ አጥልቆ ይቀብረዋል። ድንድን ብሎ እንዲቆር፣ ቦሌ በኩል ዘረኝነትን የሚጠላ ይመስላል።

እንዲያውም የፀረ ቅኝ ግዛት ትግል ስኬት፤ እንዲሁም በመጨረሻ የፀረ አፓርታይድ ትግል ውጤት የዘር ልዩነትን በሚያቀነቅኑ ዘንድሞ ሆነ የጋራ የጾታነት ትግልን በሚያወድሱት ዘንድ ከዚህ ዕሳቤ የተነሣ የትግል ስልቶችን ዳግም ወደ መቃኘት መርታል። ለስኬትም ረድቷል ማለት ይቻላል። ቢያንስ በአሜሪካን አገር የጥቁሮች የጋራ ትግል ላይ ጉልህ ጫና አስከትሏል። እንዲያ ሲባሉ አይወዱም እንጂ ዘመናይ ስቶይኮችን ይመስላሉ።

መድልዎ ያለበትን ሥርዓት ታግሎ ሙሉ በሙሉ ለመጣል ብሎ ከመላላጥ ይልቅ በግል መቃወምን፤ ይህ ሊሰጥ የሚችለውን ጥቃቅን ስኬቶችን ማጣጣም ያበረታታሉና። ጥቁር ምሁራን፤ በተለያየ ዘርፍ ዕውቅና ያተረፉ ጥቁሮች፤ (ለምሳሌ በስነ ጥበብ፤ ሥነ ጽሑፍና ስፖርት)፤ እንዲሁም በቤተሰብ ኤኮኖሚ ረገድ ማለፊያ ብሥራት ያገኙ ጥቁሮች፤ "አፍሪካዊ አንድነት ሳይጎዳ በውስጥ ሆኖ መታገልን" ወደ መምረጥ ወስደ ቸዋል። 92

ይህ ጥርት ፍሬ አፍርቶ በከፊል ጥቁር የሆኑ ባራክ አባማ ወደ ፕሬዝዳንትነት እንዲደርሱ ረድቷል። ይህም ደግሞ፤ እያደገ የመጣው ጭቆናና፤ በተጨቋኝ ተጋድሎ ብቻ ሊደመሰስ ይችል ይሆናል የሚለውን ዕሳቤ የበለጠ እንዲደረጅ ረድቷል። ይህን ዕሳቤ በተሻለ መንገድ ያቀናበረችው ደግሞ በብዕር ስሟ ቤል ሁክስ እየተባለች የምትጠራው ታዋቂዋ የእንስታይነት93 አቀንቃኝ ግሎሪያ ጄንክንስ (1952-2021) ናት።

በእርስዋ ዕሳቤ፤ ጥቁሮች፤ ሴቶች፤ የአካል ጉዳተኞች፤ እና በተመሳሳይ መልክ በአንድና በሌላ ነገር ከማንኘበሰው የሚገለሉ ሁሉ በጋራ ተሰብስበው ሥርዓትን ለመጣል ሁከት ያዘለ ትግልን መምረጥ የለባቸውም። ከዚህ ይልቅ ለኅብረተሰቡ ያበረከቱትን ነገሮች በማጉላት፤ መልካም ምሳሌ ሆኖ በመገኘት፤ የተሻለ ውጤት ይገኛል ባይ ናት።

በአስፈላጊ ቦታዎች ጊዜና ሁኔታን እየመረጡ፤ መድልዎን በቃልም ሆነ በሥራ አልቀበልም ማለትን መጨመር ይቻላል። ይህ ሲደረግ ግን "በዘር" ተመሳሳይ ከሆነ ጋር ብቻ ሳይሆን ሌሎችንም እንደ አጋዥ መጠቀም ያስፈልጋል። 94 በጭፉ፤ ባቡሩ ሃዲዱን እንዲስት አታድርጉ እንደ ማለት ነው። አደጋ ሊያስከትል ስለሚችል።

ዘመን ቀደምነት ነገሮችን ሁሉ በአንድ ዐይን፤ በቁንጽል ዕሳቤ ማየት ይቀናዋል። የቤል ሁክስ ትንታኔ ከፀረ ዘር መድልዎ ትግል ይልቅ በሴላም መንገድ ተገለልን ለሚሉ ጥሩ መድረክ የሆነው ከዚያ የተነሣ ነው። ዘው አሉበት። እንስታውያን ስለ ያታ እኩልነት፤ የአካል ጉዳተኞች ስለ ተደራሽ አገልግሎትና እኩል ዕድል፤ በተለይም ግብረ

---

92 Dube, M. (2003). Postmodernism as Postnationalism? Racial Representation in U.S. Black Cultural Studies. The Black Scholar; Vol 33. No. 1, Black Film and Culture (Spring 2003; pp 2–18).

93 ፌምኒስት የሚለውን እንዲተካ ነው።

94 Hooks, B. (1994). Postmodern Blackness. University of Pennsylvania. African Studies Center.

ሰደማውያንና መሰል ልዩ ያታዊ ግልጠት ተግባሪዎች፤ ሁሉ የቤል ሁክስን ትንታኔ
አስተጋቡት። [95]

ሠላማዊ ተቃውሞ ወይንም በየዋኅነት፤ ግን ባለማቋረጥ፤ ለውጥን መግፋት አለብን
ባዮች ናቸው። ይህ ዕሳቤ፤ በፀረ አፓርታይድ ትግል ተፈትኖ ባለፈው በደቡብ አፍሪካ
ምሁራንና ጸሐፊዎች[96] ጭምር ምንኛ የናና መሆኑን ስንመለከት የዘመን ቀደም ዕሳቤ
ምንም እንኳ ወጥ የድርጊት መርሆ ግብር ማስቀመጥ ባይችል ፈጣንና ምቹ የንድፈ ዐሳብ
ማራመጃ መስክ መሆኑን እናስተውላለን። [97] የማንዴላን የትትቅ ትግል ዐሳብ የተቃወሙ
ከንዶቹም ስለ ነበሩ።

ዘመን ቀደምነት፤ ለብዙኃን ብሔር ፖለቲካዊ ዕሳቤም ወሳኝ ዐሳቦችን የሚያበረክት
ሆኖ እናገኘዋለን። በተለይም፤ የዘር ልዩነትን ከምክንያታዊነት አውጥተን በአንዳርዊነት
እንዯዉ የሚለው መሠረታዊ ዕሳቤው ጭራሽ የዘርም ሆነ የብሔር ልዩነት ከነባራዊ
እውነታ ይልቅ ዐሳባዊ ነው ወደሚል መደምደሚያ የሚያደርስ ሊሆን ይችላል።

ሰፍ ብለው ላቀፉት መውጫ ቀዳዳ እንዳይከለከለባቸው ያስፈራል። ከዘር ልዩነት
ሌላ የጾታ እኩልነት አርማጆች፤ ሥራችንን ሊያዳፍኑ ይችላል ይላሉ። [98] የጥቁሮች
መብት አቀንቃኞት ግን ይህ እውነተኛ ፍካት ነው ብለው ያምናሉ። ከመተፋፈግ ይልቅ
መተጋገዝን ስለሚያስበልጥ። [99]

በሌላ በኩል ይህ የበለጠ ያስፈራቸው ዘረኛ የሳይንስ ጠበብትም የዘር ልዩነትን
በሳይንሳዊ መንገድ ለማረጋገጥና የዘር ፖለቲካ በነባራዊ አመክንዮ እንዲመሠረት ደፋ
ቀና ማለት ጀምሯዋል። የዘመኑን የሳይንስና ቴክኖሎጂ ዕድገት በመጠቀም። ሳይንስም፤
ቴክኖሎጂም መርበሽ አለባቸው ያለባትስ የጊዜው ፍልስፍና አይደል?

ማለትም፤ ከተለመደው የሳይንስ አካሄድ ወጣ ባለ መልክ ሙከራን ከትግበራ ጋር
በማቀናጀት የዘር ልዩነትን ሳይንሳዊ ለማድረግ ጉዞውን ተያይዘውታል። አነሥሁ በታሪክ
ሃያላንና ታላላቅ የተባሉ ሰዎች እና ዘሮቻቸውን ከማጥናት ይጀምራሉ። ለምን፤ እንዴት፤
እና በምን ሃያል ሆኑ? ምክንያቱ ከተገኘ በሰው አካል ውስጥ ማባዛት ይቻል ይሆን?

95 Kubota, R. (2003). New approaches to gender, class, and race in second language writing.
    ournal of Second Language Writing 12 (2003) 31–47. Pergamon.

96 Stevens, G. (2003). Academic representations of 'race' and racism in psychology: Knowledge
    production, historical context, and dialectics in transitional South Africa. International
    Journal of Intercultural Relations 27 (2003) 189–207. Pergamon.

97 Schnieder, C. S. (2004). Integrating Critical Race Theory and Postmodernism Implications
    of Race, Class, and Gender. Critical Criminology; 12, pages87–103 (2004)

98 Beckett, C., & Macey, M. (2001). Race, Gender and Sexuality: The Oppression of
    Multiculturalism. Women's Studies International Forum, Vol. 24, No. 3/4, pp. 309–319, 2001

99 Keith, N. W. (1998). It Is a Truly New Dawn: Blacks and the Politics of the Postmodern Age.
    Race & Society, Volume 1, Number 1, pages 33-61. Copyright 0 1998 by JAI Press Inc.

ከሥነ ፍጥረት፤ ከነርቭ፤ አዕምሮና የባሕርይ ሳይንስ፤ ከዘረ መል (ጄኔቲክስ) ጥናት፤ ከመልክዐ ምድር ሳይንስ፤ ከባሕል፤ ከሕዝብ አሠፋፈር እና ፍልሰት ጥናት እንዲሁም ከሥልጣኔና ዕድገት ጥናት ጋር በማዋሐድ የአንድ ሰው ማንነት ካለበት ኅብረተሰብ ጋራ ያለውን ቁርኝት ለመለወጥ ደፋ ቀና ማለት ተጀምሯል። ይህ ልፋት ገና ከጅምሩ ጽንፍ መርገጡ ጎኃድ እየወጣ ነው።[100]

ገና ከጅምሩ፤ የጥናቱ ትክክለኛነት እንኳን ሳይረጋገጥ፤ ከዘር መል ምህንድስና ጋር በማቀናበር ታላላቅ ሰዎችን "መፍጠር" ወደሚል የለየለት ዘረኝነት እንዳያመራ ያሰጋል። ጭራሽ ከተሳካም ያልተፈለገ ሕዝብ ካለ ለማጥፋትም ሊጠቀሙበት ይችላሉ።

ለምሳሌ:- እንገምት። የሲ.ጋራ አጫሽነት ከልምድ ወደ ባሕርይ እንዴት እንደሚሸጋገር በጥናት አውቅን እንበል። ይህንንም አስቀድመው የሚወስኑ የዘረ መል እና ነርቭ ክሮችንም ለየን እንበል። ሳይንሱ ሁለቱን ግኝቶች ማጣመር ከፈቀደ፤ እንዲጠፋ በተወሰነው ሕዝብ ሽል ላይ ከማስረጽ የሚያግድ ነገር የለም። ዘረኝነት ብቻ ሳይሆን ክፉትም ጦዝ ማለት ነው። ሌላ ሥጋት።

---

100 MacMahon, R. (2020). Resurecting raciology? Genetic ethnology and pre-1945 anthropological race classification. Studies in History and Philosophy of Biology & Biomedical Sciences 83 (2020) 101242

ዘርና ብዝጎ ብሔር ፖለቲካ

"የመጀመሪያው የኤኮኖሚክስ ትምህርት እጥረት ነው፤ ሁሉም ያሻውን
ለማርካት በቂ ነገር የለም፡፡ በፖለቲካ የመጀመሪያው ትምህርት ደግሞ፤
ይህን የኤኮኖሚክስ የመጀመሪ ትምህርት ችላ ማለት ነው፡፡ "

ቶማስ ሶዌል
አሜሪካዊ ኤኮኖሚስት፤ ሁቨር ኢንስቲትዩት፤ መምህር፤
ደራሲና የማኅበራዊ ገዳዮች ወግ አጥባቂ ተንታኝ

ሁለት መላጦች ... የቀጠላ

አንድ ቀን ሽኩቻው በርትቶ ወደ ጸብ ተሸጋገረና ለህንጻ ሥራ በያዙት የእጅ
መሣሪያ ሊደባደቡ ሲሉ በአካባቢው የሚገኙ ሁሉ እያተቦራጩ ተሰባሰበው ገላገሏቸው፡፡
ነገረ ሥራቸው እንደ ድሮው እንዳይቀጥል ግን አመላካች ነበር፡፡

የእንጀራ ነገር ነውና "አንተም ተው፤ አንተም ተው" ተባብለው የተለመደ
ኑሮአቸውን ቀጠሉ፡ ገንፈል፡ ረገብ የሚለው ጸባቸው ግን ማብቂያው አይታይም ነበር፤
የተፈራው አልቀረም፡ ከዕለታት አንድ ቀን ከረር አለ፡ ቀድም አለመግባባት ሲኖር፤
አንዱ ሌላውን ለማስፈራራት ሲያነሳው የነበረው አካፋና ዶማ የዚያን ቀን በቅርብ
አልነበረም፡፡

በእርግጥም የዚያን ዕለት በሁለቱም እጅ፡ ወይም በቅርብ ርቀት፡ ስለት ያለው
ዕቃ አልነበረም፡ ምን ዋጋ አለው? በግንባታ ቦታዎች ባላንጣን ለመጉዳት የሚረዳ
ነገር አይታጣ፡ ወዲያው እጃቸው ከፍት እንዳመጣ በማይታወቅ፡ አንዳች በሚያህል
አጣና አንድ ለአንድ ተቀማመሱ፡ ከተንዳኝ ጨዄት ጋር፡ ወዲያውም፡ ጉዳያቸውን
ሲከታተሉ የነበሩ "ተመልካቾች" ሳይጠሩ ከተፍ አሉ፡፡

55

"አረ ተው!" የሚለው በርካታ ቢሆንም፤ ነገር ለማብረድ ከተሰበሰበው መኳል በሥላም የቀረብ እየመሠለ ለካ ነገር የጠገበም አልታጣም። አልቀረም፤ ከሁለት በላይ ሰው ሆነ፤ ጎራ ለይቶ፤ እርስ በርስ መሠናዘር ተጀመረ።

ምንም ሳይጋበዙ፤ ከዐንደበታቸውም፤ ከዱላውም ማዋጣት ጀመሩ። ጨጫታው በረታ፤ አንዱ 'አብዲ፤ አብዲ' ሲል፤ ሌላው 'ሙሐ ወንድሜ' እያለ።

"አንተ፤ ተው እንጂ!"

"አንተስ ለምን አትተውም?!"

"አንተኛው ደግሞ ምን አገባህ?"

"ምንትስ ... አገባና" (መቼስ እነሱ ያሉትን ሁሉ ቃል በቃል እዚህ አንደግምም)።

". . . እንዴት አያገባኝም?"

ጨኸቱ፤ 'የጨበራ ተዝካር' ሆኖ ቁጣጭ። ማንም ማንንም አይሰማም። "አንተ" እየተባባሉ ይሰዳደቡ የነበሩ የቀድሞ ወዳጆች ጥል ሳይጠፉ የተቀላቀሉትን አካተተ።

ታዲያ "አሳታፊ" ጥል አይመችም እናንተዬ?

"ድሮም እናንተ፤ ... እንዲህና እንዲህ ያደረጋችሁ፤ ... ይህ የኛ እንጂ፤ ... ዘመናችሁ እኮ አለቀ፤ ... ወዘተ" ወደ መባባል ከምኔውና እንዴት እንደ ተሸጋገረ ራሳቸውም አያውቁትም! እህል ውሃ ፍለጋ የተሰባሰቡ ሳይሆኑ፤ ጥል የሚያከፉ፤ የለየላቸው ባላንጣዎች ስብስብ መሰለ።

አንዳንድ ጊዜ እንዲህ ዐይነት ስብስብና እንካ ሰላንቲያው ሳያምረው ሲቀር አምላክ ዝናብ ልኮ ይበትን ነበር። የቀን ጉዶሉ ሆነና የዚያን ቀን ዝናቡም አልወረደ። ለግንባታ የተሰበሰበው ድንጋይና አጣና መሬትና ሲሚንቶ፤ ምስማርና ብረት ማገናት እንዳለበት ረስቶ የሰው ጭንቅላት ይፈልግ ገባ። ዋይታው ደራ።

የደማው ደምቶ፤ የሞተው ሞቶ፤ የቆሰለው ቆስሎ፤ አካባቢው በዑዉታ ሲናጥ ሁለት ቆመጥ የያዙ "ጸዮታ አስከባሪዎች" ግርግሩ ጠርቷቸው መጡ። ትኩስ የጥላቻ ጢስ እየተግተለተለ ነበርና ፈጥነው አልተቀላቀሉም።

"ጉመን በጤና" ወዳጄ። ራቅ ብለው ቆመው የሚሆነውን ይመለከቱ ነበር። የቦሌ ቡልቡላ አካባቢ ልጆችም ሆነ ሰዎች አልመሰል ብዒቸው እንደሆን አይታወቅም።

ከጸዮታ አስከባሪዎች አንዱ ስልክ ለመደወል ይታገላል። ለበላይ ኃላፊያቸው ለማስታወቅ፤ ለክፉም፤ ለደጉም፤ "ይኼ ነገር አላማረኝም፤ ቢር ልደውል።"

ሌላኛው አልሰማውም። ልቡ በከረረው ጥልና በቡን ተከፍፍለው የማይመስል ጨዋታ ባደሩ ባላንጣዎች ላይ ነው። ራሱ የያዘውን የጸዮታ አስከባር ቆመጥ በአንዳንዶች እጅ ካለው አጣና ጋር ያስተያይ ይመስል ደጋግሞ ይመለከታል።

ቀርቦ ላየው፤ ከልጅነቱ ጋር ፍርሃቱ ዐብሮ ሳይነብብት አይቀርም። ዓይኑን ከግርግሩ አላነሣም። ሁለት ብቻ ሆነው እዚያ ከተጠጉ ሊሆን የሚችለውን በልቡ እያሰበ ርቆ የነጉደ ይመስላል። እንደ እግር ኳስ ጨዋታ፤ በሬሽካ አይቆም ነገር!

ታዲያ በገላጋይ ብርታት ወይም የጸጥታ ኃይል በመፍራት ሳይነን ከሁለቱም ባላንጦች በኩል ከባድ ጉዳት ደርሶ ኖሮ፤ የተንተከተከው አቦል ተግ፤ ግርግሩም ጋብ ወደ ማለት ቀረበ። የደከመው አንድ ሁለት ጊዜ ትንፋሽ ለመሳብ ዐይነት። ወዲያውም፤ ማን ይበልጥ እንደ ተጎዳ፤ የጎይል ሚዛኑ ወደ የት እንዳጋደለ ለማመዛዘን ያህል፤ ጥቂት ረጭ አለ።

በዚህች አጋጣሚ፤ አንዱ ባለ አጣና እግረ አውጪኝ ይላል፤ አጣናውን እንደ ያዘ፤ እየተጣጻረም ራቅ ብለው ሁኔታውን ወደሚከታተሉ ጸጥታ አስከባሪዎች መጠጋት ጀመረ። ወጠምሻ ነው፤ የያዘው አጣና እህል ውሃ አያሰኝም።

ወጣቱ ጸጥታ አስከባሪ ሁኔታው አላማረውም። ቀድሞም የፈራ የሚመስለው ልጅ እግር ነገር፤ ቆመጡን ማስተካከል ጀመረ።

አይይይ! የያዘት ቆመጥ ጭራሮ አከለችበት። እርሱም በተራው እግሬ አውጪኝ ማለት እንደሚሻለው ገባው። ዞር ወደ ጓደኛው ለመሮጥ ሲዳዳው በዚያች ቅጽበት ተኩስ ተሰማ።

ለካ ጓደኛው ስልክ መደወል ተሳክቶለት ኖሮ አንድ ፒክ አፕ መኪና ሙሉ ጠብመንጃ ያነገቱ ተጨማሪ "ጸጥታ አስከባሪዎች" ከሥፍራው ደርሰው ነበር።

"ከድርን! ከድርን ገደሉት!"

"አላልኳችሁም? እነርሱ እኮ እኛን ለመጨረስ ተዘጋጅተው ነበር።"

"መቼስ ቆመን እያየን አናልቅም!"

ከግርግሩ ለማምለጥ የሮጠው ሰው ስም ከድር ነበር። ጸጥታ አስከባሪው ያድነኝ እንደሁ ብሎ፤ መሸሿጊያ ፍለጋ ነበር ወደ እርሱ ያቀናው። ሸሽት ሳይሆን፤ የሚያሳድድ ስለ መሰላቸው የወጣቱ ጸጥታ አስከባሪ የሥራ ባለደረቦች ከድር ሆዬ "ሳይቀድም" ቀደሙት። ምድር ቀውጢ።

አብዲና ሙሔ 'ግለሰቦች' ሳይሆኑ 'ብሔር' የሚሆኑት ከዚያ በኋላ ነው።

የብዝኃ ብሔር ዕሳቤ

ትርጉም

ስለ ብሔርስ ምን ትረዳለህ ብለን ጎዳና ላይ ወጥተን ሰዎችን ብንጠይቅ ምን መልስ እናገኛለን? በቅድሚያ፣ ያለ ጥርጥር ሰው ብሔርና ዘር ልዩነታቸውን አያስተውልም። በአገራችን ስለ ዘር፣ አገር፣ ብሔር፣ ጎይማኖትም ጭምር ያለን መረዳት እንዳንዴ ፈገግ ያስብላል። ለብዙዎች ዘር፣ ብሔር፣ አገር፣ ጎይማኖት፣ ሁሉም ትርጉማቸው አንድ ነው።

'እርሷ እስላም አይደለችም አማራ ናት' እንደምንለው ሁሉ፣ 'እኔ አገሬ እዚሁ ጎንደር ነው' እንደምንል ሁሉ፣ 'እኔ እንኳን ክርስቲያን አይደለሁም፣ ቃለ ሕይወት ነኝ' እንደሚባል ሁሉ፣ ዘር፣ ብሔር፣ አገር፣ ጎይማኖት፣ ይመሰቃቀልብናል። ከባሌ ክርስቲያን፣ ከአክሱም ሙስሊም የሚገኝ አይመሰለንም። ደቡብ ውስጥ የኦርቶዶክስ እምነት ተከታይ ስለ መኖሩ የሚጠይቅ ዛሬም አይጠፉም። ስለ ንግግራችን እንኳን አጥልቀን ማሰብ የተላመድነው አይደለምና።

የዘር ልዩነት በፍጹም እግዚአብሔር የፈጠረው ልዩነት እንዳይደለ ለማየት ሞክረናል። ፈጣሪስ ሲፈጥር ሰውን አንድ ዘር አድርጎ እንጂ ሌላ አልፈጠረም፤ ይህ ከሆነ ደግሞ ብሔርን፣ ጎሣን፣ ነገድንም እርሱ አልፈጠረም። እንደ መጽሐፍ ቅዱስ ከሆነ እግዚአብሔር አንድ ሰው ብቻ ፈጠረ፣ ወንድና ሴት አድርጎ ፈጠረ፣ ተባዙም። በፍጥረት አንድ ከሆንን ይህ ሁሉ በብሔር መለያያት ከየት መጣ? መጽሐፍ ቅዱስ ራሱ የእሥራኤል ልጆች 12 ነገድ ናቸው ይል የለም?

ልክ እንደ ዘር ልዩነት ዕሳቤ አቀንቃኞች፣ የብሔር ልዩነትም ተፈጥሮአዊ ነው የሚሉ አሉ። ነገር ግን፣ የዘር ልዩነት ሆን ተብሎ የተፈጠረ እንደሆነ ተመልክተናል። የብሔር ልዩነት ግን ማኅበራዊና ፖለቲካዊ መለያያትን የበለጠ የሚያመለክት እንደሆነ እናስተውላለን። ሰው እየበዛ ሲሄድ፣ ልማዱም እየተለያየ ሄደ፣ ጭፍራ በጭፍራ ተሰባስቦ መኖር ሲጀምር የጋራ የሚያስብል ወይም ከሌላው ለየት ያለ ባሕል፣ ጎይማኖት፣ ቋንቋ መቅረጽ ቻለ። "የአንተና የእኔ" መባባል ተጀመረ።

የብሔርን ነገር ጥቂት የሚያወሳስበው፣ በብሔር ውስጥ ጎሣ፣ ነገድ፣ ሌላም ስም የምንሰጣቸው "ልዩነቶች" መኖራቸው ነው። የዘር ዕሳቤ ማኅበራዊም፣ መልክዓ ምድራዊም ገጽታ ቢኖረውም፣ በአብዛኛው ፖለቲካዊ መቀቅራዊ ነው ብለን እንደ ተነጋን ሁሉ ብዝኃ ብሔርም እንደዚሁ ነው። የፍጥረት ልዩነት ሳይሆን የማኅበራዊ ትስስርና ትፍፍግ ውጤት ነው የሚሆነው። ማኅበራዊ ስንል ግን ተፈጥሮአዊ ነገሮች የሉብትም ማለትም አይደለም።

ምክንያቱም፤ ማኅበራዊ ኑሮ የሚጀምረው ከቤተሰብ ነው፤ ተፈጥሮ ነክ ከሆነ ነገር። ልክ እንደ ዘር ዕሳቤ ምናባዊ የሚያስብልም ነን አለው። የብሔር ልዩነትን ጉዳይ የሚያቀንቅኑ የሚያነሱት ልዩነቶች ጠጣርና ወሳኝ ሳይሆኑ የዘፈቀደ የተብጀ ድንበር ያላቸው ይመስላሉ። በእርግጥም አንድን ባሕል ለክት ለእንድ ቡድን ብቻ የሰጠ የለምና።

ባሕል የሚዘመት ከመሆኑ አንጻር፤ አንድን ዘር ወይም ብሔር እንዲህ ነው ብሎ በባሕል ብቻ መገደብ አይቻልም። ደግሞም፣ ሰዎች ባሕልን ፈጠሩት እንጂ ባሕል ሰውን አልፈጠረም። ያም ሆኖ በባሕል ውስጥ ሰው ይቀረጻል። ይህ ፍረጃን አስቸጋሪ ያደርገዋል።

ለምሳሌ:- በአገራችን በስፋት ይስተዋል የነበረው የገዳ ሥርዓት በኦሮሞ ሕዝብ ብቻ የተወሰነ አይደለም። መሠል ባሕል በጌዴዎ እንዲሉ ይነገራል። በሶማሌ ውስጥም "ኡጋዝ" እየተባለ የሚጠሩ የጐሣ አባቶች አሉ። የጐሣ አስተዳደሩም ከገዳ ሥርዓት የሚዋረስበት መስመር አይታጣም።

ስለዚህ ኦሮሞ የገዳ ሥርዓት አለው ማለት እንችላለን፤ ነገር ግን የገዳ ሥርዓት የሚከተል ሁሉ ግን ኦሮሞ አይደለም። የገዳ ሥርዓት እየበለጸገ ሊሄድ የሚችል ጥሩ የሚባል ዕሴት እንዳለው ስለሚነገር መላው አፍሪካ ቢከተል አያስከፋም እያልን ነው። ያ አፍሪካን በሙሉ ኦሮሞ አያደርግም።

ብሔር ሙሉ በሙሉ ፖለቲካዊ አመለካከት፤ ብሔርተኝነትም የፖለቲካ መሠረት ነው የሚሉም አሉ። በተጨባጭም አሌክስ ዲዋል የተባለ የምሥራቅ አፍሪካ ፖለቲካ ተንታኝ እንዳመለከተው ብሔርን ለፖለቲካ ትግል የመጠቀም ፍላጎት እያጨመረ እንጂ እየቀነሰ አይደለም።[101] በእኛም አገር ብሔርተኝነት ዋና የፖለቲካ መስመር በመሆኑ አንድ ሰው በፖለቲካ ለመሳተፍ ከፈለገ የግድ ብሔር መርጦ ነው።

ትናንት ጫና ያስከተሉ ልዩነቶች ብሔርንና የብሔር ትግልን መምሪጥ እንዳስገደዱ ሁሉ ምርጫ አዳጋች የሚሆንበት ጊዜ እንዳለም አመልክተን እንለፍ። ብሔር ሲመረጥ የማይቀደደው ለመቅደድ ከዳረገስ? ከሁለት ብሔር የተወለዱትን አስቡ። እንደ አለመታደል ሆኖ የአፍሪካ ፖለቲካ የዘር ድምር ጨዋታ ነው። በፖለቲካው የረታ ይጠቀላላል። የእናትና አባት ጐሣ የተለያየ ለሆኑ ይህን ጨዋታ ተጨዋቹ ቢባል መልሳቸው መገመት አስፈላጊያችን አይሆንም።

ከዚህ በተጨማሪ፤ ብሔር ብቻ ሳይሆን በአንድ አገር ፖለቲካዊ ጥያቄ መሆን የሚችሉ ብዙ ነገሮች አሉ። የያታ እኩልነት አንዱ ነው፤ ኅይማኖትም ከማታገል አልፎ የብዙ ጦርነቶች መንሥዔ ሆኖ አልፏል። ጊዜው ያመጣቸው ሌሎችም ጥያቄዎች እንዲሁ። የብሔር ጥያቄን ለመፍታት ግጭትን ባስቀደም ፖለቲካ

101 de Waal, A. (2014). The Political Marketplace: Analyzing Political Entrepreneurs and Political Bargaining with a Business Lens. Framework and Background Seminar Memo; World Peace Foundation. https://sites.tufts.edu/reinventingpeace/files/2014/10/Political-Marketplace_de-Waal.pdf

ከዳክርን ለማያባራ የህዝብ ሥቃይ፣ መፈናቀልና ዕልቂት መንገድ ከመክፈት ውጭ የምናተርፈው ነገር የለም።

"ዘር" የሚለው ፅንሰ ዐሳብ መሆኑን በቀደሙት ክፍሎች በጥቂቱም ቢሆን ለማብራራት ተሞክሯል። "ብሔር፣ ጎሣ፣ ነገድ፣ ብሔረሰብ" የሚባላትን ነገሮች ግን መተርጎም ይኖርብናል። አንዱ የማያስማማን የእንዚህ ቃላት ፍቺ ዝብርቅርቅ መሆኑ ነው። ቢያንስ ይህንን ጽሑፍ የሚያነቡ ተመሳሳይ መረዳት እንዲያገኙ በዚህ ጽሑፍ አውዳዊ ትርጉሙን መስጠት ያሻል። መነሻ ቢሆንን እንጂ ሁሉን እንደማያስማማ ግምት መውሰዱም መልካም ነው።

ከቀላል እንጀምር፤ ከቆዳ ቀለም ልዩነት የሚነሣውን (ለምሳሌ ጥቁር እና ነጭ) 'የዘር ልዩነት' ብለው የሚከፍሉ አሉ። ይሁን እንጂ፣ ቀደም ሲል እንደተገለጠው ከቆዳ ወይም ከፀጉር ቀለም እና ዐይነት እንዲሁም ከዐይን ቀለም እና አቀማመጥ ጋር በማያያዝ በሰዎች መካከል ያለውን አለመመሳሰል "የዘር" ልዩነት ብሎ ለመጥራት የሚያበቃ ምንም ነገር የለም። የሰው ዘር በተፈጥሮ አንድ ነውና።

ደግሞም የቆዳ መንጣት ነጭ እንደማያሰኝም ይታወቃል። ጃፓንና ቻይና ምን ሊባሉ ነው? ነጭ ወይስ ጥቁር? አረብን ሀንዶችስ? የዘር ልዩነት ማኅበራዊና ፖለቲካዊ ስለሆነ ችክ ብለው የዘር ልዩነትን የሚያራግቡ ሌሎችን ጨቁኖ ለመግዛት ካላቸው ፍላጎት ብቻ እንደሆነ በሰፊው አይተናል። እነዚህ አውቀው ወይም ሳያውቁ ዘረኝነትን ያስፋፋሉ። በቀለም የተመሠረተ ልዩነት ግን ሲራገብ ውጤቱ ምን ሊሆን እንደቻለ በሰፊው ተመልክተናል።

የዘር ልዩነት ዕሳቤ እጅግ ስላስቸገረ የተባበሩት መንግሥታት ድርጅት በጥልቀት እንዲያጠናው አነሳስቶታል። በዚያውም ከጥናቱ ውጤት የተነሣ በሰዎች መካከል የሚታየውን አለመመሳሰል "ልዩነት ነው" ብሎ መጥራትን አውግዟል።[102] በዚህ ጥናት መሠረት፣ የሰው ዘር አንድ ብቻ ነው። ነጭም ሆነ ጥቁር ዘር፣ ጠጉራ ከርዳዳም ሆነ አፍንጫ ስልካካ ሌላ ዘር የለም፣ አንድ ብቻ።

የአገራችንን የብሔር ፖለቲካ አንዳንዶች "የጎሣ" ፖለቲካ ይሉታል። ይህም 'ብሔር፣ ጎሣ፣ ነገድ' የሚባሉትን ነገሮች እንዴት እንደምንረዳ አመልካች ነው። ብዙዎች ለእነዚህ ቃላት ቀጥተኛ ትርጉም መስጠት ስለሚያዳግታቸው፣ አንዱን በሌላው ይፈቱታል። በተጨማሪም፣ የብሔር ልዩነት ከባሕል ቋንቋ፣ ኃይማኖት፣ እና መሠል ልዩነቶችም የሚሰፉ አድርገው ይውስዱታል። የብሔር ዕሳቤ እየደረጀ ስለ መጣ "ጎሣ" የሚለው ቃል እየተተወ መጥቷል፣ ስለ ጎሣ ልዩነት ማውሳትም አይፈለግም።

102 United Nations (1978). Declaration on Race and Racial Prejudice. Accessed on April 23, 2021 from https://www.un.org/en/genocideprevention/documents/atrocity-crimes/Doc.11_declaration%20on%20race%20and%20racial%20prejudice.pdf

የኢትዮጵያ ቋንቋዎች ጥናት ኢንስቲትዩት በ1993 ዓመት ምህረት ባሳተመው የአማርኛ መዝገበ ቃላት[103] "ማኅበረሰብ" ለሚለው ቃል "ማኅበራዊ ትስስር ያለው"፤ በተወሰነ አካባቢ የሚኖር ሕዝብ" የሚል ትርጉም ይሰጠዋል። እንዲሁም፤ "ማኅበራዊ" ማለት "የኅብረት፤ የጋራ፤ የሕዝብ" ብሎ ይፈታዋል። ይህም መዝገብ ቃላት፤ ብሔር፤ ብሔረሰብ፤ ነገድ፤ ጎሣ ... ወዘተ የተለያዩ የማኅበረሰብ ስብስብ መገለጫዎች እንደሆኑ ያትትና ቃላቱ በጽጽር ይተረጉማቸዋል።

በዚህ መሠረት፤ "ነገድ" የሚለውን ቃል "በባሕል፤ በኤኮኖሚ እና በአካባቢ ይዞታ አንድነት ላይ የተመሠረተ ግንኙነት ያለው፤ ከጎሣ ይልቅ መጠኑ ሰፊ ማኅበረሰብ" ብሎ ይተረተመዋል። ስለዚህ "ነገድ" የሚለው ቃል "ጎሣ" ከሚለው ከፍ ያለ ስብስብ የሚወክል ቃል ነው የሚል መረዳት እናገኛለን። "ብሔረሰብ" የሚለውን ደግሞ "ከደም አንድነት ይልቅ፤ በክልል፤ በቋንቋ በባሕል አንድነት ላይ የተመሠረተ የተለያዩ ነገዶች የተዋኸዱበት ማኅበረሰብ" ይለዋል።

"ጎሣ" የሚለውን ደግሞ፤ "የባሕልና የቋንቋ አንድነት እንዲሁም፤ በደምና በሥጋ ዝምድና ላይ የተመሠረተ ግንኙነት ያለውና መጠኑ ከነገድ ያነሰ ማኅበረ ሕዝብ" ይለዋል። ስለዚህ "ነገድ" የሚለው ቃል "ብሔረሰብ" ለሚለው የቀረበ፤ ከጎሣ ከፍ ያለ የሕዝብ ሥፍር ነው ማለት ይቻላል። "ጎሣ" የሚለው ወደ ደም እና ቤተሰባዊ አንድነት ያጋደለ ትርጉም የሚሰጥ እንደሆን እንቀበል።

ታዲያ ይኸው መዝገበ ቃላት፤ የጎሣ ፖለቲካ ማለትንም "በዘር፤ በጎሣ፤ በብሔረሰብ ላይ የተመሠረተ ፖለቲካዊ እንቅስቃሴ ነው" ሲል ይገልጸዋል። ይህ እንግዲህ ነገሮችን ትንሽ ያወሳስባል። በአንድ በኩል፤ የብሔር ፖለቲካን ከዘር ፖለቲካ ጋር ማጣመሩ አነጋጋሪ ነው። በሌላ በኩል ግን ጎሣና ነገድ በብሔር ሰብ ውስጥ የሚገለጡ ከሆነ፤ የብሔር ፖለቲካን የጎሣም ነው ብለን ብንጠራው የሚያስቆጣ አይሆንም ማለት ነው።

ምንም እንኳ "ብሔረሰብ" የሚለው አገላለጥ ከደም ይልቅ ባሕል ተኮር እንደሆነ ቢገለጥም ከዘሬ የሕዝብ ትስስር እና መለያየት አንጻር ግን ፈጽሞ በደም የሆነ አንድነት የለም ማለት አይደለም። ቀድሞውኑ በአንድ አካባቢ የተሰባሰቡት በዚህ አይደል? በብሔር ዕሳቤ ውስጥ የሥጋ ዝምድና ሥፍራ እንዳለው መናፍ አይቻልም።

ሰዎች በአንድ የሚሰባሰቡት በተለያያ መንገድ ነው። ከእነዚህም ውስጥ በአምቻና ጋብቻ፤ በቤተሰባዊ አንድነት፤ በፖለቲካ ሤራ፤ በኅይልና በመስፋፋት፤ በፍቅርም በማጥመድ አንድ ማድረግ ይገኝበታል። ስለ ሆነ ባሕል ዘለል አንድነት እንዳለም ማስተዋል ያሻል።[104]

---

103 የኢትዮጵያ ቋንቋዎች ጥናት ኢንስቲትዩት (1993)። የአማርኛ መዝገበ ቃላት። አዲስ አበባ።

104 Williams, R. L. (2001). Ethnic Conflicts; in International Encyclopedia of Social and Behavioral Sciences.

ይህ መዝገበ ቃላት "ብሔር" ለሚለው ቃል ግን ቀዳሚ ትርጉም አድርጎ የሚያቀርበው "አገር" የሚለውን ነው። ይህ ትርጉም "ብሔር" የማገበራዊ ትስስርና ትፍፍግ፣ እንዲሁም ከሌሎችም ዐይነት ልዩነቶች ጋር መስተጋብር ያለው መዋቅር ውጤት ነው ከሚል ዕሳቤ የመነጨ መሆኑን እናስተውላለን። በተጨማሪም፣ ብሔርን "አንድ ዐይነት ቋንቋ፣ ባሕልና ሥነ ልቦናዊ አመለካከት ያለው፣ በታሪክ፣ በኤኮኖሚ የተሳሰረና በተወሰነ ክልል የሚኖር ሕዝብ" ብሎ ይተረጉመዋል።

"ብሔራዊ" የሚለውን ደግም "የአገር" ወይም "አገራዊ" ሲል ያትታል። በዚህ የመዝገበ ቃላት ትርጉም መሠረት "ብሔር" አገርን የሚወክል ቃል ነው። የብዙ ጎሣዎችና ነገዶች፣ የቋንቋ፣ የባሕል፣ የኤኮኖሚና፣ ሌሎች ጉዳዮች ትስስር እና ስብጥር የሚያሳይ ብለን ልንረዳው እንችላለን። ይህ በአሁኑ ጊዜ ስለ "ብሔር" ያለንን መረዳት ትንሽ ይገዳደረዋል።

በተለይም፣ በሥራ ላይ ያለው የኢትዮጵያ ሕግ መንግሥት "ብሔር፣ ብሔረሰብ ሕዝብ" የሚለውን ሲተረጉም "ሰፋ ያለ የጋራ ጠባይ የሚያንጸባርቅ ባሕል ወይም ተመሳሳይ ልምዶች ያላቸው፣ ሊግባቡት የሚችል የጋራ ቋንቋ ያላቸው፣ የጋራ ወይም የተዛመደ ሕልውና አለን ብለው የሚያምኑ፣ የሥነ ልቦና አንድነት ያላቸውና በአብዛኛው በተያያዘ መልክዐ ምድር የሚኖሩ ናቸው"[105] ብሎ ይዘጋል።

ሕግ መንግሥቱ በእነዚህ የማገበረሰብ ስብስቦች መካከል ልዩነት ስለ መኖሩ በግልጥ አልተናገረም። ስለ "ነገድ እና ጎሣ" ፈጽም አልጠቀሰም። በመጀመሪያዎቹ አራት ድንጋጌዎች ስለ ኢትዮጵያ "ስያሜ፣ ወሰን፣ ሰንደቅ ዓላማ፣ እና ብሔራዊ መዝሙር" የቀረቡት ሃረጎች "አገር" መሆኗን ቢገልጹም "ብሔር" የሚለውንም መግለጫ ተጠቅሟል። እንዲሁም የደቡብ እና አንዳንድ ሌሎች ክልሎች ልክ እንደ ኢትዮጵያ (እንደ አገር) "ብሔሮች፣ ብሔረሰቦችና ሕዝቦችን" ያቀፉ ናቸው።

ይህ አስቸጋሪ አገላለጽ ቢሆንም አንድ የምናስተውለው ወሳኝ ጉዳይ አለ። ሕግ መንግሥቱ የብሔር ጥያቄ አንግበው ሲፋለሙ በነበሩ ወገኖች የበላይ ጠባቂነት የተቀረጸ ነው። በተለይም የፌደራል መንግሥቱን አባላት ለመወሰን የተቀመጠው አንቀጽ ይህን ያሳብቃል። በዘጠኝ ክልሎች፣ ጥቂት በስም የተጠቀሱ ማገበረሰቦችን በማስቀመጥ ሌላው "ወደፊት ይታያል" የሚል ዐይነት አንቀጽ በማከል ይጨርሰዋል። ይሁን እንጂ ልዩነትን የማርገብ እንጂ የማክረር ፍላጎት ያዘለ አይመስልም።

የዘር ዕሳቤ ፖለቲካዊ ስለ ነበር ወደ ዘረኝነት እንዴት እንደ ተንደረደረ በጥቂቱ አይተናል። ብሔርተኝነትም በብዙሃ ብሔር እኩልነት ዕሳቤ ላይ ካልተመሠረተ አግላይነት ሊጠነወተው ይችላል። ሕግ መንግሥቱ ይህንን በሚገባ የተረዳ ይመስላል። ምክንያቱም፣ ፖለቲካዊ የዘር ዕሳቤ ወደ ዘር መድልዎ እንዳምራ ሁሉ፣ የብሔር

---

105 ፌደራል ነጋሪት ጋዜጣ (1995)። የኢትዮጵያ ፌደራላዊ ዴሞክራሲያዊ ሪፐብሊክ ሕግ መንግሥት አዋጅ። https:// ethiopianembassy.be/wp-content/uploads/Constitution-of-the-FDRE.pdf

ልዩነት ዕሳቤ ወደ ብሔር መድልዎ እንዳያመራ፤ የትርጉም ግልጸኝነት ቢያስቸግር እንኳ
የመብቶች እኩልነትን ማስፈን እንዲቻል ጥረት አድርጓል።

በእርግጥም ከሕገ መንግሥቱ ግማሽ ያህሉ አንቀጾች ስለ መብቶች የሚደነግጉ
ናቸው። ዘረኝነት፤ ሰዎች በአብዛኛው በተፈጥሮ፤ እንዲሁም በማኅበራዊ ወይም ፍፁም
ምናባዊ በሆነ የክፍፍል ቀመር አንዳቸው ከሌላቸው ይለያሉ ማለት ነው። ይህም ልዩነት
በሰዎች መካከል የመልክና ቀለምና ብቃ ሳይሆን የባሕርይ፤ ዐቅምና፤ የክህሎት ልዩነት
እንደሚያስከትል ያምናል። ከዚህም የተነሣ የመብት ልዩነት፤ ሲብስም የሕልውና ልዩነት
እንዳስከተለ ወይም መኖር እንዳለበት ያስባል።

የበዝጎ ብሔር ዕሳቤ፤ ብሔር ወይም ዘር ማኅበራዊ ክፍፍል ነው ወደሚለው ዕንስ
ዐሳብ በእጅጉ ያጋድለ ነው። ነገር ግን ይህንንም ጭምር አለዝበን ብናይ ይሻላ የሚል
እንድምታ አለው። በጥንቃቄ ካልተያዝ፤ ብሔርተኝነት ወደ ዘረኝነት የማያያቅብበት
ምንም ምክንያት የለምና።

የብሔርተኝነት አራማጆች "ብሔር" የሚለው ቃል ቢያንስ በአፈጻጸም ደረጃ
"ዘር" ከሚለው የሰፋ ዕይታ አለው ይላሉ። ብሔር ወይም ብሔረሰብ ቀድሞ በነበሩ
መንግሥታትም ሆነ ዛሬ ባሉ አገራት እውቅና አለው። ሥራራ ከሚሰጣቸው የአገራዊነት
ባሕርያት ወይም መገለጫዎች አንዱ ነው። መጽሐፍ ቅዱስ "ከነገድ ሁሉ፤ ከቋንቋ
ሁሉ፤ ከወገን ሁሉ፤ ከሕዝብ ሁሉ ሰዎችን ለእግዚአብሔር ዋጅተዋል" (ራእይ 5፤9)
ሲል ይህ ልዩነት የነበረ የሚኖርም ነው ለማለት ነው ይላሉ።

ቤን ራፋኤል የተባለ የማኅበረሰብ ጥናት ባለሙያ እንደገለጠው፤ ብሔር ወይም
ብሔረሰብ ወይም ነገድ ከሁሉ አስቀድሞ የማንነት መገለጫ ነው። የግል ብቃ ሳይሆን
የሚገልጸው የጋራ ማንነትን ነው። እንዲሁም የብሔር ልዩነት አገራት የማይወጡት
አጣብቂኝ ነው።[106] ሙሉ በሙሉ በሚባል ደረጃ አገራት በውስጣቸው ባሉ ነገዶች
ይከፋፈላሉ፤ ክፍፍሉ አንዱ ደመቅ፤ ሌላው ፈዘዝ ከማለቱ በስተቀር።

ይህም ክፍፍል አንዴ ያስተሳሰራቸዋል፤ ሌላ ጊዜ እርስ በርስና፤ ከራሳቸውም
ጋር፤ አንዳንድ ጊዜ በጋራ፤ ከውጪው ጋር ያላትማቻቸዋል። ይህም የሚያንበት ምክንያት
ክፍፍል በሚታይበት ሥራ ሁሉ ለብዝጎነት መቋ መጥ ስለሚያይል ነው። ወይም
ላለመዋጥ መጣር ይነበባል። ብሔር የባሕል መለያየት እስከሆነ ድረስ ግን ዘረኝነት
የሚያከትለውን ዐይነት መድልዎ፤ ንቀት፤ መገፋት፤ ጥላቻ እና የመሳሰሉት ነገሮች
እንዳያስከትል ምን መደረግ ይኖርበታል?

የብሔር ወይም ብሔረሰብ ዕንስ ዐሳብ ጥናት ከዘር ዕንስ ዐሳብ ወይም ፍልስፍና
ጋር ሲተያይ እጅግ እንጭጭ ነው። ማለትም፤ ከቅርብ ጊዜ ወዲህ የተወለደ አስተሳሰብ
ነው። የብሔር ልዩነት፤ በፍልስፍናው ዘርፍ እንደ ዘር ዕሳቤ ሥራራ የተሰጠው

---

106 Ben-Rafael, E. (2001) Sociology of Ethnicity; in the International Encyclopedia of the Social
and Behavioral Sceinces; 2001.

አልነበረም፡ የሰከነ ትርክትም ገና አላዳበረም፡ ከትርጉም ጀምሮ የሚያላጋውና ለዚያም ጭምር ነው፡

አመጣጡም፣ ግን በአብዛኛው በ20ኛው ክፍለ ዘመን አጋማሽ ነበር፡ ይህ ጊዜ ከሶሻሊዝም መጎልበት አንጻር፣ በየቦታው በምዕራባውያን አገራት የሚነሣው ግጭት እንደ መደብ ትግል ይታይ ስለ ነበር አማራጭ ፍረጃ ለመቀየስ ሲባል ነው፡ ሁሉ ተጨፍልቆ "የጭቁኗን ሕዝቦች ትግል" ይባል ነበርና፡ የብሔር ዕሳቤ፣ ለዚህ ትግል ወጥ ንድፍ ለመስጠት የተቀየሰ ዕሳብ ነው፡ ገና ያልሰከነ ቢሆንም፣ አራት የተለያዩ አመለካከቶች አሉ፡ [107]

ሀ) ብዝኃ ብሔር ጥንተ ንድፍ ነበር

የመጀመሪያው አመለካከት ብዝኃ ብሔር ተፈጥሯዊ ነው ወደ ማለት ያደላል፡ እንዲያውም፣ አምላክ የፈጠረው ነው እስከ ማለት የሚደርስ ነው፡ አርስቶትላዊ ቀኖና ያጠቃምል፣ ከኑባሬ ተነሥቶ ነገን ማስላት፡ በማንኛውም አገር የጉሣ ልዩነት አለ ከሚለው ይነሣና የጉሣዎች ልዩነት ተጨባጭና ድንበር ሊበጅለት የሚችል ነው ብሎ ያምናል፡ ይኸውም፣ ቤተሰብ ከሚባል ዋነኛ መዋቅር ተነሥቶን፣ የቤተ ዘመድ ስብስብ፣ ጎሣ፣ ጌላም እያለን ልዩነት መፍጠር እንችላለን ይላል፡

የዚህ አስተሳሰብ አንኳሩ የብሔር ልዩነት በዕቅድ፣ በንድፍ ይፈጠራል ብሎ ማመን ነው፡ ይህ የብዝኃ ብሔር ዕሳቤ ቀዳሚ፣ የጥንት ወይም መነሻ እምነት ነበር ማለት ይቻላል፡ ክርስቲያኖች፣ የዚህን ተገለባጭ ቤተ ክርስቲያን አንድ መሆኗን ለማጉላት ሲሉ፣ ይጠቀማሉ፡

በእርግጥም፣ መጽሐፍ ቅዱስ "መጽሐፉን ልትወስድ ማኅተሞቹንም ልትፈታ ይገባሃል፣ ምክንያቱም ታርደኻል፣ በደምህም ከነገድ ሁሉ፣ ከቋንቋ ሁሉ፣ ከወገን ሁሉ፣ ከሕዝብ ሁሉ ሰዎችን ለእግዚአብሔር ዋጅተሃል፡ ለአምላካችንም መንግሥትና ካህናት አድርገኃቸዋል፡ እነርሱም በምድር ላይ ይነግሣሉ" (ራእይ 5፥9) ይላል፡ ከተለያየ ሥፍራ የተሰባሰቡ፣ ነገር ግን አንድ መንግሥት፣ አንድ የካህናት ጉባዔ - ማለትም፣ አንድ ሕዝብ፡

ብዝኃ ብሔር ጥንተ ንድፍ ነው የሚሉ ግን ይህን ክፍል ሁልጊዜ ይጠቅሳሉ፡ በዚህ ቃል መሠረት ነገድ፣ ቋንቋ፣ ወገን፣ የሚባል ከጥንት የነበር፣ እግዚአብሔር የሚያውቀው ልዩነት ነው ይላሉ፡ ይህ አመለካከት ጽንሰ ሲይዝ ኅይማኖቶችንም ወደ ጉሣ ያደላ ትርጉም ያስሰጣቸዋል፡ ለምሳሌ፦ ምዕራቡ በአብዛኛው ክርስቲያን ሕዝብ ሲባል ዓረቡ ዓለም እስላም ሕዝብ ይሆናል፡ ምሥራቁ ደግሞ ሺንቶ ወይም ሕንዱ፡

107 Adlparvar, N. and Tadros, M. (2016). The Evolution of Ethnicity Theory: Intersectionality, Geopolitics and Development. IDS Bulletin Vol. 47 No. 2 May 2016: 'Development Studies – Past, Present and Future' 123–136

እንግዲህ ይህ ርእዮት፤ በሰዎች መካከል የዘር ልዩነት ባይኖር እንኳ የጉሣ መከፋፈልን ማስወገድ የማንችለው እንደሆነ ብንቀበለው የተሻለ እንደሆነ ያስገነዝባል። እንዲሁም የብሔረሰብ ወይም የጉሣ ልዩነት በደም ሊሆን እንደሚችልም ያስገነዝባል። ጉሣ በቅድሚያ ማኅበራዊ፤ በአብዛኛውም የባሕልና ቋንቋ አንድነት ብቻ ነው። ሰው የራሴ የሚለው ባሕል እና ቋንቋ ፍለጋ ሲሰባሰብ ይህ ልዩነት መልክዐ ምድራዊ እንዲሁም መዋቅራዊ መሆን ቻለ።

ጉሣ የደም አንድነት ወይም ልዩነት ጉዳይ ነው። አንድ ሰው በትውልድ ወይም በደም የአንድ ጉሣ አባል ይሆናል። ጉሣዎችም በደም አንድነት ካላቸው ጋር የመተባበር፤ አንድነት የለንም ብለው ከሚያምኗቸው ጋር ደግሞ የመቃቃር፤ ካልሆነም ቢያንስ የመጠባበቅ ባሕርይ ይታይባቸዋል። ስለዚህ ብዝኃ ብሔር ያለባቸው አገራት ግጭት አያጣቸውም።[108]

የዚህ አመለካከት ትልቁ ችግር አንድ ሰው ውስጥ ስንት ዐይነት ደም አለ የሚለው ጥያቄ መልስ ዐልባ መሆኑ ነው። በእናቱ ከአንድ ጉሣ ከሆነ፤ በአባቱ ደግሞ ከሌላ ከሆነ ምን ውስጥ ይመደባል? በእርግጥስ ከአንድ ንጹህ ጉሣ የተወለደ ሰው አለን? ባሕልና ቋንቋም ቢሆን የእኔ የብቻ የሚባል ነገር የለውም። መወራረስ፤ መተሻሸት የተለመደ ነውና፤ የብሔር ጥያቄን ለመፍታት ግጭት ብቸኛ መንገድ ሲሆን ፍትሐዊነት የሚጎድለው ከዚህ የተነሣ ነው። በሥላም ሲሆን ሁሉም ተፈላጊ ነው።

ኃይማኖቶች ጋ ስናመጣውም ይህ አመለካከት ይበልጥ ይወሳከፋል። ነጭ እስላም፤ ዓረብ ክርስቲያን ሞልቷል። ይብሱን እንዲደክም ያደረገው ግን የዚህ አመለካከት ድምዳሜ ነው። ይህም በጉሣዎች መካከል ጥርት ያለውን ድንበር ለማስጠበቅ ግጭት አይቀሬ ነው ማለቱ ነው። ጉሣዎች ልዩነትን በግጭት የመፍታት አባዜ ስላላቸው አንድ አገር ብዝኃ ብሔር ሆና በሰላም የመዝለቅ ተስፋው የመነመነ ነው የሚል ዕይታ አለው። ይህም ከኑባሬ የተቀዳ አስተሳሰብ ነው።

በደም፤ በቋንቋ፤ በባሕል፤ በኃይማኖት፤ በመልክዐ ምድር፤ እና በመሣሠሉት አንድን አካባቢ ከሌላው ጋር የሚያለያዩ ነገሮች ከመብዛታቸው የተነሣ በአንድም ሆነ በሌላ ግጭት አይታጣም። ይሁን እንጂ፤ ግድ አይደለም። እንደ ስዊዘርላንድ ያሉ አገራት በአውሮፓ፤ እንደ ናሚቢያ፤ ካሜሩንና ቦትስዋና የመሳሰሉት አገራት በአፍሪካ ብዝኃ ብሔር ሆነው የውስጥ ግጭት እምብዛም ሳይታይባቸው መዝለቃቸው ሊስተዋል ይገባል።[109]

---

108 Geertz, Clifford. 1963. 'The Integrative Revolution: Primordial Sentiments and Politics in the New States'. In Clifford Geertz, ed. Old Societies and New States: The Quest for Modernity in Asia and Africa. London: London Free Press, 255–310.

109 Che, A. M. (2016). Linking Instrumentalist and Primordialist Theories of Ethnic Conflict. E-International Relations; June 1, 2016. https://www.e-ir.info/pdf/64013

ለ) ብዝኃ ብሔር የመደብ ቅራኔ ነጸብራቅ ነው

ጎሣ የደም ወይም የተፈጥሮ አንድነትና ልዩነት ነው ከሚል አመለካከት ጋራ ዐብሮ የበቀለው አስተሳሰብ ማርክሳዊው የጎሣ ርእዮት ነው። በዚህ መሠረት ጎሣም የመደብ ቅራኔ አካል ነው። በተለይም ባሕልና ቋንቋ ገርውን መደብ የሚወክሉ፣ አንዳዴም እስከ ኅይማኖት ድረስ ዘልቀው ቅራኔ የሚፈጥሩ ስለሆነ፣ ገገርው መደብ የሚጠቀምበት መሣሪያ ነው ይላሉ። ወዛደሩም አዲስ የወዛደር ገገርነትን የሚያሥርጽ ርእዮት መፍጠር ይኖርበታል።

የዚህ አስተሳሰብ አቀንቃኝ ከተባሉት ዋና የሆነው ሚካዔል ሄክተር የተናቱን ትኩረት ያደረገው በሶሻሊስት አገራት ሳይሆን በአሜሪካ ነበር። ሄክተር ጥናቱን ያካሄደው በ1970^{ዎቹ} የነበሩ 17 የአሜሪካ ጎሣዎች ላይ ነው። በጎሣዎቹ ውስጥ ያለው የውስጥ መሳሳብና መለያየት አንድ ሰው ከጎሣው በሚያገኘው ጥቅም ልክ ይወሰናል የሚለው ሄክተር፣ አስተሳሰቡ በጥናቱ ተደጋፍነትን እንዳገኘ አውስቶ፣ በመደብ ትግል ተመሳሳይ ጥቅም የሚገኘባትን ማስላት ያስፈልጋል ብሏል።[110]

የዚህም አመለካከት እንድምታ ማዕከል ደግሞ ምን እንደሆነ ለመፈተሽ እምብዛም አያስቸግርም። ዓለም የፉክክር ብቻ ሳይሆን የቅራኔም ቤት ናት። ለመፎካከር ደግሞ ብቁ፣ ብቁውን ፈልጎ በመጎዳናት ሊሆን ይገባል። ይሁን እንጂ ይህ አስተሳሰብ ሳይደረጅ ጠወለገ። ወቅቱ በምዕራባውያን የነጻ ኤኮኖሚና ፀረ ኮምኒዝም ትግል ጣራ የደረሰበት ስለ ነበር ማርክሳዊ ርእዮት በአገሪቱ ለማስረጽ የመጣ አስተሳሰብ ነው በማለት ጥናቱንም፣ የወዛደር አብዮትንም አጣጣሉት።

ሐ) ብዝኃ ብሔር በምርጫ ነው

ጎሣ ተፈጥሮዊ ልዩነት ነው ለሚለው ፅንሰ ዐሳብ በተጻራሪነት የቆመ ሁለት ዋና ዋና ዐሳቦች አሉ። ሲዳሙ የብሔር ብሔረሰብ አባልነታችን በምርጫችን ይወሰናል የሚለውን አጠቃላይ ዐሳቤ ይሰጣሉ። ምርጫውም የሚወሰነው እንደ ግለሰቦችና ብሔር ብሔረሰቦች አሁናዊ እና ነባራዊ ሁኔታ ነው።

ከዚህ ዐሳቤ ጠንሳሾች አንዱ ፍሬዴሪክ ባርዝ ይባላል።[111] የጎሣ ፅንስ ዐሳብ ጥናት መሠረታዊ ግንዛቤ እንዳበረከተ ይጬጠራል። በእርሱ ዐሳብ መሠረት በጎሣዎች መካከል የሚታየው ማንኛውም ልዩነት ገደል የማይበጅለት፣ ስውር፣ ተንኮል የማያጣው ትስስር ነው። በጎሣዎች መካከል ያለውም ድንበር ፈዛዛ እንጂ ጠንካራ ስላይደለ ሰዎች ሁኔታን

---

110 Hechther, M. (1978). Group Formation and the Cultural Division of Labor. American Journal of Scoilogy. Volume 84 Number 2 1978 by The University of Chicago.

111 Barth, F. (1969). Introduction. In: Fredrik Barth (ed.), Ethnic Groups and Boundaries: The Social Organization of Culture Differences. Bergen: Universitetsforlaget, pp. 9–38.

እየቃኙ በውዴታቸው ከአንዱ ወደ ሌላው ይሸጋገሩ። ደግሞ አሥሬ ይሸጋገሩ እንጂ ደብዛዛው የድንበር ምልክት ጨርሶ አይጠፋም።[112]

ከግለሰቦች አልፎ በብሔረሰቦች መካከል ጥሩ ትስስርና መደጋገፍ ቢኖር ስንኳ ድንበሩ የማይጠፋበት ምክንያት ደግሞ በእያንዳንዱ ብሔር ይህ ድንበር የሚጸናበት ተቋማዊ፣ መዋቅራዊ፣ ፖለቲካዊ፣ እና የሥልጣን ክፍፍል ጉዳዮች ስላሉ ነው።[113] ለምሳሌ:- ለአንድ ጉዳይ፣ እንበልና ጋቢቻ እንዴት እንደሚፈጸም፣ ባሕላዊም ይሁን ማኅበራዊ ሕግ አለ፤ ሕጉን የሚያስፈጽሙ ዳኞች አሉ፤ ይህን ተቋማቸውን የሚያስከብሩበት መንገድ አላቸው። ስለዚህ በብሔሮች መካከል ያለ ድንበር ይደበዝዝ ይሆናል እንጂ አይደለዝም፣ አይሰረዝም።

ባርዝ ይህን መነሻ ጽሑፍ በጻፈበት ዘመን በአገራት መካከል እንጂ በብሔረሰቦች መካከል፣ ቀድሞ ከሚታወቀው ሸኩቻ የዘለለ ጦርነት አልነበረም ማለት ይቻላል። አብዛኛው አፍሪካና ጥቂት የፉሩት የእስያ እንዲሁም የደቡብ አሜሪካ አገራት ከቅኝ ግዛት የመላቀቅ ትግል ላይ ናቸው። ብሔረሰቦች ይተባበሩ ነበር እንጂ በመካከላቸው እምብዛም መናቆር አይታይም ነበር።

ይሁን እንጂ የባርዝ ጽሑፍ አንድ ሰው የብዙ ብሔረሰቦች አባል መሆን እንደሚችል ዘንግቷል። የሚለያዩበት ድንበሩም ድብዛዛ ብቻ ሳይሆን ደመቅ የሚልበትም ቦታ እንዳለ ማስተዋል ያሻል። እንዲሁም የባሕልና አንዳንድ ትውፊቶችን ጥንካሬና እያቆጠቆጠ የነበረውን የብሔር ፖለቲካ በባርዝ ሐተታ እምብዛም ሥፍራ አልተሰጠውም።[114]

ሁለተኛው የዚህ ዕሳቤ ዘርፍ "የመዳብ ቋት" ተብሎ በሚታወቀው የምዕራብና የመካከለኛው አፍሪካ ክልል፣ ጥቁር ሕዝቦች ከነጭ ቅኝ ገዢዎች ጋር ባካሄዱት የነጻነት ትግል ወቅት ከተደረጉ ጥናቶች የተቀዳ ነው። በእነዚህ ጥናቶች መሠረት ብሔር ብሔረሰብ ወይንም ነገድ የፖለቲካ ቀመር ነው። የፖለቲካ ልሂቁን ብሔር ብሔረሰብን ለትግል በሚያመች መንገድ ይቀርጹታል።

በተለይም አብኔር ኮሄን እንደ ጻፈው በናይጄሪያ የሃውሳ እና ዮሩባ ጉዛዎች የፖለቲካ ልሂቃን በአብዛኛው "የራሳችን" ብለው የደመደሙትን ሃብት ወይም አካባቢ ለማስጠበቅ ሲሉ በጉዛዎቹ መካከል ግጭት ለማስነሳት ያሉትን ጥቃትን ልዩነቶች ይጠቀሙ ነበር። በዚህ ሂደት ልዩነት ባይኖር እንኳ ይፈጥሩ ነበር ሲል ጽፏል።

112 Jakoubek, M. & Budilová, L. J. (2019). Ethnicity and the boundaries of ethnic studies. Anthropological Notebooks, XXV/1, 2019

113 Wimmer, A. (2008). The Making and Unmaking of Ethnic Boundaries: A Multilevel Process Theory. The American Journal of Sociology; Volume 113 Number 4 (January 2008): 970–1022

114 Hummell, E. (2014). Standing the Test of Time – Barth and Ethnicity. Coolabah, No.13, 2014, Australian Studies Centre, Universitat de Barcelona

የሃብት ክፍፍል ግጭቱ ከነጮች ጋር ሲሆን ግን በጉሣዎቹ መካከል ያለው መፋተግ ይተንናል።[115]

ከእነዚህ ሁለቱ አመለካከቶች የተነሣ የጉሣ ልዩነት የደም፤ የባሕል፤ የቋንቋ፤ ወይም የኅይማኖት ብቻ ሣይሆን መወቅርና ሥርዓት የያዘ፤ የአመራር ልዩነትም ሊኖረው እንደሚችል ታይቷል። ይህ አስተሳሰብ በማኅበራዊ ጥናቱ ዘርፍ ጉልህ ጫና ከማሳደሩ የተነሣ የዘርፉ ትኩረት ራሱ ሊቀየር ችሏል። ከእነዚህ አስተሳሰቦች መነሣት በኋላ "ጉሣ" የሚባለው የልዩነት መገለጫ በማኅበራዊ ሳይንሱ ዙሪያ እየከሰመ "ብሔር" ወይም "ብሔረሰብ" የሚለው እያየለ መጣ።

ከዚህም ይልቅ የዚህ አስተሳሰብ እንድምታው የበለጠ ትኩረት የሳበ ነበር። በብሔር፤ ብሔረሰቦች መካከል አለ የተባለው ልዩነትም ሆነ የተባለው መስመር ፈዛዛ ስለሆነ፤ በፈዛዛው የድንበር መስመር ሰዎች በውዴታ ወይም ሁኔታን እያዩ ገባ ወጣ ስለሚሉ። በብሔረሰቦች መካከል ወደ ጦርነት ወይም ግጭት ሊመራ የሚችል ልዩነት ወይም ቅራኔ የለም የሚል ነው። የልዩነት ፍላጎት መፋቀራዊና ፖለቲካዊ በመሆኑ፤ መፋቀሩ ካልፈለገ በስተቀር ግጭት አይኖርም።

ይህ በእርግጥም የማኅበራዊ ሳይንስ አጥኚዎችን ዐይን የከፈተ ዕሳቤ ነው። ነገር ግን በሚያሳዝን ሁኔታ፤ የፖለቲከኞችንም ዐይን የከፈተ ሆኗል። በመጀመሪያ ደረጃ ብሔረሰብ መፋቀራዊ ስለሆነ አማራሩን የያዘ ብሔረሰቡ መምራት እንደሚችል ተረዱ። እንዲሁም፤ ብሔረሰብነት በሰዎች ነጻ ፈቃድ ላይ የተመሠረተ ባለ ደብዛዛ ድንበር በመሆኑ የመፋቀር ቅጥጥሩን ለማስጠበቅ ሆነ ብሎ ግጭት መፍጠር እና የድንበር መስመሩን ማጉላት የፖለቲከኞች ቀዳሚ የሥራ ድርሻ መሆን ጀመረ።

በዚያውም፤ በተለይም የዘመናችን የአፍሪካ ዕዳ ያውም የጉሣ ወይም የብሔር ፖለቲካ ተወለደ። ይሁን እንጂ የጉሣ ፖለቲከኞች እንደሚሉት ብሔርተኝነት ዘመናት ያስቆጠረ የፖለቲካ ፍልስፍና ሳይሆን ገና ከአንድና ሁለት ትውልድ በላይ ያላስቆጠረ ዕንጭጭ ዐሳብ ነው። የታሪክ ሂደት ግን እንደጠቀመው እንመለከታለን። ይህ ጊዜ፤ የአፍሪካ አገራት ከቅኝ ግዛት መዳፍ ወጥተው የፖለቲካ ነጻነት ያገኙበት ጊዜ ነበር። የነበረው መነቃቃት፤ ለብሔርተኝነትም ምቹ ሁኔታ ስለፈጠረለት አበበ።

ታላቁ የአፍሪካ አሕጉር ከቅኝ ግዛት ሙሉ በሙሉ ነጻ ሲወጣ ተከታዩ አገዛዝ ምን መምሰል አለበት የሚለው ጥያቄ የብዙዎች ራስ ምታት ነበር። አፍሪካ አንድ ትሁን ወይስ ከቅርምት ወደ ቅርምት ትሸጋገር? ይህ ጊዜ የዓለም መንግሥታት በሁለት የቀዝቃዛው ጦርነት ቡድኖች የተከፈሉበት ሲሆን ፖለቲካውም በዚያ የተቃኘ ነበር። ኮሙኒስቶች ምሥራቃውያን በአብዛኛው፤ ለአፍሪካ ነጻ መውጣት ይከራከሩ፤ ድጋፍም ያደርጉ። አፍሪካ ምን ትሁን ለሚለው ጥያቄ መልስ ባይኖራቸውም።

115 Cohen, A. (1969) Custom and Politics in Urban Africa: A Study of Hausa Migrants in Yoruba Towns, London: Routledge

አሜሪካ ደግሞ አፍሪካውያን ነጻ መሆናቸውን ባትጠላም፤ በሶቪየቶች እጅ እንዳይወድቁ ትጥራለች። ዛሬም እንደምታደርገው፤ መሪዎችን በማጥመድ የራስዋ ማድረግን ሥራዬ ብላ ያዘች። የቀድሞ ቅኝ ገዢ አውሮፓውያን ደግሞ፤ በተለይም ፈረንሳይ፤ በእጅ አዙር አፍሪካውያን ከእጃቸው እንዳይወጡ አዳዲሶቹን መሪዎች ይወተውቱና የስምምነት ዐይነት ያስፈርሟቸውም ነበር።

አፍሪካን አንድ ለማድረግ ብቻ ሳይሆን የመላው ጥቁር ሕዝቦችን አንድነት ለማረጋገጥ በምድረ አሜሪካ እንቅስቃሴ የተጀመረው ገና በ19ኛው ምዕት ዓመት መባቻ ነው። አፍሪካ ነጻ ከመውጣቷ ከዓመታት በፊት፤ እንዲያውም በዚህ ጊዜ አፍሪካ የባርያ ንግድ ሰለባ እንጂ ገና በቅኝ ግዛት እጅም አልወደቀችም ነበር።

የአፍሪካዊነት አቀንቃኝ ሐኪምና ደራሲ ማርቲን ዴላኒ (1812–1885) እንዲሁም የጥቁሮች የትምህርት አባት በመባል የሚታወቁት ቄስ አሌክሳንደር ክሩሜል (1819–1898) በዚያን ጊዜ የተቋቋመው የፓን አፍሪካኒዝም ንቅናቄ መሪዎችም ነሩ። የዚህ እንቅስቃሴ አራማጆች የብሔርና ጉዛ ልዩነት ቀርቶ የአገራት ልዩነት የማይታይባትን አንዲት አፍሪካን መፍጠር ህልማቸው ነበር።[116]

ብዙ የአፍሪካ አገራት ከቅኝ ግዛት ነጻ መውጣት ሲጀምሩ፤ በወቅቱ የፓን አፍሪካኒዝም ንቅናቄ መሪዎች የነበሩት እነ ማርከስ ጋርቬይ፤ አሜሪካ የተማሩትን የሴኔጋል የነጻነት ትግል መሪና ፕሬዝዳንት ሴዳር ሴንግሆርን የመሳሰሉ ሰዎች በመያዝ አንዲት አፍሪካን ለመመሥረት ይጥሩ ነበር። በጊዜው የነበሩ አፍሪካውያን መሪዎች ራሳቸው ግን የተለያየ አመለካከት በያዙ ብዙ ቡድኖች ተከፋፍለው ታይተዋል።

ቢያንስ ሦስት ቡድኖች ጉልህ ነበሩ። የካዛብላንካ ቡድን በመባል የሚታወቀው በሞሮክ መሪነት የተቋቋመው የአፍሪካ ሙሉ ነጻነትና አንድነት አሁኑ የሚል ከረር ያለ መፈክር ያነገበ ነበር። የብራዛቪል 12 በመባል የሚታወቀው ቡድን ደግሞ በአብዛኛው ደቡብና መካከለኛውን አፍሪካ ያቀፈ፤ በኮት ዲቫሩ ሁፍዌት ቧኜ መሪነት ጸረ ኮሙኒስት አቋም የያዘ ሆኖ፤ አፍሪካ የኤኮኖሚ አንድነት ብቻ ያስፈልጋታል የሚል ዓላማ ያራምድ ነበር።

የሞንሮቪያ ቡድን በመባል የሚታወቀው፤ ሦስተኛው ቡድን ነበራዊ እውነታን እንመልከት ባይ ነበር። አፍሪካ እጅግ ትልቅና ግዙፍ ነች። አገራትም በተለያየ የዕድገት ደረጃ ላይ ናቸው። በዚህ ሁኔታ ፍጹም አንድነት ወዲያውኑ ማምጣት ስለማይቻል በአገራት ትብብር የሚጀመር ጠንካራ ግንኙነትን ይቅደም ይል ነበር። ይህ ቡድን ኳ ኢትዮጵያና ናይጄሪያ የመሳሰሉት ትላልቅ አገራት ገብተውበት ፈርጣማ መሆን ቻለ።

በዚህ ንትርክ መካከል፤ ጋናዊው የአፍሪካ አባት፤ ከዋሜ ንክሩማን፤ ጎኑ የሆነ አሳብ ከሰነድ ጋር አቀረብ፤ የቀረበው ሰነድ፤ አንድ የአፍሪካ ቻርተር፤ ኮንፌደራላዊ

---

116 Kuryla, Peter. "Pan-Africanism". Encyclopedia Britannica, 1 Oct. 2020, https://www. britannica.com/topic/Pan-Africanism.

አንድነት፤ የንዑስ ወይም ክፍለ አሕጉራዊ ኤኮኖሚ ውህደት፤ እና የሶቪየትን ወይንም የአሜሪካን ሞዴል የተከተለ የፖለቲካ ውቅር የሚል አራት አዕማዶችን የያዘ ነው፡፡ በዚህ ሰነድ ላይ ለመወያየት ሦስቱ ቡድኖች እና ሌሎችም በአፍሪካ አንድነት ያገባኛል የሚሉ ተሰበሰቡ፡፡

በዚያን ወቅት የኢትዮጵያ መሪ በነበሩት በብልጉ አጼ ሃይለ ሥላሴ አማካኝነት ጽንፍ የያዙ ቡድኖች ወደ ስምምነት ሊደርሱ ቻለዋል፡፡ ኢትዮጵያ፤ የሦስተኛው ቡድን ወይንም "ጊዜ እንግዛ" ባይ አገራት ወገን ነበረች፡፡ በዚህ ስብሰባ የንክፉማን አሳብ በተወሰነ ደረጃ ውሃ ተቸልሶበት፤ በእጅጉ ለዛም፡ የአፍሪካ አንድነት ድርጅት የሚባል ተቋም እውን ሆነ፡፡ አዲስ አበባም የድርጅቱ መቀመጫ ሆነች፡፡[117] ከዚያ በኋላ ግን "የአፍሪካ አንድነት" የሚባለው የመምጭ ጊዜው ረዘመ፡፡ የአንድነት ህልሙ ፈዞ አጣ፡፡

ከድርጅቱ መመሥረት በኋላ የሆነው ሁሉ አሳዛኝ ነበር፡፡ "የአፍሪካ አንድነት ድርጅት" የሚባለው ተቋም ከአፍሪካ ውጭ ላሉ ጥቁር ሕዝቦች ትርጉም ዐልባ ሆነ፡፡ ከአገራቱ አንዳንዶቹ ተከፋፍለው ይናቆሩ ጀመር፡፡ ምንም እንኳ ከዚያ በኋላ እነ ሮዴሺያ (የሁኗ ዝምባብዌ) ነጻ ሲወጡ፤ እንዲሁም በፀረ አፓርታይድ ትግሉ ላይ ጉልህ የአንድነት ሚና እና ጠንካራ አስተዋጽኦ የነበረው ቢሆንም ድርጅቱ ጥርስ ዐልባ አንበሳ ነበር፡፡

ከእርስ በርስ መናቆር ሌላ በአገራቱ ውስጥ ያሉ ፖለቲከኞች ጉሣቸውን እያነሳሱ በውስጥ ጉዳይ በነበሩ ጥቃቅን ግጭቶች ብዙ ደም ፈሰል፡፡ ከአፍሪካ አንድነት ድርጅት መመሥረቻ ውሳኔዎች አንዱ በውስጥ ጉዳይ ጣልቃ አለ መግባት የሚል ነበር፡፡ ይህ ውሳኔ ድርጅቱን ስላሳሰረ፤ ለብሔር ፖለቲከኞችና ለወታደራዊ መፈንቅለ መንግሥት አላሚዎች ምቹ ሜዳ ሆነላቸው፡፡ አፍሪካ የውጭ ኃይሎች ከንዴት በላይ የእርስ በርስ ግጭት የበለጠ አዳከማት፡፡[118]

መ) ብዝኃ ብሔር ለዓላማ የበለጸገ ውቅር ነው

አፍሪካ፤ ከላይ ከተጠቀሱት ነገሮች የተነሣ አጣብቂኝ ውስጥ ገባች፡፡ መሪ ያጣ መርከብ ሆና ዓመታት ተቆጠሩ፡፡ የችግሩ መኖር አስቃቂ ከመሆኑም በላይ ከችግሩ መውጣት አለ መቻል ደግሞ የባሰ ነው፡፡ ይህንን አፍሪካ ራሷ የፈጠረችው ችግር አልነበረም፤ ታሪክ ፈቷን አዙራባት እንጂ፡፡ ታዲያ ምን ይደረግ? ብዝኃ ብሔርን በውጥን ማበልጸግ ወይም ማክሰም ይቻል ይሆን?

117 Bowen, J. S. (1994). Power and Authority in the African Context: Why Somalia did Not Have to Starve - The Organization of African Unity (OAU) as an Example of the Constitutive Process. National Black Law Journal, 14(1)

118 Deng, F. M. (1997). Ethnicity: An African Predicament. Brookings Institution; June 1997. https://www.brookings.edu/articles/ethnicity-an-african-predicament/

ይህን ለመረዳት የአፍሪካ ምሳሌ ፍንጭ ሊሰጠን ይችላ ይሆናል። ታሪክ ስትጨክን፣ በውጭ ኃይላት ሴራና ጉልበት ምክንያት የአፍሪካዊ ባህሎችና አሻራዎች ፈጽሞ በሚባል ደረጃ ተደመሰሱ። ልጆቻዋ አንድም በባርነት፣ አሊያም በስደት ተበተኑ፣ የቀሩት የተለያየ ባሕልና ወግ እያሎቸው ሆነ ተበሎ በአንድ አገር መዋቀር ውስጥ ተጨፈለቁ።

ሌሎች እንደ ሱማሊያውያን በአራትና አምስት አገራት ጣላ ስር ተቦጫጨቁ። ይህ ሳይወዱ በአፍሪካ ነባራዊ የብሔር መዋቀር የተጫነባቸው ነው። በዚሁ እንዳይቀጥሉ ግጭት አሃዛቸውን አበላቸው። ወደ ድሮ የአባቶች ሥርዓት ትትው እንዳይመለሱ ተቀድዶ የሚሰፋውና የሚቦጫቀው እጅግ ብዙ ስለ ሆነ የአገራት ብቻ ሳይሆን የሕዝቡም ሕልውና አስጊ ደረጃ ላይ ይወድቃል።

አንዳንዶች ሠፈር ደግሞ በአገር ደረጃ ብቻ ሳይሆን በቤተሰብ ደረጃ ጭምር ክራ ካላረፈ መነጣጠል አስቸጋሪ ሆነ። አጠብቂኝ ማለት ይህ ነው፣ መቆየትም፣ ጥሎ መውጣትም ጭንቅ አገሪቱ ለዚህ የተለያየ ምላሽ ነበራቸው።

እንደ ኢትዮጵያ ያሉ ቀድሞም የቅኝ ግዛት በትር እምብዛም ያላዩ በጥቂቱ ቅኝ አገዛዝ ስር ከወደቀቻው ኤርትራ ጋራ በአንድነት ለመቆየት ያደረጉት ደም አፍሳሽ ጦርነት በመለያየት ተቋጨ። ቢሆንም፣ የኢትዮጵያና የኤርትራ ሕዝብ እስከ ዛሬ አንድነቱንና ወንድማማችነቱን አልለቅ ብሎ ተስፋ እንዳመቀ ዘልቋል። የመዋቅሩ ጥንካሬ ግን ከዚያ ተስፋ በላይ ገዝቶ በሁለት የተለያዩ አገራት እንዲተዳደሩ ግድ ሆነ።

ግጭትን የመረጡ አገራት ኢኮኖሚ ዕድገት አንዴ ከፍ ሌላ ጊዜ ዝቅ የሚል ነበር። እንደ ቦተስዋና ያሉ ጥቂት ወይም በአብዛኛው ተመሳሳይ ባሕልና ቋንቋ ያላቸው አገራት ግጭትን ማስወገድ ቻሉ። የዴሞክራሲ ባሕልን መርጠው የተረጋጋ ዕድገት ነዳና ላይ ናቸው። አንድ ዐይነትነት ግን ሶማሊያን ወይንም ካሜሩንን በእርሱ ልክ አልጠቀመም።

ኬንያ፣ አንዳንድ የደቡብ እና የምዕራብ አፍሪካ አገራት ብዝን ብሔርን እንደ ጸጋ ቆጠሩት። አገራዊ አንድነትንም፣ የብሔር መገለጫዎችንም በተስማማ ደረጃ ማክበር ቻሉ። አንዳንድ ጊዜ ብቅ እያለ ከሚያስቸግራቸው። በአብዛኛው ከብሔር ፖለቲከዎ በሚነሃ ብጥብጥ በቀር እንኒህም ሕበረ ብሔራዊ አንድነታቸው እየጎለበተ የሚያስቀና ጉዞ ላይ ናቸው ቢባል ያስሄዳል።

ለምሳሌ:- ኬንያ የአገሪቱን ሁሉንም ቋንቋዎችና ባሕል ዕድገት እያበረታታች የማናቸውም ብሔር ቋንቋ ያልሆነትን እንግሊዝኛና ስዋሂሊ ብሔራዊ መግባቢያ አደረገች። ሁሉም ኬንያዊ በሚባል ደረጃ ከሁለት በአንዱ ይግባባል። ከሕግ መንግሥትዋም ውስጥ በብሔር የሚደራጁ ፖለቲካ ፓርቲዎችን አገደች።

ደቡብ አፍሪካና ናይጄሪያ ለዚያ አልታደሉም። አንዴ በዘር፣ አንዴ በጎሣ፣ ሌላ ጊዜ በንያማኖት በሚደረግ ግጭት ምክንያት እነዚህ ጋቱፍ የአፍሪካ ኢኮኖሚዎች ቀስ

በቀስ ትልቅነታቸውን ለግብፅ በማስረከብ ላይ ናቸው። ይህ ሁኔታቸው ካልተለወጠ ግብፅ በሚቀጥሉት አምስትና አሥር ዓመታት ውስጥ የአፍሪካ ግዙፍ ኤኮኖሚ ባለቤት ትሆናለች።

እነ ዚምባብዌ፣ ሱዳን፣ ቡሩንዲና ሩዋንዳና የመሳሰሉት አገራት የብሔር ብሔረሰቦች ክፍልና መድልዋ ዐይን ያወጣና ጫፍ የደረሰ ስለሆነ ግጭትን ቤተኛ አደረጉት። ስለዚህ ዕድገትን ቢመኙአት እንጂ እስከ ዛሬ በአመርቂ ሁኔታ አላዩአትም። የአሕጉሩ ውራ ኤኮኖሚ በመሆን ከመዝለቅ የሚታደጋቸው ቀጥሎ የተዘረዘሩት ብቻ ናቸው።

ውራዎቹ፣ የባዶ ድምር ፖለቲካ የሚያራምዱ አገራት፣ መቻቻል የሚባል ነገር የማያውቃቸው። ሁሉ ለእኔ ካልሆነም ማናችንም ባንጠቀም ይመረጣል የሚል ዕኩይ ፖለቲካን የሚያራምዱ ፖለቲከኛ ነን ባዮች ያሉባቸው አገራት። የዝነኛው የ ጋን አፍሪካዊነት አቀንቃኝ የፓትሪስ ሉሙምባዋ ኮንጎ የዚህ ቡድን መሪ ናት።

ኮንጎ፣ የዓለምን አንድ ሦስተኛ ያህል ዳይመንድ በውስጧ ይዛ፣ የሚያሰደምም ዕምቅ ሃብት ባለቤት ሆና፣ ባለፉት ሃያና ሠላሣ ዓመታት ውስጥ ለሕዝቢ ዕድገት ልታወርስ አልቻለችም። እንኳንና ዕድገት፣ በምዕተ ዓመቱ መጀመሪያ ባሉት አምስት ዓመታት ከ5 ሚሊዮን በላይ ዜጎቿን በእርስ በርስ ጦርነት ምክንያት አጥታለች። በየቀኑ አንድ ሺ ህ ዜጎች እየሞቱ ማለት ነው። [119] እነ ሱማሊያ፣ ደቡብ ሱዳንና ቻድ የመሳሰሉት የዚህ ክለብ አባላት ናቸው።

የእነዚህ አገራት ችግር ምንጩ የቅኝ ግዛት ድንበሮችን ያለ መቀበል ነው። ይሁን እንጂ፣ ከበሔር ፖለቲካ በዘለለ አንድም የረባ አገራዊ ራእይ መውለድ የሚችልና የአንድነት ተምሳሌት የሚሆን የፖለቲካ ቡድንና ሥርዓት ማጣታቸው ዋናው ድክመት ነው። ስለዚህ ከመተባበር ይልቅ፣ እርስ በርስ መናቆር መፍትሔ ይመስላቸዋል፣ ተስማምተው መከፋፈልም ራቃቸው።

የአፍሪካ አንድነት ድርጅት ከ60 ያህል ዓመታት እንቅልፍ አከል መንገላጀጅ በኋላ ወደ "አፍሪካ ኅብረት" ሲያድግ፣ አንድ ያሻለው ነገር ቢኖር በውስጥ ጉዳይ ጣልቃ አንገባም የሚለውን ቻርተር ነው። "ለአፍሪካዊ ችግር አፍሪካዊ መፍትሔ" በሚል አዲስ ዕሳቤ ቢያንስ በእነዚህ አገራት መካከል ሲከሰት የነበረውን መፈንቅለ መንግሥት እውቅና በመንፈግ ጥቂት ገትታዋል። እንደ በፊቱ ቢሆን ኖሮ ዉት አንድ መንግሥት ከሰዓት ሌላ እናይ ነበር።

አራተኛውና የመጨረሻው የብሔር ፅንስ ዐሳብ ታዲያ ለእንደዚህ ዐይነት የአፍሪካና እንዲሁም የሌሎች አገራት ችግር መፍትሔ ለማምጣት ሲባል ከዘመን ቀደማዊ ዕሳቤ የተጎነቆለ ምልክታ ነው። ይህ ዕሳቤም ምርጫን መሠረት ያደረገ ሆኖ፣ ጉሣ ወይም ብሔር ወይም የብዝኃ ብሔርነት መዋቅር በሂደት አስበን በመረጥነው መንገድ የምንገነባው

119 IRC. (2007). Mortality in the Democratic Republic of Congo: An ongoing crisis. An IRC Report. https://www.rescue.org/sites/default/files/document/661/2006-7congomortalitysurvey.pdf

ነው ይለናል። ማለትም፤ ብሔረሰብ በሚመቹን መንገድ በጊዜ ሂደት ውስጥ ሆነ ብለን
የምንቀርጸው መዋቅር ነው።

አንድ ነገር ካልተስማማን አፍርሶ መገንባት፤ ወይም እንዲመቹን አድርጐ
ማበልጸግ፤ ወይም በድጋሚ ማዋቀር የዘመን ቀደሞች ዋና ዕሳቤ ነው። ብሔር፤
ብሔረሰቦችም አዲስ መሪ ነኝ ያለ በመጣ ቁጥር ከሚያነታርኩን ለምን አፍርሰን
አንሠራቸውም? ለክፋት ከመፈላለግ ይልቅ በመደጋገፍ ላይ የተመሠረተ የዐብሮነት
ርእዮት እንዲያራምዱ ለምን በሌላ መልክ ብሔርነታቸውን አናበልጽግም?

ይህ የዋዘ ዕሳቤ ቢመስልም፤ ሃይለኛ ዐቅም ያለው ምልከታ ነው። በተግባር
ሊገለጥ የሚፈልግ ሊጠቀምበት የሚችል። በዚህ ዘርፍ ደጋፊዎች ሥራ የተሰጣቸው
ሦስት ዋና ዋና ዕሳቦች በሰፈው ተንሽራሽረዋል።

የመጀመሪያው፤ ከብሔር መሪዎች በተጨማሪ ማንም ሰው ምርጫ ስላለው፤
መልካም እንዲሆን በአዲስ መልክ የተቀረጸውን መዋቅር እንዲመርጥ በስፋት ብንገፋፋ
በሂደት የሚናቆሩ ሳይሆን የሚደጋገፉ ብሔሮች መፍጠር ይቻላል ይለናል። ይህን ዐሳብ
ሲሰነዝሩ፤ ፌሮንና ሌይቲን የተባሉ የማኅበራዊ ጥናት ባለሙያዎች በዓለማችን እጅግ
አስከፊ የተባሉ አምስት የጐሣ ጦርነቶችን በጥልቀት ከማጥናት በመነሳት ነው።

በጥናቱ መሠረት የጐሣ ውቅሮች ለመልካም የመቀየር ዐቅም እንዳላቸው
ተገንዝበናል ይላሉ። ሰዎች በተፈጥሮ ዐብሮነት ይቀናቸዋል። ይህን ቀድመን አውቀን
ቢሆን ኖሮ የሰዎችን መልካም ነገር የመምረጥ ባሕርያትን በመደገፍ፤ ግጭቶችን ማስወገድ
ይቻል ነበር ይላሉ።[120]

እንዚህ ጥናቶች የተካሄዱት ደግሞ አስከፊ የዘር ጭፍጨፋ በታየባቸው ቦታዎች
ነው። ሩዋንዳ፤ ደቡብና ሰሜን ሱዳን ጦርነት፤ የሰሜን አየርላንድ ግጭት፤ ስሪላንካና
የታሚል ነብሮች ያስከተሉት ዕልቂት፤ እንዲሁም የባልካን አገራት ዘግናኝ የመለያየት
ጦርነቶች ይገኙበታል። በእነዚህ ቦታዎች በሙሉ የሚስተዋል፤ አንድ የሚያደርጋቸው
ነገር አለ። ይኸውም፤ ሁሉም ግጭቶች የሚነሡት "ተገፋን" የሚሉ የብሔረሰብ አባላት
በመኖራቸው ነው።

ይህንን ሁኔታ ለመቀየር ሲሉ ተገፋን ባዮች ግጭትን እንደ መፍትሔ ይወስዳሉ።
ነገር ግን የሚጋጩት የራሴ ከሚሉት ጋር ነው። ታዲያ በግጭት አሸናፊ ለመሆን ብዙ
ደጋፊ ያሻል። በዚህ ምክንያት ለዓላማቸው ስኬት፤ አዲስ ትርክት ተሠርቶ ማንነትም
በአዲስ መልክ ይዋቀራል፤ ይጐለብታል፤ ወይም ይበለጽጋል። በብሔር መለያየትም
በሂደት መዋቅራዊ ይሆናል።

120 Fearon, D.J. and Laitin, D.D. (2000) 'Violence and the Social Construction of Identity', International Organization 54.4: 845–77

ተመራማሪዎቺ፤ ብሔርን ለይቶ ለመውጋት እና እርስ በርስ ለመጠፋፋት ሰፈ የሉላ ብሔር ፀር የሚሆን የማንነት ትርክት መሠራት ከተቻለ፤ ተቃራኒው የማይፀራበት ምክንያት የለም ይላሉ። ለግጭት የተዋቀረን ግለሰቦቺ ከተቀበሉት፤ በብሔር መካከል መደጋገፍና ወንድማማችነት እንዲኖር ዐቃፊ ደጋፊ ማንነት በዚያው ልክ ከተሠራ የማይቀበሉት ምክንያት የለም ይላሉ። ይህ ሰፈው ዐሳብ ቢሆንም ሌላም ይታክልበታል።

በሉላ በኩል፤ ከግለሰቦቺ በተጨማሪ የብሔርን ማንነት በሂደት ለመገንባት የሚረዱ ስውር ባሕላዊና ሌሎችም ቅኔዎችን መጠቀም ይቻላል ይላሉ። በአንድ ብሔረሰብም ውስጥ ሆኖ በስውር በተለያየ መልክ መዋቅራዊ ጭቆናና ቅኔ ሊከሰት ይችላል። ይህን ለመልካም ብንለውጠው፤ የተሻለ መደጋገፍ ያላቸው የብሔር ማንነቶችን እንገነባን እንዜዳለን።

ባሕልና ኅይማኖት በብሔር ውቅር ውስጥ ከገባ ብሔረሰብነት ጥንት ንድፍ ነው ወደሚል አመለካከት ይመልሰናል፤ እንዳይገቡ ማድረግም ከባድ ነው። ብዙ ብሔሮች የሚጋሩት ኅይማኖትና ባሕል እንኳ በተለያየ ምክንያት በአንዱ ማኅበረሰብ ከሌላው የበለጠ አይሉ ይታያልና። እንዲሁም ቅኔነ በድርድር እየፈታን ሻል ያለ መተሳሰብና አንድነት ያለው ብሔር እንፈጥራለን ማለትም የቅኔዎችን ብዛት፤ አንዱ ሲፈታ ሌላ የመውለድ ምትሃታዊ ብቃቶችን ያላገናዘበ ዐይታ ነው።

በሦስተኛ ደረጃ ያሉት ዐሳቢዎች ግለሰቦችንም፤ የውስጥ ቅኔንም ከመጠቀም ይልቅ ውጫዊ የሆነ መዋቅራዊና ተቋማዊ ግፈቶችን በመጠቀም የብሔር ማንነቶችን ለበን በሚሆን መገንባት እንችላለን የሚሉ ናቸው። ለምሳሌ ልክ የቅኝ ግዛት በሰዎች ስነ ልቡና እንዲሁም ማንነት ላይ ለውጥ እንዳመጣ ሁሉ አሁን ያለው አለም ዓቀፋዊነት፤ የቴክኖሎጂ መስፋፋት፤ የዐውቀትና መረጃ ፍስት መሳለጥ የምንፈልገውን ግጭት ጠል የብሔር ማንነት ለመገንባት ያስችላል ባይ ናቸው።

የብሔር ዐሳቤ ጭንቀ፤ በአንድ አገር ያሉ ወይም ተቀራራቢ ሥፍራ ላይ የሰፈሩ ብሔሮች እርስ በርስ ሳይጋጩ መተሳሰብንና መደጋገፍን እንዴት ማምጣት ይችላሉ የሚለው ነው። ነገር ግን ስምምነት ማግኘት ከባድ ነው። እንዲያውም እያደር የብሔር ዐሳቤ ልክ እንደ ዘር ዐሳቤ በነገር ሁሉ ውስጥ ጣልቃ የመግባት ኅይሉን ማስተዋል ተችጓል።

ያለ ምክንያት አይደለም። ቀድሞም የብሔር ጥያቄ የተነሣው ከጥንት ንድፍ ዐይታ በመነሣት ዐቅል የሳተ መገፋፋት እንዲበራከት በመደረጉ ነው። ስለዚህ፤ ማንኛውም ነገር ሲደረግ፤ ለምሳሌ ጽሑፍ ቢሆን ወይም ተውኔት፤ የፈጠራ ሥራም ሆነ አዲስ ገበያ ማቋቋም፤ ሁሉ ነገር ከብሔር ዐይታ አንጻር መቃኘት አለበት እየተባለ መጣ።

በአንጹሩ መገፋፋትም ሆነ ከዚህ የተነሣ የተጎዱ የሉም የሚለውም ዐሳቤ ፈጽሞ አልሞተም። እንዲያውም፤ ዘመን ቀደማዊ የብሔር አመለካከቶች እየተቀየሩ በመምጣት ከቅርብ ጊዜ ወዲህ ብሔር ብሔረሰብ የሚባል ነገር ያለም፤ የሌለም ነገር ነው ወደ ማለት ደርሰዋል። ነገር ሲፈለግ ይኖራል። ወይም እንዲኖር ይደረጋል። ችግር ከሌለ ማንም

አያስተውሉውም። ይህን በመጥቀስ፣ ፆታ ዐሳቡ ራሱ ዕዳ ሳይሆን አይቀርም ወደ ማለት ያመሩ አሉ።

ይህም ከዘመን ቀደሞች ዕሳቤ የተቀዳ ዐሳብ ነው። ልክ እንደ ዘር ልዩነት፣ የብሔር ልዩነትንም በተናጠል ማየት የለብንም ባይ ነው። የዚህ ዐሳብ አመንጪ ተብላ የምትጠቀሰው የጥቁር አሜሪካ ሴቶች ጉዳይ ተሟጋችና በካሊፎርኒያ ዩኒቨርሲቲ የሕግ መምህር የሆነችው ኪምበርሊይ ክሬንሾው ናት። የዘርም ሆነ የብሔር ጥያቄ ይዘው የተነሡ ቡድኖች እንደ ጋራ ፈረስ አንድ አቅጣጫ ብቻ የሚያዩዋ፣ ሌሎችን ጥያቄዎችና ልዩነቶች የማይረዱ፣ በተለይም የሴቶችን እኩልነት የዘነጉ ናቸው።[121]

ይህ ክስ፣ ሰላም የሰፈነበት ሕብረተሰብ መምራት ይቻል ዘንድ፣ ለሁሉም ግፉዓን መልስ መስጠት የሚችል ሥርዓት መገንባት ያስፈልጋል ከሚል መነሾ ቢሰነዘርም፣ ብሶትን ገሸሽ ያደረገ ነው። የቀደመ ታሪክና ትርክት ያስከተለውን ሁኔታ መናቅም ሆነ መካድ፣ ብሔሮችን በሚያገናኙ ድልድዮች ላይ ከማተኮር ይልቅ "ስሙኝ" የሚል ጩኸት እያዳመጡ ጊዜ መፍጀትን ያስከትላል። የዘር፣ የብሔር፣ ሌሎችም የማንነትና የመብት እንዲሁም የፍትሕ ጥያቄዎች አሉ፣ ወደፊትም ይኖራሉ።

ጥያቄዎች በፖለቲካ መልክ ቢወጡም ባይወጡም፣ በአንድ አገር ውስጥ ያሉትን የዜግነት፣ የሠላም፣ የባሕልና ግዛማኖት፣ የልማት ወይም ሌሎች ማኅበራዊና ኤኮኖሚያዊ ኩነቶች የመወሰን ዐቅም አላቸው። ጥያቄዎች አይነሱ ማለት አይቻልም። ለተነሱ ጥያቄዎች ሁሉ ግጭት ብቻውን መፍትሔ ነው ማለት ግን አይጠቅምም። በግጭት የሚገኝ መፍትሔ ጠባሳ ትቶ ማለፉ የግድ ነው።

ስለዚህ፣ ምናልባትም አንዳንድ ጥያቄዎች ከጀርባቸው ካለው ትብትብ ያለ መነሾ አንጻር በደረስንበት የዐሳብና ዐቅም ደረጃም ሁሉን በሚያረካ መንገድ ላይፈቱ ይችላሉ ብሎ ማሰብንም ይጠይቃል። ምናልባትም ጊዜ ይፈታዋል ብሎ አማራጭ መንገዶችን መንደፍ ብልኃት ነው። ይህን ለማድረግ ግን ተሰሚነትና የአመራር ሚና ያላቸው ወይም የሚመኙ ወደ ሠላም አድልቶ መውደቅን ማስቀደም ይኖርባቸዋል።[122]

ይህን ማድረግ ይቻላል። በመጀመሪያ ደረጃ በታሪክ መካከል የተለያየ ጠባሳ ያስከተሉ መገፋፋቶች መኖራቸውን ተቀብሎ ለወደፊት ይህ ዐይነት ነገር እንዳይከሰት ከልብ መሥራት ያስፈልጋል። ብሔሮች የሚኮሩባቸውን እሴቶች ለማደብዘዝ ጥረት ማድረግም ሞኝነት ነው። ከዚህ ይልቅ መከባበር የተሞላበትን አንድነት፣ የጋራ የሆነ ህልምንም ልማት ማምጣት ላይ ትኩረት ማድረግ የተሻለ ትርፍ አለው። የምንኩራባቸውንም ሆነ የምናፍርባቸውን የታሪክ ምዕራፎች የጋራ ማድረግ የግድ ነው።

121 Crenshaw, K. (1989) 'Demarginalizing the Intersection of Race and Sex: A Black Feminist Critique of Antidiscrimination Doctrine, Feminist Theory and Antiracist Politics', University of Chicago Legal Forum 1989.1: 139–67

122 Deng, F. M. (1997). Ethnicity: An African Predicament. Brookings Institution; June 1997. https://www.brookings.edu/articles/ethnicity-an-african-predicament/

የአገራችንን ጉዳይ በዚሁ እያቃኘን ስለሆነ ይህን በአፅንዖት ብንድገመው ጥሩ ነው። የትላንቱ የኢትዮጵያ ታሪክ፤ የተጻፈውም ሆነ በትውፊት የተወረሰው፤ እንደ መኪና የኅላ መስተዋት ድንገት ደራሽ አደጋ የምንከላከልበት እንጂ መኪናውን ወደፊት የምንነዳበት ሊሆን አይገባውም። ለመጥቀስ የምናፍርባቸውን የኅላ ታሪኮች፤ በተጨባጭ የተፈጠሩም ሆነ እንደተፈጠሩ ተደርገው የተወሰዱ ትርክቶችንም በዚህ መልክ መቃኘት ግድ ነው።

ይህም ማለት፤ የትላንት ችግሮች (በእርግጥ የተከሰቱትም፤ ከትርክት የመነጩትም) ያሳደሩትን ጠባሳ እውቅና ሰጥቶ፤ ትላንትን በራሱ ማዕቀፍ ተመልክቶ፤ ዛሬ ላይ ሆነን ለነገ ምን ይበጃል የሚል የጋራ ትርክት መቅረጽ ያስፈልጋል ማለት ነው። የውዬታ ግዴታችን ነው፤ ከዚያ ውጭ ሲሆን ከአጽም ጋራ የምንነታረክ ያስመስልብናል። ልዩነት ከፈለጉት አይጠፋም። ከቋንቋ ወይም ባሕል የከፉ ሌሎች የልዩነት ነጥቦችም ሊኖሩ ይችላሉ። እነዚህን በጋራ ለይቶ፤ አንዱ ሌላውን በጥልቀት ተረድቶ፤ መከባበር መፍጠሔ ነው።

ከዚያ ውጭ ልዩነትን ማስረዳት እንኳ ከባድ ነው። እጅግ ጥቃቅን ልዩነቶችን በማስፋት በማንነት ፍለጋ ስም አገርን ማፍረስ ወይም ሰላምን ማደፍረስ የሚፈልጉ ወገኖች ይህን መጣታት ይኖርባቸዋል። እስካሁን ካለው ልምድ ለአገራት ምንም ትርፍ አላስገኘም። ለምሳሌ:- አንድ ቋንቋ እንኳ በሁሉ ሥፍራ በወጥነት አይነገርም፤ የቀበልኛ ልዩነቶች በቃላትና በአነጋገር ይስተዋላሉ። ይህን ለቋንቋው ማድለቢያ መጠቀም እንጂ ለልዩነት ማስረያ አጋጣሚ አድርጎ ማሰብ አያስፈልግም።

ባለፉት ጥቂት ዓመታት የተስተዋለው ነገራዊው ሁኔታ ግን ይህ አይደለም። በብዙ ቦታዎች ልዩነት እጅግ ተራግቧል። በሕዝብ መካከል በአሰፋፈር፤ በቋንቋ፤ በባሕል ወይም በሌላ ነገር ልዩነት እንዲነላ ተለፍቷል። ይህን በማገርም የብዝጎን ብሔር መዋቅር ፈጥሮ፤ ልዩነቶችን ተቀብሎ፤ እና አንድ የሚያደርጋቸው ነገሮች ላይ አተኩሮ መሥራት ያስፈልጋል። ይህ ሲደረግ ብሔሮች የራሳቸውን ማንነት የሚያጎሉበት ፈርጅ ከፖለቲካውና ከመተጋገል ውጭ ባለ አስተዳደራዊ፤ ሚዛናዊና መተባበርን ባስቀደመ ፉክክር እንዲያስተናግዱ ግልፅ መንገድ ሊበጅ ይችላል።

ብዝኃ ብሔር እና ብሔርተኝነት

ብሔር የሚለውን ቃልና ስብስብ ከአገር አሳኅሰን፤ ወደ ነገድ ቀረብ አድርገን ከተመለከትነው ዘንዳ መሠረቱንም ልንረዳ ግድ ነው። የሥነ ሰብዓት ጥናት ባለሙያዎች ብሔርን ወይንም ነገድን የምንረዳበት ትክክለኛ ሳይንሳዊ መንገድ የእነርሱ እንደሆን ያትቱና "ነገድ"ን የምንረዳበት አራት[123] መገለጫዎችን ይደረድራሉ።

123 Jenkins, R. (2001). Ethnicity: Anthrological Aspects; in International Encyclopedia of Social and Behavioral Sciences.

በቅድሚያ ብሔር፣ ብሔረሰብ፣ ወይም ነገድ ስንል ዋናው መሠረት የደም ወይም የውልደት ጉዳይ ሳይሆን በአብዛኛው የባሕል መለያየት ነው። አንዱ ባሕልና ትውፊት ከሌላው ልዩነት ካሳየ የብሔረሰብ ልዩነት ተንጸባረቀ ማለት ነው። ባሕል ስንል ቋንቋ፣ ትውፊት፣ የአኗኗር ዘይቤ፣ የውስጥ ግንኙነት፣ ማኅበራዊ የሐዘንና ደስታ ሥርዓት ልዩነት ወይም አንድነት ነው። ባሕል የሕዝብ ግንኙነት ነጸብራቅ በመሆኑ፣ ስለ አንድነቱ ወይም ልዩነቱ፣ አንዳንድ ጊዜ፣ ጥርት ያለ መስመር የለውም።

ሁለተኛው የብሔር፣ ብሔረሰብ፣ ወይም ነገድ ልዩነት መገለጫ፣ ማኅበራዊ ትስስር እና ግንኙነት ነው። መሠረቱ የጋራ የሚያደርግ ባሕል ቢሆንም "ሌላ" ብሎ ከሚጠራው ማኅበረሰብ ጋር ያለው የጋራ ግንኙነት አንዱን ከሌላው መለየት ያስችላል። ይህ ግንኙነት ሻካራም ሆነ ልዝብ ሊሆን ይችላል።

ለምሳሌ፦ ኢትዮጵያዊ የሆነ የባሕል ዕሴቶች ያሉት ማኅበረሰብ ብራዚል ውስጥ የሚንፀባረቁ ተመሳሳይ ዕሴቶችን ከያዘው ጋር ለመለየት እምብዛም አይከብድም፤ ምንም ትስስር የለውምና። ግንኙነት የሌለው ባሕል፣ ተመሳሳይ እንኳን ቢሆን ተገርሞ ከማለፍ በቀር የሚፈይድልን ነገር የለም። ስለዚህ ልዩነት የሚገልጠውን ያህል አንድነትም፣ ከአንድነት የሚነሣ ሽኩቻ፣ እና ፍቅርም፣ ብሔረሰቦችን ያሳያል ማለት ነው።

እንዲሁም ስለ ባሕል ሲነሣ በሦስተኛ ደረጃ ልናውቀው የሚገባ ሐቅ አለ። የባሕል አንዳንድ ገጽታዎች ከዘመን ጋር ይቀያየራሉ፤ ያድጋሉ፤ አንዳንድ ገጽታዎችም ይከስማሉ። ስለዚህ ባሕል ለውጥን አይፈራም፤ ይታቀፈዋል እንጂ።

"ባሕላችን ልዩ አደረገን" የሚሉ ማኅበረሰቦች የራሳቸውን የሚመስል ባሕል በሌላው ውስጥ የማግኘት ዕድላቸው ሰፊ ነው። ቢያንስ በአንዳንድ ገጽታቸው ከሌላው እየተመሳሰሉ የመሄድ ዕድል ሰፊ ነው። በአጭር ቃል፣ ባሕል ይቀያየራል። ባሕል ደግሞ የብሔር መለያየት መሠረት ከሆነ፣ ባሕል እንደሚቀያየር ሁሉ የብሔረሰብነት መገለጫም ይቀያያራል። ትንሽ ዘርጠጥ ብናደርገው፣ ከጊዜ እና ከግንኙነት ብዛት፣ ትላንትና እንዲህ ነኝ ያለ ብሔር ዛሬ እንዲያም ነኝ ሊል ይችላል ማለት ነው።

በመጨረሻም፣ ብሔር ወይም ብሔረሰብ ስንል የማኅበራዊ ማንነት ማመልከቻ ሆኖ፣ በወል የግንኙነት መገለጫ፣ በግልም የእኔነት መቀበያ ሆኖ እናገኘዋለን። በአብሮነት "እኛ ከዚህ ብሔር ጋር አንድ ስንሆን ከዚህ ጋር እንለያለን" ይባላል። በወል ሲነገር የሚገለጠውን ልዩነት ወይም አንድነት ለመልካም ዓላማ መጠቀም የሚፈልጉ እንዳሉ ሁሉ ወደ ክፉ የሚጠመዝዙ አይታጡም። እንደ አለመታደል ሆኖ ይህ ልዩነትን ለማጉላት ፖለቲከኞች የሚጠቀሙት መሠረታዊ ትርክት ነው።

"እኛ" እና "እናንተ" የሚለው ክፍፍል ከተራ መገለጫነት አልፎ ለመለያየት የሚያበቢድን ሲሆን አደገኛ ይሆናል። በግልም "እኔ የዚህ ብሔረሰብ አባል ነኝ" ስንል እንድምታ አለው። በብሔርም በግልም ራሳችንን በሆነ ዐጥር ውስጥ እንወስናለን። ዐጥር

ስንሠራ እሾህ የተሞላ ከሆነ፣ ወይም መግቢያውን ድፍን ያደረግን እንደሆነ፣ በልባችን “ሌሎች” ለምንለው ንቀት ወይም ፍርኃት ካደረብን አስከፊ ነው። በድምሩ የሚወለደው በጭንቀት የታጨቀ የልብ ቅዝቃዜ፣ “የእኛ” በምንለው በበቂ አይሞቅልንም።

ይሁንና ታሪክ የሚያስተምረን ሰዎች ብሔርንም ሆነ ባሕልን አጥር አበጅተው፣ ልዩነትን በጉልህ አስምረው ለማጥናትና ለመሸከም በቋመጡ ቍጥር ልዩነቱ እየገዘፈ ሳይሆን ይበልጥ እየላላ፣ እየደበዘዘ፣ የማይጨበጥ እየሆነ ማስቸገሩን ነው። ሌላው ቀርቶ የዘር ልዩነት ይስተዋላል ተብሎ የሚነገርበት ነጭና ጥቍር ወይም እስያዊ፣ ካለው የቴክኖሎጂ፣ የባሕል እና ትምህርት አንድነት የተነሣ የባሕል ድንበሩ ተንዷል። የፍላጐት እና እውነታ ተቃርኖ።

ይባስ ብሎ የደም ትስስሩ ሳይቀር ይጣሳል። ጋብቻና መዋለድ ከባሕል ውሳኔ ይልቅ የግል እየሆኑ በመጡ ቍጥር፣ የብሔረሰብ ልዩነት እየደበዘዘ፣ በፍለጋና በፍረጃ ካልሆነ “የጠራ” የሚባል የለም። ይህ ማለት ግን አንድ ዐይነትነት ሰፍኗል ማለት አይደለም። በምድር ላይ ሰው መኖር ከጀመረበት ጊዜ አንሥቶ የቋንቋና ባሕል ልዩነቶች አሉ፤ ይኖራሉም። “የአንተ ጠፍቶ የእኔ ብቻ ይለምልም” የሚል ሲበራከት ግን የጐሣ ፖለቲካ አጫዋች ያገኛል።

በሌላ በኩል፣ ጭራሽ፣ የብሔር ማንነትን ከመገንባት ይልቅ የአገር ማንነትን መገንባት ይሻላል ብለው የሚነሡም ይኖራሉ። ባሕል ያለያያል፤ ያስተሳስራልም። የመቀራረብ ትስስር ጉልህ በሆኑባቸው አገራት ውስጥ የብሔር ፖለቲካ የሚያራምዱ የብሔሩን አባላት ማስከተል የሚቸግራቸው ጊዜ አለ። በአንድ አገር ጥላ መኖርን የሚመርቱ አባላት ራሳቸውን በሌላውም ውስጥ ያያሉና።

ግንኙነትን ከማጉላት ይልቅ ልዩነትን እናጥፋ የሚለው ካየለ ግን መልሱ በጉልበት መሰንጠቅ ይሆናል። ይህ ሲሆን፣ “አገር ነን” ወይንም “እንገነጠላለን” የሚሉ የብሔር ፖለቲከኞች ፍላጐት አሸነፈ ማለት ነው። ወዲያው “አገር ነን” ብለው የሚነሡበትም ዋናው ምክንያት፣ በፓስፖርት፣ በሕግ፣ በውጭ ግንኙነት፣ በጦር ኀይል፣ በትምህርት እና በመሣሰሉት ቶሎ የማይበገር አጥር ለመገንባት ስለሚያስችላቸው ነው። በእርግጥም፣ ቅልጥፍ ያለ ልዩነት በቶሎ ለመፍጠር ቀላል መንገድ ነው።

አንድ ሰው ወይም ማኅበረሰብ “እንዲህ ዐይነት የነጠረ ባሕል አለኝ” ወይንም “ይህን የመሰልኩ ብሔር ነኝ” ለማለት የሚያስቸግሩ ነገሮች ሞልተዋል። ልዩነቱ ደማቅ መስመር አይሆንም። ማኅበረሰቡ የሚኮራበትን ማንነት ገንብቶ፣ የእኛ የሚሉት ብሔር ከሌላ ጋር ተስማምቶና ተከባብሮ መኖር እንዲችል ማድረግ አማራጭ መንገድ ነው። ምክንያቱም፣ “ሌላ” ከተባለው ጋርም የሚያለያይ ሳይሆን የሚያገናኘው ዕድል መብዛቱ እጅግ ሰፊ ነውና። ይህ ባይሆን እንኳ ሠላም የሚሻል ምርጫ አይሆንም?

አንድን ባሕል፤ ጥፍር አድርጎ አሥሮ የራስ ብቻ ማድረግ አይቻልም። ባሕል
ይተምማል፤ ይራመዳል። በአገራችን "እሳት ከተጫረበት፤ እንረቤት" እንደሚባለው
ተመንትፎርም ሆኖ ተሸሎክሎኩ በሄደበት ይበልጥ ይደምቅና የባሀሉ መሥራች ነኝ ባዩን
ኩም ያደርገዋል። አንድ ማንበረሰብ "ከዚያኛው እለያለሁ" ባለበት ቅፅበት ከአባላቱ
ውስጥ ጥቂት ያይደሉ "ሌሎችም ውስጥ አለንበት" ቢሉ ሊገርመን አይገባም። ከእነዚያም
ውስጥ ማንበረሰቡን ለመቅረብ ወይንም ለመሆን የሚዳዱ ብዙ አሉና።

ይህም ከሁለት ነገሮች የተነሣ ነው። በመጀመሪያ፤ ምንም እንኳ የብሔር
መለያየት ዋና መገለጫ ባሕል ቢሆንም የደም ትስስርም እንዳለበት ተሰምሮበታል።
የደም አንድነትና ልዩነት ደግሞ ጠንካራ ነው። አንድ ሰው የአባትና የእናት ውሁድ
ነው። የአባት ወገን በሚጠነክርባቸው ቦታዎች አንድን ሰው የአባትህን ባሕልና ሕዝብ
ብቻ ተቀበል ብሎ ጫና ማሳደር ቢቻልም ከውስጡ የእናቱን ደም ጠርነ ማውጣት
አይቻልም። ሁሌም የእናቱ ዘመዶች፤ የእርሱ ዘመዶች ሆነው ይኖራሉ።

እንዲሁም፤ አንዳንድ ጊዜ የእናት ወገን ጠንክሮ ይል ይሆናል። ከቅርበት አንጻር፤
ወይም በሌላ ምክንያት። እናም፤ የእናቱን ወገን ባሕል ተቀብሎ ያደገ ሰው ከአባት ደም
የተነሣ መሳሳብን አስወግድ ማለት ፈጽሞ አይቻልም። የወላጆቻችንን ዘመዶች ማራቅ
ከቶ አይሆንልንም።

በሁለተኛ ደረጃ፤ በየቀኑ በምንሠራው ሥራና በኑሯችን ቋንቋን፤ ትውፊትን፤
ባሕልን እንጠቀማለን እንጂ አንሆነውም። በማድረግ ወይም በመተግበር "ብሔሬ"
በምንለው ለመሳተፍ እንጥራለን እንጂ እርሱን አይደለንም። ለመሆን ብንምክርም
በፍጹምነት ልንገለጥ አንችልም። የእኛን ያህል ባይሆንም፤ በተወሰነ ደረጃ ደግሞ
"ሌላ" የምንለውም "በብሔራችን" ይሳተፋል። ስለዚህ "ድርጊት" እንጂ "መሆን"
የሚለው ትርክት የስምምነት ካልሆነ በቀር ሳይንሳዊ ሊሆን አይችልም።

በድርጊት ደግሞ መመሳሰልን ማስወገድ አይቻልም። የብሔር (ነገድ፤
ብሔረሰብ፤ ጎሣ) ፖለቲካ መሠረት ዐልባ የሚሆነው ከዚህ የተነሣ ነው። ለማግዘፍ
ብለን ካልሻላለምነው ወይም በእርግጥም አገር የመሆን ፍላጎት አይሎብን ካልሆነ
በስተቀር በአንድ አገር ውስጥ በሕዝብ መካከል የሚታየውን ልዩነት ለፖለቲካ ብንጠቀም
የማይቋረጥ ምስቅልቅል የሚፈጠረው ለዚህ ነው።

አውዳዊ ትርጉማችንን ለማጠቃለል ያህል፤ ባለፉት ሦስትና አራት አሥርት
ዓመታት "ብሔር" የሚለው ቃል "አገር" የሚለውን ትርጉም እየሸሸ፤ "ነገድ"
ለሚለው ትርጉም እጅግ እየቀረበ እንዲሄድ ስለ ተደረገ በቀላሉ ከሰው ኅዕምሮ ሊፋቅ
አይችልም። ስለዚህ፦ እንደ ሕገ መንግሥቱ "ብሔር፤ ብሔረሰብ፤ እና ሕዝብ"

የሚለውን በእኩልነት አይተን፤ [124] ብሔር፤ ብሔረሰቦችና ሕዝብን "ነገድ ወይም ጐሣ" ብለን ብንጠራ ንትርክን የሚያስከትል እንደሆን ተረድተን እንለፍ፡፡

ኢትዮጵያ ውስጥ ብሔርተኝነት አለ ወይስ የለም የሚለው ክርክር ፋይዳ ቢስ ነው፡፡ የብሔር ፖለቲካ የአገሪቱ ብቸኛው የአስተዳደር ሥርዓት ነው፡፡ "ዴሞክራሲያዊ ነውና ብሔርተኝነት ይለምልም" እየተባለ ለረኽም ዘመን ተለፈፈ፡፡ ያ ብቻ ሳይሆን የጐሣ ልዩነትን ለማስፋት ያለሙ የሚመሰሉ የብሔር ክልሎች በመፍጠር፤ ወፍራም ድንበር፤ አገርን አከል ሕልውና፤ ለመገንባት ሰፊ ጥረት ተደርጓል፡፡ ጽንፍ ሲይዝ፤ ሲገን፤ እና ሲጦዝ ወደ ዘረኝነት አያመራም ማለትስ እንችላለን ወይ?

የብሔረሰብ ፖለቲካ

ይህን ጥያቄ እስኪ በድጋሚ እንጠይቅ፡፡ ብሔርተኝነት ወደ ዘረኝነት ያመራል? ብሔርተኝነት በፖለቲካ መልክ ሲገለጥ ምን ጥቅም እና ጉዳት አለው? ከሆነስ፤ ይህ የመለያየት ዙሪያ ጥምጥም ወደ የት ያደርሳል?

የብሔርተኝነት ፅንስ ዐሳብ ከዘረኝነት ዕሳቤ ጋር ሲነጻጸር እምብዛም የዳበረ አይደለም፡፡ ገና አዲስ ከመሆን አንጻር እንደ ዘረኝነት ዕሳቤ ፍልስፍናው እያደነ የመጣና ጥርት ያለ ነው ማለት አይቻልም፡፡ በብሔረሰቦች መካከል ያለ ልዩነት የቆየ ይሆን እንጂ ፅንስ ዐሳቡ በግጭት ኑባሬ ከተነሣ ገና አንድ ምዕተ ዓመት እንኳን አልሞላውም፡፡

ስለዚህ ብሔርተኝነት ወደ የት ያመራል የሚለውን ለማየት ምሳሌዎች ብቻ ወስደን ሌላውን ለጥልቅ ጥናት ልንተወው ግድ ይለናል፡፡ የሚከተሉት ጥቂት ገጽታዎች ከታሪክ ቀለስ እውነታዎች የተቀነጨቡ ሲሆኑ፤ ሙሉ የብሔርተኝነት ፍልስፍና ባይሆኑም ብሔርተኝነት ፖለቲካ ሲሆን ወደ የት ሊያመራ እንደሚችል ፍንጭ ይሰጡናል፡፡

ብሶት የወለደው

የብሔርተኝነት ወይም የብሔር ፖለቲካ የመጀመሪያው አመለካከት የሚመነጨው "ተገፍን" ከሚሉ ወገኖች ነው፡፡ ይህ መገፋት ከተለያየ ምክንያት ሊነሣ ይችላል፡፡ በአብዛኛው ግን በታሪክ አጋጣሚ በአንድ አገር ግዛት ውስጥ ያሉ ነገር ግን በቁጥር ከሌሎች ጋር ሲነጻጸሩ "አናሣ" ከሚባሉ ብሔረሰቦች የሚነሣ ጥያቄ ነው፡፡ መገፋት በቁጥር ማነስ ብቻ የሚከሰት እንዳልሆነ ግን ልናሰምር ይገባል፡፡

ጥያቄውን የሚያነሡት በትላልቆች ላይ ወይንም እነርሱ ይመሩታል ተብሎ በሚታሰበው አገረ መንግሥት ላይ ነው፡፡ ከብሔር ማንነታችን የተነሣ፤ ወይም ከቁጥር

---

[124] በኢትዮጵያ ሕገ መንግሥቱ መሠረት "እኩልነት" ሉዓላዊነትን በመጋራት እንጂ በቁጥር አይወሰንም፡፡ በደፈናው ስንወስድ ግን "ብሔር፤ ብሔረሰብ፤ ሕዝብ" የሚለው አገላለጥ በቁጥር ልዩነት እንዳለ ለማመልከት እንደሆን መገንዘብ እንችላለን፡፡ ሕገ መንግሥቱ ግን ይህ ዴሞግ ሌላ ንትርክ እንዳያስከትል አጌ ብሔር ነው፤ ሌላው ደግሞ ሕዝብ ነው ብሎ በጽሐፍ ማስቀመጥ አልፈለገም፡፡

አናሳነት የተነሣ ሥፍራ ተነፈግን፣ ወይም ባሕል ኀይማኖታችንን እንዳንጠቀም ወይንም እንዳናሳድገው ተከለከልን የሚል ስሞታ ነው።

አንድና ጥቂት ሰዎች፣ ወይም አንድና ጥቂት ጊዜ አይደለም። ያለ ዐረፍት ይደጋገማል። እየጠፉ ብልጭ ይላል። እያለም የብሔረሰብ ጥቆና መዋቅራዊ ነው ወደሚል ያድጋል። ታዲያ እነዚህ እሮሮ የሚያቀርቡ ወገኖች መፍትሔም ስለሚጠቁሙ መዋቅራዊ መልስ ብቻ አምጡልን ሲሉ ይደመጣሉ።

መዋቅራዊ መልስ የማይሰጥ ወይንም የሚዘገይ ከሆነ መዋቅራዊ ጬና ነው ተብሎ ይደመደማል። ስለዚህ ይህን መዋቅራዊ ጬና መቋቋም፣ ሲያስፈልግም በማንኛውም መንገድ መታገል፣ ጥቆናንም ከጬንታችን ላይ መጣል መብታችን ነው ይላሉ። ግጭት ይጀመራል።

አንድ ወይም ሁለት ዓመት ሳይሆን ምዕተ ዓመታትን ካስቆጠረ ግጭት በኃላ እ.ኤ.አ. በ1921 ደቡባዊ የአየር ላንድ ክፍል ከታላቋ ብሪታኒያ መዳፍ ነጻ በመውጣት ካቶሊካውያን ክርስቲያኖች የሚበዙባት አየር ላንድ የምትባል አገር ተመሠረቱች። የሰሜኑ አየር ላንድ ክፍል ግን ፕሮቴስታንት ክርስቲያኖች ስለ ነበሩ፣ ራስ ገዝ ሆኖ በብሪታኒያ ሥር የመቆየት ፍላጎት በረታ።

መቼም በአንድ አገር አስተዳደር ውስጥ የኖሩ ሰዎችን ከመቀላቀል ማገድ አይቻልም። በአንዴም ተነስቶ ቀጥተኛ መስመር አስምሮ ማለያየት እንዲሁ። ስለዚህ፣ በሰሜን አየር ላንድም ጥቂት ካቶሊካውያን ነበሩ። እነዚህም ካቶሊኮች፣ የሰሜን አየር ላንድ መንግሥት መድልዎ ያደርግብናል ሲሉ ማጉረምረም ጀመሩ። አሃዝ እየጠቀሱ በመንግሥት ሥራ፣ በኀላፊነት ሥፍራዎች፣ ... ወዘተ ካቶሊካውያን በቂ ቦታ አልተሰጣቸውም ማለትን አበዙ።

ፍላጎታቸው በመጀመሪያ ከደቡብ አየር ላንድ ጋር ለመዋሃድ ነበር። ነገር ግን የሰሜን አየር ላንድ ክፍል በአብዛኛው ፕሮቴስታንት ስለ ሆነ ይህ የማይቻል ሆነ። እምብዛም መፍትሔ ሳያገኝ፣ የስብዓዊ መብቶች ንቅናቄ ወዳያለበት ወደ 1960ዎቹ ደረሰ። በአሜሪካ ጥቁር ሕዝቦች ላይ ያለውን መዋቅራዊ በደል የሚቃወሙ ወጣት መሪዎች እነ ጆን ሂዩም፣ ጀስቲን ኩሪ፣ እና ቤርናዴት ዳቭሊን የተጠቀሙብትን የነጻነት ትግል ስልት ለመኮረጅ ቆረጡ፣ ልክ እንደ ማርቲን ሉተር፣ ሠላማዊ ሰልፍ።

ወዲያው ካቶሊኮች "የአይሪሽ ብሔርተኞች" ሲባሉ፣ በራስ ገዝ አስተዳደር እየተመራን ከታላቋ ብሪታኒያ ጋር እንቆይ ያሉ ፕሮቴስታንቶች "ታማኞች" ተባሉ። የንቅናቄዎች ስም አስያየም ጥምር ሕዝብ ለሕዝብ በዓይን ቁሥቋኝ ወደ መተያየት እንዲያድግ ምክንያት ሆነ። በእርግጥም ብሔረኛ ወጣቶቹ የመሯቸው ሠላማዊ ሰልፎች ላይ "ታማኞች" የተባሉት ለማደናቀፍ ይወጡ ነበር።

ለትንኮሣ መውጣታቸው እየታወቀ፤ "ታማኞች" በአይሪሽ ብሔርተኛ ሰልፈኞች ላይ የድንጋይ ናዳ ሲያዘንቡ ፖሊሶች ዝም ብለው ተመልካች ሆኑ። ይህም፤ በአሜሪካን የጥቁሮች ነጻነት ትግል ጊዜ ነጭ ብሔርተኞች ሰልፈኛውን ሲያንገላቱ የአሜሪካ ፖሊሶች ያልተመለከቱ መስለው የዘለሉትን ይመስል ነበር። እንዲህ ዐይነት ድርጊት ከሕዝቡ አዕምሮ ቶሎ ያለተፋቀ፤ ነገር ግን ልዩነትን የሚያጎላ ተጫማሪ ክስተት ሆነ።

ወዲያውም ታጣቂዎች ተፈጠሩ። የካቶሊካውያን የአየር ላንድ ሪፐብሊክ ሠራዊት እና የአልስተር (ፕሮቴስታንቶች የሚበዙባት የሰሜን አየር ዋና ከተማ) አንድነት ጎይሎች የሚባሉ። የትጥቅ ትግል ሲኖር ግጭት እየከፋ እንጂ እየረገበ አይመጣም። ሲከፋም የታላቋ ብሪታኒያ ወታደሮች ጭምር ይሳተፉ ጀመር፤ ለመዳኘት። ግና እንርሱም ለፕሮቴስታንቶች ማዳላታቸው አልቀረም። 125

ለሦስት አሥርተ ዓመታት የዘለቀው አስከፊው የእርስ በርስ ግጭት እስከ 3700 ያህል ዜጎች ሕይወት ቀጥፏል። በአሥር ሺህ የሚገመቱ ደግሞ ቆስለዋል። ይህ በዘመናችን ምናልባት የመጀመሪያው የብሔር ግጭት የተስተዋለበት ሲሆን ከጎይማኖት ጋር የተቆራኘ መሆኑ አስገራሚ ያደርገዋል። በክፍለ ዘመኑ መጨረሻ አካባቢ ዕርቅ አስከሚፈታታው ድረስ።

በስምምነቱም የሰሜን አየር ላንድ ግዛት ቀድሞ እንደ ነበረች ራስ ገዝ አስተዳደር ሆና ከታላቋ ብሪታኒያ ጋር እንድትሆን ፖለቲካዊ መፍትሔ ተበጀለት። የሪፓብሊካኑም ሆነ የአልስተር ጦር አባላት ምህረት እና የፖለቲካ ሥፍራ ተሰጣቸው። ለአቅም ግጭት የሚያደርስ በቂ ምክንያት አይጠፋም። ጎይማኖት፤ ቋንቋ፤ መልካም አስተዳደር፤ ሌላም የመብት ጥያቄ። ግጭቶችን በስምምነት ማስወገድ፤ ከእልህ ይልቅ ውይይት፤ ንግግር መቅደም ይገባው ይሆን?

ከማን አንሼ

ሁለተኛው የብሔርተኝነት አመለካከት "ሌላው ያገኘው ሁሉ ለእኔም ይገባኛል" ከሚል የሚመነጭ ነው። መገፋት ቢኖርም፤ ባይኖርም፤ ራስን አግዘር ከማየት ይህ ይከሠታል። የፍትሐዊነት ጥያቄም ይመሥላል። ከቱጥር ብዛት፤ ከባሕል ወይም ጎይማኖታዊ ዘመናዊነት፤ በገንዘብ ወይም በትምህርት ከሌሎች ሻል ብዬ እገኛለሁ ከማለት ... ወዘተ "እኛ ትልቅ ነን፤ ወይም ከማን እናንሳለን" የሚል አስተሰሰብ ሊሰርፅ ይችላል። ይህ ችግር ባልሆነ፤ ማን ትልቅነትን ይጠላል?

ነገር ግን አክራሪዎች የትልቅነቱ መሠረት ትዕቢት፤ መንገዱንም ግጭት ያደርጉታል። በዚህ ምሳሌ የሚሆኑት ደግሞ ከብሶቶች እጅግ ይበዛሉ። በዓለም ላይ

125 Smyth, J. (ed). (2017). Remembering the Troubles: Contesting the Recent Past in Northern Ireland. Notre Dame Press, University of Notre Dame.

ከ195 በላይ ነጻ አገራት እንዳሉ የአገራት የተለያየ መረጃ የሚያጋራው የወርልዶሜተር[126] ድረ ገጽ ያስነብብናል። አብዛኞቹ የተመሠረቱት በሃያኛው መቶ ምዕተ ዓመት ሁለተኛው አጋማሽ ላይ ነው። ከ1960 ዓ.ም ጀምሮ በዓለም ላይ 134 የተለያዩ አገራት ነጻ መንግሥት ሆነው ተመሥርተዋል።

ከእነዚህ አብዛኞቹ ከቅኝ ግዛት የወጡ ናቸው። ነገር ግን የቀድሞዋ ሶቪየት ኅብረት ስትፈርስ 16 አገራት በአንድ ቀን መፈጠራቸውም ይታወቃል። ከ1990 ዓ.ም ወዲህ ግን ከሶቭየቶች መፍረስ በተጨማሪ 18 አገራት ተፈጥረዋል። ከእነዚህ ሁለቱ ምሥራቅ አፍሪካውያን ደቡብ ሱዳንና ኤርትራ ናቸው። በዚህ ጊዜ፣ ማለትም ከ1960 ዓ.ም ወዲህ የተዋኸዱት አገራት ቁጥር ግን እጅግ ጥቂት ነው፤ ጀርመን፣ ታንዚኒያና የመን ብቻ። ስምምነት ብርቅ ነው፤ መለያየት መንገድዋ ቀላል።

የአገርነት አባዜ፣ ከተልቅነት ይልቅ ትንሽነትን የወለደላቸውም አሉ። አገር ተብለው ከሚጠሩት ውስጥ ደግሞ አሥሩ በአማካይ 30ሺህ ሕዝብ ብቻ አላቸው። አንድ ወፈር ያለ ቀበሌ፤ በእኛ ቀመር። "ነጻ" ወጥነን ይበሉ እንጂ በዓለም ደረጃ ቀርቶ በቀጣናቸው ትርጉም ያለው ተጽዕኖ የማያደርሱ ናቸው።

የታሚል ሕዝብ ረዥም ታሪክ ያለው ነው። ትልቅ ቁጥር ካላቸው የዓለማችን ሕዝብ ውስጥ ሊመደብ ይችላል። በአብዛኛው የሂንዱ እምነት ተከታዮች ቢሆኑ፣ ከቀጥራቸው ትልቅነት የተነሣ ሁሉንም ዐይነት ኃይማኖት የሚከተሉ አይታጡም። በአሁኑ ጊዜ በግምት ወደ 70 ሚሊዮን ያህል ይሆናሉ።

ታሚሎች በደቡባዊ ህንድ (ታሚል ናዱ፣ ከሬላ፣ አንድራ ፕራዴሽ፣ ካርናታካ) ግዛቶች፣ በስሪ ላንካ፣ በማዳጋስካር፣ በቻይንና ሌሎችም የምሥራቅ እስያ አገራት፣ እንዲሁም በምሥራቅና ደቡባዊ አፍሪካ አገራት በብዛት ይገኛሉ። ብዙዎችም በዳያስፖራ መልክ በበርካታ አገራት ውስጥ ተበትነው አሉ።[127] ረዥም ታሪክ ያላቸውና ወጣ ማለት የለመዱ ስለሆኑ ሃብታሞችና የተማሩ ሴዎች ይበዙባቸዋል።

ስሪላንካ ደግሞ 21 ሚሊዮን ያህል ሕዝብ ያላት ደሴት አገር ናት። ከዚህ ውስጥ ሲሦው ያህል በሰሜን ክፍላተ አገር የሚኖሩ ታሚሎች ናቸው። ሌሎች ስሪ ላንካውያን በአብዛኛው የቡዲሂስት ኃይማኖት ተከታይ፤ ስንሃላውያን በመባል የሚታወቁ ናቸው። ከደሴቲቱ እምብዛም ርቀው ወደ ሌላ አገር አይሄዱም።

እ. ኤ. አ. በ1976 ቬሎፕላይ ፕራባካራን የተባለ ሰው ታሚሎች ትልቅ ሆነው ሳለ ለምን አገር አይገባቸውም ብሎ ተነሣ። የኤላም ታሚሎች የነጻነት ነብሮች፣ በተለምዶ ስሙ የታሚል ነብሮች የሚባል እጅግ ጽንፈኛ የነጻነት ትግል ቡድን መሠረተ። ከነጻ

126 Worldometers. (2021). Countries of the World. https://www.worldometers.info/geography/ how-many-countries-are-there-in-the-world/

127 Britannica, The Editors of Encyclopaedia. "Tamil". Encyclopedia Britannica, 13 Dec. 2017, https://www.britannica.com/topic/Tamil.

መንግሥት ይልቅ የረባ ሴላ ጥያቄ አልነበረውም። ጮካኔና ጽንፈኝነት መታወቂያቸው ነበር።

ይህ ጥያቄያቸው ግን በስሪላንካ ብቻ ተገድቦ ይቀራል ወይ የሚል ዐሳብ ታሚሎች ባሉባቸው አገራት ሁሉ መነሣቱ አልቀረም። በአብዛኛው የሺበር ጥቃትን፣ ሲመችም በሀቡዕ የትጥቅ ትግል፣ አካሂዶ ከተማ በማስለቀቅ ሃይለኛ መሆን የጀመረው ድርጅት፣ ገቢው ሕገ ወጥ ከሆነ ንግድ፣ በአብዛኛው አደንዛዥ ዕጾች፣ ባንኮችን በመዝረፍና ከሃብታም ዳያስፖራው በሚሰጥ ድጋፍ ነበር።

ጮካኔው በአካባቢው አገራት ፍርጋታ ለቀቀ። ከአሥር ዓመታት ግርግር በኋላ አገረ ሀንድ ነገሩ አላማራትም። አፍንጫዋ ስር የሚካሄድ አደጋኛ እንቅስቃሴ መታገስ አልሆነላትም። የሡላም ስምምነት በማደራደር በ1987 ዓ.ም የሡላም አስከባሪ ጦር ወደ ስሪላንካ ላከች።

በዚህ እርምጃ የተዳከመው የታሚል ነብሮች ቡድን በዓይነቱ የመጀመሪያም፣ እጅግ ጨካኛም የሆነ ነውስ ቡድን ያዋቅር ነበር። ጥቁር ነብሮች የሚባል፣ አዲስ የትግል ሥልትም ይዘው ብቅ አሉ። አጥፍቶ መጥፋት ይባላል። በዚህ ስልት፣ የሀንድ ጠቅላይ ሚንስትር ራጂብ ጋንዲን በታሚል ናዱ የምርጫ ዘመቻ ሲያካሂዱ በ1991 ዓ.ም ይዘው ጠፉ። ይህ አስደንጋጭ እርምጃ ዓለምን ያነጋገረ፣ ፖለቲከኞችንም ያናወዘ ጉዳይ ነበር።

አገረ ሀንድም የሰላም ስምምነቱን አፍርሳ፣ ከስሪላንካ ጦርን ለማስወጣት ተገደደች። ነብሮቹ ለጊዜውም ቢሆን የተሳካላቸው መሰለ። በተመሳሳይ የአጥፍቶ መጥፋት ጥቃት 10 የስሪላንካ ከፍተኛ የጦር አማራኖችን በ1992 ዓ.ም አስወገዱ። አገሪቱ የጦር መሪ ዐልባ ሆነች። እንዲሁም በ1993 ዓ.ም የአገሪቱን ዋና መሪ፣ ፕሬዝዳንት ራናሲንጌ ፕሬሜዳሳን፣ በስሪላንካ ማዕከላዊ ባንክ በተደረገ ጥቃትም 100 ንጹሓንን ገደሉ። በዚህ ብቻም አላቆሙም።

ወደ ኤኮኖሚው በሰፈው በመዞር፣ በ2001 ዓ.ም የኮሎምቦ (ዋና ከተማ) ዓለም አቀፍ የአውሮፕላን ማረፊያን በመቆጣጠር ግማሽ ያህል የአገሪቱን አውሮፕላኖች አወደሙ። ስሪላንክ ተሸመደመደች። በአጠቃላይ በዚህ አስከሪ ጦርነት እስከ 80 ሺህ ሰዎች እንደሞቱ ይገመታል። ይህ አስከፌ ቡድን "ሺበርተኛ" ተብሎ በዓለም ዙሪያ ለመፈረጅ ከቀዳሚዎች መካከል ነበር።

ብዙ የሡላም ስምምነቶች ሊሳኩ ስላልቻሉ የአገሪቱ መንግሥት በ2008 ዓ.ም ከፍተኛ ዘመቻ በማድረግ ፕራባካራንን ጨምሮ ዋና ዋናዎቹን መሪዎች ደመሰሳቸው። እስከ 16 ሺህ ይደርሳል ተብሎ የተገመተው በጥብቅ የሠለጠነው የነብሮች ጦር፣

እያንዳንዳቸው በአንጻታቸው ዙሪያ የሳይናይድ እንክብሎችን አሥረው የሚዞሩ አጥፍቶ ጠፊዎች፤ ሙሉ በሙሉ በሚባል ደረጃ በከንቱ አለቁ።[128]

የብዙዎች አገር መንግሥት አወቃቀር ለአንዳንድ ሕዝቦች ተስማሚ አይደለም። በተለይም የቅኝ ግዜ በነበረባቸው አካባቢዎች፤ አፍሪካ በዚህ ዋነኛ ተጎጂ ናት። ከትልቅነትዋ አንጻር ቅኝ ገዢዎች ሁሉን ሥፍራ "ተቆጣጥረው" አልነበርም የተከፋፈሉት፤ አንድ ሥፍራ በመቆም ዝም ብሎ ቀጥተኛ መስመር በማስመር እንጂ። ሆን ተብሎ ተመሳሳይ ባሕልና ቋንቋ ያላቸው ሕዝቦች ተከፍለዋል። ጌሎች ደግሞ በተንኮል ወይም በሰፈራ ስም የሰዎችን ከቦታ ወደ ቦታ መዘዋወር አስከትለዋል።

ለምሳሌ:- ታሚሎችን መጀመሪያ በስሪላንካ ያሰፈሩ እንግሊዞች ነፍ። የቅኝ ግዜ ውርስን በሰከነ መንገድ ካልያዙት አሃሩ ለቅኝ ገዢዎች ሳይሆን በግዛቶቹ ለሚቀሩት ሕዝብ ነው። ለምሳሌ:- ሶማሊያውያን ቢያንስ በአራት አገራት ይገኛሉ። ዚያድ ባሬ አስተባብሮ አንድ ታላቅ ሶማሊያ ካልፈጠርኩ ብለው ተነሡ። ራሷ ሶማሊያ እስከ ዛሬ ፈርሳ ቀረች። አገረ መንግሥትን መነካካት ይቻል ይሆናል። ውጤቱን ግን መተንበይ አይቻልም።

ኩርዶች በኢራቅ፣ በቱርክ፣ በኢራንም ይገኛሉ። እነዚህን የኩርድ ግዛቶች ለማዋሃድ፣ የኩርድ ነጻ አውጪ ግንባር ተቋቁም። ይህ ትግል ለኩርድ ሕዝብ እስከ ዛሬ አሥር በመሸመት ላይ ነው። ወትሮ የሚጣሉት ሦስት አገራት በኩርድ ነጻነት ጉዳይ ሲሆን አይቻልም በማለት ይስማማሉ። እናም ተባብረው፣ ወይም በተራ ይደቁሲቸዋል።

አንጎላ ዴሞክራቲክ ኮንጎን የሚያያዋል አገር ዘላ አልፋ ግዜ አላት። ለኮንጎ የባሕር በር ፍለጋ የተሳለ ካርታ እንደሆን ያስታውቃል። በአንጻሩ ግን ኮንጎ ራሷ የዛምቢያን ልብ በማንኪያ የሚጫልፍ መሳይ ካርታ ተሰጥቷታል።

ጋምቢያ ደግሞ በሴኔጋል ጎሮ የተሰካች ስንጥር ትመሥላለች። ሴኔጋሉውያን ወደ ደቡብና ሰሜን የአገራቸው ክፍል የሚመላለሱት ጋምቢያን አቋርጠው ነው። የዓለም አቀፍ ድንበር ማቋረጫ መስፈርቶችን አሟልተው፣ ካልሆነ ስዓታት የሚፈጅ ጉዞ ያውም በጠረፍ ክፍላተ አገር፣ ምናልባትም ከሽፍታ ጋር እየታገሉ ማድረግ ግዴታቸው ነው።

በዚህ ዙሪያ ብዙ ስሞታ እንጂ መፍትሔ አልተገኘም። ተመሳሳይ ሕዝቦች በሁለት ወይም ሦስት የተለያዩ አገራት መታፈናቸውን ማስቀረት አልተቻለም። የአገር መንግሥታትን ካርታ፣ በተለይም በቅኝ የተያዙትን ዳግም ለመሣል መጣርም፤ እንዳለ መተውም ይሰብሻል።

---

128 Britannica, The Editors of Encyclopaedia. "Tamil Tigers". Encyclopedia Britannica, 22 Oct. 2020, https://www.britannica.com/topic/Tamil-Tigers.

በማንኛውም ረገድ ግን ግጭት መፍትሔ አይሆንም። አፍሪካ ሆን ተብሎ በተሸረበ
ሴራ ፈጽማ ከራስዋ ጋር እየተጣላች እንድትኖር የተፈረደባት ትመስላለች። መፍትሔው
ግን ሴራ ለምን ተሸረብብን እያሉ ማላዘን ሳይሆን ኃላፊነትን ወስዶ በሰከነ መንገድ
የሚበጀውን መፍጠር ነው። በግልም፤ በጋራም ይህ ኃላፊነት በአፍሪካውያን ሁሉ ላይ
አርፉል።

የወጋ ቢረሳ

የብሔር ፖለቲካ መለያየትን ሊሰብክ የገባበት ጥልቀት ግን በቀላሉ ለመወጣት
አስቸጋሪ መሆኑን ማንሳት እጅግ አስፈላጊ ነው። "አለባብሰው ቢያርሱ" እንደሚባለው
እንዳይሆን። ዘመናትን የፈጀ መለያየት በሰዎች ልጆች መካከል ያለ መታከት ተዘርቷል።
በጥንቃቄም፤ በመዋቅር ተደግፎ ድርጅቷል። ይህንን ግጭት ቀስቃሽ ልዩነት መሠረቱን
ስንመርምር የብሔር ፖለቲካ የሚባለውን አሽቀንጥረን መጣል፤ ካልሆነም ሥርዓት
ማስያዝ እንዳለብን ግን አመላካች ነገሮች አሉ።

የቂም በቀል ትርክት ሦስተኛው የብሔር ፖለቲካ አምድ ነው። ሩዋንዳንና
ቡሩንዲን እንመልከት። በዓለማችን ውስጥ ከተከሰቱት የብሔር ግጭቶች ውስጥ
ምናልባታም እጅግ አስከፊው በእነዚህ አገራት የታየው ነው። እጅግ አስከፊ።

ለጕሣ ጥናት ባለሙያዎች ራስ ምታት የሆነው ነገር ደግሞ የአስከፊነቱ ብዛት ብቻ
አልነበረም። በግጭቱ ውስጥ የተካፈሉት ሁለት የተባሉት ብሔረሰቦች (ሁቱና ቱትሲ)
ፍጹም አንድ መሆናቸው ነው። [129] በቋንቂ አይለያዩም፤ ባሕላቸው ፈጽሞ አንድ ነው፤
የመልክዐ ምድር ልዩነትም የለም። [130]

በአሠፋፈር እንኳ አንዱ ለሌላው ጎረቤት ነው። ለየት ያለ ክፍለ አገር፤ ለየት
ያለ ቀበሌ እንኳን እምብዛም ነው። ይጋባሉ። ለዘመናት እርስ በርስ ተዋለደዋል።
ስለዚህ፤ አባት ሁቱ ቢሆን እናት ቱትሲ የመሆናቸው ዕድል እጅግ ከፍተኛ ነው።
በጎይማኖትም ልዩነት የለም። አብዛኞቹ ካቶሊካውያን ሲሆኑ ጥቂት ፕሮቴስታንቶችም
አሉባቸው።

ቀድሞ የጀርመን ቅኝ ግዛት ነበሩ። ጀርመን በአንደኛው የዓለም ጦርነት ስትሸነፍ
ወደ ቤልጂየም ዞሩ። እንኳን እነዚህ ሁለቱ ብሔረሰቦች ሩዋንዳና ቡሩንዲ ታሪካቸው
በሙሉ የተያያዘ፤ የአንድ አገር ታሪክ ነው። [131]

---

129 Gourevitch, P. (1998). We Wish to Inform You that Tomorrow We Will Be Killed with Our Families. New York: Picador, 1998

130 Fornace, K. (2009). The Rwandan Genocide. Beyond Intractability. https://www.beyondintractability.org/casestudy/fornace-rwandan

131 Uvin, P. (1999). Ethnicity and Power in Burundi and Rwanda: Different Paths to Mass Violence. Comparative Politics. Vol. 31; No. 3. (Aprl., 1999); pp. 253-271

ለኢትዮጵያ ፖለቲካ ቀረብ ስለሚል የእነዚህን አገራት እንጂ ከንቱ የብሔር ፖለቲካ ጥቂት ዘርዘር አድርገን መመልከት ይኖርብናል። ለትንበያ ወይን፣ ለማስፈራራት አይደለም። ነገር ግን በአፍሪካ አሕጉር፣ በዘመናችን የተከናወነ፣ በተሻለ ደረጃም ተጽፎ የተቀመጠ የግጭት ታሪክ ስላለው የብሔር ፖለቲካን አስከፊነት ለመረዳት ጥሩ ምንጭ ስለሚሆን ነው።

ሩዋንዳም ሆነ ቡሩንዲ በአፍሪካ እምብርት የሚገኙ አገራት ናቸው። ምድራቸው ተዳፋት የሚበዛው ሆኖ እንጂ ያምራል። በተለምዶ ሩዋንዳ የአንድ ሺህ ኮረብቶች አገር ተብላ ስትታወቅ፣ ቡሩንዲ የአፍሪካ ልብ ትባላለች። በሁለቱ አገራት በእርግጥ ኮረብቶች ለቀኑጥር ይታክታሉ። የሩዋንዳው የቢሩንጋ የተራሮች ሰንሰለት አካል የሆነው የካሪሲንቢ ተራራ በአፍሪካ አሥረኛው ትልቁ ተራራ ሲሆን ለራስ ዳሽን ጥቂት ፈሪ ነው፤ እስከ 4507 ሜትር ከፍታ ይደርሳል።

ከታላቁ ዴሞክራቲክ ኮንጎ ጋር የሚያዋስናቸው እነዚህ የተራራ ሰንሰለቶችና የአፍሪካ ታላላቅ ሐይቆች ማለትም ታንጋኒካና ኪቩ ናቸው። መካከለኛው አፍሪካ እንደ መሆናቸው ምድራቸው እንጂ ለም ነው። ኪቩ የነዳጅ እምቅ ሀብት እንዳለው ይነገራል። እንዲያውም ሜቴን የሚባል ጋዝ እያሰለሰ ፈንድቶ ሰው ይገድላል። ሥራ ላይ ቢውል ሀብት ነው።

ሁለት የዝናብ ወራት አሏቸው ቢባልም፣ ዝናብና የጸሐይ ወራቶች በእኩል ስለሚፈራረቁ በጋና ክረምቱ እምብዛም አይታወቅም። ለእርሻ፣ በተለይም ለአትክልትና ፍራፍሬ እንደ ሁለቱ አገራት የተመቸ ሥፍራ ጥቂት ነው። ኮንጎ አቅራቢያም ስለሆኑ ከርሰ ምድራቸው በማዕድን የታጨቀ እንደሆነ ይገመታል።

ከአገራቱ የቆዳ ስፋት አንጻር ጠቅጣቃ የሕዝብ አሥፋፈር የሚታይባቸው ካልሆኑ በቀር እግዚአብሔር አምላክ መፍጠር ብቻ ሳይሆን እንትፍ፣ እንትፍ ብሎ የባረካቸው ያህል መልካም ምድር ተሰጥቷቸዋል። በታሪክም እምብዛም አዳዲስ አገራት አይደሉም። በአስፋፈር ቢቪዎች የሚቆጠር ዓመታት፤ ከ1300 ዓ.ም ጀምሮ ደግሞ ጠንካራ መዋቅር ያለው የጎሣ አማራ በሁለቱም እንደ ነበረ ይታወቃል። የደረጀ ባሕልም አላቸው።[132]

ሁቱና ቱትሲ ተብለው የተለያዩ "ጎሣዎች" አሉ የሚል ትርክት መጀመሪያ የጠነሰሰው ጆን ሃኒንግ ስፔክ (1827–1864)[133] የተባለ "የጥቁ አባይን ምንጭ ያገኘ" እየተባለ የሚወራለት እንግሊዛዊ አገር አሳሽ ነበር። በጎልማስነቱ ከመሞቱ በፊት ይህንን ምድር አየ፣ ጻፈም። በእርሱ ግምት የአገራቱ የመጀመሪያ ሰፋሪዎች ከምዕራብ

---

132 Lemarchand, R. & Clay, D. (2021). "Rwanda". Encyclopedia Britannica, 10 Aug. 2021, https://www.britannica.com/place/Rwanda.

133 Britannica, The Editors of Encyclopaedia. "John Hanning Speke". Encyclopedia Britannica, 11 Sep. 2021, https://www.britannica.com/biography/John-Hanning-Speke. .

ምናልባትም ከኮንጎና ቻድ ከአራተኛው ምዕተ ዓመት ጀምሮ የመጡ ጐሣዎች ናቸው። እርሻ አዋቂ፣ አጣር ብለው፣ ሰውነታቸው ደልደል ያለ።

እንደ ስቴክ ገለጻ፣ እነዚህ ጠቆር ብለው አፍንጫቸው ጠፍጠፍ ያለ ስለሆነ ቀዳሚ (ማለትም፣ ኋላ ቀር) እውነተኛ አፍሪካውያን ናቸው አለ፣ ሁቱ ተባሉ። ጥቂት ቆየት ብሎ ከብት አርቢ የሆኑ፣ ጐሣዎች ከሰሜን በኩል ደግሞ መጡ። ምናልባትም ከምሥራቅ አፍሪካ፣ በተለይም ከኢትዮጵያ የመጡ የሐማይት ጐሣ አባላት ከ1300 እስከ 1800 ድረስ ተቀላቀሉ ሲል መላ ምት አስቀመጠ።

እንዚህ ደግሞ ረዝዥም፣ ቀጫጭን ለማየት የሚመቹ ሲል አከለበት። ቱትሲ ተባሉ። [134] ልዩነታን ሆን ብሎ መፈለግ ጊላጋ አለው። ይህ የመጤ ሐማይት (ሐማውያን) ትርክት ለጐሣ ክፍፍሉ ጠንሳሽ ዐሳብ ሆኖ እስከ ዛሬ ያፋጃል። የአንድ ወጣት አሳሽ ነኝ ባይ መላ ምት።

ስለዚህም ነው፣ በእብደቱ ሳምንታት፣ ምንም እንኳ ከቡሩንዲ የሚነዋወው ሩሲዚ ወንዝ ወደ ኪቩ ሐይቅ እንጂ ወደ ዓባይ የማይፈስ ቢሆንም፣ አንጋታቸውን እየተቀሉ የተገደሉት ቱትሲዎች በድን "ወደ አገራችሁ ኢትዮጵያ ሂዱ" እየተባለ ይጣልበት ነበር። በሁለቱም አገራት። በብቀላ ትርክት፣ ምድርም፣ ወንዞች፣ እና ሐይቆችም በሰው ደም ረከሱ።

የቾገረው ነገር ግን እስከ ዛሬ ድረስ በአንድ ቤት ውስጥ ዐጭርና ረዥም መገናታቸው ነው። ከእነዚህ ውጭ እጅግ ጥቂትም ቢሆን ቱዋ የሚባል ፈጽሞ ኑሮአቸው ከጫካ በአደን ከሚገኝ ነገር ላይ የተመሠረተ ጐሣዎችም አሉ። እውነቱን ለመናገር ብዙ የታሪክ ጸሐፍት እንደሚስማሙበት ቀዳሚዎች ሠፋሪዎች፣ እነዚህም ሌሎች ምናልባትም ከካሜሩን ጀምሮ ካሉ የአፍሪካ አገራት ሁሉ የዘለቁ፣ የባንቱ ሕዝቦች ናቸው። [135]

ለየት ያለ የጐሣ ጭቆና አለ ከተባለም፣ እስከ ዛሬም ድረስ ከሥልጣኔ ርቀው፣ ተጠቂ ሆነው የሚገኙት በቁጥር እጅግ አናሳ የሆኑ ባቱዋ የሚባሉ ጐሣዎች ናቸው። በተረፈ፣ በእነዚህ ጐሣ በተባሉ መካከል "ጐሣ" የሚያሰኝ ምንም ልዩነት የለም። ልዩነት ቢኖር ምናልባት የኤኮኖሚ ዐቅም ብቻ ነው። ንጉሡ (በሁቱዎች ቡሂዚ በቱትሲዎች ሙዋሚ) ቀንጐጫ የሆነበት ሁለቱም ጐሣዎች በመሪነት የተፈራረቁበት የአስተዳደር ታሪክ ነበራቸው።

ነገሥታቱ እንደ ጐሦ መደብ የሚኖሩ፣ ፈውዳላዊ ነበሩ። ነገር ግን አገራቱ፣ እስከ <u>1800ዎቹ</u> ድረስም በአንጻራዊ ሠላም ይኖሩ ነበር። የፈውዳሉ ሥርዓት ከሚታወቅበት

134 Speke, J. H. (2013). The Discovery of the Source of the Nile. February 6, 2013; https://www.gutenberg.org/files/3284/3284-h/3284-h.htm .

135 Sellstrom, T., and Wohlgemuth, L. (2022). The International Response to Conflict and Genocide: Lessons from the Rwanda Experience; Study 1 Historical Perspective: Some Explanatory Factors; The Nordic Africa Institute Uppsala, Sweden. https://www.oecd.org/derec/unitedstates/50189653.pdf

አንዱ በነገሥታት እና መሣፍንቱ ቅጥጡ ኑር ነው። ወደ ነገሥታት የሚጠጉ ሁሉ ተመሳሳይ ኑሮ የቀመጡ ወይም ይህን በአንድ ወይም በሌላ መንገድ ያገኙ ናቸው። በእከከኝ ልከክልህ የተጠጋጉ።

የቡሩንዲና ሩዋንዳ የፊውዳል ሥርዓት መሠረት ግን በመተማመን ላይ የተመሠረተ የከብትና የመሬት ከበርቴዎች የማኅበራዊ ኑር ድልድል ነበር። ሁቱና ቱትሲ የሚባለው ክፍፍል ከቅኝ ግዛት በፊት የነበረ ቢሆንም የጐሣ ክፍፍል አልነበረም። የፊውዳሉ ሥርዓት የመሬትና ከብት ከበርቴዎችን ለመለየት የተጠቀመበት እንጂ።

ከብት በብዛት ያላቸው ከበርቴዎች ቱትሲ፣ ሌሎች የመሬትና እርሻ ከበርቴዎች ሁቱ ይባላሉ። ይህ የማኅበራዊ ኑር ግንኙነት በተሻለ ጥራት በሚታይበት ሩዋንዳ ንቱሡ (ሙዋሚ) ቱትሲ ሆኖ የአስተዳደርና ፍትሕ ቁንጮ ነበር። የመሬትና የከብት ከበርቴዎች በፍጹም መተማመን ይተጋገዙ።

የከብት ከበርቴው አለቃ ሆኖ ከብቱን የመሬት ከበርቴው እንዲጠቀም ሲፈቅድ፣ ባለ መሬቱ በተጠቀመበት ልክ ምርትና ሲያስፈልግም ጉልበቱን ያስረክባል። የከብትና ግጦሽ ከበርቴዎች በአብዛኛው ቱትሲ ቢሆኑም፣ ጥቂት ሁቱዎችም ይህ ጓላፊነት ነበራቸው። በዚያን ጊዜ ሁቱና ቱትሲ የሚባለው ክፍፍል፣ የኤኮኖሚ ግንኙነት ብቻ ነበር። ሌላው ቀርቶ ጨቋኝ ሥርዓት ተደርጎ አይወሰድም ነበር።

ደግሞም ሁቱ የሆኑ የከብት ከበርቴዎች እንዳሉ ሁሉ ብዙ ቱትሲዎችም የመሬት ባለቤትነት ነበራቸው። እነዚህም ከሌሎች ቱትሲዎች ጋር፣ ቱትሲ - ለቱትሲ፣ በተመሳሳይ ማኅበራዊ ትስስር ይኖሩ ነበር። ይህ የአለቃና ደጋፊ ትስስር ሠላማዊ በፍጹም መተማመን ይከወን ነበር። ሥርዓቱ የፊውዳል ሥርዓት መሆኑ አንዝነጋ፣ የፊውዳሉ ሥርዓት በአምቾ ጋብቻ፣ ራሱን በራሱ የመጠበቅም የደረጀ መንገድ ነበረው።

ጨንነት የበሽታ አለ መኖር ብቻ እንዳይደለም እናስተውል። ምክንያቱም፣ እያደር፣ ቱትሲዎች የአገር አስተዳደር ጓላፊነትንም ደርበው ይይዙ ጀመር። ስለሆነም ከቱትሲዎች የወጡ ነገሥታት በጦር ስልት የላቁ። በአስተዳደር የበረቱ መሆናቸው አልቀረም። ከዚህ ጋር ተያይዞ የከብቶች ባለቤትነትም እንደ ክብር ይታይ ጀመር። ሰዎች መሬት ሸጠው ከብት ገዝተው ቱትሲ መሆንን ጥምር ይፈልጉ ጀመር። ይቻልም ነበር።

ይህ ብቻ ሳይሆን፣ የከብት ባለቤትነት፣ ከግጦሽ መሬት በተጨማሪ የእርሻ መሬትንም አስፋፍቶ ለመያዝ ዐቅም ፈጠረላቸው። ይሁን እንጂ፣ ቱትሲ ሆነውም ላቅ ላሉት ሌሎች ቱትሲዎች ደጋፊ የመሆን ሥርዓት አልቀረም። በተጨማሪም የበረቱ ሁቱዎች እስክ አሥር ከብት ድረስ ማግኘት ከቻሉ ከደጋፊነት ወጥተው ወደ ቱትሲነት መለወጥ ይችሉ ነበር። ማንም አለቃና ደጋፊ መሆኑ የሚችልበት፣ መንገዱም ግልፅ የሆነ ሥርዓት ነው።

ስለዚህ ሁቱና ቱትሲ የገጠር መደብ አባልነትን የሚያመለክት እንጂ "ጐሣ" አልነበረም። እንዲያውም፣ ቤዚ እና ባታሬ የሚባሉ እንደ ገኈ መደብ የሚታዩ ጐሣዎች የሁለቱ፣ ማለትም የሁቱና ቱትሲ ጥምረቶች ነበሩ።[136] ጥምረት በጠነከረ ቁጥር ገኈነታቸው እየጎላ መጣ። ቱትሲዎች የከብትና ግጦሽ ከበርቴዎች፣ ሌሎቹ ደግሞ የመሬት ከበርቴዎች ሆነው አንድ ላይ የገጠር መደብነትን ጥምረት ካበጁ እልቅናን ከእነዚህ ቤተሰቦች እጅ ማውጣት ከባድ ነበር።

ሌላው ሕዝብ ግን እስከ ዛሬ ያለ ገደብ ተቀላቅሎ ይኖራል። ጥቂት ልዩነት ያለው ሩዋንዳ ውስጥ የሚነገረው ቋንቋ ኪኛ ሩዋንዳ የሚባል ሲሆን ቡሩንዲ ውስጥ በስፋት የሚነገረው ኪሩንዲ ይባላል። ይሁን እንጂ ያለ አስተርጓሚ ይግባባሉ። ጀርመን በ1800 ዓ.ም ሁለቱንም አገራት ቅኝ ስትይዛቸው ሩዋንዳ ኡሩንዲ ብላ እንደ አንድ አገር ታስዳድር ነበር። የሕዝቡን የተለምዶ የመቻቻል ኑሮ ግን ለአስተዳደር ጥንካሬ ተጠቀመችበት። መተማመን እየተፍረከረከ የሄደው ከዚያ ጊዜ በኋላ ነው።

ቅኝ ገዢዎች ያላስጠጉ̂ቸው "ጐሣዎች" የተገፉ መሠላቸው። ቂምና ቁርሾ ማደር ያዙ። በ1900ዎቹ መጀመሪያ አካባቢ ጀርመን በመጀመሪያው የዓለም ጦርነት ስትሸነፍ ቤልጂየም ተሽቀዳድማ ጀርመን ታስተዳድር የነበረውን የምሥራቅና መካከለኛ አፍሪካ ግዛቶች ያዘች። በ1921 ዓ.ም በጊዜው የተሰየመው ሊግ ኦፍ ኔሽንስ መርቆ አጸደቀላት። እርሲም ቱትሲዎችንም አቀረበች፤ የሥራ አመራር ዕውቀት አላቸውና፤ ወዲያውም ልዩነት እያደረጀ ሄደ።

እንዲያውም ልዩነታቸውን ማስፋት ይቻል ዘንድ ከ1933 ዓ.ም ጀምሮ በአፍሪካውያኑ መታወቂያ ወረቀቶች ከየትኛው ጐሣ እንደ ሆኑ መለያ እንዲጻፍ አስገደደች። ብሔር ጠቀስ መታወቂያ የሚታደለው የግለሰቡ ቁመት፤ የአፍንጫ ርዝመት እና የሰውነት ውፍረት እንደ መለኪያ ተወስዶ ነበር። ረዘም፣ ቀጠን ያሉትን ቱትሲ፣ አጠር፣ ወፈር ያሉትን ደግሞ ሁቱ፣ እንዲሁም በጣም አጭሮችን ቴዋ።[137] ይህ የግፍ ክፍፍል የአፍሪካውያኑን ዐይን ይከፍት ዘንድ ይገባው ነበር። በዚያ ብቻ ግን አልቆመም።

ቤልጂየም፣ እጅግ ብዙ የነበሩ "የጐሣ መሪዎችን" በሙሉ አጥፍታ ጥቂት ብቻ ከእነርሱ ጋር እንዲያብሩ አደረገች። እነዚህ ጥቂቱ በአብላጫው የናሳው "ጐሣ" አባላት የሆኑ ቱትሲዎች ናቸው የሚሉ አሉ። ይሁን እንጂ እንደ ቤዚና ባታሬ ያሉ ጥምረታውያን በእርግጥ ይበዙ ነበር።[138]

---

136 Digital Collections. (2022). Les Clans Indigenes au Burundi. George A. Smarthers Libraries; University of Florida. https://ufdc.ufl.edu/aa00001884/00001/images/0

137 Fornace, K. (2009). The Rwandan Genocide. Beyond Intractability. https://www.beyondintractability.org/casestudy/fornace-rwandan

138 Lemarchand, René and Eggers, Ellen Kahan. "Burundi". Encyclopedia Britannica, 10 Mar. 2021, https://www.britannica.com/place/Burundi.

ጉሥኝነትን ምዕራባውያን ይጸነሱት እንጂ ተወልዶ እንዲያድግ ያደረግነው እኛው አፍሪካውያን እንደሆንን ማመንና ኃላፊነት ልንወስድ የግድ ይላል። አለዚያ ዘወትር የውጭዎችን ብቻ እየኮነንን፤ የእኛን አስተዋጽኦ እንዳሳነስን እንኖራለን። በሩዋንዳና ቡሩንዲ የአንድ አገር ሕዝብ የሚያህል ሰው በዕጥፍ ቀነٽ ውስጥ ተጨፍጭፎ ያለቀው ቅኝ ገዥዎች ከተከሉት ክፉ ዘር የተነሳ ቢሆንም ቡቃያውን ኮትኩተው ያሳደጉት የአገሬው ሕዝቦች ናቸው።

ቤልጂየም የእጅ አዙር ቅኝ አገዛዝ ስልት ስለምትከተል በቡሩንዲም ሆነ በሩዋንዳ የٽትሲው ነገሥታት በሥልጣን ላይ ሆነው የቅኝ አገዛዝ አጋዥ ነበሩ። ነገር መጠንሰስ የጀመረው በሩዋንዳ የሁٽ ጉٽ በተባለት ዘንድ በ1950ዎቹ ጀምሮ ቀٽ ተቀስቅሶ በ1961 ዓ.ም ንጉሣዊው ሥርዓት በሪፐብሊክ ሲٽካ ነበር። በእነዚያ ዓመታት ቤልጂየም ፍጹም ተቀይራ፤ የሁٽዎችን ዓመፅ ٽደግፍ ነበር።

በሩዋንዳ ከተነሣው ዓመፅ የተነሳ በርካታ ٽትሲዎች ወደ ቡሩንዲ ሲሰደዱ እዚያም ይኸው ٽግር ጀመረ። በተለይም በ1961 ዓ.ም ٽትሲው የሩዋንዳ ንጉሥ ታመው በቤልጂየም ሃኪም በመታየት ላይ ሳሉ ሕይወታቸው በማለፉ ጥርጣሬ ነገሠ። አንድ የٽትሲ ጉٽ አባል የሆነ ወጣት ልጅ፤ ስለ ንጉሡ ሞት ኃላፊነٽን የሁٽ መሪዎች መውሰድ ይገባቸዋል በማለት ይፋ ዘመቻ ጀመረ።

አልፎም ይኸው ወጣት ሌላ የሁٽ ታዋቂ መሪ በበቀል ስሜት ተነሣሥቶ ገደላቸው። ፖለቲካው ከዚያ በኋላ የጉٽ ማለትም የበቀል ሆነ፤ ቤልጂየምም አልቻሌችውም። ከብٽብٽ በኋላ የሥርዓት ለውጥና ምርጫ ተካሂዶ ٽትሲ መራሹ ንጉሣዊ ሥርዓት በሁٽ መራሽ ሪፐብሊክ ተቀየረ።

ቡሩንዲና ሩዋንዳ በአፍሪካ ሙሉ ነጻነታቸውን በማግኘት ቀዳሚ ከሆኑት ውስጥ ይመደባሉ። ሩዋንዳ በ1962 ዓ.ም በቤልጂየም ሙሉ ድጋፍ፤ በሁٽ መራሽ ሪፐብሊክ ነጻነٽዋን አወጀች። ቡሩንዲም ሩዋንዳን ተከٽላ ነጻነٽዋን አገኘች። ነገር ግን ዘውዳዊ ሥርዓٽን አልٽወٽም ነበር። [139]

በቡሩንዲም ምርጫ ተካሄዶ ሁٽ ጠቅላይ ሚኒስትር ተመረጡ። በዚያው ዓመت፤ የተባዛ\ውት መንግሥٽታት ድርጅٽ ሁለٽ አገራٽ ተለያይٽው በየራሳٽው ሙሉ የድርጅٽ አባል አገራٽ መሆናٽውን ተቀበለ። ቡሩንዲ ٽትሲ ንጉሥዋን ስላልٽወٽ የመጫጫስ ምልክٽ ٽደርጐ ይወሰድ ነበር። ቀድሞም እንደ ጉٽ መሪ አይታዮም ነበርና።

የመሪዎች መገደል ጦስ ግን ወደ ቡሩንዲም ዘለቀ። ከሽግግር ወቅٽ በኋላ በከፍٽኛ ድምፅ በድጋሚ የአገሪٽ ጠቅላٽ ሚኒስٽር ሆነው የٽመረٽٽ ሁٽው የፖለቲካ ሰው ፒየር ንጌንዳዱሜ በٽመረٽ በስምንٽኛ ቀናٽው ጽህፈٽ ቤٽቸው እያሉ ከሩዋንዳ በመጣ የٽትሲ ጉٽ አባል በሆነ አንድ ስደٽኛ ٽገደሉ።

139 Refworld (2004). Minorities at Risk Project, Chronology for Hutus in Burundi, 2004, available at: https://www.refworld.org/docid/469f38731e.html

የቡሩንዲ መንግሥትና እና ሕዝብም ጭምር፤ የቱትሲ የጦር መሪዎችና ጸዋታ ኅላፊዎች እጅ እንዳለበት ጠረጠሩ። ስለዚህም፤ ቱትሲዎችን ማሳደድ በቡሩንዲም ውስጥ ተቀጣጠለ።[140] እንግዲህ ከዚያ በኋላ የእርስ በርስ መገዳደል በረከተ፤ በቀል ናረ።

በተለይም በሩዋንዳ ያለ ማቋረጥ ቱትሲዎች ይሰደዱ ጀመር። ጭራሹንም፤ መምህርና የጐሣ ፖለቲካ አቀንቃኝ የነበሩት ግሬጐሪ ካዩባንዳ በሩዋንዳ ፕሬዝዳንት ሲሆኑ የአገሪቱን የተለያዩ ተቋማትና መወቅር ጭምር በመጠቀም ቱትሲዎችን ማሳደድ ያዙ። ፖለቲካ ሁሉ የቱትሲ ሜራ ወደ መባል ተሻጋገረ። ሕዝብ ይነሣና አሥርም፤ ሃያም ሺህ ቱትሲዎች፤ በአብዛኛው በአስቃቂ ሁኔታ ይገደሉ ነበር።

ሞትን የሸሹ ቱትሲዎችም ወደ ጐረቤት አገር ተሰድደው የትጥቅ ትግል ጀመሩ። በተለይም ወደ ዩጋንዳ የዘለቁት በአሁኑ የሩዋንዳ ፕሬዝዳንት ፖል ካጋሜ አማራ የሩዋንዳ አርበኞች ግንባርን መሠረቱ። በድርጅቱ ውስጥ ቁጭት ያበገናቸው ወጣቶች ያይሉበት ነበር።

በአንጻሩ በቡሩንዲ የቱትሲ መሪዎች እጅ ብርቱ ነበረች። እነርሱም ግን ተመሳሳይ ስጋተት ሠሩ። በምርጫ ሥልጣን ያገኙ ጠቅላይ ሚንስትር ሲገደሉ ሌላ ምርጫ ተካሄደ አሁንም ሁቱው የፖለቲካ ሰው አሸነፉ። ንትሁ ግን ድጋሚ ችግር ይከሠታል በሚል ሽፋን በፈቃዳቸው ቱትሲ ጠቅላይ ሚንስትር ሾሙ። እንደ እውነቱ ከሆነ ግን ንትሁንም ያስገደዱት የቱትሲ ጐሣ የሆነ የጸዋታ ኅይሉ መሪዎች ነበሩ።

ምርጫው እንዳልሠራ ባዩ ጊዜ ሁቱ የሆነ የጸዋታ ኅይል አባላት አፈንግጠው የመንግሥት ግልበጣ ሙከራ አድርገው ነበር። ይህን ሙከራ በማክሸፍ ሰበብ በጸዋታ ኅይሉ ውስጥ ያሉ ሁቱዎች በሙሉ እየተለቀሙ ተገደሉ። የበቀል እርምጃው ወደ ምሁራኑም ጭምር ዞረ። የቡሩንዲ ሁቱዎች በመንግሥት የሥራ መደቦች እንዳያገኙ፤ የውጭ ትምህርትና ዕድገት ዕድል እንዳይሰጣቸው ተደረገ። ሁቱዎች ዳግመኛ መሪ ዐልባ ተደረጉ። በዚያውም ጐሠኝነት ደርጅትጀት አለ።

ክፍሉና ከዚሁ ጋር የተያያዘው ዓመፅ ወደ ሕዝቡ ዘልቆ፤ መገዳደል ተንሠራፋ። ይሁን እንጂ መሪ ዐልባ ሁቱዎች ቱትሲ በበዛበት የጦር ኅይል በሚመራ አዱ ምክንያት ብዙ ዋጋ ከፈሉ። የቡሩንዲ ሁቱዎች በበኩላቸው ቂም የቋጠረ የፖለቲካ ኅይል መሆን የጀመሩት ከዚያ በኋላ ነው።

የቱትሲ ሥልጣን ቀንጭጮትን ለማጠንከር ሲሉ የቡሩንዲ መከላከያ መሪዎች ሙሉ በሙሉ በሚባል ደረጃ የጸዋታ ኅይሉን በቶነጥጥራቸው ስር አድርገው ነበር። በዚያው ዓመት (1965) ንትሁም በጦር ኅይል እንጂ ስለ ተገፋ ልጃቸውን ሾመው ከሥልጣን ወረዱና ወደ ቤልጂየም ሸሹ። የቡሩንዲ የጦር መሪዎች በቀላሉ የዘውድ

---

140 Fornace, K. (2009). The Rwandan Genocide. Beyond Intractability. https://www.beyondintractability.org/casestudy/fornace-rwandan

ሥርዓትን ገርስሰው የቡሩንዲ ፕሬዚዳንታዊ ሪፐብሊክ አወጁ። የአገሪቱ የመቻቻል
ምልክትም ደብዛው ጠፋ።

የጐሣ ፖለቲካ ወግ ወጉን የያዘባቸው ከ1960ዎች በኋላ ያሉ ዓመታት ለቡሩንዲና
ሩዋንዳ የርግማን ዓመታት ነበሩ ማለት ይቻላል። ሁቱዎች የበላይነት በጨበጡባት
ሩዋንዳና ቱትሲዎች አንጻራዊ የበላይነት በተቀዳጁባት ቡሩንዲ አንዱ ጐሣ ሌላውን
በክፉ ዐይን ማየት፣ ቂም በቀል፣ መዋቅራዊና ተቋማዊ ጫና ዋና ተግባራቸው ሆነ።

ስለሆነም፣ ቱትሲዎች ከሩዋንዳ፣ ሁቱዎች ከቡሩንዲ ወደ ጐረቤት አገራት
ተሰደዱ። ወደ ኮንጎ፣ ታንዛኒያ፣ ዩጋንዳ በየተሰደዱበትም ግጭት እየዘሩ። በተለይ
በቡሩንዲ ሁቱዎች ላይ በጦር ኃይል የተደገፈ ሥልጣዊ መገፋት ስለበረታ፣ በስደት ላይ
ባሉበትም ይጠነክርባቸው ነበር። በዚህ ዘመን ምናልባት በትንሹ እስከ 100 ሺህ የሚሆኑ
ሁቱዎች እንዳለቁ ይገመታል።

የቡሩንዲ ሁቱዎች ከጫና ብዛት ለጊዜው ዐንጋታቸውን ደፉ። ነገር ግን የጐሣ
ፖለቲካ ግጭትን ካልፈለፈለ ውሎ አያድርምና ቍርቦ ፍለጋው በየፈርጁ ነበር። የቱትሲ
ጦር መሪዎች አሳሬ አግዳሚው ያስፈራቸው ጀመር። የሚያሳድዳቸው ግን ሥራቸው
እንደሆነ አላወቁም። ፈሪ ደግሞ ወደ ፊትም፣ ወደ ኋላም መተኮስ ልማዱ ነው።
ወዳጅና ጠላት ይቀላቀልበታልና።

በ1970ዎቹ መባቻ ላይ የቡሩንዲው ፕሬዚዳንት ሚኮምቤሮ ኛሩንጉሩ የተባሉ
የቱትሲ ንዑስ ጐሣ አባላት ተነሱብኝ በማለት መሪያቻቸውን ከመንግሥት መዋቅር
ውስጥ ልክ እንደ ሁቱዎች አስወገዱ። ቱትሲዎች በቱትሲዎች ላይ መነሣሣት ጀመሩ
ማለት ነው። አጋጣሚውንም በመጠቀም ተቃዋሚ የሚባለውን ሁሉ አጠፋ።በዚህ
መልክ፣ ሚኮምቤሮ በቡሩንዲ የአንድ ፓርቲ አገዛዝን መሠረቱ። ቡሩንዲ፣ የተሻለ
የዐሳብ መንሸራሸር የሚታይባት አገር ነበረች። አምባገነንነት በጐሣኝነት ላይ ተደረበባት።

ጀነራል ባጋዛ በ1976 ዓ.ም መፈንቅለ መንግሥት አድርገው ሚኮምቤሮን
ሲያስወግዱ፣ ጥራሽ ያዜኑ አንድ ፓርቲ በማጥፋት ወታደራዊ አገዛዝ መሠረቱ።
የቡሩንዲ ሁቱዎች ሰቆቃ በፕሬዝዳንት ባጋዛም ጊዜ አላረፈም ነበር። ምንም እንኳ አዲስ
የመሬት ሥሪት ፖሊሲ በማጽደቅ ቱትሲዎች በእርሻ መሬት ላይ ያለውን የበላይነት
ቢያስታግሱም የካቶሊክ ቤተ ክርስቲያንን ነጻነት ጥምር እጅግ በመጫን ሁቱዎችን
አስቆጡ። ምዕመኑን እንዳትረዳ አደረጉት።

አብዛኞቹ ሁቱዎች ካቶሊካውያን ናቸው። ሁቱዎቹ የውጭ አገር ከፍተኛ
ትምህርትም ሆነ በአገሪቱ ባሉ ትምህርት ቤቶች እንዳይገቡ የትምህርት ዕቃባ
ተደረጉባቸው ነበር። ቤተ ክርስቲያኒቱ ሁቱዎችን ሳታገልል ለማስተማር ትምህርት

ቤት በመክፈት፣ የተሻለ ጥራት ያለው ትምህርት መስጠት በመጀመሯ የሥርዓቱ ቀጥተኛ ተግዳሮት ሆና ብቅ አለች።[141]

በ1980ዎቹ መባቻ ፕሬዝዳንት ባጋዛም በሌላ የጦር መሪ፣ ሻለቃ ቡዮያ፣ ተገለበጡ። ገልባጩ ቡዮያ ግን ለፕሬዝዳንቱና ለሌሎች የጦር መሪዎችን ምህረት አደረጉላቸው። እየበረታ የመጣውን የሁቱ ትግል ለማርገብም ሥልጣን ለመጋራት ጅምር ጣሉ። በካቶሊክ ቤተ ክርስቲያን ላይ የተጣሉትም ገደቦች ተነሡ።

ፕሬዝዳንት ቡዮያ ግን ተንኮለኛ ፖለቲከኛም ነበሩ። ለመጀመሪያ ጊዜ በእርሳቸው ዘመን ሁቱዎችም ወደ ጸጥታ ኀይላት እንደ ገና ተመልምለው መግባት ጀመሩ። ይሁን እንጂ ዐልፎ ዐልፎ በሚነሣው የሁቱዎች ቍጣ ለማርገብ በሚል ምክንያት የክልል አመራሩን ቆንጥጠው በያዙ ቱትሲዎች አማካይነት በእነዚህ ዓመታትም ሌሎች 100 ሺህ ያህል ሁቱዎች እንዳለቁ ይገመታል።

በተለይም በ1988 ዓ.ም ብቻ እስከ 50 ሺህ ሳይሞቱ እንዳልቀረ ይገመታል። አንዳንድ ግምቶች እስከ 300 ሺህ እንዳለቁ ያስቀምጣሉ።[142] በፕሬዝዳንት ቡዮያ መልካም ፈቃድና በወዳጅ መንግሥታት ትብብር፣ ምንም እንኳ ፍጹም እኩልነትን የሚያንጸባርቅ ባይሆንም፣ እጅግ የተሻለ የሚባል፣ የእኩልነት ፅንሰ ዐሳብ ያዘለ ሕገ መንግሥት በ1990ዎቹ መባቻ ጸድቆ ወታደራዊው መንግሥት ከሰመ።

ይሁን እንጂ፣ ይህ በጐ ርምጃ ፓሊፔሁቱ የሚባል አክራሪ የሁቱ ዐማፂ ቡድን ከመመሥረት አላገደም። ይህ ቡድን ከጐረቤት ሩዋንዳና ከኮንጎ እየተነሣ ብዙ ጥፋት አደረሰ። በቡሩንዲና በሩዋንዳ መካከል መቃቃር እንዲነግሥ ምክንያት ሆነ። የሁቱና ቱትሲ ሽኩቻ ድንበር ዘለል ከመሆን አልፎ፣ "የታላላቅ ሐይቆች አገራት ችግር" ተብሎ ለሚጠራው ብሔር ተኮር የፖለቲካ ውጥንቅጥ ቁንጮ ሆነ፤ መካከለኛውን አፍሪካ አመሳቀለ።

የቡሩንዲ እና የሩዋንዳ ሰቆቃ ዓለምን አላስቀምጥ አለ። በአንድ በኩል፣ በጐ ለሚያስቡ የአፍሪካ መሪዎችም የኅሊና ዕረፍት ነሣ። በሌላ በኩል ደግሞ በግጭቱ የተዘፈቁ ልዩ ልዩ አገራት መሪዎች ሌላ ዓላማ ነበራቸው። ነገሩ የሁቱና ቱትሲ ግጭት ይምሰል እንጂ በአገራቱ ባለው ግርግር ውስጥ እጃቸውን የነከሩ እጅግ ብዙ ነበሩ። ነገሩ የአካባቢውን አገራት፣ የቀድሞ ቅኝ ገዢዎችን፣ እንዲሁም ከመካከለኛው አፍሪካ የከርሰ ምድር ሃብት ለመቆንጠር የቋመጡትን ሁሉ ያነካካ ነበር።

141 Refworld (2004). Minorities at Risk Project, Chronology for Hutus in Burundi, 2004, available at: https://www.refworld.org/docid/469f38731e.html

142 Augustyn, A. (2022). Britannica, The Editors of Encyclopaedia. "Third Republic". *Encyclopedia Britannica*, 10 Mar. 2020, https://www.britannica.com/topic/Third-Republic-French-history

ለምሳሌ:- በሩዋንዳ የነበሩት የሁቱ መሪዎች ከኮንጎው አምባገነንና በአገር ሃብት ዝርፊያ የሚታወቁ መሪ ሙቡቶ ሴሴኮ ጋር ጥብቅ ወዳጅነት ነበራቸው። የኮንጎ ሃብት አማላይ ነው። ቱትሲዎቹ የሩዋንዳ ዐማፂያን ግን ወደ እንግሊዝኛ ቋንቋ ተናጋሪ የአካባቢ አገራት አደሉ፤ ኬንያ፣ ዶጋንዳ። ወደ ኮንጎ የሚወስዱ መንገዶች በቡሩንዲ ወይም በሩዋንዳ በኩል መሆናቸው ይታወቃል።

በተለይም የዶጋንዳ ገዢዎች የጉሬቤታቸው ኮንጎ ሃብት ያማልላቸው ስለነበር እጃቸው አይታጣም። ዶጋንዳ የሩዋንዳውን አርበኞች ግንባር አስጠግታ ነበረ። በጦርነት የተፈተኑ፣ በሥነ ምግባር የታነፁ መሆናቸውን ታውቃለች። ጥልቅ ፍቅራቸውም "የጋጭቱን ወጪ ለመሸፈን ተጋግዘ መበዝበዝ" ብለው የተስማሙ ያስመስልባቸው ነበር።

በዚህ አላበቃም፣ ፈረንሳይኛ ተናጋሪ የአውሮፓ አገራት በዶጋንዳ በኩል የሚስፋፋውን የእንግሊዝኛ ተናጋሪዎች መንሠራራትን ስለማይወዱ ለሙቡቱ እና ለሁቱዎቹ ጥብቅ ድጋፍ ነበራቸው። ሙቡቱም ለፈረንሳይኛ ተናጋሪ ምዕራባውያን የማይነጥፍ የገንዘብና ማዕድን ምንጭ ነበሩ። ቤልጅየም ከጊዜ በኋላ ጥራሽ የሁቱዎች ጠበቃ ሆነች።

ፈረንሳይም የእንግሊዝኛን መስፋፋትን ፍራቻ ፖል ካጋሜንና ጦራቸውን አጥብቃ ጠላች። ስለዚህ በቱትሲዎች ላይ ለሚደርሰው ስቃይ ጆሮ ዳባ ልበስ አለች። እስከ ዛሬም የሩዋንዳ መሪዎችና ፈረንሳይ የጉሪጥ ይተያያሉ። የሩዋንዳ ቱትሲዎች ግፍ ሲደርስባቸው፣ ወታደሮች በሥፍራው እያዩት፣ ለነፍስ አድን ጥሪ እንኳን ፈረንሳይ መልስ ትነፍግ ነበር።

የተባበሩት መንግሥታትም ሆነ የአፍሪካ አንድነት ድርጅት በማዕከላዊው አፍሪካ ያለውን ግጭት ለመፍታት ያለ ልክ ዳተኛ ሆኑ። አሜሪካም አንዳንድ ጊዜ ትገባና ጥናት አካሂዳ ትወጣለች፤ የጥናቱ ውጤት ግን ግጭትን ከመፍታት ይልቅ የሚያባብስ ሆኖ ይገኛል። በዚህ መካከል፣ በተለይም በቡሩንዲ ያለው የቱትሲ የጦር መሪዎች ኅይልና ድምፅ ከአገሪቱ አስተዳደር እየበለጠ ሄደ።[143]

በጉረቤት ሩዋንዳም የክፋት እርሾ ይጠነሰስ ነበር። ከላይ እንደተጠቀሰው፣ በ1970ዎቹ ከፕሬዝዳንት ካዩባንዳ ጥቃት አምልጠው የሸሹ ወጣት ቱትሲዎች፣ በዶጋንዳ መሠረታቸውን አድርገው በፖል ካጋሜ መሪነት፤ የሩዋንዳ አርበኞች ግንባርን አቋቋሙ። ካጋሜ በዚያን ጊዜ በጣም ወጣት ስለነበሩ ብዙም ታዋቂ አልነበሩም። ካዩባንዳ ግን እጅግ የተጠሉ ሰው ነበሩ።

---

143 Nkurunziza, J. D. (2018). The origin and persistence of state fragility in Burundi. The LSE-Oxford Commission on State Fragility, Growth and Development and the United Nations Conference on Trade and Development (UNCTAD). https://www.theigc.org/wp-content/uploads/2018/04/Burundi-report-v2.pdf

በዚህ ጊዜ ሁቱው የሒሳብና የአክምና ትምህርት ያላቸው የጦር ሰው ጀኔራል ጁቬናና ሃባሪማና ከጥቂት ወታደሮች ጋር በመሆን ካቦባንዳን ከሥልጣን አወረዱቸው። በ1973 ዓ.ም ሥልጣን ሲቆጣጠሩ ገና የ36 ዓመት ጉልማሳ ነበሩ፤ መላዋ ሩዋንዳ ተደሰተች። በቱትሲዎች ጭምር የተወደዱት ሃባሪማና ጥቂት ጸጥታን መግዛት ችለው ለ21 ዓመታት ሩዋንዳን መርተዋት ነበር። [144]

ነገር ግን መሪዎች በሥፍራቸው ያለ መርህ ከክራረሙ ቀስ በቀስ ጉድና ጅራት ከወደ ኋላ እንደሚባለው መሆኑ አይቀሬ ነው። እያደር፤ ቱትሲዎችን ማግለል ሕጋዊ መምሰል ጀመረ። መልካም ስምና ሥራ ይዞ በመሪነት ሥፍራ ለረኸረም ጊዜ መቆየት ከባድ ነው።

በ1990ዎቹ መባቻ ቡሩንዲ ወደ መረጋጋት ለመምጣት ስትምክር፤ የሩዋንዳ አርበኞች ግንባር ከዩጋንዳ ድንበር አካባቢ ተነሥተው ወደ ሩዋንዳ ግዛቶች መዝለቅ ጀመሩ። ቀጣናው ሌላ ትርምስ ውስጥ ገባ። በዚህ የደነገጡት ሃባሪማና፤ አሁን በብዙዎች ዘንድ እየታመነ እንደመጣው በዋና ከተማዋ ኪጋሊ ላይ ጥራቸው ጥቃት እንዲሰነዘር አዘዙ።

ዓላማቸው፤ ጥቃቱን በቱትሲ ዐማፂያን ላይ አላክከው ሕዝቡን ለማነሣሣት ነበር። ተሳካላቸውም። ቱትሲዎች ይበልጥ ተጠሉ።

በአንጻሩ፤ በቡሩንዲም የፕሬዝዳንት ቡዮያ መንግሥት በ1990ዎቹ የመጀመሪያ ሦስት ዓመታት ያደረገው የመረጋጋት ሙከራ ምንም አልተሳካም ነበር። በ1993 ዓ.ም አዲስ አበባ በተደረገ የአፍሪካ መሪዎች ስብሰባ ላይ በቡሩንዲ ሚንስትሮች ጥያቄ መሠረት የአፍሪካ የሠላም አስከባሪ ኃይል ከፍተኛ የመንግሥት ባለ ሥልጣናትን እንዲጠብቅ ወደ ቡሩንዲ እንዲላክ ስምምነት ላይ ተደረሰ።

ከእነዚህ ወታደሮች ውስጥ ጥቂቶቹ ወደ ሩዋንዳም ቢሠማሩም ወዲያው እንዲወጡ ተደረገ። በዚህ መካከል በቡሩንዲ ምርጫ ታወጀና በአንጻራዊነት ነጻ የሆነ ምርጫ ተካሄደ። ሁቱዎች የሚበዙበት የፍሮዴቡ ፓርቲ ቱትሲዎች የሚበዙበትን የቡዮያን ዩፕሮና ፓርቲ አሸነፈ። አብላጫውን ድምፅ ያገኙት ፓርቲ መሪ ሜልኳየር እንዳንዳዬ የመጀመሪያው ሁቱ ፕሬዝዳንት በመሆን ሥልጣን ያዙ።

ከነበረው የሠላም ስምምነት የተነሣ ሲሆው የካቢኔ አባላትም ከቱትሲዎች ተመረጡ። ጥቂት የሠላም ጭላንጭል የተገኘ መሰለ። [145] ምንም ሳይቆይ ግን ቱትሲ መራሽ በሆነው የጸጥታ ኃይል የተቀነባበረ የመፈንቅለ መንግሥት ሙከራና የተማሪዎች ሰልፍ ዐረፍት ነሳቸው። ፕሬዝዳንትም በመፈንቅለ መንግሥቱ ግርግር ተገደሉ። ጦሩ

144 Foyart, P. (2018, March 25). Juvénal Habyarimana (1937-1994). BlackPast.org. https://www.blackpast.org/global-african-history/habyarimana-juvenal-1937-1994/

145 Refworld (2004). Minorities at Risk Project, Chronology for Hutus in Burundi, 2004. https://www.refworld.org/docid/469f38731e.html

ከክልል መሪዎች ጋር በመሆን ከሌላው ጊዜ ይበልጥ ሁቱዎችን መጨፍጨፍ ሥራዬ ብሎ ያዘ። አንድ ሚሊዮን የሚጠጉም ተሰደዱ።

በምርጫ ሥልጣን የያዘው ፍሮዱቡ ፓርቲ መሪያቸው ቢገደልም በአገሪቱ ሡላም ለማውረድ ጣረ፤ ግን አልቻለም። የጦሩ መሪዎች ቱትሲዎች ነበሩና። ዓላማቸውም የሁቱ ፕሬዝዳንት ወይም ፓርቲ ሥልጣን ላይ መሆን ለሁቱዎች ምንም እንደማይጠቅም ለማሣየት ነበር።

ለጥቂት ጊዜያት የዓለም መንግሥታት ኅይላት ትኩረት ቡሩንዲ ላይ አረፈ። ዲፕሎማሲ ዕድል እንዲሰጠው ለመማጸን ተሯሯጡ። የቡሩንዲ ካቶሊክ ቤተ ክርስቲያን አሁንም ለሕዝቡ ታዳጊ ሆና ቆመች። ከብዙ ልፋት በኋላ ሁለቱን ፓርቲዎች አስማምታ የጥምረት መንግሥት እንዲቋቋም ረዳች። የሁቱው ፍሮዱቡ ተወካይ ሲፕሪያን እንታርያሚራ ፕሬዝዳንት ሆነው ተሾሙ።

የዲፕሎማሲውም ጥረት ተሳክቶ፤ ምንም እንኳ የቡሩንዲ መንግሥት ፍላጐት ባይኖረውም፤ በአብዛኛው የኢትዮጵያ ወታደሮች የሚገኙበት የሡላም አስከባሪ ኅይል በቡሩንዲ ተሰማራ። [146] ጥቂት ቢሆንም ይህ ኅይል አመርቂ የሡላም ማስከበር ሥራ ሠራ። ዕፍይታ የተገኘ መሠለ።

ይሁን እንጂ እንታርያሚራም ከቱትሲ የጦር መሪዎች ጋር ብርቱ ትግል ላይ ነበሩ፤ ትግላቸው ግን አልተቋጨም። ሚያዝያ 6 ቀን በ1994 ዓ.ም የሩዋንዳው ፕሬዝዳንት ሃባሪማና እና የቡሩንዲው ፕሬዝዳንት እንታርያሚራ ስብሰባ ተካፍለው ከዳሬሥላም፤ ታንዛኒያ ሲመለሱ አውሮፕላናቸው ተመታ። ሁለት አፍሪካውያን ፕሬዝዳንቶች በአንድ ጊዜ ሞቱ። [147]

ሎስ አንጀለስ ታይምስ የተባለው ጋዜጣ በጊዜው እንዳስከበው፤ ፕሬዝዳንቶቹ ስብሰባ የኔዱት በአገራቸው ያለውን ችግር ለመፍታት መውሰድ ስለሚገባቸው ርምጃዎች ከቀጣናው አገራት ጋር ለመምከር ነበር። [148] እስከ ዛሬ ድረስ አፍሪካውያን ምን እንደ ዞረብን እንኳን አላ ማወቃችን የሚገርም ነው። በየትኛውም አገር ታሪክ ሁለት መሪዎች በአንድ ጊዜ በግፍ አልተገደሉም። ያውም ከወገን በተተከስ ጥይት።

ምክንያትና ተጠያቂ ፍለጋ መዳከር ምንም ዋጋ የለውም። መሪዎቹ የሞቱት በእኛው ምድር፤ ከእኛው በተተከስ ጥይት መሆኑ የጐሣ ፖለቲካ ምን ዐይነት ጨለማ

146 Refworld (2004). Minorities at Risk Project, Chronology for Hutus in Burundi, 2004, https://www.refworld.org/docid/469f38731e.html

147 NEWS. (1994). International Journal on World Peace, 11(2), 67–72. http://www.jstor.org/stable/20751975

148 LA Times (1994). Two African Presidents Die in Plane Crash. https://www.latimes.com/archives/la-xpm-1994-04-07-mn-43287-story.html

ውስጥ እን ጣለን ለማወቅ በቂ ነው፤ ይህ ግን አልሆነም። ፕሬዝዳንት ሃባሪማና መልካም ሰው ነበሩ። ምሁር፤ የጦር ሰውና ልምድ ያላቸው መሪ። በብሔር ልዩነት ጉዳይ ለዘብተኛ አቋም ያራምዱ ነበር። ልዩነትን ማክረር አይወድዱም።

ከእርሳቸው ግድያ በኋላ በሩዋንዳ እሳት ነደደ። ቱትሲዎች ገደዲቸው ተብሎ ተወራ። ሕዝቡ በነቂስ ወጥቶ ቱትሲዎችን እንዲበቀል ተቀሰቀሰ። ቱትሲ የማይገድል ሁቱ ዕጣው ዐባሮ መሞት ነበር። "ለዘብተኛ" ቦታ የለውም፡ና። እስከ አንድ ሚሊዮን የሚሆኑ ዜጎች፤ በአብላጫው ቱትሲና ለዘብተኛ የተባሉ ሁቱዎች በ100 ቀናት ብቻ ተጨፈጨፉ።

ይህ ዘመናኝ ድርጊት ምናልባትም በዓለም ታሪክ ሕዝብ የተካፈለበት የመጀመሪያው የዘር ጭፍጨፋ ሆኖ ተመዘገበ። በቤተሰብ ደረጃ ወርዶ አባትና እናት የልጆቻቸውን ወይንም የራሳቸውን ሕይወት እንዲመርጡ የተገደዱበት ነበር። ከዚህም የተነሣ ብዙ ወላጆች አዕምሮቸውን እንደ ሳቱ ጭዓምር ይነገራል። አገሪቱ ብቻ ሳትሆን ዓለም በድርጊቱ አፈረበት። [149]

ከ100 የእብደት ቀናት በኋላ የካጋሜ ጦር ኪጋሊን ተቆጣጠረ። በዚህ ጊዜ ደግሞ ሌላ ብቀላ ፈርተው እጅግ ብዙዎች ሸሹ። ከሸሹት አብዛኞ ሁቱዎች ነበሩ። በመንገድም ሆነ በሽሹበት የስደተኞች ካምፕ በርጎብና በሽታ ብዙ ሁቱዎች አለቁ። [150]

በቡሩንዲም እንደ ተገመተው የሕዝብ ለሕዝብ ዕልቂት ተከሰተ። ነገር ግን በዚያች አገር ያለቁት በአብዛኛው ሁቱዎች ነበሩ። ምክንያቱም ቱትሲ መራሽ ጦር ኅይሉ ግጭት በተነሣ ቁጥር ሥላማዊውን ሕዝብ አጭዶ ስለሚመለስ ነው። የሚገርመው ይህ እንደሚሆን እያወቁ ነገሮችን ቆስቁሰው የሚሸሹት ሁቱ የፖለቲካ ጽንፈኞችም ነበሩ።

በተለይም "ሕዝባዊ ኅይል" እየተባለ የሚጠራው አክራሪ የሁቱ ዐማጺያን ቡድን ሥልጣን የሚገኘው ሁቱዎች በነቂስ ተነስተው ሲቃወሙ ነው ብሎ ስለሚያምን ቦታ እየቀያየረ ቱትሲዎችን በመግደል ነገር ያነሳሳል። በዚህ ጊዜ ቱትሲ መራሹ ጦር ይደርስና በርካታ ሁቱዎችን ገድሎ፤ አሥርና ወደ ስደት ሸኝቶ ይመለሳል። [151]

እንዲህ እያለ የመበቃቀል ፖለቲካ የአካባቢውን አገራትም ጭምር የለበለበ ሆነ። የጎጓ እና ሌላም የማንነት ጥያቄ በፖለቲካ ውስጥ ፈጽሞ መግባት እንደሌለበት ከሩዋንዳና ቡሩንዲ የተሻለ አስረጂ የለም። ከካጋሜ በኋላ አንጸራዊ ሥላም በሩዋንዳ ተገኘ ቢባልም የቂም በቀል ታሪኩ በቀላሉ ይረሳል ማለት ያስቸግራል።

149 Fornace, K. (2009). The Rwandan Genocide. Beyond Intractability. https://www.beyondintractability.org/casestudy/fornace-rwanda

150 William Mitchell College of Law. (2012). "Rwandan Genocide." World Without Genocide. Accessed on 29 Oct 2013 https://www.eriesd.org/site/handlers/filedownload.ashx?moduleinstanceid=9515&dataid=14415&FileName=Rwandan%20Genocide.pdf

151 Refworld (2004). Minorities at Risk Project, Chronology for Hutus in Burundi, 2004, https://www.refworld.org/docid/469f38731e.html

በቡሩንዲማ ታላላቅ የአፍሪካ መሪዎች ጭምር ብዙ ለፋ። እንደ ታንዛኒያው ፕሬዝዳንት ጁሊየስ ኔሬሬ እና የደቡብ አፍሪካው መሪ ኔልሰን ማንዴላ ጭምር ገብተውና አምጠው የወለዱት የሠላም ፍኖተ ካርታ እስከ ዛሬ ሙሉ ሰላም አላመጣም። ጥቂት መረጋጋት፤ ጥቂት መቻቻል እንጂ ዘላቂ ለውጥ አልመጣም። [152]

እኛሳ?

በኢትዮጵያ ጉሠኝነት የለም ብንል እውነታን መካድ ይሆናል። ነገሩ እንዴት እንዳቆጠቆጠ፣ ወደ ጎሣ ፖለቲካ ሥርዓት እንዴት እንደ ገባን፣ እንዲሁም የፖለቲካውን እንቅ ሰላንቲያና ውጤቱን እጅግ በተሻለ ሁኔታ የሚያስረፉ ስላሉ በዚህ ረገድ ግን ብዙ ጊዜ አናፈሱም። ከላይ የተጠቀሱት የጎሣ ፖለቲካ መገለጫ መንገዶች ግን በጥቂቱም ቢሆን በአገራችን ተገልጠው ነበር ብለን ብቻ እንዝዝለቅ።

ይህም ማለት የብሔር ልዩነቶችን ለማስተናገድ የመረጥነው መንገድ፣ ከክረሪ ልክ ከላይ እንደ ተጠቀሱት ሁሉ የሠላም ጠንቅ ነው ማለት ነው። ይብቃን? ሌሎችንም የጎሣ ፖለቲካ መንገዶች ብንቃኝ ከዚህ የተለዩ መደምደሚያ አይሰጡንም። ጎሣ ብቻ ሳይሆን ሌሎችንም የማንነት መገለጫዎች ለአገር ውስጥ ፖለቲካ አካሄድ መሣሪያ ብናደርግ ዕልቂት እንጂ ሌላ ትርፍ አይኖረውም። ለምሳሌ የጎይማኖት አክራሪነት በአፍሪካም ሆነ በሌሎች አገራት ያስከተለውን ግጭት መቃኘት ይቻላል።

የኢትዮጵያ ፖለቲከኞች ግን ተዓምራዊ የፖለቲካ መንገድ የተገኘ ይመስል ብሔርተኝነትን የሙጥኝ ብለዋል። አዲስ ዐይነት ወይም "ምርጥ" የብሔር ፖለቲካ የለም። የሙጥኝ ያሉትም የተሻለ ወይም የተለየ መልክ አግኝተውበትም አይደለም።

ከአውሮፓ፣ ከእስያ እና ከጎረቤት አገራት ሩዋንዳንና ቡሩንዲን አየን። የጎሣ ፖለቲካ መልኩ እጅግ ተመሳሳይ ነው። ያውም፤ የጎሣ ፖለቲካ፣ በተለይም ሲከር እና ያለ ቅጥ ጊዜ ሲደማመርበት፣ ሲበዛ መልክ ጥፉ፣ መራራ፣ የሚጎፈንን፣ መሆኑ ነው። በብዙ አገራት የተወለን ምሳሌ ዕልቂት ነው። ይህን መልክ ጥፉ መንገድ መርጠን ብቻ ሳይሆን አጡዘን ለመከተል መወሰናችን አስደማሚ ነው፤ ዋጋ ያስከፍለናል። እያስከፈለንም ይገኛል።

152 Nkurunziza, J. D. (2018). The origin and persistence of state fragility in Burundi. The LSE-Oxford Commission on State Fragility, Growth and Development and the United Nations Conference on Trade and Development (UNCTAD). https://www.theigc.org/wp-content/uploads/2018/04/Burundi-report-v2.pdf

ዋለልኝና አጼው

የዚህ ጽሑፍ ዋና ዓላማ የጐሣን ፖለቲካዊ ኤኮኖሚ መዳሰስ ስለሆነ ወደዚያ ከመመለሳችን በፊት ግን የኢትዮጵያን ነባራዊ፣ የማኅበራዊና ፖለቲካዊ ሁኔታ ተከትለው የሚሰነዘሩ ጥቂት መሠረታዊ አመለካከቶችን መቃኘት አስፈላጊ ነው። በአገሪቱ የብሔር ፖለቲካ ጽንፍ የያዙ አመለካካቶች እንዳሉ ግልፅ ነው። ነገር ግን ሁለት ጽንፎች ብቻ እንዳሉ የሚወሳውም ህጸጽን የተሞላ ነው። "ዋለልኝ እና አጼው" እንበላቸው።

ፖለቲካ እህል ውሃቸው ያልሆነ፣ ከንትርክ ለመራቅ የወሰኑ ስንኳ የብሔር ፖለቲካውን ጥቅም ወይም አስከፊነት ከውጤቱ በመነሣት መጠቆም ቢሞክሩ፣ በፍጥነት ከሁለት በአንዱ ያስፈረጃቸዋል። 'የአጼው ወይም የዋለልኝ ናፋቂ' ይሆናሉ፣ ብሔርተኝነት አስከፊ ነው ያለ ሁሉ "አጓዳዊ" እየተባለ ወደሚገለጸው ጐራ ይደመራል። ይህ አመለካከት፣ የአገሪቱ ማዕከላዊ አንድነት የነበረ፣ ያለ፣ እና የሚኖር አድርጐ የሚያሳትት፣ ለኢትዮጵያዊነትም መስፈርት ያወጣ ተብሎ የሚታማ ነው።

ሌሎች ደግሞ ብሔርተኞች ወይም ጐሣኞች፣ ሲያሻም ዘረኞች ተብለው ይፈረጃሉ። ከአማርኛ ውጭ ቋንቋ፣ ከማዕከላዊነት ውጭ አስተዳደር አለ የሚል ከተገኘ "ዘረኛ" ተብሎ ይፈረጃል። ብሔርተኞቹ፣ 'ዘረኛ' የሚለውን ባይወዱትም፣ "ብሔርተኞች" በሚለው ይመጻደቁበታል። ይህ አመለካከት፣ ላለፉት ጥፋቶች ሁሉ አንድን ወይም ጥቂት ብሔሮችን ተጠያቂ በማድረግ፣ 'አገራችን በብሔሮች ፈቃድ ከተናነት ወዲያ ተከስተች ይላል' በሚል ይከሰሳል። [153]

ከእነዚህ ሁለት ጽንፍ የያዙ አመለካከቶች የተነሣ በሰከነ መንገድ መወያየት ብርቅ ሆኗል። ዳርና ዳር ቆመን የሚያስማማ መፍትሔ ፍለጋ እንዳክራለን። በቅድሚያ፣ የብሔርተኞች ጠንካራ አሻራ ያለበት በሥራ ላይ ያለው የኢትዮጵ ሕገ መንግሥት፣ ገና በመግቢያው ላይ "አንድ የፖለቲካ ማኅበረሰብ በጋራ ለመገንባት"[154] ሲል ይህን የአመለካከት ልዩነት በአሉታዊ ጐኑ ብቻ ማጉላቱን እናስተውላለን።

ይህም የብሔር ፖለቲከኞች ጽን ፍላጐት መሆኑ አይካድም። 'አንድ አይደለንም' በሂደት አንድ ለመሆን እንሠራለን' የሚል እንድምታ ያዘለ ነው። የቀደመው ዐሳብ ግን ኢትዮጵያ የበርካታ ብሔሮች መገኛ አገር መሆኗን ማጉላጽ ነበር። በዐሳቡ ጠንሳሽነት የሚወደሰው ወጣት ዋለልኝ መኮንን (1945–1972) ለተማሪዎች የሶሻሊስት እንቅስቃሴ

153 Taye, B. A. (2017). Ethnic federalism and conflict in Ethiopia. Africa Journal of Conflict Resolution. Volume 17; No. 2. https://www.ajol.info/index.php/ajcr/article/view/167170

154 ፌዴራል ነጋሪት ጋዜጣ፡ (1986)። የኢትዮጵያ ፌዴራላዊ፣ ዴሞክራሲያዊ ሪፐብሊክ ሕገ መንግሥት አዋጅ። https://ethiopianembassy.be/wp-content/uploads/Constitution-of-the-FDRE.pdf

ድጋፍ ይህን ዘንድ እ.ኤ.አ. በ1962 ዓ.ም በጸፈው ጽሑፉ ብሔሮች መብታቸውን ማስከበር እንዳለባቸው በአፅንዖት ገልጾ ነበር።[155]

አገራችን የብዙ ማኅበረሰቦች ስብስብ አገር መሆኗ አይካድም። ጠንካራ የታሪክ፣ የባሕል፣ የኅይማኖት፣ የሕግ እና ሞራል፣ እንዲሁም የአንትሮፖሎጂ ማጣቀሻዎችን ማቅረብ ይቻላል፣ እንዲሁም፣ የኢትዮጵያ አገር መንግሥት በረኸም ጊዜ ታሪኩ አንዱ ብሔር በሌላው ላይ፣ አንዱም አካባቢ በጎረቤቱ ላይ በሚያሳድረው የተለያየ ጫና የተሞላ መሆኑም ይታወቃል። የተጽዕኖው ዐይነት እንደ ብዛታችን ውጥንቅጥ፣ እንደ መልካችንም ኸንጉርጉር ሆነ እንጂ።

የዋለልኝን ዐሳብ ይዘናል የሚሉ ጸሐፍትና ፖለቲከኞች እነዚህ ተጽዕኖዎች የፈጠሩትን ቀዳዳዎች ይበልጥ አነፈነፉ። የማይካደውን የዘመናት የሰው ልጅ ልቅ ክፋት ከራሳቸው ጉዳት አኳያ ብቻ መቃኘት ተመቻቸው። መሪው ጥያቄ፣ "እኔ እውነተኛ ኢትዮጵያዊ የምባለው መቼ ነው?"[156] የሚል ይሆናና፣ መልሱ አከራካሪ ይሆናል። ውጥረትን፣ መራራቅን፣ መሳሳብን የሚፈጥር።

በዚህ መካከል፣ ለሁሉም ብሔሮች "የራስን ዕድል በራስ የመወሰን መብት" ብታጉናጽፉ ይበጃችኋል የሚሉን እንደ ሔርማን ኮኄን ዐይነት "መካሪዎችም" አላጣን።[157] መብት ማን ይጠላል? ወዲያው "እስከ መገንጠል" የሚል ጫመርንበትና ይህ መብት ሕገ መንግሥታዊ ሆነ፣ በተግባር ደግሞ አጥልቀን ስንቀብረው። የፖለቲካ ፓርቲ በብሔር መስመር ብቻ ማደራጀት፣ የአገሪቱ የውስጥ አስተዳደር ክፍፍልም ብሔር ተኮር እንዲሆን ተደረገ።

ይህ ግን ምናልባት ዋለልኝ ራሱ ያላሰበው፣ ምናልባትም የማይደግፈው ነው። ምክንያቱም፣ ብዙ ጊዜ በማጣቀሻነት በሚቀርበው ጽሑፉ፣ 'ብሔሮች ለመብታቸው የሚያደርጉት ትግል የአጄውን ሥርዓት ቢያዳክም የምንጋነባትን ሶሻሊስት ኢትዮጵያ መዳረሻ ያፋጥንልናል' ሲል በመጻፍ ነው።[158] ሶሻሊዝም ለብሔር ጭቆና መልስ አለው ብሎ ቢያምን እንኳ የጽሑፉ መነሻ የ'ጠላቴ ጠላት ወዳጄ' የሚለውን ብሂል የታከከ ይመስላል።

የዋለልኝ ተከታይ ነን የሚሉ ጸሐፍት በዚህ ግምገማ አይስማሙ ይሆናል። ለዚህም ነው፣ የኤርሱን ዐሳቦች በጥልቀት መመርመር እምብዛም የሆነው። በተቃራኒው፣

155 Mekonnen, W. (1962). On the Question of Nationalities in Ethiopia. Arts IV, HSIU Nov. 17, 1969. https://www.marxists.org/history/erol/ethiopia/nationalities.pdf

156 Bulcha, M. (2013). Walelign Mekonnen, the Question of Nationalities and Ethiopia's Persistent Crisis. Oromia Today, 28/06/10. https://oromia.today/history/walelign-mekonnen-the-question-of-nationalities-and-ethiopias-persistent-crisis/

157 Cohen, J. H. (1995). Ethinic Federalism in Ethiopia. Northeast African Studies; New Serises, Vol. 2. No. 2. pp. 157-188 (32 pages)

158 Mekonnen, W. (1962). On the Question of Nationalities

የብሔርተኝነትን ትርክት ለማዳበር፤ ከቋንቋ እና ባሕል ብዝኃነት ይልቅ ሌላ ጠንካራ ምክንያት ተፈለገ። በረጂሙ የኢትዮጵያ ታሪክ ውስጥ ጥቂት ጦዝ ቢደረግ ለዚህ እማኝ የሚሆን ክስተት ማግኘት እምብዛም አይቸግርም። ስለሆነም፤ በኢትዮጵያ የተሰተዋለው የብሔር ሽኩቻ የቅኝ ግዛት ፍላጎት ነው የሚል ትርክት ተሠራ።

አለም ሀብቱ የተባለ ጸሐፊ እንደገለጠው፤ በሕዝብ ቁጥር ትልልቅ የሚባሉ ኦሮሞ፤ አማራ፤ እና ትግራዋይ ብሔሮች ብቻ የአገሪቱን ሁለት - ሦስተኛ ሕዝብ ይወክላሉ። [159] የሱማሌ፤ የሲዳማ፤ የወላይታ፤ እና የጉራጌ ብሔሮች ሲጨመሩ ሰባቱ የአገሪቱን 85 ከመቶ ሕዝብ ይይዛሉ። ሌሎች ከፍተኛ ቁጥር ያላቸው አምስት ከተጨመሩ ደግሞ 92 ከመቶው ሕዝብ ከ12 ብሔሮች ይሆናል። በእርግጥ፤ በዚህ ዐይነት ስብጥር፤ 85 ብሔሮች ባሉባት አገር የቅኝ ግዛት ትርክት ሊሠራ ይችላል?

ይልቅ፤ አንዱ ሌላውን ለመንቆር፤ እያንዳንዳቸው የማይኖናቅ ዐቅም አላቸው ቢባል የበለጠ ያስኼዳል። ደግሞም ነቀራ በየርጀ ነበር። ግና በዘመናት መካከል ጸሐፍትም፤ አፌ ታሪኮችም አልረዱንም። የብሔርተኝነት እሳት በሰው ልቦና ሁሉ እንዲቆሰቆስ የጥቆናን ቀንበር ማክበድ ተፈለገና፤ የቀን ቅዠት የሚመሥሉ አፌ ታሪኮች ተሰባሰቡ፤ አደሙብን። አንዱን ጭራቅ ሌላውን መልአክ አድርጎ መሳል ማለፊያ ሆነ።

እስከ ዛሬም ዘለቀ፤ በአፌ ታሪክ ላይ የፈጠራ ትርክት በዘፈቀደ እንደ ተሰደረ ሁሉ፤ የቅኝ ግዛትነት ትርክትንም ለማጦዝ ብዙ ፈጠራዎች በነባር አፌ ታሪኮች ላይ ታከሉ። ቅኝ የተገዛ ደግሞ ነጻ ሊወጣ ስብዓዊና ሞራላዊ ግዴታ ነው። ምክንያቱም፤ ዛሬ ያለንበት ፖለቲካዊ ዓለም ቅኝ ግዛትን አይታገስም።

"የራስን ዕድል በራስ መወሰን" የሚባለው ንድፈ ዐሳብና ተግባር ተጣሉ። በመረጡት የአስተዳደር ሥርዓትና መሪ መተዳደር፤ በራስ ቋንቋ መማር፤ ወይም መዳኘት፤ እና ባሕልን ማሳደግ መሠረታዊ የፖለቲካ መብት ነው፤ የትንሹም የትልቁም፤ የሃያላን መንግሥታት፤ የዓለም አቀፋዊ መድረኮችም ድጋፍ እና ይሁንታ ያለው። [160] ድጋፉ ግን በሁለት ይከፈላል።

አንዱ በቅኝ ግዛት ስር ያሉ የፖለቲካ ነጻነትን እንዲያገኙ የሞራል፤ የማቴሪያልና ፖለቲካዊ ድጋፍ መስጠት ነው። በቅርቡ እንኳ የዝምባብዌን የነጻነት ትግል ስንደግፍ ከዚህ አኳያ ነው። ሌላው በአንድ አገር ውስጥ ያሉ እና ጭቆና እና መገለል የከረረባቸው አካባቢዎች፤ ከሚነጠሉ ይልቅ ሰፊ መብት ተሰጥቷቸው በጋራ እንዲኖሩ መርዳት ነው።

159 Habtu, A. (2003). Ethnic F Ethnic Federalism in Ethiopia: Back alism in Ethiopia: Background, Pr ound, Present Conditions esent Conditions and Future Prospects. International Conference on African Development Archives. 57. https://scholarworks.wmich.edu/africancenter_icad_archive/57

160 Carley, P. (1996). Self-Determination Sovereignty, Territorial Integrity, and the Right to Secession. Report From a Roundtable Held in Conjunction with the U.S. Department of State's Policy Planning Staff. https://www.usip.org/sites/default/files/pwks7.pdf

ይህ ሁለተኛው መንገድ በብዙ አገራት ተሞክሮ የፌደራሊዝምን ሥርዓት በመውለዱ ይሠራበታል።

በብዙ አገራት ይሁንታ ካለው የፌደራል ሥርዓት የኢትዮጵያ ለየት የሚለው ሁለቱን አጣምሮ በመያዙ ነው። የኢትዮጵያ መንግሥታዊ ሥርዓት፣ የትም አገር የሌለ፤ የውስጥም፣ የውጭም ነጻነት ለሁሉ ብሔሮች በአንድ ጊዜ ለማጉናጸፍ የሚፍጨረጨር መሆኑ ልዩ ያደርገዋል። ለሁሉም ብሔሮች በራስ መተዳደርን እስከ መገንጠል በመፍቀዱ፤ ውስጡን ታዲያ ለቂስ፡ ዝርዝሩን ፖለቲከኞች ይጨነቁበት።

ከተግባር አንጻር ሲታይ ግን፣ ከጅምር 9 "ክልሎች" ብቻ መደራጀታቸውን እናውቃለን። ከአንድ ማዕከል ወደ 9 ማዕከል፡ ሥራ ላይ ሲውልም፣ ፌደራሊዝም፣ እንዳለተገባበጠ ቂጣ በአንድ በኩል አርርር ሌላው ሊጥ ሆነ፡ እንዲያው ዘጠኝ ይባል እንጂ እጅግ ማዕከላዊነትን የተላበሰ አግላይ ብሔርተኝነትን ማስቀደሙ ታየ፡ [161] እንኳን መገንጠልን፡ የራስን ዕድል በሙላት ለመወስን በቅቻለሁ የሚል ክልል እስኪታጣ ድረስ ጥብቅ የዕዝ አስተዳደርን የተላበሰ መሰለ። [162]

እስከ ዛሬም፣ "የክልል እንሁን፣ ዞን፣ ወረዳ፣ ወይም ቀበሌ እንሁን" ጥያቄዎች መልስ የሚያገኙት በጎይል ወይም በእጅ ጥምዘዛ ነው። ስለዚህ፣ ማዕከላዊነትን የሚከስሱ፣ የባሱ "አዬ" ሆነው አረፉት የሚሉ ሐያሲያን ጥቂት አይደሉም። [163] በአንደበታቸው ጠልተውት፡ በሥራቸው "አኃዳዊነትን" ናፈቁ። በተለይም ከለውጡ በፊት፣ ይህን አካሄድ "ወራጅ አለ" ያለ ከተገኘ፣ እንቢ ያለ ከተፈጠረ፡ ደህና ተድርጎ መደፈቅ ለዚህ በእማኝነት ይቀርባል። [164]

ይህ ጉዳይ እንደሚባለው የአፈጻጸም ችግር [165] ወይስ በእርግጥም ብሔርተኝነት የፖለቲካ ጥያቄን ለመመለስ ትክክለኛ መንገድ ስላልሆነ? ጥያቄውን በጥያቄ እንመልስ። ብሔርተኝነት ትርምስ ያስከተለው መስሪሩ ትክክል ሆኖ ለሦስት ዐሠርት ዓመታት

161 Abbinl, J. (2011). Ethnic-based federalism and ethnicity in Ethiopia: reassessing the experiment after 20 years. Journal of East African Studies. Volume 5, Issue 4. https://doi.org/10.1080/17531055.2011.642516

162 Cats-Barill, A. (2018). Self-determination. International IDEA, Constitution Brief. September 2018. https://www.idea.int/sites/default/files/publications/self-determination-constitution-brief.pdf

163 Gedamu, Y. (2017). "Ethnic Federalism and Authoritarian Survival in Ethiopia." Dissertation, Georgia State University, 2017. doi: https://doi.org/10.57709/10995588

164 International Crisis Group. (2009). Ethiopia: Ethnic Federalism and its Discontents. Africa Report N°153 – 4 September 2009. https://www.crisisgroup.org/africa/horn-africa/ethiopia/ethiopia-ethnic-federalism-and-its-discontents

165 Abraha, A. H. (2019). Ethnic Federalism and Conflict in Ethiopia. Research on humanities and social sciences}, Volume 9, pages 16-22. https://www.semanticscholar.org/paper/Ethnic-Federalism-and-Conflict-in-Ethiopia-Abrha/01e583950a19ef042344a5181bc985563083f833

መፍቻው ጠፍቶን ዳከርን ወይስ ቀድሞውኑ ቁላፉን የዋጠ ጉዳና ሆኖ? ይህን ያህል ሞትና ዕልቂት ሲያስከትል በርህራሔ ስንኳ ቁላፉን ለምን አልተፋም?

ምናልባት መንገዱን መፈተሽ ግድ ይለናል የሚሉ ብዙ ናቸው።[166] ለጊዜው በተለይም ፖለቲከኞች በሕዝብ ጥቅም ስም የራሳቸውን ቤት ለመገንባት የነደፉት መንገድ ነው ቢባል ሚዛን ይደፋል፤ የኢትዮጵያ ፌዴራሊዝም እና እርሱን ተከትሎ የመጣው ግርግር ለዚህ ዓይነተኛ ምሳሌ ነው።[167] ለሕዝቦች ሮሮ ጥቄት መልስ የሚሰጥ መስሎ አዲስ ዐይነት "አኃዳዊነትን" የወለደ፤ አካሄድ ነውና።[168]

አገሪቱን ለመበታተን የታሰበ ተንኮል አድርገው የሚመለከቱም ሞልተዋል።[169] እንዳይሰፋበን ግን አሁንም አንለፈው። በሌላው ጽንፍ፤ "እኃዳዊ" የተባሉት፤ በብሔሮች መካከል የነበረውን መነቋቆር አክሶሰው በማየታቸው ይከስሳሉ።[170] ምንም እንዳተከሰተ፤ ከፍቅር እና ከማቀፍ ሌላ አንዳችንም በሌላችን ላይ አርጪሜ እንኳን እንዳላገሳን የሚነገር ጣፋጭ ወግ ይዘዋል።

አገሪቱ ፍቅር በፍቅር የተሞላች፤ መጋባት፤ መሿሿም፤ አንዱ የሌላውን ልብስ፤ ባሕል፤ ምግብ፤ ቋንቋ ሳይጸየፍ የሚጠቀምበት፤ ለመንግሥተ ሰማይ ሩብ ጉዳይ የሆነች ምድር እንደሆነች ያምናሉ። ስለ አንድነት ሲነሳም ፈጽሞ አንድ ዐይነት ካልሆንን የሚል አስተሳሰብ። ይህ በእርግጥ አየደከም የመጣ ዐሳብ ቢሆንም ክርክር የማስነሣት ጉልበቱ አልሞተም። በእርግጥም ለሥላማዊ ኑሮና የሕዝብ መደጋገፍ አዳጋች የሆነ ዐሳብ ነው።

ከላይ እንደ ተገለጠው፤ በአገሪቱ ውስጥ ያሉ ብሔሮች አንዱ ሌላውን ለመጉዳት ቢፈልግ የማይናቅ ዐቅም እንደነበረው ማስተዋል ያሻል። በታሪክ መካከልም፤ ሌላውን ለማስገበር ሲል፤ የማይከላ መንግሥትን ሥልጣን ለመቆጣጠር ሲል፤ ጥካኔ የተሞሉ ጦርነቶችና ርምጃዎች እንደ ነበሩ አይካድም። እጅ ለእጅ ተያይዘው አገሪቱን ከውጭ ጥቃት የተከላከሉ መሪዎች እንዱ ሁሉ ለሥልጣናቸው ሳስተው ጊዜ ጠብቆ የሚፈነዳ ፈንጂ የቀበሩ እንደነበሩም ብዙዎች ይስማማሉ።[171]

166 Bayu, T. B. (2022). Is Federalism the Source of Ethnic Identity-Based Conflict in Ethiopia? Insight on Africa, 14(1), 104–125. https://doi.org/10.1177/09750878211057125

167 Birru, D. T. (2018). Ethnic Federalism Implementation in Ethiopia: The Paradox. Journal of Political Sciences & Public Affairs. Analysis - (2018) Volume 6, Issue 4. https://www.longdom.org/open-access/ethnic-federalism-implementation-in-ethiopia-the-paradox-37377.html

168 Taye, Ibid.

169 Miheretu, A. (2009). Ethnic federalism and its potential to dismember the Ethiopian state. Progress in Deelopment Studies. Volume 12; Issue 2 – 3. https://journals.sagepub.com/doi/10.1177/146499341101200303

170 Ogbazghi, P. B. (2022). Ethiopia and the Running Sores of Ethnic Federalism: The Antithetical Forces of Statehood and Nationhood. African Studies Quarterly; Volume 21, Issue 2; August 2022. https://asq.africa.ufl.edu/wp-content/uploads/sites/168/V21i2a3.pdf

171 ባይሳ ገመቹ (2008) የዘረኝነት አውራቂስ። ሁለተኛ እትም። ፍንፍኔ ማተሚያ ቤት

በተለይም፣ በ16ኛው እና በ17ኛው መቶ ክፍለ ዘመናት በኢትዮጵያ ያሉ ጐሣዎች አንዱ በሌላው ላይ ከፍተኛ ዘመቻ ያደርግ እንደ ነበር በታሪክ ይወሳል። ዘመቻው ጭካኔ የተሞላበት ቢሆንም፣ የመቀላቀል፣ የመወራረስ እና የመወዳጀት ባሕርይም እንዳለው በብዙ የተዘገበ ከመሆኑም በላይ እስከ ዛሬ ድረስ ይህን የሚያመላክቱ የታሪክ አሻራዎችም ይገኛሉ። ከዚህም ጋር፣ ራስ ገዝነት ባየለበት ጊዜ ስንኳ በጐሣዎች መካከል ያለው ድንበር ሽንቍር የበዛበት ስለነበር ግንኙነቱ ያለመዘጋቱ አገሪቱን ልዩ ያደርጋታል።[172]

ባይከዳኝ

ጭካኔ ደግሞ ቅሬታን ይፈጥራል። ከመደጋገፍ እና ከመተሳሰብ ይልቅ ቍርሾ እና በቀልን ያከማቻል። ያለፉት አባቶቻችን ያለሙትን ብቻ አጉልቶ፣ እገረ መንገድ በአንዳንድ ሥፍራዎች ያጠፉትን ለመጥቀስ ማፈር ከታሪክ ለመማር መሸማቀቅ ብቻ ሳይሆን "ተጐዳሁ" የሚለውን አከታትሎ ማፈን ይሆናል። የታፈነ ደግሞ ጊዜ ጠብቆ መፈንዳቱ ግድ ነው።

ሲፈነዳ ለማንም አይጠቅምም። በተለይም የፖለቲካ ንቃት አጥጋቢ ባልሆኑባቸው ቦታዎች፣ በብሔር ጥያቄ ስም ለተደራጁ ብልጣ ብልጦች የአንባገነንነት መለማመጃ ይሆናል እንጂ ትርፍ የለውም።[173] በጐሣዎች መካከል ለሚከሰት ክፍፍል እና መገፋፋት መፍትሔው የጐሣ ፖለቲካ ማራመድ የማይሆነው ለዚህ ነው።

"የራስን ዕድል በራስ መወሰን" ሲባልም መልክ አለው። ወይ ፍጹም ፖለቲካዊ ነጻነት፤ አለያም በአንድ ሉዓላዊ አገር ስር በመከባበር እና በመተሳሰብ ዐብሮ መኖር። "ከከፋኝ እገነጠላለሁ" በሚል አስፈራርቶ ለዳግመኛ አፄነት መዘጋጀት ግን ሰው ሰራሽ፣ በተለይም ሥልጣን የተራቡ ፖለቲከኞች ሠራሽ የፖለቲካ መስመር ነው። መዘጋት አለበት እንጂ መኮትኮት የለበትም። ከጥላቻ ስለሚጀምር፣ የግል ጥቅምን ስለሚያስቀድም፣ መፍትሔን ሊያመነጭ አይችልም።

ለብዝኃ ብሔርነት፣ ከብሔር ፖለቲካ ውጭ በእርግጥ ምንም መፍትሔ የለም? ሞትና ዕልቂትንስ እያበረከተ ዘላቂ መፍትሔ መሆን ቀርቶ ጊዜያዊ መንገድ እንኳን ሊሆን እንዴት ቻለ? አሁንም የተሻለ መልስ አለን የሚሉ ይጨነቁበት። የዚህ ጽሑፍ ዓላማ ለፖለቲካዊ ጥያቄ መልስ ማግኘት ሳይሆን የተመረጠው የፖለቲካ መስመር ኤኮኖሚውን ምን ያህል ሊረዳ ወይም ሊጐዳ እንደሚችል ማመልከት ነው።

---

172 Poluha, E. (2004). The Power of Continuity Ethiopia Through the Eyes of Its Children, Nordiska Afrikainstitut, January 2004. https://www.researchgate.net/publication/44833599_The_Power_of_Continuity_Ethiopia_Through_the_Eyes_of_Its_Children

173 Holdo, M. (2019). Power Games: Elites, Movements, and Strategic Cooperation. Political Studies Review. Bolume 18; Issue 2. https://doi.org/10.1177/1478929919864778

ትውልዳቸው ዓድዋ፤ ትግራይ፤ ዕድገታቸው፤ አንድ በድንንት በተፈጠረ አጋጣሚ አስትሪያ፤ በዚያውም ወደ ጀርመን ዘልቀው ጥንቅቅ ካለ የጀርመንኛ ቋንቋ ትምህርት ጋር በበርሊን ዩኒቨርሲቲ ሕክምናን አጥንተዋል። ትንታግ ወጣት ሳሉ ወደ አገራቸው ተመልሰው ለጃንሆይ ምኒልክ የግል ጸሐፊና የጀርመንኛ ቋንቋ አስተርጓሚ ከመሆናቸውም በላይ የኢትዮ-ጁቡቲ የባቡር መስመር ሥራ እና የውጭ ንግድም ተቆጣጣሪ ሆነው ሠርተዋል። [174]

ኃይለ ሥላሴ ንቱዉ ነገሥት ከመሆናቸው በፊትም በእርሳቸው ስር አገልግለዋል። በአዜዎች ተከብበው፤ ግን "አዳነትን" ሳይሆን ብዝጎ ብሔር የሚንጸባረቅባት ኢትዮጵያ እኩልነትንና አንድነትን ባጣመረ ሥልጣኔ እና የኤኮኖሚ እመርታ እንድትጓዝ አዲስ የኤኮኖሚ ፍልስፍና እንዳበረከቱ ይነገርላቸዋል። [175] ኢትዮጵያ በዓለም የረቀቁ ከሚባሉ አገራት ተርታ እንዴት መራመድ እንደምትችል ካመለከቱት ብርቅ ኢትዮጵያዊ የኤኮኖሚ ዕይታ ባለቤቶች ምናልባት ቀዳሚው ናቸው። [176]

ነጋድራስ ገብረ ሕይወት ባይከዳኝ (1876-1919) በምዕራቡ ክፍለ ዓለም ይማሩ እንጂ፤ የኤኮኖሚ ዕድገት ፖሊሲ ዕይታቸው ፕሮፌሰር መሳይ ከበደ ስለ ታሪክ ዕይታቸው እንዳነሱት[177] ከምዕራባውያን የተቀዳ አልነበረም። በአፍሪካም ጭምር ቀዳሚ የኤኮኖሚ ፈላሳፊ አድርገው የሚወስዱ አሉ። በተለምዶ "ጃፓን ወዳድ" እየተባሉ ከሚጠቀሱ ሌሎችም ጋር አብረው ይጠቀሳሉ። ኢትዮጵያዊ የልማት ኤኮኖሚክስን ያፈለቁ ቢባል ያስሄዳል። [178]

አመለካከታቸውን በዐጭር ለማስቀመጥ ያህል፤ የኢትዮጵያም ሆነ የሌሎችን አፍሪካ አገራት የልማት ችግር በሁለት ይመድቡታል። አንድም፤ የእርስ በርስ እና ከውጭ ከሚመጣ ጠላት ጋር የሚደረግ አውዳሚ ግጭት፤ ሌላም፤ ኤኮኖሚውን

174 Zewde, B. (2002). Pioneers of Change in Ethiopia: The Reformist Intellectuals of the Early Twentieth Century (Eastern African Studies) Paperback – November 30, 2002. Ohio State University.

175 Geda, Ae. (2003). Ethiopian Macroeconomic Modeling in Historical Perspective: Bringing Gebre-Hiwot and His Contemporaries to Ethiopian Macroeconomics Realm. International Conference on African Development Archives; Center for African Development Policy Development Archives Research. Scholarly Works at Weetern Michagan University. https://scholarworks.wmich.edu/cgi/viewcontent.cgi?article=1066&context=africancenter_icad_archive

176 Haile, A. (2011). Book Review: 'Negadras Baikedagn Serawoch.' https://www.alemayehu.com/TradeGraduate/Book%20Review%20YeGebrhiwotSerawotchAbebe.pdf

177 Kebede, M. (2006). Gebrehiwot Baykedagn, Eurocentrism, And the Decentering of Ethiopia. Journal Of Black Studies, Vol. 36 No. 6, July 2006 815-832. https://journals.sagepub.com/doi/pdf/10.1177/0021934705280086

178 Rekiso, E, Z. (2015). Economics of Late Development and Industrialization: Putting Gebrehiwot Baykedgn (1886-1919) in Context. http://etdiscussion.worldeconomicsassociation.org/wp-content/uploads/Rekiso-20-june-15.pdf

በአገር በቀል ዕውቀት መምራት ካለመቻል የተነሣ በእኩልነት ላይ ያልተመሠረተ
ግንኙነት ከሃያላን አገራት ጋር ማድረግ ናቸው። [179] መፍትሔአቸውም በእነዚህ ዙሪያ
ያጠነጥናል።

የኤኮኖሚ ዕድገትን በጥብቅ ኢንዱስትሪ ግንባታ ዐቅም ከማዳበር ጋር፣
የባሕል ሽኩቻዎችን በማስታረቅ፣ የሰው ኃይል ዕድገትን፣ እንዲሁም በእኩልነት
ላይ የተመሠረተ የእርስ በርስ ግንኙነትን ማዳበር እንደሚያስፈልግ አትተዋል።
ይህም በእርግጥ ከጊዜው የቀደመ አስተሳሰብ ነበር። [180] እርስ በርስ በመሻኮት አገር
አይገነባም። እንዲሁም ከመለያየት ይልቅ በጋራ በመቆም የሃያላንን ጫና መቋቋም
ይቻላል ብለው ያምኑ ነበር።

ይህንኑ አስተሳሰባቸውን በአገር አስተዳደር ገና ሲሞክሩ በጊዜው ከፉ ደዌ
ተጠልፈው በወጣትነታቸው አለፉ። [181] የኢትዮጵያ ሕዝብና መንግሥት ያላቸው
የፖለቲካዊ ኤኮኖሚ ግንኙነት ዛሬም ቢሆን ከነጋድራስ አስተሳሰብ እምብዛም የራቀ
አይደለም። የእርሳቸውን፣ ብዝጎ ባሕልን ያጣጣመ፣ በእኩልነት ላይ የተመሠረተ፣
የሰውን ኃይል ልማት (ሰብዓዊ ልማት) ያስቀደመ መፍትሔ፣ ከዚያን ጊዜ ጀምሮ
ፈልገነው፣ ሞክረነው ቢሆን በእርግጥም እመርታ አይታጣም ነበር።

ዛሬም ቢሆን የሕዝብና መንግሥት ፖለቲካዊ ኤኮኖሚ ግንኙነቶች የሚያጠነጥኑት
በሦስት መሠረታዊ ጉዳዮች ላይ ነው። እነዚህም፣ የንብረት ባለቤትነት መብት፣
ተስማሚ የፖለቲካ ውክልና፣ እና ምናልባትም አያደግ የመጣው የገጠርና ከተማ
ልዩነቶችን ማጥበብ ተብለው ሊጠቀሱ ይችላሉ። [182] በተለይ ስለ ንብረት ባለቤትነት
ጉዳይ ሲነሣ፣ የመሬት ባለቤትነትን ጉዳይ ልዩ ትኩረት ይሻል። ሁለት ዋና ዋና
ህጸጾችን ያስተናገደው የአገራችን የመሬት አስተዳደር ጉዳይ ለብሔር ፖለቲካ ዋና
መዘውር መሆኑን እናስተውላለን።

የመጀመሪያው ህጸጽ መሬትን "የማይሸጥ፣ የማይለወጥ" አድርጎ መደንገግ
ነው። ከዚህ ሕግ የተነሣ ብቻ የመሬት ዋጋ የማይላስ የማይቀመስ ሆነ። በዚህ ዘመን
የአንድ ኤኮኖሚ አገልግሎት ወይም የምርት መገልገያ ዋጋው ከንቱ ነው እንደ ማለት

179 Geda, A. & Abebe, A. (2011). A Dynamic Macroeconomic Modelling of Gebre-Hiwot's
   Idea about Early 20th Century Ethiopia's Development Problems. Conference: Paper
   Presented at Western Michigan University and Adma University Conference on Ethiopian
   Development Problems; Adma-Nazareth, Ethiopia. https://www.researchgate.net/
   publication/283307703_A_Dynamic_Macroeconomic_Modeling_of_Gebre-Hiwot's_Idea_
   about_Early_20th_Century_Ethiopia's_Development_Problems

180 Haile, Ibid.

181 Zewde, Ibid.

182 Bekele, Y. W., Kjosavik, D. J. & Shanmugaratnam, N. (2016). State-Society Relations
   in Ethiopia: A Political- Economy Perspective of the Post-1991 Order. Journal of Social
   Sciences. Volume 5, No. 48. https://www.mdpi.com/2076-0760/5/3/48

ትልቅ የዋሳነት የለም። ገበያው፤ የትክክለኛውን ዋጋ ብዙ እጥፍ በመክፈልም ቢሆን የራስ ለማድረግ መሯሯጡ አልቀረም።

ሁለተኛው፤ ህጸጽ የዚህ "ዋጋ ዐልባ" ሃብት ባለቤትነት ጉዳይ ነው። በሕገ መንግሥቱ፤ "የሕዝብና የመንግሥት" ይሆናል ተብሎ ተደንግጓል። ቃል በቃልም፤ "የገጠርና የከተማ መሬትና የተፈጥሮ ሃብት፤ የባለቤትነት መብት የሕዝብና የመንግሥት ብቻ ነው። መሬት የማይሸጥ፤ የማይለወጥ የኢትዮጵያ ብሔሮች፤ ብሔረሰቦችና ሕዝቦች የጋራ ንብረት ነው።"[183] በማለት ቁጥርት ያለ ቃል ይናገራል።

ብሔርተኛው ፖለቲካችን ለሕገ መንግሥቱም ተገዝ አለመሆኑ የሚታወቀው በተግባር ይህ ድንጋጌ ሲሠራ "መሬት የብሔር ነው" ብሎ ሽምጥ በመጋለቡ ነው። በሕጉ መሠረት የትኛውም መሬት ለብሔር አልተሰጠም። የትኛውም መሬት፤ ለየትኛውም ብሔር አልተከለከለም። ምክንያቱም የአገሪቱ "ብሔሮች፤ ብሔረሰቦችና ሕዝቦች" በጋራ እንጂ በግል ሉዓላዊ ስላይደሉ ነው። አንድ አገር በሕልውና ለመቆየት አስፈላጊ ከሆኑ ነገሮች ውስጥ ሉዓላዊ ሥልጣን ዋንኛው ነው። ድርብ ሉዓላዊነትም የለም።

በሕገ መንግሥቱ መሠረት አሮማው በባሕር ዳር ከተማ ላይ ከሌሎች እኩል ፍጹም ሉዓላዊ የባለቤትነት መብት አለው። ለትግራዋይ፤ ጋምቤላም አገሩ ነው። ወላይታው፤ ነቀምት ቤቱ ነው። ሱማሌው ስለ ቤንሻንጉል ያገባዋል። የጋራ እንጂ ለብሔር ተነጥሎ የተሰጠ ባለቤትነት የለም።

ይህ የኢትዮጵያውያን ሁሉ የአገራቸው እኩል ባለቤትነት መብት፤ በነጋድራስ ገብረ ሕይወት ዕይታ ከተቃኙ ነገሮች ውስጥ ዋንኛው ነበር። የኢትዮጵያ ሕገ መንግሥት አርቃቂዎችም፤ ምንም እንኳ የጊዜው ፖለቲካ እየተተታም ቢሆን፤ ይህን ግዙፍ የሉዓላዊነት ጥያቄ ሳይንሳዊ መልክ ለማስያዝ መጣራቸው ይታያል። ትልቁ ችግር ግን በአጻጻም ደረጃ፤ "ይህ የእኔ፤ ያ የአንተ" እየተባለ፤ በግልፅ ሌላ አሠራር ተቀርጾ "የዚህ ክልል ባለቤት 'እገሌ' የሚባል ብሔር ነው እስከ ማለት ተደርሷል።

ለምሳሌ:- የተሻሻለው የአማራ ክልል ሕገ መንግሥት 'ማንም ሰው፤ አማርኛ ቋንቋ እስከ ቻለ ድረስ በክልሉ የመኖር፤ የመምረጥና የመመረጥ፤ የመሥራት፤ ንብረት የማፍራት፤ ወዘተ መብት' ይፈቅድና 'መሬት የክልሉ ሕዝብ የጋራ ንብረት ነው' ይላል።[184] የኦሮሚያም ተመሳሳይ ነው።[185] ስለዚህ፤ በሌላ የኢትዮጵያ ክልል የሚኖር

183 ፌዴራል ነጋሪት ጋዜጣ፡ (1995)። የኢትዮጵያ ፌዴራላዊ ዴሞክራሲያዊ ሪፐብሊክ ሕገ መንግሥት አዋጅ። አንቀጽ 40/3። https://ethiopianembassy.be/wp-content/uploads/Constitution-of-the-FDRE.pdf

184 አማራ ብሔራዊ ክልላዊ መንግሥት ምክር ቤት ዝክረ ሕግ፡ (2001)። የአማራ ብሔራዊ ክልላዊ ሕገ መንግሥት ለማጽደቅ የወጣ አዋጅ። http://knowledge-uclga.org/IMG/pdf/amhara-national-regional-state-constitution_1_.pdf

185 ጨፌ ኦሮሚያ፡ (1994)። የተሻሻለው የ1994 የኦሮሚያ ሕገ መንግሥት ማጽደቂያ አዋጅ። https://chilot.me/wp-content/uploads/2012/02/oromia-national-regional-state-constitution.pdf

ሕዝብ የአማራ ወይም የኦሮሚያ ክልል መሬት ላይ የባለቤትነት መብት የፌደራሉ ሕግ መንግሥት ቢፈቅድለትም በክልሎች ሕግ መንግሥት ተከልክሏል።

የቤንሻንጉል ክልል የተሻሻለው ሕግ መንግሥት[186] ይህን ላቅ ወዳለ ደረጃ ያደርሰዋል። "በክልሉ ውስጥ የሚኖሩ ሌሎች ሕዝቦች የሚታወቁ ቢሆንም፤ የክልሉ ባለቤት ብሔር፤ ብሔረሰቦች በርታ፤ ጉሙዝ፤ ሽናሻ፤ ማኦ እና ኮሞ ናቸው" ይላል። አንዱ የመኖር እውቅና፤ ሌላው የባለቤትነት እውቅና ተሰጣቸው። እኮልነትን በዐንደበታችን ሰበክን፤ በተግባር ግን ናቅነው። እነዚህ ብሔሮች ስለ ሌላው ኢትዮጵያ ያገባቸዋል? የብሔርተኛ ፖለቲካዊ ኤኮኖሚ ህጸጽ ጅማሬው በዚህ ነው ማለት ይቻላል።

ሌሎችንም ክልላዊ የመንግሥት ሕጎች ብንመለከት የተለየ ቅርጽ አይሰጡንም። የንብረት መብቱ ያልተጠበቀለት ዜጋ ስለ ክልሉ ብሎም ስለ አገሩ ደንታ ሊኖረው አይችልም። ስለ ንብረት መብት ብቻ አወራን እንጂ፤ የግለሰቦችና ቡድኖች የፖለቲካ ተሳትፎ፣ የገጠርና ከተማ መለያየትና መያያዝን ብንመለከት ምን ሥዐል ይሰጠን ይሆን? አገር እየገነባን ወይስ ቀስ በቀስ እያፈረስን?

---

186 የቤንሻንጉል ጉሙዝ ክልል ምክር ቤት። (1995)። የተሻሻለው የቤንሻንጉል ጉሙዝ ክልል ሕገ መንግሥት ማጽደቂያ አዋጅ። http://www.ethcriminallawnetwork.com/system/files/BENSHANGULE%5B1%5D.pdf

ብሔርተኛ ኢኮኖሚ

የሳሃራን በረሃ በፌዴራል መንግሥቱ ቍጥጥር ስር ብናውለው፣ በአምስት ዓመት ውስጥ የአሸዋ እጥረት ያጋጥመናል።
ሚልተን ፍሪድማን፣ አሜሪካዊ ሥነ ገንዘብ ኢኮኖሚስት

ሁለት መላጦች ... የቀጠለ

ማታ፣ ዜና ላይ ነው። ለካስ በአብዲና ሙሔ ፀብ ከድርና ለጊዜው ስማቸውን የማናውቅ ሌሎችም ሰዎች ሞተዋል። ከድር በጥይት ይሙት እንጂ ሌሎች ጥቂቶችም ጉዳት የደረሰባቸው አሉ። ፊታቸው፣ ጭንቅላታቸው አይታወቅም። በዱላና በስለት ብዙ ሥፍራ ተወጋግተዋል። በሞትና በሕይወት መካከል ካሉት በተጨማሪ እጅግ ብዙዎች ደግሞ በመለስተኛ ደረጃ ቆስለዋል።

እንዲህ ዐይነት ዜና በዝርዝር በራዲዮም ሆነ በቴሌቪዥን አይቀርብም። የብሔር ፖለቲከኞች የማይወድዱት ዐይነት ዜና ነው። ተራ ብጥብጥ ይሉታል። እንዲህ ዐይነት ብጥብጥ በሰዎች መካከል ሲቀሰቀስ ዜና አይሆንም።

መቼውም ተመቺውም ታፍሶ ይታሠርና ነገሩ ይልኮፈኮፋል። የዚያን ዕለት ግን ሌላም ጉንጭ የሚሞላ ዜና ስለታጣ፣ ዜና አቅራቢው ጥቂት መናገር ፈለገ።

አንዱን ጓደኛውን "የስልክ ጥሪ ደርሶኛልና እስቲ ተከታትለህ በሥፍራው ያለውን ዘግብልኝ" ብሎ እየላከው። የተላከውም ጋዜጠኛ ተጎጂዎቹ ሃኪም ቤት በመወሰዳቸው ወደዚያ ከነፈ። በስልክ ቀጥታ ሥርጭት ላይ ማስተላለፍ ዓላማቸው ነበር።

እናም ጀመሩ፤ ዜና አቅራቢውም፣ ሆስፒታል የተገኘ ጋዜጠኛ ጓደኛው ነገሩን ይበልጥ እንዲያራግብለት የፈለገ ይመስል፣ "እስቲ ከቍስለኞች አንዱን አነጋግረህ ከሆነ"...።

ወቼ ጉድ። ያንንማ እርሱ ከመጠየቁ በፊት ተዘጋጅቶ አልነበር! ተገኝቶ ነው? በእርግጥም ሆስፒታል ደርሶ አንድ ሦስቱን ቢያናግርም "አንጀት አርስ" መልስ የሰጠው አንድም የለም።

ትንሽ ሻል ያለ ነገር ያላቸው የሚመስል፤ ጭንቅላታቸውን በፊሻ አሥረው ሲያቃስቱ የነበሩ፣ ጠና ያሉ የቀን ሠራተኛ ናቸው። 'ምራቃቸውን ዋጥ ያደረጉ' ስለ ሆኑ የሆነውን ሁሉ ያስረዱኛል የሚል እምነት አደረብት፤ ጋዜጠኛው።

"አባባ፤ እንዴት ነዎት? በምን መሣሪያ ነው የተጎዱት?"

"በጀራ። አንዳች በሚያሃል ዱላ አናቴን፤ ማለትም በድንጋይ!" እያቃስቱ።

"ማለት አባባ፤ በምን መሣሪያ ነው ያሉኝ?"

"እነርሱ ያልያዙት ምን ነገር አለና?! ሁሉንም፤ እኛ እኩ ባዶ እጃችንን ነበርን?"

"ማን ናቸው እነሱ፤ አባባ?"

"አንተም ከእነርሱ ነህ መሰለኝ! ይሀች ነርስም ከእነርሱ መሆኗን አውቄአለሁ።"

እምብዛም የማያስሄድ፤ በተለይ በቀጥታ ሥርጭት ሊዘገብ የማይገባው መሆኑን ሲያውቅ፤ "እሺ አባባ፤ እግዜር በፍጥነት ይማርዎት" ብሎ ዞጋው።

የከበሮው ቆዳ

እስካሁን ባሉት ሁለት ክፍሎች የዘርና የብሔር ዕሳቤ ዳራ ተመልክቷል። የብሔርተኝነት ፖለቲካውም መነሻና እንድምታ ተቃኝቷል። ሦስተኛውና የመጨረሻው ክፍል የብሔር ፖለቲካው በኤኮኖሚው ላይ ምን ተጽዕኖ ያስከትል ይሆን የሚለውን አንሥቶ ይቋጫል።

ከበሮ ከጅብ ቆዳ ቢሠራ፤ "በላሁ፤ በላሁ!" ይላል አሉ ሲመቱት። የአበው ምሳሌያዊ ንግግር ነው። ፖለቲካ ከመርህ ወጥቶ መተማመን በሌለው የግጭት ኑባሬ ላይ ብቻ ሲያተኩር ሌላው የኑሮ መስክ ሁሉ ይመሰቃቀላል። ሁሉም ነገር በግጭት ቅኝት እንዴት ይቻላል?

ኤኮኖሚ ደግሞ ከፖለቲካ እርምጃዎች ጋር በጥብቅ የተቄራኝ ስለሆን ማንኛውም ዐይነት የፖለቲካ ውዥኔና እርምጃ በተጨባጭ ተጽዕና ያሳድርበታል። የያዝነው ዓመት (2023 እ.ኤ.አ.) ጅማሬ ካለፋት ጥቂት ዐመታት ይሻላል። አስከፊ ዕልቂት ያስከተለው ግጭት አባርቷል። ነገር ግን አንድ ሰው፤ ማንኛውንም በአገሪቱ ውስጥ የሚታተም ጋዜጣ ቢያነብ ወይም በሬዲዮና በቴሌቪዥን ወዬ ቢያዳምጥ ስለ ኤኮኖሚያችን የሚከተለውን ምንባዊ ሥዕል ማየቱ ወይም መስማቱ አይቀርም።

የሰሜኑ የእርስ በርስ ጦርነት እንዲያበቃ ስምምነት ላይ ተደርሷል። ይሁን እንጂ፤ በትግራይ ያለው የክልል መንግሥት ቢጠየቅ የሚለው አንድ ነገር ነው። የክልሉ ኤኮኖሚ ተንኮታኩቷል። ወደ ክልሉ ዘልቀው ከገቡ የአገር መከላከያ፤ የአማራ ልዩ ኃይልና

የኤርትራ ወታደሮች ጋር በነበረው ግጭት የኤኮኖሚ አውታሮች ሙሉ በሙሉ በሚባል ደረጃ ወድመዋል።

ከአየር ድብደባው የተነሣ ሰዎች በሠላም ወጥተው ለመግባት ይፈሩ ነበር። የኤርትራ ጦር ሙሉ በሙሉ ስላልወጣ ይህ ስጋት አሁንም አልተወገደም። በትግራይ ይኖራሉ ተብለው ከሚገመቱ 6 ሚሊዮን ያህል ዜጎች ውስጥ ሰባ ከመቶው ያህል የመኖር ተስፋቸው በቂ የምግብ ዕርዳታ በማግኘት ላይ የተንጠለጠለ ነው። ማለትም 4 ወይም 5 ሚሊዮን ሕዝብ።

ባለፉት ዓመታት አንበጣ የወረረውን ማሣ በትክልል ገልብጦ እንዳያርስ ግጭቱ ገበሬውን ከቤት እንዳይወጣ ስላደረገው እህል የለም። የዕርዳታ እህል በገፍ እንዳይገባ የመሠረት ልማት መንደል ተጽዕኖ እያሳደረ ነው። በአውሮፓላን የሚደርግ የሕክምና መገልገያዎች ድጋፍ እጅግ የዘገየም፤ ከፍለጎት አንጻር ሲታይ እጅግም አናሣ ነው። በሥፍራው ሁሉ የነዳጅና ተሽከርካሪ እጥረት ስላለ የመጣውን ያህል ዕርዳታ ማዳረስ ስላልተቻለ ሕዝቡ ወደ መቀሌና ሌሎች ትላልቅ ከተሞች በመፍለስ ላይ ይገኛል።

የአፋር መንግሥትን የጠየቃችሁ እንደሆነ፣ ተመሳሳይ ስቆቃ ትሰማላችሁ። በሕዝባዊ ወያኔ ሓርነት ትግራይ (ሕወሓት) ወረራ ምክንያት የኤኮኖሚ ተቋማት ሙሉ በሙሉ ወድመዋል። ዛሬም ድረስ በአፋር ደቡብ ምሥራቅ ወረዳዎች ሌላ ግጭት ስላለ፤ ቀድሞ ከነበረው ጋር ተደምሮ እስከ ግማሽ ሚሊዮን የሚደርሱ ወገኖች ተፈናቅለው መጠለያ ጣቢያ ናቸው።

የጤናና ትምህርት ተቋማት ስለ ተደመሰሱ ትግራይን በሚያዋስነው የአፋር ክፍሎች በሙሉ ለጊዜው አገልግሎቱ ቆሟል። ሌላው አካባቢ ወቅቱ የድርቅ ችግር ያጠላበት በመሆኑ በታላቅ ሥጋት ይኖራል። ከግጭቶችም የተነሣ እንደ ፈለጉ ከቦታ ወደ ቦታ መንቀሳቀስ አዳጋች ነው። የድርቅ ነገር ከተነሣ የሶማሌ ክልል የእኔ ችግር የባሰ ነው ይላል። ግመሎችና ከብቶች፤ ትናንሽ እንስሳትም ሳይቀር በድርቁ ሞተዋል። የግጦሽና የውሃ እጥረት ያሉትንም አንገዋቂሏል። ለሕጻናት የሚሆን ወተት የለም።

በዚያ ላይ በሶማሌና ኦሮሞ ጐሣዎች ግጭት ምክንያትና በተለያዩ የሶማሌ ጐሣዎች መካከልም ካለው ግጭት ሽሽተው በመጠለያ ያሉ እጅግ ብዙ ወገኖች አሉ። የሶማሌ ክልል ከአፋር ጋር በሚያዋስናቸው ቦታዎች አልፎ አልፎ በአርብቶ አደሮች መካከል ግጭት ስለሚከሰት ሕዝቡ ተረጋግቶ መኖር አልቻለም። የውስጥ ሽኩቻም ሰከን ያለ ሕይወት ለመምራት አላስቻለም።

አማራ ክልልም ሮሮ አለው። የግጭቱ ዋናው ገፈት ቀማሽ ነው። ሰዎች ሞተዋል። ኤኮኖሚው ደቅቋል። የሕዝብ አገልግሎት መስጫ ተቋሞች ወድመዋል። ሴቶችና ሕጻናት ተደፍረዋል።

ከግጭቱ የተነሣ በክልሉ የደረሰውን ጉዳት ለመጠገን ከ7000 ቢሊዮን ብር በላይ[187] ያስፈልግ ይሆናል። ማለትም ከጠቅላላው የአገሪቱ ዓመታዊ በጀት ውስጥ ግማሽ ያህሉ ቢመደብ ስንኳ የማይሸፈን ኪሣራ ደርሷል። ዛሬ 12 ሚሊዮን ሕዝብ ለምግብ እጥረት ተዳርጓል።

ኦሮሚያ የአገሪቱ ትልቁ ክልል ሲሆን ከሰሜኑ ግጭት ጋር ተያይዞ በቀጥታ የደረሰበት ጉዳት ባይኖርም የአገሪቱ ፖለቲካ የማይጥማቸው ወገኖች አሉ። አንዳንዶች ነፍጥ አንስተው፣ ህቡዕም፣ ሸምቅም፣ ግልፅም ጦርነት እያካሄዱ ነው። በያንዳንዱ ዞን ውስጥ ሰፊ መሠረት ያለው የሚመስል ትንኮሳ "ከህዋሃት እና ሌሎች ጽንፈኛ ኃይሎች" ጋር በጣ6ር በጠቅ6 ኃይል የፖለቲካ ዓላማ ለማሳካት የተነሣ "ሽብርተኛ" በመባል የተፈረጀው "አኔግ ሽኔ" ይላከካል።

እዚህም እዚያም ጥቃት የማድረስ ዐቅም ያላቸው ቡድኖች ተፈጥረዋል የሚል እምነት አይሩን ሞልቶታል። ሰዎች ይታጣታሉ፣ ይገደላሉ፣ መንገድ ይዘጋል። መሠረት ልማት በበቂ ያልተሟላባት ቢሆንም የአገሪቱ የደም ስር የሚባሉ መንገዶች በሙሉ ኦሮሚያን ሳያቋርጡ የትም አይዘለቀንም። ታዲያ እንዚህን ጨምሮ በተለይም በክልሉ የውስጥ ለውስጥ መንገዶች ጥቁት በማይባል ሥፍራዎች በተለያዩ ቡድኖች ተቆፍረው ወይም ተዘግተው ከጠቅም ውጭ ሆነዋል።

ሌሎች የኤኮኖሚ አውታሮችም ላይ ጥቃት ደርሷል። የአገሪቱ የውጭ ንግድ የጀርባ አጥንት ከሆኑት ውስጥ የሚመደበው ቡና በበቂ መጠን ከኦሮሚያ አካባቢዎች መቅረብ ባለመቻሉ የውጭ ምንዛሪ ገቢ በሙሉ ዐቅም ሊያድግ አልቻለም። የአገር ውስጥ የቡና ዋጋ እንኳን ጨምሯል። ድርቁም ከሶማሌ ክልል ባልተናነሰ ጉድቶታል። በተለይም ቦረና እና ሌሎችም አርብቶ አደር አካባቢዎች እጅግ ተጉድተዋል። ሰባ ሺህ ከብቶች ሞተው 1 ሚሊዮን ያህሉ እጅግ ተጉሣቀላዋል።[188]

ቤንሻንጉል ጉሙዝ ክልል በደቡብ በኮል በአነግ ሽኔ፣ በውስጥ ደግሞ በህዋሃት ይደገፋሉ ተብለው በሚገመቱ የጉሙዝ ነጻ አውጭ አባላት፣ ጥቃት ዘር ተኮር ጭፍጨፋ አላቋረጠም። መንግድም ስለ ተዘጋ ነዳጅና ሌሎች አስፈላጊ ቀሳቁስ አቅርቦት ችግር ይስተዋላል። ወይም ለማሳለፍ እጅግ አዳጋች ሆኗል። ብዙ ሕዝብ ግጭት ፈርቶ በጫካ ያድራል። ክልሉ ገና ታዳጊ ቢሆንም በግጭት ምክንያት ያሉትም የኤኮኖሚ አውታሮች ላይ ጉዳት ደርሷል።

እያለ ይቀጥላል። ለምን? የፖለቲካው መሠረት ብሔር፣ ግጭት ደግሞ የፖለቲካ <u>ጥያቄ ሁሉ መመለሻ</u> መንገድ ተደርጎ ስለ ተወሰደ ነው። በአገሪቱ ከ100 በላይ

187 Endale, A. (2022). "Reconstruction of Amhara region requires over 700-billion-birr, study." Reporter, December 17, 2022. https://www.thereporterethiopia.com/28667/

188 FAO. (2021). Rapid drought assessment report for Borena and Dawa zones (November 2021). Reliefweb; 23 Nov 2021. https://reliefweb.int/report/ethiopia/rapid-drought-assessment-report-borena-and-dawa-zones-november-2021

ፓርቲዎች ተመዝግበው ይገኛሉ። ያልተመዘገቡ፣ ዓላማቸውን በጦር ኀይል ለማሳካት የተነሡም ብዙ እንዳሉ ይገመታል። ሁሉ በሚባል ደረጃ እነዚህ ኀይሎች በብሔር እዝ የተዋቀሩ ናቸው። "በላሁ፣ በላሁ!" የሚል የአንድ ጅብ ቆዳ።

ዕሳቤ ሥርዓት

አይመስለንም እንጂ ፍጥረት በአብዛኛው ዑደታዊ ነው። ቀንና ሌሊት ሲፈራረቁ፣ ዝም ብሎ መሽቶ የሚነጋ ይመስለናል። አይደለም፤ ሥርዓት አለው። የሚመላለስ የሚመስለው ቅርጽና ይዘቱ ፍጹም ልዩ ነው።

ዝናብ ይዘንብና በትነት መልክ ወደ ላይ ተንሳፍፎ ሲቀዘቅዝ መልሶ ይዘንባል። ወንዞች ወደ ባሕር ይንቀለቀላሉ። ምንጭ ከመሬት ውስጥ ተፍለቅልቆ ወንዝ የሚሆንበት ገሚሱን ኀይል የሚያገኘው ደግሞ ባሕሩ ጠግቦ ካቀረሸው ውሃ ነው።

ተክሎች ኦክሲጅን ይሰጡናል። እንስሳት ደግሞ ለተክሎች ሕይወት መሠረታዊ የሆነውን ካርቦን ዳዮክሳይድ እናመነጫለን። በሬ ሣር ሲግጥ የተወው እዳሪ ከከብት ጥርስ ላመለጠው የሰርዶ ጉራጅ መንደላቀቂያ ነው።

የማይሰጥ አይኖርም፤ የማይቀበል አይዘልቅም። ዑደቱን መስበር መሰበር ነው። ይህ በፍጥረት የተደራጀልን ጥቂት ዓይናችንን ስንከፍት የምናየው ሥርዓት ነው። ሥርዓት ከሕግ ይጠነክራል። ቅጣቱ ፍጹም ነውና፤ አያወላዳም፤ አያዳግምም።

ትንፋሼን ለተክሎች እነፍጋለሁ ያለ ይታፈናል። ተክሎች እንዳይኖሩ የሚተጋም ለሳንባው አበሣ ያከማቻል። መታፈን በሁለቱም በኩል ይመጣል። የማያስፈልጉን የሚመስሉ የበለጠ የምንሻቸው ይሆናሉ። ሰድዶ ማሳደድ ሥርዓታዊ ነው። ግድ።

ተላላው ግን ይፋንናል። እኔነትን ብቻ ያጎላል። በበላይነት ስሜት ይንጐማለላል። ናቅኩኝ እያለ ይናቃል። ሌላው ድኩም ዕሳቤ የተቸረው ደግሞ መስደድ ብቻ ሳይሆን ያባርራል። ይገፋተራል። እናም ራሱን እንደ ገደለ ስላልገባው ለከናፍሩ ድንበር ሳይሟሟ ይስቃል። በተከፈተው አፍ ታልፎ ልቡ ሲትታይ በሥፍራዋ የለችም።

ሁሉም ነገር ሥርዓት አለው። ፖለቲካም ጭምር። የዘሩት ይበቅላል። ተግተው የሠሩት ነገር ፍሬ ማፍራቱ አይቀርም። ዕሳቤ ሥርዓት ታዲያ የተፈጥሮን ዑደታዊ ሕግ የማክበር እና ዐብሮ የመሥራት ብልኀት ነው። አንዳንድ ዑደት የፈጠነ፣ አንዳንድ የዘገየ ቢመስልም አይቀሬ መሆኑን ይገነዘባል።

ዕሳቤ ሥርዓት የዘለቀው፣ የፈጠኑትን አንብቦ ለዘገዩት ጥበብ ይቀስማል። ለምሳሌ፦ የዘሩትን ማጨድ የማይሻር ሕግ መሆኑን ይረዳል። መራራ ዛፍ ጣፋጭ ፍሬ እንደማይገኝበት ፈጽሞ ያውቀዋል። እንዲሁም መሶብና እዳሪ ከአንድ በላይ በሆነ

መንገድ ሊገናኙ እንደሚችሉ ያስባል። እናም ያገኘውን ሁሉ በተሻለ መልክ አጉልብቶ ለመጨው ለማስረከብ ይጥራል እንጂ ለማጥፋት አይጣደፍም።

ይህን የናቀ፤ አይጠረቃም። ዕሳቤ ሥርዓትን የዘነጋ ዕቅድ አውጪ ፊት ለፊት የታየውን ብቻ ሰብስቦ ቢተልም ውጥን ተልካሻ ይሆናል። ሥርዓትን የናቀ ማንበረሰብም ሆነ ግለሰብ ይናቃል ብቻ ሳይሆን ይጠፋል። ያልፋል።

ሰውን የሚያሃል ነገር፤ ባሕልና እምነትን፤ ቋንቋና ዘርን የሚያሃል የተፈጥሮ ውብት በቍንጽል የሚተነትን የዕሳቤ ድኽነት የተጠናወተው ነው። የራስን ነገር በሌላው ላይ ለመጫን መራወጥም ሆን ሌላውን ሰው 'እኔን አይመስልም' በሚል ወራዳ ዕሳቤ 'ወግድልኝ፤ ውጣልኝ' የሚል ጠፍቶ አጥፊ እንደሆን ልናስተውል ግድ ነው።

ሰው ሁሉ ከፋብሪካ እንደ ወጣ ዕቃ ተመሳሳይ ነው ብሎ ማሰብም ሆን እኔን ያልመሰለ መጥፋት አለበት ማለትም አድራሻቸው አንድ ነው። ጉሥጓነት፤ ዘረኝነት ይባላል። እንደዚህ ዓይነቶች ከፍተው የለቀቁት ጂኒ አገር ያጠፋል። ሕዝብ ይሰለቅጣል። ጠፍተው የሚያፋፉን ገታ አድርጉት ልንላቸው ይገባል።

በኤኮሚ ረገድ ዕሳቤ ሥርዓት ልዩ ሚና ይይዛል። ገቢያን አዳምጦ ምርቱን ከሚጨምር ወይም ከሚቀንስ የኤኮሚ ሕዋስ አንሥሦ እስከ አገር ኤኮሚ አመራር ድረስ መሠረታዊ የሆነ የኤኮሚ ሥርዓቶችን ማክበር የግዴታ አስፈላጊ ነው። ሥርዓትን ላከበሩ ወይም ለናቁ ኤኮሚ ትርፍ ወይም ኪሣራ ስትከፍል በፍጥነት ነው።

እንድገመው እንዴ? ጤናማ ኤኮሚ እንዲኖር፤ ለኤኮሚ ሥርዓቶች መገዛት ግድ ነው። ሕዝብ እያደገ፤ ፍላጎት እያጨመረ ሲሄድ ሕጉንና ሥርዓቱን ተከትሎ ማስተናገድ የአንድ አገር ወይም ሕዝብ የሕልውና ጉዳይ ነው። የአገራችን የብሔር ፖለቲካዊ ኤኮሚ በዚህ ረገድ ሥርዓት አልበኛ ከሆነ ይብዛም ይነስ ዋጋ ለመክፈል መዘጋጀት ይኖርብናል።

ዳቦው

የኢትዮጵያ ኤኮሚ ምን ያህላል ከሚለው ጥያቄ እንጀምር። ሥርጭቱና ክፍፍሉስ ምን ይመስላል? ኤኮሚያችን በመጠ ከምሥራቅ አፍሪካ ግዙፍ ኤኮሚዎች አንዱ ነው። በአፍሪካም ካሉ አሥር ትልልቅ ኤኮሚ ካላቸው አገራት ተርታ እንመደባለን። የማያከፋ ዳቦ ነው። ነገር ግን ይህ ዳቦ ለእያንዳንዳችን ሲሆን ምን ማለት ነው?

የአገራትን ዓመታዊ የኤኮኖሚ ጤንነት የሚመረምረው የዓለም ባንክ[189] ባስቀመጠው አኃዝ መሠረት የኢትዮጵያ ኤኮኖሚ ጠቅላላ ግምቱ በ2022 ዓ.ም በወቅቱ ምንዛሬ ወደ 111 ቢሊዮን ዶላር ገደማ ደርሷል። ሕዝባችን ደግሞ 121 ሚሊዮን ገደማ። ከአፍሪካ አኅጉር በሕዝብ ብዛት ሁለተኛ ደረጃ።

ይህም ማለት ለአገራቱ ሕዝብ ሲከፋፈል የእያንዳንዳችን ዓመታዊ ገቢ 925 ዶላር ይደርሳል። ወይንም በ2023 ዓ.ም መነሻ ወራት አካባቢ ባለው የብር ምንዛሬ መጠን የነፍስ ወከፍ ገቢያችን በዓመት 50ሺ ብር ያህል ይሆናል፣ በወር ሲሰሊ 4100 ብር አካባቢ። ማለትም፣ የአንድ ኢትዮጵያዊ የቀን ገቢ ከ130 ብር እምብዛም ፈቀቅ አይልም።

እንጂግ ብዙ የመሠለው ሲከፋፈል ኢምንት ነው፣ ያ ብቻ ሳይሆን ከዓለምም ሆነ ከአካባቢያችን አገራት ጋር ሲታይ እዚህ ግባ የሚባል አይደለም። እንዲያው ለንጽጽር ያህል ግን ከአፍሪካ 3 ትሪሊዮን ኤኮኖሚ የእኛ ድርሻ 3 በመቶ ብቻ ነው። ለነገሩ አፍሪካ ራስዋ፣ በምርት ብዛት ሲለካ፣ ለዓለም በኤኮኖሚ አቅም ደረጃ የሚታበረከተው አስተዋጾ እምብዛም አይደለም። የዓለም ኤኮኖሚ አጠቃላይ ምርት ዛሬ 106 ትሪሊዮን ዘልቋል። አፍሪካ ድርሻዋ 3 በመቶ ብቻ።

የኢትዮጵያን ድርሻ ከዓለም ላይ ለማስላት አትሞክሩ፣ 0ደራ፣ ቀጥር አይኖረውም። እዚሁ በዙ ማንጻጸር ይሻላል። ጉሬቤት ኬንያ 110 ቢሊዮን ዶላር ያህል አጠቃላይ ምርት ሲኖራት ሕዝቧ ግን 53 ሚሊዮን ብቻ ስለሆነ በነፍስ ወከፍ ገቢያቸው ያስከነዱናል። የእያንዳንዱ ኬንያዊ ዓመታዊ ምርት ወይም ገቢ 2100 ዶላር አካባቢ ወይም 112 ሺህ ብር ነው። የእኛ በሁለት ተባዝቶ እንኳን አይደርስበትም ማለት ነው።

በዚህ ስሌት የኬንያ ዜጋ የቀን ገቢ፣ ማለትም ወደ 315 ብር ገደማ፣ በእኛ አገር ዶክትሬት ድግሪ ድረስ ተምሮ እየሠራ ላለ ሐኪም ከሚከፈለ ደመወዝ የሚተካከል መሆኑን ስናይ የዳቦ ነገር የቸገረን መሆኑ ግልጥ ይሆንልናል። ከሕዝብ ብዛት አንጻር ሲታያ አጠቃላይ ምርታችን እንጂ ዝቅተኛ ስለሆነ። የድኻ ድኻ ከሚባሉ አገራት የምንመደበው ስለዚህ ነው።

መቼም ወዳጆቻችንን ምድረ ምጽራይም (ግብጽ) ካላነሳን ንጽጽሩ ሙሉ አይሆንም። የሰሜን አፍሪካዊቷ እነት አገር በሕዝብ ብዛት ተቀናቃኛችን ናት። ከጥቂት ዓመታት በፊት በሕዝብ ብዛት ቀድመናታል። በ2023 ዓ.ም 110 ሚሊዮን ሕዝብ ሲኖራት አጠቃላይ ምርቷ፣ 404 ቢሊዮን ዶላር ያህል ደርሷል። ማለትም የእያንዳንዱ ግብጻዊ ዓመታዊ ገቢ 3700 ዶላር ወይንም 200ሺ ብር ገደማ ነው። የእኛን አራት እጥፍ ማለት ነው።

---

189 The World Bank. (2023). Data. https://data.worldbank.org/country በዚህ ክፍል የተጠቀሱት አኃዞች በልዩነት ካልተገለጡ በቀር በሙሉ የተሰባሰዱት ከዚህ ምንጭ ነው።

የሕዝብ ብዛት ዐቅም ቢሆንም ያለ በቂ ኤኮኖሚ የሰው ብዛት ብቻውን ሸክም ነው። ማምረት የማይችሉ ወይንም የማይፈልጉ እጅና እግሮች በረከትነታቸው ያጠያይቃል። ለነገሩ፣ እንኳን አገራት፣ በበለጸጉ አገራት ያሉ አንዳንድ ኩባንያዎች የምርት መጠናቸው ከአፍሪካ አገራት ጋር ሲነጻጸር በላጠ ይታያል። ለምሳሌ፡- በቅርብ የወጡ መረጃዎች እንደሚያሳልክቱ የአፕል ኮምፒውተሮች አምራቹ ግዙፍ ድርጅት በዚህ ዓመት ከወጪ ገቢ የተጣራ ትርፍ ያገኘው ሙሉ የኢትዮጵያን ኤኮኖሚ ያህላል። [190]

ስቲቭ ጄብስ አርፉል እንጂ ነሸጥ ብሎት በዘንድሮ ትርፍ መላ የኢትዮጵያን ዓመታዊ ምርት ልግዛ ቢል ይችላል ማለት ነው፤ አንድ ሳያስቀር፣ በትርፍ ብቻ። ለነገሩ የስቲቭ ጄብስ አፕል ወይንም የወዳጃቻን የቢ ጌትሱ ማይክሮ ሶፍት ሃብታችንን በዛሬ ዋጋ ሸጠን የአፍሪካን ዓመታዊ ምርት በሙሉ እንግዛ ቢሉ የአንዳቸው ሃብት ብቻ መላ የአፍሪካን ምርት ገዝቶ ጥቂት የተረፈ ይኖረዋል።

ስቲቭ ጄብስም ሆነ ቢል ጌትስ ግለሰቦች ናቸው። በመካከለኛው ዕድሜ ክልል የሚገኙ፣ ሁለቱም አሜሪካውያን። በአፍሪካ ካሉ "እኔ ነኝ" ካሉ ሙሉ አገራት በላይ ሃብት ማፍራት የቻሉት ለምን እንደሆነ ማሰብ ካቃተን ከፍተኛ ችግር ላይ ነን። ለድኅነታችን የሚጠቀሰውን ምንም ዐይነት ምክንያትንም እንደ ምክንያት ከተቀበልን ከእኛ የበለጠ ምስኪን የለም።

ለነገሩ አፕል እና ማይክሮ ሶፍት እጅግ ግዙፍ ኩባንያዎች ናቸው። የሁለቱም ሃብት በዛሬ የገበያ ዋጋ ተምኖ የአሜሪካ ኤኮኖሚ ላይ ብንቀንስ በአጠቃላይ ምርት አሜሪካ አንደኛነትዋን ጠብቃ ከቻይና፣ ጃፓን፣ ጀርመን፣ እንግሊዝ፣ ህንድና ፈረንሳይ ቀጥሎ በሰባተኛና በስምንተኛ ደረጃ ሊቀመጡ የሚችሉ አሕጉር-አክል ድርጅቶች ናቸው። በአንድ ወይም ጥቂት ግለሰቦች የተገነቡ።

በቁጭት ለሥራ የሚያነሳሳን ነገር ደግሞ እንደ ማይክሮ ሶፍት ያሉ ድርጅቶችን መገንባት የቻሉ ሰዎች ከምንም ተነስተው እዚህ መድረስ መቻላቸውን ስንመለከት ነው። የገነቡትንም ሃብት መሬት ምሰው ማዕድን አውጥተው ያገኙት ሳይሆን አዕምሮአቸውን ተጠቅመው አዲስ ነገር ፈጥረው ብቻ እንደሆነ ስንገነዘብ ተስፋን የሚያጭር ነገር አለው።

ችግሩ፣ አዕምሮአችንን ለምን ተጠቀምን የሚለውን ነገር ስናስተውል ነው። ይባስ ብሎ ባለፉት ሁለትና ሦስት ዓመታት የደፋነው ዳቦ መጠኑ እየቀነሰ መሆኑ አይካድም። ኮቪድ አንዱ ችግር ሆኖ ሌላም የቀነሰበት ምክንያት ጊዜና ጉልበታችንን ለመገዳደል እና ለማፍራረስ ስላዋልነው እንደሆነ ምንም ጥርጥር የለውም። ከኮቪድ መልስ ዓለሙ ሁሉ ባደገበት በ2022 ዓ.ም እኛ ጭራሽ ተንሸራተትን።

በ1928 ዓ.ም ቻርልስ ኮብ እና ፖል ዳግላስ የተባሉ የኤኮኖሚ ጠበብት የአንድ __አገር ኤኮኖሚ__ የምርት ዕድገትን ቅልብጭ ባለ ሁኔታ በመግለጥ እስከ ዛሬ ድረስ እውቅ

190 Statista. (2023). Apple's net income in the company's fiscal years from 2005 to 2022(in billion U.S. dollars). https://www.statista.com/statistics/267728/apples-net-income-since-2005/

የሆነውን ንድፈ ዐሳብና ቀመር አበረከቱ። [191] የኮብ-ዳግላስ የምርት ንድፈ ዐሳብ ተብሎ በሚታወቀው በዚህ ቀመር መሠረት የአንድ አገር ምርት መጠን የሚወሰነው ካፒታል ወይም ጥሪት እና የሰው ኃይል (ጉልበት፣ ላብ) ባላቸው የእርስ በርስ ግንኙነት ነው።

ካፒታል ወይም ጥሪት በትክክለኛው መንገድ የሰው ኃይል ሲታከልበት ተጨማሪ ምርት ይፈጥራል። ጥሪትና የሰው ኃይል ያልተቀላቀለበት ምርት ወይም አገልግሎት የለም። ምንልባት ከዚህ ተጨማሪ የሚሆነው፣ በአንድ አገር ውስጥ ያለ ቀደሞ የነበረ የቴክኖሎጂ እምቅ ሀብትና የሰው ኃይል የዕድገት ደረጃ ብቻ ነው። ላብን የረገጠ የዘነጋ ካፒታል አይጠረቃም። በላብ ብቻም ዳገት አይገፋም።

ቴክኖሎጂም ቢሆን ከሁለቱ ውጭ ፍጹም ፍሬ የለውም። ጥሪትና ላብ ለቴክኖሎጂ ውም ዕድገት መሠረት ይሆናሉ። በኢትዮጵያ ያለው 'ሦስት ሺህ ዓመታትን ያስቆጠረ' ብለን የምንመጻደቅበት የእርሻ ቴክኖሎጂ በካፒታልም፣ በሰው ኃይልም ስለተዘነጋ ለዛሬው የዕድገት ውጤት አበቃን። እርሻን ጠቀስን እንጂ ሁሉም በሚባል ደረጃ የአገራችን ጥሪትና የሰው ሀብት ወደ መንኮራኩር ቴክኖሎጂ (ሽርክርቦ ሽ፣ ነማ፣ ሞተር) ያደረገው ሽግግር ያልነበረ ወይም የተገታ መሆኑ ሊያሳስበን ይገባል።

እርሻ ከማረሻ ወደ ትራክተር (መንኮራኩር)፣ አሁን ደግሞ ወደ ድሮን፣ ወይም አፈር ዐልባ ምርት ባደገበት ዘመን ከሁለት በሬና ማንኪያ እምታክል ማረሻ ጋር የሙጥኝ ማለት አያዋልቅም። ጥሪትና የሰው ኃይል በአግባቡ አንዱ ሌላውን በሚያጉለብት መልክ ሥራ ላይ ሊውሉ ይገባልና። ይህ ቀላል የሚመስል አገላለጥ ከፍተኛ አስተውሎትን ይጋብዛል። አንዲት አገር ዕድገትን ከተመኘች ለሁለት ነገሮች ትኩረት ትሰጣለች፤ ካፒታልና የሰው ኃይል።

ትኩረትን መስጠት ደግሞ አጠቃላይ ፖለቲካዊና ማኅበራዊ መልካም አስተዳደርን ማስፈን ይጨምራል። የአንድ አገር አስተዳደር በመልካም መያዙን ለማወቅ፣ የዓለም ባንክ ስድስት ዋና ዋና አመልካቾችን ይጠቀማል። [192] በየዓመቱም 200 አገራት ያሉበትን የአስተዳደር ዐይነትና ደረጃ እነዚህን አመልካቾች በመጠቀም በንጽጽር ያስቀምጣል። አስተዳደር ካፒታልን፣ የሰው ኃይልንም በእጅጉ ይወስናል። የቴክኖሎጂ ደረጃና ልቀትንም ይወስናል። መልካም ከሆነ በጉ ተጽዕኖ ያሳድራል።

የመልካምነት ቀዳሚው መለኪያ የአንድ አገር ዜጎች በአገሩቱ አስተዳደር ላይ ያላቸው ድምፅ እና ተጠያቂነት ነው። ሰዎች መሪዎቻቸውን ለመምረጥ ያላቸው ነጻነት እና ተሳትፎ ምን ያህል ነው የሚለውንም ይጨምራል። መንግሥት ለዜጎች ምን ያህል

---
191 Cob, C. & Douglas, P. (1928). A theory of production. The American Economic Review. Vol. 18; No. 1. https://www.jstor.org/stable/1811556

192 The World Bank. (2023). Worldwide Governance Indicators. https://info.worldbank.org/governance/wgi/

ነጻነት ይሰጣል? ሐሳብን በነፃነት የመግለጽ ነፃነት፤ የመደራጀት ነፃነት፤ እና ነፃ ሚዲያ በዚህ መለኪያ ስር ይጠቃለላሉ።

ሁለተኛው አመልካች የፖለቲካ መረጋጋትና የግጭት ወይም ሽብርተኝነት ጥቃትን መቆጣጠር መቻል ነው። ሰዎች ስለ ፖለቲካዊ ወይም ሽብርተኝነት ጥቃት ያላቸው ግንዛቤ ጥራትንና የሰው ኃይልን በአገሪቱ ወይም በተወሰኑ ክፍሎች ከማፍሰስ ሊያቀባቸው ይችላል። ዜጎች በራስ ላይ ወይም በንብረት ላይ ጥቃት ይደርሳል ብለው ይፈራሉ? ጥቃት ከደረሰ የመንግሥት የመከላከል ዐቅምና ፍላጎት ምን ያህል ነው? በግጭት ጉዳይ ዜጎችና መንግሥት ይተማመናሉ? ይግባባሉ?

ሦስተኛው አመልካች የመንግሥት ውጤታማነትን ይመለከታል። ይህም የሕዝብ አገልግሎቶችን በጥራት እና በብቃት፤ ያለማዳላትም ማዳረስን፤ የሲቪል ሰርቪሱን ጥራት እና የአገልግሎት ተነሳሽነት፤ እንዲሁም የፍትሐዊነት ግንዛቤ ይጨምራል። ሰዎች ከፖለቲካዊ ጫናዎች ነፃ ሆነው በአገራቸው ኤኮኖሚ መሳተፍን፤ የመንግሥት ፖሊሲ ቀረፃ እና ትግበራ ጥራት እና ታማኝነት፤ እንዲሁም ለፖሊሲያች አፈጻጸም መንግሥት የሚያሳየው ቁርጠኝነት ከዚህ ይመደባል።

ሌላው ደግሞ መንግሥት ኤኮኖሚውን በመቆጣጠር የሚጫወተው ሚና ነው። የቁጥጥር ጥራት ትክክለኛ ፖሊሲዎችን እና ደንቦችን ለመቅረፅ እና ለመተግበር መንግሥት ያለውን ችሎታ የሚለካ ነው። በተጨማሪም መንግሥት የግል ዘርፍ ልማትን የመፍቀድ እና የማስተዋወቅ ኃላፊነትን በብቃት እየተወጣ መሆኑን ይህ አመልካች ያረጋግጣል።

ከፍተኛ ትኩረት ከሚሰጣቸው አመልካቾች አንዱ የሕግ የበላይነት ነው። መንግሥትና አሠራሩ የሕግ የበላይነትን እንዴት ያስጠብቃሉ? የመንግሥት መዋቅርና ወኪሎች በፍትሕ ጉዳይ ላይ ምን ያህል እምነት ይጣልባቸዋል? ሕግን ከማስጠበቅ ጎን መንግሥትና ወኪሎቹ የጎብረተሰቡን ሕግጋት እንደሚያከብሩ፤ የወንጀልና አመፅን መከላከል ሥራ፤ የኮንትራት ወይም ውል ማስፈጸሚያ ጥራት፤ የንብረት ባለቤትነት መብት፤ ፖሊስ እና የፍርድ ቤቶች ነጻነት በዚህ ውስጥ ይካተታል።

በመጨረሻም፤ የሙስና ቁጥጥር ሌላው አመልካች ነው። ከጥቃቅን ማጭበርበር እና ጉቦ ጀምሮ ሕዝብ በሰጠው ሥልጣን መባለግ ወይም ሥልጣንን ተገን በማድረግ ለግል ጥቅም መሥራት ካለ መልካም አስተዳደር ይነደላል፤ አገር አያድግም። ምዝበራና ጥራትን የማሸሽ የመሰሉ ታላላቅ የሙስና ዓይነቶች ሲበራከቱ፤ በተለይም የመንግሥት ሥልጣን በልሂቃን በጎ ፈቃድ ስር ሲወድቅ፤ ከዚህም የተነሣ ለግል ፍላጎቶች እንደፈለጉ መጠምዘዝ ሲቻል አገር አለቀላት።

እነዚህ ሁሉ አመልካቾችና ሌሎችም የመልካም አስተዳደር መገለጫዎች በግልና በጋራ በኤኮኖሚው ላይ ያላቸውን ተጽዕኖ በሙሉ ለመዘርዘር ይህ መጽሐፍ አይበቃም። ነገር ግን ፖለቲካ በመልካም አስተዳደር በኩል በጥራትና የሰው ኃይል ልማት፤

እንቅስቃሴና ምርታማነት ላይ ምን ያህል ተጽዕኖ እንደሚያደርስ ለማመልከት ያህል ጥቂቶች ተነስተዋል። ፖለቲካው ብሔርተኛ ሲሆን አመልካቾቹ ምን እንደሚጠቁሙ ለማወቅም ጥረት ተደርጓል።

ልምዓተ ሰብዕ[193]

ገና በመጽሐፉ ጅምር ላይ የሚያጣላን ዳቦ እዚህ ግባ የሚባል እንዳልሆነ ተመልክቷል። ከምጣዱ ያስታውቃል ይሉ የለ? የዳቦው ውፍረት ከዓመታዊ የገቢ ዕድገት ውጭ የሚለካበት ሌላ መንገድም አለ። ያለፉት ሃያ ዓመታት አገራት፤ በተለይም ታዳጊ የሚባሉ አገራት ብዙ እመርታ ያሳዩበት ጊዜ ነበር። በአገራችንም ኢትዮጵያ ብዙ ባይባልም መልካም ለውጦች የታዩበት ዘመን ነው። ዕድገቱ የሚያስጉመኘሽ ሲሆን ዳቦው ትንሽ ቢሆንም ተስፋ ያጭራል።

ያለፈው መንግሥት በአገሪቱ ያልተለመደ የሁለት አኃዝ ዕድገት አሳይተናል እያለ ይመጻደቅ ነበር። ራሱን ከራሱ ጋር በማወዳደር። እንደፈለገው፤ ሁሉ ሰው አላመነም እንጂ ፈጽሞም ዕድገት ዐል[ነ]ነ ተብሎ አልተካደም። የሁለት አኃዝ ዕድገቱን ባይቀበሉም፤ ዓለም አቀፍ ድርጅቶች ጭምር ኢትዮጵያ የሚያስቀና የዕድገት ጉዞ ላይ እንዳለች መስክረዋል።

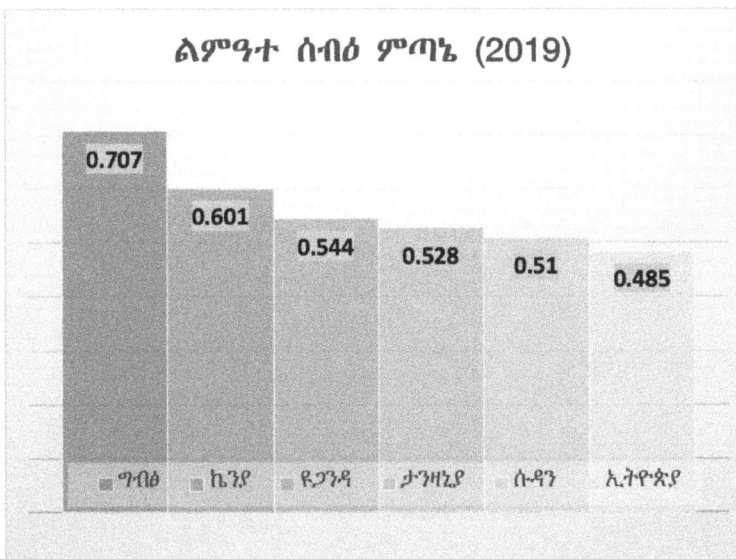

ልምዓተ ሰብዕ ምጣኔ (2019)

ግብፅ	ኬንያ	ዩጋንዳ	ታንዛኒያ	ሱዳን	ኢትዮጵያ
0.707	0.601	0.544	0.528	0.51	0.485

ምንጭ:- የተባበሩት መንግሥታት የልማት ፕሮግራም፤ 2020

---

193 ልምዓተ ሰብዕ ወይም ልማተሰብዕ የአንድን አገር ወይም ከፍል አገር የሰውን ሁለንተናዊ ዕድገት የሚያመልከት ሲሆን፤ ረኽም ዕድሜና ጤና፤ የዕውቀት ደረጃ፤ እና አጠቃላይ የኑሮ ደረጃ ጥራትን አጣምሮ የሚለካ ምጣኔ ነው።

ይሁን እንጂ፤ ዕድገቱ ወደ ሁለንተናዊ የሰው ልማት ተቀየረ ወይ? ኢትዮጵያ ከጉረቤት አገራት ስትወዳደር እንኳ፤ ዕድገትዋ ለኩራት የሚዳርግ እንዳይደለ መረጃዎች ያመለክታሉ። በተለይም፤ የአገሪቱን ሁለንተናዊ ልማት ስንመለከት ዕድገት ምኑ ላይ ነው ያስብላል። ለውጥ በሰው ሁለንተናዊ ዐቅምና አቋም ላይ ሲታይ በእርግጥም ዕድገት ተገኘ ቢባል ያስሄዳል። በዚህ ረገድ አገራችን እጅግ ዝቅ ብላ ትታያለችና።

ብዙ ጊዜ ስለ ኤኮኖሚ ዕድገት ሲወራ ከምን ተነስተን የት እንደ ደረስን ብቻ ይነገራል። ከራሳችን፤ በተለይም ከቀደሙት አስተዳደሮች ጋር ብቻ በማስተያየት። ጉረቤት የሚሆኑን እንዳናይ የሚደረገው ምን ተፈርቶ ነው? አዳኝ ፈርታ አንገቷን አሸዋ ውስጥ እንደ ቀበረችው ሰጉን መሆን መልካም አይደለም። ሌሎች ከእኛ ይልቅ ፈጥነው አድገው እንደሆነስ?

ይህን አስፈሪ እውነታ ስንሸሽ ዘመናት አለፉ። እውነታው ይህን ይመስላል። ሌሎች እኮ አላደጉም፤ መንድገዋል የተሻለ በማደጋቸው። ወይም ቀድሞም ሲነሱ በተሻለ ቦታ ስለ ነበሩ የባሰ ወደ ኋላ ጥለውን ሄደዋል። ይህን አናውቅም፤ ወይም እያወቅን ጆሮ ዳባ ልበስ ብለናል። የኤኮኖሚውን ልዕልና እንደማስጠበቅ በፖለቲካው እና በፕሮፓጋንዳው ጠገብን።

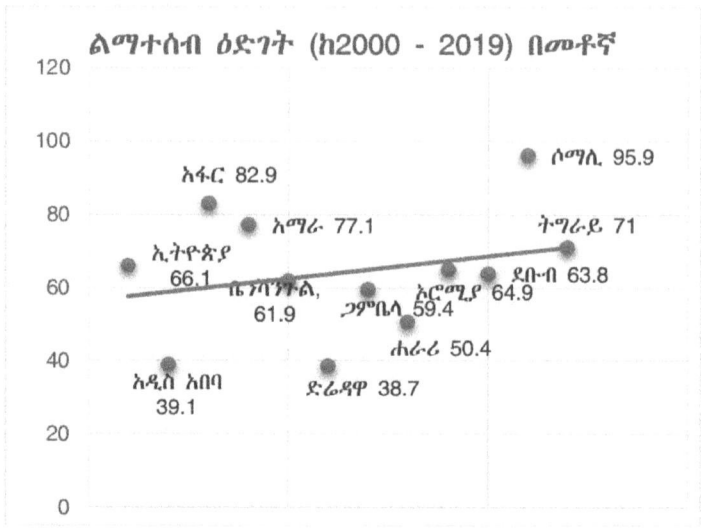

ልማተሰብ ዕድገት (ከ2000 - 2019) በመቶኛ

ለምሳሌ የተባበሩት መንግሥታት የልማት ፕሮግራም፤ በ2022 ዓ.ም ባወጣው የልማተሰብዕ ምጣኔ ቀመር መሠረት በ2019 እ. ኤ. አ. የኢትዮጵያ 0.485 ነው። [194] ከሃያ ዓመት በፊት 0.292 ብቻ ስለ ነበር ለውጡ ይበል ያሰኛል። ችግሩ ግን ጉረቤቶቻችን

---

194 UNDP. (2020). Human Development Index.

ታንዛኒያና ዩጋንዳ እንኳ ሳይቀሩ በልማተሰብዕ ከእኛ እጅግ በለጠው ይታያሉ። ወዳጆችን ግብዕግ ያለችበትን የ0.707 የልማተሰብዕ ምጣኔ ላይ ለመድረስ አሁን እያደገንበት ያለ ፍጥነት ሳይቀንስ ለ20 ተጨማሪ ዓመታት መኪተን ይጠበቅብናል።

ከፍ እያለ ሲሄድ የአሁኑን ያህል የዕድገት ምጣኔ ማስጠበቅ አዳጋች እየሆነ እንደሚሄድም ማስተዋል ያሻል። ሴላው፤ አለ የተባለው ለውጥ እንኳን በሁሉም የአገሪቱ ክፍሎች በእኩልነት የተዳረሰ አለመሆን ነው። ዓመታዊ ዕድገቱም ዝብርቅርቅ ነው።

ይህም፤ የጥሪት ክፍፍል ላይ ህጸጽ እንዳለ የሚያመለክት ነው። ቀደም ሲል ከተጠቀሰው በመነሣት፤ ባለፉት ሁለት አሥርት ዓመታት የኢትዮጵያ ልማተሰብዕ ዕድገት ጠቋሚ በ66 ከመቶ መሻሻል ማሳየቱን እንረዳለን። ነገር ግን በእኩልነት አላደገንም። ማለትም፤ ይህ ዕድገት በተለያዩ የአገሪቱ ክፍሎች ሁሉ ተመሳሳይ አልነበረም።[195]

ሁልጊዜ ሲባል እንደምንሰማው አራት ታዳጊ ክልሎች አሉ። ጋምቤላ፤ ቤኒሻንጉል፤ አፋርና፤ ሶማሌ። እነዚህ ልዩ ትኩረት ተደርጎባቸው ከተቀመጡ የሃብት ክፍል ቀመር በተጨማሪ እገዛ ይደረግላቸዋል። አራቱ ክልሎች ሴሎችን በልማት ቶሎ እንዲደርሱባቸው ማድረግ ይገባል ብሎ ማሰብ ትክክል ይሆናል። ከእነዚህ አራቱ ጋር በዕድገት ተመሳሳይ ደረጃ ላይ ያሉ በሴሎችም ክልሎች እንደማይታጡ ያስተውሏል።

ይሁን እንጂ ከእነዚህ ውስጥ ሁለቱ ብቻ (ማለትም አፋርና ሶማሌ) የተፈለገውን ፈጣን ለውጥ ያስመዘገቡ ሲሆን ጋምቤላና ቤንሻንጉል ከላይ ከተጠቀሰው አማካይ ዕድገት በታች ነው ያስመዘገቡት። ለምን? ሰውን ለማልማት ከፋይናንስና መሰል ሃብት ሴላ ዐቅም፤ የምርት መገለገያዎች ክፍልና መልካም አስተዳደር ወሳኝ ናቸው። ልማት ሃብት ስለ ተመደበ ብቻ የሚገኝ አይደለም።

ጋምቤላና ቤንሻንጉል እንደ ሴሎች ታዳጊ ክልሎች ትኩረት ተሰጥቷቸዋል ቢባልም የሃብት አስተዳደር ሥርዓታቸው ከላይ በተጠቀሱት ነገሮች ዙሪያ ብዙ ችግሮች ነበሩባቸው። ጋምቤላ በጉሣዎች መካከል እንዲከሰት በተደረገ ክፍፍል ምክንያት መረጋጋት አልቻለም። ቤንሻንጉልም እንደዚሁ፤ ሕዝቡ ዳር ዳሩን፤ ዋና ከተማዋ ሕዝቡን ትታ ፎቅ ፎቁን።

ከልማት ይልቅ፤ በሁለቱም ክልሎች የተገለጠ፤ ግን መነገር የማይፈልግ ህጸጽ አለ። ፈረንጆች "የሳሎን ውስጥ ዝሆን" ይሉታል። ክልሎቹ ራሳቸውን በራሳቸው አስተዳደሩ ተባለ። በአንጻሩ ስፊ የምሬት ሃብት ያላቸው ስለሆነ፤ ለኢንቨስትመንት እንዲያጋጁና ለፌደራል መንግሥቱ "ውክልና" እንዲሰጡ ታዘዙ። የተሻለ የማስተዳደር ዐቅም አለኝ ባይ ነውና።

---

195 UNDP. (2020). Ethiopia: Sub National Human Development Index.

በዚህ ዐይነት አሠራር ብቻ፤ ለምሳሌ፡- በጋምቤላ ክልል ብቻ ወደ 370 ሺህ ሄክታር የሚጠጋ መሬት በዚህ መልክ 400 ለሚደርሱ "ባለ ሀብቶች" ተከፋፍሏል። ለእያንዳንዱ በአማካይ ወደ አንድ ሺህ ሄክታር ገደማ። ይህ ከክልሉ ጠቅላላ ስፋት ውስጥ አምስተኛ እጅ እንደ ማለት ነው።[196]

ካሩቱሪ ግሎባል ይባላል። ህንድ ውስጥ የተመዘገበ ኩባንያ ነው። በኢትዮጵያ የአበባ ምርት እንቅስቃሴ ሲጀመር አበባ ለማምረት ከኬንያ ተነሥተው ከገቡት ኩባንያዎች መካከል ነው። በሆላታ እና ወሊሶ ያሉት 80 ሄክታር በሚያህል መሬት የተተከሉ የኩባንያው አበባ ምርቶች በመጠኑ ወደ ውጭ ይላካሉ።

ካሩቱሪ ጋምቤላን አስገድደው ከደፈሩ የውጭ አገራት ኩባንያዎች ውስጥ ቀንደኛው ነው። በአፍሪካ ውስጥ እስከ 400 ሺህ ሄክታር መሬት ለማልማት ተነስቻለሁ፤ ከዚህም ውስጥ ግማሽ ያህሉን ኢትዮጵያ፤ በጋምቤላ ክልል ሰጠችኝ ሲል ለዓለም ነዛ፤ እውነትም፤ በሄክታር እጅግ አናሳ በሚባል ኪራይ፤ የቤልጅየምን ያህል የቆዳ ስፋት ያለው መሬት አበረከተችለት። ከባንክ ብድርና እስከ 100 ፐርሰንት ከሚደርስ የቀረጥ ነጻ መብት ጋር።[197]

ምንም ሳይከፍል ካገኘው መሬት ግማሽ ደን ጨፍጭፎ፤ ወና አድርጎ ሲያበቃ፤ የረባ ነገር ሳያመርት ቆይቶ፤ በጥሪት ገበያው ሀብቱ ይመንደግ ጀመር። ምን አለፋው? የኢትዮጵያ መንግሥት ከብዙ ንትርክ በኋላ መሬቱን ቀማው። ባጉራስኩ፤ ተነክስኩ የሚባለው አልቀረም። ይባስ ብሎ አገሪቱን በኢንቨስትመንት ግዴታ ባለሚሚላት ከሰሳት። ጉዳዩ እስከ ዛሬ (2022 ዓ.ም) ድረስ አልተቋጨም።

ይህና መሠል ኢንቨስትመንቶች በእርግጥ አገር ለመጥቀም ነው ወይ ብሎ መጠየቁ አስፈላጊ ነው። የውጭ ኢንቨስትመንት ይፈለጋል። አገር እያከሰሰ ለራሱ የሚጠረቃ ግን አያስፈልግም። ይህ የውድድር ሜዳ ነው። በፍትሐዊነት የተወዳደረ ቢያተርፍ ችግር የለውም። መሠረቱ በውል ሳይታወቅ የአገር ሃብትን የተቆናጠጡ ግን ምርታቸው ድኽነት ነው።

ካሩቱሪ ግሎባል ወደ ኢትዮጵያ በ2004 ዓ.ም ሲገባ በገበያ የነበረው የድርጅቱ የአንድ ሼር ዋጋ በሙምባይ የካፒታል ገበያ 1.06 ብቻ ነበር። በ2009 ዓ.ም የጋምቤላን መሬት እንዳገኘ ምንም ነገር ሳያመርት መሬቱ ብቻ በሥራለት የገበያ ማስታወቂያ የሼር ዋጋው አራት እጥፍ ያህል ጣሪያ በርቅሶ በመውጣት ወደ 22.95 ደርሶ ነበር። ጋምቤላ ከዚህ ትርፉት ምንም አልደረሳትም።

196 Gebresenbet F. Land Acquisitions, the Politics of Dispossession, and State-Remaking in Gambella, Western Ethiopia. Africa Spectrum. 2016;51(1):5-28.

197 IDE. (2022). Karuturi Global Limited. Institute of Developing Economies; African Growing Enterprises. Accessed on January 10, 2022, from https://www.ide.go.jp/English/Data/Africa_file/Company/ethiopia03.html

ጠቅላይ ሚንስትር ሃይለ ማርያም ሥልጣን ከያዙ ጀምሮ በሙስና ላይ ከተነሣው ያዝ ለቀቅ ዘመቻ ተከትሎ ካራቱሪም ሠርቶ እንዲከብርና እንዲያስከብር ጫና ተደረገበት። በዚህ መካከል በተነሣው አተካራ፣ በ2017 ዓ.ም ድርጅቱ ከኢትዮጵያ መንግሥት ጋር ተጣላ። በዚህ መሠረት መሬቱን ሲቀማ የድርጅቱ ሼር ተመልሶ ከ15 ዓመት በፊት ወደ ነበረበት ወደቀ።

ዛሬ የኩባንያው ሼር በሙምባይ የካፒታል ገበያ 0.24 ብቻ ቢሸጥም ገዢ የለውም።[198] እንደ እነዚህ ካሉ ኩባንያዎች ጋር የሚያወዳጅ የአገር ዕድገት ትልም ሊሆን አይችልም። ጉርሻ ፍለጋ እንዳይሆን ያስብላል።

የፌደራል መንግሥት "ውክልና" በመውሰድ፣ ልማትን ሳይሆን የመሬት ቅርምትን ያስፋፋ እንደ ነበር ቆይቶ የተገለጠ ሀቅ ነበር። ካሩቱሪ ግዙፍ ስለ ነበር ታየ እንጂ የማይታይ ብዙ ዘረፋ ተከናውኗል። ያለውን የተፈጥሮ ሃብት የመቀራመት ዘመቻ ሃብትን ከማሳደግ ይልቅ የበለጠ ትኩረት ተሰጠው። ዳቦው እየሰፋ እንዲሄድ ከማድረግ ይልቅ ያለውን ለመቦጥቦጥ ቅድሚያ ተሰጠ።

በእነዚህ ክልሎች፣ ሰከን ያለ ልማት ለመሥራት ዕድል እስከማይገኝ ድረስ የመሬት ዝርፊያው ገናና ነበር። በተለይም የሰው ሃብት ልማት በእነዚህ ክልሎች ትኩረት ተነፍጎት ቆይቷል። ለነገሩ ሰው ከለማ ነገሮችን ማሰላሰል ይጀምራል፤ ይጠይቃልም። ኮሳሳ ሆኖ ቢቆይ ለብዝበዛ ይመቻል።

የፌደራሉም መንግሥት እምብዛም አልጠረቃ። የተቦጨቀው የሄደበት ሌላ ሥፍራ ነበርና። በተለይም፣ የእርሻ ኢንቨስትመንት አለን የሚሉ ሁሉ በልዩ ሁኔታ ከኢትዮጵያ ልማት ባንክ ብድር ይመቻችላቸው ነበርና። ይህ ባንክ ደግሞ በኢትዮጵያ የፋይናንስ ዘርፍ ልቅ ብድርን ያስተማረ ነው እየተባለ ይታማል።

ምክንያቱም የሌሎች ባንኮች ሁሉ የማይሠራ ወይም የተበላሸ ብድር ተደምሮ ካበደሩት ገንዘብ 2.7 በመቶ ብቻ እንደሆነ መረጃዎች ያመለክታሉ። ጥንቁቅ እና ጽኑ የብድር ፖሊሲ እንደሚከተሉ አመልካች ነው። የልማት ባንክ ሲጨመርበት የአገሪቱ የማይሠራ ወይም የተበላሸ ብድር ምጣኔ ወደ 5.5 በመቶ ያሻቅባል።[199] ከእጥፍ በላይ። ሌሎች ባንኮች ሁሉ ተደምረው አንድ ሲያበላሹ ልማት ባንክ ሁለት ብድር ያበላሽ ዘንድ ፈቃድ ተሰጥቶት ይሆን?

---

198 Money Central. (2022). Karuturi Global Ltd. Historical Data for the Period 2004-22 on BSE. www.moneycontrol.com/stocks/hist_stock_result.php?ex=B&sc_id=KF10&mycomp=Karuturi%20Global

199 IMF. (2019). The Federal Democratic Republic of Ethiopia: Technical Assistance Report-Financial Soundness Indicators Mission. Volume 2020, Issue 323. Accessed on March 19, 2022, from https://www.elibrary.imf.org/view/journals/002/2020/323/article-A001-en.xml

ፈርጀ ብዙ ድኽነት

ልማትንም ሆነ ድኽነትን በአንድ ጠቋሚ መገለጫ ብቻ ገልጠን አንጨርሰውም፤ ሌሎችን እንዩ። ዓመታዊው የኦክስፎርድ ድኽነትና ልማተሰብዕ ጥናት እንደሚጠቁመው፣ በአሥር የተለያዩ የድኽነት መስፈርቶች ሲመዘን ከኢትዮጵያ ሕዝብ 70 በመቶ[200] ያህሉ በፈርጀ ብዙ ድኽነት ይማቅቃል። ሰማንያ ሚሊዮን ድኽ ሕዝብ፤ ማለትም በፈርጀ ብዙ ድኽነት የሚማቅቅ ሕዝብ።

በአንጻሩ ግብፅ ከኢትዮጵያ ተቀራራቢ ጠቅላላ ሕዝብ ሲኖራት በፈርጀ ብዙ ድኽነት መዳፍ የሚገኙት ከ 6 ሚሊዮን አይበልጡም። እኛ ከአራትና ከዚያ በላይ እጥፍ ከግብፅ ወደ ኋላ ነን ማለት ነው። ጉረቤታችን ኬንያ የእኛ ግማሽ ያህል ሕዝብ አላት። ከላይ በተጠቀሰው ቀመር መሠረት የኬንያ ፈርጀ ብዙ ድኽነት ጠቋሚ 0.171 ብቻ ነው።

ይህን ከኢትዮጵያ ጠቋሚ 0.367 ጋር ስናነሰታያይ አንድ ኢትዮጵያዊ ከአንድ ኬንያዊ ጋር ሲነፃፀር በድኽነት የመማቀቅ ዕድሉ መቶ በመቶ ይጨምራል። በኍጥርም ደረጃ፣ ኬንያ አንድ ድኽ ቢኖራት ኢትዮጵያ አራት አላት ማለት ነው። ግብፅ አንድ ድኽ ቢኖራት ኢትዮጵያ ሃያ የሚጠጋ ታስፈልፈች። ይህ ቀላል ተደርጎ መወሰድ የለበትም።

ፈርጀ ብዙ ድኽነት ስንል፣ የሰውን ልጅ መሠረታዊ የመኖር መብቶች ለማሟላት አለመቻል ማለት ነው። በልቶ ማደር፣ ልጅ ወልዶ ማሳደግ መቻል፣ መደበኛ ትምህርት ማግኘትና ምቹ የመኖሪያ ሥፍራና መገለገያዎች የማግኘት እና የመሳሰሉ ጉዳዮች እንጂ ቅንጦት እያወራን አይደለም። ለሕዝባችን ይህንን ማሟላት አልቻልንም። ሰባ በመቶ ሕዝባችን ይህ መብት የለውም።

የሕዝብ ቁጥራቸው ብዙ ስለሆነ፣ በፈርጀ ብዙ ድኽነት መዳፍ ከሚገኙት ሰዎች ውስጥ አብዛኞች የሚገኙት በኦሮሚያ፣ አማራና ደቡብ ሕዝቦች (የቀድሞው) ክልል ነው። ይህ ደግሞ ይበልጥ አሳሳቢው ነው። እንዚህ የአገሪቱ "ዋና ዋና" የሚባሉ ክልሎች ናቸው። ያለ ምንም ጥያቄ በሌሎች ክልሎች ይብሳል ማለት ነው። ለምሳሌ፦ በሶማሊና በአፋር 90 ከመቶ ሕዝብ ከፈርጀ ብዙ ድኽነት ወለል በታች ይገኛል።

በኦሮሚያ ብቻ ያለው ያጣ የነጣ ድኽ ቁጥር ጠቅላላውን የኬንያ ሕዝብ ብዛት ይጠጋል። ጉረቤትስ እንዴት ያየናል ወገን? ኦሮሚያ የአገሪቱ ትልቅ ክልል፣ አብዛኛው የአገሪቱ ሃብት የተከማቸበት ሆኖ በክልሉ ያሉ ሰዎች ለምን ከሌላው የተሻለ

200 Alkire, S., Kanagaratnam, U. and Suppa, N. (2021). 'The Global Multidimensional Poverty Index (MPI) 2021', OPHI MPI Methodological Notes 51, Oxford Poverty and Human Development Initiative, University of Oxford.

የልማተሰብ ዕድገት ደረጃ መድረስ አልቻሉም ብሎ መጠየቅ ያስፈልጋል። ደግሞ እንጌሌ ይሻላል በማይባልበት ሕዝብ እርስ በርሱ እንዲባላ ፖለቲካውን ማጫቅየት ምን የሚሉት ድኸነት ነው?

ሌላ አንድ መመዘኛ እናክል። የነፍስ ወከፍ ገቢ ዕድገትን በተመለከተ የአክስፎርድ ድኸነት ጥናት ኢንስቲትዩት እንደሚያስቀምጠው፣ ባለፉት 20 ዓመታት በኢ.ትዮጵያ የግል ገቢ በ17 ከመቶ ብቻ ነው የጨመረው። ሻል ያለ ዕድገት በታየባቸው በአዲስ አበባና ሐረር ከተሞች ብቻ ይህ ዕድገት ወደ 20 ከመቶ ተጠግቷል። ማለትም፣ በየዓመቱ የአንድ ሰው ደመወዝ 1 ከመቶ ብቻ ሲጨምር በሉት።

እጅግ አናሣ የገቢ ዕድገት የተመዘገበው ደግሞ ደቡብና ሶማሊ ክልል ነው። ደቡብ አንድ ከመቶ ዓመታዊ ዕድገትም ብርቅ ሆኖበታል። በዚህ መስፈርት መሠረት ደቡብ ምናልባት እየደኸየ ሂዷል ቢባል ያስኬዳል። ሶማሊ እንኳን በተደጋጋሚ በድርቅ እየተመታ፣ በዚያውም የጸጥታ እና የመልካም አስተዳደር ችግር እያጋጠመው በመሆኑ ነው እንበል። የደቡብን ምን እንበለው?

ባለፉት ጥቂት ዓመታት የኢትዮጵያ ፖለቲካዊ ኤኮኖሚ ዳቦውን በማሳደግ እና በማወፈር ላይ የረባ ነገር አልሠራም። በዳቦው ክፍል ላይ ከፍተኛ ትኩረት በሚጥል ፖሊሲ የኤኮኖሚው አሠራር እና አመራር ተቃኝቷል። ያጣላን የነበረው ምን ያህል ተመረተ የሚለው ሳይሆን ማን ምን አገኘ የሚለው ብቻ እንደ ነበር እናስተውል።

የሃብትና በተለይም የምርት መገልገያዎች ክፍል በብሔር ብቻ ተብሎ በአንድ ትንፋሽ በመወሰን ድኸነትን በተዓምራዊ መንገድ ለማስወገድ አይቻልም። አገራዊ ፋይዳ ያለው ልማት እንዲኖር የልማት ችግሮችን በውል ባገነዘበ። አንዱ ከሌላው ጋር በምን መልክ እንደ ተቄዋሩን እያጤኑ መሆን እንዳለበት ማስረጽ አስፈላጊ ነው። ሃብትና ክህሎት በጎነት መንቀሳቀስ በማይችልበት ሥፍራ ሁሉ የኤኮኖሚ ቅሸባ (ቅልጥፍና ማጣት) አይቀሬ ነውና።

ክልሎች አንዱ ከሌላው ጋር በልማት ሲወዳደሩ ወይም ሲተባበሩ አናይም። የተሻለ መዋዕለ ንዋይ ለማጋበዝ፣ የተሻለ አገልግሎት ለመስጠት፣ ዐቅም ፈጥሮ የመገናኘት፣ ደህንነትና ጥበቃ፣ የሃብት ከለላን አስቀድሞ መሥራት፣ ... ወዘተርፈ የሚባል ነገር አይስተዋልም። ወይንም ሰጥቶ መቀበልና መተጋገዝ አይዘወተርም። ይልቁንም፣ በደቡ ተነስቶ የሰው ሃብት መዝረፍ፣ ማቃጠል፣ በቢሮክራሲያዊ ጫና ሥራ እንዳይፈጠር፣ ወይም እንዲተጓጎል ጉልቶ ይወራል።

ዓለትና ድቡሸት

የአንድ አገር ኤኮኖሚ ፖሊሲ ግብ ዕድገትንና አጠቃላይ ልማትን ማምጣት ነው። ርቱዕ ፖሊሲ ደግሞ ከፖለቲካ አመለካከት፣ ከሥራ አመራር ብልኃት፣ የወደፊቱን አጥርቶ ከማየት ጥበብ፣ እንዲሁም ከፍትሐዊ አስተዋይነት የሚመነጭ ገፅ ዕሳብ ነው። ፖሊሲ ከሰማይ የወረደ ብቻኛ መንገድ አይደለም፣ ከአግራሮች የተመረጠ፣ ሊተገበር የሚችል፣ የተስፋ ፍኖት ያለው መርኆ ግብር እንጂ።

በኤኮኖሚ ፖሊሲ አስተሳሰብ የደረጀው ጥበብ አጠቃላይ ልማትንና ዕድገትን የሚያመጣ የኤኮኖሚ ፖሊሲ ጥቂቶችን በአብላጫነት የሚጠቅም እንኳን ቢሆን ተመራጭ ነው የሚል ነው።[201] ዕድገትና ክፍፍል አይመሳቀሉም፣ ይልቁንም፣ በአብላጫው ከተጠቀሙት ላይ ጥቂት ተቆንጥሮ ትሩፋቱ ላልደረሳቸው ማቃመስ ወይም ማካፈል አስተዳደራዊ ኃላፊነት ስለሆነ።

ስለዚህ በጤናማ የኤኮኖሚ ፖሊሲ ቅኝት የራስ ጥቅምን ብቻ የሚፈጥር ወይም የሚያነላ አድርጐ መቅረዝ ነውር ነው። ጥቅም አይጠላም፣ ይሁን እንጂ አንድንም አካል ያለ አግባብ ከጉዳ፣ ፖሊሲው ውድቅ ነው። የፖለቲካዊ ኤኮኖሚው ፍትሐዊነት ጥርነት የሚጀምረው ከዚህ ነው። በመጀመሪያ የትኛውም ቡድን ጉዳት እንዲያገናው አይፈልግም፣ ቢቻል ተጠቃሚ ለመሆን እንጂ።

በእርግጥ 'እኔን ብቻ እንዲጠቅም ፖሊሲ ቀርጭለሁ' የሚል የፖለቲካዊ ኤኮኖሚ ጐይል የለም። በብዙ አገራት፣ ዋናው የፍትሐዊነት ችግር የተሻለ ያገኙ ወገኖች ቀርጦ መክፈል አለመፈለጋቸው ነው። ብቻቸውን ሥርተው ያመጡ ስለሚመስላቸው ማካፈል አይሆንላቸውም፣ መንግሥትን የደጐሙ ይመስላቸዋል። በተለይም፣ ጥቅም ሲያገኙ ሌላውን አለመጉዳታቸውን ካረጋገጡ፣ አካኪ ዘራፍ ይላሉ። ፍትሕ አሳንደሉም።

መንግሥትም ከዚህ የተነሣ አጣብቂኝ ውስጥ ይገባል። የ''ስጠኝ' አልሰጥህም'' እስጥ አገባ። አገራዊ ራእይ ላነገበ ፖለቲከኛ ቀዳሚው ጥያቄ ''ለየትኛው ቡድን ባደላ አገርን እንደ ፖለቲካ ፕሮጀክት ማስቀጠል እችላለሁ?'' የሚለው ይሆናል። የበረታም ለሕዝብ የሚጠቅም ፖሊሲ ከመቅረጽ አንጻር ማን ምን ያግኝ የሚለውን ያሰላስላል። አብዛኛውን ጊዜ ግን መልካም የሆኑ የፖሊሲ አማራጮች በበረቱ ጥቅም ፈላጊዎች በጐ ፈቃድ ይጠለፋሉ።

የፖለቲካው አመለካከት ወደ ዘረኝነት ወይም ጐሠኝነት ካዘመመ የፖሊሲ ምርጫ መልሱ ቀላል ነው። የእኔ የሆነው ጐሣ ያገኛል። ሌላው ያፈጣል፣ ዘረኝነት የፖለቲካ

---

201 Stigler, G. J. (1975). The Goals of Economic Policy. The Henry Simons Lecture; The University of Chicago Law School. The Journal of Law & Economics, Vol. 18. No. 2. October 1975. pp. 283-292. Accessed on March 19, 2022, from https://chicagounbound. uchicago.edu/cgi/viewcontent.cgi?article=1625&context=lsr

ኤኮኖሚውን የሚያዛንፈው ከመሠረቱ ላይ ነው። ከፖሊሲ መነሻነት ፍትሕ ዐልባነትን ይገነባል። እንዳይዘዘምም ለማድረግ ውሳኔ፣ ፍላጎት እና ዐቅም ካለ ግን ቅጫ ብሎ በመወያየት፣ ለዛሬም ባይሆን በረኸም ጊዜም ቢሆን የጉንጮሽ ጉዳትን የሚቀንስ ፖሊሲ መቅረጽ ይቻላል።

ብሔር ማለት አገር ቢሆን ኖሮ ብሔርተኛ የኤኮኖሚ ፖሊሲን ትክክለኝነት ማስረዳት ከባድ አይሆንም። የአንድ አገር ኤኮኖሚ ፖሊሲ የአገር ውስጥ ምርትና ሃብትን ማሳደግን ያስቀድማልና። ነገር የሚመሳቀለው በአንድ አገር ክልዩነት ዕሳቤ በመነሣት የሚያስማማ ፖሊሲ ለመንደፍ ሲሞከር ነው። 'አንተ ትንሽ ቆይና እኔ ልደግ' ሲባል ውሉ ይጠፋል።

ለምሳሌ፦ የውጭ ንግድን ብንመለከት፣ ለአገር ጠቃሚ ፖሊሲ እንዴት እንደሚቀረጽ ማስረዳት ቀላል ነው። የነጻ ገበያ ሥርዓትን የሚከተሉ እንኳን በነጻ ገበያ ውስጥ አገርን የሚጠቅም ፖሊሲ መቅረጽ እንዴት ጠቃሚ እንደሆነ ማሳየት አይቸግራቸውም። ብዙ ሰዎች በአገር ውስጥም ሆነ ከውጭ ገበያ ጋር ነጻ የኤኮኖሚ ውድድር እንዲኖር የውድድር ብልጫ ማለትም ፍጹም የበላይነት ያለው ምርት ወይም አገልግሎት ሊኖር የሚገባ ይመስላቸዋል።

ይህ ግን አስፈላጊ አይሆንም። ቀደምት ኤኮኖሚ ሊቆች እንዳመለከቱት፣ ፍጹም ብልጫ ሳይሆን ተነጻጻሪ ጥቅም የሚያስገኝ ብልጫ ካለ ለነጻ ውድድር በቂ መሥፈርት ነው። ለምሳሌ፦ የአልማዝ ማዕድን ያለው አገር ወደ ሌላ የአልማዝ ማዕድን የማይገኝበት አገር ምርትን መሸጥ መቻል ነጻ ውድድር አለ አያስብልም። ከተፈጥሮ የተነሣ ፍጹም የውድድር ብልጫ የሚገኝበት ንግድ ነውና።

ፍጹም ሳይሆን፣ ተነጻጻሪ ብልጫ ለንግድ በቂ ነው። ተነጻጻሪ ብልጫን ለማስረዳት ምሳሌ እንውሰድ። አንድ አገር በቆሎ ያመርታል እንበል። ነገር ግን በቆሎ በርካሽ የሚያመርት ጉራቤት አገር ካለ ከዚያ ለማግኘት ሲወስን፣ በአንጻሩ ደግሞ ሌላ በንጽጽር ሻል ባለ ዋጋ የሚያመርተውን ነገር በልዋጭ ቢሰጥ ተነጻጻሪ ጥቅም ፈለገ ይባላል። ይህ ምርት ስንዴ ነው ብንል፣ አንዱ ስንዴ ላይ፣ ሌላው በቆሎ በማምረት ቢያተኩሩ የጋራ ተጠቃሚ ይሆናሉ።[202]

በገበያ ውስጥ ተዋናይ ሲበዛ ግን ነገሮች ሁሉ እንዲህ ቀላል አይኑም። የጋራ ተጠቃሚነትን ባጉላ ነጻ ውድድር ውስጥ የአንድን ሉዓላዊ አገር ጥቅም ለማስከበር፣ አጥርቶ መደምደም፣ ለይቶ ማጠርም ይጠበቃል። ገና ብቅ ሲል እንዳይደፈቅ የጨቅላ ኢንዱስትሪዎች ጥበቃ ተብሎ የሚታወቀው ሥርዓት ከዚህ ዕሳቤ የመነጨ ነው።

202 Siddiqui, K. (2018). David Ricardo's Comparative Advantage and Developing Countries: Myth and Reality. International Critical Thought, Vol 8, issue 3. Pages: 426-452. Accesed on February 28, 2022, from https://pure.hud.ac.uk/ws/files/14132571/David_Ricardo_s_Comparative_Trade_Theory.pdf

ለምሳሌ፡- ኢትዮጵያ ከውጭ የሚመጣውን የምግብ ዘይት ሙሉ በሙሉ በአገር ውስጥ ለማምረት ፖሊሲ ቀረጸች እንበል። ይህን እንዱስትሪ ለመጠበቅና ለመከላል፣ ከውጭ በሚመጡ ዘይትና የዘይት ተዋጽዖዎች ላይ ከፍተኛ ቀረጥና አስተዳደራዊ አሽክላዎች ማድረጃ ያስፈልግ ይሆናል። በተጨማሪም ለአገር ውስጥ አምራቾች የገንዘብና ሌሎችም ድጎማዎች በመስጠት ጉልበታቸውን ማፈርጠም ይቻላል።

ይህ አሠራር በተለይ በከፍተኛ ኢንዱስትሪዎች ደረጃ በብዙ አገራት፣ የነጻ ገበያ ሥርዓት እንከተላለን በሚሉም ጭምር፣ በጠራ ፀሐይ የሚከወን ድርጊት ነው። ይህ ግን ፈር እንዳይለቅ ዓለም አቀፍ ሕግ አለ፣ የዓለም የንግድ ድርጅት ብዙ የቁጥጥር ተግባራትን ያከናውናል። ምክንያቱም፣ የአገራት የንግድ ሚዛን ጉዳት በሚያስከትል መጠን እጅግም እንዳይዛባ ማድረጃ እምብዛም ክርክር አያስነሳም።[203]

በአገራት መካከል፣ የንግድንም ሆነ ዲፕሎማሲያዊ ልውውጥ የሚቃኝ ሥርዓት እና ድንበር ማበጀት ይቻላል። እንዲያውም፣ አንድ አገር ሆነ ብሎ የንግድ ጥቅም ለማግኘት ሲል ልዩ ጥበቃ የሚያደርግበት የኤኮኖሚ አቅጣጫ ሊያበጅ እንደሚችል ብዙዎች ይስማማሉ። ነጹ ውድድር የሚደገፉ ሊቃውንት እንኳን ሳይቀሩ ይህን መሰል ጥበቃ የጨቅላ ወይም የታዳጊ ኢንዱስትሪዎች ከለላ ሲሉ ያሞካሹታል።[204]

በአንድ አገር የውስጥ ፖለቲካ ብሔርተኝነት አለ ሲባልሳ? የጎሣ ፖለቲካ በሚያራምዱ አገራት፣ ማንኛውም የአገሪቱ መገለጫ በብሔር የተቃኘ ይሆናል። ወደ አፈጻጸም ሲወርድ፣ የኤኮኖሚውን ሥሪት በብሔር ቅኝት መቀየር ዋናው ግብ ይሆናል። ብሔር ለሁሉ ነገር ቅድሚያ ተሰጥቶ የሚሰደር ዐሳብ ነው ተብሎ ስለሚታሰብ፣ ኤኮኖሚው በተለመዱት ሕግጋት እንዲመራ ዕድል አይሰጠውም።

በተለይም፣ በጎሣ ፖለቲካ ሥርዓት አንድ ጎሣ አሸንፎ ሥልጣን ሲይዝ ኤኮኖሚውንም ሥልጣን ለያዘው አካል በሚመች እንደሚቀረጽ ይጠበቃል። ባያደርገው ስንኳ እንደዚያ ይጌጠራል። ይህ ደግሞ "በስምህ ሥልጣን ያዝኩልህ" የተባለት ቡድኖች ሁሉ የሚፈልጉት አካሄድ ስለሆነ የአንድ አገር የጋራ ስምምነት ይናፋል። የፖለቲካ መሠረት ከሚሆኑት ነገሮች መካካል ዋነኛው ተጣሰ ማለት ነው።

በጎሣዎች መካከል ፋክክርን (ይባስ ብሎም ጥላቻን) ዘርቶ ከሚመነጭ ድል የሚነሣ ፖለቲካ ኤኮኖሚውን ደግሞ በጎሣዎች መካከል ባል ድርድር ወይም ዲፕሎማሲ መምራት አይችልም። ያለው አማራጭ አግላይነት ብቻ ነው። አግላይነት ደግሞ ፍትሕ ያዛባል። ስለዚህ በኤኮኖሚ ዕይታ ረገድ ጎሠኝነትና ዘረኝነት እምብዛም ልዩነት የላቸውም <u>የሚባለው ከዚህ የተነሣ ነው።</u>

203 Rodrik, D. (2021). A Primer on Trade and Inequality Working Paper 29507 National Bureau of Economic Research 1050 Massachusetts Avenue Cambridge, MA 02138 November 2021. Http://Www.Nber.Org/Papers/W29507

204 Grubel, H. G. (1966). The Anatomy of Classical and Modern Infant Industry Arguments. Weltwirtschaftliches Archiv Bd. 97 (1966); pp. 325-344; Springer

የዘረኝነት ፖለቲካዊ ኤኮኖሚ አንድን ሰው በቆዳ ቀለም ለይቶ የምርት መገልገያዎችና አገልግሎቶች ተደራሽ ወይም ተነፋጊ ማድረግ ነው። ጉሠኝነትም ቅኝቱ በጉሣ ከፍሎ መንፈግ እስከሆነ ድረስ ከዚህ አይለይም። የቆዳ ቀለም የሚለው መመዘኛ ይቀራል። ነገር ግን በሌሎች አግላይ መለኪያዎች ከሰዎች መካከል የእኔ ነው ያሉትን ለይቶ ተደራሽ ወይም ተጠቃሚ ያደርጋል።

ብሔርተኞች ዋንኛ ስብከታቸው የብሔር ማንነት (በተለይም ቋንቋና ባሕል) ቀዳሚ የፖለቲካ መገለጫ ነው የሚል ነው። ነገር ግን የብሔሮች ልዩነት ፖለቲካን ወለደ የሚለው ዐሳብ በጭንቅላቱ የቆመ ነው፤ እግርን ወደ ሰማይ አንሥቶ። ማንነት የፖለቲካ መሠረት ሳይሆን፤ ማንነትን ለፖለቲካ መሣሪያ አድርጎ መጠቀም የተለመደው መንገድ ነው። ሆኖም፤ የትናንቱን ስብራት እናስተካክለን እያሉ መልሶ በማዘባት የቀደመውን ስንተት የሚደግሙም መልስ ዐልባ ናቸው።

የፖለቲካ ትንተና ዓላማችን ስላይደለ ይህን እንለፈው። መሠመር ያለበት ነገር ግን፤ የኤኮኖሚ ጥቅም ተደራሽነት ወይም ተነፋጊነት ከቆዳ ቀለም ይልቅ በተውልድ ሥፍራ ወይም በባሕል ልዩነት መሆኑ አሥራሩን የተሻለ ስም አያሰጠውም፤ ያው ዘረኝነት ነው፤ አግላይነት ነው። ምንም መልካም ስም ልንሰጠው ብንሞክር፤ በፖለቲካዊ ኤኮኖሚ ዐይታ ጉሠኝነት (ማለትም ብሔርተኝነት) እና ዘረኝነት እምብዛም ልዩነት የላቸውም።

ታዲያ ይህን ጠንካራ ትችት ለመሸሽ ሲሉ አንዳንዶች ጉሠኝነት ለኤኮኖሚ ጠቃሚ ነው የሚል ክርክር ያቀርባሉ።[205] ኤኮኖሚው በጉሣ ፖለቲካ መስመር ሲመራ፤ ማንነትን ለማሳለጥ በሚደረግ ቅንነት የተሞላ ፉክክር ስለሚታጀብ ዕድገትና ልማትን ያፋጥናል የሚል ዕይታ አላቸው።[206] መከባበር ሲኖር ኢንቨስትመንት ድፍረት ያገኛል፤ ያተርፋልም፤ ይላሉ።[207]

እንዲሁም፤ በውድድር መንፈስ ኤኮኖሚን ከማነቃቃት ዐልፎ የተሻለ የሃብት ክፍፍል ስለሚኖር በተረሱ አካባቢዎች የመንግሥት አገልግሎትን ለማዳረስ ስለሚረዳ፤ በአጠቃላይ ጥሩ ነው የሚሉ አሉ። በእርግጥ ብሔርተኝነት ዕድገትን ያሳልጣል? "አዎን" የሚሉ፤ ኢትዮጵያን ጭምር እንደ ምሳሌ ይወስዳሉ። ለምሣሌ በታዳጊ

205 Weingast, B. R. (1995). The Economic Role of Political Institutions: MarketPreserving Federalism and Economic Development; Journal of Law, Economics & Organizations; Volume1, 5-8 (1995).

206 Gebre Selassie, A. (2003). Ethnic Federalism: Its Promise and Pitfalls for Africa. College of William & Mary Law School William & Mary Law School Scholarship Repository. Faculty Publications. 88. Accessed on March 19, 2022; from https://scholarship.law.wm.edu/facpubs/88

207 Rodden, J. & Rose-Ackerman, S. (1997). Does Federalism Preserve Markets? 83 Virginia Law Reviews; 1521 (1997).

ክልሎች የሚታየው አንጻራዊ የአገልግሎት መሻሻል በዚህ ፖሊሲ ምክንያት ነው ብለው ለማስረዳት ምክረዋል።[208]

የብሔር ጥያቄን በመገፋት እውነታ መነሻነት አንግበው፣ ሥፍራ ሲያገኙ ፖለቲካውን በመግፋት እውነታ ላይ ለመመሥረት የሚፈልጉ ፖለቲከኞች ሲኖሩ ጥቂት ያስከፋል። ምክንያቱም፣ ይህ የሚሆነው የተሻለ ፍኖት በማጣት ሳይሆን ጥያቄውን የግል ጥቅም ለማሳደድ ስለሚጠቀሙ ነው። በጭቆና ቀንበር ስር ያለፉ፣ ለተወሰነ ጊዜ የጥቅም ማስተካከያ ማድረግ ቢያስፈልግና ቢተገበር እንኳን፣ ከአግላይነት ይልቅ፣ መተጋገዝንና መተቃቀፍን ቢመርጡ ልዕልና ነበር።

ጥልቅ ጥናቶች እንደሚያመለክቱት አግላይነት አሉታዊ ውጤት አለው፤ እንዲያውም ዘላቂ አሉታዊ ውጤት። በ2013 ዓ.ም በደቡብ አፍሪካ የተደረገ አንድ ትልቅ የኢኮኖሚ ጉባዔ ላይ በቀረቡ በርካታ ትልቅ ጥናቶች በመመርኮዝ በተደረሰው መደምደሚያ፣ አግላይ የኢኮኖሚ ተደራሽነት ዘላቂ የኢኮኖሚ ልዩነትን ያስከትላል።[209] ይህ ደግሞ በደቡብ አፍሪካ ብቻ አይደለም።

በአሜሪካ ከጥቁሮች ሴቶች የሚወለዱ ሕጻናት ክብደታቸው ከነጭ ሴቶች ልጆች ጋር ሲነጻጸር እናሳ ነው። አልፎ ተርፎም፣ ጥቁር ሴቶች እና ልጆቻቸው አነስተኛውን የክብደት መጠን እንኳ ሳያሟሉ የሚወለዱ እንደሆን ከተረጋገጠ ቆይቷል። ያለ በቂ የክብደት መጠን የሚወለዱ ሕጻናት ደግሞ ዕድሜያቸውን በሙሉ በተለያዩ በሽታዎች ይጠቃሉ።

እንግዲህ በአካልም ሆነ በአዕምሮ መቀንጨር ብቻ ሳይሆን፣ እድሜ ልክ ችግር ተከናንቦ መወለድ የዘረኝነት ትሩፋት መሆኑ እሙን ነው። የዘር ጭቆናና ለዘላቂ ዘር ተኮር ችግር እንደሚዳርግ ሳይታለም የተፈታ ነውና። የቀነጨረ፣ ምናልባትም በአዕምሮም ጭምር ዘገምተኛ የሆነ፣ በሽተኛ፣ ሲያድግም የሥራ በር የሚከፈትለት እጅግ በጠባብ ነው።

ይህ ደግሞ በጥናት ተረጋግጧል። በቅርቡ ጥቁሮችን በማግለል ረገድ እስከ ዛሬ ድረስ ከሌላው እኩል መሻሻል ባልታየበት የደቡባዊ አሜሪካ ግዛቶች በተደረገ ጥናት፣ የጨቅላ ሕጻናት ክብደት መጠን እናቶች ለሥራ ካላቸው ተደራሽነት ጋር የተቄራኛ

208 Zimmermann-Steinhart, P. & Bekele, Y. (2012). The implications of federalism and decentralisation on socio-economic conditions in Ethiopia. Potchefstroom Electronic Law Journal; PER vol.15 n.2; Potchefstroom August 2012. Accessed on March 19, 2022; from http://www.scielo.org.za/scielo.php?script=sci_arttext&pid=S1727-37812012000200006

209 Mariotti, M. and Fourie, J. (2014). The economics of apartheid: An introduction. Economic History of Developing Regions; Volume 29, 2014 - Issue 2; Pages 113-125 | Published online: 29 Sep 2014

መሆኑ ታውቋል። [210] እንግዲህ ምግብ ማጣት አይደለም። ሥራ ማጣትም ከመዋቅራዊ አግላይነት ይነሣል።

ዘረኝነት ያስከተለው ጠንቅ ለትውልድ መቀንጨር ምክንያት ሆኖ ሳለ፤ አግላዮቹ የማይረዱት ነገር አለ። ችግሩ ዞሮ የማይነድፋቸው፣ ለእንዴም፤ ለመጨረሻም የተገባገሉት ይመስላቸዋል፣ አላስተዋሉም። የጥቁሮች ልጆች ይቀንጭሩ እንጂ፣ በእኛ እስካልደረሰ ድረስ ምን አገባን ብለው፤ እግር ዘርግተው፣ መቀመጥ እንደማይችሉ አልተረዱም።

ከማሕጸን ጀምሮ የተገለሉ ሕጻናትን ሰዎች ናቸውና ሲያድጉ፤ የሚያድግ አዕምሮ አላቸው። ያስባሉም። አግላይነት ጉልቶ፤ ባደጉም ጊዜ መዋቅራዊ ዘረኝነት እንደሚጠብቃቸው ይረዳሉ። እናም፤ ከዚህ ያፈጠጠ ጥቆና የመላቀቅ ፍላጉቱም አብዞቸው ያድጋል። ይህ ማለት ግን የተገለሉ ስለሆን ቅሣጣ የወለደው ሥርዓተ ወልበኝነት ያጠቃቸዋል ማለት አይደለም፤ ጥቂቶች ሊገቡበት ቢችሉም።

በአሜሪካን አገር በተደጋጋሚ ከሚነሣው የጸጥታ ችግር አብላጫው፤ ከጥቁሮች የተነሣ አለያም በጥቁሮች ላይ እንደሆን ይታወቃል። የሚገርመው ነገር፤ በቅርቡ በተጠና ሌላ ጥናት መሠረት፤ የጸጥታውን ችግር ያባባሱት፣ ከመድልዎ የተነሣ ጥቁሮች ተናድደው፣ እልህና ብቀላ ተስፋፍቶ አይደለም። ከዚህ ይልቅ፣ ከመዋቅራዊ ዘረኝነት ከራሱ ጋር የተቄራኘ ችግር እንደሆነም ተመላክቷል።

አካሄዱ እንዲህ ነው። መዋቅራዊ ዘረኝነት በሰዎች መካከል ፍቅርን ሳይሆን ጥላቻንና ጥርጣሬን ይዘራል ይልቁንም፤ ከመዋቅራዊ ዘረኝነት ጋራ "ሌላው ሊገድልህ ነውና ቅደመው" የሚል ትርክት ዐብሮ ተስፋፍቶ ተገኝቷል። አግላይነት የሚከርመው፣ ፍርሃትን በመዝራት ነው። መዋቅሩን ከመገርሰስ ይልቅ በሕዝብ መካከል ፍርሃትን ይሰነቅራል። [211]

እንዲያውም፣ ጥቁሮች ተገፍተዋል ብለው የሚያምኑ እንኳ ሳይቀሩ፤ ስለተገፉ መራር ሆነዋል ብለው እስኪያምኑ ድረስ ፍርሃት በማኅበረሰቡ መካከል አዪኔል። ከዚህ የተነሣ ነጮች፤ በተለይም ጠብመንጃ የያዙ፤ እና ጸጥታ አስከባሪዎች ገና ጥቁር ሲያዩ መቅደም እንዳለባቸው ያስባሉ፤ ምህረት የለሽ እርምጃ ይቀናቸዋል። ፍርሃት ከራስ ወዳድነት ጋር ሲቃናጅ ደግሞ ያለ ጥርጥር ገዳይ ነው።

ጥቁሮችም ተመሳሳይ ችግር ውስጥ ናቸው። ፈሪ አግላዮች ድንገት አጉል ሥፍራ ላይ ፈት ለፈት ከተገጣጠሙ እንደማይምሯቸው ይሰማቸዋል። ሕግ አስከባሪ

210 Chantarat, T., Mentzer, K. M., Van riper, D. C., Rachel, M. and Hardeman, R. (2022). Where are the labor markets? Examining the association between structural racism in labor markets and infant birth weight. Health and Place, Volume 74, March 2022, 102742

211 Burrel, M., Whiite, A. M., Frerichs, L., Funchess, M, Cerulli, C., DiGiovanni, L. and Lich, H. (2021). Depicting "the system": How structural racism and disenfranchisement in the United States can cause dynamics in community violence among males in urban black communities. Social Science & Medicine, Volume 271, March 2021, 113469

በሥላም እንኳ ቢጠይቅ ዐይናቸው ይቀላል። ዐሳባቸው ሌላጋ ነው። እቀደማለሁ ብለው ስለሚያሰቡ ሕግ ተላላፊ ይሆናሉ።

በቅርቡ ዓለሙን ሁሉ ያንቀጠቀጠው የኮሮና ወረርሽኝ ዓለም ያስተናገደችበት መንገድ ዘረኝነት ጉልቶ የወጣበት ነበር ማለት ይቻላል። በኮቪድ 19 በቫታ ምክንያት ብዙዎች ሞተዋል። አሜሪካን አገር፤ መረጃዎች የሚያመለክቱት፤ በአብላጫው ይሞቱ የነበሩት፤ ጥቁሮች፤ ውፍረት ያጠቃቸው ሰዎች፤ ቅልቅል ዘሮች፤ እና አነስተኛ ገቢ ያላቸው ሰዎች ናቸው። የእነዚህ የሞት ምጣኔ፤ ልክ መሠረታዊ የጤና ችግር እንዳለባቸው ሰዎች የታከክ የመሆን አዝማሚያ እየተስተዋለ መጣ።

ጥናትም ተደረገ፤ እንደተረፈራውም መሠረታዊ የጤና ችግር በአርግጥ የሞት መንሥኤ ነበር። ነገር ግን ድኽነት እና አግላይ የዘረኝነት መዋቅር ዋና ምክንያት ሆኖ ብቅ አለ። ጥቁሮችና ቅልቅል ሕዝቦች ያሉባቸው አካባቢዎች ቀድሞውንም በረቀቀ መዋቅራዊ አሠራር የጤና አገልግሎት ተደራሽነታቸው ደካማ ነበር። በሽታው ሲስፋፋ ተጨማሪ አገልግሎቶችም ወደ ድሆች ሳይሆን ወደ ሌሎች እንዲሄዱ ተደረገ።[212]

ቶሎ የተጎዱ አካባቢዎችን ለይቶ፤ በቂ ሃብት በመመደብ መቆጣጠር ቢቻል ኖሮ የበሽታውን ሥርጭት መግታት፤ ቢያንስ ፍጥነቱን መቀነስ ይችሉ ነበር። በራስ ወዳድነት፤ ቀድሞውኑ ከአፍ እስከ ገደፍ በጤና ባለሙያዎች በተጠቀጠቁ አካባቢዎች ሥራ ብዙ ሆኑ። በሽታው የድሆች አካባቢዎችን ምሽግ አድርጎ ከዚያ እየተነሣ ወረራቸው፤ ሥራ አበዛባቸው።

አሜሪካም፤ ኮሮና መጀመሪያ ከተገኘባት ከቻይና ይልቅ እጅግ ተጠቂ የሆነችበት ምስጢር በከፊል ከዚህ ጋር የተያያዘ ነው። ቻይና ሥፍራ ሳትመርጥ ዜጎች ባሉበት ሁሉ ገብታ ሬዳች፤ ተቆጣጠረች። መዋቅራዊ አግላይነት በአሜሪካ ዕድል ተሰጠው፤ ኮሮና መላዋን አገር ገረፈት፤ ለበለባት።

በዓለማችን ውስጥ ዛሬ (በ2022 ዓ.ም መጨረሻ) በኮሮና ቫይረስ መያዛቸው ከተረጋገጡ ግማሽ ቢሊዮን ሰዎች ውስጥ አንድ አምስተኛ እጅ አሜሪካውያን ናቸው። ከሕዝባቸው አንድ ሦስተኛ ሊደርስ ጥቂት የሚቀረው። በበሽታው በዓለም ዙሪያ ሞቱ ከተባሉት 5 ሚሊዮን ውስጥ፤ በተመሳሳይ ሁኔታ፤ አንድ ሚሊዮን ያህሉ በማዋጣት አሜሪካ ተወዳዳሪ አልተገኘላትም።[213] መዋቅራዊ አግላይነት ለሁሉ የሚተርፍ ዕዳ።

212 Ramprasad, A., Qureshi, F., Lee, B. R. and Jones, B. L. (2022). The relationship between structural racism and COVID-19 related health disparities across 10 metropolitan cities in the United States. Journal of the National Medical Asssociation, Available online 25 February 2022

213 Worldodometer. (2022). COVID-19 Corona virus Pandemic. Accessed on March 1, 2022, from https://www.worldometers.info/coronavirus/

እናጠቃልለው፤ በመጀመሪያ፣ ብሔርን የፖለቲካ መሠረት እንዲሁም የኤኮኖሚ ፖሊሲ ምንጭ አድርጎ መጠቀም የጊዜው ፖለቲካ ነው። በሁለት ትይዩ ዕሳቦች ምክንያት የተፈጠረ አሳዛኝ ክስተት። አንዱ የብሔር ልዩነትን የሚጠየፍና ከዚህ የተነሣ በገሃድም ሆነ በትርክት ደረጃ የደረሰ ግፍ ስለመኖሩ የሚክድ ወይም የሚያራክስ፤ ሌላው የብሔር ልዩነት ኑባሬዎችን ከጭቆናና መገፋት ጋር እንጂ ከሌላ አንጻር ለማየት ችላ ያለ። ሁለቱም የሚያስማማ ሳይሆን የግጭት መንገድ መረጡ።

ግጭትን የዕሳብ ልዩነት መፍቻ ማድረግ የፈለጉ ፖለቲከኞች የብሔር ፖለቲካን ለመለያየት ተጠቀሙበት። እንጂ የብሔር ልዩነት የፖለቲካ መሠረት አይደለም። ብሔርተኛ ኤኮኖሚም የተሻለ ፋክክር፣ የተሻለ ዕድገትም የሚያመጣበት አስማት የለውም። ኤኮኖሚው ይበልጥ ይኮስሳል እንጂ አያድግም። ብሔርተኝነት የተሻለ የኤኮኖሚ ውድድር ያስከትላል የሚለውም አከራካሪ ነው።

የፖለቲካ ኤኮኖሚው በአግላይ ዘረኝነት ሲቃኝ በእኔነት ስሜት ውድድር ስለሚጦፍ አጠቃላይ የአገር ምርትም ሆነ ዕድገት ላይ በጎ ተጽዕኖ ይኖረዋል የሚለውም ዕሳብ ፋርሽ እንደሆነ ብዙዎች ታሪክን፣ እውነታን፣ ልምድን አገላብጠው ጽፈዋል። አግላይነት መዋቅራዊ ሲሆን ለማንም የማይመች አገር እና ሁኔታ ይፈጠራል እንጂ ፈቅ አይባልም። የቆምክበት ሥፍራ መቀመጫህንም ይወስናል ይባላል። መሠረት ከላላ፣ ድቡሽት ወይም አሸዋማ ከሆነ አቋቋም ይበላሻል።

ኀብረ ብሔራዊነት ማለትም ብዝኃነት ራሱ በታህታይ ኤኮኖሚው ሥሉጥነት አሉታዊ ተጽዕኖ የሚያሳድር፣ በላዕላይ[214] ኤኮኖሚውም ቅሸባ የሚጭን ነው። ይህ የሚሆነው በብሔር ፖለቲካ ኤኮኖሚ ቅኝት መላ ዐልባ የኤኮኖሚ ፖሊሲ ሕጸጾች ያለ ብቁ ውይይት፣ ያለ ማካካሻ፣ በግዴታ ስለሚታከሉ ነው። ከዚህ የተነሣ ለምሳሌ:- ሙስናን ማስወገድ ፈጽሞ መላ ዐልባ ነው፤ አይቻልም። ለማስወገድ የሚወሰዱ እርምጃዎች ጭራሽ አባብሰውት ይገኛሉና።

ዳቦ ሲቆርሱ

ከወገንተኝነት የነጻ የኤኮኖሚ ሥርዓት ጥረትን ደግፎ፣ አበረታቶ፣ ውጤትን በመጋራት ላይ የተመሠረተ እንዲሆን ይቀረጻል። ምንም ፍጹም ባይሆን ሃብታምና ድኻን እስከ ዛሬ አቅፎ የኖረው አመዛኝ የኤኮኖሚ ሥርዓት ይህ ነው። "ስውር እጅ"ም ሆነች "ጣልቃ ገብ እጅ" በዐይነትና ብዛት ይጣሉ እንደሆነ እንጂ መሠረታዊ ዕሳባቸው ይኸው ነው።

በኢትዮጵያ የታየው የብሔር ፖለቲካ ሥርዓት የኤኮኖሚውን ዳቦ ለዜጎች የከፋፈለበት መንገድ እጅግ ውስብስብ ነው። የዚህንም የመጀመሪያውን ፍንጭ ከሕገ

214 "ላዕላይ ኤኮኖሚ" የሚለው መግለጫ በዚህ ጽሑፍ አጠቃላይ ወይም ማክሮ ኤኮኖሚ የሚባለውን ያመለክታል። ከዚያ በታች ያለው፣ የሴክተር፣ ኢንዱስትሪ፣ ወይም የኤኮኖሚ ሕዋስ (ማይክሮ) ደረጃ ያለው "ታህታህ ኤኮኖሚ" በሚል ተገልጿል።

መንግሥቱ እናገኛለን። በአንቀጽ 32 ለዜጎች የመዘዋወር መብት፣ በአንቀጽ 40 ደግሞ ንብረት የማፍራት መብት ያጎናጸፈው ሕገ መንግሥት፣ ንብረት የሚፈራበትን የአገሪቱን የገጠር እና የከተማ መሬት በሙሉ "የመንግሥትና የሕዝብ" ሲል ፍጹም ገደበው። [215]

በእርግጥ ይህን ሕገ መንግሥቱ አልፈጠረውም። ይህ የሆነበት ሌላ ታሪካዊ እውነታ አለው። የአገሪቱ የመሬት ሃብት በመንግሥት እጅ የወደቀው በደርግ ዘመን ነበር። ወደ ግል ይዞታ ይመለስ ቢባል በአንድ በኩል ግጭት ባየለበት እውነታ፣ በሌላም በኩል ሕጋዊ ሥፍርና የይዞታ መካለል ባለነበረበት ሕዝቡን እርስ በርስ ማባላት መስሎ ታየ። ገበሬው ሽጦ ወደ ከተማ ከነረፈስ ደግሞ? ምን ሥርቶ ይብላ? ኤኮኖሚው ከግጭት በማገገም ላይ የነበረ፣ የመዋቅር ለውጥ የናፈቀው ነበርን።

ግና "መንግሥት" የሚባለው በአዲሱ ሥርዓት ብዙ ሆነ። "የፌዴራል፣ እና የክልል መንግሥታት" ተብሎ ተለየ። የሕዝብ ሉዓላዊ የሥልጣን ባለቤትነት ተሸራረፈ። ሁለቱ ለወደዱት ያከፋፍላሉ። አንዱ ሲሰጥ ሌላው ሊነሣም የሚችልበት ክፍተት ተፈጠረ። ከፉክክር ይልቅ መጋፋትን 'ሂድልኝ፣ ውጣልኝ' የሚል መስፈርት ሕግ ሆና ጸድቃ ይተገበራል።

የብሔር ነጻነት ጥያቄ አንገበው በጦር ሜዳ ድል የቀናቸው ኃይላት ኢትዮጵያ አገር እንዳልነበረች እንዲቆጥር ሕገ መንግሥቱን ተጫኑት፣ ጥያቄ ስለነበራቸው። "በአገሪቱ አንድ የኤኮኖሚ ማኅበረሰብ ለመፍጠር" የሚል ትርክት ታክለበት። "የለም፣ አልነበረም" ማለት ብቻ ሳይሆን "እስከሚፈጠር ጠብቁኝ" የሚል እንድታታ እንዳለው ያስተውሷል። ይህንን በተግባር የአገር ውስጥ ሃብትና ክህሎት ዝውውርን ፈጽሞ በሚባል ደረጃ ለሚገድብ አካሄድ እንደ ሽፋን ተጠቀሙ።

ጥረት፣ የምርት መገልገያዎች ክፍፍል መሠረት መሆኑ አክትሞ ፖለቲካ ሲረከበው ነገር ይበላሻል። የጤናማ ኤኮኖሚ ዕድገት ሥርዓት ጥቂት ደንቦች ይበሻቀጣሉ። የብሔር ፖለቲካ ይህንን የኤኮኖሚ መሠረት አይቶት ይሆን? ቀዳሚ ምልክቶቹ ያስፈራሉ። ጉሥኝነት፣ የባጡንም የቆጡንም ለእኔ እና ለመሰሎቹ ብቻ የሚል አባዜ የተጠናወተው ስለሆነ።

በዚህም አያቆምም፣ ከጉርሻው መንፈት ሳያንስ በኩርኩምም አይታማም። ሲማታ ደግሞ ነገን አያውቅም። ቢቻል መዋቅራዊ፣ ሳይሆን ሲቀር ደግሞ በህቡዕና በመንጋ ደንብ በተደራጁ ኃይላት የሃብትና ክህሎት ሥርጭትና ከቦታ ወደ ቦታ በነጻነት የመዘዋወር መብት ይገደባል። የፖለቲካና የፍትሕ ሥርዓቱ አማራም ግልፅ የሆኑ የሕግና መብት ጥሰቶችን እንዳላዩ በማለፍ ወይንም ስውር ከለላ በመስጠት ይከናል።

215 Federal Negarit Gazeta. (1995). Proclamation No. 1/1995 - Proclamation of the Constitution of the Federal Democratic Republic of Ethiopia. August 21, 1995. Accessed on March 11, 2022 from https://ethiopianembassy.be/wp-content/uploads/Constitution-of-the-FDRE.pdf

ታዲያ አይታፈርበትም፤ መድልዎ ያደረግኩት የራሴን ቡድን ለመጥቀም ነው ተብሎ በግልጥ ይነገራል። ይህን ይበል እንጂ "የእኔ" ወደ ተባለው ቡድን ቀረብ ተብሎ ሲጠየቅ ከብሔርተኛ ፖለቲከኞች በሚደርስ ኤኮኖሚያዊ እንግልት እኩል ያላዘናሉ። ይህም ያለ ምክንያት አይደለም። በመጀመሪያ ደረጃ ለአንድ ሰው ወይም የኤኮኖሚ ሕዋስ፤ ብሔር ብቸኛ ፖለቲካዊ ማንነት መሆኑ ይቅርና ቀዳሚ ማንነትም እንኳን አይደለም። ሰው የፖለቲካዊ ኤኮኖሚ እንስሳነቱ መጀመሪያ ለራስ ነውና።

የገዝ ወንድሙን ጉቦ አስከፍሎ ሥራ የሚሰጥ ታዲያ ምን ሊባል ነው? የጉቦ ምጣኔስ በብሔር አባልነት ይለያያል ወይ? የምርት መገልገያዎች ክፍፍልና ድርሻ በዘር ቀረቤታ ወይስ ብዙ በኪፈል የሚል ተመን ወጥቶለት? ከክልል ውጭ ያላችሁና በክልሌ ተብሎ የጉቦ ስብጥር ይለካል?

በእርግጥ አሁን በሥራ ላይ ያለው ሕግ መንግሥት ከመጽደቁም በፊት ባሉት ሁለት አሥርት ዓመታት የከተማና የገጠር ቦታ በግል መያዝ በሕግ የተደገፈ አልነበረም። በሶሻሊዝም አቀንቃኝ አገራት እንደሚታየውም ሃብትን ሳይሆን ድኽነትን መጋራት የተለመደ ነው። የገጠር መሬትን ለሕዝብ ያካፈለው አዋጅ ሃብታሞችን እጥፍቶ መላ አገሪቱ ከሞላ ጉደል እኩል፤ ጎላ ቀር ድሆች የሚኖሩበት አድርጎ ነበር የሚሉ ምልከታዎች አሉ። [216]

ከምዕተ ዓመቱ መለወጫ ዓመታት አካባቢ ጀምሮ ለጥቂት ዓመታት የታየው ፈጣን የኤኮኖሚ ዕድገት ያስከተለው የሃብት ክፍፍል ብዙዎችን ግራ የሚያጋባቸው ይህን መነሻ ስለማያጤኑት ነው። በኢትዮጵያ ከፍተኛ ገቢ አላቸው የሚባሉ ከሕዝቡ 10 ከመቶ የሚሆኑ የጎብረትሰብ ክፍሎች የሚቆጣጠሩት የሃብት መጠን ከአጠቃላይ ሃብት ላይ ከፉቡ እምብዛም ፈቅ ብሎ አያውቅም።

ያጡ የነጡ የሚባሉ 10 ከመቶ የሚሆኑ የጎብረትሰብ ክፍሎችም ቢሆን እስክ 3 ከመቶ የሚደርስ የአገሪን ሃብት ይቆጣጠራሉ። ለምሳሌ፡- ይህንን እጅግ ከፍተኛ የሃብት መዘነፍ ከሚታይበቸው ከማዕከላዊ ወይም ደቡባዊ አፍሪካ ጋር ማነጻጸር ይቻላል። ድኻ የሚባሉ አሥረኞች በእነዚህ አገራት ከአገሪቱ ሃብት የሚደርሳቸው በጣም አንድ በመቶ ያህል ብቻ ነው። ሃብታሞች ግን ግማሽ ያህሉን ይቀራመቱታል። [217]

ስለዚህ፡ በኢትዮጵያ የሃብት ክፍፍል እጅግ በመዛነፍ የብሔር ፖለቲካን ወለደ ለማለትም አያስኬድም። ክፍሎች አገራት አንጻር ሁሉ ከሞላ ጉደል እኩል ድኻ ስለሆነ፤ ይሁን እንጂ የብሔር ፖለቲከኞች የሥርጭት መቀራረብን መፍጠር ዓላማቸው እንደሆነ

---

216 Baye, T. G. (2017). Poverty, peasantry, and agriculture in Ethiopia. Annals of Agrarian Sceince. Volume 15, Issue 3; September 2017, Pages 420-430

217 UNU (WIDER). (2022). World Inequalities Database. Accessed on August 16, 2022 from https://wid.world/world/#sptinc_p90p100_z/US;FR;DE;CN;ZA;GB;WO/last/eu/k/p/yearly/s/false/23.469/80/curve/false/country

ይናገራሉ። ፖስክርንና አድሷዊ ክፍፍልን በማሥረጽ በሕዝቡ መካከል "ፍትሐዊ" ተደራሽነት ለማምጣት ያልማሉ። ይቻል ይሆን?

ቤተልሔም አርጋው የተባሉት አጥኚ፣ ከተባበሩት መንግሥታት ዩኒቨርሲቲ ጋር በ2017 የኢኮኖሚ ዕድገት ፖሊሲ በክልሎች እና በሰዎችም መካከል ያለውን የሃብት ሥርጭት አሻሻሎ እንደሆን ለማየት ጥናት አድርገው ነበር። በአገሪቱ ከተከሠተው የኢኮኖሚ ዕድገት፣ በክልሎች መካከል የነበረው የትምህርት፣ የሥራ ዕድልና የመጠጥ ውሃ ተደራሽነት ክፍተት በመጥበቡ ነው የሚል መላምት በመሠንዘር።

ጥናቱ በአጠቃላይ በክልሎች መካከል ያለው አንጻራዊ የድኽነት መጠን ከተጠቀሱት መመዘኛዎች አንጸር ሲታይ ቀነሶ መታየቱን አብስሯል። ይህ ብቻ ሳይሆን፣ በትውልድ መካከል ያለውም የተደራሽነት ክፍተትም በመጥበብ ላይ ይገኛል። ማለትም፣ ትላንት በአንድ ክልል ላይ የነበሩ ሰዎች ከሌላው ጋር ራሳቸውን ሲያስተያዩ ድኻ አድርገው የሚመለከቱበት ምክንያት ቀርቷል። [218]

ይህም ማለት እንግዲህ፣ ከምዕተ ዓመቱ መባቻ ጀምሮ ባሉት ዓመታት ከታየው ዕድገትና ለውጥ የተነሣ ትውልድ ከትላንት ይልቅ ዛሬ ካለሁበት ክልል የተነሣ ወደ ጓላ ቀረሁ የሚልበት ምክንያት እየከሰመ ሄዷል ማለት ነው፤ እሰዬው። በአንድ አካባቢ ያለ ሕዝብ በሌላ አካባቢ ከሚገኘው ወገኑ ጋር የተስተካከለ ኑሮ እመራለሁ ብሎ የማሰብ ጀምሮ እንኳን ቢኖር ትልቅ እመርታ ነው። እውነታው ግን ያንን ለማገመልከቱ ከፍተኛ ጥርጣሬ አለ።

በእርግጥ የአገራችን የኢኮኖሚ ዕድገት፣ በሌሎች አገራት እንደሚከሰተው የኢኮኖሚ ዕድገት የተደራሽነት ልዩነትን ቢያስከትልም እንኳን፣ የተጋነነ የድርኻ አለመስተካከልን አልወለደም። መነሻው ኢምንት በመሆኑም በሕዝብ ደረጃ ልዩነቱ አይጎላም። በዕድገቱም ሆነ በድርኻ የሚነሣው ክርክር ግን ከጥቂት ዓመታት በፊት መንግሥትን የሚያሃል ነገር ከሥልጣን መገርሰሱን ስንመለከት ሌላ ጥያቄ እንድናነሳ ያስገድዳል።

ዕድገቱ እኩል ያልተዳረሰ የመሰለበት ምክንያያ ምንድር ነው? ለዚህ ጥያቄ መልስ የሚሆን ነገር በእነዚህ የለውጥ ዓመታት ኩዝነር በሚባል ሰው የተደረገ ሌላ ጥናት ጥቂት ፍንጭ ይሰጣል። የኢትዮጵያ ፈጣን የኢኮኖሚ ዕድገት እንደ ሌላው አገር የክፍፍል መዛባትን ያልፈጠረ ቢመስልም እውነታው ሌላ ነው። [219]

በኩዝነር ጥናት መሠረት፣ የኢኮኖሚው ዕድገትና ተጠቃሚነት ከተለያዩ የማኅበራዊና ኤኮኖሚያዊ ምድቦች አንጻር ሲተነተን ከፍተኛ ዝብጠት ያሳያል። ለምሳሌ፦-

218 Argaw, B. A. (2017). Regional inequality of economic outcomes and opportunities in Ethiopia A tale of two periods. UNU-WIDER Working Paper 2017/118. Accessed on March 11, 2022, from file:///Users/simonheliso/Desktop/Regional%20inequalities%20in%20ethiopia.pdf

219 Kuzner, L. A. (2019). Ethiopia Inequality Report. NSI Agreieved Population Report, 2019. Accessed on March 11, 2022, from https://nsiteam.com/ethiopia-country-report-an-nsi-aggrieved-populations-analysis/

ዕድገቱ ወደ ከተሞች ያደላ ስለነበር ገጠራማ ክፍሎች ወደ ድኽነት አሽቆልቁለዋል። በከተሞችም ውስጥ ባረጁ መንደሮችና እና በተለይም ዳር ዳሩ እጅግ የተረሱና መፈናቀል የተፈረረደባቸው ይኖራሉ። ጥቂቶች ግን ባልተመጣጠነ ዋጋ የከተማ መሬትን በመቀራመት ከመቅጽበት ተመንድገዋል።

በትምህርት ደረጃም ሲተነተን ተመሳሳይ ልዩነቶች ይስተዋላሉ። ቀድሞ በትምህርት ተደራሽነት ሻል ያለ ያሰ ሥፍራዎች ሥራ ዕድገትን የመቀራመት አዝማሚያ ታይቷል። መማር ብቻውን ሀብት ለማጋበስ አይረዳም። በጥናቱ መሰረት የኢትዮጵያ ፈጣን የኤኮኖሚ ዕድገት ያመጣውን ትሩፋት የተቀራመቱት በደንብ የተማሩ ብቻ ሳይሆኑ፣ የተዘጋጁበትና የተደራጁ አካላት ናቸው።

ቀድመው የተደራጁ፣ ብልህ ልሂቃን፣ ትሩፋቱን ተቀራምተዋል። እንዲሁም፣ ከተሜ እና የፖለቲካ ሥልጣን የሙጥኝ ያለ ልሂቃን፣ እነርሱንም በአምቻ ጋብቻም ሆነ በሌላ የተጠጉት ሁሉ አብረው ተመንድገዋል። ይህ የጥናት ሪፖርት ብዙዎች እንደሚስማሙበት አሌ አይባልም።

ያልተደራጁ ተመነጠሩ፤ የትም ይኑሩ የት። ለአንዳንዶች ድርብ መገለል ሆነባቸው። በእርግጥም በቅርቡ በጤና አገልግሎት ተደራሽነት ላይ የተደረገ ጥናት፣ ምንም እንኳ የጤና ተቋማት በየሥፍራው ቢገነቡም፣ በመድኃኒት፣ የውስጥ ዕደራጆት፣ እና የጤና ባለሙያ አመዳደብን ስንመለከት ልዩነቱ እንደ ገጠጠ ታውቋል።[220] ከላይ እንደ ተገለጸውም የተደራሽነት ችግር ሲኖር ዘላቂ ጉዳት ያመጣል።

በሕጻናት ዕድገት ላይ ትኩረት ተደርጎ በተካሄደ ጥናት፣ ከጤና ተደራሽነት እንዲሁም ከተወለዱበት ክልል የኤኮኖሚ ሁኔታ የተሳ በልጆች ሁለንትናዊ ዕድገት ላይ ጉልህ ልዩነት መታየቱም ተረጋግጧል።[221] በስተትም ሆነ በገሃድ ተደራሽነትን መንፈግ ዘላቂ ልዩነት ስለሚፈጥር መጠንቀቅ ይበጃል። እንዲያውም የኤኮኖሚ ፖሊሲ ይህን መሳይ ልዩነት ተከታትሎ ካልቀረፈ ፋይዳው እምብዛም ነው። አድዒዊ ተብሎ የሚፈረጀውም ከዚህ የተነሣ ነው።

አያሳንሱ

የሚያሳዝነው፣ ዳቦ ቆራሾች እየተገበሩ ያሉት ይህን መሠረታዊ የአገር ብሂል ነው። ሲቆርሱ ለራስ ማሳነስን ይህ ብሂል አይደግፈውም። ስጦቶ፣ ሰጥቶ ባዶ የሚቀሩ

---

220 Woldemichael, A., Takina, A., Sari, A. A. & Olyaeemanes, A. (2019). Inequalities in healthcare resources and outcomes threatening sustainable health development in Ethiopia: panel data analysis. Health Policy Research BMJ Journal, Volume 9; issue 1.

221 Bekele, T., Rawstorne, P., Rahman, B. (2021). Socioeconomic inequalities in child growth failure in Ethiopia: findings from the 2000 and 2016 Demographic and Health Surveys. BMJ Open 2021. Accessed on March 11, 2022, from https://bmjopen.bmj.com/content/bmjopen/11/12/e051304.full.pdf

ወይም የማስተዛዘኛ ብጤ ቤት የሚያስቀረውን እንደ ምኝ ይቆጥረዋል። እናም ብሔርተኛ ከተሸመ ማግሥት ጀምሮ "ለብሔሬ" እንዳለ ይኖራል። በአገር ደረጃ ማሰብ ጥረት ይጠይቃል፣ ምናልባትም ዋጋም ያስከፍላል። ስለዚህም ጥረቱ ሁሉ ለራስ ማግበስበስ፣ ሌላውን ደግሞ መጉዳት ላይ ይሆናል።

በኢኮኖሚክስ ዕይታ ግን ሲቀርሱ ያሳነሱት ዳቦ ጦስ አምራች ነው፣ ልክ እንደ ኮሮና፣ በሮጡ ልክ ሱሪ እያስፈረ ይሄዳል እንጂ ይሉኝታ አያውቅም። የተሸነቆረበት ሥፍራ ምን ቢጠገን ማፍሰሱ አይቀርም። የሚገባውን ያጣ የራሱን ባያገኝ የሌላውን የመበተን ወይም የማምከን ዐቅም በለሆሳስ፣ ሲመችም በገሃድ ያበጀና የጠቅላላ ኤኮኖሚውን ዕድገት ይጎተታል።

ሁሉንም ወገን በፍትሐዊነት እና በእኩልነት ለመጥቀም ተብሎ ያልተሠራ ሥራ ሽቀባን መውለዱ አይቀሬ ነው። ተንጎዦ ያጠራቸው ወይም እስከን አካቴው የሌላቸው መንገዶች፣ በሬ በሌለበት የተቋቋመ የቆዳ ፋብሪካ፣ እንዲሁም ከማን አንሼ በሚል ኩረጃ የሚሠሩ ነገሮች ሁሉ የቅሽባ ምሳሌዎች ናቸው። ሲብስም በመሥራት ሳይሆን በመከልከል ይገለጣል። አንዳንዱ ጥቂት የክልከላ ምክንያት ሊኖረው ይችላል። ሌላው ያው የብሔር አባዜ ስለያዘው ብቻ።

በአገራችንም በአንድም በሌላም ምክንያት የቆመ፣ ሳይሠሩ ዕድሜአቸውን የፈጁ ተቋማት፣ ፋብሪካዎች፣ የእርሻ ድርጅቶችና የተለያዩ መገልገያዎች ምልተዋል። ምክንያታቸው ከሞላ ጉደል ብሔሬን ጉዳህ ወይም በበቂ አልጠቀምሽንም የሚል ነው። ለምሳሌ፦ የኢትዮጵያ የወርቅ ምርት እያደገ መጥቶ በ2012 ዓ.ም በዓመት ወደ 13 ቶን አካባቢ ደርሶ ነበር። ይህ መጠን በእጅጉ አሽቆልቁሎ፣ በ2019 ዓ.ም በዓመት 3 ቶን ብቻ ሆኗል። [222]

ይህ የሆነው በአብዛኛው የሻኪሶ፣ አዶላና ለገደንቢ የወርቅ ማዕድን ቁፋሮ ባጋጣማቸው ንትርክ ምክንያት ነው። ችግሩ የተነሣው ፋብሪካዎቹ የአካባቢ ብክለትን ለመቋቋም ያደረጉት ጥረት እናዣ ከመሆኑ የተነሣ ሰዎች ላይ ጉዳት በመድረሱ እንደሆነ ሲነገር እንሰማለን። ይሁን እንጂ ለጉዳዩ መፍትሔ ሳይሰጥ ዓመታትን አስቆጥሯል። ሠራተኛውም በሥራ ገበታው ላይ እንዳለ ይነገራል፣ ምርት ግን የለም። ወርቁስ ከአምላክ የተሰጠን በረከታችን ነበር። ፍሬ ዐልባ የጭቅጭቁ የጉዳት ምንጭ ይሁን?

ከላይ እንደተጠቀሰው ልማትን የሚያሳልጠው፣ የተቀየሰው የኤኮኖሚ ፖሊሲ ማንንም ሳይጎዳ ቢያንስ አንድን የኤኮኖሚ ተዋናይ መጥቀም ሲችል ነው። ይህን ውጤት ሆነ ብሎ በመቀስ ማምጣት የሚቻል ቢሆንም፣ ኤኮኖሚው በጸነት ተነስቶ የሚያደርገው ቢሆን ይመረጣል። ያለ ጣልቃ ገብነት እንዲሠራ የሚፈለግበት ዋና

---

222 Meralis Plaza-Toledo (USGS). (2022). The Mineral Industry of Ethiopia. Accessed on August 16, 2022 from https://pubs.usgs.gov/myb/vol3/2019/myb3-2019-ethiopia.pdf

ምክንያትም፤ የራስን ብሔር መጥቀም ወይንም ተመሳሳይ ቀዳሚ ዓላማ ያነገቡ የሥራ መሪዎች ኤኮኖሚውን አቅጣጫ እንዳያስቱ ሲባል ነው።

በእርግጥ፤ ኤኮኖሚ ሙሉ በሙሉ በጸ ገበያ ሥርዓት እንዲመራ ተፈቅዶ መንግሥት ዋነኛ ሥራው ወደ ሆነው ሕግና ሥርዓትን ማስከበር፤ ወይንም፤ ደህንነትና ጥበቃ ላይ ብቻ ቢያተኩር ተዓምራዊ እኩልነት ሊገኝ አይችልም። ለዚህም ነው መንግሥት በኤኮኖሚ አመራር ጣልቃ መግባት ያለበት። ጣልቃ መግባት ሲባል ግን ዝንተ ዓለም በማይቀየር፤ መዘንፍን በሚያስቀድም ፖሊሲ መወዘፍ አይደለም። የጋራ ዕድገትን ባማከለ መልኩ ግልዕና የማያሻማ የዳቦ ቆረሳ ያካሂድ ማለት እንጂ።

በኤኮኖሚ ውድድሩ ካተረፈው ላይ በቀረጥ መልክ መሰብሰብ የመንግሥትን ኃላፊነት ለመወጣት ይረዳል፤ ተገቢ ሥልጣን ነው። ይህ ሥልጣን ሆነ ተብሎ አንድን ቡድን ለመጥቀም ወይም ለመጉዳት ጥቅም ላይ ከዋለ ኃላፊነትን ያወሳስባል። አድሏዊ ጥቅማ ጥቅም ከጀመራት ለማቆም አዳጋች ነው። ምክንያቱም፤ ድጓማ በባህርያው ቀጣይነት ያለው፤ ነገር ግን ቀሻቢ አሠራር ስለሆነ። ፍትሐዊነትን ለማስቀድም በድኅማ ላይ የተመረኮዘ ፖሊሲ አይመከርም።

የተሻለው አሠራር የኤኮኖሚ ሕዋሳት የሚወዳደሩበትን ሜዳ ማስተካከል ነው። የሀብት ክፍፍል የግድ አስፈላጊ ከሆነ ግን በመስማማት የአንድ ጊዜ ማስተላለፊያ መንገድ ማበጀት ይሻላል። በእንም አገር ቆይት ተቀለበሰ እንጂ እንደ መሬት ለአራሹ ዐይነት ርምጃዎች ኤኮኖሚያዊ ድጋፍ አላቸው። የሥፈራና የኮንዶምኒየም ዕጣ ተመሳሳይ ዐሳቦችን ያዘሉ ዕቅዶች ነበሩ። ከአሠራር ግድፈት የተነሣ የታለመላቸውን ዒላማ ሳይመቱ የቀሩ ይመስላል እንጂ።

ዳቦ ቆረሳው ሌላ መመልከት ያለበት ነገር አለ። ሕዝባዊ የኑሮ ዕድገት፤ ደስተኝነትና ርካታ ገንዘብ በማግኘትና ሃብት በማፍራት ብቻ የሚገኝ አይደለም። የኤኮኖሚ ፖሊሲ ርካታን በብቃት የሚሸምተው ገንዘብና ሃብት ከማሳደግ ጎን፤ በቂ የትምህርትና ሥልጠና ዕድል፤ የጤና ክብካቤ፤ የአገልግሎት ተደራሽነት፤ መኖሪያ ቤት እና ንጹህ የመኖሪያ አካባቢ ማግኘት፤ መልካም እስተዳደር፤ ጥበቃና ከለላ የማግኘት፤ ሕዝባዊ ተሳትፎና አስተዋጽዖ ሁሉ ላይ ሲያተኩር ነው። [223] ይህ የበለጸጉት አገራት የፖሊሲ መርሕ ነው።

በኤኮኖሚ ፖሊሲ ጣልቃ ገብነት ካስፈለገ እንዚህን ፍትሐዊ በሆነ መልክ ከማግኘት አንጻር ብቻ ሊሆን ይገባል። ብሔርተኛ የኤኮኖሚ ፖሊሲ ግን እንዲህ በጥልቀት የማሰብ ዐቅሙ በሌላ ጉዳይ ይያዛል። ቀልጣፋ ኤኮኖሚ ዕድገትን ያለም ክፍፍል እና ማንበራዊ እርካታን ለማምጣት ካልተደረ በቀር ማንኛውም ብሔርተኛ የሃብት ክፍፍል ሽቀባን በማስፋፋት የዕድገት ጠንቆችን ያበዛል።

---

223 OECD. (2022). Regional Wellbeing Index. Accessed on August 16, 2022, from https://www.oecdregionalwellbeing.org/index.html

ውሃ በልባ ደመና

"የኢኮኖሚ ፍትሕ ለሥላምና ነጻነት ዋና ቁልፍ ነው።"

ማኅትማ ጋንዲ

ሁለት መላጦች ... የቀጠለ

የዘነበው ሁሉ አባርቶ መሐመድ ወደ አዕምሮው ሲመለስ፣ ቁስሉ ትንሽ የጠገገለት መሰለው። ወዲያው የቀነ ግርግር በአዕምሮው እንደ ብልጭታ መጣና ዘገነነው። ማሰብ አይቀርምና ጎደኛውን አስታወሰው።

ንዴቱ ግን ገና አልበረደለትም ነበር። በተለይ፣ አብዲ እጁን አንሥቶ የመታው ነገር ወደ አዕምሮው መጣ፤ እንደ ትልቅ ወንድም ያየው ስለነበር እንዲህ ይጨክንብኛል ብሎ አላሰበም።

እናም፣ ለረኸም ዘመን አብረው ሲሠሩ ያሳለፈበትን ጊዜ ረገመው። አብረው የሠሩ ሳይሆን በእሩሱ ላብ ብቻ አብዲ የከበረ መሠለው።

እናም ይቆጥር ጀመር፤

"ቆይ እስቲ። ከቅርቡ ልጀምር። ባለፈው ያ የአገራቸው ባለ ሃብት ከከፈለን ገንዘብ የሰጠኝ ድርሻ ትክክል ነበር?"

በአዕምሮው ሊያሰላ ሞከረ።

"ብሎኬት መደርደር፣ ሦስቱንም ቀን በአብዛኛው የሠራሁ እኔ ነበርኩ። ያውም በውጭ ተንጠላጥዬ በፀሐይ። እሩሱ በውስጥ በኩል፣ ከእነዚያ መሠሪዎች ጋራ ይኸኔ ነገር እያነሳ። እሩሱ በጥላ ውስጥ። እኔ በፀሐይ።

ምን እንደ ሥራ እንኳን አላየሁም። ገንዘቡን ደግሞ ወስጄ በሥራችን መጣን ያከፋፈልኩት እኔው ነኝ። እንዴት አባታው አድርጎ እንዳጭበረበሩኝ እኔ ምን አውቁ?

እኔው ነኝ ሞኙ! ስንት ነበር ያስቀረሁት?"

ትንሽ ራሱን ያመመው መሠለው። ጠዝጠዝም አደረገውና ራሱን በእጁ ለመንካት አሰበ ሲምክር፤ ለካስ እጁ አይነሣም። ለመንቀሳቀስ ሲምክር ምንም ዐቅም አጣ።

ወገቡ ከአልጋው ጋር የተሳፋ መሠለው። አንገቱን ቀና አድርጎ ለመመልከት ሲምክር፤ የማይንቀሳቀስ ሆነ፤ ወዲያውም አንዳች ነገር ጉሮሮውን ዘጋቶ፤ ትኩስ እንባ ከዐይኑ ኮለል ብሎ ሲወርድ ታወቀው።

"ውይህ ነቃህ እንዴ?"

ፈገግታም፤ ኀዘኔታም የተቀላቀለበት፤ ከአሁን በፊት አይቶ የማያውቀው የለግላጋ ቤት ፈት ቁልቁል ያያዋል። ማቃሰቱ እርሱ ባይታወቀውም፤ በሆስፒታሉ ተረኛ የነበረችው ነርስ ሰምታው ኖሯል።

"አታልቅስ፤ አይዞህ፤ ለመናገር አትሞክር፤ ግዴለም፤ አሁን ተርፈሃል። የተቻለንን ሁሉ እናደርጋለን፤ አንተ አሁን ዕረፍ፤ ገና እኩለ ሌሊት ነው።"

ዔሊና ጥንቸል

አንዳች ያህል መጅ ተሸክማ የምትንፈቀቅ ፍጥረት ጥፍሯ መሬት ከማይቆነጥጥ ፌንጣ ጋር ለእሽቅድምድም ማሰለፍን የመሠለ አሣር አይገጠማችሁ፤ ምጥ ነው። ጦጣና ዓሣ ዛፍ ላይ የመውጣት ውድድር እንዲያደርጉ ቢታለም ሜዳሊያው ለማን እንደሚገባ አስቀድሞ ተወስኖ የለምን? ለጫናማ ውድድር ሳይሆን ለአጫፋሪነት ብቻ እንደመታደም አስከፊ ነገርስ አለን?

የዘረኝነት ፖለቲካ ኤኮኖሚ ሲገን ታህታይ ኤኮኖሚው በብቃት ላይ ሳይሆን በወገንተኝነት ላይ የተመሠረተ ክፍፍል እና ተደራሽነት እንዲያስፋፋ ይገደዳል። አማራጩ አጥቶ ውድድር ለገባም ትርፋማነቱ እንደዚሁ፤ ገደብ፤ በገደብ፤ ያደላለት ሲመነደግ፤ የተነፈገው የበይ ተመልካች ይሆናል።

ለምሳሌ፦ የስኳር ፋብሪካ ማቋቋም ፈለግሁ፤ መንግሥት በ10 ቢሊዮን ብር አሥር ፋብሪካዎች እሥራለሁ ብሎ የተነሳበት ሰሞን የተወለድኩ ባለ ሃብት ነኝ በሉ። ብሆን ምኔ ሞኝ ነው? መሬት የምወስደው ከመንግሥት ለምኔ፤ ማለት የሊዝ ክፍዬ። እርሱ ግን ይህ ክፍያ የለበትም፤ አይመለከተውም። የተሻለ ጮጮማ መሬት፤ ለገበያ ተደራሽነት በሚመች ሥፍራ ያቋቁማል። የእኔ ፋብሪካ የት ትሁን?

ምን ይህ ብቻ። ፋብሪካውና መለዋወጫዎችን ከውጭ አገር የማመጣው መንግሥት ሆዬ ሲፈቅድ፤ ይህን ሁሉ አልፌ ምርት ካመረትሁ በኋላ እንኳን ክፍፍሉን በቀበሌ ሱቆች በኩል የሚያካሂደው ያው መንግሥት። ዋጋ ወሳኝ፤ 'ለሕዝብ መዳረስ አለበት'

ብሎ ሥርጭትና ጊዜ ተቆጣጣሪ፤ የአከፋፈል ሥርዓት የሚያበጅ፤ ሌላው ቀርቶ ምን ያህል ማምረት እንዳለብኝ የሚያዝዘው መንግሥት ሆኖ ሥራ እንዴት ይሠራል?

እንበልና ይህ "መንግሥት" ደግሞ የብሔር ክልል መንግሥት ነው። ወይም በብሔር ስም የተደራጀ ግዙፍ ቤተሰብ ያቀፈ፤ ብዙ ሥልጣን ቆንጥጦ በእጁ የያዘ ድርጅት! እኔ ደግሞ "ከሌላ ክልል" የመጣሁ። ባለ ሃብት አለመሆኔ በጀኝ ልበል? እንዲህ ዐይነት ክስተት አይበዛም እንበልና ይቆይ።

በቅርቡ የብሔር ዳር እንዱስትሪ ፓርክ ሲመረቅ በፓርኩ የሥራ ቅድሚያ የሚያገኙ ፓርኩ ያረፈበት ሥፍራ ያሉ ባለቤቶች ናቸው ተብሏል። እምብዛም አስከፊ ውሳኔ አይደለም። መሬቱን ያጣ ሰውስ ሥራም አያገኝ? እናስ ሁሉም በደፈናው የፋብሪካ ሠራተኛ ይሆናሉ ማለት ነው? ላይሆን ይችላል። ግን ምርጫው በብቃት ምዘና ሳይሆን ከቀረስ? የሚያያጋጥሙን ጥያቄዎች ቀላል ወይም የዘፈቀደ መልስ ያላቸው እንዳይመስለን።

እንበልና የባስክሌት ጠጋኝ በሥፍራው ነበር። ሥራ ማሳነስ ከእኛ ይራቅ፤ መካኒክ እንበለው። በኢንዱስትሪ ፓርኩ ውስጥ ደግሞ የኤሌክትሮኒክ ፋብሪካ ተቋቋመ እንበል። ፋብሪካው መካኒክ ለኤሌክትሮኒክስ ባለሙያነት የመቅጠር ግዳጅ ወደቀበት ማለት ነው። ወይንም፤ በጉዞ ተፈናቃይ ነኝ ባይ፤ አለያም እንዲያ ብሎ እንዲያምን የተደረገ የኤሌክትሮኒክስ ባለሙያ ከጉንደር ወይም ቢቸና ፈልጐ ለማምጣት ይገደዳል። ሆሮ ጉድሩ አላልኩም!

ይህ "ከየት ነህ" ሳይባል፤ ሥራ ጠርቶት፤ ዐውቀት በር ከፍቶለት ስላልመጣ ለፋብሪካው አላስፈላጊ፤ ድርብ ወጪ ይሆንበታል። ሃብት ክህሎትን እንዴትና ከየት መግዛት እንዳለበት ራሱ ያውቃል። ለማዘዝ መምከር ውሃን ሸቅብ ፍሰስ እንደ ማለት ነው። በኤኮኖሚ ሥርዓት ውስጥ መንግሥት ገበያውን ለመምራት መሞከሩ ክፋት የለውም። ብዙዎች ያደርጉታል።

ነገር ግን ማዘዝን መሞከር፤ ወይም ገበያው ትክክል በሚሆንበት ጊዜ አለ መታዘዝ፤ ትልቅ ዕዳ ነው። ገበያን የማያገናዝብ ፖለቲካዊ ኤኮኖሚ ያለ ዐውቀት ሲሆን አስከፊ ነው። ሆን ተብሎ፤ የብሔር ፖለቲካችን መገለጫ እንዲሆን መቀረጹ፤ ግን የኤኮኖሚው ውድቀት መነሻ መሆኑ አሌ አይባልም።

በቅርቡ በእንጦጦ ፓርክ ሥራ ሂደት ድኩም ሥራቸው ለተቀማ የተሻለ ሥራ በፓርኩ ተሰጣቸው ሲባል እሳይ አልን፤ በቅጽበት ፤ 'እኛ ግን ተመሳሳይ ዕድል ሲገባን ተከለከልን' ባዮች መነሳታቸውን ሰማን። ገበያው ያውቃቸው ይሆን? የትስ ይገቡ? ፓርኩ ውስጥ በሥራ ስም ገብተው ሥራ በመፍታት ሊተዳደሩ? በሥራ ፈትነት ገንዘብ አይገኝ ነገር።

አዲስ አበባ ትደግ ተባለና በውስጧና ዳር አካባቢ ያሉት ተፈናቅለው ሥፍራቸው ዐቅም ላላቸው፤ ወይም ከመቅጽበት ዐቅም ለተፈጠረላቸው፤ ተሸነሸነ። የተሻለ ነገር

መጣ ብለን አልተከፋንም። ያላቸውን የተቀሙ "ገበሬዎች" የነበሩ ተፈናቃዮች ግን የተሰጣቸው ካሣ ፍትሕ ዐልባ ነበር። ሲያጉረመርሙ ቆይና ድምጻቸው ይሰማ ጀመር። ለለውጡ እሳት አንድ የክብሪት እንጨት።

ጉርምርምታው እውነትነት ስለነበረው ብዙዎች ለፍትሕ ጮኹ። ፍትሐዊ ኤኮኖሚ ለሥላጤ ዋስትና ነውና። ጨዥኽን የሚሰማ አምላክ ሰማና ለ20 ሺህ ተፈናቃዮችና ወራሾቻቸው ኮንዶምኒየምና በከተማው ውስጥ የእርሻ መሬት ታደለ ሲባል ደግሞ ሰማን። እሰይ አልን።

ነገር ግን እኛ ተፈናቃዮች፣ 60 ሺህ እንጂ 20 ሺህ ብቻ አይደለንም የሚሉ ተነሡ። ሌላ መልክም ያዘ፣ "ገበሬዎች" ከመቼው ብሔሮች እንደሆኑ ሳይገለጥልን ፖለቲካዊ ሆነ። የሚታደል ሲገኝ ያልተሰለፈ ሞኝ ነው። ገበያ ወደ ዳር ሲይዝ፣ ብሔርተኝነትም ኤኮኖሚውን ልምራ ሲል፣ እንዲህ ዐይነት የማያቋርጥ ፍላጎት ማስተናገድ ግድ ይላል።

በእርግጠኝነት እነዚያ ሁሉም ተፈናቀልን ባዮች ቤት ወይም መሬት ቢሰጣቸው ተጨማሪ 600 ሺህ የሚሆኑ የአያቴ፣ የምንጅላቴ መሬት እያሉ መምጣታቸው አይቀርም። ወዲያውም፣ ከቤተሰብ ይገባኛልነት ወደ ብሔር ይገባኛልነት ሲያድግ ውስብስብነቱ ይጉላል። የአገር ሃብት ከገበያ ውጭ በሆነ መንገድ ሲደለደል አድኂዊነቱ ቢቀር ትርፋማነትን በሚቀንስ መልኩ መሆኑ ግድ ነው።

ከዚህ በበለጠ ግን፣ ሃብት በገበያው፣ በኤኮኖሚ ሕዋሳት መካከል በሚደረግ ነጻ ድርድር በማይከፋፈልበት ሁኔታ ሁሉ ቅሽባን ማስቀረት አይቻልም። የተቀሸ ማለት፣ ማምረት ከሚገባው በታች ያመረተ ማለት ነው። ዐቅሙን የደበቀ፣ ወይም ዕምቅ ጉልበትን መጠቀም ያልቻለ ማለት ነው።

ለምሳሌ፦ ከዛሓይ ከለላ አጥቶ አናት አናቱን በሐሩር የተጠበሰ የቡና ዛፍ ማምረት ከሚገባው ፍሬ በታች ይሰጣል። በአንጻሩ፣ በዛፎች መካከል በቀሎ ዐፀይ ያላየ የበቆሎ ተክል ወገቡ እንደ ዘመኑ የከተማ ልጃገረድ ቀጥኖ አበባ ቢዘረዝር እንኳ፣ መሽራውን መሸከም አይችልም፣ ይቀነጠሳል። ለአንድ አገር ኤኮኖሚ እንዲሁም ለማንኛውም የኤኮኖሚ ተዋናይ ገበያ እንደ ፀሓይ ነው፣ በአግባቡ ማግኘት አለበት። የገበያ ውድድር ቢበዛ ያሳርዋል። ሲያንስ ደግሞ በአያት እጅ እንዳደገ ልጅ ጭንቅ አይችልም።

ያለ ገበያ ውድድር የተደለደለ የምርት መገልገያ ትርፋማነቱ የተቀሸ ብቻ ሳይሆን ለብክነትም የተጋለጠ ነው። የመንግሥት የልማት ድርጅቶችን፣ በተለይም ተጠያቂነትን ማስፈን አስፈሪ በሚሆንባቸው፣ የጉሥ ፓርቲ የልማት አውታሮችን መመልከት ይቻላል። ሜቴክንና ጥሪትን ያየ ይገነዘባዋል። ትዕምትና ገዳ፣ ዲንሾና መሰሎቹ የብክነት ጉተራዎች ናቸው። ያለ ምንም ጥያቄ።

እናም ዛሬ ኤኮኖሚው ዳገት ላይ ጉልበቱ የለገመው፤ አገሪቱ ብዝጎ ብሔር አገር ከመሆኗ ጋር የተያያዘ አይደለም። ፀሐይን በአግባቡ ካለ መጠቀም እንጂ፤ ገበያውን ናቅን። ገበያ የኤኮኖሚ ዋልታና ወጋግራ ነው። እርሱን ስንንቅ፤ ቤታችን አይቆምም።

አብዛኞቹ ጥናቶች ያለ ምንም ልዩነት የሚስማሙበት ብዝጎነት ከዴሞክራሲያዊ ውድድር ጋር በተጣመረበባቸው ቦታዎች ሁሉ የምጣኔ ሃብት ዕድገትም ሆነ የአጠቃላይ ምርት ምጣኔ ላቅ ብሎ መገኘቱ ነው። [224] እንኳንና አንድ ላይ የኖረ ሕዝብ ቀርቶ በፍልሰት ምክንያት ብዝጎነት ሲጨምር ለኤኮኖሚ ዕድገት በጉ እንደሆነ ጥናቶች አሳይተዋል። [225]

የታላቁ ብሪታኒያ ልማት ታሪክ እንደሚያመለክተው አገሪቱ ከፈውዳላዊ አግላይነት ወደ ዴሞክራሲያዊ አንድነት ስትሸጋገር ዌልስ፤ ስኮትላንድና ሰሜን አየርላንድ የተሻለ ዕድገት አስመዝግበዋል። አሜሪካ ቅድም እና ድኅረ አንድነት ፍጹም ልዩነት ያለው ዕድገት አስመዝግባለች። በአፍሪካ ስንኳ ብዝጎነትን ከውድድር ጋር በተቀበሉ አገራት ዘላቂ ዕድገት ታይቷል።

የአገራችንን ልማት ቀስፎ የያዘው ልዩነትን አስማምቶ መያዝ ያልቻለ የብሔር ፖለቲካ ኤኮኖሚ ውቅር ሙስናን፤ ብሶትን፤ ቅሸባንና፤ የዋጋ ንረትን እንዳንቋቋም ያደረገ ዋናው ምክንያት ነው። ይሁን እንጂ ልማት ሠናይ የኤኮኖሚ አመራርንም ይጠይቃል። ብዙ ብሔረሰብ ስላለ ብቻ ለልማት መልካም ይሆናል ማለት አይደለም።

ደቡብ አፍሪካ "ቀስተ ዳመናዊ አገር" በመባል ትታወቃለች፤ ብዙ ብሔረሰቦች አቅፋለችና፤ የኤኮኖሚ አመራሯ ግን ባለፉት 50 ዓመታት፤ አንዴ ላይ፤ አንዴ ደግሞ ታች ያደረገፀዋል፤ የዓለም ባንክ መረጃ እንደሚያመለክተው፤ [226] ከአፓርታይድ መውደቅ በኋላ "ዴሞክራሲያዊ" በተባለው ዘመን ያለው የኤኮኖሚ ዕድገት፤ ከዚያ በፊት ከነበረው ጋር ሲተያይ እምብዛም ልዩነት የለውም።

በቁጥር ደረጃ፤ ከአፓርታይድ ውድቀት በኋላ የአገሪቱ ሃብት በሦስት እጥፍ አድጓል። ዓመታዊ ዕድገቱ፤ በተለይም ከዋጋ ግሽበት አንጻር ሲታይ ግን እምብዛም ነው። ከአፓርታይድ ውድቀት 20 ዓመታት ቀደም ብሎ የጀመረው የአንጡራ ጠቢ.[227]

224 Alhendi, O., József, T., Péter, L., and Péter B. (2021). Tolerance, Cultural Diversity and Economic Growth: Evidence from Dynamic Panel Data Analysis. Economies 9: 20

225 Rodriguez-Pose, A. and Belepsch, V. (2019). Does Population Diversity Matter for Economic Development in the Very Long Term? Historic Migration, Diversity and County Wealth in the US. European Journal of Population; volume 35, pages873–911 (2019)

226 The World Bank. (2022). South Africa Open Data. Accessed from https://data.worldbank. org/country/ZA

227 አንጡራ ጠቢ የዋጋ ግሽበትን ታሳቢ ያደረገ እውነተኛው ወይም ሃቀኛ ጠቢ. ማለት ነው።

ደረጃ መዝቀጥ ሂደት ዛሬም በአስተማማኝ መንገድ ገና አልተቀየረም። ሃብትንና የሰውን ኃይል ፈራ ተባ እያለ የሚያከብር ፖሊሲ ሰንጥቆ አይወጣም።

የተከለከለ

እኛ ዐጥር እንወዳለን። የራስ የሆነን ነገር ለመከለል ዐጥርን ከፍ፣ ጥቅጥቅ አድርጉ መሥራት በብዙ የአገራችን ክፍሎች እንደ ባሕል ነው። መተላለፍ፣ ማየት፣ ክልክል ነው የምንልበት የራሳችን ቋንቋ ነው። ብዙ፣ ሌሎች አገራት ዐጥር አያስፈልጋቸውም። "መተላለፍ ክልክል ነው" ወይም "የተከለከለ" ብቻ የሚል ጽሑፍ ለምልክት አስቀምጠው ይከበርላቸዋል።

እንዲያው እንዴት አመጡት? የታደሉ። እሾህና ቆንጥር ፍልጋ ሳይዳክሩ፣ ወጪ በማያስከትል ዐጥር ንብረታቸው ይከበርላቸዋል። የራሱ ያልሆነውን የሚነካ በራሱ ላይ መፍረዱን በሁሉ ዘንድ ግንዛቤ አግኝቷል።

በሕይወት የመጀመር፣ ነጻነት፣ እና የንብረት ባለቤትነት መብቶች የሰው ተፈጥሯዊ መብቶች ናቸው። የአንድ ሰው የንብረት ባለቤትነት መብት፣ በሕይወት ከመጀመር መብት እና ከሌሎች ሰብዓዊ መብቶች ጋር በሕገ መንግሥታችን በወጉ ተሰድሯል፤ መብቶች መሻራፍ የለባቸውም። የሰው ነጻነት፣ የንብረት ባለቤትነት መብት ካልታከለበት ትርጉም ዐልባ መብት ነው፤ ዋጋ የለውም።

የንብረት ባለቤትነት መብት የሌለው ሰው ሌሎችን መብቶች ማስጠበቅ አይችልም። ልክ እንደ ሞት ይቈጠራል። ንብረት ማፍራት፣ ያፈራውን ሃብት ማስጠበቅ የማይችል ሰው ነጻነትን ተጉናጽፎ ማለት አይቻልም።

ስለዚህም፣ የመንግሥት መኖር ትርጉሙ ሰዎች በሕይወት የመኖር መብትን መጠበቅ እና ማስጠበቅ ብቻ አይደለም። መንግሥት የሚያስፈልገው ነጻነትንና የንብረት ባለቤትነት መብትንም ለመጠበቅ፣ ለማስከበር፣ እና ለማስፈጸም ነው። መንግሥት ባይኖር ወይም ባይችል አንድ ሰው እነዚህን የግሉን መብቶች ቢያስጠብቅ ጥፋት አይኖርበትም።

በጣም የሚገርመው ግን ብዙ ጊዜ ሰብዓዊ መብት ሲባል ቶሎ ማሰብ የሚቀናን፣ የነሲና፣ የዐሳብና፣ የንግግር ነጻነትን በተመለከተ ብቻ ነው። የንብረት መብት የሌለው፣ ሰብዓዊ መብቱም ጉዶሎ ነው። መጠየቅም ማስጠበቅም አይችልምና።

ትልቁ ስንተት ደግሞ እነዚህ መብቶች ግለሰብን ብቻ ይመለከታሉ ብሎ መደምደም ነው። ዐሳብን በነጻነት መግለጥም ሆነ ሰው ጥሮ ግሮ በላቡ ባገኘው ንብረት ላይ ኃላፊ ባለ መብት መሆን ሰውየውን ብቻ የሚመለከት አይደለም። ቤተሰብን፣ እንዲሁም ደግሞ ኅብረተሰቡንም ጥምር የሚጠቅም እንደሆነ ማስተዋል ያሻል።

በራስም ሆነ የሌሎች መብት መከበር ጉዳይ ላይ መናገር የሚችሉ ሰዎች፤ በቅድሚያ ማሰብ የቻሉ ናቸው፤ የነሊና ነጻነታቸውን የተቀዳጁ ሰዎች። በራስ ጉዳይ እንኳ ሲናገሩ ለራሳቸው ብቻ አይደለም። መናገር የተሳናቸውን ወይም የማይችሉትን፤ ወይም የመናገር ዕድልና ሥፍራ ያልተሰጣቸውን ብዙዎች ሰዎች ይወክላሉ። ከራሳቸው በላይ ለሌላው እጅግ ይጠቅማሉ።

መጽሐፍ ቅዱስ ለተገፋት መናገር እንድንችል ያዛናል፦ "አፍህን ስለ ዲዳው ክፈት፤ ተስፋ ስለ ሌላቸውም ሁሉ ተፋረድ፤...» ይላል (ምሳሌ 31፤ 8)። በመጽሐፍ ቅዱስ ምልከታ የመናገር ነጻነት ለራስ ብቻ አይደለም ማለት ነው። ለድኻ፤ ለምስኪን፤ ለዲዳ፤ የእኛ አፍ በጽድቅ መከፈቱ አስፈላጊ ነው። ክርስቲያን ጨዋና ጭምት ብቻ አይደለም ማለት ነው። ፍትሕ ሲዛባ ይጮኻል! በሌሎች እምነቶችም ተመሳሳይ ነገር እንዳለ መገመት ይቻላል።

ልክ እንደዚሁ፤ ንብረት አፍርተው በእርሱ ላይ የማዘዝ መብትም የተጎናጸፉት ለራሳቸው ብቻ አይጠቀሙበትም። ዐሳብን በጸነት እንደ መግለጥ፤ የንብረት ባለቤትነትም ጥቅሙ ማንበራዊ ነው። በላቡ ውጤት ላይ ማዘዝ የማይችል፤ የተጎዳ ካለ ቢራራ ትርጉም የለውም፤ ቀንጥቦ መስጠት ካልቻለ።

ከዚህም ባለፈ፤ ትልልቅ ድርጅቶች የሚመሠርቱ ሰዎች በሁሉም የድርጅቱ ሥራ ኃላፊነት ቦታዎች ራሳቸው ገብተው ለመሥራት አይደለም። አይችሉም፤ ሌሎች እንደ አግባቡ ይሠራሉ እንጂ። ገለጥ አድርገው አይተው፤ ለሚመቻቸው ዐደራ ይሰጣሉ። ራሱን ያዘጋጀ የሥራ ዕድል አገኘ ማለት ነው። ሰው በንብረቱ በተከክል ሲያዝና ተጠቃሚ ሲሆን የሥራ ዕድል ይፈጥራል። ካልቻለ፤ ወደሚችልበት ይንዛል። ሃብትና የሰው ኃይልን በጉልበት ማቀብ አይቻልም፤ ወደ ተመቻቸው ይንዛሉ።

የንብረት መብት መጽሐፍ ቅዱሳዊም ነው። ታላቁ መጽሐፍ፤ የፍጥረት ሁሉ አለቃና ባለቤት እግዚአብሔር መሆኑን ይናገራል። "ሰማያት የአንተ ናቸው። ምድርም የአንተ ናት፤ ዓለምና ሞላዋንም አንተ መሠረትህ" (መዝሙር 89፤ 11) ይላናል።

ይህ የሁሉ ባለቤት፤ ምድርና ሞላዋን ለሰው ሰጠ። የሰው ልጅ እንዲዋለድባት፤ እንዲሰለጥንባት፤ እንዲሁም እንዲንከባከብ፤ እንዲያበጅና እንዲጠብቃቅ ያዘዘዋል ማለትም ዐደራ ይሰጠዋል (ዘፍጥረት 1፤ 28 እና 2፤ 15)። የተንከባከበና ያበጀ ደግሞ ፍሬዋን ሳይሸማቀቅ ይበላል።

ስለዚህ በፍጥረት ላይ መሰልጠን፤ ማስዋብ፤ መንከባከብና መጠበቅ ከእግዚአብሔር የተሰጠን የግልም የጋራም ኃላፊነት እና ዕደራ እንደሆነ እንገነዘባለን፤ በእርግጥ፤ በግል ለእያንዳንዱ ሰው ድርሻ አላካፈለም። አንዳንድ ሥፍራ ብቻ በጋራ ሲሰጥ ከምንመለከት በቀር በምድር ላይ ያሉ ሕልቆ መሣፍርት ብሔሮችን ሁሉ 'አንተ በዚህ፤ አንተ በዚያ

እያለ ሲያደላድልም አይገኝ። ፍትሕ ሲዛባ ከተገፉት ጐን መቆም ግን እርግጥ ነው። የእጁ ሥራዎች ናቸውና ይራራላቸዋል።

ነገር ግን፤ ምድርና ሰው ከተገናኙ ጀምሮ እያንዳንዱ ሰው የድርሻውን የማበጀት አባዜም ተፈጥሯል። ሰዎች እየበዙ በሄዱ ቁጥርም ድርሻ ማበጀቱ እጅግ ዋጋ የሚያስከፍል እየሆነ ከመምጣቱም ጋር የባለቤትነት ስሜቱም ጠዋርነት አበጅቷል። ሰው ድርሻው ሲከበር ችግር አይኖርም። ችግር ሲፈጠርም የመፍታት ዘዴዎች በእጅጉ አዳብሯል።

መብት ስንልም፤ በዚህ ጣር ታልፎ የተገኘን ነገር ማክበር ማለት ነው። ለእኔ የተሰጠኝ (ወይም በሰውም በእግዚአብሔርም ዐይን ፍትሐዊ በሆነ መንገድ ያገኙት)፤ የእኔ ነው ማለት ነው፤ በላዩ ላይ የመሰልጠን መብት አለኝ፤ ዕሴት እጨምርበታለሁ፤ አቅሜ በፈቀደ መጠን ሁሉ፤ ውብና ማራኪ፤ ጠንካራና የሚሰፋ፤ ብርቱና የማይደፈር፤ የማድረግ ተፈጥሯዊ ሥልጣን እና መብት አለኝ።

እንደዚሁም፤ የመጠበቅና የመንከባከብ ኃላፊነትም የእኔ ነው። ዐደራ ስለሆነ በጥንቃቄ እይዘዋለሁ። ምክንያቱም፤ እንደ መጽሐፍ ቅዱስ፤ በመስጠቱ የእኔ ይሁን እንጂ በቅድሚያ ባለቤት አለው። እርሱ ፈጣሪ ስለሆነ ፍጥረቱን አሳልፎ ሰጥቶ ጥሎ አልሄደም። ያያዋል፤ ይቆጣጠረዋማል።

ምክንያቱም:- የእኔ የሆነው ከእኔ አልፎ ለሌላው ማኅበራዊ ጥቅም አለው። ከመብቴ ጋር ሳይጋጭ፤ "ሁለት ልብስ ያለው ለሌላው ያካፍል፤ ምግብም ያለው እንዲሁ ያድርግ" (ሉቃስ 3፤ 11) ስለሚል ለማካፈልም ጮምር የተሰጠኝ ነው። የማስተዳድረው ይሆንንም ስለማውቅ ነው።

መስጠት የፍቅር ዕዳ እንጂ ግዴታ አይሆንም። "ነገር ግን የዚህ ዓለም ገንዘብ ያለው፤ ወንድሙም የሚያስፈልገው ሲያጣ አይቶ ያልራራለት ማንም ቢሆን፤ የእግዚአብሔር ፍቅር በእርሱ እንዴት ይኖራል? ልጆቼ ሆይ፤ በሥራና በእውነት እንጂ በቃልና በአንደበት አንዋደድ" ይላልና (1ኛ ዮሐንስ 3፤ 17) እንሰጣለን። የእግዚአብሔር ፍቅር በእርሱ የሌለው ዐደራ በላ ተወካይ ነው። ግፍ ሲያይል፤ ቅጥፈት ሲበዛ፤ ዐደራ ሲጫ ውክልናውን የማንሣት ሙሉ ሥልጣን አለው።

በፈጣሪ እግዚአብሔርና በአስተዳዳሪ ተወካይ (ሰው) መካከል ሰዎች መንግሥት የሚባል ተቋም ፈጠሩ። አስተዳደርን፤ በተለይም ማኅበራዊ ጐኑን ሥርዓት ማስያዝ ስለሚያስፈልግ። ታዲያ መንግሥትም የቀማኛነት ባሕርይ ያለው ተቋም ነው። ካልተገራ፤ ገደብ ካልተበጀለት፤ ከመቀማት ወደ ጓላ አይልም። ተላሎች መንግሥትን እንደ ቅዱስ አባት ይቆጥሩታል። ልጉሙንም ጅራፉንም ያስረክቡታል። እናም ልጓሙን አውልቆ ሲጋጥ፤ ባለቤቶችንም ሲገርፍ ይኖራል።

ነገር ግን፡ መንግሥት ሥራውን መሥራት ካለበት፣ ከገደብ ጋራ የሚገባውን ማግኘት ይኖርበታል። ስለዚህም፣ በአንድ አገር ያሉ ዜጎች በሚስማሙበት መሠረት "የቄሣርን ለቄሣር የእግዚአብሔርንም ለእግዚአብሔር አስረክቡ" (ማቴዎስ 22፡ 21) እንደሚል "የሚገባውን" ብቻ የሚያገኘበት መንገድ ሊቀየስ ይገባል። ይህን ካላገኘ ማስተዳደር አይችልምና። ይህ ትዕዛዝም ባይሆን የሰብዓዊነት፣ የግብረ ገብነትም መለኪያ ሊሆን በተገባው ነበር፡ ማኅበራዊ እሴታችንም መነሻው እንጂ።

ሰው ማኅበራዊ እንስሳቱ በጋራ የሚያኖረው ከሆነ፣ አንድ ላይ መኗዝ የድርሻውን መወጣት እንዳለበትም ያስረዳዋል። ነገር ግን ዜጎች የሚገባውን ሁሉ ከደረጉ በኃላ የሚቀረው ከማንም ተጽዕኖ ፍጹም ነጻ የሆነ የግል ሃብት ነው። ድንበር አለው፤ ሊከበር ይገባል። በኢትዮጵያ ይህ ድንበር በእጅጉ ተገፍቷል። በተለይም የሶሻሊዝም ዕሳቤ በአገሪቱ ከተጠነሰሰበት ከ20ኛው መቶ ክፍለ ዘመን አጋማሽ ጀምሮ የግል ንብረት እንደ ጠላት ንብረት ይታያል።

ዓለም አቀፉ የንብረት መብት ኑብረት ተቋም በየዓመቱ የአገራት የንብረት መብትና አስተዳደር የሚጠቆሙ ቀመር ያወጣል። በዚህ ቀመር መሠረት በኢትዮጵያ የንብረት መብት ጥበቃ በመጠኑም ቢሆን እየተሻሻለ የመጣ ቢሆንም አሁንም እጅግ ዝቅተኛ ከሚባሉ አገራት ውስጥ ትገኛለች። ጠቅሚ ከተዘጋጃላቸው 129 አገራት ውስጥ 115ኛ ደረጃ ይዛ ትገኛለች። በአፍሪካ ጠቅሚው ከተገመተላቸው 30 አገራት ውስጥ 20ኛ ደረጃ ይዛለች።

በኢትዮጵያ ሕግ መንግሥት እንደ ተደነገገው፣ አንድ ሰው በኢትዮጵያ ውስጥ የትም ቦታ ንብረት የማፍራት መብት አለው። ምን ፋይዳ አለው? ሰው ሁሉ ንብረት ሲያፈራ እየራ ነው። ከአሁን አሁን ይወሰድብኛል፣ ይፈርስብኛል ወይም አንዳች ነገር ይከሠታል የሚል ሥጋት አለውና።

ይህ ፍርሃት በአብዛኛው ከፖለቲካው አለ መረጋጋት ጋር የተያያዘ ቢሆንም የንብረት ጥበቃ ሕጎችም ምሉዕ አይደሉም። እንደ ኮፒ ሌብነት ዐይነት ያሉ ያልተገሩ፣ ልቅ ሥርቆቶች የባለቤትነት መብትን አሳንሰውታል። በንብረት ላይ ማንም ተነሥቶ ጉዳት ካደረሰ ሕግ አያዋጣም።

በተለይ ደግሞ "ስለ ብሔር ጥቅም" ተብሎ የንብረት ዘረፋ ከተደረገ እንደ ጀግንነት፣ እንደ ነጻ አውጭነት ይቄጠራል። ይህ ደግሞ የለየለት ዕብደት ነው። የዜጎችን የንብረት ባለቤትነት መብት ይደረምሳል። ፍርሃቱ እጅግ አይሎ በብሔረ ክልል ንብረት አፈራሁ የሚሉትን ጭምር እያርገበገበ ነው፤ ዋስትና የለምና። ዘመድ ቢጠብቅ ጉረቤት እንደማያፈርስ እርግጠኞች አይደለንምና።

ጥቂት እያተሻሻለ የመጣው የንብረት ምዝገባ ብቻ እንደሆነ መረጃዎች ይጠቁማሉ። በተለይም ቋሚ ንብረት በተሻለ መንገድ በአገባቡ ይመዘገባል። ይሁን

እንጂ በብሔር ፖለቲካ የተቃኘው አስተዳደር ሲያሰኝው በጉቦ መዝገብን ይለውጣል፤ ሲብስም መዝገብና መዝገብ ቤቱን ጭምር ያቃጥላል።

የአገራችን የብሔር ፖለቲካ ጽንፈኝነትን መውለዱ የታለመም ባይሆን በግልፅ መታየቱን መካድ አይቻልም። ጽንፈኝነት የብሔር ፖለቲካው ራሱ በፈጠረው መዋቅር ተሸክሞት ከሚዘልቀው በላይ ሆኗል። ከገደብ በላይ ሆኖ ፈሷል። የመልካም አስተዳደር ዕጦት ዋና ችግር ሆኗል።

በቅርቡ የተከሰተው የሶሜን ኢትዮጵያ ችግር፣ ቋሚ ብቻ ሳይሆን ተንቀሳቃሽም፣ የአዕምሮ ንብረትንም መብት አቃጥሎ አልፏል። ሕጻናት ስንኳ ሳይቀሩ የትምህርት ቤት መረጃቸው ወድሟል። ፖለቲካችን የዛሬ ዜጎችን ብቻ ሳይሆን ትውልድን ማረድ መጀመሩን እናያለን።

ፖለቲካዊ ኤኮኖሚው በብሔርተኝነት ሲታኝ የሰው ላብ ጥበቃው ድንበር ድንብርብሩ ይወጣል። በምድራችን ከቅርብ ጊዜ ወዲህ እየታየ ያለው የ"ይገባኛል" እንቅስቃሴ የዚህ ድንብርብር አካል ነው። ላብ ባልፈሰሰበት፣ በብሔር ስም የግለሰብ ንብረትን የራስ የማድረግ፣ ካልተቻለም የመዝረፍና የማውደም ባሕል የጽንፍ ረገጥ ብሔርተኝነት አስተዋጽኦ ነው።

ንብረት የማግኛትና የማፍራት መብት ስንል በቀጥታ የሚመለከተው የግል ንብረትን ነው። የግል ንብረት ጥበቃና እንክብካቤ የኤኮኖሚ ዕድገት መሠረት ነው። በታዳጊ አገራትና በተለይም በብሔርተኝነት ኤኮኖሚው የታጠረባቸው አገራት ይህ መሠረት በመናጋቱ፣ የዕድገት ተጠቃሚ አይሆኑም። አስተማማኝ የግል ንብረት ጥበቃና እንክብካቤ ልማትንና ዕድገትን እንደሚያፋጥን በሰፊው ተመልክቷል። [228]

የግል ንብረት ጥበቃና እንክብካቤ እንዴት ልማትን ያመጣል የሚል ጥያቄ ሊነሣ ይችላል። በዚህ ረገድ የተደረጉ ጥናቶች እንደሚያመለክቱት፣ ሰዎች የንብረታቸው ደህንነት ሲረጋገጥ በሚወስዱቸው እርምጃዎች የዕድገትና ልማት ሞተር ይሆናሉ። ለጥበቃና ደህንነት ሳያስቡ በሃብታቸው ዕድገት ላይ ብቻ ያተኮረ እርምጃ ስለሚያስቡ፣ የንብረት ጥበቃ ከተጓደለበት ሁኔታ ይልቅ ለልማት ዝግጁ ይሆናሉ።

በመጀመሪያ ደረጃ፣ ንብረት የማፍራት መብት ወደ ልማት እንዲሸጋገር አንድ ሰው ጥሮ ግሮ ያፈራውን ንብረት ማንም በዘፈቀደ የማይቀማው መሆኑ ማረጋገጥ ያስፈልጋል። ይህን ሲያውቁ ባለ ሃብቶች ለዛሬ ከመኖር አልፈው ነገን ያልማሉ።

---

228 Haydaroglu, C. (2015). The relationship between property rights and economic growth: An analysis of OECD and EU countries, DANUBE: Law, Economics and Social Issues Review, ISSN 1804-8285, De Gruyter, Warsaw, Vol. 6, Iss. 4, pp. 217-239, https://doi.org/10.1515/danb-2015-0014

ተረካቢያዎችን፣ (ቤተሰብንና ሌሎችን) ስለሚያስቡ በሃብት ማፍራቱ ላይ ተረጋግተው እንደሚሠሩ በጥናት ተረጋግጧል።[229]

ሰዎች ያካበቱትን ንብረት ብቻቸውን እንደማይበሉት ይገባቸዋል። ነገር ግን ወራሾችን ራሳቸው መርጠው ማስተላለፍ ይፈልጋሉ። ልጅም ይሁን ሌላ፣ በግልዕም ሆነ በሀቡዕ "ትቀማለህ" እየተባለ ማን ሊሠራ ይነሳል?

እንዲሁም፣ ንብረታቸው ሠላማዊ ሥፍራ መኖሩን ሲያረጋግጡ፣ ባለ ሀብቶች ገንዘብም ሆነ ሌላ ሃብት ከማሽሽ ይቆጠባሉ። ተረጋግተው ከመሥራት ባለፈ፣ ጥልቅ፣ ቋሚና ዘላቂ መዋዕለ ንዋይ ማፍሰስንም ተግባራዊ ያደርጉታል። ይህ በሌለበት ግን ሃብትን በተገኘው አጋጣሚ ሁሉ ሊያሸሹ ይምክራሉ።

ሃብት ብሔር የለውም። ብዙ ጊዜ 'እንጌ ከዚህ ብሔር ስላይደለ እዚህ ሥርቶ ያፈራውን ሃብት ብሔሩ ወዳለበት ያሸሻል' ሲባል እንሰማለን። ምን ጥያቄ አለው? ብሔሩን ፍለጋ የሸሸው ግሁዙ ገንዘብ ሳይሆን ልቡ እንዲሸፍት ያደረግነው ሰው፣ ባለ ገንዘቡ ነው።[230]

ሦስተኛም መንገድ እለው። መንግሥት የሃብት ጥበቃን 'ሳላሴት ሲወስድ ሰዎች ለራሳቸውና ለሃብታቸው ጥበቃ የሚያወጡትን የጊዜ፣ የጉልበት፣ የአዕምሮና የገንዘብ ጎይል ያድናሉ። ይህንም ወደ ልማት ሊያውሉ የሚችሉበት ስፌ ዕድል ይፈጠርላቸዋል። ማንም በሕጋዊ መንገድ ሃብት ያፈራ ሰው ዝርፊያና ቅሚያ የሚጋብዝ ጥበቃ ማድረግ አይፈልግም።

በአፍሪካ እንኳ የተደረጉ ጥናቶች እንደሚያመለክቱት፣ ሰዎች ሃብታቸውን የሚጠብቅ ጠንካራ መንግሥታዊ መዋቅር ሲያጡ ራሳቸው የጥበቃ ዐቅም ለመፍጠር ይምክራሉ። ይህ ደግሞ የሕጋዊነት አተካራ ውስጥ ይከትታቸዋል። አልፎ ተርፎም ዐቅምን የሚጎዳ ከመሆኑም በላይ ከመንግሥት ጋር ድብብቆሽ፣ እያደርም ለከፉ ሥርዓተ ዐልበኝነትም ሊዳርግ ይችላል።[231]

---

229 Besley, T. & Gathak, M. (2009). Property Rights and Economic Development. The Suntory Centre Suntory and Toyota International Centres for Economics and Related Disciplines; London School of Economics and Political Science. Accessed on August 17, 2022, from https://ideas.repec.org/h/eee/devchp/v5y2010icp4525-4595.html

230 Locke, A. (2013). Briefing Paper Property Rights and Development: Property Rights and Economic Growth. ODI, UKAID. Accessed on August 17, 2022 from https://assets.publishing.service.gov.uk/media/57a08a3be5274a27b20004c5/61055-Growth_and_property_rights_PUBLISHED_FINAL.pdf

231 Asoungu, S. A. & Kodila-Tedika, O. (2016). Determinants of Property Rights Protection in Sub-Saharan Africa. Journal of the Knowledge Economy, November 2016. African Governance and Development Institute. Accessed on August 17, 2022, from https://mpra.ub.uni-muenchen.de/76587/

በመጨረሻም፣ ጥርት ያለ ምዝገባ፣ የማያሻማ የባለቤትነት መብት፣ እንዲሁም ዋስትና እና ጥበቃ ያለው ሃብት የባለቤቱ ብቻ ሳይሆን ንግድና ልማትን ለማሳለጥ ለሚፈልጉ ሁሉ መከታ ነው። ለምሳሌ፦ ባንኮች የጠራ ባለቤትነት ሳይኖር ብድር አይፈቅዱም። እንዲሁም፣ የአገራት የፖለቲካ መዋቅር ለሃብት ምዝገባና ጥበቃ ዋነኛ መሠረት መሆኑ ተመልክቷል። [232]

በአፍሪካ ግን፣ ለብድር አቅርቦትና ተደራሽነት ትልቁ ማነቁ ለመያዣ የሚሆን ጥርት ያለ ሃብት ያለ መኖሩ ነው። በፖለቲከኞች በተሻበበ የኤኮኖሚ መዋቅር ደግሞ፣ የግል ሃብት ዋስትና እና ክብካቤ አይቀድምም። በፖለቲካዊ መንገድ በተሠራ ድልድል ወይም መብት ተጠቃሚ የሚሆነው ሕዝብ ሳይሆን መዋቅሩን የሠሩ የፖለቲካ ልሂቃን ናቸው። [233]

በተለይም ሕብረ ብሔራዊ በሆኑ አገራት የግል ሃብት ዋስትና እና ጥበቃን ለማጠናከር አድልዎ የሌለበት ብርቱ መዋቅር መፍጠር ያስፈልጋል። ይሁን እንጂ፣ በእንደዚህ ዐይነት አገራት መንግሥትን በያዘው ጎሳል ብዙ ድክመቶች እንደሚገለጥበት ጥናቶች ይጠቁማሉ። እርስ በራሱ የተከፋፈለ፣ እርስ በራሱ የተጣረሰ ስለሆነ ሰከን ያለ መዋቅር መሥራት አዳጋች ነው።

ፖል ዛክ የተባሉ የካሊፎርኒያ ዩኒቨርሲቲ የኤኮኖሚክስ አስተማሪ እንደሚያነሱት ከሆነ በዚህ ረገድ ሦስት ዋና ዋና ድክመቶችን መለየት ይቻላል። [234] በመጀመሪያ ደረጃ፣ እጅግ የከፋ የሚባለው እንዲህ ነው፦ ደካማ ማዕከላዊ መንግሥት ያጋጥምና በየክፍላተ አገሩቱ በየጫካው፣ የየብሔሩ ተወካይ ነኝ ባዮች የሚያደራጁት ትይዩ መዋቅር ይፈለፈላል። ይህ ትርፍ አንጀት የሆነ መዋቅር ለባለ ሃብት አበሳ ይሆናል።

ባለ ትይዩ መዋቅሮችን ሕግ አይገዛቸውም፣ የሠፈር ጦር እያደራጁ የሕዝብ ጣር ይሆናሉ። እነርሱ በሚንቀሳቀሱባቸው አካባቢዎች፣ የጉብዝ አለቆች ካልፈቀዱ ምንም መሥራት አይቻልም። ይባስ ብሎ የመዘዋወር፣ የቅጥር፣ የምርት ማከፋፈል እና የግብዓቶች ግብይት በጉብዝ አለቆች መልካም ፈቃድ ላይ የተመሰረተ ይሆናል። ይህ የከፋው ደረጃ ነው።

232 Mijiyawa, A, G. (2013). Determinants of property rights institutions: survey of literature and new evidence. May 2013, Volume 14, Issue 2. Accessed on August 17, 2022, from https://journals.scholarsportal.info/details/14356104/v14i0002/127_doprisolane.xml&sub=all

233 Miller, T. (1997). The Role of Property Rights in Economic Development that Benefits the Poor. Accessed on August 17, 2022 from https://www.researchgate.net/publication/228434733_The_Role_of_Property_Rights_in_Economic_Development_that_Benefits_the_Poor

234 Zak, P. J. (2002). Institutions, Property Rights, and Growth. Recherches economiques de Louvain; 2002/1-2 (vol. 68; pages 55 – 73. Accessed on August 17, 2022, from https://www.cairn.info/revue-recherches-economiques-de-louvain-2002-1-page-55.htm

ሁለተኛው ጽንፍም ቢሆን ለባለ ሀብቶች ዕዳ ነው። ትይዩ መዋቅር ቀርቶ አንገቱን
ቀና ማድረግ የሚችል ቀርቶ የሚፈልግ እንኳ የሌለበት የአምባገነኖች ሥርዓት። ፈላጭ
ቆራጭ የሆነ ጠንካራ ማዕከላዊ መንግሥት ሲኖር ይህ ይከሠታል።

ይህም ግን ሠላምን ይሰጣል ማለት አይደለም። ጡንቸኛ መሆኑን ሲያውቅ፣
በባለ ሀብቶች ላይ እንደ መሿገር ተጣብቆ የሚጠባ፣ ሳይጮቅ የማይነቀል ዕልቂት
ይሆናል። "ጥበቃና ከለላ ሰጠሁህ" እያለ መጠን ራሱ ወስኖ "አካፍለኝ" ይላል።
"ተካፍሎ ያልበላን" ይገድላል። "ማካፈል" ተባለ እንጂ፣ ያካፈለም ቢሆን ደሙ
ተመጥጦ ይሞታል።

መኃል ሠፋሪውም ለንብረት ደህንነትና ጥበቃ መብቃ አይበጅ። የሠፈር
ጉልበተኞችን የማንበርከክ ዐቅም ያለው፣ ነገር ግን ልግመኝነት የተጠናወተው
መንግሥት የሚያጋጋምበትም ጊዜ አያሌ ነው። የዚህም ቅኚቱ ብሔርተኝነት ሲሆን፣
አጿም ሲዋኸቅ በግልፅ ይነበባል።

እነዚህ ሦስቱ ብሔርተኛ ፖለቲካ የሚወልዳቸው የመንግሥት ዐይነቶች ናቸው።
ሃብትና ላብ ከእነዚህ አንዱ መከሰታቸውን ባወቁ ጊዜ በፍጹም መታመን በመንግሥታዊ
መዋቅሮችና ሕጎች ላይ መደገፍ አይሆንላቸውም። ይህ ደግሞ ሃብትንና ንብረትን
ማፍራት የሚፈልጉ ዝነት ዓለም ፈራ ተባ እንዳሉ እንዲኖሩ የሚያደርግ ነው። ደፍሮ
የቢዝነስ አደጋና ስጋትን መጋፈጥንና ፈጠራን ያዳፍናል።

መዋቅራዊ ወንጀል?

ለግል ንብረትና ሃብት መዋቅራዊ ጥበቃና ዋስትና ያስፈልጋል ለሚለው ከዚህ
የበለጠ ምክንያት መደርደር ይቻላል። ይሁን እንጂ፣ ብሔርተኝነት ባየለባቸው የአፍሪካ
አገራት ከጥበቃ ይልቅ መዋቅራዊ ወንጀል ሊባል የሚችል ሥራ በኤኮኖሚ ፖሊሲ ስም
እንደሚሠራ ልንገነዘብ ይገባል የሚሉ ያጋጥማሉ። ስለዚህ ይህንንም ደግሞ በጨረፍታም
ቢሆን እንየው።

መንግሥት የሚባለው አካል፣ የሚያስተዳድረውን ሕዝብ ደህንነት ይጠብቅልኛል
ብሎ ካሰበ፣ ከፍተኛ ጎሣል እስከ መጠቀም የሚያስችለው ሕጋዊ ፈቃድና ጉልበት
የተሰጠው ብቸኛ ተቋም ነው። ይገባዋልም። ከሕግ አፈንጋጭ ሲበዛ የንብረት መብት
ጥሪሽ ይጠፋልና። አስተዳደር ዐቅም ይፈልጋል።

መንግሥት የሚያወጣቸው ፖሊሲዎችም ስንተት እንኳ ቢሆኑ፣ መብት እንደ
ተሰጠው አካል ያደረገው እስከ ሆነ ድረስ "ወንጀል" ማለት ከባድ አገላለፅ ነው።
ፖለቲካዊ ኤኮኖሚው ፈቅዶ ወይም አስፈልጎት ሳይሆን፣ አንድን ከመንግሥት ጋር

ይበልጥ የተቄራኗ አካል ለማበልጸግ ሲባል እጅግ ያፈነገጠ ፖሊሲ ቢቀረድ ግን የወንጀል
ድርጊት ሊባል ይችላል የሚሉም ሞልተዋል።

ጊዜው የ1960ዎቹ መገባደጃ እና የ1970ዎቹ መጀቻ አካባቢ ነው። በኤኮኖሚ ላይ
የመንግሥት ጣልቃ ገብነት እንነደ አማራጭ ዐልባ መንገድ ብቻ ሳይሆን እንደ አሸናፊ
ዐሳብ የተወሰደበት ጊዜ ነበር። ሶሻሊዝም ተንሠራፍቷል፤ ተደላድሏልም። ወይም
እንዲያ ተብሎ ታስቧል።

በተለይም በቅርብ ከፖለቲካ ጥገኛነት ነጻ የወጡ የአፍሪካ አገራት መንግሥት
መር ኤኮኖሚን የሙጥኝ ብለዋል። ምዕራባውያኑ ይህ የሚፈጥረውን የጥራት ዕጦት፤
ብክንነትና ጫና አስልተው፤ የእንርሱን የካፒታል የበላይነት እስካልነካ ድረስ በመቻቻል
ለመኖር ይዳዱ ነበር። ቀዝቃዛውን ጦርነት ይበልጥ ማቀዝቀዝ ይበጃል እንደ ማለት።

ልክ በዚህ ጊዜ ፕሮፌሰር ጉርደን ቱሎክ (1922–2014)[235] የተባሉ በጆርጅ
ሜሰን ዩኒቨርሲቲ የሕግ ትምህርት ቤት የኤኮኖሚክስ መምህር የሆኑ ሰው ብቅ አሉ።
ከኖቤል ተሸላሚ ጓደኛቸው ጄምስ ቡካናን ጋር በመሆን "ሕዝባዊ ምርጫ" የተሰኘ
አዲስ ንድፈ ዐሳብ ይዘው። ብዙዎች፤ ለጄምስ ቡካናን የተሰጠው የኖቤል ሽልማት
የጋራቸው ቢሆን ይሻል ነበር ይላሉ። እኒህ ሰው፤ በረኸም ዕድሜአቸው አዳዲስ ዐሳብ
በመፈንጠቅ ይታወቃሉ።

የመንግሥት ጣልቃ ገብነት የሚያስከትለው የኤኮኖሚ ቀውስ በቀሞር ተሰልቶ
በሚታወቅበት በዚያ ዘመን ቀሞሩ ሕዝባዊ ወይም ማነባራዊ ኪሣራን የማይቆጥር ስለሆነ
መሠረታዊ ግድፈት እንዳለበት አመለክቱ። ይህ ሕዝባዊ ወይም ማነባራዊ ቀውስ
ሲካተትበት፤ የመንግሥት ጣልቃ ገብነት ከልክ በላይ ዋጋ የሚያስከፍል መሆኑ ፍንትው
እያለ መጣ።

አንድ የኤኮኖሚ ውሳኔ አካል እጅግ ብዙ ሥፍራ ወይም ጎይል ሲሰጠው፤
በውሳኔው ከሚያበላሸው ነገር ይልቅ፤ ያን አካል ተደግፎ ለመቦጥቦጥ ወይም ከውድቀቱ
ትርፋት ለማግኘት መሯሯጥ የሕዝብ ድርሻ ይሆናል። በቱሎክ ዕሳቤ ሰው ወይም አንድ
የኤኮኖሚ ሕዋስ ማዕከላዊ ውሳኔው 'ከራስ በላይ ንፋስ" የሚል ነውና። አጋጣሚ ሲገኝ
ማንም አይምርም።

ይህ "ሲሾም ያልበላ" የሚባለውን ብቻ ያካተተ አይደለም። በእርግጥ ይህም
አለ፤ የባሰው ግን የኤኮኖሚ ባለ ድርሻዎች በሙሉ የፖሊሲ ክፍተትን በመመገስ ሲማስኑ
የሚፈጥሩት ውድቀት ነው። ከውድቀቱ በፌት ደግሞ ጥልፍልፉ ይበዛል። "እከከኝ

---

235 Forte, F., & Brady, G. L. (2021). Remembering Gordon Tullock—The Unconventional
Economist: Beyond *Homo Economicus* and *"Economist Borne."* Alternative Traditons in
Public Service; Vol. 11 No. 1; 2021. Accessed on September 29, 2022, from https://journals.
openedition.org/oeconomia/10819

ልከክህ›› በሚያስብል ቁኖርኝት የመንግሥት እና የግለሰቦች ወይም የኤኮኖሚ ሕዋሳት ድንበር ይደበላለቃል።

ስለሆነም፣ በአንድ አገር የመንግሥት እጅ በኤኮኖሚ ላይ እጅግ በጠነከረች ቁጥር መንግሥት ሳይሆን፣ አፈ ትብ ደላሎች፣ አማላጆች፣ የሕግ ትርጉም አጣማሚዎች፣ እንዲሁም ደፋሮች የአገሪቱን ኤኮኖሚ ይጆምራሉ። ባለ ሥልጣናት፣ አውቀውም ሆነ ተታልለው በወጥመዱ ይያዛሉ። ይህ ታዲያ ኤኮኖሚን ብቻ ሳይሆን ተቋማትን፣ ሕዝባዊ ዕሴትን፣ ብሎም አገርን የመገደል ዐቅም ያለው ክፉ ጥምረት ነው፤ እናም ወንጀል ነው።

ምሳሌ እንውሰድ፦ በአገራችን መሬት መሸጥ በሕግ የተከለከለ ነው። መሬት "የማይሸጥ፣ የማይለወጥ፣ የመንግሥትና የሕዝብ እንዲሁም የብሔር ብሔረሰቦች ሃብት ነው" ይላል ሕገ መንግሥቱ።[236] ይህ ገና ከጅምሩ ጥያቄ ያስነሳል። ይህ አራት ባለቤቶች የሚሻኮቱበት ሃብት በእርግጥ የማን ነው? በዚህ ሃብት ላይ ሌላ ሃብት ለምሳሌ ቤት የገነባስ ሰው ከመሬት ሀብቱ ድርሻ አለው?

መሬት ግንባታ ሲታከልበት ዕሴት ይጨምራል። ይህ ዕሴት የማን ነው? ቤት ግን መሸጥ ይቻላል። እንድ ሰው ቤቱን ሲሸጥ ዕሴት የታከለበት መሬት ጭምር ስለሚያስተላልፍ፣ ትርፉ ወደ ማን ይሄዳል? ደግም ዕሴት በመሬቱ ላይ የጨመረው፣ በባለ ንብረቱ ብቻ ሳይሆን፣ በአጠገቡ ቤት በሠሩ ሰዎች፣ በተቋቋሙ የመሠረተ ልማት ዓይነቶች፣ እንደ ዕድል ሆኖ ሰፈሩ ጥሩና ነፋሻማ አየር ካለው ጭምር። አሊያም እንደ ዘመኑ ቀልድ የመብራት ኃይልና ወይም ውሃና ፍሳሽ መሠሪያ ቤቶች ኃላፊዎች ጉርብትና።

የማን ሃብት እንደሆን ግልፅ ባልሆነ ነገር ላይ የበቀለ ፍሬ ሲያስጎመጅ፣ ሁሉም የራስ ለማድረግ ይፈልጋል። ሽርክናም፣ ሽኩቻም ይጆምራል። መንግሥት፣ ሕዝብ፣ ብሔር ብሔረሰቦች እና ግለሰቦች ወይም መሰል ሕጋዊ ዕውቅና የተሰጣቸው የኤኮኖሚ ሕዋሳት ይሻረኩሉ፣ ይሻኩታሉም። ይህ ሽኩቻና ሽርክና ኪራይ ሰብሳቢነት ይባላል።

ኪራይ መሰብሰብ በራሱ ችግር አይደለም። ሰው በለፋበት ነገር ላይ የተጨመረ ዕሴት ሲሆን፣ ሰብሳቢነቱ የሚገለጥበት መልክ ግን አስቀያሚ የሚሆንበት አጋጣሚ ይበዛል። ቴሎክ መልክ ጥፋውን የኪራይ ሰብሳቢነት መንገድ፣ በቀደም ጽሐፎቻቸው "ያልተበረዘ ክፋት" ብለውታል።[237] በእርግጥም፣ ክፋትን ያዘለ ስለሆነ፣ እያደረጀ ሲሄድ ለሰውም፣ ለአገር ሕልውናም ጠንቅ ስለ ሆነ።

236 Conistitute. (2022). Ethiopian Consitiution 1994. Accessed on September 29, 2022, from https://www.constituteproject.org/constitution/Ethiopia_1994.pdf

237 Tullock, G. (1988). Rents and Rent-Seeking. In: Rowley, C.K., Tollison, R.D., Tullock, G. (eds) The Political Economy of Rent-Seeking. Topics in Regulatory Economics and Policy, vol 1. Springer, Boston, MA. https://doi.org/10.1007/978-1-4757-1963-5_4

መንግሥት ኪራይ ሰብሳቢነትን ለመዋጋት ተጨማሪ ሕግ ማውጣቱ ግድ ይሆናል። ችግሩ ግን በሕግም፣ በመለማመጥም መቆጣጠር አይችልም። አሳሪ ሕግ ቢያወጣ፣ መልሶ ሌላ ኪራይ ሰብሳቢነትን ይወልዳል። ኪራይ ሰብሳቢነትን የሚከታታሉና የሚያስወግዱ ተቋማትን ቢያደራጅም አይጠረቅንም። ቀድመው በመርዙ ይነደፋሉ።

ለምሳሌ፦ 'መሬት በሊዝ ይተዳደር፣ የሊዝ ገቢው ለመንግሥት ይሁን፣ የሚል ሕግ ያወጣል እንበል። ሕግ ስለሆነ ከላይ፣ ከላይ ሲታይ ሕጋዊ ይመስላል፣ ውስጡ ግን። "ያልተበረዘ ክፋት" በመርጨት የተከኑ ኪራይ ሰብሳቢዎች ከሊዝ አስተዳደር ሥርዓት አንስተው መላ መዋቅሩን ይበክሉታል። በጉቦ ያለ ሊዝ ንብረትን ማስተላለፍ እና በእጅ ማስገባት እጅግ ጥቂቱ ነው። ወንጀሉን ማኅበራዊ ያደርጉታል። ሕዝብ የሚሳተፍበት።

ብዙኃኑ ሲሳተፍበት ደግሞ ወንጀልነቱ አጠራጣሪ ይሆናል። ይልቁን፣ የተቸገረ የሚያልፍበት፣ "የማሪያም መንገድ ነው" ብሎ እንዲያምን ይደረጋል። ካላመነም ያስገድዳሉ ወይም ይወተውታሉ። ሕግን የመጣስ ወይም የማጣመም ድፍረት እያለ ሲመጣ፣ ማኅበራዊ ወይም ሕዝባዊ መተላለፍ ስለሚያስከትል ዝቅጠቱ የጅምላ ይሆናል።

መልካም ዕሴት መገንባት ጊዜ ይፈጃል። ሙስናን መዋቅራዊ ማድረግ ግን ቀላል ነው። የሊዙን ዋጋ በሼርክና ውድድር ከፍና ዝቅ ከማድረግ አንሥቶ፣ በማስተላለፍ ባልተወጠነ ሥራ ላይ በማዋል፣ ወይም ጥራሽ መሬትን ያለ ሥራ በማስቀመጥ፣ ... ወዘተ ከፍተኛ ሃብት ማጋበስ ስለሚቻል ሙሰኞች ሳይሆን "ጤነኛውም" ይቀላቀላል። እንዲያ እያለ በርካታ ተከታይ ሲገኝ ጠንሳሾች ሌላ የመጠቀ የወንጀል አካሄድ ያብሰለስላሉ።

ስለዚህ፣ ሠንድ ዐልባ ቤቶች ይበራከታሉ፣ ሠንድ ቢኖር ባይኖር ግድ የማይሰጠው ሹማች ይበራከታል። ሙሰኞች ደግሞ ዘሩን ያከሩታል። ሕዝብን አደራጅተው በሠንድ ላይ ወንጀል ከመሥራት ዐልፎ ሕግ ከተሞከረ፣ ሁከት ወደ መፍጠር ይሸጋገራል። ገበያው እቅል ይስታል፣ የመሬት አጠቃቀም ይሳከራል። ከተሞች ሕዝብ የሰፈረባቸውን ለም የእርሻ ሥፍራ መርጠው ያድጋሉ። ለእርሻ ምቹ የሆኑ ሥፍራዎች ቀድሞውት ተፈላጊ ስለሆኑ። ችግሩ፣ ለእርሻትን ሳይሆን ለሌላ ዓላማ ይውላሉ።

እያንዳንዱ ገበሬ፣ በተለይም ከተማ አካባቢ ያለው ግን ውስጥ ለውስጥ መሬቱን አስረክቦ ጨርጓል። ችግሩ፣ የሸጠው ያው ለምጭላፊች መሆኑ ነው። የመሬት ትክክለኛ ዋጋ ስለማይታወቅ ባገኘው ሽጦ ከተማ ይገባል። ወይም ከተሞችን ወደ ራሱ ይስባል። የተረፈም የእርሻ መሬት ካለ በባሕር ዛፍ ችግኝ ያጭቅና የከተሞችን ዕድገት እንደ ክርስቶስ መምጫ ይጠባበቃል።

ገበሬው ጥቂት ገንዘብ ቋጥሮ "ከተማ" ሲገባ ግን ሁሉ ነገር እንዳሰበው ላይሆን ይችላል። ኑሮውን ገና አላለመደውም። ከተሜነት፣ ቋጥር ከማያውቀው ገንዘብ ጋር ሲዳመር ባሕሪይ ይቀይራል። የቋጠረውን በቱሎ ይቀማዋል፣ ሲደማመር ሕግ ሳይፈርስ፣ የአገር ሕግጋት መሠረት የሆነው ማኅበራዊ ዕሴት ይሸረሽራል። ይህ ታዲያ ምን ይባል?

"መሬት የእኔ ነው" ያለው መንግሥት፣ ከእንቅልፍ እንደሚነቃ ሰው በርግጎ ሰው የማይኖርባቸውን ሕጋዊ ያልሆኑ ቤቶች በማፍረስና በጎይል ርምጃ ይጠመዳል። ታዲያ "ቤት" የፈረሰባቸው ሰዎች ዋይታና ጩኸት "ብሔሬ ተጎዳብኝ" ወደሚለው ስሞታና ሽብር ለመድረስ ያለው ርቀት የአፍና የአፍንጫ ያክል ብቻ ነው። ብሔር ተከር ጥቃት አይሰነዘርም ማለትም አይቻልም። 'ግርግር ለሌባ ያመቻልና' በርምጃ መካከል ግርግር መቀላቀል የኪራይ ሰብሳቢዎች ወግ ነው።

ወንጀል የሚያስብለውም ይኸው ነው። በዚህ የአገር ሃብት ቅርምት ሽኩቻ ውስጥ የተሻለ መንበር ያላቸው እጃቸውን እስክ ትከሻ ነክረውት ስለሚገኙ ነው። ሠነድ ይመሳቀላል፣ ሕግ ይውጣ እንጂ የይስሙላ ብቻ ይሆናል፣ ወይም አተገባበሩ ሆን ተብሎ ይዛነፋል፣ ገና ሲረቀቅ 'ይህቺን ክፍተት እንተዋት" የተባለ ይመስል፣ ሕቱ የታተመበተ ጋዜጣ ሳይደርቅ ተቃራኒው ይሠራል፣ ይህ ወንጀል ነው፣ መዋቅራዊ ወንጀል።

መሬትን እንደ ምሳሌ አነሳን እንጂ ኪራይ ሰብሳቢነት በየሠርጁ ሞልቷል፣ በማንበራዊ፣ በፖለቲካውም፣ በሕግና አስተዳደርም ዘርፍ ይስተዋላል። ወንጀል መሆኑን እያወቁ በዚህ ክንዳቸውን ያፈረጠሙ እንኳንና ለሌላው ለመንግሥት ለራሱ ሥጋት ናቸው፣ እንዲያውም ከዚህም አልፈዋል፣ አንዳንዶች መንግሥትን የራሳቸው ንብረት እስከ ማድረግ ደርሰዋል፣ ይህ አዝማሚያ አስፈሪ ነው።

በብዙ የአፍሪካ አገራት ያልተለፋበት ዕሴት የመዛቅ መዋቅራዊ መሆኑ እያየለ መጥቶ፣ ጠንካራ አካላት ገብተውበታል። የውጭና የውስጥ አካላት፣ የውጭው ይቆይና፣ ከውስጥ ለምሳሌ:- የአገር መከላከያ ጎይሎ እና ተመሳሳይ ድርብ ዕቅም ያላቸው ጎይላት ኤኮኖሚውን ተቆጣጥረዋል። የአገር ጦር መሪዎች፣ በየሥፍራው የተደራጁ የጎጥ ሚሊሺያ አዛዦች፣ ግዙፍ ማንበራዊና ፖለቲካዊ ግንኙነት ያላቸው ተቋማት አለቆች ሥራቸው ኤኮኖሚውን መዘወር ይሆናል።

በእኛም አገር ይህ አዝማሚያ ታይቶ ነበር። ሙሉ በሙሉ ለመወገዱ እርግጠኛ መሆን ባይቻልም። መከላከያም ግዙፍ የኤኮኖሚ አውታሮችን ተቆጣጥሮ አንቱ የተባሉ ኮንትራቶችን ተቀብሎ መሥራቱ ተያይዞት ነበር። በለውጡ ሰሞን የጦር መሪዎቹ በተቋሙ ስም "የሠራት" ሌላ ሆኖ ተገኝቷል መባሉ ሰማን እንጂ።

ከዚህም የባሰው ልምድ ግን የፖለቲካ ድርጅቶች ዋና የአገሪቱ ባለ ሃብት የሆኑበት እውነታ ነው። ፖለቲካና ኤኮኖሚ አጣቃልሎ የያዘ ጎይል ታማኝነቱ ለአገር እና ለሕዝብ ነው ወይስ ለሃብቱ? በተለይም የፖለቲካ ድርጅቶቹ ዘርና ጎይማኖትን ተከትለው በተዋቀሩበት አገር፣ ሁሉን በመንግሥት እጅ አሳልፎ መስጠት ምንኛ ችግር ደጋሽ ይሆን?

በቱሎክ ዕይታ፤ ኪራይ ሰብሳቢነት ቀድሞ ከሚታወቀው ከሞኖፖሊ ወይም ጉቦ ጋር በተያያዘ ከሚከሰተው የኤኮኖሚ ዐቅም ሽቀባ በእጥፍ የሚበልጥ ዋጋ ያስከፍላል። [238] ይህ ዕይታ ግን የ1960ዎቹ ነው፤ አሁን ብሶበታል። ተጨማሪ ዋጋ ማስከፈል ብቻ ሳይሆን ሕልውና ይዳፈራል።

የኪራይ ሰብሳቢነትን አደገኛነት የምንገነዘበው ከብዙ ምክንያቶቹ አንጻር ስናይ ነው። የኪራይ ዕድል ሰብሳቢነትን ይፈጥራል። በመጀመሪያ ተርታ የሚመደበው መመዘኛ በቻዋታው ተርታ የሚገቡት ተጫዋቾች ብዛትና ማንነት ነው። እነማን ናቸው?

የፖለቲካ ጉላፈዎች፤ የመንግሥት ባለ ሥልጣናት፤ የጦር መሪዎች፤ እና መሰሎች መቺም አሉበት። እንዚህ ታዲያ ጥቅቱና ማዕከላዊነቱ በጠበቀ አስተዳደር የተጠረነፉ ናቸው ወይስ የተበታተኑ? እንደ ኢትዮጵያ ባለ የብሔር ድርጅትና ፖለቲካ ባለ ብዙ ሻኛ ግመል በፈጠሩበት ሥፍራ መገፋፋትም፤ መተቃቀፍም እንዲሁ መገመት ይቻላል። በጥቅም ሠንስለት መተሳሰርም፤ መጠላለፍም።

በተጨማሪም፤ እነዚህ ተሳታፊዎች በአገር ውጭና ውስጥ ካሉ ኪራይ አነፍናፊዎች ወይም ሌሎች ባለ ሀብቶች ጋር ሽርክናም፤ ሽኩቻም ገጥመው እንደሚሠሩ መገመት ይቻላል። ገንዘብ ለማሻገር ወይም ለመደበቅ ብቻ ሳይሆን ሕጋዊ ሥራ ለመሥራትም ይህ የግድ ነው። ግና፤ ምንልባት፤ ከተሳታፊ ጉዞዎች ውስጥ ገንዘብን ግልጥ ባልሆነ መንገድ ያካባቱ የሚገኙበት ከሆንስ?

አጠያያቂ የገንዘብ ምንጭ ካላቸው ውስጥ ደግሞ ምንልባት ዓለም አቀፍ የዕፅ አመላላሽ ወይንም የመሣሪያ ሽያጭ የሚያከናውኑ ወገኖች ያሉበት ከሆንስ? ንጹሕ እጅ ያፈራው ገንዘብ ከክፋት ጋር ሲመሳጠር በሉት፤ አውቀውም ሆነ ሳያውቁት። ምንልባትም "ዓለም አቀፍ የሽብር ቡድን" ተብሎ የተፈረጀትስ የበግ ለምድ ለብሰው ተቀላቅለውበ ቢሆን? አንዳንዱ ሲያስቡት ያስፈራል።

ሌላው የኪራይ ምክንያት የኪራይ ምንጭ ራሱ ነው። መሬትና ሌላ በግልጥ የሚታይ ሀብት መሆኑ ቀርቶ፤ ሊሸሽግ የሚችል፤ ክርስ ምድራዊ፤ ረቂቅ፤ ደግሞ በሌላ አገር የሚገኝ ከሆንስ? ማዕድናቷ ከክርስ ምድር ሀብትነት ይልቅ ከጥልቁ የሚወጣ የሞት ድግስ የሆነባት ኮንጎ ይህን በደንብ ትረዳዋለች። ኪራይ ሰብሳቢነት ከጉሚ ጽንፈኝነት ጋር ሲቀላቀል የሚንቀለቀል እሳት ይሆናል።

ብዙ ምንጮች የተለያየ የሰብሳቢነት ዕድልና ባሕርይ ይፈጥራሉ። የእርሻ መሬት እና ሕጋዊነቱ አጠራጣሪ ወይንም ሕዝብን ሊጎዳ የሚችል እንደ ዕፅና የጦር መሣሪያ አዘዋዋሪነት ከሆነ ውጤቱ እንዲሁ ይለያያል። በምንዛሬና ወለድ ምጣኔ ላይ ከሆነ አዘዋዋሪውም ስንኳ አይታይም።

238 Tullock, G. (1967). The Welfare Costs of Tariffs, Monopolies, and Theft, Western Economic Journal, 5:3 (1967: June) p.224. Accessed on September 29, 2022, from https://cameroneconomics.com/tullock%201967.pdf

ኪራይ ስብሳቢነትን፣ ደህንኛውም ቢሆን፣ ማንንም በፍቅር ዐይን አያይም። ከሕጋዊነት በቶሎ ወደ ግራጫነት የመቀየር አባዜ አለበት። ድብብቆሹ እያየለ ሲመጣ፣ የኪራይ መጠኑም እየጨመረ ይሄዳል፣ ሽሽቱኝ ይላል። መሸሻግ ደግሞ ብዙ አደጋ ይወልዳል። አደጋ በበዛ ቁጥር ደግሞ የመሰወር ዋጋ ያሻቅባል። ሌላ የኪራይ ምንጭ።

የተሳታፊዎች ባሕርይም ወሳኝ ነው። የኤኮኖሚ ሕዋሳት የእነነት ባሕርይ ያይልባቸው እንደሆን እንጂ ሁሉም ሌባ አይድሉም። በሌላ ጽንፍ ግን ጥራሽ በዱር በገደሉ ጦር ይዘው የኪራይ ምንጫቸውን ለመጠበቅ የወጡ ሞልተዋል። ይህ ባሕርይ የኪራዩን ምንጭ የሚያሰፋ ሲሆን በእርግጥ ዋጋውም ከፍ ይላል። በተለይም፣ "የእኔ፣ የብሔሬ" እያለ ጫካ የገባ ሁሉ የኪራይ ስብሳቢዎችን ጡት ገና ያላጣለ ነው። ጫካም ይሁን ቤተ መንግሥት "ከእኔ በላይ ለአሥር" ማለቱ አይቀርምና።

የጋራ ያሉትና የግል ፍላጎት ሲጓኮት ባሕርይ ይመሳቀላል። ለኪራይ ስብሳቢነት ምክንያት ከሚሆኑት ነገሮች አንዱን፣ ማለትም ግጭትን ይወልዳል። በተለይም በአንድ አገር ውስጥ ያለ የእርስ በርስ ግጭት ለኪራይ ስብሳቢነት መንስዔም ውጤትም ሆኖ እናገኘዋለን። "ብሶት" የወለዳቸው፣ ብሶትን መወለዳቸው አያላዳም፣ በየወንዙ ቢማማሉ እንኳ ኪራይ ሰብሳቢ ስለሆኑ ብቻ ተስማምተው ይሠሩ ማለት አይደለም። እጅግ የሚቀዋወሙ ሊሆኑ ይችላሉ።

እናም ጦር የሚያማግዝ ልዩነት ቢከሰትስ? በተለይ በብሔር ፖለቲካው ማዶ ለማዶ የቆሙ፣ የጉሪጥ የሚተያዩ ባላንጣዎች ከፈጠረ ይህ አይቀርም። ይህ ሁሉ የዘመናችንን ኪራይ ስብሳቢነት የአልዓዉና ጥያቄ ያደርገዋል።

እማኝ አናጣም፣ በቅርብ ጊዜ (2015 ዓ.ም) በዩክሬን አገር የተካሄደ አንድ ጥናት መጠቀስ ይቻላል። ጥናቱ፣ ኪራይ ስብሳቢነትን ለመዋጋት የሚያስችሉ ስፈ ርምጃዎች ካልተወሰዱ በቀር ለአገሪቱ አንድነትና ዘላቂነት አስጊ እንደሚሆን ፍንጭ ስጥቶ ነበር። የዩክሬን ንትርክ አንዱ ምንጭ መዋቅራዊ ወንጀል የወለደው ትሩፋት ነው። በአገሪቱ ኪራይ ስብሳቢነት የተገለጠበት መንገድ፣ ተብሎ የተቀመጠው ደግሞ በጣም አስተማሪ ነው።[239]

ከሞላ ጉደል የምናውቃቸው ናቸው። የቢሮክራሲው መንዛዛት፣ የመልካም አስተዳደር ዕጦት፣ የመንግሥት ቢሮዎችና ጎላፊዎች የመረጃ አሰጣጥ ቁጥብነት ወይንም መዛባት፣ የግል ንብረት ሕጎች ወጥነት መታጣት፣ የሕግ የበላይነት ዕጦት፣ የመንግሥት በጀትና ገንዘብ አጠቃቀም ልቅ መሆን፣ በመንግሥት ሃብት ላልተፈቀዱ ጉዳዮች ያለ ገደብ መገልገል። ብላ ከጉሪቤት ይማራል።

239 Grazhevskaa, N., Virchenkob, A., Grazhevskaa, A. (2015). The Effects of Rent-Seeking Behavior on the Efficiency of Fiscal Policy in Ukraine; Procedia Economics and Finance 27 (2015) 274 – 287.

ዮክሬን ይህ ጥናት በወጣበት ጊዜ ሲንተከተክ የነበረው ያለ መረጋጋት ፈንድቶ እስከ ዛሬ ያምሳታል። የፉሲያ ሲዛይ ሆና በቅድሚያ ክራይሚያን፣ በቅርቡ ደግሞ ምናልባት የምዕራባውያኑ ድጋፍ የጦርነቱን አካሄድ ካልቀየረ፣ አራት ሌሎች ግዛቶችን ታስረክባለች። በጦርነቱ ውስጥ ያለቀው የሰው ኀይል ሳይጠር፣ ወደ 20 ሚሊዮን የሚጠጋ ሕዝቡ[240] በአገር ውስጥና በውጭ አገራት ተፈናቃይ ሆኖ ዕርዳታ በመለመን ይተዳደር ዘንድ ተገዷል።

የእምነት ዕዳ

በአገራችን ኢትዮጵያ ቅርጽ ይዞ የተደራጀ መንግሥትና ግዛት እንግዳ አይደለም። እየጠበበ፣ እየሰፋም፣ እየጠፋም ቢሆን፣ መንግሥታት፣ ለረኽም ዘመን ይታወቃሉ። በተለያዩ የአገሪቱ ክፍሎች፣ የራሳቸው ገንዘብና የውጭ ግንኙነት ጭምር የሚያካሂዱ ሥርወ መንግሥት የነበራቸው አካላት ነበሩ። ከዚህ የተነሣ ሕግ ይታወቃል።

እንዲሁም፤ ነገሮችን በሕግ ማዕቀፍ የመፍታት ልምድ የዳበረ ነው። ሕጉም ለክፉ አይሰጥም። በተለይም የንግድ ሕቱ በቅርብ እስኪካለስ ድረስም ቢሆን የሕዝቡን ዕለታዊ ኑሮ በመቃኘትና በመዳኘት አይታማም ነበር፤ በእርግጥም የዓለም ባንክ በሚያወጣው ደረጃ መሠረት፤ የንግድ ሕቱ አለ መግባባትን በመፍታት ረገድ የተሻለ ከሚባሉት የሚመደብ ነው።

ለምሳሌ፦ ከአምስት ዓመታት በፊት (2019 ዓ.ም) የወጣው ደረጃ[241] እንደሚያመላክተው ደረጃ ከተሰባቸው የዓለም አገራት መካከል ኢትዮጵያ 67ኛ ደረጃ ላይ ተቀምጣለች። የአፍሪካ አጠቃላይ ደረጃ 126 ከመሆኑ አንጻር እጅግ ሻል ያለ መሆኑን ማስተዋል ይቻላል። በእርግጥ እንደ ሩዋንዳ ያሉ አገራት፣ በ32ኛ ደረጃ ላይ በመቀመጥ ቢበልጡንም።

የንግድ አለመግባባቶችን በፍትሕ ብሔር ለመቋጨት አፍሪካ ውስጥ 655 ቀናት ሲያስፈልጉ በኢትዮጵያ 530 ቀናት ያህል ይበቃል። በእርግጥ በፍትሕዊነት ከተደመደም ይህም ለክፉ አይሰጥም። ለድርድር የሚያስልገው ቀን ተስፋ የሚያስቆርጥ ቢሆንም ለሕግ ሒደት የሚከፈለው ክፍ (ዳኝነትና ጥብቅናን ጨምር) ለክርክር ካበቃው ክፍያ ዋጋ ላይ 15 በመቶ ብቻ በመሆን ሰዎች ፍርድ ቤትን ሊመርጡ ይችላሉ።

የፍርድ ሒደት ክፍ በአፍሪካ ክርክር ካስነሳው ሃብት እስከ 42 በመቶ ይደርሳል። በአንዳንድ አገራት ይህ ክፍያ ክርክር ካስከተለው ዕሴት በላb ስለሚገኝ ፍርድ ቤt

---

240 UNOCHA. (2022). Ukraine Sitaution Report. September 21, 2022. Accessed on September 29, 2022 from https://reliefweb.int/country/ukr?gclid=CjwKCAjwhNWZBhB_EiwAPzlhNv lLESvWY1q2Etw0YR7vwjficv0o50Ibr9KqXGh36EJiSdxk4MDnhoCyaAQAvD_BwE

241 World Bank. (2019). Doing Business. Accessed on September 29, 2022, from https://archive. doingbusiness.org/en/data/exploretopics/enforcing-contracts

እንደ መፍትሔ አይቆጠርም። የመንግሥት ዐቅም ደካማ በሆነባቸው እንደ ቡርኪና ፋሶ
እና መካከለኛው አፍሪካ የመሳሰሉት አገራት ክፍያው ለክርክር ከዳረገው መጠን በላይ
ሊሆን ስለሚችል እስከነአካቴው ፍትሕ ፍለጋ አያዋጣም።

ፍትሕ ፍለጋ የሚኪደው እምነት ሲንደል ነው። እንደ መጨረሻ መፍትሔ
ይቄጠራል። በብዙ የኢትዮጵያ ሕዝቦች መካከል ግን የደረጀ፣ የተጓድሶ ፍትሕ ሊሰ
የሚችል ባሕላዊ የግጭት አፈታት ዘዴ መኖሩን፤ ነገር ግን እነዚህ ዘዴዎች በአገሪቱ
ሕጎች እና በአንዳንድ ክልሎች እውቅና ቢሰጣቸውም ፈጽሞ ያልተቆራኙ መሆኑን
ጥናቶች ይጠቁማሉ። [242]

እንዲሁም የብሔር ፖለቲካው የማንነትና ባሕላዊ እሴቶችን ከማጉላቱ የተነሣ
የአካባቢ ሽምግልና እና ግልግል ወጎችን የመፈለግ አዝማሚያ እየጨመረ መጥቷል። [243]
ይሁን እንጂ ለፍትሐዊነቱ እና ለዕኮልነቱ ደረጃ አልተሰጠውም። ወጥነት የጎደለው፣
እንደ ምሉዕ የፍትሕ ሥርዓት ሁሉም በምርጫ እንዲጠቀምበት ሆኖ የተዘጋጀ
አይደለም። [244]

እንዲሁም፣ በተለይ የብሔር ስብጥር ባለባት አገር፣ ይህን ጠቃሚ የፍትሕ
ሥርዓት ሕዝቦችን ሊያቀራርብ በሚችል መልኩ ለማዘመን ምንም ዐይነት ማዕቀፍ
አልተዘጋጀም። [245] ትኩረቱ "የእኔ" የሚባለውን ቆፍሮም ቢሆን በማውጣት እንጂ
ከጊዜውና ከአገሪቱ ፍላጎት ጋር እንዴት ይጣጣማል በሚለው ላይ አይደለም።
እንዲያውም ሌላውን ለመጉዳት ሆነ ተብሎ ይጣመማል ተብሎ ይታማል።

ይህ ከሆነ፣ ከአንድነት ይልቅ የማንነት እና የመለያየት ድርሻ እየጎላ ከመምጣቱ
ጋራ ፍትሕ እየተሸረሸረ መሄዱን ማስተዋል ይቻላል። ያም ባይሆን፣ ባሕላዊ ብቻ
ሳይሆን ጥንታዊ፣ ከትውፊት ጋር ብቻ ሳይሆን ከአምልኮም ጋር የተያያዘ በመሆኑ

242 Eniyew, E. L. (2014). Ethiopian customary dispute resolution mechanisms: Forms of
restorative justice? Accessed on September 29, 2022, from https://www.accord.org.za/ajcr-
issues/ethiopian-customary-dispute-resolution-mechanisms/

243 Gowok, S. M. (2008). Alternative Dispute Resolution in Ethiopia - A Legal Framework.
AFRR Vol 2 No. 2 April 2008; Improved Version pp. 265-285.

244 Dezo, M. E. (2020). Traditional Conflict Resolution Mechanism in Ethiopia: (The case
of Enashma of the BoroShinasha Community, BenisahngulGumuz Regional State).
Accessed on September 29, 2022 from https://www.ijser.org/researchpaper/Traditional-
Conflict-Resolution-Mechanism-in-Ethiopia-The-case-of-Enashma-of-the-Boro-Shinasha-
Community-Benisahngul-Gumuz-Regional-State.pdf

245 Alemie, A. & Mandefro, H. (2018). Roles of Indigenous Conflict Resolution Mechanisms for
Maintaining Social Solidarity and Strengthening Communities in Alefa District, Northwest
of Ethiopia. Journal of Indigenious social development. Volume 7, Issue 2 (2018). Accessed
on September 29, 2022, from http://umanitoba.ca/faculties/social_work/research/jisd/

ተገቢ ሥፍራ እያገኘ አይደለም። [246] ባሕል፣ አባቶች፣ ወይም የአገር ሽማግሌዎች ተሰሚነታቸው ሲቀንስ የእምነት ዕዳም ሥፍራ ያጣል።

የጉርሻ ፍትሕ

የመንግሥት መኖር አንዱ ምክንያት በሕዝቦች መካከል ፍትሐዊ የሃብት ሥርጭት እንዲኖር ለማርዳት ነው። ይህ ግን ሁል ጊዜ የሚሳካ እንዳልሆነም ይታወቃል። ከዚህ የተነሳ መንግሥታት ተጉጂ ወይም ድጋፍ ለሚሹ ቦታዎችና የኅብረተሰብ ክፍሎች "ጉርሻ" ያዘጋጃሉ። አንዳንዱ ጉርሻ በሕግና ፖሊሲ ተደንግጎ፣ ለረኂም ጊዜ፣ አንዳንዱ ደግሞ እንደየ አስፈላጊነቱ።

ለምሳሌ፦ በኢትዮጵያ የማኅበራዊ ልማት ዕሳቤ በፖሊሲ ደረጃ የመጀመሪያ ደረጃ የኅብረተሰብ ጤና አጠባበቅ ድጋፍ የኤኮኖሚ አቅማቸው ደካማ ለሆኑት፣ ለገጠራማ ቦታዎች እና አዳጊ ክልሎች እንዲያደላ ተደርጓል። በእርግጥም ጥናቶች እንደሚጠቁሙት፣ የመጀመሪያ ደረጃ የኅብረተሰብ ጤና አጠባበቅ በጤና ጣቢያ ደረጃ ተመላላሽ ታካሚ ለሆኑት ያደላ ነው። [247]

ይኼው ጥናት እንደ ጠቆመው፣ ተሻተው ለሚታከሙ የሚሰጠው ድጋፍ በሃብታሞች ይጠለፋል። ማለትም፣ ክድኻው ይልቅ የተሻለ የኤኮኖሚ ዐቅም ያላቸውን ይጠቅማል። ድኻ ተሻቶ የመታከም፣ በተለይ ራቅ ብለው በሚገኙ የጤና ተቋማት የመጠቀም ቅንጦት አይነካካውም። ድኻን ለመጥቀም ታስበው አድራሻቸው ሌላ የሆነ የጉርሻ ዓይነቶች ብዙ ናቸው።

ምክንያቱም፣ ድጎማ ለድኻ ተብሎ ይደረግ እንጂ ሃብታምን የመጥቀም አባዜ አለበት፣ በተለይም ዒላማው ቀጥተኛ ካልሆነ። ለዚህ ተጨማሪ እማኝ የሚሆነው፣ በ2019 በአዲስ አበባ ከተማ የተደረገ አንድ ጥናት ነው። በውሃና መብራት ላይ ከሚደረገው ድጎማ ሦስተ አንድ በመቶው ወደ ሃብታም ቤተሰቦች የሄደ ሲሆን እጅግ ድኻ የሆነት የተጠቀሙት 15 በመቶውን ብቻ ነው። [248]

246 Wolde. B. G. (20918). Traditional Conflict Resolution Mechanisms in Kaffa Society of Ethiopia. Universitepark bulletin, Vol 7. Issue 2. pp. 128-142; Published Online: July 2018. Accessed on September 29, 2022 from https://www.unibulletin.com/index/arsiv/28/138/traditional-conflict-resolution-mechanisms-in-kaffa-society-of-ethiopia

247 Hailu, A., Gebreyes, R. & Norheim, O. F. (2021). Equity in public health spending in Ethiopia: a benefit incidence analysis. *Health Policy and Planning*, Volume 36, Issue Supplement_1, December 2021, Pages i4–i13. Accessed on September 29, 2022; from https://doi.org/10.1093/heapol/czab060

248 Cardenas, H. & Whitington, D. (2019). Magnitude and Distribution of Electricity and Water Subsidies for Households in Addis Ababa, Ethiopia. World Bank Policy and Research Working Papers. Open Knowledge Repository. Accessed on September 29, 2022; from https://openknowledge.worldbank.org/handle/10986/32455

በዓለም ባንክ ጥናት መሠረት በኢትዮጵያ በተለያዩ ደረጃ እና መጠን ድጐማ የሚሰጥባቸው የኤኮኖሚ ክፍሎች አሉ። እንዚህም፤ ስንዴ፤ ነዳጅ፤ መብራት ኃይል፤ ጤና፤ ትምህርትና የምግብ ዕርዳታ የመሳሰሉት ናቸው። [249] ይሁን እንጂ ከምግብ ዕርዳታና በተለምዶ የሴፍቲ ኔት መርጐ ግብር ተብሎ ከሚጠራው በቀር ሁሉም የድጐማ ዓይነቶች አስፈላጊ ቢሆንም ድኻው ላይ ያተኮሩ አልነበሩም።

የጉርሻ ፍትሐዊነት ግን ከብሔረ የፖለቲካ ኤኮኖሚ ጋር ምን ያገናኛዋል? ድጐማ በአገሪቱ ውስጥ እጅግ የተለመደ እና ሰዎችም የሙጥኝ ብለው የያዙት ነገር ነው። እስክ 2012 ዓ.ም ድረስ በከፍተኛ ፍጥነት እያደገ መጥቶ ከመንግሥት ወጪ እስክ ሰባ ሁለት በመቶ የሚደርሰው በአንድም ሆነ በሌላ "ድጐማ" ሊባል በሚችል መንገድ ይጠፋ እንደ ነበር መረጃዎች አሉ። [250]

የመንግሥት ወጪ አመዳደብ የብሔረ ክልልን በጠባቁ መልኩ በተለይም የሕዝብ ቁጥር እንደ አንድ መመዘኛ ተወስዶ እንደሆነ ስንገነዘብ፤ የመንግሥት አካላት ጭማር ድጐማን እንዲህ የወደዱበት ምክንያት ይገባናል። በቀጥታ፤ ለሚመለከተው ሰው፤ ስም ተጠርቶ ያልተሰጠ ድጐማ ከድኻ ይልቅ ሃብታሙን (ወይንም ሻል ያለ የኤኮኖሚ ዐቅም ያላቸውን) ይጠቅማል።

ለምሳሌ፦ በኢትዮጵያ የእርሻ ምርት ዕድገት ፖሊሲ ምክንያት (የእርሻ ትራንስፎርሜሽን ፕሮግራም) የማዳበሪያ አጠቃቀም ላይ ልዩ ትኩረት ተደርጓል። በጥቂት ዓመታት ውስጥ የአፈር ማዳበሪያ አጠቃቀም በአምስት እጥፍ ያደገ ሲሆን ከመንግሥት ጐን የገበሬዎች የጐብረት ሥራ ማህበራትም በማከፋፍል የገበያው ተሳታፊ ሆነዋል። [251]

ይሁን እንጂ መንግሥት በይፋ ለማዳበሪያ ግዥ ድጐማ አይሰጥም። በ2012 ዓ.ም የተደረገ ጥናት እንደሚያመለክተው ግን ገበያውን በማሳለጥ፤ ወይም ለትራንስፖርት ምቹ ሁኔታ በመፍጠር እና በመሣሠሉት በማዳበሪያ ዋጋ ላይ ተጫማሪ ያልተደረገ እስክ 1 ቢሊዮን ብር በዓመት ወጪ አውጥቷል። ይህ ለማዳበሪያ ግዥ በልዩ ሁኔታ የሚፈቀድለውን የውጭ ምንዛሬ ሳይጨምር ነው።

የማዳበሪያ ሥርጭት ቀድሞውኑ በንጽጽር ሻል ያለ የእርሻ ገቢ ወዳለባቸው፤ ሰፋፊ የእርሻ መሬት ወዳላቸው የአዝርእት ልማት ላይ በሚያተኩሩ ቦታዎች ትኩረት ተደርጐ እንደሚከፋፈልም ይታወቃል። ይህ ስውር ድጐማ ልዩነትን የሚፈጥር መሆኑ

249 World Bank. (2016). Ethiopia Public Expenditure Review. Accessed on September 29, 2022 from https://documents1.worldbank.org/curated/en/176471468178145744/pdf/ACS14541-WP-OUO-9-Ethiopia-PER-final-May-12.pdf

250 Fedec, A. & Sousa, A. (2022). Ethiopia – Subsidies and Transfers (as % of government expenditures). Trading Economics. Accessed on September 29, 2022; from https://tradingeconomics.com/ethiopia/subsidies-and-other-transfers-percent-of-expense-wb-data.html

251 Rashid, S., Tefera, N., Minot, N. & Ayele, G. (2013). Fertilizer in Ethiopia: An Assessment of Policies, Value Chain, and Profitability. IFPRI.

እየታወቀ መከናወን ቀጥሏል። በሌሎች ዘርፎች ግን፤ ቀስ በቀስም ቢሆን፤ በተለይም ከ2014 ዓ.ም ጀምሮ ድጓማ እየቀነሰ መምጣቱ በጐ ጅምር ነው።

የታመነ ምንዛሬ

በመስከረም 2024 ዓ.ም አንድ የአሜሪካ ዶላር በአማራጭ ገበያ መንግሥት በየዕለቱ ከሚያውጀው ዋጋ በእጥፍ እንደሚሸመት መረጃዎች አሉ። የውጭ ምንዛሬ ዋጋን ብልቃጥ ውስጥ ማፈን ትርፉ ዕዳ ነው። ምንዛሬ በገበያ ዋጋ ሳይወሰን ሲቀር፤ ዛሬ የምናየው ሁኔታ ሊፈጠር እንደሚችል ብዙዎች አስጠንቅቀው ነበር።[252] የተፈራው አልቀረም።

ዶላር በእንዲህ መታፈኑ ከቀጠለ ከሰሜኑ ውጥረት ጋር ካጋጠመን የአሜሪካ መንግሥት ጫና ይልቅ ምትኃተኛ ወረቀታቸው የበለጠ ዋጋ ታስከፍለናለች። ከአንድ ዓመት በፊት የሸቀጦች ዋጋ መናር ጭራው አልያዝ ማለት ሲጀምር እንኳን ምንዛሬው ለገበያ ተለቅቆ ቢሆን ዛሬ እንደሚታየው የአገር ውስጥ ገበያ ዋጋውን ወደ መምራት አይዘልቅም ነበር።

ምንዛሬ፤ ከብዙ በጥቂቱ፤ በሸቀጦች እና አገልግሎቶች ዋጋ ዕገታት ምጣኔ፤ በወለድ ምጣኔ፤ እና በሰዎች የነገ ግንዛቤ፤ ግምት፤ ወይም ጥበቃ ላይ ይመሠረታል። ኢትዮጵያ ውስጥ ምንዛሬ ከሸቀጦች ዋጋ ጋር እንዲዋልል ሲፈቀድ ታይቶ አይታወቅም። በምንዛሬ ገበያ የኤኮኖሚ አካላት ፈጽሞ ማይም፤ ለማኝ ሆነዋል። ዋጋውን በመወሰን ስሌት የሉበትም። መንግሥት የሰጠውን፤ ወገብ የሚቆርጥ ወረፋ ጠብቀው፤ ወይም አማራጭ ገበያው የወሰነውን ዋጋ ከፍለው ይወስዳሉ፤ ያስረክባሉም።

በተለይም ባለፉት 50 ዓመታት ውስጥ መሬት እንደ ግል ንብረት ተሸጦና ተለውጦ ስለማይታወቅና ምንዛሬ በገበያ ዋጋ የወደደው ሁሉ መግዛት ስለማይችል እንዲህ የሚያደርጉት አገራት እንዱ እንኳ የማይገኝበብ ትውልድ ሞልቷል። ስለሆነም፤ መሬት ይሸጥ፤ ወይም ምንዛሬ በገበያ ዋጋ ይወሰን ሲባል ይደነብራሉ። "መሬት ይሸጣል እንዴ?" ወይንም "ዶላር ማንም እንዲይዘው ይፈቀዳል እንዴ?" የሚሉ ያጋጥማሉ፤ አይፈረድባቸውም።

ስለዚህ ስለ ውጭ ምንዛሬ ዋጋ አወሳሰን በጥቂቱ ልንመለከት እንገደዳለን። ምክንያቱም፤ የውጭ ምንዛሬ አስተዳደር በበሔር ፖለቲካዊ ሔኖሚው እንዴት እንደ ተቃኛ ለመረዳት ያግዘናል። እንደ ምንዛሬ ዐይነት ወሳኝ ግብዓቶች ላይ ከውሳኔው

252 Haile, F. (2019). The Exchange Rate Why It Matters for Structural Transformation and Growth in Ethiopia. Policy Research Working Paper 8868; World Bank Group; Macroeconomics, Trade and Investment Global Practice May 2019. Accessed on September 30, 2022; from https://documents1.worldbank.org/curated/en/898821559134798352/pdf/The-Exchange-Rate-Why-It-Matters-for-Structural-Transformation-and-Growth-in-Ethiopia.pdf

ጠረጴዛ የተገለለ ባለ ሃብት ወይም የኤኮኖሚ አካል በአንድ እጁ እንዲያጨበጭብ የተፈረደበት ነው።

ከዚያ በፊት ስለ ኢትዮጵያ የውጭ ምንዛሬ አስተዳደር እና መንግሥት የደነገገው የውጭ ምንዛሬ ዋጋ ከአማራጭ ገበያው ዋጋ ያለውን ልዩነት በተመለከተ ጥቂት እንበል። ከአይ ኤም ኤፍ በተገኘው መረጃ መሠረት፤ ምንም እንኳ የውጭ ምንዛሬ በመንግሥት ቁጥጥር ስር ቢሆንም እስከ 2012 ዓ.ም አካባቢ ድረስ ልዩነት የለም በሚያስብል ደረጃ ምጣኔአቸው ተመጣጣኝ ነበር።

ይህ ልዩነት ቀስ በቀስ እያሻቀበ መጥቶ በ2020 ዓ.ም ወደ 40 ከመቶ የሚደርስ የዋጋ ክፍተት በመንግሥት ጥሪ በአማራጭ ገበያ ይታይ ጀመር፤ በያዝነው ዓመት (2023 ዓ.ም) ዕጥፍ ከመሆኑ በላይ በአስፈሪ ፍጥነት ልዩነቱ እየሰፋ ሄዶአል።[253] ነገሮች የተረጋጉ በሚመስል ጊዜ፤ ዕድሎችን ተጠቅሞ ዋጋውን ከገበያው ጋር ለማስተካከል ሙከራ አለመደረጉ ለምን ይሆን?

የኢትዮጵያ የውጭ ምንዛሬ አስተዳደር ፈጽሞ የተገደበ ወይም ቋሚ ዋጋ የተቆረጠለት የሚባል አይደለም። አፍሪሳዊ የውጭ ምንዛሬ ዋጋ የሚወሰነው፤ በየቀኑ ባንኮች ከብሔራዊ ባንክ ጋር ባላቸው የምንዛሬ ገበያ ጨረታ ካቀረቡት ዋጋ ላይ፤ የውጭ ምንዛሬ በተሸጠበት ዝቅተኛ ተመን ላይ ተመርኩዞ በሚደነገግ ዋጋ ነው።[254] ጨረታም፤ የአስተዳደር ገደብም ያለበት ማለት ነው።

ይሁን እንጂ ለሸያጭ የሚቀርበው የውጭ ምንዛሬ እነስተኛ መጠን ያለው ብቻ ሳይሆን፤ በዝቅተኛ ዋጋ ላይ የተመሠረተ ተመን በመሆኑ ገና ከጅምሩ ልዩነት እንዲዮርጽበት ሆኗል። በተገደበ ዋጋ አስተዳደርም ይሁን በነጻ ገበያ፤ የውጭ ምንዛሬ ዋጋ ዋነኛ ወሳኝ የሆነው የሸቀጦችና አገልግሎቶች ዋጋ ንረት ነው። የሸቀጦች ዋጋ ደግሞ የሚወሰነው በአቅርቦትና ፍላጎት መመጣጠን ላይ ነው።

እንደ ኢትዮጵያ ያሉ ብዙ አስፈላጊ ሸቀጥና ሌሎች አገልግሎቶችን ከውጭ የሚያስገቡ አገራት፤ የአገር ውስጥ የዋጋ ድባብ ቢያንስ በሁለት በኩል ከፍተኛ ግሬት ያጋጥመዋል። በመጀመሪያ፤ ማንኛውም ከውጭ የገባ ምርት በተገዛበት ሥፍራ ዋጋው ንር ከሆነ፤ ዕቃው ብቻ ሳይሆን ዋጋውንም ዕዳ ለማስገባት ይገደዳሉ።

253 Gray, S. T. (2021). Recognizing Reality: Unificatopn of the Offical and Parallel Market Exchange Rates. IMF Working Paper; Monetary Capital Markets; WP.21/25. February 2021. https://www.imf.org/en/Publications/WP/Issues/2021/02/06/Recognizing-Reality-Unification-of-Official-and-Parallel-Market-Exchange-Rates-50047

254 Deressa, A. (2007). Exchange Market Pressure and Monetary Policy in Ethiopia. NBE Working Papers. Accessed on September 30, 2022; from https://nbebank.com/wp-content/uploads/pdf/staff%20working%20paper/Exchange%20Market%20Pressure%20and%20Monetary%20Policy%20in%20Ethiopia.pdf

ለምሳሌ:- ኢትዮጵያ ነዳጅ አታመርትም፤ የነዳጅ ዋጋ በዓለም ገበያ ከጨመረ፤ ዋጋ ከፍ አድርጋ ከመግዛት በስተቀር አማራጭ የላትም። ይህ የውጭ የዋጋ ንረት ከምላ ጉደል በቀጥታ የሚገባበት ዓይነተኛው መንገድ ነው። ማምለጥ አይቻልም፤ ዋጋ ለማረጋጋት ድጎማ ቢስት እንኳ ዘላቂነት አይኖረውም። ከ2022 ዓ.ም መገባደጃ ጀምሮ በነዳጅ ዋጋ ላይ ያለውን ድጎማ ደረጃ በደረጃ ለማንሣት መንግሥት የተገደደው በዚህ ምክንያት ነው።

ሁለተኛው መንገድ ከዚህም የበለጠ አጣብቂኝ ነው። የውጭ ምንዛሬ ግኝት ወይም አቅርቦት ከፍላጎት ጋር መመጣጠን ይኖርበታል። አቅርቦት ደግሞ የሚገኘው ከውጭ ንግድ፤ ዜጎች ከውጭ ከሚልኩት ገንዘብ፤ እና ከዕርዳታ ወይም ብድር ብቻ ነው። ከዓለም ባንክ የተገኘው መረጃ እንደሚያመለክተው፤ ከ1980 ዓ.ም ጀምሮ ባለት 50 ዓመታት ኢትዮጵያ ውስጥ ከውጭ ንግድ የተገኘ ገቢ ከውጭ ለምናስገባቸው ዕቃዎች የሚያስፈልገውን ያሀል የሸፈነበት ጊዜ የለም።

እስክ ሚሊኒየሙ መጨረሻ ድረስ አንድና ሁለት ቢሊዮን ዶላር ገደማ ጉድለት ያጋጥመን ነበር። ዓመታዊ የገቢ ጉድለት ግን ከ2000 ዓ.ም ጀምሮ እጅግ በከፍተኛ ፍጥነት አድንል። ስለሆነም፤ የጉድለቱ መጠን በ2016 ወደ 15 ቢሊዮን ዶላር ደርሶ ነበር።[255] በ2020 ጥቂት ተሻሽሎ ወደ 10 ቢሊዮን ገደማ ጉድለት ያሳያል። ይህ ሁሉ ጉድለት እንዴት ተሞላ? በዕርዳታና ብድር የተወሰነው እየተሸፈነ ዘልቋል። ለቀረው፤ ምስጢሩ ያለው በአማራጭ የውጭ ምንዛሬ ገበያ ላይ ነው።

የውጭ ምንዛሬ በጉን በከፍተኛ ዋጋ ተገዝቶ ይገባል። ወይም በከፍተኛ ዋጋ የተገዙ የውጭ ሸቀጦች ገበያ ውስጥ ይገባሉ፤ እንዚህ ደግሞ የአገር ውስጥ የሸቀጦች ዋጋ እንዲነር ምክንያት ይሆናሉ። ዋጋ ስነር ፍላጎት ባይጨምር እንኳ ለማሟላት ብዙ የውጭ ምንዛሬ ያስፈልጋል። ፍላጎት ሲያይል ዋጋው ይነራል፤ አዙሪት፤ የማያባራ የዋጋ ንረት ዑደት በሉት።

የውጭ ምንዛሬ ዋጋ መቆጣጠር እምብዛም ፋይዳ ቢስ የሚሆነው ከዚህ የተነሣ ነው። የአማራጭ ገበያው ዋጋ እየጨመረ ሲመጣ የውጭ ምንዛሬ ሊያገኙ የሚችሉ ሁሉ እንደ ዜጋ ሳይሆን እንደ ባዕድ መሆን ይጀምራሉ። ትርፍ አይጠላም፤ መቼም። በአፌሴላዊ ዋጋ ከመሸጥ አማራጭ ገበያውን ቢጠቅሙ ሳይሆፉ አጋበሱ ማለት አይደል? አማራጫቸን "ጥቁር ገበያ" ማለት ፋይዳ የለውም።

ቁጥጥሩ ቢላሳ፤ ቢያንስ በዚህ መልክ ውጭ አገር የሚቀር የውጭ ምንዛሬ አገር ውስጥ ገብቶ በአገር ምርት ዋጋ ላይ እንዲሳተፍ ያስችል ነበር። ሁሉቱም ካራ

255 World Bank. (2022). Net Trade in Goods and Services (Balance of Payments, Current Dollars, Ethiopia). International Monetary Fund, Balance of Payments Statistics Yearbook and data files. Accessed on September 30, 2022; from https://data.worldbank.org/indicator/BN.GSR.GNFS.CD?locations=ET

አልቀረልን፡፡ የውጭ ምርት ዋጋ በማሻቀቡ እጅግ ትርፉ ከፈልን፡፡ እኛ ያመረትነውም ለአገር ውስጥ ፍጆታ አልዳረስ በማለቱ ብቻ ወደ ውጭ ሸጠን ምንዛሬ ከማምጣት ይልቅ እዚሁ መጠቀም ጀመርን፤ ያውም ከተመረተ፡፡

መንግሥትም ከማፈን ብዛት ሊያገኝ የሚገባውን ጥቅም አጣ፡፡ የምንዛሬን ዋጋ ለማፈን መንግሥት የቆረጠበት ምክንያት ግልፅ ነው፡፡ በተለይም እንደ ነዳጅና ቅባት፣ መድኃኒትና የመሳሰሉ የፍጆታ ዕቃዎች ወደ አገር ውስጥ ሲገቡ መሸጫቸው በአማራጭ ገበያ ዋጋ ከታሰበ ለዕድገት ጸር፣ ለሕዝባዊ ኑሮ ክብደትም ይዳርጋል የሚል አቅል የሳተ ፍራቻ ነው፡፡

ባለፉት 20 ዓመታት ውስጥ በመጠኑም ቢሆን የኢትዮጵያ ኤኮኖሚ እያደገ መምጣቱን ከዚህ በፊት ጠቅሰናል፡፡ ዕድገቱን ያፋጠነው ደግሞ መንግሥት በተለያዩ የኤኮኖሚ አገልግሎት ግንባታ ላይ ያደረገው አስተዋጽኦ ነው፡፡ በተለይም ፌደራል መንግሥት ከወጭው ውስጥ ሁሌም በሚባል ደረጃ ከግማሹ በላይ በካፒታል ፕሮጀክቶች ላይ ያጠፋል፡፡[256] ለእነዚህ ካፒታል ፕሮጀክቶች ማስፈጸሚያ የውጭ ምንዛሬ በማስፈለጉ ቁጥጥሩን መርጧል፡፡

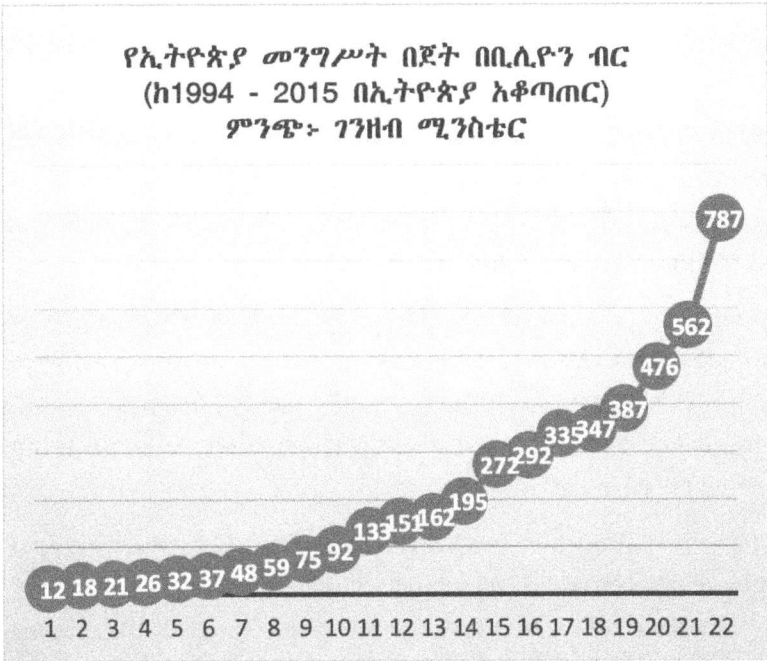

የኢትዮጵያ መንግሥት በጀት በቢሊዮን ብር
(ከ1994 - 2015 በኢትዮጵያ አቆጣጠር)
ምንጭ፦ ገንዘብ ሚንስቴር

787
562
476
387
333 347
272 292
195
133 151 162
12 18 21 26 32 37 48 59 75 92
1 2 3 4 5 6 7 8 9 10 11 12 13 14 15 16 17 18 19 20 21 22

256 UNICEF. (2022). Highlights of the 2021/22 Federal Government Budget Proclamation. Accessed on September 30, 2022, from https://www.unicef.org/ethiopia/media/5006/file/ screenshot%20of%20the%20Highlights%20federal%20budget%20proclamation%20 document.pdf

ከዚህ ጋር ተያይዞ ግን አንድ መነሣት ያለበት የምንዛሬ መወሰኛ ኮነት አለ። መንግሥት በኤኮኖሚው ላይ በሰፈው ሲሳተፍ የዜጉችን የውጭ ምንዛሬን ፍላጉት ብቻ ሳይሆን የብድር ፍላጎትንም ያጣብባል። ከገንዘብ ሚንስቴር የተገኘ መረጃ እንደሚያመለክተው[257] ከ1994 ጀምሮ የመንግሥት ወጪ በፍተኛ ፍጥነት እያደገ መጥቷል። ስለዚህ የመንግሥት በጀት ከዜጉች በቀረጥ መልክ የሚሰበሰበው ብቻ የሚሸፍነው አልሆነም።

የበጀት ዕድገት ፍላጉቱን መንግሥት በብድርም ጭምር እንዲደግም ይህ አስገድዶታል። የቀረጥ ገቢም፣ ብድርም፣ ዕርዳታም ታክሎበት ግን የመንግሥት በጀት ጉድለት ከአጠቃላይ ኤኮኖሚው እስከ 4 በመቶ የሚደርስበት አጋጣሚዎች በርካታ ነበሩ።[258] ለምሳሌ በያዝነው ዓመት (2015 ዓመት ምህረት እንደ ኢትዮጵያ አቆጣጠር) ወደ 800 ቢሊዮን የሚጠጋ በጀት ተይዟል። ከአምናው ወደ ሃያ በመቶ ያህል ዕድገት ማሳየቱ አንድ ልዩ ክስተት ነው።

ይህ የዕድገት ፍጥነቱን ያመላክታል። የበጀት ጉድለቱ 112 ቢሊዮን ዶላር ከሚገመተው አጠቃላይ ኤኮኖሚ 4 በመቶ ይደርሳል ብነል ወደ 250 ቢሊዮን የሚጠጋ ገንዘብ ይፈልጋል ማለት ነው። ከአገር ውስጥና ከውጭ አገር የሚገኝ ዕርዳታና ብድር ከዚህ የተወሰነውን ቢሞላ ቀሪው ብቻኛ ገንዘብ የማተም ሥልጣን ያለው ተቋም እንደ መሆኑ በአንድም በሌላም መንገድ ይሸፈናል።

መንግሥት ከዜጉች ጋር ተሻምቶ ሲበደር፤ የወለድ ምጣኔን ያንራል። ወይንም ብድር ለማግኘት ለሌላው ከባድ ስለሚሆን የብድር ዋጋ ከፍ ይላል። የጎዳ ድርድር ሥፍራውን ስለሚረከብ። ከፍ አድርጉ ከፍሎ፤ ለምሳሌ ምርት ያመረተ የኤኮኖሚ ሕዋስ፤ ለማካካስ ሲል በምርት ላይ ዋጋ ይጨምራል።

ገንዘብም ሆነ ሌላ ገንዘብ ነክ ሃብት (ለምሳሌ:- ወርቅ፤ ወይንም የመንግሥት ግምጃ ቤት ሰነድ) ወደ አንጡራ ጥሪት (ለምሳሌ ፋብሪካ ወይም ቤት) ከመቀየሩ በፊት ኤኮኖሚስቶች ስለ-ገንዘብ ይሉታል። መንግሥት ብድር ተሻምቶ አግኝቶም ቀዳዳውን መድፈን ቢያቅተው ዝም ብሎ አይቀመጥም። የስለ-ገንዘብ ባለቤትነት ስላላው ይህንን ሃብቱን መጠቀም ይጀምራል።

የስለ-ገንዘብ ሃብት ለመጠቀም ሲል መንግሥት ድንገት የወረቀት ገንዘብ ቢያትም በኤኮኖሚው ውስጥ የሚንሸራሸረው የገንዘብ መጠን ይጨምራል። ይህም ደግሞ ዓይነተኛ የሸቀጦችና አገልግሎቶች ዋጋ ግሸበት ምንጭ ነው። ከላይ እንደ ጠቀስነው፤ የዋጋ

---

257 Ministry of Finance Ethiopia. (2022). Budget Resources. Accessed on October 1, 2022; from https://www.mofed.gov.et/resources/budget/

258 Fedec, A. & Sousa, A. (2022). Ethiopia – Government Budget. Trading Economics. Accessed on September 29, 2022; from https://tradingeconomics.com/ethiopia/government-budget

ግሽበት የውጭ ምንዛሬ ዋጋ እያሻቀብ እንዲሄድ ከፍተኛ አስተዋጽኦ የሚያደርግ ወሳኝ ነገር ነው።

የአንድ አገር የውጭ ምንዛሬ መሠረት የሆነ በርካታ ነገሮች አሉ። ሁለት ሦስቱን በጥልቀት አይተናል። የዋጋ ግሽበት፣ የመንግሥት ወጪ እና ከዚህ ጋር ተያይዞ የሚመጣ የውጭና ውስጥ ሂሳብ ጉድለት። ሌላ አንድ ዋና መሠረት የሆነ ነገር ላይ ጥቂት እንበልና እናብቃ።

የውጭ ምንዛሬ ዋጋ ለመወሰን እጅግ አስቸጋሪ ከሆነት ነገሮች አንዱና ዋነኛው የአገሪቱ ሕዝብና በኤኮኖሚው የሚሳተፍ ሕዋስ ሁሉ ስለ ምንዛሬው ሁኔታና ሂደት ያለው አመለካከት ነው። ገበያው ስለ ምንዛሬው ምን ይጠብቃል? ምንዛሬ እንዲጠናከር ወይስ እየሞተ እንዲሄድ?

መጠበቅ ሲባል ቁጭ ብሎ የመጸለይ ወይም ጸጉር የመንጨት ጉዳይ ሳይሆን፣ ማንኛውም ተሳታፊ የኤኮኖሚ ሕዋስ አነሰም በዛ ከተበቃው እንጻር የሚሠራው ሥራ ማለት ነው። ግማሹ እንደ አካል የራሱን ድርሻ ለማበርከት፣ ሌላው የግል ፍላጎትን ብቻ በማስቀደም። ከዚህም ውጭ በሌላው ዕዳ የመክበር ፍላጎት ያላቸውም በየፈናቸው።

ይህ "ጥበቃ" ምናልባት ከዚህ በላይ ከተጠቀሱትም ወሳኝ እውነታዎች የላቀ ሊሆን የሚችልበት አጋጣሚ ሞልቷል። የኤኮኖሚ ሕዋሳት ስለ ምንዛሬው ሂደት ያላቸው ጥበቃ በራሱ ደግሞ በአመዛኙ በሁለት ነገር ላይ የተመሠረተ ነው። አንደኛው የኤኮኖሚው አጠቃላይ ጤንነት ሲሆን፣ ሌላው የኤኮኖሚውን አመራር የሚያዩበት መንገድ ነው።

ሰዎች ስለ ኤኮኖሚው ጤንነት ለማወቅ የግድ የኤኮኖሚ ሊቅ መሆን አያስፈልጋቸውም። የዕለት ተዕለት ኑሮ የሚያስተምረው ብዙ ነገር አለ። በእርግጥ፣ ስለ አካሄዱ በጥልቀት አጥንተው "ጥበቃቸውን" የሚያስተካክሉም አሉ።

እንደ ማንኛውም ሰው ሆኖ ለማየት ግን የአገራችን ኤኮኖሚ ጤንነት የማያሳስበው እንደሌለ መገመት አያዳግትም። በተለይም፣ ግራ የገባው፣ ከዚህም የተነሣ ስለ አካሄዱ ተስፋ የቆረጠው በየዕለቱ እየበዛ ስለ መምጣቱ ፍንጭ ሞልቷል። ይሁን እንጂ በጥልቀት ተረድቶ የመተንተን ነገር ይጎድላል።

ኤኮኖሚያችን ሁለት መንታ ጋሬጣዎች የተደቀኑበት ይመስላል። በአንድ በኩል ከፍተኛ የዋጋ ግሽበት እየተስተዋለ ሲሆን፣ በሌላ በኩል ደግሞ የዕድገት ምጣኔው፣ በተለይም ባለፉት አራትና አምስት ዓመታት ከጊዜ ወደ ጊዜ፣ በተጨባጭ እያሽቆለቆለ ይገኛል።

በአንድ አገር የኤኮኖሚ ዕድገት ሂደት ውስጥ ፍጥነቱ ሞቅና ቀዝቀዝ ማለቱ እንደ ዑደት የሚፈራረቁ ነገሮች ናቸው። የተረጋጋ ኤኮኖሚ ማግኘት የውሃ ዋና

እንደ መለማመድ ዐይነት ነው። እጅም እግርም እየተወራጨ መስጠም አለ። እኛ መወራጨትም አልቻልን።

የኤኮኖሚ ዕድገት፣ በዐጭርና መካከለኛ ጊዜ ትልም፣ በአብዛኛው ሥራ አጥነትን በመቀነስ ይገለጣል። ይህ ሲከሰት፣ ፌሽታ ነው። በተለምዶ፣ ምርት ሲኖር ዕቃ ይረክሳል። ግና ኤኮኖሚው ሲያድግ፣ ምርትም ቢኖር፣ ሰው ሥራና ገንዘብ ስለሚያጋኝ የዋጋ ግሽበት ዐብሮ የማደግ አዝማሚያ አለው። ብዙ ሰው መግዛት ይችላልና።

የተገዳቢጦሹም ተለምዶአዊ ነው። ምርት ስለ ተትረፈረፈ ብቻ ሳይሆን የኤኮኖሚ ዕድገትም ሲዳከም ዋጋ ይቀንሳል። ምክንያቱም ሥራ አጥ ይበዛል። ሥራ የሌለው ሕዝብ የመግዛት አቅሙ ስለሚወድቅ የዋጋ ግሽበቱ ሊቀንስ ይችላል።

ዋጋ ከመቀነሱ በላይ ግን ዕቃዎች ጋር ስለሚያጠጡ ፈጽሞም አይመረቱም። ይህ ደግሞ የጉን ውጋት አለው! ኤኮኖሚው ራሱ ይኮራመታል! ማለትም፣ ቀበቶአችንን መብላት እንጀምራለን። ኤኮኖሚ ሲኮራመት በሁሉም ዘርፍ ውድቀት ይስተዋላል።

እነዚህ ሁለት ተቃራኒ ኮንቶች የተለመዱ ናቸው። ነገር ግን በታሪክ የኤኮኖሚ ውድቀት እና የዋጋ ንረት አንድ ላይ የተከሰቱበት አጋጣሚም ታይቷል! አይብዛ እንጂ። ለድኻ ሰማይ ነሐስ፣ ምድር ብረት ሆኖ የሚግልበት ዘመን ማለት ነው። ዐቅም እየወደቀ፣ ለመግዛት የፈለጉት ነገር ዋጋው አልቀመስ እያለ።

ይህን ባለ ሁለት ጫፍ አርጩሜ መንግሥታት፣ በተለይም ያደገ ኤኮኖሚ ያላቸው አገራት፣ መከላከል የሚችሉበትን ብቃት ስላዳበሩ በብዛት አይታየም ነበር። የኤኮኖሚ ድቀትንና የዋጋ ንረትን አጣምረን "ድቅረት" እንበለውና ዛሬ በአገራችን የሚታየው ነገር የድቅረት ሽታ ያለው ሳይሆን አይቀርም የሚያስብሉ ብዙ ነገሮች አሉ። አንዱን ብቻ እናንሣ፦

እንደ አይ ኤም ኤፍ ጥናት ኮቪድ የዓለም ጠንቅ ነው ተብሎ ከታወጀበት ከ2020 ዓ.ም መባቻ ጀምሮ አጠቃላይ የዓለም ሃብት በ3.1 ከመቶ ተኮማትሯል። የበለጸጉት አገራት ሃብት በጋራ 5 በመቶ ያህል ወደ ኋላ ሸሽቷል። ይህ ግን በ2021 ዓ.ም ሙሉ በሙሉ በሚባል ደረጃ ተቀልብሶ የዓለም ኤኮኖሚ ዕድገት እስከ 6 በመቶ መድረሱ የዓለም የገንዘብ ድርጅት ዘግቧል። [259]

ይህ ደግሞ ያለፈውን ዓመት እንጂ ጥሩ ዕድገት ተገኘቶባቸዋል ከሚባሉ ዓመታት ጋር ይደምረዋል። ድርጅቱ በዚያው ዓመት፣ የኢትዮጵያን ኤኮኖሚ በሚመለከት ግን ያለ ወትሮው በዝምታ ማለፍ መርጧል። ዕድገትም ውድቀትም አልነገርን።

የሆነ ሆኖ፣ ያላቸውን የመረጃ ቋት ስንበረብር የኢትዮጵያ አጠቃላይ ምርት በጊዜው የገንዘብ ምንዛሬ በ2020 ዓ.ም ከነበረበት 97 ቢሊዮን ዶላር በ2021 ዓ.ም ወደ 92 ቢሊዮን ወርዷል። ምክንያቱ፣ ምንም ይሁን ምን፣ ደህና ተደርጐ መከርከሙን

---

259 IMF. (2022). World Economic Outlook Database 2022. Accessed on October 5, 2022, from https://www.imf.org/en/Publications/WEO/weo-database/2021/October

መረጃዎች ያረጁናል። አይ ኤም ኤፍ “ራርቶልን” በግላጭ አልዘረገፈውም እንጂ፣ የኢኮኖሚ ድቀት ያለ ማወላወል ጐብኝቶናል።[260]

መንግሥት የ3 በመቶ ዕድገት አስቆጥረናል ቢለንም የአይ ኤም ኤፍ መረጃ አይደግፍም። በ2021 ዓ.ም ብቻ ገና በጥሬ ዋጋ ቢያንስ የ 5 በመቶ ያህል ኩርኩም ቀምሰናል። ይህ ግን የዋጋ ግሽበት ሳይታከልበት ነው። እያንዳንዱ ሰው ኪሱ ካለው ብር 5 በመቶ ይቀንስና የቀረውን ለዋጋ ግሽበቱ አጋፍጦ ሲያይ ምን ይሰማው ይሆን?

ዓመታዊ የዋጋ ግሽበት በመቶኛ (በጐርጐሮሳውያን ዘመን አቆጣጠር)

አገር	2017	2018	2019	2020	2021
ኢትዮጵያ	10.7	13.8	15.8	20.4	25.2
ያደጉ አገራት	1.7	2	1.4	0.7	2.8
በማደግ ላይ ያሉ አገራት	4.4	4.9	5.1	5.1	5.5
የዓለም አጠቃላይ	3.2	3.6	3.5	3.2	4.3

ምንጭ፣ አይ ኤም ኤፍ፤ 2021

በዚህም ከላይ የተጠቀሰው የአይ ኤም ኤፍ መረጃ አያወላዳም። የኢትዮጵያ ኢኮኖሚ ከዋጋ ግሽበቱ አንጻር ሲታይ፤ ከ2005 ጀምሮ ኢኮኖሚው ገባ ወጣ እያለ አኃዛዊ ዕድገት ቢያስመዘግብም፣ እውነተኛ ጉዞው ባለፉት 20 አመታት አመርቂ አልነበረም። ይህ የግሽበት መረጃ መንግሥት ደረሰብኝ ከሚለው ስንኳ ያነሰ መሆኑን ያስተውሏል።

በእርግጥም በታኅሳሥ 2021 ከማዕከላዊ ስታቲክስ ባለ ሥልጣን አገኘን ያሉትን የዋጋ ግሽበት ወሬ ከተለያዩ ሚድያ ሰማን። በታህሣስ (2021 ዓ.ም) ወር መጨረሻ አጠቃላይ የዋጋ ግሽበቱ 35 ከመቶ እንደ ደረሰና የምግብ ነክ ሸቀጦች ግሽበት 42 ከመቶ መሆኑ። ይህ የአገራችንን ኢኮኖሚ ጤንነት ከአሳሳቢ በላይ ያደርገዋል።

የታኅሳሥ ወር ዋነኛ የመኸር ወቅት መሆኑን አንርሣ። ቢያንስ የምግብ ዋጋ ረገብ ማለት ነበረበት፤ ግን አልሆነም። እንደገና ወደ መረጃ ምንጫችን እንመለስ። አይ ኤም ኤፍ በ2021 ዓ.ም መጨረሻ አጠቃላይ የዋጋ ግሽበት 25 በመቶ ነው ይለናል። እንግዲህ ኪስህ ያለው ገንዘብ ላይ በተጨማሪ አንድ አራተኛው ተራ ወረቀት ነው ማለት እንደሆነ አስተውል።

ዓለም 5 በመቶ ወደ ላይ ሲመነደግ እኛ 5 በመቶ ያክል ከደረጃ ወርደን፣ የቀረችውንም ለመቀራመት አምና ከምንከፍለው ገንዘብ ላይ አንድ አራተኛ ተጨማሪ

260 IMF. (2022). Ethiopia: Economic outlook at a glance. Accessed on October 5, 2022, from https://www.imf.org/en/Countries/ETH

አድርገን እየከፈልን ገና የዓመቱ እርሻ ወቅት ላይ እንኳን አል መድረሳችን ማንንም በእጅጉ ሊያሳስብ ይገባል። በዚያ ላይ ጦርነቱ በሰሜን ቢቆምም በሌሎች የአገሪቱ ክፍሎች ያለው መተነኳኮስ ገና ሙሉ በሙሉ አላባራም። የመልሶ ግንባታው ወጪብ የሚቆርጥ እንደሚሆን ከአሁን በርካታ ምልክቶች አሉ።

በእንቅርት ላይ ጆሮ ደግፍ እንዲሉ ድርቅ በተለይም የከብት ሃብታችን ላይ ጉዳት እያደረሰ ነው። በልግ አብቃይ የአገራችን ክፍሎች ወቅታዊ ዝናብ ያላገኙ ሲሆን የ2022 ዓ.ም የክረምቱም ዝናብም እጅግ ዘግይቷል። በመጣ ጊዜ መጠኑ አስከፊ ባይሆንም ስርጭቱ ችግር ነበረበት። ሔኮኖሚያችን እያየን ደቀረተ (ደክረተ)። ይህን በብሔር ፖለቲካ በኮል ለመቅረፍ የሚመኙ ግን አሁንም ገና ሙቅ በማንነክ ላይ ናቸው።

ይህና ተመሳሳይ መረዳት በውጭ ምንዛሬ ሂደት "ጥበቃ" ላይ ከፍተኛ አስተዋጽኦ አለው። ሔኮኖሚው የደክረተ ከሆነ ብር መያዙ ምን ትርጉም አለው? ስለዚህ፣ ሰው ሁሉ ወይ ብርን በሌላ የተሻለ አመለካከት ሊያገኝ በቻለ የገንዘብ ዐይነት፣ ካልሆነም ወደ ሌላ አንጡራ ጥሪት ለመቀየር ይጣደፋል። ይህ ሲሆን ብር የውጭ ምንዛሬ ዋጋው ወደቀ ይባላል። የውጭው ውድ፣ የእኛው ርካሽ።

ሌላው ሰዎች ስለ ውጭ ምንዛሬ ሂደት ያላቸውን ጥበቃ የሚወስነው ስለ ሔኮኖሚው አጠቃላይ አመራር ያላቸው ዕይታ ወይም አመለካከት ነው። አመራሩ ለሔኮኖሚ ሕግጋት ያለው ታማኝነት ምን ይመሥላል? የብሔር ፖለቲካ በሔኮኖሚ ፖሊሲና አመራር ላይ ጣልቃ ሲገባ፣ አንድ የሔኮኖሚ ሕዋስ የገበያው አስተዳደር እና ፍትሕ የሚወስነው በገበያ ሕግ ሳይሆን በዘር ቤጠራ ነው ብሎ ሲያምን፣ ሰዎች በሔኮኖሚ ወጋግራዎች ላይ ያላቸውን እምነት ክፉኛ ይሸረሽረዋል።

ለብያኔው፣ በአገራችን እንዲህ ዐይነት ተስፋ መቁረጥ ለመክሰቱ ማስረጃ ማግኘት ያስፈልጋል ከባድም ነው። ነገር ግን፣ አመላካች የሆኑ ነገሮች እንዳሉ መጠቆም አይከፋም። በተለይም፣ ከፖለቲካው አለመረጋጋት ጋር የተከሰቱ ፍኖጎቻችን ልብ ልንላቸው ይገባል።

የኢትዮጵያ ሔኮኖሚ አኃዛዊ ዕድገቱ ለክፉ እንደማይሰጥ ደጋግመን ገልጠናል። ይህ ለምሳሌ መልካም ዕይታ እንዲኖረው ያደርጋል። ነገር ግን አንድ ሰው ስለ ሔኮኖሚው ያለውን ፍርጋት ለመረዳት ከአንድ ሌላ አቅጣጫ ልንመለከት አስፈላጊያችን ይሆናል። ለምሳሌ፦ የውጭ ቀጥታ ኢንቨስትመንትን ስንመለከት ይህን በተሻለ መንገድ ያሳየናል።

ልክ እንደ ዕድገቱ፣ አንድ የውጭ ኢንቨስተር የሕዝቡን ብዛት ሲመለከት፣ ገበያ እንደሚገኝ ሊያስብ ይችላል። የሕዝባችን ብዛት፣ በአፍሪካ ሁለተኛ፣ በዓለምም የማይናቅ ነው። ከሕዝብ ብዛት ጋራ የሰው ጉይል እጥረት የሚባል ሊያጋጥም እንደማይችልም ያስባል። የአገሪቱ የቆዳ ስፋት፣ በአፍሪካ ቀንድ መገኛቱ፣ ለም መሬት፣ እምብዛም

ያልተበዘበዘ የተፈጥሮ ሃብት መልካም የስበት ጎይል አለው። የመንግሥት ፖሊሲም የውጭ ባለ ሃብትን ለመጋበዝ ብዙ መከራ መደረጉን ያሳያል።

የውጭ ቀጥታ ኢንቨስትመንት በኢትዮጵያ
(በቢሊዮን ዶላር ከ1992 - 2021 ዓ.ም)

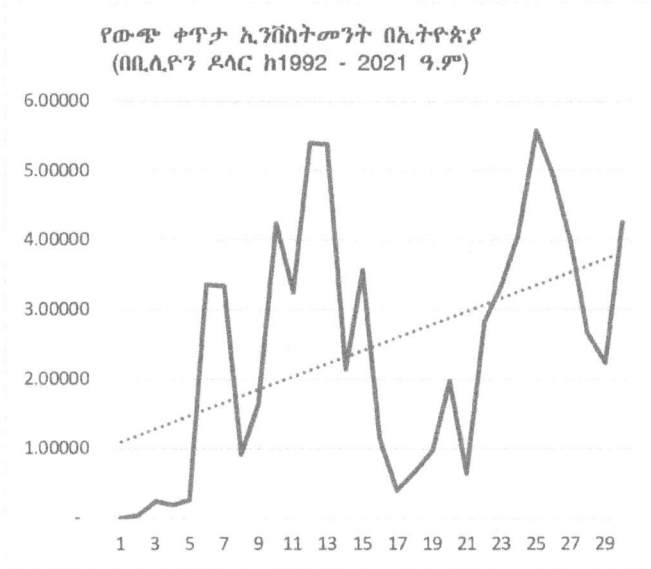

ይህ ሁሉ ያስነመጃል፤ ቢያንስ ሌላ ጥያቄም እንዲያነሳ ይገፋፋል። ታዲያ የእያንዳንዱን ሰው ዐቅም ሲያይስ? ምን ያህል ገንዘብ አለው? ሀብቱስ ምን ይመስላል? የሕዝቡ የትምህርት ደረጃ፤ የሥራ ዝንባሌው፤ የሥራተኛ አስተዳደር፤ ታማኝነት እና ክህሎት ምን ይመስል ይሆን?

እንዲያ አድጎ የነበረው ተስፋ ወዲያው ይሟሽሻል። የድኸ ድኸ ከሚባሉ አገራት ተርታ ሲያየን በአገር ውስጥ በቁ ገበያ የማግኘት ተስፋው ይዳከማል። በተለይም ውድ እና ትልቅ ዋጋ ያላቸውን ዕቃዎች ለማምረት ወይም ለማስመጣት ያሰበ ከሆነ በድጋሚ ያጤናል። ምናልባት መሠረታዊ የፍጆታ ዕቃዎች ካልሆነ በቀር ሌላ ትርጉም ያለው ሥራ ለመሥራት አይነሳሳ ይሆናል።

ሠራተኛውም እንደዚሁ። ከሕዝቡ ግማሽ ማንበብና መጻፍ ይቸገረዋል። አንድም በአፍሪካ እንኳ ስም ያለው የትምህርትና ምርምር ተቋም ጎልቶ አይታይም። አልወጣም ወይስ በበቁ አልተነገረም? ከራስ ቋንቋና የደረጃ ግን የተበታተነ ባሕል በስተቀር ከዓለም ኤኮኖሚ ጋር፤ ቢያንስ ከአሕጉራዊ ቋንቋና አረዳር ጋር እንኳ ንክኪው ገና እንደሆነ ያስተውላል።

ኤኮኖሚውና አስተዳዳሩም አያጠረቃም። ብቸኛ የኤሌክትሪክ ኃይል ኩባንያ፣ ብቸኛ የስልክና መገናኛ ኩባንያ፣ ብቸኛ አየር መንገድ፣ ብቸኛ በሚባል ደረጃ የብዙ የግል ባንኮች ድምር የማይትካከለው የመንግሥት ባንክ። በተፈጥሮ ዝናብ ላይ የተመረከዘ እርሻ፣ ኋላ ቀር እና የተበጣጠሰ የአስተራረስ ዘዴ፣ በመንግሥት ብቻ የሚዘወር የመሬት ሃብት።

በዚህ ሁሉ ላይ እርስ በርስ የሚናቆር ወደብ ዐልባ አገር መሆኗንም ጨምሮ ይመለከታል። የረኸገም ጊዜ ታሪክ እያላት አገሪቱ ከራሷ የመጣላቲ ምስጢር ዐሳብን ይገዳደራል። ከውጭ ጠላት እና እርስ በርስ እጅግ ብዙ ፍትጊያ ባስተናገዱ ዘመናት የታጨቀው ታሪኳ ዕረፍት ይነሳል። እናም ለማወቅ ካለ ጉጉት ይልቅ፣ ድንገት ከገባ፣ በምን መልክ በሰላም መውጣት እንዳለበት እንዲያሰላስል ይገደዳል።

ይሁን እንጂ፣ በአጠቃላይ ሲታይ፣ በኢትዮጵያ የመንግሥት ለውጥ ከተደረገበት ከ1990ዎቹ መጀመሪያ አካባቢ አንጻር ከፍተኛ የውጭ ኢንቨስትመንት ዕድገት ተመዝግቧል። መረጃዎች እንደሚያመለክቱት፣ ከውጭ የሚገባ ኢንቨስትመንት ከጥቂት ሚልዮኖች ተነስቶ በአንድ ዓመት ብቻ እስከ 5 ቢሊዮን (2003፣ 2004፣ 2016) የተገኘበት ጊዜም ነበር። [261]

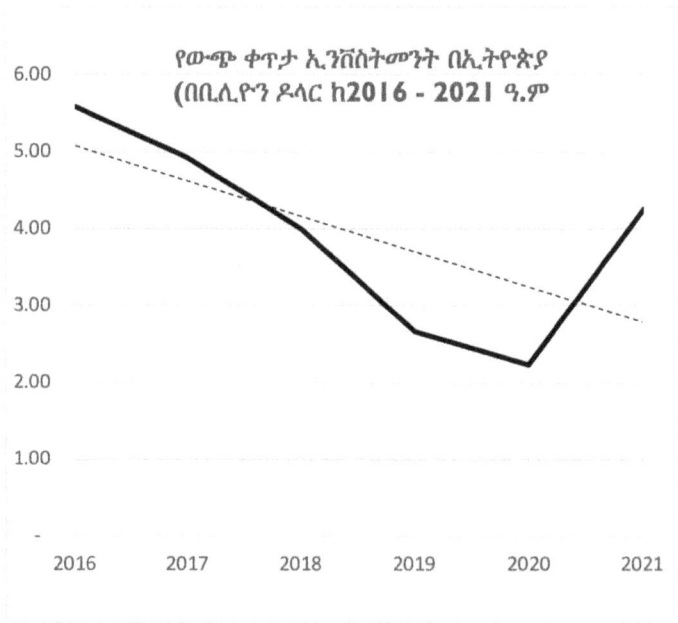

የውጭ ቀጥታ ኢንቨስትመንት በኢትዮጵያ (በቢሊዮን ዶላር ከ2016 - 2021 ዓ.ም

261 Macrotrends. (2022). Ethiopia Foreign Direct Investment (1977 – 2022). Accessed on October 5, 2022; from https://www.macrotrends.net/countries/ETH/ethiopia/foreign-direct-investment

ኤኮኖሚው ላይ አንዳች ተጨማሪ ተጽዕኖ የሚያሳድር አንድ ነገር ሲጠረጥር ግን የውጭ ኢንቨስተሮች እጃቸውን ይሰበስባሉ። በተለምዶ 1997ቱ ምርጫ (2003) እየተባለ የሚጠራው የፖለቲካ አለ መረጋጋት በተከሰተ ጊዜ ይህን ከፍተኛ ድንጋጤ ያዘለ እርምጃ ማስተዋል ተችሏል።

መረጃዎች እንደሚያመለክቱት፣ 5 ቢሊዮን ደርሶ የነበረው ዓመታዊ ኢንቨስትመንት ተንኮታኩቶ ግማሽ ቢሊዮን እንኳ ለመሙላት ሲግደረደር አንድ ዓመት አልፈጀበትም። እንዲህ ዐይነት እጅ የመሰብሰብ ያዘለ "ጥበቃ" በውጭ ምንዛሬው ላይም ከፍተኛ ተጽዕኖ ያሳድራል። ዋጋው ያሽቆልቁላል። የውጭ ገንዘብ ያለው ከመሸጥ ይልቅ ማቀብ እንደሚሻለው ይበይናል።

ከ2017 ዓ.ም ወዲህ ደግሞ ተመሳሳይ ድንጋጤ በኤኮኖሚ ሕዋሳት ላይ እንደ ደረሰ እናያለን። ሌላ የመንግሥት ለውጥ ያዘለ ጉምጉም፤ ተስፋና ግራ መጋባት አንድ ላይ። ግልፅ ሥርዓተ አልበኝነት፤ ሆኖም ግን የሠላምና የዴሞክራሲ ተስፋ፤ ተከትሎም ቅልጥ ያለ የእርስ በርስ ጦርነት። አጠቃላይ ማኅበራዊና ፖለቲካዊ ቀውስ እስኪመስል ድረስ ለውጡ ጥቅጥቅ ያለ ጭጋግማ ሆነ።

የውጭ ኢንቨስትመንት በኢትዮጵያ (ቢሊዮን ዶላር)

ዓ.ም	2019	2020	2021
የኢንቨስትመንት ገቢ	2.66	2.23	4.26
ከምችት እስከ ዛሬ	24.956	27.337	31.596
ተጨማሪ ኢንቨስትመንት ያመጡ ፕሮጀክቶች ብዛት	32	11	7
የተጨመረው ኢንቨስትመንት መጠን	1.909	0.503	0.132

ምንጭ፣ ሎይድስ ባንክ

ወዲያው የውጭ ኢንቨስትመንት ግኝት ማሽቆልቆል ጀመረ። በያዝነው ዓመት ከቴሌኮም ኩባንያ ሽያጭ ጋር በተያያዘ ጥቂት መሻሻል ያሳየ ቢመስልም በግማሽ የወረደው የኢንቨስትመንት መጠን ከወደቀበት ለማንሣት ሥራ ይጠይቃል።

ለምሳሌ ከሎይድስ ባንክ ድረ ገጽ ያገኘነው መረጃ እንደሚያመለክተው፣ ባለፉት ሦስት ዓመታት ከውጭ የሚገባ ቀጥተኛ ኢንቨስትመንት ከማሽቆልቆሉ በተጨማሪ አሳሳቢ ነገሮችም ይስተዋላሉ።[262] አዳዲስ ኢንቨስትመንት ብቻ ሳይሆን ነባሮችም ተጨማሪ ሃብት ለማስገባት የፈሩ ይመስላሉ።

262 Lloyds Bank. (2022). Foreign direct investment (FDI) in Ethiopia. Accessed on October 5, 2022, from https://www.lloydsbanktrade.com/en/market-potential/ethiopia/investment

በነባር ፕሮጀክቶቻቸው ላይ ተጨማሪ የውጭ ሃብት ለማስገባት ፈቃደኛ የሆኑ 32 ኢንቨስተሮች በ2019 ዓ.ም ነበሩ። በዚህ ዓመት ከተገኘው 2 ቢሊዮን 7 መቶ ሚሊዮን የውጭ ኢንቨስትመንት ውስጥ ሦስት አራተኛው የተገኘው በዚህ መልክ ነው። አገሪቱንና ኤኮኖሚውን የተሻለ ስለሚያውቁ አልፈሩም እንበል።

በ2020 ዓ.ም ግን ነባሮች ይበልጥ የፈሩ ይመስላል። ከሦስት ፕሮጀክቶች ሁለቱ ይህን ለማድረግ ፈቃደኛ አልነበሩም። በአጠቃላይ 11 ፕሮጀክቶች ብቻ ተጨማሪ ሃብት አመጡ። በሚቀጥለው ዓመት ደግሞ ሰባት ነባር ፕሮጀክቶች ብቻ ተጨማሪ የውጭ ኢንቨስትመንት የሳቡ ሲሆን ድምሩ ከአንድ መቶ ሚሊዮን አልዘለለም።

የአገሪቱን ኤኮኖሚ ከቀፈደዱት ነገሮች አንዱ ይህ እንደሆነ ጥርጥር የለውም። የውጭ ምንዛሬ ከሚያስገቡት ዋነኛ ምንጮች ውስጥ ኢንቨስትመንት ቀዳሚውን ድርሻ ይይዛልና። የብሔር ፖለቲካው ያስከተለው አለመረጋጋት ለዚህ እጅ መስብሰብ፤ ብሎም ለምንዛሬው መንኮታኮት ቀዳሚ አስተዋጽኦ እንዳለው መገንዘብ ይቻላል።

የፖለቲካው አለመረጋጋት ባሕሪው ሲሆን ኤኮኖሚው ላይ ክፋኛ ጥላሽት ስለሚጥል፤ የለውጥ ዓመታት ክፍተኛ ጥንቃቄ ይሻሉ። በአገራችን የብሔር ፖለቲካ የሚቀነቀንበት አንዱ ምክንያት "ውክልና ለማግኘት" በሚል ምክንያት ነው። ከአሥር ዓመታት በፊት በደቡብ ኢትዮጵያ የተደረገ አንድ ጥናት እንደ ጠቆመው ከሆነ፤[263] የብሔር ፖለቲካው የአገሪቱ አስተዳደር መሠረት በመሆኑ፤ በቁጥር አናሳ የሆኑ ብሔሮች ፖለቲካዊ ውክልና የማግኘት ዕድላቸው እንዲሰፋ አስተዋጽኦ አድርጓል።

ይህ ፍጹም መረጋጋትን የፈጠረ ባይሆንም ትላልቅ የሚባሉ ግጭቶችን ለማስወገድ ችሎ ነበር። ቀደም ሲል በመንግሥት ሥራና ሥልጣን እምብዛም ተሳትፎ ያልነበራቸው በመጠኑም ቢሆን ጠጋ እንዲሉ ምክንያት ሆኗልና። ቀስ በቀስ ግን በዚያው ልክ መላ ቅጣቸው የጠፋ ማኅበራዊና ኤኮኖሚያዊ ውጥረቶች እየተስተዋሉ መጡ።

ይህ ብቻ ሳይሆን፤ ውጥረቶቹ፣ የብሔር ሽኩቻዎች መልክ ያዙ። ይህን አስከሬ መልክ መያዛቸው ብቻ ሳይሆን ቀድሞ የነበሩ መተፋፈጎችን አጉልተው በርካታ ወደ ሆነ ግልፅ ግጭቶች እንዲያመሩ አደረገ። ቀጥተኛም፤ ተዘዋዋሪም አስተዋጽኦ በማበርከት። ያ ብቻ ሳይሆን ጥራሽ መካረር።

በደቡብ የሆነው ጥንታቄ የሚሻ ክስተት ነበር። አጠቃላይ የአገሪቱን ሁኔታ ሊያስረዳ የሚችል፤ የልብ ትርታ ማዳመጫ ሊሆን ይገባ ነበር። ባለፉት ጥቂት ዓመታት ኤኮኖሚውና የፖለቲካው ሥልጣን አናሳ ቁጥር ባላቸው ብሔሮች ተይዘል በሚል ሌላ እንቅስቃሴ እየበረታ መምጣቱ አልቀረም። ይህ በሌሎችም የብሔር ፖለቲካ በሚያይልባቸው የታያ እንቅስቃሴ ነው።

263 Aalen, L. (2011). The Politics of Ethnicity in Ethiopia (African Social Studies) Illustrated Edition. Amazon.

ሰፊ የሕዝብ ድርሻ ያላቸው ብሔሮች ሥልጣን ሲይዙና የሃብት ክፍፍል ከአናሳዎች ወደ ብዙኃን ሲደረግ ጥንቃቄ የተሞላበት ቢሆን ኤኮኖሚው አይጐዳም። በደቡብ አፍሪካ የነበረው የዘር መድልዎ የማስወገድ ትግል ሲቋጭ፣ ቀሪው አካሄድ የተያዘበት ስልት ትምህርት አለው። ምንም እንኳ ያ የፀረ ዘረኝነት እንቅስቃሴ ቢሆንም፣ ዚምባብዌና ደቡብ አፍሪካ ከጸነት ማግሥት የተከተሉት እጅግ ልዩነት ያለው ፖሊሲ በኤኮኖሚያቸው ላይ ከፍተኛ ተጽዕኖ ነበረው።

ሃብት ወደ ብዙኃን ሲከፋፈል ጥንቃቄ ይሻል። ከእንዚህ ይልቅ ይበልጥ አስተማሪው የማሌዥያ አካሄድ ነው። በአገሪቱ ሃብት የቻይና ዘር ያላቸው ማሌዥያውያን ቁጥጥር ነበር። የብዙሃኑን የማሌይ ብሔሮች ፖለቲካዊ እንቅስቃሴ አይሎ፣ ሥልጣንም ወደ ብዙሃኑ የማሌይ ዜጐች ሲተላለፍ፣ በሃብት ክፍፍል ላይ ጥንቃቄ ስለነበረው ኤኮኖሚው እድገቱ አለተገታም።[264] በአንድና በሌላ መንገድ ሃብት ያፈሩ፣ አልተዘረፉም፣ ያለ ዝርፊያ ሃብት ማከፋፈል ይቻላል።

ሃብት ለብዙሃኑ ሲከፋፈል፣ ከባለሃብቶች ላይ በዘፈቀደ መቀራመትን የሚያስከትል ከሆነ ይበላሻል። የማሌዥያ አካሄድ ትምህርት የሚሰጥ ቢሆን፣ የተገፋት ሥፍራ እንዲያገኙ መርዳት ለክፉት አይሰጥም። ይህ ቢሆን ግን፣ ከባለ ሃብት፣ ለምሳሌ:- መሬትና የመሳሰሉ ነገሮችን መቀማት እንኳን አስፈላጊ ቢሆን ካሃ ተከፍሎ መሆን ይኖርበታል። ለወደፊትም ልዩነት እየሰፋ እንዳይሄድ የመወዳደሪያ ሜዳውን ምቹ በማድረግና በትምህርትና ሥልጠና መደገፍ የተሻለ ይሆናል።

በኢትዮጵያ ግን ባለፉት አምስት የለውጥ ዓመታት ከእንዚህ አካሄዶች የረባ ትምህርት የቀሰምን አይመስልም። ከሌላው ያልተማረ፣ በራሱ ላይ በሚደርስ ግዙፍ ኪሣራ ልብ ይገዛል፣ ከገዛ በበሔር ፖለቲካ የታገዘ ሌብነት ከፍተኛ የሃብት ቅርምት ማስከተሉ የማይታበል ቢሆንም፣ ይህን የተዛባ አካሄድ ለመፍታት አንዱኑ ነጥሎ ሌባና ቀማኛ በማስመሰል፣ ያለ ሕግ አግባብ ዝርፊያ መሰል ውርስ አያዋጣም። መዋቅራዊ ሌብነት በምን መልክ ይስተካከል ለሚለው ሕዝብን ያሳተፈ የሰከነ ውይይት አያስፈልግም?

አንድ አቅጣጫ ብቻ የተመለከተ እንቅስቃሴ ዘላቂ መፍትሔ አይወልድም፣ እናም እንጠይቅ። የለየለት ጦርነት በትግራይ፣ የከፋ የህቡዕ ድርጅቶች እንቅስቃሴ በምዕራብና ደቡባዊ የአገሪቱ ክፍሎች መከሰቱ ከዚህ ጋር ግንኙነት አይኖረው ይሆን? አልታረቅ ያለ ከራራ የፖለቲካ አቋም የበረከተውስ በእርግጥ እንደ ሰው ልዩነታችን ገንኖ ወይስ ልዩነትን ላለተገበ ጥቅም ማጋበሻ እንዲውል ከሚያውጠነጥኑ? ሌቦች የእኛው ልጆች ናቸው ወይስ ከጨረቃ ላይ ዱብ ያሉ?

264 Esman, M. J. (1987). Ethnic Politics and Economic Power. Comparative Politics; Vol. 19, No. 4 (July 1987) pp. 395-418 (24 pages). Accessed on October 5, 2022, from https://www.jstor.org/stable/421814

መልሱ አዎንታዊም ይሆን አሉታዊ፤ በውጭ ምንዛሬ ሂደት ግምት ላይ ትልቅ ጫና ማሳደሩን መመልከት ይቻላል፡፡ የኤኮኖሚ ሕዋሳት የውጭ ምንዛሬ ዋጋ ሳይሆን የሚገምቱት፤ የአገሪቱን የኤኮኖሚ አማራር ነው፡፡ በዘፈቀደ፣ በሰፈር አለቃ የሚመራ ኤኮኖሚ ጠንካራ የውጭ ግምት፤ ማለትም ጠንካራ የምንዛሬ ግምት አይኖረውም፡፡

የዕዳ ምጣኔ

የማይበደር አገር የለም ማለት ይቻላል፡፡ ታላላቆችም፤ ትናንሽ አገራትም ይበደራሉ፤ አንዱ ከሌላው፡፡ አበዳሪ ተቀማጭም ሞልተዋል፡፡ ብድር፤ ንግድም ጮምር ነው፡፡ በአገራት መካከል ሲሆን ደግሞ፤ የፖለቲካና የኤኮኖሚ ጥቅም ያስገኛል፡፡ ለአበዳሪ፤ ከወለድ ጥቅም ጋር የፖለቲካ ዓላማ ማስፈጸሚያ ሲዉል፤ ለተበዳሪ የውጭ ምንዛሬ ምንጭ፣ የኢንቨስትመንት ድጋፍ ይሆናል፡፡

ዕዳ ተሸክሞ አለመንገታገት ግን አይቻልም፡፡ መጽሐፍ ቅዱስ፤ ተበዳሪ የአበዳሪ ባርያ ነው ይላል (ምሳሌ 22፥ 7)፡፡ ባለዕዳ ሳይፍል፤ አበዳሪ ሳያስፍል አይተውም፡፡ በገንዘብ መልክ ባይመለስ በሌላ፤ ምህረት እንኳን ሲደረግ በከንቱ አይሆንም፡፡

ስለዚህ የዕዳ ምጣኔ ዓይነተኛ የኤኮኖሚ ደህንነት መለኪያ ነው፡፡ አንድ አገር ዕዳውን በሙሉ ዛሬውኑ መክፈል ካለበት ከሀብቱ ምን ያህል ለዕዳ ክፍያ ይውላል? ብዙዎቻችን እንደምንገምተው ሳይሆን፤ በዚህ መለኪያ የባሳ ዕዳ የተከማቸባቸው አገራት "የበለጸጉ" የምንላቸው ናቸው፡፡

ለምሳሌ፦ ጃፓን ያላትን ሃብት በሦስት እጥፍ ያህል የሚበልጥ ዕዳ በመሸከም የዓለማችን መሪ ናት፡፡ ግሪክ የሀብቷን ሁለት እጥፍ ያህል ዕዳ አለባት፡፡ ታላቂቱ አሜሪካም ያለባትን ዕዳ ሁሉ ዛሬ ትክፈል ቢባል ያላትን ሃብት አሟጥጣ ከፍላ፣ ቤሳ ቤስቲን አይተርፍትም፡፡ [265]

በዚህ የመረጃ ምንጭ መሠረት፤ እንደ አሜሪካ ሁሉ የኤኮኖሚያቸውን መጠን ያህል የተበደሩ የአፍሪካ አገራት በርካታ ናቸው፡፡ ከፖ ቬርዴ፤ አንጎላ፤ ሞዛምቢክ፤ ጁቡቲና ግብፅ፤ ኢትዮጵያ ግን ዕዳ በማከማቸት በኩል ፈሪ ነች፡፡ ግማሽ ያህል ሀብቷን ብትሸጥ ሙሉ ዕዳዋን ዛሬ መዝጋት ትችላለች፡፡

ነገር ግን የዕዳ ምጣኔ ዋና መለኪያ ብዛቱ ወይም የዕዳው መጠን አይደለም፡፡ መልሶ የመክፈል ዐቅም እንጂ፡፡ የመክፈል ዐቅም ደግሞ የሚወሰነው በኤኮኖሚ ትልቅነት

---

265 World Population Review (2022). Debt to GDP Ratio by Country, 2022. Accessed on November 18, 2022 from https://worldpopulationreview.com/country-rankings/countries-by-national-debt

ብቻ ሳይሆን በሌሎች መስፈርቶችም ጭምር ነው። ኤኮኖሚው ያለው የውጭ ምንዛሬ የማስገኘት ዐቅም ዋናው ነው።

እንዲሁም የዕዳው ዐይነት አከፋፈሉን ይወስነዋል። ለምሳሌ፦ ከጸ ገበያ የተገኘ ዕዳ፣ በአገራት የጋራ ስምምነት፣ በተስማሚ ወይም ተመራጭ የወለድ ምጣኔ ከተገኘው ጋር ሲመዘን፣ ወደድ ይላል። የአከፋፈል ሁኔታና (የጊዜ ርዝመትና ፍጥነት)፣ እና የገንዘቡ ምንጭ (ከአገር ውስጥ ወይስ ውጭ፣ እንዲሁም በዐይነት ወይስ በገንዘብ) የሚለው የክፍያን ዐቅም ይወስናል።

ዘላቂ፣ ምቹ ዕዳ የሚባለው አንድ አገር ሌላ ብድር ሳይኖርበት፣ ወይም ዕርዳታ ሳያስፈልገው የተበደረውን ከነወለዱ በተስማማው ጊዜ ውስጥ መክፈል ሲችል ብቻ ነው።[266] የክፍያ ዐቅም መለካት ግን ያስቸግራል። በተለይ በአገራት መካከል የሚደረግ ውል ያወሳስበዋል። ይሁን እንጂ፣ በዕዳ ክፍያ ምጣኔነት በስፋት ጥቅም ላይ የዋሉ መለኪያዎች አሉ።

ከእነዚህም አንዱ፣ በአንድ ዘመን የሚከፈል ዕዳ አገሪቱ ከምታገኘው የውጭ ምንዛሬ አንጻር ምን ያህል ይሆናል የሚለው ነው። ማለትም፣ ለምሳሌ በአንድ ወር ውስጥ ዕቃና አገልግሎት ለውጭ ገበያ አቅርቦት ከምናገኘው የውጭ ምንዛሬ ምን ያህሉን መልሰን ለዕዳ ክፍያ እናውለዋለን? በቂ ባይሆንም ቀለል ያለ አመልካች ስለሆነ በስፋት ጥቅም ላይ የዋለ መለኪያ ነው።

የዓለም ባንክ መረጃ እንደሚያመለክተው ባለፈው ዓመት (2022) ኢትዮጵያ ሸቀጦችና አገልግሎት ለውጭ ገበያ ሸጣ ካገኘችው የውጭ ምንዛሬ፣ ከአራት እጅ አንዱን ለአበዳሪ ስጥታ ተመልሳለች። ጂቡቲ የኤኮኖሚዋን ያህል ዕዳ አለባት፦ ነገር ግን፣ በዚህ መለኪያ መሠረት፣ ከውጭ ምንዛሬዋ ገቢዋ ሁለት ከመቶ ብቻ ለዕዳ ክፍያ ታስረክባለች።

ግብፅ የኢትዮጵያን ኤኮኖሚ በአራት እጥፍ የሚበልጥ ሃብት አላት። ኢትዮጵያ ካለባት የዕዳ መጠን ጋር ሲወዳደር፣ በስድስት እና በሰባት እጥፍ በሚበልጥ መጠን ዕዳ ታቅፋለች። ነገር ግን ግብፅም ለዕዳ ክፍያ የምታውለው ከውጭ ምንዛሬ ግኝቷ አንድ አራተኛውን ያህል ብቻ ነው።

ከእነዚህ ሁሉ አንጸር ሲታይ፣ ከዕዳ መጠን ይልቅ ብድርን መልሶ የመክፈል ዐቅም የሚወስነው የኤኮኖሚው አማራ መሆን እናስተውላለን። ተመራጭ ብድር፣ ወለድና የአከፋፈል ሥርዓት ከመደራደር ጋራ የአገር ውስጥ ዋና ዋና የኤኮኖሚ ትንፋሽ

---

266 Dalia Hakura. (2020). What Is Debt Sustainability? Accessed on November 18, 2022 from https://www.imf.org/en/Publications/fandd/issues/2020/09/what-is-debt-sustainability-basics#:~:text=A%20country's%20public%20debt%20is,assistance%20or%20going%20into%20default.

መለኪ.ያዎችን (ማለትም፤ የውጭ ምንዛሬ ምጣኔ፤ የባንክ ወለድ ምጣኔ፤ የአገር ውስጥ እዳ ምጣኔ፤ እና በተለይም የሸቀጦች ዋጋ ግሽበትን) በአስተማማኝ መምራት እጅግ ወሳኝ ነው።

በብሔርተኝነት የተቃኛ ኤኮኖሚ ግን እነዚህን ነገሮች የኤኮኖሚ ሕግጋትን ተከትሎ በመምራት ረገድ ከባድ በሽታ ያለበት እንደሆነ በጥልቀት ከላይ ተመልክተናል። በዓለም ገበያ የውጭ ምንዛሬ ዋጋ ሲወሰንም፤ በውጭ ምንዛሬ ግኝት ዐቅም እየታየ ብድር ሲሰጥም፤ ብድሩን የመመለስ ዐቅም ሲገመገምም፤ ብቻ በማንኛውም የዓለም ገበያ እንቅስቃሴ ውስጥ "የኤኮኖሚው አመራር እንዴት ነው?" የሚለው ወሳኝ ጥያቄ ነው።

በያዝነው ክፍለ ዘመን መጀመሪያ አካባቢ የአፍሪካ አገራት በዕዳ ስረዛ ምክንያት ጫና በመቀነሱና፣ በአጋጣሚው በተገኘ የተረጋጋ የኤኮኖሚ ዕድገት በመደፋፈር ብዙ ብድር የወሰዱበት ጊዜ ነበር። ከጥቂት ዓመታት በኋላ ግን ዋጋ ያስከፍላቸው ጀመር፤ በተለይም የኤኮኖሚ ዕድገት ምጣኔ ወረድ ሲል ከግማሽ በላይ የሚሆኑት ችግር ውስጥ መግባታቸው በጥናት ተረጋግጧል። [267]

ኢትዮጵያን ጨምሮ ከእርስ በርስ ግጭት ጋራ ተቋማዊና ማኅበራዊ ብልሽት ባለባቸው 17 አገራትና ግጭትም ባይሆን ተቋማዊና ማኅበራዊ ቀውስ ባለባቸው ተጨማሪ 20 አገራት ላይ በቅርቡ በተካሄደ ጥናት እንደተመለከተው፤ ከክፍለ ዘመኑ መባቻ ዓመታት ይልቅ በያዝነው አሥርት ዓመታት የዕዳ ክፍያ ምጣኔ በእጅጉ አሽቆልቁሏል። [268]

እንዲያውም፤ ኢትዮጵያ በዚህ ረገድ ትሻላለች የሚሉ አሉ። [269] ብድርን፣ በተለይም የውጭ ብድርን፣ ፈራ፣ ተባ በማለት ማስተናገድዋ ይታወቃል። [270] ስለዚህ የክፍያ ጫና ቢኖርባትም፣ ከቁጥጥር ውጭ አልወጣም። ወይም፣ ጫናውን ተገንዝቦ ከአበዳሪዎች ጋር በመደራደር ጊዜያዊ ትንፋሽ እየተገዛ በመነገዳገድ ላይ እንገኛለን። ጫናው ግን ዛሬም አልተወገደም።

267 Ncube, M. & Brixiová, Z. (2015). Public Debt Sustainability in Africa: Building Resilience and Challenges Ahead. Africa Deevlopment Bank Group; Working Papers; No 227 – July 2015. Accessed on November 18, 2022 from https://www.afdb.org/fileadmin/uploads/afdb/Documents/Publications/WPS_No_227_Public_Debt_Sustainability_in_Africa_Building_Resilience_and_Challenges_Ahead_H.pdf

268 Keller, J. & Nogueira-Budnym, D. (2020). Debt sustainability in fragile and conflict-affected states: heightened risks and needs. The World Bank Group. Accessed on November 18, 2022 from https://ieg.worldbankgroup.org/blog/debt-sustainability-fragile-and-conflict-affected-states-heightened-risks-and-needs

269 Martin, M. (2010). Ethiopian Debt Policy: The Long Road from Paris Club to the MDGs. In Herman, B. et al (ed.). Overcoming Developing country Debt Crisis. Pages 277–297. Oxford.

270 Estevão, M., Zeidane, Z. & Nolan, S. (2019). Ethiopia - Joint World Bank-IMF Debt Sustainability Analysis. IDA & IMF. Accessed on November 18, 2022 from, https://documents1.worldbank.org/curated/en/346081586457062642/pdf/Ethiopia-Joint-World-Bank-IMF-Debt-Sustainability-Analysis.pdf

በዘላቂነት እንዳይወገድ፣ አሁንም የኤኮኖሚው አመራር የታሰበውን ያህል አልሆነም። የኢትዮጵያ የዕዳ ጫና አመራር ከቻይና አመራር ጋር በማነጻጸር ጥናት የሠሩት ፍሬው በቀለ ወልደየስ[271] የተባሉ የተባበሩት መንግሥታት የንግድና ልማት ድርጅት ባለሙያ እንደገለጡት ከሆነ፣ በፖሊሲ ደረጃ ጫናውን ለመምራት ጥፉ የሚባል ማዕቀፍ ቢቀመጥም በተግባር አፍራሽ እንቅስቃሴዎች ይታያሉ።

ሦስት ነገሮች ትኩረት አላገኙም። በመጀመሪያ ደረጃ፣ የዕዳ ጫና በጥብቅ ለመቆጣጠር መስፈርቶቹን በዓይነ ቁራኛ መከታተል ቢያስፈልግም ይህ አይታይም። አንዱን ይዞ፣ ሌላውን መልቀቅ ይስተዋላል። ለምሳሌ:- ዕዳ እጅግ ያሻቀበው ከ1997 ዓ.ም እስከ 2017 ዓ.ም ድረስ ባሉት፣ ቻይናን በተወዳጀንበት ዓመታት ነው። በመጠንም፣ በፍጥነትም እጅግ አድጓል። በአጠቃላይ ከ7 ቢሊዮን ወደ 53 ቢሊዮን፣ በነፍስ ወከፍ ደግሞ፣ ከ200 ዶላር በሦስት ዕጥፍ አድጎ ወደ 600 ዶላር ደርሷል።[272]

ሌላው፣ የአገር ውስጥ ብድር አመራር አድልዎን ያማከለ መሆኑ ነው። የአገሪቱ የገንዘብ ተቋማት ሆነ ዜጎች ከሚካፈሉበት የብድር ስሌት ውስጥ ሁለት የመንግሥት ተቋማት ማለትም የኢትዮጵያ መብራታ ኃይል ባለሥልጣንና የምድር ባቡር ድርጅት ብቻ 90 በመቶውን ይጠቃታል። የቀረችውን የሚወስደው አዲስ አበባ ከተማ አስተዳደር ነው።

ሁለቱ ድርጅቶች ለኤኮኖሚው ከሚያደርጉት አስተዋጽኦ አንጻር ይገባቸዋል ብንልም እንኳ፣ ያሉንን እንቁላሎች በሙሉ ሰብስቦ አንድ ቅርጫት መከተት ያስመስልብናል። ሙስና እና የአመራር ድክመት በእነዚህ ድርጅቶች ውስጥ ከታየ ምን ይኮናል? ደግሞስ ይህን መሰል ብክነት በድርጅቶቹ የኢንቨስትመንትም ሆነ የገንዘብ አጠቃቀም አልታየም ይሆን?

በመጨረሻም፣ በ2016 ዓ.ም ከቻይና ብቻ የተገኘው ብድር ከአጠቃላዩ እስከ 40 በመቶ ሆኖ ነበር። የቻይና ብድር በአብዛኛው በመሠረተ ልማት ላይ የሚውል እና ከፕሮጀክት ጋር የተያያዘ ብድር ነው። ነገር ግን ፕሮጀክቱንም በመሥራትና፣ ገንዘቡን በማግኘት የቻይና ኩባንያዎች የሚካፈሉ ስለሆነ ተስማሚ ብድር አይገኝበትም። ሁለት ወዶ አይሆንም የተባለ ይመስላል።

በኢትዮጵያ መንግሥት የብድር ፖሊሲ መሠረት ተስማሚ ብድር የሚባለው ከተገኘው ገንዘብ ውስጥ 35 በመቶ ያህሉ ዕርዳታ አክል ሲሆን ነው። ለፕሮጀክቶችም

271 Woldeyes, F. B. (2021). Debt Sustainability and Management in Ethiopia Lessons from China. South South Integration and the SDGs: Enhancing Structural Transformation in Key Partner Countries of the Belt and Road Initiative UNCTAD/BRI PROJECT/RP 20. Accessed on November 21, 2022, from https://unctad.org/system/files/official-document/BRI-Project_RP20_en.pdf

272 Countryeconomy.com (2022). Ethiopia: Evolution of Debt. Accessed on November 21, 2022, from https://countryeconomy.com/national-debt/ethiopia

ሆን ለሌላ የመንግሥት በጀት የሚፈቀደው የልማት ብድር መጠንና ቅንብር 35 በመቶ ዕርዳታ አከል እንዲሆን በሕግ ተወስኗል፡፡ ቢሆንም ትላልቅ የልማት ፕሮጀክቶች ይህን ቅንብር ፈጽመው ጥሰው ተገኝተዋል፡፡ [273]

ዓለም አቀፉ የገንዘብ ድርጅት የአንድ አገር የዕዳ ክፍያ ምጣኔ (በአንድ ዘመን ለዕዳ ክፍያ የሚውለው ገንዘብ ከውጭ ምንዛሬ ግኝት አንጻር ሲታይ) ከአንድ ስድስተኛ ወይም 15 በመቶ ባይበልጥ ይደግፋል፡፡ ከዚህ ካለፈ የዕዳ አያያዝ ጥንቃቄ የጐደለው ይሆናል፡፡ የኢትዮጵያ ከሩብ በላይ ማለትም 27 በመቶ ደርሷል፡፡

በሌሎችም የዕዳ ጫና ምዘናዎች ድንበር ጥሰናል፡፡ ለምሳሌ፡- ጠቅላላ ከውጭ የተገኘ ብድር ክምችት ከዓመታዊ የውጭ ምንዛሬ ግኝት ጋር ሲነጻጸር ከ180 በመቶ በላይ (ማለትም እጥፍ ያህል) ከሆነ አገሪቱ ያለ ጥርጥር ችግር ላይ ናት፡፡ አበዳሪዎች በዓይነ ቁራኛ መመልከት ይጀምራሉ፡፡ የኢትዮጵያ ወደ 250 በመቶ ደርሷል፡፡ እጥፍና ከዚያ በላይ ማለት ነው፡፡

---

273 Woldeyes, F. B. (2021). Ibid.

በነፋስ ሲወሰድ

ሩጫ ምናልባት ከስፖርቶች ዓይነቶች ሁሉ በጣም መሠረታዊው ነው። በኢኮኖሚ ረገድም አነስተኛውን ወጪ የሚጠይቅ። በውጤቱም፤ ከስፖርቶች ሁሉ የበለጠ ዴሞክራሲያዊ እና ተወዳዳሪነትን ያማከለ ... ግለሰቦች በብቃታቸው የሚያሸንፉበት፤ የሰው ሁሉ፤ የዓለም ሁሉ የሆነ ስፖርት።

ፕሮፌሰር ቤርን ኃይንረከ፤ የቨርሞንት ዩኒቨርሲቲ የባዮሎጂ መምህርና የእንሰሳትና ሥነ ፍጥረት መላመድ ዓለም አቀፍ ሊቅ

ሁለት መላጦች ... የቀጠለ

"ፖሊስ ጣቢያ ክስ መስርቼብህ ነበር። ትቼዋለሁ ልልህ ነው የመጣሁት።"

ባለፉት ስድስት ወራት ላይና ታች ሲለው የነበረ ሃሳብ ነበረ። መሐመድ ቀና ብሎ እስከሚያየው እንኳ አልጠበቀውም። አፈረጠው።

"ደግሞ ባንተ ብሶ ልተከስሰኝ?"

አብዱልቃድር እንደሆን አውቆታል፤ ድፍረቱ ደግሞ ገርሞታል። ፍርሃትም ያዘው።

"እርሱ ቆም እየተራመደ፤ በእግሩ እየሄደ ነው። እኔ ከወገብ በታች ሽባ ሆኛለሁ። አንዳች ቢያደርገኝስ? ለነገሩ ከዚህ በላይ ምን ያደርገኛል? እንዲያው በጨረሰኝ፤ አብዱልቃድር መጣ አይሉኝም እንዴ? ለምን ሰው ሊጠይቅህ መጣ ይሉኛል?"

ይህን እያሰበ ዞር ሲል ጤናውን የሚከታተል ሐኪም እምብዛም ሳይርቅ እያያ ስለነበር ትንሽ ተረጋጋ።

አብዱልቃድር መሐመድ ወደተቀመጠበት ሥፍራ እንደ ደረሰ ነበር የተናገረው። ብዙ አስቦበት ስለመጣ፤ አልተቻገረም። የቀድሞ ጓደኛው እንደ ወትሮው ሠላም ባይሆኑ እንኳ ከራሱ ጋር ታርቆ እንዲኖር ምኞቱ ነበር። የፈለገ የጐጣ ቃል ቢናገር እችላለሁ ብሎ ራሱን አጽናንቶ ነበር የመጣው።

185

"እርሱን አሁን እንተወው። አንተ እንዴት እየሆነክ ነው ሙሔ?"

መሐመድም ቀድሞ በሚጠራበት መንገድ ስለጠራው ንዴቱ ለአፍታ መለስ እንደማለት አለና ቁጣው ይበልጥ ጨሰ።

"መጀመሪያ መነጽርህን ከፊትህ ገለል አድርገውና አናግረኝ። ከሰው ለማትቆጥረኝ!" አንባረቀበት።

አብዱልቃድር ጥቁር መነጽር አድርጐ ወደ ተቀመጠበት ስለ ተጠጋ ነበር።

የጉዳታቸው ልክ እንደ ታወቀ፤ ሁለቱ ዋነኛ ፀበኞች እንደ ነፍሩም ስለ ተነገረ፤ የሆስፒታል ጓላፌዎች ተነጋገሩ በተለያዩ ሆስፒታሎች የሕክምና ክትትል እንዲያደርጉ አመቻችተውላቸው ነበርና። አንዱ፤ ሌላው ላይ የደረሰውን ጉዳት መጠን በውል አያውቁም።

አብዲ አንድ ዓይኑን ክፋኛ ተመታ እንጂ ሌላ የሰውነት ክፍል እምብዛም ስላልተጐዳ ብዙ ሳይቆይ ከሆስፒታል ወጣ። ቀኝ ዓይኑ ግን የለም። ስለዚህ መነጽር አድርጐ ይዞራል። ጓደኛው የደረሰበትን ሙሉ ጉዳት የሰማው ፖሊስ ጣቢያ ክስ ለመመሥረት በሄደ ጊዜ ነበር።

ለካ መሐመድ አከርካሪው ክፋኛ ተመትቶ ኖሮ ቆም የሚ/ድ ተስፋው አክትሞ ነበር። ከሆስፒታል ሳይወጣ የዘገየውም አንድ የመጫሪሻ ምርመራ ለማድረግ እና ተሸከርካሪ ወንበር ልትገዛለት ቃል የገባችው አንዲት ሴት እስከታስመጣለት ጊዜ ስለ ወሰደ ነበር።

"ሙሔ፤ እኔ ሁሉን ሰምቻለሁ። ለደረሰብህ ጉዳት በጣም አዝናለሁ። መነጽር ያደረግኩት ግን አንድ ዓይኔ በግርግሩ ቀን ስለጠፋ እንዳይታወቅብኝ ብዬ ነው።" ከመቅጸበት እያወለቀው።

ሌላ ድንጋጤ።

"ቀኝ ዐይንህን? ውይ በሞትኩት። ለነገሩ ከእኔ የሞተ ውሻ አይሻልም?"

"አይሻልም። በአንድ ዓይኔም ቢሆን እያየሁ ኑሮ ለመግፋት ቆርጫለሁ። አንተም ቁጭ ባልከበት ቢሆንም የምትሥራውን አታጣም። ክስ ልመሥርትብህ ሂጄ፤ ተነሥቶ መራመድ እንኳ አይችልም ሲሉኝ፤ የተመታሁ ቀን ያለቅስኩትን ያህል አንብቻለሁ። አሁን ግን ይቅር ተባበለን፤ የመጣብንን ቀ/ጣ ችለነው ልንኖር ይገባል። በራስህ ላይ ክፉ እንዳታደርግ፤ ተስፋ እንደማትቆርጥ ከነገርሽኝ ይቅር እንዳልከኝ አምናለሁ። "

የድሮው አብዲ። እንደ ታላቅ ወንድም የሚመክረው አብዲ።

ባሕላዊ ጨዋታ

እንስሳትና ዕፅዋት ያሉበትን አካባቢ ይለመዳሉ። ወይም ካልተላመዱ ይጠፋሉ። ከባድ ማለትም፣ ወይ እጅግ ብርድ፣ አለያም እጅግ ሞቃትና ደረቅ በሆነ፣ የአየር ንብረት ባለበት አካባቢ ለመኖር ራሳቸውን መቀየር፣ መላመድ መቻል አለባቸው። ሰውስ ለማዳ ይሆን?

ካሉበት የአየር ንብረት ጋር ለመላመድ እንስሳትና ዕፅዋት በአብዛኛው የሚቀይሩት የውጭውን አካላቸውን ነው። ሰው ግን ውጩም፤ ውስጡም ውስብስብ ነው። መላመድ ብቻ ሳይሆን ያላምዳል። ባሕል፣ ጎይማኖትና መሰል የማይዳሰሱ ነገሮች ከፖለቲካ ጋር ይመሳቀሉና ኤኮኖሚውን አሣር ያሳይታል። ኤኮኖሚውም፣ ቀጥታ ባልሆነ መንገድ ፖለቲካውን መንካት ሲፈልግ እንኝህን ይጠቀማል።

ባሕል የበሔር ማንነትን ለመስከምም ሆነ ለመሸጥ እምብዛም እንደማይረባ ስለ ዘር ባነሳንበት ምዕራፍ ተመልክተናል። ይህ የሚሆንበት ዋናው ምክንያት፣ ባሕል ተቀያሪ ስለሆነ ነው። ይሁን እንጂ የማንነት ፖለቲካ የሙጥኝ ብሎ የሚያራግበው የባሕል ልዩነትን ነው። ሽሚያው አይጣል።

ማንነትም ዐብር ይለወጥ ካልተባለ በቀር፣ ባሕል የፖለቲካ፣ በተለይም ዘላቂ የአገር ወጋግራዎች የሚቲከለብብ ፖለቲካ መሠረት መሆኑ ግራ ነው። ባሕል አይረጋም፤ ይሠረጋል እንጂ፣ ሲሠርግም፣ ተቀባይ አንድም እንደ ወራሽ የራሱ የማድረግ መብቱ ፍጹም ስለሆነ ይጠርበዋል። አለያም ወደ ሌላ አጮልቆ ማየቱን ስለማይተው እና "ሌላው" ከጣፈጠው ጨልፎ ይመርጣታል።

ባሕልን ለማዛደግ ይባልና ግን ኤኮኖሚው አጫፋሪ ይሆናል። ወይንም፣ ወሳኝ የኤኮኖሚ ጉልቻዎች ይቀያየራሉ። በባሕል፣ በጎይማኖት፣ በዐመት በዐል ወዘተ ስም እንዚህን ጉልቻዎች መቀየር ለፖለቲካው ምትጎታዊ እርካታ ይሰጣል። ለምሳሌ፦ ቋንቋን እንመልከት።

አንድ ሰሞን (2022 ዓ.ም አጋማሽ ገደማ) አፋን ኦሮሞ የማይችል ሐኪም በኦሮሚያ ይቀጠር አይቀጠር በሚል ንትርክ ተነሣ። መንሥኤው፣ የኦሮሚያ ክልላዊ መንግሥት ለሥራ ፈላጊዎች ያወጣው ማስታወቂያ ሐኪም ተፈለገ ይልና አፋን ኦሮሞ የሚችል ብቻ የሚል ነው በሚል ወሬ በመነዛቱ ነው። ፖለቲካዊ ክርክሩን እናቆየውና የቋንቋ ችሎታ ከሕክምናው ችሎታ የሚገዝፍ የሚያስመስል ማስታወቂያ ለምን ተለጠፈ የሚለው አከራከረ።

የብሔር ፌደራሊዝሙ ፍኖተ ካርታ ውስጥ የቋንቋ ብዝኃነት ይገኝበታል። ሕክምና ግን በቋንቋ ችሎታ ሳይሆን በሙያው ዕውቀት ቢሆን አይሻልም? በመሠረቱ ሕክምናም ሆነ ሌላ አገልግሎት ለተገልጋይ በሚመቸው ቋንቋ ቢሰጥ ውጤቱ ቀና ነው።

ይህን ማበረታታት ወንጀል የለውም። ቅድሚያ ሊሰጠው የሚገባው ሕክምና መቻል ቢሆንም ለአንድ የጤና ባለ *ሙያ* መልካም ተግባበት የሕክምና እምብርት ነው። ይህን ማን ከቁ..ብ ቆጥሮት?

ንትርኩ ፖለቲካዊ እንድምታ እንዲይዝ ስለ ተፈለገ ማስታወቂያው የኤኮኖሚ ፍትሐዊነት ነፈገ የሚሉ አየሉ። የከፋት መፍትሔ እንኳን አይጠቀሙም። ማስታወቂያው "የአፋን አሮሞ ችሎታ እንደ ተጨማሪ ነጥብ ይታያል" ቢል ኖሮ አንድም ለፖለቲካ ንትርክ ማስነሻ ምን ባገኝ ብለው አሰፍስፈው የሚጠብቁ አጀንዳ ለቃሚዎችን ያሳፍር ነበር። እንዲሁም፣ ወጣቶች ከአንድ በላይ ቋንቋ መናገር ፋይዳ እንዳለው ያውቁ ነበር።

አልሆነም፣ ኢትዮጵያዊ ሁሉ ቢያንስ ሁለተኛ ቋንቋ መቻልን ግቡ ማድረግ ነበረበት። ቱባና እጅግ ብዙ ባህሎቻችን ቢዋረሱ ቢጠቅም እንጂ አይጎዳም። በአዋንታዊ መልክ ብንመለከተው፣ ራሳችንን በተለያየ መልክ እንድንገልጥ ይረዳን ነበር። በአሉታዊው እንኳ ብንፈፍ፣ ከአንድ በላይ ቋንቋ ብናውቅ፣ የየብሔሩ ፈተና አውጪ በሰርቀለት ውጤት ዩኒቨርሲቲ የገባ፣ የብሔሩ "መምህር" በመረቀለት ከፍተኛ ውጤት በማዕረግ የጨረሰ "ሐኪም" በእንክፍ እጁ ሲነካን ልንመለስለት እንችል ነበር።

ሐኪም ሁሉ በተሰረቀ ውጤት ተማረ አልተባለም። ነገር የተበላሸው ክስር መሠረቱ መሆኑን ለማመልከት እንጂ። የተባበሩት መንግሥታት የትምህርት፣ የሳይንስና የባሕል ድርጅት፣ ዩኔስኮ፣ የጨቅላ ልጆች ትምህርት በአፍ መፍቻ ቋንቋ ቢሆን ይመረጣል ይላል። [274] ልጆች በአፍ መፍቻ ቋንቻቸው ሲማሩ የማንበብና መጻፍ እንዲሁም የቁጥሮች ቅመራ መሠረታዊ ዕውቀታቸው በሰዉ ይሻሻላል። [275]

የብሔር ፖለቲካው በዚህ ሳይንሳዊ ዕውቀት ዘው ሲልበት ግን፣ ከአፍሪካዊ ፊደል ይልቅ የፈረንጆቹ ስለሚቀርበን በሚል ብዙ ገንዘብና ጉልበት ፈሶ ፊደል እንዲቀየር ይደረጋል። ቋንቋ ከማግባባት ይልቅ የማለያየት ሚና እንዲጫወት ተደርጎ። ከአፍ መፍቻ ተጨማሪ ሌላ አፍ ለመናገር የሞከረ ሁላ በአደባባይ እንዲሳለቅበት ሆነ።

ብዝኃነትን ማክበር፣ የዕድገት፣ የምሉዕ ማንነትም ምልክት ነው። በግልም፣ በጋራም ስንነጋገር ለአፋችን (ለንግግራችን) ጥራት፣ ለአንደበታችን ልዝብነት መጨነቅ አለብን እንጂ በምን ቋንቋ አወራን የሚለው ባይሆን ይሻል ነበር። የብሔር ፖለቲካ ሹል

274 UNESCO. (2022). Why mother language-based education is essential. Accessed on November 23, 2022; from https://www.unesco.org/en/articles/why-mother-language-based-education-essential

275 Alimi, F. O., Tella, A., Adeyemo, G. O. & Oyoweso, M. O. (2020). Impact of Mother Tongue on Primary Pupils' Literacy and Numeracy Skills in Osun State. International Online Journal of Primary Education. 2020, volume 9, issue 2. Accessed on November 23, 2022; from https://files.eric.ed.gov/fulltext/EJ1283007.pdf

እንደበት ይጠቀምና ጒራዴ ያስጨብጠናል። ሕይወትም ሞትም በምላስ እጅ ነውና ምላሳችንን ከተመዘዘው ሰይፋችን ጋር ወደ ስገባዋ ብትገባስ?

የትምህርት ዘርፍ የአንድ አገር መሰረት፣ የኤኮኖሚም አምድ እና ድምድማት ነው። ትምህርት የነገው አገር ተረካቢ ትውልድ የሚቀረጽበት፣ በዚህ ውድድር እና መቀራመት በበዛበት ዓለም የትናንትን ጠብቆ፣ ዛሬን ተቆናጥጦ፣ ነገን የሚፈጥር ዜጋ ተረግዞ በምጥ የሚወለድበት፣ የአንድ አገር እና በግለሰብም ደረጃ የዕድገት ብቻ ሳይሆን የሕልውና መስክ ነው።

ይሁንና እንደ ማንኛውም ቍልፍ የኤኮኖሚ መስክ የትምህርት ዘርፍ ከፖለቲካው ውጭ አይሆንም። እንዲያውም በፖለቲካው ተጠቃሚ ወይም ሰለባ የመሆን ዕድሉ ከፍተኛ ነው። ከዚህ የተነሣ የብሔር ፖለቲካ መስመር ዕቅዱንና ተግባሩን ከሚገልጥባቸው መንገዶች ውስጥ ዓይነተኛው የትምህርት መስክ ነው።

በእኛ አገር ይህ ፖለቲካ የተገለጠበት ቀዳሚው መንገድ 'የብሔሮችን ቋንቋ እና ባሕል ለማሳደግ' በሚል የመጀመሪያ ደረጃ ትምህርት፣ በአንዳንድ ሥፍራዎችም እስከ ከፍተኛ ትምህርት ድረስ በብሔረሰብ ቋንቋ ብቻ ይሰጥ በሚል ፖለቲካዊ ውሳኔ ተሰጥቶ ነው። እናም ልጅ ሁሉ ወላጅ በመረጠው ሳይሆን ካድሬዎች በመረጡለት ቋንቋ መማር ግድ ሆነበት።

በአፍ መፍቻ ቋንቋ የመጀመሪያ ደረጃ ትምህርት መማር በባለሙያዎች የሚደገፍ፣ ተገቢ የትምህርት አሰጣጥ ነው። ቅርብ ጊዜ በኢትዮጵያ በተደረገ ጥናት[276] ሕጻናት እስከ 4ኛ ክፍል ድረስ በአፍ መፍቻና በሌላ ሁለተኛ ቋንቋ ተምረው 5ኛ፣ 7ኛ ወይም 9ኛ ክፍል ላይ እንግሊዝኛን እንዲመርጡ ተደረጎ ነበር። በመጀመሪያ፣ ብዙ ወላጆችና ልጆች 5ኛ ክፍል ላይ ወደ እንግሊዝኛ መዛወሩን ወደዱት።

እንዲሁም፣ ከሥር ጀምሮ በአፍ መፍቻ የተማሩ፣ ከ5ኛ ክፍል ጀምሮ በእንግሊዝኛ ቋንቋ የሚሰጠውን መርጠው ሲገቡ፣ በሌላ ቋንቋ ከተማሩ ይልቅ፣ በሒሳብ ትምህርት የተሻለ ውጤት እንዳገኙ ተረጋገጠ። ነገር ግን መለያየትን ሰንቆ የተነሣው የጐሣ ፖለቲካ ይህን በጐ ፈቃድ ለፖለቲካ ዓላማ ማስፈጸሚያ ተጠቀመበት።

በወላጆችና ልጆች ላይ ያለ ውዴታ ከጨቅላነት ዕድሜ ባለፉትም ላይ የአፍ መፍቻ ቋንቋ ብቻ ተጫነባቸው። ተለቅ ባሉ ከተሞች እና የተለያዩ ብሔሮች በሰፈሩባቸው የገጠር አካባቢዎች ጭምር ምርጫ ተከለከለ። የጥናት ውጤትን የተመረኮዘ ሥርዓት መከተል አልሆነልንም።

276 Seid, Y. (2019). The impact of learning first in mother tongue: evidence from a natural experiment in Ethiopia. Applied Economics, Volume 51, Issue 6; 2019. Accessed on November 24, 2022; from https://www.tandfonline.com/doi/abs/10.1080/00036846.2018.1497852?journalCode=raec20#2b85d6ca-6520-4a3d-8e4a-aa9f2ee3f33d-b6de7b7c-de82-45a5-9538-313dd15c6659

የከተሞች የአና መፍቻ ቋንቋ አካባቢው በፖለቲካዊ ውሳኔ እንዲናገር ግዴታ የተጣለበት ቋንቋ ላይሆን ይችላል። ለምሳሌ፡- ሾኔ በሃዲያ ክልል ያለች አካባቢ ብትሆንም ሃዲይኛ፣ ካምባትኛ፣ ወላይትኛ እና አማርኛ እኩል ይነገሩባታል። ወለጆችም ሆነ ልጆች ግን ምርጫ አልተሰጣቸውም። አዲስ አበባ፣ ሐዋሳ እና ድሬ ዳዋ ያለው ትክትክ ያልተፈታው ይህ ውሳኔ ወላጆችንና ልጆችን ስለሚያንገሸግሽ ነው።

የትምህርት ፖሊሲው፣ እያደርም የከፍተኛ ትምህርት ፈተና፣ ውጤቱና ምደባው የብሔር ፖለቲካው ጥገኛ እንዲሆን ተሠርቷል። የዩኒቨርሲቲ መግቢያ ፈተና ንትርክ ዝቅጠቱ የከፋ ደረጃ ላይ ለመድረሱ አመላካች ነበር። በ2022 ዓ.ም ተማሪዎች ላይ ተፈርዶ በካምፕ ታጉረው ተፈተኑ።

እንደ ሕዝብ ይህን መዘርክርክ እና አገራዊ ውድቀት ስንኮንነው፣ ተፈልነ በዕቅድ የተሰራ መሆን ካላስተዋልን ጨኻታችን 'ላም ባልዋለበት ኩበት ለቀማ' ይሆንብናል። ልጆች ፈተና እንዳይወስዱ ከአንድም ሁለቴ "የተሰረቀው" ፈተናውን ለማላፍ የተደረገ ኩረጃ ወይንም መልሱን ሾጦ ገንዘብ ለማግኛት የተከናወነ ተራ ሌብነት እንዳልነበረ ግልፅ ነው።

ይህ ስንክሳር፣ ከፍተኛ እና የተሳካ የብሔር ፖለቲካ ቀመር ለመሆን ግን በቂ ጠቋሚዎች ነበሩ። በዚያም አያቆምም። በተማሪዎች ምደባ እና ኮታ፣ ከአንዱ ክልል ወደ ሌላ እንዲሄዱ ወይም እንዳይሄዱ ሲደረግ፣ ከዬዱም በኋላ እግራቸው የዩኒቨርሲቲውን ደጅ ከመርገጡ የብሔር ድርጆቶችን ካባ በማልበስ፣ ከእስክርብቶ ቀድሞ ዱላ የማስያዝ ተከታታይ የማጋደል እና የመበጣበጥ ድራማ።

እንዲሁም የተማሪዎች ውጤት ከስማቸው ወይም ከተወለዱበት ብሔር አንጸር መታየቱ በሰፈው የምንሰማው ነው። ማስረጃ ማግኛት ግን ከባድ ነው። ጽንፈኛ ብሔርተኝነት እንዳዋው ሲናኛ ስለነበር ተከድኖ መብሰልሰል እንጂ መፍትሔ የለውም። እስከ መቼ? ልክ ያታዊ ጥቃት እንደ ደረሰባት ሴት ደብቆ መቃጠልም፣ ገልጦ መንጋፈጥም ዕዳ። ለብቻዋ ከተጋፈጠች ከጥቃቱ ይልቅ ተከታዩ ሥቃይ ይበረታል። ልዩ ርዳታ ትሻለች። የኢትዮጵያ ሕዝብ አንዱ ሌላውን መርዳት ያለበት ዘመን ነው።

ሰርቆትን አጀግነን አገር ማዋረዳችንም ሆነ የመላውን ተፈታኝ የፈተና ውጤት እንዲሰረዝ ወይም እንዲሻሻል የፖለቲካ መሪዎች ጣልቃ እንዲገቡ ማድረጋ አሳዛኝ ነው። ነገር ግን የአንዳች ዕኩይ ውጥን አካል ነው ያሰኛል። ምርጫው ግልፅ ነው። የምንኮራባትን አንዲት አገር ለኛ እንኳን ባይሆን ለልጆቻች የመፍጠር ዒላማ ካለን የኤኮኖሚ አውታሮችን ከብሔር ፖለቲካ ማነቆ መፍታት ነው።

የኤኮኖሚ ሕዋሳት የሚያደርጉትን ምርጫ የማያከብር ወይም የሚገድብ ፖሊሲ በጉና ዘላቂ ለውጥ አያመጣም። ለምሳሌ የንግድ ቋንቋ ምርጫ ከዐቅም ጋር የሚያያዝ ቢሆንም ታሪክ፣ መልክዓ ምድር፣ እና የኤኮኖሚ ሕዋሳት የትርፍ ማነቀነፍ ሃሞት

ይወስነዋል። በአዋጅ 'ከዛሬ ጀምሮ ይህን ቋንቋ ለንግድ ተጠቀሙ' ቢባል እንግልትን እንሸምት እንደሁ እንጂ ትርፉ አያጠረቃ።

በነባራዊው የዓለም ሁኔታ፣ የእንግሊዝኛ ቋንቋን ወድደን አንማርም። ታሪካዊ ሥርጭቱ ቅድሚያ ሰጥቶታል። የትርፋማነት ሃሞት የጠነከረበት ይማረዋል። ለመማር ያወጣው ገንዘብም ሆነ ልፋት ግብረ መልስ ትርፍ አለው። የባሕል ውርርስ ትርፍ እስካለው ድረስ ፖለቲካው ምን ቢዳክር አይቀይረውም።

በመልክንጵ ምድር ስንኩ የማይቀራረቡት አገሬ፣ ሺናሻና ወላይታ እጅግ ተቀራራቢ ባሕላዊ ጥፈራ አላቸው። ይህ የባሕል መወራረስ አንዱ ሌላውን ስለ ጨቆነ የተገኘ አይደለም። ወራሽ የራሱ አድርጎት ነው እንጂ። ነገር ግን ለረኸም ጊዜ አብረው ኖረው፣ ከወላይታ እስከ ሺናሻ በመሃ ያሉት ሕዝቦችም ለምን እስከ ዛሬ አልተማሩትም? ትርፉን ስለሚያሳሱ ነው።

በአንጻሩ፣ ዛሬ የወላይታ ማሕበረሰብ ልዩ ልዩ ባሕላዊ ጥፈራዎች የወላይታ ናቸው ማለቱ እስኪከብድ ድረስ ሁሉም ባሕል ውስጥ መሰባጠራቸውስ ለምንድነው? የነገሮች ነጃ ትርፍ ነው። ወላይታዎች የባሕል ወረራን አቅደው ስለ ዘመቱብን አይደለም። እንዲሁም ከትር የከተሜውን ሁላ ቤት ቤተኛ ያደረጋቸው ጉራጌ ነፍጥ አንሥቶ ስላንበረከከን አይደለም። የበላይነት በጉልበት ሲጫን ብቻ የዕድገት ፀር ይሆናል።

ግጭት

አስተዳደር በጥሪትና ላብ መስተጋብር ላይ ተጽዕኖ ከሚያሳድርባቸው መንገዶች አንድ ግለጥ ነገር እናንሳና ክፍሉን ለመቋጨት እንሞክር። ግለጥ የተባለው ሰውና ሃብት ግጭት ወደሚያያይልበት ስለማይስፍር ነው። ለግጭት የሚዳርጉ በርካታ ነገሮች አሉ። ምን ያህል ጥንቃቄ ሊደረግበት እንደሚገባ ለማስረዳት ስንል አንድ ምሳሌ ብቻ እንጠቀም። በአገራችን ግጭት የተብራከተው እንደሚወራው የሕዝብ ፍልሰት አንድነ ወይም ሌላውን ሥፍራ ስላሰጫነቀ ነውን?

የሕዝብ ፍልሰት ዓለም አቀፋዊ ክስተት ነው። በያዝነው ዓመት፣ በዓለም ዙሪያ ወደ 281 ሚሊዮን የሚጠጉ ሰዎች ፍልሰት ላይ መሆናቸውን ዓለም አቀፉ የሰዎች ፍልሰት ክትትል ድርጅት[277] አስታውቋል። ይህ ማለት አብዛኛው ሰው በተወለደበት አካባቢ ይኖራል ማለት ነው። ምክንያቱም 8 ቢሊዮን ደርሰን የለ? ከመቶ ሰው ውስጥ አራት ያህሉ፣ ያውም በጉልበት የተፈናቀለውን ጨምሮ፣ ሥፍራቸውን ለቀቀው ቢሰደዱ ምን ይገርማል?

---

277 IOM. (2022). World Migration Report 2022. Accessed on November 24, 2022; from https://publications.iom.int/books/world-migration-report-2022

በየሥፍራው የሚታየው ግጭት፤ ከፍልሰት ጋር የተያያዘ እንደሆነ በሰፈው ይወራል። መረጃዎች ግን ይህን አይደግፉም። በቅርቡ ሐዋሳ ላይ ከታየው አስቃቂ ግጭት በመነሣት ችግሩ የተከሰተው፤ የወላይታ አካባቢ ሰዎች ሥራ ፍለጋ የትውልድ ሥፍራቸውን ጥለው ሐዋሳ ስለ ከታሙ ነው የሚ አስተሳሰብ በሰፈው ይነገራል፤ ፍልሰትማ አለ። ግን፤ እንደሚባለው ነው ወይ?

ቢሆንስ በዉነ ፍልሰት ለግጭት፤ በተለይም እንዳያነው ዐይነት እብደት የቀላቀለ ግጭት መንስዔ ይሆናል ወይ? በአገራችን የፍልሰቱ ልክ በውል አልተጠናም። እንደ ለመድነው በደፈናው የልምድ ከበሮ እንደልቃለን፤ ጥናት ባይኖርም መነሻ ዐሳቦች ለማንሣት ቁጥር ፍለጋ መዳከር ግድ ነው፤ ብዙም የለም እንጂ።

የተገኘው ያው የምንነቁረው የሕዝብ ቤጠራ ውጤት ነው። በእርግጥም በፈረንጆቹ አቆጣጠር በ2007 ዓ.ም የተካሄደው አገር አቀፍ የሕዝብ ቤጠራ ሪፖርት[278] ስለ ፍልሰት አንዳንድ ነገሮችን አንሥቶ እንደ ነበር ማየት ይቻላል። የቤጠራውን የቀድሞ ደቡብ ክልል ሪፖርት በጥልቀት ስንመለከት ክልሉ 56 ብሔሮች፤ ሕዝቦች፤ ... ወዘተ ያሉበት ነው ቢባልም የጉረቤት አገራት ዜጎችንና የሌላ አገር ዜግነት ካላቸው አባት ወይንም እናት ከተወለዱት ጋር 93 የተለያዩ ብሔሮችና ሕዝቦች ይገኙበታል።

ኢትዮጵያውያን የሚባሉ ከነዚህ 86[+] ናቸው። በአጭሩ ኢትዮጵያዊ ሆኖ ደቡብ ክልል የማይገኝ ዘር ወይም ጎሣ የለም። ቤጠራው በተካሄደበት ጊዜ ከክልሉ ሕዝብ አሥር ከመቶ ያህሉ ከሌሎች የኢትዮጵያ ሕዝቦች፤ በተለይም ከአማራና ኦሮሞ የፈለሱና ኑሮአቸውን በክልሉ የተለያዩ አካባቢዎች የመሠረቱ መሆናቸው ታውቋል። በቤጠራው ወቅት "የፈለሰ" ወይም "መጤ" ማለት በተቆጠረበት ቀበሌ ያልተወለደ በሚለው ከተወሰደ በኋላ፤ በሶስት ጥያቄዎች ተጠንቷል።

ጥናቱ መጤውን መች መጣህ? ከየት አካባቢ መጣህ? ከከተማ ወይስ ከገጠር መጣህ? የሚሉ ሦስት ጥያቄዎች ጠይቆ ነበር። ይሁን እንጂ ከየትኛው ዞን ወይም አካባቢ እንደ መጡ የመለሱበት በሪፖርቱ አልተካተተም። ለምን አልተካተተም የሚለው ጥያቄ ማንሣት ቢገባም እንተወው።

በሪፖርቱ ካለው ስንነሳ ግን በተቆጠሩበት ሥፍራ አልተወለድኩም ያሉ የክልሉ ነዋሪዎች 14 ከመቶ ያህሉ ብቻ ነበሩ። ማለትም ይህን በአሥር አመት ብናከፋፍለው እንኳ በዓመት 1.4 በመቶ አካባቢ የምናገኘው የፍልሰት ምጣኔ እጅግ የሚባል አይደለም። ከዓለም አቀፉ ሪፖርት ጋርም ይስማማል። ይህ ቁጥር ከሐዋሳ ከተማ በስተቀር በደቡብ ባሉ ዞኖችና ልዩ ወረዳዎች ሁሉ ተቀራራቢ ነው። ሲዳማም ሆነ ወላይታ እምብዛም በማይራራቅ ደረጃ ፍልሰት አስመዝግበዋል።

---

278 CSA. (2012). The 2007 Population and Housing Census of Ethiopia: Administrative Report. Accessed on November 24, 2022; from https://rise.esmap.org/data/files/library/ethiopia/Documents/Clean%20Cooking/Ethiopia_Census%202007.pdf

ባሉበት ቦታ "መጤ" ነኝ (ማለትም በዥኑ አልተወለድኩም) ካሉት 17 ከመቶ
ሲዳማ ሲሆኑ 9 ከመቶዎቹ ወላይታ ናቸው። የኢትዮጵያ ሕዝብ የተወለደበትን ቦታ
ያለ በቂ ምክንያት ጥሎ የሚሰደድ ነው ለማለት አያስደፍርም። ይህ ብቻ ሳይሆን
በደቡቡ የአገራችን ክፍል ያለው ፍልሰት ወደ ከተማ ግር ብሎ መግባትም እንዳልነበር
እናያለን። ከመጤዎቹ አንድ ሦስተኛው ብቻ ከተማ የገቡ ሲሆን ሌላው ከገጠር ወደ
ገጠር የሄደ ነው።

በጊዜው ያለውን የገጠር መሬት ሥሪት ስንመለከት ደቡብ ውስጥ በአብዛኞቹ
ዞኖች ሕዝቡ ጥቅጥቅ ብሎ የሰፈረ ከመሆኑ ጋር ዐዳዲስና የተሚካለ የሰፋራ ፕሮግራም
የለበትም። ማለትም፣ ለገበሬው መሬት የማዳረስ ሥራ በአካባቢው ጎላፊዎች እጅ
ባለበት ከአንድ ዞን ገጠራማ ቀበሌዎች ወደ ሌላ ዞን አርሶ አደሮች ፈለሱ ማለት
የማይመስል ነገር ነው። ስለሆነም ባጭሩ ሁለት - ሦስተኛው ፍልሰት እዚያው በዚያው
ነው። ይፍለስ እንጂ አብዛኛው ከዥኑ አልወጣም።

ይህም የተወለደበትን ሥፍራ ለሚወድ የአገራችን ሕዝብ አስደናቂ ወይም ልዩ
የሚገባ ሊሆን አይችልም። ቄጠራ ከተካሄደበት ዓመት በፊት ባሉት ሦስት ተከታታይ
ዓመታት ያለውንም የፍልሰት መጠን ስናይ ሥዕሉ ብዙ አይቀየርም። ከቄጠራው በፊት
ባሉት ሦስት ዓመታት ሥፍራቸውን የቀየሩት በገጠርም፣ በከተማም ከሦስት ሰዎች
አንዱ ያህሉ ብቻ ናቸው። የከተሞች ጥቂቱ ከፍ ብሎ ቢታይም።

ወደ ሐዋሳ ከተማ ስንመለስ፣ በከተማዋ፣ በቄጠራው ወቅት ግማሽ ያህል ሕዝቢ
በተቆጠረበት ቀበሌ ያልተወለደ ሕዝብ ነበር። ከተማዋ በዐይሚዋ ለጋ፣ በከፍተኛ ፍጥነት
እያደገች ያለች ከተማ መሆኗን ያስተውሿል። በዚህ መነጽር ሲታይ፣ በርካታ ዐዳዲስ
ሰው ቢሂርባት አስደናቂ ሊባል አይችልም። ያም ሆኖ ከቄጠራው ሦስት ዓመታት
ቀደም ብሎ ባሉት ጊዜያት ወደ ከተማዋ የገቡትን ስንመለከት፣ ሰው ወደ ሐዋሳ ጉረፈ
አያሰኝም፣ ከአጠቃላዩ የፍልሰት መጠን ጋር ተቀራራቢ ነበር።

ከዚህም በላይ ከቀድሞ የደቡብ ክልል አጠቃላዩ የፍልሰት መጠን ውስጥ ሐዋሳ
ከተማ ያስተናገደችው 6 ከመቶውን ብቻ ነበር። ስለዚህ አብዛኞች ነዋሪዎች ከዚያ በፊት
ወደ ከተማዋ የገቡ ነበሩ። ከሲዳማና ከወላይታ ወደ ከተሞች ከፈለሱ ሰዎች ውስጥ
ግማሽ የሚሆኑት ወደ ሐዋሳ ከተማ ገቡ የሚል ግምት ብንወስድ እንኳን ጠቅላላ ድምሩ
ከዚህ ቁጥር (ከ6 ከመቶ) በታች ይሆናል። የፈለሱ ሁሉ ሐዋሳ ገቡ ማለት የማይቻል
ነው። ይህ ሆኖ ቢሆን ስብጥሩን እጅግ ያዛባው ነበር።

ምክንያቱም በቄጠራው ወቅት በከተማይቱ ከነበሩት ሕዝቦች ውስጥ አብዛኛዎች
የሲዳማ ብሔር ተወላጆች ነበሩ። የሐዋሳ ከተማ ገጠር ቀበሌያትን ሕዝብ ጨምሮ 48
ከመቶ የሚሆኑት ሲዳማዎች ሲሆኑ፣ አማራ 16 ከመቶ፣ ወላይታ 14 ከመቶ አሮሞ

6 ከመቶ ነበሩ። የተቀሩት ከጉራጌ፣ ከከምባታ፣ ከሃዲያና ከስልጤ የመጡ ሕዝቦች ተደምረው 10 ከመቶ፣ ሌሎች ደግሞ ወደ 5 ከመቶ ነበር።

ቢያንስ የደቡቡን የአገራችንን ክፍል ስናይ አጠቃላይ የፍልሰት መጠን 1.4 ከመቶ ብቻ ነው። ከዚህም ውስጥ ሲሶው ብቻ ወደ ከተሞች የገባ ነው። ሌላው ከገጠር ወደ ገጠር የሄደ ነው። በዞኖችም፣ ፈጣን ዕድገት አላቸው እንኳ በሚባሉትም ከተሞች ከሌላ ሥፍራ የገባው ሕዝብ መጠን እጅግ ጥቂት ነው። ይልቁንም፣ ቀድሞውኑ የኢትዮጵያ ሕዝብ አንድም ጎሣ እንኳ ሳይቀር በሁሉም አካባቢ ይገኝል የሚለው የተሻለ ተዓማኒ ነው።

እና ፍልሰት፣ የሕዝቦች ዐብሮ የመኖር ውበት የሚጨምርበት እንጂ የግጭት መንስዔ እንዴት ይሆናል? ግጭቶችን ለማባባስ፣ በተለይም ሕዝብን ከሕዝብ ጋር ለማጋጨት የሚፈልጉ የሚያናፍሱትን ወሬ ጠርጥረን፣ መንዘረን ልንሰማ ይገባል። አብዛኛው አረፋ ብቻ ነው። አንኳርም ሆነ ጥብጥ የለውም የፈሰሰ ሁሉ ከአገሩ ወጥቶ፣ የራሱ ባልሆነ ሥፍራ ዓለሙን ይቀጭል ብሎ ማሰብም ስንተት ነው።

ይህ የብሔር ፖለቲካው የሚያራግበው ህጸጽ ነው። በበለጸጉም፣ በድኻ አገራትም ይስተዋላል። የፈሰሰ ሁሉ ግጭት ጠማቂ የሰው ነጋቂ አይደለም። ይልቁንም፣ ከሌላ ሥፍራ ፈለሰው የሚመጡ፣ ኑር ለማሽነፍ ሲሉ ጠንክረው የመሥራት ዝንባሌ ስላላቸው ጠቃሚ የሚሆኑበት አጋጣሚ እንደምሚበዛ የሚያስተውል የለም። የዓለም ባንክ፣ ባለፉት ጥቂት ዓመታት በፍልሰት ላይ እየጨመረ ከመጣው ጉርምርምታ የተነሣ ጥናት አካሂዶ አራት ቁልፍ ጥብጦችን ይሰነዝራል። [279]

በመጀመሪያ ደረጃ፣ ፍልሰት መንሥዔው ግጭት ነው እንጂ ፍልሰት ራሱ የግጭት ምክንያት አይሆንም። ነገር ግን እያደር ፍልሰት ራሱ ብዙ ዋጋ የሚያስከፍል እየሆነ መጥቷል። በገንዘብም፣ በጉልበትም፣ በማኅበራዊ ኑሮም ውድ ዋጋ ያስከፍላል። ይሁን እንጂ ፍልሰት የማይቆም ነገር ነው። ግጭቶች በበዙ ቁጥር ሕዝብ ከሥፍራ ወደ ሥፍራ ይፈልሳል።

ሁለተኛው፣ በሚቀጥሉት 30 ዓመታት የሕዝብ ዕድገት የሚቀጥል ስለሆነ ዓለም አቀፉ ፍልሰትም እየጨመረ ይሄዳል። ነገር ግን ሁሉም ወደ ምዕራብ ማለትም ያደገ

279 IMF. (2020). The macroeconomic effects of global migration. World Econoic Outlook – A Long and Difficult Ascent. Accessed on November 24, 2022; from https://www.imf.org/en/ Publications/WEO/Issues/2020/09/30/world-economic-outlook-october-2020

ኤኮኖሚ ወዳለባቸው አገራት አይጓዝም። ይልቅ በማደግ ላይ ያሉ ሥፍራዎች ብዙ ተቀባይ የሚሆኑበት ዕድል ይፈጠራል።

በተጨማሪም፣ ወደፊት ከግጭት ጋር የአየር ንብረት ለውጥ የሚያስከትለው ፍልሰት ተጨማሪ ምክንያት ይሆናል፣ ድርቅ፣ ጎርፍ፣ ወይንም በበረዶ መቅለጥ ምክንያት ደሴታማና ከፍታቸው ከባሕር ጠለል እምብዛም የሆኑ ሥፍራዎች ላይ ያሉ ሰዎች ወደ ሌላ ሥፍራ መንቀሳቀሳቸው አይቀሬ ነው።

በመጨረሻ ግን፣ በተጨባጭ የታየው ብዙ የፈለሱ ሰዎች ያስተናገዱ አገራት ኤኮኖሚያቸው የተሻለ እንቅስቃሴ እንዳለው ተረጋግጧል። ስለዚህ ብዙ ሰዎች ለፍልሰት በሚመርጡባቸው አካባቢዎች ያሉ የኤኮኖሚ ፖሊሲ አውጭዎች ውህደትንና መደጋገፍን ያለም ሥርዓት ቢዘረጉ ለዕድገትና ፍትሐዊ የሃብት ክፍፍል መልካም አስተዋጽኦ ሊያደርጉ ይችላሉ።

ለመሆኑ ስንት ነን?

አናውቅም፣ የመጨረሻው የሕዝብ ቆጠራ የተካሄደው ከ15 ዓመት በፊት ነው። ለዚያውም ከብዙ ጉርምርምታ ጋር፣ እውነትነቱ አጠራጣሪ ስለነበር። ሕግ መንግሥቱ በ10 ዓመት አንድ ጊዜ ቆጠራ የማድረግ ግዴታ ይጥላል፣ አልታዘዝነውም። ስለዚህ ቁጥር በዘፈቀደ ይቀመራል። መሪዎቻችን ስለ ቁጥር አገራዊ ንስሓ እንድናደርግ ቢያስተባብሩን ጥሩ ነው። ንስሓ ማለት ስንታትን አምኖ በመቀበል ይቅርታ መጠየቅና ያንን ስነታት ደግሞ አለ መሥራት፣ ወይም ላለመሥራት መወሰን ማለት ነው።

ከተቻለ ለስነታቱ በቂ ማካካሻ ብናደርግም ጥሩ ነው። የአንድን አገር የሕዝብ ብዛትና ስብጥር ማወቅ ለኤኮኖሚ ፖሊሲ አጀግ ወሳኝ ነው። የሕዝብ ብዛት፣ ጥራት፣ አወቃቀር፣ ሥርጭትና እንቅስቃሴ ከኤኮኖሚ ልማት ጋር ጥብቅ ቁርኝት እንዳለው በሰፊው ይታቃል።[280] ካልቆጠርን እና በጥልቀት ካላጠናን ግን ምን ያህል ተጽዕኖ እንዳለው፣ በምን እናውቀዋለን?

ብዙ አገራዊ በደሎች አሉብን። በወጣት መሥዋዕትነት ሥልጣን ጨብጠu አንለቅም ያልንበት፣ አንድ ትውልድ ክፍተት እስኪፈጠር በ"ሽብር" ስም ያረድንበት፣ ሌላውን "አድኻሪ" ብለን ያለ ፍርድ የገደልንበት፣ እልከኝነትንና መናናቅን ያነገስንበት፣ የልሂቃን ልጆች የባሕር ማዶ ቋንቋ እንዲያላጥፉ መርቀን የደኻውን ልጅ ግን ባሕል ማሳደግ በሚል ሰበብ እርስ በራሱ እንኳን እንዳይግባባ ያደረግንበት።

---
280 Behrman, J. R. & Kohler, H. (2014). Population Quantity, Quality, and Mobility. In Allen, F. (ed.). Towards a Better Global Economy: Policy Implications for Citizens Worldwide in the 21st Century. Chapter 3. Pages 138–215, Accessed on November 24, 2022; from https://academic.oup.com/book/11948/chapter-abstract/161155739?redirectedFrom=fulltext

ሥራና ምግብ በማጣቱ የደረሰበትን በደል ለመናገር ወረቀት አንግቦ የወጣውን ሕጻን በቆሎ ፋንታ ጥይት ያስቃምንበት፤ በሰፈራ ስም ሰዎችንና ዛፎችን አንድ ላይ የጨረስንበት፤ ድኻ ወገኑን በመጣፋት ነጻነት ይገኛል ብለን ድፍን ሕዝብ ያሳሳትንበት፤ በልማት ስም ሰውን ከቀዬው አፈናቅለን መሠረቱን ያናጋንበት። ... አረ ስንቱ።

ከእነዚህ ጋር ሲተያይ በኍጥር ላይ ስለፈጸምነው በደል ይቅርታ መጠየቅ ቅንጦት አይምሰለን። የምናወራው የሕዝብ ቁጥር ስለሆነ ጉዳዩ ይለያል። ለምሳሌ በኍጥር ስም ቀድሞ ድኽነት ባጠበጣቸው እናቶች ላይ የሞት ፍርድ የሚያሀል ጫና አስተላልፈናል። ይህ ፍርድ ገምድልነት አገራዊ በደል ነው። የማንኛውም በደል ማረፊያው ደግሞ ሰው ላይ ነው።

በኍጥር ላይ የፈጸምነው በደል ገፈት ቀማሽ ደግሞ በገጠር ያለችው እናት ናት። በአሁን ሰዓት ማንኛዋም ድኻ እናት ማሳደግ የማትችላቸውን ልጆች መውለድ አትፈልግም፤ እጅዋ ለወለደቻቸው ልጆች እንኳ እያጠረ እንዳለ ትገነባለች። ራሷም በቂ ምግብና እንክብካቤ ስለማታገኝ የመጸነስና የመውለድ አቅሚ እየከዳት እንዳለ ታውቃለች። ቤተሰቢን መጥና መኖር ትወዳለች።

ፖለቲከኞች ግን የብሔራችን ቁጥር ቀነሰብን ብለው በድኻ እናቶች ላይ የሞት ፍርድ አስተላልፈዋል። ግፈኝነት ነው። የብሔር ፖለቲካ በኍጥር ብዛት ስለሚታመን ቤተሰብን መመጠን እንደ ጥቃት በመቁጠር ተገልጿል። በበዙ ክልሎች፤ በሁሉም ማለት ይቻላ፤ የቤተሰብ ምጣኔ አገልግሎት መስጠት እንደ ነውር ከተቆጠረ ውሎ አድሯል።

አክቲቪስቶች፤ ፖለቲከኞች እና መሪዎች ራሳቸው አንድ ወይም ሁለት ልጅ ብቻ እየወለዱ ለማገዶ የሚውል ልጅ በመውለድ እንድትሞት የፈረዱባት ድኽዋ የገጠር እመቤት ሆነች፤ የብሔራቸው ቁጥር እንዲጨምር እናታቸው፤ ሚስታቸው፤ እኃታቸው፤ ወይም ቤት ልጃቸው ላይ ይህ ጫና እንዲወድቅ የማይፈቅዱ ሁሉ በገጠር እመቤት ሕይወት ላይ ፈረደዋል።

እርሷ በከፈለችው ቀረጥ በተገነባ የተመቾ ቢሮቻቸው ላይ ቁጭ ብለው፤ ከመዳፉ ከተሰበሰበው ላይ ደመወዛቸውን እየበሉ፤ ይህን ክፉ ፍርድ ይፈርዳሉ። ይህ ጋጢአት ነው፤ በደል ነው፤ እናም ስለዚህ ድኻ እናት ሲባል አገራዊ ንስሐ ያስፈልጋል።

አንዳንድ ጥናቶች እንደሚያመለክቱት በአገራችን የቤተሰብ ምጣኔ አገልግሎት አጠቃቀም እያሽቆለቆለ ነው። ምክንያቱ ግልፅ ነው። ወላዶች ባለ መፈለጋቸው አይደለም። የኍጥር አምላኪዎች ስለሚያሸማቅቋቸውና አገልግሎቱን ቢፈልጉ እንኳ እንዳያገኙ ስለሚያደርጉ ነው።

ቤተሰብን መመጠን ለእናት ጤንነት እጅግ አስፈላጊ ነው። ይህ ብቻ ሳይሆን ለተወለዱት ልጆች በቂ ፍቅርና እንክብካቤ ለመስጠት፤ እንዲሁም ብዙ ዜጋ ለማፍራት

ወሳኝ ነው። ይህን በትክክል የሚያውቁ ሰዎች፤ የመንግሥት ባለሥልጣናት፤ እና ፖለቲከኞች በቀጥር ኃጢአት ተይዘው አፋቸው ሲሸበብ ማየት ያሻማቅቃል፤ ያሳዝናልም።

በአገር መሪ ደረጃ "ሰው ሲወለድ እጅና እግር እንጂ አፍ ብቻ ይዞ አይወለድም" እስኪባል ተደርሷል። ሰው በጊዜና አገሪቱ ያፈራችው ሃብት ይበቃናል ወይ ተብለው ሲጠየቁ ነው። ለማብቃቃት እያዳገተ መሆኑ ማስተዋል ተስኖናል፤ ያለን ካልጉለበተ አይበቃንም። አሥር እግርና አሥር እጅ ይዞን ብንወለድ እንኳ ማጉልበቻውን ካላወቅን ጥቅሙ ምንድን ነው?

የሕዝብ ቁጥር ዕድገትን ብቻ እንመልከት። ዊዝሊ ፓተርሰን[281] የተባሉ የኔብራስካ ዩኒቨርሲቲ የኤኮኖሚክስ መምህር፤ ያለፉትን 200 ዓመታት የሕዝብና የኤኮኖሚ ዕድገትን በማነጻጸር ሁለት ዓይነተኛ ግኝቶችን አሥፍረዋል። ባደጉት አገራት ዝቅተኛ የሕዝብ ዕድገት ምጣኔ ማኅበራዊና ኤኮኖሚያዊ ችግር ይፈጥራል። ከፍተኛ ዕድገት ደግሞ በማደግ ላይ ያሉ ኤኮኖሚዎችን ያቀጭጫል።

የሕዝብ ብዛት ኤኮኖሚ ስለሚያቀጭጭ አንውለድ ወደሚል ድምዳሜ ለመድረስ አይደለም። መውለድማ አለብን፤ ግን በኅላፊነት ስሜት ይሁን። ኤኮኖሚ በማጉልበቱ ሂደት ላይ ግንባር ቀደም ሥራ ያላቸውን የአገሩን እናቶች ትኩረት የሚነፍጉ ልጆች ደራርበው እንዲወልዱ፤ ጤናቸውም እንዲጎዳ ፈርደንባቸው ዕድገትን አንመኝ። የቁጥር አምልኮአችን ከልክ በላይ ስለሆነ፤ መቋጠር ስንኳ ስላልፈለግን የሕዝብ ቆጠራውን ለተደጋጋሚ ጊዜ ስናስተላልፍ አይታወቀንም።

በማይበቃ ነገር ላይ ተጫማሪ አፍችን ማብዛት በትውልድ ላይ የሚፈጸም አገራዊ በደል ነው። የጉሣ ፖለቲካ ስናስብ ይህን በጥልቀት ከመመርመር እንታቀባለን፤ ሥልጣን ለማግኘት ወይም ለማደላደል የሚረዳን ቁጥር ስለሆነ፤ በራሳችን ላይ እንዲሆን የማንፈልገውን ቀንበር በሌሎች ላይ ስለጫንንበት ነገር ከሰውም ከአምላክም ይቅርታን እንለምን።

ጥናቶች እንደሚያመለክቱት፤ ብዝኃ ብሔርነትን ማራገብ በኤኮኖሚው ላይ ተጫማሪ አሉሎ[282] የሚሆንበት ምክንያት የሕዝብ ዕድገትን ከኤኮኖሚ ዕድገት ጋር ማመጣጠን አዳጋች ስለሚሆን ነው። በሁሉም በሚባል ደረጃ ብዝኃ ብሔር አገራት መዋለድን ይደግፋሉ፤ ታላቅነት በቁጥር ስለሚመስላቸው። በጥቂቶች እንደ ኢትዮጵያ ባሉ አገራት የቁጥር ልቀት የኤኮኖሚ ተደራሽነትን እንዲወስን በመዋቅር ጫምም ይደገፋል።

281 Patterson. E. W. F. (2017). The Role of Population in Economic Growth. SAGE Journals. Accessed on November 24, 2022; from https://journals.sagepub.com/doi/full/10.1177/2158244017736094

282 Goren, E. (2014) How Ethnic Diversity Affects Economic Growth. World Development; Volume 59; July 2014, Pages 275-297

ቁኖጥር ከፍ እንዲል የቤተሰብ ምጣኔ አገልግሎቶች እንዳይካሄዱ፤ የሕዝብ ፖሊሲም እንዳይኖር፤ ቢኖርም አፈጻጸሙ እንዲለዝብ መዋቅራዊ ተጽዕኖ ይደረጋል። "ልጅ ሲወለድ ሆድ ብቻ ሳይሆን እጅና እግርም ይዞ ይወለዳል" የሚለው ተወዳጅ አባባል የሆነው ከዚህ የተነሣ ነው። ኤኮኖሚ ግን አንድ ሰው እጅና እግር መታደሉን አያስተውልም፤ ሥራ መሥራቱን እንጂ።

በእጅም፤ በእግርም ከተሠራ፤ በእርግጥ ጸጋ ነው። በእጅም፤ በእግርም ጥሪት ከቢጫሩ ግን አይጣል። ውጤቱ እጅም እግርም ያሳጣልና።

ድምድማት

ለሌሎች ማካፈል የምትነፍገው ምንም ነገር፤
ፈጽሞ በሙላት የአንተ አይሆንም።
ክላይቭ ስቴፕልስ ሉዊስ፤ ክርስቲያን አቃቤ እምነትና ፈላስፋ

ሁለት መላጦች ... የቀጠለ

"አብዲ፤ እኔንም፤ አንተንም ራስ ወዳድነት አሸነፈን፤ የሚያየንን የሰፈሩ ሰው ሁሉ እንዚህስ ከአንድ ማሕጸን የወጡ ነው የሚመስሉት ይለን ነበር።"

መሐመድ ነበር። በመካከላቸው የሰፈነውን ጸጥታ ለመስበር ያህል። ቀና ብሎ በዓይኑ ከአድማስ ባሻገር የሚቃኝ እየመሰለ።

"እኔስ ልክ እንደ ድሮ ሰዎች የምንተካቸው ልጆች ጭምር ፍቅራችንን በማይበጠስ ገመድ ያስተሳስሩልናል ብዬ እመኝ ነበር።"

የምሩን ነበር። አብዲን በጣም ይወድደው ስለነበር፤ ልጅ ብንወልድ፤ ልክ እንደ ድሮ አባቶች 'ልጅህን ለልጄ እለዋለሁ' ብሎ ያስብና 'ደግሞ የዘንድሮ ልጅ፤ መች ወላጅን ይሰማና' ብሎ በራሱ ስቆ ይተዋል። ከሆስፒታል ወጥቶ በተከራያት ትንሽ ቤት ውስጥ ደጋግሞ መጥቶ ሲጎበኘው፤ ያ ምጮቱ ተቀስቀሰበት። አብዲ በመጣ ቁጥር ሁሉ እጁ አንዳች ይዞ፤ በድሮው ፈገግታውና ርህራሄው ታጅቦ ነበር።

"እውነት ነው ሙሔ። ራስ ወዳድነታችን በልጦ፤ ነገን አሻግረን ማየት ተስኖን፤ ምንም ባልነበረን ጊዜ የገነባነውን የፍቅር ግንብ ሰርተን ማግኘት ስንጀምር የተሻለ ማድረግ ሲገባን አፈራረስነው። ያሳዝናል። እኛ በቀሰቀስነው ፀብ ለሰው ሕይወት መጥፋት፤ እና የአካል መጉደል ሰበብ ሆንን። በጉብኙሁህ ቁጥር በዋሳብህ እየጠነከርክ መምጣትህን ሳይ እጸናናለሁ።"

በሥራ ታታሪ ከመሆን በላይ በአስተዋይነቱ የሚወደደው አብዲ ሁሌም ይቅር መባባል መልካም እንደሆነ ያምናል። በጠንካራ መንፈስ ከዜሮ መጀመር ምንም አያጉድልም ብሎ ስለሚያምን፤ በመሐመድ መበረታታት እጅግ ተደስቶ ነበር።

"ገና መጀመሪያ ስንገናኝ፤ ከየት መጣህ? ከማን ወገን ነህ? ከማን ዘር ነህ? ሳንባባል ሌሎች እስኪደነቁ፤ በጅሩህ ወንድማማችነት አብረን እንደ አንድ ሠርተን ኖርን። ከፉ ዕጣ ሆነና ዛሬንም አየን። ትላንትና ያልጠየቅነውን ዘር መጠየቅ በጀመርን ማግስት፤ ሁሉም የወደፊት ጉዟችን በአንድ ጊዜ ወደ ኋላ መንሽራተት ጀመረ። ታዲያ ወድቆ መነሳትን ልናውቅ ይገባል። ስንሰማ ያደግነውን መጥፎ ነገር ላለመድገም፤ ከኛም አልፎ ለነገ ቤተሰቦቻችን ጥሩ ምሳሌ ብንሆን ደስታዬ ነው። "

"ይልቅስ አብዲ፤ ቁጭ ባልኩበት አንድ የአክስቴ ልጅ ኮምፒውተር እንዳስተማረኝ ታውቃለህ? "

"ኮምፒውተር ምንድነው? እኔ አላውቅም። ማለት ኮምፒውተር ምን እንደሆን አውቃለሁ፤ ግን ምን ይሠራበታል? መሥሪያ ቤት ልትቀጠር ነው? "

"የለም። አብዲ፤ አብረን እንሥራበታለን። በምናውቀው፤ በሕንጻ ሥራ ዙሪያ አብረን እንሥራለን። አንተ ወተተህ መንቀሳቀስ ትችላለህ። እኔ እንደምታየኝ ይህችን ተሸከርካሪ ወንበር የሙጥኝ ብዬ ነው የምኖረው። አንተ እግር ትሆነኛለህ፤ እኔ ዐይንህ ለነገሩ ትምህርቱን ግን ሙሉ በሙሉ ገና አልጨረስኩም። ይኸው ያልሁ የአክስቴ ልጅም መጣ። ያሰብነውን እርሱ የተሻለ ያስረዳሃል። "

ክፉና ደጉን አብረው ያሳለፉት፤ ተባብረው ሠርተው ከባዶ በመነሳት ወደ ጥሩ ደረጃ መንደርደር የጀመሩት፤ ከምንም በላይ ወንድምነትን ያጣጣሙት መሐመድና አብዲ፤ ድንገት ውሉን ስቶ ከቀጥጥር በወጣ ትርጉም ዐልባ ግጭት ብዙ ጉዳት አስተናገዱ። በእነርሱም ሰበብ ሌሎች ሕይወታቸውን ጭምር አጡ። ለእነርሱም ቢሆኑ ከደረሰባቸው የአካል ጉዳት በላይ የመንፈስ ስብራቱ ቀላል አልነበርም።

ስብራታቸውን ራሳቸው ለማከም ቆረጡ።

"በኮምፒውተር የሕንጻ ሥራ ይሠራል ነው የምትለኝ?" አብዱልቃዲር ነበር። በትምህርቱ የተሻለ የገፋ እንደ ነበር ስለ መሐመድ ያውቃል። እጁ ከአርማታ ሥራ ተላቅቆ ልክ ቢሮ እንደሚሠራ ሰው ይህናል ብሎ ፈጽሞ አስቦ አያውቅም።

"አይ አብዲ፤ የሕንጻ ሥራ እኮ ግድግዳና ወለል፤ ጣሪያን ልስን ብቻ አይደለም። ዲዛይን የሚባል አለ። ከዚያ ማሻሻጥ ወይም ማከራየት አለ። አንተ ስፖችን፤ በተለይም ባለሃብቶችን ስለምታውቅ መጀመሪያ በማሻሻጥ ሥራ፤ በኮሚሽን እንሥራለን። ኮምፒውተር መጠቀም ለዚህ ያግዘናል። ገቢያ እናስፋበታለን። ዲዛይንም እየተማርኩ ስለ ሆን ቀስ በቀስ ከፍ ያለውንም አብረን እንሥራዋለን። "

ዘዳግም

በዚህ ጽሑፍ የብሔር ፖለቲካ በኤኮኖሚው ላይ ከሚያሳድረው በጐ ተጽዕኖ ይልቅ አስቸጋሪነቱ እንደሚያይል ለማሳየት ተሞክሯል። ከዚህ የተነሣ፤ ጽሑፉ፣ በተቃራኒ አሰላለፍ የሚወሰደውን "የዜግነት ፖለቲካ" የሚያወድስ ተደርጐ እንዳይወሰድ በመጨረሻ ቢሆን ጥቂት እንበል። ይህ መጽሐፍ ለብሔርተኝነትም ሆነ ሌላ የፖለቲካ አሰላለፍ ድጋፍ ለመስጠት የተጻፈ አይደለም። የብሔርም ይሁን የዜግነት ፖለቲካ፣ ቀዳሚ ትኩረታቸው የሕዝብ አስተዳደር እንጂ ለድኸነት እልባት መስጠት አይደለም።

ድኸነትን መቅረፍ፤ እንዲሁም የአገር ዕድገትና ለውጥ ከፖለቲካው ይልቅ የኤኮኖሚው ፖሊሲ ቅንነት፣ የእያንዳንዱን ሰው የገል ባሕርይ ለውጥና፤ ሕዝባዊ፣ ማኀበራዊ ተሃድሶ ይጠይቃል። ምክንያቱም፣ ድኸነት፤ ሥራ ማጣት፣ ተስፋ ቢስነት፣ ... ወዘተ አንዱ ብሔር ሌላውን ስለጨቆነ ብቻ የመጡ ሳይሆን ውስብስብ የሆኑ የገል፣ ማኀበራዊና ከባቢያዊ ነገሮች ውሁድ የፈጠራቸው ክስተቶች ናቸው።

የሚከተለው እውነተኛ ታሪክ ነው፡ ለባለታሪኮቹ ሰብዓዊ ክብር ሲባል ስማቸውና የታሪኩ መቼት (ጊዜውና በታውም ጭምር) ተቀይሯል። ለንባብ እንዲመችም በልበ ወለድ መልክ ተደርጓል።

ባለ ታሪካችን ማለፊያ አንተነህ ትባላለች። አያቷ ሙሲሳ ከከሚሴ ተነስተው ከራስ ጋር ስድስት ቤተሰቦች አስከትለው ባሕር ዳር ጐጆ ሲቀልሱ ገና በአባቷ ጉልበት ነበረች። አንተነህ በእድሜ ታናሽ ስለነበር ከቤት አይጠፋም ነበር።

ገና ለጋ ቢሆንም ከሙሲሳ ጭቅጭቅ ለመትረፍ እንዲሁም የእህል ውሃ ነገር ሆነና ጠጁቱ ከሚትባል አንዲት ከብቹና ከመጣች ኮረዳ ጋር ተዋውቀው ተጣመሩ። ሙሲሳም ደስ አላቸው። ሁለት ልጆች አክታትለው ሲወልዱላቸው ቤቲን የልጅ ልጆቻቸውን "የዓይኔ ማረፊያ" ለማለት በልባቸው አስበው "ማረፊያ" ያሏት አያቷ ነበሩ።

ሙሲሳም ጥቂት ሳይቆዩ፣ ሳየርፉባት፣ በጓይናቸው ሙሉ አይተው ሳይጠግቧት አረፉ። እናም ቤተሰቡና ሠፈሩ ሁሉ "ማለፊያ" እያሉ ይጠሯት ጀመር። አባቷ ግን ልክ እንደ አያቷ ባያንቆለጳጵሳትም አልፎ አልፎ በሙሉ የጨቅላነት ስሚ "ያይኔ ማረፊያ" ይላት ነበር፡ የማለፊያም ልብ ከአባቷ ጋር ነበር።

አንተነህ፣ ከአባቷ ሞት በኋላ መጠጦ አዘውታሪ ከመሆን ጋር በሚኖርበት ሠፈር ባለው ማኀበረሰብ ተጠላ። ጠጁቱም ፀባዩን መሸከም ስላቃታት እስከ መለያየት የሚያደርስ ፀብ ሆነ፡ ጨከነችበትም። ማለፊያ የአባቷ ነገር እንደማይሆንላት ስላወቀች ትታት ትልቅ ወንድሟን ይዛ አካባቢውን ለቅቃ መኖር ጀመረች።

አንተነህ በዚህ በጣም ተበሳጨ፤ እጅግም አዘነ፡፡ አንድ ቀን፣ እንዳበደ ሰው፣ ማለፊያን አንጠልጥሎ ባሕር ዳርን ተሰናበተ፤ ያደገበትን ቀዬ ጥሎ ሸሸ፡፡ እነ አንተነህ ልጆች ሆነው ከእነርሱ ከፍ ያሉ ወጣቶች መተከል ወደሚባል አገር ሄደው፣ ሲመለሱ ገንዘብ አጋኝተው፣ ለብሰውና አጊጠው ስላያቸው ሕይወትን በዚያ ልምክር ብሎ ፈቱን ወደ ምዕራብ አዞረ፡፡

መተከል ሲደርስ ግን የአምስት ዓመት ሕጻን ይዞ፣ ሥራ ሠርቶ፣ ምግብ አብስሎ አብልቷት ኖርን መግፋት እንደማይችል ገና በመጀሪያዎቹ ሁለት ቀናት ውስጥ ገባው፡፡ ያ ገጣሚ ሆኖ አንድ መጠጥ ቤት ያላቸው ኮማሪት የዕቃ አጣቢነት ሥራ ሰጡት፡፡ ልጁንም እኪያው እንድታድር ፈቀዱ፡፡

እርሱ ግን ዉት መጠጥ ቤቱ ከተከፈተበት ሰዓት አንሥቶ እስኪዘጋ ድረስ ሠርቶ በውድቅት ሌሊት ይወጣና የባሕር ዳር ልጆች አሉበት ወደተባሉ ሥፍራዎች እየተመላለሰ ያድር ጀመር፡፡ ታዲያ ገና ቀዬ ስላሳበጀ ያስጠጉትን የአገሩ ልጆች ከመጋበዝ ጋር የተጣባውን የመጠጥ ሱስ ለማስታገስ ሲል በጭንቅ ውስጥ ያገኛትን ጥቂት ገንዘብ ያጠፋታል፡፡

መጀመሪያ ከጠላው፤ ከጥቂት ጣሳ በኋላም አረቂ፡፡ ከዚያ በኋላ አያውቀውም፡፡ ካልሰከረ ወደፊት ማለፊያ ሊገጥማት የሚችለውን ሕይወት እያሰበ ያለ እንቅልፍ ስለሚያድር በማግሥቱ ወፈ እያደረገው እንደሆነ አስተውሎታል፡፡ የታላቅ ልጁም ናፍቆት ከልክ አልፎል፡፡ ስለዚህ መጠጥ ሱስ ብቻ ሳይሆነ መሸሽጊያም ሆነው፡፡

መሰለው እንጂ ወፈፈኑቱ ለሌሎች ይበልጥ እየተገለጠ መጣ፡፡ ሳያስበው ቀናት ከነፋ፡፡ ዓመትም፣ ሁለት ዓመትም፣ ለውጥ የለም፡፡ የባሳ ነገር እንጂ ይህን ሁሉ የሚያሰሳው፣ ማለፊያን ሁል ጊዜ ዉት ስለሚያገኛት ከርሲ ጋር የሚጫወተ ጨዋታ ነው፡፡ ሕጻኑም ብትሆን አባቷን ትረዳለች፣ ትወደዋለች፣ ደግሞም ትምህርት ቤት አስገብተዋት ጉብዝ ተማሪ እንደሆነች ነገሩታል፡፡

ይሁን እንጂ ሰክሮ እያደረ፣ በሥራው ላይ እንደ በፈቱ ስላልሆነ የቤቱ ባለቤት "ማለፊያን አሳድግልሃለሁ አንተ ግን ከሥራህ ተሰናብተሃል" ሲሉት ምድር ተሰንትቃ የዋጠች መሰለው፡፡ በቀጥታ ያመራው ወደ ጠላ ቤት ነበር፤ መጠጥ ቤት ኑሮው ሆነ አንድ ቀን ከተኛበት ሲነቃ ሥፍራውን አያውቀውም፡ ጓዳ ብዉ ነው፡፡ ጀሮውን ጣል ሲያደርግ ከዋናው ክፍል የሚወራው አማርኛም የአገሩን ቋንቋ ድብልቅ ነበር፡፡

መንቀሳቀሱን ሰምታ አጠገቡ የመጣችው ዐልፍ ዐልፍ ለአረቄ ፍራንክ ሲቸግረው ቦርዴ የሚጠጣበት ቤት ባለቤት ነበረች፤ የአካባቢው ተወላጅ ናት፡፡ ከርሲ ጋር ለመጫወት ሲልም ቋንቋውን እስክ መልመድ ደርሶ ነበር፡፡

"ተኛ፣ ሰው እያየ ከጎዳዬ ከወጣህ ምን ይሉኛል?"

ወዲያውም በላስቲክ ሰሃን በተመሳሳይ ላስቲክ ሰሃን የተከደነ ምግብ ሰጠችው። በላ፣ ተኛም።

"ያለ ዐሳብ የተኛሁበት ቀን ያን ቀን ነበር" አለ ቀኑ ዳግመኛ የመጣበት ይመስል አሳቅ እያተመለከተ።

ሲነታ በአጠገቡ ቤት ነበረች።

"ማን ነው? ማን ነሽ? ምን ትሠሪያለሽ?" በጥያቄ አጣደፋት።

'አንት ደግሞ ሳትጠጣ ትሰክራለህ? እንቅልፍ ያሰክርሃል? ሁሌም እንዲህ እንቅልፋም ነህ?'

የእርሷ ተራ። ጠጋ ብላ አቀፈችው።

"በል ተኛ።"

'ምን ማድረግሽ ነው?'

"ምን አደረግሁ? ቤቴ መጥተህ ላገባሽ ነው፣ አልወጣም አልክ፣ አሳደርኩህ። የልብህን ካደርስክ በኋላ ቤተኛ አዳሪ መሰልኩህ እንዴ ጥለሽኝ የምትሄድ? በአልጋዬ፣ በጭኔ አድረህ ልትገፋኝ? ከዛሬ ማለት ከተናንት ጀምሮ ባሌ ነህ፣ ልጄቹስ 'አንተነህ እናታችሁን አስነውሮ ሄዳል' የሚለውን አሽሙርና ስድብ ከሰው አፍ ይስሙ?"

ካንዴም ሁለት ልጆችዋን አግኝቷቸዋል። ቦርዷ በቁማታው ጠጥተው በቀሉ ዓይኖቻቸው ታዳሚውን ሁሉ ገርፈው ውልቅ ይላሉ። "ቀስት በመወርወር የሚችላቸው የለም" እያለች ትመጻደቅባቸዋለች። በይወረሱ ለሥስት እንደ ቅርጫ ሥጋ ይከፋፈሉታል። "የሞት ሞቴን 'ባል ብሆንሽስ ይለቅቁኛል ወይ' ሲላት እንዳገሩ ባሕል ካደረግክ ችግር የለም" ብላ አረጋጋችው። ፈገግታ የማያውቀውን ፊቱን ለማፈገግ እያሞከረ።

የእርሱ ከባሕር ዳር መሰደድ ሲገርመው፣ በምን ምክንያት እንደሆን ከቻይና የተሰደዱ አንድ መዓት ሰዎች ባሉበት ግቢ ዘበኛ ሆኖ ተቀጠረ። መሪያቸው የነበረ፣ ፈቱን ሲጋራ ያበለዘበት አንድ ቻይናዊ ግን ካልሲውን ከማሳጠብ አንሥቶ ሲጋራ እስከ መግዛት የሚልከው እርሱን ነበር። በርግጥ ምግብ ሲተርፈውም ያጋራዋል። የሲጋራ ቁራጭም እየሰጠ በሌላ ጥሮ በፈገግታ "ሞክር" ይለዋል።

ሲጋራም ለመደ፣ ከዚህ በኋላማ ግቢ ውስጥ የተጣሉ ቁራጭ ሲጋራዎች ፍለጋ ያልተቀጠረበትን የግቢ ጽዳት ተያያዘው። አንድ ቀን ግን ከሚስቱ ልጆች ታናሹ ከሩቅ ቀስት ሲለጥብበት፣ ሰዎች ለመከላከል ሲጯጯሁ ድንገት አየ። በደም ነፍሱ ዘሎ ወደ ውስጥ በመግባት አመለጠ።

ሲነጋም የመሸታ ቤት ባለቤት ወደ ሆነችው ሚስቱ ሲያፍና እሳት ጉርሻ ጠበቀችው።

"በአገሬ፤ በልጇቼ ፊት አዋረድከኝ። ሥራ ሠራሁ ስትል አልነበረም? ዘበኝነት ሥራ ነው? ቻይና ካልሲውን አጉርሶ የገረፈውን ቂጥህን ታቅፈ ልደር? ድሮም እናንተ ክብር አይወድላችሁም ሲባል ሰምቼ ነበር። ደግሞስ የትም አድረህ በዚህ ሰዓት እየመጣህ ሚስትነቴ እንዴት ነው? ትወጣ እንደሁ ውጣልኝ፤ ካልሆነ አርፈህ ተቀመጥ።"

ማለፊያን አሰባት። እጇን አንጠልጥሎ ወጥቶ፤ ከቤት ጉርቤቷ ነጥሎ በዚህ እሳት ውስጥ መጨመሩ ወንጀለኝነት ተሰማው፤ ሆድ ባሰው። ሳያስበው እንባው ካይኑ ዱብ ዱብ ሲል ከሚስቱ ፊት ዘወር ለማለት ሲነሣ በንዴል ቃል 'ቀጭጭ በል!' አለቸው፤ አማራጭ አልነበረውም።

ሲመሽ ቢተኛም እንቅልፍ አለወሰደውም፤ በውድቅት ሌሊት ተነሥቶ ማለፊያን ወደተወበት ቤት አቀና። አስጠርቷት 'ወደ ባሕር ዳር እንሂ዗ር" የሚል ድንገተኛ ጥያቄ አቀረበላት። እጇን ጭምድድ አድርጎ ይዞ ታገላት። ጉንጭዋ በእንባ እየራስ የዘንድሮ ትምህርቲን እስክትጨርስ እንዲተዋት ተማጸነችው።

ግርግሩን ሰምተው የወጡ የቤቱ ባለቤት በቀጣ ሊያግባቡ ሞከሩ። አንድ ሁለት እያለ የተሰበሰበውም ሰው ማለፊያንና አባቷን እያስተያየ 'እንደ አንተ ልታጉሣቁላት ነው?' ሲለት አንጀቱን በጨጨ የተዘከዘከ ያህል ተሰማው። እንባ ባቁረሩ አይኖቹ ትክ ብሎ ተመልክቷት እጇን ለአሳዳጊዋ ሰጠ። ባትወልዳትም፤ ሆዷንና ልብሷን ትምህርቲንም ችላለችና።

ነገር ግን፤ ከዚያች ቅጽበት ጀምሮ ያቺ ትንሽ ከተማ ሲያል ሆነችበት። ጉዳናዎቿ ተቀበሉት። ሳያቋርጥ ከመለፍለፉ ጋር በየምሽቱ "ማለፊያ፤ የአይኔ ማረፊያ" እያለ ሲጮህ ያድራል።

የእኛም ጨኸት እንደ አንተነህ ብስጭት ጭንቅላታችን ላይ ሲወጣ የተወለደ ከቱ ጫጫታ እንዳይሆን ሰከን ያለ ማጠቃለያ እንስጥና እናብቃ። ጨኸትን አስምቶ ብቻ መዝጋት ምን ፋይዳ አለው? መፍትሔ ሊሆኑ የሚችሉ መንገዶችም እናነሳ።

ሰው ሥራሽ ልዩነት

በቅድሚያ፤ አገራችን ብዝኀ ብሔርም፤ የብሔር ስብጥርም የሚታይባት መሆኑን መቀበል ያሻል። ይህ ሲሆን የብሔር ፖለቲካም ሆነ የብሔር ክልል ሰከን ያለ የኤኮኖሚ ዕድገት ለሚያስፈልጋት አገር በገዛ እጃችን ዳገት እንደ ማቆም፤ መሆኑን እንረዳለን። ብሔርተኝነት ሲከርር ቀድሞም በማይመች ጉዳና ላይ ጉድባ እንደ መቆፈር ነው። አከራሪ ብሔርተኝነት መሠረቱ የተዘነፈ ከመሆኑ የተነሣ አመለካከቱ ሊወገድ እንጂ ሊሸሻል እንኳ አይችልም።

ከዚያ በመለስ ግን አገር ገና ቀርቶን ከሆነ እንደ አንድ አገር ሰዎች በጋራ ልንመካከርበት ይገባል። የፖለቲካው አሰላለፍ እየተካረረ ስለመጣ ብሔርተኝነትን በማጠዝ

መዳን ከዚያ ይገኛል ብሎ ማሰብ እያዳገተን ነው። የብሔር ፖለቲካ "ቅዱስ ላም" ከሆነችም ሰከን ባለ ውይይት ግጦሽ እንፈልግላት እንጂ ታርዳ አለመበላቷ ሳያንስ ማሳውንም፤ ጉዳናውንም እየፋነነችበት ለምን ታስጨንቀናለች?

ኩሬ ላይ እንደሚንሳፈፍ ፌኛም ባንዋልል ጥሩ ነው። በአንድ በኩል፤ ምናልባትም በቀኝ ጉኖችን በነቃን ዕለት፤ እንደ ገብሩ ሕይወት ባይከዳኝ ዐይነት ዘመንን የዋጁ አስተሳሰቦች እናፈልቅና፤ እጅግ ተራማጅ ከሚባሉ ሕገ መንግሥታት ተርታ የሚመደብ መመሪያ እንቀርጸለን፤ በሌላ በኩል፤ ለመልካም የታሰበውን አፈጻጸሙን አወሳሰበን፤ ወይም ፈጽሞ አፈራርሰን እናርፈዋለን።

አገር "ናን ወይስ አይደለንም? እንሁን ወይስ አንሁን" እያተባላ፤ በፈራ ተባ የምንንገዘበት ዘመን ሊበቃ ይገባዋል። የምንስማው ወይም ተጽፎ የተላለፈልን ታሪክ ሁሉ በአንድ ጀምበር ወይም በአንድ ብሔር የተከወነ አይደለም። የመስባጠር፤ የመፈቃቀር፤ የመጋፋፋትም ውጤት ነው። ለታሪካችን ተጠቢውን ሥፍራ ስጥተን፤ ልዩነትን አክብረን፤ በአንድነት መዘለቅ የውዴታ ግዴታችን ነው። ይህ ሲሆን ብሔርተኝነት ከፖለቲካዊ ኤኮኖሚ ጉራ ይለቅና ትክክለኛ ሥፍራውን ይይዛል።

አንዱን ብሔር አግዝፈን፤ ሌላውን አኮስምነን ፖለቲካ ልንሠራ አንችልም፤ ጥልና ግጭትን እንጂ። አንድነታችንን እንደምንወደው ሁሉ ልዩነታችንንም ልንወደው ይገባል። ልዩነት ድምቀት እና ውበት የሚሆንበትን ሕጋዊ ሥርዓት መገንባት ይቻላል። ሕጋዊ እንጂ ፖለቲካዊ ሊሆን ግን አይገባውም።

ቤታችንን እያየነው በራሳችን ላይ ማፍረስ ፋይዳው ምንድነው? የአንድ ባልና ሚስት ቤት መፍረስ ስንኳ ከባድ ዋጋ ያስከፍላል። በዘመናት መካከል ሲዋደዱ፤ ሲነታረኩም የቆዩ፤ በአንድነት ተጓምR የሩ፤ በተዋደዱ መጠን የተሰባጠሩ፤ በተራራቁ መጠን ልዩነታቸው ውበትን የተላበሰ፤ አኩሪ ማንነት ያላቸው ልዩ ልዩ ማሕበረሰቦች አሉን። ይህ ልንኮራበት እንጂ ልንንሻማቀቅበት የሚገባ ነገር አይደለም።

ወይንም "እወቀኝ፤ እወቅልኝ" ብሎ የራስን ባሕልና ወግ በግድ ሌላውን መጋት አስፈላጊያኝን አይደለም። ይህ ካልሆነ ለመቦጫጨቅ እንሳለሁ ማለትንም ሰከን ብለን ልናየው ይገባል። ውይይት የሚኖር ከሆነም፤ መለያየት የሕዝብ ምርጫ እንዳይደለ ፖለቲከኞች በውል ሊረዱት ይገባል። በእርግጥ ሕዝብ የሚወያይ ከሆነ፤ በድፍረት ሊነሱ የሚገባቸው ጉዳዮችንም ማጥራት ያስፈልጋል።

መለያየት ይቅር የሚባለው "ትንሽ አገር" መሆን ተፈርቶም አይደለም። በቆዳ ስፋትና በሕዝብ ብዛት "ትንሽ" አገር" ሆኖ መኖር ይቻላል። ትንሻዬ ሆነው እዚህ ግብ የማይበሉ አገራት እንዳሉ ሁሉ ትንሽ እና ሃብታም የሆኑ ጥቂት አገራትም አሉ። ትንሻዬ ግን ዓለምን የሚገዙ። ቫቲካን በሮም ውስጥ ያለች የ8 እግር ኪስ ሜዳዎች ስፋት ያላት ነጻ ከተማ ናት። ጿጿሳቱ የዓለም መሪዎች ናቸው።

ትንኳነት ባይፈራም የእኛ እንደ ቫቲካን እንደማይሆን መናገር አያቅትም። ነጋድራስ ከዛሬ 120 ዓመት በፊት እንደተገነበቱት በሌሎች እጅግ ተቀድመን ሳለ ጉዞን ማስተካከል ካላወቅንበት እዚያው ስንዳክር ሌላ 120 ዓመት ይፈጅብናል። በዚህ ዘመን ትንሽ ያው ትንሽ ነው። በሕዝብ ቁጥር እና በቆዳ ስፋት አናሳ የሆኑ፤ በተለይም ደሴትማ አገራት ጭንቃችው ብዙ ነው።

ለምሳሌ ሚጢጢዬ ከሆኑ አገራት አንዷ አሽኒያ ውስጥ የሚትገኘው ናኡሩ[283] ናት። አሥር ሺህ ሰዎች በ20 ካሬ ኪሎ ሜትር አሥፍራለች። አሥራ ዘጠኝ የፓርላማ አባላትና ፕሬዝዳንቱ ከሦስት ፓርቲዎች፤ ለሦስት ዓመታት በሕዝብ ቀጥተኛ ድምፅ ይመረጣሉ። ከመሬት ወለል 4 ሜትር ብቻ የሆነው መሬቷ ፎስፌት በስፋት ቢቆረርበትም ለእርሻ እምብዛም ነው። አንድ አውሮፕላን ማረፊያና 3 ኪሜ የባቡር እንዲሁም 30 ኪሜ የመኪና መንገድ ብቻ አላት።

በነፍስ ወከፍ 12 ሺህ ዶላር የሆነው ገቢዋ ከናጠጡ አገራት ተርታ ቢመድባትም ጠቅላላ ህብቲ ሌላ 30 ኪሜ መንገድ ልሥራ ብትል አይበቃትም። በአንድ ወቅት የፎስፌት ህብቲ ተሟጥጦ ሌላ ከምችት ሥራ ላይ እስኪውል ድረስ ሕዝቡ በሙሉ ሥራ አጥ ነበር። ዛሬም የወጪና የገቢ ንግዱ ከጠቅላላ ህብቲ ጋር የተመጣጠነ ነው። ማለትም እምብዛም ሌላ ምርት ስለሌለ በሼጠችው የሚያሰፈልጋትን ትገዛና ነገር አለሙ ያልቃል።

ከማዕድን ቀጓፈርና ዓሣ ማስገር ውጭ ሥራ የለም። ከሕዝቡ 70 ከመቶው የውፍረት በሽተኛ ነው። የቴለቪዥን ጣቢያ የማቆም ዐቅም ስለሌላት የመንግሥት ሚዲያ የአየር ሰዓት የሚገዛው ከአውስትራሊያ ነው። በውቅያኖስ ተከብባ ሳል ጎብኚም ሆነ ወደብ የላትም። ወታደርም ሆነ የሙር ኃይል አታውቅም።

የቤንሻንጉል ክልል ሕዝብ 1.2 ሚሊዮን እንደሚሆን ይገመታል። ናኡሩን በ120 እጥፍ ይበልጣል። የኢትዮጵያ አማካይ የነፍስ ወከፍ ገቢ አንድ ሺህ ዶላር ነው ብንል የቤንሻንጉል ጠቅላላ ዓመታዊ ምርት፤ የናኡሩን በ10 ሲባዝ፤ ማለትም 1.2 ቢሊዮን ዶላር ይሆናል። ከዚህ ህብት ውስጥ የቤንሻንጉል መንግሥት ገቢ ባለው የኢትዮጵያ የቀረጥ ገቢ ቀመር 10 ከመቶ ቢሆን 120 ሚሊዮን ብር ይሆናል።

የሕዳሴ ግድብ ገና ሲታቀድ ወደ 5 ቢሊዮን ዶላር ገደማ እንደሚፈጅ ታስቦ ነበር፤ አሁን ብዙ ወጭ ቢያስወጣም፤ የቤንሻንጉል ሕዝብ ብቻውን የሕዳሴን ግድብ ይገነባ ብንል እና፤ የቤንሻንጉል መንግሥት በጀት እያንዳንዱ ሳንቲም ግድቡን ለመገንባት እንድትውል ቢደረግ 40 ድፍን ዓመታት ያስፈልጋቸዋል። በአጭሩ፤ ባለበት ሁኔታ በቤንሻንጉል ዐቅም ብቻ መቼም አይገነባም። ዐብሮነት ጥቅም ያስገኛል ስንል ከንቱ ንግግር ማሳመሪያ አይደለም።

---

283 Foster, S. (2022). Nauru: Island Country, Pacific Ocean. Encyclopedia Britanica. https://www.britannica.com/place/Nauru

ትንንሽ አገራት እንሁን ብን፤ ስንኴ ለሥላም ዋስትና የለንም። ታሪካችን፣ የጂኦፖለቲካ አቀማመጣችን ለዚህ አይበጅም። የመገፋፋት እና የመሳሳብ እውነታችን በቀላሉ የሚቀየር አይደለም። ኤርትራ ከኢትዮጵያ ከተገነጠለች በኋላ ከጉራቤቶቿ፣ ከኢትዮጵያም ጥምር የገባችበት አተካራ መጥፎ መሪዎች ስለነበሩ ብቻ አይደለም። የመገፋፋት እና የመሳሳብ እውነታችን ውጤት ነው። በክልሎች መካከል ያለው አተካራም የዚሁ እውነታ ነጸብራቅ ነው።

አባካኝነት

መድልዎ በዚያው ልክ አባካኝ ነው። የሚበጀው ልዩነትና ውጥረት አውነታ መሆኑን ተቀብሎ፣ ውጥረት ግጭትን እንዳይወልድ፣ የታሰበበት የሕግ ማዕቀፍ ማደራጀት ነው። ለውጥረት ቤንዚን የሚጨምር ሕጋዊ ከሌላ ግን ሊነሃ ይገባል። ውጥረትን በመድልዎ በማራገብ መልካም ውጤት እናገኛለን ብለን ስንዳክር ዓመታት ተቆጥረዋል።

በግጭት የጠፋውን የሰው ሕይወት እና የአካል ጉዳት ትተን በሃብት ደረጃ ብቻ ምን ያህል እንዳጣን መገንዘብ ካልቻልን አሳፋሪ ነው። የኢትዮጵያ የአገር መከላከያ ወጪ ባለፉት 10 ዓመታት፣ በአማካይ 500 ሚሊዮን ዶላር እንደ ነበር መረጃዎች ያመለክታሉ፣ በፌደራል ደረጃ። በእነዚህ ዓመታት ከፖትኛውም የውጭ ጠላት ጋር እንዲህ የሚጠቀስ ውጊያ አልተደረገም።

አንድ ሌላ የሕዳሴ ግድብ የሚገነባ ሃብት ግን አባክነናል። ይህ ብቻም አይደለም። እጅግ ብዙው ወጪ በግጭት መንስዔነት የሚታመው የክልል ጸጥታ አካላትን ለማቋቋምና ለማስነበት ምን ያህል ወጥቶ ይሆን? ከፍተኛ የሰው ዕልቂት፣ የአካልና የአዕምሮ ጉዳት፣ ዓለም እስኪሳላቅብን ድረስ ቅጥ ያጣ ጥፋኔ ግን አይተናል። ይብቃን ማለት ያለበት ሕዝብ ነው። ድጋሚ ፖለቲከኛ መድህን ሆኖ ሊገለጥ ቢል ነሁሳላ የምንባል እያንዳንዳችን እንጂ ብላጋ ብልጦቹ አይደሉም።

ዘርፈ ብዙ እርምጃ ያስፈልግ ይሆናል። ዝነተ ዓለም በመንግሥት ተሿሚዎች እና በፖለቲካ ካድሬዎች ቁኖጥሮ ስር የወደቀውን የኢኮኖሚ ፖሊሲ ለዕድገት በሚመቸ መልኩ ለመቃኘት የኢኮኖሚ ሕዋሳት ሁሉ ሊንቀሳቀሱ ያስፈልጋል። መንግሥት "ሁሉ የራሴ" የማለት አባዜ ያለበት አካል ነው። ድንበር ሊበጅለት ይገባል። ኬላ ሲያልፍም ሊነገረው ይገባል። ጥሮ ግሮ ሃብት ካፈራው የኢኮኖሚ ሕዋስ የበለጠ በጥንቃቄ ለመጠቀም የሚችል ማንም የለም።

ቀኝ ጓላ ዙር

"በአካለ ስንኩልነትም ቢሆን ይመዝገብልኝ!"

ስትናገር እንባዋ ይቀድማታል። የደረቀው ከንፈራ ይንቀጠቀጣል፤ ዝርግፍግፍ የሚለው እንባዋ ከሆድ ያፈተለከ የብሶት ዘለላ እንጂ ከዐይን ብቻ አለ መሆኑ ለማወቅ አፍታ አይፈጅም። ዐይኔም እንባ እቅርር ስለ ነበር በደንብ አላያኋትም፤ አስፍቼ ልሰማትም ጊዜ አልነበረኝም።

ግን ከዐይኔ አትጠፋም፤ ድምፅዋም በጆሮዬ አለ። ከልጆቼ ምናልባት ከትንን̄ ጋር የዕድሜ እኩያ ብትሆን ነው። ሁለት ልጆች ይዛለች፤ መንትያ። አንዱ ታዝዒል፤ ሌላው ጣቷን አጥብቆ ይዞ በቀሚሷ ተሸፍኗል።

"ይኸው ምግብ በትክክል ስለማያገኝ አልራመድ አለኝ"

በጀርባዋ ወዳለው ልጅ እያመለከተችን ነበር የምትናገረው።

"ቢተርፍልኝ፤ በአካለ ስንኩልነትም ቢሆን ይመዝገብልኝና ምግብ ቢያገኝ!"

እግሬ ሲከዳኝ፤ ጉልበቴም ሲንቀጠቀጥ ስለ ተሰማኝ ከፈትዋ ዘወር አልኩ። እንግዳ ፊት ስላዩ ከበውን ከሚያዩወሩት ነገር አንዳንዱ ልብ ብቻ ሳይሆን ቅስምም ይሰብራል። ኢትዮጵያዊነቱን ብቻ ሳይሆን ሰብዐዊነቱን ይፈታተናል።

"ባሌ ከሞቱት ውስጥ ነው። ምን ማድረግ እንዳለብኝ አላውቅም" አለችን ሌላኛዋ።

"ቀኝ ዐይኔን በዱላ ተመትቼ ጠፍቷል። በወደቅሁበት ምንነቱን በማላውቀው ስለት አናቴን ብለውኛል። መትረፉንስ ተረፍኩ፤ እየተሰቃየሁ፤ እየለመንኩ ልኑር?" አሉን ሌላው።

ጠና ያሉ ናቸው። ጠንከር፤ ሻከር ያሉት እጆቻቸው ራሳቸውን መግበው ለሌላ እንደ ተረፉ መስካሪ የማያሻቸው።

"ለመሆኑ ምን ይዛችሁ መጣችሁ? ከየት ናችሁ? ከየትም ብትሆኑ ቢያንስ ያለንበትን ሁኔታ አድርሱልን። ተጨማሪ ሻራ እንኳን እንጣ? በእያንዳንዱ ድንኳን ብዙ ሰዎች ታጉረናል። ውጭ እንዳናድር ብርድ ነው።"

"እዚሁ ተወልጄ ነው ያደግሁት፤ አባቴና እናቴን እዚሁ ቀብርያለሁ። ወዴት ሂድ ይሉኛል? የአያትህ አገር ሂድ ቢሉኝ የት ብዬ?" ሌላው ግራ የተጋባ ብሶተኛ።

"ዞር ዞር እያላችሁ እዩአቸው" አሉን ተፈናቃዮቹ ያሉበትን ሁኔታና ልፋታችንን ሳትጉበኙ እንዳትሄዱ ያሉን የመንግሥት ተወካይ።

አየንም፤ ብዙ ናቸው። የዡና የወረዳው መንግሥት ከጴሎች አካላት ጋር በመተባበር ተፈናቃዮቹን ከከተማዋ ወጣ ባለ ሥፍራ ተቀብሎ ለማስተናገድ እየጣረ ይገኛል።

"በእጃችን ያለውን ጥቂት ነገር ሰጥተናቸዋል። ከሕዝብም የተገኘውን ያህል ለማግኘት እያሰባሰብን ነው። ጥቂት የማይባሉ የዕርዳታ ድርጅቶችም ወደ ሥፍራው ደርሰዋል።"

እንዳነውም ሁሉም ያላቸውን እፍኝ ታህል ይዘው እነኺህ ቀን የጨለመባቸውን ሰዎች ለማገዝ ይራራጡ። ለምግብነት የሚውል እህል ከመንግሥት፤ የካቶሊክ ቤተ ክርስቲያን እና ጴሎች በቦቴ የመጠጥ ውሃ፤ ዩኒሴፍ የሚል የተፃፈበት የሸራ ድንኳን፤ የሕክምናም ድጋፍ ተጀምሯል። ግን ጠብ አላለም።

"ከጓላ ያሉ ድንኳኖች ምዝገባ እንኺን አልደረሰም" አለን አንዱ ወጣት።

"ጴሎች አሁንም እየመጡ እንዲያው በሚዳ ፈሰዋል።" ይለናል ትከሻውን ግማሽ ቅጠሏ ቢያልቅም ብቻኛ የገቢው ጥላ በሆነት በአንዲት ዛፍ ያስደገፈ ሌላ ወጣት።

"በዚህ መጠለያ እስከ 40 ሺህ የሚሆኑ መዘግበናል። በከተማዋ ዙሪያ ባሉት መንደሮች ተጨማሪ 20 ሺህ ያህል ይገኙ። በአጠቃላይ በወረዳችን ወደ 90 ሺህ የሚጠጉ ተፈናቃዮች ተጠልለዋል" አሉን የመንግሥት ተወካይ።

አርባ ዓመት ያህል ወደ ኋላ ተጓዝኩ። ቻግኒ ያን ጊዜ የመተከል አውራጃ ዋና ከተማ ነበረች። መንግሥት "በድርቅ ምክንያት የተጎዱ" ወገኖችን ለም ወደ ሆኑ ሥፍራዎች በሠፈራ ለማዘወር ለነደፈው ዕቅድ ማስፈፀሚያ ትምህርት ቤታችንን ዘግቶ ቤተ ሥፍላቸው ብሎ ሲያዘምተን አንድ ቀን አልፌባታለሁ። ተፈናቃዮቹ የተለያየ ቋንቋ ያወራሉ። አብዛኞቹ በአማርኛና በአገውኛ ቢግባቡም ትግርኛ፤ ምንልባትም ሌላ ቋንቋ የሚናገሩም አሉባቸው።

መተከልን ቤታቸው ካደረጉ እንግዲህ ቢያንስ 30 ዓመት። ምናልባት ከአያት ቅድመ አያት ጀምሮ። የብሔር ፖለቲካ ሕዝብን በዘር ፈርጆ መፍጀት ትክክለኛ እርምጃ አድርጉ ሳለልን። ልጆቻችን ከጨቅላነታቸው ጀምሮ እንዲማሩት ጥብቅ ድጋፍ ተደረገ። ክርፋቱን በነቂስ ዝም ስላልን ያገኘን ፍርድ ነው። መተከል ቁንፅልዋ ናት። በባሌ፤ ቦረና፤ ሀረር፤ ድሬዳዋ፤ መኃል አዲስ አበባ፤ መስቃንና ማረቆ፤ መላ ሱማሌ ክልል፤ ወዘተ ከግጭት ጋር በተያያዘ 1200 ያህል የተፈናቃይ መጠለያዎች አሉ።

በዓለም የአገር ውስጥ ተፈናቃዮች ተርታ ቀዳሚዎች ነን። ወደ 2.5 ሚሊዮን ገደማ ሕዝብ ተፈናቅሏል። ዛሬ ደግሞ መላው ትግራይ፤ አማራና አፋር የዚህን እጥፍ ያህል ሕዝብ ይዞ የአበሣ ማዕከል ሆኗል። ለዘረኛው የጥላቻ ትርክት እጥፍ በእጥፍ፤ ነዶ

በነዶ የእጃችንን አግኘንተናል። ዛሬም የብሔር ጥላቻ በማራገብ ሥልጣን እይዛለሁ፤ እንጀራም እበላለሁ የምትል ወገኔ የዚህ ሕዝብ ዕጣ እንዲያገኝህ አልመኝም። ነገር ግን የዚህን ሕዝብ ዕጣ ዐይንህ ተከፍቶ እንድታይ አምላኬን አማፀናለሁ።

ከአድማስ ባሻገር

ዶክተር ሲሞን ሔሊዮ "የብሔርተኝነት ፖለቲካዊ ኤኮኖሚ" በሚል ርእስ የአገራችንን ፖለቲካዊ ኤኮኖሚ አሁናዊ ሁኔታ በምሳሌ እያዋዛ ተንትኗል። ርእሱ ብዙ ያልተለመደ ብቻ ሳይሆን ብዙም ያልተደፈረ ነው። የፖለቲካዊ ኤኮኖሚ በብሔርተኝነት ጽንፍ በሚዘወርበት አገር እንዲህ "መዳፈር" ቀላል አይሆንም። ብሔርተኝነት በኤኮኖሚው ላይ ተፅዕኖ ማሳደሩን በድፍረት ብቻ ሳይሆን በበቂ ዕውቀትና ማስረጃ ለመተንተን አስተውሎት ይጠይቃል።

የመፅሐፉን ጭብጥ ለመረዳት ግን የግድ ኤኮኖሚስት መሆን የሚጠይቅ አይደለም። ለሁሉም ሰው በሚገባ አቀራረብ የፖለቲካ አካሄዳችን ከኤኮኖሚ ዕድጋዎች በላይ ለአገር ሕልውና ቀጣይነትም አስኪ መሆኑ ማሳየት ችሏል። "የሁለት መላጦች" ግሩም ወግ ነገራችንን ቀስ በቀስ ለአስታራቂ ወደማይመች ግጭት ሊያደርስ እንደሚችል ቁም ነገር አስጨብጦናል። እኛስ ምን እንበል?

በአገራችን ተዘውትሮ ለክርክርና ለውይይት የተጋለጠው ርእስ ዘረኝነት፣ ብሔርተኝነት፣ እና ጉሥኝነት የተባለው ነው። ይህ መጽሐፍ አንድነትና ልዩነታቸውን በተመለከተ የተሻለ መረዳትን ፈጥሯል። ትንታኔው የሰውን ክቡርነት የሚያስረግጥ አቋም ያንጸባርቃል። የሰውን ክቡርነት የሚቀበል አስተሳሰብ ለማንበራዊ መፍትሔዎች ቅርብ ነው። መፍትሔ ካሰብን ከዚህ መንደርደሪያ ላይ መነሣት እንዳለብን አመልካች ነው።

እንደ ጸሐፊው አገላለጽ "ውሉ በጠፋበት ዘመን" ላይ ያለን ነን። ውል መያዝ አቅቶን ወይም አልያዝልን እንዳለን በጋራ ዕሴቶቻችን፣ በተጠጥሮ ሃብታችን፣ በማኅበራዊ ግንኙነታችን፣ እና በገል የኖሮ ዘዴቤአችን ላይ ምስክልቅል እንደ ተፈጠረብን ማስተዋልም የመፍትሔው መጀመሪያ ነው። ምስክልቅሎሹ የዐሳብ ድኽነትንም ይፈጥራል። በዐሳብ መከራከር ቀርቶ በዘር ወይም በማንነት ላይ ብቻ የተመሰረተ ይሆንና ርእዮትና አመንክዮ ማሳጣቱ ትልቅ ስጋት ነው።

ይህ መጽሐፍ ብሔርተኝነት ፖለቲካዊ ኤኮኖሚውን ሲዘውር የሚያስከትለውን አደጋ አመላከተን እንጂ በበሔር ብሔረሶች መብትና እኩልነት ላይ ግልፅ አቋም ያራምዳል።

ለሰው ዘር ሁሉ ክቡርነት ሥፍራ የማይሰጥ ፖለቲካዊ ኤኮኖሚ ብሔሮችንም እንደማያከብር ልንገነዳ ይገባል። ፖለቲካዊ ኤኮኖሚው በብሔረተኝነት ላይ የተመሰረተ ሲሆን ለመተንተን ማስቸገሩ ብቻ ሳይሆን ወደ ሳይንሳዊ ተፈጥሮው ካልተመለሰ አደጋ አለው።

ከአደጋዎችም አንዱ፣ ሙስና ይስፋፋል። ሌብነትና ዝቅጠትን ለመከላከልም ያሰቸግራል። በውድድር ላይ ለተመሰረተ የኤኮኖሚ እንቅስቃሴ ብዙ ቦታ አይሰጥም። በውድድር ማትረፍ፣ ገበያን ማወቅና መቆጣጠር፣ እና ከቦታ ቦታ ሄዶ ሃብት መፍጠር ተፈጥሮአዊ ስለሆነ ወደዚህ የሚመልሰንን ነገር መፈለግ ይኖርብናል። ይህ ሲሆን ታዲያ የብሔር ጉዳዮችንን በሰከነ መንገድ መፍታትም አለብን።

በመሰረቱ የብሔር ጉዳይ ከመብት፣ ከፍትሕ፣ እና ከእስኮነት አንጻር በፖለቲካው ውስጥ አጀንዳ መሆን ተገቢ ነው። ችግሩ ከመብትም፣ ከፍትሕም፣ ከእስኮነትም ሳይሆን ቀርቶ ልዩነትን ለማስፋት እንደ አዋጪ መስመር ሲያዝ ነው። እንጂ በአንድ አገር ውስጥ የሚኖሩ ብሔሮች ስለ እውነተኛ መብት፣ እኩልነት፣ እና ነጻነት መነጋገርም መታገልም ተገቢ ነው። ለአንድ ብሔር መብት ለመታገልም የግድ ከዚያው ብሔር መፈጠርን አይጠይቅም።

በአንድነት ውስጥ ያሉ ልዩነቶች በጤናማ መንገድ ካልተጠበቁ አንድነት አደጋ ይገጥመዋል። በእኔ እምነት በአንድነት ውስጥ ስላሉ ልዩነቶች እንጂ በልዩነቶች ውስጥ ስላለ አንድነት ብቻ እንድናወራ መፈለግ ተገቢ አይደለም። ልዩነቶችን ብቻ እንድናወራ መፈለግ አንድነትን ባለማስቀደምና ባለማክበር የሚመጣ ዕይታ ነው። ክርክሩ 'ዶሮዋ ወይስ እንቁላሏ' እንዲሉት ቢመስልም በምንም ዐይነትመንገድ ቢሆን ዜጐች በአንድ አገር መኖራቸው እና ለታሪካዊ መስተጋብሮቻቸው ትልቅ ፋይዳ መስጠት ይገባል።

ልዩነቶች ግን እንደሚባለው ውብት እንጂ ለጥፋት ሊውሉ አይገባም። በአንድነታችን ውስጥ ያገኛናቸውን ልዩነቶች ማክበር ይገባል። አንድ ባንሆን ግን ልዩነቶቻችን ምን ትርጉም ይሰጡናል? አንድ ስለሆንን ነው ልዩነታችን መከበር ያለበት። ስለዚህም በአንድነት ውስጥ ያሉ ልዩነቶቻችን ሊከበሩ ይገባል። ይህም የሁሉም ዜጐች ግዴታ መሆን አለበት።

ጽንፈኛ ብሔርተኝነትን የየኮነንን "የምርጥ ዘር ዕሳቤ" የምናራምድ ከሆነም ናዚያችን እንዳሰባደ ይሞከረናል። በጊዜው ቤተ ክርስቲያንን ጭምር እንዴት እንዳፈዘዘ በፀሃፊው የተገለጸው ዕሳብ ከምንኖርበት ዘመን ጋር እጅጉን ተመሳሰለብኝ። "የምርጥ ዘር" ዕሳቤም አክራሪ ብሔርተኝነትም ሁለቱም ጽንፈኛ ዕሳቦች ናቸው፣ አይጠቅሙም። ከሁለቱ አንዱ ወይም ሁለቱም በአንድ ጊዜ ፖለቲካዊ ኤኮኖሚን ሲቆጣጠሩ አገር ከፍተኛ አደጋ ላይ ትወድቃለች። ችግሩ ያ ዘመን አሁን የተደገመ ይመስላል።

በአገራችን ያለውን 'ፖለቲካ' በበኩሌ 'ቦለቲካ' ነው የምለው። የቡንተኝነትና ጅምለኝነትን አካሄድ ስለሚታይበት። የዐሳብ ፋክክር እስኪለመድ ድረስ ፖለቲካ የለም

ማለቴ የችግር ነው። ችግራችን ይሄ መሆኑን ተረድተን ወዲያ ወዲህ ሳንል ለአገራችን ችግሮች የመፍትሔ መጀመሪያ እዚህ ላይ እንደሆነ መቀበል ይገባል።

የአገራችን ኤኮኖሚ ተግዳሮቶች ይበዙበታል። ኤኮኖሚ ተግዳሮት ማጋጠሙ በብዙ አገራት የተለመደ፣ ተፈጥሯዊ ነው። የእኛ ፖለቲካዊ ኤኮኖሚ በብሔርተኝነት የተጠለፈ ከመሆኑ ጋራ አሌክስ ዴዋል የተባለ ተመራማሪ እንደጻፈው "የፖለቲካ ገበያው" ተስማሚና ምቹ ሁኔታ የማግኘቱ ነገር ያስፈራል። "ፖለቲካ ነው" ስንል፣ ፍልስፍናውና አስተዳደሩ ለግል ወይም በጥንቃቄ ለተቀናጀ ቡድን ጥቅም ገበያ ላይ ከዋለ ሙስና፣ ሥርዓት አልበኝነት፣ ሁከት መቀስቀስ፣ እና ተቋማዊ ሙስና በመፍጠር የሌብነት አገዛዝ ፈጥሮ አገርን ያምሳል።

ዝም ከተባለም፣ ወደለየለት ፖለቲካዊም ማኅበራዊም ምስቅልቅል ማምራቱ የማይቀር ይሆናል። ይህን መከላከል የኢትዮጵያዊ ሁሉ ኃላፊነት ነው። ይህ መጽሐፍ የአገራችንን ትንሣዔ ለሚሹ ብቻ የተጻፈ አይደለም። ፖለቲካዊ ኤኮኖሚን መረዳት ለሚፈልጉም ሆነ በዕለቱ ለሚያጋጥሙን ያልተለመዱ ቀውሶች ከግራ መጋባት ተላቅቀው ሰከን ያለ ትንተና መስጠት ለሚፈልጉም ይጠቅማል።

በተለያዩ አገራት ያጋጠሙ በፖለቲካዊ ኤኮኖሚያዊ መዛባት ምክንያት የተከሰቱ ቀውሶች ለምንድነው ለትምህርታችን የማይሆኑ ብሎ መጠየቅ አይገባንም? ለምንስ በአንድ የዓለም ክፍል የተደረገ ጥፋት በሌላው አገር እንዲደገም እንፈቅዳለን? የየአገሩ ነባራዊ ሁኔታ ልዩ ልዩ መሆኑ ቢታወቅም፣ መነሻው የተለያየም ቢሆን አንኳ፣ ጥፋቱ በሰው ልጆች ላይ ምን ያህል የከፋ እንደሆነ መረዳት አያስቸግርም። በታሪክ በሰው ልጆች ላይ የደረሱ ጥፋቶችን ለትምህርታችን እንዲሆኑ አዋቂዎች ሊፈሩ ሊመክሩ ይገባል።

ይህ መጽሐፍ አስቀድሞ ችግርን ማየትና መከላከልን ያበረታታል። ልንነጋገርበት ይገባል። ፖለቲካዊ ኤኮኖሚው እየተወላገደ አቅጣጫውን ሲስት እንዴት ዝም ይባላል?! እንነጋገር።

በአንድ በኩል ለሰዎች ሁሉ እኩልነትን ለማምጣት እየደከምን በሌላ በኩል የኤኮኖሚም የመብትም ልዩነት እንዲስፋፋ መፍቀድ ወይም ሲሆን ማየት ተገቢ ነገር አይደለም። ዜጎች ሁሉ በእኩልነትና በተገቢው ነጻነት ያለ አድሎ የተፈጠሩለትን ምክንያት ኖረው እንዲያልፉ የፖለቲካ ኤኮኖሚያችን በብሔርተኝነትና በጽንፈኛ አስተሳሰብ እንዳይጠለፍ እንደአቅማችን ልንጽፍና ልንመራመር ይገባል። የዚህ መጽሐፍ ዐሳሬ ጥሪ ያቀረብልን መስሎ ይሰማኛል። የምንችለውን ሁሉ በማድረግ እንመካከር። ምክክር ነው መፍትሔው።

መመካከር ባለመቻል በታሪክ የተመዘገቡ እጅግ የሚፀፅቱ በሰው ላይ የደረሱ ጥፋቶችን መርሳት ተገቢ አይደለም። ካረሰሳን በእኛ እንዲደገም መፍቀድ የለብንም።

የተመሰቃቀለው ፖለቲካዊ ኤኮኖሚያችን ጤናም ሆኖ እንዲቀጥል ምን እናድርግ? አዋቂዎች፤ ጠቢባን ሆይ ወዴት አላችሁ? በጉ ነገርን ችላ ባልነው ቁጥር ክፋት አያደገች ትሄዳለች። ዐሳብ እናዋጣና ለፀሃፊው የጭንቀት ጥሪ ምላሽ እንስጥ።

ፖለቲካዊ ኤኮኖሚያችን ከብሄርተኝነት መላቀቅ ይኖርበታል። ይህ ሲሆን ኤኮኖሚያችንም ምንም ተገዳሮቶች ቢበዛበት በመነጋገር ያለንን ሃብት በፍትሕና በእኩልነት መጠቀም ይቻለናል። ደህና ነገር ማሰብ ማንንም አይጎዳም። በዐሳብ መከባበር ጤና ነው። ለሁሉም ይጠቅማል።

አበበ ንጋቱ እንዳለው (ዶ/ር)

ዋቢ መጻሕፍት

የኢትዮጵያ መጽሐፍ ቅዱስ ማሕበር (1954)። መጽሐፍ ቅዱስ፤ የብሉይና የሐዲስ ኪዳን መጻሕፍት። ብርሃንና ሰላም ማተሚያ ቤት። 1954 ዓ.ም እንደ ኢትዮጵያ አቆጣጠር። UBS. (1962). The Bible in Amharic. United Bible Societies. Africa Regional Centre; Nairobi, Kenya.

ሲሞን ሔሊሶ ኩካ (2019)። ዘመን ቀደምነትና የዛሬይቱ ቤተ ክርስቲያን። አማዞን።

ባይሳ ገመቹ (2008)። የዘረኝነት አውራቂስ። ሁለተኛ እትም። ፍንፍኔ ማተሚያ ቤት

አማራ ብሔራዊ ክልላዊ መንግሥት ምክር ቤት ዝክረ ሕግ (2001)። የአማራ ብሔራዊ ክልላዊ ሕገ መንግሥት ለማጽደቅ የወጣ አዋጅ። http://knowledge-uclga.org/IMG/pdf/amhara-national-regional-state-constitution_1_.pdf

የቤንሻንጉል ጉሙዝ ክልል ምክር ቤት። (1995)። የተሻሻለው የቤንሻንጉል ጉሙዝ ክልል ሕገ መንግሥት ማጽደቂያ አዋጅ። http://www.ethcriminalawnetwork.com/system/files/BENSHANGULE%5B1%5D.pdf

የኢትዮጵያ ቋንቋዎች ጥናት ኢንስቲትዩት (1993)። የአማርኛ መዝገበ ቃላት። አዲስ አበባ።

ጨፌ ኦሮሚያ (1994)። የተሻሻለው የ1994 የኦሮሚያ ሕገ መንግሥት ማጽደቂያ አዋጅ። https://chilot.me/wp-content/uploads/2012/02/oromia-national-regional-state-constitution.pdf

ፌደራል ነጋሪት ጋዜጣ (1995)። የኢትዮጵያ ፌደራላዊ ዴሞክራሲያዊ ሪፐብሊክ ሕገ መንግሥት አዋጅ። https://ethiopianembassy.be/wp-content/uploads/Constitution-of-the-FDRE.pdf

Aalen, L. (2011). *The Politics of Ethnicity in Ethiopia* (African Social Studies) Illustrated Edition. Amazon.

Abbinl, J. (2011). Ethnic-based federalism and ethnicity in Ethiopia: reassessing the experiment after 20 years. *Journal of East African Studies*. Volume 5, Issue 4. https://doi.org/10.1080/17531055.2011.642516

Abraha, A. H. (2019). Ethnic Federalism and Conflict in Ethiopia. *Research on humanities and social sciences*, Volume 9, pages 16-22. https://www.semanticscholar.org/paper/Ethnic-Federalism-and-Conflict-in-Ethiopia-Abrha/01e583950a19ef042344a5181bc985563083f833

Abyssinian Baptist Church. (2023). History of the Abyssinan Baptist Church. https://abyssinian.org/about-us/history/

Adlparvar, N. and Tadros, M. (2016). The Evolution of Ethnicity Theory: Intersectionality, Geopolitics and Development. *IDS Bulletin* Vol. 47 No. 2 May 2016: 'Development Studies – Past, Present and Future' 123–136

Alemie, A. & Mandefro, H. (2018). Roles of Indigenous Conflict Resolution Mechanisms for Maintaining Social Solidarity and Strengthening Communities in Alefa District, Northwest of Ethiopia. *Journal of Indigenous Social Development*. Volume 7, Issue 2 (2018).

Alhendi, O., József, T., Péter, L., and Péter B. (2021). Tolerance, Cultural Diversity and Economic Growth: Evidence from Dynamic Panel Data Analysis. *Economies* 9: 20

Alimi, F. O., Tella, A., Adeyemo, G. O. & Oyoweso, M. O. (2020). Impact of Mother Tongue on Primary Pupils' Literacy and Numeracy Skills in Osun State. *International Online Journal of Primary Education*. 2020, volume 9, issue 2. Accessed on November 23, 2022; from https://files.eric.ed.gov/fulltext/EJ1283007.pdf

Alkire, S., Kanagaratnam, U. and Suppa, N. (2021). 'The Global Multidimensional Poverty Index (MPI) 2021', OPHI MPI Methodological Notes 51, Oxford Poverty and Human Development Initiative, University of Oxford.

Anderson, R. Lanier, "Friedrich Nietzsche", *The Stanford Encyclopedia of Philosophy* (Winter 2021 Edition), Edward N. Zalta (ed.), https://plato.stanford.edu/archives/win2021/entries/nietzsche/

Argaw, B. A. (2017). Regional inequality of economic outcomes and opportunities in Ethiopia A tale of two periods. UNU-WIDER Working Paper 2017/118.

Aspinall, Arthur C. V. D. "William Pitt, the Younger". *Encyclopedia Britannica*, 19 Jan. 2022, https://www.britannica.com/biography/William-Pitt-the-Younger.

Asoungu, S. A. & Kodila-Tedika, O. (2016). Determinants of Property Rights Protection in Sub-Saharan Africa. Journal of the Knowledge Economy, November 2016. African Governance and Development Institute.

Augustyn, A. (2022). Britannica, The Editors of Encyclopaedia. "Third Republic". *Encyclopedia Britannica*, 10 Mar. 2020, https://www.britannica.com/topic/Third-Republic-French-history

Baltzly, Dirk, "Stoicism", *The Stanford Encyclopedia of Philosophy* (Spring 2019 Edition), Edward N. Zalta (ed.), https://plato.stanford.edu/archives/spr2019/entries/stoicism/

Barth, F. (1969). Introduction. In: Fredrik Barth (ed.), *Ethnic Groups and Boundaries: The Social Organization of Culture Differences*. Bergen: Universitetsforlaget, pp. 9–38.

Baudrillard, Jean (1995). *Simulacra and Simulation*. Translated by Sheila Faria Glaser. Ann Arbor: University of Michigan Press.

Baye, T. G. (2017). Poverty, peasantry, and agriculture in Ethiopia. *Annals of Agrarian Science*. Volume 15, Issue 3; September 2017, Pages 420-430

Bayu, T. B. (2022). Is Federalism the Source of Ethnic Identity-Based Conflict in Ethiopia? *Insight on Africa, 14*(1), 104–125. https://doi.org/10.1177/09750878211057125

Beckett, C., & Macey, M. (2001). Race, Gender and Sexuality: The Oppression of Multiculturalism. *Women's Studies International Forum*, Vol. 24, No. 3/4, pp. 309–319, 2001

Bekele, T., Rawstorne, P., Rahman, B. (2021). Socioeconomic inequalities in child growth failure in Ethiopia: findings from the 2000 and 2016 Demographic and Health Surveys. BMJ Open 2021.

Bekele, Y. W., Kjosavik, D. J. & Shanmugaratnam, N. (2016). State-Society Relations in Ethiopia: A Political- Economy Perspective of the Post-1991 Order. *Journal of Social Sciences*. Volume 5, No. 48. https://www.mdpi.com/2076-0760/5/3/48

Behrman, J. R. & Kohler, H. (2014). Population Quantity, Quality, and Mobility. In Allen, F. (ed.). *Towards a Better Global Economy: Policy Implications for Citizens Worldwide in the 21st Century*. Chapter 3. Pages 138–215, Accessed on November 24, 2022; from https://academic.oup.com/book/11948/chapter-abstract/161155739?redirectedFrom=fulltext

Besley, T. & Gathak, M. (2009). Property Rights and Economic Development. The Suntory Centre Suntory and Toyota International Centres for Economics and Related Disciplines; London School of Economics and Political Science.

Ben-Rafael, E. (2001) Sociology of Ethnicity; in the *International Encyclopedia of the Social and Behavioral Sciences*; 2001.

Birru, D. T. (2018). Ethnic Federalism Implementation in Ethiopia: The Paradox. *Journal of Political Sciences & Public Affairs*. Analysis - (2018) Volume 6, Issue 4. https://www.longdom.org/open-access/ethnic-federalism-implementation-in-ethiopia-the-paradox-37377.html

Bloch, E, and Wong, R. (2020). When Did Women Get the Right to Vote in the United States? A Timeline. *Teen Vogue*; August 17, 2020.

Bonnoil, J., Edward-Grossi, E. & Wang, S. (2021). Introduction to *Race and Biology*. https://journals.openedition.org/alterites/338

Bowen, J. S. (1994). Power and Authority in the African Context: Why Somalia did Not Have to Starve - The Organization of African Unity (OAU) as an Example of the Constitutive Process. *National Black Law Journal*, 14(1)

Britannica (2022). The Editors of Encyclopedia. *Encyclopedia Britannica*, 24 Jan. 2022,

Brooks, T. (2021). "Hegel's Social and Political Philosophy", *The Stanford Encyclopedia of Philosophy* (Summer 2021 Edition), Edward N. Zalta (ed.), https://plato.stanford.edu/archives/sum2021/entries/hegel-social-political/

Brown, C. L. (2007). Evangelicals and the origins of anti-slavery in England. *Oxford Dictionary of National Biography*. 04 January 2007.

Bulcha, M. (2013). Walelign Mekonnen, the Question of Nationalities and Ethiopia's Persistent Crisis. *Oromia Today*, 28/06/10. https://oromia.today/history/walelign-mekonnen-the-question-of-nationalities-and-ethiopias-persistent-crisis/

Burrel, M., Whiite, A. M., Frerichs, L., Funchess, M, Cerulli, C., DiGiovanni, L. and Lich, H. (2021). Depicting "the system": How structural racism and disenfranchisement in the United States can cause dynamics in community violence among males in urban black communities. *Social Science & Medicine,* Volume 271, March 2021, 113469

Cardenas, H. & Whitington, D. (2019). Magnitude and Distribution of Electricity and Water Subsidies for Households in Addis Ababa, Ethiopia. *World Bank Policy and Research Working Papers*. Open Knowledge Repository.

Carley, P. (1996). Self-Determination Sovereignty, Territorial Integrity, and the Right to Secession. Report From a Roundtable Held in Conjunction with the U.S. Department of State's Policy Planning Staff. https://www.usip.org/sites/default/files/pwks7.pdf

Cartwrght, M. (2013). Slavery in the Roman World. *World History Encyclopedia.*

Cats-Barill, A. (2018). Self-determination. International IDEA, Constitution Brief. September 2018. https://www.idea.int/sites/default/files/publications/self-determination-constitution-brief.pdf

Chantarat, T., Mentzer, K. M., Van riper, D. C., Rachel, M. and Hardeman, R. (2022). Where are the labor markets? Examining the association between structural racism in labor markets and infant birth weight. *Health and Place*, Volume 74, March 2022, 102742

Che, A. M. (2016). Linking Instrumentalist and Primordialist Theories of Ethnic Conflict. E-International Relations; June 1, 2016.

Chenu, M. (2021). St. Thomas Aquinas: Italian Christian theologian and philosopher. *Encyclopedia Beritanninca.* https://www.britannica.com/biography/Saint-Thomas-Aquinas

Cob, C. & Douglas, P. (1928). A theory of production. *The American Economic Review.* Vol. 18; No. 1. https://www.jstor.org/stable/1811556

Cohen, A. (1969) *Custom and Politics in Urban Africa: A Study of Hausa Migrants in Yoruba Towns*, London: Routledge

Cohen, J. H. (1995). Ethinic Federalism in Ethiopia. Northeast African Studies; *New Serises*, Vol. 2. No. 2. pp. 157-188 (32 pages)

Conistitute. (2022). Ethiopian Consitiution 1994.

Cornish, P. J. (2011). Marriage, Slavery, and Natural Rights in the Political Thought of Aquinas. *The Review of Politics*; Vol. 60; No. 3; pp. 545-56

Countryeconomy.com (2022). Ethiopia: Evolution of Debt.

Crenshaw, K. (1989) 'Demarginalizing the Intersection of Race and Sex: A Black Feminist Critique of Antidiscrimination Doctrine, Feminist Theory and Antiracist Politics', *University of Chicago Legal Forum* 1989.1: 139–67

Deng, F. M. (1997). *Ethnicity: An African Predicament.* Brookings Institution; June 1997.

Deressa, A. (2007). Exchange Market Pressure and Monetary Policy in Ethiopia. NBE Working Papers. A

Derrida, J. (1997). Of Grammatology. Corrected ed. Baltimore: Johns Hopkins University Press

Dezo, M. E. (2020). Traditional Conflict Resolution Mechanism in Ethiopia: (The case of Enashma of the BoroShinasha Community, Benisahngul Gumuz Regional State).

de Waal, A. (2014). The Political Marketplace: Analyzing Political Entrepreneurs and Political Bargaining with a Business Lens. Framework and Background Seminar Memo; World Peace Foundation. https://sites.tufts.edu/reinventingpeace/files/2014/10/Political-Marketplace_de-Waal.pdf

Digital Collections. (2022). Les Clans Indigenes au Burundi. George A. Smarthers Libraries; University of Florida.

Dube, M. (2003). Postmodernism as Post nationalism? Racial Representation in U.S. Black Cultural Studies. *The Black Scholar*; Vol 33. No. 1, Black Film and Culture (Spring 2003; pp 2 – 18).

Duignan, B. (2022). rian. "Richard Thaler". *Encyclopedia Britannica*, 8 Sep. 2022, https://www.britannica.com/biography/Richard-Thaler

Dunn, S. P. & Pressman, S. (2005). The Economic Contributions of John, K. Galbraith. *Review of Political Economy*, Volume 17, Number 2; 160 – 209. https://www.researchgate.net/publication/24088369_The_Economic_Contributions_of_John_Kenneth_Galbraith

Eniyew, E. L. (2014). Ethiopian customary dispute resolution mechanisms: Forms of restorative justice? *African Journal on Conflict Resolution*. Volume 14; No. 1. https://www.ajol.info/index.php/ajcr/article/view/108898

Esman, M. J. (1987). (Ethnic Politics and Economic Power. *Comparative Politics*; Vol. 19, No. 4 (July 1987) pp. 395-418 (24 pages).

Estevão, M., Zeidane, Z. & Nolan, S. (2019). Ethiopia - Joint World Bank-IMF Debt Sustainability Analysis. IDA & IMF.

Fearon, D.J. and Laitin, D.D. (2000) 'Violence and the Social Construction of Identity', *International Organization* 54.4: 845–77

Fedec, A. & Sousa, A. (2022). Ethiopia – Subsidies and Transfers (as % of government expenditures). Trading Economics.

Fedec, A. & Sousa, A. (2022). Ethiopia – Government Budget. Trading Economics.

Federal Negarit Gazeta. (1995). Proclamation No. 1/1995 - Proclamation of the Constitution of the Federal Democratic Republic of Ethiopia. August 21, 1995.

Fornace, K. (2009). The Rwandan Genocide. Beyond Intractability.

Forte, F., & Brady, G. L. (2021). Remembering Gordon Tullock—The Unconventional Economist: Beyond *Homo Economicus* and *"Economist Borne."* Alternative Traditons in Public Service; Vol. 11 No. 1; 2021.

Foster, S. (2022). Nauru: Island Country, Pacific Ocean. *Encyclopedia Britanica.* https://www.britannica.com/place/Nauru

Foucault, Michel (1970). *The Order of Things: An Archaeology of the Human Sciences*. New York: Pantheon.

Foyart, P. (2018, March 25). *Juvénal Habyarimana (1937-1994).*

Frantz, R. (2020). The Beginings of Behavioral Economics: Katona, Simon, and Leibenstein's X-efficiency theory. London.

Galbraith, J. K. (1976) Conservative majority myth, Dissent, 23, pp. 123–126.

Gebre Selassie, A. (2003). Ethnic Federalism: Its Promise and Pitfalls for Africa. College of William & Mary Law School William & Mary Law School Scholarship Repository. *Faculty Publications. 88.*

Gebresenbet F. Land Acquisitions, the Politics of Dispossession, and State-Remaking in Gambella, Western Ethiopia. *Africa Spectrum*. 2016;51(1):5-28.

Geda, A. (2003). Ethiopian Macroeconomic Modeling in Historical Perspective: Bringing Gebre-Hiwot and His Contemporaries to Ethiopian Macroeconomics Realm. International Conference on African Development Archives; Western Michigan University Center for African Development Policy Research. https://scholarworks.wmich.edu/cgi/viewcontent.cgi?article=1066&context=africancenter_icad_archive

Geda, A. & Abebe, A. (2011). A Dynamic Macroeconomic Modelling of Gebre-Hiwot's Idea about Early 20th Century Ethiopia's Development Problems. Conference: Paper Presented at Western Michigan University and Adma University Conference on Ethiopian Development Problems; Adma-Nazareth, Ethiopia. https://www.researchgate.

net/publication/283307703_A_Dynamic_Macroeconomic_Modeling_of_Gebre-Hiwot's_Idea_about_Early_20th_Century_Ethiopia's_Development_Problems.

Gedamu, Y. (2017). "Ethnic Federalism and Authoritarian Survival in Ethiopia." Dissertation, Georgia State University, 2017. doi: https://doi.org/10.57709/10995588

Geertz, Clifford. 1963. 'The Integrative Revolution: Primordial Sentiments and Politics in the New States'. In Clifford Geertz, ed. *Old Societies and New States: The Quest for Modernity in Asia and Africa.* London: London Free Press, 255–310.

Glasgow, J., Haslanger, S., Jeffers, C. & Spencer, Q. (2019). *What is Race: Four Philosophical Views.* Oxford University Press.

Glasgow, J. (2019). Is Race an Illusion of a (very) Basic Reality? in What is Race; Glasgow, et al. OUP.

Goren, E. (2014) How Ethnic Diversity Affects Economic Growth. World Development; Volume 59; July 2014, Pages 275-297

Gourevitch, Philip. *We Wish to Inform You that Tomorrow We Will Be Killed with Our Families.* New York: Picador, 1998

Gowok, S. M. (2008). Alternative Dispute Resolution in Ethiopia - A Legal Framework. AFRR Vol 2 No. 2 April 2008; Improved Version pp. 265-285.

Grazhevskaa, N., Virchenkob, A., Grazhevskaa, A. (2015). The Effects of Rent-Seeking Behavior on the Efficiency of Fiscal Policy in Ukraine; Procedia Economics and Finance 27 (2015) 274 – 287.

Grubel, H. G. (1966). The Anatomy of Classical and Modern Infant Industry Arguments. Weltwirtschaftliches Archiv Bd. 97 (1966); pp. 325-344; Springer

Habtu, A. (2003). Ethnic Federalism in Ethiopia: Background, Present Conditions and Future Prospects. International Conference on African Development Archives. 57. https://scholarworks.wmich.edu/africancenter_icad_archive/57

Haile, A. (2011). Book Review: 'Negadras Baikedagn Serawoch.' https://www.alemayehu.com/TradeGraduate/Book%20Review%20YeGebrhiwotSerawotchAbebe.pdf

Haile, F. (2019). The Exchange Rate Why It Matters for Structural Transformation and Growth in Ethiopia. Policy Research Working Paper 8868; World Bank Group; Macroeconomics, Trade and Investment Global Practice May 2019.

Hailu, A., Gebreyes, R. & Norheim, O. F. (2021). Equity in public health spending in Ethiopia: a benefit incidence analysis. *Health Policy and Planning*, Volume 36, Issue Supplement_1, December 2021, Pages i4–i13.

Hakura, D. (2020). What Is Debt Sustainability? Finance and Development. September 2020. https://www.imf.org/en/Publications/fandd/issues/2020/09/what-is-debt-sustainability-basics

Hansson, S. O. (2022). John Stuart Mill and the Conflicts of Equality. *Journal of Ethics*. Volume 26, pages 433–453 (2022). https://link.springer.com/article/10.1007/s10892-022-09393-7

Haslanger, S. (2019). Tracing the Sociopolitical Reality of Race; in What is Race; Glasgow, et al. OUP.

Haydaroglu, C. (2015). The relationship between property rights and economic growth: An analysis of OECD and EU countries, *DANUBE: Law, Economics and Social Issues Review*, De Gruyter, *Warsaw*, Vol. 6, Iss. 4, pp. 217-239,

Hechter, M. (1978). Group Formation and the Cultural Division of Labor. *American Journal of Sociology*. Volume 84 Number 2 1978 by The University of Chicago.

Holdo, M. (2019). Power Games: Elites, Movements, and Strategic Cooperation. *Political Studies Review*. Bolume 18; Issue 2. https://doi.org/10.1177/1478929919864778

Hooks, B. (1994). Postmodern Blackness. University of Pennsylvania. African Studies Center.

Hummell, E. (2014). Standing the Test of Time – Barth and Ethnicity. *Coolabah*, No.13, 2014, Australian Studies Centre, Universitat de Barcelona

Hutcheon, L. (1987). The Politics of Postmodernism. *Cultural Critique* No. 5, Modernity and Modernism Postmodernity and Postmodernism (Winter, 1986-1987), pp. 179-207

IDE. (2022). Karuturi Global Limited. Institute of Developing Economies; African Growing Enterprises.

IMF. (2019). The Federal Democratic Republic of Ethiopia: Technical Assistance Report-Financial Soundness Indicators Mission. Volume 2020, Issue 323.

IMF. (2021). World Economic Outlook.

IMF. (2022). World Economic Outlook Database 2022.

IMF. (2022). Ethiopia: Economic outlook at a glance.

Immerwahr, I. (1992) Hume's Revised Racism. *Journal of the History of Ideas*; Vol. 53; No. 3 (July – Sept 1992).

International Crisis Group. (2009). Ethiopia: Ethnic Federalism and its Discontents. *Africa Report* N°153 – 4 September 2009. https://www.crisisgroup.org/africa/horn-africa/ethiopia/ethiopia-ethnic-federalism-and-its-discontents

IRC. (2007). Mortality in the Democratic Republic of Congo: An ongoing crisis. An IRC Report.

Jakoubek, M. & Budilová, L. J. (2019). Ethnicity and the boundaries of ethnic studies. *Anthropological Notebooks*, XXV/1, 2019

Jeffers, C. (2019). Cultural Constructionism: in What is Race; Glasgow, et al. OUP.

Jevons, S. W. (1871). *The Theory of Political Economy*, first edition, London and New York: MacMillan and Co. https://socialsciences.mcmaster.ca/econ/ugcm/3ll3/jevons/TheoryPoliticalEconomy.pdf

Jordan, A. (2017). Thomas Carlyle and Political Economy: The 'Dismal Science' in Context. *The English Historical Review*, Volume 132, Issue 555, April 2017, Pages 286–317, https://doi.org/10.1093/ehr/cex068

Kebede, M. (2006). Gebrehiwot Baykedagn, Eurocentrism, And the Decentering of Ethiopia. *Journal Of Black Studies*, Volume 36 No. 6, July 2006 815-832. https://journals.sagepub.com/doi/pdf/10.1177/0021934705280086

Keith, N. W. (1998). It Is a Truly New Dawn: Blacks and the Politics of the Postmodern Age. *Race & Society*, Volume 1, Number 1, pages 33-61. Copyright 0 1998 by JAI Press Inc.

Keller, J. & Nogueira-Budnym, D. (2020). Debt sustainability in fragile and conflict-affected states: heightened risks and needs. The World Bank Group.

Kenny, A. J. P. (2021). Aristotle: Greek Philosopher. https://www.britannica.com/biography/Aristotle

Keyenes, J. M. (1935). The General Theory of Employment, Interest and Money. International Relations and Security Network; Primary Soruces. https://www.files.ethz.ch/isn/125515/1366_KeynesTheoryofEmployment.pdf

Kirchschlaeger, P. G. (2016). Slavery And Early Christianity – A Reflection from a Human Rights Perspective. *Acta Theologica* 2016 Suppl 23: 66-93

Kleingeld, P. (2019). On Dealing with Kant's Sexism and Racism. *SGIR Review* 2, no. 2, 3-22, 2019

Kubota, R. (2003). New approaches to gender, class, and race in second language writing. *Journal of Second Language Writing* 12 (2003) 31–47. Pergamon.

Kuryla, Peter. "Pan-Africanism". *Encyclopedia Britannica*, 1 Oct. 2020, https://www.britannica.com/topic/Pan-Africanism.

Kuzner, L. A. (2019). Ethiopia Inequality Report. *NSI Agreieved Population Report*, 2019.

LA Times (1994). Two African Presidents Die in Plane Crash.

Lemarchand, René and Eggers, Ellen Kahan. "Burundi". *Encyclopedia Britannica*, 10 Mar. 2021, https://www.britannica.com/place/Burundi.

Lemarchand, R. & Clay, D. (2021). "Rwanda". *Encyclopedia Britannica*, 10 Aug. 2021, https://www.britannica.com/place/Rwanda.

Lloyds Bank. (2022). Foreign direct investment (FDI) in Ethiopia.

Locke, A. (2013). Briefing Paper Property Rights and Development: Property Rights and Economic Growth. ODI, UKAID.

Lyotard, J. F. (1979). La condition postmoderne: rapport sur le savoir (Paris: Minuit, 1979).

Macleod, C. (2021). "John Stuart Mill", *The Stanford Encyclopedia of Philosophy* (Summer 2020 Edition), Edward N. Zalta (ed.), https://plato.stanford.edu/archives/sum2020/entries/mill/

MacMahon, R. (2020). Resurecting raciology? Genetic ethnology and pre-1945 *anthropological race classification. Studies in History and Philosophy of Biology & Biomedical Sciences 83 (2020) 101242*

Macrotrends. (2022). Ethiopia Foreign Direct Investment (1977 – 2022).

Mariotti, M. and Fourie, J. (2014). The economics of apartheid: An introduction. *Economic History of Developing Regions*; Volume 29, 2014 - Issue 2; Pages 113-125 | Publihed online: 29 Sep 2014

Martin, M. (2010). Ethiopian Debt Policy: The Long Road from Paris Club to the MDGs. In Herman, B. et al (ed.). Overcoming Developing country Debt Crisis. Pages 277–297. Oxford.

McInerney, D. J. (1991). "A Faith for Freedom": The Political Gospel of Abolition. *Journal of the Early Republic.* Vol. 11. No. 3 (Autumn, 1991; pp. 371-393 (23 pages). University of Pennsylvania Press

Meinwald, C. C. (2021). Plato: Greek Philospher. *Encyclopedia Britanica.* https://www.britannica.com/biography/Plato

Mekonnen, W. (1962). On the Question of Nationalities in Ethiopia. Arts IV, HSIU Nov. 17, 1969. https://www.marxists.org/history/erol/ethiopia/nationalities.pdf

Menger, C. (1871). Principles of Economics. https://cdn.mises.org/principles_of_economics.pdf

Meralis Plaza-Toledo (USGS). (2022). The Mineral Industry of Ethiopia.

Merriam Webster. (2021), Definition of Racism.

Miheretu, A. (2009). Ethnic federalism and its potential to dismember the Ethiopian state. *Progress in Deelopment Studies.* Volume 12; Issue 2 – 3. https://journals.sagepub.com/doi/10.1177/146499341101200303

Mijiyawa, A, G. (2013). Determinants of property rights institutions: survey of literature and new evidence. May 2013, Volume 14, Issue 2.

Miller, T. (1997). The Role of Property Rights in Economic Development that Benefits the Poor.

Ministry of Finance Ethiopia. (2022). Budget Resources.

Miyasaki, D. (2014). Nietzsche's Naturalist Moraloty of Breeding: A Critique of Eugenics as Taming; in Vanessa Lemm (ed.), *Neitzsche and the Becoming of Life.* Fordham University Press. pp. 194-213 (2014)

Mises Institute. (2023). Ludwig Heinrich Edler von Mises (1881–1973). https://mises.org/profile/ludwig-von-mises?page=29

Moellendorf, D. (1992). Racism And Rationality in Hegel's Philosophy of Subjective Spirit. *History of Political Thought* vol. 13, No, 2; Summer 1992.

Morris, W. E. and Charlotte R. B. (2021), "David Hume", *The Stanford Encyclopedia of Philosophy* (Spring 2021 Edition), Edward N. Zalta (ed.), https://plato.stanford.edu/archives/spr2021/entries/hume/

National Archives, (2016). America's Historical Documents: 13th Amendment to the U.S. Constitution: Abolition of Slavery.

Ncube, M. & Brixiová, Z. (2015). Public Debt Sustainability in Africa: Building Resilience and Challenges Ahead. Africa Deevlopment Bank Group; Working Papers; No 227 – July 2015.

NEWS. (1994). *International Journal on World Peace*, *11*(2), 67–72.

Nkurunziza, J. d. (2018). The origin and persistence of state fragility in Burundi. The LSE-Oxford Commission on State Fragility, Growth and Development and the United Nations Conference on Trade and Development (UNCTAD).

Nunn, N. (2008). The Long-Term Effects of Africa's Slave Trades. *The Quarterly Journal of Economics*. February 2008. https://scholar.harvard.edu/files/nunn/files/empirical_slavery.pdf

OECD. (2022). Regional Wellbeing Index.

Ogbazghi, P. B. (2022). Ethiopia and the Running Sores of Ethnic Federalism: The Antithetical Forces of Statehood and Nationhood. *African Studies Quarterly*; Volume 21, Issue 2; August 2022. https://asq.africa.ufl.edu/wp-content/uploads/sites/168/V21i2a3.pdf

Patterson. E. W. F. (2017). The Role of Population in Economic Growth. *SAGE Journals*. Accessed on November 24, 2022; from https://journals.sagepub.com/doi/full/10.1177/2158244017736094

Petruzzello, M. (2021). "John Newton". *Encyclopedia Britannica*, 17 Dec. 2021, https://www.britannica.com/biography/John-Newton.

Pierce, F. S. (2022). "Thorstein Veblen". *Encyclopedia Britannica*, 30 Jul. 2022, https://www.britannica.com/biography/Thorstein-Veblen. Accessed 3 February 2023.

Poluha, E. (2004). The Power of Continuity Ethiopia Through the Eyes of Its Children, Nordiska Afrikainstitut, January 2004. https://www.researchgate.net/publication/44833599_The_Power_of_Continuity_Ethiopia_Through_the_Eyes_of_Its_Children

Ramprasad, A., Qureshi, F., Lee, B. R. and Jones, B. L. (2022). The relationship between structural racism and COVID-19 related health disparities across 10 metropolitan cities in the United States. *Journal of the National Medical Association*, Available online 25 February 2022.

Raymer, A. J. (1940). Slavery-The Graeco-Roman Defense. *Greece & Rome*; Vol. 10; No. 28 (Oct. 1940; pp. 17 – 21)

Rashid, S., Tefera, N., Minot, N. & Ayele, G. (2013). Fertilizer in Ethiopia: An Assessment of Policies, Value Chain, and Profitability. IFPRI.

Rediker, M. (2017). Benjamin Lay: The "Quaker Comet" Was the Greatest Abolitionist You've Never Heard of. History; Secrets of American History; Smithsonian Magazine. September 2017.

Refworld (2004). Minorities at Risk Project, *Chronology for Hutus in Burundi*, 2004,

Rekiso, E, Z. (2015). Economics of Late Development and Industrialization: Putting Gebrehiwot Baykedgn (1886-1919) in Context. http://etdiscussion. worldeconomicsassociation.org/wp-content/uploads/Rekiso-20-june-15.pdf

Rodden, J. & Rose-Ackerman, S. (1997). Does Federalism Preserve Markets? 83 *Virginia Law Reviews*; 1521 (1997).

Rodriguez-Pose, A. and Belepsch, V. (2019). Does Population Diversity Matter for Economic Development in the Very Long Term? Historic Migration, Diversity and County Wealth in the US. *European Journal of Population*; volume **35**, pages873–911 (2019)

Rodrik, D. (2021). A Primer on Trade and Inequality Working Paper 29507 National Bureau of Economic Research 1050 Massachusetts Avenue Cambridge, MA 02138 November 2021.

Rohlf, M. (2021). "Immanuel Kant", *The Stanford Encyclopedia of Philosophy* (Fall 2020 Edition), Edward N. Zalta (ed.), https://plato.stanford.edu/archives/fall2020/entries/kant/

Schnieder, C. S. (2004). Integrating Critical Race Theory and Postmodernism Implications of Race, Class, and Gender. Critical Criminology; 12, pages87–103 (2004)

Seid, Y. (2019). The impact of learning first in mother tongue: evidence from a natural experiment in Ethiopia. *Applied Economics*, Volume 51, Issue 6; 2019. Accessed on November 24, 2022; from https://www.tandfonline.com/doi/abs/10.1080/00036 846.2018.1497852?journalCode=raec20#2b85d6ca-6520-4a3d-8e4a-aa9f2ee3f33d-b6de7b7c-de82-45a5-9538-313dd15c6659

Sellstrom, T., and Wohlgemuth, L. (2022). The International Response to Conflict and Genocide: Lessons from the Rwanda Experience; Study 1 Historical Perspective: Some Explanatory Factors; The Nordic Africa Institute Uppsala, Sweden.

Siddiqui, K. (2018). David Ricardo's Comparative Advantage and Developing Countries: Myth and Reality. *International Critical Thought*, Vol 8, issue 3. Pages: 426-452.

Smyth, J. (ed). (2017). Remembering the Troubles: Contesting the Recent Past in Northern Ireland. Notre Dame Press, University of Notre Dame.

Speke, J. H. (2013). The Discovery of the Source of the Nile. February 6, 2013

Spencer, Q. (2019). How to be a Biological Realist; in What is Race; Glasgow, et al. OUP.

Spengler, J. J. "David Ricardo". *Encyclopedia Britannica*, 22 Dec. 2021, https://www.britannica.com/biography/David-Ricardo.

Statista. (2023). Apple's net income in the company's fiscal years from 2005 to 2022 (in *billion U.S. dollars). https://www.statista.com/statistics/267728/apples-net-income-since-2005/

Stevens, G. (2003). Academic representations of 'race' and racism in psychology: Knowledge production, historical context, and dialectics in transitional South Africa. *International Journal of Intercultural Relations* 27 (2003) 189–207. Pergamon.

Stein, M. M. (2015). *Measuring Manhood: Race and the Science of Masculinity, 1830–1934.* Minneapolis, Minnesota, University of Minnesota Press, 2015

Stigler, G. J. (1975). The Goals of Economic Policy. The Henry Simons Lecture; The University of Chicago Law School. *The Journal of Law & Economics*, Vol. 18. No. 2. October 1975. pp. 283-292.

Taye, B. A. (2017). Ethnic federalism and conflict in Ethiopia. *Africa Journal of Conflict Resolution*. Volume 17; No. 2. https://www.ajol.info/index.php/ajcr/article/view/167170

Thermitus, F. (2021). A Stoic Approach to Racism. Philosophy Now: *A Magazine of Ideas*. Volume 144, June/July 2021

Tornau, C. (2019). "Saint Augustine", *The Stanford Encyclopedia of Philosophy* (Summer 2020 Edition), Edward N. Zalta (ed.), https://plato.stanford.edu/archives/sum2020/entries/augustine/

Tullock, G. (1988). Rents and Rent-Seeking. In: Rowley, C.K., Tollison, R.D., Tullock, G. (eds) The Political Economy of Rent-Seeking. Topics in Regulatory Economics and Policy, vol 1. Springer, Boston, MA.

Tullock, G. (1967). The Welfare Costs of Tariffs, Monopolies, and Theft, *Western Economic Journal*, 5:3 (1967: June) p.224.

Tunick, M. (2006). Tolerant Imperialism: John Stuart Mill's Defense of British Rule in India. *The Review of Politics* 68 (2006), 1 –26.

UNDP. (2020). Human Development Index.

UNDP. (2020). Ethiopia: Sub National Human Development Index.

UNESCO. (2022). Why mother language-based education is essential. Accessed on November 23, 2022; from https://www.unesco.org/en/articles/why-mother-language-based-education-essential

UNICEF. (2022). Highlights of the 2021/22 Federal Government Budget Proclamation.

United Nations (1978). Declaration on Race and Racial Prejudice.

United Nations (1978). Declaration on Race and Racial Prejudice. Accessed on April 23, 2021 from https://www.un.org/en/genocideprevention/documents/atrocity-crimes/Doc.11_declaration%20on%20race%20and%20racial%20prejudice.pdf

UNOCHA. (2022). Ukraine Sitaution Report. September 21, 2022.

UNU (WIDER). (2022). World Inequalities Database.

Uzgalis, W. (2017). John Locke, Racism, Slavery, and Indian Lands. The Oxford Handbook of Philosophy and Race (ed. Naomi Zack), Oxford,

Uvin, P. (1999). Ethnicity and Power in Burundi and Rwanda: Different Paths to Mass Violence. *Comparative Politics*. Vol. 31; No. 3. (Aprl., 1999); pp. 253-271

Vablen, T. (1899). The Theory of Leisurly Class. http://moglen.law.columbia.edu/LCS/theoryleisureclass.pdf

Wagner, J. K., Yu, J., Ifekwunigwe, J. O., Harrell, T. M., Bamshad, M. J. & Royal, C. D. (2017). Anthropologists' views on race, ancestry, and genetics. *American Journal of*

Physical Anthropology. 2017 Feb; 162(2): 318–327. https://www.ncbi.nlm.nih.gov/pmc/articles/PMC5299519/

Wiedemann, T. (1981). *Greek and Roman Slavery*; Routledge; London, New York.

Weingast, B. R. (1995). The Economic Role of Political Institutions: MarketPreserving Federalism and Economic Development; Development; *Journal of Law, Economics & Organizations*; Volume1, 5-8 (1995).

Weinstein, J. R. (2001). Adam Smith (1723-1790). Internet *Encyclopedia of Philosophy*.

William Mitchell College of Law. (2012). "Rwandan Genocide." World Without Genocide.

Williams, R. L. (2001). Ethnic Conflicts; in International Encyclopedia of Social and Behavioral Sciences.

Wimmer, A. (2008). The Making and Unmaking of Ethnic Boundaries: A Multilevel Process Theory. *The American Journal of Sociology*; Volume 113 Number 4 (January 2008): 970–1022

Wolde. B. G. (20918). Traditional Conflict Resolution Mechanisms in Kaffa Society of Ethiopia. *Universitepark Bulletin,* Vol 7. Issue 2. pp. 128-142; Published Online: July 2018.

Woldemichael, A., Takina, A., Sari, A. A. & Olyaeemanes, A. (2019). Inequalities in healthcare resources and outcomes threatening sustainable health development in Ethiopia: panel data analysis. *Health Policy Research* BMJ Journal, Volume 9; issue 1.

Woldeyes, F. B. (2021). Debt Sustainability and Management in Ethiopia Lessons from China. South South Integration and the SDGs: Enhancing Structural Transformation in Key Partner Countries of the Belt and Road Initiative UNCTAD/BRI PROJECT/RP 20.

Wolff, J. and Leopold, D. (2003). "Karl Marx", *The Stanford Encyclopedia of Philosophy* (Spring 2021 Edition), Edward N. Zalta (ed.); https://plato.stanford.edu/archives/spr2021/entries/marx/

World Bank. (2016). Ethiopia Public Expenditure Review.

World Bank. (2019). Doing Business.

World Bank. (2022). Net Trade in Goods and Services (Balance of Payments, Current Dollars, Ethiopia). International Monetary Fund, Balance of Payments Statistics Yearbook and data files.

World Bank. (2022). South Africa Open Data.

Worldometers. (2021). Countries of the World.

World Population Review (2022). Debt to GDP Ratio by Country, 2022

Wyatt-Brown, Bertram. "American Abolitionism and Religion." Divining America, TeacherServe®. National Humanities Center.

Zak, P. J. (2002). Institutions, Property Rights, and Growth. Recherches economiques de Louvain; 2002/1-2 (vol. 68; pages 55 – 73.

Zack, N. (2018). The Philosophy of Race. *Palgrave Philosophy Today*. McMillan.

Zalta, E. N. (ed.). (2022). *The Stanford Encyclopedia of Philosophy. Summer 2020 Edition.*

Zewde, B. (2002). *Pioneers of Change in Ethiopia: The Reformist Intellectuals of the Early Twentieth Century*; Ohio University Press, 2022.

Zimmermann-Steinhart, P. & Bekele, Y. (2012). The implications of federalism and decentralisation on socio-economic conditions in Ethiopia. *Potchefstroom Electronic Law Journal;* PER vol.15 n.2; Potchefstroom August 2012.

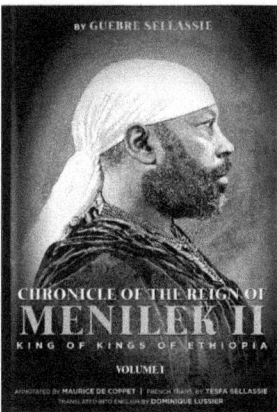

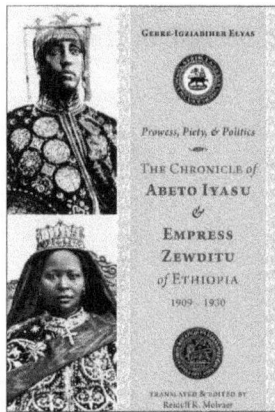

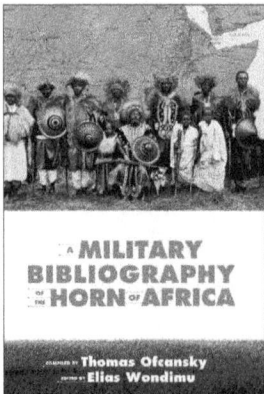

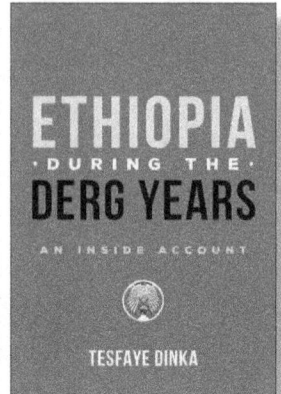

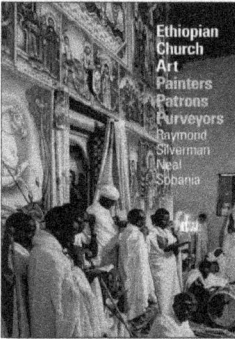

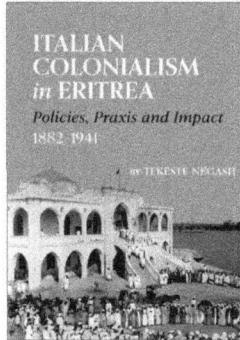

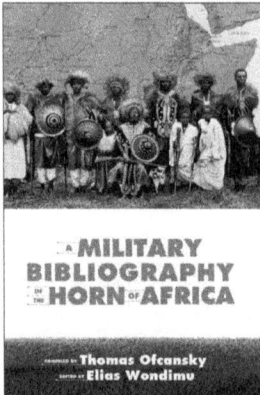

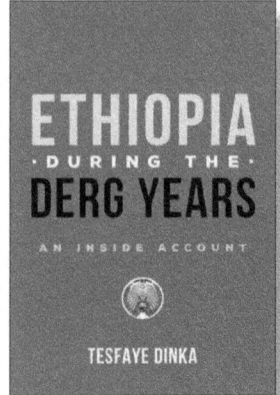

www.ingramcontent.com/pod-product-compliance
Lightning Source LLC
Chambersburg PA
CBHW020402100426
42812CB00001B/166